Prepare, Apply, and Confirm

- **Enhanced eText Features**—Keep students engaged in learning on their own time, while helping them achieve greater conceptual understanding of course material through author-created solutions videos and opportunities to Try It!

- **Dynamic Study Modules**—Work by continuously assessing student performance and activity, then using data and analytics to provide personalized content in real time to reinforce concepts that target each student's particular strengths and weaknesses.

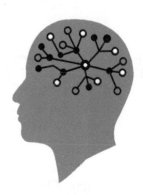

- **Hallmark Features**—Personalized Learning Aids, like Help Me Solve This, View an Example, and instant feedback are available for further practice and mastery when students need the help most!

- **Learning Catalytics**—Generates classroom discussion, guides lecture, and promotes peer-to-peer learning with real-time analytics. Now, students can use any device to interact in the classroom.

- **Study Plan for Self-Paced Learning**—MyOMLab generates a personalized Study Plan for each student based on his or her test results. The Study Plan links directly to interactive tutorial exercises for topics the student has not mastered.

with MyOMLab™

- **Worked Solutions**—Provide step-by-step explanations on how to solve select problems using the exact numbers and data that were presented in the problem. Instructors will have access to the Worked Solutions in preview and review mode.

- **Test Manager**—Choose from the hundreds of available questions correlated to the textbook and AACSB standards to create and manage tests.

- **Reporting Dashboard**—View, analyze, and report learning outcomes clearly and easily. Available via the Gradebook and fully mobile-ready, the Reporting Dashboard presents student performance data at the class, section, and program levels in an accessible, visual manner.

- **LMS Integration**—Link from any LMS platform to access assignments, rosters, and resources, and synchronize MyLab grades with your LMS gradebook. For students, new direct, single sign-on provides access to all the personalized learning MyLab resources that make studying more efficient and effective.

- **Mobile Ready**—Students and instructors can access multimedia resources and complete assessments right at their fingertips, on any mobile device.

PEARSON

Lee J. Krajewski • Manoj K. Malhotra • Larry P. Ritzman

Operations Management
Processes and Supply Chains

Custom Edition for University of Oregon

Taken from:
Operations Management: Processes and Supply Chains, Eleventh Edition
by Lee J. Krajewski, Manoj K. Malhotra, and Larry P. Ritzman

Taken from:

Operations Management: Processes and Supply Chains, Eleventh Edition
by Lee J. Krajewski, Manoj K. Malhotra, and Larry P. Ritzman
Copyright © 2016, 2013, 2010 by Pearson Education, Inc.
New York, New York 10013

This special edition published in cooperation with Pearson Learning Solutions.

All trademarks, service marks, registered trademarks, and registered service marks are the property of their respective owners and are used herein for identification purposes only.

Pearson Learning Solutions, 330 Hudson Street, New York, New York 10013
A Pearson Education Company
www.pearsoned.com

Printed in the United States of America

8   17

000200010271988408

IM

ISBN 10: 1-323-26527-9
ISBN 13: 978-1-323-26527-7

Brief Contents

Contents

MyOMLab **SUPPLEMENTS**

USING OPERATIONS TO CREATE VALUE

Characters perform at Cinderella's Castle in Magic Kingdom, Orlando, Florida, USA.

Disney

Disney Corporation is an internationally diversified entertainment and media enterprise comprising of five business segments of media networks (e.g., ABC, ESPN networks), parks and resorts (e.g., Disneyland and Disneyworld), studio entertainment (e.g., Pixar and Marvel studios), consumer products (e.g., toys, apparel, and books), and interactive media (e.g., Disney.com). It is one of the 30 companies that has been a part of the Dow Jones Industrial Average since 1991. With annual revenues of $45 billion in 2013, Disney is particularly well known for its theme parks that had a 17 percent increase in operating income to $2.2 billion in the last fiscal year alone. Its largest park, Walt Disney World Resort opened in Orlando, Florida, in 1971 and includes the Magic Kingdom, Epcot Center, Disney Studios, and Animal Kingdom.

Disney constantly evaluates and improves its processes to enhance customer experience. One of its recent innovations is a $1 billion comprehensive reservation and ride-planning system that can allow guests to book rides months in advance through a website or a smartphone app. Dubbed as MyMagic+, it works through a radio-frequency identification (RFID) chip embedded inside electronic wristbands or bracelets that guests wear once they check into a Disney theme park. Called MagicBands, they link electronically to centralized databases and can be used as admission tickets, credit or debit cards, or hotel room keys. Just by tapping them against electronic sensors, these MagicBands also become a form of payment for food, entertainment, and merchandise. Data from these wristbands can help Disney determine when to add more staff to which rides, decide how many employees in costumes should roam around at which locations in the park, determine restaurant menus and which souvenirs should be stocked based on customer preferences, and even send e-mail or text message alerts to guests when space opens up in an expedited queue at that guest's favorite ride such as Space Mountain or Pirates of the Caribbean. Apart from facilitating crowd control and data collection, this wearable technology helps Disney seamlessly personalize each guest's experience and change how they play and spend at the oft-advertised "Most Magical Place on Earth."

Despite some privacy concerns surrounding the use of RFID chips that can track a guest's identity and location within the theme parks, the new MyMagic+ system has multiple advantages. First, when visitors have well-planned schedules and forward visibility on what they are going to do on a given day on an hourly basis, they are less likely to jump ship to other theme parks in the area such as the Sea World or the popular Wizarding World of Harry Potter by Universal Studios. Second, when the logistics of moving from one attraction to another are simplified, guests have additional opportunities to spend more time and money in Disney restaurants and shops. Finally, by using this new RFID-enabled technology, Disney can effectively increase its capacity when it is needed the most. For instance, this new system allowed Disney to handle 3,000 additional visitors to the Magic Kingdom in Orlando during the Christmas rush. With other costs more or less fixed, the incremental revenues from additional guests flow directly to the bottom line. Increased profitability through technological and operational innovations help Disney provide more value to its guests as well as maintain its leadership position in the entertainment industry on multiple dimensions. It is also one among many other reasons why despite the price of entrance tickets crossing an average of $100 per day inclusive of taxes, an increase of 45 percent since 2005, there is no end in sight to the large crowds flooding Disney's theme parks.

Sources: Christopher Palmeri, "Disney Bets $1 Billion on Technology to Track Theme Park Visitors," *Bloomberg Business Week* (March 7, 2014); Justin Bachman, "Disney's Magic Kingdom Nears $100 Tickets, and the Crowds Keep Coming," *Bloomberg Business Week* (February 25, 2014); **http://thewaltdisneycompany.com/about-disney/company-overview**; **http://en.wikipedia.org/wiki/Disney** (August 18, 2014).

LEARNING GOALS *After reading this chapter, you should be able to:*

1. Describe the role of operations in an organization and its historical evolution over time.

2. Describe the process view of operations in terms of inputs, processes, outputs, information flows, suppliers, and customers.

3. Describe the supply chain view of operations in terms of linkages between core and support processes.

4. Define an operations strategy and its linkage to corporate strategy and market analysis.

5. Identify nine competitive priorities used in operations strategy, and explain how a consistent pattern of decisions can develop organizational capabilities.

6. Identify the latest trends in operations management, and understand how given these trends, firms can address the challenges facing operations and supply chain managers in a firm.

Operations management refers to the systematic design, direction, and control of processes that transform inputs into services and products for internal, as well as external customers. As exemplified by Disney, it can be a source of competitive advantage for firms in both service as well as manufacturing sectors.

This book deals with managing those fundamental activities and processes that organizations use to produce goods and services that people use every day. A **process** is any activity or group of activities that takes one or more inputs, transforms them, and provides one or more outputs for its customers. For organizational purposes, processes tend to be clustered together into operations. An **operation** is a group of resources performing all or part of one or more processes. Processes can be linked together to form a **supply chain**, which is the interrelated series of processes within a firm and across different firms that produce a service or product to the satisfaction of customers.[1] A firm can have multiple supply chains, which vary by the product or service provided. **Supply chain management** is the synchronization of a firm's processes with those of its suppliers and customers to match the flow of materials, services, and information with customer demand. As we will learn throughout this book, all firms have processes and supply chains. Sound operational planning and design of these processes, along with internal and external coordination within its supply chain, can create wealth and value for a firm's diverse stakeholders.

Role of Operations in an Organization

Broadly speaking, operations and supply chain management underlie all departments and functions in a business. Whether you aspire to manage a department or a particular process within it, or you just want to understand how the process you are a part of fits into the overall fabric of the business, you need to understand the principles of operations and supply chain management.

Operations serve as an excellent career path to upper management positions in many organizations. The reason is that operations managers are responsible for key decisions that affect the success of the organization. In manufacturing firms, the head of operations usually holds the title chief operations officer (COO) or vice president of manufacturing (or of production or operations). The corresponding title in a service organization might be COO or vice president (or director) of operations. Reporting to the head of operations are the managers of departments such as customer service, production and inventory control, and quality assurance.

Figure 1.1 shows operations as one of the key functions within an organization. The circular relationships in Figure 1.1 highlight the importance of the coordination among the three mainline functions of any business, namely, (1) operations, (2) marketing, and (3) finance. Each function is unique and has its own knowledge and skill areas, primary responsibilities, processes, and decision domains. From an external perspective, finance generates resources, capital, and funds from investors and sales of its goods and services in the marketplace. Based on business strategy, the finance and operations functions then decide how to invest these resources and convert them into physical assets and material inputs. Operations subsequently transforms these material and service inputs into product and service outputs. These outputs must match the characteristics that can be sold in the selected markets by marketing. Marketing is responsible for producing sales revenue of the outputs, which become returns to investors and capital for supporting operations. Functions such as accounting, information systems, human resources, and engineering make the firm complete by providing essential information, services, and other managerial support.

These relationships provide direction for the business as a whole and are aligned to the same strategic intent. It is important to understand the entire circle, and not just the individual functional areas. How well these functions work together determines the effectiveness of the organization. Functions should be integrated and should pursue a common strategy. Success depends on how well they are able to do so. No part of this circle can be dismissed or minimized without loss of effectiveness, and regardless of how departments and functions are individually managed; they are always linked together through processes. Thus, a firm competes not only by offering new services and products, creative marketing, and skillful finance but also through its unique competencies in operations and sound management of core processes.

Sidebar definitions

operations management
The systematic design, direction, and control of processes that transform inputs into services and products for internal, as well as external, customers.

process
Any activity or group of activities that takes one or more inputs, transforms them, and provides one or more outputs for its customers.

operation
A group of resources performing all or part of one or more processes.

supply chain
An interrelated series of processes within and across firms that produces a service or product to the satisfaction of customers.

supply chain management
The synchronization of a firm's processes with those of its suppliers and customers to match the flow of materials, services, and information with customer demand.

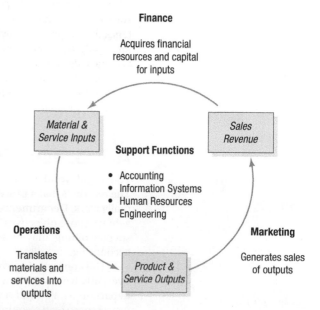

▲ FIGURE 1.1
Integration between Different Functional Areas of a Business

[1]The terms *supply chain* and *value chain* are sometimes used interchangeably.

Historical Evolution and Perspectives

The history of modern operations and supply chain management is rich and over two hundred years old, even though its practice has been around in one form or another for centuries. James Watt invented the steam engine in 1785. The subsequent establishment of railroads facilitated efficient movement of goods throughout Europe, and eventually even in distant colonies such as India. With the invention of the cotton gin in 1794, Eli Whitney introduced the concept of interchangeable parts. It revolutionized the art of machine-based manufacturing, and coupled with the invention of the steam engine, lead to the great industrial revolution in England and the rest of Europe. The textile industry was one of the earliest industries to be mechanized. The industrial revolution gradually spread to the United States and the rest of the world in the nineteenth century and was accompanied by such great innovations as the internal combustion engine, steam-powered ships, metallurgy of iron making, large-scale production of chemicals, and invention of machine tools, among others. The foundations of modern manufacturing and technological breakthroughs were also inspired by the creation of a mechanical computer by Charles Babbage in the early part of the nineteenth century. He also pioneered the concept of division of labor, which laid the foundation for scientific management of operations and supply chain management that was further improved upon by Frederick Taylor in 1911.

The Ford Motor Company, founded in 1903, produced about one million Model T's in 1921 alone.

Martyn Goddard/Corbis

Three other landmark events from the twentieth century define the history of operations and supply chain management. First is the invention of the assembly line for the Model T car by Henry Ford in 1909. The era of mass production was born, where complex products like automobiles could be manufactured in large numbers at affordable prices through repetitive manufacturing. Second, Alfred Sloan in the 1930s introduced the idea of strategic planning for achieving product proliferation and variety, with the newly founded General Motors Corporation offering "a car for every purse and purpose." Finally, with the publication of the Toyota Production System book in Japanese in 1978, Taiichi Ohno laid the groundwork for removing wasteful activities from an organization, a concept that we explore further in this book while learning about lean systems.

The recent history of operations and supply chains over the past three decades has been steeped in technological advances. The 1980s were characterized by wide availability of computer-aided design (CAD), computer-aided manufacturing (CAM), and automation. Information technology applications started playing an increasingly important role in the 1990s and started connecting the firm with its extended enterprise through Enterprise Resource Planning Systems and outsourced technology hosting for supply chain solutions. Service organizations like Federal Express, United Parcel Service (UPS), and Walmart also became sophisticated users of information technology in operations, logistics, and management of supply chains. The new millennium has seen an acceleration of this trend, along with an increased focus on sustainability and the natural environment. We cover all these ideas and topical areas in greater detail throughout this book.

A Process View

You might wonder why we begin by looking at processes rather than at departments or even the firm. The reason is that a process view of the firm provides a much more relevant picture of the way firms actually work. Departments typically have their own set of objectives, a set of resources with capabilities to achieve those objectives, and managers and employees responsible for performance. Some processes, such as billing, may be so specific that they are contained wholly within a single department, such as accounting.

The concept of a process, however, can be much broader. A process can have its own set of objectives, involve a work flow that cuts across departmental boundaries, and require resources from several departments. You will see examples throughout this text of companies that discovered how to use their processes to gain a competitive advantage. You will notice that the key to success in many organizations is a keen understanding of how their processes work, since an organization is only as effective as its processes. Therefore, operations management is relevant and important for all students, regardless of major, because all departments have processes that must be managed effectively to gain a competitive advantage.

How Processes Work

Figure 1.2 shows how processes work in an organization. Any process has inputs and outputs. Inputs can include a combination of human resources (workers and managers), capital (equipment and facilities), purchased materials and services, land, and energy. The numbered circles in Figure 1.2 represent operations through which services, products, or customers pass and where processes are performed. The arrows represent flows and can cross because one job or customer can have different requirements (and thus a different flow pattern) than the next job or customer.

Processes provide outputs to customers. These outputs may often be services (that can take the form of information) or tangible products. Every process and every person in an organization has customers. Some are **external customers**, who may be end users or intermediaries (e.g., manufacturers, financial institutions, or retailers) buying the firm's finished services or products. Others are **internal customers**, who may be employees in the firm whose process inputs are actually the outputs of earlier processes managed within the firm. Either way, processes must be managed with the customer in mind.

In a similar fashion, every process and every person in an organization relies on suppliers. **External suppliers** may be other businesses or individuals who provide the resources, services, products, and materials for the firm's short-term and long-term needs. Processes also have **internal suppliers**, who may be employees or processes that supply important information or materials.

Inputs and outputs vary depending on the service or product provided. For example, inputs at a jewelry store include merchandise, the store building, registers, the jeweler, and customers; outputs to external customers are services and sold merchandise. Inputs to a factory manufacturing blue jeans include denim, machines, the plant, workers, managers, and services provided by outside consultants; outputs are clothing and supporting services. The fundamental role of inputs, processes, and customer outputs holds true for processes at all organizations.

Figure 1.2 can represent a whole firm, a department, a small group, or even a single individual. Each one has inputs and uses processes at various operations to provide outputs. The dashed lines represent two special types of input: participation by customers and information on performance from both internal and external sources. Participation by customers occurs not only when they receive outputs but also when they take an active part in the processes, such as when students participate in a class discussion. Information on performance includes internal reports on customer service or inventory levels and external information from market research, government reports, or telephone calls from suppliers. Managers need all types of information to manage processes most effectively.

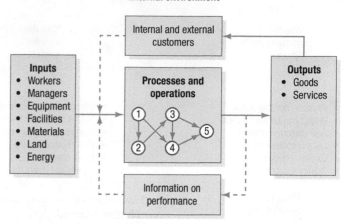

▲ **FIGURE 1.2**
Processes and Operations

external customers

A customer who is either an end user or an intermediary (e.g., manufacturers, financial institutions, or retailers) buying the firm's finished services or products.

internal customers

One or more employees or processes that rely on inputs from other employees or processes to perform their work.

external suppliers

The businesses or individuals who provide the resources, services, products, and materials for the firm's short-term and long-term needs.

internal suppliers

The employees or processes that supply important information or materials to a firm's processes.

nested process

The concept of a process within a process.

Nested Processes

Processes can be broken down into subprocesses, which in turn can be broken down further into still more subprocesses. We refer to this concept of a process within a process as a **nested process**. It may be helpful to separate one part of a process from another for several reasons. One person or one department may be unable to perform all parts of the process, or different parts of the process may require different skills. Some parts of the process may be designed for routine work while other parts may be geared for customized work. The concept of nested processes is illustrated in greater detail in Chapter 2, "Process Strategy and Analysis," where we reinforce the need to understand and improve activities within a business and each process's inputs and outputs.

Service and Manufacturing Processes

Two major types of processes are (1) service and (2) manufacturing. Service processes pervade the business world and have a prominent place in our discussion of operations management. Manufacturing processes are also important; without them the products we enjoy as part of our daily lives would not exist. In addition, manufacturing gives rise to service opportunities.

Differences   Why do we distinguish between service and manufacturing processes? The answer lies at the heart of the design of competitive processes. While Figure 1.3 shows several distinctions between service and manufacturing processes along a continuum, the two key differences that we discuss in detail are (1) the nature of their output and (2) the degree of customer contact. In general, manufacturing processes also have longer response times, are more capital intensive, and their quality can be measured more easily than those of service processes.

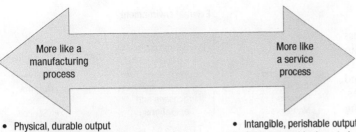

- Physical, durable output
- Output can be inventoried
- Low customer contact
- Long response time
- Capital intensive
- Quality easily measured

- Intangible, perishable output
- Output cannot be inventoried
- High customer contact
- Short response time
- Labor intensive
- Quality not easily measured

▲ **FIGURE 1.3**
Continuum of Characteristics of Manufacturing and Service Processes

Manufacturing processes convert materials into goods that have a physical form we call products. For example, an assembly line produces a 370 Z sports car, and a tailor produces an outfit for the rack of an upscale clothing store. The transformation processes change the materials on one or more of the following dimensions:

1. Physical properties
2. Shape
3. Size (e.g., length, breadth, and height of a rectangular block of wood)
4. Surface finish
5. Joining parts and materials

The outputs from manufacturing processes can be produced, stored, and transported in anticipation of future demand.

If a process does not change the properties of materials on at least one of these five dimensions, it is considered a service (or nonmanufacturing) process. Service processes tend to produce intangible, perishable outputs. For example, the output from the auto loan process of a bank would be a car loan, and an output of the order fulfillment process of the U.S. Postal Service is the delivery of your letter. The outputs of service processes typically cannot be held in a finished goods inventory to insulate the process from erratic customer demands.

A second key difference between service processes and manufacturing processes is degree of customer contact. Service processes tend to have a higher degree of customer contact. Customers may take an active role in the process itself, as in the case of shopping in a supermarket, or they may be in close contact with the service provider to communicate specific needs, as in the case of a medical clinic. Manufacturing processes tend to have less customer contact. For example, washing machines are ultimately produced to meet retail forecasts. The process requires little information from the ultimate consumers (you and me), except indirectly through market surveys and market focus groups. Even though the distinction between service and manufacturing processes on the basis of customer contact is not perfect, the important point is that managers must recognize the degree of customer contact required when designing processes.

Similarities   At the level of the firm, service providers do not just offer services and manufacturers do not just offer products. Patrons of a restaurant expect good service and good food. A customer purchasing a new computer expects a good product as well as a good warranty, maintenance, replacement, and financial services.

Further, even though service processes do not keep finished goods inventories, they do inventory their inputs. For example, hospitals keep inventories of medical supplies and materials needed for day-to-day operations. Some manufacturing processes, on the other hand, do not inventory their outputs because they are too costly. Such would be the case with low-volume customized products (e.g., tailored suits) or products with short shelf lives (e,g., daily newspapers).

When you look at what is being done at the process level, it is much easier to see whether the *process* is providing a service or manufacturing a product. However, this clarity is lost when the whole company is classified as either a manufacturer or a service provider because it often performs both types of processes. For example, the process of cooking a hamburger at a McDonald's is a manufacturing process because it changes the material's physical properties (dimension 1), as is the process of assembling the hamburger with the bun (dimension 5). However, most of the other processes visible or invisible to McDonald's customers are service processes. You can debate whether to call the whole McDonald's organization a service provider or a manufacturer, whereas classifications at the process level are much less ambiguous.

A Supply Chain View

Most services or products are produced through a series of interrelated business activities. Each activity in a process should add value to the preceding activities; waste and unnecessary cost should be eliminated. Our process view of a firm is helpful for understanding how services or products are produced and why cross-functional coordination is important, but it does not shed any light on the strategic benefits of the processes. The missing strategic insight is that processes must add value for customers throughout the supply chain. The concept of supply chains reinforces the link between processes and performance, which includes a firm's internal processes as well as those of its external customers and suppliers. It also focuses attention on the two main types of processes in the supply chain, namely (1) core processes and (2) support processes. Figure 1.4 shows the links between the core and support processes in a firm and a firm's external customers and suppliers within its supply chain.

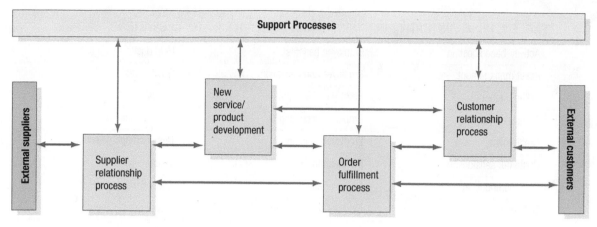

▲ **FIGURE 1.4**
Supply Chain Linkages Showing Work and Information Flows

MyOMLab Animation

Core Processes

A **core process** is a set of activities that delivers value to external customers. Managers of these processes and their employees interact with external customers and build relationships with them, develop new services and products, interact with external suppliers, and produce the service or product for the external customer. Examples include a hotel's reservation handling, a new car design for an auto manufacturer, or Web-based purchasing for an online retailer like amazon.com. Of course, each of the core processes has nested processes within it.

In this text we focus on four core processes:

1. *Supplier Relationship Process.* Employees in the **supplier relationship process** select the suppliers of services, materials, and information and facilitate the timely and efficient flow of these items into the firm. Working effectively with suppliers can add significant value to the services or products of the firm. For example, negotiating fair prices, scheduling on-time deliveries, and gaining ideas and insights from critical suppliers are just a few of the ways to create value.

2. *New Service/Product Development Process.* Employees in the **new service/product development process** design and develop new services or products. The services or products may be developed to external customer specifications or conceived from inputs received from the market in general.

3. *Order Fulfillment Process.* The **order fulfillment process** includes the activities required to produce and deliver the service or product to the external customer.

4. *Customer Relationship Process,* sometimes referred to as *customer relationship management.* Employees involved in the **customer relationship process** identify, attract, and build relationships with external customers and facilitate the placement of orders by customers. Traditional functions, such as marketing and sales, may be a part of this process.

Support Processes

A **support process** provides vital resources and inputs to the core processes and is essential to the management of the business. Processes as such are not just in operations but are found in accounting, finance, human resources, management information systems, and marketing. The human resources function in an organization provides many support processes such as recruiting and hiring workers who are needed at different levels of the organization, training the workers for skills and knowledge needed to properly execute their assigned responsibilities, and establishing incentive and compensation plans that reward employees for their performance. The legal department puts in place support processes that ensure that the firm is in compliance with the rules and regulations under which the business operates. The accounting function supports processes that track how the firm's financial resources are being created and allocated over time, while the information systems function is responsible for the movement and processing of data and information needed to make business decisions. Organizational structure throughout the many diverse industries varies, but for the most part, all organizations perform similar business processes. Table 1.1 lists a sample of them that are outside the operations area.

All of these support processes must be managed to create as much value for the firm and its customers and are therefore vital to the execution of core processes highlighted in Figure 1.4. Managers of these processes must understand that they cut across the organization, regardless of whether the firm is organized along functional, product, regional, or process lines.

core process
A set of activities that delivers value to external customers.

supplier relationship process
A process that selects the suppliers of services, materials, and information and facilitates the timely and efficient flow of these items into the firm.

new service/product development process
A process that designs and develops new services or products from inputs received from external customer specifications or from the market in general through the customer relationship process.

order fulfillment process
A process that includes the activities required to produce and deliver the service or product to the external customer.

customer relationship process
A process that identifies, attracts, and builds relationships with external customers and facilitates the placement of orders by customers, sometimes referred to as *customer relationship management.*

support process
A process that provides vital resources and inputs to the core processes and therefore is essential to the management of the business.

TABLE 1.1 | ILLUSTRATIVE BUSINESS PROCESSES OUTSIDE OF OPERATIONS

Activity-based costing	Employee benefits	Help desks
Asset management	Employee compensation	IT networks
Billing budget	Employee development	Payroll
Complaint handling	Employee recruiting	Records management
Credit management	Employee training	Research and development
Customer satisfaction	Engineering	Sales
Data warehousing	Environment	Security management
Data mining	External communications	Waste management
Disaster recovery	Finance	Warranty

Supply Chain Processes

supply chain processes

Business processes that have external customers or suppliers.

Supply chain processes are business processes that have external customers or suppliers. Table 1.2 illustrates some common supply chain processes.

TABLE 1.2 | SUPPLY CHAIN PROCESS EXAMPLES

Process	Description	Process	Description
Outsourcing	Exploring available suppliers for the best options to perform processes in terms of price, quality, delivery time, environmental issues	**Customer Service**	Providing information to answer questions or resolve problems using automated information services as well as voice-to-voice contact with customers
Warehousing	Receiving shipments from suppliers, verifying quality, placing in inventory, and reporting receipt for inventory records	**Logistics**	Selecting transportation mode (train, ship, truck, airplane, or pipeline) scheduling both inbound and outbound shipments, and providing intermediate inventory storage
Sourcing	Selecting, certifying, and evaluating suppliers and managing supplier contracts	**Cross-docking**	Packing of products of incoming shipments so they can be easily sorted more economically at intermediate warehouses for outgoing shipments to their final destination

These supply chain processes should be documented and analyzed for improvement, examined for quality improvement and control, and assessed in terms of capacity and bottlenecks. Supply chain processes will be only as good as the processes within the organization that have only internal suppliers and customers. Each process in the chain, from suppliers to customers, must be designed and managed to add value to the work performed.

Operations Strategy

operations strategy

The means by which operations implements the firm's corporate strategy and helps to build a customer-driven firm.

Operations strategy specifies the means by which operations implements corporate strategy and helps to build a customer-driven firm. It links long-term and short-term operations decisions to corporate strategy and develops the capabilities the firm needs to be competitive. It is at the heart of managing processes and supply chains. A firm's internal processes are only building blocks: They need to be organized to ultimately be effective in a competitive environment. Operations strategy is the linchpin that brings these processes together to form supply chains that extend beyond the walls of the firm, encompassing suppliers as well as customers. Since customers constantly desire change, the firm's operations strategy must be driven by the needs of its customers.

Developing a customer-driven operations strategy is a process that begins with *corporate strategy*, which, as shown in Figure 1.5, coordinates the firm's overall goals with its core processes. It determines the markets the firm will serve and the responses the firm will make to changes in the environment. It provides the resources to develop the firm's core competencies and core processes, and it identifies the strategy the firm will employ in international markets. Based on corporate strategy, a *market analysis* categorizes the firm's customers, identifies their needs, and assesses competitors' strengths. This information is used to develop *competitive priorities*. These priorities help managers develop the services or products and the

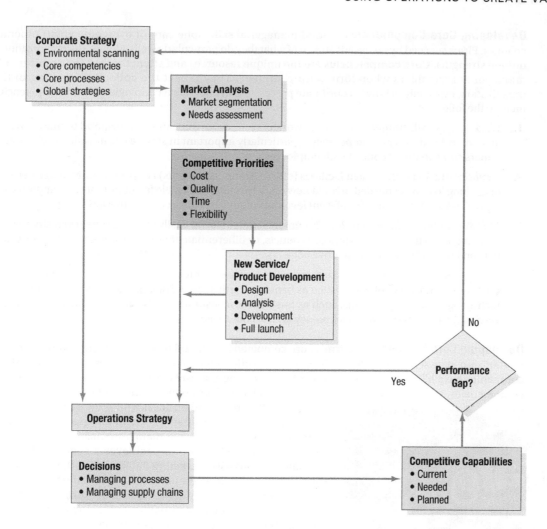

◀ **FIGURE 1.5**
Connection Between
Corporate Strategy and Key
Operations Management
Decisions

MyOMLab Animation

processes needed to be competitive in the marketplace. Competitive priorities are important to the design of existing as well as new services or products, the processes that will deliver them, and the operations strategy that will develop the firm's capabilities to fulfill them. Developing a firm's operations strategy is a continuous process because the firm's capabilities to meet the competitive priorities must be periodically checked, and any gaps in performance must be addressed in the operations strategy.

Corporate Strategy

Corporate strategy provides an overall direction that serves as the framework for carrying out all the organization's functions. It specifies the business or businesses the company will pursue, isolates new opportunities and threats in the environment, and identifies growth objectives.

Developing a corporate strategy involves four considerations: (1) environmental scanning: monitoring and adjusting to changes in the business environment, (2) identifying and developing the firm's core competencies, (3) developing the firm's core processes, and (4) developing the firm's global strategies.

Environmental Scanning   The external business environment in which a firm competes changes continually and an organization needs to adapt to those changes. Adaptation begins with *environmental scanning*, the process by which managers monitor trends in the environment (e.g., the industry, the marketplace, and society) for potential opportunities or threats. A crucial reason for environmental scanning is to stay ahead of the competition. Competitors may be gaining an edge by broadening service or product lines, improving quality, or lowering costs. New entrants into the market or competitors that offer substitutes for a firm's service or product may threaten continued profitability. Other important environmental concerns include economic trends, technological changes, political conditions, social changes (i.e., attitudes toward work), and the availability of vital resources. For example, car manufacturers recognize that dwindling oil reserves will eventually require alternative fuels for their cars. Consequently, they have designed prototype cars that use hydrogen or electric power as supplements to gasoline as a fuel.

core competencies

The unique resources and strengths that an organization's management considers when formulating strategy.

lead time

The elapsed time between the receipt of a customer order and filling it.

Developing Core Competencies Good managerial skill alone cannot overcome environmental changes. Firms succeed by taking advantage of what they do particularly well—that is, the organization's unique strengths. **Core competencies** are the unique resources and strengths that an organization's management considers when formulating strategy. They reflect the collective learning of the organization, especially in how to coordinate processes and integrate technologies. These competencies include the following:

1. *Workforce.* A well-trained and flexible workforce allows organizations to respond to market needs in a timely fashion. This competency is particularly important in service organizations, where customers come in direct contact with employees.

2. *Facilities.* Having well-located facilities (offices, stores, and plants) is a primary advantage because of the long **lead time** needed to build new ones. In addition, flexible facilities that can handle a variety of services or products at different levels of volume provide a competitive advantage.

3. *Market and Financial Know-How.* An organization that can easily attract capital from stock sales, market and distribute its services or products, or differentiate them from similar services or products on the market has a competitive edge.

4. *Systems and Technology.* Organizations with expertise in information systems have an edge in industries that are data intensive, such as banking. Particularly advantageous is expertise in Internet technologies and applications, such as business-to-consumer and business-to-business systems. Having the patents on a new technology is also a big advantage.

Developing Core Processes A firm's core competencies should drive its core processes: customer relationship, new service or product development, order fulfillment, and supplier relationship. Many companies have all four processes, while others focus on a subset of them to better match their core competencies, since they find it difficult to be good at all four processes and still be competitive. For instance, in the credit card business within the banking industry, some companies primarily specialize in finding customers and maintaining relationships with them. American Airlines's credit card program reaches out and achieves a special affinity to customers through its marketing database. On the other hand, specialized credit card companies, such as Capital One, focus on service innovation by creating new features and pricing programs. Finally, many companies are taking over the order fulfillment process by managing the processing of credit card transactions and call centers. The important point is that every firm must evaluate its core competencies and choose to focus on those processes that provide it the greatest competitive strength.

Developing Global Strategies Identifying opportunities and threats today requires a global perspective. A global strategy may include buying foreign services or parts, combating threats from foreign competitors, or planning ways to enter markets beyond traditional national boundaries. Although warding off threats from global competitors is necessary, firms should also actively seek to penetrate foreign markets. Two effective global strategies are (1) strategic alliances and (2) locating abroad.

One way for a firm to open foreign markets is to create a *strategic alliance*. A strategic alliance is an agreement with another firm that may take one of three forms. One form of strategic alliance is the *collaborative effort*, which often arises when one firm has core competencies that another needs but is unwilling (or unable) to duplicate. Such arrangements commonly arise out of buyer–supplier relationships. Another form of strategic alliance is the *joint venture*, in which two firms agree to produce a service or product jointly. This approach is often used by firms to gain access to foreign markets. Finally, *technology licensing* is a form of strategic alliance in which one company licenses its service or production methods to another. Licenses may be used to gain access to foreign markets.

Another way to enter global markets is to locate operations in a foreign country. However, managers must recognize that what works well in their home country might not work well elsewhere. The economic and political environment or customers' needs may be

Peter Foley/Bloomberg/Getty Images

Capital One Financial Corp. is a U.S.-based bank holding company specializing in credit cards, home loans, auto loans, banking, and savings products.

significantly different. For example, the family-owned chain Jollibee Foods Corporation became the dominant fast-food chain in the Philippines by catering to a local preference for sweet and spicy flavors, which it incorporates into its fried chicken, spaghetti, and burgers. Jollibee's strength is its creative marketing programs and an understanding of local tastes; it claims that its burger is similar to the one a Filipino would cook at home. McDonald's responded by introducing its own Filipino-style spicy burger, but competition is stiff. This example shows that to be successful, corporate strategies must recognize customs, preferences, and economic conditions in other countries.

Locating abroad is a key decision in the design of supply chains because it affects the flow of materials, information, and employees in support of the firm's core processes. Chapter 12, "Supply Chain Design," and Chapter 13, "Supply Chain Logistic Networks," offer more in-depth discussion of these other implications.

Market Analysis

One key to successfully formulating a customer-driven operations strategy for both service and manufacturing firms is to understand what the customer wants and how to provide it. A *market analysis* first divides the firm's customers into market segments and then identifies the needs of each segment. In this section, we examine the process of market analysis, and we define and discuss the concepts of market segmentation and needs assessment.

Market Segmentation   *Market segmentation* is the process of identifying groups of customers with enough in common to warrant the design and provision of services or products that the group wants and needs. To identify market segments, the analyst must determine the characteristics that clearly differentiate each segment. The company can then develop a sound marketing program and an effective operating strategy to support it. For instance, The Gap, Inc., a major provider of casual clothes, targets teenagers and young adults while the parents or guardians of infants to 12-year-olds are the primary targets for its GapKids stores. At one time, managers thought of customers as a homogeneous mass market but now realize that two customers may use the same product for different reasons. Identifying the key factors in each market segment is the starting point in devising a customer-driven operations strategy.

Needs Assessment   The second step in market analysis is to make a *needs assessment*, which identifies the needs of each segment and assesses how well competitors are addressing those needs. Each market segment's needs can be related to the service or product and its supply chain. Market needs should include both the tangible and intangible attributes and features of products and services that a customer desires. Market needs may be grouped as follows:

- *Service or Product Needs.* Attributes of the service or product, such as price, quality, and degree of customization.
- *Delivery System Needs.* Attributes of the processes and the supporting systems, and resources needed to deliver the service or product, such as availability, convenience, courtesy, safety, accuracy, reliability, delivery speed, and delivery dependability.
- *Volume Needs.* Attributes of the demand for the service or product, such as high or low volume, degree of variability in volume, and degree of predictability in volume.
- *Other Needs.* Other attributes, such as reputation and number of years in business, after-sale technical support, ability to invest in international financial markets, and competent legal services.

Once it makes this assessment, the firm can incorporate the needs of customers into the design of the service or product and the supply chain that must deliver it. We further discuss these new service and product development-related issues in Chapter 14, "Supply Chain Integration."

Competitive Priorities and Capabilities

A customer-driven operations strategy requires a cross-functional effort by all areas of the firm to understand the needs of the firm's external customers and to specify the operating capabilities the firm requires to outperform its competitors. Such a strategy also addresses the needs of internal customers because the overall performance of the firm depends upon the performance of its core and supporting processes, which must be coordinated to provide the overall desirable outcome for the external customer.

Competitive priorities are the critical operational dimensions a process or supply chain must possess to satisfy internal or external customers, both now and in the future. Competitive priorities are planned for processes and the supply chain created from them. They must be present to maintain or build market share or to allow other internal processes to be successful. Not all competitive priorities are critical for a given process; management selects those that are most important. **Competitive capabilities** are the cost, quality, time, and flexibility dimensions that a process or supply chain actually

competitive priorities

The critical dimensions that a process or supply chain must possess to satisfy its internal or external customers, both now and in the future.

competitive capabilities

The cost, quality, time, and flexibility dimensions that a process or supply chain actually possesses and is able to deliver.

possesses and is able to deliver. When the capability falls short of the priority attached to it, management must find ways to close the gap or else revise the priority.

We focus on nine broad competitive priorities that fall into the four capability groups of cost, quality, time, and flexibility. Table 1.3 provides definitions and examples of these competitive priorities, as well as how firms achieve them at the process level.

TABLE 1.3 | DEFINITIONS, PROCESS CONSIDERATIONS, AND EXAMPLES OF COMPETITIVE PRIORITIES

Cost	Definition	Processes Considerations	Example
1. **Low-cost operations**	Delivering a service or a product at the lowest possible cost to the satisfaction of external or internal customers of the process or supply chain	To reduce costs, processes must be designed and operated to make them efficient using rigorous process analysis that addresses workforce, methods, scrap or rework, overhead, and other factors, such as investments in new automated facilities or technologies to lower the cost per unit of the service or product.	**Costco** achieves low costs by designing all processes for efficiency, stacking products on pallets in warehouse-type stores, and negotiating aggressively with their suppliers. Costco can provide low prices to its customers because they have designed operations for low cost.
Quality			
2. **Top quality**	Delivering an outstanding service or product	To deliver top quality, a service process may require a high level of customer contact, and high levels of helpfulness, courtesy, and availability of servers. It may require superior product features, close tolerances, and greater durability from a manufacturing process.	**Rolex** is known globally for creating precision timepieces.
3. **Consistent quality**	Producing services or products that meet design specifications on a consistent basis	Processes must be designed and monitored to reduce errors, prevent defects, and achieve similar outcomes over time, regardless of the "level" of quality.	**McDonald's** standardizes work methods, staff training processes, and procurement of raw materials to achieve the same consistent product and process quality from one store to the next.
Time			
4. **Delivery speed**	Quickly filling a customer's order	Design processes to reduce lead time (elapsed time between the receipt of a customer order and filling it) through keeping backup capacity cushions, storing inventory, and using premier transportation options.	**Netflix** engineered its customer relationship, order fulfillment and supplier relationship processes to create an integrated Web-based system that allows its customers to watch multiple episodes of a TV program or movies in rapid succession.
5. **On-time delivery**	Meeting delivery-time promises	Along with processes that reduce lead time, planning processes (forecasting, appointments, order promising, scheduling, and capacity planning) are used to increase percent of customer orders shipped when promised (95% is often a typical goal).	**United Parcel Services (UPS)** uses its expertise in logistics and warehousing processes to deliver a very large volume of shipments on-time across the globe.
6. **Development speed**	Quickly introducing a new service or a product	Processes aim to achieve cross-functional integration and involvement of critical external suppliers in the service or product development process.	**Zara** is known for its ability to bring fashionable clothing designs from the runway to market quickly.
Flexibility			
7. **Customization**	Satisfying the unique needs of each customer by changing service or product designs	Processes with a customization strategy typically have low volume, close customer contact, and an ability to reconfigure processes to meet diverse types of customer needs.	**Ritz Carlton** customizes services to individual guest preferences.
8. **Variety**	Handling a wide assortment of services or products efficiently	Processes supporting variety must be capable of larger volumes than processes supporting customization. Services or products are not necessarily unique to specific customers and may have repetitive demands.	**Amazon.com** uses information technology and streamlined customer relationship and order fulfillment processes to reliably deliver a vast variety of items to its customers.
9. **Volume flexibility**	Accelerating or decelerating the rate of production of services or products quickly to handle large fluctuations in demand	Processes must be designed for excess capacity and excess inventory to handle demand fluctuations that can vary in cycles from days to months. This priority could also be met with a strategy that adjusts capacity without accumulation of inventory or excess capacity.	The **United States Post Office (USPS)** can have severe demand peak fluctuations at large postal facilities where processes are flexibly designed for receiving, sorting, and dispatching mail to numerous branch locations.

At times, management may emphasize a cluster of competitive priorities together. For example, many companies focus on the competitive priorities of delivery speed and development speed for their processes, a strategy called **time-based competition**. To implement the strategy, managers carefully define the steps and time needed to deliver a service or produce a product and then critically analyze each step to determine whether they can save time without hurting quality.

To link to corporate strategy, management assigns selected competitive priorities to each process (and the supply chains created from them) that are consistent with the needs of external as well as internal customers. Competitive priorities may change over time. For example, consider a high-volume standardized product, such as color ink-jet desktop printers. In the early stages of the ramp-up period when the printers had just entered the mass market, the manufacturing processes required consistent quality, delivery speed, and volume flexibility. In the later stages of the ramp-up when demand was high, the competitive priorities became low-cost operations, consistent quality, and on-time delivery. Competitive priorities must change and evolve over time along with changing business conditions and customer preferences.

The lavish interior lobby decor of the Ritz Carlton resort in Palm Beach, Florida, USA

America/Alamy

Order Winners and Qualifiers

Competitive priorities focus on what operations can do to help a firm be more competitive and are in response to what the market wants. Another useful way to examine a firm's ability to be successful in the marketplace is to identify the order winners and order qualifiers. An **order winner** is a criterion that customers use to differentiate the services or products of one firm from those of another. Order winners can include price (which is supported by low-cost operations) and other dimensions of quality, time, and flexibility. However, order winners also include criteria not directly related to the firm's operations, such as after-sale support (Are maintenance service contracts available? Is there a return policy?); technical support (What help do I get if something goes wrong? How knowledgeable are the technicians?); and reputation (How long has this company been in business? Have other customers been satisfied with the service or product?). It may take good performance on a subset of the order-winner criteria, cutting across operational as well as nonoperational criteria, to make a sale.

Order winners are derived from the considerations customers use when deciding which firm to purchase a service or product from in a given market segment. Sometimes customers demand a certain level of demonstrated performance before even contemplating a service or product. Minimal level required from a set of criteria for a firm to do business in a particular market segment is called an **order qualifier**. Fulfilling the order qualifier will not ensure competitive success; it will only position the firm to compete in the market. From an operations perspective, understanding which competitive priorities are order qualifiers and which ones are order winners is important for the investments made in the design and management of processes and supply chains.

Figure 1.6 shows how order winners and qualifiers are related to achieving the competitive priorities of a firm. If a minimum threshold level is not met for an order-qualifying dimension (consistent quality, for example) by a firm, then it would get disqualified from even being considered further by its customers. For example, there is a level of quality consistency that is minimally tolerable by customers in the auto industry. When the subcompact car Yugo built by Zastava Corporation could not sustain the minimal level of quality, consistency, and reliability expected by customers, it had to exit the U.S. car market in 1991 despite offering very low prices (order winner) of under $4,000. However, once the

time-based competition

A strategy that focuses on the competitive priorities of delivery speed and development speed.

order winner

A criterion customers use to differentiate the services or products of one firm from those of another.

order qualifier

Minimal level required from a set of criteria for a firm to do business in a particular market segment.

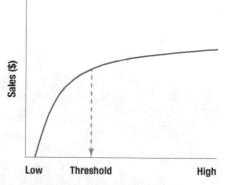

Order Winner

Sales ($)

Low   High

Achievement of competitive priority

Order Qualifier

Sales ($)

Low   Threshold   High

Achievement of competitive priority

▲ **FIGURE 1.6**

Relationship of Order Winners and Order Qualifiers to Competitive Priorities

MyOMLab Animation

firm qualifies by attaining consistent quality beyond the threshold, it may only gain additional sales at a very low rate by investing further in improving that order-qualifying dimension. In contrast, for an order-winning dimension (i.e., low price driven by low-cost operations), a firm can reasonably expect to gain appreciably greater sales and market share by continuously lowering its prices as long as the order qualifier (i.e., consistent quality) is being adequately met. Toyota Corolla and Honda Civic have successfully followed this route in the marketplace to become leaders in their target market segment.

Order winners and qualifiers are often used in competitive bidding. For example, before a buyer considers a bid, suppliers may be required to document their ability to provide consistent quality as measured by adherence to the design specifications for the service or component they are supplying (order qualifier). Once qualified, the supplier may eventually be selected by the buyer on the basis of low prices (order winner) and the reputation of the supplier (order winner).

Using Competitive Priorities: An Airline Example

To get a better understanding of how companies use competitive priorities, let us look at a major airline. We will consider two market segments: (1) first-class passengers and (2) coach passengers. Core services for both market segments are ticketing and seat selection, baggage handling, and transportation to the customer's destination. The peripheral services are quite different across the two market segments. First-class passengers require separate airport lounges; preferred treatment during check-in, boarding, and deplaning; more comfortable seats; better meals and beverages; more personal attention (cabin attendants who refer to customers by name); more frequent service from attendants; high levels of courtesy; and low volumes of passengers (adding to the feeling of being special). Coach passengers are satisfied with standardized services (no surprises), courteous flight attendants, and low prices. Both market segments expect the airline to hold to its schedule. Consequently, we can say that the competitive priorities for the first-class segment are *top quality* and *on-time delivery*, whereas the competitive priorities for the coach segment are *low-cost operations*, *consistent quality*, and *on-time delivery*.

The airline knows what its collective capabilities must be as a firm, but how does that get communicated to each of its core processes? Let us focus on the four core processes: (1) customer relationship, (2) new service or product development, (3) order fulfillment, and (4) supplier relationship. Competitive priorities are assigned to each core process to achieve the service required to provide complete customer satisfaction. Table 1.4 shows some possible assignments just to give you an idea of how this works.

Identifying Gaps between Competitive Priorities and Capabilities

Operations strategy translates service or product plans and competitive priorities for each market segment into decisions affecting the supply chains that support those market segments. Even if it is not formally stated, the current operations strategy for any firm is really the pattern of decisions that have been made for its processes and supply chains. As we have previously seen in Figure 1.5, corporate strategy provides the umbrella for key operations management decisions that contribute to the development of the firm's ability to compete successfully in the marketplace. Once managers determine the competitive priorities for a process, it is necessary to assess the *competitive capabilities* of the process. Any gap between a competitive priority and the capability to achieve that competitive priority must be closed by an effective operations strategy.

Developing capabilities and closing gaps is the thrust of operations strategy. To demonstrate how this works, suppose the management of a bank's credit card division decides to embark on a marketing campaign to significantly increase its business, while keeping costs low. A key process in this division is billing and payments. The division receives credit transactions from the merchants, pays the merchants, assembles and sends the bills to the credit card holders, and processes payments. The new marketing effort is expected to significantly increase the volume of bills and payments. In assessing the capabilities, the process must have to serve the bank's customers and to meet the

Flight attendants welcoming passengers aboard a commercial airline.

TABLE 1.4 | COMPETITIVE PRIORITIES ACROSS DIFFERENT CORE PROCESSES FOR AN AIRLINE

	CORE PROCESSES			
Priority	**Supplier Relationship**	**New Service Development**	**Order Fulfillment**	**Customer Relationship**
Low Cost Operations	Costs of acquiring inputs must be kept to a minimum to allow for competitive pricing.		Airlines compete on price and must keep operating costs in check.	
Top Quality		New services must be carefully designed because the future of the airline industry depends on them.	High quality meal and beverage service delivered by experienced cabin attendants ensures that the service provided to first-class passengers is kept top notch.	High levels of customer contact and lounge service for the first-class passengers.
Consistent Quality	Quality of the inputs must adhere to the required specifications. In addition, information provided to suppliers must be accurate.		Once the quality level is set, it is important to achieve it every time.	The information and service must be error free.
Delivery Speed				Customers want immediate information regarding flight schedules and other ticketing information.
On time delivery	Inputs must be delivered to tight schedules.		The airline strives to arrive at destinations on schedule, otherwise passengers might miss connections to other flights.	
Development Speed		It is important to get to the market fast to preempt the competition.		
Customization		The process must be able to create unique services.		
Variety	Many different inputs must be acquired, including maintenance items, meals and beverages.		Maintenance operations are required for a variety of aircraft models.	The process must be capable of handling the service needs of all market segments and promotional programs.
Volume Flexibility	The process must be able to handle variations in supply quantities efficiently.			

challenges of the new market campaign; management assigns the following competitive priorities for the billing and payments process:

- *Low-Cost Operations.* It is important to maintain low costs in the processing of the bills because profit margins are tight.
- *Consistent Quality.* The process must consistently produce bills, make payments to the merchants, and record payments from the credit card holders accurately.
- *Delivery Speed.* Merchants want to be paid for the credit purchases quickly.
- *Volume Flexibility.* The marketing campaign is expected to generate many more transactions in a shorter period of time.

Management assumed that customers would avoid doing business with a bank that could not produce accurate bills or payments. Consequently, consistent quality is an order qualifier for this process.

TABLE 1.5 | OPERATIONS STRATEGY ASSESSMENT OF THE BILLING AND PAYMENT PROCESS

Competitive Priority	Measure	Capability	Gap	Action
Low-cost operations	■ Cost per billing statement ■ Weekly postage	■ $0.0813 ■ $17,000	■ Target is $0.06 ■ Target is $14,000	■ Eliminate microfilming and storage of billing statements ■ Develop Web-based process for posting bills
Consistent quality	■ Percent errors in bill information ■ Percent errors in posting payments	■ 0.90% ■ 0.74%	■ Acceptable ■ Acceptable	■ No action ■ No action
Delivery speed	■ Lead time to process merchant payments	■ 48 hours	■ Acceptable	■ No action
Volume flexibility	■ Utilization	■ 98%	■ Too high to support rapid increase in volumes	■ Acquire temporary employees ■ Improve work methods

Is the billing and payment process up to the competitive challenge? Table 1.5 shows how to match capabilities to priorities and uncover any gaps in the credit card division's operations strategy. The procedure for assessing an operations strategy begins with identifying good measures for each priority. The more quantitative the measures are, the better. Data are gathered for each measure to determine the current capabilities of the process. Gaps are identified by comparing each capability to management's target values for the measures, and unacceptable gaps are closed by appropriate actions.

The credit card division shows significant gaps in the process's capability for low-cost operations. Management's remedy is to redesign the process in ways that reduce costs but will not impair the other competitive priorities. Likewise, for volume flexibility, management realized that a high level of utilization is not conducive for processing quick surges in volumes while maintaining delivery speed. The recommended actions will help build a capability for meeting more volatile demands.

Addressing the Trends and Challenges in Operations Management

Several trends are currently having a great impact on operations management: productivity improvement; global competition; and ethical, workforce diversity, and environmental issues. Accelerating change in the form of information technology, e-commerce, robotics, and the Internet is dramatically affecting the design of new services and products as well as a firm's sales, order fulfillment, and purchasing processes. In this section, we look at these trends and their challenges for operations managers.

Productivity Improvement

Productivity is a basic measure of performance for economies, industries, firms, and processes. Improving productivity is a major trend in operations management because all firms face pressures to improve their processes and supply chains so as to compete with their domestic and foreign competitors. **Productivity** is the value of outputs (services and products) produced divided by the values of input resources (wages, cost of equipment, etc.) used:

productivity

The value of outputs (services and products) produced divided by the values of input resources (wages, costs of equipment, etc.).

$$\text{Productivity} = \frac{\text{Output}}{\text{Input}}$$

Manufacturing employment peaked at just below 20 million in mid-1979, and shrunk by nearly 8 million from 1979 to 2011.[2] However, the manufacturing productivity in the United States has climbed steadily, as more manufacturing capacity and output has been achieved efficiently with a leaner work force. It is interesting and even surprising to compare productivity improvements in the service and manufacturing sectors. In the United States, employment in the service sector has grown rapidly, outstripping the manufacturing sector. It now employs about 90 percent of the workforce. But service-sector

[2]Paul Wiseman, "Despite China's Might, US Factories Maintain Edge," *The State* and *The Associated Press* (January 31, 2011).

productivity gains have been much lower. If productivity growth in the service sector stagnates, so does the overall standard of living regardless of which part of the world you live in. Other major industrial countries, such as Japan and Germany, are experiencing the same problem. Yet signs of improvement are appearing. The surge of investment across national boundaries can stimulate productivity gains by exposing firms to greater competition. Increased investment in information technology by service providers also increases productivity.

Measuring Productivity   As a manager, how do you measure the productivity of your processes? Many measures are available. For example, value of output can be measured by what the customer pays or simply by the number of units produced or customers served. The value of inputs can be judged by their cost or simply by the number of hours worked.

Managers usually pick several reasonable measures and monitor trends to spot areas needing improvement. For example, a manager at an insurance firm might measure office productivity as the number of insurance policies processed per employee per week. A manager at a carpet company might measure the productivity of installers as the number of square yards of carpet installed per hour. Both measures reflect *labor productivity*, which is an index of the output per person or per hour worked. Similar measures may be used for *machine productivity*, where the denominator is the number of machines. Accounting for several inputs simultaneously is also possible. *Multifactor productivity* is an index of the output provided by more than one of the resources used in production; it may be the value of the output divided by the sum of labor, materials, and overhead costs. Here is an example:

EXAMPLE 1.1	**Productivity Calculations**

Calculate the productivity for the following operations:

a.   Three employees process 600 insurance policies in a week. They work 8 hours per day, 5 days per week.

b.   A team of workers makes 400 units of a product, which is sold in the market for $10 each. The accounting department reports that for this job the actual costs are $400 for labor, $1,000 for materials, and $300 for overhead.

MyOMLab
Tutor 1.1 in MyOMLab provides a new example for calculating productivity.

SOLUTION

a.   Labor productivity $= \dfrac{\text{Policies processed}}{\text{Employee hours}}$

$$= \dfrac{600 \text{ policies}}{(3 \text{ employees})(40 \text{ hours/employee})} = \textbf{5} \text{ policies/hour}$$

b.   Multifactor productivity $= \dfrac{\text{Value of output}}{\text{Labor cost + Materials cost + Overhead cost}}$

$$= \dfrac{(400 \text{ units})(\$10/\text{unit})}{\$400 + \$1,000 + \$300} = \dfrac{\$4,000}{\$1,700} = \textbf{2.35}$$

DECISION POINT

We want multifactor productivity to be as high as possible. These measures must be compared with performance levels in prior periods and with future goals. If they do not live up to expectations, the process should be investigated for improvement opportunities.

The Role of Management   The way processes are managed plays a key role in productivity improvement. Managers must examine productivity from the level of the supply chain because it is the collective performance of individual processes that makes the difference. The challenge is to increase the value of output relative to the cost of input. If processes can generate more output or output of better quality using the same amount of input, productivity increases. If they can maintain the same level of output while reducing the use of resources, productivity also increases.

Global Competition

Most businesses realize that, to prosper, they must view customers, suppliers, facility locations, and competitors in global terms. Firms have found that they can increase their market penetration by locating their production facilities in foreign countries because it gives them a local presence that reduces customer

wsr/Alamy

Sonoco is a global supplier of innovative packaging solutions including packages for Chips Ahoy cookies, M&M's, Pringles Potato Crisps, flexible brick packs for coffee, and many other products.

aversion to buying imports. Globalization also allows firms to balance cash flows from other regions of the world when economic conditions are less robust in the home country. Sonoco, a $5-billion-a-year industrial and consumer packaging company in Hartsville, South Carolina, has nearly 20,000 employees in 335 locations worldwide spread across 33 countries. These global operations resulted in international sales and income growth even as domestic sales were stumbling during 2007. How did Sonoco do it?[3] Locating operations in countries with favorable tax laws is one reason. Lower tax rates in Italy and Canada helped in padding the earnings margin. Another reason was a weak dollar, whereby a $46 million boost came from turning foreign currencies into dollars as Sonoco exported such items as snack bag packaging, and tubes and cores used to hold tape and textiles, to operations it owned in foreign countries. The exchange rate difference was more than enough to counter the added expense of increased raw materials, shipping, and energy costs in the United States.

Most products today are composites of materials and services from all over the world. Your Gap polo shirt is sewn in Honduras from cloth cut in the United States. Sitting in a Cineplex theater (Canadian), you munch a Nestle's Crunch bar (Swiss) while watching a Columbia Pictures movie (Japanese). Five developments spurred the need for sound global strategies: (1) improved transportation and communications technologies; (2) loosened regulations on financial institutions; (3) increased demand for imported services and goods; (4) reduced import quotas and other international trade barriers due to the formation of regional trading blocks, such as the European Union (EU) and the North American Free Trade Agreement (NAFTA); and (5) comparative cost advantages.

Comparative Cost Advantages   China and India have traditionally been the sources for low-cost, but skilled, labor, even though the cost advantage is diminishing as these countries become economically stronger. In the late 1990s, companies manufactured products in China to grab a foothold in a huge market, or to get cheap labor to produce low-tech products despite doubts about the quality of the workforce and poor roads and rail systems. Today, however, China's new factories, such as those in the Pudong industrial zone in Shanghai, produce a wide variety of products that are sold overseas in the United States and other regions of the world. U.S. manufacturers have increasingly abandoned low profit margin sectors like consumer electronics, shoes, and toys to emerging nations such as China and Indonesia. Instead, they are focusing on making expensive goods like computer chips, advanced machinery, and health care products that are complex and which require specialized labor.

Foreign companies have opened tens of thousands of new facilities in China over the past decade. Many goods the United States imports from China now come from foreign-owned companies with operations there. These companies include telephone makers, such as Nokia and Motorola, and nearly all of the big footwear and clothing brands. Many more major manufacturers are there as well. The implications for competition are enormous. Companies that do not have operations in China are finding it difficult to compete on the basis of low prices with companies that do. Instead, they must focus on speed and small production runs.

What China is to manufacturing, India is to service. As with the manufacturing companies, the cost of labor is a key factor. Indian software companies have grown sophisticated in their applications and offer a big advantage in cost. The computer services industry is also affected. Back-office operations are affected for the same reason. Many firms are using Indian companies for accounting and bookkeeping, preparing tax returns, and processing insurance claims. Many tech companies, such as Intel and Microsoft, are opening significant research and development (R&D) operations in India.

---

[3]Ben Werner, "Sonoco Holding Its Own," *The State* (February 7, 2008); **http://www.sonoco.com**, 2008.

Disadvantages of Globalization   Of course, operations in other countries can have disadvantages. A firm may have to relinquish proprietary technology if it turns over some of its component manufacturing to offshore suppliers or if suppliers need the firm's technology to achieve desired quality and cost goals. Political risks may also be involved. Each nation can exercise its sovereignty over the people and property within its borders. The extreme case is nationalization, in which a government may take over a firm's assets without paying compensation. Exxon and other large multinational oil firms are scaling back operations in Venezuela due to nationalization concerns. Further, a firm may actually alienate customers back home if jobs are lost to offshore operations.

Employee skills may be lower in foreign countries, requiring additional training time. South Korean firms moved much of their sports shoe production to low-wage Indonesia and China, but they still manufacture hiking shoes and in-line roller skates in South Korea because of the greater skills required. In addition, when a firm's operations are scattered globally, customer response times can be longer. We discuss these issues in more depth in Chapter 12, "Supply Chain Design," because they should be considered when making decisions about outsourcing. Coordinating components from a wide array of suppliers can be challenging. In addition, as Managerial Practice 1.1 shows, catastrophic events such as the Japanese earthquake affect production and operations in Europe and United States because connected supply chains can spread disruptions rapidly and quickly across international borders.

MANAGERIAL PRACTICE 1.1   Japanese Earthquake and Its Supply Chain Impact

Northeast Touhoku district of Japan was struck by a set of massive earthquakes on the afternoon of March 11, 2011, which were soon followed by a huge tsunami that sent waves higher than 33 feet in the port city of Sendai 80 miles away and traveling at the speed of a jetliner. At nearly 9.0 on the Richter scale, it was one of the largest recorded earthquakes to hit Japan. It shifted the Earth's axis by 6 inches with an impact that was felt 250 miles inland in Tokyo, and which moved Eastern Japan 13 feet toward North America. Apart from huge loss of life and hazards of nuclear radiation arising from the crippled Daiichi nuclear reactors in Fukushima, the damage to the manufacturing plants in Japan exposed the hazards of interconnected global supply chains and their impact on factories located half way around the globe.

The impact of the earthquake was particularly acute on industries that rely on cutting edge electronic parts sourced from Japan. Shin-Etsu Chemical Company is the world's largest producer of silicon wafers and supplies 20 percent of the global capacity. Its centralized plant located 40 miles from the Fukushima nuclear facility was damaged in the earthquake, causing ripple effects at Intel and Toshiba that purchase wafers from Shin-Etsu. Similarly, a shortage of automotive sensors from Hitachi slowed or halted production of vehicles in Germany, Spain, and France, while Chrysler reduced overtime at factories in Mexico and Canada to conserve parts from Japan. Even worse, General Motors stopped production altogether at a plant in Louisiana and Ford closed a truck plant in Kentucky due to the quake. The supply of vehicles such as Toyota's Prius and Lexus were limited in the United States because of production disruptions in its Japanese factories. China was affected too, where ZTE Corporation faced shortages of batteries and LCD screens for its cell phones. Similarly, Lenovo in China faced reduced supplies of components

Daro Mifidieri/Getty Images

Devastation caused by the strong earthquake in Kobe, the sixth-largest city in Japan located approximately 19 miles west of Osaka on the north shore of Osaka Bay.

from Japan for assembly of its tablet computers. These disruptions due to reliance on small concentrated network of suppliers in Japan and globally connected production and logistics systems have caused worker layoffs an increase in prices of affected products, and economic losses that have been felt around the world.

Sources: Don Lee and David Pearson, "Disaster in Japan Exposes Supply Chain Weakness," *The State* (April 8, 2011), B6-B7; "Chrysler Reduces Overtime to Help Japan," *The Associated Press* (April 8, 2011) printed in *The State* (April 6, 2011), B7; Krishna Dhir, "From the Editor," *Decision Line*, vol. 42, no. 2, 3.

Strong global competition affects industries everywhere. For example, U.S. manufacturers of steel, appliances, household durable goods, machinery, and chemicals have seen their market share decline in both domestic and international markets. With the value of world trade in commercial services now at more than $4.3 trillion per year, banking, data processing, airlines, and consulting services are beginning to face many of the same international pressures. Regional trading blocs, such as EU and NAFTA, further change the competitive landscape in both services and manufacturing. Regardless of which area of the world you live in, the challenge is to produce services or products that can compete in a global market and to design the processes that can make it happen.

Ethical, Workforce Diversity, and Environmental Issues

Businesses face more ethical quandaries than ever before, intensified by an increasing global presence and rapid technological change. As companies locate new operations and acquire more suppliers and customers in other countries, potential ethical dilemmas arise when business is conducted by different rules. Some countries are more sensitive than others about conflicts of interest, bribery, discrimination against minorities and women, minimum-wage levels, and unsafe workplaces. Managers must decide whether to design and operate processes that do more than just meet local standards. In addition, technological change brings debates about data protection and customer privacy. In an electronic world, businesses are geographically far from their customers, so a reputation of trust is paramount.

In the past, many people viewed environmental problems, such as toxic waste, poisoned drinking water, poor air quality, and climate change as quality-of-life issues; now, many people and businesses see them as survival issues. The automobile industry has seen innovation in electric and hybrid cars in response to environmental concerns and economic benefits arising from using less expensive fuels. Industrial nations face a particular burden because their combined populations consume proportionally much larger resources. Just seven nations, including the United States and Japan, produce almost half of all greenhouse gases. Now China and India have added to that total carbon footprint because of their vast economic and manufacturing expansion over the past decade.

Apart from government initiatives, large multinational companies have a responsibility as well for creating environmentally conscious practices, and can do so profitably. For instance, Timberland has over 110 stores in China because of strong demand for its boots, shoes, clothes, and outdoor gear in that country. It highlights its environmental credentials and corporate social responsibility through investments such as the reforestation efforts in northern China's Horqin Desert. Timberland hopes to double the number of stores over the next 3 years by environmentally differentiating itself from the competition. We discuss these issues in greater detail in Chapter 15, "Supply Chain Sustainability."

The challenge is clear: Issues of ethics, workforce diversity, and the environment are becoming part of every manager's job. When designing and operating processes, managers should consider integrity, respect for the individual, and customer satisfaction along with more conventional performance measures such as productivity, quality, cost, and profit.

A Chinese consumer looks at Timberland products at a department store in Shanghai, China, November 11, 2010. Timberland seeks to benefit from rising incomes in the worlds fastest-growing major economy, and will also invest in its Hong Kong shops.

Weng lei/AP Photos

Designing and Operating Processes and Supply Chains

How can firms meet challenges today and in the future to adequately recognize these trends and take advantage of opportunities in a global market place? One way is to recognize challenges as opportunities to improve existing processes and supply chains or to create new, innovative ones. The management of processes and supply chains goes beyond designing them; it requires the ability to ensure they achieve their goals. Firms should manage their processes and supply chains to maximize their competitiveness in the markets they serve. We share this philosophy of operations management, as illustrated in Figure 1.7. We use this figure at the start of each chapter to show how the topic of the chapter fits into our philosophy of operations management. In addition, this text also contains several chapter supplements that are not explicitly shown in Figure 1.7.

Figure 1.7 shows that all effective operations decisions follow from a sound operations strategy. Consequently, our text has three major parts: "Part 1: Managing Processes," Part 2: "Managing Customer Demand," and "Part 3: Managing Supply Chains." The flow of topics reflects our approach of first understanding how a firm's operations can help provide a solid foundation for competitiveness before tackling the essential process design decisions that will support its strategies. Each part begins with a strategy discussion to support the decisions in that part. Once it is clear how firms design and improve processes, we try to understand how they implement those designs to satisfactorily meet customer demand. Finally we examine the design and operation of supply chains that link processes, whether they are internal or external to the firm. The performance of the supply chains determines the firm's outcomes, which include the services or products the firm produces, the financial results, and feedback from the firm's customers. These outcomes, which are considered in the firm's strategic plan, are discussed throughout this text.

Part 1: Managing Processes   In Part 1, we focus on analyzing processes and how they can be improved to meet the goals of the operations strategy. We begin by addressing the strategic aspects of process design and then present a six-step systematic approach to process analysis. Each chapter in this part deals with some aspect of that approach. We discuss the tools that help managers analyze processes, and we reveal the methods firms use to measure process performance and quality. These

➤ **Using Operations to Create Value**

MANAGING PROCESSES

Process Strategy and Analysis
Quality and Performance
Capacity Planning
Constraint Management
Lean Systems
Project Management

MANAGING CUSTOMER DEMAND

Forecasting
Inventory Management
Operations Planning and
   Scheduling
Resource Planning

MANAGING SUPPLY CHAINS

Supply Chain Design
Supply Chain Logistic Networks
Supply Chain Integration
Supply Chain Sustainability

▲ **FIGURE 1.7**
Managing Processes, Customer Demand, and Supply Chains

methods provide the foundation for programs such as Six Sigma and total quality management. We also look at long-term capacity planning of firms, and shorter-term tactical decisions aimed at better identification and management of system constraints and bottlenecks.

Determining the best process capacity with effective constraint management and making processes "lean" by eliminating activities that do not add value while improving those that do are also key decisions in the redesign of processes. The activities involved in managing processes are essential for providing significant benefits to the firm. Effective management of its processes can allow a firm to reduce its costs and also increase customer satisfaction.

The concluding chapter of Part 1 is a discussion of the methods and tools of project management. Project management is an effective approach to implementing operations strategy through the introduction of new services or products as well as any changes to a firm's processes or supply chains.

Part 2: Managing Customer Demand   The focus of this part of the book is on effectively forecasting and managing customer demand. Therefore we begin by taking a look at forecasting methods and their accuracy, followed by managing inventory such that enough is kept on hand for satisfying customer demand but without tying up excessive resources in it. We follow that with chapters focused on two key planning activities for the effective operations (1) operations planning and scheduling, and (2) resource planning. Together, these planning activities allow for the creation of goods and services that would meet customer demand in a cost effective fashion.

Part 3: Managing Supply Chains   The focus of Part 3 is on supply chains involving processes both internal and external to the firm and the tools that enhance their execution. We follow that with understanding how the design of supply chains and major strategic decisions, such as outsourcing and locating facilities affect performance. We also look at contemporary issues surrounding supply chain integration and the impact of supply chains on the environment.

Adding Value with Process Innovation

It is important to note that the effective operation of a firm and its supply chain is as important as the design and implementation of its processes. Process innovation can make a big difference even in a low-growth industry. Examining processes from the perspective of the value they add is an important part of a successful manager's agenda, as is gaining an understanding of how core processes and related supply chains are linked to their competitive priorities, markets, and the operations strategy of a firm. Who says operations management does not make a difference?

In the long run, the operations manager's decisions should reflect corporate strategy. At the strategic level, operations managers are involved in the development of new capabilities and the maintenance of existing capabilities to best serve the firm's external customers. Operations managers design new processes that have strategic implications, and they are deeply involved in the development and organization of supply chains that link external suppliers and external customers to the firm's internal processes. Operations managers are often responsible for key performance measures such as cost and quality. These decisions have strategic impact because they affect the processes the firm uses to gain a competitive edge.

Via operational innovations that add value to its products, and catchy promotional advertisements, Progressive Insurance has been able to achieve amazing growth in a low-growth industry.

David Adame/AP Images

Plans, policies, and actions should be linked to those in other functional areas to support the firm's overall goals and objectives. Taking a process view of a firm facilitates these links. Regardless of whether you aspire to be an operations manager, or you just want to use the principles of operations management to become a more effective manager, remember that effective management of people, capital, information, and materials is critical to the success of any process and any supply chain.

As you study operations management, keep two principles in mind:

1. Each part of an organization, not just the operations function, must design and operate processes that are part of a supply chain and deal with quality, technology, and staffing issues.

2. Each function of an organization has its own identity and yet is connected with operations through shared processes.

Great strategic decisions lead nowhere if the tactical decisions that support them are wrong. Operations managers are also involved in tactical decisions, including process improvement and performance measurement, managing and planning projects, generating production and staffing plans, managing inventories, and scheduling resources. You will find numerous examples of these decisions, and the implications of making them, throughout this text. You will also learn about the decision-making tools practicing managers use to recognize and define the problem and then choose the best solution. The topics in this text will help you meet operations challenges and achieve operational innovation regardless of your chosen career path.

LEARNING GOALS IN REVIEW

	Learning Goal	Guidelines for Review	MyOMLab Resources
❶	Describe the role of operations in an organization and its historical evolution over time.	The section "Role of Operations in an Organization," pp. 3–4, shows how different functional areas of business come together to create value for a firm.	
❷	Describe the process view of operations in terms of inputs, processes, outputs, information flows, suppliers, and customers.	See the section "A Process View," pp. 4–6, which focuses on how nested and other processes work. Understand the key differences between manufacturing and service processes. Review Figure 1.2 for the important inputs, outputs, and information flows associated with any process.	
❸	Describe the supply chain view of operations in terms of linkages between core and support processes.	Review Figure 1.4 for the important supply chain linkage and information flows.	
❹	Define an operations strategy and its linkage to corporate strategy and market analysis.	See the section on "Operations Strategy" and sub-section on "Corporate Strategy," pp. 8–11, and review Figure 1.5.	
❺	Identify nine competitive priorities used in operations strategy, and explain how a consistent pattern of decisions can develop organizational capabilities.	The section "Competitive Priorities and Capabilities," pp. 11–16, discusses the important concept of order winners and qualifiers. Review Table 1.3 for important illustrations and examples of how leading edge firms implemented different competitive priorities to create a unique positioning in the marketplace. Review Table 1.5 that provides a nice illustrative example of how firms must identify gaps in their competitive priorities and build capabilities through related process and operational changes.	
❻	Identify the latest trends in operations management, and understand how given these trends, firms can address the challenges facing operations and supply chain managers in a firm.	The section "Addressing the Trends and Challenges in Operations Management," pp. 16–22, describes the pressures managers face for achieving productivity improvements, along with managing sustainability and work force diversity related issues in the face of global competition. Also review the section "Adding Value with Process Innovation" on p. 21.	**OM Explorer Tutor:** Productivity Measures **Active Model Exercise:** Productivity

Key Equations

Addressing the Trends and Challenges in Operations Management

1. Productivity is the ratio of output to input:

$$\text{Productivity} = \frac{\text{Output}}{\text{Input}}$$

Key Terms

competitive capabilities 11
competitive priorities 11
consistent quality 12
core competencies 10
core process 7
customer relationship process 7
customization 12
delivery speed 12
development speed 12
external customers 5
external suppliers 5
internal customers 5

internal suppliers 5
lead time 10
low-cost operations 12
nested process 5
new service/product development
    process 7
on-time delivery 12
operation 3
operations management 3
operations strategy 8
order fulfillment process 7
order qualifier 13

order winner 13
process 3
productivity 16
supplier relationship process 7
supply chain 3
supply chain management 3
supply chain processes 8
support process 7
time-based competition 13
top quality 12
variety 12
volume flexibility 12

Solved Problem 1

Student tuition at Boehring University is $150 per semester credit hour. The state supplements school revenue by $100 per semester credit hour. Average class size for a typical 3-credit course is 50 students. Labor costs are $4,000 per class, materials costs are $20 per student per class, and overhead costs are $25,000 per class.

MyOMLab Video

a. What is the *multifactor* productivity ratio for this course process?
b. If instructors work an average of 14 hours per week for 16 weeks for each 3-credit class of 50 students, what is the *labor* productivity ratio?

SOLUTION

a. Multifactor productivity is the ratio of the value of output to the value of input resources.

$$\text{Value of output} = \left(\frac{50 \text{ students}}{\text{class}}\right)\left(\frac{3 \text{ credit hours}}{\text{students}}\right)\left(\frac{\$150 \text{ tuition} + \$100 \text{ state support}}{\text{credit hour}}\right)$$

$$= \$37,500/\text{class}$$

$$\text{Value of inputs} = \text{Labor} + \text{Materials} + \text{Overhead}$$

$$= \$4,000 + (\$20/\text{student} \times 50 \text{ students/class}) + \$25,000$$

$$= \$30,000/\text{class}$$

$$\frac{\text{Multifactor}}{\text{productivity}} = \frac{\text{Output}}{\text{Input}} = \frac{\$37,500/\text{class}}{\$30,000/\text{class}} = \textbf{1.25}$$

b. Labor productivity is the ratio of the value of output to labor hours. The value of output is the same as in part (a), or $37,500/class, so

$$\text{Labor hours of input} = \left(\frac{14 \text{ hours}}{\text{week}}\right)\left(\frac{16 \text{ weeks}}{\text{class}}\right) = 224 \text{ hours/class}$$

$$\text{Labor productivity} = \frac{\text{Output}}{\text{Input}} = \frac{\$37,500/\text{class}}{224 \text{ hours/class}}$$

$$= \textbf{\$167.41}/\text{hour}$$

Solved Problem 2

Natalie Attire makes fashionable garments. During a particular week, employees worked 360 hours to produce a batch of 132 garments, of which 52 were "seconds" (meaning that they were flawed). Seconds are sold for $90 each at Attire's Factory Outlet Store. The remaining 80 garments are sold to retail distribution at $200 each. What is the *labor* productivity ratio of this manufacturing process?

SOLUTION

$$\text{Value of output} = (52 \text{ defective} \times \$90 / \text{defective}) + (80 \text{ garments} \times \$200 / \text{garment})$$

$$= \$20,680$$

$$\text{Labor hours of input} = 360 \text{ hours}$$

$$\text{Labor productivity} = \frac{\text{Output}}{\text{Input}} = \frac{\$20,680}{360 \text{ hours}}$$

$$= \$57.44 \text{ in sales per hour}$$

Discussion Questions

1. Consider your last (or current) job.

   a. What activities did you perform?

   b. Who were your customers (internal and external), and how did you interact with them?

   c. How could you measure the customer value you were adding by performing your activities?

   d. Was your position in accounting, finance, human resources, management information systems, marketing, operations, or other? Explain.

2. Consider amazon.com, whose Web site enjoys millions of "hits" each day and puts customers in touch with millions of services and products. What are amazon.com's competitive priorities and what should its operations strategy focus on?

3. A local hospital declares that it is committed to provide *care* to patients arriving at the emergency unit in less than 15 minutes and that it will never turn away patients who need to be hospitalized for further medical care. What implications does this commitment have for strategic operations management decisions (i.e., decisions relating to capacity and workforce)?

4. FedEx built its business on quick, dependable delivery of items being shipped by air from one business to another. Its early advantages included global tracking of shipments using Web technology. The advancement of Internet technology enabled competitors to become much more sophisticated in order tracking. In addition, the advent of Web-based businesses put pressure on increased ground transportation deliveries. Explain how this change in the environment has affected FedEx's operations strategy, especially relative to UPS, which has a strong hold on the business-to-consumer ground delivery business.

5. Suppose that you were conducting a market analysis for a new textbook about technology management. What would you need to know to identify a market segment? How would you make a needs assessment? What should be the collection of services and products?

6. Although all nine of the competitive priorities discussed in this chapter are relevant to a company's success in the marketplace, explain why a company should not necessarily try to excel in all of them. What determines the choice of the competitive priorities that a company should emphasize for its key processes?

7. Choosing which processes are core to a firm's competitive position is a key strategic decision. For example, Nike, a popular sports shoe company, focuses on the customer relationship, new product development, and supplier relationship processes and leaves the order fulfillment process to others. Allen Edmonds, a top-quality shoe company, considers all four processes to be core processes. What considerations would you make in determining which processes should be core to your manufacturing company?

8. A local fast-food restaurant processes several customer orders at once. Service clerks cross paths, sometimes nearly colliding, while they trace different paths to fill customer orders. If customers order a special combination of toppings on their hamburgers, they must wait quite some time while the special order is cooked. How would you modify the restaurant's operations to achieve competitive advantage? Because demand surges at lunchtime, volume flexibility is a competitive priority in the fast-food business. How would you achieve volume flexibility?

9. Kathryn Shoemaker established Grandmother's Chicken Restaurant in Middlesburg 5 years ago. It features a unique recipe for chicken, "just like grandmother used to make." The facility is homey, with relaxed and friendly service. Business has been good during the past 2 years, for both lunch and dinner. Customers normally wait about 15 minutes to be served, although complaints about service delays have increased recently. Shoemaker is currently considering whether to expand the current facility or open a similar restaurant in neighboring Uniontown, which has been growing rapidly.

   a. What types of strategic plans must Shoemaker make?

   b. What environmental forces could be at work in Middlesburg and Uniontown that Shoemaker should consider?

   c. What are the possible distinctive competencies of Grandmother's?

10. Wild West, Inc., is a regional telephone company that inherited nearly 100,000 employees and 50,000 retirees from AT&T. Wild West has a new mission: to diversify. It calls for a 10-year effort to enter the financial services, real estate, cable TV, home shopping, entertainment, and cellular communication services markets—and to compete with other telephone companies. Wild West plans to provide cellular and fiber-optic communications services in markets with established competitors, such as the United Kingdom, and in markets with essentially no competition, such as Russia and former Eastern Bloc countries.

    a. What types of strategic plans must Wild West make? Is the "do-nothing" option viable? If Wild West's mission appears too broad, which businesses would you trim first?

b. What environmental forces could be at work that Wild West should consider?

c. What are the possible core competencies of Wild West? What weaknesses should it avoid or mitigate?

11. You are designing a grocery delivery business. Via the Internet, your company will offer staples and frozen foods in a large metropolitan area and then deliver them within a customer-defined window of time. You plan to partner with two major food stores in the area. What should be your competitive priorities and what capabilities do you want to develop in your core and support processes?

Problems

The OM Explorer and POM for Windows software is available to all students using the 11th edition of this textbook. Go to **http://www.pearsonhighered.com/krajewski** to download these computer packages. If you purchased MyOMLab, you also have access to Active Models software and significant help in doing the following problems. Check with your instructor on how best to use these resources. In many cases, the instructor wants you to understand how to do the calculations by hand. At the least, the software provides a check on your calculations. When calculations are particularly complex and the goal is interpreting the results in making decision, the software entirely replaces the manual calculations.

Addressing the Trends and Challenges in Operations Management

1. (Refer to Solved Problem 1.) Coach Bjourn Toulouse led the Big Red Herrings to several disappointing football seasons. Only better recruiting will return the Big Red Herrings to winning form. Because of the current state of the program, Boehring University fans are unlikely to support increases in the $192 season ticket price. Improved recruitment will increase overhead costs to $30,000 per class section from the current $25,000 per class section. The university's budget plan is to cover recruitment costs by increasing the average class size to 75 students. Labor costs will increase to $6,500 per 3-credit course. Material costs will be about $25 per student for each 3-credit course. Tuition will be $200 per semester credit, which is supplemented by state support of $100 per semester credit.

a. What is the multifactor productivity ratio? Compared to the result obtained in Solved Problem 1, did productivity increase or decrease for the course process?

b. If instructors work an average of 20 hours per week for 16 weeks for each 3-credit class of 75 students, what is the *labor* productivity ratio?

2. Suds and Duds Laundry washed and pressed the following numbers of dress shirts per week.

Week	Work Crew	Total Hours	Shirts
1	Sud and Dud	24	68
2	Sud and Jud	46	130
3	Sud, Dud, and Jud	62	152
4	Sud, Dud, and Jud	51	125
5	Dud and Jud	45	131

a. Calculate the *labor* productivity ratio for each week.

b. Explain the labor productivity pattern exhibited by the data.

3. White Tiger Electronics produces CD players using an automated assembly line process. The standard cost of CD players is $150 per unit (labor, $30; materials, $70; and overhead, $50). The sales price is $300 per unit.

a. To achieve a 10 percent multifactor productivity improvement by reducing materials costs only, by what percentage must these costs be reduced?

b. To achieve a 10 percent multifactor productivity improvement by reducing labor costs only, by what percentage must these costs be reduced?

c. To achieve a 10 percent multifactor productivity improvement by reducing overhead costs only, by what percentage must these costs be reduced?

4. At Symtecks, the output of a specific process is valued at $100 per unit. The cost of labor is $50 per hour including benefits. The accounting department provided the following information about the process for the past four weeks:

	Week 1	Week 2	Week 3	Week 4
Units Produced	1,124	1,310	1,092	981
Labor ($)	12,735	14,842	10,603	9,526
Material ($)	21,041	24,523	20,442	18,364
Overhead ($)	8,992	10,480	8,736	7,848

a. Use the multifactor productivity ratio to see whether recent process improvements had any effect and, if so, when the effect was noticeable.

b. Has labor productivity changed? Use the labor productivity ratio to support your answer.

5. Alyssa's Custom Cakes currently sells 5 birthday, 2 wedding, and 3 specialty cakes each month for $50, $150, and $100 each, respectively. The cost of labor is $50 per hour including benefits. It takes 90 minutes to produce a birthday cake, 240 minutes to produce a wedding cake, and 60 minutes to produce a specialty cake. Alyssa's current multifactor productivity ratio is 1.25.

a. Use the multifactor productivity ratio provided to calculate the average cost of the cakes produced.

b. Calculate Alyssa's labor productivity ratio in dollars per hour for each type of cake.

c. Based solely on the labor productivity ratio, which cake should Alyssa try to sell the most?

d. Based on your answer in part (a), is there a type of cake Alyssa should stop selling?

6. The Big Black Bird Company (BBBC) has a large order for special plastic-lined military uniforms to be used in an urgent military operation. Working the normal two shifts of 40 hours each per week, the BBBC production process usually produces 2,500 uniforms per week at a standard cost of $120 each. Seventy employees work the first shift and 30 employees work the second. The contract price is $200 per uniform. Because of the urgent need, BBBC is authorized to use around-the-clock production, 6 days per week. When each of the two shifts works 72 hours per week, production increases to 4,000 uniforms per week but at a cost of $144 each.

a. Did the multifactor productivity ratio increase, decrease, or remain the same? If it changed, by what percentage did it change?

b. Did the labor productivity ratio increase, decrease, or remain the same? If it changed, by what percentage did it change?

c. Did weekly profits increase, decrease, or remain the same?

7. Mack's guitar fabrication shop produces low-cost, highly durable guitars for beginners. Typically, out of the 100 guitars that begin production each month, only 80 percent are considered good enough to sell. The other 20 percent are scrapped due to quality problems that are identified after they have completed the production process. Each guitar sells for $250. Because some of the production process is automated, each guitar only requires 10 labor hours. Each employee works an average 160 hours per month. Labor is paid at $10/hour, materials cost is $40/guitar, and overhead is $4,000.

a. Calculate the labor and multifactor productivity ratios.

b. After some study, the operations manager Darren Funk recommends three options to improve the company's multifactor productivity: (1) increase the sales price by 10 percent, (2) improve quality so that only 10 percent are defective, or (3) reduce labor, material, and overhead costs by 10 percent. Which option has the greatest impact on the multifactor productivity measure?

8. Mariah Enterprises makes a variety of consumer electronic products. Its camera manufacturing plant is considering choosing between two different processes, named Alpha and Beta, which can be used to make two component parts A and B. To make the correct decision, the managers would like to compare the labor and multifactor productivity of process Alpha with that of process Beta. The value of process output for component A and B are $175 and $140 per unit, respectively. The corresponding overhead costs are $6,000 and $5,000, respectively.

Product	PROCESS ALPHA A	PROCESS ALPHA B	PROCESS BETA A	PROCESS BETA B
Output (units)	50	60	30	80
Labor ($)	$1,200	$1,400	$1,000	$2,000
Material ($)	$2,500	$3,000	$1,400	$3,500

a. Which process, Alpha or Beta, is more productive?

b. What conclusions can you draw from your analysis?

9. The Morning Brew Coffee Shop sells Regular, Cappuccino, and Vienna blends of coffee. The shop's current daily labor cost is $320, the equipment cost is $125, and the overhead cost is $225. Daily demands, along with selling price and material costs per beverage, are given below.

	Regular Coffee	Cappuccino	Vienna Coffee
Beverages sold	350	100	150
Price per beverage	$2.00	$3.00	$4.00
Material ($)	$0.50	$0.75	$1.25

Harald Luckerbauer, the manager at Morning Brew Coffee Shop, would like to understand how adding Eiskaffee (a German coffee beverage of chilled coffee, milk, sweetener, and vanilla ice cream) will alter the shop's productivity. His market research shows that Eiskaffee will bring in new customers and not cannibalize current demand. Assuming that the new equipment is purchased before Eiskaffee is added to the menu, Harald has developed new average daily demand and cost projections. The new equipment cost is $200, and the overhead cost is $350. Modified daily demands, as well as selling price and material costs per beverage for the new product line, are given below.

	Regular Coffee	Cappuccino	Vienna Coffee	Eiskaffee
Beverages sold	350	100	150	75
Price per beverage	$2.00	$3.00	$4.00	$5.00
Material ($)	$0.50	$0.75	$1.25	$1.50

a. Calculate the change in labor and multifactor productivity if Eiskaffee is added to the menu.

b. If everything else remains unchanged, how many units of Eiskaffee would have to be sold to ensure that the multifactor productivity increases from its current level?

Active Model Exercise

This Active Model appears in MyOMLab. It allows you to evaluate the important elements of labor productivity.

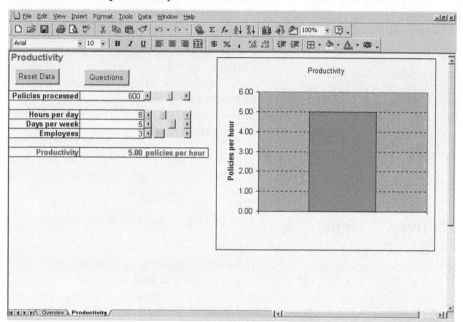

◄ **ACTIVE MODEL 1.1**
Labor Productivity Using Data from Example 1.1

QUESTIONS

1. If the insurance company can process 60 (10 percent) more policies per week, by what percentage will the productivity measure rise?

2. Suppose the 8-hour day includes a 45-minute lunch. What is the revised productivity measure, excluding lunch?

3. If an employee is hired, what will be the weekly number of policies processed if the productivity of five policies per hour is maintained?

4. Suppose that, during the summer, the company works for only 4 days per week. What will be the weekly number of policies processed if the productivity of five policies per hour is maintained?

VIDEO CASE   Using Operations to Create Value at Crayola

Operations processes are at the heart of Crayola, the Easton, Pennsylvania maker of crayons, markers, and paints loved by children of all ages around the world. Since 1903, the company has been taking wax, dyes, and other raw materials and turning them into a colorful array of products sold through an extensive network of distributors and retailers such as Walmart and Target stores. Each day, the company produces 13 million crayons, 2 million markers, 500,000 jars of paint, 170,000 pounds of modeling compounds, and 22,000 Silly Putty© eggs from its three manufacturing plants.

Crayola derives much of its own inspiration and creativity by asking, "What would a kid do?"—especially when focusing on innovation. Not that kids have the knowledge to create complex systems and operational processes. Rather, the question leads to creative solutions by freeing employees to think about the company's competitive priorities in new ways. In the supply chain, the company maintains five "pillars" of operational leadership. These pillars focus attention on differentiating the company on (1) innovation, (2) sustainability, (3) agility and resilience, (4) cost, and (5) quality and ethical responsibility.

The company has a history of innovation. They were the first to introduce an art education program called Dream-Makers, into the nation's elementary schools. Washable markers and crayons also were firsts for the industry and continue to be best-sellers for the company. Recently, the language on crayon paper packaging changed to include three languages—French,

Crayola, headquartered in Pennsylvania, has become a leader in its industry by focusing on operational excellence and innovation.

English and Spanish—instead of one. This change alone saved $400,000 in paper and printing costs since the packaging could now be used across multiple markets.

In the area of sustainability, Crayola built a solar farm on a 20-acre site adjacent to its manufacturing plant in Easton. The farm produces enough energy to completely run the plant as well as the headquarters building nearby. The 850 million colored pencils produced each year only use reforested wood, with one tree planted for every tree harvested. Sourcing for paraffin wax used in crayons recently moved from Louisiana to western Pennsylvania, saving 5,000 barrels of oil annually related to wax transportation. All plastic components are made with recycled plastics. And any excess wax from the production of crayons is reintroduced into the manufacturing process so no waste is produced.

The company is aggressively pursuing new markets outside the United States. China's market of children ages 0–14 is larger than all the other global markets combined, with more than half the world's child population. Yet only 14 percent of the company's total sales come from international markets. So, particular attention is being devoted to growing the company's

manufacturing and distribution presences there. As you can imagine, this means operations managers must think about how to grow the current supply chain beyond the boundaries of existing domestic and international borders if additional expansion is to occur.

QUESTIONS

1. Map Crayola's five pillars of operational leadership to the competitive priorities in Table 1.3.
2. Create an assessment of Crayola's competitive priorities as it relates to their Asian expansion plans.
3. Which of the competitive priorities might present the biggest challenge to Crayola as it expands internationally?

CASE | Chad's Creative Concepts

Chad's Creative Concepts designs and manufactures wood furniture. Founded by Chad Thomas on the banks of Lake Erie in Sandusky, Ohio, the company began by producing custom-made wooden furniture for vacation cabins located along the coast of Lake Erie and on nearby Kelly's Island and Bass Island. Being an "outdoors" type himself, Thomas originally wanted to bring "a bit of the outdoors" inside. Chad's Creative Concepts developed a solid reputation for creative designs and high-quality workmanship. Sales eventually encompassed the entire Great Lakes region. Along with growth came additional opportunities.

Traditionally, the company focused entirely on custom-made furniture, with the customer specifying the kind of wood from which the piece would be made. As the company's reputation grew and sales increased, the sales force began selling some of the more popular pieces to retail furniture outlets. This move into retail outlets led Chad's Creative Concepts into the production of a more standard line of furniture. Buyers of this line were much more price-sensitive and imposed more stringent delivery requirements than did clients for the custom line. Custom-designed furniture, however, continued to dominate sales, accounting for 60 percent of volume and 75 percent of dollar sales. Currently, the company operates a single manufacturing process in Sandusky, where both custom furniture and standard furniture are manufactured. The equipment is mainly general purpose in nature to provide the flexibility needed for producing custom pieces of furniture. The layout puts together saws in one section of the facility, lathes in another, and so on. The quality of the finished product reflects the quality of the wood chosen and the craftsmanship of individual workers. Both custom and standard furniture compete for processing time on the same equipment by the same craftspeople.

During the past few months, sales of the standard line steadily increased, leading to more regular scheduling of this product line. However,

when scheduling trade-offs had to be made, custom furniture was always given priority because of its higher sales and profit margins. Thus, scheduled lots of standard furniture pieces were left sitting around the plant in various stages of completion.

As he reviews the progress of Chad's Creative Concepts, Thomas is pleased to note that the company has grown. Sales of custom furniture remain strong, and sales of standard pieces are steadily increasing. However, finance and accounting indicate that profits are not what they should be. Costs associated with the standard line are rising. Dollars are being tied up in inventory, both in raw materials and work-in-process. Expensive public warehouse space has to be rented to accommodate the inventory volume. Thomas also is concerned with increased lead times for both custom and standard orders, which are causing longer promised delivery times. Capacity is being pushed, and no space is left in the plant for expansion. Thomas begins a careful assessment of the overall impact that the new standard line is having on his manufacturing process.

QUESTIONS

1. What types of decisions must Chad Thomas make daily for his company's operations to run effectively? Over the long run?
2. How did sales and marketing affect operations when they began to sell standard pieces to retail outlets?
3. How has the move to producing standard furniture affected the company's financial structure?
4. What might Chad Thomas have done differently to avoid some of the problems he now faces?

Source: This case was prepared by Dr. Brooke Saladin, Wake Forest University, as a basis for classroom discussion. Copyright © Brooke Saladin. Reprinted by permission.

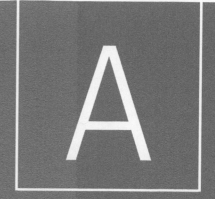
Operations managers make many decisions as they manage processes and supply chains. Although the specifics of each situation vary, decision making generally involves the same basic steps: (1) recognize and clearly define the problem, (2) collect the information needed to analyze possible alternatives, and (3) choose and implement the most feasible alternative.

Sometimes, hard thinking in a quiet room is sufficient. At other times, interacting with others or using more formal procedures are needed. Here, we present four such formal procedures: break-even analysis, the preference matrix, decision theory, and the decision tree.

- Break-even analysis helps the manager identify how much change in volume or demand is necessary before a second alternative becomes better than the first alternative.

- The preference matrix helps a manager deal with multiple criteria that cannot be evaluated with a single measure of merit, such as total profit or cost.

- Decision theory helps the manager choose the best alternative when outcomes are uncertain.

- A decision tree helps the manager when decisions are made sequentially—when today's best decision depends on tomorrow's decisions and events.

Break-Even Analysis

To evaluate an idea for a new service or product, or to assess the performance of an existing one, determining the volume of sales at which the service or product breaks even is useful. The **break-even quantity** is the volume at which total revenues equal total costs. Use of this technique is known as **break-even analysis**. Break-even analysis can also be used to compare processes by finding the volume at which two different processes have equal total costs.

break-even quantity

The volume at which total revenues equal total costs.

break-even analysis

The use of the break-even quantity; it can be used to compare processes by finding the volume at which two different processes have equal total costs.

LEARNING GOALS *After reading this supplement, you should be able to:*

1. Explain break-even analysis, using both the graphic and algebraic approaches.

2. Define and construct a preference matrix.

3. Explain how decision theory can be used to make decisions under conditions of certainty, uncertainty, and risk.

4. Describe how to draw and analyze a decision tree.

A manager is doing some hard thinking and analysis on his computer before reaching a final decision.

Evaluating Services or Products

We begin with the first purpose: to evaluate the profit potential of a new or existing service or product. This technique helps the manager answer questions, such as the following:

- Is the predicted sales volume of the service or product sufficient to break even (neither earning a profit nor sustaining a loss)?
- How low must the variable cost per unit be to break even, based on current prices and sales forecasts?
- How low must the fixed cost be to break even?
- How do price levels affect the break-even volume?

Break-even analysis is based on the assumption that all costs related to the production of a specific service or product can be divided into two categories: (1) variable costs and (2) fixed costs.

The **variable cost**, c, is the portion of the total cost that varies directly with volume of output: costs per unit for materials, labor, and usually some fraction of overhead. If we let Q equal the number of customers served or units produced per year, total variable cost = cQ. The **fixed cost**, F, is the portion of the total cost that remains constant regardless of changes in levels of output: the annual cost of renting or buying new equipment and facilities (including depreciation, interest, taxes, and insurance); salaries; utilities; and portions of the sales or advertising budget. Thus, the total cost of producing a service or good equals fixed costs plus variable costs multiplied by volume, or

$$\text{Total cost} = F + cQ$$

The variable cost per unit is assumed to be the same no matter how small or large Q is, and thus, total cost is linear. If we assume that all units produced are sold, total annual revenues equal revenue per unit sold, p, multiplied by the quantity sold, or

$$\text{Total revenue} = pQ$$

If we set total revenue equal to total cost, we get the break-even quantity point as

$$pQ = F + cQ$$
$$(p - c)Q = F$$
$$Q = \frac{F}{p - c}$$

variable cost

The portion of the total cost that varies directly with volume of output.

fixed cost

The portion of the total cost that remains constant regardless of changes in levels of output.

We can also find this break-even quantity graphically. Because both costs and revenues are linear relationships, the break-even quantity is where the total revenue line crosses the total cost line.

EXAMPLE A.1	Finding the Break-Even Quantity

A hospital is considering a new procedure to be offered at $200 per patient. The fixed cost per year would be $100,000, with total variable costs of $100 per patient. What is the break-even quantity for this service? Use both algebraic and graphic approaches to get the answer.

SOLUTION

The formula for the break-even quantity yields

$$Q = \frac{F}{p - c} = \frac{100,000}{200 - 100} = 1,000 \text{ patients}$$

To solve graphically we plot two lines: one for costs and one for revenues. Two points determine a line, so we begin by calculating costs and revenues for two different output levels. The following table shows the results for $Q = 0$ and $Q = 2,000$. We selected zero as the first point because of the ease of plotting total revenue (0) and total cost (F). However, we could have used any two reasonably spaced output levels.

Quantity (patients) (Q)	Total Annual Cost ($) (100,000 + 100$Q$)	Total Annual Revenue ($) (200$Q$)
0	100,000	0
2,000	300,000	400,000

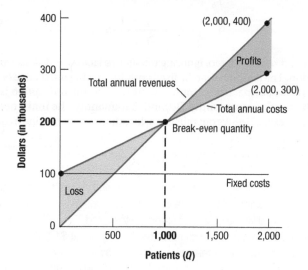

◀ **FIGURE A.1**
Graphic Approach to
Break-Even Analysis

We can now draw the cost line through points (0, 100,000) and (2,000, 300,000). The revenue line goes between (0, 0) and (2,000, 400,000). As Figure A.1 indicates, these two lines intersect at 1,000 patients, the break-even quantity.

DECISION POINT
Management expects the number of patients needing the new procedure will exceed the 1,000-patient break-even quantity but first wants to learn how sensitive the decision is to demand levels before making a final choice.

Break-even analysis cannot tell a manager whether to pursue a new service or product idea or drop an existing line. The technique can only show what is likely to happen for various forecasts of costs and sales volumes. To evaluate a variety of "what-if" questions, we use an approach called **sensitivity analysis**, a technique for systematically changing parameters in a model to determine the effects of such changes. The concept can be applied later to other techniques, such as linear programming. Here we assess the sensitivity of total profit to different pricing strategies, sales volume forecasts, or cost estimates.

sensitivity analysis
A technique for systematically changing parameters in a model to determine the effects of such changes.

EXAMPLE A.2	**Sensitivity Analysis of Sales Forecasts**

If the most pessimistic sales forecast for the proposed service in Figure A.1 were 1,500 patients, what would be the procedure's total contribution to profit and overhead per year?

SOLUTION
The graph shows that even the pessimistic forecast lies above the break-even volume, which is encouraging. The procedure's total contribution, found by subtracting total costs from total revenues, is

$$pQ - (F + cQ) = 200(1,500) - [100,000 + 100(1,500)]$$
$$= \$50,000$$

DECISION POINT
Even with the pessimistic forecast, the new procedure contributes $50,000 per year. After evaluating the proposal with the present value method (see MyOMLab Supplement F), management added the new procedure to the hospital's services.

MyOMLab

Evaluating Processes

Often, choices must be made between two processes or between an internal process and buying services or materials on the outside. In such cases, we assume that the decision does not affect revenues. The manager must study all the costs and advantages of each approach. Rather than find the quantity at which total costs equal total revenues, the analyst finds the quantity for which the total costs for two alternatives are equal. For the make-or-buy decision, it is the quantity for which the total "buy" cost equals the total "make" cost. Let F_b equal the fixed cost (per year) of the buy option, F_m equal the fixed cost of the make option, c_b equal the variable cost (per unit) of the buy option, and c_m equal the variable cost of the make option. Thus, the total cost to buy is $F_b + c_b Q$ and the total cost to make is $F_m + c_m Q$. To find the break-even quantity, we set the two cost functions equal and solve for Q:

$$F_b + c_b Q = F_m + c_m Q$$

$$Q = \frac{F_m - F_b}{c_b - c_m}$$

The make option should be considered, ignoring qualitative factors, only if its variable costs are lower than those of the buy option. The reason is that the fixed costs for making the service or product are typically higher than the fixed costs for buying. Under these circumstances, the buy option is better if production volumes are less than the break-even quantity. Beyond that quantity, the make option becomes better. Chapter 12, "Supply Chain Design," brings out other considerations when making make-or-buy decisions.

EXAMPLE A.3	**Break-Even Analysis for Make-or-Buy Decisions**

MyOMLab

Active Model A.2 in MyOMLab provides additional insight on this make-or-buy example and its extensions.

The manager of a fast-food restaurant featuring hamburgers is adding salads to the menu. For each of the two new options, the price to the customer will be the same. The make option is to install a salad bar stocked with vegetables, fruits, and toppings and let the customer assemble the salad. The salad bar would have to be leased and a part-time employee hired. The manager estimates the fixed costs at $12,000 and variable costs totaling $1.50 per salad. The buy option is to have preassembled salads available for sale. They would be purchased from a local supplier at $2.00 per salad. Offering preassembled salads would require installation and operation of additional refrigeration, with an annual fixed cost of $2,400. The manager expects to sell 25,000 salads per year. What is the make-or-buy quantity?

MyOMLab

Tutor A.2 in MyOMLab provides a new example to practice break-even analysis on make-or-buy decisions.

SOLUTION

The formula for the break-even quantity yields the following:

$$Q = \frac{F_m - F_b}{c_b - c_m}$$

$$= \frac{12,000 - 2,400}{2.0 - 1.5} = 19,200 \text{ salads}$$

FIGURE A.2 ▶
Break-Even Analysis Solver of OM Explorer for Example A.3

	Process 1	Process 2
Fixed costs (F)	$12,000	$2,400
Variable costs (c)	$1.50	$2.00
Expected demand	25,000	
Break-even quantity	19,200.0	

Decision: Process 1

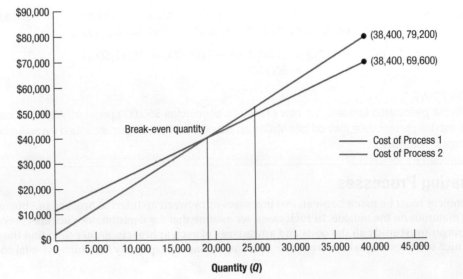

Figure A.2 shows the solution from OM Explorer's *Break-Even Analysis* Solver. The break-even quantity is 19,200 salads. As the 25,000-salad sales forecast exceeds this amount, the make option is preferred. Only if the restaurant expected to sell fewer than 19,200 salads would the buy option be better.

DECISION POINT

Management chose the make option after considering other qualitative factors, such as customer preferences and demand uncertainty. A deciding factor was that the 25,000-salad sales forecast is well above the 19,200-salad break-even quantity.

Ministr-84/Shutterstock

A drive-through only restaurant that does not have seating capacity will have lower fixed costs than a full service restaurant, and therefore will need a lower number of customers to reach the break-even point.

Preference Matrix

Decisions often must be made in situations where multiple criteria cannot be naturally merged into a single measure (such as dollars). For example, a manager deciding in which of two cities to locate a new plant would have to consider such unquantifiable factors as quality of life, worker attitudes toward work, and community reception in the two cities. These important factors cannot be ignored. A **preference matrix** is a table that allows the manager to rate an alternative according to several performance criteria. The criteria can be scored on any scale, such as from 1 (worst possible) to 10 (best possible) or from 0 to 1, as long as the same scale is applied to all the alternatives being compared. Each score is weighted according to its perceived importance, with the total of these weights typically equaling 100. The total score is the sum of the weighted scores (weight $\times$ score) for all the criteria. The manager can compare the scores for alternatives against one another or against a predetermined threshold. We use the preference matrix technique extensively in this text to address decisions where there are qualitative, as well as quantitative, factors to consider.

preference matrix

A table that allows the manager to rate an alternative according to several performance criteria.

EXAMPLE A.4	Evaluating an Alternative with a Preference Matrix

The following table shows the performance criteria, weights, and scores (1 = worst, 10 = best) for a new product: a thermal storage air conditioner. If management wants to introduce just one new product and the highest total score of any of the other product ideas is 800, should the firm pursue making the air conditioner?

MyOMLab

Tutor A.3 in MyOMLab provides a new example to practice with preference matrixes.

Performance Criterion	Weight (*A*)	Score (*B*)	Weighted Score (*A* $\times$ *B*)
Market potential	30	8	240
Unit profit margin	20	10	200
Operations compatibility	20	6	120
Competitive advantage	15	10	150
Investment requirement	10	2	20
Project risk	5	4	20
			Weighted score = 750

SOLUTION

Because the sum of the weighted scores is 750, it falls short of the score of 800 for another product. This result is confirmed by the output from OM Explorer's *Preference Matrix* Solver in Figure A.3.

	Insert a Criterion	Add a Criterion	Remove a Criterion

	Weight (A)	Score (B)	Weighted Score (A x B)
Market potential	30	8	240
Unit profit margin	20	10	200
Operations compatability	20	6	120
Competitive advantage	15	10	150
Investment requirement	10	2	20
Project risk	5	4	20

Final Weighted Score   750

DECISION POINT

Management should drop the thermal storage air-conditioner idea. Another new product idea is better, considering the multiple criteria, and management only wanted to introduce one new product at the time.

Not all managers are comfortable with the preference matrix technique. It requires the manager to state criteria weights before examining the alternatives, although the proper weights may not be readily apparent. Perhaps, only after seeing the scores for several alternatives can the manager decide what is important and what is not. Because a low score on one criterion can be compensated for or overridden by high scores on others, the preference matrix method also may cause managers to ignore important signals. In Example A.4, the investment required for the thermal storage air conditioner might exceed the firm's financial capability. In that case, the manager should not even be considering the alternative no matter how high its score.

Decision Theory

Decision theory is a general approach to decision making when the outcomes associated with alternatives are often in doubt. It helps operations managers with decisions on process, capacity, location, and inventory because such decisions are about an uncertain future. Decision theory can also be used by managers in other functional areas. With decision theory, a manager makes choices using the following process:

decision theory

A general approach to decision making when the outcomes associated with alternatives are often in doubt.

1. List the feasible *alternatives*. One alternative that should always be considered as a basis for reference is to do nothing. A basic assumption is that the number of alternatives is finite. For example, in deciding where to locate a new retail store in a certain part of the city, a manager could theoretically consider every grid coordinate on the city's map. Realistically, however, the manager must narrow the number of choices to a reasonable number.

2. List the *events* (sometimes called *chance events* or *states of nature*) that have an impact on the outcome of the choice but are not under the manager's control. For example, the demand experienced by the new facility could be low or high, depending not only on whether the location is convenient to many customers but also on what the competition does and general retail trends. Then, group events into reasonable categories. For example, suppose that the average number of sales per day could be anywhere from 1 to 500. Rather than have 500 events, the manager could represent demand with just three events: 100 sales/day, 300 sales/day, or 500 sales/day. The events must be mutually exclusive and collectively exhaustive, meaning that they do not overlap and that they cover all eventualities.

payoff table

A table that shows the amount for each alternative if each possible event occurs.

MyOMLab

3. Calculate the *payoff* for each alternative in each event. Typically, the payoff is total profit or total cost. These payoffs can be entered into a **payoff table**, which shows the amount for each alternative if each possible event occurs. For three alternatives and four events, the table would have 12 payoffs (3 × 4). If significant distortions will occur if the time value of money is not recognized, the payoffs should be expressed as present values or internal rates of return (see MyOMLab Supplement F.) For multiple criteria with important qualitative factors, use the weighted scores of a preference matrix approach as the payoffs.

4. Estimate the likelihood of each event, using past data, executive opinion, or other forecasting methods. Express it as a *probability*, making sure that the probabilities sum to 1.0. Develop probability estimates from past data if the past is considered a good indicator of the future.

5. Select a *decision rule* to evaluate the alternatives, such as choosing the alternative with the lowest expected cost. The rule chosen depends on the amount of information the manager has on the event probabilities and the manager's attitudes toward risk.

Using this process, we examine decisions under three different situations: certainty, uncertainty, and risk.

Decision Making under Certainty

The simplest situation is when the manager knows which event will occur. Here the decision rule is to pick the alternative with the best payoff for the known event. The best alternative is the highest payoff if the payoffs are expressed as profits. If the payoffs are expressed as costs, the best alternative is the lowest payoff.

EXAMPLE A.5	Decisions under Certainty

A manager is deciding whether to build a small or a large facility. Much depends on the future demand that the facility must serve, and demand may be small or large. The manager knows with certainty the payoffs that will result under each alternative, shown in the following payoff table. The payoffs (in $000) are the present values of future revenues minus costs for each alternative in each event.

	POSSIBLE FUTURE DEMAND	
Alternative	**Low**	**High**
Small facility	200	270
Large facility	160	800
Do nothing	0	0

What is the best choice if future demand will be low?

SOLUTION

In this example, the best choice is the one with the highest payoff. If the manager knows that future demand will be low, the company should build a small facility and enjoy a payoff of $200,000. The larger facility has a payoff of only $160,000. The "do nothing" alternative is dominated by the other alternatives; that is, the outcome of one alternative is no better than the outcome of another alternative for each event. Because the "do nothing" alternative is dominated, the manager does not consider it further.

DECISION POINT

If management really knows future demand, it would build the small facility if demand will be low and the large facility if demand will be high. If demand is uncertain, it should consider other decision rules.

Decision Making under Uncertainty

Here, we assume that the manager can list the possible events but cannot estimate their probabilities. Perhaps, a lack of prior experience makes it difficult for the firm to estimate probabilities. In such a situation, the manager can use one of four decision rules:

1. *Maximin.* Choose the alternative that is the "best of the worst." This rule is for the *pessimist*, who anticipates the "worst case" for each alternative.

2. *Maximax.* Choose the alternative that is the "best of the best." This rule is for the *optimist* who has high expectations and prefers to "go for broke."

3. *Laplace.* Choose the alternative with the best *weighted payoff*. To find the weighted payoff, give equal importance (or, alternatively, equal probability) to each event. If there are n events, the importance (or probability) of each is $1/n$, so they add up to 1.0. This rule is for the *realist*.

4. *Minimax Regret.* Choose the alternative with the best "worst regret." Calculate a table of regrets (or opportunity losses), in which the rows represent the alternatives and the columns represent the events. A regret is the difference between a given payoff and the best payoff in the same column. For an event, it shows how much is lost by picking an alternative to the one that is best for this event. The regret can be lost profit or increased cost, depending on the situation.

EXAMPLE A.6	Decisions under Uncertainty

MyOMLab

Tutor A.4 in MyOMLab provides a new example to make decisions under uncertainty.

Reconsider the payoff matrix in Example A.5. What is the best alternative for each decision rule?

SOLUTION

a. *Maximin.* An alternative's worst payoff is the *lowest* number in its row of the payoff matrix because the payoffs are profits. The worst payoffs ($000) are

Alternative	Worst Payoff
Small facility	200
Large facility	160

The best of these worst numbers is $200,000, so the pessimist would build a small facility.

b. *Maximax.* An alternative's best payoff ($000) is the *highest* number in its row of the payoff matrix, or

Alternative	Best Payoff
Small facility	270
Large facility	800

The best of these best numbers is $800,000, so the optimist would build a large facility.

c. *Laplace.* With two events, we assign each a probability of 0.5. Thus, the weighted payoffs ($000) are

Alternative	Weighted Payoff
Small facility	$0.5(200) + 0.5(270) = \textbf{235}$
Large facility	$0.5(160) + 0.5(800) = \textbf{480}$

The best of these weighted payoffs is $480,000, so the realist would build a large facility.

d. *Minimax Regret.* If demand turns out to be low, the best alternative is a small facility and its regret is 0 (or 200 − 200). If a large facility is built when demand turns out to be low, the regret is 40 (or 200 − 160).

Alternative	REGRET		Maximum Regret
	Low Demand	High Demand	
Small facility	$200 - 200 = \textbf{0}$	$800 - 270 = \textbf{530}$	530
Large facility	$200 - 160 = \textbf{40}$	$800 - 800 = \textbf{0}$	40

The column on the right shows the worst regret for each alternative. To minimize the maximum regret, pick a large facility. The biggest regret is associated with having only a small facility and high demand.

DECISION POINT

The pessimist would choose the small facility. The realist, optimist, and manager choosing to minimize the maximum regret would build the large facility.

Decision Making under Risk

Here we assume that the manager can list the events and estimate their probabilities. The manager has less information than with decision making under certainty, but more information than with decision making under uncertainty. For this intermediate situation, the *expected value* decision rule is widely used (both in practice and in this book). The expected value for an alternative is found by weighting each payoff with its associated probability and then adding the weighted payoff scores. The alternative with the best expected value (highest for profits and lowest for costs) is chosen.

This rule is much like the Laplace decision rule, except that the events are no longer assumed to be equally likely (or equally important). The expected value is what the *average* payoff would be if the decision could be repeated time after time. Of course, the expected value decision rule can result in a bad outcome if the wrong event occurs. However, it gives the best results if applied consistently over a long period of time. The rule should not be used if the manager is inclined to avoid risk.

EXAMPLE A.7	Decisions under Risk

Reconsider the payoff matrix in Example A.5. For the expected value decision rule, which is the best alternative if the probability of small demand is estimated to be 0.4 and the probability of large demand is estimated to be 0.6?

MyOMLab

Tutor A.5 in MyOMLab provides a new example to make decisions under risk.

SOLUTION

The expected value for each alternative is as follows:

Alternative	Expected Value
Small facility	$0.4(200) + 0.6(270) =$ **242**
Large facility	$0.4(160) + 0.6(800) =$ **544**

DECISION POINT

Management would choose a large facility if it used this expected value decision rule because it provides the best long-term results if consistently applied over time.

Decision Trees

The decision tree method is a general approach to a wide range of processes and supply chain decisions, such as product planning, process analysis, process capacity, and location. It is particularly valuable for evaluating different capacity expansion alternatives when demand is uncertain and sequential decisions are involved. For example, a company may expand a facility in 2015 only to discover in 2018 that demand is much higher than forecasted. In that case, a second decision may be necessary to determine whether to expand again or build a second facility.

A **decision tree** is a schematic model of alternatives available to the decision maker along with their possible consequences. The name derives from the tree-like appearance of the model. It consists of a number of square *nodes*, representing decision points, which are left by *branches* (which should be read from left to right), representing the alternatives. Branches leaving circular, or chance, nodes represent the events. The probability of each chance event, *P(E)*, is shown above each branch. The probabilities for all branches leaving a chance node must sum to 1.0. The conditional payoff, which is the payoff for each possible alternative–event combination, is shown at the end of each combination. Payoffs are given only at the outset, before the analysis begins, for the end points of each alternative–event combination. In Figure A.4, for example, payoff 1 is the financial outcome the manager expects if alternative 1 is chosen and then chance event 1 occurs.

No payoff can be associated yet with any branches farther to the left, such as alternative 1 as a whole because it is followed by a chance event and is not an end point. Payoffs often are expressed as the present value of net profits. If revenues are not affected by the decision, the payoff is expressed as net costs.

decision tree

A schematic model of alternatives available to the decision maker, along with their possible consequences.

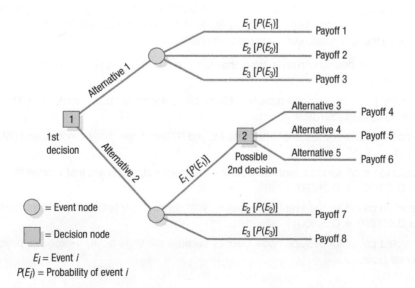

◀ **FIGURE A.4**

A Decision Tree Model

After drawing a decision tree, we solve it by working from right to left, calculating the *expected payoff* for each node as follows:

1. For an event node, we multiply the payoff of each event branch by the event's probability. We add these products to get the event node's expected payoff.

2. For a decision node, we pick the alternative that has the best expected payoff. If an alternative leads to an event node, its payoff is equal to that node's expected payoff (already calculated). We "saw off," or "prune," the other branches not chosen by marking two short lines through them. The decision node's expected payoff is the one associated with the single remaining unpruned branch. We continue this process until the leftmost decision node is reached. The unpruned branch extending from it is the best alternative to pursue. If multistage decisions are involved, we must await subsequent events before deciding what to do next. If new probability or payoff estimates are obtained, we repeat the process.

Various software applications are available for drawing decision trees. PowerPoint can be used to draw decision trees, although it does not have the capability to analyze the decision tree. More extensive capabilities, in addition to POM for Windows, are found with SmartDraw (**http://www.smartdraw .com**), PrecisionTree decision analysis from Palisade Corporation (**http://www.palisade.com**), and TreePlan (**http://www.treeplan.com/treeplan.htm**).

EXAMPLE A.8	Analyzing a Decision Tree

MyOMLab

Active Model A.3 in MyOMLab provides additional insight on this decision tree example and its extensions.

A retailer must decide whether to build a small or a large facility at a new location. Demand at the location can be either low or high, with probabilities estimated to be 0.4 and 0.6, respectively. If a small facility is built and demand proves to be high, the manager may choose not to expand (payoff = $223,000) or to expand (payoff = $270,000). If a small facility is built and demand is low, there is no reason to expand and the payoff is $200,000. If a large facility is built and demand proves to be low, the choice is to do nothing ($40,000) or to stimulate demand through local advertising. The response to advertising may be either modest or sizable, with their probabilities estimated to be 0.3 and 0.7, respectively. If it is modest, the payoff is estimated to be only $20,000; the payoff grows to $220,000 if the response is sizable. Finally, if a large facility is built and demand turns out to be high, the payoff is $800,000.

Draw a decision tree. Then analyze it to determine the expected payoff for each decision and event node. Which alternative—building a small facility or building a large facility—has the higher expected payoff?

SOLUTION

The decision tree in Figure A.5 shows the event probability and the payoff for each of the seven alternative-event combinations. The first decision is whether to build a small or a large facility. Its node is shown first, to the left, because it is the decision the retailer must make now. The second decision node—whether to expand at a later date—is reached only if a small facility is built and demand turns out to be high. Finally, the third decision point—whether to advertise—is reached only if the retailer builds a large facility and demand turns out to be low.

Analysis of the decision tree begins with calculation of the expected payoffs from right to left, shown on Figure A.5 beneath the appropriate event and decision nodes.

1. For the event node dealing with advertising, the expected payoff is 160, or the sum of each event's payoff weighted by its probability $[0.3(20) + 0.7(220)]$.

2. The expected payoff for decision node 3 is 160 because *Advertise* (160) is better than *Do nothing* (40). Prune the *Do nothing* alternative.

3. The payoff for decision node 2 is 270 because *Expand* (270) is better than *Do not expand* (223). Prune *Do not expand*.

4. The expected payoff for the event node dealing with demand, assuming that a small facility is built, is 242 [or $0.4(200) + 0.6(270)$].

5. The expected payoff for the event node dealing with demand, assuming that a large facility is built, is 544 [or $0.4(160) + 0.6(800)$].

6. The expected payoff for decision node 1 is 544 because the large facility's expected payoff is largest. Prune *Small facility*.

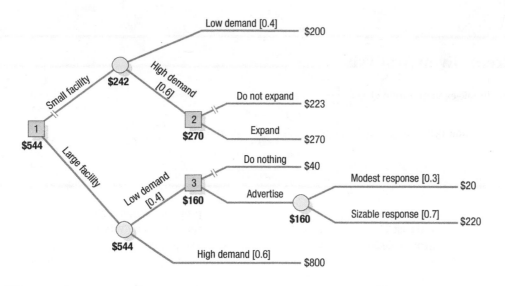

◄ **FIGURE A.5**
Decision Tree for Retailer
(in $000)

MyOMLab Animation

DECISION POINT

The retailer should build the large facility. This initial decision is the only one made now. Subsequent decisions are made after learning whether demand actually is low or high.

LEARNING GOALS IN REVIEW

Learning Goal	Guidelines for Review	MyOMLab Resources
❶ Explain break-even analysis using both the graphic and algebraic approaches.	The section "Break-Even Analysis," pp. 29–33, covers this analysis. Example A.1 and Solved Problem 1 demonstrate both approaches. Example A.3 shows its use in evaluating different processes.	**Active Model Exercises:** A.1: Break-Even Analysis; A.2: Make-or-Buy Decision **OM Explorer Solver:** Break-Even Analysis **OM Explorer Tutors:** A.1: Break-Even Analysis; Evaluating Services and Products; A.2: Break-Even Analysis; Evaluating Processes **POM for Windows:** Break-Even Analysis; Cost-Volume Analysis
❷ Define and construct a preference matrix.	See the section "Preference Matrix," pp. 33–34, for making decisions involving unquantifiable factors, where some factors are rated more important than others. Example A.4 and Solved Problem 2 demonstrate the calculations.	**OM Explorer Solver:** Preference Matrix **OM Explorer Tutor:** A3: Preference Matrix **POM for Windows:** Preference Matrix
❸ Explain how decision theory can be used to make decisions under conditions of certainty, uncertainty, and risk.	The section "Decision Theory," pp. 34–37, begins with the construction of a payoff table that shows the payoff for each feasible alternative and each event. See the table in Example A.5. In addition, the sections "Decision Making under Uncertainty" and "Decision Making under Risk," pp. 36–37, cover these decision rules for when the outcomes associated with alternatives are in doubt. Examples A.6 and A.7 demonstrate how these rules work and so does Solved Problem 3.	**OM Explorer Solver:** Decision Theory **OM Explorer Tutors:** A.4: Decisions under Uncertainty; A.5: Decisions under Risk; A.6: Location Decisions under Uncertainty **POM for Windows:** Decision Tables
❹ Describe how to draw and analyze a decision tree.	The section "Decision Trees," pp. 37–39, shows how to draw and analyze decision trees where several alternatives are available over time. Example A.8 and Solved Problem 4 shows how to work back from right to left, pruning as you go, until the best alternative is found for decision node 1.	**Active Model Exercise:** A.3: Decision Tree **POM for Windows:** Decision Trees (graphical)

Key Equations

Break-Even Analysis

1. Break-even quantity: $Q = \dfrac{F}{p - c}$

2. Evaluating processes, make-or-buy indifference quantity: $Q = \dfrac{F_m - F_b}{c_b - c_m}$

Key Terms

break-even analysis 29
break-even quantity 29
decision theory 34

decision tree 37
fixed cost 30
payoff table 34

preference matrix 33
sensitivity analysis 31
variable cost 30

Solved Problem 1

The owner of a small manufacturing business has patented a new device for washing dishes and cleaning dirty kitchen sinks. Before trying to commercialize the device and add it to his or her existing product line, the owner wants reasonable assurance of success. Variable costs are estimated at $7 per unit produced and sold. Fixed costs are about $56,000 per year.

a. If the selling price is set at $25, how many units must be produced and sold to break even? Use both algebraic and graphic approaches.

b. Forecasted sales for the first year are 10,000 units if the price is reduced to $15. With this pricing strategy, what would be the product's total contribution to profits in the first year?

SOLUTION

a. Beginning with the algebraic approach, we get

$$Q = \frac{F}{p - c} = \frac{56,000}{25 - 7}$$
$$= 3,111 \text{ units}$$

FIGURE A.6 ▶

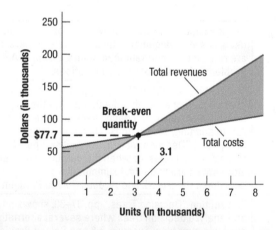

Using the graphic approach, shown in Figure A.6, we first draw two lines:

$$\text{Total revenue} = 25Q$$
$$\text{Total cost} = 56,000 + 7Q$$

The two lines intersect at $Q = 3,111$ units, the break-even quantity.

b. Total profit contribution = Total revenue − Total cost

$$= pQ - (F + cQ)$$
$$= 15(10,000) - [56,000 + 7(10,000)]$$
$$= \$24,000$$

Solved Problem 2

Herron Company is screening three new product ideas: A, B, and C. Resource constraints allow only one of them to be commercialized. The performance criteria and ratings, on a scale of 1 (worst) to 10 (best), are shown in the following table. The Herron managers give equal weights to the performance criteria. Which is the best alternative, as indicated by the preference matrix method?

MyOMLab Video

Performance Criterion	RATING		
	Product A	Product B	Product C
1. Demand uncertainty and project risk	3	9	2
2. Similarity to present products	7	8	6
3. Expected return on investment (ROI)	10	4	8
4. Compatibility with current manufacturing process	4	7	6
5. Competitive advantage	4	6	5

SOLUTION

Each of the five criteria receives a weight of 1/5 or 0.20.

Product	Calculation	Total Score
A	$(0.20 \times 3) + (0.20 \times 7) + (0.20 \times 10) + (0.20 \times 4) + (0.20 \times 4)$	= 5.6
B	$(0 \times 9) + (0.20 \times 8) + (0.20 \times 4) + (0.20 \times 7) + (0.20 \times 6)$	= **6.8**
C	$(0.20 \times 2) + (0.20 \times 6) + (0.20 \times 8) + (0.20 \times 6) + (0.20 \times 5)$	= 5.4

The best choice is Product B. Products A and C are well behind in terms of total weighted score.

Solved Problem 3

Adele Weiss manages the campus flower shop. Flowers must be ordered three days in advance from her supplier in Mexico. Although Valentine's Day is fast approaching, sales are almost entirely last-minute, impulse purchases. Advance sales are so small that Weiss has no way to estimate the probability of low (25 dozen), medium (60 dozen), or high (130 dozen) demand for red roses on the big day. She buys roses for $15 per dozen and sells them for $40 per dozen. Construct a payoff table. Which decision is indicated by each of the following decision criteria?

a. Maximin
b. Maximax
c. Laplace
d. Minimax regret

MyOMLab

Tutor A.6 in MyOMLab examines decisions under uncertainty for a location example.

SOLUTION

The payoff table for this problem is

Alternative	DEMAND FOR RED ROSES		
	Low (25 dozen)	Medium (60 dozen)	High (130 dozen)
Order 25 dozen	$625	$625	$625
Order 60 dozen	$100	$1,500	$1,500
Order 130 dozen	($950)	$450	$3,250
Do nothing	$0	$0	$0

a. Under the maximin criteria, Weiss should order **25** dozen, because if demand is low, Weiss's profits are $625, the best of the worst payoffs.

b. Under the maximax criteria, Weiss should order **130** dozen. The greatest possible payoff, $3,250, is associated with the largest order.

c. Under the Laplace criteria, Weiss should order **60** dozen. Equally weighted payoffs for ordering 25, 60, and 130 dozen are about $625, $1,033, and $917, respectively.

d. Under the minimax regret criteria, Weiss should order **130** dozen. The maximum regret of ordering 25 dozen occurs if demand is high: $3,250 − $625 = $2,625. The maximum regret of ordering 60 dozen occurs if demand is high: $3,250 − $1,500 = $1,750. The maximum regret of ordering 130 dozen occurs if demand is low: $625 − (−$950) = **$1,575**.

Solved Problem 4

White Valley Ski Resort is planning the ski lift operation for its new ski resort. Management is trying to determine whether one or two lifts will be necessary; each lift can accommodate 250 people per day. Skiing normally occurs in the 14-week period from December to April, during which the lift will operate seven days per week. The first lift will operate at 90 percent capacity if economic conditions are bad, the probability of which is believed to be about a 0.3. During normal times the first lift will be utilized at 100 percent capacity, and the excess crowd will provide 50 percent utilization of the second lift. The probability of normal times is 0.5. Finally, if times are really good, the probability of which is 0.2, the utilization of the second lift will increase to 90 percent. The equivalent annual cost of installing a new lift, recognizing the time value of money and the lift's economic life, is $50,000. The annual cost of installing two lifts is only $90,000 if both are purchased at the same time. If used at all, each lift costs $200,000 to operate, no matter how low or high its utilization rate. Lift tickets cost $20 per customer per day.

Should the resort purchase one lift or two?

SOLUTION

The decision tree is shown in Figure A.7. The payoff ($000) for each alternative-event branch is shown in the following table. The total revenues from one lift operating at 100 percent capacity are **$490,000** (or 250 customers × 98 days × $20/customer-day).

Alternative	Economic Condition	Payoff Calculation (Revenue − Cost)
One lift	Bad times	0.9(490) − (50 + 200) = 191
	Normal times	1.0(490) − (50 + 200) = 240
	Good times	1.0(490) − (50 + 200) = 240
Two lifts	Bad times	0.9(490) − (90 + 200) = 151
	Normal times	1.5(490) − (90 + 400) = 245
	Good times	1.9(490) − (90 + 400) = 441

FIGURE A.7 ▶

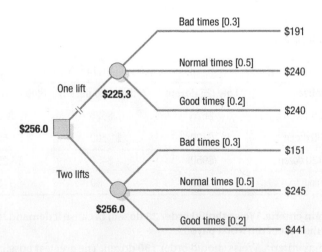

Problems

The OM Explorer and POM for Windows software is available to all students using the 11th edition of this textbook. Go to **http://www.pearsonhighered.com/krajewski** to download these computer packages. If you purchased MyOMLab, you also have access to Active Models software and significant help in doing the following problems. Check with your instructor on how best to use these resources. In many cases, the instructor wants you to understand how to do the calculations by hand. At the least, the software provides a check on your calculations. When calculations are particularly complex and the goal is interpreting the results in making decisions, the software entirely replaces the manual calculations.

Break-Even Analysis

1. Mary Williams, owner of Williams Products, is evaluating whether to introduce a new product line. After thinking through the production process and the costs of raw materials and new equipment, Williams estimates the variable costs of each unit produced and sold at $6 and the fixed costs per year at $60,000.

    a. If the selling price is set at $18 each, how many units must be produced and sold for Williams to break even? Use both graphic and algebraic approaches to get your answer.

    b. Williams forecasts sales of 10,000 units for the first year if the selling price is set at $14 each. What would be the total contribution to profits from this new product during the first year?

    c. If the selling price is set at $12.50, Williams forecasts that first-year sales would increase to 15,000 units. Which pricing strategy ($14.00 or $12.50) would result in the greater total contribution to profits?

    d. What other considerations would be crucial to the final decision about making and marketing the new product?

2. A product at the Jennings Company enjoyed reasonable sales volumes, but its contributions to profits were disappointing. Last year, 17,500 units were produced and sold. The selling price is $22 per unit, the variable cost is $18 per unit, and the fixed cost is $80,000.

    a. What is the break-even quantity for this product? Use both graphic and algebraic approaches to get your answer.

    b. If sales were not expected to increase, by how much would Jennings have to reduce their variable cost to break even?

    c. Jennings believes that a $1 reduction in price will increase sales by 50 percent. Is this enough for Jennings to break even? If not, by how much would sales have to increase?

    d. Jennings is considering ways to either stimulate sales volume or decrease variable cost. Management believes that either sales can be increased by 30 percent or that variable cost can be reduced to 85 percent of its current level. Which alternative leads to higher contributions to profits, assuming that each is equally costly to implement? (*Hint:* Calculate profits for both alternatives and identify the one having the greatest profits.)

    e. What is the percent change in the per-unit profit contribution generated by each alternative in part (d)?

3. An interactive television service that costs $10 per *month* to provide can be sold on the information highway for $15 per client per *month*. If a service area includes a potential of 15,000 customers, what is the most a company could spend on *annual* fixed costs to acquire and maintain the equipment?

4. A restaurant is considering adding fresh brook trout to its menu. Customers would have the choice of catching their own trout from a simulated mountain stream or simply asking the waiter to net the trout for them. Operating the stream would require $10,600 in fixed costs per year. Variable costs are estimated to be $6.70 per trout. The firm wants to break even if 800 trout dinners are sold per year. What should be the price of the new item?

5. Spartan Castings must implement a manufacturing process that reduces the amount of particulates emitted into the atmosphere. Two processes have been identified that provide the same level of particulate reduction. The first process is expected to incur $350,000 of fixed cost and add $50 of variable cost to each casting Spartan produces. The second process has fixed costs of $150,000 and adds $90 of variable cost per casting.

    a. What is the break-even quantity beyond which the first process is more attractive?

    b. What is the difference in total cost if the quantity produced is 10,000?

6. A news clipping service is considering modernization. Rather than manually clipping and photocopying articles of interest and mailing them to its clients, employees electronically input stories from most widely circulated publications into a database. Each new issue is searched for key words, such as a client's company name, competitors' names, type of business, and the company's products, services, and officers. When matches occur, affected clients are instantly notified via an online network. If the story is of interest, it is electronically transmitted, so the client often has the story and can prepare comments for follow-up interviews before the publication hits the street. The manual process has fixed costs of $400,000 per year and variable costs of $6.20 per clipping mailed. The price charged the client is $8.00 per clipping. The computerized process has fixed costs of $1,300,000 per year and variable costs of $2.25 per story electronically transmitted to the client.

    a. If the same price is charged for either process, what is the annual volume beyond which the automated process is more attractive?

    b. The present volume of business is 225,000 clippings per year. Many of the clippings sent with the current process are not of interest to the client or are multiple copies of the same story appearing in several publications. The news clipping service believes that by improving service and by lowering the price to $4.00 per story, modernization will increase volume to 900,000 stories transmitted per year. Should the clipping service modernize?

c. If the forecasted increase in business is too optimistic, at what volume will the new process (with the $4.00 price) break even?

7. Hahn Manufacturing purchases a key component of one of its products from a local supplier. The current purchase price is $1,500 per unit. Efforts to standardize parts succeeded to the point that this same component can now be used in five different products. Annual component usage should increase from 150 to 750 units. Management wonders whether it is time to make the component in-house rather than to continue buying it from the supplier. Fixed costs would increase by about $40,000 per year for the new equipment and tooling needed. The cost of raw materials and variable overhead would be about $1,100 per unit, and labor costs would be $300 per unit produced.

a. Should Hahn make rather than buy?

b. What is the break-even quantity?

c. What other considerations might be important?

8. Techno Corporation is currently manufacturing an item at variable costs of $5 per unit. Annual fixed costs of manufacturing this item are $140,000. The current selling price of the item is $10 per unit, and the annual sales volume is 30,000 units.

a. Techno can substantially improve the item's quality by installing new equipment at additional annual fixed costs of $60,000. Variable costs per unit would increase by $1, but, as more of the better-quality product could be sold, the annual volume would increase to 50,000 units. Should Techno buy the new equipment and maintain the current price of the item? Why or why not?

b. Alternatively, Techno could increase the selling price to $11 per unit. However, the annual sales volume would be limited to 45,000 units. Should Techno buy the new equipment and raise the price of the item? Why or why not?

9. The Tri-County Generation and Transmission Association is a nonprofit cooperative organization that provides electrical service to rural customers. Based on a faulty long-range demand forecast, Tri-County overbuilt its generation and distribution system. Tri-County now has much more capacity than it needs to serve its customers. Fixed costs, mostly debt service on investment in plant and equipment, are $82.5 million per year. Variable costs, mostly fossil fuel costs, are $25 per megawatt-hour (MWh, or million watts of power used for one hour). The new person in charge of demand forecasting prepared a short-range forecast for use in next year's budgeting process. That forecast calls for Tri-County customers to consume 1 million MWh of energy next year.

a. How much will Tri-County need to charge its customers per MWh to break even next year?

b. The Tri-County customers balk at that price and conserve electrical energy. Only 95 percent of forecasted demand materializes. What is the resulting surplus or loss for this nonprofit organization?

10. Earthquake, drought, fire, economic famine, flood, and a pestilence of TV court reporters have caused an exodus from the City of Angels to Boulder, Colorado. The sudden increase in demand is straining the capacity of Boulder's electrical system. Boulder's alternatives have been reduced to buying 150,000 MWh of electric power from Tri-County G&T at a price of $75 per MWh, or refurbishing and recommissioning the abandoned Pearl Street Power Station in downtown Boulder. Fixed costs of that project are $10 million per year, and variable costs would be $35 per MWh. Should Boulder build or buy?

11. Tri-County G&T sells 150,000 MWh per year of electrical power to Boulder at $75 per MWh, has fixed costs of $82.5 million per year, and has variable costs of $25 per MWh. If Tri-County has 1,000,000 MWh of demand from its customers (other than Boulder), what will Tri-County have to charge to break even?

Preference Matrix

12. The Forsite Company is screening three ideas for new services. Resource constraints allow only one idea to be commercialized at the present time. The following estimates have been made for the five performance criteria that management believes to be most important:

Performance Criterion	RATING		
	Service A	Service B	Service C
Capital equipment investment required	0.6	0.8	0.3
Expected return on investment (ROI)	0.7	0.3	0.9
Compatibility with current workforce skills	0.4	0.7	0.5
Competitive advantage	1.0	0.4	0.6
Compatibility with EPA requirements	0.2	1.0	0.5

a. Calculate a total weighted score for each alternative. Use a preference matrix and assume equal weights for each performance criterion. Which alternative is best? Worst?

b. Suppose that the expected ROI is given twice the weight assigned to each of the remaining criteria. (The sum of weights should remain the same as in part (a).) Does this modification affect the ranking of the three potential services?

13. You are in charge of analyzing five new suppliers of an important raw material and have been given the information shown below (1 = worst, 10 = best). Management has decided that criteria 2 and 3 are equally important and that criteria 1 and 4 are each four times as important as criterion 2. No more than two new suppliers are required but each new vendor must exceed a total score of 70 percent of the maximum total points to be considered.

Performance Criterion	Vendor A	Vendor B	Vendor C	Vendor D	Vendor E
			RATING		
Quality of raw material	8	7	3	6	9
Environmental impact	3	8	4	7	7
Responsiveness to order changes	9	5	7	6	5
Cost of raw material	7	6	9	2	7

a. Which new vendors do you recommend?

b. Would your decision change if the criteria were considered equally important?

14. Accel Express, Inc., collected the following information on where to locate a warehouse (1 = poor, 10 = excellent):

Location Factor	Factor Weight	A	B
		LOCATION SCORE	
Construction costs	10	8	5
Utilities available	10	7	7
Business services	10	4	7
Real estate cost	20	7	4
Quality of life	20	4	8
Transportation	30	7	6

a. Which location, A or B, should be chosen on the basis of the total weighted score?

Decision Theory

16. Build-Rite Construction has received favorable publicity from guest appearances on a public TV home improvement program. Public TV programming decisions seem to be unpredictable, so Build-Rite cannot estimate the probability of continued benefits from its relationship with the show. Demand for home improvements next year may be either low or high. But Build-Rite must decide now whether to hire more employees, do nothing, or develop subcontracts with other home improvement contractors. Build-Rite has developed the following payoff table:

Alternative	Low	Moderate	High
	DEMAND FOR HOME IMPROVEMENTS		
Hire	($250,000)	$100,000	$625,000
Subcontract	$100,000	$150,000	$415,000
Do nothing	$50,000	$80,000	$300,000

Which alternative is best, according to each of the following decision criteria?

a. Maximin

b. Maximax

c. Laplace

d. Minimax regret

b. If the factors were weighted equally, would the choice change?

15. Janice Gould of Krebs Consulting is in the process of making a recommendation to a client regarding the corporate-wide purchase of an analytical software platform. She has made the following estimates on management's most important performance criteria and has rated three Software packages across these criteria.

Performance Criterion	Factor Weight	Software A	Software B	Software C
		RATING		
Functionality	25	9	8	9
Vendor reliability	10	7	5	9
Compatibility with current systems	20	6	8	6
Maintenance & support	10	5	5	8
Total cost	25	4	8	5
Speed of implementation	10	8	4	7

a. Which software platform would you recommend?

b. Assume that the client changes their mind and now argues that the maintenance and support criterion is already accounted for by the total cost criterion. Further, the client asks Ms. Gould to drop maintenance and support and add its factor weight to total cost. Will this client request alter the recommendation?

17. Robert Ragsdale is trying to decide if he should purchase repair and replacement insurance on a new laptop computer that he is planning to purchase. The policy costs $400.00 at the time of purchase, and over the next three years will replace the laptop if it is stolen or repair it if it is broken. The following table contains the total costs of this decision.

Alternative	Computer Is Stolen	Computer Breaks	Computer Neither Breaks Nor Is Stolen
Buy the Insurance	$2,900.00	$2,900.00	$2,900.00
Do Not Buy the Insurance	$5,000.00	$3,100.00	$2,500.00

Which alternative is best, according to each of the following decision criteria?

a. Maximin

b. Maximax

c. Laplace

d. Minimax regret

18. Benjamin Moses, chief engineer of Offshore Chemicals, Inc., must decide whether to build a new processing facility based on an experimental technology. If the new facility works, the company will realize a net profit of $20 million. If the new facility fails, the company will lose $10 million. Benjamin's best guess is that there is a 40 percent chance that the new facility will work.

What decision should Benjamin Moses make?

19. A manager is trying to decide whether to build a small, medium, or large facility. Demand can be low, average, or high, with the estimated probabilities being 0.25, 0.40, and 0.35, respectively.

A small facility is expected to earn an after-tax net present value of just $18,000 if demand is low. If demand is average, the small facility is expected to earn $75,000; it can be increased to medium size to earn a net present value of $60,000. If demand is high, the small facility is expected to

earn $75,000 and can be expanded to medium size to earn $60,000 or to large size to earn $125,000.

A medium-sized facility is expected to lose an estimated $25,000 if demand is low and earn $140,000 if demand is average. If demand is high, the medium-sized facility is expected to earn a net present value of $150,000; it can be expanded to a large size for a net payoff of $145,000.

If a large facility is built and demand is high, earnings are expected to be $220,000. If demand is average for the large facility, the present value is expected to be $125,000; if demand is low, the facility is expected to lose $60,000.

Which alternative is best, according to each of the following decision criterion?

a. Maximin

b. Maximax

c. Minimax regret

Decision Trees

20. Draw a decision tree for the three options described in problem 19. What should management do to achieve the highest expected payoff?

21. The owner of Pearl Automotive Dealers is trying to decide whether to expand his current facility. If he expands and customer demand turns weak, there is a chance he could lease part of his newly constructed facility to another dealer. If he doesn't expand and strong demand occurs, he could attempt to lease another facility across town. Analyze the decision tree in Figure A8. What is the best set of decisions and the expected payoff?

22. Analyze the decision tree in the figure below. What is the expected payoff for the best alternative? First, be sure to infer the missing probabilities.

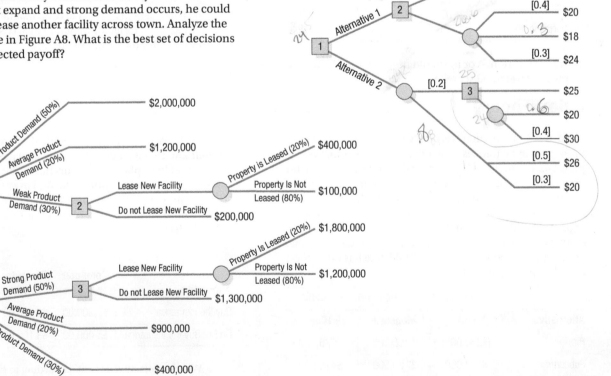

▼ **FIGURE A.8**

23. A manager is trying to decide whether to buy one machine or two. If only one is purchased and demand proves to be excessive, the second machine can be purchased later. Some sales will be lost, however, because the lead time for producing this type of machine is six months. In addition, the cost per machine will be lower if both are purchased at the same time. The probability of low demand is estimated to be 0.20. The after-tax net present value of the benefits from purchasing the two machines together is $90,000 if demand is low and $180,000 if demand is high.

   If one machine is purchased and demand is low, the net present value is $120,000. If demand is high, the manager has three options. Doing nothing has a net present value of $120,000; subcontracting, $160,000; and buying the second machine, $140,000.

a. Draw a decision tree for this problem.

b. How many machines should the company buy initially? What is the expected payoff for this alternative?

24. A manufacturing plant has reached full capacity. The company must build a second plant—either small or large—at a nearby location. The demand is likely to be high or low. The probability of low demand is 0.3. If demand is low, the large plant has a present value of $5 million and the small plant, a present value of $8 million. If demand is high, the large plant pays off with a present value of $18 million, and the small plant with a present value of only $10 million. However, the small plant can be expanded later if demand proves to be high for a present value of $14 million.

a. Draw a decision tree for this problem.

b. What should management do to achieve the highest expected payoff?

PROCESS STRATEGY AND ANALYSIS

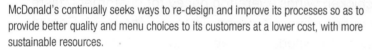

McDonald's continually seeks ways to re-design and improve its processes so as to provide better quality and menu choices to its customers at a lower cost, with more sustainable resources.

McDonald's Corporation

As a global food service retailer, McDonald's has more than 35,000 restaurants around the world, and 70 million customers visit them each day. It employs 1.9 million people who work for McDonald's and its franchisees across more than 100 countries. Even though the company is a leader in its industry, things were not so good in 2002, when customer complaints were growing more frequent and bitter. McDonald's began listening to the customers again and changed its processes to reflect it. The board brought on a new CEO who had spent 20 years on the operational side of the business. With a zeal for measuring customer satisfaction and sharing the data freely with operators, he pulled off a turnaround that stunned everyone in the business with its speed and scope. Initiatives were launched to collect performance measures and re-vamp McDonald's processes to meet customer expectations. Data on speed of service; food temperature; presentation and taste; cleanliness of the counter, tables and condiment islands; even whether the counter crewperson smiles at diners, was collected using mystery shoppers. Operators could pinpoint lingering problems, and performance measures focused operators' attention on needed process changes. Customers were encouraged to report their experience at a particular U.S. restaurant by e-mail, regular mail, or toll-free telephone call.

Another initiative was to send 900 operations missionaries into the field, each visiting stores multiple times to fine-tune processes while also conducting day-long seminars where store managers could share tips from corporate kitchen gurus—such as where to place staff—that would shave precious seconds off average service times. The process was changed back to toasting buns rather than microwaving them, giving them an even sweeter caramelized flavor. Other initiatives were taken on McDonald's fast lane. Outdoor menu boards were placed with more pictures and fewer words. An LED display confirmed what customers ordered, reducing confusion later on. Premium sandwiches were put in boxes rather than paper wrappers, saving a few seconds, and boxes were color coded by sandwich to improve speed and accuracy. Processes were also changed to become environment friendly, all the way from the counters of McDonald's restaurants into its supply chain. All these changes resulted in greater profitability and share price over ten years, as performance measurement and process analysis increased customer value and the bottom line.

Lately, however, the growth has stagnated. Same-store sales slipped 0.1 percent, which marked a second quarterly decline in 2013. The menu got overly complicated as more items were added to suit a wider range of tastes. This created bottlenecks in the kitchen, which slowed service and turned off customers. Some items, like chicken wings, were too pricey for customers' taste and resulted in 10 million pounds of unsold wings. To regain focus, McDonalds is now redesigning its kitchens to include prep tables that would give employees more space for assembling food. In addition, $3 billion in capital expenditures is being budgeted in 2014 for opening new restaurants and refurbishing existing ones. Apart from making the menu more relevant to closely reflect customer preferences, more employees would also be hired at peak hours and weekends to increase speed of service.

Even at successful firms like McDonald's, it is easy to lose touch over time. Careful design and execution of processes that appropriately reflect product designs and market trends ultimately drive business outcomes and financial success.

Source: Julie Jargon, "McDonald's Says Its Restaurants Got Too Complicated," *Wall Street Journal*, January 24, 2014; Daniel Kruger, "You Want Data with That?" *Forbes*, vol. 173, no. 6 (March 2004), pp. 58–60; **http://www.mcdonalds.com**, June 26, 2014.

LEARNING GOALS *After reading this chapter, you should be able to:*

1. Understand the process structure in services and how to position a service process on the customer-contact matrix.

2. Understand the process structure in manufacturing and how to position a manufacturing process on the product-process matrix.

3. Explain the major process strategy decisions and their implications for operations.

4. Discuss how process decisions should strategically fit together.

5. Compare and contrast the two commonly used strategies for change, and understand a systematic way to analyze and improve processes.

6. Discuss how to document and evaluate processes.

7. Identify the commonly used approaches for effectively redesigning and managing processes.

Processes involve the use of an organization's resources to provide something of value and are perhaps the least understood and managed aspect of a business. No service can be provided and no product can be made without a process, and no process can exist without at least one service or product. Even with talented and motivated people, a firm cannot gain competitive advantage with faulty processes. Process decisions as such are strategic in nature. As we saw in Chapter 1, they should further a company's long-term competitive goals. In making process decisions, managers focus on controlling such competitive priorities as quality, flexibility, time, and cost. As exemplified by McDonald's, process management is an ongoing activity, with the same principles applying to both first-time and redesign choices. Many different choices are available in selecting human resources, equipment, outsourced services, materials, work flows, and methods that transform inputs into outputs. Another choice is which processes are to be done in-house and which processes are to be outsourced—that is, done outside the firm and purchased as materials and services. This decision helps to define the supply chain, and is covered more fully in subsequent chapters.

In this chapter, we focus on **process strategy**, which specifies the pattern of decisions made in managing processes so that the processes will achieve their competitive priorities, as well as **process analysis**, which is the documentation and detailed understanding of how work is performed and how it can be redesigned. Process decisions directly affect the process itself and indirectly the services and the products that it provides. All parts of an organization, as well as external suppliers and customers across the supply chain, need to be involved to ensure that processes are providing the most value to their internal and external customers.

Process strategy guides a variety of process decisions, and in turn is guided by operations strategy and the organization's ability to obtain the resources necessary to support them. We begin by defining four basic process decisions: (1) process structure, (2) customer involvement, (3) resource flexibility, and (4) capital intensity. We discuss these decisions for both service and manufacturing processes. We pay particular attention to ways in which these decisions fit together, depending on factors such as competitive priorities, customer contact, and volume, which in turn lead to two basic change strategies for analyzing and modifying processes: (1) process reengineering and (2) process improvement. Both these approaches need process analysis to identify and implement changes.

Three principles concerning process strategy are particularly important:

1. The key to successful process decisions is to make choices that fit the situation and that make sense together. They should not work at cross-purposes, with one process optimized at the expense of other processes. A more effective process is one that matches key process characteristics and has a close *strategic fit*.

2. Although this section of the text focuses on individual processes, they are the building blocks that eventually create the firm's whole supply chain. The cumulative effect on customer satisfaction and competitive advantage is huge.

3. Whether processes in the supply chain are performed internally or by outside suppliers and customers, management must pay particular attention to the interfaces between processes. Dealing with these interfaces underscores the need for cross-functional coordination.

Whether dealing with processes for offices, service providers, or manufacturers, operations managers must consider four common process decisions. Figure 2.1 shows that they are all important steps toward an effective process design. These four decisions are best understood at the process or subprocess level rather than at the firm level.

- **Process structure** determines the process type relative to the kinds of resources needed, how resources are partitioned between them, and their key characteristics. A **layout** is the physical arrangement of operations (or departments) relative to each other.

- **Customer involvement** reflects the ways in which customers become part of the process and the extent of their participation.

- **Resource flexibility** is the ease with which employees and equipment can handle a wide variety of products, output levels, duties, and functions.

- **Capital intensity** is the mix of equipment and human skills in a process. The greater the cost of equipment relative to the cost of labor, the greater is the capital intensity.

The concepts that we develop around these four decisions establish a framework within which we can address the appropriate process design in every situation. We establish the patterns of choices

process strategy

The pattern of decisions made in managing processes so that they will achieve their competitive priorities.

process analysis

The documentation and detailed understanding of how work is performed and how it can be redesigned.

process structure

The process type relative to the kinds of resources needed, how resources are partitioned between them, and their key characteristics.

layout

The physical arrangement of operations (or departments) relative to each other.

customer involvement

The ways in which customers become part of the process and the extent of their participation.

resource flexibility

The ease with which employees and equipment can handle a wide variety of products, output levels, duties, and functions.

▼ **FIGURE 2.1**
Major Decisions for Effective Processes

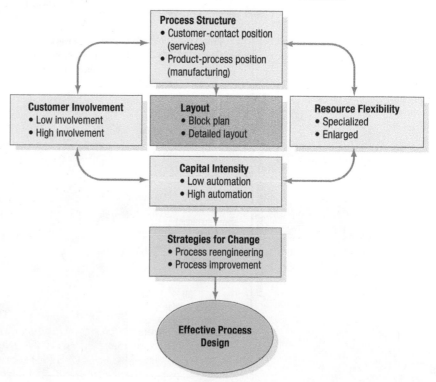

capital intensity

The mix of equipment and human skills in a process.

that create a good fit between the four decisions. For example, if you walk through a manufacturing facility where materials flow smoothly from one work station to the next (which we will define later to be a *line* process), you would be tempted to conclude that all processes should be line processes. They seem so efficient and organized. However, converting to a line process would be a big mistake if volumes are low and the products made are customized. Resources must be more flexible to handle a variety of products in such a situation. The result is a more disorganized appearance with jobs crisscrossing in many different directions depending on the product being made. Despite appearances, this process is the best choice.

Process Structure in Services

One of the first decisions a manager makes in designing a well-functioning process is to choose a process type that best achieves the competitive priorities for that process. Strategies for designing processes can be quite different, depending on whether a service is being provided or a product is being manufactured. We begin with service processes, given their huge implication for workforce resources in industrialized countries.

A process strategy that gets customers in and out of a fast-food restaurant quickly would not be the right process strategy for a five-star restaurant, where customers seek a leisurely dining experience. To gain insights, we must start at the process level and recognize key contextual variables associated with the process. A good process strategy for a service process depends first and foremost on the type and amount of customer contact. **Customer contact** is the extent to which the customer is present, is actively involved, and receives personal attention during the service process. Face-to-face interaction, sometimes called a *moment of truth* or *service encounter*, brings the customer and service providers together. At that time, customer attitudes about the quality of the service provided are shaped. Table 2.1 shows several dimensions of customer contact. Many levels are possible on each of the five dimensions. Also, some parts of a process can have low contact and other parts of a process can have high contact.

customer contact

The extent to which the customer is present, is actively involved, and receives personal attention during the service process.

TABLE 2.1 | DIMENSIONS OF CUSTOMER CONTACT IN SERVICE PROCESSES

Dimension	High Contact	Low Contact
Physical presence	Present	Absent
What is processed	People	Possessions or information
Contact intensity	Active, visible	Passive, out of sight
Personal attention	Personal	Impersonal
Method of delivery	Face-to-face	Regular mail or e-mail

Customer-Contact Matrix

The customer-contact matrix, shown in Figure 2.2, brings together three elements: (1) the degree of customer contact, (2) customization, and (3) process characteristics. The matrix is the starting point for evaluating and improving a process.

FIGURE 2.2 ▶

Customer-Contact Matrix for Service Processes

MyOMLab Animation

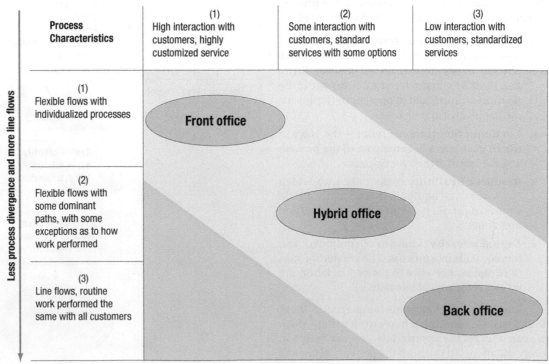

Customer Contact and Customization   The horizontal dimension of the matrix represents the service provided to the customer in terms of customer contact and competitive priorities. A key competitive priority is how much customization is needed. Positions on the left side of the matrix represent high customer contact and highly customized services. The customer is more likely to be present and active. The process is more likely to be visible to the customer, who receives more personal attention. The right side of the matrix represents low customer contact, passive involvement, less personalized attention, and a process out of the customer's sight.

Process Divergence and Flow   The vertical dimension of the customer-contact matrix deals with two characteristics of the process itself: (1) process divergence and (2) flow. Each process can be analyzed on these two dimensions.

Process divergence is the extent to which the process is highly customized with considerable latitude as to how its tasks are performed. If the process changes with each customer, virtually every performance of the service is unique. Examples of highly divergent service processes where many steps in them change with each customer are found in consulting, law, and architecture. A service with low divergence, on the other hand, is repetitive and standardized. The work is performed exactly the same with all customers and tends to be less complex. Certain hotel services and telephone services are highly standardized to ensure uniformity.

Closely related to divergence is how the customer, object, or information being processed flows through the service facility. Work progresses through the sequence of steps in a process, which could range from highly diverse to linear. When divergence is considerable, the work flow tends to be more flexible. A **flexible flow** means that the customers, materials, or information move in diverse ways, with the path of one customer or job often crisscrossing the path that the next one takes. Each one can follow a carefully preplanned path, even though the first impression is one of disorganized, jumbled flows. Such an appearance goes naturally with high process divergence. A **line flow** means that the customers, materials, or information move linearly from one operation to the next, according to a fixed sequence. When diversity is low and the process standardized, line flows are a natural consequence.

Service Process Structuring

Figure 2.2 shows several desirable positions in the matrix that effectively connect the service product with the process. The manager has three process structures, which form a continuum, to choose from: (1) front office, (2) hybrid office, and (3) back office. It is unlikely that a process can be a top performer if a process lies too far from one of these diagonal positions, occupying instead one of the extreme positions represented by the light blue triangles in the matrix (refer to Figure 2.2). Such positions represent too much of a disconnect between the service provided and process characteristics.

Front Office   A **front-office** process has high customer contact where the service provider interacts directly with the internal or external customer. Because of the customization of the service and variety of service options, many of the steps in it have considerable divergence. Work flows are flexible, and they vary from one customer to the next. The high-contact service process tends to be adapted or tailored to each customer.

Hybrid Office   A hybrid office tends to be in the middle of the five dimensions in Table 2.1, or perhaps high on some contact measures and low on others. A **hybrid-office** process has moderate levels of customer contact and standard services, with some options available from which the customer chooses. The work flow progresses from one workstation to the next, with some dominant paths apparent.

process divergence

The extent to which the process is highly customized with considerable latitude as to how its tasks are performed.

flexible flow

The customers, materials, or information move in diverse ways, with the path of one customer or job often crisscrossing the path that the next one takes.

line flow

The customers, materials, or information move linearly from one operation to the next, according to a fixed sequence.

front office

A process with high customer contact where the service provider interacts directly with the internal or external customer.

hybrid office

A process with moderate levels of customer contact and standard services with some options available.

A financial consultant discusses options with a couple at their home. This process scores high on customer contact, because the customers are present, take an active part in creating the service, receive personal attention, and have a face-to-face meeting.

Monkey Business/Fotolia

back office

A process with low customer contact and little service customization.

Back Office A **back-office** process has low customer contact and little service customization. The work is standardized and routine, with line flows from one service provider to the next until the service is completed. Preparing the monthly client fund balance reports in the financial services industry is a good example. It has low customer contact, low divergence, and a line flow.

Process Structure in Manufacturing

Many processes at a manufacturing firm are actually services to internal or external customers, and so the previous discussion on services applies to them. Similarly, manufacturing processes can be found in service firms. Clarity comes when viewing work at the process level, rather than the organizational level. Here we focus instead on the manufacturing processes. Because of the differences between service and manufacturing processes, we need a different view on process structure.

Product–Process Matrix

The product–process matrix, shown in Figure 2.3, brings together three elements: (1) volume, (2) product customization, and (3) process characteristics. It synchronizes the product to be manufactured with the manufacturing process itself.

A good strategy for a manufacturing process depends first and foremost on volume. Customer contact, a primary feature of the customer-contact matrix for services, normally is not a consideration for manufacturing processes (although it *is* a factor for the many service processes throughout manufacturing firms). For many manufacturing processes, high product customization means lower volumes for many of the steps in the process. The vertical dimension of the product–process matrix deals with the same two characteristics in the customer-contact matrix: process divergence and flow. Each manufacturing process should be analyzed on these two dimensions, just as was done for a service process.

Serge Kozak/Corbis

Employees discuss work with one another and their supervisor. Employees in these work stations are in a back office, because they have low customer contact and little service customization.

FIGURE 2.3 ▶
Product-Process Matrix for
Manufacturing Processes
MyOMLab Animation

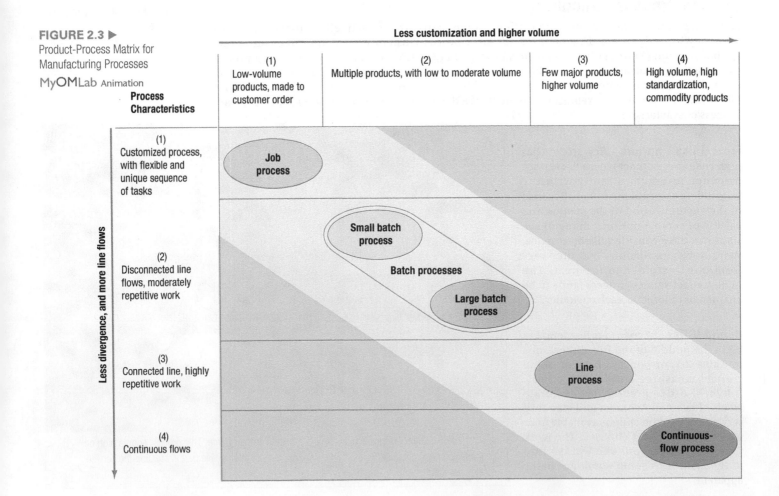

Manufacturing Process Structuring

Figure 2.3 shows several desirable positions (often called *process choices*) in the product–process matrix that effectively connect the manufactured product with the process. **Process choice** is the way of structuring the process by organizing resources around the process or organizing them around the products. Organizing around the process means, for example, that all milling machines are grouped together and process all products or parts needing that kind of transformation. Organizing around the product means bringing together all the different human resources and equipment needed for a specific product and dedicating them to producing just that product. The manager has four process choices, which form a continuum, to choose from: (1) job process, (2) batch process, (3) line process, and (4) continuous-flow process. As with the customer-contact matrix, it is unlikely that a manufacturing process can be a top performer if its position is too far from the diagonal. The fundamental message in Figure 2.3 is that the best choice for a manufacturing process depends on the volume and degree of customization required of the process. The process choice might apply to an entire manufacturing process or just one subprocess nested within it.

process choice

A way of structuring the process by organizing resources around the process or organizing them around the products.

Job Process   A **job process** creates the flexibility needed to produce a wide variety of products in significant quantities, with considerable divergence in the steps performed. Customization is high and volume for any one product is low. The workforce and equipment are flexible to handle considerable task divergence. Companies choosing job processes often bid for work. Typically, they make products to order and do not produce them ahead of time. Each new order is handled as a single unit—as a job. Examples are machining a metal casting for a customized order or producing customized cabinets.

job process

A process with the flexibility needed to produce a wide variety of products in significant quantities, with considerable divergence in the steps performed.

With a job process, all equipment and workers capable of certain types of work are positioned together. Because customization is high and most jobs have a different sequence of steps, this process choice creates flexible flows through the operations rather than a line flow.

Batch Process   The batch process is by far the most common process choice found in practice, leading to terms such as *small batch* or *large batch* to further distinguish one process choice from another. A **batch process** differs from the job process with respect to volume, variety, and quantity. The primary difference is that volumes are higher because the same or similar products or parts going into them are produced repeatedly. Some of the components going into the final product may be processed in advance. Production lots are handled in larger quantities (or *batches*) than they are with job processes. A batch of one product (or component part going into it or perhaps other products) is processed, and then production is switched to the next one. Eventually, the first product is produced again. A batch process has average or moderate volumes, but process divergence is still too great to warrant dedicating a separate process for each product. The process flow is flexible, but more dominant paths emerge than at a job process, and some segments of the process have a line flow. Examples of a batch process are making standard components that feed an assembly line or some processes that manufacture capital equipment.

batch process

A process that differs from the job process with respect to volume, variety, and quantity.

Line Process   A **line process** lies between the batch and continuous processes on the continuum; volumes are high and products are standardized, which allows resources to be organized around particular products. Divergence is minimal in the process or line flows, and little inventory is held between the processing steps. Each step performs the same process over and over, with little variability in the products manufactured. Production and material handling equipment is specialized. Products created by a line process include the assembly of computers, automobiles, appliances, and toys.

line process

A process that lies between the batch and continuous processes on the continuum; volumes are high and products are standardized, which allows resources to be organized around particular products.

Standard products are produced in advance of their need and held in inventory so that they are ready when a customer places an order. Product variety is possible by careful control of the addition of standard options to the main product.

Continuous-Flow Process   A **continuous-flow process** is the extreme end of high-volume standardized production, with rigid line flows. Process divergence is negligible. Its name derives from the way materials move through the process. Usually, one primary material (such as a liquid, a gas, or a powder) moves without stopping through the process. A continuous-flow process differs from a line process in one important respect: Materials (be they undifferentiated or discrete) flow through the process without stopping until the whole batch is finished. The time span can be several shifts or even several months. Examples of a continuous-flow process are petroleum refining; chemical processes; paper manufacturing; and processes making steel, soft drinks, and food.

continuous-flow process

The extreme end of high-volume standardized production and rigid line flows, with production not starting and stopping for long time intervals.

Production and Inventory Strategies

Strategies for manufacturing processes differ from those in services not only because of low customer contact and involvement but also because of the ability to use inventories not only as purchased materials but also in the form of subassemblies or finished products. As we learned in Chapter 1, there are clearly exceptions to this rule as Avis has an inventory of autos to rent, and FedEx has an inventory of in-process parcels. Design-to-order, make-to-order, assemble-to-order, and make-to-stock strategies are four approaches to inventory that should be coordinated with process choice.

design-to-order strategy

A strategy that involves designing new products that do not currently exist, and then manufacturing them to meet unique customer specifications.

make-to-order strategy

A strategy used by manufacturers that make products to customer specifications in low volumes.

assemble-to-order strategy

A strategy for producing a wide variety of products from relatively few subassemblies and components after the customer orders are received.

postponement

The strategy of delaying final activities in the provision of a product until the orders are received.

mass customization

The strategy that uses highly divergent processes to generate a wide variety of customized products at reasonably low costs.

make-to-stock strategy

A strategy that involves holding items in stock for immediate delivery, thereby minimizing customer delivery times.

mass production

A term sometimes used in the popular press for a line process that uses the make-to-stock strategy.

Design-to-Order Strategy   A firm uses a **design-to-order strategy** when it can design new products that do not currently exist, and then manufacture them to meet unique customer specifications. Typically a job process is employed to create a highly customized product, such as a designer pair of shoes for a particular client.

Make-to-Order Strategy   Manufacturers that make products to customer specifications in low volumes tend to use the **make-to-order strategy**, coupling it with job or small batch processes. Even though the product is based on a standard design, it is a more complex process than assembling a final product from standard components. This strategy provides a high degree of customization and typically uses job or small batch processes. The processes have high divergence. Specialized medical equipment, castings, and expensive homes are suited to the make-to-order strategy.

Assemble-to-Order Strategy   The **assemble-to-order strategy** is an approach to producing a wide variety of products from relatively few subassemblies and components after the customer orders are received. Typical competitive priorities are variety and fast delivery times. The assemble-to-order strategy often involves a line process for assembly and a batch process for fabrication. Because they are devoted to manufacturing standardized components and subassemblies in high volumes, the fabrication processes focus on creating appropriate amounts of component inventories for the assembly processes. Once the specific order from the customer is received, the assembly processes create the product from standardized components and subassemblies produced by the fabrication processes.

Stocking finished products would be economically prohibitive because the numerous possible options make forecasting relatively inaccurate. Thus, the principle of **postponement** is applied, whereby the final activities in the provision of a product are delayed until the orders are received. The assemble-to-order strategy is also linked to **mass customization**, where highly divergent processes generate a wide variety of customized products at reasonably low costs. Both postponement and mass customization are covered more fully in Chapter 12, "Supply Chain Design."

Make-to-Stock Strategy   Manufacturing firms that hold items in stock for immediate delivery, thereby minimizing customer delivery times, use a **make-to-stock strategy**. This strategy is feasible for standardized products with high volumes and reasonably accurate forecasts. It is the inventory strategy of choice for line or continuous-flow processes. Examples of products produced with a make-to-stock strategy include garden tools, electronic components, soft drinks, and chemicals.

Combining a line process with the make-to-stock strategy is sometimes called **mass production**. It is what the popular press commonly envisions as the classical manufacturing process, because the environment is stable and predictable, with workers repeating narrowly defined tasks with low divergence.

Layout

Selecting process structures for the various processes housed in a facility is a strategic decision, but must be followed by a more tactical decision—creating a layout. A *layout* is the physical arrangement of operations (or departments) created from the various processes and puts them in tangible form. For organizational purposes, processes tend to be clustered together into operations or departments. An *operation* is a group of human and capital resources performing all or part of one or more processes. For example, an operation could be several customer service representatives in a customer reception area; a group of machines and workers producing cell phones; or a marketing department. Regardless of how processes are grouped together organizationally, many of them cut across departmental boundaries. The flows across departmental lines could be informational, services, or products. Process structures that create more flows across departmental lines, as with job or batch processes, are the most challenging layout problems. Supplement K, "Layout," provides a more in-depth analysis of how to gather information and develop detailed layout plans.

Process Strategy Decisions

Having covered process structure decisions in both service and manufacturing organizations, we turn our attention now to the other three major process strategy decisions shown in Figure 2.1—customer involvement, resource flexibility, and capital intensity.

Customer Involvement

Customer involvement reflects the ways in which customers become part of the process and the extent of their participation. As illustrated in Managerial Practice 2.1, it is especially important for many service processes such as eBay, particularly if customer contact is (or should be) high.

Possible Advantages   The advantages of a more customer-focused process might increase the net value to the customer. Some customers seek active participation in and control over the service process, particularly if they will enjoy savings in both price and time. The manager must assess whether advantages outweigh disadvantages, judging them in terms of the competitive priorities and customer satisfaction. More customer

MANAGERIAL PRACTICE 2.1   Customer Involvement at eBay

Most manufacturers do not have to contend with customers waltzing around their shop floors, showing up intermittently and unannounced. Such customer contact can introduce considerable variability, disrupting carefully designed production processes. Costs and quality can be adversely affected. While customer contact is an issue even with manufacturers (each process does have at least one customer), extensive customer contact and involvement are business as usual for many processes of service providers. Customers at restaurants or rental car agencies are directly involved in performing the processes. The area where the sales person interacts with the customer *is* the shop floor.

How much should customers be involved in a process, so as to provide timely delivery and consistent quality, and at sustainable cost? Various ways are available—some accommodate customer-introduced variability and some reduce it. eBay provides two services: It provides sellers a platform for selling their goods or services, and it provides buyers a platform to find the goods and services they want. From a business perspective, providing these two services generates a high degree of variability in the demands for the company's resources. eBay illustrates one way to accommodate that kind of variability—provide an online auction house. As an online auction house, eBay accommodates high volumes as well as service order variability from customers seeking to buy and sell an endless number of items. eBay customers also have variability in technological capability, some with considerable Internet experience and some needing more handholding. Such variability would greatly complicate workforce scheduling if eBay's customers were not involved in many of its processes. eBay's process strategy utilizing customer involvement has been successful. Founded in 1995 in California, it now has 145 million active buyers globally buying and selling more than 650 million

At any given time eBay has approximately 650 million listings worldwide, and yet its workforce consists of just 31,800 employees. The explanation? Customers do most of the work in eBay's buying and selling processes.

listed items with revenue of about $16.5 billion per year. It connects hundreds of millions of people around the world every day with only 31,800 employees. This relatively small workforce is possible in the face of customer-induced variability because its customers perform virtually all of the selling and buying processes through the e-commerce platform eBay.com and other vertical shopping sites. When the customer is responsible for much of the work, the right labor is provided at the right moment.

Source: Frances X. Frei, "Breaking the Trade-Off between Efficiency and Service," *Harvard Business Review* (November 2006), pp. 93–101; **http://en.wikipedia.org/wiki/Ebay** (May 31, 2014); **https://finance.yahoo.com/q/pr?s=EBAY+Profile** (May 31, 2014); **http://www.ebayinc.com/who_we_are/one_company** (May 31, 2014).

involvement can mean better quality, faster delivery, greater flexibility, and even lower cost. Self-service is the choice of many retailers, such as gasoline stations, supermarkets, and bank services. Manufacturers of products (such as toys, bicycles, and furniture) may also prefer to let the customer perform the final assembly because product, shipping, and inventory costs frequently are lower. In fact, IKEA Furniture Company's business model is based on customers being actively involved in its processes.

Customer involvement can also help coordinate across the supply chain (see Chapter 14, "Supply Chain Integration"). Emerging technologies allow companies to engage in an active dialogue with customers and make them partners in creating value and forecasting future demand. Suppliers to automobile companies can be close collaborators in the process of developing new vehicles and are no longer passive providers of materials and services. The same is true for distributors. Walmart does more than just distribute Procter & Gamble's products: It shares daily sales information and works with Procter & Gamble in managing inventories and warehousing operations.

A customer at Starbucks, a large coffee shop chain, places his order in the correct way. By structuring the ordering process for counter clerks and customers, Starbucks can deal efficiently with the variety in products offered, and with no hit on the service experience.

A car mechanic must be flexibly cross-trained at many different tasks in order to repair a wide variety of cars from different manufacturers.

Possible Disadvantages   Customer involvement is not always a good idea. In some cases, giving the customer more active contact in a service process will just be disruptive, making the process less efficient. Managing the timing and volume of customer demands becomes more challenging if the customer is physically present and expects prompt delivery. Exposing the facilities and employees to the customer can have important quality implications (favorable or unfavorable). Such changes make interpersonal skills a prerequisite to the service provider's job, but higher skill levels come at a cost. It also might mean having many smaller decentralized facilities closer to the various customer concentration areas if the customer comes to the service providers.

Resource Flexibility

Just as managers must account for customer contact when making customer involvement decisions, so must they account for process divergence and diverse process flows when making resource flexibility decisions in Figure 2.1. For example, high task divergence and flexible process flows require more flexibility of the process's resources—its employees, facilities, and equipment. Employees need to perform a broad range of duties, and equipment must be general purpose. Otherwise, resource utilization will be too low for economical operations.

flexible workforce

A workforce whose members are capable of doing many tasks, either at their own workstations or as they move from one workstation to another.

Workforce   Operations managers must decide whether to have a **flexible workforce**. Members of a flexible workforce are capable of doing many tasks, either at their own workstations or as they move from one workstation to another. However, such flexibility often comes at a cost, requiring greater skills and thus more training and education. Nevertheless, benefits can be large: Worker flexibility can be one of the best ways to achieve reliable customer service and alleviate capacity bottlenecks. Resource flexibility helps to absorb the feast-or-famine workloads in individual operations that are caused by low-volume production, divergent tasks, flexible flows, and fluid scheduling.

The type of workforce required also depends on the need for volume flexibility. When conditions allow for a smooth, steady rate of output, the likely choice is a permanent workforce that expects regular full-time employment. If the process is subject to hourly, daily, or seasonal peaks and valleys in demand, the use of part-time or temporary employees to supplement a smaller core of full-time employees may be the best solution. However, this approach may not be practical if knowledge and skill requirements are too high for a temporary worker to grasp quickly.

MyOMLab

Tutor 2.1 in MyOMLab demonstrates how to do break-even analysis for equipment selection.

Equipment   Low volumes mean that process designers should select flexible, general-purpose equipment. Figure 2.4 illustrates this relationship by showing the total cost lines for two different types of equipment that can be chosen for a process. Each line represents the total annual cost of the process at different volume levels. It is the sum of fixed costs and variable costs (see Supplement A, "Decision Making"). When volumes are low (because customization is high), process 1 is the better choice. It calls for inexpensive general-purpose equipment, which keeps investment in equipment low and makes fixed costs (F_1) small. Its variable unit cost is high, which gives its total cost line a relatively steep slope. Process 1 does the job, but not at peak efficiency.

Conversely, process 2 is the better choice when volumes are high and customization is low. Its advantage is low variable unit cost, as reflected in the flatter total cost line. This efficiency is possible when customization is low because the equipment can be designed for a narrow range of products or tasks. Its disadvantage is high equipment investment and, thus, high fixed costs (F_2). When annual volume produced is high enough, spreading these fixed costs over more units produced, the advantage of low variable costs more than compensates for the high fixed costs.

The break-even quantity in Figure 2.4 is the quantity at which the total costs for the two alternatives are equal. At quantities beyond this point, the cost of process 1 exceeds that of process 2. Unless the firm expects to sell more than the break-even amount, which is unlikely with high customization and low volume, the capital investment of process 2 is not warranted.

▼ **FIGURE 2.4**

Relationship between Process Costs and Product Volume

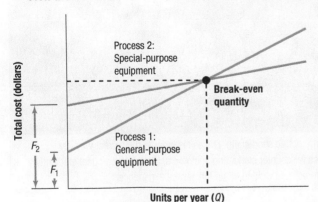

Capital Intensity

Capital intensity is the mix of equipment and human skills in the process; the greater the cost of equipment relative to the cost of labor, the greater is the capital intensity. As the capabilities of technology increase and its costs decrease, managers face an ever-widening range of choices, from operations utilizing very little automation to those requiring task-specific equipment and little human intervention. **Automation** is a system, process, or piece of equipment that is self-acting and self-regulating. Although automation is often thought to be necessary to gain competitive advantage, it has both advantages and disadvantages. Thus, the automation decision requires careful examination.

Automating Manufacturing Processes Substituting labor-saving capital equipment and technology for labor has been a classic way of improving productivity and quality consistency in manufacturing processes. If investment costs are large, automation works best when volume is high, because more customization typically means reduced volume. Gillette, for example, spent $750 million on the production lines and robotics that gave it a capacity to make 1.2 billion razor cartridges a year. The equipment is complicated and expensive. Only with such high volumes could this line process produce the product at a price low enough that consumers could afford to buy it.

One big disadvantage of capital intensity can be the prohibitive investment cost for low-volume operations (see Figure 2.4). Generally, capital-intensive operations must have high utilization to be justifiable. Also, automation does not always align with a company's competitive priorities. If a firm offers a unique product or high-quality service, competitive priorities may indicate the need for hand labor and individual attention rather than new technology. A case in point is the downstream processes in Gillette's supply chain that package and store the razor cartridges. It customizes the packaging for different regions of the world, so that volumes for any one type of package are much lower. As a result of the low volumes, Gillette does not use expensive automation for these processes. In fact, it outsources them. It produces razor cartridges to stock using highly automated processes and then packages them in customized fashion at remote locations on demand.

Manufacturers use two types of automation: (1) fixed and (2) flexible (or programmable). Particularly appropriate for line and continuous-flow process choices, **fixed automation** produces one type of part or product in a fixed sequence of simple operations. Operations managers favor fixed automation when demand volumes are high, product designs are stable, and product life cycles are long. These conditions compensate for the process's two primary drawbacks: (1) large initial investment cost and (2) relative inflexibility. However, fixed automation maximizes efficiency and yields the lowest variable cost per unit if volumes are high.

Flexible (or programmable) automation can be changed easily to handle various products. The ability to reprogram machines is useful for both low-customization and high-customization processes. In the case of high customization, a machine that makes a variety of products in small batches can be programmed to alternate between products. When a machine has been dedicated to a particular product or family of products, as in the case of low customization and a line flow, and the product is at the end of its life cycle, the machine can simply be reprogrammed with a new sequence of tasks for a new product. An **industrial robot**, which is a versatile, computer-controlled machine programmed to perform various tasks, is a classic example of flexible automation. These "steel-collar" workers operate independently of human control. A robot's arm has up to six standard movements. The robot's "hand" can be changed to perform different tasks, such as materials handling, assembly, and testing.

Automating Service Processes Using capital inputs as a labor-saving device is also possible for service processes. In educational services, for example, long-distance learning technology now can supplement or even replace the traditional classroom experience by using books, computers, Web sites, and videos as facilitating goods that go with the service. Justifying technology need not be limited to cost reduction. Sometimes, it can actually allow more task divergence by making available a wide menu of choices to the customer. It can also improve quality by being more consistent.

automation
A system, process, or piece of equipment that is self-acting and self-regulating.

fixed automation
A manufacturing process that produces one type of part or product in a fixed sequence of simple operations.

flexible (or programmable) automation
A manufacturing process that can be changed easily to handle various products.

industrial robot
Versatile, computer-controlled machine programmed to perform various tasks.

R.R. Donnelly has been able to achieve flexible automation by receiving books digitally and preparing them to go to press electronically. This allows the company to put books on press more quickly and print smaller more manageable quantities in a single print run.

James Hardy/PhotoAlto/Alamy

David R. Frazier/Newscom

Regional automated mail sorting facility in Boise, Idaho. Automating service processes in high volume environments such as these save labor and justify expensive capital investments.

The need for volume to justify expensive automation is just as valid for service processes as for manufacturing processes. Increasing the volume lowers the cost per dollar of sales. Volume is essential for many capital-intensive processes in the transportation, communications, and utilities industries.

Economies of Scope   If capital intensity is high, resource flexibility usually is low. In certain types of manufacturing operations, such as machining and assembly, programmable automation breaks this inverse relationship between resource flexibility and capital intensity. It makes possible both high capital intensity and high resource flexibility, creating economies of scope. **Economies of scope** reflect the ability to produce multiple products more cheaply in combination than separately. In such situations, two conflicting competitive priorities—customization and low price—become more compatible. However, taking advantage of economies of scope requires that a family of parts or products have enough collective volume to utilize equipment fully.

economies of scope

Economies that reflect the ability to produce multiple products more cheaply in combination than separately.

Economies of scope also apply to service processes. Consider, for example, Disney whose managers used the Internet to reap the benefits of economies of scope. They aggressively linked their Internet processes with one another and with other parts of Disney. A flexible technology that handles many services together can be less expensive than handling each one separately, particularly when the markets are not too volatile.

Strategic Fit

The manager should understand how the four major process decisions tie together, so as to spot ways of improving poorly designed processes. The choices should fit the situation and each other. When the fit is more *strategic*, the process will be more effective. We examine services and manufacturing processes, looking for ways to test for strategic fit.

Decision Patterns for Service Processes

After analyzing a process and determining its position on the customer-contact matrix in Figure 2.2, it may be apparent that it is improperly positioned, either too far to the left or right, or too far to the top or bottom. Opportunities for improvement become apparent. Perhaps, more customization and customer contact is needed than the process currently provides. Perhaps, instead, the process is too divergent, with unnecessarily flexible flows. Reducing divergence might reduce costs and improve productivity.

The process should reflect its desired competitive priorities. Front offices generally emphasize top quality and customization, whereas back offices are more likely to emphasize low-cost operation, consistent quality, and on-time delivery. The process structure selected then points the way to appropriate choices on customer involvement, resource flexibility, and capital intensity. High customer contact at a front-office service process means:

1. *Process Structure.* The customer (internal or external) is present, actively involved, and receives personal attention. These conditions create processes with high divergence and flexible process flows.

2. *Customer Involvement.* When customer contact is high, customers are more likely to become part of the process. The service created for each customer is unique.

3. *Resource Flexibility.* High process divergence and flexible process flows fit with more flexibility from the process's resources—its workforce, facilities, and equipment.

4. *Capital Intensity.* When volume is higher, automation and capital intensity are more likely. Even though higher volume is usually assumed in the back office, it is just as likely to be in the front office for financial services. Information technology is a major type of automation at many service processes, which brings together both resource flexibility and automation.

Of course, this list provides general tendencies rather than rigid prescriptions. Exceptions can be found, but these relationships provide a way of understanding how service process decisions can be linked coherently.

Decision Patterns for Manufacturing Processes

Just as a service process can be repositioned in the customer-contact matrix, a manufacturing process can also be moved in the product–process matrix. Changes can be made either in the horizontal direction of Figure 2.3 by changing the degree of customization and volume, or they can be moved in the vertical direction by changing process divergence. Competitive priorities must be considered when translating strategy into specific manufacturing processes. Figure 2.5 shows some usual tendencies found in practice. Job and small batch processes are usual choices if top quality, on-time delivery, and flexibility (customization, variety, and volume flexibility) are given primary emphasis. Large batch, line, and continuous-flow processes match up with an emphasis on low-cost operations, consistent quality, and delivery speed.

The production and inventory strategy should also be chosen to be consistent with the competitive priorities emphasized. As shown in Figure 2.5, the design-to-order strategy is consistent with top quality, customization, and variety. The focus is on meeting the unique needs of the customers by specifically designing a variety of products according to the customer specifications. The make-to-order strategy matches up with flexibility (particularly customization) and top quality. Because delivery speed is more difficult, meeting due dates and on-time delivery get the emphasis on the time dimension. The assemble-to-order strategy allows delivery speed and flexibility (particularly variety) to be achieved, whereas the make-to-stock strategy is the usual choice if delivery speed and low-cost operations are emphasized. Keeping an item in stock ensures quick delivery because it is generally available when needed, without delays in producing it. High volumes open up opportunities to reduce costs.

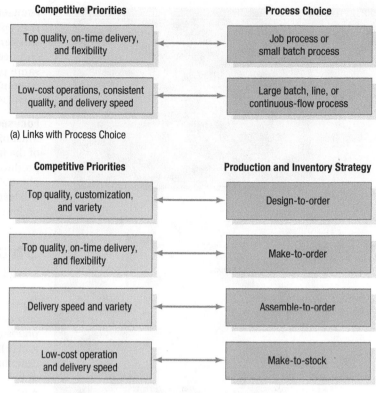

(a) Links with Process Choice

(b) Links with Production and Inventory Strategy

▲ **FIGURE 2.5**
Links of Competitive Priorities with Manufacturing Strategy

The process structure selected once again points the way to appropriate choices on customer involvement, resource flexibility, and capital intensity. High volumes per part type at a manufacturing process typically mean:

1. *Process Structure.* High volumes, combined with a standard product, make a line flow possible. It is just the opposite where a job process produces to specific customer orders.

2. *Customer Involvement.* Customer involvement is not a factor in most manufacturing processes, except for choices made on product variety and customization. Less discretion is allowed with line or continuous-flow processes to avoid the unpredictable demands required by customized orders.

3. *Resource Flexibility.* When volumes are high and process divergence is low, flexibility is not needed to utilize resources effectively, and specialization can lead to more efficient processes.

4. *Capital Intensity.* High volumes justify the large fixed costs of an efficient operation.

Gaining Focus

In the past, new services or products often were added to a facility in the name of better utilizing fixed costs and keeping everything under the same roof. The result was a jumble of competitive priorities, process structures, and technologies. In the effort to do everything, nothing was done well.

Focus by Process Segments   A facility's operations often can neither be characterized nor actually designed for one set of competitive priorities and one process choice. At a services facility, some parts of the process might seem like a front office and other parts like a back office. Such arrangements can be effective, provided that sufficient focus is given to each process by the management segmenting them into separate operations that are relatively autonomous.

Plants within plants (PWPs) are different operations within a facility with individualized competitive priorities, processes, and workforces under the same roof. Boundaries for PWPs may be established by physically separating subunits or simply by revising organizational relationships. At each PWP, customization, capital intensity volume, and other relationships are crucial and must be complementary. The advantages of PWPs are fewer layers of management, greater ability to rely on team problem solving, and shorter lines of communication between departments.

plants within plants (PWPs)

Different operations within a facility with individualized competitive priorities, processes, and workforces under the same roof.

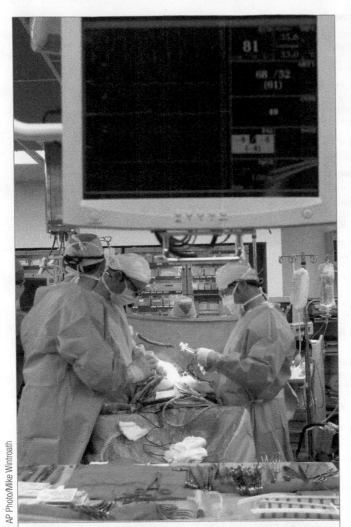

AP Photo/Mike Wintroath

Focused factories are not just found in manufacturing. This single-specialty facility focuses just on heart surgery and has all the advanced resources need that cannot be provided by a general hospital. Another example is the Toronto-based Shouldice Clinic, which focuses just on hernias.

Focused Service Operations   Service industries also implement the concepts of focus and PWPs. Specialty retailers opened stores with smaller, more accessible spaces. These focused facilities generally chipped away at the business of large department stores. Using the same philosophy, some department stores now focus on specific customers or products. Remodeled stores create the effect of many small boutiques under one roof.

Focused Factories   Hewlett-Packard, Rolls-Royce, Japan's Ricoh and Mitsubishi, and Britain's Imperial Chemical Industries PLC are some of the firms that created **focused factories**, splitting large plants that produced all the company's products into several specialized smaller plants. The theory is that narrowing the range of demands on a facility will lead to better performance because management can concentrate on fewer tasks and lead a workforce toward a single goal.

Strategies for Change

The four major process decisions represent broad, strategic issues and define the nature of the processes a firm needs to compete effectively. However, decisions that are made must be translated into actual process designs or redesigns. There are two different but complementary philosophies for process design and change: (1) process reengineering and (2) process improvement. Process analysis, supported by the tools described later, is needed regardless of whether reengineering or process improvement is attempted. An individual or a whole team examines the process and looks for ways to streamline tasks, eliminate whole processes entirely, cut expensive materials or services, improve the environment, or make jobs safer. By comprehensively analyzing the process, one must find the ways to trim costs and delays and to improve customer satisfaction.

Process Reengineering

Reengineering is the fundamental rethinking and radical redesign of processes to improve performance dramatically in terms of cost, quality, service, and speed. Process reengineering is about reinvention rather than incremental improvement. It is strong medicine and not always needed or successful. Pain, in the form of layoffs and large cash outflows for investments in information technology, almost always accompanies massive change. However, reengineering processes can have big payoffs. Table 2.2 lists the key elements of the overall approach.

focused factories

The result of a firm's splitting large plants that produced all the company's products into several specialized smaller plants.

reengineering

The fundamental rethinking and radical redesign of processes to improve performance dramatically in terms of cost, quality, service, and speed.

TABLE 2.2 | KEY ELEMENTS OF REENGINEERING

Element	Description
Critical processes	The emphasis of reengineering should be on core business processes. Normal process-improvement activities can be continued with the other processes.
Strong leadership	Senior executives must provide strong leadership for reengineering to be successful. Otherwise, cynicism, resistance ("we tried that before"), and boundaries between departments can block radical changes.
Cross-functional teams	A team, consisting of members from each functional area affected by the process change, is charged with carrying out a reengineering project. Self-managing teams and employee empowerment are the rule rather than the exception.
Information technology	Information technology is a primary enabler of process engineering. Most reengineering projects design processes around information flows, such as customer order fulfillment.
Clean-slate philosophy	Reengineering requires a "clean-slate" philosophy—that is, starting with the way the customer wants to deal with the company. To ensure a customer orientation, teams begin with internal and external customer objectives for the process.
Process analysis	Despite the clean-slate philosophy, a reengineering team must understand things about the current process: what it does, how well it performs, and what factors affect it. The team must look at every procedure involved in the process throughout the organization.

Reengineering has led to many successes and will continue to do so. However, it is not simple or easily done, nor is it appropriate for all processes or all organizations. The best understanding of a process, and how to improve it, often lies with the people who perform the work each day, not with cross-functional teams or top management.

Process Improvement

Process improvement is the systematic study of the activities and flows of each process to improve it. Its purpose is to "learn the numbers," understand the process, and dig out the details. Once a process is really understood, it can be improved. The relentless pressure to provide better quality at a lower price means that companies must continually review all aspects of their operations. Process improvement goes on, whether or not a process is reengineered. There is always a better way. Most processes can be improved if someone thinks of a way and implements it effectively. Indeed, companies will either adapt processes to the changing needs of customers or cease to exist. Long-term success comes from managers and employees who really understand their businesses. But all too often, highly publicized efforts that seem to offer quick-fix solutions fail to live up to expectations over the long haul, be they programs for conceptualizing a business vision, conducting culture transformation campaigns, or providing leadership training.

process improvement
The systematic study of the activities and flows of each process to improve it.

Process Analysis

Process analysis is the documentation and detailed understanding of how work is performed and how it can be redesigned. Looking at the strategic issues can help identify opportunities for improvement. Do gaps exist between a process's competitive priorities and its current competitive capabilities, as was found for the assessment of operations strategy at a credit card division in Chapter 1, "Using Operations to Create Value"? Do multiple measures of cost, top quality, quality consistency, delivery speed, and on-time delivery meet or exceed expectations? Is there a good *strategic fit* in the process? If the process provides a service, does its position on the customer-contact matrix (see Figure 2.2) seem appropriate? How does the degree of customer contact match up with process structure, customer involvement, resource flexibility, and capital intensity? Similar questions should be asked about manufacturing processes regarding the strategic fit between process choice, volume, and product customization.

Process analysis begins with identifying and defining a new opportunity for improvement and ends with implementing and controlling a revised process, and which we capture through the Six Sigma Process Improvement Model. Other approaches to process improvement are statistical process control and process capability analysis, discussed in Chapter 3, "Quality and Performance," and value stream mapping, discussed in Chapter 6, "Lean Systems." We avoid overlap by covering each technique just once, while bringing out the essence of the approach covered in each chapter. The chapters do have a shared goal: better processes.

Six Sigma Process Improvement Model   Figure 2.6 shows the Six Sigma Process Improvement Model, a five-step procedure that leads to improvements in-process performance. This model can be applied to projects involving incremental improvements to processes or to projects requiring major changes, including a redesign of an existing process or the development of a new process.

The following steps comprise the model:

- *Define.* The scope and boundaries of the process to be analyzed are first established. Is it a broad process that stretches across the whole organization, involving many steps and many employees, or is it a more narrowly bracketed nested subprocess that is just part of one person's job? A process's scope can be too narrow or too broad. For example, a broadly defined process that outstrips the resources available, sometimes called "trying to boil the ocean," is doomed because it will increase employee frustration without producing any results. The resources that management assigns to improving or reengineering a process should match the scope of the process. Once scope is established, determine the characteristics of the process's output that are critical to customer satisfaction and identify any gaps between these characteristics and the process's capabilities. Get a picture of the current process by documenting it using techniques outlined in this chapter.

- *Measure.* It is important to have good performance measures to evaluate a process for clues on how to improve it. **Metrics** are performance measures for the process and the steps within it. A good place to start is with competitive priorities, but they need to be specific. The analyst creates multiple measures of quality, customer satisfaction, time to perform each step or the whole process, cost, errors, safety, environmental measures, on-time delivery, flexibility, and the like. Once the metrics are identified, it is time to collect information on how the process is currently performing on each one. Measurement can be rough-cut estimates or quite extensive. It is important to quantify the work the process does that affects the gap. Select what to measure, identify data sources, and prepare a data collection plan.

- *Analyze.* Use the data on measures to perform process analysis to determine where improvements are necessary. A careful analysis of the process and its performance on the selected metrics should

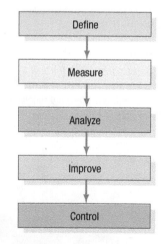

▲ **FIGURE 2.6**
Six Sigma Process Improvement Model

metrics
Performance measures that are established for a process and the steps within it.

uncover *disconnects*, or gaps, between actual and desired performance. Illogical, missing, or extraneous steps can cause performance gaps. They can also be caused by metrics that reinforce the silo mentality of individual departments when the process spans across several departments. The analyst or design team should dig deep to find the root causes of performance gaps. For instance, techniques for analyzing wait times and delays can provide important information (see Supplement B, "Waiting Lines" and MyOMLab Supplement E, "Simulation"). Whether or not major redesign is necessary, establish procedures to make the desired outcome routine.

- *Improve*. Using analytical and creative thinking, the design team generates a long list of ideas for improvements. These ideas are then sifted and analyzed. Ideas that are justifiable, where benefits outweigh costs, are reflected in a new process design that can meet the new performance objectives. The new design should be documented "as proposed." Combining the new process design with the documentation of the current process gives the analysts clear before and after pictures. The new documentation should make clear how the revised process will work and the performance expected for the various metrics used. Implement the changes.

- *Control*. After the implementation, monitor the process to make sure that high performance levels are maintained. Once again, data analysis tools can be used to control the process. Implementation is more than developing a plan and carrying it out. Many processes have been redesigned effectively, but never get implemented. People resist change: "We have always done it that way" or "we tried that before." Widespread participation in process analysis is essential, not only because of the work involved but also because it builds commitment. It is much easier to implement something that is partly your own idea. In addition, special expertise may be needed, such as for developing software. New jobs and skills may be needed, involving training and investments in new technology. Implementation and control brings to life the steps needed to bring the redesigned process online. Management or the steering committee must make sure that the implementation project goes according to schedule.

Successful users have found that it is essential to rigorously follow the steps in the Six Sigma Improvement Model, which is sometimes referred to as the *DMAIC process* (whose name comes from using the first letter of each step in the model). To accomplish the goals of Six Sigma, employees must be trained in the "whys" and the "how-tos" of process performance and what it means to customers, both internal and external. Successful firms using Six Sigma develop a cadre of internal teachers who then are responsible for teaching and assisting teams involved in a process-improvement project. These teachers have different titles depending on their experience and level of achievement. "**Green Belts**" devote part of their time to teaching and helping teams with their projects and the rest of their time to their normally assigned duties. "**Black Belts**" are full-time teachers and leaders of teams involved in Six Sigma projects. Finally, "**Master Black Belts**" are full-time teachers who review and mentor "Black Belts."

Green Belt

An employee who achieved the first level of training in a Six Sigma program and spends part of his or her time teaching and helping teams with their projects.

Black Belt

An employee who reached the highest level of training in a Six Sigma program and spends all of his or her time teaching and leading teams involved in Six Sigma projects.

Master Black Belt

Full-time teachers and mentors to several Black Belts.

flowchart

A diagram that traces the flow of information, customers, equipment, or materials through the various steps of a process.

Documenting and Evaluating the Process

Three major techniques for effectively documenting and evaluating processes are (1) flowcharts, (2) work measurement techniques, and (3) process charts. They allow you to "lift the lid and peer inside" to see how an organization does its work. You can see how a process operates, at any level of detail, and how well it is performing. Trying to create one of these charts might even reveal a lack of any established process. It may not be a pretty picture, but it is how work actually gets done. Techniques for documenting the process lend themselves to finding performance gaps, generating ideas for process improvements, and documenting the look of a redesigned process.

Flowcharts

A **flowchart** traces the flow of information, customers, equipment, or materials through the various steps of a process. Flowcharts are also known as flow diagrams, process maps, relationship maps, or blueprints. Flowcharts have no precise format and typically are drawn with boxes (with a brief description of the step inside), and with lines and arrows to show sequencing. The rectangle ($\square$) shape is the usual choice for a box, although other shapes ($\bigcirc, \bigcirc, \bigcirc,$ $\bigtriangledown,$ or $\square$) can differentiate between different types of steps (e.g., operation, delay, storage, and inspection). Colors and shading can also call attention to different

Young designer presenting a flow chat during a meeting. The use of flowcharts can help in documenting and evaluating processes.

types of steps, such as those particularly high on process divergence. Divergence is also communicated when an outgoing arrow from a step splits into two or more arrows that lead to different boxes. Although many representations are acceptable, there must be agreement on the conventions used. They can be given as a key somewhere in the flowchart, and/or described in accompanying text. It is also important to communicate *what* (e.g., information, customer order, customer, and materials) is being tracked.

You can create flowcharts with several programs. Microsoft PowerPoint offers many different formatting choices for flowcharts (see the Flowchart submenu under AutoShapes). The tutorials "Flowcharting in Excel" and "Flowcharting in PowerPoint" in MyOMLab offer other options. Other powerful software packages for flowcharting and drawing diagrams (such as organization charts and decision trees) are SmartDraw (**http://www.smartdraw.com**), Microsoft Visio (**http://www.microsoft.com/office/visio**), and Micrografx (**http://www.micrografx.com**). Often, free downloads are available at such sites on a trial basis.

MyOMLab

Flowcharts can be created for several levels in the organization. For example, at the strategic level, they could show the core processes and their linkages, as in Figure 1.4 in Chapter 1. At this level, the flowcharts do not have much detail; however, they give a bird's eye view of the overall business. Just identifying a core process is often helpful. However, in this chapter, we focus at the process level, where we get into the details of the process being analyzed. Many steps may have subprocesses nested within them. Rather than representing everything in one flowchart, an overview of the whole process can first be created. Subsequently flowcharts can be developed to flesh out nested processes. This nesting approach often becomes a practical necessity because only so much detail can be shown in any single flowchart.

Swim Lane Flowchart   One of the most commonly used forms of a flowchart is the **swim lane flowchart**. It is a visual representation that groups functional areas responsible for different subprocesses into lanes. It is most appropriate when the business process spans several department boundaries, and where parallel lines similar to lanes in a swimming pool separate each department or a functional area. Swim lanes are labeled according to the functional groups they represent and can be arranged either horizontally or vertically.

The swim lane flowchart in Figure 2.7 illustrates the order placement and acceptance process at a manufacturing company. The process starts when an order is generated by a customer and ends when

swim lane flowchart

A visual representation that groups functional areas responsible for different subprocesses into lanes. It is most appropriate when the business process spans several department boundaries.

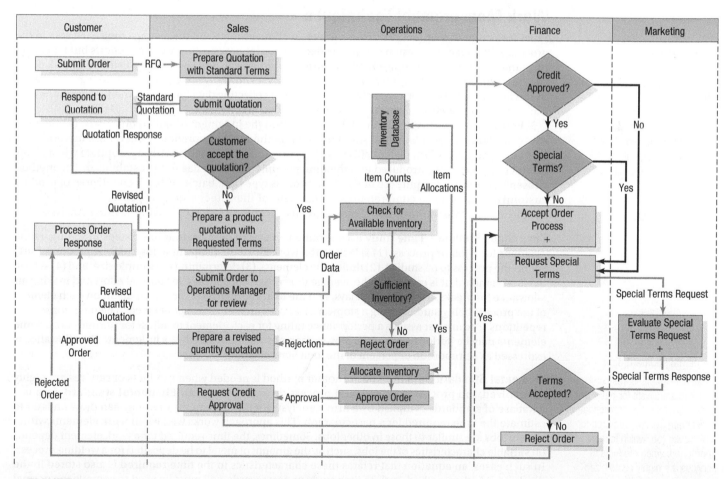

▲ **FIGURE 2.7**

Swim Lane Flowchart of the Order-Filling Process Showing Handoffs between Departments

Source: D. Kroenke, *Using MIS*, 4th ed., © 2012. Reprinted and electronically reproduced by permission of Pearson Education, Inc., Upper Saddle River, New Jersey.

the order is actually rejected, modified, or approved by the company in consultation with the customer. All functions contributing to this process are included in the flowchart. The columns represent different departments or functional areas, and the steps appear in the department column where they are performed. The customer is also shown as one of the column headings. This approach shows the *handoffs* from one department to another when the outgoing arrow from a step goes to another column. Special dotted-line arrows are one way to show handoffs. Handoffs are points where cross-functional coordination is at particular risk due to the silo mentality. Misunderstandings, backlogs, and errors are more likely at these points.

Figure 2.7 illustrates one other feature. The diamond shape (◊) represents a yes/no decision or outcome, such as the results of an inspection or recognition of different kinds of customer requirements. In Figure 2.7, the diamond represents three yes/no decision points within finance, and one each within sales and operations. These yes/no decision points are more likely to appear when a process is high in divergence.

Swim lane flowcharts allow the process analyst and managers to look at the horizontal organization rather than the vertical organization and departmental boundaries implied by a typical organizational chart. Swim lane flowcharts show how organizations produce their outputs through cross-functional work processes and allow the design team to see all the critical interfaces between functions and departments.

service blueprint

A special flowchart of a service process that shows which steps have high customer contact.

Service Blueprint   A **service blueprint** is a special flowchart of a service process that shows which steps have high customer contact. It uses a dotted line of visibility to identify which steps are visible to the customer (and thus are more of a front-office process) and those that are not (back-office process). Of course, visibility is just one aspect of customer contact, and it may not adequately capture how actively the customer is involved or how much personal attention is required. A service blueprint can use colors, shading, or box shapes, instead of the lines of visibility, to show the extent and type of customer contact. Another approach to service blueprinting is to tag each step with a number, and then have an accompanying table that describes in detail the customer contact for each numbered step. There is no one "right way" to create a flow chart or service blueprint.

Work Measurement Techniques

time study

A work measurement method using a trained analyst to perform four basic steps in setting a time standard for a job or process: selecting the work elements (or nested processes) within the process to be studied, timing the elements, determining the sample size, and setting the final standard.

MyOMLab

Process documentation would not be complete without estimates of the average time each step in the process would take. Time estimates are needed not just for process-improvement efforts but for capacity planning, constraint management, performance appraisal, and scheduling. Estimating task times can be as simple as making a reasoned guess, asking a knowledgeable person, or taking notes while observing the process. More extensive studies involve collecting data for several weeks, consulting cost accounting data, or checking data recorded in information systems.

Formal techniques are also available that rely on the judgment of skilled observers: (1) the time study method, (2) the elemental standard data method, (3) the predetermined data method, and (4) work sampling. A fifth method, (5) learning curve analysis, is particularly appropriate when a new product or process is introduced and the time per unit produced has not yet stabilized. The method chosen depends on the purpose of the data, process type (job, batch, or line), and degree of product customization. A more comprehensive treatment of these techniques is provided in MyOMLab Supplement H, "Measuring Output Rates" and MyOMLab Supplement I, "Learning Curve Analysis."

Time Study Method   **Time study** uses a trained analyst to perform four basic steps in setting a time standard for a job or process: (1) selecting the work elements (steps in a flowchart or process chart) within the process to be studied, (2) timing the elements, (3) determining the sample size, and (4) setting the final standard. It is essentially the average time observed, adjusted for normal effort and making an allowance for breaks, unavoidable delays, and the like. The analyst records time spent on each element of the process being studied using a stopwatch, and records the time spent on each element for several repetitions. The analyst assigns a performance rating for each element to adjust for normal effort. Some elements may be performed faster or slower than normal, in the analyst's judgment. The allowance is expressed as a proportion or percent of the total *normal* time.

elemental standard data

A database of standards compiled by a firm's analysts for basic elements that they can draw on later to estimate the time required for a particular job, which is most appropriate when products or services are highly customized, job processes prevail, and process divergence is great.

Elemental Standard Data Method   Another method is needed when products or services are highly customized, job processes prevail, and process divergence is great. **Elemental standard data** is a database of standards compiled by a firm's analysts for basic elements that they can draw on later to estimate the time required for a particular job. This approach works well when work elements within certain jobs are similar to those in other jobs. Sometimes, the time required for a work element depends on variable characteristics of the jobs, such as the amount of metal to be deposited for a welding process. In such cases, an equation that relates these characteristics to the time required is also stored in the database. Another method, such as time study or past records, still must be used to compile the normal times (before the allowance is added) stored in the database.

| EXAMPLE 2.1 | Time Study of Watch Assembly Process |

A process at a watch assembly plant has been changed. The process is divided into three work elements. A time study has been performed with the following results. The time standard for the process previously was 14.5 minutes. Based on the new time study, should the time standard be revised?

SOLUTION

The new time study had an initial sample of four observations, with the results shown in the following table. The performance rating factor (RF) is shown for each element (to adjust for normal effort), and the allowance for the whole process is 18 percent of the total *normal* time.

Workers seen on a watch assembly line at the Jaeger-LeCoultre factory in Le Sentier, Switzerland.

Christopher Bosset/Bloomberg/Getty Images

	Obs 1	Obs 2	Obs 3	Obs 4	Average (min)	RF	Normal Time
Element 1	2.60	2.34	3.12	2.86	2.730	1.0	2.730
Element 2	4.94	4.78	5.10	4.68	4.875	1.1	5.363
Element 3	2.18	1.98	2.13	2.25	2.135	0.9	1.922
					Total Normal Time = **10.015 minutes**		

The normal time for an element in the table is its average time, multiplied by the RF. The total normal time for the whole process is the sum of the normal times for the three elements, or 10.015 minutes. To get the standard time (ST) for the process, just add in the allowance, or

$$ST = 10.015(1 + 0.18) = \mathbf{11.82}\text{ minutes/watch}$$

DECISION POINT

The time to assemble a watch appears to have decreased considerably. However, based on the precision that management wants, the analyst decided to increase the sample size before setting a new standard. MyOMLab Supplement H, "Measuring Output Rates," gives more information on determining the number of additional observations needed.

MyOMLab

Predetermined Data Method   The **predetermined data method** divides each work element even more, into a series of micromotions that make up the element. The analyst then consults a published database that contains the normal times for the full array of possible micromotions. A process's normal time can then be calculated as the sum of the times given in the database for the elements performed in the process. This approach makes most sense for highly repetitive processes with little process divergence and line flows. The micromotions (such as reach, move, or apply pressure) are very detailed.

Work Sampling Method   **Work sampling** estimates the proportion of time spent by people or machines on different activities, based on observations randomized over time. Examples of these activities include working on a service or product, doing paperwork, waiting for instructions, waiting for maintenance, or being idle. Such data can then be used to assess a process's productivity, estimate the allowances needed to set standards for other work measurement methods, and spot areas for process improvement. It is best used when the processes are highly divergent with flexible flows. Figure 2.8 shows the input data and numerical results for one week of observations. It shows an idle time of 23.81 percent for the week and also reports that 237 more observations are needed to achieve the confidence and precision levels required with the input data. How these conclusions are reached is explained in MyOMLab Supplement H, "Measuring Output Rates."

Learning Curve Analysis   The time estimation techniques just covered assume that the process is stable. If the process is revised, then just repeat the method for the revised process after it stabilizes. Learning curve analysis, on the other hand, takes into account that learning takes place on an ongoing basis, such as when new products or services are introduced frequently. With instruction and repetition,

predetermined data method

A database approach that divides each work element into a series of micromotions that make up the element. The analyst then consults a published database that contains the normal times for the full array of possible micromotions.

work sampling

A process that estimates the proportion of time spent by people or machines on different activities, based on observations randomized over time.

MyOMLab

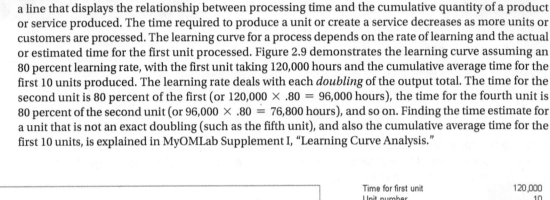

(a) Input Data and Numerical Results			
Increase Observations		Remove An Observation	
Confidence *z*	1.96	Precision *p*	0.05
Observation Period	**Times Busy**	**Times Idle**	**Observations**
Monday	6	1	7
Tuesday	5	2	7
Wednesday	7	0	7
Thursday	9	2	11
Friday	5	5	10
Total	32	10	42

(b) Idle Time and Observations Required	
Portion of idle times	0.2381
Total observations required	279
Additional observations required	237

▲ **FIGURE 2.8**

Work Sampling Study of Admission Clerk at Health Clinic Using OM Explorer's *Time Study* Solver.

learning curve

A line that displays the relationship between processing time and the cumulative quantity of a product or service produced.

MyOMLab

workers learn to perform jobs more efficiently, process improvements are identified, and better administration methods are created. These learning effects can be anticipated with a **learning curve**, a line that displays the relationship between processing time and the cumulative quantity of a product or service produced. The time required to produce a unit or create a service decreases as more units or customers are processed. The learning curve for a process depends on the rate of learning and the actual or estimated time for the first unit processed. Figure 2.9 demonstrates the learning curve assuming an 80 percent learning rate, with the first unit taking 120,000 hours and the cumulative average time for the first 10 units produced. The learning rate deals with each *doubling* of the output total. The time for the second unit is 80 percent of the first (or 120,000 × .80 = 96,000 hours), the time for the fourth unit is 80 percent of the second (or 96,000 × .80 = 76,800 hours), and so on. Finding the time estimate for a unit that is not an exact doubling (such as the fifth unit), and also the cumulative average time for the first 10 units, is explained in MyOMLab Supplement I, "Learning Curve Analysis."

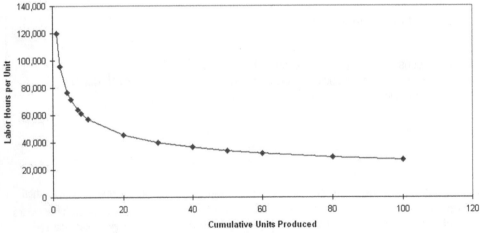

Time for first unit	120,000
Unit number	10
Time for unit 10	57,172
Cumulative average time per unit	75,784

▲ **FIGURE 2.9**

Learning Curve with 80% Learning Rate Using OM Explorer's *Learning Curves* Solver.

process chart

An organized way of documenting all the activities performed by a person or group of people, at a workstation, with a customer, or on materials.

Process Charts

A **process chart** is an organized way of documenting all the activities performed by a person or group of people at a workstation, with a customer, or working with certain materials. It analyzes a process using a table, and provides information about each step in the process. In contrast to flowcharts, swim lane flowcharts, and service blueprints, it requires the time estimates (see work measurement techniques covered in the last section). Often it is used to drill down to the job level for an individual person, a team, or a focused nested process. It can have many formats. Here, we group the type of activities for a typical process into five categories:

- *Operation.* Changes, creates, or adds something. Drilling a hole or serving a customer are examples of operations.
- *Transportation.* Moves the study's subject from one place to another (sometimes called *materials handling*). The subject can be a person, a material, a tool, or a piece of equipment. A customer walking from one end of a counter to the other, a crane hoisting a steel beam to a location, and a conveyor carrying a partially completed product from one workstation to the next are examples of transportation. It could also be the shipment of a finished product to the customer or a warehouse.

- *Inspection.* Checks or verifies something but does not change it. Getting customer feedback, checking for blemishes on a surface, weighing a product, and taking a temperature reading are examples of inspections.

- *Delay.* Occurs when the subject is held up awaiting further action. Time spent waiting for a server; time spent waiting for materials or equipment; cleanup time; and time that workers, machines, or workstations are idle because they have no work to complete are examples of delays.

- *Storage.* Occurs when something is put away until a later time. Supplies unloaded and placed in a storeroom as inventory, equipment put away after use, and papers put in a file cabinet are examples of storage.

Depending on the situation, other categories can be used. For example, subcontracting for outside services might be a category, temporary storage and permanent storage, or environmental waste might be three separate categories. Choosing the right category for each activity requires taking the perspective of the subject charted. A delay for the equipment could be inspection or transportation for the operator.

To complete a chart for a new process, the analyst must identify each step performed. If the process is an existing one, the analyst can actually observe the steps and categorize each step according to the subject being studied. The analyst then records the distance traveled and the time taken to perform each step. After recording all the activities and steps, the analyst summarizes the steps, times, and distances data. Figure 2.10 shows a process chart prepared using OM Explorer's *Process Chart* Solver. It is for a patient with a twisted ankle being treated at a hospital. The process begins at the entrance and ends with the patient exiting after picking up the prescription.

After a process is charted, the analyst sometimes estimates the annual cost of the entire process. It becomes a benchmark against which other methods for performing the process can be evaluated. Annual labor cost can be estimated by finding the product of (1) time in hours to perform the process each time, (2) variable costs per hour, and (3) number of times the process is performed each year, or

$$\frac{\text{Annual}}{\text{labor cost}} = \left(\begin{array}{c}\text{Time to perform}\\ \text{the process in hours}\end{array}\right)\left(\begin{array}{c}\text{Variable costs}\\ \text{per hour}\end{array}\right)\left(\begin{array}{c}\text{Number of times process}\\ \text{is performed per year}\end{array}\right)$$

MyOMLab

Tutor 2.2 in MyOMLab provides a new example to practice creating process charts.

Process:	Emergency room admission
Subject:	Ankle injury patient
Beginning:	Enter emergency room
Ending:	Leave hospital

Insert Step

Append Step

Remove Step

Summary

Activity	Number of Steps	Time (min)	Distance (ft)
Operation ●	5	23.00	
Transport ➡	9	11.00	815
Inspect ■	2	8.00	
Delay ◗	3	8.00	
Store ▼	—	—	—

◀ **FIGURE 2.10**
Process Chart for Emergency Room Admission

MyOMLab Animation

Step No.	Time (min)	Distance (ft)	●	➡	■	◗	▼	Step Description
1	0.50	15.0		X				Enter emergency room, approach patient window
2	10.00		X					Sit down and fill out patient history
3	0.75	40.0		X				Nurse escorts patient to ER triage room
4	3.00				X			Nurse inspects injury
5	0.75	40.0		X				Return to waiting room
6	1.00					X		Wait for available bed
7	1.00	60.0		X				Go to ER bed
8	4.00					X		Wait for doctor
9	5.00				X			Doctor inspects injury and questions patient
10	2.00	200.0		X				Nurse takes patient to radiology
11	3.00		X					Technician x-rays patient
12	2.00	200.0		X				Return to bed in ER
13	3.00					X		Wait for doctor to return
14	2.00		X					Doctor provides diagnosis and advice
15	1.00	60.0		X				Return to emergency entrance area
16	4.00		X					Check out
17	2.00	180.0		X				Walk to pharmacy
18	4.00		X					Pick up prescription
19	1.00	20.0		X				Leave the building

For example, if the average time to serve a customer is 4 hours, the variable cost is $25 per hour, and 40 customers are served per year, then the labor cost is $4,000 per year (or 4 hrs/customer × $25/hr × 40 customers/yr).

In the case of the patient in Figure 2.10, this conversion would not be necessary, with total patient time being sufficient. What is being tracked is the patient's time, not the time and costs of the service providers.

You can design your own process chart spreadsheets to bring out issues that are particularly important for the process you are analyzing, such as categories for customer contact, process divergence, and the like. You can also track performance measures other than time and distance traveled, such as error rates. In addition, you can also create a different version of the process chart spreadsheet that examines processes much as done with flowcharts, except now in the form of a table. The columns that categorize the activity type could be replaced by one or more columns reporting different metrics of interest, rather than trying to fit them into a flowchart. Although it might not look as elegant, it could be just as informative—and easier to create.

The leader of a design team presents several charts that document a process in their office that they are analyzing. He is identifying several areas of substandard performance across a range of different metrics. The next step will be to redesign the process. The flipchart on the right will be quite useful in generating rapid fire ideas from the team on how the process might be improved.

Data Analysis Tools

Metrics and performance information complete the documentation of a process. The specific metrics analysts choose depends on the process being analyzed and on the competitive priorities. Good starting points are the per-unit processing time and cost at each step, and the time elapsed from beginning to end of the process. Capacity utilization, environmental issues, and customer (or job) waiting times reveal where in the process delays are most likely to occur. Customer satisfaction measures, error rates, and scrap rates identify possible quality problems. We introduce many such metrics in subsequent chapters. Only when these subsequent chapters are understood do we really complete our discussion of process analysis.

Metrics can be displayed in various ways. Sometimes, they can be added directly on the flowchart or process chart. When the number of metrics gets unwieldy, another approach is to create a supporting table for the chart. Its rows are the steps in the flowchart, swim lane flowchart, service blueprint, or process chart. The columns are the current performance, goals, and performance gaps for various metrics. Various tools are available to help you understand the causes of these performance gaps and problems[1]. Here we present six tools: (1) checklists, (2) histograms and bar charts, (3) Pareto charts, (4) scatter diagrams, (5) cause-and-effect diagrams, and (6) graphs. Many of them were developed initially to analyze quality issues, but they apply equally well to process analysis in general.

checklist

A form used to record the frequency of occurrence of certain process failures.

process failure

Any performance shortfall, such as error, delay, environmental waste, rework, and the like.

histogram

A summarization of data measured on a continuous scale, showing the frequency distribution of some process failure (in statistical terms, the central tendency and dispersion of the data).

bar chart

A series of bars representing the frequency of occurrence of data characteristics measured on a yes-or-no basis.

Checklists Data collection through the use of a checklist is often the first step in the analysis of a metric. A **checklist** is a form used to record the frequency of occurrence of certain process failures. A **process failure** is any performance shortfall, such as error, delay, environmental waste, rework, and the like. The characteristics may be measurable on a continuous scale (e.g., weight, customer satisfaction on a 1 to 7 scale, unit cost, scrap loss percentage, time, or length) or on a yes-or-no basis (e.g., customer complaint, posting error, paint discoloration, or inattentive servers).

Histograms and Bar Charts Data from a checklist often can be presented succinctly and clearly with histograms or bar charts. A **histogram** summarizes data measured on a continuous scale, showing the frequency distribution of some process failure (in statistical terms, the central tendency and dispersion of the data). Often the mean of the data is indicated on the histogram. A **bar chart** (see Figure 2.11) is a series of bars representing the frequency of occurrence of data characteristics measured on a yes-or-no basis. The bar height indicates the number of times a particular process failure was observed.

---

[1]Several of these tools, particularly Pareto charts and cause-and-effect diagrams, are closely affiliated with Chapter 3, "Quality and Performance." We introduce them here because they apply to process failures in general and not just to quality rejects.

Pareto Charts   When managers discover several process problems that need to be addressed, they have to decide which should be attacked first. Vilfredo Pareto, a nineteenth-century Italian scientist whose statistical work focused on inequalities in data, proposed that most of an "activity" is caused by relatively few of its factors. In a restaurant quality problem, the activity could be customer complaints and the factor could be "discourteous server." For a manufacturer, the activity could be product defects and the factor could be "missing part." Pareto's concept, called the 80–20 rule, is that 80 percent of the activity is caused by 20 percent of the factors. By concentrating on the 20 percent of the factors (the "vital few"), managers can attack 80 percent of the process failure problems. Of course, the exact percentages vary with each situation, but inevitably relatively few factors cause most of the performance shortfalls.

The few vital factors can be identified with a **Pareto chart**, a bar chart on which the factors are plotted along the horizontal axis in decreasing order of frequency (see Figure 2.12). The chart has two vertical axes, the one on the left showing frequency (as in a histogram) and the one on the right showing the cumulative percentage of frequency. The cumulative frequency curve identifies the few vital factors that warrant immediate managerial attention.

Pareto chart

A bar chart on which factors are plotted along the horizontal axis in decreasing order of frequency.

EXAMPLE 2.2   **Pareto Chart for a Restaurant**

The manager of a neighborhood restaurant is concerned about the lower numbers of customers patronizing his eatery. Complaints have been rising, and he would like to find out what issues to address and present the findings in a way his employees can understand.

SOLUTION

The manager surveyed his customers over several weeks and collected the following data:

Complaint	Frequency
Discourteous server	12
Slow service	42
Cold dinner	5
Cramped tables	20
Atmosphere	10

MyOMLab

Active Model 2.1 in MyOMLab provides additional insights on this Pareto chart example and its extensions.

MyOMLab

Tutor 2.3 in MyOMLab provides a new example on creating Pareto charts.

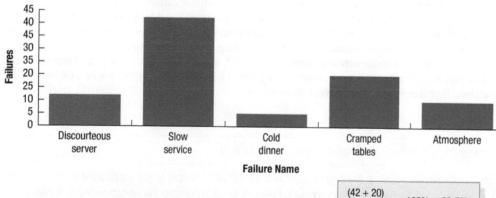

◄ **FIGURE 2.11**
Bar Chart

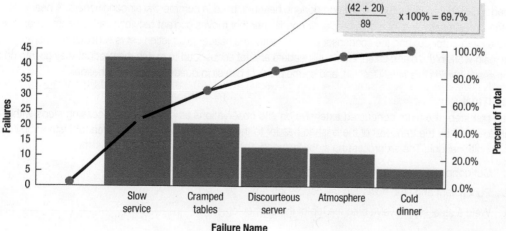

◄ **FIGURE 2.12**
Pareto Chart

Figure 2.11 is a bar chart and Figure 2.12 is a Pareto chart, both created with OM Explorer's *Bar, Pareto, and Line Charts* Solver. They present the data in a way that shows which complaints are more prevalent (the vital few). You can reformat these charts for any yes-or-no metrics by unprotecting the spreadsheet and then making your revisions. Another approach is to create your own spreadsheets from scratch. More advanced software with point-and-click interfaces include Minitab (**http://www.minitab.com/index.htm**), SAS (**http://www.sas.com/rnd/app/qc.html**), and Microsoft Visio (**http://www.microsoft.com/office/visio**).

DECISION POINT

It was clear to the manager (and all employees) which complaints, if rectified, would cover most of the process failure problems in the restaurant. First, slow service will be addressed by training the existing staff, adding another server, and improving the food preparation process. Removing some decorative furniture from the dining area and spacing the tables better will solve the problem with cramped tables. The Pareto chart shows that these two problems, if rectified, will account for almost 70 percent of the complaints.

---

scatter diagram

A plot of two variables showing whether they are related.

Scatter Diagrams   Sometimes managers suspect that a certain factor is causing a particular process failure. A **scatter diagram**, which is a plot of two variables showing whether they are related, can be used to verify or negate the suspicion. Each point on the scatter diagram represents one data observation. For example, the manager of a castings shop may suspect that casting defects are a function of the diameter of the casting. A scatter diagram could be constructed by plotting the number of defective castings found for each diameter of casting produced. After the diagram is completed, any relationship between diameter and number of process failures will be clear.

cause-and-effect diagram

A diagram that relates a key performance problem to its potential causes.

Cause-and-Effect Diagrams   An important aspect of process analysis is linking each metric to the inputs, methods, and process steps that build a particular attribute into the service or product. One way to identify a design problem is to develop a **cause-and-effect diagram** that relates a key performance problem to its potential causes. First developed by Kaoru Ishikawa, the diagram helps management trace disconnects directly to the operations involved. Processes that have no bearing on a particular problem are not shown on the diagram.

The cause-and-effect diagram sometimes is called a *fishbone diagram*. The main performance gap is labeled as the fish's "head," the major categories of potential causes as structural "bones," and the likely specific causes as "ribs." When constructing and using a cause-and-effect diagram, an analyst identifies all the major categories of potential causes for the problem. These might be personnel, machines, materials, and processes. For each major category, the analyst lists all the likely causes of the performance gap. Under personnel might be listed "lack of training," "poor communication," and "absenteeism." Creative thinking helps the analyst identify and properly classify all suspected causes. The analyst then systematically investigates the causes listed on the diagram for each major category, updating the chart as new causes become apparent. The process of constructing a cause-and-effect diagram calls management and worker attention to the primary factors affecting process failures. Example 2.3 demonstrates the use of a cause-and-effect diagram by a firm manufacturing air conditioners.

EXAMPLE 2.3	**Analysis of Inadequate Production of Headers**

A process improvement team is working to improve the production output at the Johnson Manufacturing plant's Header Cell that manufactures a key component, headers, used in commercial air conditioners. A header is part of the circulatory system of a commercial air conditioner that moves coolant between various components such as the evaporator coil and the condenser coil. Currently, the header production cell is scheduled separately from the main work in the plant. Often, individual headers are not sequenced to match the product they go into on the final assembly line in a timely fashion, and so the product can sit in queue waiting for a header.

SOLUTION

As a first step, the team conducted extensive on-site observations across the six processing steps within the cell, followed by the transport of the finished header to the air conditioner assembly area for installation into an air conditioner unit. The six processing steps included:

1. Cut copper pipes to the appropriate length.
2. Punch vent and stub holes into the copper log.
3. Weld a steel supply valve onto the top of the copper log.

4. Braze end caps and vent plugs to the copper log.

5. Braze stub tubes into each stub hole in the copper log.

6. Add plastic end caps to protect the newly created header.

To analyze all the possible causes of the problem, the team constructed a cause-and-effect diagram, shown in Figure 2.13. The main problem, inadequate header production, is the head of the diagram. The team brainstormed all possible causes, and together they identified several major categories: management, manpower, method, measurement, machine, and materials, or the 6 M's. Several suspected causes were identified for each major category.

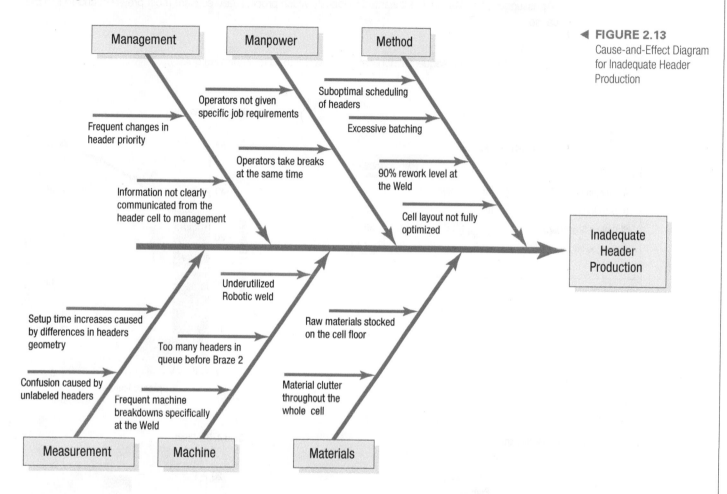

◀ **FIGURE 2.13**
Cause-and-Effect Diagram for Inadequate Header Production

DECISION POINT

The improvement team noted several immediate issues that were slowing down production of headers. These issues included operators batching individual jobs (method branch) into groups to save walking time, which was further exasperated by the availability of raw materials stocked on the shop floor (materials branch) and the lack of specific job requirement (management branch). Further, there were many instances of individual tasks not being done correctly, and thus having to be redone; such as the 90 percent rework rate at weld (method branch). The next step in this process improvement was to eliminate the raw material on the floor, improve quality at the weld machine, and move each header individually using a header-specific cart.

Graphs   Visualizing data in user-friendly ways can greatly enhance process analysis. **Graphs** represent data in a variety of pictorial formats, such as line charts and pie charts. *Line charts* represent data sequentially with data points connected by line segments to highlight trends in the data. Line charts are used in control charts (see Chapter 3, "Quality and Performance") and forecasting (see Chapter 8, "Forecasting"). Pie charts represent process factors as slices of a pie; the size of each slice is in proportion to the number of occurrences of the factor. Pie charts are useful for showing data from *a group of factors* that can be represented as percentages totaling 100 percent.

graphs

Representations of data in a variety of pictorial forms, such as line charts and pie charts.

Each of the tools for improving quality may be used independently, but their power is greatest when they are used together. In solving a process-related problem, managers often must act as detectives, sifting data to clarify the issues involved and deducing the causes. We call this process *data snooping*. Example 2.4 demonstrates how the tools for improving quality can be used for data snooping.

EXAMPLE 2.4   **Identifying Causes of Poor Headliner Process Failures**

The Wellington Fiber Board Company produces headliners, the fiberglass components that form the inner roof of passenger cars. Management wanted to identify which process failures were most prevalent and to find the cause.

SOLUTION

Figure 2.14 shows the sequential application of several tools for improving quality.

▼ **FIGURE 2.14**
Application of the Tools for Improving Quality

Step 1. Checklist

Process failure	Tally	Total
A. Tears in fabric	IIII	4
B. Discolored fabric	III	3
C. Broken fiber board	卅 卅 卅 卅 卅 卅 I	36
D. Ragged edges	卅 II	7
		Total 50

Headliner failures

Step 2. Pareto Chart

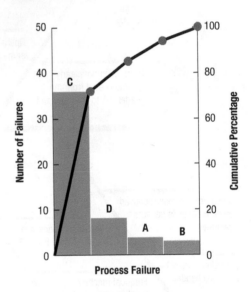

Step 3. Cause-and-Effect Diagram

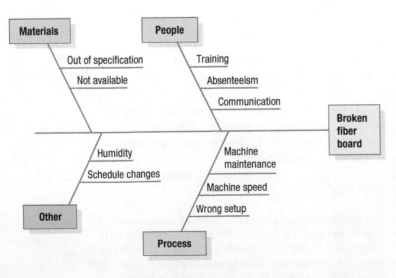

Step 4. Bar Chart

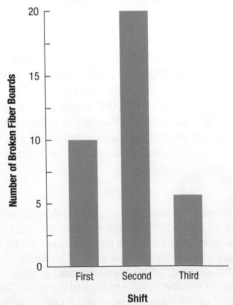

Step 1. A checklist of different types of process failures was constructed from last month's production records.

Step 2. A Pareto chart prepared from the checklist data indicated that broken fiber board accounted for 72 percent of the process failures.

Step 3. A cause-and-effect diagram for broken fiber board identified several potential causes for the problem. The one strongly suspected by the manager was employee training.

Step 4. The manager reorganized the production reports into a bar chart according to shift because the personnel on the three shifts had varied amounts of experience.

DECISION POINT

The bar chart indicated that the second shift, with the least experienced workforce, had most of the process failures. Further investigation revealed that workers were not using proper procedures for stacking the fiber boards after the press operation, which caused cracking and chipping. The manager set up additional training sessions focused on board handling. Although the second shift was not responsible for all the process failures, finding the source of many of the failures enabled the manager to improve the performance of her operations.

A simulation model goes one step further than static data analysis tools, because it can show how the process dynamically changes over time. **Process simulation** is the act of reproducing the behavior of a process, using a model that describes each step. Once the process is modeled, the analyst can make changes in the model to measure the impact on certain metrics, such as response time, waiting lines, resource utilization, and the like. To learn more about how simulation works, see MyOMLab Supplement E, "Simulation."

process simulation

The act of reproducing the behavior of a process, using a model that describes each step.

Redesigning and Managing Process Improvements

A doctor pinpoints an illness after a thorough examination of the patient, and then the doctor recommends treatments based on the diagnosis; so it is with processes. After a process is documented, metrics data are collected, and disconnects are identified, the process analyst or design team puts together a set of changes that will make the process better. At this step, people directly involved in the process are brought in to get their ideas and inputs.

brainstorming

Letting a group of people, knowledgeable about the process, propose ideas for change by saying whatever comes to mind.

Questioning and Brainstorming

Sometimes, ideas for reengineering or improving a process become apparent after documenting the process and carefully examining the areas of substandard performance, handoffs between departments, and steps where customer contact is high. Example 2.4 illustrated how such documentation pointed to a better way of handling the fiber boards through better training. In other cases, the better solution is less evident. Ideas can be uncovered (because there is always a better way) by asking six questions about each step in the process, and a final series of questions about the process as a whole:

1. *What* is being done?
2. *When* is it being done?
3. *Who* is doing it?
4. *Where* is it being done?
5. *How* is it being done?
6. *How* well does it do on the various metrics of importance?

Answers to these questions are challenged by asking still another series of questions. *Why* is the process even being done? *Why* is it being done where it is being done? *Why* is it being done when it is being done?

Creativity can also be stimulated by **brainstorming**, letting a group of people knowledgeable about the process propose ideas for change by saying whatever comes to mind. A facilitator records the ideas on a flipchart, so that all can see. Participants are discouraged from evaluating any of the ideas generated during the session. The purpose is

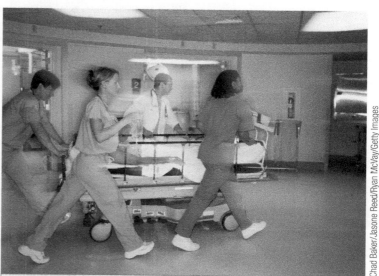

Baptist Memorial Hospital in Memphis, Tennessee, holds "huddle meetings" at least three times a day seeking out process improvements. The meetings bring together the hospital's house supervisor, housekeeping supervisor, and key nurses. Improvements have been dramatic. In 2011, the hospital was ranked in the top 5 percent nationally for emergency medicine.

Chad Baker/Jasone Reed/Ryan McVay/Getty Images

to encourage creativity and to get as many ideas as possible, no matter how far-fetched the ideas may seem. The participants of a brainstorming session need not be limited to the design team as long as they have seen or heard the process documentation. A growing number of big companies are taking advantage of the Internet and specially designed software to run brainstorming sessions that allow people at far-flung locations to "meet" online and hash out solutions to particular problems. The technology lets employees see, and build on, one another's ideas, so that one person's seed of a notion can grow into a practical plan.

After the brainstorming session is over, the design team moves into the "get real" phase: They evaluate the different ideas. The team identifies the changes that give the best payoffs for process redesign. The redesign could involve issues of capacity, technology, or even location, all of which are discussed in more detail in the following chapters.

The redesigned process is documented once again, this time as the "after" view of the process. Expected payoffs are carefully estimated, along with risks. For changes involving investments, the time value of money must be considered (see MyOMLab Supplement F, "Financial Analysis"). The impact on people (skills, degree of change, training requirements, and resistance to change) must also be factored into the evaluation of the new design.

MyOMLab

Benchmarking

benchmarking

A systematic procedure that measures a firm's processes, services, and products against those of industry leaders.

Benchmarking can be another valuable source for process redesign. **Benchmarking** is a systematic procedure that measures a firm's processes, services, and products against those of industry leaders. Companies use benchmarking to better understand how outstanding companies do things so that they can improve their own processes.

Benchmarking focuses on setting quantitative goals for improvement. *Competitive* benchmarking is based on comparisons with a direct industry competitor. *Functional* benchmarking compares areas such as administration, customer service, and sales operations with those of outstanding firms in any industry. For instance, Xerox benchmarked its distribution function against L.L. Bean's because L.L. Bean is renowned as a leading retailer in distribution efficiency and customer service. *Internal* benchmarking involves using an organizational unit with superior performance as the benchmark for other units. This form of benchmarking can be advantageous for firms that have several business units or divisions. All forms of benchmarking are best applied in situations where you are looking for a long-term program of continuous improvement.

Typical measures used in benchmarking include cost per unit, service upsets (breakdowns) per customer, processing time per unit, customer retention rates, revenue per unit, return on investment, and customer satisfaction levels.

Collecting benchmarking data can sometimes be a challenge. Internal benchmarking data is surely the most accessible. One way of benchmarking is always available—tracking the performance of a process over time. Functional benchmarking data are often collected by professional associations or consulting firms. Several corporations and government organizations have agreed to share and standardize performance benchmarks. The American Productivity and Quality Center, a nonprofit organization, created thousands of measures, as Figure 2.15 illustrates. A full range of metrics can be explored at **http://www.apqc.org**. Another source is the Supply Chain Council, which has defined key metrics in its Supply Chain Operations Reference (SCOR) model (See Chapter 14, "Supply Chain Integration.").

Implementing

Implementing a beautifully redesigned process is only the beginning to continually monitoring and improving processes. Metrics goals must be continually evaluated and reset to fit changing requirements. Avoid the following seven mistakes when managing processes:[2]

1. *Not Connecting with Strategic Issues.* Is particular attention being paid to core processes, competitive priorities, impact of customer contact and volume, and strategic fit during process analysis?

2. *Not Involving the Right People in the Right Way.* Does process analysis closely involve the people performing the process, or those closely connected to it as internal customers and suppliers?

3. *Not Giving the Design Teams and Process Analysts a Clear Charter, and then Holding Them Accountable.* Does management set expectations for change and maintain pressure for results? Does it allow paralysis in process-improvement efforts by requiring excessive analysis?

4. *Not Being Satisfied Unless Fundamental "Reengineering" Changes Are Made.* Is the radical change from process reengineering the expectation? If so, the cumulative effect of many small improvements that could be made incrementally could be lost. Process management efforts should not be

---

[2]Geary A. Rummler and Alan P. Brache, *Improving Performance*, 2nd ed. (San Francisco: Jossey-Bass, 1995), pp. 126–133.

Customer Relationship Process

- Total cost of "enter, process, and track orders" per $1,000 revenue
- System costs of process per $100,000 revenue
- Value of sales order line item not fulfilled due to stockouts, as percentage of revenue
- Percentage of finished goods sales value that is returned
- Average time from sales order receipt until manufacturing or logistics is notified
- Average time in direct contact with customer per sales order line item
- Energy consumed in transporting product
- Total distance traveled for products
- Green house gas emissions

Order Fulfillment Process

- Value of plant shipments per employee
- Finished goods inventory turnover
- Reject rate as percentage of total orders processed
- Percentage of orders returned by customers due to quality problems
- Standard customer lead time from order entry to shipment
- Percentage of orders shipped on time
- Use of non-renewable energy sources
- Use of toxic ingredients
- Safe and healthy work environment

New Service/Product Development Process

- Percentage of sales due to services/products launched last year
- Cost of "generate new services/products" process per $1,000 revenue
- Ratio of projects entering the process to projects completing the process
- Time to market for existing service/product improvement project
- Time to market for new service/product project
- Time to profitability for existing service/product improvement project

Supplier Relationship Process

- Cost of "select suppliers and develop/maintain contracts" process per $1,000 revenue
- Number of employees per $1,000 of purchases
- Percentage of purchase orders approved electronically
- Average time to place a purchase order
- Total number of active vendors per $1,000 of purchases
- Percentage of value of purchased material that is supplier certified
- Amount of toxic chemicals used in supplies production process
- Energy consumed in transporting raw materials and parts
- Total distance traveled for raw materials and parts
- Green house gas emissions
- Supplier's use of toxic chemicals in production process
- Percentage of child labor used by supplier

Support Process

- Systems cost of finance function per $1,000 revenue
- Percentage of finance staff devoted to internal audit
- Total cost of payroll processes per $1,000 revenue
- Number of accepted jobs as percentage of job offers
- Total cost of "source, recruit, and select" process per $1,000 revenue
- Average employee turnover rate

◀ **FIGURE 2.15**
Illustrative Benchmarking
Metrics by Type of Process

limited to downsizing or to reorganization only, even though jobs may be eliminated or the structure changed. It should not be limited to big technological innovation projects, even though technological change occurs often.

5. *Not Considering the Impact on People.* Are the changes aligned with the attitudes and skills of the people who must implement the redesigned process? It is crucial to understand and deal with the *people side* of process changes.

6. *Not Giving Attention to Implementation.* Are processes redesigned but never implemented? A great job of flowcharting and benchmarking is of only academic interest if the proposed changes are not implemented. Sound project management practices are required.

7. *Not Creating an Infrastructure for Continuous Process Improvement.* Is a measurement system in place to monitor key metrics over time? Is anyone checking to see whether anticipated benefits of a redesigned process are actually being realized?

Failure to manage processes is failure to manage the business. Managers must make sure that their organization spots new performance gaps in the continual search for process improvements. Process redesign efforts need to be part of periodic reviews and even annual plans. Measurement is the particular focus of the next chapter. It covers how a performance tracking system is the basis for feedback and improvement efforts. The essence of a learning organization is the intelligent use of such feedback.

LEARNING GOALS IN REVIEW

Learning Goal	Guidelines for Review	MyOMLab Resources
1 Understand the process structure in services and how to position a service process on the customer-contact matrix	The section "Process Structure in Services," pp. 52–54, shows at the process level the key contextual variables associated with service processes and how they relate to each other. There is a key figure in this section: Figure 2.2 brings together three key elements: (1) the degree of customer contact, (2) customization, and (3) process characteristics. It shows how the degree of customer contact and customization are linked with process divergence and line flows.	**Video:** Manufacturing Process Structure Choices
2 Understand the process structure in manufacturing and how to position a manufacturing process on the product-process matrix.	See the section "Process Structure in Manufacturing," pp. 54–56, which focuses on the manufacturing processes. Figure 2.3 brings together three key elements: (1) volume, (2) product customization, and (3) process characteristics. The key drivers are customization and volume, which are linked with line flows and the extent of repetitive work. See the video "Manufacturing Process Structure Choices" to understand how SOME BURROS Mexican Restaurant, WT Graphix Custom Embroidery and Silk Screening, and Crayola make trade-offs between customization and volume in designing their processes.	**Video:** Manufacturing Process Structure Choices
3 Explain the major process strategy decisions and their implications for operations.	"Process Strategy Decisions," pp. 56–60, explains three major process strategy decisions shown in Figure 2.1. Apart from process structure, these include customer involvement, resource flexibility, and capital intensity. Note that customer involvement has advantages and disadvantages, resource flexibility applies to both workforce and equipment, and economies of scope in certain situations can break the inverse relationship between resource flexibility and capital intensity.	**OM Explorer Tutor:** Break-Even for Equipment Selection **POM for Windows:** Break-Even Analysis
4 Discuss how process decisions should strategically fit together.	See "Strategic Fit," pp. 60–62, for a detailed discussion of how managers should understand how the four major process decisions tie together in service and manufacturing firms, so as to spot ways of improving poorly designed processes.	
5 Compare and contrast the two commonly used strategies for change, and understand a systematic way to analyze and improve processes.	The section "Strategies for Change," pp. 62–64, explains two different but complementary philosophies for process design and change: (1) process reengineering and (2) process improvement. The Six Sigma DMAIC model for process improvement then shows a systematic way in which processes can be defined, measured, analyzed, improved, and controlled.	
6 Discuss how to document and evaluate processes.	The section "Documenting and Evaluating the Process," pp. 64–75, discusses three major techniques for effectively documenting and evaluating processes including (1) flowcharts, (2) work measurement techniques, and (3) process charts. Review the Solved Problems for examples of flowchart, process chart, and Pareto chart construction. The time study method, elemental standard data method, predetermined data method, work sampling method, and learning curve analysis are briefly described in the "Work Measurement Techniques" section, pp. 66–68. Pareto charts and cause-and-effect diagrams help you to understand the causes of performance gaps.	**Video:** Process Analysis at Starwood **Cases:** Custom Molds, Inc.; José's Authentic Mexican Restaurant **OM Explorer Solvers:** Learning Curve Analysis; Measuring Output Rates; Process Charts; Pareto Charts **OM Explorer Tutors:** Process Charts; Pareto Charts **POM for Windows:** Learning Curve Analysis; Measuring Output Rates **Supplement I:** Learning Curve Analysis
7 Identify the commonly used approaches for effectively redesigning and managing processes.	The section "Redesigning and Managing Process Improvements," pp. 75–78, discusses how the process analyst puts together a set of changes that will make the process better. Then seven mistakes to avoid when managing processes are discussed at the end. There must be a continual search for process improvements.	

Key Terms

assemble-to-order strategy 56
automation 59
back office 54
bar chart 70
batch process 55
benchmarking 76
Black Belt 64
brainstorming 75
capital intensity 52
cause-and-effect diagram 72
checklist 70
continuous-flow process 55
customer contact 52
customer involvement 51
design-to-order strategy 56
economies of scope 60
elemental standard data 66
fixed automation 59
flexible (or programmable)
    automation 59
flexible flow 53

flexible workforce 58
flowchart 64
focused factories 62
front office 53
graphs 73
Green Belt 64
histogram 70
hybrid office 53
industrial robot 59
job process 55
layout 51
learning curve 68
line flow 53
line process 55
make-to-order strategy 56
make-to-stock strategy 56
mass customization 56
mass production 56
Master Black Belt 64
metrics 63
Pareto chart 71

plants within plants (PWPs) 61
postponement 56
predetermined data method 67
process analysis 51
process chart 68
process choice 55
process divergence 53
process failure 70
process improvement 63
process simulation 75
process strategy 51
process structure 51
reengineering 62
resource flexibility 51
scatter diagram 72
service blueprint 66
swim lane flowchart 65
time study 66
work sampling 67

Solved Problem 1

Create a flowchart for the following telephone-ordering process at a retail chain that specializes in selling books and music CDs. It provides an ordering system via the telephone to its time-sensitive customers besides its regular store sales.

MyOMLab Video

First, the automated system greets customers and identifies whether they have a tone or pulse phone. Customers choose 1 if they have a tone phone; otherwise, they wait for the first available service representative to process their request. If customers have a tone phone, they complete their request by choosing options on the phone. First, the system checks to see whether customers have an existing account. Customers choose 1 if they have an existing account or choose 2 if they want to open a new account. Customers wait for the service representative to open a new account if they choose 2.

Next, customers choose between the options of making an order, canceling an order, or talking to a customer representative for questions and/or complaints. If customers choose to make an order, then they specify the order type as a book or a music CD, and a specialized customer representative for books or music CDs picks up the phone to get the order details. If customers choose to cancel an order, then they wait for the automated response. By entering the order code via phone, customers can cancel the order. The automated system says the name of the ordered item and asks for the confirmation of the customer. If the customer validates the cancellation of the order, then the system cancels the order; otherwise, the system asks the customer to input the order code again. After responding to the request, the system asks whether the customer has additional requests; if not, the process terminates.

SOLUTION

Figure 2.16 shows the flowchart.

FIGURE 2.16 ▶
Flowchart of Telephone
Ordering Process

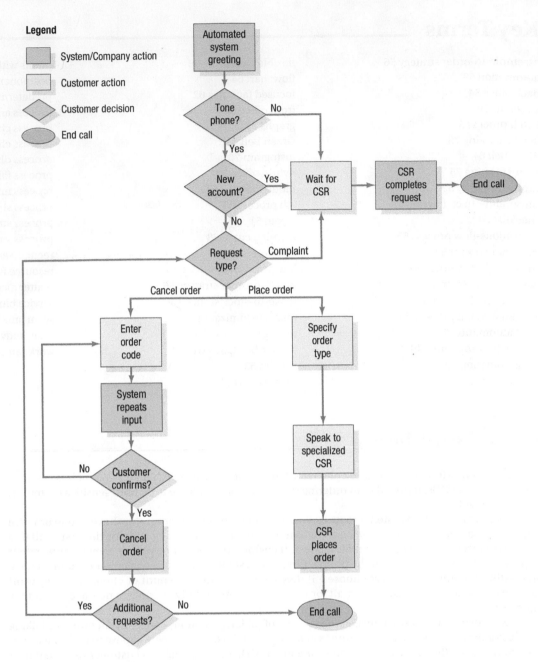

Solved Problem 2

An automobile service is having difficulty providing oil changes in the 29 minutes or less mentioned in its advertising. You are to analyze the process of changing automobile engine oil. The subject of the study is the service mechanic. The process begins when the mechanic directs the customer's arrival and ends when the customer pays for the services.

SOLUTION

Figure 2.17 shows the completed process chart. The process is broken into 21 steps. A summary of the times and distances traveled is shown in the upper right-hand corner of the process chart.

The times add up to 28 minutes, which does not allow much room for error if the 29-minute guarantee is to be met and the mechanic travels a total of 420 feet.

Process:	Changing engine oil
Subject:	Mechanic
Beginning:	Direct customer arrival
Ending:	Total charges, receive payment

Insert Step

Append Step

Remove Step

Summary

Activity		Number of Steps	Time (min)	Distance (ft)
Operation	●	7	16.50	
Transport	➡	8	5.50	420
Inspect	■	4	5.00	
Delay	❱	1	0.70	
Store	▼	1	0.30	

Step No.	Time (min)	Distance (ft)	●	➡	■	❱	▼	Step Description
1	0.80	50.0		X				Direct customer into service bay
2	1.80		X					Record name and desired service
3	2.30				X			Open hood, verify engine type, inspect hoses, check fluids
4	0.80	30.0		X				Walk to customer in waiting area
5	0.60		X					Recommend additional services
6	0.70					X		Wait for customer decision
7	0.90	70.0		X				Walk to storeroom
8	1.90		X					Look up filter number(s), find filter(s)
9	0.40				X			Check filter number(s)
10	0.60	50.0		X				Carry filter(s) to service pit
11	4.20		X					Perform under-car services
12	0.70	40.0		X				Climb from pit, walk to automobile
13	2.70		X					Fill engine with oil, start engine
14	1.30				X			Inspect for leaks
15	0.50	40.0		X				Walk to pit
16	1.00				X			Inspect for leaks
17	3.00		X					Clean and organize work area
18	0.70	80.0		X				Return to auto, drive from bay
19	0.30						X	Park the car
20	0.50	60.0		X				Walk to customer waiting area
21	2.30		X					Total charges, receive payment

Solved Problem 3

What improvement can you make in the process shown in Figure 2.17?

SOLUTION

Your analysis should verify the following three ideas for improvement. You may also be able to come up with others.

a. **Move Step 17 to Step 21.** Customers should not have to wait while the mechanic cleans the work area.

b. **Store Small Inventories of Frequently Used Filters in the Pit.** Steps 7 and 10 involve travel to and from the storeroom. If the filters are moved to the pit, a copy of the reference material must also be placed in the pit. The pit will have to be organized and well lighted.

c. **Use Two Mechanics.** Steps 10, 12, 15, and 17 involve running up and down the steps to the pit. Much of this travel could be eliminated. The service time could be shortened by having one mechanic in the pit working simultaneously with another working under the hood.

Solved Problem 4

Vera Johnson and Merris Williams manufacture vanishing cream. Their packaging process has four steps: (1) mix, (2) fill, (3) cap, and (4) label. They have had the reported process failures analyzed, which shows the following:

Process failure	Frequency
Lumps of unmixed product	7
Over- or underfilled jars	18
Jar lids did not seal	6
Labels rumpled or missing	29
Total	60

Draw a Pareto chart to identify the vital failures.

SOLUTION

Defective labels account for 48.33 percent of the total number of failures:

$$\frac{29}{60} \times 100\% = 48.33\%$$

Improperly filled jars account for 30 percent of the total number of failures:

$$\frac{18}{60} \times 100\% = 30.00\%$$

The cumulative percent for the two most frequent failures is

$$48.33\% + 30.00\% = 78.33\%$$

Lumps represent $\frac{7}{60} \times 100\% = 11.67\%$ of failures; the cumulative percentage is

$$78.33\% + 11.67\% = 90.00\%$$

Defective seals represent $\frac{6}{60} \times 100\% = 10\%$ of failures; the cumulative percentage is

$$10\% + 90\% = 100.00\%$$

The Pareto chart is shown in Figure 2.18.

FIGURE 2.18 ▶
Pareto Chart

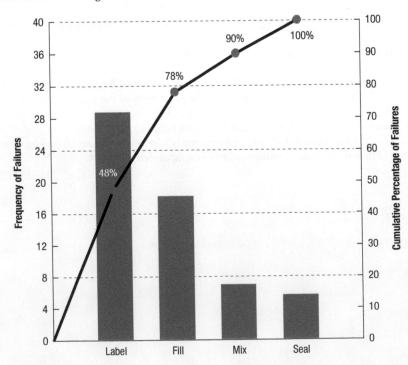

Discussion Questions

1. What processes at manufacturing firms are really service processes that involve considerable customer contact? Can customer contact be high, even if the process only has internal customers?

2. Consider this sign seen in a local restaurant: "To-go orders do NOT include complimentary chips and salsa. If you have any questions, see our management, NOT our employees." What impact does this message have on its employees, their service processes, and customer satisfaction? Contrast this approach with the one taken by a five-star restaurant. Are the differences primarily due to different competitive priorities?

3. How do the process strategies of eBay and McDonald's differ, and how do their choices relate to customer-introduced variability?

4. Medical technology can outfit a patient with an artificial heart or cure vision defects with the touch of a laser. However, hospitals still struggle with their back-office processes, such as getting X-ray files from radiology on the fourth floor to the first-floor view boxes in the emergency room without having to send a runner. More than 90 percent of the estimated 30 billion health transactions each year are conducted by telephone, fax, or mail. To what extent, and how, can information technology improve productivity and quality for such processes? Remember that some doctors are not ready to give up their pads and pencils, and many hospitals have strong lines drawn around its departments, such as pharmacy, cardiology, radiology, and pediatrics.

5. Consider the range of processes in the financial services industry. What position on the customer-contact matrix would the process of selling financial services to municipalities occupy? The process of preparing monthly fund balance reports? Explain why they would differ.

6. Rate operators at a call center, who respond to queries from customers who call in about the company's product, on each of the five dimensions of customer contact in Table 2.1. Use a seven-point scale, where 1 = very low and 7 = very high. For example, the operators newer are physically present with the customer, and so they would get a score of 1 for physical presence. Explain your ratings, and then calculate a combined score for the overall customer contact. Did you use equal weights in calculating the combined score? Why or why not? Where is your process positioned on the customer-contact matrix? Is it properly aligned? Why or why not?

7. Continuous improvement recognizes that many small improvements add up to sizable benefits. Will continuous improvement take a company at the bottom of an industry to the top? Explain.

8. The Hydro-Electric Company (HEC) has three sources of power. A small amount of hydroelectric power is generated by damming wild and scenic rivers; a second source of power comes from burning coal, with emissions that create acid rain and contribute to global warming; the third source of power comes from nuclear fission. HEC's coal-fired plants use obsolete pollution-control technology, and an investment of several hundred million dollars would be required to update it. Environmentalists urge HEC to promote conservation and purchase power from suppliers that use the cleanest fuels and technology.

   However, HEC is already suffering from declining sales, which have resulted in billions of dollars invested in idle equipment. Its large customers are taking advantage of laws that permit them to buy power from low-cost suppliers. HEC must cover the fixed costs of idle capacity by raising rates charged to its remaining customers or face defaulting on bonds (bankruptcy). The increased rates motivate even more customers to seek low-cost suppliers, the start of a death spiral for HEC. To prevent additional rate increases, HEC implements a cost-cutting program and puts its plans to update pollution controls on hold.

   Form sides and discuss the ethical, environmental, and political issues and trade-offs associated with HEC's strategy.

9. Paul O'Neill, former U.S. Treasury Secretary, estimated that arguably half of the $2 trillion a year that Americans spend on health care is needlessly wasted. Brainstorm up to 10 blue-sky ideas to solve the following problems:

   a. A typical retail pharmacy spends 20 percent of its time playing telephone tag with doctors trying to find out what the intent was for a given prescription.

   b. After the person responsible for filling the prescription determines what they think they are supposed to do, errors can be made even in filling the prescription. For example, administering an adult dose (rather than the dose for a premature baby) of Heparin in a preemie ICU is fatal.

   c. Drugs get distributed at a hospital on a batch basis. For example, carts can be filled on Monday, Wednesday, and Friday. A huge volume of drugs can come back on Monday because they are not consumed on the wards between Friday and Monday, patient conditions changed, or the doctor decided on a different intervention. A technician spends the rest of the day restocking the shelves with the returns and 40 percent of the intravenous materials prepared on Friday morning are poured down the drain.

   d. Sometimes the administration of the drug was not done on the agreed schedule, because the nurses were busy doing something else.

   e. For every bed in an acute care hospital system, someone falls during the year. Most falls occur after 11 P.M. and before 6 A.M. Sometimes a bone is fractured, leading to immobilization and then pneumonia.

   f. One in every 14 people who goes to a U.S. hospital gets an infection they did not bring with them.

Problems

The OM Explorer and POM for Windows software is available to all students using the 11th edition of this textbook. Go to **http://www.pearsonhighered.com/krajewski** to download these computer packages. If you purchased MyOMLab, you also have access to Active Models software and significant help in doing the following problems. Check with your instructor on how best to use these resources. In many cases, the instructor wants you to understand how to do the calculations by hand. At the least, the software provides a check on your calculations. When calculations are particularly complex and the goal is interpreting the results in making decisions, the software replaces entirely the manual calculations.

Process Strategy Decisions

Problems 1, 2, and 3 apply break-even analysis (discussed in Supplement A, "Decision Making") to process decisions.

1. Dr. Gulakowicz is an orthodontist. She estimates that adding two new chairs will increase fixed costs by $150,000, including the annual equivalent cost of the capital investment and the salary of one more technician. Each new patient is expected to bring in $3,000 per year in additional revenue, with variable costs estimated at $1,000 per patient. The two new chairs will allow Dr. Gulakowicz to expand her practice by as many as 200 patients annually. How many patients would have to be added for the new process to break even?

2. Two different manufacturing processes are being considered for making a new product. The first process is less capital-intensive, with fixed costs of only $50,000 per year and variable costs of $700 per unit. The second process has fixed costs of $400,000 but has variable costs of only $200 per unit.

   a. What is the break-even quantity beyond which the second process becomes more attractive than the first?

   b. If the expected annual sales for the product is 800 units, which process would you choose?

3. The operations manager at Sebago Manufacturing is considering three proposals for supplying a critical component for its new line of electric watercraft. Proposal one is to purchase the component, proposal two is make the component in-house using rebuilt equipment, and proposal three is to purchase new, highly automated equipment. The costs associated with each proposal are provided in the table below.

Proposal	Annual cost of capital required	Variable cost of each component
One: purchase	$0.00	$22.00
Two: make with rebuilt equipment	$150,000.00	$14.00
Three: make with new equipment	$450,000.00	$12.50

At what quantity range will each option be preferred?

Documenting and Evaluating the Process

4. Consider the Custom Molds, Inc., case at the end of this chapter. Prepare a flowchart of the mold fabrication process and the parts manufacturing process, showing how they are linked. For a good tutorial on how to create flowcharts, see **http://www.hci.com.au/hcisite5/library/materials/Flowcharting.htm**. Also check out the Flowcharting Tutor in Excel in MyOMLab.

5. Do Problem 4 using a process chart spreadsheet of your own design, one that differs from the *Process Chart* Solver in OM Explorer. It should have one or more columns to record information or metrics that you think are relevant, be they external customer contacts, time delays, completion times, percent rework, costs, capacity, or demand rates. Your entries should show what information you would collect, even though only part of it is available in the case.

6. Founded in 1970, ABC is one of the world's largest insurance companies with locations in 28 countries. Given the following description, flowchart the new policy setup process as it existed in 1970:

   Individual customers who wanted to set up a new policy would visit one of ABC's 70 branch offices or make contact with an agent. They would then fill out an application and sometimes attach a check. The branch office then sent the application package through company mail to the XYZ division in London. In addition, a customer might also fill out the application at home and send it directly to any number of ABC locations, which would then transfer it to the London operation. Once received, XYZ separated the various parts of the application, then scanned and digitized it. The electronic image was then retrieved from a server and delivered to an associate's desktop client computer. The associate was responsible for entering the information on the form into the appropriate database. If the information supplied on the application was complete, a confirmation notice was automatically printed and sent to the customer. If the information was incomplete, then another associate, trained to deal with customers on the telephone, would call the customer to obtain the additional information. If the customer noticed something wrong on the confirmation notice received, she or he would either call a toll-free number or send in a letter describing the problem. The Customer Problem Resolution division dealt with problems arising at this point. An updated confirmation notice was sent to the customer. If the information was correct, the application transaction was complete.

7. Do Problem 6 using a process chart spreadsheet of your own design, one that differs from the *Process Chart* Solver in OM Explorer. It should have one or more columns to record information or metrics that you think should be collected to analyze the process (see Problem 5).

8. Prepare a flowchart of the field service division process at DEF, as described here. Start from the point where a call is received and end when a technician finishes the job.

   DEF was a multibillion dollar company that manufactured and distributed a wide variety of electronic, photographic, and reprographic equipment used in many engineering and medical system applications. The Field Service Division employed 475 field service technicians, who performed maintenance and warranty repairs on the equipment sold by DEF. Customers would call DEF's National Service Center (NSC), which received about 3,000 calls per day. The NSC staffed its call center with about 40 call-takers. A typical incoming service call was received at the NSC and routed to one of the call-takers, who entered information about the machine, the caller's name, and the type of problem into DEF's mainframe computer. In some cases, the call-taker attempted to help the customer fix the problem. However, call-takers were currently only able to avoid about 10 percent of the incoming emergency maintenance service calls. If the service call could not be avoided, the call-taker usually stated the following script: "Depending upon the availability of our technicians, you should expect to see a technician sometime between now and (now +X)." ("X" was the target response time based on the model number and the zone.) This information was given to the customer because many customers wanted to know when a tech would arrive on site.

   Call-takers entered service call information on DEF's computer system, which then sent the information electronically to the regional dispatch center assigned to that customer location. (DEF had four regional dispatch centers with a total of about 20 dispatchers.) Service call information was printed on a small card at the dispatch center. About every hour, cards were ripped off the printer and given to the dispatcher assigned to that customer location. The dispatcher placed each card on a magnetic board under the name of a tech that the dispatcher believed would be the most likely candidate for the service call, given the location of the machine, the current location of the tech, and the tech's training profile. After completing a service call, techs called the dispatcher in the regional dispatch center, cleared the call, and received a new call assigned by the dispatcher. After getting the service call from a dispatcher, a tech called the customer to give an expected time of arrival, drove to the customer site, diagnosed the problem, repaired the machine if parts were available in the van, and then telephoned the dispatcher for the next call. If the tech did not have the right parts for a repair, the tech informed the NSC, and the part was express mailed to the customer; the repair was done the next morning.

9. Big Bob's Burger Barn would like to graphically depict the interaction among its lunch-ordering customers and its three employees. Customers come into the restaurant and eat there rather than drive through and eat in the car. Using the brief process descriptions below, develop a service blueprint.

   Fry Employee: receive customer order from counter employee, retrieve uncooked food, drop food into fry vat, wrap cooked food into special packaging, place wrapped items on service counter.

   Grill Employee: receive customer order from counter employee, retrieve uncooked food, place food onto grill, build sandwich with requested condiments, deliver sandwich to Counter Employee.

   Counter Employee: take order from customer, transmit appropriate orders to Fry and Grill Employee, transact payment, retrieve drinks, wrap sandwich, package order, and deliver order to customer.

10. Your class has volunteered to work for Referendum 13 on the November ballot, which calls for free tuition and books for all college courses except Operations Management. Support for the referendum includes assembling 10,000 yard signs (pre-printed water-resistant paper signs to be glued and stapled to a wooden stake) on a fall Saturday. Construct a flowchart and a process chart for yard sign assembly. What inputs in terms of materials, human effort, and equipment are involved? Estimate the amount of volunteers, staples, glue, equipment, lawn and garage space, and pizza required.

11. Suppose you are in charge of a large mailing to the alumni of your college inviting them to contribute to a scholarship fund. The letters and envelopes have been individually addressed (mailing labels were not used). The letters are to be processed (matched with correct envelope, time estimated to be 0.2 minutes each), folded (0.12 minutes each), and stuffed into the correct envelope (0.10 minutes each). The envelopes are to be sealed (0.05 minutes each), and a large commemorative stamp is to be placed in the upper right-hand corner of each envelope (0.10 minutes each).

    a. Make a process chart for this activity, assuming that it is a one-person operation.

    b. Estimate how long it will take to stuff, seal, and stamp 2,000 envelopes. Assume that the person doing this work is paid $8 per hour. How much will it cost to process 2,000 letters?

    c. Consider each of the following process changes. Which changes would reduce the time and cost of the current process?

    ■ Each letter has the same greeting, "Dear Alumnus or Alumna," instead of the person's name.

    ■ Mailing labels are used and have to be put on the envelopes (0.10 minutes each).

    ■ Prestamped envelopes are used.

    ■ Envelopes are stamped by a postage meter which can stamp 200 letters per minute.

    ■ Window envelopes are used.

    ■ A preaddressed envelope is included with each letter for contributions (adds 0.05 minutes to stuffing step).

    d. Would any of these changes be likely to reduce the effectiveness of the mailing? If so, which ones? Why?

    e. Would the changes that increase time and cost be likely to increase the effectiveness of the mailing? Why or why not?

12. Diagrams of two self-service gasoline stations, both located on corners, are shown in Figure 2.19(a) and (b). Both have two rows of four pumps and a booth at which an attendant receives payment for the gasoline. At neither station is it necessary for the customer to pay in advance. The exits and entrances are marked on the diagrams. Analyze the flows of cars and people through each station.

    a. Which station has the more efficient flows from the standpoint of the customer?

    b. Which station is likely to lose more potential customers who cannot gain access to the pumps because another car is headed in the other direction?

    c. At which station can a customer pay without getting out of the car?

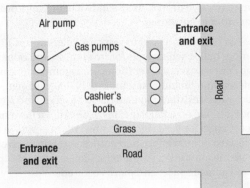

(a)

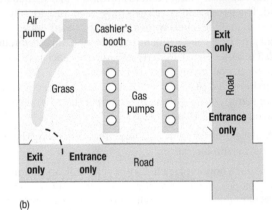

(b)

▲ **FIGURE 2.19**
Two Self-Service Gasoline Stations

13. The management of the Just Like Home Restaurant has asked you to analyze some of its processes. One of these processes is making a single-scoop ice cream cone. Cones can be ordered by a server (for table service) or by a customer (for takeout).

Figure 2.20 illustrates the process chart for this operation.

- The ice cream counter server earns $10 per hour (including variable fringe benefits).
- The process is performed 10 times per hour (on average).
- The restaurant is open 363 days a year, 10 hours a day.

a. Complete the Summary (top-right) portion of the chart.

b. What is the total labor cost associated with the process?

c. How can this operation be made more efficient? Make a process chart using OM Explorer's *Process Charts* Solver of the improved process. What are the annual labor savings if this new process is implemented?

14. As a graduate assistant, your duties include grading and keeping records for Operations Management course homework assignments. Five sections for 40 students each are offered each semester. A few graduate students attend sections 3 and 4. Graduate students must complete some extra work to higher standards for each assignment. Every student delivers (or is supposed to deliver) directly to (under) the door of your office one homework assignment every Tuesday. Your job is to correct the homework, record grades, sort the papers by class section, sort by student last name in

FIGURE 2.20 ▶
Process Chart for
Making Ice Cream
Cones

Process:	Making one ice cream cone
Subject:	Server at counter
Beginning:	Walk to cone storage area
Ending:	Give it to server or customer

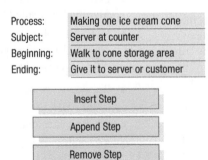

	Summary		
Activity	Number of Steps	Time (min)	Distance (ft)
Operation ●			
Transport ➡			
Inspect ■			
Delay ❭			
Store ▼			

Step No.	Time (min)	Distance (ft)	●	➡	■	❭	▼	Step Description
1	0.20	5.0		X				Walk to cone storage area
2	0.05		X					Remove empty cone
3	0.10	5.0		X				Walk to counter
4	0.05		X					Place cone in holder
5	0.20	8.0		X				Walk to sink area
6	0.50					X		Ask dishwasher to wash scoop
7	0.15	8.0		X				Walk to counter with clean scoop
8	0.05		X					Pick up empty cone
9	0.10	2.5		X				Walk to flavor ordered
10	0.75		X					Scoop ice cream from container
11	0.75		X					Place ice cream in cone
12	0.25				X			Check for stability
13	0.05	2.5		X				Walk to order placement area
14	0.05		X					Give server or customer the cone

alphabetical order, and return the homework papers to the appropriate instructors (not necessarily in that order). There are some complications. A fair majority of the students sign their names legibly, others identify work with their correct ID number, and a few do neither. Rarely do students identify their section number or graduate status. Prepare a list of process chart steps and place them in an efficient sequence.

15. At the Department of Motor Vehicles (DMV), the process of getting license plates for your car begins when you enter the facility and take a number. You walk 50 feet to the waiting area. During your wait, you count about 30 customers waiting for service. You notice that many customers become discouraged and leave. When a number is called, if a customer stands, the ticket is checked by a uniformed person, and the customer is directed to the available clerk. If no one stands, several minutes are lost while the same number is called repeatedly. Eventually, the next number is called, and more often than not, that customer has left too. The DMV clerk has now been idle for several minutes but does not seem to mind.

After 4 hours, your number is called and checked by the uniformed person. You walk 60 feet to the clerk, and the process of paying city sales taxes is completed in four minutes. The clerk then directs you to the waiting area for paying state personal property tax, 80 feet away. You take a different number and sit down with some different customers who are just renewing licenses. There is a 1-hour, 40-minute wait this time, and after a walk of 25 feet you pay property taxes in a process that takes two minutes. Now that you have paid taxes, you are eligible to pay registration and license fees. That department is 50 feet away, beyond the employees' cafeteria.

The registration and license customers are called in the same order in which personal property taxes were paid. There is only a 10-minute wait and a 3-minute process. You receive your license plates, take a minute to abuse the license clerk, and leave exactly 6 hours after arriving.

Make a process chart using OM Explorer's *Process Charts* Solver to depict this process, and suggest improvements.

16. Refer to the process chart for the automobile oil change in Solved Problem 2. Calculate the annual labor cost if:

■ The mechanic earns $40 per hour (including variable fringe benefits).

■ The process is performed twice per hour (on average).

■ The shop is open 300 days a year, 10 hours a day.

a. What is the total labor cost associated with the process?

b. If steps 7, 10, 12, and 15 were eliminated, estimate the annual labor savings associated with implementing this new process.

17. A time study of an employee assembling peanut valves resulted in the following set of observations. What is the standard time, given a performance rating of 95 percent and an allowance of 20 percent of the total normal time?

Average Time (seconds)	Observations
15	14
20	12
25	15

18. An initial time study was done on a process with the following results (in minutes). Based on the data obtained so far, assuming an allowance of 20 percent of the normal time, what do you estimate for the time per customer served, based on this preliminary sample?

Element	Performance Rating	Obs 1	Obs 2	Obs 3	Obs 4	Obs 5
Element 1	70	4	3	5	4	3
Element 2	110	8	10	9	11	10
Element 3	90	6	8	7	7	6

19. A work sampling study was conducted to determine the proportion of the time a worker is idle. The following information was gathered on a random basis:

Day	Number of Times Worker Idle	Total Number of Observations
Monday	17	44
Tuesday	18	56
Wednesday	14	48
Thursday	16	60

a. Based on these preliminary results, what percent of the time is the worker working?

b. If idle time is judged to be excessive, what additional categories might you add to a follow-up work sampling study to identify the root causes?

20. A contractor is preparing a bid to install swimming pools at a new housing addition. The estimated time to build the first pool is 35 hours. The contractor estimates an 85 percent learning rate. Without using the computer:

a. How long do you estimate the time required to install the second pool?

b. How long do you estimate the time required to install the fourth pool?

21. Return to Problem 20. Using OM Explorer's Learning Curves Solver, how long do you estimate the time required to install the fifth pool? What is your estimate of the total time for all five pools?

22. On RainTite Window's manual assembly line, a new employee can usually assemble their first window unit in 30 minutes. Management assumes a 90 percent learning rate.

a. How long should a new employee take to assemble their second window if management is correct in their assumption? How long should the 16th window take?

b. On RainTite's semi-automated line, a new employee takes 45 minutes to assemble their first window; however, the learning rate is 75 percent. At how many windows produced will the semi-automated line's employee take less time to produce a window than an employee on the manual line?

23. The manager of Perrotti's Pizza collects data concerning customer complaints about pizza delivery. Either the pizza arrives late, or the wrong pizza is delivered.

Problem	Frequency
Topping is stuck to box lid	17
Pizza arrives late	35
Wrong topping or combination	9
Wrong style of crust	6
Wrong size	4
Pizza is partially eaten	3
Pizza never arrives	6

a. Use a Pareto chart to identify the "vital few" delivery problems. Comment on potential root causes of these problems and identify any especially egregious quality failures.

b. The manager of Perrotti's Pizza is attempting to understand the root causes of late pizza delivery and has asked each driver to keep a log of specific difficulties that create late deliveries. After one week, the logs included the following entries:

delivery vehicle broke down, couldn't make it across town to deliver second pizza in time, couldn't deliver four pizzas to four different customers in time, kitchen was late in producing order, got lost, order ticket was lost in production, couldn't read address on ticket and went to wrong house.

Organize these causes into a cause-and-effect diagram.

24. Smith, Schroeder, and Torn (SST) is a short-haul household furniture moving company. SST's labor force, selected from the local community college football team, is temporary and part-time. SST is concerned with recent complaints, as tabulated on the following tally sheet:

Complaint	Tally
Broken glass	ЖЖ ЖЖ III
Delivered to wrong address	ЖЖ IIII
Furniture rubbed together while on truck	ЖЖ ЖЖ ЖЖ ЖЖ
Late delivery	ЖЖ
Late arrival for pickup	ЖЖ ЖЖ ЖЖ III
Missing items	ЖЖ ЖЖ ЖЖ ЖЖ ЖЖ I
Nicks and scratches from rough handling	ЖЖ ЖЖ
Soiled upholstery	ЖЖ III

a. Draw a bar chart and a Pareto chart using OM Explorer to identify the most serious moving problems.

b. The manager of Smith, Schroeder, and Torn is attempting to understand the root causes of complaints. He has compiled the following list of issues that occurred during problem deliveries:

truck broke down, ran out of packing boxes, multiple deliveries in one day caused truck to be late, no furniture pads, employee dropped several items, drive got lost on route to address, ramp into truck was bent, no packing

tape, new employee doesn't know how to pack, moving dolly has broken wheel, employee late to work

Organize these causes into a cause-and-effect diagram.

25. Rick DeNeefe, manager of the Golden Valley Bank credit authorization department, recently noticed that a major competitor was advertising that applications for equity loans could be approved within two working days. Because fast credit approval was a competitive priority, DeNeefe wanted to see how well his department was doing relative to the competitor's. Golden Valley stamps each application with the date and time it is received and again when a decision is made. A total of 104 applications were received in March. The time required for each decision, rounded to the nearest hour, is shown in the following table. Golden Valley's employees work 8 hours per day.

Decision Process Time (hours)	Frequency
8	8
11	19
14	28
17	10
20	25
23	4
26	10
Total	104

a. Draw a bar chart for these data.

b. Analyze the data. How is Golden Valley Bank doing with regard to this competitive priority?

26. Last year, the manager of the service department at East Woods Ford instituted a customer opinion program to find out how to improve service. One week after service on a vehicle was performed, an assistant would call the customer to find out whether the work had been done satisfactorily and how service could be improved. After one year of gathering data, the assistant discovered that the complaints could be grouped into the following five categories:

Complaint	Frequency
Unfriendly atmosphere	5
Long wait for service	17
Price too high	20
Incorrect bill	8
Needed to return to correct problem	50
Total	100

a. Use OM Explorer to draw a bar chart and a Pareto chart to identify the significant service problems.

b. Categorize the following causes of complaints into a cause-and-effect diagram: tools, scheduling, defective parts, training, billing system, performance measures, diagnostic equipment, and communications.

27. Oregon Fiber Board makes roof liners for the automotive industry. The manufacturing manager is concerned about product quality. She suspects that one particular failure, tears

in the fabric, is related to production-run size. An assistant gathers the following data from production records:

Run	Size	Failures (%)	Run	Size	Failures (%)
1	1,000	3.5	11	6,500	1.5
2	4,100	3.8	12	1,000	5.5
3	2,000	5.5	13	7,000	1.0
4	6,000	1.9	14	3,000	4.5
5	6,800	2.0	15	2,200	4.2
6	3,000	3.2	16	1,800	6.0
7	2,000	3.8	17	5,400	2.0
8	1,200	4.2	18	5,800	2.0
9	5,000	3.8	19	1,000	6.2
10	3,800	3.0	20	1,500	7.0

a. Draw a scatter diagram for these data.

b. Does there appear to be a relationship between run size and percent failures? What implications does this data have for Oregon Fiber Board's business?

28. Grindwell, Inc., a manufacturer of grinding tools, is concerned about the durability of its products, which depends on the permeability of the sinter mixtures used in production. Suspecting that the carbon content might be the source of the problem, the plant manager collected the following data:

Carbon Content (%)	Permeability Index
5.5	16
3.0	31
4.5	21
4.8	19
4.2	16
4.7	23
5.1	20
4.4	11
3.6	20

a. Draw a scatter diagram for these data.

b. Is there a relationship between permeability and carbon content?

c. If low permeability is desirable, what does the scatter diagram suggest with regard to the carbon content?

29. The operations manager for Superfast Airlines at Chicago's O'Hare Airport noticed an increase in the number of delayed flight departures. She brainstormed possible causes with her staff:

- Aircraft late to gate
- Acceptance of late passengers
- Passengers arriving late at gate
- Passenger processing delays at gate
- Late baggage to aircraft

- Other late personnel or unavailable items
- Mechanical failures

Draw a cause-and-effect diagram to organize the possible causes of delayed flight departures into the following major categories: equipment, personnel, material, procedures, and other factors beyond managerial control. Provide a detailed set of causes for each major cause identified by the operations manager, and incorporate them in your cause-and-effect diagram.

30. Plastomer, Inc., specializes in the manufacture of high-grade plastic film used to wrap food products. Film is rejected and scrapped for a variety of reasons (e.g., opacity, high carbon content, incorrect thickness or gauge, scratches, etc.). During the past month, management collected data on the types of rejects and the amount of scrap generated by each type. The following table presents the results:

Type of Failure	Amount of Scrap (lbs.)
Air bubbles	500
Bubble breaks	19,650
Carbon content	150
Unevenness	3,810
Thickness or gauge	27,600
Opacity	450
Scratches	3,840
Trim	500
Wrinkles	10,650

Draw a Pareto chart to identify which type of failure management should attempt to eliminate first.

31. Management of a shampoo bottling company introduced a new 13.5-ounce pack and used an existing machine, with some modifications, to fill it. To measure filling consistency by the modified machine (set to fill 13.85 ounces), an analyst collected the following data (volume in ounces) for a random sample of 100 bottles:

a. Draw a histogram for these data.

b. Bottles with less than 12.85 ounces or more than 14.85 ounces are considered to be out of specification. Based on the sample data, what percentage of the bottles filled by the machine will be out of specification?

Bottle Volume (ounces)									
13.0	13.3	13.6	13.2	14.0	12.9	14.2	12.9	14.5	13.5
14.1	14.0	13.7	13.4	14.4	14.3	14.8	13.9	13.5	14.3
14.2	14.1	14.0	13.9	13.9	14.0	14.5	13.6	13.3	12.9
12.8	13.1	13.6	14.5	14.6	12.9	13.1	14.4	14.0	14.4
13.1	14.1	14.2	12.9	13.3	14.0	14.1	13.1	13.6	13.7
14.0	13.6	13.2	13.4	13.9	14.5	14.0	14.4	13.9	14.6
12.9	14.3	14.0	12.9	14.2	14.8	14.5	13.1	12.7	13.9
13.6	14.4	13.1	14.5	13.5	13.3	14.0	13.6	13.5	14.3
13.2	13.8	13.7	12.8	13.4	13.8	13.3	13.7	14.1	13.7
13.7	13.8	13.4	13.7	14.1	12.8	13.7	13.8	14.1	14.3

32. This problem should be solved as a team exercise:

Shaving is a process that most men perform each morning. Assume that the process begins at the bathroom sink with the shaver walking (say, 5 feet) to the cabinet (where his shaving supplies are stored) to pick up bowl, soap, brush, and razor. He walks back to the sink, runs the water until it gets warm, lathers his face, shaves, and inspects the results. Then he rinses the razor; dries his face; walks over to the cabinet to return the bowl, soap, brush, and razor; and comes back to the sink to clean it up and complete the process.

a. Develop a process chart for shaving. (Assume suitable values for the time required for the various activities involved in the process.)

b. Brainstorm to generate ideas for improving the shaving process. Having fewer than 20 ideas is unacceptable. (Do not try to evaluate the ideas until the group has compiled as complete a list as possible. Otherwise, judgment will block creativity.)

33. At Conner Company, a custom manufacturer of printed circuit boards, the finished boards are subjected to a final inspection prior to shipment to its customers. As Conner's quality assurance manager, you are responsible for making a presentation to management on quality problems at the beginning of each month. Your assistant has analyzed the reject memos for all the circuit boards that were rejected during the past month. He has given you a summary statement listing the reference number of the circuit board and the reason for rejection from one of the following categories:

A = Poor electrolyte coverage

B = Improper lamination

C = Low copper plating

D = Plating separation

E = Improper etching

For 50 circuit boards that had been rejected last month, the summary statement showed the following:

C B C C D E C C B A D A C C C B C A C D C A C C B
A C A C B C C A C A A C C D A C C C E C C A B A C

a. Prepare a tally sheet (or checklist) of the different reasons for rejection.

b. Develop a Pareto chart to identify the more significant types of rejection.

c. Examine the causes of the most significant type of defect, using a cause-and-effect diagram.

Active Model Exercise

This Active Model appears in MyOMLab. Continuing on with Example 2.2, it allows you to evaluate the structure of a Pareto chart.

QUESTIONS

1. What percentage of overall complaints does discourteous service account for?

2. What percentage of overall complaints do the three most common complaints account for?

3. How does it affect the chart if we eliminate discourteous service?

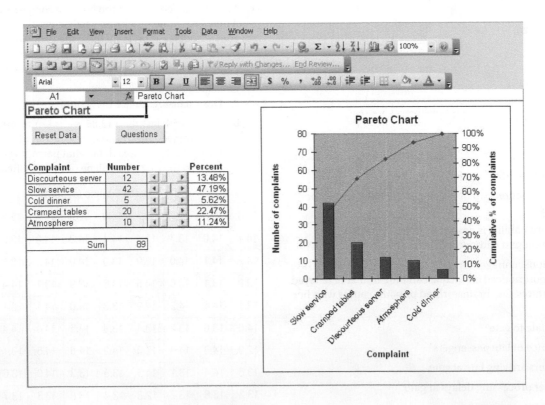

VIDEO CASE   Process Analysis at Starwood

The features and layout of The Phoenician property of Starwood Hotels and Resorts at Scottsdale, Arizona, are shown in the following figure. Starwood Hotels and Resorts is no stranger to process improvement. In fact, the president's letter in a recent annual report stated that through "…benchmarking, Six Sigma, and recognition of excellence, [Starwood is] driving results in a virtual cycle of self-improvement at all levels of the Company." Recognizing that improved processes in one department of a single hotel, if rolled out across the organization, could lead to significant improvements, the company recently created a program called Power of Innovation, or POI.

The Power of Innovation program in Starwood seeks to capture best practices that exist throughout hotels across all brands in North America. An internal team with expertise in kitchen preparation and production, laundry, stewarding, front office, and housekeeping works with individual properties to build upon and maximize the existing knowledge of local property management teams. The team usually spends about a week on property entrenched in operations to really see day-to-day activity over an extended period. Of particular interest is scheduling the workforce to meet the demand of each hotel's individual operations while streamlining operations processes.

At the Westin Galleria-Oaks in Houston, Texas, for example, the POI team helped management achieve a 6 percent productivity improvement in the kitchen preparation and production job, with a reduction of 2,404 hours used and $23,320 in annual payroll savings alone. At the same time, other POI projects at the hotel generated an additional $14,400 in annual payroll savings.

The Phoenician in Scottsdale also had a visit from the POI team. One area the team focused on was stewarding. The typical stewarding process includes the following duties: dishwashing, kitchen trash removal, polishing silver, and assisting with banquet meal food prep lines. Stewards support eight kitchens and two bakeries and work with housekeeping in keeping public areas, such as restrooms and pool cabanas, clean.

A flowchart that diagrams the existing stewarding process that the team documented is shown in the figure. In any given day, a particular steward may provide support to more than one kitchen and be called upon to do a variety of tasks.

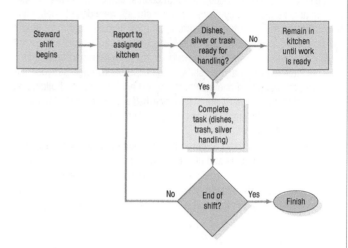

Before the POI team arrived, stewards were dedicated to a particular kitchen or area during their shift. Each kitchen required stewarding coverage as outlined by the executive chef, so more than one steward may be assigned to an area. A certain amount of stewarding work could be forecast by the food and beverage manager, based on scheduled banquets, afternoon teas, conference buffets, and restaurant reservations. Considerable uncertainty also arose from traffic generated by leisure travelers and local clientele, meaning that stewards assigned to designated areas periodically did not have a steady flow of work.

On a weekly basis, activity levels for the dedicated stewarding staff were determined, based on executive chef input. Other factors considered in the weekly planning included prior year activity, special events and holidays, and

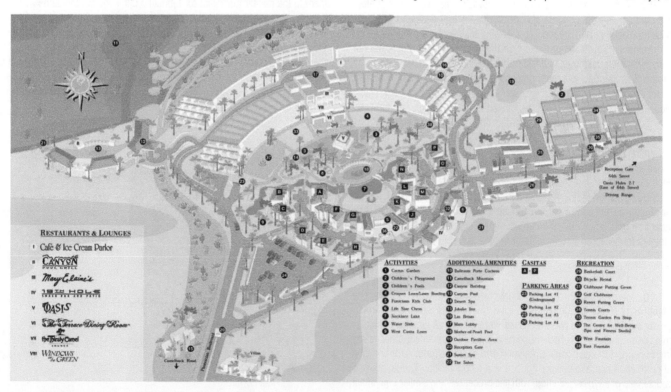

RESTAURANTS & LOUNGES
i Café & Ice Cream Parlor
ii CANYON POOL GRILL
iii Mary Elaine's
iv 19TH HOLE
v OASIS
vi The Terrace Dining Room
vii the Thirsty Camel LOUNGE
viii WINDOWS on the GREEN

ACTIVITIES
1 Cactus Garden
2 Children's Playground
3 Children's Pools
4 Croquet Lawn/Lawn Bowling
5 Funicians Kids Club
6 Life Size Chess
7 Necklace Lake
8 Water Slide
9 West Casita Lawn

ADDITIONAL AMENITIES
10 Ballroom Porte Cochere
11 Camelback Mountain
12 Canyon Building
13 Canyon Pool
14 Desert Spa
15 Jokake Inn
16 Las Brisas
17 Main Lobby
18 Mother-of-Pearl Pool
19 Outdoor Pavilion Area
20 Reception Gate
21 Sunset Spa
22 The Salon

CASITAS
A - P

PARKING AREAS
23 Parking Lot #1 (Underground)
24 Parking Lot #2
25 Parking Lot #3
26 Parking Lot #4

RECREATION
29 Basketball Court
30 Bicycle Rental
31 Clubhouse Putting Green
32 Golf Clubhouse
33 Resort Putting Green
34 Tennis Courts
35 Tennis Garden Pro Shop
36 The Centre for Well-Being (Spa and Fitness Studio)
37 West Fountain
38 East Fountain

number of children. With this information, the executive steward created a summary of all meals, called covers, by location, date, and time of day. Then an Excel spreadsheet template was used to create the schedule for deployment of stewarding staff throughout the resort's kitchens and restaurants.

In performing its analysis, the POI team examined staff availability, banquet events, restaurants, occupied room counts, and other drivers of business to areas supported by stewards. Time studies were done to determine how far stewards were traveling throughout the property, and how long it took to perform each stewarding task. Some restaurants and kitchens did not require full-time coverage by a steward, so the steward would be assigned multiple kitchens to fill a work shift. In the case of coverage between the 19th Hole restaurant on one side of the resort and the Canyon Building on the other side, that steward would walk one-half mile, one way, to take care of duties in both locations because they lacked enough work for a dedicated steward in each location.

Often, stewards had downtime as they waited for banquet dishes to be cleared, or kitchen pots and utensils to be brought in for cleaning. Some restaurants had china with special cleaning requirements, meaning those dishes had to be handwashed instead of being placed in an automated sanitizing dishwasher. This situation required a dedicated steward to perform that task.

Time studies revealed how long it took stewards to move from one kitchen to the next. The studies also helped the POI team understand how long it took to wash dishes in the five-star restaurant versus the casual poolside dining area's kitchen. Additionally, the studies uncovered building design and landscaping limitations that prevented staff from moving between kitchens quickly. In some cases, a maze of corridors added miles to the distances covered each day, and thick privacy hedges barred entry to sidewalk shortcuts.

QUESTIONS

1. How can the management specifically improve the stewarding process at The Phoenician? Using the information provided, create a flowchart illustrating the new process.

2. What are the benefits that the POI program can bring to Starwood? Can these benefits be extended to other processes and properties within the Starwood system?

3. Of the seven mistakes organizations can make when managing processes (see last section of this chapter), which ones might Starwood be most at risk of making? Why?

CASE   Custom Molds, Inc.

Custom Molds, Inc., manufactures custom-designed molds for plastic parts and produces custom-made plastic connectors for the electronics industry. Located in Tucson, Arizona, Custom Molds was founded by the father-and-son team of Tom and Mason Miller in 1997. Tom Miller, a mechanical engineer, had more than 20 years of experience in the connector industry with AMP, Inc., a large multinational producer of electronic connectors. Mason Miller graduated from the Arizona State University in 1996 with joint degrees in chemistry and chemical engineering.

The company was originally formed to provide manufacturers of electronic connectors with a source of high-quality, custom-designed molds for producing plastic parts. The market consisted mainly of the product design and development divisions of those manufacturers. Custom Molds worked closely with each customer to design and develop molds to be used in the customer's product development processes. Thus, virtually every mold had to meet exacting standards and was somewhat unique. Orders for multiple molds would arrive when customers moved from the design and pilot-run stage of development to large-scale production of newly designed parts.

As the years went by, Custom Molds's reputation grew as a designer and fabricator of precision molds. Building on this reputation, the Millers decided to expand into the limited manufacture of plastic parts. Ingredient-mixing facilities and injection-molding equipment were added, and by the mid-2000s, Custom Molds developed its reputation to include being a supplier of high-quality plastic parts. Because of limited capacity, the company concentrated its sales efforts on supplying parts that were used in limited quantities for research and development efforts and in preproduction pilot runs.

Production Processes

By 2010, operations at Custom Molds involved two distinct processes: one for fabricating molds and one for producing plastic parts. Although different, in many instances these two processes were linked, as when a customer would have Custom Molds both fabricate a mold and produce the necessary parts to support the customer's research and design efforts. All fabrication and production operations were housed in a single facility. The layout was characteristic of a typical job shop, with like processes and similar equipment grouped in various places in the plant. Figure 2.21 shows a layout of the plant floor. Multiple pieces of various types of high-precision machinery, including milling, turning, cutting, and drilling equipment, were located in the mold-fabrication area.

Fabricating molds is a skill-oriented, craftsman-driven process. When an order is received, a design team, comprising a design engineer and one of 13 master machinists, reviews the design specifications. Working closely with the customer, the team establishes the final specifications for the mold and gives them to the master machinist for fabrication. It is always the same machinist who was assigned to the design team. At the same time, the purchasing department is given a copy of the design specifications, from which it orders the appropriate raw materials and special tooling. The time needed to receive the ordered materials is usually three to four weeks. When the materials are received for a particular mold, the plant master scheduler reviews the workload of the assigned master machinist and schedules the mold for fabrication.

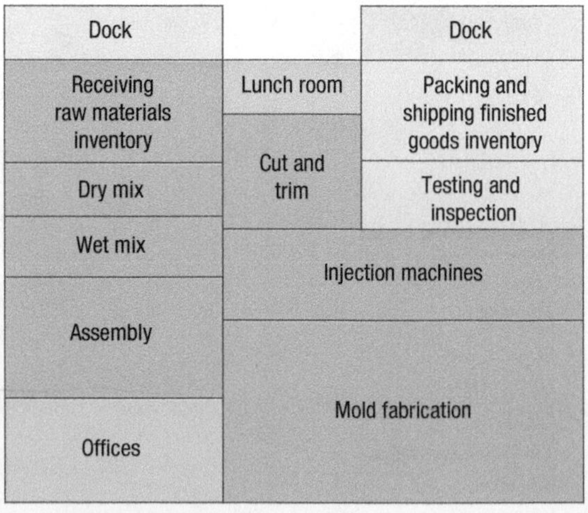

▲ **FIGURE 2.21**
Plant Layout

Fabricating a mold takes from two to four weeks, depending on the amount of work the machinist already has scheduled. The fabrication process itself takes only three to five days. Upon completion, the mold is sent to the testing and inspection area, where it is used to produce a small number of parts on one of the injection-molding machines. If the parts meet the design specifications established by the design team, the mold is passed on to be cleaned and polished. It is then packed and shipped to the customer. One day is spent inspecting and testing the mold and a second day cleaning, polishing, packing, and shipping it to the customer. If the parts made by the mold do not meet design specifications, the mold is returned to the master machinist for retooling and the process starts over. Currently, Custom Molds has a published lead time of nine weeks for delivery of custom-fabricated molds.

The manufacturing process for plastic parts is somewhat different from that for mold fabrication. An order for parts may be received in conjunction with an order for a mold to be fabricated. In instances where Custom Molds has previously fabricated the mold and maintains it in inventory, an order may be just for parts. If the mold is already available, the order is reviewed by a design engineer, who verifies the part and raw material specifications. If the design engineer has any questions concerning the specifications, the customer is contacted and any revisions to specifications are mutually worked out and agreed upon.

Upon acceptance of the part and raw material specifications, raw material orders are placed and production is scheduled for the order. Chemicals and compounds that support plastic-parts manufacturing are typically ordered and received within one week. Upon receipt, the compounds are first dry-mixed and blended to achieve the correct composition. Then the mixture is wet-mixed to the desired consistency (called *slurry*) for injection into molding machines. When ready, the slurry is transferred to the injection-molding area by an overhead pipeline and deposited in holding tanks adjacent to the injection machines. The entire mixing process takes only one day.

When the slurry is staged and ready, the proper molds are secured—from inventory or from the clean and polish operation if new molds were fabricated for the order—and the parts are manufactured. Although different parts require different temperature and pressure settings, the time to produce a part is relatively constant. Custom Molds has the capacity to produce 5,000 parts per day in the injection-molding department; historically, however, the lead time for handling orders in this department has averaged one week. Upon completion of molding, the parts are taken to the cut and trim operation, where they are disconnected and leftover flashing is removed. After being inspected, the parts may be taken to assembly or transferred to the packing and shipping area for shipment to the customer. If assembly of the final parts is not required, the parts can be on their way to the customer two days after being molded.

Sometimes, the final product requires some assembly. Typically, this entails attaching metal leads to plastic connectors. If assembly is necessary, an additional three days are needed before the order can be shipped. Custom Molds is currently quoting a three-week lead time for parts not requiring fabricated molds.

The Changing Environment

In early 2015, Tom and Mason Miller began to realize that the electronics industry they supplied, along with their own business, was changing. Electronics manufacturers had traditionally manufactured their own component parts to reduce costs and ensure a timely supply of parts. By the mid-1990s, this trend had changed. Manufacturers were developing strategic partnerships with parts suppliers to ensure the timely delivery of high-quality, cost-effective parts. This approach allowed funds to be diverted to other uses that could provide a larger return on investment.

The impact on Custom Molds could be seen in sales figures over the past three years. The sales mix was changing. Although the number of orders per year for mold fabrication remained virtually constant, orders for multiple molds were declining, as shown in the following table:

	NUMBER OF ORDERS		
Order Size	Molds 2012	Molds 2013	Molds 2014
1	80	74	72
2	60	70	75
3	40	51	55
4	5	6	5
5	3	5	4
6	4	8	5
7	2	0	1
8	10	6	4
9	11	8	5
10	15	10	5
Total orders	230	238	231

The reverse was true for plastic parts, for which the number of orders per year had declined, but for which the order sizes were becoming larger, as illustrated in the following table:

	NUMBER OF ORDERS		
Order Size	Parts 2012	Parts 2013	Parts 2014
50	100	93	70
100	70	72	65
150	40	30	35
200	36	34	38
250	25	27	25
500	10	12	14
750	1	3	5
1,000	2	2	8
3,000	1	4	9
5,000	1	3	8
Total orders	286	280	277

During this same period, Custom Molds began having delivery problems. Customers were complaining that parts orders were taking four to five weeks instead of the stated three weeks and that the delays were disrupting production schedules. When asked about the situation, the master scheduler said that determining when a particular order could be promised for delivery was difficult. Bottlenecks were occurring during the production process, but where or when they would occur could not be predicted. The bottlenecks always seemed to be moving from one operation to another.

Tom Miller thought that he had excess labor capacity in the mold-fabrication area. So, to help push through those orders that were behind schedule, he assigned one of the master machinists the job of identifying and expediting those late orders. However, that tactic did not seem to help much. Complaints about late deliveries were still being received. To add to the problems, two orders had been returned recently because of the number of defective parts. The Millers knew that something had to be done. The question was, "What?"

QUESTIONS

1. What are the major issues facing Tom and Mason Miller?
2. What are the competitive priorities for Custom Molds's processes and the changing nature of the industry?
3. What alternatives might the Millers pursue? What key factors should they consider as they evaluate these alternatives?

Source: This case was prepared by Dr. Brooke Saladin, Wake Forest University, as a basis for classroom discussion. Copyright © Brooke Saladin. Reprinted by permission.

CASE José's Authentic Mexican Restaurant

"Two bean tacos, a chicken burrito grande, and a side order of Spanish rice, please." Ivan Karetski called his table's order into the kitchen as he prepared the beverage orders. Business was brisk. Karetski liked it that way. Lots of customers meant lots of tips and, as a struggling graduate student, the extra income was greatly appreciated. Lately, however, his tips had been declining.

José's is a small, 58-seat restaurant that offers a reasonably broad range of Mexican food prepared and presented in a traditional Mexican style. It is located in New England in a mature business district on the edge of a large metropolitan area. The site is adjacent to a central artery and offers limited free off-street parking. The restaurant's interior decoration promotes the Mexican theme: The walls appear to be made of adobe and are draped with serapes, the furniture is Spanish–Mexican style, and flamenco guitar and mariachi alternate as background music.

Patrons enter the restaurant through a small vestibule that opens directly into the dining area; there is no separate waiting area. Upon arrival, patrons are greeted by a hostess and either seated directly or apprised of the expected wait. Seating at José's is usually immediate except for Friday and Saturday nights when waits of as long as 45 minutes can be encountered. Because space inside for waiting is very limited, patrons must remain outside until their party is called. José's does not take reservations.

After seating patrons, the hostess distributes menus and fills glasses with water. If standards are being met, the waiter assigned to the table greets the patrons within one minute of their being seated. (Being a traditional Mexican restaurant, its entire wait staff is male.) The waiter introduces himself, announces the daily specials, and takes the beverage orders. After delivering the beverages, the waiter takes the meal orders.

The menu consists of 23 main entrees assembled from eight basic stocks (chicken, beef, beans, rice, corn tortillas, flour tortillas, tomatoes, and lettuce) and a variety of other ingredients (fruits, vegetables, sauces, herbs, and spices). Before the dining hours begin, the cook prepares the basic stocks so that they can be quickly combined and finished off to complete the requested meals. The typical amount of time needed to complete a meal once it has been ordered is 12 minutes. A good portion of this time is for final cooking, so several meals may be in preparation at the same time. As can be imagined, one of the skills a good cook needs is to be able to schedule production of the various meals ordered at a table so that they are ready at approximately the same time. Once all the meals and any side dishes have been completed by the cook, the waiter checks to see that all meals are correct and pleasing to the eye, corrects any mistakes, and adds any finishing touches. When everything is in order, he assembles them on a tray and delivers them to the table. From this point on, the waiter keeps an eye on the table to detect when any additional service or assistance is needed.

When the diners at the table appear to be substantially finished with their main meal, the waiter approaches, asks if he can clear away any dishes, and takes any requests for dessert or coffee. When the entire meal has been completed, the waiter presents the bill and shortly thereafter collects payment. José's accepts cash or major credit card but no checks.

Karetski feels that his relationship with the cook is important. As the cook largely controls the quality of the food, Karetski wants to stay on good terms with him. He treats the cook with respect, tries to place the items on his order slip in the sequence of longest preparation time, and makes sure to write clearly so that the orders are easy to read. Although it is not his job, he helps out by fetching food stocks from the refrigerator or the storage area when the cook is busy and by doing some of the food preparation himself. The cook has been irritable lately, complaining of the poor quality of some of the ingredients that have been delivered. Last week, for example, he received lettuce that appeared wilted and chicken that was tough and more bone than meat. During peak times, it can take more than 20 minutes to get good meals delivered to the table.

Karetski had been shown the results of a customer survey that management conducted last Friday and Saturday during the evening mealtime. The following table shows a summary of the responses:

Customer Survey Results		
Were you seated promptly?	Yes: 70	No: 13
Was your waiter satisfactory?	Yes: 73	No: 10
Were you served in a reasonable time?	Yes: 58	No: 25
Was your food enjoyable?	Yes: 72	No: 11
Was your dining experience worth the cost?	Yes: 67	No: 16

As Karetski carried the tray of drinks to the table, he wondered whether the recent falloff in tips was due to anything that he could control.

QUESTIONS

1. How should process outcomes and quality be defined at this restaurant?
2. What are the restaurant's costs of process failures?
3. Use some of the tools for process analysis to assess the situation at José's.

Source: This case was prepared by Larry Meile, Boston College, as a basis for classroom discussion. Reprinted by permission.

David J. Green/Alamy

A customer buying from QVC shopping TV channel.

QVC

Quality and performance is everyone's concern at QVC Inc., one of the largest multimedia retailers in the world. Headquartered in Pennsylvania since 1986, its name is a short form for its customer-focused principles of Quality, Value, and Convenience (QVC). Well prepared hosts, who thoroughly research and understand every product, showcase more than 1000 products per week, with a quarter of them being new ones on a weekly basis. Using some of the most technologically advanced studios, QVC airs 24 hours a day, seven days a week, all year round in the United States, UK, Italy, Japan, Germany, and China. It sells a variety of items ranging from jewelry, tools, cookware, beauty products, apparel, and accessories to electronics. In 2013, QVC shipped more than 169 million products worldwide.

QVC's processes, which span all the functional areas, spring into action with a customer order: Order taking and delivery date promising, billing, and order delivery all ensue once an order is placed. In the United States, QVC operates three call centers in Virginia, Florida, and Texas that handle hundreds of million calls annually from customers who want to order something, complain about a problem, or just get product information. In-house representatives who answer customer calls have an average of seven years of in-house QVC experience. The call center representative's demeanor and skill are critical to achieving a success-ful customer encounter. QVC management keeps track of productivity, quality, and customer satisfaction measures for all processes. When the measures slip, problems are addressed aggressively. As a result, QVC has achieved a customer satisfaction rating of 95 percent and has been recognized as a top 10 retailer for customer service. Knowing how to assess whether the process is performing well and when to take action are key skills QVC managers must have.

QVC's relentless focus on quality and exceeding customer expectations by placing them at the center of its business processes has paid off handsomely. Either through its on-air programming, mobile platforms, or QVC.com shopping website, it reaches nearly 300 million homes worldwide, with about 100 million of them in the United States alone. With a workforce of 17,000 employees across six countries and revenues in excess of $8.6 billion in 2013, QVC is one of the top mass merchandize retailers globally.

Sources: Anne Schwarz, "Listening to the Voice of the Customer is the Key to QVC's Success," *Journal of Organizational Excellence* (Winter 2004), pp. 3–11; **http://en.wikipedia.org/wiki/Qvc**; **http://www.qvc.com/AboutQVCFacts.content .html** (August 6, 2014).

LEARNING GOALS *After reading this chapter, you should be able to:*

① Define the four major costs of quality, and their relationship to the role of ethics in determining the overall costs of delivering products and services.

② Explain the basic principles of Total Quality Management (TQM) and Six Sigma.

③ Understand how acceptance sampling and process performance approaches interface in a supply chain.

④ Describe how to construct process control charts and use them to determine whether a process is out of statistical control.

⑤ Explain how to determine whether a process is capable of producing a service or product to specifications.

⑥ Describe International Quality Documentation Standards and the Baldridge Performance Excellence Program.

Using Operations to Create Value

MANAGING PROCESSES

Process Strategy and Analysis
→ **Quality and Performance**
Capacity Planning
Constraint Management
Lean Systems
Project Management

MANAGING CUSTOMER DEMAND

Forecasting
Inventory Management
Operations Planning and
   Scheduling
Resource Planning

MANAGING SUPPLY CHAINS

Supply Chain Design
Supply Chain Logistic Networks
Supply Chain Integration
Supply Chain Sustainability

The challenge for businesses today is to satisfy their customers through the exceptional performance of their processes. QVC is one example of a company that met the challenge by designing and managing processes that provide customers with total satisfaction. Evaluating process performance is important if this is to happen.

Evaluating process performance is also necessary for managing supply chains. Take for example the telecommunications giant AT&T, which delivers phone, Internet, and cellular data service to millions of commercial and residential customers around the globe. At AT&T, the process of delivering cell phone communications to the customer might be measured on the consistency of service and the sound quality of the voice transmissions. The procurement process, which involves selecting the suppliers for the cell phones and evaluating how they deliver their products, might be measured in terms of the quality of the cell phones delivered to AT&T, the on-time delivery performance of the suppliers, and the cost of the cell phones. Ultimately, the evaluation of the supply chain consisting of these two processes and many others will depend on how well it satisfies the customers of AT&T, who consider the value of the service to be how well it meets or exceeds expectations. The performance of these individual processes must be consistent with the performance measures for the supply chain.

Quality and performance should be everybody's concern. Therefore in this chapter, we first address the costs of quality and then focus on Total Quality Management and Six Sigma, two philosophies and supporting tools that many companies embrace to evaluate and improve quality and performance. We subsequently describe how acceptance sampling and process performance approaches interface in a supply chain, and the role played by process variation in determining whether a process is in statistical control or not. We finally conclude with techniques that can be used to measure and improve quality such that the product or service meets the customers' needs and specifications.

Costs of Quality

defect

Any instance when a process fails to satisfy its customer.

When a process fails to satisfy a customer, the failure is considered a **defect**. For example, according to the California Academy of Family Physicians, defects for the processes in a doctor's practice are defined as "anything that happened in my office that should not have happened, and that I absolutely do not want to happen again." Obviously, this definition covers process failures that the patient sees, such as poor communication and errors in prescription dosages. It also includes failures the patient does not see, such as incorrect charting.

Closely tied to the notion of defects is the question of determining how much quality is enough. There is a greater societal effect that also must be factored into decision making involving the production of services or products that often requires balancing the costs of quality with the overall benefits to society. For example, in the health care industry, aiming for zero complications in cardiac surgery might sound good; however, if it comes at the cost of turning down high-risk patients, is society being served in the best way? Or how much time, energy, and money should go into delivering vaccines or preventing complications? These are questions that often do not have clear answers.

Many companies spend significant time, effort, and expense on systems, training, and organizational changes to improve the quality and performance of their processes. They believe that it is important to be able to gauge current levels of performance so that any process gaps can be determined. Gaps reflect potential dissatisfied customers and additional costs for the firm. Most experts estimate that the costs of quality range from 20 to 30 percent of gross sales. These costs can be broken down into four major categories: (1) prevention, (2) appraisal, (3) internal failure, and (4) external failure. In addition, there is a fifth category of costs associated with unethical behavior in making quality decisions, and which can be significantly higher than all the other four costs combined.

Prevention Costs

Prevention costs are associated with preventing defects before they happen. They include the costs of redesigning the process to remove the causes of poor performance, redesigning the service or product to make it simpler to produce, training employees in the methods of continuous improvement, and working with suppliers to increase the quality of purchased items or contracted services. To prevent problems from happening, firms must invest additional time, effort, and money.

prevention costs
Costs associated with preventing defects before they happen.

Appraisal Costs

Appraisal costs are incurred when the firm assesses the level of performance of its processes. As the costs of prevention increase and performance improves, appraisal costs decrease because fewer resources are needed for quality inspections and the subsequent search for causes of any problems that are detected.

appraisal costs
Costs incurred when the firm assess the performance level of its processes.

Internal Failure Costs

Internal failure costs result from defects that are discovered during the production of a service or product. Defects fall into two main categories: (1) *rework*, which is incurred if some aspect of a service must be performed again or if a defective item must be rerouted to some previous operation(s) to correct the defect; and (2) *scrap*, which is incurred if a defective item is unfit for further processing. For example, an analysis of the viability of acquiring a company might be sent back to the mergers and acquisitions department if an assessment of the company's history of environmental compliance is missing. The proposal for the purchase of the company may be delayed, which may result in the loss of the purchase opportunity.

internal failure costs
Costs resulting from defects that are discovered during the production of a service or product.

External Failure Costs

External failure costs arise when a defect is discovered after the customer receives the service or product. Dissatisfied customers talk about bad service or products to their friends, who in turn tell others. If the problem is bad enough, consumer protection groups may even alert the media. The potential impact on future profits is difficult to assess, but without doubt external failure costs erode market share and profits. Encountering defects and correcting them after the product is in the customer's hands is costly.

External failure costs also include warranty service and litigation costs. A **warranty** is a written guarantee that the producer will replace or repair defective parts or perform the service to the customer's satisfaction. Usually, a warranty is given for some specified period. For example, television repairs are usually guaranteed for 90 days and new automobiles for five years or 50,000 miles, whichever comes first. Warranty costs must be considered in the design of new services or products.

external failure costs
Costs that arise when a defect is discovered after the customer receives the service or product.

warranty
A written guarantee that the producer will replace or repair defective parts or perform the service to the customer's satisfaction.

ethical failure costs
Societal and monetary costs associated with *deceptively* passing defective services or products to internal or external customers such that it jeopardizes the well being of stockholders, customers, employees, partners, and creditors.

Ethical Failure Costs

The costs of quality go far beyond the out-of-pocket costs associated with training, appraisal, scrap, rework, warranties, litigation, or the lost sales from dissatisfied customers. **Ethical failure costs** are the societal and monetary costs associated with *deceptively* passing defective services or products to internal or external customers such that it jeopardizes the well-being of stockholders, customers, employees, partners, and creditors.

A young boy plays with Fisher-Price toys of Mattel at a store in Shanghai.

Imaginechina/Corbis

As a practical matter, ethical costs arise from internal or external failures. The main difference is that somebody tries to "cover them up" and knowingly passes the defects along to the customer knowing that they can do harm. What makes the nature of ethical failure costs different from internal failure or external failure costs already mentioned is the punitive costs of litigation once the ethical lapses are discovered, the extraordinary magnitude of the fines and penalties, the loss of goodwill that can literally damage the firm for a long time, and the hidden costs of employee morale and attitude. Ethical costs are tied to deception and shifting the blame to other partners in the supply chain and go beyond the internal or external failure costs associated with fixing the quality problems in an organization. Mattel, with brands like Fisher Price, Barbie Dolls, and Hot Wheels among others, had to issue multiple product recalls in 2007 due to the presence of cheaper but toxic lead paint in its toys. Problems also existed with loosely attached small magnets in its toys, which if swallowed could cause injuries to the children. Despite exerting downward pressures on costs, Mattel initially denied knowledge and responsibility for the use of lead paint, and instead placed the blame on the suppliers to its manufacturing plants in China. But later on, after stockholder lawsuits claiming the withholding of timely information and misleading financial statements, and also government and media pressure, Mattel instituted stringent inspection and quality programs to prevent the recurrence of such incidents. As a result, Mattel has significantly repaired its corporate image over time.

Deceptive business practices are a source of major concern for service or product quality. Deceptive business practice involves three elements: (1) the conduct of the provider is intentional and motivated by a desire to exploit the customer; (2) the provider conceals the truth based upon what is actually known to the provider; and (3) the transaction is intended to generate a disproportionate economic benefit to the provider at the expense of the customer. This behavior is unethical, diminishes the quality of the customers' experience, and may impose a substantial cost on society. Quality is all about increasing the satisfaction of customers. When a firm engages in unethical behavior and the customer finds out about it, the customer is unlikely to favorably assess the quality of his or her experience with that firm or to return as a customer. Under these conditions, employees of firms that attempt to profit by deceiving customers are less likely to be motivated to put forth their best effort to create true value for customers; they erode a firm's ability to compete now and in the future. Therefore ethical behavior falls on the shoulders of all employees of an organization.

Overall, management must put in place the appropriate processes and approaches to manage the quality costs of prevention, assessment, internal failure, external failure, and ethical failure. Developing the cultural environment for ethical behavior is not cost-free. Employees must be educated in how ethics interfaces with their jobs. The firm may organize an ethics task force or an ethics public relations group to provide an interface between the firm and society. Documentation may be required.

total quality management (TQM)

A philosophy that stresses three principles for achieving high levels of process performance and quality: (1) customer satisfaction, (2) employee involvement, and (3) continuous improvement in performance.

Total Quality Management and Six Sigma

We now turn to a discussion of Total Quality Management and Six Sigma, two philosophies companies use to evaluate and improve quality and process performance along technical, service, and ethical dimensions.

Total Quality Management

Total quality management (TQM) is a philosophy that stresses three principles for achieving high levels of process performance and quality. These principles

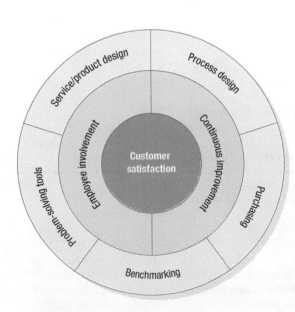

▲ **FIGURE 3.1**
TQM Wheel

are related to (1) customer satisfaction, (2) employee involvement, and (3) continuous improvement in performance. As Figure 3.1 indicates, TQM also involves a number of other important elements. We have covered tools and process analysis techniques useful for process problem solving, redesign, and improvement in Chapter 2. Service or product design and purchasing are covered later in this text. Here, we just focus on the three main principles of TQM.

Customer Satisfaction   Customers, internal or external, are satisfied when their expectations regarding a service or product have been met or exceeded. Often, customers use the general term **quality** to describe their level of satisfaction with a service or product. Quality has multiple dimensions in the mind of the customer, which cut across the nine competitive priorities we introduced in Chapter 1, "Using Operations to Create Value." One or more of the following five definitions apply at any one time.

quality
A term used by customers to describe their general satisfaction with a service or product.

- **Conformance to Specifications** Although customers evaluate the service or product they receive, it is the processes that produced the service or product that are really being judged. In this case, a process failure would be the process's inability to meet certain advertised or implied performance standards. Conformance to specifications may relate to consistent quality, on-time delivery, or delivery speed.

- **Value** Another way customers define quality is through value, or how well the service or product serves its intended purpose at a price customers are willing to pay. The service or product development process plays a role here, as do the firm's competitive priorities relating to top quality versus low-cost operations. The two factors must be balanced to produce value for the customer. How much value a service or product has in the mind of the customer depends on the customer's expectations before purchasing it.

- **Fitness for Use** When assessing how well a service or product performs its intended purpose, the customer may consider the convenience of a service, the mechanical features of a product, or other aspects such as appearance, style, durability, reliability, craftsmanship, and serviceability. For example, you may define the quality of the entertainment center you purchased on the basis of how easy it was to assemble and its appearance and styling.

- **Support** Often the service or product support provided by the company is as important to customers as the quality of the service or product itself. Customers get upset with a company if its financial statements are incorrect, responses to its warranty claims are delayed, its advertising is misleading, or its employees are not helpful when problems are incurred. Good support once the sale has been made can reduce the consequences of quality failures.

- **Psychological Impressions** People often evaluate the quality of a service or product on the basis of psychological impressions: atmosphere, image, or aesthetics. In the provision of services where the customer is in close contact with the provider, the appearance and actions of the provider are especially important. Nicely dressed, courteous, friendly, and sympathetic employees can affect the customer's perception of service quality.

Attaining quality in all areas of a business is a difficult task. To make things even more difficult, consumers change their perceptions of quality. In general, a business's success depends on the accuracy of its perceptions of consumer expectations and its ability to bridge the gap between those expectations and operating capabilities. Good quality pays off in higher profits. High-quality services and products can be priced higher and yield a greater return. Poor quality erodes the firm's ability to compete in the marketplace and increases the costs of producing its service or product. Managerial Practice 3.1 shows how Verizon Wireless aims to improve customer satisfaction by emphasizing many of the quality dimensions outlined above.

Employee Involvement   One of the important elements of TQM is employee involvement, as shown in Figure 3.1. A program in employee involvement includes changing organizational culture and encouraging teamwork.

- **Cultural Change** One of the main challenges in developing the proper culture for TQM is to define *customer* for each employee. In general, customers are internal or external. *External customers* are the people or firms who buy the service or product. Some employees, especially those having little contact with external customers, may have difficulty seeing how their jobs contribute to the whole effort.

    It is helpful to point out to employees that each employee also has one or more *internal customers*—employees in the firm who rely on the output of other employees. All employees must do a good job of serving their internal customers if external customers ultimately are to be satisfied. They will be satisfied only if each internal customer demands value be added that the external customer will recognize and pay for. The notion of internal customers applies to all parts of a firm and enhances cross-functional coordination. For example, accounting must prepare accurate and

<table>
<tr><td>MANAGERIAL PRACTICE 3.1</td><td>Quality at Verizon Wireless</td></tr>
</table>

MANAGERIAL PRACTICE 3.1 — Quality at Verizon Wireless

Anyone who owns a cell phone knows the agony of a dropped call. Did you know that the reason for the dropped call may be the phone itself and not the strength of the signal? With annual revenues of $81 billion and 74,000 employees in 2013, Verizon Wireless serves more than 105 million retail connections in the United States. Along with the other major carriers, it knows that if the phone does not work, the company, and not the manufacturer, will likely take the blame from the customer. With major investments in its technologically advanced 4G-LTE networks in the United States, Verizon touts the reliability of its services and can ill afford the failure of cell phones due to the quality of manufacture. Verizon expects manufacturers such as Motorola, Apple, Samsung, and LG Electronics to provide defect-free phones; however, experience has indicated that extensive testing by Verizon employees is also needed.

In addition to a tear-down analysis that looks for weaknesses in a phone's hardware and components, the device is tested for its ability to withstand temperature extremes, vibration, and stress. Beyond these physical tests, Verizon uses two approaches to assess a phone's capability to receive cellular signals and clearly communicate to the caller. First, Verizon hires 98 test personnel who drive $300,000 specially equipped vans more than 1 million miles a year to measure network performance using prospective new cell phones. They make more than 3 million voice call attempts and 16 million data tests annually. The tests check the coverage of the network as well as the capability of the cell phones to pick up the signals and clearly communicate to the caller. Second, Verizon uses Mr. Head, a robotic mannequin, who has a recorded voice and is electronically equipped with a rubber ear that evaluates how well the phone's mouthpiece transmits certain phonetics. Mr. Head utters what sounds like gibberish; however, it actually covers the range of sounds in normal speech patterns. Other systems monitor the tests and summarize results. Some phones spend so much time in the test phase that ultimately they never make it to the market. Clearly, in those cases, the cost of poor quality to the manufacturer is very high.

Along with testing the quality of its hardware and wireless service, Verizon also provides extensive training to its customer service representatives. Quality checks are done through company executives visiting retail stores and each of its 34 customer service center operations. With its focus on quality in operations, products, services, and technology, it is not surprising that Verizon Wireless has built a great reputation with its customer base and has also been recognized through several best wireless service awards.

ZUMA Press/Newscom

A baseline technician for Verizon Wireless checks boxes of cell phones wired to his computer used to check reception in different areas and also competition's reception and signal as he drives about Sacramento territory.

Sources: Amol Sharma, "Testing, Testing," *Wall Street Journal* (October 23, 2007); Janet Hefler, "Verizon Tester Checks Vineyard Networks," *The Martha's Vineyard Times* (August 30, 2007); Jon Gales, "Ride Along With a Verizon Wireless Test Man," *Mobile Tracker* (April 4, 2005); **http://www.verizonwireless.com/aboutus/company/story .html** (August 6, 2014).

---

quality at the source

A philosophy whereby defects are caught and corrected where they were created.

teams

Small groups of people who have a common purpose, set their own performance goals and approaches, and hold themselves accountable for success.

employee empowerment

An approach to teamwork that moves responsibility for decisions further down the organizational chart—to the level of the employee actually doing the job.

timely reports for management, and purchasing must provide high-quality materials on time for operations.

In TQM, everyone in the organization must share the view that quality control is an end in itself. Errors or defects should be caught and corrected at the source, not passed along to an internal or external customer. For example, a consulting team should make sure its billable hours are correct before submitting them to the accounting department. This philosophy is called **quality at the source**. In addition, firms should avoid trying to "inspect quality into the product" by using inspectors to weed out unsatisfactory services or defective products after all operations have been performed. By contrast, in some manufacturing firms, workers have the authority to stop a production line if they spot quality problems.

■ **Teams** Employee involvement is a key tactic for improving processes and quality. One way to achieve employee involvement is by the use of **teams**, which are small groups of people who have a common purpose, set their own performance goals and approaches, and hold themselves accountable for success. The three approaches to teamwork most often used are (1) problem-solving teams, (2) special-purpose teams, and (3) self-managed teams. All three use some amount of **employee**

empowerment, which moves responsibility for decisions further down the organizational chart—to the level of the employee actually doing the job.

Continuous Improvement Based on a Japanese concept called *kaizen*, **continuous improvement** is the philosophy of continually seeking ways to improve processes. Continuous improvement involves identifying benchmarks of excellent practice and instilling a sense of employee ownership in the process. The focus of continuous improvement projects is to reduce waste, such as reducing the length of time required to process requests for loans at a bank, the amount of scrap generated at a milling machine, or the number of employee injuries at a construction site. The basis of the continuous improvement philosophy is the belief that virtually any aspect of a process can be improved and that the people most closely associated with a process are in the best position to identify the changes that should be made. The idea is not to wait until a massive problem occurs before acting.

Employees should be given problem-solving tools, such as the statistical process control (SPC) methods we discuss later in this chapter, and a sense of ownership of the process to be improved. A sense of operator ownership emerges when employees feel a responsibility for the processes and methods they use and take pride in the quality of the service or product they produce. It comes from participation on work teams and in problem-solving activities, which instill in employees a feeling that they have some control over their workplace and tasks.

Most firms actively engaged in continuous improvement train their work teams to use the **plan-do-study-act cycle** for problem solving. Another name for this approach is the Deming Wheel, named after the renowned statistician W. Edwards Deming who taught quality improvement techniques to the Japanese after World War II. Figure 3.2 shows this cycle, which lies at the heart of the continuous improvement philosophy. The cycle comprises the following steps:

1. *Plan.* The team selects a process (an activity, method, machine, or policy) that needs improvement. The team then documents the selected process, usually by analyzing related data; sets qualitative goals for improvement; and discusses various ways to achieve the goals. After assessing the benefits and costs of the alternatives, the team develops a plan with quantifiable measures for improvement.

2. *Do.* The team implements the plan and monitors progress. Data are collected continuously to measure the improvements in the process. Any changes in the process are documented, and further revisions are made as needed.

3. *Study.* The team analyzes the data collected during the *do* step to find out how closely the results correspond to the goals set in the *plan* step. If major shortcomings exist, the team reevaluates the plan or stops the project.

4. *Act.* If the results are successful, the team documents the revised process so that it becomes the standard procedure for all who may use it. The team may then instruct other employees in the use of the revised process.

Problem-solving projects often focus on those aspects of processes that do not add value to the service or product. Value is added in processes such as machining a part or serving a customer through a Web page. No value is added in activities such as inspecting parts for defects or routing requests for loan approvals to several different departments. The idea of continuous improvement is to reduce or eliminate activities that do not add value and, thus, are wasteful.

Six Sigma

Six Sigma, which relies heavily on the principles of TQM, is a comprehensive and flexible system for achieving, sustaining, and maximizing business success by minimizing defects and variability in processes. Six Sigma has a different focus than TQM: It is driven by a close understanding of customer needs; the disciplined use of facts, data, and statistical analysis; and diligent attention to managing, improving, and reinventing business processes. Figure 3.3 shows how Six Sigma focuses on reducing variation in processes as well as centering processes on their target measures of performance. Either flaw—too much variation or an off-target process—degrades performance of the process. For example, a mortgage loan department of a bank might advertise loan

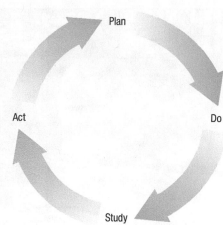

▲ **FIGURE 3.2**
Plan-Do-Study-Act Cycle

continuous improvement

The philosophy of continually seeking ways to improve processes based on a Japanese concept called *kaizen*.

plan-do-study-act cycle

A cycle, also called the Deming Wheel, used by firms actively engaged in continuous improvement to train their work teams in problem solving.

Six Sigma

A comprehensive and flexible system for achieving, sustaining, and maximizing business success by minimizing defects and variability in processes.

MyOMLab *Animation*

▼ **FIGURE 3.3**
Six Sigma Approach Focuses on Reducing Spread and Centering the Process

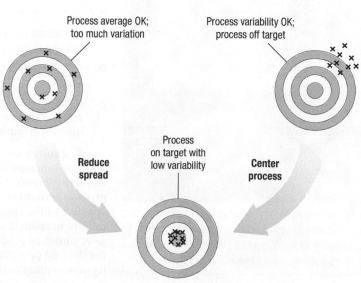

Process average OK; too much variation

Process variability OK; process off target

Process on target with low variability

Reduce spread

Center process

Harley Davidson uses Statistical Process Control techniques to enhance the quality of its motorcycles in different areas of the plant where the motorcycles are assembled.

Rick Friedman/Corbis

approval decisions in two days. If the actual performance ranges from one day to five days, with an average of two days, those customers who had to wait longer than two days would be upset. Process variability causes customer dissatisfaction. Similarly, if actual performance consistently produced loan decisions in three days, all customers would be dissatisfied. In this case, the process is consistent, but off the target. Six Sigma is a rigorous approach to align processes with their target performance measures with low variability.

The name Six Sigma, originally developed by Motorola for its manufacturing operations, relates to the goal of achieving low rates of defective output by developing processes whose mean output for a performance measure is $\pm$ six standard deviations (sigma) from the limits of the design specifications for the service or product. We will discuss variability and its implications on the capability of a process to perform at acceptable levels when we present the tools of statistical process control.

Although Six Sigma was rooted in an effort to improve manufacturing processes, credit General Electric with popularizing the application of the approach to non-manufacturing processes such as sales, human resources, customer service, and financial services. The concept of eliminating defects is the same, although the definition of "defect" depends on the process involved. For example, a human resource department's failure to meet a hiring target counts as a defect. Using the DMAIC approach within the Six Sigma Improvement model highlighted in Chapter 2, "Process Strategy and Analysis," Six Sigma process improvement specialists with black belts have been able to mentor employees and successfully apply Six Sigma to improve a host of service processes, including financial services, human resource processes, marketing processes, and health care administrative processes.

Acceptance Sampling

Before any internal process can be evaluated for performance, the inputs to that process must be of good quality. **Acceptance sampling**, which is the application of statistical techniques to determine if a quantity of material from a supplier should be accepted or rejected based on the inspection or test of one or more samples, limits the buyer's risk of rejecting good-quality materials (and unnecessarily delaying the production of goods or services) or accepting bad-quality materials (and incurring downtime due to defective materials or passing bad products to customers). Relative to the specifications for the material the buyer is purchasing, the buyer specifies an **acceptable quality level (AQL)**, which is a statement of the proportion of defective items (outside of specifications) that the buyer will accept in a shipment. These days, that proportion is getting very small, often measured in parts per ten-thousand. The idea of acceptance sampling is to take a sample, rather than testing the entire quantity of material, because that is often less expensive. Therein lies the risk—the sample may not be representative of the entire lot of goods from the supplier. The basic procedure is straightforward.

Wine production is an example of a situation where complete inspection is not an option. Here a quality inspector draws a sample of white wine from a stainless steel maturation tank.

Ian Shraw/Alamy

1. A random sample is taken from a large quantity of items and tested or measured relative to the specifications or quality measures of interest.

2. If the sample passes the test (low number of defects), the entire quantity of items is accepted.

3. If the sample fails the test, either (a) the entire quantity of items is subjected to 100 percent inspection and all defective items repaired or replaced or (b) the entire quantity is returned to the supplier.

In a supply chain, any company can be both a producer of goods purchased by another company and a consumer of goods or raw materials supplied by another company. Figure 3.4 shows a flowchart of how acceptance sampling and internal process performance (TQM or Six Sigma) interface in a supply chain. From the perspective of the supply chain, the buyer's specifications for various dimensions of quality become the targets the supplier shoots for in a supply contract. The supplier's internal processes must be up to the task; TQM or Six Sigma can help achieve the desired performance. The buyer's sampling plan will provide a high probability of accepting AQL (or better). MyOMLab Supplement G, "Acceptance Sampling

Plans," shows how to design an acceptance sampling plan that meets the level of risk desired.

Statistical Process Control

Regardless of whether a firm is producing a service or a product, it is important to ensure that the firm's processes are providing the quality that customers want. A key element of TQM or Six Sigma is building the capability to monitor the performance of processes so that corrective action can be initiated in a timely fashion. Evaluating the performance of processes requires a variety of data gathering approaches. We already discussed checklists, histograms and bar charts, Pareto charts, scatter diagrams, cause-and-effect diagrams, and graphs (see Chapter 2, "Process Strategy and Analysis"). All of these tools can be used with TQM or Six Sigma. Here, we focus on the powerful statistical tools that can be used to monitor and manage repetitive processes.

Statistical process control (SPC) is the application of statistical techniques to determine whether a process is delivering what customers want. In SPC, tools called control charts are used primarily to detect defective services or products or to indicate that the process has changed and that services or products will deviate from their design specifications, unless something is done to correct the situation. SPC can also be used to inform management of improved process changes. Examples of process changes that can be detected by SPC include the following:

- A decrease in the average number of complaints per day at a hotel
- A sudden increase in the proportion of defective gear boxes
- An increase in the time to process a mortgage application
- A decline in the number of scrapped units at a milling machine
- An increase in the number of claimants receiving late payment from an insurance company

Let us consider the last situation. Suppose that the manager of the accounts payable department of an insurance company notices that the proportion of claimants receiving late payments rose from an average of 0.01 to 0.03. The first question is whether the rise is a cause for alarm or just a random occurrence. Statistical process control can help the manager decide whether further action should be taken. If the rise in the proportion is not just a random occurrence, the manager should seek explanations of the poor performance. Perhaps the number of claims significantly increased causing an overload on the employees in the department. The decision might be to hire more personnel. Or perhaps the procedures being used are ineffective or the training of employees is inadequate. SPC is an integral part of TQM and Six Sigma.

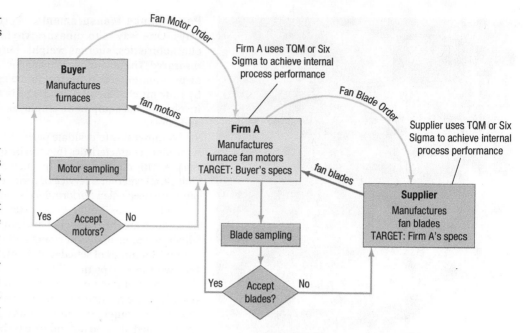

▲ **FIGURE 3.4**
Interface of Acceptance Sampling and Process Performance Approaches in a Supply Chain

MyOMLab Animation

acceptance sampling

The application of statistical techniques to determine whether a quantity of material should be accepted or rejected based on the inspection or test of a sample.

acceptable quality level (AQL)

The quality level desired by the consumer.

statistical process control (SPC)

The application of statistical techniques to determine whether a process is delivering what the customer wants.

Variation of Outputs

No two services or products are exactly alike because the processes used to produce them contain many sources of variation, even if the processes are working as intended. Nonetheless, it is important to minimize the variation in outputs because frequently variation is what the customer sees and feels. Suppose a physicians' clinic submits claims on behalf of its patients to a particular insurance company. In this situation, the physicians' clinic is the customer of the insurance company's bill payment process. In some cases, the clinic receives payment in 4 weeks, and in other cases 20 weeks. The time to process a request for payment varies because of the load on the insurance company's processes, the medical history of the patient, and the skills and attitudes of the employees. Meanwhile, the clinic must cover its expenses while it waits for payment. Regardless of whether the process is producing services or products, nothing can be done to eliminate variation in output completely; however, management should investigate the *causes* of the variation in order to minimize it.

Process measurement is the key to quality improvement. Here a quality inspector measures the diameter of holes in a machined part.

Performance Measurements   Performance can be evaluated in two ways. One way is to measure **variables**—that is, service or product characteristics, such as weight, length, volume, or time, that can be *measured*. The advantage of using performance variables is that if a service or product misses its performance specifications, the inspector knows by how much. The disadvantage is that such measurements typically involve special equipment, employee skills, exacting procedures, and time and effort.

Another way to evaluate performance is to measure **attributes**; service or product characteristics that can be quickly *counted* for acceptable performance. This method allows inspectors to make a simple "yes or no" decision about whether a service or product meets the specifications. Attributes often are used when performance specifications are complex and measurement of variables is difficult or costly. Some examples of attributes that can be counted are the number of insurance forms containing errors that cause underpayments or overpayments, the proportion of airline flights arriving within 15 minutes of scheduled times, and the number of stove-top assemblies with spotted paint.

The advantage of counting attributes is that less effort and fewer resources are needed than for measuring variables. The disadvantage is that, even though attribute counts can reveal that process performance has changed, they do not indicate by how much. For example, a count may determine that the proportion of airline flights arriving within 15 minutes of their scheduled times declined, but the result does not show how much beyond the 15-minute allowance the flights are arriving. For that, the actual deviation from the scheduled arrival, a variable, would have to be measured.

Sampling   The most thorough approach to inspection is to inspect each service or product at each stage of the process for quality. This method, called *complete inspection*, is used when the costs of passing defects to an internal or external customer outweigh the inspection costs. Firms often use automated inspection equipment that can record, summarize, and display data. Many companies find that automated inspection equipment can pay for itself in a reasonably short time.

A well-conceived **sampling plan** can approach the same degree of protection as complete inspection. A sampling plan specifies a **sample size**, which is a quantity of randomly selected observations of process outputs, the time between successive samples, and decision rules that determine when action should be taken. Sampling is appropriate when inspection costs are high because of the special knowledge, skills, procedures, and expensive equipment that are required to perform the inspections, or because the tests are destructive.

Sampling Distributions   Relative to a performance measure, a process will produce output that can be described by a *process distribution*, with a mean and variance that will be known only with a complete inspection with 100 percent accuracy. The purpose of sampling, however, is to estimate a variable or attribute measure for the output of the process without doing a complete inspection. That measure is then used to assess the performance of the process itself. For example, the time required to process specimens at an intensive care unit lab in a hospital (a variable measure) will vary. If you measured the time to complete an analysis of a large number of patients and plotted the results, the data would tend to form a pattern that can be described as a process distribution. With sampling, we try to estimate the parameters of the process distribution using statistics such as the sample mean and the sample range or standard deviation.

1. The *sample mean* is the sum of the observations divided by the total number of observations:

$$\bar{x} = \frac{\sum\limits_{i=1}^{n} x_i}{n}$$

where

x_i = observation of a quality characteristic (such as time)

n = total number of observations

$\bar{x}$ = mean

---

variables

Service or product characteristics, such as weight, length, volume, or time, that can be measured.

attributes

Service or product characteristics that can be quickly counted for acceptable performance.

sampling plan

A plan that specifies a sample size, the time between successive samples, and decision rules that determine when action should be taken.

sample size

A quantity of randomly selected observations of process outputs.

2. The *range* is the difference between the largest observation in a sample and the smallest. The *standard deviation* is the square root of the variance of a distribution. An estimate of the process standard deviation based on a sample is given by

$$\sigma = \sqrt{\frac{\sum_{i=1}^{n}(x_i - \bar{x})^2}{n - 1}} \quad \text{or} \quad \sigma = \sqrt{\frac{\sum_{i=1}^{n}x^2 - \frac{\left(\sum_{i=1}^{n}x_i\right)^2}{n}}{n - 1}}$$

where

σ = standard deviation of a sample

n = total number of observations in the sample

$\bar{x}$ = mean

x_i = observation of a quality characteristic

Relatively small values for the range or the standard deviation imply that the observations are clustered near the mean.

These sample statistics have their own distribution, which we call a *sampling distribution*. For example, in the lab analysis process, an important performance variable is the time it takes to get results to the critical care unit. Suppose that management wants results available in an average of 25 minutes. That is, it wants the process distribution to have a mean of 25 minutes. An inspector periodically taking a sample of five analyses and calculating the sample mean could use it to determine how well the process is doing. Suppose that the process is actually producing the analyses with a mean of 25 minutes. Plotting a large number of these sample means would show that they have their own sampling distribution with a mean centered on 25 minutes, as does the process distribution mean, but with much less variability. The reason is that the sample means offset the highs and lows of the individual times in each sample. Figure 3.5 shows the relationship between the sampling distribution of sample means and the process distribution for the analysis times.

Some sampling distributions (e.g., for means with sample sizes of four or more and proportions with sample sizes of 20 or more) can be approximated by the normal distribution, allowing the use of the normal tables (see Appendix 1, "Normal Distribution"). For example, suppose you wanted to determine the probability that a sample mean will be more than 2.0 standard deviations higher than the process mean. Go to Appendix 1 and note that the entry in the table for $z = 2.0$ standard deviations is 0.9772. Consequently, the probability is $1.0000 - 0.9772 = 0.0228$, or 2.28 percent. The probability that the sample mean will be more than 2.0 standard deviations lower than the process mean is also 2.28 percent because the normal distribution is symmetric to the mean. The ability to assign probabilities to sample results is important for the construction and use of control charts.

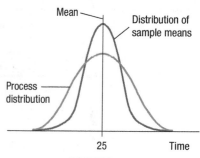

▲ **FIGURE 3.5**

Relationship Between the Distribution of Sample Means and the Process Distribution

Common Causes   The two basic categories of variation in output include common causes and assignable causes. **Common causes of variation** are the purely random, unidentifiable sources of variation that are unavoidable with the current process. A process distribution can be characterized by its *location*, *spread*, and *shape*. Location is measured by the *mean* of the distribution, while spread is measured by the *range* or *standard deviation*. The shape of process distributions can be characterized as either symmetric or skewed. A *symmetric* distribution has the same number of observations above and below the mean. A *skewed* distribution has a greater number of observations either above or below the mean. If process variability results solely from common causes of variation, a typical assumption is that the distribution is symmetric, with most observations near the center.

common causes of variation

The purely random, unidentifiable sources of variation that are unavoidable with the current process.

Assignable Causes   The second category of variation, **assignable causes of variation**, also known as *special causes*, includes any variation-causing factors that can be identified and eliminated. Assignable causes of variation include an employee needing training or a machine needing repair. Let us return to the example of the lab analysis process. Figure 3.6 shows how assignable causes can change the

assignable causes of variation

Any variation-causing factors that can be identified and eliminated.

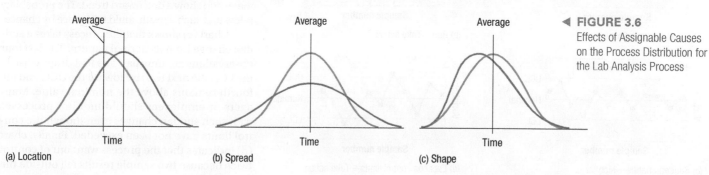

◀ **FIGURE 3.6**

Effects of Assignable Causes on the Process Distribution for the Lab Analysis Process

distribution of output for the analysis process. The **green** curve is the process distribution when only common causes of variation are present. The **purple** curves depict a change in the distribution because of assignable causes. In Figure 3.6(a), the **purple** curve indicates that the process took more time than planned in many of the cases, thereby increasing the average time of each analysis. In Figure 3.6(b), an increase in the variability of the time for each case affected the spread of the distribution. Finally, in Figure 3.6(c), the **purple** curve indicates that the process produced a preponderance of the tests in less than average time. Such a distribution is skewed, or no longer symmetric to the average value. A process is said to be in statistical control when the location, spread, or shape of its distribution does not change over time. After the process is in statistical control, managers use SPC procedures to detect the onset of assignable causes so that they can be addressed.

control chart

A time-ordered diagram that is used to determine whether observed variations are abnormal.

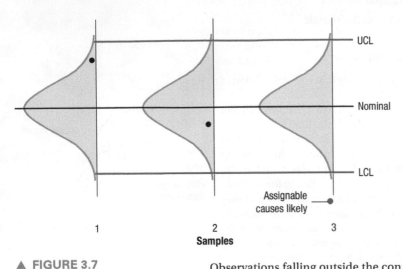

▲ **FIGURE 3.7**
How Control Limits Relate to the Sampling Distribution: Observations from Three Samples

My**OM**Lab Animation

Control Charts

To determine whether observed variations are abnormal, we can measure and plot the performance measure taken from the sample on a time-ordered diagram called a **control chart**. A control chart has a nominal value, or central line, which can be the process's historic average or a target that managers would like the process to achieve, and two control limits based on the sampling distribution of the quality measure. The control limits are used to judge whether action is required. The larger value represents the *upper control limit* (UCL), and the smaller value represents the *lower control limit* (LCL). Figure 3.7 shows how the control limits relate to the sampling distribution. A sample statistic that falls between the UCL and the LCL indicates that the process is exhibiting common causes of variation. A statistic that falls outside the control limits indicates that the process is exhibiting assignable causes of variation.

Observations falling outside the control limits do not always mean poor quality. For example, in Figure 3.7 the assignable cause may be a new billing process introduced to reduce the number of incorrect bills sent to customers. If the proportion of incorrect bills, that is, the performance measure from a sample of bills, falls *below* the LCL of the control chart, the new procedure likely changed the billing process for the better, and a new control chart should be constructed.

Managers or employees responsible for evaluating a process can use control charts in the following way:

1. Take a random sample from the process and calculate a variable or attribute performance measure.

2. If the statistic falls outside the chart's control limits or exhibits unusual behavior, look for an assignable cause.

3. Eliminate the cause if it degrades performance; incorporate the cause if it improves performance. Reconstruct the control chart with new data.

4. Repeat the procedure periodically.

Sometimes, problems with a process can be detected even though the control limits have not been exceeded. Figure 3.8 contains four examples of control charts. Chart (a) shows a process that is in statistical control. No action is needed. However, chart (b) shows a pattern called a *run* or a sequence of observations with a certain characteristic. A typical rule is to take remedial action when five or more observations show a downward or upward trend, even if the points have not yet exceeded the control limits. Here, nine sequential observations are below the mean and show a downward trend. The probability is low that such a result could take place by chance.

Chart (c) shows that the process takes a sudden change from its normal pattern. The last four observations are unusual: The first drops close to the LCL, the next two rise toward the UCL, and the fourth remains above the nominal value. Managers or employees should monitor processes with such sudden changes even though the control limits have not been exceeded. Finally, chart (d) indicates that the process went out of control twice because two sample results fell outside the

▼ **FIGURE 3.8**
Control Chart Examples

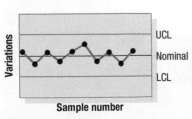

(a) Normal—No action

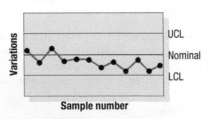

(b) Run—Take action

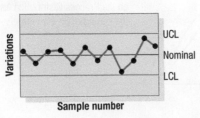

(c) Sudden change—Monitor

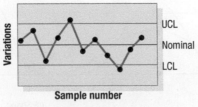

(d) Exceeds control limits—Take action

control limits. The probability that the process distribution has changed is high. We discuss more implications of being out of statistical control when we discuss process capability later in this chapter.

Control charts are not perfect tools for detecting shifts in the process distribution because they are based on sampling distributions. Two types of error are possible with the use of control charts. A **type I error** occurs when the conclusion is made that the process is out of control based on a sample result that falls outside the control limits, when in fact it was due to pure randomness. A **type II error** occurs when the conclusion is that the process is in control and only randomness is present, when actually the process is out of statistical control.

These errors can be controlled by the choice of control limits. The choice would depend on the costs of looking for assignable causes when none exist versus the cost of not detecting a shift in the process. For example, setting control limits at $\pm$ three standard deviations from the mean reduces the type I error because chances are only 0.26 percent that a sample result will fall outside of the control limits unless the process is out of statistical control. However, the type II error may be significant; more subtle shifts in the nature of the process distribution will go undetected because of the wide spread in the control limits. Alternatively, the spread in the control limits can be reduced to $\pm$ two standard deviations, thereby increasing the likelihood of sample results from a non-faulty process falling outside of the control limits to 4.56 percent. Now, the type II error is smaller, but the type I error is larger because employees are likely to search for assignable causes when the sample result occurred solely by chance. As a general rule, use wider limits when the cost for searching for assignable causes is large relative to the cost of not detecting a shift in the process distribution.

SPC methods are useful for both measuring the current process performance and detecting whether the process has changed in a way that will affect future performance. Consequently, we first discuss mean and range charts for variable measures of performance and then consider control charts for attributes measures.

Control Charts for Variables

Control charts for variables are used to monitor the mean and the variability of the process distribution.

R-Chart   A range chart, or **R-chart**, is used to monitor process variability. To calculate the range of a set of sample data, the analyst subtracts the smallest from the largest measurement in each sample. If any of the ranges fall outside the control limits, the process variability is not in control.

The control limits for the R-chart are

$$\text{UCL}_R = D_4\overline{R} \quad \text{and} \quad \text{LCL}_R = D_3\overline{R}$$

where

$\overline{R}$ = average of several past R values and the central line of the control chart

D_3, D_4 = constants that provide three standard deviation (three-sigma) limits for a given sample size

Notice that the values for D_3 and D_4 shown in Table 3.1 change as a function of the sample size. Notice, too, that the spread between the control limits narrows as the sample size increases. This change is a consequence of having more information on which to base an estimate for the process range.

type I error

An error that occurs when the employee concludes that the process is out of control based on a sample result that falls outside the control limits, when in fact it was due to pure randomness.

type II error

An error that occurs when the employee concludes that the process is in control and only randomness is present, when actually the process is out of statistical control.

R-chart

A chart used to monitor process variability.

TABLE 3.1 | FACTORS FOR CALCULATING THREE SIGMA LIMITS FOR THE $\overline{x}$-CHART AND R-CHART

Size of Sample (n)	Factor for UCL and LCL for $\overline{x}$-Chart (A_2)	Factor for LCL for R-Chart (D_3)	Factor for UCL for R-Chart (D_4)
2	1.880	0	3.267
3	1.023	0	2.575
4	0.729	0	2.282
5	0.577	0	2.115
6	0.483	0	2.004
7	0.419	0.076	1.924
8	0.373	0.136	1.864
9	0.337	0.184	1.816
10	0.308	0.223	1.777

Source: Reprinted with permission from *ASTM Manual on Quality Control of Materials,* copyright © ASTM International, 100 Barr Harbor Drive, West Conshohocken, PA 19428.

$\bar{x}$-chart

A chart used to see whether the process is generating output, on average, consistent with a target value set by management for the process or whether its current performance, with respect to the average of the performance measure, is consistent with past performance.

$\bar{x}$-Chart An $\bar{x}$-Chart (read "x-bar chart") is used to see whether the process is generating output, on average, consistent with a target value set by management for the process or whether its current performance, with respect to the average of the performance measure, is consistent with its past performance. A target value is useful when a process is completely redesigned and past performance is no longer relevant. When the assignable causes of process variability have been identified and the process variability is in statistical control, the analyst can then construct an $\bar{x}$-chart. The control limits for the $\bar{x}$-chart are

$$UCL_{\bar{x}} = \bar{\bar{x}} + A_2\bar{R} \quad \text{and} \quad LCL_{\bar{x}} = \bar{\bar{x}} - A_2\bar{R}$$

where

$\bar{\bar{x}}$ = central line of the chart, which can be either the average of past sample means or a target value set for the process

A_2 = constant to provide three-sigma limits for the sample mean

The values for A_2 are contained in Table 3.1. Note that the control limits use the value of $\bar{R}$; therefore, the $\bar{x}$-chart must be constructed *after* the process variability is in control.

To develop and use $\bar{x}$- and R-charts, do the following:

Step 1. Collect data on the variable quality measurement (such as time, weight, or diameter) and organize the data by sample number. Preferably, at least 20 samples of size n should be taken for use in constructing a control chart.

Step 2. Compute the range for each sample and the average range, $\bar{R}$, for the set of samples.

Step 3. Use Table 3.1 to determine the upper and lower control limits of the R-chart.

Step 4. Plot the sample ranges. If all are in control, proceed to step 5. Otherwise, find the assignable causes, correct them, and return to step 1.

Step 5. Calculate $\bar{x}$ for each sample and determine the central line of the chart, $\bar{\bar{x}}$.

Step 6. Use Table 3.1 to determinew the parameters for $UCL_{\bar{x}}$ and $LCL_{\bar{x}}$ and construct the $\bar{x}$-chart.

Step 7. Plot the sample means. If all are in control, the process is in statistical control in terms of the process average and process variability. Continue to take samples and monitor the process. If any are out of control, find the assignable causes, address them, and return to step 1. If no assignable causes are found after a diligent search, assume that the out-of-control points represent common causes of variation and continue to monitor the process.

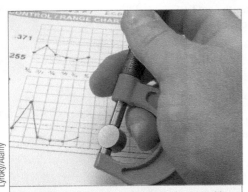

An analyst measures the diameter of a part with a micrometer. After he measures the sample, he plots the range on the control chart.

Lyroky/Alamy

| EXAMPLE 3.1 | **Using $\bar{x}$ and R-Charts to Monitor a Process** |

MyOMLab

Tutor 3.1 in MyOMLab provides a new example to practice the use of x-bar and R-charts.

MyOMLab

Active Model 3.1 in MyOMLab provides additional insight on the x-bar and R-charts and their uses for the metal screw problem.

The management of West Allis Industries is concerned about the production of a special metal screw used by several of the company's largest customers. The diameter of the screw is critical to the customers. Data from five samples appear in the accompanying table. The sample size is 4. Is the process in statistical control?

SOLUTION

Step 1. For simplicity, we use only 5 samples. In practice, more than 20 samples would be desirable. The data are shown in the following table.

DATA FOR THE $\bar{x}$- AND R-CHARTS: OBSERVATIONS OF SCREW DIAMETER (INCH)

Sample Number	OBSERVATIONS				R	$\bar{x}$
	1	**2**	**3**	**4**		
1	0.5014	0.5022	0.5009	0.5027	0.0018	0.5018
2	0.5021	0.5041	0.5024	0.5020	0.0021	0.5027
3	0.5018	0.5026	0.5035	0.5023	0.0017	0.5026
4	0.5008	0.5034	0.5024	0.5015	0.0026	0.5020
5	0.5041	0.5056	0.5034	0.5047	0.0022	0.5045
				Average	0.0021	0.5027

Step 2. Compute the range for each sample by subtracting the lowest value from the highest value. For example, in sample 1 the range is $0.5027 - 0.5009 = 0.0018$ inch. Similarly, the ranges for samples 2, 3, 4, and 5 are 0.0021, 0.0017, 0.0026, and 0.0022 inch, respectively. As shown in the table, $\bar{R} = 0.0021$.

Step 3. To construct the R-chart, select the appropriate constants from Table 3.1 for a sample size of 4. The control limits are

$$UCL_R = D_4\bar{R} = 2.282(0.0021) = 0.00479 \text{ inch}$$

$$LCL_R = D_3\bar{R} = 0(0.0021) = 0 \text{ inch}$$

Step 4. Plot the ranges on the R-chart, as shown in Figure 3.9. None of the sample ranges falls outside the control limits. Consequently, the process variability is in statistical control. If any of the sample ranges fall outside of the limits, or an unusual pattern appears (see Figure 3.9), we would search for the causes of the excessive variability, address them, and repeat step 1.

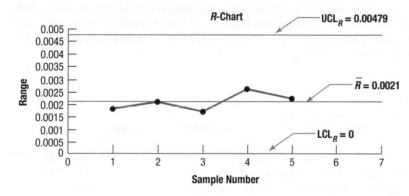

◀ **FIGURE 3.9**
Range Chart from the *OM Explorer* $\bar{x}$- and *R-Chart* Solver, Showing that the Process Variability Is In Control

Step 5. Compute the mean for each sample. For example, the mean for sample 1 is

$$\frac{0.5014 + 0.5022 + 0.5009 + 0.5027}{4} = 0.5018 \text{ inch}$$

Similarly, the means of samples 2, 3, 4, and 5 are 0.5027, 0.5026, 0.5020, and 0.5045 inch, respectively. As shown in the table, $\bar{\bar{x}} = 0.5027$.

Step 6. Now, construct the $\bar{x}$-chart for the process average. The average screw diameter is 0.5027 inch, and the average range is 0.0021 inch, so use $\bar{\bar{x}} = 0.5027, \bar{R} = 0.0021$, and A_2 from Table 3.1 for a sample size of 4 to construct the control limits:

$$UCL_{\bar{x}} = \bar{\bar{x}} + A_2\bar{R} = 0.5027 + 0.729(0.0021) = 0.5042 \text{ inch}$$

$$LCL_{\bar{x}} = \bar{\bar{x}} - A_2\bar{R} = 0.5027 - 0.729(0.0021) = 0.5012 \text{ inch}$$

Step 7. Plot the sample means on the control chart, as shown in Figure 3.10.

The mean of sample 5 falls above the UCL, indicating that the process average is out of statistical control and that assignable causes must be explored, perhaps using a cause-and-effect diagram.

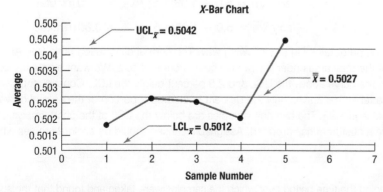

◀ **FIGURE 3.10**
The $\bar{x}$-Chart from the *OM Explorer* $\bar{x}$- and *R-Chart* Solver for the Metal Screw, Showing that Sample 3 Is Out of Control

DECISION POINT

A new employee operated the lathe machine that makes the screw on the day sample 5 was taken. To solve the problem, management initiated a training session for the employee. Subsequent samples showed that the process was back in statistical control.

If the standard deviation of the process distribution is known, another form of the $\bar{x}$-chart may be used:

$$\text{UCL}_{\bar{x}} = \bar{\bar{x}} + z\sigma_{\bar{x}} \text{ and } \text{LCL}_{\bar{x}} = \bar{\bar{x}} - z\sigma_{\bar{x}}$$

where

$\sigma_{\bar{x}} = \sigma / \sqrt{n} = $ standard deviation of sample means

$\sigma = $ standard deviation of the process distribution

$n = $ sample size

$\bar{\bar{x}} = $ central line of the chart, which can be either the average of past sample means or a target value set for the process

$z = $ normal deviate (number of standard deviations from the average)

The analyst can use an R-chart to be sure that the process variability is in control before constructing the $\bar{x}$-chart. The advantage of using this form of the $\bar{x}$-chart is that the analyst can adjust the spread of the control limits by changing the value of z. This approach can be useful for balancing the effects of type I and type II errors.

EXAMPLE 3.2	**Designing an $\bar{x}$-Chart Using the Process Standard Deviation**

The Sunny Dale Bank monitors the time required to serve customers at the drive-through window because it is an important quality factor in competing with other banks in the city. After analyzing the data gathered in an extensive study of the window operation, bank management determined that the mean time to process a customer at the peak demand period is 5 minutes, with a standard deviation of 1.5 minutes. Management wants to monitor the mean time to process a customer by periodically using a sample size of six customers. Assume that the process variability is in statistical control. Design an $\bar{x}$-chart that has a type I error of 5 percent. That is, set the control limits so that there is a 2.5 percent chance a sample result will fall below the LCL and a 2.5 percent chance that a sample result will fall above the UCL. After several weeks of sampling, two successive samples came in at 3.70 and 3.68 minutes, respectively. Is the customer service process in statistical control?

SOLUTION

$$\bar{\bar{x}} = 5.0 \text{ minutes}$$

$$\sigma = 1.5 \text{ minutes}$$

$$n = 6 \text{ customers}$$

$$z = 1.96$$

The process variability is in statistical control, so we proceed directly to the $\bar{x}$-chart. The control limits are

$$\text{UCL}_{\bar{x}} = \bar{\bar{x}} + z\sigma / \sqrt{n} = 5.0 + 1.96(1.5) / \sqrt{6} = 6.20 \text{ minutes}$$

$$\text{LCL}_{\bar{x}} = \bar{\bar{x}} - z\sigma / \sqrt{n} = 5.0 - 1.96(1.5) / \sqrt{6} = 3.80 \text{ minutes}$$

The value for z can be obtained in the following way. The normal distribution table (see Appendix 1) gives the proportion of the total area under the normal curve from $-\infty$ to z. We want a type I error of 5 percent, or 2.5 percent of the curve above the UCL and 2.5 percent below the LCL. Consequently, we need to find the z value in the table that leaves only 2.5 percent in the upper portion of the normal curve (or 0.9750 in the table). The value is 1.96. The two new samples are below the LCL of the chart, implying that the average time to serve a customer has dropped. Assignable causes should be explored to see what caused the improvement.

DECISION POINT

Management studied the time period over which the samples were taken and found that the supervisor of the process was experimenting with some new procedures. Management decided to make the new procedures a permanent part of the customer service process. After all employees were trained in the new procedures, new samples were taken and the control chart reconstructed.

Control Charts for Attributes

Two charts commonly used for performance measures based on attributes measures are the *p*- and *c*-chart. The *p*-chart is used for controlling the proportion of defects generated by the process. The *c*-chart is used for controlling the number of defects when more than one defect can be present in a service or product.

p-Charts   The ***p*-chart** is a commonly used control chart for attributes. The performance characteristic is counted rather than measured, and the entire service or item can be declared good or defective. For example, in the banking industry, the attributes counted might be the number of nonendorsed deposits or the number of incorrect financial statements sent to customers. The method involves selecting a random sample, inspecting each item in it, and calculating the sample proportion defective, *p*, which is the number of defective units divided by the sample size.

Sampling for a *p*-chart involves a "yes or no" decision: The process output either is or is not defective. The underlying statistical distribution is based on the binomial distribution. However, for large sample sizes, the normal distribution provides a good approximation to it. The standard deviation of the distribution of proportion defectives, σ_p, is

$$\sigma_p = \sqrt{\overline{p}(1 - \overline{p})/n}$$

where

n = sample size
$\overline{p}$ = central line on the chart, which can be either the historical average population proportion defective or a target value

We can use σ_p to arrive at the upper and lower control limits for a *p*-chart:

$$\text{UCL}_p = \overline{p} + z\sigma_p \quad \text{and} \quad \text{LCL}_p = \overline{p} - z\sigma_p$$

where

z = normal deviate (number of standard deviations from the average)

The chart is used in the following way. Periodically, a random sample of size n is taken, and the number of defective services or products is counted. The number of defectives is divided by the sample size to get a sample proportion defective, p, which is plotted on the chart. When a sample proportion defective falls outside the control limits, the analyst assumes that the proportion defective generated by the process has changed and searches for the assignable cause. Observations falling below the LCL_p indicate that the process may actually have improved. The analyst may find no assignable cause because it is always possible that an out-of-control proportion occurred randomly. However, if the analyst discovers assignable causes, those sample data should not be used to calculate the control limits for the chart.

p-chart

A chart used for controlling the proportion of defective services or products generated by the process.

EXAMPLE 3.3	**Using a *p*-Chart to Monitor a Process**

The operations manager of the booking services department of Hometown Bank is concerned about the number of wrong customer account numbers recorded by Hometown personnel. Each week a random sample of 2,500 deposits is taken, and the number of incorrect account numbers is recorded. The results for the past 12 weeks are shown in the following table. Is the booking process out of statistical control? Use three-sigma control limits, which will provide a type I error of 0.26 percent.

A customer making a bank deposit in Boise, Idaho, USA.

MyOMLab
Active Model 6.2 in MyOMLab provides additional insight on the *p*-chart and its uses for the booking services department.

MyOMLab
Tutor 6.2 in MyOMLab provides a new example to practice the use of the *p*-chart.

Sample Number	Wrong Account Numbers	Sample Number	Wrong Account Numbers
1	15	7	24
2	12	8	7
3	19	9	10
4	2	10	17
5	19	11	15
6	4	12	3
			Total 147

SOLUTION

Step 1. Using this sample data to calculate $\bar{p}$

$$\bar{p} = \frac{\text{Total defectives}}{\text{Total number of observations}} = \frac{147}{12(2,500)} = 0.0049$$

$$\sigma_p = \sqrt{\bar{p}(1-\bar{p})/n} = \sqrt{0.0049(1-0.0049)/2,500} = 0.0014$$

$$\text{UCL}_p = \bar{p} + z\sigma_p = 0.0049 + 3(0.0014) = 0.0091$$

$$\text{LCL}_p = \bar{p} - z\sigma_p = 0.0049 - 3(0.0014) = 0.0007$$

Step 2. Calculate each sample proportion defective. For sample 1, the proportion of defectives is $15/2,500 = 0.0060$.

Step 3. Plot each sample proportion defective on the chart, as shown in Figure 3.11.

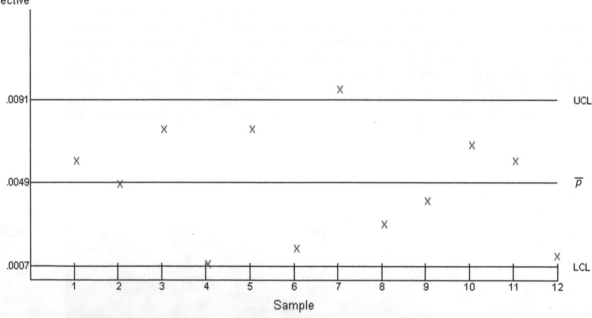

Fraction Defective

▲ **FIGURE 3.11**
The p-Chart from POM for Windows for Wrong Account Numbers, Showing that Sample 7 Is Out of Control

Sample 7 exceeds the UCL; thus, the process is out of control and the reasons for the poor performance that week should be determined.

DECISION POINT

Management explored the circumstances when sample 7 was taken. The encoding machine used to print the account numbers on the checks was defective that week. The following week the machine was repaired; however, the recommended preventive maintenance on the machine was not performed for months prior to the failure. Management reviewed the performance of the maintenance department and instituted changes to the maintenance procedures for the encoding machine. After the problem was corrected, an analyst recalculated the control limits using the data without sample 7. Subsequent weeks were sampled, and the booking process was determined to be in statistical control. Consequently, the p-chart provides a tool to indicate when a process needs adjustment.

***c*-Charts**   Sometimes services or products have more than one defect. For example, a roll of carpeting may have several defects, such as tufted or discolored fibers or stains from the production process. Other situations in which more than one defect may occur include accidents at a particular intersection, bubbles in a television picture face panel, and complaints from a patron at a hotel. When management is interested in reducing the number of defects per unit or service encounter, another type of control chart, the ***c*-chart**, is useful.

> **c-chart**
> A chart used for controlling the number of defects when more than one defect can be present in a service or product.

The underlying sampling distribution for a *c*-chart is the Poisson distribution. The Poisson distribution is based on the assumption that defects occur over a continuous region on the surface of a product or a continuous time interval during the provision of a service. It further assumes that the probability of two or more defects at any one location on the surface or at any instant of time is negligible. The mean of the distribution is $\bar{c}$ and the standard deviation is $\sqrt{\bar{c}}$. A useful tactic is to use the normal approximation to the Poisson so that the central line of the chart is $\bar{c}$ and the control limits are

$$\text{UCL}_c = \bar{c} + z\sqrt{\bar{c}} \quad \text{and} \quad \text{LCL}_c = \bar{c} - z\sqrt{\bar{c}}$$

EXAMPLE 3.4	**Using a *c*-Chart to Monitor Defects per Unit**

The Woodland Paper Company produces paper for the newspaper industry. As a final step in the process, the paper passes through a machine that measures various product quality characteristics. When the paper production process is in control, it averages 20 defects per roll.

a. Set up a control chart for the number of defects per roll. For this example, use two-sigma control limits.

b. Five rolls had the following number of defects: 16, 21, 17, 22, and 24, respectively. The sixth roll, using pulp from a different supplier, had 5 defects. Is the paper production process in control?

A worker at a paper roll manufacturing facility.

> **MyOMLab**
> Tutor 3.3 in MyOMLab provides a new example to practice the use of the *c*-chart.

SOLUTION

a. The average number of defects per roll is 20. Therefore

$$\text{UCL}_c = \bar{c} + z\sqrt{\bar{c}} = 20 + 2(\sqrt{20}) = 28.94$$

$$\text{LCL}_c = \bar{c} - z\sqrt{\bar{c}} = 20 - 2(\sqrt{20}) = 11.06$$

The control chart is shown in Figure 3.12.

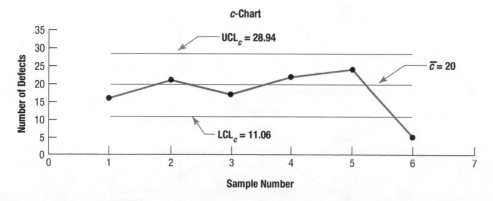

c-Chart

UCL$_c$ = 28.94

$\bar{c}$ = 20

LCL$_c$ = 11.06

Number of Defects / Sample Number

> ◀ **FIGURE 3.12**
> The *c*-Chart from the *OM Explorer c-Chart* Solver for Defects per Roll of Paper

b. Because the first five rolls had defects that fell within the control limits, the process is still in control. The sixth roll's five defects, however, is below than the LCL, and therefore, the process is technically "out of control." The control chart indicates that something good has happened.

H. Mark Weidman Photography/Alamy

Process Capability

Statistical process control techniques help managers achieve and maintain a process distribution that does not change in terms of its mean and variance. The control limits on the control charts signal when the mean or variability of the process changes. However, a process that is in statistical control may not be producing services or products according to their design specifications, because the control limits are based on the mean and variability of the *sampling distribution*, not the design specifications. **Process capability** refers to the ability of the process to meet the design specifications for a service or product. Design specifications often are expressed as a **nominal value**, or target, and a **tolerance**, or allowance above or below the nominal value.

For example, the administrator of an intensive care unit lab might have a nominal value for the turnaround time of results to the attending physicians of 25 minutes and a tolerance of ±5 minutes because of the need for speed under life-threatening conditions. The tolerance gives an *upper specification* of 30 minutes and a *lower specification* of 20 minutes. The lab process must be capable of providing the results of analyses within these specifications; otherwise, it will produce a certain proportion of "defects." The administrator is also interested in detecting occurrences of turnaround times of less than 20 minutes because something might be learned that can be built into the lab process in the future. For the present, the physicians are pleased with results that arrive within 20 to 30 minutes.

Defining Process Capability

Figure 3.13 shows the relationship between a process distribution and the upper and lower specifications for the lab process turnaround time under two conditions. In Figure 3.13(a), the process is capable because the extremes of the process distribution fall within the upper and lower specifications. In Figure 3.13(b), the process is not capable because the lab process produces too many reports with long turnaround times.

Figure 3.13 shows clearly why managers are so concerned with reducing process variability. The less variability—represented by lower standard deviations—the less frequently bad output is produced. Figure 3.14 shows what reducing variability implies for a process distribution that is a normal probability

process capability

The ability of the process to meet the design specifications for a service or product.

nominal value

A target for design specifications.

tolerance

An allowance above or below the nominal value.

FIGURE 3.13 ▶

The Relationship Between a Process Distribution and Upper and Lower Specifications

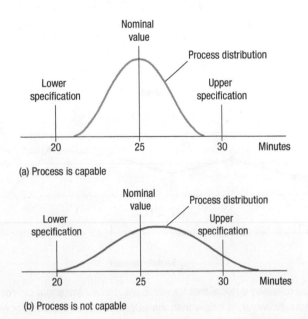

(a) Process is capable

(b) Process is not capable

distribution. The firm with two-sigma performance (the specification limits equal the process distribution mean ± 2 standard deviations) produces 4.56 percent defects, or 45,600 defects per million. The firm with four-sigma performance produces only 0.0063 percent defects, or 63 defects per million. Finally, the firm with six-sigma performance produces only 0.0000002 percent defects, or 0.002 defects per million.[1]

How can a manager determine quantitatively whether a process is capable? Two measures commonly are used in practice to assess the capability of a process: the process capability index and the process capability ratio.

Process Capability Index   The **process capability index**, C_{pk}, is defined as

$$C_{pk} = \text{Minimum of}\left[\frac{\bar{\bar{x}} - \text{Lower specification}}{3\sigma}, \frac{\text{Upper specification} - \bar{\bar{x}}}{3\sigma}\right]$$

where

$$\sigma = \text{standard deviation of the process distribution}$$

The process capability index measures how well the process is centered as well as whether the variability is acceptable. As a general rule, most values of any process distribution fall within ± 3 standard deviations of the mean. Consequently, ± 3 standard deviations are used as the benchmark. Because the process capability index is concerned with how well the process distribution is centered relative to the specifications, it checks to see if the process average is at least three standard deviations from the upper and lower specifications. We take the minimum of the two ratios because it gives the *worst-case* situation.

The process capability index must be compared to a critical value to judge whether a process is capable. Firms striving to achieve three-sigma performance use a critical value for the ratio of 1.0. A firm targeting four-sigma performance will use 1.33 (or 4/3), a firm targeting five-sigma performance will use 1.67 (or 5/3), and a firm striving for six-sigma performance will use 2.00 (or 6/3). Processes producing services or products with less than three-sigma performance will have C_{pk} values less than 1.0.

If a process passes the process capability index test, we can declare the process is capable. Suppose a firm desires its processes to produce at the level of four-sigma performance. If C_{pk} is greater than or equal to the critical value of 1.33, we can say the process is capable. If C_{pk} is less than the critical value, either the process average is too close to one of the tolerance limits and is generating defective output, or the process variability is too large. To find out whether the variability is the culprit, we need another test.

Process Capability Ratio   If a process fails the process capability *index* test, we need a quick test to see if the process variability is causing the problem. If a process is *capable*, it has a process distribution whose extreme values fall within the upper and lower specifications for a service or product. For example, if the process distribution is normal, 99.74 percent of the values fall within ± 3 standard deviations. In other words, the range of values of the quality measure generated by a process is approximately six standard deviations of the process distribution. Hence, if a process is capable at the three-sigma level, the difference between the upper and lower specification, called the *tolerance width*, must be greater than six standard deviations. The **process capability ratio, C_p**, is defined as

$$C_p = \frac{\text{Upper specification} - \text{Lower specification}}{6\sigma}$$

Suppose management wants four-sigma capability in their processes, and a process just failed the process capability index test at that level. A C_p value of 1.33, say, implies that the variability of the process is at the level of four-sigma quality and that the process is capable of consistently producing outputs within specifications, assuming that the process is centered. Because C_p passed the test, but C_{pk} did not, we can assume that the problem is that the process is not centered adequately.

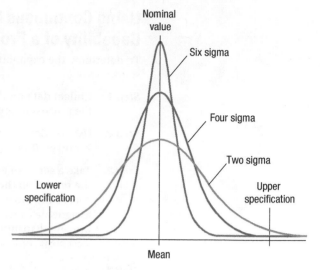

▲ **FIGURE 3.14**
Effects of Reducing Variability on Process Capability

process capability index, C_{pk}

An index that measures the potential for a process to generate defective outputs relative to either upper or lower specifications.

process capability ratio, C_p

The tolerance width divided by six standard deviations.

---

[1] Our discussion assumes that the process distribution has no assignable causes. Six Sigma programs, however, define defect performance with the assumption that the process average has moved 1.5 standard deviations. In such a case, there would be 3.4 defects per million. See **http://www.isixsigma.com** for the rationale behind that assumption.

Using Continuous Improvement to Determine the Capability of a Process

To determine the capability of a process to produce outputs within the tolerances, use the following steps.

Step 1.   Collect data on the process output, and calculate the mean and the standard deviation of the process output distribution.

Step 2.   Use the data from the process distribution to compute process control charts, such as an $\bar{x}$- and an R-chart.

Step 3.   Take a series of at least 20 consecutive random samples of size n from the process and plot the results on the control charts. If the sample statistics are within the control limits of the charts, the process is in statistical control. If the process is not in statistical control, look for assignable causes and eliminate them. Recalculate the mean and standard deviation of the process distribution and the control limits for the charts. Continue until the process is in statistical control.

Step 4.   Calculate the process capability *index*. If the results are acceptable, the process is capable and document any changes made to the process; continue to monitor the output by using the control charts. If the results are unacceptable, calculate the process capability *ratio*. If the results are acceptable, the process variability is fine and management should focus on centering the process. If the results of the process capability ratio are unacceptable, management should focus on reducing the variability in the process until it passes the test. As changes are made, recalculate the mean and standard deviation of the process distribution and the control limits for the charts and return to step 3.

EXAMPLE 3.5	Assessing the Process Capability of the Intensive Care Unit Lab

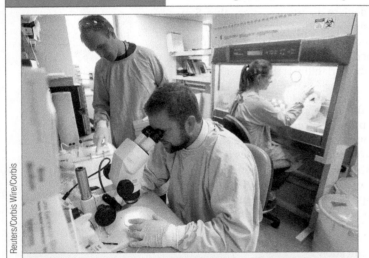

Reuters/Corbis Wire/Corbis

A doctor examines a specimen through his microscope in a lab at St. Vincent's Hospital.

The intensive care unit lab process has an average turnaround time of 26.2 minutes and a standard deviation of 1.35 minutes. The nominal value for this service is 25 minutes with an upper specification limit of 30 minutes and a lower specification limit of 20 minutes. The administrator of the lab wants to have four-sigma performance for her lab. Is the lab process capable of this level of performance?

SOLUTION

The administrator began by taking a quick check to see if the process is capable by applying the process capability index:

$$\text{Lower specification calculation} = \frac{26.2 - 20.0}{3(1.35)} = 1.53$$

$$\text{Upper specification calculation} = \frac{30.0 - 26.2}{3(1.35)} = 0.94$$

$$C_{pk} = \text{Minimum of } [1.53, 0.94] = 0.94$$

Since the target value for four-sigma performance is 1.33, the process capability index told her that the process was not capable. However, she did not know whether the problem was the variability of the process, the centering of the process, or both. The options available to improve the process depended on what is wrong.

She next checked the process variability with the process capability ratio:

$$C_p = \frac{30.0 - 20.0}{6(1.35)} = 1.23$$

The process variability did not meet the four-sigma target of 1.33. Consequently, she initiated a study to see where variability was introduced into the process. Two activities, report preparation and specimen slide preparation, were identified as having inconsistent procedures. These procedures were modified to provide consistent performance. New data were collected and the average turnaround was now 26.1 minutes with

MyOMLab

Active Model 3.3 in MyOMLab provides additional insight on the process capability problem at the intensive care unit lab.

MyOMLab

Tutor 3.4 in MyOMLab provides a new example to practice the process capability measures.

a standard deviation of 1.20 minutes. She now had the process variability at the four-sigma level of performance, as indicated by the process capability ratio:

$$C_p = \frac{30.0 - 20.0}{6(1.20)} = 1.39$$

However, the process capability index indicated additional problems to resolve:

$$C_{pk} = \text{Minimum of} \left[\frac{(26.1 - 20.0)}{3(1.20)}, \frac{(30.0 - 26.1)}{3(1.20)} \right] = 1.08$$

DECISION POINT

The lab process was still not at the level of four-sigma performance on turnaround time. The lab administrator searched for the causes of the off-center turnaround time distribution. She discovered periodic backlogs at a key piece of testing equipment. Acquiring a second machine provided the capacity to reduce the turnaround times to four-sigma capability.

International Quality Documentation Standards and Awards

Once a company has gone through the effort of making its processes capable, it must document its level of quality so as to better market its services or products. This documentation of quality is especially important in international trade. However, if each country had its own set of standards, companies selling in international markets would have difficulty complying with quality documentation standards in each country where they did business. To overcome this problem, the International Organization for Standardization devised a family of standards called ISO 9000 for companies doing business in the European Union. Subsequently, ISO 14000 was devised for environmental management systems and ISO 26000 for guidance on social responsibility.

The ISO 9001:2008 Documentation Standards

ISO 9001:2008 is the latest update of the ISO 9000 standards governing documentation of a quality program. According to the International Organization for Standardization, the ISO 9001:2008 standards address *quality management* by specifying what the firm does to fulfill the customer's quality requirements and applicable regulatory requirements, while aiming to enhance customer satisfaction and achieve continual improvement of its performance in pursuit of these objectives. Companies become certified by proving to a qualified external examiner that they comply with all the requirements. Once certified, companies are listed in a directory so that potential customers can see which companies are certified and to what level. Compliance with ISO 9001:2008 standards says *nothing* about the actual quality of a product. Rather, it indicates to customers that companies can provide documentation to support whatever claims they make about quality. As of 2009, more than 1 million organizations worldwide have been certified in the ISO 9000 family of documentation standards.

ISO 9001:2008

A set of standards governing documentation of a quality program.

The ISO 140001:2004 Environmental Management System

The **ISO 140001:2004** standards require documentation of a firm's environmental program. According to the International Organization for Standardization, the ISO 140001:2004 family addresses *environmental management* by specifying what the firm does to minimize harmful effects on the environment caused by its activities, and to achieve continual improvement of its environmental performance. The documentation standards require participating companies to keep track of their raw materials use and their generation, treatment, and disposal of hazardous wastes. Although not specifying what each company is allowed to emit, the standards require companies to prepare a plan for ongoing improvement in their environmental performance. ISO 140001:2004 covers a number of areas, including the following:

ISO 140001:2004

Documentation standards that require participating companies to keep track of their raw materials use and their generation, treatment, and disposal of hazardous wastes.

- *Environmental Management System.* Requires a plan to improve performance in resource use and pollutant output.

- *Environmental Performance Evaluation.* Specifies guidelines for the certification of companies.

- *Environmental Labeling.* Defines terms such as *recyclable, energy efficient,* and *safe for the ozone layer.*

- *Life-Cycle Assessment.* Evaluates the lifetime environmental impact from the manufacture, use, and disposal of a product.

To maintain their certification, companies must be inspected by outside, private auditors on a regular basis. Apart from large US based companies like Ford, General Motors, IBM, Honda of America, and Xerox, approximately 10,000 firms worldwide have registered for ISO 140001:2004.

Benefits of ISO Certification

Completing the certification process can take as long as 18 months and involve many hours of management and employee time. The cost of certification can exceed $1 million for large companies. Despite the expense and commitment involved in ISO certification, it bestows significant external and internal benefits. The external benefits come from the potential sales advantage that companies in compliance have. Companies looking for a supplier will more likely select a company that has demonstrated compliance with ISO documentation standards, all other factors being equal. Consequently, more and more firms are seeking certification to gain a competitive advantage.

Internal benefits can be substantial. Registered companies report an average of 48 percent increased profitability and 76 percent improvement in marketing. The British Standards Institute, a leading third-party auditor, estimates that most ISO 9001-registered companies experience a 10 percent reduction in the cost of producing a product because of the quality improvements they make while striving to meet the documentation requirements. Certification in ISO 9001:2008 requires a company to analyze and document its procedures, which is necessary in any event for implementing continuous improvement, employee involvement, and similar programs. The guidelines and requirements of the ISO documentation standards provide companies with a jump-start in pursuing TQM programs.

Benefits of the Baldrige Performance Excellence Program

Baldrige Performance Excellence Program

A program named for the late secretary of commerce, Malcolm Baldrige, who was a strong proponent of enhancing quality as a means of reducing the trade deficit; organizations vie for an award that promotes, recognizes, and publicizes quality strategies and achievements.

Regardless of where a company does business, it is clear that all organizations have to produce high-quality products and services if they are to be competitive. To emphasize that point, in August 1987 the U.S. Congress signed into law the Malcolm Baldrige National Quality Improvement Act, creating the Malcolm Baldrige National Quality Award, which is now entitled the **Baldrige Performance Excellence Program (www.quality.nist.gov).** Named for the late secretary of commerce, who was a strong proponent of enhancing quality as a means of reducing the trade deficit, the award promotes, recognizes, and publicizes quality strategies and achievements.

The application and review process for the Baldrige award is rigorous. However, the act of preparing the application itself is often a major benefit to organizations because it helps firms define what *quality* means for them. According to the U.S. Commerce Department's National Institute of Standards and Technology (NIST), investing in quality principles and performance excellence pays off in increased productivity, satisfied employees and customers, and improved profitability, both for customers and investors. The seven major criteria for the award are the following:

1. *Leadership.* Describes how senior leaders' actions guide and sustain the organization and how they communicate with the workforce and encourage high performance.

2. *Strategic Planning.* Describes how the organization establishes its strategy to address its strategic challenges, leverage its strategic advantages, and summarizes the organization's key strategic objectives and their related goals.

3. *Customer Focus.* Describes how the organization determines its service or product offerings and the mechanisms to support the customers' use of them.

4. *Measurement, Analysis, and Knowledge Management.* Describes how the organization measures, analyzes, reviews, and improves its performance through the use of data and information at all levels of the organization.

5. *Workforce Focus.* Describes how the organization engages, compensates, and rewards its workers and how they are developed to achieve high performance.

6. *Operations Focus.* Describes how the organization designs its work systems and determines its key processes to deliver customer value, prepare for potential emergencies, and achieve organizational success and sustainability.

7. *Results.* Describe the organization's performance and improvement in five categories: products and processes, customer focus, workforce focus, leadership and governance, and financial and market.

Customer satisfaction underpins these seven criteria. Criterion 7, "Results," is given the most weight in selecting winners.

LEARNING GOALS IN REVIEW

Learning Goal	Guidelines for Review	MyOMLab Resources
1 Define the four major costs of quality, and their relationship to the role of ethics in determining the overall costs of delivering products and services.	See the section "Costs of Quality," pp. 96–98, and understand how deceptive business practices can affect a customer's experiences and why the costs of quality should be balanced with ethical considerations.	**Video:** Process Performance and Quality at Starwood Hotels & Resorts
2 Explain the basic principles of Total Quality Management (TQM) and Six Sigma.	See the section "Total Quality Management and Six Sigma," pp. 98–102. Focus on the five customer definitions of quality, and the key Figures 3.1 and 3.2. Be sure to understand Figure 3.3, which shows the goals of Six Sigma.	**Video:** Process Performance and Quality at Starwood Hotels & Resorts
3 Understand how acceptance sampling and process performance approaches interface in a supply chain.	See the section "Acceptance Sampling," pp. 102–103. Figure 3.4 shows how TQM or Six Sigma works in a supply chain through the tactic of acceptance sampling.	**POM for Windows:** Acceptance Sampling **Supplement G:** Acceptance Sampling Plans
4 Describe how to construct process control charts and use them to determine whether a process is out of statistical control.	See the section "Statistical Process Control," pp. 103–114. Understanding Figures 3.5 and 3.6 is key to understanding the methods to follow. The subsections on "Control Charts," "Control Charts for Variables," and "Control Charts for Attributes," pp. 106–114, show you how to determine if a process is in statistical control. Study Examples 3.1 to 3.4 as well as Solved Problems 1 to 3.	**Active Model Exercises:** 3.1: x-bar and R-Charts; 3.2: p-Charts **OM Explorer Solvers:** R- and x-bar Charts; c-Charts; p-Charts **OM Explorer Tutors:** 3.1: x-bar and R-Charts; 3.2: p-Charts; 3.3: c-Charts **POM for Windows:** x-bar Charts; p-Charts; c-Charts
5 Explain how to determine whether a process is capable of producing a service or product to specifications.	The major take-away in the chapter is found in the section "Process Capability," pp. 114–117. Be sure you understand Figures 3.13 and 3.14; study Example 3.5 and Solved Problem 4.	**Active Model Exercise:** 3.3: Process Capability **OM Explorer Solver:** Process Capability **OM Explorer Tutor:** 3.4: Process Capability **POM for Windows:** Process Capability
6 Describe International Quality Documentation Standards and the Baldridge Performance Excellence Program.	The section "International Quality Documentation Standards and Awards," pp. 117–118, reviews details of different ISO standards and the Baldridge Award Program.	

Key Equations

Statistical Process Control

1. Sample mean:

$$\bar{x} = \frac{\sum\limits_{i=1}^{n} x_i}{n}$$

2. Standard deviation of a sample:

$$\sigma = \sqrt{\frac{\sum\limits_{i=1}^{n}(x_i - \bar{x})^2}{n-1}} \text{ or } \sigma = \sqrt{\frac{\sum\limits_{i=1}^{n} x_i^2 - \frac{(\sum x_i)^2}{n}}{n-1}}$$

3. Control limits for variable process control charts

   a. R-chart, range of sample:

$$\text{Upper control limit} = \text{UCL}_R = D_4\bar{R}$$
$$\text{Lower control limit} = \text{LCL}_R = D_3\bar{R}$$

b. $\bar{x}$-chart, sample mean:

$$\text{Upper control limit} = \text{UCL}_{\bar{x}} = \bar{\bar{x}} + A_2\bar{R}$$
$$\text{Lower control limit} = \text{LCL}_{\bar{x}} = \bar{\bar{x}} - A_2\bar{R}$$

c. When the standard deviation of the process distribution, σ, is known:

$$\text{Upper control limit} = \text{UCL}_{\bar{x}} = \bar{\bar{x}} + z\sigma_{\bar{x}}$$
$$\text{Lower control limit} = \text{LCL}_{\bar{x}} = \bar{\bar{x}} - z\sigma_{\bar{x}}$$

where

$$\sigma_{\bar{x}} = \frac{\sigma}{\sqrt{n}}$$

4. Control limits for attribute process control charts

a. p-chart, proportion defective:

$$\text{Upper control limit} = \text{UCL}_p = \bar{p} + z\sigma_p$$
$$\text{Lower control limit} = \text{LCL}_p = \bar{p} - z\sigma_p$$

where

$$\sigma_p = \sqrt{\bar{p}(1 - \bar{p})/n}$$

b. c-chart, number of defects:

$$\text{Upper control limit} = \text{UCL}_c = \bar{c} + z\sqrt{\bar{c}}$$
$$\text{Lower control limit} = \text{LCL}_c = \bar{c} - z\sqrt{\bar{c}}$$

Process Capability

5. Process capability index:

$$C_{pk} = \text{Minimum of} \left[\frac{\bar{\bar{x}} - \text{Lower specification}}{3\sigma}, \frac{\text{Upper specification} - \bar{\bar{x}}}{3\sigma} \right]$$

6. Process capability ratio:

$$C_p = \frac{\text{Upper specification} - \text{Lower specification}}{6\sigma}$$

Key Terms

acceptable quality level (AQL) 103
acceptance sampling 103
appraisal costs 97
assignable causes of variation 105
attributes 104
Baldrige Performance Excellence
    Program 118
c-chart 113
common causes of variation 105
continuous improvement 101
control chart 106
defect 96
employee empowerment 100
ethical failure costs 97

external failure costs 97
internal failure costs 97
ISO 9001:2008 117
ISO 140001:2004 117
nominal value 114
p-chart 111
plan-do-study-act cycle 101
prevention costs 97
process capability 114
process capability index, C_{pk} 115
process capability ratio, C_p 115
quality 99
quality at the source 100
R-chart 107

sample size 104
sampling plan 104
Six Sigma 101
statistical process control (SPC) 103
teams 100
tolerance 114
total quality management (TQM) 98
type I error 107
type II error 107
variables 104
warranty 97
$\bar{x}$-chart 108

Solved Problem 1

The Watson Electric Company produces incandescent light bulbs. The following data on the number of   MyOMLab Video
lumens for 40-watt light bulbs were collected when the process was in control.

Sample	OBSERVATION			
	1	2	3	4
1	604	612	588	600
2	597	601	607	603
3	581	570	585	592
4	620	605	595	588
5	590	614	608	604

a. Calculate control limits for an R-chart and an $\bar{x}$-chart.

b. Since these data were collected, some new employees were hired. A new sample obtained the following readings: 625, 592, 612, and 635. Is the process still in control?

SOLUTION

a. To calculate $\bar{x}$, compute the mean for each sample. To calculate R, subtract the lowest value in the sample from the highest value in the sample. For example, for sample 1,

$$\bar{x} = \frac{604 + 612 + 588 + 600}{4} = 601$$

$$R = 612 - 588 = 24$$

Sample	$\bar{X}$	R
1	601	24
2	602	10
3	582	22
4	602	32
5	604	24
Total	2,991	112
Average	$\bar{\bar{x}} = 598.2$	$\bar{R} = 22.4$

The R-chart control limits are

$$\text{UCL}_R = D_4\bar{R} = 2.282(22.4) = 51.12$$
$$\text{LCL}_R = D_3\bar{R} = 0(22.4) = 0$$

The $\bar{x}$-chart control limits are

$$\text{UCL}_{\bar{x}} = \bar{\bar{x}} + A_2\bar{R} = 598.2 + 0.729(22.4) = 614.53$$
$$\text{LCL}_{\bar{x}} = \bar{\bar{x}} - A_2\bar{R} = 598.2 - 0.729(22.4) = 581.87$$

b. First check to see whether the variability is still in control based on the new data. The range is 43 (or $635 - 592$), which is inside the UCL and LCL for the R-chart. Since the process variability is in control, we test for the process average using the current estimate for $\bar{R}$. The average is 616 (or $(625 + 592 + 612 + 635)/4$), which is above the UCL for the $\bar{x}$-chart. Since the process average is out of control, a search for assignable causes inducing excessive average lumens must be conducted.

Solved Problem 2

The data processing department of the Arizona Bank has five data entry clerks. Each working day their supervisor verifies the accuracy of a random sample of 250 records. A record containing one or more errors is considered defective and must be redone. The results of the last 30 samples are shown in the table. All were checked to make sure that none was out of control.

Sample	Number of Defective Records	Sample	Number of Defective Records	Sample	Number of Defective Records	Sample	Number of Defective Records
1	7	9	6	17	12	24	7
2	5	10	13	18	4	25	13
3	19	11	18	19	6	26	10
4	10	12	5	20	11	27	14
5	11	13	16	21	17	28	6
6	8	14	4	22	12	29	11
7	12	15	11	23	6	30	9
8	9	16	8				
						Total	300

a. Based on these historical data, set up a p-chart using $z = 3$.

b. Samples for the next 4 days showed the following:

Sample	Number of Defective Records
Tues	17
Wed	15
Thurs	22
Fri	21

What is the supervisor's assessment of the data-entry process likely to be?

SOLUTION

a. From the table, the supervisor knows that the total number of defective records is 300 out of a total sample of 7,500 [or 30(250)]. Therefore, the central line of the chart is

$$\bar{p} = \frac{300}{7,500} = 0.04$$

The control limits are

$$\text{UCL}_p = \bar{p} + z\sqrt{\frac{\bar{p}(1 - \bar{p})}{n}} = 0.04 + 3\sqrt{\frac{0.04(0.96)}{250}} = 0.077$$

$$\text{LCL}_p = \bar{p} - z\sqrt{\frac{\bar{p}(1 - \bar{p})}{n}} = 0.04 - 3\sqrt{\frac{0.04(0.96)}{250}} = 0.003$$

b. Samples for the next 4 days showed the following:

Sample	Number of Defective Records	Proportion
Tues	17	0.068
Wed	15	0.060
Thurs	22	0.088
Fri	21	0.084

Samples for Thursday and Friday are out of control. The supervisor should look for the problem and, upon identifying it, take corrective action.

Solved Problem 3

The Minnow County Highway Safety Department monitors accidents at the intersection of Routes 123 and 14. Accidents at the intersection have averaged three per month.

a. Which type of control chart should be used? Construct a control chart with three-sigma control limits.

b. Last month, seven accidents occurred at the intersection. Is this sufficient evidence to justify a claim that something has changed at the intersection?

SOLUTION

a. The safety department cannot determine the number of accidents that did *not* occur, so it has no way to compute a proportion defective at the intersection. Therefore, the administrators must use a c-chart for which

$$\text{UCL}_c = \bar{c} + z\sqrt{\bar{c}} = 3 + 3\sqrt{3} = 8.20$$

$$\text{LCL}_c = \bar{c} - z\sqrt{\bar{c}} = 3 - 3\sqrt{3} = -2.196, \text{ adjusted to } 0$$

There cannot be a negative number of accidents, so the LCL in this case is adjusted to zero.

b. The number of accidents last month falls within the UCL and LCL of the chart. We conclude that no assignable causes are present and that the increase in accidents was due to chance.

Solved Problem 4

Pioneer Chicken advertises "lite" chicken with 30 percent fewer calories. (The pieces are 33 percent smaller.) The process average distribution for "lite" chicken breasts is 420 calories, with a standard deviation of the population of 25 calories. Pioneer randomly takes samples of six chicken breasts to measure calorie content.

a. Design an $\bar{x}$-chart using the process standard deviation. Use three-sigma limits.

b. The product design calls for the average chicken breast to contain 400 ± 100 calories. Calculate the process capability index (target $= 1.33$) and the process capability ratio. Interpret the results.

SOLUTION

a. For the process standard deviation of 25 calories, the standard deviation of the sample mean is

$$\sigma_{\bar{x}} = \frac{\sigma}{\sqrt{n}} = \frac{25}{\sqrt{6}} = 10.2 \text{ calories}$$

$$\text{UCL}_{\bar{x}} = \bar{\bar{x}} + z\sigma_{\bar{x}} = 420 + 3(10.2) = 450.6 \text{ calories}$$

$$\text{LCL}_{\bar{x}} = \bar{\bar{x}} - z\sigma_{\bar{x}} = 420 - 3(10.2) = 389.4 \text{ calories}$$

b. The process capability index is

$$C_{pk} = \text{Minimum of} \left[\frac{\bar{\bar{x}} - \text{Lower specification}}{3\sigma}, \frac{\text{Upper specification} - \bar{\bar{x}}}{3\sigma} \right]$$

$$= \text{Minimum of} \left[\frac{420 - 300}{3(25)} = 1.60, \frac{500 - 420}{3(25)} = 1.07 \right] = 1.07$$

The process capability ratio is

$$C_p = \frac{\text{Upper specification} - \text{Lower specification}}{6\sigma} = \frac{500 \text{ calories} - 300 \text{ calories}}{6(25)} = 1.33$$

Because the process capability ratio is 1.33, the process should be able to produce the product reliably within specifications. However, the process capability index is 1.07, so the current process is not centered properly for four-sigma performance. The mean of the process distribution is too close to the upper specification.

Discussion Questions

1. Should a very pricey hand-crafted object of beauty, use automated equipment for manufacturing some of its component parts needed for assembling the object? Do you think it is a mistake to use automation in this way?

2. Recently, the Polish General Corporation, well-known for manufacturing appliances and automobile parts, initiated a $13 billion project to produce automobiles. A great deal of learning on the part of management and employees was required. Even though pressure was mounting to get a new product to market in early 2012, the production manager of

the newly formed automobile division insisted on almost a year of trial runs before sales started because workers have to do their jobs 60 to 100 times before they can memorize the right sequence. The launch date was set for early 2013. What are the consequences of using this approach to enter the market with a new product?

3. Explain how unethical business practices degrade the quality of the experience a customer has with a service or product. How is the International Organization for Standardization trying to encourage ethical business behavior?

Problems

The OM Explorer and POM for Windows software is available to all students using the 11th edition of this textbook. Go to **http://www.pearsonhighered.com/krajewski** to download these computer packages. If you purchased MyOMLab, you also have access to Active Models software and significant help in doing the following problems. Check with your instructor on how best to use these resources. In many cases, the

instructor wants you to understand how to do the calculations by hand. At the least, the software provides a check on your calculations. When calculations are particularly complex and the goal is interpreting the results in making decisions, the software replaces entirely the manual calculations. The software also can be a valuable resource well after your course is completed.

Statistical Process Control

1. At Quickie Car Wash, the wash process is advertised to take less than 7 minutes. Consequently, management has set a target average of 390 seconds for the wash process. Suppose the average range for a sample of 9 cars is 10 seconds. Use Table 3.1 to establish control limits for sample means and ranges for the car wash process.

2. At Isogen Pharmaceuticals, the filling process for its asthma inhaler is set to dispense 150 milliliters (ml) of steroid solution per container. The average range for a sample of 4 containers is 3 ml. Use Table 3.1 to establish control limits for sample means and ranges for the filling process.

3. The Canine Gourmet Company produces delicious dog treats for canines with discriminating tastes. Management wants the box-filling line to be set so that the process average weight per packet is 45 grams. To make sure that the process is in control, an inspector at the end of the filling line periodically selects a random box of 10 packets and weighs each packet. When the process is in control, the range in the weight of each sample has averaged 6 grams.

   a. Design an R- and an $\bar{x}$-chart for this process.

   b. The results from the last 5 samples of 10 packets are

Sample	$\bar{x}$	R
1	44	9
2	40	2
3	46	5
4	39	8
5	48	3

   Is the process in control? Explain.

4. Aspen Plastics produces plastic bottles to customer order. The quality inspector randomly selects four bottles from the bottle machine and measures the outside diameter of the bottle neck, a critical quality dimension that determines whether the bottle cap will fit properly. The dimensions (inch) from the last six samples are

Sample	BOTTLE			
	1	2	3	4
1	0.594	0.622	0.598	0.590
2	0.587	0.611	0.597	0.613
3	0.571	0.580	0.595	0.602
4	0.610	0.615	0.585	0.578
5	0.580	0.624	0.618	0.614
6	0.585	0.593	0.607	0.569

   Assume that only these six samples are sufficient, and use the data to determine control limits for an R- and an $\bar{x}$-chart.

5. In an attempt to judge and monitor the quality of instruction, the administration of Mega-Byte Academy devised an examination to test students on the basic concepts that all should have learned. Each year, a random sample of 10 graduating students is selected for the test. The average score is used to track the quality of the educational process. Test results for the past 10 years are shown in Table 3.2.

   Use these data to estimate the center and standard deviation for this distribution. Then, calculate the two-sigma control limits for the process average. What comments would you make to the administration of the Mega-Byte Academy?

TABLE 3.2 | TEST SCORES ON EXIT EXAM

Year	STUDENT										Average
	1	2	3	4	5	6	7	8	9	10	
1	63	57	92	87	70	61	75	58	63	71	69.7
2	90	77	59	88	48	83	63	94	72	70	74.4
3	67	81	93	55	71	71	86	98	60	90	77.2
4	62	67	78	61	89	93	71	59	93	84	75.7
5	85	88	77	69	58	90	97	72	64	60	76.0
6	60	57	79	83	64	94	86	64	92	74	75.3
7	94	85	56	77	89	72	71	61	92	97	79.4
8	97	86	83	88	65	87	76	84	81	71	81.8
9	94	90	76	88	65	93	86	87	94	63	83.6
10	88	91	71	89	97	79	93	87	69	85	84.9

6. The Money Pit Mortgage Company is interested in monitoring the performance of the mortgage process. Fifteen samples of five completed mortgage transactions each were taken during a period when the process was believed to be in control. The times to complete the transactions were measured. The means and ranges of the mortgage process transaction times, measured in days, are as follows:

Sample	1	2	3	4	5	6	7	8	9	10	11	12	13	14	15
Mean	17	14	8	17	12	13	15	16	13	14	16	9	11	9	12
Range	6	11	4	8	9	14	12	15	10	10	11	6	9	11	13

Subsequently, samples of size 5 were taken from the process every week for the next 10 weeks. The times were measured and the following results obtained:

Sample	16	17	18	19	20	21	22	23	24	25
Mean	11	14	9	15	17	19	13	22	20	18
Range	7	11	6	4	12	14	11	10	8	6

a. Construct the control charts for the mean and the range, using the original 15 samples.

b. On the control charts developed in part (a), plot the values from samples 16 through 25 and comment on whether the process is in control.

c. In part (b), if you concluded that the process was out of control, would you attribute it to a drift in the mean, an increase in the variability, or both? Explain your answer.

7. Webster Chemical Company produces mastics and caulking for the construction industry. The product is blended in large mixers and then pumped into tubes and capped. Management is concerned about whether the filling process for tubes of caulking is in statistical control. The process should be centered on 8 ounces per tube. Several samples of eight tubes were taken, each tube was weighed, and the weights in Table 3.3 were obtained.

TABLE 3.3 | OUNCES OF CAULKING PER TUBE

Sample	TUBE NUMBER							
	1	2	3	4	5	6	7	8
1	7.98	8.34	8.02	7.94	8.44	7.68	7.81	8.11
2	8.33	8.22	8.08	8.51	8.41	8.28	8.09	8.16
3	7.89	7.77	7.91	8.04	8.00	7.89	7.93	8.09
4	8.24	8.18	7.83	8.05	7.90	8.16	7.97	8.07
5	7.87	8.13	7.92	7.99	8.10	7.81	8.14	7.88
6	8.13	8.14	8.11	8.13	8.14	8.12	8.13	8.14

a. Assume that only six samples are sufficient and develop the control charts for the mean and the range.

b. Plot the observations on the control chart and comment on your findings.

8. The Digital Guardian Company issues policies that protect clients from downtime costs due to computer system failures. It is very important to process the policies quickly because long cycle times not only put the client at risk, they could also lose business for Digital Guardian. Management is concerned that customer service is degrading because of long cycle times, measured in days. The following table contains the data from five samples, each sample consisting of eight random observations.

Sample	OBSERVATION (DAYS)							
	1	2	3	4	5	6	7	8
1	13	9	4	8	8	15	8	6
2	7	15	8	10	10	14	10	15
3	8	11	4	11	8	12	9	15
4	12	7	12	9	11	8	12	8
5	8	12	6	12	11	5	12	8

a. What is your estimate of the process average?

b. What is your estimate of the average range?

c. Construct an R- and an $\bar{x}$-chart for this process. Are assignable causes present?

9. The Precision Machining Company makes hand-held tools on an assembly line that produces one product every minute. On one of the products, the critical quality dimension is the diameter (measured in thousandths of an inch) of a hole bored in one of the assemblies. Management wants to detect any shift in the process average diameter from 0.015 inch. Management considers the variance in the process to be in control. Historically, the average range has been 0.002 inch, regardless of the process average. Design an $\bar{x}$-chart to control this process, with a center line at 0.015 inch and the control limits set at three sigmas from the center line.

Management provided the results of 80 minutes of output from the production line, as shown in Table 3.4. During these 80 minutes, the process average changed once. All measurements are in thousandths of an inch.

a. Set up an $\bar{x}$-chart with $n = 4$. The frequency should be sample four and then skip four. Thus, your first sample would be for minutes $1 - 4$, the second would be for minutes $9 - 12$, and so on. When would you stop the process to check for a change in the process average?

b. Set up an $\bar{x}$-chart with $n = 8$. The frequency should be sample eight and then skip four. When would you stop the process now? What can you say about the desirability of large samples on a frequent sampling interval?

10. Using the data from Problem 9, continue your analysis of sample size and frequency by trying the following plans.

a. Using the $\bar{x}$-chart for $n = 4$, try the frequency sample four, then skip eight. When would you stop the process in this case?

b. Using the $\bar{x}$-chart for $n = 8$, try the frequency sample eight, then skip eight. When would you consider the process to be out of control?

c. Using your results from parts (a) and (b), determine what trade-offs you would consider in choosing between them.

TABLE 3.4 | SAMPLE DATA FOR PRECISION MACHINING COMPANY

Minutes	Diameter (thousandths of an inch)										
1–12	15	16	18	14	16	17	15	14	14	13	16	17
13–24	15	16	17	16	14	14	13	14	15	16	15	17
25–36	14	13	15	17	18	15	16	15	14	15	16	17
37–48	18	16	15	16	16	14	17	18	19	15	16	15
49–60	12	17	16	14	15	17	14	16	15	17	18	14
61–72	15	16	17	18	13	15	14	14	16	15	17	18
73–80	16	16	17	18	16	15	14	17				

11. Garcia's Garage desires to create some colorful charts and graphs to illustrate how reliably its mechanics "get under the hood and fix the problem." The historic average for the proportion of customers that return for the same repair within the 30-day warranty period is 0.10. Each month, Garcia tracks 100 customers to see whether they return for warranty repairs. The results are plotted as a proportion to report progress toward the goal. If the control limits are to be set at two standard deviations on either side of the goal, determine the control limits for this chart. In March, 8 of the 100 customers in the sample group returned for warranty repairs. Is the repair process in control?

12. As a hospital administrator of a large hospital, you are concerned with the absenteeism among nurses' aides. The issue has been raised by registered nurses, who feel they often have to perform work normally done by their aides. To get the facts, absenteeism data were gathered for the last 3 weeks, which is considered a representative period for future conditions. After taking random samples of 64 personnel files each day, the following data were produced:

Day	Aides Absent	Day	Aides Absent
1	4	9	7
2	3	10	2
3	2	11	3
4	4	12	2
5	2	13	1
6	5	14	3
7	3	15	4
8	4		

Because your assessment of absenteeism is likely to come under careful scrutiny, you would like a type I error of only 1 percent. You want to be sure to identify any instances of unusual absences. If some are present, you will have to explore them on behalf of the registered nurses.

a. Design a *p*-chart.

b. Based on your *p*-chart and the data from the last 3 weeks, what can you conclude about the absenteeism of nurses' aides?

13. The IRS is concerned with improving the accuracy of tax information given by its representatives over the telephone. Previous studies involved asking a set of 25 questions of a large number of IRS telephone representatives to determine the proportion of correct responses. Historically, the average proportion of correct responses has been 72 percent. Recently, IRS representatives have been receiving more training. On April 26, the set of 25 tax questions were again asked of 20 randomly selected IRS telephone representatives. The numbers of correct answers were 18, 16, 19, 21, 20, 16, 21, 16, 17, 10, 25, 18, 25, 16, 20, 15, 23, 19, 21, and 19.

   a. What are the upper and lower control limits for the appropriate *p*-chart for the IRS? Use $z = 3$.

   b. Is the tax information process in statistical control?

14. Management at Webster, in Problem 7, is now concerned as to whether caulking tubes are being properly capped. If a significant proportion of the tubes are not being sealed, Webster is placing its customers in a messy situation. Tubes are packaged in large boxes of 144. Several boxes are inspected, and the following numbers of leaking tubes are found:

Sample	Tubes	Sample	Tubes	Sample	Tubes
1	3	8	6	15	5
2	5	9	4	16	0
3	3	10	9	17	2
4	4	11	2	18	6
5	2	12	6	19	2
6	4	13	5	20	1
7	2	14	1	Total	72

Calculate *p*-chart three-sigma control limits to assess whether the capping process is in statistical control.

15. Janice Sanders, CEO of Pine Crest Medical Clinic, is concerned over the number of times patients must wait more than 30 minutes beyond their scheduled appointments. She asked her assistant to take random samples of 64 patients to see how many in each sample had to wait more than 30 minutes. Each instance is considered a defect in the clinic process. The table below contains the data for 15 samples.

Sample	Number of Defects
1	5
2	2
3	1
4	3
5	1
6	5
7	2

Sample	Number of Defects
8	3
9	6
10	3
11	9
12	9
13	5
14	2
15	3

   a. Assuming Janice Sanders is willing to use three-sigma control limits, construct a *p*-chart.

   b. Based on your *p*-chart and the data in the table, what can you conclude about the waiting time of the patients?

16. Representatives of the Patriot Insurance Company take medical information over the telephone from prospective policy applicants prior to a visit to the applicant's place of residence by a registered nurse who takes vital sign measurements. When the telephone interview has incorrect or incomplete information, the entire process of approving the application is unnecessarily delayed and has the potential of causing loss of business. The following data were collected to see how many applications contain errors. Each sample has 200 randomly selected applications.

Sample	Defects	Sample	Defects
1	20	16	15
2	18	17	40
3	29	18	35
4	12	19	21
5	14	20	24
6	11	21	9
7	30	22	20
8	25	23	17
9	27	24	28
10	16	25	10
11	25	26	17
12	18	27	22
13	25	28	14
14	16	29	19
15	20	30	20

   a. What are the upper and lower control limits of a *p*-chart for the number of defective applications? Use $z = 3$.

   b. Is the process in statistical control?

17. The manager of the customer service department of Data Tech Credit Card Service Company is concerned about the number of defects produced by the billing process. Every day a random sample of 250 statements was inspected for errors

regarding incorrect entries involving account numbers, transactions on the customer's account, interest charges, and penalty charges. Any statement with one or more of these errors was considered a defect. The study lasted 30 days and yielded the data in Table 3.5.

a. Construct a p-chart for the billing process.

b. Is there any nonrandom behavior in the billing process that would require management attention?

18. Red Baron Airlines serves hundreds of cities each day, but competition is increasing from smaller companies affiliated with major carriers. One of the key competitive priorities is on-time arrivals and departures. Red Baron defines *on time*

as any arrival or departure that takes place within 15 minutes of the scheduled time. To stay on top of the market, management set the high standard of 98 percent on-time performance. The operations department was put in charge of monitoring the performance of the airline. Each week, a random sample of 300 flight arrivals and departures was checked for schedule performance. Table 3.6 contains the numbers of arrivals and departures over the last 30 weeks that did not meet Red Baron's definition of on-time service. Using three-sigma control limits based on 98 percent on time arrivals or departures, what can you tell the management about the quality of service? Can you identify any nonrandom behavior in the process? If so, what might cause the behavior?

TABLE 3.5 | SAMPLE DATA FOR DATA TECH CREDIT CARD SERVICE

Samples	Number of Errors in Sample of 250									
1–10	3	8	5	11	7	1	12	9	0	8
11–20	3	5	7	9	11	3	2	9	13	4
21–30	12	10	6	2	1	7	10	5	8	4

TABLE 3.6 | SAMPLE DATA FOR RED BARON AIRLINES

Samples	Number of Late Planes in Sample of 300 Arrivals and Departures									
1–10	3	8	5	11	7	2	12	9	1	8
11–20	3	5	7	9	12	5	4	9	13	4
21–30	12	10	6	2	1	8	4	5	8	2

19. A textile manufacturer wants to set up a control chart for irregularities (e.g., oil stains, shop soil, loose threads, and tears) per 100 square yards of carpet. The following data were collected from a sample of twenty 100-square-yard pieces of carpet:

Sample	1	2	3	4	5	6	7	8	9	10
Irregularities	11	8	9	12	4	16	5	8	17	10
Sample	11	12	13	14	15	16	17	18	19	20
Irregularities	11	5	7	12	13	8	19	11	9	10

a. Using these data, set up a c-chart with $z = 3$.

b. Suppose that the next five samples had 15, 18, 12, 22, and 21 irregularities. What do you conclude?

20. A travel agency is concerned with the accuracy and appearance of itineraries prepared for its clients. Defects can include errors in times, airlines, flight numbers, prices, car rental information, lodging, charge card numbers, and reservation numbers, as well as typographical errors. As the possible number of errors is nearly infinite, the agency measures the number of errors that do occur. The current process results in an average of three errors per itinerary.

a. What are the two-sigma control limits for these defects?

b. A client scheduled a trip to Dallas. Her itinerary contained six errors. Interpret this information.

21. Jim's Outfitters, Inc., makes custom fancy shirts for cowboys. The shirts could be flawed in various ways, including flaws in the weave or color of the fabric, loose buttons or decorations, wrong dimensions, and uneven stitches. Jim randomly examined 10 shirts, with the following results:

Shirt	Defects
1	8
2	0
3	7
4	12
5	5
6	10
7	2
8	4
9	6
10	6

a. Assuming that 10 observations are adequate for these purposes, determine the three-sigma control limits for defects per shirt.

b. Suppose that the next shirt has 13 flaws. What can you say about the process now?

22. The Big Black Bird Company produces fiberglass camper tops. The process for producing the tops must be controlled so as to keep the number of dimples low. When the process was in control, the following defects were found in 10 randomly selected camper tops over an extended period of time:

Top	Dimples
1	7
2	9
3	14
4	11
5	3
6	12
7	8
8	4
9	7
10	6

a. Assuming 10 observations are adequate for this purpose, determine the three-sigma control limits for dimples per camper top.

b. Suppose that the next camper top has 15 dimples. What can you say about the process now?

23. At Webster Chemical Company, lumps in the caulking compound could cause difficulties in dispensing a smooth bead from the tube. Even when the process is in control, an average of four lumps per tube of caulk will remain. Testing for the presence of lumps destroys the product, so an analyst takes random samples. The following results are obtained:

Tube No.	Lumps	Tube No.	Lumps	Tube No.	Lumps
1	6	5	6	9	5
2	5	6	4	10	0
3	0	7	1	11	9
4	4	8	6	12	2

Determine the c-chart two-sigma upper and lower control limits for this process. Is the process in statistical control?

Process Capability

24. The production manager at Sunny Soda, Inc., is interested in tracking the quality of the company's 12-ounce bottle filling line. The bottles must be filled within the tolerances set for this product because the dietary information on the label shows 12 ounces as the serving size. The design standard for the product calls for a fill level of 12.00 ± 0.10 ounces. The manager collected the following sample data (in fluid ounces per bottle) on the production process:

Sample	OBSERVATION			
	1	**2**	**3**	**4**
1	12.00	11.97	12.10	12.08
2	11.91	11.94	12.10	11.96
3	11.89	12.02	11.97	11.99
4	12.10	12.09	12.05	11.95
5	12.08	11.92	12.12	12.05
6	11.94	11.98	12.06	12.08
7	12.09	12.00	12.00	12.03
8	12.01	12.04	11.99	11.95
9	12.00	11.96	11.97	12.03
10	11.92	11.94	12.09	12.00
11	11.91	11.99	12.05	12.10
12	12.01	12.00	12.06	11.97
13	11.98	11.99	12.06	12.03
14	12.02	12.00	12.05	11.95
15	12.00	12.05	12.01	11.97

a. Are the process average and range in statistical control?

b. Is the process capable of meeting the design standard at four-sigma quality? Explain.

25. The Money Pit Mortgage Company of Problem 6 made some changes to the process and undertook a process capability study. The following data were obtained for 15 samples of size 5. Based on the individual observations, management estimated the process standard deviation to be 4.21 (days) for use in the process capability analysis. The lower and upper specification limits (in days) for the mortgage process times were 5 and 25.

Sample	1	2	3	4	5	6	7	8	9	10	11	12	13	14	15
Mean	11	12	8	16	13	12	17	16	13	14	17	9	15	14	9
Range	9	13	4	11	10	9	8	15	14	11	6	6	12	10	11

a. Calculate the process capability index and the process capability ratio values.

b. Suppose management would be happy with three-sigma performance. What conclusions is management likely to draw from the capability analysis? Can valid conclusions about the process be drawn from the analysis?

c. What remedial actions, if any, do you suggest that management take?

26. The Farley Manufacturing Company prides itself on the quality of its products. The company is engaged in competition for a very important project. A key element is a part that ultimately goes into precision testing equipment. The specifications are 8.000 ± 3.000 millimeters. Management is concerned about the capability of the process to produce that part. The following data (shown below) were randomly collected during test runs of the process:

Sample	OBSERVATION (MILLIMETERS)							
	1	2	3	4	5	6	7	8
1	9.100	8.900	8.800	9.200	8.100	6.900	9.300	9.100
2	7.600	8.000	9.000	10.100	7.900	9.000	8.000	8.800
3	8.200	9.100	8.200	8.700	9.000	7.000	8.800	10.800
4	8.200	8.300	7.900	7.500	8.900	7.800	10.100	7.700
5	10.000	8.100	8.900	9.000	9.300	9.000	8.700	10.000

Assume that the process is in statistical control. Is the process capable of producing the part at the three-sigma level? Explain.

27. A critical dimension of the service quality of a call center is the wait time of a caller to get to a sales representative. Periodically, random samples of three customer calls are measured for time. The results of the last four samples are in the following table:

Sample	Time (Sec)		
1	495	501	498
2	512	508	504
3	505	497	501
4	496	503	492

a. Assuming that management is willing to use three-sigma control limits, and using only the historical information contained in the four samples, show that the call center access time is in statistical control.

b. Suppose that the standard deviation of the process distribution is 5.77. If the specifications for the access time are 500 ± 18 sec., is the process capable? Why or why not? Assume three-sigma performance is desired.

28. An automatic lathe produces rollers for roller bearings, and statistical process control charts are used to monitor the process. The central line of the chart for the sample means is set at 8.50 and for the range at 0.31 mm. The process is in control, as established by samples of size 5. The upper and lower specifications for the diameter of the rollers are $(8.50 + 0.25)$ and $(8.50 - 0.25)$ mm, respectively.

a. Calculate the control limits for the mean and range charts.

b. If the standard deviation of the process distribution is estimated to be 0.13 mm, is the process capable of meeting specifications? Assume four-sigma performance is desired.

c. If the process is not capable, what percent of the output will fall outside the specification limits? (*Hint*: Use the normal distribution.)

29. Canine Gourmet Super Breath dog treats are sold in boxes labeled with a net weight of 12 ounces (340 grams) per box. Each box contains 8 individual 1.5-ounce packets. To reduce the chances of shorting the customer, product design specifications call for the packet-filling process average to be set at 43.5 grams so that the average net weight per box of 8 packets will be 348 grams. Tolerances are set for the box to weigh 348 ± 12 grams. The standard deviation for the *packet-filling* process is 1.01 grams. The target process capability ratio is 1.33. One day, the packet-filling process average weight drifts down to 43.0 grams. Is the packaging process capable? Is an adjustment needed?

30. Return to Problem 4 relating to Aspen Plastics producing plastic bottles to customer order. Suppose that the specification for the bottleneck diameter is 0.600 ± 0.050 and the population standard deviation is 0.013 inch.

a. What is the Process Capability Index?

b. What is the Process Capability Ratio?

c. If the firm is seeking four-sigma performance, is the process capable of producing the bottle?

31. Beaver Brothers, Inc., is conducting a study to assess the capability of its 150-gram bar soap production line. A critical quality measure is the weight of the soap bars after stamping. The lower and upper specification limits are 162 and 170 grams, respectively. As a part of an initial capability study, 25 samples of size 5 were collected by the quality assurance group and the observations in Table 3.7 were recorded.

After analyzing the data by using statistical control charts, the quality assurance group calculated the process capability ratio, C_p, and the process capability index, C_{pk}. It then decided to improve the stamping process, especially the feeder mechanism. After making all the changes that were deemed necessary, 18 additional samples were collected. The summary data for these samples are

$$\bar{\bar{x}} = 163 \text{ grams}$$
$$\bar{R} = 2.326 \text{ grams}$$
$$\sigma = 1 \text{ gram}$$

All sample observations were within the control chart limits. With the new data, the quality assurance group recalculated the process capability measures. It was pleased with the improved C_p but felt that the process should be centered at 166 grams to ensure that everything was in order. Its decision concluded the study.

a. Draw the control charts for the data obtained in the initial study and verify that the process was in statistical control.

b. What were the values obtained by the group for C_p and C_{pk} for the initial capability study? Comment on your findings and explain why further improvements were necessary.

c. What are the C_p and C_{pk} after the improvements? Comment on your findings, indicating why the group decided to change the centering of the process.

d. What are the C_p and C_{pk} if the process were centered at 166? Comment on your findings.

TABLE 3.7 | SAMPLE DATA FOR BEAVER BROTHERS, INC.

Sample	OBS.1	OBS.2	OBS.3	OBS.4	OBS.5
1	167.0	159.6	161.6	164.0	165.3
2	156.2	159.5	161.7	164.0	165.3
3	167.0	162.9	162.9	164.0	165.4
4	167.0	159.6	163.7	164.1	165.4
5	156.3	160.0	162.9	164.1	165.5
6	164.0	164.2	163.0	164.2	163.9
7	161.3	163.0	164.2	157.0	160.6
8	163.1	164.2	156.9	160.1	163.1
9	164.3	157.0	161.2	163.2	164.4
10	156.9	161.0	163.2	164.3	157.3
11	161.0	163.3	164.4	157.6	160.6
12	163.3	164.5	158.4	160.1	163.3
13	158.2	161.3	163.5	164.6	158.7
14	161.5	163.5	164.7	158.6	162.5
15	163.6	164.8	158.0	162.4	163.6
16	164.5	158.5	160.3	163.4	164.6
17	164.9	157.9	162.3	163.7	165.1
18	155.0	162.2	163.7	164.8	159.6
19	162.1	163.9	165.1	159.3	162.0
20	165.2	159.1	161.6	163.9	165.2
21	164.9	165.1	159.9	162.0	163.7
22	167.6	165.6	165.6	156.7	165.7
23	167.7	165.8	165.9	156.9	165.9
24	166.0	166.0	165.6	165.6	165.5
25	163.7	163.7	165.6	165.6	166.2

Active Model Exercise

This Active Model appears in MyOMLab. It allows you to see the effects of sample size and z-values on control charts.

QUESTIONS

1. Has the booking process been in statistical control?

2. Suppose we use a 95 percent p-chart. How do the upper and lower control limits change? What are your conclusions about the booking process?

3. Suppose that the sample size is reduced to 2,000 instead of 2,500. How does this affect the chart?

4. What happens to the chart as we reduce the z-value?

5. What happens to the chart as we reduce the confidence level?

p-Chart

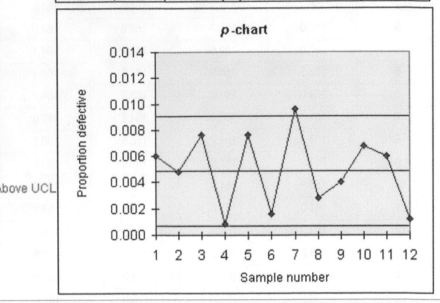

	Reset Data	Questions

Number of samples	12
Sample size	2500 ◀ ☐ ▶
z value	3.0000 ◀ ☐ ▶
Confidence	99.73% ◀ ☐▶

Total sample size	30000	Upper Control Limit	0.0091
Total defects	147	Center Line	0.0049
Percentage defects	0.0049	Lower Control Limit	0.0007
Std dev of *p*-bar	0.0014		

	# Defects	Fraction Defective
Sample 1	15	0.0060
Sample 2	12	0.0048
Sample 3	19	0.0076
Sample 4	2	0.0008
Sample 5	19	0.0076
Sample 6	4	0.0016
Sample 7	24	0.0096 Above UCL
Sample 8	7	0.0028
Sample 9	10	0.0040
Sample 10	17	0.0068
Sample 11	15	0.0060
Sample 12	3	0.0012

p-Chart Using Data from Example 3.3

VIDEO CASE	Process Performance and Quality at Starwood Hotels & Resorts

Starwood Hotels & Resorts is no stranger to quality measurement. In the most recent year, Starwood properties around the globe held 51 of approximately 700 spots on Condé Nast's Gold List of the world's best places to stay. Its spa and golf programs have consistently been ranked among the best in the world.

At Starwood, processes and programs are driven by the work of its team of Six Sigma experts, called Black Belts. Developed by Motorola more than 20 years ago, Six Sigma is a comprehensive and flexible system for achieving, sustaining, and maximizing business success by driving out defects and variability in a process. Starwood uses the five-step DMAIC process: (1) define, (2) measure, (3) analyze, (4) improve, and (5) control.

Clearly, understanding customer needs is paramount. To this end, Starwood collects data from customers on its Guest Satisfaction Index survey, called the "Voice of the Customer." The survey covers every department guests may have encountered during their stay, from the front desk and hotel room, to restaurants and concierge. Past surveys indicated that how well problems were resolved during the guest stay was a key driver in high guest satisfaction scores. To increase its scores for problem resolution, the Sheraton brand of Starwood launched the Sheraton Service Promise program in the United States and Canada. The program was designed to give guests a single point of contact for reporting any problems. It was intended to focus associate (employee) attention on taking care of service issues during the guest's stay within 15 minutes of first receiving notice.

However, although scores did increase, they did not increase by enough. Consequently, Sheraton brought in its Six Sigma team to see what it could do. The team employed the basic Six Sigma model of define-measure-analyze-improve-control to guide its work. To define the problem, the Six Sigma team worked with data collected and analyzed by an independent

Pearson

Starwood has implemented Six Sigma quality programs to efficiently resolve guest problems at its properties around the globe.

survey organization, National Family Opinion. The study indicated that three key factors are needed in problem resolution: (1) speed, (2) empathy, and (3) efficiency. All three must be met in order for the guests to be satisfied and the Sheraton Service Promise fulfilled. Then, the team looked at the specific processes that affected performance: Telephone operators' handling of requests, procedures for determining who to call, engineering workloads, and so on. The work identified in each area was measured. For example, call logs were established to track speed, empathy of associate handling the call, and efficiency of the staff charged with fixing the problem. The data collected were analyzed to determine why guests' problems were not resolved within the 15-minute standard. Pareto charts and other techniques were used for the analysis.

The final step involved control and monitoring to be sure that the improved processes developed by the Six Sigma team became part of the property's culture, and that they were not abandoned after the team's work was finished. Tracking continues for 12 to 18 months, with monthly feedback to the manager or department head responsible for the improvement of the Sheraton Service Promise program. The improvement effort also receives visibility through the company's intranet so the rest of the organization sees the benefits—including service levels and financial performance—and can use the experience to improve their own operations.

QUESTIONS

1. Implementing Six Sigma programs takes considerable time and commitment from an organization. In terms of top-down commitment, measurement systems to track progress, tough goal setting, education, communication, and customer priorities, evaluate the degree to which Starwood successfully addressed each with the redesign of the Sheraton Service Promise program.

2. How might the new Sheraton Service Promise process help Starwood avoid the four costs of poor process performance and quality (prevention, appraisal, internal failure, and external failure)?

3. Starwood is the first major hotel brand to commit to a dedicated Six Sigma program for improving quality. Why might an organization be reluctant to follow this type of formalized methodology? What other approaches could Starwood or its competitors use?

EXPERIENTIAL LEARNING   Statistical Process Control with a Coin Catapult

Exercise A: Control Charts for Variables

Materials

1 ruler

1 pen or pencil

1 coin (a quarter will do nicely)

1 yardstick

An exercise worksheet

Access to a calculator

Tasks

Divide into teams of two to four. If four people are on a team,

one person holds the yardstick and observes the action,

one person adjusts the catapult and launches the coin,

one person observes the maximum height for each trial, and

one person records the results.

If teams of fewer than four are formed, provide a support for the yardstick and combine the other tasks as appropriate.

Practice

To catapult the coin, put a pen or pencil under the 6-inch mark of the ruler. Put the coin over the 11-inch mark. Press both ends of the ruler down as far as they will go. Let the end that holds the coin snap up, catapulting the coin into the air. The person holding the yardstick should place the stick so that it is adjacent to, but does not interfere with, the trajectory of the coin. To observe the maximum height reached by the coin, the observer should stand back with his or her eye at about the same level as the top of the coin's trajectory. Practice until each person is comfortable with his or her role. The person operating the catapult should be sure that the pen or pencil fulcrum has not moved between shots and that the launch is done as consistently as possible.

Step 1. *Gather data.* Take four samples of five observations (launches) each. Record the maximum height reached by the coin in the first data table on the worksheet. When you have finished, determine the mean and range for each sample, and compute the mean of the means $\bar{\bar{x}}$ and the mean of the ranges $\bar{R}$.

Step 2. *Develop an R-chart.* Using the data gathered and the appropriate D_3 and D_4 values, compute the upper and lower three-sigma control limits for the range. Enter these values and plot the range for each of the four samples on the range chart on the worksheet. Be sure to indicate an appropriate scale for range on the y-axis.

Step 3. *Develop an $\bar{x}$-chart.* Now, using the data gathered and the appropriate value for A_2, compute the upper and lower three-sigma control limits for the sample means. Enter these values and plot the mean for each of the four samples on the $\bar{x}$-chart on the worksheet. Again, indicate an appropriate scale for the y-axis.

Step 4. *Observe the process.* Once a control chart has been established for a process, it is used to monitor the process and to identify when it is not running normally. Collect two more samples of five trials each, as you did to collect the first set of data. Plot the range and the sample mean on the charts you constructed on the worksheet each time you collect a sample. What have you observed that affects the process? Does the chart indicate that the process is operating the way it did when you first collected data?

Step 5. *Observe a changed process.* Now change something (for instance, move the pencil out to the 8-inch mark). Collect data for samples 7 and 8. Plot the range and the sample mean on the charts you constructed on the worksheet as you complete each sample. Can you detect a change in the process from your control chart? If the process has changed, how sure are you that this change is real and not just due to the particular sample you chose?

Exercise B: Control Charts for Attributes

Materials

1 ruler

1 pen or pencil

1 coin (a quarter will do nicely)

1 paper or plastic cup (with a 4-inch mouth)

An exercise worksheet

Access to a calculator

Tasks

Divide into teams of two or three. If three people are on a team,

one person adjusts the catapult and launches the coin,

one person observes the results and fetches the coin, and

one person records the results.

If teams of two are formed, combine the tasks as appropriate.

Practice

The object is to flip a coin into a cup using a ruler. To catapult the coin, put a pen or pencil under the 6-inch mark of the ruler.

Put a coin over the 11-inch mark and let its weight hold that end of the ruler on the tabletop. Strike the raised end of the ruler with your hand to flip the coin into the air. Position a cup at the place where the coin lands so that on the next flip, the coin will land inside. You will have to practice several times until you find out how hard to hit the ruler and the best position for the cup. Be sure that the pen or pencil fulcrum has not moved between shots and that the launch is done as consistently as possible.

Step 1. *Gather data.* Try to catapult the coin into the cup 10 times for each sample. Record each trial in the data table on the worksheet as a hit (H) when the coin lands inside or a miss (M) when it does not. The proportion of misses will be the number of misses divided by the sample size, n, in this case 10. A miss is a "defect," so the proportion of misses is the proportion defective, p.

Step 2. *Develop a p-chart.* Compute the upper and lower three-sigma control limits for the average fraction defective. Plot these values and the mean for each of the four samples on the p-chart on the worksheet.

Step 3. *Observe the process.* Once a chart has been established for a process, it is used to monitor the process and to identify abnormal behavior. Exchange tasks so that someone else is catapulting the coin. After several practice launches, take four more samples of 10. Plot the proportion defective for this person's output. Is the process still in control? If it is not, how sure are you that it is out of control? Can you determine the control limits for a 95 percent confidence level? With these limits, was your revised process still in control?

Source: The basis for Exercise A was written by J. Christopher Sandvig, Western Washington University, as a variation of the "Catapulting Coins" exercise from *Games and Exercises for Operations Management* by Janelle Heinke and Larry Meile (Prentice Hall, 1995). Given these foundations, Larry Meile of Boston College wrote Exercise A. He also wrote Exercise B as a new extension. Reprinted by permission of Larry Meile.

Stan Honda/AFP/Getty Images/Newscom

Tesla's battery charging station emphasizes the close connection between the electric car and the batteries that serve as the main source of energy for this new generation automobile. Tesla's long-term growth strategies are therefore tied to also expanding its battery manufacturing capacity.

CAPACITY PLANNING

Tesla Motors

Driven by a need to reduce dependence on petroleum-based transportation, a new automobile manufacturing company, Tesla Motors, was formed by Silicon Valley engineers in 2003 with the idea of making fuel efficient electric cars that do not have an internal combustion engine and that run only on rechargeable batteries. Headquartered in Palo Alto, California, Tesla has over 600 employees and an expected revenue of over $3 billion in 2014. Its premium sedan Model S and cross-over utility vehicle Model X are sold through a network of 125 company-owned stores and service locations in North America, Europe, and Asia. Apart from a planned European Research and Development Center in the United Kingdom in 2015 or 2016, Tesla plans to open manufacturing plants in China and Europe once global sales pass 500,000 vehicles a year.

In order to meet the growing energy needs of its next-generation automobiles, Tesla announced plans in 2014 to build the world's largest battery factory at an expense of $4–5 billion. This gigantic Gigafactory would occupy 10 million square feet and employ about 6,500 workers once completed. It would manufacture the 18/650 cell, a cylindrical battery format that is 18 mm wide and 65 mm tall and favored by Tesla and some laptop manufacturers. About 8000 such cells, modified with Tesla's own proprietary chemistry, are needed to power the 85 kWh drive model S car. The completion of this plant in 2016–2017 is slated to coincide with the production of a third-generation Tesla car that would be a smaller version of model S but half priced at $35,000. Along with reduced raw material usage and a more efficient design, much of the price reduction of the new vehicle would come from a significant decrease in the cost of the battery pack made possible by the scale economies that arise with the construction of the Gigafactory. The supplier partner Panasonic, which expects to be the sole manufacturer in Tesla's Gigafactory, agrees that a reduction in battery pack cost of as much as 30 percent or higher may be possible. Having a car model that could potentially gain a large market share for electric vehicles at a lower price point could be a huge strategic advantage for Tesla Motors in the years to come. By expanding capacity beyond its immediate needs, Tesla could become a leading source for battery power if electric car sales continue to climb.

But the move by Tesla to expand capacity so dramatically for cylindrical cell batteries in such a large plant is not without its own perils. The plant's excess capacity may be underutilized in the first three years, as global production of Tesla cars starts gradually ramping up towards the 500,000 vehicles mark in 2020. In addition, other car manufacturers such as GM and Nissan use larger flat cell batteries that are not compatible with the cylindrical cells. So who would consume Tesla's excess battery capacity? While transition to a flat cell battery format may still be possible later on, productive use of such an expanded capacity may prove to be a challenging task for Tesla Motors in the near future.

Source: Mike Ramsey, "Will Tesla's $5 Billion Gigafactory Make a Battery Nobody Else Wants?" *Wall Street Journal* (April 14, 2014); **http://wardsauto.com/report-ceo-says-tesla-plans-european-plant** (July 16, 2014); **http://seekingalpha.com/article/2295695-teslas-gigafactory-and-why-competitors-should-worry** (July 1, 2014); **http://wardsauto.com/tesla-eyeing-third-li-ion-battery-factory-us** (June 3, 2014); **http://www.teslamotors.com/about** (July 18, 2014).

LEARNING GOALS *After reading this chapter, you should be able to:*

1. Define long-term capacity and its relationship with economies and diseconomies of scale.

2. Understand the main differences between the expansionist and wait-and-see capacity timing and sizing strategies.

3. Identify a systematic four-step approach for determining long-term capacity requirements and associated cash flows.

4. Describe how the common tools for capacity planning such as waiting-line models, simulation, and decision trees assist in capacity decisions.

capacity

The maximum rate of output of a process or a system.

Capacity is the maximum rate of output of a process or a system. Managers are responsible for ensuring that the firm has the capacity to meet current and future demand. Otherwise, the organization will miss out on opportunities for growth and profits. Making adjustments to decrease capacity, or to increase it to facilitate the launch of an expanded product line as Tesla Motors did when planning a lower priced car model, is therefore an important part of the job. Acquisition of new capacity requires extensive planning and often involves significant expenditure of resources and time. Bringing new capacity online can take several years, for instance, in the semiconductor industry or in the construction of new nuclear power plants.

Capacity decisions related to a process need to be made in light of the role the process plays within the organization and the supply chain as a whole, because changing the capacity of a process will have an impact on other processes within the firm and across the chain. As such, capacity decisions have implications for different functional areas throughout the organization. Accounting needs to provide the cost information needed to evaluate capacity expansion decisions. Finance performs the financial analysis of proposed capacity expansion investments and raises funds to support them. Marketing provides demand forecasts needed to identify capacity gaps. Management information systems design the electronic infrastructure that is needed to make data such as cost information, financial performance measures, demand forecasts, and work standards available to those needing it to analyze capacity options. Operations is involved in the selection of capacity strategies that can be implemented to effectively meet future demand. Purchasing facilitates acquisition of outside capacity from suppliers. Finally, human resources focuses on hiring and training employees needed to support internal capacity plans. So all departments in a firm get involved with and are affected by long-term capacity planning decisions.

Increasing or decreasing capacity by itself is not as important as ensuring that the entire supply chain, from order entry to delivery, is designed for effectiveness. Capacity decisions must be made in light of several long-term issues such as the firm's economies and diseconomies of scale, capacity cushions, timing and sizing strategies, and trade-offs between customer service and capacity utilization. Therefore this chapter focuses on how managers can best revise capacity levels and best determine when to add or reduce capacity for the long term. The type of capacity decisions differ for different time horizons. Both long-term as well as short-term issues associated with planning capacity and managing constraints are important and must be understood in conjunction with one another. While we deal here with the long-term decisions shown below in the capacity management framework, short-term decisions centered on making the most of existing capacity by managing constraints are more fully explored in Chapter 5, "Constraint Management."

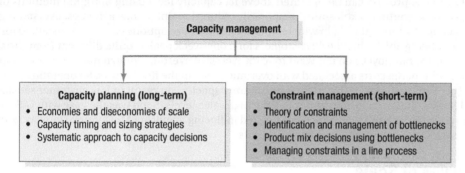

Planning Long-Term Capacity

Long-term capacity plans deal with investments in new facilities and equipment at the organizational level and require top management participation and approval because they are not easily reversed. These plans cover at least two years into the future, but construction lead times can sometimes be longer and result in longer planning time horizons.

As already seen in our opening vignette, long-term capacity planning is central to the success of an organization. Too much capacity can be as agonizing as too little. Often entire industries can fluctuate over time between too much and too little capacity, as evidenced in the airline and cruise ship industry over the past 20 years. When choosing a capacity strategy, managers must consider questions such as the following: How much of a cushion is needed to handle variable, or uncertain, demand? Should we expand capacity ahead of demand, as Tesla did with battery production, or wait until demand is more certain? Even before these questions can be answered, a manager needs to be able to measure a process's capacity. So a systematic approach is needed to answer these and similar questions and to develop a capacity strategy appropriate for each situation.

Measures of Capacity and Utilization

No single capacity measure is best for all situations. A retailer measures capacity as annual sales dollars generated per square foot, whereas an airline measures capacity as available seat-miles (ASMs) per month. A theater measures capacity as number of seats, while a job shop measures capacity as number of machine hours. In general, capacity can be expressed in one of two ways: in terms of output measures or input measures.

Output Measures of Capacity   *Output measures* of capacity are best utilized when applied to individual processes within the firm or when the firm provides a relatively small number of standardized services and products. High-volume processes, such as those in a car manufacturing plant, are a good example. In this case, capacity would be measured in terms of the number of cars produced per day. However, many processes produce more than one service or product. As the amount of customization and variety in the product mix increases, output-based capacity measures become less useful. Then input measures of capacity become the usual choice for measuring capacity.

Input Measures of Capacity   *Input measures* are generally used for low-volume, flexible processes, such as those associated with a custom furniture maker. In this case, the furniture maker might measure capacity in terms of inputs such as number of workstations or number of workers. The problem with input measures is that demand is invariably expressed as an output rate. If the furniture maker wants to keep up with demand, he or she must convert the business's annual demand for furniture into labor hours and number of employees required to fulfill those hours. We will explain precisely how this input–output conversion is done later in the chapter.

utilization

The degree to which equipment, space, or the workforce is currently being used, and is measured as the ratio of average output rate to maximum capacity (expressed as a percent).

Utilization   **Utilization** is the degree to which a resource such as equipment, space, or the workforce is currently being used and is measured as the ratio of average output rate to maximum capacity (expressed as a percent). The average output rate and the capacity must be measured in the same terms—that is, time, customers, units, or dollars. The utilization rate indicates the need for adding extra capacity or eliminating unneeded capacity.

$$\text{Utilization} = \frac{\text{Average output rate}}{\text{Maximum capacity}} \times 100\%$$

Here, we refer to maximum capacity as the greatest level of output that a process can reasonably sustain for a longer period, using realistic employee work schedules and the equipment currently in place. In some processes, this capacity level implies a one-shift operation; in others, it implies a three-shift operation. A process can be operated above its capacity level using marginal methods of production, such as overtime, extra shifts, temporarily reduced maintenance activities, overstaffing, and subcontracting. Although they help with temporary peaks, these options cannot be sustained for long. For instance, being able to handle 40 customers for a one-week peak is quite different from sustaining it for six months. Employees do not want to work excessive overtime for extended periods, so quality drops. In addition, the costs associated with overtime drive up the firm's costs. So operating processes close to (or even temporarily above) their maximum capacity can result in low customer satisfaction, minimal profits, and even losing money despite high sales levels. Such was the case with U.S. aircraft manufacturers in the late 1980s, which culminated in Boeing acquiring McDonnell Douglas in 1997 to shore up skyrocketing costs and plummeting profits.

Economies of Scale

economies of scale

A concept that states that the average unit cost of a service or good can be reduced by increasing its output rate.

Deciding on the best level of capacity involves consideration for the efficiency of the operations. A concept known as **economies of scale** states that the average unit cost of a service or good can be reduced by increasing its output rate. Four principal reasons explain why economies of scale can drive costs down when output increases: (1) Fixed costs are spread over more units; (2) construction costs are reduced; (3) costs of purchased materials are cut; and (4) process advantages are found.

Spreading Fixed Costs   In the short term, certain costs do not vary with changes in the output rate. These fixed costs include heating costs, debt service, and managers' salaries. The depreciation of plant and equipment already owned is also a fixed cost in the accounting sense. When the average output rate—and, therefore, the facility's utilization rate—increases, the average unit cost drops because fixed costs are spread over more units.

Reducing Construction Costs   Certain activities and expenses are required to build small and large facilities alike: building permits, architects' fees, and rental of building equipment. Doubling the size of the facility usually does not double construction costs.

Cutting Costs of Purchased Materials   Higher volumes can reduce the costs of purchased materials and services. They give the purchaser a better bargaining position and the opportunity to take advantage of quantity discounts. Retailers such as Walmart reap significant economies of scale because their national and international stores buy and sell huge volumes of each item.

Finding Process Advantages   High-volume production provides many opportunities for cost reduction. At a higher output rate, the process shifts toward a line process, with resources dedicated to individual products. Firms may be able to justify the expense of more efficient technology or more specialized equipment. The benefits from dedicating resources to individual services or products may include speeding up the learning effect, lowering inventory, improving process and job designs, and reducing the number of changeovers.

Diseconomies of Scale

diseconomies of scale

Occurs when the average cost per unit increases as the facility's size increases.

Bigger is not always better, however. At some point, a facility can become so large that **diseconomies of scale** set in; that is, the average cost per unit increases as the facility's size increases. The reason is that excessive size can bring complexity, loss of focus, and inefficiencies that raise the average unit cost of a service or product. Too many layers of employees and bureaucracy can cause management to lose touch with employees and customers. A less agile organization loses the flexibility needed to respond to changing demand. Many large companies become so involved in analysis and planning that they innovate less and avoid risks. The result is that small companies outperform corporate giants in numerous industries.

Figure 4.1 illustrates the transition from economies of scale to diseconomies of scale. The 500-bed hospital shows economies of scale because the average unit cost at its *best operating level*, represented by the blue dot, is less than that of the 250-bed hospital. However, assuming that sufficient demand exists, further expansion to a 750-bed hospital leads to higher average unit costs and diseconomies of scale. One reason the 500-bed hospital enjoys greater economies of scale than the 250-bed hospital is that the cost of building and equipping it is less than twice the cost for the smaller hospital. The 750-bed facility would enjoy similar savings. Its higher average unit costs can be explained only by diseconomies of scale, which outweigh the savings realized in construction costs.

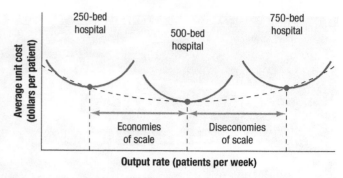

▲ **FIGURE 4.1**
Economies and Diseconomies of Scale

Figure 4.1 does not mean that the optimal size for all hospitals is 500 beds. Optimal size depends on the number of patients per week to be served. On the one hand, a hospital serving a small community could have lower costs by choosing a 250-bed capacity rather than the 500-bed capacity. On the other hand, a large community might be served more efficiently by two 500-bed hospitals than by one 1,000-bed facility if diseconomies of scale exist at the bigger size.

Capacity Timing and Sizing Strategies

Operations managers must examine three dimensions of capacity strategy before making capacity decisions: (1) sizing capacity cushions, (2) timing and sizing expansion, and (3) linking process capacity and other operating decisions.

Sizing Capacity Cushions

Average utilization rates for any resource should not get too close to 100 percent over the long term, though it may occur for some processes from time to time in the short run. If the demand keeps increasing over time, then long-term capacity must be increased as well to provide some buffer against uncertainties. When average utilization rates approach 100 percent, it is usually a signal to increase capacity or decrease order acceptance to avoid declining productivity. The **capacity cushion** is the amount of reserve capacity a process uses to handle sudden increases in demand or temporary losses of production capacity; it measures the amount by which the average utilization (in terms of total capacity) falls below 100 percent. Specifically,

capacity cushion

The amount of reserve capacity a process uses to handle sudden increases in demand or temporary losses of production capacity; it measures the amount by which the average utilization (in terms of total capacity) falls below 100 percent.

$$\text{Capacity cushion, } C = 100\ (\%) - \text{Average Utilization rate}\ (\%)$$

The appropriate size of the cushion varies by industry. In the capital-intensive paper industry, where machines can cost hundreds of millions of dollars each, cushions well under 10 percent are preferred. The less capital-intensive hotel industry breaks even with a 60 to 70 percent utilization (40 to 30 percent cushion), and begins to suffer customer-service problems when the cushion drops to 20 percent. The more capital-intensive cruise ship industry prefers cushions as small as 5 percent. Large cushions are particularly vital for front-office processes where customers expect fast service times.

Businesses find large cushions appropriate when demand varies. In certain service industries (the grocery industry, for example), demand on some days of the week is predictably higher than on other days, and even hour-to-hour changes are typical. Long customer waiting times are not acceptable because customers grow impatient if they have to wait in a supermarket checkout line for more than a few minutes. Prompt customer service requires supermarkets to maintain a capacity cushion large enough to handle peak demand. Large cushions also are necessary when future demand is uncertain, particularly if resource flexibility is low. Simulation and waiting-line analysis (see Supplement B, "Waiting Lines") can help managers better anticipate the relationship between capacity cushion and customer service.

Another type of demand uncertainty occurs with a changing product mix. Though total demand measured in monetary terms might remain stable, the load can shift unpredictably from one workstation to another as the product mix changes. Supply uncertainty tied to delivery of purchased materials also makes large capacity cushions helpful. Capacity often comes in large increments because a complete machine has to be purchased even if only a fraction of its available capacity is needed, which in turn creates a large cushion. Firms also need to build in excess capacity to allow for employee absenteeism, vacations, holidays, and any other delays. If a firm is experiencing high overtime costs and frequently needs to rely on subcontractors, it perhaps needs to increase its capacity cushions.

The argument in favor of small cushions is simple: Unused capacity costs money. For capital-intensive firms, minimizing the capacity cushion is vital. Studies indicate that businesses with high capital intensity achieve a low return on investment when the capacity cushion is high. This strong

Paul Vernon/Reuters

Accord ready to come off the line during a tour of the Honda automobile plant in Marysville, Ohio, October 11, 2012. The factory produces the Acura and Accord models and has an annual production of 440,000 vehicles. According to Green Car Reports, Honda will also move production of the 2014 Accord Hybrid from Sayama, Japan to Marysville, Ohio, and invest about $23 million more and hire 50 additional workers to accommodate this move.

correlation does not exist for labor-intensive firms, however. Their return on investment is about the same because the lower investment in equipment makes high utilization less critical. Small cushions have other advantages. By implementing a small cushion, a company can sometimes uncover inefficiencies that were difficult to detect when cushions were larger. These inefficiencies might include employee absenteeism or unreliable suppliers. Once managers and workers identify such problems, they often can find ways to correct them.

Timing and Sizing Expansion

The second issue of capacity strategy concerns when to adjust capacity levels and by how much. At times, capacity expansion can be done in response to changing market trends. General Motors decided to increase production capacity of the four-seat series hybrid car Chevrolet Volt from 30,000 units to 45,000 units in 2012 because of strong public interest. While we deal with this issue from the perspective of capacity expansion in greater detail here, it must be noted that firms may not always be looking to expand capacity but at times may be forced to retrench as evidenced by the situation in the airlines industry, where all major airlines have consolidated routes and reduced the total number of flights in the face of increasing oil costs. Some of this consolidation has been achieved through mergers like United Airlines and Continental to create the world's largest airline company, as well as the merger between Delta and Northwest Airlines.

Figure 4.2 illustrates two extreme strategies for expanding capacity: the *expansionist strategy*, which involves large, infrequent jumps in capacity, and the *wait-and-see strategy*, which involves smaller, more frequent jumps.

FIGURE 4.2 ▶
Two Capacity Strategies

MyOMLab Animation

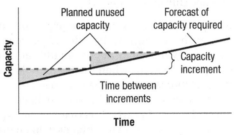

(a) Expansionist strategy

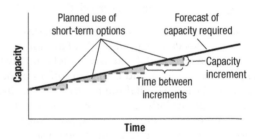

(b) Wait-and-see strategy

Expansionist Strategy   The timing and sizing of expansion are related; that is, if demand is increasing and the time between increments increases, the size of the increments must also increase. The expansionist strategy, which stays ahead of demand, minimizes the chance of sales lost to insufficient capacity.

Several factors favor the expansionist strategy. Expansion can result in economies of scale and a faster rate of learning, thus helping a firm reduce its costs and compete on price. This strategy might increase the firm's market share or act as a form of preemptive marketing. By making a large capacity expansion or announcing that one is imminent, the firm can preempt the expansion of other firms. These other firms must sacrifice some of their market share or risk burdening the industry with overcapacity. To be successful, however, the preempting firm must have the credibility to convince the competition that it will carry out its plans—and must signal its plans before the competition can act. Managerial Practice 4.1 illustrates the use of expansionist strategy by Sharp Corporation for its LCD panels and shows that using such a strategy can be both risky as well as potentially rewarding if correct judgments are made about its future use.

Wait-and-See Strategy   The conservative wait-and-see strategy is to expand in smaller increments, such as by renovating existing facilities rather than building new ones. The wait-and-see strategy lags behind demand. To meet any shortfalls, it relies on short-term options, such as use of overtime,

MANAGERIAL PRACTICE 4.1 Expansionist Capacity Strategy by Sharp Corporation

Sharp Corporation, founded in 1912 in Japan, is a global manufacturer and distributor of consumer and information products such as LCD TVs and projectors, DVD recorders, mobile communication handsets, point-of-sale systems, home appliances such as refrigerators and microwave ovens, and electronic components such as flash memories, LCD panels, and optical sensors, among others. With over 50,000 employees, it has manufacturing, sales, and R&D presence in 25 different countries and regions of the world. For production of its large-size LCDs needed in television sets, Sharp increased the capacity of its Kameyama No. 2 plant in Japan from 15,000 LCD sheets per month in August 2006 to 30,000 LCD sheets per month during the second phase in January 2007. Capacity enhancements in the third phase (July 2007) were 60,000 LCD sheets per month. The world's largest LCD TV screen at that time, measuring 108 inch, was made at the Kameyama plant No. 2 from eighth-generation glass substrates.

Is such a rapid expansion of long-term capacity a good idea? Opinions vary. Even though Sharp had thrived in recent years due to its LCD business, the decision to expand was made because production capacity had reached its limit and Sharp was unable to meet its market demand. As a result, Sharp had been overtaken in global LCD television sales, and its share in the second quarter of 2006 was only 10.8 percent, fourth behind Sony, Samsung, and Philips Electronics. However, the competition did not stay idle even as Sharp quickly expanded its capacity for LCD sheets. A joint company of Sony and Samsung planned for opening a new plant in autumn of 2007 that would have the same capacity as Sharp's Kameyama plant. Critics feared that if all three major players continue to add capacity faster than the rate at which the market can grow, it would lead to a mature industry with too much capacity and too little profitability.

Meanwhile, Sharp's bet that large capacity investments in LCD sheets will help enhance its leadership position in the LCD industry well into the future seems to be paying off. With a newly launched IZGO display technology in March 2012 that was based on using eighth-generation glass substrates already being produced at Kameyama Plant No. 2, Sharp will become the first company in the world during 2013–2014 to achieve commercial production of high definition LCD panels for smartphones, tablets, and notebook PCs. Optimized production processes using the existing capacity for eighth-generation glass substrates, coupled with IGZO technology's ability to enable smaller thin-film transistors and increased light transmittance, will enable

STR/AFP/Getty Images

Sharp's Kameyama plant No. 2 in Japan

Sharp to meet vigorously growing demand for high definition LCD panels in market segments that are quite different from the television set segment for which the original Kameyama plant No. 2 was established in 2006 and then subsequently expanded.

Source: William Trent, "LCD Producers Continue to Add Too Much Capacity as They Battle for Market Share," http://seekingalpha.com/article/19038-lcd-producers-continue-to-add-too-much-capacity-as-they-battle-for-market-share (October 2006); http://www.sharp-world.com/corporate/info/ci/g_organization/index .html, and http://www.sharp-world.com/corporate/ir/event/policy_meeting/pdf/shar080108e_1.pdf (May 31, 2011); http://www.sharp-world.com/corporate/ news/131017.html (July 17, 2014), "Sharp to Begin Production of IZGO LCD Panels for Smartphones at Kameyama Plant No.2" (October 17, 2013).

temporary workers, subcontractors, stockouts, and the postponement of preventive maintenance on equipment. It reduces the risks of overexpansion based on overly optimistic demand forecasts, obsolete technology, or inaccurate assumptions regarding the competition.

However, this strategy has its own risks, such as being preempted by a competitor or being unable to respond if demand is unexpectedly high. Critics claim the wait-and-see strategy is a short-term strategy typical of some U.S. management styles. Managers on the fast track to corporate advancement tend to take fewer risks. They earn promotions by avoiding the big mistakes and maximizing short-term profits and return on investment. The wait-and-see strategy fits this short-term outlook but can erode market share over the long run.

Management may choose one of these two strategies or one of the many between these extremes. With strategies in the more moderate middle, firms can expand more frequently (on a smaller scale) than they can with the expansionist strategy without lagging behind demand as with the wait-and-see strategy. An intermediate strategy could be to *follow the leader*, expanding when others do. If others are right, so are you, and nobody gains a competitive advantage. If others make a mistake and over expand, so do you, but everyone shares in the agony of overcapacity. Such a situation was noted for the airlines industry, and may yet occur in the LCD industry due to large capacity expansions by Sharp Corporation, Sony, and Samsung as described in Managerial Practice 4.1.

Linking Capacity and Other Decisions

Capacity decisions should be closely linked to processes and supply chains throughout the organization. When managers make decisions about designing processes, determining degree of resource flexibility and inventory, and locating facilities, they must consider its impact on capacity cushions. Capacity cushions in the long run buffer the organization against uncertainty, as do resource flexibility, inventory, and longer customer lead times. If a change is made in any one decision area, the capacity cushion may also need to be changed to compensate. For example, capacity cushions for a process can be lowered if less emphasis is placed on fast deliveries (*competitive priorities*), yield losses (*quality*) drop, or if investment in capital-intensive equipment increases or worker flexibility increases (*process design*). Capacity cushions can also be lowered if the company is willing to smooth the output rate by raising prices when inventory is low and decreasing prices when it is high.

A Systematic Approach to Long-Term Capacity Decisions

Long-term decisions for capacity would typically include whether to add a new plant or warehouse or to reduce the number of existing ones, how many workstations a given department should have, or how many workers are needed to staff a given process. Some of these decisions can take years to become operational. Hence, a systematic approach is needed to plan for long-term capacity decisions.

Although each situation is somewhat different, a four-step procedure generally can help managers make sound capacity decisions. (In describing this procedure, we assume that management already performed the preliminary steps of determining the process's existing capacity and assessing whether its current capacity cushion is appropriate.)

1. Estimate future capacity requirements.

2. Identify gaps by comparing requirements with available capacity.

3. Develop alternative plans for reducing the gaps.

4. Evaluate each alternative, both qualitatively and quantitatively, and make a final choice.

Step 1: Estimate Capacity Requirements

A process's **capacity requirement** is what its capacity should be for some future time period to meet the forecasted demand of the firm's customers (external or internal), given the firm's desired capacity cushion. Larger cushions than normal should be planned for those processes or workstations that could potentially become bottlenecks in the future.

Capacity requirements can be expressed in one of two ways: with an output measure or with an input measure. Either way, the foundation for the estimate is forecasts of demand, productivity, competition, and technological change. These forecasts normally need to be made for several time periods in a **planning horizon**, which is the set of consecutive time periods considered for planning purposes. Long-term capacity plans need to consider more of the future (perhaps, a whole decade) than do short-term plans. Unfortunately, the further ahead you look, the more chance you have of making an inaccurate forecast. See Chapter 8, "Forecasting," for a complete discussion of forecast errors and their origins.

Using Output Measures   The simplest way to express capacity requirements is as an output rate. As discussed earlier, output measures are appropriate for high-volume processes with little product variety or process divergence. Here, demand forecasts for future years are used as a basis for extrapolating capacity requirements into the future. If demand is expected to double in the next five years, then the capacity requirements also double. For example, if a process's current demand is 50 customers per day, then the demand in five years would be 100 customers per day. If the desired capacity cushion is 20 percent, management should plan for enough capacity to serve $[100/(1 - 0.2)] = 125$ customers in five years.

Using Input Measures   Output measures may be insufficient in the following situations:

- Product variety and process divergence is high.
- The product or service mix is changing.
- Productivity rates are expected to change.
- Significant learning effects are expected.

---

capacity requirement

What a process's capacity should be for some future time period to meet the demand of customers (external or internal), given the firm's desired capacity cushion.

planning horizon

The set of consecutive time periods considered for planning purposes.

In such cases, it is more appropriate to calculate capacity requirements using an input measure, such as the number of employees, machines, computers, or trucks. Using an input measure for the capacity requirement brings together demand forecasts, process time estimates, and the desired capacity cushion. When just one service or product is processed at an operation and the time period is a particular year, the capacity requirement, M, is

$$\text{Capacity requirement} = \frac{\text{Processing hours required for year's demand}}{\text{Hours available from a single capacity unit (such as an employee or machine) per year, after deducting desired cushion}}$$

$$M = \frac{Dp}{N[1 - (C/100)]}$$

where

D = demand forecast for the year (number of customers served or units produced)

p = processing time (in hours per customer served or unit produced)

N = total number of hours per year during which the process operates

C = desired capacity cushion (expressed as a percent)

M = the number of input units required

M should be calculated for each year in the time horizon. The processing time, p, depends on the process and methods selected to do the work. The denominator is the total number of hours, N, available for the year from one unit of capacity (an employee or machine), multiplied by a proportion that accounts for the desired capacity cushion, C. The proportion is simply $1.0 - C/100$, where C is converted from a percent to a proportion by dividing by 100. For example, a 20 percent capacity cushion means that $1.0 - C/100 = 0.80$.

Setups may be involved if multiple products are being manufactured. **Setup time** is the time required to change a process or an operation from making one service or product to making another. The total setup time is found by dividing the number of units forecast per year, D, by the number of units made in each lot, Q, (number of units processed between setups), which gives the number of setups per year, and then multiplying by the time per setup, s. For example, if the annual demand is 1,200 units and the average lot size is 100, there are $1,200/100 = 12$ setups per year. Accounting for both processing and setup times for multiple services (products), we get

setup time

The time required to change a process or an operation from making one service or product to making another.

$$\text{Capacity requirement} = \frac{\text{Processing and setup hours required for year's demand, summed over all services or products}}{\text{Hours available from a single capacity unit per year, after deducting desired cushion}}$$

$$M = \frac{[Dp + (D/Q)s]_{\text{product 1}} + [Dp + (D/Q)s]_{\text{product 2}} + \cdots + [Dp + (D/Q)s]_{\text{product } n}}{N[1 - (C/100)]}$$

where

Q = number of units in each lot

s = setup time in hours per lot

What to do when M is not an integer depends on the situation. For example, it is impossible to buy a fractional machine. In this case, round up the fractional part, unless it is cost efficient to use short-term options, such as overtime or stockouts, to cover any shortfalls. If, instead, the capacity unit is the number of employees at a process, a value of 23.6 may be achieved using just 23 employees and a modest use of overtime (equivalent to having 60 percent of another full-time person). Here, the fractional value should be retained as useful information.

EXAMPLE 4.1   **Estimating Capacity Requirements When Using Input Measures**

A copy center in an office building prepares bound reports for two clients. The center makes multiple copies (the lot size) of each report. The processing time to run, collate, and bind each copy depends on, among other factors, the number of pages. The center operates 250 days per year, with one 8-hour shift. Management believes that a capacity cushion of 15 percent (beyond the allowance built into time standards) is best. It currently has three copy machines. Based on the following table of information, determine how many machines are needed at the copy center.

Item	Client X	Client Y
Annual demand forecast (copies)	2,000	6,000
Standard processing time (hour/copy)	0.5	0.7
Average lot size (copies per report)	20	30
Standard setup time (hours)	0.25	0.40

SOLUTION

$$M = \frac{[Dp + (D/Q)s]_{\text{product 1}} + [Dp + (D/Q)s]_{\text{product 2}} + \cdots + [Dp + (D/Q)s]_{\text{product } n}}{N[1 - (C/100)]}$$

$$= \frac{[2,000(0.5) + (2,000/20)(0.25)]_{\text{client X}} + [6,000(0.7) + (6,000/30)(0.40)]_{\text{client Y}}}{[(250 \text{ day/year})(1 \text{ shift/day})(8 \text{ hours/day})][1.0 - (15/100)]}$$

$$= \frac{5,305}{1,700} = \mathbf{3.12}$$

Rounding up to the next integer gives a requirement of **four** machines.

DECISION POINT

The copy center's capacity is being stretched and no longer has the desired 15 percent capacity cushion with the existing three machines. Not wanting customer service to suffer, management decided to use overtime as a short-term solution to handle past-due orders. If demand continues at the current level or grows, it will acquire a fourth machine.

Step 2: Identify Gaps

capacity gap

Positive or negative difference between projected demand and current capacity.

A **capacity gap** is any difference (positive or negative) between projected capacity requirements (M) and current capacity. Complications arise when multiple operations and several resource inputs are involved. Expanding the capacity of some operations may increase overall capacity. However, as we will learn later in Chapter 5, "Constraint Management," if one operation is more constrained than others, total process capacity can be expanded only if the capacity of the constrained operation is expanded.

Step 3: Develop Alternatives

base case

The act of doing nothing and losing orders from any demand that exceeds current capacity, or incur costs because capacity is too large.

The next step is to develop alternative plans to cope with projected gaps. One alternative, called the **base case**, is to do nothing and simply lose orders from any demand that exceeds current capacity or incur costs because capacity is too large. Other alternatives if expected demand exceeds current capacity are various timing and sizing options for adding new capacity, including the expansionist and wait-and-see strategies illustrated in Figure 4.2. Additional possibilities include expanding at a different location and using short-term options, such as overtime, temporary workers, and subcontracting. Alternatives for reducing capacity include the closing of plants or warehouses, laying off employees, or reducing the days or hours of operation.

Step 4: Evaluate the Alternatives

In this final step, the manager evaluates each alternative, both qualitatively and quantitatively.

Qualitative Concerns Qualitatively, the manager looks at how each alternative fits the overall capacity strategy and other aspects of the business not covered by the financial analysis. Of particular concern might be uncertainties about demand, competitive reaction, technological change, and cost estimates. Some of these factors cannot be quantified and must be assessed on the basis of judgment and experience. Others can be quantified, and the manager can analyze each alternative by using different assumptions about the future. One set of assumptions could represent a worst case, in which demand is less, competition is greater, and construction costs are higher than expected. Another set of assumptions could represent the most optimistic view of the future. This type of "what-if" analysis allows the manager to get an idea of each alternative's implications before making a final choice.

Qualitative factors would tend to dominate when a business is trying to enter new markets or change the focus of its business strategy. For instance, Dell opened a data center in Shanghai in 2011 as part of its plans for a $1 billion investment in cloud computing (on-demand provision of computational resources for data and software through computer networks rather than local computers) and virtualization (creating a virtual rather than an actual version of an operating system or a storage device) and open other data centers around the world. Little hard data was available to guide the exact size and timing of the significant expansion of data center capacity that must be undertaken to support this diversification strategy, which will also include a deeper focus on sales training and expertise.

Quantitative Concerns   Quantitatively, the manager estimates the change in cash flows for each alternative over the forecast time horizon compared to the base case. **Cash flow** is the difference between the flows of funds into and out of an organization over a period of time, including revenues, costs, and changes in assets and liabilities. The manager is concerned here only with calculating the cash flows attributable to the project.

Dell's Green Energy-saving and Environment-protecting Data Center will monitor the energy consumption index of 54 government offices in Beijing, China

cash flow

The difference between the flows of funds into and out of an organization over a period of time, including revenues, costs, and changes in assets and liabilities.

EXAMPLE 4.2	**Evaluating the Alternatives**

Grandmother's Chicken Restaurant is experiencing a boom in business. The owner expects to serve 80,000 meals this year. Although the kitchen is operating at 100 percent capacity, the dining room can handle 105,000 diners per year. Forecasted demand for the next five years is 90,000 meals for next year, followed by a 10,000-meal increase in each of the succeeding years. One alternative is to expand both the kitchen and the dining room now, bringing their capacities up to 130,000 meals per year. The initial investment would be $200,000, made at the end of this year (year 0). The average meal is priced at $10, and the before-tax profit margin is 20 percent. The 20 percent figure was arrived at by determining that, for each $10 meal, $8 covers variable costs and the remaining $2 goes to pretax profit.

What are the pretax cash flows from this project for the next five years compared to those of the base case of doing nothing?

MyOMLab

Tutor 4.2 in MyOMLab provides a new example to practice projecting cash flows for capacity decisions.

SOLUTION

Recall that the base case of doing nothing results in losing all potential sales beyond 80,000 meals. With the new capacity, the cash flow would equal the extra meals served by having a 130,000-meal capacity, multiplied by a profit of $2 per meal. In year 0, the only cash flow is –$200,000 for the initial investment. In year 1, the 90,000-meal demand will be completely satisfied by the expanded capacity, so the incremental cash flow is $(90,000 - 80,000)(\$2) = \$20,000$. For subsequent years, the figures are as follows:

Year 2: Demand = 100,000; Cash flow = $(100,000 - 80,000)\$2 = \$40,000$

Year 3: Demand = 110,000; Cash flow = $(110,000 - 80,000)\$2 = \$60,000$

Year 4: Demand = 120,000; Cash flow = $(120,000 - 80,000)\$2 = \$80,000$

Year 5: Demand = 130,000; Cash flow = $(130,000 - 80,000)\$2 = \$100,000$

If the new capacity were smaller than the expected demand in any year, we would subtract the base case capacity from the new capacity (rather than the demand). The owner should account for the time value of money, applying such techniques as the net present value or internal rate of return methods (see MyOMLab Supplement F, "Financial Analysis"). For instance, the net present value (NPV) of this project at a discount rate of 10 percent is calculated here, and equals $13,051.76.

MyOMLab

$NPV = -200,000 + [(20,000/1.1)] + [40,000/(1.1)^2] + [60,000/(1.1)^3] + [80,000/(1.1)^4] + [100,000/(1.1)^5]$

$= -\$200,000 + \$18,181.82 + \$33,057.85 + \$45,078.89 + \$54,641.07 + \$62,092.13$

$= \mathbf{\$13,051.76}$

DECISION POINT

Before deciding on this capacity alternative, the owner should also examine the qualitative concerns, such as future location of competitors. In addition, the homey atmosphere of the restaurant may be lost with expansion. Furthermore, other alternatives should be considered (see Solved Problem 2).

Tools for Capacity Planning

Capacity planning requires demand forecasts for an extended period of time. Unfortunately, forecast accuracy declines as the forecasting horizon lengthens. In addition, anticipating what competitors will do increases the uncertainty of demand forecasts. Demand during any period of time may not be evenly distributed; peaks and valleys of demand may (and often do) occur within the time period. These realities necessitate the use of capacity cushions. In this section, we introduce three tools that deal more formally with demand uncertainty and variability: (1) waiting-line models, (2) simulation, and (3) decision trees. Waiting-line models and simulation account for the random, independent behavior of many customers, in terms of both their time of arrival and their processing needs. Decision trees allow anticipation of events, such as competitors' actions, which requires a sequence of decisions regarding capacities.

Waiting-Line Models

Waiting-line models often are useful in capacity planning, such as selecting an appropriate capacity cushion for a high customer-contact process. Waiting lines tend to develop in front of a work center, such as an airport ticket counter, a machine center, or a central computer. The reason is that the arrival time between jobs or customers varies, and the processing time may vary from one customer to the next. Waiting-line models use probability distributions to provide estimates of average customer wait time, average length of waiting lines, and utilization of the work center. Managers can use this information to choose the most cost-effective capacity, balancing customer service and the cost of adding capacity.

Supplement B, "Waiting Lines," follows this chapter and provides a fuller treatment of these models. It introduces formulas for estimating important characteristics of a waiting line, such as average customer waiting time and average facility utilization for different facility designs. For example, a facility might be designed to have one or multiple lines at each operation and to route customers through one or multiple operations. Given the estimating capability of these formulas and cost estimates for waiting and idle time, managers can select cost-effective designs and capacity levels that also provide the desired level of customer service.

Figure 4.3 shows output from POM for Windows for waiting lines. A professor meeting students during office hours has an arrival rate of three students per hour and a service rate of six students per hour. The output shows that the capacity cushion is 50 percent (1 − average server utilization of 0.50). This result is expected because the processing rate is double the arrival rate. What might not be expected is that a typical student spends 20 minutes either in line or talking with the professor, and the probability of having two or more students at the office is 0.25. These numbers might be surprisingly high, given such a large capacity cushion.

▼ **FIGURE 4.3**
POM for Windows Output for Waiting Lines during Office Hours

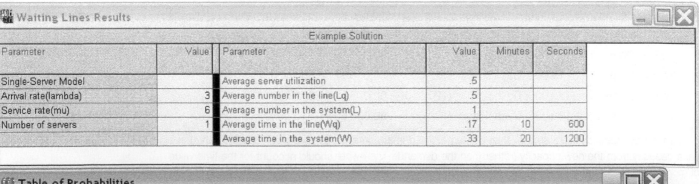

Waiting Lines Results

Example Solution

Parameter	Value	Parameter	Value	Minutes	Seconds
Single-Server Model		Average server utilization	.5		
Arrival rate(lambda)	3	Average number in the line(Lq)	.5		
Service rate(mu)	6	Average number in the system(L)	1		
Number of servers	1	Average time in the line(Wq)	.17	10	600
		Average time in the system(W)	.33	20	1200

Table of Probabilities

Example Solution

k	Prob (num in sys = k)	Prob (num in sys <= k)	Prob (num in sys >k)
0	.5	.5	.5
1	.25	.75	.25
2	.13	.88	.13
3	.06	.94	.06
4	.03	.97	.03
5	.02	.98	.02
6	.01	1	.01
7	.0	1	.0

Simulation

More complex waiting-line problems must be analyzed with simulation. It can identify the process's bottlenecks and appropriate capacity cushions, even for complex processes with random demand patterns and predictable surges in demand during a typical day. The SimQuick simulation package, provided in MyOMLab, allows you to build dynamic models and systems. Other simulation packages can be found with Extend, Simprocess, ProModel, and Witness.

MyOMLab

Decision Trees

A decision tree can be particularly valuable for evaluating different capacity expansion alternatives when demand is uncertain and sequential decisions are involved (see Supplement A, "Decision Making"). For example, the owner of Grandmother's Chicken Restaurant (see Example 4.2) may expand the restaurant now, only to discover in year 4 that demand growth is much higher than forecasted. In that case, she needs to decide whether to expand further. In terms of construction costs and downtime, expanding twice is likely to be much more expensive than building a larger facility from the outset. However, making a large expansion now, when demand growth is low, means poor facility utilization. Much depends on the demand.

Figure 4.4 shows a decision tree for this view of the problem, with new information provided. Demand growth can be either low or high, with probabilities of 0.40 and 0.60, respectively. The initial expansion in year 1 (square node 1) can either be small or large. The second decision node (square node 2), whether to expand at a later date, is reached only if the initial expansion is small and demand turns out to be high. If demand is high and if the initial expansion was small, a decision must be made about a second expansion in year 4. Payoffs for each branch of the tree are estimated. For example, if the initial expansion is large, the financial benefit is either $40,000 or $220,000, depending on whether demand is low or high. Weighting these payoffs by the probabilities yields an expected value of $148,000. This expected payoff is higher than the $109,000 payoff for the small initial expansion, so the better choice is to make a large expansion in year 1.

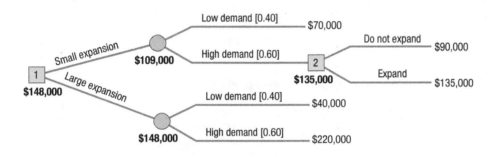

◀ **FIGURE 4.4**
A Decision Tree for Capacity Expansion

LEARNING GOALS IN REVIEW

	Learning Goal	Guidelines for Review	MyOMLab Resources
❶	Define long-term capacity and its relationship with economies and diseconomies of scale.	Review the section "Measures of Capacity and Utilization," pp. 137–138, and understand why and how capacity is measured in high-volume processes is different from its measurement in low-volume, flexible processes. Also see the section on "Economies of Scale" and "Diseconomies of Scale," pp. 138–139. Figure 4.1 illustrates the relationship between average unit cost and output rate, and shows different output ranges over which economies and diseconomies of scale can occur.	**Video:** Gate Turnaround at Southwest Airlines
❷	Understand the main differences between the expansionist and wait-and-see capacity timing and sizing strategies.	The section "Capacity Timing and Sizing Strategies," pp. 139–142, and Figure 4.2 differentiates between the expansionist and wait-and-see strategies. Understand the notion of capacity cushions, and how they link to other decisions in the firm.	
❸	Identify a systematic four-step approach for determining long-term capacity requirements and associated cash flows.	The section "A Systematic Approach to Long-Term Capacity Decisions," pp. 142–145, shows you how capacity requirements can be estimated for both input-based as well as output-based measures. Focus on how different alternatives can be developed to fill the capacity gaps between requirements and current capacity.	**OM Explorer Solvers:** Capacity Requirements **OM Explorer Tutors:** 4.1: Capacity Requirements; 4.2: Projecting Cash Flows **MyOMLab Supplements:** F. Financial Analysis; H. Measuring Output Rates; I. Learning Curve Analysis **Additional Case:** Fitness Plus B

Learning Goal	Guidelines for Review	MyOMLab Resources
4 Describe how the common tools for capacity planning such as waiting-line models, simulation, and decision trees assist in capacity decisions.	The section "Tools for Capacity Planning," pp. 146–147, illustrates how several different methods can be used to arrive at capacity decisions.	

Key Equations

Planning Long-Term Capacity

1. Utilization, expressed as a percent:

$$\text{Utilization} = \frac{\text{Average output rate}}{\text{Maximum capacity}} \times 100\%$$

Capacity Timing and Sizing Strategies

2. Capacity cushion, C, expressed as a percent:

$$C = 100\% - \text{Average Utilization rate} (\%)$$

A Systematic Approach to Long-Term Capacity Decisions

3. Capacity requirement for one service or product:

$$M = \frac{Dp}{N[1 - (C/100)]}$$

4. Capacity requirement for multiple services or products:

$$M = \frac{[Dp + (D/Q)s]_{\text{product 1}} + [Dp + (D/Q)s]_{\text{product 2}} + \cdots + [Dp + (D/Q)s]_{\text{product } n}}{N[1 - (C/100)]}$$

Key Terms

base case 144
capacity 136
capacity cushion 139
capacity gap 144

capacity requirement 142
cash flow 145
diseconomies of scale 138
economies of scale 138

planning horizon 142
setup time 143
utilization 138

Solved Problem 1

MyOMLab Video

You have been asked to put together a capacity plan for a critical operation at the Surefoot Sandal Company. Your capacity measure is number of machines. Three products (men's, women's, and children's sandals) are manufactured. The time standards (processing and setup), lot sizes, and demand forecasts are given in the following table. The firm operates two 8-hour shifts, 5 days per week, 50 weeks per year. Experience shows that a capacity cushion of 5 percent is sufficient.

Product	TIME STANDARDS Processing (hr/pair)	Setup (hr/pair)	Lot Size (pairs/lot)	Demand Forecast (pairs/yr)
Men's sandals	0.05	0.5	240	80,000
Women's sandals	0.10	2.2	180	60,000
Children's sandals	0.02	3.8	360	120,000

a. How many machines are needed?

b. If the operation currently has two machines, what is the capacity gap?

SOLUTION

a. The number of hours of operation per year, N, is $N =$ (2 shifts/day)(8 hours/shifts)(250 days/machine-year) $= 4{,}000$ hours/machine-year

The number of machines required, M, is the sum of machine-hour requirements for all three products divided by the number of productive hours available for one machine:

$$M = \frac{[Dp + (D/Q)s]_{\text{men}} + [Dp + (D/Q)s]_{\text{women}} + [Dp + (D/Q)s]_{\text{children}}}{N[1 - (C/100)]}$$

$$= \frac{\begin{array}{c}[80{,}000(0.05) + (80{,}000/240)0.5] + [60{,}000(0.10) + (60{,}000/180)2.2] \\ + [120{,}000(0.02) + (120{,}000/360)3.8]\end{array}}{4{,}000[1 - (5/100)]}$$

$$= \frac{14{,}567 \text{ hours/year}}{3{,}800 \text{ hours/machine} - \text{year}} = \textbf{3.83 or 4} \text{ machines}$$

b. The capacity gap is 1.83 machines (3.83 − 2). Two more machines should be purchased, unless management decides to use short-term options to fill the gap.

The *Capacity Requirements* Solver in OM Explorer confirms these calculations, as Figure 4.5 shows, using only the "Expected" scenario for the demand forecasts.

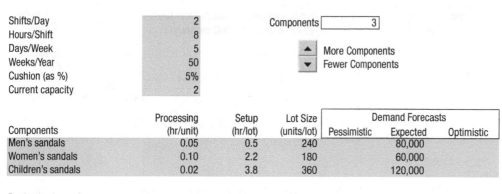

◀ **FIGURE 4.5**
Using the *Capacity Requirements* Solver for Solved Problem 1

Shifts/Day	2
Hours/Shift	8
Days/Week	5
Weeks/Year	50
Cushion (as %)	5%
Current capacity	2

Components [3]

▲ More Components
▼ Fewer Components

Components	Processing (hr/unit)	Setup (hr/lot)	Lot Size (units/lot)	Pessimistic	Expected	Optimistic
					Demand Forecasts	
Men's sandals	0.05	0.5	240		80,000	
Women's sandals	0.10	2.2	180		60,000	
Children's sandals	0.02	3.8	360		120,000	

Productive hours from one capacity unit for a year   3,800

	Pessimistic		Expected		Optimistic	
	Process	Setup	Process	Setup	Process	Setup
Men's sandals	0	0.0	4,000	166.7	0	0.0
Women's sandals	0	0.0	6,000	733.3	0	0.0
Children's sandals	0	0.0	2,400	1,266.7	0	0.0
	0	0.0	12,400	2,166.7	0	0.0
Total hours required		0.0		14,566.7		0.0

Total capacity requirements (M)	0.00	3.83	0.00
Rounded	0	4	0
Scenarios that can be met with current system/capacity:		Pessimistic, Optimistic	

| If capacity increased by | 0% | | |
| Expanded current capacity | 3,800 | | |

Total capacity requirements (M)	0.00	3.83	0.00
Rounded	0	4	0
Scenarios that can be met with expanded current capacity:		Pessimistic, Optimistic	

Solved Problem 2

The base case for Grandmother's Chicken Restaurant (see Example 4.2) is to do nothing. The capacity of the kitchen in the base case is 80,000 meals per year. A capacity alternative for Grandmother's Chicken Restaurant is a two-stage expansion. This alternative expands the kitchen at the end of year 0, raising its capacity from 80,000 meals per year to that of the dining area (105,000 meals per year). If sales in year 1 and 2 live up to expectations, the capacities of both the kitchen and the dining room will be expanded at the *end* of year 3 to 130,000 meals per year. This upgraded capacity level should suffice up through year 5. The initial investment would be $80,000 at the end of year 0 and an additional investment of

$170,000 at the end of year 3. The pretax profit is $2 per meal. What are the pretax cash flows for this alternative through year 5, compared with the base case?

SOLUTION

Table 4.1 shows the cash inflows and outflows. The year 3 cash flow is unusual in two respects. First, the cash inflow from sales is $50,000 rather than $60,000. The increase in sales over the base is 25,000 meals (105,000 − 10,000) instead of 30,000 meals (110,000 − 80,000) because the restaurant's capacity falls somewhat short of demand. Second, a cash outflow of $170,000 occurs at the end of year 3, when the second-stage expansion occurs. The net cash flow for year 3 is $50,000 − $170,000 = −$120,000.

For comparison purposes, the NPV of this project at a discount rate of 10 percent is calculated as follows, and equals negative $2,184.90.

$$\text{NPV} = -80{,}000 + (20{,}000/1.1) + [40{,}000/(1.1)^2] - [120{,}000/(1.1)^3] + [80{,}000/(1.1)^4] + [100{,}000/(1.1)^5]$$

$$= -\$80{,}000 + \$18{,}181.82 + \$33{,}057.85 - \$90{,}157.77 + \$54{,}641.07 + \$62{,}092.13$$

$$= -\$2{,}184.90$$

On a purely monetary basis, a single-stage expansion seems to be a better alternative than this two-stage expansion. However, other qualitative factors as mentioned earlier must be considered as well.

TABLE 4.1 | CASH FLOWS FOR TWO-STAGE EXPANSION AT GRANDMOTHER'S CHICKEN RESTAURANT

Year	Projected Demand (meals/yr)	Projected Capacity (meals/yr)	Calculation of Incremental Cash Flow Compared to Base Case (80,000 meals/yr)	Cash Inflow (outflow)
0	80,000	80,000	Increase kitchen capacity to 105,000 meals =	($80,000)
1	90,000	105,000	90,000 − 80,000 = (10,000 meals)($2/meal) =	$20,000
2	100,000	105,000	100,000 − 80,000 = (20,000 meals)($2/meal) =	$40,000
3	110,000	105,000	105,000 − 80,000 = (25,000 meals)($2/meal) =	$50,000
			Increase total capacity to 130,000 meals =	(($170,000))
				($120,000)
4	120,000	130,000	120,000 − 80,000 = (40,000 meals)($2/meal) =	$80,000
5	130,000	130,000	130,000 − 80,000 = (50,000 meals)($2/meal) =	$100,000

Discussion Questions

1. What are the economies of scale in college class size? As class size increases, what symptoms of diseconomies of scale appear? How are these symptoms related to customer contact?

2. A young boy sets up a lemonade stand on the corner of College Street and Air Park Boulevard. Temperatures in the area climb to 100°F during the summer. The intersection is near a major university and a large construction site. Explain to this young entrepreneur how his business might benefit from economies of scale. Explain also some conditions that might lead to diseconomies of scale.

3. Identify an industry in which expansionist strategy has generally been followed by most firms in the past. Under which conditions will it be better for a firm to follow the wait-and-see strategy rather than the expansionist strategy? Then identify a firm or an industry that has done so successfully.

Problems

The OM Explorer and POM for Windows software is available to all students using the 11th edition of this textbook. Go to http://www.pearsonhighered.com/krajewski to download these computer packages. If you purchased MyOMLab, you also have access to Active Models software and significant help in doing the following problems. Check with your instructor on how best to use these resources. In many cases, the instructor wants you to understand how to do the calculations by hand. At the least, the software provides a check on your calculations. When calculations are particularly complex and the goal is interpreting the results in making decisions, the software replaces entirely the manual calculations.

Problems 20, 21, 22, 23, 24, and 25 require reading of Supplement A, "Decision Making." Problems 15, 16, 17, 24, and 25 require reading of MyOMLab Supplement F, "Financial Analysis."

Planning Long-Term Capacity

1. The Dahlia Medical Center has 30 labor rooms, 15 combination labor and delivery rooms, 3 delivery rooms, and 1 special delivery room reserved for complicated births. All of these facilities operate around the clock. Time spent in labor rooms varies from hours to days, with an average of about a day. The average uncomplicated delivery requires about 1 hour in a delivery room.

   During an exceptionally busy 3-day period, 109 healthy babies were born at Dahlia Medical Center. Sixty babies were born in separate labor and delivery rooms, 45 were born in combined labor and delivery rooms, and only 4 babies required a labor room and the complicated delivery room. Which of the facilities (labor rooms, combination labor and delivery rooms, or delivery rooms) had the greatest utilization rate?

2. A process currently services an average of 50 customers per day. Observations in recent weeks show that its utilization is about 90 percent, allowing for just a 10 percent capacity cushion. If demand is expected to be 75 percent of the current level in five years and management wants to have a capacity cushion of just 5 percent, what capacity requirement should be planned?

3. An airline company must plan its fleet capacity and its long-term schedule of aircraft usage. For one flight segment, the average number of customers per day is 70, which represents a 65 percent utilization rate of the equipment assigned to the flight segment. If demand is expected to increase to 84 customers for this flight segment in three years, what capacity requirement should be planned? Assume that management deems that a capacity cushion of 25 percent is appropriate.

4. Food Goblin Supermarkets use both cashiers and baggers to serve customers at check out. During the first 6 hours of each workday (Monday–Friday), 4 cashiers and 2 baggers serve approximately 20 customers per hour. A cashier and a bagger who require approximately 5 minutes at checkout and 5 minutes at bagging serve each customer.

   a. Calculate the utilization of both cashiers and baggers.

   b. Assume that both baggers and cashiers are cross-trained to perform both activities so that they can serve customers independently. Customers are now both checked and their groceries bagged by one individual. Further, assume that it takes 12 minutes for one individual to both cash out and bag each customer's groceries. Calculate the utilization of this new group of 6 cross-trained employees.

5. Returning to Problem 4, under both assumption of cashiers and baggers working together (part a.) and, cross-trained, working independently (part b.) how many employees should Food Goblin Supermarket schedule if it requires a 10 percent capacity cushion?

A Systematic Approach to Long-Term Capacity Decisions

6. Purple Swift manufactures birdhouses in lots of 10. Each birdhouse takes 45 minutes to paint. After 10 birdhouses are painted, the company switches paint color which requires a one hour changeover. The company works 8 hours per shift, one shift per day, 220 days per year. Currently the company has one paint booth. What is Purple Swift's paint capacity cushion if it builds 2,000 birdhouses per year?

7. Macon Controls produces three different types of control units used to protect industrial equipment from overheating.

   Each of these units must be processed by a machine that Macon considers to be their process bottleneck. The plant operates on two 8-hour shifts, 5 days per week, 52 weeks per year. Table 4.2 provides the time standards at the bottleneck, lot sizes, and demand forecasts for the three units. Because of demand uncertainties, the operations manager obtained three demand forecasts (pessimistic, expected, and optimistic). The manager believes that a 20 percent capacity cushion is best.

TABLE 4.2 | CAPACITY INFORMATION FOR MACON CONTROLS

	TIME STANDARD			DEMAND FORECAST		
Component	Processing (hr/unit)	Setup (hr/lot)	Lot Size (units/lot)	Pessimistic	Expected	Optimistic
A	0.05	1.0	60	15,000	18,000	25,000
B	0.20	4.5	80	10,000	13,000	17,000
C	0.05	8.2	120	17,000	25,000	40,000

   a. How many machines are required to meet minimum (pessimistic) demand, expected demand, and maximum (optimistic) demand?

   b. How many machines are required if the operations manager decides to double lot sizes?

   c. If the operations manager has three machines and believes that the plant can reduce setup time by 20 percent through process improvement initiatives, does that plant have adequate capacity to meet all demand scenarios without increasing lot sizes?

8. Up, Up, and Away is a producer of kites and wind socks. Relevant data on a bottleneck operation in the shop for the upcoming fiscal year are given in the following table:

Item	Kites	Wind Socks
Demand forecast	30,000 units/year	12,000 units/year
Lot size	20 units	70 units
Standard processing time	0.3 hour/unit	1.0 hour/unit
Standard setup time	3.0 hours/lot	4.0 hours/lot

The shop works two shifts per day, 8 hours per shift, 200 days per year. Currently, the company operates four machines, and desires a 25 percent capacity cushion. How many machines should be purchased to meet the upcoming year's demand without resorting to any short-term capacity solutions?

9. Tuff-Rider, Inc., manufactures touring bikes and mountain bikes in a variety of frame sizes, colors, and component combinations. Identical bicycles are produced in lots of 100. The projected demand, lot size, and time standards are shown in the following table:

Item	Touring	Mountain
Demand forecast	5,000 units/year	10,000 units/year
Lot size	100 units	100 units
Standard processing time	.25 hour/unit	.50 hour/unit
Standard setup time	2 hours/lot	3 hours/lot

The shop currently works 8 hours a day, 5 days a week, 50 weeks a year. It operates five workstations, each producing one bicycle in the time shown in the table. The shop maintains a 15 percent capacity cushion. How many workstations will be required next year to meet expected demand without using overtime and without decreasing the firm's current capacity cushion?

10. Knott's Industries manufactures standard and super premium backyard swing sets. Currently it has four identical swing-set-making machines, which are operated 250 days per year and 8 hours each day. A capacity cushion of 20 percent is desired. The following information is also known:

	Standard Model	Super Premium Model
Annual Demand	20,000	10,000
Standard Processing Time	7 min	20 min
Average Lot Size	50	30
Standard Setup Time per Lot	30 min	45 min

a. Does Knott's have sufficient capacity to meet annual demand?

b. If Knott's was able to reduce the setup time for the Super Premium Model from 45 minutes to 30 minutes, would there be enough current capacity to produce 20,000 units of each type of swing set?

11. Arabelle is considering expanding the floor area of her high-fashion import clothing store, The French Prints of Arabelle, by increasing her leased space in the upscale Cherry Creek Mall from 2,000 square feet to 3,000 square feet. The Cherry Creek Mall boasts one of the country's highest ratios of sales value per square foot. Rents (including utilities, security, and similar costs) are $110 per square foot per year. Salary increases related to French Prints' expansion are shown in the following table, along with projections of sales per square foot. The purchase cost of goods sold averages 70 percent of the sales price. Sales are seasonal, with an important peak during the year-end holiday season.

Year	Quarter	Sales (per sq ft)	Incremental Salaries
1	1	$90	$12,000
	2	60	8,000
	3	110	12,000
	4	240	24,000
2	1	99	12,000
	2	66	8,000
	3	121	12,000
	4	264	24,000

a. If Arabelle expands French Prints at the end of year 0, what will her quarterly pretax cash flows be through year 2?

b. Project the quarterly pretax cash flows assuming that the sales pattern (10 percent annually compounded increase) continues through year 3.

12. The Astro World amusement park has the opportunity to expand its size now (the end of year 0) by purchasing adjacent property for $250,000 and adding attractions at a cost of $550,000. This expansion is expected to increase attendance by 30 percent over projected attendance without expansion. The price of admission is $30, with a $5 increase planned for the beginning of year 3. Additional operating costs are expected to be $100,000 per year. Estimated attendance for the next five years, *without expansion*, is as follows:

Year	1	2	3	4	5
Attendance	30,000	34,000	36,250	38,500	41,000

a. What are the pretax combined cash flows for years 0 through 5 that are attributable to the park's expansion?

b. Ignoring tax, depreciation, and the time value of money, determine how long it will take to recover (pay back) the investment.

13. Kim Epson operates a full-service car wash, which operates from 8 A.M. to 8 P.M., 7 days a week. The car wash has two stations: an automatic washing and drying station and a manual interior cleaning station. The automatic washing and drying station can handle 30 cars per hour. The interior cleaning station can handle 200 cars per day. Based on a recent year-end review of operations, Kim estimates that future demand for the interior cleaning station for the 7 days of the week,

expressed in average number of cars per day, would be as follows:

Day	Mon.	Tues.	Wed.	Thurs.	Fri.	Sat.	Sun.
Cars	160	180	150	140	280	300	250

By installing additional equipment (at a cost of $50,000), Kim can increase the capacity of the interior cleaning station to 300 cars per day. Each car wash generates a pretax contribution of $4.00. Should Kim install the additional equipment if she expects a pretax payback period of three years or less?

14. Roche Brothers is considering a capacity expansion of its supermarket. The landowner will build the addition to suit in return for $200,000 upon completion and a 5-year lease. The increase in rent for the addition is $10,000 per month. The annual sales projected through year 5 follow. The current effective capacity is equivalent to 500,000 customers per year. Assume a 2 percent pretax profit on sales.

Year	1	2	3	4	5
Customers	560,000	600,000	685,000	700,000	715,000
Average Sales per Customer	$50.00	$53.00	$56.00	$60.00	$64.00

a. If Roche expands its capacity to serve 700,000 customers per year now (end of year 0), what are the projected annual incremental pretax cash flows attributable to this expansion?

b. If Roche expands its capacity to serve 700,000 customers per year at the end of year 2, the landowner will build the same addition for $240,000 and a 3-year lease at $12,000 per month. What are the projected annual incremental pretax cash flows attributable to this expansion alternative?

15. MKM International is seeking to purchase a new CNC machine in order to reduce costs. Two alternative machines are in consideration. Machine 1 costs $500,000 but yields a 15 percent savings over the current machine used. Machine 2 costs $900,000 but yields a 25 percent savings over the current machine used. In order to meet demand, the following forecasted cost information for the current machine is also provided.

a. Based on the NPV of the cash flows for these five years, which machine should MKM International Purchase? Assume a discount rate of 12 percent.

b. If MKM International lowered its required discount rate to 8 percent, what machine would it purchase?

Year	Projected Cost
1	1,000,000
2	1,350,000
3	1,400,000
4	1,450,000
5	2,550,000

16. Several years ago, River City built a water purification plant to remove toxins and filter the city's drinking water. Because of population growth, the demand for water next year will be more than the plant's capacity of 120 million gallons per year. Therefore, the city must expand the facility. The estimated demand over the next 20 years is given in Table 4.3.

The city planning commission is considering three alternatives.

- *Alternative 1:* Expand enough at the end of year 0 to last 20 years, which means an 80 million gallon increase (200 – 120).
- *Alternative 2:* Expand at the end of year 0 and at the end of year 10.
- *Alternative 3:* Expand at the end of years 0, 5, 10, and 15.

Each alternative would provide the needed 200 million gallons per year at the end of 20 years, when the value of the plant would be the same regardless of the alternative chosen. Significant economies of scale can be achieved in construction costs: A 20 million gallon expansion would cost $18 million; a 40 million gallon expansion, $30 million; and an 80 million gallon expansion, only $50 million. The level of future interest rates is uncertain, leading to uncertainty about the hurdle rate. The city believes that it could be as low as 12 percent and as high as 16 percent (see MyOMLab Supplement F, "Financial Analysis").

a. Compute the cash flows for each alternative, compared to a base case of doing nothing. (*Note*: As a municipal utility, the operation pays no taxes.)

b. Which alternative minimizes the present value of construction costs over the next 20 years if the discount rate is 12 percent? 16 percent?

c. Because the decision involves public policy and compromise, what political considerations does the planning commission face?

TABLE 4.3 | WATER DEMAND

Year	Demand	Year	Demand	Year	Demand
0	120	7	148	14	176
1	124	8	152	15	180
2	128	9	156	16	184
3	132	10	160	17	188
4	136	11	164	18	192
5	140	12	168	19	196
6	144	13	172	20	200

17. Mars Incorporated is interested in going to market with a new fuel savings device that attaches to electrically powered industrial vehicles. The device, code named "Python," promises to save up to 15 percent of the electrical power required to operate the average electric forklift. Mars expects that modest demand expected during the introductory year will be followed by a steady increase in demand in subsequent years. The extent of this increase in demand will be based on customer's expectations regarding the future cost of electricity and which is shown in Table 4.4. Mars expects to sell the device for $500 each, and does not expect to be able to raise its price over the foreseeable future.

TABLE 4.4 | DEMAND FOR PYTHON POWER SAVING DEVICE

EXPECTED DEMAND OF THE DEVICE IN UNITS/YEAR

Year	Small Increases in the Cost of Electrical Power	Large Increases in the Cost of Electrical Power
1	1,000	10,000
2	5,000	8,000
3	1,000	15,000
4	15,000	20,000
5	18,000	30,000

Mars is faced with two alternatives:

- *Alternative 1:* Make the device themselves, which requires an initial outlay of $250,000 in plant and equipment and a variable cost of $75 per unit.

- *Alternative 2:* Outsource the production, which requires no initial investment, but incurs a per unit cost of $300.

a. Assuming small increases in the cost of electrical power, compute the cash flows for each alternative. Over the next five years, which alternative maximizes the NPV of this project if the discount rate is 10 percent?

b. Assuming large increases in the cost of electrical power, compute the cash flows for each alternative. Over the next five years, which alternative maximizes the NPV of this project if the discount rate is 10 percent?

18. Mackelprang, Inc., is in the initial stages of building the premier planned community in the greater Phoenix, Arizona, metropolitan area. The main selling point will be the community's lush golf courses. Homes with golf course views will generate premiums far larger than homes with no golf course views, but building golf courses is expensive and takes up valuable space that non-view homes could be built upon. Mackelprang, Inc., has limited land capacity. In order to maximize its profits, it is faced with a decision as to how many golf courses it should build, which, in turn, will impact how many homes with and without golf course views it will be able to construct. Mackelprang, Inc., realizes that this decision is directly related to the premium buyers will be willing to spend to buy homes with golf course views. Mackelprang, Inc., is required to build at least one golf course but has enough space to build up to three golf courses. The following table indicates the costs and potential revenues for each course:

	Indian River	The Cactus	Wildwood
Cost	$2.6M	$1.25M	$2.5M
Highest Possible Revenue	$4M	$2M	$2M
Probability of High Revenue	0.3	0.2	0.3
Likely Revenue	$2.5M	$1.5M	$4M
Probability of Likely Revenue	0.4	0.5	0.5
Lowest Possible Revenue	$1M	$1M	$1M
Probability of Low Revenue	0.3	0.3	0.2

a. Which golf course or courses should Mackelprang, Inc., build?

b. What is the expected payoff for this project?

19. Two new alternatives have come up for expanding Grandmother's Chicken Restaurant (see Solved Problem 2). They involve more automation in the kitchen and feature a special cooking process that retains the original-recipe taste of the chicken. Although the process is more capital-intensive, it would drive down labor costs, so the pretax profit for *all* sales (not just the sales from the capacity added) would go up from 20 to 22 percent. This gain would increase the pretax profit by 2 percent of each sales dollar through $800,000 (80,000 meals × $10) and by 22 percent of each sales dollar between $800,000 and the new capacity limit. Otherwise, the new alternatives are much the same as those in Example 4.2 and Solved Problem 2.

- *Alternative 1:* Expand both the kitchen and the dining area now (at the end of year 0), raising the capacity to 130,000 meals per year. The cost of construction, including the new automation, would be $336,000 (rather than the earlier $200,000).

- *Alternative 2:* Expand only the kitchen now, raising its capacity to 105,000 meals per year. At the end of year 3, expand both the kitchen and the dining area to the 130,000 meals-per-year volume. Construction and equipment costs would be $424,000, with $220,000 at the end of year 0 and the remainder at the end of year 3. As with alternative 1, the contribution margin would go up to 22 percent.

With both new alternatives, the salvage value would be negligible. Compare the cash flows of all alternatives. Should Grandmother's Chicken Restaurant expand with the new or the old technology? Should it expand now or later?

Tools for Capacity Planning

20. Dawson Electronics is a manufacturer of high-tech control modules for lawn sprinkler systems. Denise, the CEO, is trying to decide if the company should develop one of the two potential new products, the Water Saver 1000 or the Greener Grass 5000. With each product, Dawson can capture a bigger market share if it chooses to expand capacity by buying additional machines. Given different demand scenarios, their probabilities of occurrence, and capacity expansion versus no change in capacity, the potential sales of each product are summarized in Table 4.5.

TABLE 4.5 | DEMAND AND SALES INFORMATION FOR DAWSON ELECTRONICS

	Water Saver 1000 Dollar Sales ($1,000)	Greener Grass 5000 Dollar Sales ($1,000)	Probability of Occurrence
With Capacity Expansion			
Low Demand	1,000	2,500	0.25
Medium Demand	2,000	3,000	0.50
High Demand	3,000	5,000	0.25
Without Capacity Expansion			
Low Demand	700	1,000	0.25
Medium Demand	1,000	2,000	0.50
High Demand	2,000	3,000	0.25

   a. What is the expected payoff for Water Saver 1000 and the Greener Grass 5000, with and without capacity expansion?

   b. Which product should Denise choose to produce, and with which capacity expansion option?

21. A manager is trying to decide whether to buy one machine or two. If only one machine is purchased and demand proves to be excessive, the second machine can be purchased later. Some sales would be lost, however, because the lead time for delivery of this type of machine is 6 months. In addition, the cost per machine will be lower if both machines are purchased at the same time. The probability of low demand is estimated to be 0.30 and that of high demand to be 0.70. The after-tax NPV of the benefits from purchasing two machines together is $90,000 if demand is low and $170,000 if demand is high.

   If one machine is purchased and demand is low, the NPV is $120,000. If demand is high, the manager has three options: (1) doing nothing, which has an NPV of $120,000; (2) subcontracting, with an NPV of $140,000; and (3) buying the second machine, with an NPV of $130,000.

   a. Draw a decision tree for this problem.

   b. What is the best decision and what is its expected payoff?

22. Acme Steel Fabricators experienced booming business for the past five years. The company fabricates a wide range of steel products, such as railings, ladders, and light structural steel framing. The current manual method of materials handling is causing excessive inventories and congestion. Acme is considering the purchase of an overhead rail-mounted hoist system or a forklift truck to increase capacity and improve manufacturing efficiency.

   The annual pretax payoff from the system depends on future demand. If demand stays at the current level, the probability of which is 0.50, annual savings from the overhead hoist will be $10,000. If demand rises, the hoist will save $25,000 annually because of operating efficiencies in addition to new sales. Finally, if demand falls, the hoist will result in an estimated annual loss of $65,000. The probability is estimated to be 0.30 for higher demand and 0.20 for lower demand.

If the forklift is purchased, annual payoffs will be $5,000 if demand is unchanged, $10,000 if demand rises, and −$25,000 if demand falls.

   a. Draw a decision tree for this problem and compute the expected value of the payoff for each alternative.

   b. Which is the best alternative, based on the expected values?

23. Referring to Problem 7, the operations manager at Macon Controls believes that pessimistic demand has a probability of 20 percent, expected demand has a probability of 50 percent, and optimistic demand has a probability of 30 percent. Currently, new machines must be purchased at a cost of $500,000 a piece, the price charged for each control unit is $110, and the variable cost of production is $50 per unit. (Hint: since the price and variable cost for each control unit are the same, the profit maximizing product mix will be the same as the mix that maximizes the total number of units produced.)

   a. Draw a decision tree for this problem.

   b. How many machines should the company purchase, and what is the expected payoff?

24. Darren Mack owns the Gas n' Go convenience store and gas station. After hearing a marketing lecture, he realizes that it might be possible to draw more customers to his high-margin convenience store by selling his gasoline at a lower price. However, the Gas n' Go is unable to qualify for volume discounts on its gasoline purchases, and therefore cannot sell gasoline for profit if the price is lowered. Each new pump will cost $95,000 to install, but will increase customer traffic in the store by 1,000 customers per year. Also, because the Gas n' Go would be selling its gasoline at no profit, Darren plans on increasing the profit margin on convenience store items incrementally over the next five years. Assume a discount rate of 8 percent. The projected convenience store sales per customer and the projected profit margin for the next five years are as follows:

Year	Projected Convenience Store Sales Per Customer	Projected Profit Margin
1	$5.00	20%
2	$6.50	25%
3	$8.00	30%
4	$10.00	35%
5	$11.00	40%

   a. What is the NPV of the next five years of cash flows if Darren had four new pumps installed?

   b. If Darren required a payback period of four years, should he go ahead with the installation of the new pumps?

25. The vice president of operations at Dintell Corporation, a major supplier of passenger-side automotive air bags, is considering a $50 million expansion at the firm's Fort Worth, Texas, production complex. The most recent economic projections indicate a 0.60 probability that the overall market will be $400 million per

year over the next five years and a 0.40 probability that the market will be only $200 million per year during the same period. The marketing department estimates that Dintell has a 0.50 probability of capturing 40 percent of the market and an equal probability of obtaining only 30 percent of the market. The cost of goods sold is estimated to be 70 percent of sales. For planning purposes, the company currently uses a 12 percent discount rate, a 40 percent tax rate, and the MACRS depreciation schedule. The criteria for investment decisions at Dintell are (1) the net expected present value must be greater than zero; (2) there must be at least a 70 percent chance that the net present value will be positive; and (3) there must be no more than a 10 percent

chance that the firm will lose more than 20 percent of the initial value.

a. Based on the stated criteria, determine whether Dintell should fund the project.

b. What effect will a probability of 0.70 of capturing 40 percent of the market have on the decision?

c. What effect will an increase in the discount rate to 15 percent have on the decision? A decrease to 10 percent?

d. What effect will the need for another $10 million in the third year have on the decision?

VIDEO CASE   Gate Turnaround at Southwest Airlines

Rollin King and Herb Kelleher started Southwest Airlines in 1971 with this idea: If they could take airline passengers where they want to go, on time, at the lowest possible price, and have a good time while doing it, people would love to fly their airline. The result? No other airline in the industry's history has enjoyed the customer loyalty and extended profitability for which Southwest is now famous. The company now flies more than 3,400 times each day to over 64 destinations across the United States.

There's more to the story, however, than making promises and hoping to fulfill them. A large part of Southwest Airlines' success lies in its ability to plan long-term capacity to better match demand and also improving the utilization of its fleet by turning around an aircraft at the gate faster than its competitors. Capacity at Southwest is measured in seat-miles, and even a single minute reduction in aircraft turnaround time system wide means additional seat-miles being added to the available capacity of Southwest Airlines.

As soon as an aircraft calls "in range" at one of Southwest's airport locations, called a station, the local operations manager notifies the ground operations team so that they can start mobilizing all the parties involved in servicing the aircraft in preparation for its next departure. The grounds operations team consists of a baggage transfer driver who has responsibility for getting connecting flight bags to their proper planes, a local baggage driver who moves bags to baggage claim for passenger pick-up, a lavatory truck driver who handles restroom receptacle drainage, a lead gate agent to handle

Baggage transfer starts less than 40 seconds after engine shutdown at Southwest Airlines.

baggage carts and track incoming and outgoing bag counts, and a bin agent to manage baggage and cargo inside the plane. The ground operations team knows it must turn the plane around in 25 minutes or less. The clock starts when the pilot sets the wheel brakes.

Inbound and outbound flights are coordinated by the supervisors between Southwest's 64 airport stations through the company's Operations Terminal Information System (OTIS). Each local supervisor is able to keep track of their flights and manage any delays or problems that may have crept into the system by keeping in touch with headquarters in Dallas for system-wide issues that may impact a local station, along with using the OTIS information coming from stations sending flights their way.

Just what, exactly, does it take to turn around an aircraft? In-bound flight 3155 from Phoenix to Dallas' Love Field is a good example. In Phoenix, the operations coordinators and ground operations team push back the plane as scheduled at 9:50 A.M. The flight is scheduled to arrive at 3:35 P.M. in Dallas. The Phoenix team enters into OTIS the information the ground operations team will need in Dallas, such as wheelchairs, gate-checked baggage, cargo bin locator data, and other data needed to close out the flight on their end. This action lets the Dallas station know what to expect when the plane lands.

In Dallas, the local ground operations coordinators have been monitoring all 110 inbound flights and now see Phoenix flight 3155 in the system, scheduled for an on-time arrival. When the pilot calls "in range" as it nears Dallas, the ground crew prepares for action.

As the plane is guided to its "stop mark" at the gate, the lead agent waits for the captain's signal that the engines have been turned off and brakes set. Within just 10 seconds, the provisioning truck pulls up to open the back door for restocking supplies such as drinks and snacks. The waiting fuel truck extends its hose to the underwing connection and in less than 2 minutes picks up refueling instructions and starts to load fuel. As soon as the aircraft is in position, the operations team steers the jetway into position and locks it against the aircraft. The door is opened, the in-flight crew is greeted, and passengers start to deplane.

Outside, less than 40 seconds after engine shutdown, baggage is rolling off the plane and gets placed onto the first cart. Any transfer bags get sent to their next destination, and gate-checked bags are delivered to the top of the jetway stairs for passenger pick-up.

While passengers make their way out of the plane, the in-flight crew helps clean up and prepare the cabin for the next flight. If all goes well, the last passenger will leave the plane after only 8 minutes. By this time, passengers waiting to board have already lined up in their designated positions for boarding. The gate agent confirms that the plane is ready for passenger boarding and calls for the first group to turn in their boarding passes and file down the jetway.

At the completion of boarding, the operations agent checks the fuel invoice, cargo bin loading schedule with actual bag counts in their bins from the baggage agents, and a lavatory service record confirming that cleaning has taken place. Final paperwork is given to the captain. The door to the aircraft is closed, and the jetway is retracted. Thirty seconds later, the plane is pushed back and the operations agent gives a traditional salute to the captain to send the flight on its way. Total elapsed time: less than 25 minutes.

Managing Southwest's capacity has been somewhat simplified by strategic decisions made early on in the company's life. First, the company's fleet of aircraft is all Boeing 737's. This single decision impacts all areas of operations—from crew training to aircraft maintenance. The single-plane configuration also provides Southwest with crew scheduling flexibility. Since pilots and flight crews can be deployed across the entire fleet, there are no constraints with regard to training and certification pegged to specific aircraft types.

The way Southwest has streamlined its operations for tight turnarounds means it must maintain a high capacity cushion to accommodate variability in its daily operations. Anything from weather delays to unexpected maintenance issues at the gate can slow down the flow of operations to a crawl. To handle these unplanned but anticipated challenges, Southwest builds into its schedules enough cushion to manage these delays yet not so much that employees and planes are idle. Additionally, the company encourages discussion to keep on top of what's working and where improvements can be made. If a problem is noted at a downstream station, say bags were not properly loaded, this information quickly travels back up to the originating station for correction so that it does not happen again.

Even with the tightly managed operations Southwest Airlines enjoys, company executives know that continued improvement is necessary if the company is to remain profitable into the future. Company executives know when they have achieved their goals when internal and external metrics are reached. For example, the Department of Transportation (DOT) tracks on-time departures, customer complaints, and mishandled baggage for all airlines. The company sets targets for achievement on these dimensions and lets employees know on a monthly basis how the company is doing against those metrics and the rest of the industry. Regular communication with all employees is delivered via meetings, posters, and newsletters. Rewards such as prizes and profit sharing are given for successful achievement.

As for the future, Bob Jordan, Southwest's executive vice president for strategy and planning, puts it this way: "We make money when our planes are in the air, not on the ground. If we can save one minute off every turn system-wide, that's like putting five additional planes in the air. If a single plane generates annual revenue of $25 million, there's $125 million in profit potential from those time savings."

QUESTIONS

1. How can capacity and utilization be measured at an airline such as Southwest Airlines?

2. Which factors can adversely impact turnaround times at Southwest Airlines?

3. How does Southwest Airlines know they are achieving their goals?

4. What are the important long-term issues relevant for managing capacity, revenue, and customer satisfaction for Southwest Airlines?

CASE   Fitness Plus, Part A

Fitness Plus, Part B, explores alternatives to expanding a new downtown facility and is included in the Instructor's Resource Manual. If you are interested in this topic, ask your instructor for a preview.

Fitness Plus is a full-service health and sports club in Greensboro, North Carolina. The club provides a range of facilities and services to support three primary activities: fitness, recreation, and relaxation. Fitness activities generally take place in four areas of the club: the (1) aerobics room, which can accommodate 35 people per class; a (2) room equipped with free weights; a (3) workout room with 24 pieces of Nautilus equipment; and a (4) large workout room containing 29 pieces of cardiovascular equipment. This equipment includes nine stairsteppers, six treadmills, six life-cycle bikes, three Airdyne bikes, two cross-aerobics machines, two rowing machines, and one climber. Recreational facilities comprise eight racquetball courts, six tennis courts, and a large outdoor pool. Fitness Plus also sponsors softball, volleyball, and swim teams in city recreation leagues. Relaxation is accomplished through yoga classes held twice a week in the aerobics room, whirlpool tubs located in each locker room, and a trained massage therapist.

Situated in a large suburban office park, Fitness Plus opened its doors in 1995. During the first two years, membership was small and use of the facilities was light. By 1997, membership had grown as fitness began to play a large role in more and more people's lives. Along with this growth came increased use of club facilities. Records indicate that in 2000, an average of 15 members per hour checked into the club during a typical day. Of course, the actual number of members per hour varied by both day and time. On some days during a slow period, only six to eight members would check in per hour. At a peak time, such as Mondays from 4:00 P.M. to 7:00 P.M., the number would be as high as 40 per hour.

The club was open from 6:30 A.M. to 11:00 P.M. Monday through Thursday. On Friday and Saturday, the club closed at 8:00 P.M., and on Sunday the hours were 12:00 P.M. to 8:00 P.M.

As the popularity of health and fitness continued to grow, so did Fitness Plus. By May 2005, the average number of members arriving per hour during a typical day had increased to 25. The lowest period had a rate of 10 members per hour; during peak periods, 80 members per hour checked in to use the facilities. This growth brought complaints from members about overcrowding and unavailability of equipment. Most of these complaints centered on the Nautilus, cardiovascular, and aerobics fitness areas. The owners began to wonder whether the club was indeed too small for its membership. Past research indicated that individuals work out an average of 60 minutes per visit. Data collected from member surveys showed the following facilities usage pattern: 30 percent of the members do aerobics, 40 percent use the cardiovascular equipment, 25 percent use the Nautilus machines, 20 percent use the free weights, 15 percent use the racquetball courts, and 10 percent use the tennis courts. The owners wondered whether they could use this information to estimate how well existing capacity was being utilized.

If capacity levels were being stretched, now was the time to decide what to do. It was already May, and any expansion of the existing facility would take at least four months. The owners knew that January was always a peak membership enrollment month and that any new capacity needed to be ready by then. However, other factors had to be considered. The area was growing both in terms of population and geographically. The downtown area just received a major facelift, and many new offices and businesses were moving back to it, causing a resurgence in activity.

With this growth came increased competition. A new YMCA was offering a full range of services at a low cost. Two new health and fitness facilities had opened within the past year in locations 10 to 15 minutes from Fitness Plus. The first, called the Oasis, catered to the young adult crowd and restricted the access of children under 16 years old. The other facility, Gold's Gym, provided excellent weight and cardiovascular training only.

As the owners thought about the situation, they had many questions: Were the capacities of the existing facilities constrained, and if so, where? If capacity expansion was necessary, should the existing facility be expanded? Because of the limited amount of land at the current site, expansion of some services might require reducing the capacity of others. Finally, owing to increased competition and growth downtown, was now the time to open a facility to serve that market? A new facility would take 6 months to renovate, and the financial resources were not available to do both.

QUESTIONS

1. What method would you use to measure the capacity of Fitness Plus? Has Fitness Plus reached its capacity?

2. Which capacity strategy would be appropriate for Fitness Plus? Justify your answer.

3. How would you link the capacity decision being made by Fitness Plus to other types of operating decisions?

SUPPLEMENT

B

WAITING LINES

Anyone who has ever waited at a stoplight, at McDonald's, or at the registrar's office has experienced the dynamics of waiting lines. Perhaps one of the best examples of effective management of waiting lines is that of Walt Disney World. One day the park may have only 25,000 customers, but on another day the numbers may top 90,000. Careful analysis of process flows, technology for people-mover (materials handling) equipment, capacity, and layout keeps the waiting times for attractions to acceptable levels.

A **waiting line** is one or more "customers" waiting for service. The customers can be people or inanimate objects, such as machines requiring maintenance, sales orders waiting for shipping, or inventory items waiting to be used. A waiting line forms because of a temporary imbalance between the demand for service and the capacity of the system to provide the service. In most real-life waiting-line problems, the demand rate varies; that is, customers arrive at unpredictable intervals. Most often, the rate of producing the service also varies, depending on customer needs. Suppose that bank customers arrive at an average rate of 15 per hour throughout the day and that the bank can process an average of 20 customers per hour. Why would a waiting line ever develop? The answers are that the customer arrival rate varies throughout the day and the time required to process a customer can vary. During the noon hour, 30 customers may arrive at the bank. Some of them may have complicated transactions requiring above-average process times. The waiting line may grow to 15 customers for a period of time before it eventually disappears. Even though the bank manager provided for more than enough capacity on average, waiting lines can still develop.

In a similar fashion, waiting lines can develop even if the time to process a customer is constant. For example, a subway train is computer controlled to arrive at stations along its route. Each train is programmed to arrive at a station, say, every 15 minutes. Even with the constant service time, waiting lines develop while riders wait for the next train or cannot get on a train because of the size of the crowd at a busy time of the day. Consequently, variability in the rate of demand determines the sizes of the waiting

waiting line

One or more "customers" waiting for service.

LEARNING GOALS *After reading this supplement, you should be able to:*

1. Identify the structure of waiting lines in real situations.
2. Use the single-server, multiple-server, and finite-source models to analyze operations and estimate the operating characteristics of a process.
3. Describe the situations where simulation should be used for waiting-line analysis and the nature of the information that can be obtained.
4. Explain how waiting-line models can be used to make managerial decisions.

lines in this case. In general, if no variability in the demand or service rate occurs and enough capacity is provided, no waiting lines form.

Waiting-line theory applies to service as well as manufacturing firms, relating customer arrival and service-system processing characteristics to service-system output characteristics. In our discussion, we use the term *service* broadly—the act of doing work for a customer. The service system might be hair cutting at a hair salon, satisfying customer complaints, or processing a production order of parts on a certain machine. Other examples of customers and services include lines of theatergoers waiting to purchase tickets, trucks waiting to be unloaded at a warehouse, machines waiting to be repaired by a maintenance crew, and patients waiting to be examined by a physician. Regardless of the situation, waiting-line problems have several common elements.

The analysis of waiting lines is of concern to managers because it affects process design, capacity planning, process performance, and ultimately, supply chain performance. In this supplement we discuss why waiting lines form, the uses of waiting-line models in operations management, and the structure of waiting-line models. We also discuss the decisions managers address with these models. Waiting lines can also be analyzed using computer simulation. Software such as SimQuick or Excel spreadsheets can be used to analyze the problems in this supplement.

Structure of Waiting-Line Problems

Analyzing waiting-line problems begins with a description of the situation's basic elements. Each specific situation will have different characteristics, but four elements are common to all situations:

customer population

An input that generates potential customers.

1. An input, or **customer population**, that generates potential customers

2. A waiting line of customers

service facility

A person (or crew), a machine (or group of machines), or both necessary to perform the service for the customer.

3. The **service facility**, consisting of a person (or crew), a machine (or group of machines), or both necessary to perform the service for the customer

4. A **priority rule**, which selects the next customer to be served by the service facility

priority rule

A rule that selects the next customer to be served by the service facility.

Figure B.1 shows these basic elements. The triangles, circles, and squares are intended to show a diversity of customers with different needs. The **service system** describes the number of lines and the arrangement of the facilities. After the service has been performed, the served customers leave the system.

service system

The number of lines and the arrangement of the facilities.

Customer Population

A customer population is the source of input to the service system. If the potential number of new customers for the service system is appreciably affected by the number of customers already in the system, the input source is said to be *finite*. For example, suppose that a maintenance crew is assigned responsibility for the repair of 10 machines. The customer population for the maintenance crew is 10 machines in working order. The population generates customers for the maintenance crew as a function of the failure rates for the machines. As more machines fail and enter the service system, either waiting for service or for being repaired, the customer population becomes smaller or the rate at which it can generate another customer falls. Consequently, the customer population is said to be finite.

Alternatively, an *infinite* customer population is one in which the number of customers in the system does not affect the rate at which the population generates new customers. For example,

FIGURE B.1 ▶
Basic Elements of Waiting-Line Models

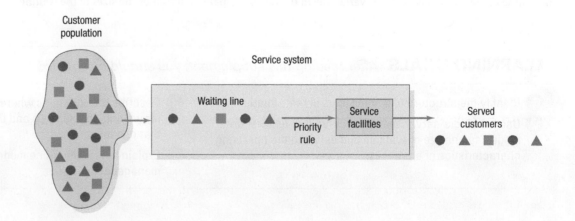

consider a mail-order operation for which the customer population consists of shoppers who have received a catalog of products sold by the company. Because the customer population is so large and only a small fraction of the shoppers place orders at any one time, the number of new orders it generates is not appreciably affected by the number of orders waiting for service or being processed by the service system. In this case, the customer population is said to be infinite.

Customers in waiting lines may be *patient* or *impatient*, which has nothing to do with the colorful language a customer may use while waiting in line for a long time on a hot day. In the context of waiting-line problems, a patient customer is one who enters the system and remains there until being served; an impatient customer is one who either decides not to enter the system (balks) or leaves the system before being served (reneges). For the methods used in this supplement, we make the simplifying assumption that all customers are patient.

The Service System

The service system may be described by the number of lines and the arrangement of facilities.

Number of Lines   Waiting lines may be designed to be a *single line* or *multiple lines.* Figure B.2 shows an example of each arrangement. Generally, single lines are utilized at airline counters, inside banks, and at some fast-food restaurants whereas multiple lines are utilized in grocery stores, at drive-in bank operations, and in discount stores. When multiple servers are available and each one can handle general transactions, the single-line arrangement keeps servers uniformly busy and gives customers a sense of fairness. Customers believe that they are being served on the basis of when they arrived and not on how well they guessed their waiting time when selecting a particular line. The multiple-line design is best when some of the servers provide a limited set of services. In this arrangement, customers select the services they need and wait in the line where that service is provided, such as at a grocery store that provides special lines for customers paying with cash or having fewer than 10 items.

Sometimes customers are not organized neatly into lines. Here ships wait to use the port facilities in Victoria Harbor, West Kowloon, Hong Kong.

Islemount Images/Alamy

Sometimes customers are not organized neatly into "lines." Machines that need repair on the production floor of a factory may be left in place, and the maintenance crew comes to them. Nonetheless, we can think of such machines as forming a single line or multiple lines, depending on the number of repair crews and their specialties. Likewise, passengers who telephone for a taxi also form a line even though they may wait at different locations.

Arrangement of Service Facilities   Service facilities consist of the personnel and equipment necessary to perform the service for the customer. Service facility arrangement is described by the number of channels and phases. A **channel** is one or more facilities required to perform a given service. A **phase** is a single step in providing the service. Some services require a single phase, while others require a sequence of phases. Consequently, a service facility uses some combination of channels and phases. Managers should choose an arrangement based on customer volume and the nature of services provided. Figure B.3 shows examples of the five basic types of service facility arrangements.

In the *single-channel, single-phase* system, all services demanded by a customer can be performed by a single-server facility. Customers form a single line and go through the service facility one at a time. Examples are a drive-through car wash and a machine that must process several batches of parts.

channel

One or more facilities required to perform a given service.

phase

A single step in providing a service.

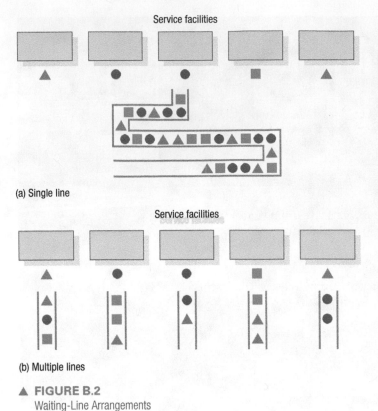

(a) Single line

(b) Multiple lines

▲ **FIGURE B.2**
Waiting-Line Arrangements

The *single-channel, multiple-phase* arrangement is used when the services are best performed in sequence by more than one facility, yet customer volume or other constraints limit the design to one channel. Customers form a single line and proceed sequentially from one service facility to the next. An example of this arrangement is a McDonald's drive-through, where the first facility takes the order, the second takes the money, and the third provides the food.

The *multiple-channel, single-phase* arrangement is used when demand is large enough to warrant providing the same service at more than one facility or when the services offered by the facilities are different. Customers form one or more lines, depending on the design. In the single-line design, the first available server serves customers, just as it is usually done in the lobby of a bank. If each channel has its own waiting line, customers wait until the server for their line can serve them, as at a bank's drive-through facilities.

The *multiple-channel, multiple-phase* arrangement occurs when customers can be served by one of the first-phase facilities but then require service from a second-phase facility, and so on. In some cases, customers cannot switch channels after service has begun; in others they can. An example of this arrangement is a laundromat. Washing machines are the first-phase facilities, and dryers are the second-phase facilities. Some of the washing machines and dryers may be designed for extra-large loads, thereby providing the customer a choice of channels.

The most complex waiting-line problem involves customers who have unique sequences of required services; consequently, service cannot be described neatly in phases. A *mixed* arrangement is used in such a case. In the mixed arrangement, waiting lines can develop in front of each facility, as in a medical center, where a patient goes to an exam room for a nurse to take his or her blood pressure and weight, goes back to the waiting room until the doctor can see him or her, and after consultation proceeds to the laboratory to give a blood sample, radiology to have an X-ray taken, or the pharmacy for prescribed drugs, depending on specific needs.

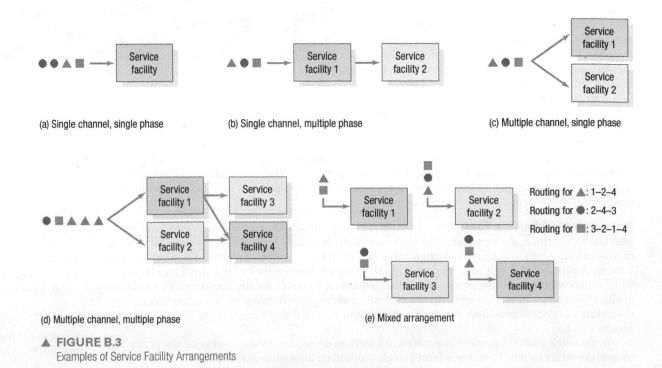

(a) Single channel, single phase

(b) Single channel, multiple phase

(c) Multiple channel, single phase

(d) Multiple channel, multiple phase

(e) Mixed arrangement

Routing for ▲: 1–2–4
Routing for ●: 2–4–3
Routing for ■: 3–2–1–4

▲ **FIGURE B.3**
Examples of Service Facility Arrangements

Priority Rule

The priority rule determines which customer to serve next. Most service systems that you encounter use the first-come, first-served (FCFS) rule. The customer at the head of the waiting line has the highest priority, and the customer who arrived last has the lowest priority. Other priority disciplines might take the customer with the earliest promised due date (EDD) or the customer with the shortest expected processing time (SPT).[1]

A **preemptive discipline** is a rule that allows a customer of higher priority to interrupt the service of another customer. For example, in a hospital emergency room, patients with the most life-threatening injuries receive treatment first, regardless of their order of arrival. Modeling of systems having complex priority disciplines is usually done using computer simulation.

preemptive discipline

A rule that allows a customer of higher priority to interrupt the service of another customer.

Probability Distributions

The sources of variation in waiting-line problems come from the random arrivals of customers and the variations in service times. Each of these sources can be described with a probability distribution.

Arrival Distribution

Customers arrive at service facilities randomly. The variability of customer arrivals often can be described by a Poisson distribution, which specifies the probability that n customers will arrive in T time periods:

$$P_n = \frac{(\lambda T)^n}{n!} e^{-\lambda T} \text{ for } n = 0,1,2, \ldots$$

where

P_n = probability of n arrivals in T time periods
λ = average number of customer arrivals per period
e = 2.7183

The mean of the Poisson distribution is λT, and the variance also is λT. The Poisson distribution is a discrete distribution; that is, the probabilities are for a specific number of arrivals per unit of time.

EXAMPLE B.1	Calculating the Probability of Customer Arrivals

Management is redesigning the customer service process in a large department store. Accommodating four customers is important. Customers arrive at the desk at the rate of two customers per hour. What is the probability that four customers will arrive during any hour?

SOLUTION

In this case $\lambda = 2$ customers per hour, $T = 1$ hour, and $n = 4$ customers. The probability that four customers will arrive in any hour is

$$P_4 = \frac{[2(1)]^4}{4!} e^{-2(1)} = \frac{16}{24} e^{-2} = \mathbf{0.090}$$

DECISION POINT

The manager of the customer service desk can use this information to determine the space requirements for the desk and waiting area. There is a relatively small probability that four customers will arrive in any hour. Consequently, seating capacity for two or three customers should be more than adequate unless the time to service each customer is lengthy. Further analysis on service times is warranted.

Another way to specify the arrival distribution is to do it in terms of customer **interarrival times**—that is, the time between customer arrivals. If the customer population generates customers according to a Poisson distribution, the *exponential distribution* describes the probability that the next customer will arrive, or that service to a customer will conclude, in the next T time periods.

interarrival times

The time between customer arrivals.

---

[1]We focus on FCFS in this supplement. See Chapter 10, "Operations Planning and Scheduling," for additional discussion of FCFS and EDD. See also Supplement J, "Operations Scheduling," for SPT and additional rules.

Service Time Distribution

The exponential distribution describes the probability that the service time of the customer at a particular facility will be no more than T time periods. The probability can be calculated by using the formula

$$P(t \leq T) = 1 - e^{-\mu T}$$

where

μ = average number of customers completing service per period

t = service time of the customer

T = target service time

The mean of the service time distribution is $1/\mu$, and the variance is $(1/\mu)^2$. As T increases, the probability that the customer's service time will be less than T approaches 1.0.

For simplicity, let us look at a single-channel, single-phase arrangement.

EXAMPLE B.2	Calculating the Service Time Probability

The management of the large department store in Example B.1 must determine whether more training is needed for the customer service clerk. The clerk at the customer service desk can serve an average of three customers per hour. What is the probability that a customer will require 10 minutes or less of service?

SOLUTION

We must have all the data in the same time units. Because $\mu = 3$ customers per hour, we convert minutes of time to hours, or $T = 10$ minutes = 10/60 hour = 0.167 hour. Then

$$P(t \leq T) = 1 - e^{-\mu T}$$

$$P(t \leq 0.167 \text{ hour}) = 1 - e^{-3(0.167)} = 1 - 0.61 = \textbf{0.39}$$

DECISION POINT

The probability that the customer will require only 10 minutes or less is not high, which leaves the possibility that customers may experience lengthy delays. Management should consider additional training for the clerk so as to reduce the time it takes to process a customer request.

Some characteristics of the exponential distribution do not always conform to an actual situation. The exponential distribution model is based on the assumption that each service time is independent of those that preceded it. In real life, however, productivity may improve as human servers learn about the work. Another assumption underlying the model is that very small, as well as very large, service times are possible. However, real-life situations often require a fixed-length start-up time, some cutoff on total service time, or nearly constant service time.

Using Waiting-Line Models to Analyze Operations

Operations managers can use waiting-line models to balance the gains that might be made by increasing the efficiency of the service system against the costs of doing so. In addition, managers should consider the costs of *not* making improvements to the system: Long waiting lines or long waiting times may cause customers to balk or renege. Managers should therefore be concerned about the following operating characteristics of the system.

1. *Line Length.* The number of customers in the waiting line reflects one of two conditions. Short lines could mean either good customer service or too much capacity. Similarly, long lines could indicate either low server efficiency or the need to increase capacity.

2. *Number of Customers in System.* The number of customers in line and being served also relates to service efficiency and capacity. A large number of customers in the system causes congestion and may result in customer dissatisfaction, unless more capacity is added.

3. *Waiting Time in Line.* Long lines do not always mean long waiting times. If the service rate is fast, a long line can be served efficiently. However, when waiting time seems long, customers perceive

the quality of service to be poor. Managers may try to change the arrival rate of customers or design the system to make long wait times seem shorter than they really are. For example, at Walt Disney World, customers in line for an attraction are entertained by videos and also are informed about expected waiting times, which seems to help them endure the wait.

4. *Total Time in System.* The total elapsed time from entry into the system until exit from the system may indicate problems with customers, server efficiency, or capacity. If some customers are spending too much time in the service system, it may be necessary to change the priority discipline, increase productivity, or adjust capacity in some way.

5. *Service Facility Utilization.* The collective utilization of service facilities reflects the percentage of time that they are busy. Management's goal is to maintain high utilization and profitability without adversely affecting the other operating characteristics.

The best method for analyzing a waiting-line problem is to relate the five operating characteristics and their alternatives to dollars. However, placing a dollar figure on certain characteristics (such as the waiting time of a shopper in a grocery store) is difficult. In such cases, an analyst must weigh the cost of implementing the alternative under consideration against a subjective assessment of the cost of *not* making the change.

We now present three models and some examples showing how waiting-line models can help operations managers make decisions. We analyze problems requiring the single-server, multiple-server, and finite-source models, all of which are single phase. References to more advanced models are cited at the end of this supplement.

Single-Server Model

The simplest waiting-line model involves a single server and a single line of customers, commonly referred to as a single-channel, single-phase system. To further specify the single-server model, we make the following assumptions:

Visitors to Disney MGM Studios, Disney World, Orlando, Florida patiently wait in line for the Aerosmith Rock N Roller Coaster ride, which is an example of a single-channel, single-phase system.

1. The customer population is infinite and all customers are patient.

2. The customers arrive according to a Poisson distribution, with a mean arrival rate of λ.

3. The service distribution is exponential, with a mean service rate of μ.

4. The mean service rate exceeds the mean arrival rate.

5. Customers are served on a first-come, first-served basis.

6. The length of the waiting line is unlimited.

With these assumptions, we can apply various formulas to describe the operating characteristics of the system:

$$\rho = \text{Average utilization of the system}$$
$$= \frac{\lambda}{\mu}$$

$$P_n = \text{Probability that } n \text{ customers are in the system}$$
$$= (1 - \rho)\rho^n$$

$$P_0 = \text{Probability that zero customers are in the system}$$
$$= 1 - \rho$$

$$L = \text{Average number of customers in the service system}$$
$$= \frac{\lambda}{\mu - \lambda}$$

$$L_q = \text{Average number of customers in the waiting line}$$
$$= \rho L$$

$$W = \text{Average time spent in the system, including service}$$
$$= \frac{1}{\mu - \lambda}$$

$$W_q = \text{Average waiting time in line}$$
$$= \rho W$$

EXAMPLE B.3	Calculating the Operating Characteristics of a Single-Channel, Single-Phase System with the Single-Server Model

The manager of a grocery store in the retirement community of Sunnyville is interested in providing good service to the senior citizens who shop in her store. Currently, the store has a separate checkout counter for senior citizens. On average, 30 senior citizens per hour arrive at the counter, according to a Poisson distribution, and are served at an average rate of 35 customers per hour, with exponential service times. Find the following operating characteristics:

a. Probability of zero customers in the system

b. Average utilization of the checkout clerk

c. Average number of customers in the system

d. Average number of customers in line

e. Average time spent in the system

f. Average waiting time in line

SOLUTION

The checkout counter can be modeled as a single-channel, single-phase system. Figure B.4 shows the results from the *Waiting-Lines* Solver from OM Explorer. Manual calculations of the equations for the *single-server model* are demonstrated in the Solved Problem at the end of the supplement.

FIGURE B.4 ▶
Waiting-Lines Solver for Single-Channel, Single-Phase System

Servers		(Number of servers s assumed to be 1 in single-serve model)
Arrival Rate (λ)	30	
Service Rate (μ)	35	

Probability of zero customers in the system (P_0)	0.1429
Probability of exactly ▼ 0 customers in the system	0.1429
Average utilization of the server (ρ)	0.8571
Average number of customers in the system (L)	6.0000
Average number of customers in line (L_q)	5.1429
Average waiting/service time in the system (W)	0.2000
Average waiting time in line (W_q)	0.1714

Both the average waiting time in the system (W) and the average time spent waiting in line (W_q) are expressed in hours. To convert the results to minutes, simply multiply by 60 minutes/hour. For example, $W = 0.20(60) = $ **12.00** minutes, and $W_q = 0.1714(60) = $ **10.28** minutes.

EXAMPLE B.4	Analyzing Service Rates with the Single-Server Model

The manager of the Sunnyville grocery in Example B.3 wants answers to the following questions:

a. What service rate would be required so that customers averaged only 8 minutes in the system?

b. For that service rate, what is the probability of having more than four customers in the system?

c. What service rate would be required to have only a 10 percent chance of exceeding four customers in the system?

SOLUTION

The *Waiting-Lines* Solver from OM Explorer could be used iteratively to answer the questions. Here we show how to solve the problem manually.

a. We use the equation for the average time in the system and solve for μ.

$$W = \frac{1}{\mu - \lambda}$$

$$8 \text{ minutes} = 0.133 \text{ hour} = \frac{1}{\mu - 30}$$

$$0.133\mu - 0.133(30) = 1$$

$$\mu = \textbf{37.52 customers/hour}$$

b. The probability of more than four customers in the system equals 1 minus the probability of four or fewer customers in the system.

$$P = 1 - \sum_{n=0}^{4} P_n$$

$$= 1 - \sum_{n=0}^{4} (1 - \rho)\rho^n$$

and

$$\rho = \frac{30}{37.52} = 0.80$$

Then,

$$P = 1 - 0.2(1 + 0.8 + 0.8^2 + 0.8^3 + 0.8^4)$$
$$= 1 - 0.672 = \mathbf{0.328}$$

Therefore, there is a nearly 33 percent chance that more than four customers will be in the system.

c. We use the same logic as in part (b), except that μ is now a decision variable. The easiest way to proceed is to find the correct average utilization first, and then solve for the service rate.

$$P = 1 - (1 - \rho)(1 + \rho + \rho^2 + \rho^3 + \rho^4)$$
$$= 1 - (1 + \rho + \rho^2 + \rho^3 + \rho^4) + \rho(1 + \rho + \rho^2 + \rho^3 + \rho^4)$$
$$= 1 - 1 - \rho - \rho^2 - \rho^3 - \rho^4 + \rho + \rho^2 + \rho^3 + \rho^4 + \rho^5$$
$$= \rho^5$$

or

$$\rho = P^{1/5}$$

If $P = 0.10$,

$$\rho = (0.10)^{1/5} = 0.63$$

Therefore, for a utilization rate of 63 percent, the probability of more than four customers in the system is 10 percent. For $\lambda = 30$, the mean service rate must be

$$\frac{30}{\mu} = 0.63$$

$$\mu = \mathbf{47.62} \text{ customers/hour}$$

DECISION POINT
The service rate would only have to increase modestly to achieve the 8-minute target. However, the probability of having more than four customers in the system is too high. The manager must now find a way to increase the service rate from 35 per hour to approximately 48 per hour. She can increase the service rate in several different ways, ranging from employing a high school student to help bag the groceries to installing self-checkout stations.

Multiple-Server Model

With the multiple-server model, customers form a single line and choose one of s servers when one is available. The service system has only one phase; consequently, we are focusing our discussion on multiple-channel, single phase systems. We make the following assumptions in addition to those for the single-server model: There are s identical servers, and the service distribution for each server is exponential, with a mean service time of $1/\mu$. It should always be the case that $s\mu$ exceeds λ.

| EXAMPLE B.5 | Estimating Idle Time and Hourly Operating Costs with the Multiple-Server Model |

The management of the American Parcel Service terminal in Verona, Wisconsin, is concerned about the amount of time the company's trucks are idle (not delivering on the road), which the company defines as waiting to be unloaded and being unloaded at the terminal. The terminal operates with four unloading bays. Each bay requires a crew of two employees, and each crew costs $30 per hour. The estimated cost of an idle truck is $50 per hour. Trucks arrive at an average rate of three per hour, according to a Poisson distribution. On average, a crew can unload a semitrailer rig in one hour, with exponential service times. What is the total hourly cost of operating the system?

MyOMLab

Tutor B.2 in MyOMLab provides a new example to practice the multiple-server model.

MyOMLab

Active Model B.2 in MyOMLab provides additional insight on the multiple-server model and its uses for this problem.

SOLUTION

The *multiple-server model* for $s = 4$, $\mu = 1$, and $\lambda = 3$ is appropriate. To find the total cost of labor and idle trucks, we must calculate the average number of trucks in the system at all times.

Figure B.5 shows the results for the American Parcel Service problem using the *Waiting-Lines* Solver from OM Explorer. The results show that the four-bay design will be utilized 75 percent of the time and that the average number of trucks either being serviced or waiting in line is 4.53 trucks. That is, on average at any point in time, we have 4.53 idle trucks. We can now calculate the hourly costs of labor and idle trucks:

Labor cost:	$30(s) = $30(4) = $120.00
Idle truck cost:	$50(L) = $50(4.53) = $226.50
	Total hourly cost = **$346.50**

FIGURE B.5 ▶

Waiting-Lines Solver for Multiple-Server Model

Servers	4
Arrival Rate (λ)	3
Service Rate (μ)	1

Probability of zero customers in the system (P_0)	0.0377
Probability of [exactly ▼] 0 customers in the system	0.0377
Average utilization of the servers (p)	0.7500
Average number of customers in the system (L)	4.5283
Average number of customers in line (L_q)	1.5283
Average waiting/service time in the system (W)	1.5094
Average waiting time in line (W_q)	0.5094

DECISION POINT

Management must now assess whether $346.50 per day for this operation is acceptable. Attempting to reduce costs by eliminating crews will only increase the waiting time of the trucks, which is more expensive per hour than the crews. However, the service rate can be increased through better work methods; for example, L can be reduced and daily operating costs will be less.

Little's Law

Little's law

A fundamental law that relates the number of customers in a waiting-line system to the arrival rate and waiting time of customers.

One of the most practical and fundamental laws in waiting-line theory is **Little's law**, which relates the number of customers in a waiting-line system to the arrival rate and the waiting time of customers. Using the same notation we used for the single-server model, Little's law can be expressed as $L = \lambda W$ or $L_q = \lambda W_q$. However, this relationship holds for a wide variety of arrival processes, service-time distributions, and numbers of servers. The practical advantage of Little's law is that you only need to know two of the parameters to estimate the third. For example, consider the manager of a motor vehicle licensing facility who receives many complaints about the time people must spend either having their licenses renewed or getting new license plates. It would be difficult to obtain data on the times individual customers spend at the facility. However, the manager can have an assistant monitor the number of people who arrive at the facility each hour and compute the average (λ). The manager also could periodically count the number of people in the sitting area and at the stations being served and compute the average (L). Using Little's law, the manager can then estimate W, the average time each customer spent in the facility. For example, if 40 customers arrive per hour and the average number of customers being served or waiting is 30, the average time each customer spends in the facility can be computed as

$$\text{Average time in the facility} = W = \frac{L \text{ customers}}{\lambda \text{ customers/hour}} = \frac{30}{40} = 0.75 \text{ hour, or } \textbf{45} \text{ minutes}$$

If the time a customer spends at the facility is unreasonable, the manager can focus on either adding capacity or improving the work methods to reduce the time spent serving the customers.

Likewise, Little's law can be used for manufacturing processes. Suppose that a production manager knows the average time a unit of product spends at a manufacturing process (W) and the average number of units per hour that arrive at the process (λ). The production manager can then estimate the average work-in-process (L) using Little's law. *Work-in-process* (WIP) consists of items, such as components or assemblies, needed to produce a final product in manufacturing. For example, if the average time a gear case used for an outboard marine motor spends at a machine center is 3 hours,

Cars line up at the Triborough Bridge toll, New York City. This is an example of a multiple-channel, single-phase system where some channels are devoted to special services.

and an average of five gear cases arrive at the machine center per hour, the average number of gear cases waiting and being processed (or work-in-process) at the machine center can be calculated as

$$\text{Work-in-process} = L = \lambda W = (5 \text{ gear cases/hour})(3 \text{ hours}) = \textbf{15 gear cases}$$

Knowing the relationship between the arrival rate, the lead time, and the work-in-process, the manager has a basis for measuring the effects of process improvements on the work-in-process at the facility. For example, adding some capacity to a bottleneck in the process can reduce the average lead time of the product at the process, thereby reducing the work-in-process inventory.

Even though Little's law is applicable in many situations in both service and manufacturing environments, it is not applicable in situations where the customer population is finite, which we address next.

Finite-Source Model

We now consider a situation in which all but one of the assumptions of the single-server model are appropriate. In this case, the customer population is finite, having only N potential customers. If N is greater than 30 customers, the single-server model with the assumption of an infinite customer population is adequate. Otherwise, the finite-source model is the one to use.

EXAMPLE B.6	Analyzing Maintenance Costs with the Finite-Source Model

The Worthington Gear Company installed a bank of 10 robots about three years ago. The robots greatly increased the firm's labor productivity, but recently attention has focused on maintenance. The firm does no preventive maintenance on the robots because of the variability in the breakdown distribution. Each machine has an exponential breakdown (or interarrival) distribution with an average time between failures of 200 hours. Each machine hour lost to downtime costs $30, which means that the firm has to react quickly to machine failure. The firm employs one maintenance person, who needs 10 hours on average to fix a robot. Actual maintenance times are exponentially distributed. The wage rate is $10 per hour for the maintenance person, who can be put to work productively elsewhere when not fixing robots. Determine the daily cost of labor and robot downtime.

MyOMLab

Tutor B.3 in MyOMLab provides a new example to practice the finite-source model.

SOLUTION

The *finite-source model* is appropriate for this analysis because the customer population consists of only 10 machines and the other assumptions are satisfied. Here, $\lambda = 1/200$, or 0.005 break-down per hour, and $\mu = 1/10 = 0.10$ robot per hour. To calculate the cost of labor and robot downtime, we need to estimate the average utilization of the maintenance person and L, the average number of robots in the maintenance system at any time. Either OM Explorer or POM for Windows can be used to help with the calculations. Figure B.6 shows the results for the Worthington Gear Problem using the *Waiting-Lines* Solver

MyOMLab

Active Model B.3 in MyOMLab provides additional insight on the finite-source model and its uses for this problem.

from OM Explorer. The results show that the maintenance person is utilized only **46.2** percent of the time, and the average number of robots waiting in line or being repaired is **0.76** robot. However, a failed robot will spend an average of **16.43** hours in the repair system, of which 6.43 hours of that time is spent waiting for service. While an individual robot may spend more than two days with the maintenance person, the maintenance person has a lot of idle time with a utilization rate of only **42.6** percent. That is why there is only an average of 0.76 robot being maintained at any point of time.

FIGURE B.6 ▶
Waiting-Lines Solver for Finite-Source Model

Customers	10
Arrival Rate (λ)	0.005
Service Rate (μ)	0.1

Probability of zero customers in the system (P_0)	0.5380
Probability of [fewer than ▼] 0 customers in the system	#N/A
Average utilization of the server (p)	0.4620
Average number of customers in the system (L)	0.7593
Average number of customers in line (L_q)	0.2972
Average waiting/service time in the system (W)	16.4330
Average waiting time in line (W_q)	6.4330

The daily cost of labor and robot downtime is

Labor cost: ($10/hour)(8 hours/day)(0.462 utilization) $= \$ \ 36.96$

Idle robot cost: (0.76 robot)($30/robot hour)(8 hours/day) $= \underline{\ \ 182.40}$

Total daily cost $= \mathbf{\$219.36}$

DECISION POINT

The labor cost for robot repair is only 20 percent of the idle cost of the robots. Management might consider having a second repair person on call in the event two or more robots are waiting for repair at the same time.

Waiting Lines and Simulation

For each of the problems we analyzed with the waiting-line models, the arrivals had a Poisson distribution (or exponential interarrival times), the service times had an exponential distribution, the service facilities had a simple arrangement, the waiting line was unlimited, and the priority discipline was first-come, first-served. Waiting-line theory has been used to develop other models in which these criteria are not met, but these models are complex. For example, POM for Windows includes a finite system-size model in which limits can be placed on the size of the system (waiting line and server capacity). It also has several models that relax assumptions on the service time distribution. Nonetheless, many times the nature of the customer population, the constraints on the line, the priority rule, the service-time distribution, and the arrangement of the facilities are such that waiting-line theory is no longer useful. In these cases, simulation often is used. MyOMLab Supplement E, "Simulation," discusses simulation programming languages and powerful PC-based packages. Here we illustrate process simulation with the SimQuick software (also provided in MyOMLab).

SimQuick

SimQuick is an easy-to-use package that is simply an Excel spreadsheet with some macros. Models can be created for a variety of simple processes, such as waiting lines, inventory control, and projects. Here, we consider the passenger security process at one terminal of a medium-sized airport between the hours of 8 A.M. and 10 A.M. The process works as follows. Passengers arriving at the security area immediately enter a single line. After waiting in line, each passenger goes through one of two inspection stations, which involves walking through a metal detector and running any carry-on baggage through a scanner. After

Passengers go through a TSA, security checkpoint screening at Boston International Airport, Boston Massachusetts. The airport security process is a multi-channel, multi phase system.

completing this inspection, 10 percent of the passengers are randomly selected for an additional inspection, which involves a pat-down and a more thorough search of the person's carry-on baggage. Two stations handle this additional inspection, and selected passengers go through only one of them. Management is interested in examining the effect of increasing the percentage of passengers who undergo the second inspection. In particular, they want to compare the waiting times for the second inspection when 10 percent, then 15 percent, and then 20 percent of the passengers are randomly selected for this inspection. Management also wants to know how opening a third station for the second inspection would affect these waiting times.

A first step in simulating this process with SimQuick is to draw a flowchart of the process using SimQuick's building blocks. SimQuick has five building blocks that can be combined in a wide variety of ways. Four of these types are used to model this process. An *entrance* is used to model the arrival of passengers at the security process. A *buffer* is used to model each of the two waiting lines, one before each type of inspection, as well as the passengers that have finished the process. Each of the four inspection stations is modeled with a *workstation*. Finally, the random selection of passengers for the second inspection is modeled with a *decision point*. Figure B.7 shows the flowchart.

Information describing each building block is entered into SimQuick tables. In this model, three key types of information are entered: (1) when people arrive at the entrance, (2) how long inspections take at the four stations, and (3) what percentage of passengers are randomly selected for the additional inspection. All of this information must be entered into SimQuick in the form of statistical distributions. The first two types of information are determined by observing the real process from 8 A.M. and 10 A.M. The third type of information is a policy decision (10 percent, 15 percent, or 20 percent).

The original model is run 30 times, simulating the arrival of passengers during the hours from 8 A.M. to 10 A.M. Statistics are collected by SimQuick and summarized. Figure B.8 provides some key results for the model of the present process as output by SimQuick (many other statistics are collected, but not displayed here).

The numbers shown are averages across the 30 simulations. The number 237.23 is the average number of passengers that enter line 1 during the simulated two hours. The two mean inventory statistics tell us, on average, 5.97 simulated passengers were standing in line 1 and 0.10 standing in line 2. The two statistics on *cycle time*, interpreted here as the time a passenger spends in one or more SimQuick building blocks, tell us that the simulated passengers in line 1 waited an average of 3.12 minutes, while those in line 2 waited 0.53 minutes. The final inventory statistic tells us that, on average, 224.57 simulated passengers passed through the security process in the simulated two hours. The next step is to change the percentage of simulated passengers selected for the second inspection to 15 percent, and then to 20 percent, and rerun the model. Of course, these process changes will increase the average waiting time for the second inspection, but by how much? The final step is to rerun these simulations with one more workstation and see its effect on the waiting time for the second inspection. All the details for this model (as well as many others) appear in the book *SimQuick: Process Simulation with Excel*, which is included, along with the SimQuick software, in MyOMLab.

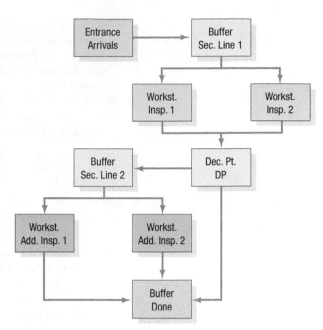

▲ **FIGURE B.7**
Flowchart of Passenger Security Process

Element Types	Element Names	Statistics	Overall Means
Entrance(s)	Door	Objects entering process	237.23
Buffer(s)	Line 1	Mean inventory	5.97
		Mean cycle time	3.12
	Line 2	Mean inventory	0.10
		Mean cycle time	0.53
	Done	Final inventory	224.57

▲ **FIGURE B.8**
Simulation Results of Passenger Security Process

MyOMLab

Decision Areas for Management

After analyzing a waiting-line problem, management can improve the service system by making changes in one or more of the following areas.

1. *Arrival Rates.* Management often can affect the rate of customer arrivals, λ, through advertising, special promotions, or differential pricing. For example, hotels in the Caribbean will reduce their room rates during the hot, rainy season to attract more customers and increase their utilization.

2. *Number of Service Facilities.* By increasing the number of service facilities, such as tool cribs, toll booths, or bank tellers, or by dedicating some facilities in a phase to a unique set of services, management can increase system capacity.

3. *Number of Phases.* Managers can decide to allocate service tasks to sequential phases if they determine that two sequential service facilities may be more efficient than one. For instance, in assembly lines a decision concerns the number of phases or workers needed along the assembly line. Determining the number of workers needed on the line also involves assigning a certain set of work elements to each one. Changing the facility arrangement can increase the service rate, μ, of each facility and the capacity of the system.

4. *Number of Servers per Facility.* Managers can influence the service rate by assigning more than one person to a service facility.

5. *Server Efficiency.* By adjusting the capital-to-labor ratio, devising improved work methods, or instituting incentive programs, management can increase the efficiency of servers assigned to a service facility. Such changes are reflected in μ.

6. *Priority Rule.* Managers set the priority rule to be used, decide whether to have a different priority rule for each service facility, and decide whether to allow preemption (and, if so, under what conditions). Such decisions affect the waiting times of the customers and the utilization of the servers.

7. *Line Arrangement.* Managers can influence customer waiting times and server utilization by deciding whether to have a single line or a line for each facility in a given phase of service.

Obviously, these factors are interrelated. An adjustment in the customer arrival rate might have to be accompanied by an increase in the service rate, λ, in some way. Decisions about the number of facilities, the number of phases, and waiting-line arrangements also are related.

LEARNING GOALS IN REVIEW

Learning Goal	Guidelines for Review	MyOMLab Resources
1 Identify the structure of waiting lines in real situations.	The section "Structure of Waiting-Line Problems," pp. 160–164, defines the four elements of every waiting-line problem. Figures B.1, B.2, and B.3 depict these elements and various service facility arrangements.	
2 Use the single-server, multiple-server, and finite-source models to analyze operations and estimate the operating characteristics of a process.	See the section "Using Waiting-Line Models to Analyze Operations," pp. 164–170, for a description and demonstration of these three models. Examples B.3, B.4, and the Solved Problem at the end of the supplement apply the single-server model. Example B.5 shows the multiple-server model and Example B.6 applies the finite-source model. In addition, Examples B.3 through B.6 show how to obtain estimates for the important operating characteristics of processes using waiting-line models.	**Active Model Exercises:** B.1: Single-Server Waiting-Line Model; B.2: Multi-Server Model with Costs; B.3: Finite Source Model with Costs **OM Explorer Solvers:** Single-Server Waiting-Line Model; Multi-Server Model; Finite Source Model **OM Explorer Tutors:** B.1: Single-Server Waiting-Line Model; B.2: Multi-Server Model; B.3: Finite Source Model **POM for Windows:** B.1: Single-Server Waiting-Line Model; B.2: Multi-Server Model with Costs; B.3: Finite Source Model with Costs; B.4: Finite System-Size Model
3 Describe the situations where simulation should be used for waiting-line analysis and the nature of the information that can be obtained.	The section "Waiting Lines and Simulation," pp. 170–171, explains when simulation must be used and discusses an example that demonstrates the nature of the managerial information that can be obtained from that analysis.	**Online Text:** SimQuick: Process Simulation with Excel, 2e
4 Explain how waiting-line models can be used to make managerial decisions.	The section "Decision Areas for Management," pp. 171–172, describes seven decision areas that can be analyzed with waiting-line models.	

Key Equations

Structure of Waiting-Line Problems

1. Customer arrival Poisson distribution:

$$P_n = \frac{(\lambda T)^n}{n!} e^{-\lambda T}$$

2. Service time exponential distribution:

$$P(t \leq T) = 1 - e^{-\mu T}$$

Using Waiting-Line Models to Analyze Operations

3. Average utilization of the system:

$$\rho = \frac{\lambda}{\mu}$$

4. Probability that n customers are in the system:

$$P_n = (1 - \rho)\rho^n$$

5. Probability that zero customers are in the system:

$$P_0 = 1 - \rho$$

6. Average number of customers in the service system:

$$L = \frac{\lambda}{\mu - \lambda}$$

7. Average number of customers in the waiting line:

$$L_q = \rho L$$

8. Average time spent in the system, including service:

$$W = \frac{1}{\mu - \lambda}$$

9. Average waiting time in line:

$$W_q = \rho W$$

10. Little's Law

$$L = \lambda W$$

Key Terms

channel 161	phase 161	service facility 160
customer population 160	preemptive discipline 163	service system 160
interarrival times 163	priority rule 160	waiting line 159
Little's law 168		

Solved Problem

MyOMLab Video

A photographer takes passport pictures at an average rate of 20 pictures per hour. The photographer must wait until the customer smiles, so the time to take a picture is exponentially distributed. Customers arrive at a Poisson-distributed average rate of 19 customers per hour.

a. What is the utilization of the photographer?

b. How much time will the average customer spend with the photographer?

SOLUTION

a. The assumptions in the problem statement are consistent with a single-server model. Utilization is

$$\rho = \frac{\lambda}{\mu} = \frac{19}{20} = \mathbf{0.95}$$

b. The average customer time spent with the photographer is

$$W = \frac{1}{\mu - \lambda} = \frac{1}{20 - 19} = \mathbf{1} \text{ hour}$$

Problems

The OM Explorer and POM for Windows software is available to all students using the 11th edition of this textbook. Go to **http://www.pearsonhighered.com/krajewski** to download these computer packages. If you purchased MyOMLab, you also have access to Active Models software and significant help in doing the following problems. Check with your instructor on how best to use these resources. In many cases, the instructor wants you to understand how to do the calculations by hand. At the least, the software provides a check on your calculations. When calculations are particularly complex and the goal is interpreting the results in making decisions, the software entirely replaces the manual calculations.

Structure of Waiting-Line Problems

1. Wingard Credit Union is redesigning the entryway into its bank of ATM machines. Management is trying to conceptually understand the interarrival of individuals, which has been described to them as following a Poisson distribution. If on an average, two customers arrive per minute randomly during busy times, calculate the probability that during a specific minute, no customers arrive. Calculate the probability that between one and four customers arrive.

2. Wingard Credit Union (from Problem 1) is also interested in understanding how long customers spend in front of the ATMs. Customer service times follow an Exponential distribution, with an average customer taking 1.5 minutes to complete a transaction. Calculate the probability that a customer will take less than half a minute. Additionally, calculate the probability that a customer will take more than 3 minutes.

Using Waiting-Line Models to Analyze Operations

3. The Solomon, Smith, and Samson law firm produces many legal documents that must be word processed for clients and the firm. Requests average eight pages of documents per hour, and they arrive according to a Poisson distribution. The secretary can word process 10 pages per hour on average according to an exponential distribution.

   a. What is the average utilization rate of the secretary?

   b. What is the probability that more than four pages are waiting or being word processed?

   c. What is the average number of pages waiting to be word processed?

4. Benny's Arcade has six video game machines. The average time between machine failures is 50 hours. Jimmy, the maintenance engineer, can repair a machine in 15 hours on average. The machines have an exponential failure distribution, and Jimmy has an exponential service-time distribution.

   a. What is Jimmy's utilization?

   b. What is the average number of machines out of service, that is, waiting to be repaired or being repaired?

   c. What is the average time a machine is out of service?

5. Moore, Aiken, and Payne is a critical care dental clinic serving the emergency needs of the general public on a first-come, first-served basis. The clinic has five dental chairs, three of which are currently staffed by a dentist. Patients in distress arrive at the rate of five per hour, according to a Poisson distribution, and do not balk or renege. The average time required for an emergency treatment is 30 minutes, according to an exponential distribution. Use POM for Windows or OM Explorer to answer the following questions:

   a. If the clinic manager would like to ensure that patients do not spend more than 15 minutes on average waiting to see the dentist, are three dentists on staff adequate? If not, how many more dentists are required?

b. From the current state of three dentists on staff, what is the change in each of the following operating characteristics when a fourth dentist is placed on staff:

■ Average utilization

■ Average number of customers in line

■ Average number of customers in the system

c. From the current state of three dentists on staff, what is the change in each of the following operating characteristics when a fifth dentist is placed on staff:

■ Average utilization

■ Average number of customers in line

■ Average number of customers in the system

6. Fantastic Styling Salon is run by three stylists, Jenny Perez, Jill Sloan, and Jerry Tiller, each capable of serving four customers per hour, on average. Use POM for Windows or OM Explorer to answer the following questions:

During busy periods of the day, when nine customers on average arrive per hour, all three stylists are on staff.

a. If all customers wait in a common line for the next available stylist, how long would a customer wait in line, on average, before being served?

b. Suppose that each customer wants to be served by a specific stylist, 1/3 want Perez, 1/3 want Sloan, 1/3 want Tiller. How long would a customer wait in line, on average, before being served?

During less busy periods of the day, when six customers on average arrive per hour, only Perez and Sloan are on staff.

c. If all customers wait in a common line for the next available stylist, how long would a customer wait in line, on average, before being served?

d. Suppose that each customer wants to be served by a specific stylist, 60 percent want Perez and 40 percent want Sloan. How long would a customer wait in line, on average, before being served by Perez? By Sloan? Overall?

7. You are the manager of a local bank where three tellers provide services to customers. On average, each teller takes 3 minutes to serve a customer. Customers arrive, on average, at a rate of 50 per hour. Having recently received complaints from some customers that they waited a long time before being served, your boss asks you to evaluate the service system. Specifically, you must provide answers to the following questions:

a. What is the average utilization of the three-teller service system?

b. What is the probability that no customers are being served by a teller or are waiting in line?

c. What is the average number of customers waiting in line?

d. On average, how long does a customer wait in line before being served?

e. On average, how many customers would be at a teller's station and in line?

8. Pasquist Water Company (PWC) operates a 24-hour facility designed to efficiently fill water-hauling tanker trucks. Trucks arrive randomly to the facility and wait in line to access a wellhead pump. Since trucks vary in size and the filling operation is manually performed by the truck driver, the time to fill a truck is also random.

a. If the manager of PWC uses the multiple-server model to calculate the operating characteristics of the facility's waiting line, list three assumptions she must make regarding the behavior of waiting trucks and the truck arrival process.

b. Suppose an average of 336 trucks arrive each day, there are four wellhead pumps, and each pump can serve an average of four trucks per hour.

■ What is the probability that exactly 10 trucks will arrive between 1:00 P.M. and 2:00 P.M. on any given day?

■ How likely is it that once a truck is in position at a wellhead, the filling time will be less than 15 minutes?

c. Contrast and comment on the performance differences between:

■ One waiting line feeding all four stations.

■ One waiting line feeding two wellhead pumps and a second waiting line feeding two other wellhead pumps. Assume that drivers cannot see each line and must choose randomly between them. Further, assume that once a choice is made, the driver cannot back out of the line.

9. The supervisor at the Precision Machine Shop wants to determine the staffing policy that minimizes total operating costs. The average arrival rate at the tool crib, where tools are dispensed to the workers, is eight machinists per hour. Each machinist's pay is $20 per hour. The supervisor can staff the crib either with a junior attendant who is paid $5 per hour and can process 10 arrivals per hour or with a senior attendant who is paid $12 per hour and can process 16 arrivals per hour. Which attendant should be selected, and what would be the total estimated hourly cost?

10. The daughter of the owner of a local hamburger restaurant is preparing to open a new fast-food restaurant called Hasty Burgers. Based on the arrival rates at her father's outlets, she expects customers to arrive at the drive-up window according to a Poisson distribution, with a mean of 20 customers per hour. The service rate is flexible; however, the service times are expected to follow an exponential distribution. The drive-in window is a single-server operation.

a. What service rate is needed to keep the average number of customers in the service system (waiting line and being served) to four?

b. For the service rate in part (a), what is the probability that more than four customers are in line and being served?

c. For the service rate in part (a), what is the average waiting time in line for each customer? Does this average seem satisfactory for a fast-food business?

11. The manager of a branch office of Banco Mexicali observed that during peak hours an average of 20 customers arrives per hour and that there is an average of four customers in the branch office at any time. How long does the average customer spend waiting in line and being serviced?

12. Paula Caplin is manager of a major electronics repair facility owned by Fisher Electronics. Recently, top management expressed concern over the growth in the number of repair jobs in process at the facility. The average arrival rate is 120 jobs per day. The average job spends four days at the facility.

a. What is the current work-in-process level at the facility?

b. Suppose that top management has put a limit of one-half the current level of work-in-process. What goal must Paula establish, and how might she accomplish it?

13. Failsafe Textiles employs three highly skilled maintenance workers who are responsible for repairing the numerous industrial robots used in its manufacturing process. A worker can fix one robot every 8 hours on average, with an exponential distribution. An average of one robot fails every 3 hours, according to a Poisson distribution. Each down robot costs the company $100.00 per hour in lost production. A new maintenance worker costs the company $80.00 per hour in salary, benefits, and equipment. Should the manager hire any new personnel? If so, how many people? What would you recommend to the manager, based on your analysis?

14. The College of Business and Public Administration at Benton University has a copy machine on each floor for faculty use. Heavy use of the five copy machines causes frequent failures. Maintenance records show that a machine fails every 2.5 days (or $\lambda = 0.40$ failure/day). The college has a maintenance contract with the authorized dealer of the copy machines. Because the copy machines fail so frequently, the dealer has assigned one person to the college to repair them. The person can repair an average of 2.5 machines per day. Using the finite-source model, answer the following questions:

a. What is the average utilization of the maintenance person?

b. On average, how many copy machines are being repaired or waiting to be repaired?

c. What is the average time spent by a copy machine in the repair system (waiting and being repaired)?

15. The manager of Vintage Time Video Machine Parlor is responsible for ensuring that all six of his machines are in good condition. Machines frequently need attention but can normally be returned to service quickly. On an average, each machine requires attention five times each hour. The manager averages 4 minutes per repair.

a. What percentage of each hour is the manager fixing machines?

b. On an average, how many machines are broken down and waiting for repair?

c. On an average, how many minutes in an hour are machines waiting for repair or being repaired?

16. Two nurses at Northwood Hospital's Cardiac Care Unit are assigned to care for eight patients. Nurses are responsible for administering medication, taking vital signs, and responding to frequent calls for assistance that can come either from the patient, or the equipment monitoring the patient's current condition. On an average, each patient requires attention three times each hour. Nurses average 6 minutes per patient visit.

a. What is the average utilization of the nursing staff?

b. On an average, how many patients are waiting for a nurse?

c. By how much would adding a third nurse reduce the patient waiting time?

17. You are in charge of a quarry that supplies sand and stone aggregates to your company's construction sites. Empty trucks from construction sites arrive at the quarry's huge piles of sand and stone aggregates and wait in line to enter the station, which can load either sand or aggregate. At the station, they are filled with material, weighed, checked out, and proceed to a construction site. Currently, nine empty trucks arrive per hour, on average. Once a truck has entered a loading station, it takes 6 minutes for it to be filled, weighed, and checked out. Concerned that trucks are spending too much time waiting and being filled, you are evaluating two alternatives to reduce the average time the trucks spend in the system. The first alternative is to add side boards to the trucks (so that more material could be loaded) and to add a helper at the loading station (so that filling time could be reduced) at a total cost of $50,000. The arrival rate of trucks would change to six per hour, and the filling time would be reduced to 4 minutes. The second alternative is to add another loading station identical to the current one at a cost of $80,000. The trucks would wait in a common line and the truck at the front of the line would move to the next available station.

Which alternative would you recommend if you want to reduce the current average time the trucks spend in the system, including service?

5

CONSTRAINT MANAGEMENT

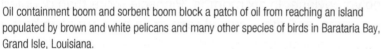

Oil containment boom and sorbent boom block a patch of oil from reaching an island populated by brown and white pelicans and many other species of birds in Barataria Bay, Grand Isle, Louisiana.

British Petroleum Oil Spill in Gulf of Mexico

British Petroleum (BP) is one of the world's leading international oil, gas, and petrochemical products company that provides a diverse range of products and services across the hydrocarbon value chain. It has operations in around 80 countries, 83,900 employees, and revenues of $377 billion. It operates over 17,500 retail sites. On April 20, 2010, there was an explosion and fire on Transocean Ltd's Deepwater Horizon drilling rig that had been licensed to BP. It sank two days later in 5,000 feet of water, and released as many as 4.9 billion barrels of oil into the Gulf of Mexico before the damaged well was finally capped in mid-July 2010. The resulting oil spill closed down fisheries and threatened the delicate coastline and its fragile ecosystems. Pinnacle Strategies was one of the firms hired by BP to help in boosting the output of spill-fighting equipment like boats, ships, and rigs, as well as supplies of critical resources like containment booms, skimmers, and decontamination suits.

A boom is an inflatable floating device that can be used to trap oil downwind on a body of water. This oil can then be pumped into containers by skimming equipment. Limited production capacities of booms, however, represented a daunting challenge. Prestige Products in Walker, Michigan, could only make 500 feet of boom a day, whereas a single order of the size requested by BP would exceed the combined capacity of every boom manufacturer in the United States. Despite increasing the staff from 5 to 75 and raising production to 12,800 feet daily, the Prestige plant felt that it had reached its limit. That is where Ed Kincer from Pinnacle Strategies stepped in. He noticed that the boom was assembled in a flurry, with little to do in-between for several minutes. Cutters sliced boom by cutting one side, then walking 100 feet to cut the other side. Workers also sat idle while waiting for a welding machine. Waste occurred in the form of excessive walks, waiting for machines, and changing production rhythms. Kincer identified the constraints in the process, found ways to manage them, and more than tripled capacity. Prestige eventually ended up making more than a million feet of boom for BP.

Theory of constraints is the scientific approach that was used by Pinnacle to boost throughput for BP's other key suppliers as well. Kvichak Marine in Seattle quadrupled output of oil skimmers, while Illinois-based Elastec increased production from four skimmers a week to 26. Abasco, a Houston-based boom manufacturer, increased production by 20 percent due to rebalancing staff such that the welding operation kept going even during the breaks. At Supply Pro, a Texan manufacturer of absorbent boom, capacity increased several fold by using cellulose instead of scarce polypropylene. In six months, Pinnacle more than doubled the supply of skimmers, booms, and other critical resources by identifying bottlenecks at dozens of factories and working around them. These capacity enhancements throughout BP's supply chain ensured that lack of materials did not end up constraining the clean-up operations in the fight against the oil spill.

Source: Brown, A. "Theory of Constraints Tapped to Accelerate BP's Gulf of Mexico Cleanup." *Industry Week* (March 18, 2011); **http://www.newsweek.com/photo/2010/05/22/oil-spill-timeline.html**; **http://www.bp.com/** (July 25, 2014).

LEARNING GOALS *After reading this chapter, you should be able to:*

1 Explain the theory of constraints.

2 Identify and manage bottlenecks in service processes.

3 Identify and manage bottlenecks in manufacturing processes.

4 Apply the theory of constraints to product mix decisions.

5 Describe how to manage constraints in line processes and balance assembly lines.

constraint

Any factor that limits the performance of a system and restricts its output. In linear programming, a limitation that restricts the permissible choices for the decision variables.

bottleneck

A capacity constraint resource (CCR) whose available capacity limits the organization's ability to meet the product volume, product mix, or demand fluctuation required by the marketplace.

Suppose one of a firm's processes was recently reengineered, and yet results were disappointing. Costs were still high or customer satisfaction still low. What could be wrong? The answer might be constraints that remain in one or more steps in the firm's processes. A **constraint** is any factor that limits the performance of a system and restricts its output, while *capacity* is the maximum rate of output of a process or a system. When constraints exist at any step, as they did at suppliers of BP, capacity can become imbalanced—too high in some departments and too low in others. As a result, the overall performance of the system suffers.

Constraints can occur up or down the supply chain, with either the firm's suppliers or customers or within one of the firm's processes like service or product development or order fulfillment. Three kinds of constraints can generally be identified: physical (usually machine, labor, or workstation capacity or material shortages, but could be space or quality), market (demand is less than capacity), or managerial (policy, metrics, or mind-sets that create constraints that impede work flow). A **bottleneck**[1] is a special type of a constraint that relates to the capacity shortage of a process and is defined as any

---

[1]Under certain conditions, a bottleneck is also called a *capacity constrained resource* (CCR). The process with the least capacity is called a bottleneck if its output is less than the market demand, or called a CCR if it is the least capable resource in the system but still has higher capacity than the market demand.

resource whose available capacity limits the organization's ability to meet the service or product volume, product mix, or fluctuating requirements demanded by the marketplace. A business system or a process would have at least one constraint or a bottleneck; otherwise, its output would be limited only by market demand.

Firms must manage their constraints and make appropriate capacity choices at the individual-process level as well as at the organization level. Hence, this process involves inter-functional cooperation. Detailed decisions and choices made within each of these levels affect where resource constraints or bottlenecks show up, both within and across departmental lines. Relieving a bottleneck in one part of an organization might not have the desired effect unless a bottleneck in another part of the organization is also addressed. A bottleneck could be the sales department not getting enough sales or the loan department not processing loans fast enough. The constraint could be a lack of capital or equipment, or it could be planning and scheduling.

The experience of BP and other firms in the health care, banking, and manufacturing industries demonstrates how important managing constraints can be to an organization's future. Therefore managers throughout the organization must understand how to identify and manage bottlenecks in all types of processes, how to relate the capacity and performance measures of one process to another, and how to use that information to determine the firm's best service or product mix. This chapter explains how managers can best make these decisions.

The Theory of Constraints

The **theory of constraints (TOC)** is a systematic management approach that focuses on actively managing those constraints that impede a firm's progress toward its goal of maximizing profits and effectively using its resources. The theory was developed nearly three decades ago by Eli Goldratt, a well-known business systems analyst. It outlines a deliberate process for identifying and overcoming constraints. The process focuses not just on the efficiency of individual processes but also on the bottlenecks that constrain the system as a whole. Pinnacle Strategies in the opening vignette followed this theory to improve BP's operations.

TOC methods increase the firm's profits more effectively by focusing on making materials flow rapidly through the entire system. They help firms look at the big picture—how processes can be improved to increase overall work flows, and how inventory and workforce levels can be reduced while still effectively utilizing critical resources. To do this, it is important to understand the relevant performance and capacity measures at the operational level, as well as their relationship to the more broadly understood financial measures at the firm level. These measures and relationships, so critical in successfully applying the principles of the TOC, are defined in Table 5.1.

theory of constraints (TOC)

A systematic management approach that focuses on actively managing those constraints that impede a firm's progress toward its goal.

TABLE 5.1 | HOW THE FIRM'S OPERATIONAL MEASURES RELATE TO ITS FINANCIAL MEASURES

Operational Measures	TOC View	Relationship to Financial Measures
Inventory (I)	All the money invested in a system in purchasing things that it intends to sell	A decrease in I leads to an increase in net profit, ROI, and cash flow.
Throughput (T)	Rate at which a system generates money through sales	An increase in T leads to an increase in net profit, ROI, and cash flows.
Operating Expense (OE)	All the money a system spends to turn inventory into throughput	A decrease in OE leads to an increase in net profit, ROI, and cash flows.
Utilization (U)	The degree to which equipment, space, or workforce is currently being used; it is measured as the ratio of average output rate to maximum capacity, expressed as a percentage	An increase in U at the bottleneck leads to an increase in net profit, ROI, and cash flows.

According to the TOC view, every capital investment in the system, including machines and work-in-process materials, represents inventory because they could all potentially be sold to make money. Producing a product or a service that does not lead to a sale will not increase a firm's throughput, but will increase its inventory and operating expenses. It is always best to manage the system so that utilization at the bottleneck resource is maximized to maximize throughput.

Key Principles of the TOC

The chief concept behind the TOC is that the bottlenecks should be scheduled to maximize their throughput of services or products while adhering to promised completion dates. The underlying assumption is that demand is greater or equal to the capacity of the process that produces the service or product, otherwise instead of internal changes, marketing must work toward promoting increasing demand. For example, manufacturing a garden rake involves attaching a bow to the rake's head. Rake heads must be processed on the blanking press, welded to the bow, cleaned, and attached to the handle to make the rake, which is packaged and finally shipped to Sears, Home Depot, or Walmart, according to a specific delivery schedule. Suppose that the delivery commitments for all styles of rakes for the next month indicate that the welding station is loaded at 105 percent of its capacity, but that the other processes will be used at only 75 percent of their capacities. According to the TOC, the welding station is the bottleneck resource, whereas the blanking, cleaning, handle attaching, packaging, and shipping processes are non-bottleneck resources. Any idle time at the welding station must be eliminated to maximize throughput. Managers should therefore focus on the welding schedule.

Seven key principles of the TOC that revolve around the efficient use and scheduling of bottlenecks and improving flow and throughput are summarized in Table 5.2.

TABLE 5.2 | SEVEN KEY PRINCIPLES OF THE THEORY OF CONSTRAINTS

1. The focus should be on balancing flow, not on balancing capacity.

2. Maximizing the output and efficiency of every resource may not maximize the throughput of the entire system.

3. An hour lost at a bottleneck or a constrained resource is an hour lost for the whole system. In contrast, an hour saved at a non-bottleneck resource is a mirage, because it does not make the whole system more productive.

4. Inventory is needed only in front of the bottlenecks to prevent them from sitting idle and in front of assembly and shipping points to protect customer schedules. Building inventories elsewhere should be avoided.

5. Work, which can be materials, information to be processed, documents, or customers, should be released into the system only as frequently as the bottlenecks need it. Bottleneck flows should be equal to the market demand. Pacing everything to the slowest resource minimizes inventory and operating expenses.

6. Activating a non-bottleneck resource (using it for improved efficiency that does not increase throughput) is not the same as utilizing a bottleneck resource (that does lead to increased throughput). Activation of non-bottleneck resources cannot increase throughput, nor promote better performance on financial measures outlined in Table 5.1.

7. Every capital investment must be viewed from the perspective of its global impact on overall throughput (T), inventory (I), and operating expense (OE).

Practical application of the TOC involves the implementation of the following steps.

1. *Identify the System Bottleneck(s).* For the rake example, the bottleneck is the welding station because it is restricting the firm's ability to meet the shipping schedule and, hence, total value-added funds. Other ways of identifying the bottleneck will be looked at in more detail a little later in this chapter.

2. *Exploit the Bottleneck(s).* Create schedules that maximize the throughput of the bottleneck(s). For the rake example, schedule the welding station to maximize its utilization while meeting the shipping commitments to the extent possible. Also make sure that only good quality parts are passed on to the bottleneck.

3. *Subordinate All Other Decisions to Step 2.* Non-bottleneck resources should be scheduled to support the schedule of the bottleneck and not produce more than the bottleneck can handle. That is, the blanking press should not produce more than the welding station can handle, and the activities of the cleaning and subsequent operations should be based on the output rate of the welding station.

4. *Elevate the Bottleneck(s).* After the scheduling improvements in steps 1–3 have been exhausted, and the bottleneck is still a constraint to throughput, management should consider increasing the capacity of the bottleneck. For example, if the welding station is still a constraint after exhausting schedule improvements, consider increasing its capacity by adding another shift or another welding machine. Other mechanisms are also available for increasing bottleneck capacity, and we address them a little later.

5. *Do Not Let Inertia Set In.* Actions taken in steps 3 and 4 will improve the welder throughput and may alter the loads on other processes. Consequently, the system constraint(s) may shift. Then, the practical application of steps 1–4 must be repeated to identify and manage the new set of constraints.

Because of its potential for improving performance dramatically, many manufacturers have applied the principles of the TOC. All manufacturers implementing TOC principles can also dramatically change the mind-set of employees and managers. Instead of focusing solely on their own functions, they can see the "big picture" and where other improvements in the system might lie. A study shows that more than one third of winners and finalists of *Industry Week's* best manufacturing plants have extensively implemented TOC, while up to 80 percent make some use of it.

Managing Bottlenecks in Service Processes

Bottlenecks can both be internal or external to the firm, and typically represent a process, a step, or a workstation with the lowest capacity. **Throughput time** is the total elapsed time from the start to the finish of a job or a customer being processed at one or more work centers. Where a bottleneck lies in a given service or manufacturing process can be identified in two ways. A workstation in a process is a bottleneck if (1) it has the highest total time per unit processed, or (2) it has the highest average utilization and total workload.

Example 5.1 illustrates how a bottleneck step or activity can be identified for a loan approval process at a bank.

throughput time

Total elapsed time from the start to the finish of a job or a customer being processed at one or more work centers.

EXAMPLE 5.1	Identifying the Bottleneck in a Service Process

Managers at the First Community Bank are attempting to shorten the time it takes customers with approved loan applications to get their paperwork processed. The flowchart for this process, consisting of several different activities, each performed by a different bank employee, is shown in Figure 5.1. Approved loan applications first arrive at activity or Step 1, where they are checked for completeness and put in order. At Step 2, the loans are categorized into different classes according to the loan amount and whether they are being requested for personal or commercial reasons. While credit checking commences at Step 3, loan application data are entered in parallel into the information system for record-keeping purposes at Step 4. Finally, all paperwork for setting up the new loan is finished at Step 5. The time taken in minutes is given in parentheses.

Which single step is the bottleneck, assuming that market demand for loan applications exceeds the capacity of the process? The management is also interested in knowing the maximum number of approved loans this system can process in a 5-hour workday.

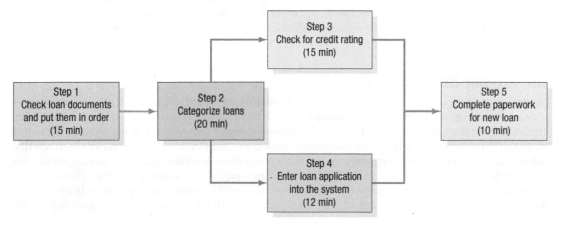

▲ FIGURE 5.1

Processing Credit Loan Applications at First Community Bank

SOLUTION

We define the bottleneck as Step 2, which has the highest time per loan processed. The throughput time to complete an approved loan application is 15 + 20 + max (15, 12) + 10 = **60** minutes. Although we assume no waiting time in front of any step, in practice such a smooth process flow is not always the case. So the actual time taken for completing an approved loan will be longer than 60 minutes due to nonuniform arrival of applications, variations in actual processing times, and the related factors.

The capacity for loan completions is derived by translating the "minutes per customer" at the bottleneck step to "customer per hour." At First Community Bank, it is three customers per hour because the bottleneck Step 2 can process only one customer every 20 minutes (60/3).

DECISION POINT

Step 2 is the bottleneck constraint. The bank will be able to complete a maximum of only three loan accounts per hour, or 15 new loan accounts in a 5-hour day. Management can increase the flow of loan applications by increasing the capacity of Step 2 up to the point where another step becomes the bottleneck.

Due to constrained resources like doctors, nurses, and equipment, patients wait for medical care in a crowded waiting room at South Central Family Health Center in Los Angeles, California.

A front-office process with high customer contact and divergence does not enjoy the simple line flows shown in Example 5.1. Its operations may serve many different customer types, and the demands on any one operation could vary considerably from one day to the next. Computing the average utilization of each operation can still identify bottlenecks. However, the variability in workload also creates *floating bottlenecks*. One week the mix of work may make operation 1 a bottleneck, and the next week it may make operation 3 the bottleneck. This type of variability increases the complexity of day-to-day scheduling. In this situation, management prefers lower utilization rates, which allow greater slack to absorb unexpected surges in demand.

TOC principles outlined here are fairly broad-based and widely applicable to many types of processes. They can be useful for evaluating individual processes as well as large systems for both manufacturers as well as service providers. Service organizations, such as Delta Airlines, United Airlines, and major hospitals across the United States, including the U.S. Air Force health care system, use the TOC to their advantage.

Managing Bottlenecks in Manufacturing Processes

Bottlenecks can exist in all types of manufacturing processes, including the job process, batch process, line process, and continuous process. Since these processes differ in their design, strategic intent, and allocation of resources (see Chapter 2, "Process Strategy and Analysis," for additional details), identification and management of bottlenecks will also differ accordingly with process type. We first discuss in this section issues surrounding management of bottlenecks in job and batch processes, while relegating constraint management in line processes for a later section.

Identifying Bottlenecks

Manufacturing processes often pose some complexities when identifying bottlenecks. If multiple services or products are involved, extra setup time at a workstation is usually needed to change over from one service or product to the next, which in turn increases the overload at the workstation being changed over. *Setup times* and their associated costs affect the size of the lots traveling through the job or batch processes. Management tries to reduce setup times because they represent unproductive time for workers or machines and thereby allow for smaller, more economic, batches. Nonetheless, whether setup times are significant or not, one way to identify a bottleneck operation is by its utilization. Example 5.2 illustrates how a bottleneck can be identified in a manufacturing setting where setups are negligible.

EXAMPLE 5.2	Identifying the Bottleneck in a Batch Process

Diablo Electronics manufactures four unique products (A, B, C, and D) that are fabricated and assembled in five different workstations (V, W, X, Y, and Z) using a small batch process. Each workstation is staffed by a worker who is dedicated to work a single shift per day at an assigned workstation. Batch setup times have been reduced to such an extent that they can be considered negligible. A flowchart denotes the path each product follows through the manufacturing process as shown in Figure 5.2, where each product's price, demand per week, and processing times per unit are indicated as well. Inverted triangles represent purchased parts and raw materials consumed per unit at different workstations. Diablo can make and sell up to the limit of its demand per week, and no penalties are incurred for not being able to meet all the demand.

Which of the five workstations (V, W, X, Y, or Z) has the highest utilization, and thus serves as the bottleneck for Diablo Electronics?

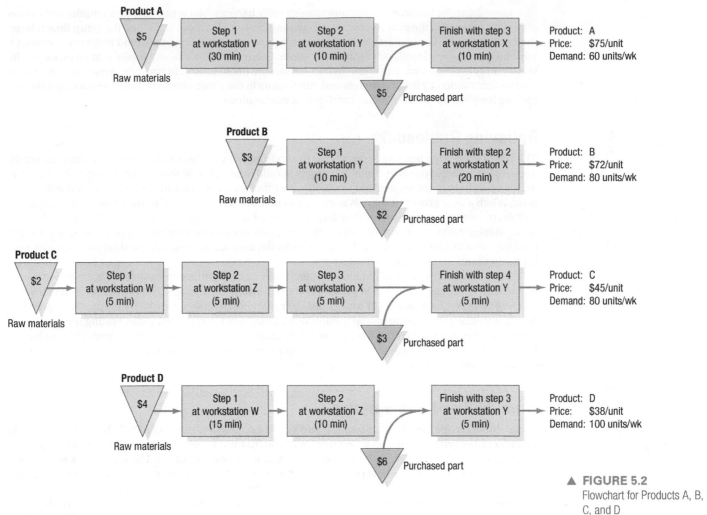

▲ FIGURE 5.2
Flowchart for Products A, B, C, and D

SOLUTION

Because the denominator in the utilization ratio is the same for every workstation, with one worker per machine at each step in the process, we can simply identify the bottleneck by computing aggregate workloads at each workstation.

The firm wants to satisfy as much of the product demand in a week as it can. Each week consists of 2,400 minutes of available production time. Multiplying the processing time at each station for a given product by the number of units demanded per week yields the workload represented by that product. These loads are summed across all products going through a workstation to arrive at the total load for the workstation, which is then compared with the others and the existing capacity of 2,400 minutes.

Workstation	Load from Product A	Load from Product B	Load from Product C	Load from Product D	Total Load (min)
V	60 × 30 = 1800	0	0	0	1,800
W	0	0	80 × 5 = 400	100 × 15 = 1,500	1,900
X	60 × 10 = 600	80 × 20 = 1,600	80 × 5 = 400	0	**2,600**
Y	60 × 10 = 600	80 × 10 = 800	80 × 5 = 400	100 × 5 = 500	2,300
Z	0	0	80 × 5 = 400	100 × 10 = 1,000	1,400

DECISION POINT

Workstation X is the bottleneck for Diablo Electronics because the aggregate workload at X is larger than the aggregate workloads of workstations V, W, Y, and Z and the maximum available capacity of 2,400 minutes per week.

Identifying the bottlenecks becomes considerably harder when setup times are lengthy and the degree of divergence in the process is greater than that shown in Example 5.2. When the setup time is large, the operation with the highest total time per unit processed would typically tend to be the bottleneck. Variability in the workloads will again likely create floating bottlenecks, especially if most processes involve multiple operations, and often their capacities are not identical. In practice, these bottlenecks can also be determined by asking workers and supervisors in the plant where the bottlenecks might lie, and looking for piled up material in front of different workstations.

Relieving Bottlenecks

The key to preserving bottleneck capacity is to carefully monitor short-term schedules and keep bottleneck resource as busy as is practical. Managers should minimize idle time at the bottlenecks caused by delays elsewhere in the system and make sure that the bottleneck has all the resources it needs to stay busy. When a changeover or setup is made at a bottleneck, the number of units or customers processed before the next changeover should be large compared to the number processed at less critical operations. Maximizing the number of units processed per setup means fewer setups per year and, thus, less total time lost to setups. The number of setups also depends on the required product variety; more variety necessitates more frequent changeovers.

The long-term capacity of bottleneck operations can be expanded in various ways. Investments can be made in new equipment and in brick-and-mortar facility expansions. The bottleneck's capacity also can be expanded by operating it more hours per week, such as by hiring more employees and going from a one-shift operation to multiple shifts, or by hiring more employees and operating the plant six or seven days per week versus five days per week. Managers also might relieve the bottleneck by redesigning the process, either through *process reengineering* or *process improvement*, or by purchasing additional machines that can handle more capacity.

Drum-Buffer-Rope Systems

drum-buffer-rope (DBR)

A planning and control system that regulates the flow of work-in-process materials at the bottleneck or the capacity constrained resource (CCR) in a productive system.

Drum-buffer-rope (DBR) is a planning and control system based on the TOC that is often used in manufacturing firms to plan and schedule production. It works by regulating the flow of work-in-process materials at the bottleneck or the capacity constrained resource (CCR). The bottleneck schedule is the *drum* because it sets the beat or the production rate for the entire plant and is linked to the market demand. The *buffer* is a time buffer that plans early flows to the bottleneck and thus protects it from disruption. It also ensures that the bottleneck is never starved for work. A finished-goods inventory buffer can also be placed in front of the shipping point to protect customer shipping schedules. Finally, the *rope* represents the tying of material release to the drumbeat, which is the rate at which the bottleneck controls the throughput of the entire plant. It is thus a communication device to ensure that raw material is not introduced into the system at a rate faster than what the bottleneck can handle. Completing the loop, *buffer management* constantly monitors the execution of incoming bottleneck work. Working together, the drum, the buffer, and the rope can help managers create a production schedule that reduces lead times and inventories while simultaneously increasing throughput and on-time delivery.

To better understand the DBR system, consider the schematic layout shown in Figure 5.3. Process B, with a capacity of only 500 units per week, is the bottleneck because the upstream Process A and downstream Process C have capacities of 800 units per week and 700 units per week, respectively, and the market demand is 650 units per week, on average. In this case, because the capacity at Process B is less than the market demand, it is the bottleneck. A constraint time buffer, which can be in the form of materials arriving earlier than needed, is placed right in front of the bottleneck (Process B). A shipping buffer, in the form of finished goods inventory, can also be placed prior to the shipping schedule to protect customer orders that are firm. Finally, a rope ties the material release schedule to match the schedule, or drum beat, at the bottleneck. The material flow is pulled forward by the drumbeat prior to the bottleneck, while it is pushed downstream toward the customer subsequent to the bottleneck.

▼ **FIGURE 5.3**
Drum-Buffer-Rope System

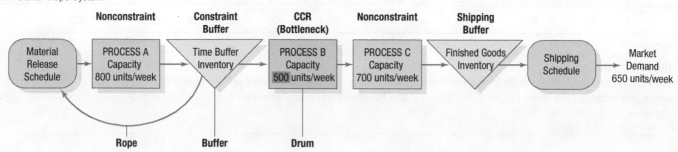

DBR specifically strives to improve throughput by better utilizing the bottleneck resource and protecting it from disruption through the time buffer and protective buffer capacity elsewhere. So while the process batch in the DBR is any size that minimizes setups and improves utilization at the bottleneck, at nonconstrained resources the process batches are equal to what is needed for production at that time. The material can consequently be released in small batches known as transfer batches at the release point, which then combine at the constraint buffer to make a full process batch at the bottleneck. Transfer batches can be as small as one unit each, to allow a downstream workstation to start work on a batch before it is completely finished at the prior process. Using transfer batches typically facilitates a reduction in overall lead time.

DBR can be an effective system to use when the product the firm produces is relatively simple and the production process has more line flows. Planning is greatly simplified in this case and primarily revolves around scheduling the constrained resource and triggering other points to meet that bottleneck's schedule. Effectively implementing a DBR system requires an understanding of the TOC principles. However, such a system can be utilized in many different kinds of manufacturing and service organizations, either by itself or in conjunction with other planning and control systems.

Applying the Theory of Constraints to Product Mix Decisions

Managers might be tempted to produce the products with the highest contribution margins or unit sales. *Contribution margin* is the amount each product contributes to profits and overhead; no fixed costs are considered when making the product mix decision. We call this approach the *traditional method*. The problem with this approach is that the firm's actual throughput and overall profitability depend more upon the contribution margin generated at the bottleneck than by the contribution margin of each individual product produced. We call this latter approach the *bottleneck method*. Example 5.3 illustrates both of these methods.

Linear programming (see Supplement D) could also be used to find the best product mix in Example 5.3. It must be noted, however, that the problem in Example 5.3 does not involve significant

EXAMPLE 5.3	Determining the Product Mix Using Contribution Margin

The senior management at Diablo Electronics (see Example 5.2) wants to improve profitability by accepting the right set of orders, and so collected some additional financial data. Variable overhead costs are $8,500 per week. Each worker is paid $18 per hour and is paid for an entire week, regardless of how much the worker is used. Consequently, labor costs are fixed expenses. The plant operates one 8-hour shift per day, or 40 hours each week. Currently, decisions are made using the traditional method, which is to accept as much of the highest contribution margin product as possible (up to the limit of its demand), followed by the next highest contribution margin product, and so on until no more capacity is available. Pedro Rodriguez, the newly hired production supervisor, is knowledgeable about the TOC and bottleneck-based scheduling. He believes that profitability can indeed be improved if bottleneck resources were exploited to determine the product mix. What is the change in profits if, instead of the traditional method used by Diablo Electronics, the bottleneck method advocated by Pedro is used to select the product mix?

SOLUTION

Decision Rule 1: Traditional Method

Select the best product mix according to the highest overall contribution margin of each product.

Step 1. Calculate the contribution margin per unit of each product as shown here.

	A	B	C	D
Price	$75.00	$72.00	$45.00	$38.00
Raw material and purchased parts	−10.00	−5.00	−5.00	−10.00
= Contribution margin	$65.00	$67.00	$40.00	$28.00

When ordered from highest to lowest, the contribution margin per unit sequence of these products is B, A, C, D.

Step 2. Allocate resources V, W, X, Y, and Z to the products in the order decided in Step 1. Satisfy each demand until the bottleneck resource (workstation X) is encountered. Subtract minutes away from 2,400 minutes available for each week at each stage.

Work Center	Minutes at the Start	Minutes Left After Making 80 B	Minutes Left After Making 60 A	Can Only Make 40 C	Can Still Make 100 D
V	2,400	2,400	600	600	600
W	2,400	2,400	2,400	2,200	700
X	2,400	800	200	0	0
Y	2,400	1,600	1,000	800	300
Z	2,400	2,400	2,400	2,200	1,200

The best product mix according to this traditional approach is then 60 A, 80 B, 40 C, and 100 D.

Step 3. Compute profitability for the selected product mix.

Profits		
Revenue	$(60 \times \$75) + (80 \times \$72) + (40 \times \$45) + (100 \times \$38)$	$= \$15,860$
Materials	$(60 \times \$10) + (80 \times \$5) + (40 \times \$5) + (100 \times \$10)$	$= -\$2,200$
Labor	$(5 \text{ workers}) \times (8 \text{ hours/day}) \times (5 \text{ days/week}) \times (18/\text{hour})$	$= -\$3,600$
Overhead		$= -\$8,500$
Profit		$= \$1,560$

Manufacturing the product mix of 60 A, 80 B, 40 C, and 100 D will yield a profit of **$1,560** per week.

Decision Rule 2: Bottleneck Method

Select the best product mix according to the dollar contribution margin per minute of processing time at the bottleneck workstation X. This method would take advantage of the principles outlined in the TOC and get the most dollar benefit from the bottleneck.

Step 1. Calculate the contribution margin/minute of processing time at bottleneck workstation X:

	Product A	Product B	Product C	Product D
Contribution margin	$65.00	$67.00	$40.00	$28.00
Time at bottleneck	10 minutes	20 minutes	5 minutes	0 minutes
Contribution margin per minute	$6.50	$3.35	$8.00	Not defined

When ordered from highest to lowest contribution margin/minute at the bottleneck, the manufacturing sequence of these products is D, C, A, B, which is reverse of the earlier order. Product D is scheduled first because it does not consume any resources at the bottleneck.

Step 2. Allocate resources V, W, X, Y, and Z to the products in the order decided in Step 1. Satisfy each demand until the bottleneck resource (workstation X) is encountered. Subtract minutes away from 2,400 minutes available for each week at each stage.

Work Center	Minutes at the Start	Minutes Left After Making 100 D	Minutes Left After Making 80 C	Minutes Left After Making 60 A	Can Only Make 70 B
V	2,400	2,400	2,400	600	600
W	2,400	900	500	500	500
X	2,400	2,400	2,000	1,400	0
Y	2,400	1,900	1,500	900	200
Z	2,400	1,400	1,000	1,000	1,000

The best product mix according to this bottleneck-based approach is then 60 A, 70 B, 80 C, and 100 D.

Step 3. Compute profitability for the selected product mix.

Profits		
Revenue	$(60 \times \$75) + (70 \times \$72) + (80 \times \$45) + (100 \times \$38)$	$= \$16,940$
Materials	$(60 \times \$10) + (70 \times \$5) + (80 \times \$5) + (100 \times \$10)$	$= -\$2,350$
Labor	$(5 \text{ workers}) \times (8 \text{ hours/day}) \times (5 \text{ days/week}) \times (18/\text{hour})$	$= -\$3,600$
Overhead		$= -\$8,500$
Profit		$= \ \ \$2,490$

Manufacturing the product mix of 60 A, 70 B, 80 C, and 100 D will yield a profit of **$2,490** per week.

DECISION POINT

By focusing on the bottleneck resources in accepting customer orders and determining the product mix, the sequence in which products are selected for production is reversed from **B, A, C, D** to **D, C, A, B**. Consequently, the product mix is changed from 60 A, 80 B, 40 C, and 100 D to 60 A, 70 B, 80 C, and 100 D. The increase in profits by using the bottleneck method is **$930,** ($2,490 − $1,560), or almost 60 percent over the traditional approach.

setup times. Otherwise, they must be taken into consideration for not only identifying the bottleneck but also in determining the product mix. The experiential learning exercise of Min-Yo Garment Company at the end of this chapter provides an interesting illustration of how the product mix can be determined when setup times are significant. In this way, the principles behind the TOC can be exploited for making better decisions about a firm's most profitable product mix.

Managing Constraints in Line Processes

As noted in Chapter 2, "Process Strategy and Analysis," products created by a line process include the assembly of computers, automobiles, appliances, and toys. Such assembly lines can exist in providing services as well. For instance, putting together a standardized hamburger with a fixed sequence of steps is akin to operating an assembly line. In this section, we explain in greater detail how constraints can be managed for line processes.

Line Balancing

Line balancing is the assignment of work to stations in a line process so as to achieve the desired output rate with the smallest number of workstations. Normally, one worker is assigned to a station. Thus, the line that produces at the desired pace with the fewest workers is the most efficient one. Achieving this goal is much like the TOC, because both approaches are concerned about bottlenecks. Line balancing differs in how it addresses bottlenecks. Rather than (1) taking on new customer orders to best use bottleneck capacity or (2) scheduling so that bottleneck resources are conserved, line balancing takes a third approach. It (3) creates workstations with workloads as evenly balanced as possible. It seeks to create workstations so that the capacity utilization for the bottleneck is not much higher than for the other workstations in the line. Another difference is that line balancing applies only to line processes that do assembly work, or to work that can be bundled in many ways to create the jobs for each workstation in the line. The latter situation can be found both in manufacturing and service settings.

The goal of line balancing is to obtain workstations with well-balanced workloads (e.g., every station takes roughly 3 minutes per customer in a cafeteria line with different food stations). The analyst begins by separating the work into **work elements**, which are the smallest units of work that can be performed independently. The analyst then obtains the time standard for each element and identifies the work elements, called **immediate predecessors**, which must be done before the next element can begin.

Precedence Diagram   Most lines must satisfy some technological precedence requirements; that is, certain work elements must be done before the next can begin. However, most lines also allow for some latitude and more than one sequence of operations. To help you better visualize immediate predecessors,

line balancing

The assignment of work to stations in a line process so as to achieve the desired output rate with the smallest number of workstations.

work elements

The smallest units of work that can be performed independently.

immediate predecessors

Work elements that must be done before the next element can begin.

FIGURE 5.4 ▶
Diagramming Activity
Relationships

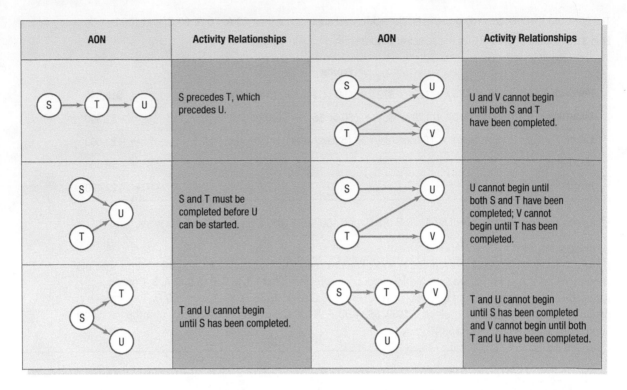

AON	Activity Relationships	AON	Activity Relationships
S → T → U	S precedes T, which precedes U.	S, T → U, V (crossed)	U and V cannot begin until both S and T have been completed.
S, T → U	S and T must be completed before U can be started.	S → U; T → U, V	U cannot begin until both S and T have been completed; V cannot begin until T has been completed.
S → T, U	T and U cannot begin until S has been completed.	S → T → V; S → U → V	T and U cannot begin until S has been completed and V cannot begin until both T and U have been completed.

precedence diagram

A diagram that allows one to visualize immediate predecessors better; work elements are denoted by circles, with the time required to perform the work shown below each circle.

let us run through the construction of a **precedence diagram**. The diagramming approach we use in this text is referred to as the **activity-on-node (AON) network**, in which nodes represent activities and arcs represent the precedence relationships between them. More specifically, we denote the work elements by nodes or circles, with the time required to perform the work shown below each circle. Arrows or arcs lead from immediate predecessors to the next work element. Some diagramming conventions must be used for AON networks. In cases of multiple activities with no predecessors, it is usual to show them emanating from a common node called *start*. For multiple activities with no successors, it is usual to show them connected to a node called *finish*. Figure 5.4 shows how to diagram several commonly encountered activity relationships.

Example 5.4 illustrates a manufacturing process, but a back office line-flow process in a service setting can be approached similarly.

EXAMPLE 5.4 | **Constructing a Precedence Diagram**

Green Grass, Inc., a manufacturer of lawn and garden equipment, is designing an assembly line to produce a new fertilizer spreader, the Big Broadcaster. Using the following information on the production process, construct a precedence diagram for the Big Broadcaster.

Work Element	Description	Time (sec)	Immediate Predecessor(s)
A	Bolt leg frame to hopper	40	None
B	Insert impeller shaft	30	A
C	Attach axle	50	A
D	Attach agitator	40	B
E	Attach drive wheel	6	B
F	Attach free wheel	25	C
G	Mount lower post	15	C
H	Attach controls	20	D, E
I	Mount nameplate	18	F, G
		Total 244	

SOLUTION

Figure 5.5 shows the complete diagram. We begin with work element A, which has no immediate predecessors. Next, we add elements B and C, for which element A is the only immediate predecessor. After entering time standards and arrows showing precedence, we add elements D and E, and so on. The diagram simplifies interpretation. Work element F, for example, can be done anywhere on the line after element C is completed. However, element I must await completion of elements F and G.

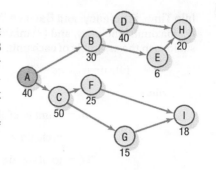

◀ **FIGURE 5.5**
Precedence Diagram for Assembling the Big Broadcaster

MyOMLab Animation

DECISION POINT

Management now has enough information to develop a line-flow layout that clusters work elements to form workstations, with a goal being to balance the workloads and, in the process, minimize the number of workstations required.

Desired Output Rate The goal of line balancing is to match the output rate to the staffing or production plan. For example, if the plan calls for 4,800 units or customers per week and the line operates 80 hours per week, the desired output rate ideally would be 60 units or customers (4,800/80) per hour. Matching output to the plan ensures on-time delivery and prevents buildup of unwanted inventory or customer delays. However, managers should avoid rebalancing a line too frequently because each time a line is rebalanced many workers' jobs on the line must be redesigned, temporarily hurting productivity and sometimes even requiring a new detailed layout for some stations.

Cycle Time After determining the desired output rate for a line, the analyst can calculate the line's cycle time. A line's **cycle time** is the maximum time allowed for work on a unit at each station.[2] If the time required for work elements at a station exceeds the line's cycle time, the station will be a bottleneck, preventing the line from reaching its desired output rate. The target cycle time is the reciprocal of the desired hourly output rate:

$$c = \frac{1}{r}$$

where

c = cycle time in hours per unit

r = desired output rate in units per hour

For example, if the line's desired output rate is 60 units per hour, the cycle time is $c = 1/60$ hour per unit, or 1 minute.

Theoretical Minimum To achieve the desired output rate, managers use line balancing to assign every work element to a station, making sure to satisfy all precedence requirements and to minimize the number of stations, n, formed. If each station is operated by a different worker, minimizing n also maximizes worker productivity. Perfect balance is achieved when the sum of the work-element times at each station equals the cycle time, c, and no station has any idle time. For example, if the sum of each station's work-element times is 1 minute, which is also the cycle time, the line achieves perfect balance. Although perfect balance usually is unachievable in practice, owing to the unevenness of work-element times and the inflexibility of precedence requirements, it sets a benchmark, or goal, for the smallest number of stations possible. The **theoretical minimum (TM)** for the number of stations is

$$\text{TM} = \frac{\Sigma t}{c}$$

where

Σt = total time required to assemble each unit (the sum of all work-element standard times)

c = cycle time

For example, if the sum of the work-element times is 15 minutes and the cycle time is 1 minute, TM = 15/1, or 15 stations. Any fractional values obtained for TM are rounded up because fractional stations are impossible.

activity-on-node (AON) network

An approach used to create a network diagram, in which nodes represent activities and arcs represent the precedence relationships between them.

cycle time

The maximum time allowed for work on a unit at each station.

theoretical minimum (TM)

A benchmark or goal for the smallest number of stations possible, where the total time required to assemble each unit (the sum of all work-element standard times) is divided by the cycle time.

---

[2]Except in the context of line balancing, *cycle time* has a different meaning. It is the elapsed time between starting and completing a job. Some researchers and practitioners prefer the term *lead time* in these non-line balancing applications.

Idle Time, Efficiency, and Balance Delay   Minimizing n automatically ensures (1) minimal idle time, (2) maximal efficiency, and (3) minimal balance delay. Idle time is the total unproductive time for all stations in the assembly of each unit:

$$\text{Idle time} = nc - \Sigma t$$

where

$$n = \text{number of stations}$$

$$c = \text{cycle time}$$

$$\Sigma t = \text{total standard time required to assemble each unit}$$

Efficiency is the ratio of productive time to total time, expressed as a percent:

$$\text{Efficiency (\%)} = \frac{\Sigma t}{nc}(100)$$

balance delay

The amount by which efficiency falls short of 100 percent.

Balance delay is the amount by which efficiency falls short of 100 percent:

$$\text{Balance delay (\%)} = 100 - \text{Efficiency}$$

As long as c is fixed, we can optimize all three goals by minimizing n.

EXAMPLE 5.5	**Calculating the Cycle Time, Theoretical Minimum, and Efficiency**

MyOMLab

Tutor 5.1 in MyOMLab provides another example to calculate these line-balancing measures.

Green Grass's plant manager just received marketing's latest forecasts of Big Broadcaster sales for the next year. She wants its production line to be designed to make 2,400 spreaders per week for at least the next three months. The plant will operate 40 hours per week.

a. What should be the line's cycle time?

b. What is the smallest number of workstations that she could hope for in designing the line for this cycle time?

c. Suppose that she finds a solution that requires only five stations. What would be the line's efficiency?

SOLUTION

a. First, convert the desired output rate (2,400 units per week) to an hourly rate by dividing the weekly output rate by 40 hours per week to get $r = 60$ units per hour. Then, the cycle time is

$$c = 1/r = 1/60 \text{ (hour/unit)} = 1 \text{ minute/unit} = \textbf{60} \text{ seconds/unit}$$

b. Now, calculate the theoretical minimum for the number of stations by dividing the total time, Σt, by the cycle time, $c = 60$ seconds. Assuming perfect balance, we have

$$\text{TM} = \frac{\Sigma t}{c} = \frac{244 \text{ seconds}}{60 \text{ seconds}} = 4.067 \text{ or } \textbf{5} \text{ stations}$$

c. Now, calculate the efficiency of a five-station solution, assuming for now that one can be found:

$$\text{Efficiency (\%)} = \frac{\Sigma t}{nc}(100) = \frac{244}{5(60)}(100) = \textbf{81.3}\%$$

DECISION POINT

If the manager finds a solution with five stations that satisfies all precedence constraints, then that is the optimal solution; it has the minimum number of stations possible. However, the efficiency (sometimes called the *theoretical maximum efficiency*) will be only 81.3 percent. Perhaps the line should be operated less than 40 hours per week (thereby adjusting the cycle time) and the employees transferred to other kinds of work when the line does not operate.

Finding a Solution   Often, many assembly-line solutions are possible, even for such simple problems as Green Grass's. The goal is to cluster the work elements into workstations so that (1) the number of workstations required is minimized, and (2) the precedence and cycle-time requirements are not violated. The idea is to assign work elements to workstations subject to the precedence requirements so that the work content for the station is equal (or nearly so, but less than) the cycle time for the line. In this way, the number of workstations will be minimized.

Here we use the trial-and-error method to find a solution, although commercial software packages are also available. Most of these packages use different decision rules in picking which work element to assign next to a workstation being created. The ones used by POM for Windows are described in Table 5.3. The solutions can be examined for improvement, because there is no guarantee that they are optimal or even feasible. Some work elements cannot be assigned to the same station, some changes can be made to reduce the number of stations, or some shifts can provide better balance between stations.

TABLE 5.3 | HEURISTIC DECISION RULES IN ASSIGNING THE NEXT WORK ELEMENT TO A WORKSTATION BEING CREATED

Create one station at a time. For the station now being created, identify the unassigned work elements that qualify for assignment: They are candidates if

1. All of their predecessors have been assigned to this station or stations already created.

2. Adding them to the workstation being created will not create a workload that exceeds the cycle time.

Decision Rule	Logic
Longest work element	Picking the candidate with the longest time to complete is an effort to fit in the most difficult elements first, leaving the ones with short times to "fill out" the station.
Shortest work element	This rule is the opposite of the longest work element rule because it gives preference in workstation assignments to those work elements that are quicker. It can be tried because no single rule guarantees the best solution. It might provide another solution for the planner to consider.
Most followers	When picking the next work element to assign to a station being created, choose the element that has the most *followers* (due to precedence requirements). In Figure 5.5, item C has three followers (F, G, and I) whereas item D has only one follower (H). This rule seeks to maintain flexibility so that good choices remain for creating the last few workstations at the end of the line.
Fewest followers	Picking the candidate with the fewest followers is the opposite of the most followers rule.

▼ **FIGURE 5.6**
Big Broadcaster Precedence Diagram Solution

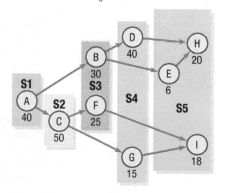

Figure 5.6 shows a solution that creates just five workstations. We know that five is the minimum possible, because five is the theoretical minimum found in Example 5.5 All of the precedence and cycle-time requirements are also satisfied. Consequently, the solution is optimal for this problem. Each worker at each station must perform the work elements in the proper sequence. For example, workstation **S5** consists of one worker who will perform work elements E, H, and I on each unit that comes along the assembly line. The processing time per unit is 44 seconds (6 + 20 + 18) which does not exceed the cycle time of 60 seconds (see Example 5.5). Furthermore, the immediate predecessors of these three work elements are assigned to this workstation or upstream workstations, so their precedence requirements are satisfied. The worker at workstation S5 can do element I at any time but will not start element H until element E is finished.

Rebalancing the Assembly Line

While the product mix or demand volumes do not change as rapidly for line processes as for job or batch processes, the load can shift between work centers in a line as the end product being assembled is changed from one product to another, or when the total output rate of the line is altered. Constraints arising out of such actions can be managed by either rebalancing the line, or as illustrated by Chrysler in Managerial Practice 5.1, by shifting workers across different lines in the manufacturing plant to reduce waste and create a more balanced allocation of workloads and available worker capacity.

Managerial Considerations

In addition to balancing a line for a given cycle time, managers have four other considerations: (1) pacing, (2) behavioral factors, (3) number of models produced, and (4) different cycle times.

MANAGERIAL PRACTICE 5.1   Assembly Line Balancing at Chrysler

Headquartered in Auburn Hills, Michigan, Chrysler Corporation was founded in 1925 and is currently owned by the Italian automaker Fiat since January 21, 2014. It is the smallest of the "Big Three" automobile manufacturers in the United States, and had sales of over 1.8 million vehicles in 2013. Especially well known for its industry leading pioneering designs of minivans, Chrysler was interested in reducing costs and improving efficiency through a better balancing of its assembly lines in the trim, chassis, and final (TCF) center. Such was the case at one of its manufacturing plants in Windsor, Ontario, which builds the popular minivan models Chrysler Town & Country and Dodge Grand Caravan among others. Instead of actually stopping the lines and experimenting with new ideas, the improvement team felt that it would be best to build simulation models that can identify system bottlenecks and evaluate the impact of line design and scheduling decisions associated with different cycle times, mean time to repair, and mean time between failures.

Using a commercially available Simul8 software, the simulation models included data on how many operators were available for each line, sequence and mix of products, cycle times for different delivery rates, and size of line buffers. After validating the model with historical data, the best performing as well as the worst performing bottlenecked lines were identified based on the process flow layouts of the system. Using different scenarios, it was determined that slowing down the best performing lines would not adversely affect the system throughput, which in turn would allow some workers to be transferred away to eliminate waste. Steve Lin, the throughput specialist at Chrysler leading the project, commented, "We reduced two people a shift on one line. So, with three shifts a day we effectively reduced manpower costs by six on that line, saving us $600,000 per year." This idea of using the simulation

Rebecca Cook/Reuters/Corbis

A Chrysler auto worker uses an ergo-arm to load the seats into Chrysler minivans during the production launch of the new 2011 Dodge Grand Caravan's and Chrysler Town & Country minivans at the Windsor Assembly Plant in Windsor, Ontario.

tool for slowing down the best performing lines to improve efficiency has now been rolled out to eight other Chrysler assembly plants, with cumulative savings projected to be around $5 million.

Understanding the impact of bottlenecks, cycle times, repair times, and product mix on the efficiency and throughputs of assembly lines can really pay off in managing line processes.

Source: http://en.wikipedia.org/wiki/Chrysler; http://en.wikipedia.org/wiki/Windsor_Assembly; http://www.simul8.com/our_customers/case_studies/Chrysler_line_balancing_case_study.pdf (July 29, 2014).

---

pacing

The movement of product from one station to the next as soon as the cycle time has elapsed.

Pacing   The movement of product from one station to the next as soon as the cycle time has elapsed is called **pacing**. Pacing manufacturing processes allows materials handling to be automated and requires less inventory storage area. However, it is less flexible in handling unexpected delays that require either slowing down the entire line or pulling the unfinished work off the line to be completed later.

Behavioral Factors   The most controversial aspect of line-flow layouts is behavioral response. Studies show that installing production lines increases absenteeism, turnover, and grievances. Paced production and high specialization (say, cycle times of less than 2 minutes) lower job satisfaction. Workers generally favor inventory buffers as a means of avoiding mechanical pacing. One study even showed that productivity increased on unpaced lines.

mixed-model line

A production line that produces several items belonging to the same family.

Number of Models Produced   A line that produces several items belonging to the same family is called a **mixed-model line**. In contrast, a single-model line produces one model with no variations. Mixed-model production enables a plant to achieve both high-volume production *and* product variety. However, it complicates scheduling and increases the need for good communication about the specific parts to be produced at each station.

Cycle Times   A line's cycle time depends on the desired output rate (or sometimes on the maximum number of workstations allowed). In turn, the maximum line efficiency varies considerably with the cycle time selected. Thus, exploring a range of cycle times makes sense. A manager might go with a particularly efficient solution even if it does not match the desired output rate. The manager can compensate for the mismatch by varying the number of hours the line operates through overtime, extending shifts, or adding shifts. Multiple lines might even be the answer.

LEARNING GOALS IN REVIEW

Learning Goal	Guidelines for Review	MyOMLab Resources
1 Explain the theory of constraints.	The section on "The Theory of Constraints (TOC)," pp. 179–181 explains that constraints or bottlenecks can exist in the form of internal resources or market demand in both manufacturing and service organizations, and in turn play an important role in determining system performance. Review opening vignette on BP Oil Spill cleanup for an application of TOC, and Table 5.2 for its key principles.	**Video:** Constraint Management at Southwest Airlines
2 Identify and manage bottlenecks in service processes	The section "Managing Bottlenecks in Service Processes," pp. 181–182, shows you how to identify bottlenecks in manufacturing firms. Review Solved Problem 1 on p. 193 for an illustration of this approach.	
3 Identify and manage bottlenecks in manufacturing processes	The section "Managing Bottlenecks in Manufacturing Processes," pp. 182–185, shows you how to identify and relieve bottlenecks in manufacturing firms, and links them to a planning and control system known as drum-buffer-rope on p. xxx.	
4 Applying the theory of constraints to product mix decisions.	The section "Applying Theory of Constraints to Product Mix Decisions," pp. 185–187, to understand how using a bottleneck based method for allocating resources and determining the product mix leads to greater profits. The experiential learning exercise Min-Yo Garment Company on p. 202 illustrates how product mix can be determined when set up times are significant.	**OM Explorer Solver:** Min-Yo Garment Company spreadsheet
5 Describe how to manage constraints in line processes and balance assembly lines.	The section "Managing Constraints in Line Processes," pp. 187–192, shows you how to balance assembly lines and create workstations. It also positions assembly line balancing is a special form of a constraint in managing a line process within both manufacturing and services, and can also be an effective mechanism for matching output to a plan and running such processes more efficiently. Review Solved Problem 2 on p. 194 for an application of line-balancing principles.	**OM Explorer Tutor:** 5.1: Calculate Line-Balancing Measures **POM for Windows:** Line Balancing

Key Equations

Managing Constraints in Line Processes

1. Cycle time: $c = \dfrac{1}{r}$

2. Theoretical minimum number of workstations: $TM = \dfrac{\Sigma t}{c}$

3. Idle time: $nc - \Sigma t$

4. Efficiency (%): $\dfrac{\Sigma t}{nc}(100)$

5. Balance delay (%): $100 - \text{Efficiency}$

Key Terms

activity-on-node (AON) network 189
balance delay 190
bottleneck 178
constraint 178
cycle time 189

drum-buffer-rope (DBR) 184
immediate predecessors 187
line balancing 187
mixed-model line 192
pacing 192

precedence diagram 188
theoretical minimum (TM) 189
theory of constraints (TOC) 179
throughput time 181
work elements 187

Solved Problem 1

Bill's Car Wash offers two types of washes: Standard and Deluxe. The process flow for both types of customers is shown in Figure 5.7. Both wash types are first processed through Steps A1 and A2. The Standard wash then goes through Steps A3 and A4 while the Deluxe is processed through Steps A5,

A6, and A7. Both offerings finish at the drying station (A8). The numbers in parentheses indicate the minutes it takes for that activity to process a customer.

FIGURE 5.7 ▶
Precedence Diagram

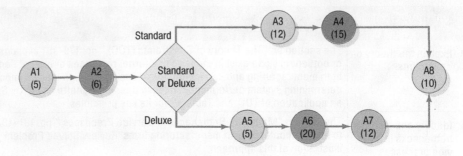

a. Which step is the bottleneck for the Standard car wash process? For the Deluxe car wash process?

b. What is the capacity (measured as customers served per hour) of Bill's Car Wash to process Standard and Deluxe customers? Assume that no customers are waiting at Step A1, A2, or A8.

c. If 60 percent of the customers are Standard and 40 percent are Deluxe, what is the average capacity of the car wash in customers per hour?

d. Where would you expect Standard wash customers to experience waiting lines, assuming that new customers are always entering the shop and that no Deluxe customers are in the shop? Where would the Deluxe customers have to wait, assuming no Standard customers?

SOLUTION

a. Step A4 is the bottleneck for the Standard car wash process, and Step A6 is the bottleneck for the Deluxe car wash process, because these steps take the longest time in the flow.

b. The capacity for Standard washes is four customers per hour because the bottleneck Step A4 can process one customer every 15 minutes (60/15). The capacity for Deluxe car washes is three customers per hour (60/20). These capacities are derived by translating the "minutes per customer" of each bottleneck activity to "customers per hour."

c. The average capacity of the car wash is $(0.60 \times 4) + (0.40 \times 3) = $ **3.6** customers per hour.

d. Standard wash customers would wait before Steps A1, A2, A3, and A4 because the activities that immediately precede them have a higher rate of output (i.e., smaller processing times). Deluxe wash customers would experience a wait in front of Steps A1, A2, and A6 for the same reasons. A1 is included for both types of washes because the arrival rate of customers could always exceed the capacity of A1.

Solved Problem 2

MyOMLab Video

A company is setting up an assembly line to produce 192 units per 8-hour shift. The following table identifies the work elements, times, and immediate predecessors:

Work Element	Time (Sec)	Immediate Predecessor(s)
A	40	None
B	80	A
C	30	D, E, F
D	25	B
E	20	B
F	15	B
G	120	A
H	145	G
I	130	H
J	115	C, I
	Total 720	

a. What is the desired cycle time (in seconds)?

b. What is the theoretical minimum number of stations?

c. Use trial and error to work out a solution, and show your solution on a precedence diagram.

d. What are the efficiency and balance delay of the solution found?

SOLUTION

a. Substituting in the cycle-time formula, we get

$$c = \frac{1}{r} = \frac{8 \text{ hours}}{192 \text{ units}}(3{,}600 \text{ seconds / hour}) = \mathbf{150} \text{ seconds / unit}$$

b. The sum of the work-element times is 720 seconds, so

$$TM = \frac{\Sigma t}{c} = \frac{720 \text{ seconds / unit}}{150 \text{ seconds / unit-station}} = 4.8 \text{ or } \mathbf{5} \text{ stations}$$

which may not be achievable.

c. The precedence diagram is shown in Figure 5.8. Each row in the following table shows work elements assigned to each of the five workstations in the proposed solution.

d. Calculating the efficiency, we get

$$\text{Efficiency} = \frac{\Sigma t}{nc}(100) = \frac{720 \text{ seconds / unit}}{5[150 \text{ seconds / unit}]}(100) = \mathbf{96\%}$$

Thus, the balance delay is only 4 percent (100–96).

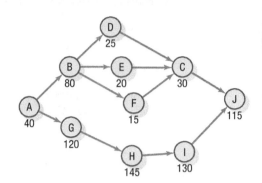

▲ FIGURE 5.8
Precedence Diagram

Station	Candidate(s)	Choice	Work-Element Time (Sec)	Cumulative Time (Sec)	Idle Time ($c = 150$ Sec)
S1	A	A	40	40	110
	B	B	80	120	30
	D, E, F	D	25	145	5
S2	E, F, G	G	120	120	30
	E, F	E	20	140	10
S3	F, H	H	145	145	5
S4	F, I	I	130	130	20
	F	F	15	145	5
S5	C	C	30	30	120
	J	J	115	145	5

Discussion Questions

1. Take a process that you encounter on a daily basis, such as the lunch cafeteria or the journey from your home to school or work, and identify the bottlenecks that limit the throughput of this process.

2. Using the same process as in question 1, identify conditions that would lead to the bottlenecks changing or shifting away from the existing bottleneck.

3. How could the efficiency of the redesigned process be improved further?

Problems

The OM Explorer and POM for Windows software is available to all students using the 11th edition of this textbook. Go to **http://www.pearsonhighered.com/krajewski** to download these computer packages. If you purchased MyOMLab, you also have access to Active Models software and significant help in doing the following problems. Check with your instructor on how best

to use these resources. In many cases, the instructor wants you to understand how to do the calculations by hand. At the least, the software provides a check on your calculations. When calculations are particularly complex and the goal is interpreting the results in making decision, the software entirely replaces the manual calculations.

Managing Bottlenecks in Service Processes

1. Bill's Barbershop has two barbers available to cut customers' hair. Both barbers provide roughly the same experience and skill, but one is just a little bit slower than the other. The process flow in Figure 5.9 shows that all customers go through Steps B1 and B2 and then can be served at either of the two barbers at Step B3. The process ends for all customers at Step B4. The numbers in parentheses indicate the minutes it takes that activity to process a customer.

   a. How long does it take the average customer to complete this process?

   b. What single activity is the bottleneck for the entire process?

   c. How many customers can this process serve in an hour?

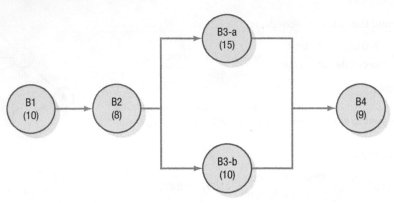

▲ **FIGURE 5.9**
Process Flow for Bill's Barbershop

2. Melissa's Photo Studio offers both individual and group portrait options. The process flow diagram in Figure 5.10 shows that all customers must first register and then pay at one of two cashiers. Then, depending on whether they want a single or group portrait they go to different rooms. Finally, everyone picks up their own finished portrait.

   a. How long does it take to complete the entire process for a group portrait?

   b. What single activity is the bottleneck for the entire process, assuming the process receives equal amounts of both groups and individuals?

   c. What is the capacity of the bottleneck for both groups and individuals?

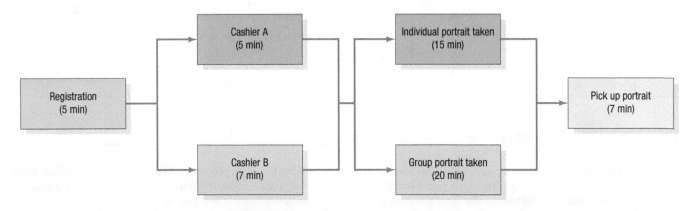

▲ **FIGURE 5.10**
Process Flow for Melissa's Photo Studio

3. Figure 5.11 details the process flow for two types of customers who enter Barbara's Boutique shop for customized dress alterations. After Step T1, Type A customers proceed to Step T2 and then to any of the three workstations at T3, followed by Steps T4 and T7. After Step T1, Type B customers proceed to Step T5 and then Steps T6 and T7. The numbers in parentheses are the minutes it takes to process a customer.

   a. What is the capacity of Barbara's shop in terms of the numbers of Type A customers who can be served in an hour? Assume no customers are waiting at Steps T1 or T7.

   b. If 30 percent of the customers are Type A customers and 70 percent are Type B customers, what is the average capacity of Barbara's shop in customers per hour?

c. Assuming that the arrival rate is greater than five customers per hour, when would you expect Type A customers to experience waiting lines, assuming no Type B customers in the shop? Where would the Type B customers have to wait, assuming no Type A customers?

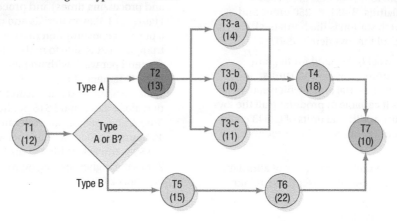

▲ **FIGURE 5.11**
Process Flow for Barbara's Boutique Customers

Managing Bottlenecks in Manufacturing Processes

4. Canine Kernels Company (CKC) manufactures two different types of dog chew toys (A and B, sold in 1,000-count boxes) that are manufactured and assembled on three different workstations (W, X, and Y) using a small-batch process (see Figure 5.12). Batch setup times are negligible. The flowchart denotes the path each product follows through the manufacturing process, and each product's price, demand per week, and processing times per unit are indicated as well. Purchased parts and raw materials consumed during production are represented by inverted triangles. CKC can make and sell up to the limit of its demand per week; no penalties are incurred for not being able to meet all the demand. Each workstation is staffed by a worker who is dedicated to work on that workstation alone, and is paid $6 per hour. Total labor costs per week are fixed. Variable overhead costs are $3,500/week. The plant operates one 8-hour shift per day, or 40 hours/week. Which of the three workstations, W, X, or Y, has the highest aggregate workload, and thus serves as the bottleneck for CKC?

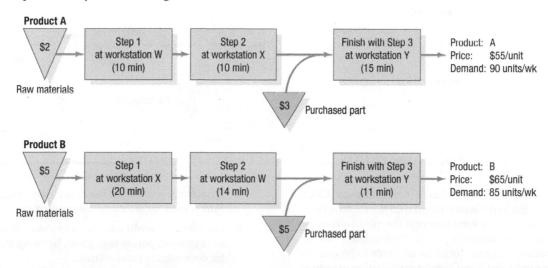

▲ **FIGURE 5.12**
Flowchart for Canine Kernels Company (CKC)

5. Super Fun Industries manufactures four top-selling toys code named A-148, B-356, B-457, and C-843. The following table shows how long it takes to process each toy through each required station. Note that all times are in minutes. Super Fun's manufacturing plant is open 16 hours a day, 5 days a week, and 8 hours on Saturday.

	A-148	B-356	B-457	C-843
Processing Time Station 1	6 min	5 min	0 min	8 min
Processing Time Station 2	4 min	4 min	5 min	2 min
Processing Time Station 3	5 min	7 min	4 min	2 min
Processing Time Station 4	3 min	0 min	10 min	1 min

a. If only toy A-148 is produced during a specific week, how many units could be produced?

b. If weekly demand for the four products are A-148 = 200 units, B-356 = 250 units, B-457 = 250 units, and C-843 = 300 units, which station is the bottleneck, and is it capable of producing all the toys demanded?

6. Returning to problem 5, if weekly demand for the four products are A-148 = 100 units, B-356 = 400 units, B-457 = 250 units, and C-843 = 100 units, which station is the bottleneck now, and is it capable of producing all the toys demanded? If so, how many additional units of C-843 could be produced? Under this condition, does the bottleneck change?

7. Yost-Perry Industries (YPI) manufactures a mix of affordable guitars (A, B, C) that are fabricated and assembled at four different processing stations (W, X, Y, Z). The operation is a batch process with small setup times that can be considered negligible. The product information (price, weekly demand, and processing times) and process sequences are shown in Figure 5.13. Raw materials and purchased parts (shown as a per-unit consumption rate) are represented by inverted triangles. YPI is able to make and sell up to the limit of its demand per week with no penalties incurred for not meeting the full demand. Each workstation is staffed by one highly skilled worker who is dedicated to work on that workstation alone and is paid $15 per hour. The plant operates one 8-hour shift per day and operates on a 5-day work week (i.e., 40 hours of production per person per week). Overhead costs are $9,000/week. Which of the four workstations, W, X, Y, or Z, has the highest aggregate workload, and thus serves as the bottleneck for YPI?

FIGURE 5.13 ▶
Flowchart for Yost-Perry Industries (YPI)

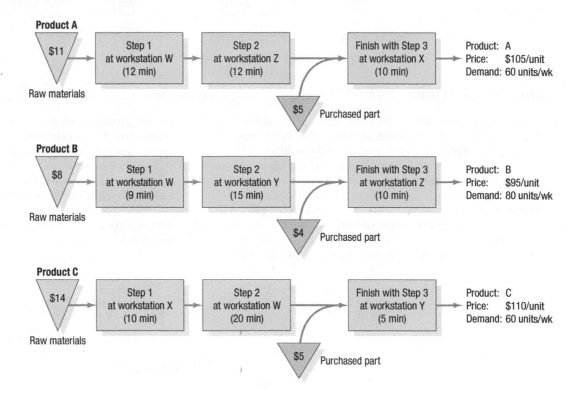

Applying the Theory of Constraints to Product Mix Decisions

8. The senior management at Canine Kernels Company (CKC) mentioned in problem 4 is concerned with the existing capacity limitation, so they want to accept the mix of orders that maximizes the company's profits. Traditionally, CKC has utilized a method whereby decisions are made to produce as much of the product with the highest contribution margin as possible (up to the limit of its demand), followed by the next highest contribution margin product, and so on until no more capacity is available. Because capacity is limited, choosing the proper product mix is crucial. Troy Hendrix, the newly hired production supervisor, is an avid follower of the TOC philosophy and the bottleneck method for scheduling. He believes that profitability can indeed be approved if bottleneck resources are exploited to determine the product mix.

a. What is the profit if the traditional contribution margin method is used for determining CKC's product mix?

b. What is the profit if the bottleneck method advocated by Troy is used for selecting the product mix?

c. Calculate the profit gain, both in absolute dollars as well as in terms of percentage gains, by using TOC principles for determining product mix.

9. Yost-Perry Industries' (YPI) senior management team wants to improve the profitability of the firm by accepting the right set of orders. Currently, decisions are made using the traditional method, which is to accept as much of the highest contribution margin product as possible (up to the limit of its demand), followed by the next highest contribution margin product, and so on until all available capacity is utilized. Because the firm cannot satisfy all the demand, the product mix must be chosen carefully. Jay Perry, the newly promoted production supervisor, is knowledgeable about the TOC and the bottleneck-based method for scheduling. He believes

that profitability can indeed be improved if bottleneck re-sources are exploited to determine the product mix. What is the change in profits if, instead of the traditional method that YPI has used thus far, the bottleneck method advocated by Jay is used for selecting the product mix?

10. A.J.'s Wildlife Emporium manufactures two unique birdfeeders (Deluxe and Super Duper) that are manufactured and assembled in up to three different workstations (X, Y, Z) using a small batch process. Each of the products is produced according to the flowchart in Figure 5.14. Additionally, the flowchart indicates each product's price, weekly demand, and processing times per unit. Batch setup times are negligible. A.J. can make and sell up to the limit of its weekly demand and there are no penalties for not being able to meet all of the demand. Each workstation is staffed by a worker who is dedicated to work on that workstation alone and is paid $16 per hour. The plant operates 40 hours per week, with no overtime. Overhead costs are $2,000 per week. Based on the information provided, as well as the information contained in the flowchart, answer the following questions.

a. Using the traditional method, which bases decisions solely on a product's contribution to profits and overhead, what is the optimal product mix and what is the overall profitability?

b. Using the bottleneck-based method, what is the optimal product mix and what is the overall profitability?

11. Cooper River Glass Works (CRGW) produces four different models of desk lamps as shown in Figure 5.15. The operations manager knows that total monthly demand exceeds the capacity available for production. Thus, she is interested in determining the product mix which will maximize profits. Each model's price, routing, processing times, and material cost are provided in Figure 5.15. Demand next month is estimated to be 200 units of model Alpha, 250 units of model Bravo, 150 units of model Charlie, and 225 units of model Delta. CRGW operates only one 8-hour shift per day and is scheduled to work 20 days next month (no overtime). Further, each station requires a 10 percent capacity cushion.

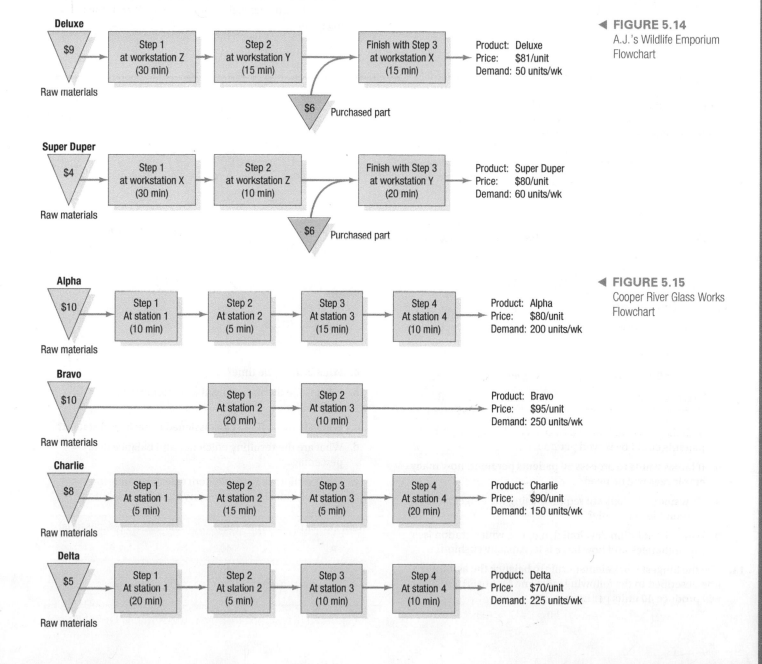

◀ **FIGURE 5.14**
A.J.'s Wildlife Emporium Flowchart

◀ **FIGURE 5.15**
Cooper River Glass Works Flowchart

a. Which station is the bottleneck?

b. Using the traditional method, which bases decisions solely on a product's contribution to profits and overhead, what is the optimal product mix and what is the overall profitability?

c. Using the bottleneck-based method, what is the optimal product mix and what is the overall profitability?

12. The senior management at Davis Watercraft would like to determine if it is possible to improve firm profitability by changing their existing product mix. Currently, the product mix is determined by giving resource priority to the highest contribution margin watercraft. Davis Watercraft always has a contingent of 10 workers on hand; each worker is paid $25 per hour. Overhead costs are $35,000 per week. The plant operates 18 hours per day and 6 days per week. Labor is considered a fixed expense because workers are paid for their time regardless of their utilization. The production manager has determined that workstation 1 is the bottleneck. Detailed production information is provided below.

	MODEL		
	A	**B**	**C**
Price	$450	$400	$500
Material Cost	$50	$40	$110
Weekly Demand	100	75	40
Processing Time Station 1	60 min	0 min	30 min
Processing Time Station 2	0 min	0 min	60 min
Processing Time Station 3	10 min	60 min	0 min
Processing Time Station 4	20 min	30 min	40 min

a. Using the traditional method, which bases decisions solely on a product's contribution to profits and overhead, what is the product mix that yields the highest total profit? What is the resulting profit?

b. Using the bottleneck-based method, what is the product mix that yields the highest total profit? What is the resulting profit?

Managing Constraints in Line Processes

13. Quick Stop Pharmacy is a small family-owned drug compounding business in Portland Oregon that is trying to perfect its customer service operations. John Suleiman, the owner wants to maximize the productivity of his staff as well as serve customers well. One area of concern is the drive-thru operation during the 7:30–8:30 morning rush hour. The process of fulfilling an order is as follows:

	Work Element	Time (Sec.)	Immediate Predecessor(s)
(A)	Greet patient and take prescription	40	—
(B)	Check patient information on system	45	A
(C)	Gather compounding materials	55	A
(D)	Perform compounding	55	C
(E)	Package and label	65	D
(F)	Instruct patient on use	40	B
(G)	Collect payment	25	B

a. If all the steps are handled by one employee, how many patients could be served per hour?

b. If James wants to process 30 patients per hour, how many employees will he need?

c. How many stations are required using the longest work element decision rule?

d. Using the solution developed in part c, which station is the bottleneck and how large is its capacity cushion?

14. Use the longest work element rule to balance the assembly line described in the following table and Figure 5.16 so that it will produce 40 units per hour.

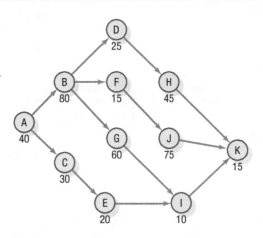

▲ **FIGURE 5.16**
Precedence Diagram

a. What is the cycle time?

b. What is the theoretical minimum number of workstations?

c. Which work elements are assigned to each workstation?

d. What are the resulting efficiency and balance delay percentages?

e. Use the shortest work element rule to balance the assembly line. Do you note any changes in solution?

Work Element	Time (Sec)	Immediate Predecessor(s)
A	40	None
B	80	A
C	30	A

Work Element	Time (Sec)	Immediate Predecessor(s)
D	25	B
E	20	C
F	15	B
G	60	B
H	45	D
I	10	E, G
J	75	F
K	15	H, I, J
	Total 415	

Work Element	Time (Sec)	Immediate Predecessor(s)
G	0.8	B
H	1.4	C
I	1.4	D
J	1.4	F, G
K	0.5	H
L	1.0	J
M	0.8	I, K, L

a. Draw a precedence diagram.

b. What cycle time (in minutes) results in the desired output rate?

c. What is the theoretical minimum number of stations?

d. Use the longest work element decision rule to balance the line and calculate the efficiency of your solution.

e. Use the most followers work element decision rule to balance the line and calculate the efficiency of your solution.

15. Johnson Cogs wants to set up a line to serve 60 customers per hour. The work elements and their precedence relationships are shown in the following table.

a. What is the theoretical minimum number of stations?

b. How many stations are required using the longest work element decision rule?

c. Suppose that a solution requiring five stations is obtained. What is its efficiency?

17. Refer back to problem 16. Suppose that in addition to the usual precedence constraints, there are two zoning constraints within the trim line. First, work elements K and L should be assigned to the same station; both use a common component, and assigning them to the same station conserves storage space. Second, work elements H and J cannot be performed at the same station.

a. Using trial and error, balance the line as best you can.

b. What is the efficiency of your solution?

Work Element	Time (Sec)	Immediate Predecessor(s)
A	40	None
B	30	A
C	50	A
D	40	B
E	6	B
F	25	C
G	15	C
H	20	D, E
I	18	F, G
J	30	H, I
	Total 274	

18. To meet holiday demand, Penny's Pie Shop requires a production line that is capable of producing 50 pecan pies per week, while operating only 40 hours per week. There are only four steps required to produce a single pecan pie with respective processing times of 5 minutes, 5 minutes, 45 minutes, and 15 minutes.

a. What should be the line's cycle time?

b. What is the smallest number of workstations Penny could hope for in designing the line considering this cycle time?

c. Suppose that Penny finds a solution that requires only four stations. What would be the efficiency of this line?

16. The *trim line* at PW is a small subassembly line that, along with other such lines, feeds into the final chassis line. The entire assembly line, which consists of more than 900 workstations, is to make PW's new E cars. The trim line itself involves only 13 work elements and must handle 20 cars per hour. Work-element data are as follows:

19. A paced assembly line has been devised to manufacture calculators, as the following data show:

Work Element	Time (Sec)	Immediate Predecessor(s)
A	1.8	None
B	0.4	None
C	1.6	None
D	1.5	A
E	0.7	A
F	0.5	E

Station	Work Element Assigned	Work Element Time (min)
S1	A	2.7
S2	D, E	0.6, 0.9
S3	C	3.0
S4	B, F, G	0.7, 0.7, 0.9
S5	H, I, J	0.7, 0.3, 1.2
S6	K	2.4

a. What is the maximum hourly output rate from this line? (*Hint:* The line can go only as fast as its slowest workstation.)

b. What cycle time corresponds to this maximum output rate?

c. If a worker is at each station and the line operates at this maximum output rate, how much idle time is lost during each 10-hour shift?

d. What is the line's efficiency?

20. Jane produces custom greeting cards using six distinct work elements. She would like to produce 10 cards in each 8-hour card-making session. Figure 5.17 details each work element and its associated durations in minutes as well as their precedence relationships.

FIGURE 5.17 ▶
Precedence Diagram for Custom Greeting Cards

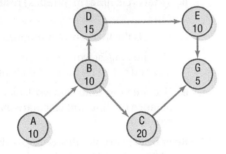

a. What cycle time is required to satisfy the required output rate?

b. What is the theoretical minimum number of workstations required?

c. If Jane identifies a five-station solution, what is the associated efficiency and balance delay?

d. If the cycle time increased by 100 percent, would the theoretical minimum number of workstations also increase by 100 percent?

21. Greg Davis, a business major at the University of South Carolina (USC), has opened Six Points Saco (SPS), a specialty subs–taco restaurant, at the rim of the USC campus. SPS has grown in popularity over the one year that it has been in operation, and Greg is trying to perfect the business model before making it into a franchise. He wants to maximize the productivity of his staff, as well as serve customers well in a timely fashion. One area of concern is the drive-thru operation during the 11:30 A.M. to 12:30 P.M. lunch hour.

The process of fulfilling an order involves fulfilling the tasks listed below.

Greg is interested in getting a better understanding of the staffing patterns that will be needed to operate his restaurant. After taking a course in operations management at the university, he knows that fulfilling a customer order at SPS is very similar to operating an assembly line. He has also used the POM for Windows software before, and wants to apply it for examining different demand scenarios for serving his customers.

a. If all the seven tasks are handled by one employee, how many customers could be served per hour?

b. If Greg wants to process 45 customers per hour, how many employees will he need during the peak period?

c. With the number of employees determined in part b, what is the maximum number of customers who could be served every hour (i.e., what is the maximum output capacity)?

d. Assuming that no task is assigned to more than one employee, what is the maximum output capacity from this assembly line? How many employees will be needed to actually accomplish this maximum output capacity?

e. Beyond the output accomplished in part d, if Greg decides to add one additional worker to help out with a bottleneck task, where should he add that worker? With that addition, would he be able to process more customers per hour? If so, what is the new maximum output capacity for the drive-thru?

Task	Time (Seconds)	Immediate Predecessors
A. Take an order at the booth. Most orders are for a taco and a sub.	25	
B. Collect money at the window.	20	A
C. Gather drinks.	35	B
D. Assemble taco order.	32	B
E. Assemble sub order.	30	B
F. Put drinks, taco, and sub in a bag.	25	C, D, E
G. Give the bag to the customer.	10	F

EXPERIENTIAL LEARNING   Min-Yo Garment Company

The Min-Yo Garment Company is a small firm in Taiwan that produces sportswear for sale in the wholesale and retail markets. Min-Yo's garments are unique because they offer fine embroidery and fabrics with a variety of striped and solid patterns. Over the 20 years of its existence, the Min-Yo Garment Company has become known as a quality producer of sports shirts with dependable deliveries. However, during that same period, the nature of the apparel industry has undergone change. In the past, firms could be successful producing standardized shirts in high volumes with few pattern or color choices and long production lead times. Currently, with the advent of regionalized merchandising and intense competition at the retail level, buyers of the shirts are looking for shorter lead times and much more variety in patterns and colors. Consequently, many more business opportunities are available today than ever before to a respected company such as Min-Yo.

Even though the opportunity for business success seemed bright, the management meeting last week was gloomy. Min-Yo Lee, president and owner of Min-Yo Garment, expressed concerns over the performance of the company: "We are facing strong competition for our products. Large apparel firms are driving prices down on high-volume licensed brands. Each day more firms enter the customized shirt business. Our profits are lower than expected, and delivery performance is deteriorating. We must reexamine our capabilities and decide what we can do best."

Products

Min-Yo has divided its product line into three categories: licensed brands, subcontracted brands, and special garments.

Licensed Brands

Licensed brands are brands that are owned by one company but, through a licensing agreement, are produced by another firm that also markets the brand in a specific geographic region. The licenser may have licensees all over the world. The licensee pays the licenser a fee for the privilege of marketing the brand in its region, and the licenser agrees to provide some advertising for the product, typically through media outlets that have international exposure. A key aspect of the licensing agreement is that the licensee must agree to provide sufficient quantities of product at the retail level. Running out of stock hurts the image of the brand name.

Currently, only one licensed brand is manufactured by Min-Yo. The brand, called the Muscle Shirt, is owned by a large "virtual corporation" in Italy that has no manufacturing facilities of its own. Min-Yo has been licensed to manufacture Muscle Shirts and sell them to large retail chains in Taiwan. The retail chains require prompt shipments at the end of each week. Because of competitive pressures from other licensed brands, low prices are important. Min-Yo sells each Muscle Shirt to retail chains for $6.

The demand for Muscle Shirts averages 900 shirts per week. The following demand for Muscle Shirts has been forecasted for the next 12 weeks.

Min-Yo's forecasts of Muscle Shirts are typically accurate to within ±200 shirts per week. If demand exceeds supply in any week, the excess demand is lost. No backorders are taken, and Min-Yo incurs no cost penalty for lost sales.

Subcontracted Brands

Manufacturers In the apparel industry often face uncertain demand. To maintain level production at their plants, many manufacturers seek subcontractors to produce their brands. Min-Yo is often considered a subcontractor because of its reputation in the industry. Although price is a consideration, the owners of subcontracted brands emphasize dependable delivery and the ability of the subcontractor to adjust order quantities on short notice.

Week	Demand	Week	Demand
1*	700	7	1,100
2	800	8	1,100
3	900	9	900
4	900	10	900
5	1,000	11	800
6	1,100	12	700

*In other words, the company expects to sell 700 Muscle Shirts at the end of week 1.

Currently, Min-Yo manufactures only one subcontracted brand, called the Thunder Shirt because of its bright colors. Thunder Shirts are manufactured to order for a company in Singapore. Min-Yo's price to this company is $7 per shirt. When orders are placed, usually twice a month, the customer specifies the delivery of certain quantities in each of the next 2 weeks. The last order the customer placed is overdue, forcing Min-Yo to pay a penalty charge. To avoid another penalty, 200 shirts must be shipped in week 1. The Singapore company is expected to specify the quantities it requires for weeks 2 and 3 at the beginning of week 1. The delivery schedule containing the orders for weeks 4 and 5 is expected to arrive at the beginning of week 3, and so on. The customer has estimated its average weekly needs for the year to be 200 shirts per week, although its estimates are frequently inaccurate.

Because of the importance of this large customer to Min-Yo and the lengthy negotiations of the sales department to get the business, management always tries to satisfy its needs. Management believes that if Min-Yo Garment ever refuses to accept an order from this customer, Min-Yo will lose the Thunder Shirt business. Under the terms of the sales contract, Min-Yo agreed to pay this customer $1 for every shirt not shipped on time for each week the shipment of the shirt is delinquent. Delinquent shipments must be made up.

Special Garments

Special garments are made only to customer order because of their low volume and specialized nature. Customers come to Min-Yo Garment to manufacture shirts for special promotions or special company occasions. Min-Yo's special garments are known as Dragon Shirts because of the elaborate embroidery and oriental flair of the designs. Because each shirt is made to a particular customer's specifications and requires a separate setup, special garments cannot be produced in advance of a firm customer order.

Although price is not a major concern for the customers of special garments, Min-Yo sells Dragon Shirts for $8 a shirt to ward off other companies seeking to enter the custom shirt market. Its customers come to Min-Yo because the company can produce almost any design with high quality and deliver an entire order on time. When placing an order for a Dragon Shirt, a customer specifies the design of the shirt (or chooses from Min-Yo's catalog), supplies specific designs for logos, and specifies the quantity of the order and the delivery date. In the past, management checked to see whether such an order would fit into the schedule, and then either accepted or rejected it on that basis. If Min-Yo accepts an order for delivery at the *end* of a certain week and fails to meet this commitment, it pays a penalty of $2 per shirt for each week delivery is delayed. This penalty is incurred weekly until the delinquent order is delivered. The company tried to forecast demand for specific designs of Dragon Shirts but has given up. Last week, Min-Yo had four Dragon Shirt opportunities of 50, 75, 200, and 60 units but chose not to accept any of the orders. Dragon Shirt orders in the past ranged from 50 units to 300 units with varying lead times.

Figure 5.18, Min-Yo's current open-order file, shows that in some prior week Min-Yo accepted an order of 400 Thunder Shirts for delivery last week. The open-order file is important because it contains the commitment management made to customers. Commitments are for a certain quantity and a date of delivery. As customer orders are accepted, management enters the quantity in the green cell representing the week that they are due. Because Dragon Shirts are unique unto themselves, they each have their own order number for future use. No Dragon Shirt orders appear in the open-order file because Min-Yo has not committed to any in the past several weeks.

Manufacturing Process

The Min-Yo Garment Company has the latest process technology in the industry—a machine, called a garment maker, that is run by one operator on each of three shifts. This single machine process can make every garment Min-Yo produces; however, the changeover times consume a substantial amount of capacity. Company policy is to run the machine three shifts a day, five days a week. If business is insufficient to keep the machine busy, the workers are idle because Min-Yo is committed to never fire or lay off a worker. By the same token, the firm has a policy of never working on weekends. Thus, the capacity of the process is 5 days × 24 hours = 120 hours per week. The hourly wage is $10 per hour, so the firm is committed to a fixed labor cost of $10 × 120 = $1,200 per week. Once the machine has been set up to make a particular type of garment, it can produce that garment at the rate of 10 garments per hour, regardless of type. The cost of the material in each garment, regardless of type, is $4. Raw materials are never a problem and can be obtained overnight.

Scheduling the Garment Maker

Scheduling at Min-Yo is done once each week, after production for the week has been completed and shipped, after new orders from customers have arrived, and before production for the next week has started. Scheduling results in two documents.

MIN-YO GARMENT COMPANY

Open Order File (Record of commitments)

Product	Week Order is Due									
	1	2	3	4	5	6	7	8	9	10
Thunder Orders	400									
Dragon Order 1										
Dragon Order 2										
Dragon Order 3										
Dragon Order 4										
Dragon Order 5										
Dragon Order 6										
Dragon Order 7										
Dragon Order 8										
Dragon Order 9										
Dragon Order 10										
Dragon Order 11										
Dragon Order 12										
Dragon Order 13										
Dragon Order 14										
Dragon Order 15										

▸ ▸| Intro / **Open Order File** / Week 1 / Week 2 / Week 3 / Week 4 / Week 5 / Week 6 / Week 7 / Week 8 / Week 9 / Week 10 / Su

▲ **FIGURE 5.18**

Min-Yo's Open Order File

Note: All orders are to be delivered at the end of the week indicated, after production for the week has been completed and before next week's production is started.

The first is a production schedule, shown in Figure 5.19. The schedule shows what management wants the garment maker process to produce in a given week. Two spreadsheet entries are required for each product that is to be produced in a given week. They are in the green shaded cells. The first is the production quantity. In Figure 5.19, the schedule shows that Min-Yo produced quantities of 800 units for Muscle and 200 units for Thunder last week. The second input is a "1" if the machine is to be set up for a given product or a "blank" if no changeover is required. Figure 5.19 shows that last week changeovers were required for the Muscle and Thunder production runs. The changeover information is important because, at the end of a week, the garment maker process will be set up for the last product produced. If the same product is to be produced first the following week, no new changeover will be required. Management must keep track of the sequence of production each week to take advantage of this savings. The only exception to this rule is Dragon Shirts, which are unique orders that always require a changeover. In week 0, Min-Yo did not produce any Dragon Shirts; however, it did produce 800 Muscle Shirts, followed by 200 Thunder Shirts. Finally, the spreadsheet calculates the hours required for the proposed schedule. Changeover times for Muscle, Thunder, and Dragon Shirts are 8, 10, and 25 hours, respectively. Because the garment maker process produces 10 garments per hour regardless of type, the production hours required for Muscle Shirts is 8 + 800/10 = 88 hours, and the production hours for Thunder Shirts is 10 + 200/10 = 30 hours, as shown in Figure 5.19. The total time spent on the garment maker process on all products in a week cannot exceed 120 hours. The spreadsheet will not allow you to proceed if this constraint is violated.

The second document is a weekly profit and loss (P&L) statement that factors in sales and production costs, including penalty charges and inventory carrying costs, as shown in Figure 5.20. The inventory carrying cost for *any type of product* is $0.10 per shirt per week left in inventory after shipments for the week have been made. The spreadsheet automatically calculates the P&L statement, which links to the open-order file and the production schedule, after the demand for Muscle Shirts is known. Figure 5.20 shows that the actual demand for Muscle Shirts last week was 750 shirts.

Notes

- The past due quantity of shirts are those shirts not shipped as promised, and appear as a negative number in the "End Inv" column.
- Available = Beginning inventory + Production
- Sales = Demand × Production < available; Available × Price, otherwise
- Inventory cost = $0.10 times number of shirts in inventory. Past due cost equals past due quantity times the penalty ($1 for Thunder Shirts; $2 for Dragon Shirts). These costs are combined in the "Inv/Past Due Costs" column.

The Simulation

At Min-Yo Garment Company, the executive committee meets weekly to discuss the new order possibilities and the load on the garment maker process. The executive committee consists of top management representatives from finance, marketing, and operations. You will be asked to participate on a team and play the role of a member of the executive committee in class. During this exercise, you must decide how far into the future to plan. Some decisions, such as the markets you want to exploit, are long-term in nature. Before class, you may want to think about the markets and their implications for manufacturing. Other decisions are short-term and have an

MIN-YO GARMENT COMPANY

PRODUCTION SCHEDULE

The two inputs to the Production Schedule table are:
1. The quantity you decide to produce this time period
2. Whether there is a setup/changover required (1 or 0)

PRODUCT	Changeover	Quantity
Muscle	1	800
Hours		88
Thunder	1	200
Hours		30

				Changeover	Quantity		Changeover	Quantity
Dragon Order 1			Dragon Order 11			Dragon Order 21		
Dragon Order 2			Dragon Order 12			Dragon Order 22		
Dragon Order 3			Dragon Order 13			Dragon Order 23		
Dragon Order 4			Dragon Order 14			Dragon Order 24		
Dragon Order 5			Dragon Order 15			Dragon Order 25		
Dragon Order 6			Dragon Order 16			Dragon Order 26		
Dragon Order 7			Dragon Order 17			Dragon Order 27		
Dragon Order 8			Dragon Order 18			Dragon Order 28		
Dragon Order 9			Dragon Order 19			Dragon Order 29		
Dragon Order 10			Dragon Order 20			Dragon Order 30		
Total Dragon Hours	0							
Total Dragon Production	0							
Total Hours scheduled	118							

Is production within capacity?   Yes

▲ FIGURE 5.19
Min-Yo's Production Schedule

P&L STATEMENT

Product	Price	Beg Inv	Production	Available	Demand	Sales	End Inv	Inv/Past due costs
Muscle	$6	550	800	1350	750	4500	600	60
Thunder	$7		200	200	400	1400	-200	200
Dragon Orders	$8		0	0	0	0	0	0
Totals			1000			5900		260

		Current	Cumulative
Sales Total		$5,900	$5,900
Labor	$1,200		
Materials	$4,000		
Inv/Past due	$260		
Total Cost		$5,460	
Profit Contribution		$440	$440

▲ FIGURE 5.20
Min-Yo's P&L Schedule

impact on the firm's ability to meet its commitments. In class, the simulation will proceed as follows.

1. Use the Min-Yo Tables spreadsheet in OM Explorer in MyOMLab. It is found in the Solver menu, under Constraint Management. You will start by specifying the production schedule for week 1, based on the forecasts for week 1 in the case narrative for Muscle Shirts and additional information on new and existing orders for the customized shirts from your instructor. *You may assume that your managerial predecessors left the garment machine set up for Thunder Shirts.* The production schedule decision is to be made in collaboration with your executive committee colleagues in class.

2. When all the teams have finalized their production plans for week 1, the instructor will supply the actual demands for Muscle Shirts in week 1. Enter that quantity in the P&L statement in the spreadsheet for week 1.

3. After the P&L statement for week 1 is completed, the instructor will announce the new order requests for Thunder Shirts and Dragon Shirts to be shipped in week 2 and the weeks beyond.

4. You should look at your order requests, accept those that you want, and reject the rest. Add those that you accept for delivery in future periods to your open-order file. Enter the quantity in the cell representing the week the order is due. You are then irrevocably committed to them and their consequences.

5. You should then make out a new production schedule, specifying what you want your garment-maker process to do in the next week (it will be for week 2 at that time).

6. The instructor will impose a time limit for each period of the simulation. When the time limit for one period has been reached, the simulation will proceed to the next week. Each week the spreadsheet will automatically update your production and financial information in the Summary Sheet.

| VIDEO CASE | Constraint Management at Southwest Airlines |

What if you could take a commercial airline flight any time and anywhere you wanted to go? Just show up at the airport without the need to consider time schedules or layovers. Aside from the potentially cost-prohibitive nature of such travel, there are also constraints in the airline system that preclude this kind of operation. From the lobby check-in process through to boarding at the gate and processing plane turnaround, the process of operating the airline is filled with constraints that must be managed in order for them to be successful and profitable. Flight schedules are tightly orchestrated and controlled, departure and arrival gates at airports are limited, and individual aircraft have seating capacities in each section of the plane, to name a few.

Southwest Airlines is one company that has figured out how to manage its constraints and generate positive customer experiences in the process. No other airline can claim the same level of profitability and customer satisfaction Southwest regularly achieves. What is its secret?

Talk to any loyal Southwest customer and you will hear rave reviews about its low fares, great customer service, and lack of assigned seating that gives customers a chance to choose who they sit next to onboard. From an operations perspective, it is much more than what the customer sees. Behind the scenes, operations managers carefully manage and execute—3,400 times a day in over 60 cities in the United States—a process designed to manage all potential bottleneck areas.

Southwest's famous rapid gate-turnaround of 25 minutes or less demonstrates how attention to the activities that ground operations must complete to clean, fuel, and prepare a plane for flight can become bottlenecks if not properly scheduled. In the terminal at the gate, passenger boarding also can be a bottleneck if the boarding process itself is not carefully managed. Since the individual mix of passengers presents a different set of issues with

Passengers boarding a Southwest Airlines flight.

each flight that often are not evident until the passengers actually arrive at the gate, ranging from families with kids and strollers to large quantities of carry-on bags and passengers needing wheelchair assistance, operations managers must be ready for any and all situations to avoid a boarding bottleneck while also ensuring a pleasant and stress-free gate experience for all passengers.

In 2007, as part of the company's continuous improvement activities, Southwest focused its attention on the passenger boarding process to determine whether there was a better way to board. Its existing process consisted of three groups, A, B, C, with no assigned seating. Depending on passenger check-in and arrival time, passengers were given a spot in a group. Those first to check-in received choice places in the A group. The last to check in ended up in the C group and usually had a choice of only middle seats in the back of the plane upon boarding. As passengers arrived at the gate, they queued up in their respective boarding group areas to await the boarding call.

Seven different alternate boarding scenarios were designed and tested. They included

- New family pre-boarding behind the "A" group of first-to-board passengers
- Family pre-boarding before anyone else, but seating choices limited on-board to behind the wing
- Six boarding groups (within A-B-C groups) instead of the original three A-B-C groups
- Assigned boarding gate line positions based on both boarding group and gate arrival time
- Single boarding chute at the gate, but up to nine groups all in one queue
- Boarding with a countdown clock to give customers an incentive to get in line and board quickly; incentives given out if everyone was on time
- Educational boarding video to make the boarding process fun, inform passengers how to board efficiently, and provide the company another way to promote its brand.

QUESTIONS

1. Analyze Southwest's passenger boarding process using the TOC.
2. Which boarding scenario among the different ones proposed would you recommend for implementation? Why?
3. How should Southwest evaluate the gate boarding and plane turnaround process?
4. How will Southwest know that the bottleneck had indeed been eliminated after the change in the boarding process?

An Aldi discount grocery store.

LEAN SYSTEMS

Aldi

Aldi is a discount supermarket chain with headquarters in Germany and over 8000 stores worldwide including Australia, Europe, Great Britain, Ireland, and the United States. With roots and distribution in several countries throughout Europe, it is a different kind of retailer that prides itself in displaying key dietary and nutritional information on the front of their packaging to enable customers to make informed choices about their food. Aldi also makes its packaging from recycled materials to keep the planet green. Its emphasis on core values of simplicity, consistency, and corporate responsibility are closely tied to the principles of lean production, which Aldi uses to keep costs down in all areas, provide customers more value for their money, and remain more competitive in a business with razor thin margins.

Aldi's waste reduction efforts start with training its employees to do many different tasks, which improves flexibility and lowers staff costs. In addition, consistent with total quality management (TQM) principles, all workers have the responsibility to get it right the first time, whether it is accurate pricing or ordering the appropriate replenishment stocks. In return, they are paid some of the better wages in the United States in the grocery industry. In the stores, all items have bar codes in a number of places to save time in finding them, which makes the checkout process more efficient. Aldi is also known for having smaller stores, which are made possible by the fact that it sells fewer variations of each product and so less space is used for display. It also means that Aldi can get quantity discounts and economies of scale in sourcing products. Holding only the stock that is needed for each product is further facilitated through a just-in-time ordering and delivery system. Products are delivered as needed in display-ready cases; some of them are even sold directly from a pallet or a platform to minimize handling and increase the efficiency of getting a large volume into the store quickly. In contrast to several of its 24-hour competitors, Aldi stores are only open from 8 A.M. to 8 P.M. on most days, which reduces the use of energy and staff salary costs. By limiting the use of credit cards, except Discover in some stores in the United States and Visa and MasterCard in Ireland, and using only cash or debit cards saves Aldi the surcharge fees levied by most credit card companies. Finally, Aldi's shopping carts utilize a 25¢ (in the United States) or a €1 (in Europe) coin system to make sure that customers return them to the parking stations near the store, which saves labor costs in collecting the carts that would otherwise be left scattered across the parking lots or potentially be lost or stolen.

Aldi's lean philosophy extends into the supply chain as well. Up to 60 percent of its fruits and vegetables are sourced locally to save on transportation costs and time. As part of its inventory reduction policies, suppliers are not allowed to hold more than one month of normal orders and requirements of Aldi's private label products in inventory at any given point of time, unless Aldi submits a written authorization for a temporary or permanent change in suppliers' inventory levels. Due to its relentless focus on lean principles, it is no wonder that Aldi is a clear leader in prices among leading grocery brands according to a study of 6,200 consumers conducted in May 2014 by Market Force Information, a customer intelligence solutions firm. Aldi's products can be as much as 30 percent cheaper than its competitors in some cases. In addition, Publix and Aldi were ranked second and third in customer satisfaction in North America after Trader Joe's due to their courteous service, fast checkouts, and the quality of their private label brand products. All these initiatives have contributed to Aldi's explosive growth globally—a new store opens roughly every week in the United Kingdom alone.

Sources: "Competitive Advantage through Efficiency: An Aldi Case Study," **http://businesscasestudies.co.uk/aldi/ competitive-advantage-through-efficiency/introduction.html#axzz39GsjgbiQ; http://en.wikipedia.org/wiki/Aldi; https://corporate.aldi.us; http://www.producenews.com/news-dep-menu/test-featured/13168-consumer-study- reveals-top-grocery-stores** (August 2, 2014).

LEARNING GOALS *After reading this chapter, you should be able to:*

1. Describe how lean systems can facilitate the continuous improvement of processes.

2. Identify the strategic supply chain and process characteristics of lean systems.

3. Explain the differences between one-worker, multiple-machine (OWMM) and group technology (GT) approaches to lean system layouts.

4. Understand value stream mapping and its role in waste reduction.

5. Understand *kanban* systems for creating a production schedule in a lean system.

6. Explain the implementation issues associated with the application of lean systems.

lean systems

Operations systems that maximize the value added by each of a company's activities by removing waste and delays from them.

Aldi is a learning organization and an excellent example of an approach for designing supply chains known as lean systems, which allow firms like Aldi to continuously improve its operations and spread the lessons learned across the entire corporation. **Lean systems** are operations systems that maximize the value added by each of a company's activities by removing waste and delays from them. They encompass the company's operations strategy, process design, quality management, constraint management, layout design, supply chain design, and technology and inventory management and can be used by both service and manufacturing firms. Like a manufacturer, each service business takes an order from a customer, delivers the service, and then collects revenue. Each service business purchases services or items, receives and pays for them, and hires and pays employees. Each of these activities bears considerable similarity to those in manufacturing firms. They also typically contain huge amounts of waste.

Lean systems affect a firm's internal linkages between its core and supporting processes and its external linkages with its customers and suppliers. The design of supply chains using the lean systems approach is important to various departments and functional areas across the organization. Marketing relies on lean systems to deliver high-quality services or products on time and at reasonable prices. Human resources must put in place the right incentive systems that reward teamwork and also recruit, train, and evaluate the employees needed to create a flexible workforce that can successfully operate a lean system. Engineering must design products that use more common parts, so that fewer setups are required and focused factories can be used. Operations is responsible for maintaining close ties with suppliers, designing the lean system, and using it in the production of services or goods. Accounting must adjust its billing and cost accounting practices to provide the support needed to manage lean systems. Finally, top management must embrace the lean philosophy and make it a part of organizational culture and learning, as was done by Aldi in the opening vignette.

Thus far in the text, we have discussed many ways to improve manufacturing and service processes. We take that further in this chapter by showing how process improvement techniques can be used to make a firm lean by first discussing the continuous improvement aspect of lean systems, followed by a discussion of the characteristics of lean systems, and the design of layouts needed to achieve these characteristics. We also address different types of lean systems used in practice and some of the implementation issues that companies face.

Continuous Improvement Using a Lean Systems Approach

just-in-time (JIT) philosophy
The belief that waste can be eliminated by cutting unnecessary capacity or inventory and removing non-value-added activities in operations.

One of the most popular systems that incorporate the generic elements of lean systems is the just-in-time (JIT) system. According to Taiichi Ohno, one of the earlier pioneers at Toyota Corporation, the **just-in-time (JIT) philosophy** is simple but powerful—eliminate waste or muda by cutting excess capacity or inventory and removing non-value-added activities. Table 6.1 shows the eight types of waste that often occur in firms in an interrelated fashion and which must be eliminated in implementing lean systems.

TABLE 6.1 | THE EIGHT TYPES OF WASTE OR *MUDA*[1]

Waste	Definition
1. Overproduction	Manufacturing an item before it is needed, making it difficult to detect defects and creating excessive lead times and inventory.
2. Inappropriate Processing	Using expensive high-precision equipment when simpler machines would suffice. It leads to overutilization of expensive capital assets. Investment in smaller flexible equipment, immaculately maintained older machines, and combining process steps where appropriate reduce the waste associated with inappropriate processing.
3. Waiting	Wasteful time incurred when product is not being moved or processed. Long production runs, poor material flows, and processes that are not tightly linked to one another can cause over 90 percent of a product's lead time to be spent waiting.
4. Transportation	Excessive movement and material handling of product between processes, which can cause damage and deterioration of product quality without adding any significant customer value.
5. Motion	Unnecessary effort related to the ergonomics of bending, stretching, reaching, lifting, and walking. Jobs with excessive motion should be redesigned.
6. Inventory	Excess inventory hides problems on the shop floor, consumes space, increases lead times, and inhibits communication. Work-in-process inventory is a direct result of overproduction and waiting.
7. Defects	Quality defects result in rework and scrap and add wasteful costs to the system in the form of lost capacity, rescheduling effort, increased inspection, and loss of customer goodwill.
8. Underutilization of Employees	Failure of the firm to learn from and capitalize on its employees' knowledge and creativity impedes long-term efforts to eliminate waste.

[1]David McBride, "The Seven Manufacturing Wastes," August 29, 2003, **http://www.emsstrategies.com** by permission of EMS Consulting Group, Inc. © 2003.

Stacks of bags at a coffee bean warehouse indicate that too much inventory can result from overproduction.

JIT system

A system that organizes the resources, information flows, and decision rules that enable a firm to realize the benefits of JIT principles.

The goals of a lean system are thus to eliminate these eight types of waste, produce services and products only as needed, and to continuously improve the value-added benefits of operations. A **JIT system** organizes the resources, information flows, and decision rules that enable a firm to realize the benefits of JIT principles.

By spotlighting areas that need improvement, lean systems lead to continuous improvement in quality and productivity. The Japanese term for this approach to process improvement is kaizen. The key to kaizen is the understanding that excess capacity or inventory hides underlying problems with the processes that produce a service or product. Lean systems provide the mechanism for management to reveal the problems by systematically lowering capacities or inventories until the problems are exposed. For example, Figure 6.1 characterizes the philosophy behind continuous improvement with lean systems. In services, the water surface represents service system capacity, such as staff levels. In manufacturing, the water surface represents product and component inventory levels. The rocks represent problems encountered in the fulfillment of services or products. When the water surface is high enough, the boat passes over the rocks because the high level of capacity or inventory covers up problems. As capacity or inventory shrinks, rocks are exposed. Ultimately, the boat will hit a rock if the water surface falls far enough. Through lean systems, workers, supervisors, engineers, and analysts apply methods for continuous improvement to demolish the exposed rock. The coordination required to achieve smooth material flows in lean systems identifies problems in time for corrective action to be taken.

Maintaining low inventories, periodically stressing the system to identify problems, and focusing on the elements of the lean system lie at the heart of continuous improvement. For example, plants may periodically cut its safety stocks almost to zero. The problems at the plant are exposed, recorded, and later assigned to employees as improvement projects. After improvements are made, inventories are permanently cut to the new level. Many firms use this trial-and-error process to develop more efficient manufacturing operations. In addition, workers using special presses often fabricate parts on the assembly line in exactly the quantities needed. Service processes, such as scheduling, billing, order taking, accounting, and financial planning, can be improved with lean systems, too. In service operations, a common approach used by managers is to place stress on the system by reducing the number of employees doing a particular activity or series of activities until the process begins to slow or come to a halt. The problems can be identified, and ways for overcoming them explored. Other kaizen tactics can be used as well.

▼ **FIGURE 6.1**
Continuous Improvement with Lean Systems

Eliminating the problem of too much scrap might require improving the firm's work processes, providing employees with additional training, or finding higher-quality suppliers. Eliminating capacity imbalances might involve revising the firm's master production schedule and improving the flexibility of its workforce. Irrespective of which problem is solved, there are always new ones that can be addressed to enhance system performance.

Oftentimes, continuous improvement occurs with the ongoing involvement and input of new ideas from employees, who play an important role in implementing the JIT philosophy. In one year alone, about 740,000 corporate-wide improvement suggestions were received at Toyota. A large majority of them got implemented, and employees making those suggestions received rewards ranging from 500 yen (about $5) to upwards of 50,000 yen (about $500) depending upon their bottom line impact.

Scrap   Unreliable suppliers   Capacity imbalance

Strategic Characteristics of Lean Systems

The philosophy of lean systems, applicable at the process level, is also applicable at the supply chain level. Factors, both within and outside the firm, arising from supply chain and process considerations that have an important impact in creating and implementing lean systems are discussed next in this section.

Supply Chain Considerations in Lean Systems

In this section, we discuss the two salient characteristics of lean systems that are related to creating and managing material flows in a supply chain: close supplier ties and small lot sizes.

Close Supplier Ties   Because lean systems operate with low levels of capacity slack or inventory, firms that use them need to have a close relationship with their suppliers. Supplies must be shipped frequently, have short lead times, arrive on schedule, and be of high quality. A contract might even require a supplier to deliver goods to a facility as often as several times per day.

The lean system philosophy is to look for ways to improve efficiency and reduce inventories throughout the supply chain. Close cooperation between companies and their suppliers can be a win-win situation for everyone. Better communication of component requirements, for example, enables more efficient inventory planning and delivery scheduling by suppliers, thereby improving supplier profit margins. Customers can then negotiate lower component prices. Close supplier relations cannot be established and maintained if companies view their suppliers as adversaries whenever contracts are negotiated. Rather, they should consider suppliers to be partners in a venture, wherein both parties have an interest in maintaining a long-term, profitable relationship. Consequently, one of the first actions undertaken when a lean system is implemented is to pare down the number of suppliers, and make sure they are located in close geographic proximity to promote strong partnerships and better synchronize product flows.

A particularly close form of supplier partnerships through lean systems is the JIT II system, which was conceived and implemented by Bose Corporation, a producer of high-quality professional sound and speaker systems. In a JIT II system, also called *vendor-managed inventories*, the supplier is brought into the plant to be an active member of the purchasing office of the customer. The in-plant representative is on site full-time at the supplier's expense and is empowered to plan and schedule the replenishment of materials from the supplier. Thus, JIT II fosters extremely close interaction with suppliers. The qualifications for a supplier to be included in the program are stringent.

In general, JIT II can offer benefits to both buyers and suppliers because it provides the organizational structure needed to improve supplier coordination by integrating the logistics, production, and purchasing processes together. We have more to say about supplier relationships and vendor-managed inventories in Chapter 14, "Supply Chain Integration."

Small Lot Sizes   Lean systems use lot sizes that are as small as possible. A **lot** is a quantity of items that are processed together. Small lots have the advantage of reducing the average level of inventory relative to large lots. Small lots pass through the system faster than large lots since they do not keep materials waiting. In addition, if any defective items are discovered, large lots cause longer delays because the entire lot must be examined to find all the items that need rework. Finally, small lots help achieve a uniform workload on the system and prevent overproduction. Large lots consume large chunks of capacity at workstations and, therefore, complicate scheduling. Small lots can be juggled more effectively, enabling schedulers to efficiently utilize capacities.

Although small lots are beneficial to operations, they have the disadvantage of increased setup frequency. A setup is the group of activities needed to change or readjust a process between successive lots of items, sometimes referred to as a changeover. This changeover in itself is a process that can be made more efficient. Setups involve trial runs, and the material waste can be substantial as the machines are fine tuned for the new parts. Typically, a setup takes the same time regardless of the size of the lot. Consequently, many small lots, in lieu of several large lots, may result in waste in the form of idle employees, equipment, and materials. Setup times must be brief to realize the benefits of small-lot production.

Achieving brief setup times often requires close cooperation among engineering, management, and labor. For example, changing dies on large presses to form automobile parts from sheet metal can take 3 to 4 hours. At Honda's Marysville, Ohio, plant—where four stamping lines stamp all the exterior and major interior body panels for Accord production—teams worked on ways to reduce the changeover time for the massive dies. As a result, a complete change of dies for a giant 2,400-ton press now takes less than 8 minutes. The goal of **single-digit setup** means having setup times of less than 10 minutes. Some techniques used to reduce setup times at the Marysville plant include using conveyors for die storage, moving large dies with cranes, simplifying dies, enacting machine controls, using microcomputers to automatically feed and position work, and preparing for changeovers while a job currently in production is still being processed.

lot
A quantity of items that are processed together.

single-digit setup
The goal of having a setup time of less than 10 minutes.

A diner at a Chinese restaurant buffet. Because the food items must be prepared in advance, the restaurant uses a push method of workflow.

Process Considerations in Lean Systems

In this section, we discuss the following characteristics of lean systems: pull method of work flow, quality at the source, uniform workstation loads, standardized components and work methods, flexible workforce, automation, Five S (5S) practices, and total preventive maintenance (TPM).

Pull Method of Work Flow   Managers have a choice as to the nature of the material flows in a process or supply chain. Most firms using lean operations use the **pull method**, in which customer demand activates the production of a good or service. In contrast, a method often used in conventional systems that do not emphasize lean systems is the **push method**, which involves using forecasts of demand and producing the item before the customer orders it. To differentiate between these two methods, let us use a service example that involves a favorite pastime, eating.

For an illustration of the pull method, consider a five-star restaurant in which you are seated at a table and offered a menu of exquisite dishes, appetizers, soups, salads, and desserts. You can choose from filet mignon, porterhouse steak, yellow fin tuna, grouper, and lamb chops. Your choice of several salads is prepared at your table. Although some appetizers, soups, and desserts can be prepared in advance and brought to temperature just before serving, the main course and salads cannot. Your order for the salad and the main course signals the chef to begin preparing your specific requests. For these items, the restaurant is using the pull method. Firms using the pull method must be able to fulfill the customer's demands within an acceptable amount of time.

For an understanding of the push method, consider a cafeteria on a busy downtown corner. During the busy periods around 12 P.M. and 5 P.M. lines develop, with hungry patrons eager to eat and then move on to other activities. The cafeteria offers choices of chicken (roasted or deep fried), roast beef, pork chops, hamburgers, hot dogs, salad, soup (chicken, pea, and clam chowder), bread (three types), beverages, and desserts (pies, ice cream, and cookies). Close coordination is required between the cafeteria's "front office," where its employees interface with customers, and its "back office," the kitchen, where the food is prepared and then placed along the cafeteria's buffet line. Because it takes substantial time to cook some of the food items, the cafeteria uses a push method. The cafeteria would have a difficult time using the pull method because it could not wait until a customer asked for an item before asking the kitchen to begin processing it. After all, shortages in food could cause riotous conditions (recall that customers are hungry), whereas preparing an excess amount of food will be wasteful because it will go uneaten. To make sure that neither of these conditions occurs, the cafeteria must accurately forecast the number of customers it expects to serve. A Chinese restaurant buffet as shown above would similarly follow a push method for serving its customers.

The choice between the push and pull methods is often situational. Firms using an assemble-to-order strategy sometimes use both methods: the push method to produce the standardized components, and the pull method to fulfill the customer's request for a particular combination of the components.

Quality at the Source   Consistently meeting the customer's expectations is an important characteristic of lean systems. One way to achieve this goal is by adhering to a practice called quality at the source, which is a philosophy whereby defects are caught and corrected where they are created. The goal for workers is to act as their own quality inspectors and never pass on defective units to the next process. Automatically stopping the process when something is wrong and then fixing the problems on the line itself as they occur is also known as *jidoka*. Jidoka tends to separate worker and machine activities by freeing workers from tending to machines all the time, thus allowing them to staff multiple operations simultaneously. Jidoka represents a visual management system whereby status of the system in terms of safety, quality, delivery, and cost performance relative to the goals for a given fabrication cell or workstation in an assembly line is clearly visible to workers on the floor at all times.

An alternative to jidoka or quality at the source is the traditional practice of pushing problems down the line to be resolved later. This approach is often ineffective. For example, a soldering operation at the Texas Instruments antenna department had a defect rate that varied from 0 to 50 percent on a daily basis, averaging about 20 percent. To compensate, production planners increased the lot sizes, which only increased inventory levels and did nothing to reduce the number of defective items. The company's

---

pull method

A method in which customer demand activates production of the service or item.

push method

A method in which production of the item begins in advance of customer needs.

jidoka

Automatically stopping the process when something is wrong and then fixing the problems on the line itself as they occur.

engineers then discovered through experimentation that gas temperature was a critical variable in producing defect-free items. They subsequently devised statistical control charts for the firm's equipment operators to use to monitor the temperature and adjust it themselves. Process yields immediately improved and stabilized at 95 percent, and Texas Instruments was eventually able to implement a lean system.

One successful approach for implementing quality at the source is to use ***poka-yoke***, or mistake-proofing methods aimed at designing fail-safe systems that attack and minimize human error. Poka-yoke systems work well in practice. Consider, for instance, a company that makes modular products. The company could use the *poka-yoke* method by making different parts of the modular product in such a way that allows them to be assembled in only one way—the correct way. Similarly, a company's shipping boxes could be designed to be packed only in a certain way to minimize damage and eliminate all chances of mistakes. At Toyota plants, every vehicle being assembled is accompanied by an RFID chip containing information on how many nuts and bolts need to be tightened on that vehicle for an operation at a given workstation. A green light comes on when the right numbers of nuts have been tightened. Only then does the vehicle move forward on the assembly line.

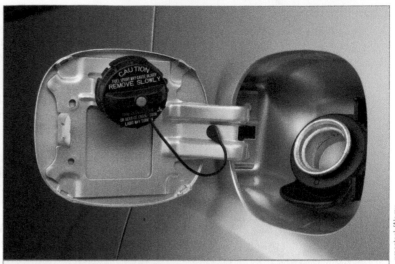

An example of poka-yoke is the design of new fuel doors in automobiles. They are mistake proof since the filling pipe insert keeps larger, leaded-fuel nozzle from being inserted. In addition, a gas cap tether does not allow the motorist to drive off without the cap, and is also fitted with a ratchet to signal proper tightness and prevent over-tightening.

poka-yoke
Mistake-proofing methods aimed at designing fail-safe systems that minimize human error.

Another tool for implementing quality at the source is *andon*, which is a system that gives machines and machine operators the ability to signal the occurrence of any abnormal condition such as tool malfunction, shortage of parts, or the product being made outside the desired specifications. It can take the form of audio alarms, blinking lights, LCD text displays, or cords that can be pulled by workers to ask for help or stop the production line if needed. Stopping a production line can, however, cost a company thousands of dollars each minute production is halted. Needless to say, management must realize the enormous responsibility this method puts on employees and must prepare them properly.

Uniform Workstation Loads   A lean system works best if the daily load on individual workstations is relatively uniform. Service processes can achieve uniform workstation loads by using reservation systems. For example, hospitals schedule surgeries in advance of the actual service so that the facilities and facilitating goods can be ready when the time comes. The load on the surgery rooms and surgeons can be evened out to make the best use of these resources. Another approach is to use differential pricing of the service to manage the demand for it. Uniform loads are the rationale behind airlines promoting weekend travel or red-eye flights that begin late in the day and end in the early morning. Efficiencies can be realized when the load on the firm's resources can be managed.

For manufacturing processes, uniform loads can be achieved by assembling the same type and number of units each day, thus creating a uniform daily demand at all workstations. Capacity planning, which recognizes capacity constraints at critical workstations, and line balancing are used to develop the master production schedule. For example, at Toyota's plant the production plan may call for 4,500 vehicles per week for the next month. That requires two full shifts, 5 days per week, producing 900 vehicles each day, or 450 per shift. Three models are produced: Camry (C), Avalon (A), and Venza (V). Suppose that Toyota needs 200 Camrys, 150 Avalons, and 100 Venzas per shift to satisfy market demand. To produce 450 units in one shift of 480 minutes, the line must roll out a vehicle every $480/450 = 1.067$ minutes. The 1.067 minutes, or 64 seconds, represents the **takt time** of the process, defined as the cycle time needed to match the rate of production to the rate of sales or consumption.

takt time
Cycle time needed to match the rate of production to the rate of sales or consumption.

With traditional big-lot production, all daily requirements of a model are produced in one batch before another model is started. The sequence of 200 Cs, 150 As, and 100 Vs would be repeated once per shift. Not only would these big lots increase the average inventory level, but they also would cause lumpy requirements on all the workstations feeding the assembly line.

But there are other two options for devising a production schedule for the vehicles. These options are based on the Japanese concept of ***heijunka***, which is the leveling of production load by both volume and product mix. It does not build products according to the actual flow of customer orders but levels out the total volume of orders in a period so that the same amount and mix are being made each day.[2]

heijunka
The leveling of production load by both volume and product mix.

---

[2]David McBride, "Heijunka, Leveling the Load," September 1, 2004, **http://www.emsstrategies.com**.

mixed-model assembly

A type of assembly that produces a mix of models in smaller lots.

Let us explore two possible heijunka options. The first option uses leveled **mixed-model assembly**, producing a mix of models in smaller lots. Note that the production requirements at Toyota are in the ratio of 4 Cs to 3 As to 2 Vs, found by dividing the model's production requirements by the greatest common divisor, or 50. Thus, the Toyota planner could develop a production cycle consisting of 9 units: 4 Cs, 3 As, and 2 Vs. The cycle would repeat in $9(1.067) = 9.60$ minutes, for a total of 50 times per shift $(480 \, \text{min}/9.60 \, \text{min} = 50)$.

The second heijunka option uses a lot size of one, such as the production sequence of C–V–C–A–C–A–C–V–A repeated 50 times per shift. The sequence would achieve the same total output as the other options; however, it is feasible only if the setup times are brief. The sequence generates a steady rate of component requirements for the various models and allows the use of small lot sizes at the feeder workstations. Consequently, the capacity requirements at those stations are greatly smoothed. These requirements can be compared to actual capacities during the planning phase, and modifications to the production cycle, production requirements, or capacities can be made as necessary.

Standardized Components and Work Methods   In highly repetitive service operations, analyzing work methods and documenting the improvements to use can gain great efficiencies. For example, UPS consistently monitors its work methods, from sorting packages to delivering them, and revises them as necessary to improve service. In manufacturing, the standardization of components increases the total quantity that must be produced for that component. For example, a firm producing 10 products from 1,000 different components could redesign its products so that they consist of only 100 different components with larger daily requirements. Because the requirements per component increase, each worker performs a standardized task or work method more often each day. Productivity tends to increase because workers learn to do their tasks more efficiently with increased repetition. Standardizing components and work methods help a firm achieve the high-productivity, low-inventory objectives of a lean system.

Flexible Workforce   The role of workers is elevated in lean systems. Workers in flexible workforces can be trained to perform more than one job. A benefit of flexibility is the ability to shift workers among workstations to help relieve bottlenecks as they arise without the need for inventory buffers—an important aspect of the uniform flow of lean systems. Also, workers can step in and do the job for those who are on vacation or who are out sick. Although assigning workers to tasks they do not usually perform can temporarily reduce their efficiency, some job rotation tends to relieve boredom and refreshes workers. At some firms that have implemented lean systems, cross-trained workers may switch jobs every 2 hours.

five S (5S)

A methodology consisting of five workplace practices—sorting, straightening, shining, standardizing, and sustaining—that are conducive to visual controls and lean production.

The more customized the service or product is, the greater the firm's need for a multiskilled workforce. For example, stereo repair shops require broadly trained personnel who can identify a wide variety of component problems when the customer brings the defective unit into the shop and who then can repair the unit. Alternatively, back-office designs, such as the mail-processing operations at a large post office, have employees with more narrowly defined jobs because of the repetitive nature of the tasks they must perform. These employees do not have to acquire as many alternative skills. In some situations, shifting workers to other jobs may require them to undergo extensive, costly training.

Automation   Automation plays a big role in lean systems and is a key to low-cost operations. Money freed up because of inventory reductions or other efficiencies can be invested in automation to reduce costs. The benefits, of course, are greater profits, greater market share (because prices can be cut), or both. Automation can play a big role when it comes to providing lean services. For example, banks offer ATMs that provide various bank services on demand 24 hours a day. Automation should be planned carefully, however. Many managers believe that if some automation is good, more is better, which is not always the case. At times, humans can do jobs better than robots and automated assembly systems. In other instances, especially when production volumes are high, automation can result in higher quality, precision, and productivity.

Five S Practices   Five S (5S) is a methodology for organizing, cleaning, developing, and sustaining a productive work environment. It represents five related terms, each beginning with an S, that describe workplace

Spirit AeroSystems' plant in Prestwick, Scotland, has seen some big changes. For one, it has invested in automation on the A320 production line.

Molly McMillin/MCT/Newscom

practices conducive to visual controls and lean production. As shown in Figure 6.2, these five practices of sort, straighten, shine, standardize, and sustain build upon one another and are done systematically to achieve lean systems. These practices are interconnected and are not something that can be done as a stand-alone program. As such, they serve as an enabler and an essential foundation of lean systems. Table 6.2 shows the terms[3] that represent the 5S and what they imply.

It is commonly accepted that 5S forms an important cornerstone of waste reduction and removal of unneeded tasks, activities, and materials. 5S practices can enable workers to visually see everything differently, prioritize tasks, and achieve a greater degree of focus. They can also be applied to a diverse range of manufacturing and service settings including organizing work spaces, offices, tool rooms, shop floors, and the like. Implementation of 5S practices have been shown to lead to lowered costs, improved on-time delivery and productivity, higher product quality, better use of floor space, and a safe working environment. It also builds the discipline needed to make the lean systems work well.

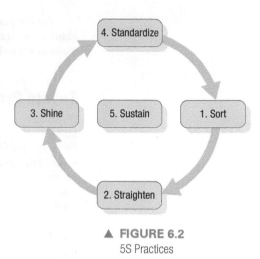

▲ **FIGURE 6.2**
5S Practices

TABLE 6.2 | 5S DEFINED

5S Term	Definition
1. Sort	Separate needed items from unneeded items (including tools, parts, materials, and paperwork), and discard the unneeded.
2. Straighten	Neatly arrange what is left, with a place for everything and everything in its place. Organize the work area so that it is easy to find what is needed.
3. Shine	Clean and wash the work area and make it shine.
4. Standardize	Establish schedules and methods of performing the cleaning and sorting. Formalize the cleanliness that results from regularly doing the first three S practices so that perpetual cleanliness and a state of readiness are maintained.
5. Sustain	Create discipline to perform the first four S practices, whereby everyone understands, obeys, and practices the rules when in the plant. Implement mechanisms to sustain the gains by involving people and recognizing them through a performance measurement system.

Total Preventive Maintenance (TPM)   Because lean systems emphasize finely tuned flows of work and little capacity slack or buffer inventory between workstations, unplanned machine downtime can be disruptive. Total Preventive Maintenance (TPM), which is also sometimes referred to as total *productive* maintenance, can reduce the frequency and duration of machine downtime. After performing their routine maintenance activities, technicians can test other machine parts that might need to be replaced. Replacing parts during regularly scheduled maintenance periods is easier and quicker than dealing with machine failures during production. Maintenance is done on a schedule that balances the cost of the preventive maintenance program against the risks and costs of machine failure. Routine preventive maintenance is important for service businesses that rely heavily on machinery, such as the rides at Walt Disney World or Universal Studios.

Another tactic is to make workers responsible for routinely maintaining their own equipment, which will develop employee pride in keeping the machines in top condition. This tactic, however, typically is limited to general housekeeping chores, minor lubrication, and adjustments. Maintaining high-tech machines requires trained specialists. Nonetheless, performing even simple maintenance tasks goes a long way toward improving the performance of machines.

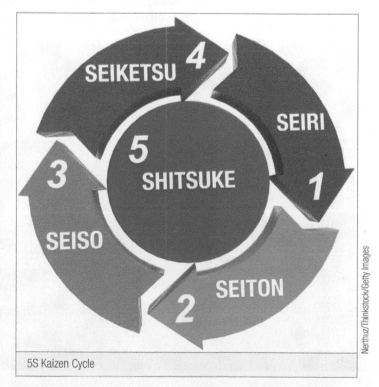

5S Kaizen Cycle

Nerthuz/Thinkstock/Getty Images

---

[3]The Japanese words for these 5S terms are *seiri, seiton, seiso, seiketsu,* and *shitsuke,* respectively.

For long-term improvements, data can be collected for establishing trends in failure pattern of machines, which can subsequently be analyzed to establish better standards and procedures for preventive maintenance. The data can also provide failure history and costs incurred to maintain the systems.

Toyota Production System

If you were to select one company that regularly invokes the above-mentioned features of lean systems and also exemplifies excellence in automobile manufacturing, it would probably be Toyota. Despite its recent problems with quality and product recalls, as well as component shortages and delayed new model launches caused by the Japanese earthquake in March 2011, Toyota has become one of the largest car manufacturers in the world and also one of its most admired. Worldwide in its presence, Toyota has 11 manufacturing plants in North America alone producing over 1.86 million vehicles per year. Much of this success is attributed to the famed Toyota Production System (TPS), which is one of the most admired lean manufacturing systems in existence. Replicating the system, however, is fraught with difficulties. What makes the system tick, and why has Toyota been able to use it so successfully in many different plants?

Most outsiders see the TPS as a set of tools and procedures that are readily visible during a plant tour. Even though they are important for the success of the TPS, they are not the key. What most people overlook is that through the process of continuous improvement, Toyota built a learning organization over the course of 50 years. Lean systems require constant improvements to increase efficiency and reduce waste. Toyota's system stimulates employees to experiment to find better ways to do their jobs. In fact, Toyota sets up all of its operations as "experiments" and teaches employees at all levels how to use the scientific method of problem solving.

Four principles form the basis of the TPS. First, all work must be completely specified as to content, sequence, timing, and outcome. Detail is important; otherwise, a foundation for improvements is missing. Second, every customer–supplier connection must be direct, unambiguously specifying the people involved, the form and quantity of the services or goods to be provided, the way the requests are made by each customer, and the expected time in which the requests will be met. Customer–supplier connections can be internal (employee to employee) or external (company to company). Third, the pathway for every service and product must be simple and direct. That is, services and goods do not flow to the next available person or machine but to a specific person or machine. With this principle, employees can determine, for example, whether a capacity problem exists at a particular workstation and then analyze ways to solve it.

The first three principles define the system in detail by specifying how employees do work and interact with each other and how the work flows are designed. However, these specifications actually are "hypotheses" about the way the system should work. For example, if something goes wrong at a workstation enough times, the hypothesis about the methods the employee uses to do work is rejected. The fourth principle, then, is that any improvement to the system must be made in accordance with the scientific method, under the guidance of a teacher, at the lowest possible organizational level. The scientific method involves clearly stating a verifiable hypothesis of the form, "If we make the following specific changes, we expect to achieve this specific outcome." The hypothesis must then be tested under a variety of conditions. Working with a teacher, who is often the employees' supervisor, is a key to becoming a learning organization. Employees learn the scientific method and eventually become teachers of others. Finally, making improvements at the lowest level of the organization means that the employees who are actually doing the work are actively involved in making the improvements. Managers are advised only to coach employees—not to fix their problems for them.

These four principles are deceptively simple. However, they are difficult but not impossible to replicate. Those organizations that successfully implement them enjoy the benefits of a lean system that adapts to change. Toyota's lean system made it an innovative leader in the auto industry and served as an important cornerstone of its success.

An employee helps assemble a vehicle in Toyota City, located in central Japan. Toyota's production system is among the most-admired lean manufacturing systems in the world.

House of Toyota   Taiichi Ohno and Eiji Toyoda created a graphic representation shown in Figure 6.3

to define the TPS to its employees and suppliers, and which is now known as the House of Toyota. It captures the four principles of TPS described above, and represents all the essential elements of lean systems that make the TPS work well. The house conveys stability. The twin pillars of JIT and *jidoka* support the roof, representing the primary goals of high quality, low cost, waste elimination, and short lead-times. Within JIT, TPS uses a pull system that focuses on one-piece work flow methods that can change and match the takt time of the process to the actual market demand because setup reductions and small changeover times are facilitated by cross-trained workers in cellular layouts. Implementing various tools of jidoka ensures that quality is built into the product rather than merely inspected at the end. Finally, within an environment of continuous improvement, operational stability to the House of Toyota is provided at the base by leveraging other lean concepts such as heijunka, standard work methods, 5S practices, total preventive maintenance, and elimination of waste throughout the supply chain within which the Toyota products flow to reach their eventual customers.

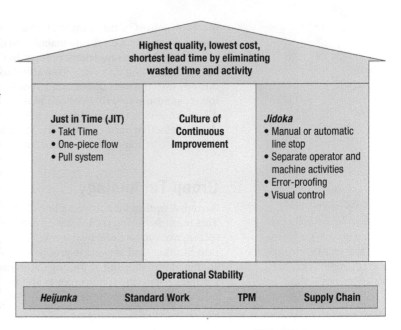

▲ **FIGURE 6.3**
House of Toyota[5]

Designing Lean System Layouts

Line flows are recommended in designing lean system layouts because they eliminate waste by reducing the frequency of setups. If volumes of specific products are large enough, groups of machines and workers can be organized into a line-flow layout to eliminate setups entirely. In a service setting, managers of back-office service processes can similarly organize their employees and equipment to provide uniform work flows through the process and, thereby, eliminate wasted employee time. Banks use this strategy in their check-processing operations, as does UPS in its parcel-sorting process.

When volumes are not high enough to justify dedicating a single line of multiple workers to a single customer type or product, managers still may be able to derive the benefits of line-flow layout—simpler materials handling, low setups, and reduced labor costs—by creating line-flow layouts in some portions of the facility. Two techniques for creating such layouts are one-worker, multiple-machines (OWMM) cells, and group technology (GT) cells.

one-worker, multiple-machines (OWMM) cell

A one-person cell in which a worker operates several different machines simultaneously to achieve a line flow.

▼ **FIGURE 6.4**
One-Worker, Multiple-Machines (OWMM) Cell

One Worker, Multiple Machines

If volumes are not sufficient to keep several workers busy on one production line, the manager might set up a line small enough to keep one worker busy. The **one-worker, multiple-machines (OWMM) cell** is a workstation in which a worker operates several different machines simultaneously to achieve a line flow. Having one worker operate several identical machines is not unusual. However, with an OWMM cell, several different machines are in the line.

Figure 6.4 illustrates a five-machine OWMM cell that is being used to produce a flanged metal part, with the machines encircling one operator in the center. (A U-shape also is common.) The operator moves around the circle, performing tasks (typically loading and unloading) that have not been automated. Different products or parts can be produced in an OWMM cell by changing the

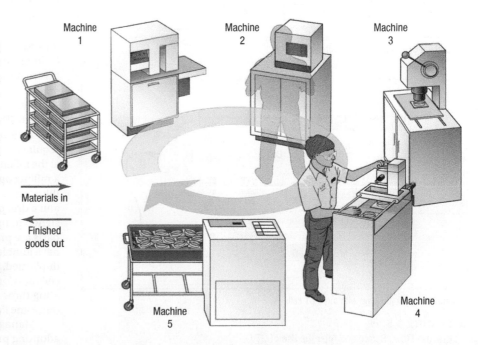

[5]TBM Consulting Group; **http://www.tbmcg.com/about/ourroots/house_toyota.php**

machine setups. If the setup on one machine is especially time-consuming for a particular part, management can add a duplicate machine to the cell for use whenever that part is being produced.

An OWMM arrangement reduces both inventory and labor requirements. Inventory is cut because, rather than piling up in queues waiting for transportation to another part of the plant, materials move directly into the next operation. Labor is cut because more work is automated. The addition of several low-cost automated devices can maximize the number of machines included in an OWMM arrangement: automatic tool changers, loaders and unloaders, start and stop devices, and fail-safe devices that detect defective parts or products. Manufacturers are applying the OWMM concept widely because of their desire to achieve low inventories.

Group Technology

group technology (GT)

An option for achieving line-flow layouts with low volume processes; this technique creates cells not limited to just one worker and has a unique way of selecting work to be done by the cell.

A second option for achieving line-flow layouts with low volume processes is **group technology (GT)**. This manufacturing technique creates cells not limited to just one worker and has a unique way of selecting work to be done by the cell. The GT method groups parts or products with similar characteristics into families and sets aside groups of machines for their production. Families may be based on size, shape, manufacturing or routing requirements, or demand. The goal is to identify a set of products with similar processing requirements and minimize machine changeover or setup. For example, all bolts might be assigned to the same family because they all require the same basic processing steps regardless of size or shape.

Once parts have been grouped into families, the next step is to organize the machine tools needed to perform the basic processes on these parts into separate cells. The machines in each cell require only minor adjustments to accommodate product changeovers from one part to the next in the same family. By simplifying product routings, GT cells reduce the time a job is in the shop. Queues of materials waiting to be worked on are shortened or eliminated. Frequently, materials handling is automated so that, after loading raw materials into the cell, a worker does not handle machined parts until the job has been completed.

Figure 6.5 compares process flows before and after creation of GT cells. Figure 6.5(a) shows a shop floor where machines are grouped according to function: lathing, milling, drilling, grinding, and assembly. After lathing, a part is moved to one of the milling machines, where it waits in line until it has a higher priority than any other job competing for the machine's capacity. When the milling operation on the part has been finished, the part is moved to a drilling machine, and so on. The queues can be long, creating significant time delays. Flows of materials are jumbled because the parts being processed in any one area of the shop have so many different routings.

By contrast, the manager of the shop shown in Figure 6.5(b) identified three product families that account for a majority of the firm's production. One family always requires two lathing operations followed by one operation at the milling machines. The second family always requires a milling operation followed by a grinding operation. The third family requires the use of a lathe, a milling machine, and a drill press. For simplicity, only the flows of parts assigned to these three families are shown. The remaining parts are produced at machines outside the cells and still have jumbled routings. Some equipment might have to be duplicated, as when a machine is required for one or more cells and for operations outside the cells. However, by creating three GT cells, the manager has definitely created more line flows and simplified routings.

Managerial Practice 6.1 illustrates how along with adopting principles of continuous flow processes, standardized work methods, and cellular layouts, Panasonic Corporation used robots and automation to increase throughput and reduce costs in its manufacturing plant.

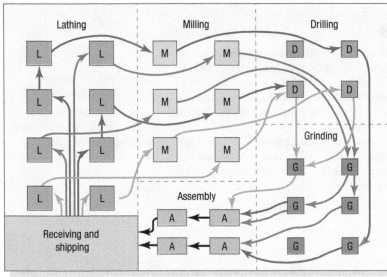

(a) Jumbled flows in a job shop without GT cells

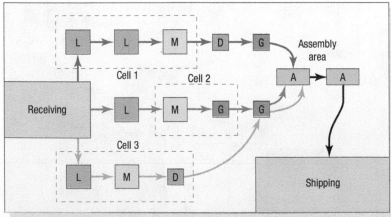

(b) Line flows in a job shop with three GT cells

▲ **FIGURE 6.5**

Process Flows Before and After the Use of GT Cells

Source: Groover, Automation, Production Systems & Computer-Aided Manufacturing, 1st Ed., © 1980. Reprinted and Electronically reproduced by permission of Pearson Education, Inc., Upper Saddle River, New Jersey.

MANAGERIAL PRACTICE 6.1   Panasonic Corporation

Panasonic Corporation, which was originally founded as Matsushita Corporation in 1918 to produce lamps, has grown to become one of the largest electronic manufacturing firms in the world. As of March 31, 2014, Panasonic had 271,789 employees and over 500 consolidated companies creating net sales of about $75 billion per year. While the last few years have been challenging in terms of reduction in sales and workforce, Panasonic continues to be one of the largest producers in Japan of electronic products. Renowned for its global focus on efficiency and lean operations, its pursuit of excellence is exemplified nowhere better than at the Matsushita Electric Company's factory in Saga on Japan's southern island of Kyushu, where cordless phones, fax machines, and security cameras are made in record time by machines in a spotless facility.

Even though the plant's efficiency had doubled over a four-year span, managers saw opportunities for "trimming the fat" and improving further. A cluster of robots that could seamlessly hand off work to one another, flexibly substitute for a broken robot, and use software to synchronize production replaced the plant's conveyor belts. As a result, throughput time declined from 2.5 days to 40 minutes, allowing the Saga plant to make twice as many phones per week, which in turn allowed a reduction in inventory because components such as chips and circuit boards spend much less time in the factory. Being able to make things faster means that the plant can quickly change the product mix even as customer demands shift and new products are introduced, thus allowing Panasonic to keep ahead of low-cost rivals in other Asian countries.

Panasonic has used the lessons learned from the Saga mother plant to change layouts and setups at six other plants in China, Malaysia, Mexico, and Great Britain. These plants have been able to similarly cut their inventories and improve productivity, even as ideas from local staff at each plant

Panasonic stand with many 3D television screens at IFA consumer electronics trade fair in Berlin, Germany.

were incorporated into the change effort. The next sets of improvements are focused on breaking assembly lines into cells and better utilizing the idle robots. In addition, standardized circuit board designs that are common to a large variety of end products are being used to minimize the retooling of robots for every type of board. By relentlessly focusing on minimizing waste and continuously improving efficiency, Panasonic has been able to weather severe business challenges and downturn better than what would have been the case otherwise.

Source: Kenji Hall, "No One Does Lean Like the Japanese," Business Week (July 10, 2006), pp. 40–41; **http://panasonic.net/corporate/info/** (August 4, 2014).

Value Stream Mapping

Value stream mapping (VSM) is a widely used qualitative lean tool aimed at eliminating waste or muda. Waste in many processes can be as high as 60 percent. Value stream mapping is helpful because it creates a visual map of every process involved in the flow of materials and information in a product's value chain. These maps consist of a current state drawing, a future state drawing, and an implementation plan. Value stream mapping spans the supply chain from the firm's receipt of raw materials or components to the delivery of the finished good to the customer. Thus, it tends to be broader in scope, displaying far more information than a typical process map or a flowchart used with Six Sigma process improvement efforts. Creating such a big picture representation helps managers identify the source of wasteful non-value-added activities.

Value stream mapping follows the steps shown in Figure 6.6. The first step is to focus on one product family for which mapping can be done. It is then followed by drawing a current state map of the existing production situation: Analysts start from the customer end and work upstream to draw the map by hand and record actual process times rather than rely on information not obtained by firsthand observation. Information for drawing the material and information flows can be gathered from the shop floor, including the data related to each process: cycle time (C/T), setup or changeover time (C/O), uptime (on-demand available machine time expressed as a percentage), production batch sizes, number of people required to operate the process, number of product variations, pack size (for moving the product to the next stage), working time (minus breaks), and scrap rate. Value stream mapping uses a standard set of icons for material flow, information flow, and general information (to denote operators, safety stock buffers, etc.). Even though the complete glossary is extensive, a representative set of these icons is shown in Figure 6.7. These icons provide a common language for describing in detail how a facility should operate to create a better flow.

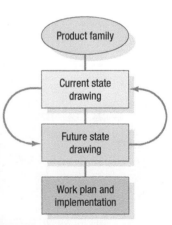

▲ **FIGURE 6.6**
Value Stream Mapping Steps
Source: © Copyright 2003 Lean Enterprise Institute, Inc. Cambridge, MA, lean.org. All rights reserved.

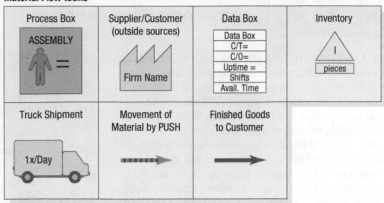

value stream mapping (VSM)

A qualitative lean tool for
eliminating waste or muda that
involves a current state drawing,
a future state drawing, and an
implementation plan.

   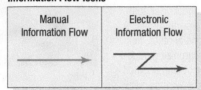 **Determining the Value Stream Map, Takt Time, and Total Capacity**

Jensen Bearings Incorporated, a ball bearing manufacturing company located in Lexington, South Carolina, receives raw material sheets from Kline Steel Company once a week every Monday for a product family of retainers (casings in which ball bearings are held), and then ships its finished product on a daily basis to a second-tier automotive manufacturing customer named GNK Enterprises. The product family of the bearing manufacturing company under consideration consists of two types of retainers—large (L) and small (S)—that are packaged for shipping in returnable trays with 40 retainers in each tray. The manufacturing process consists of a cell containing pressing operation; a piercing and forming cell, and a finish grind operation, after which the two types of retainers are staged for shipping. The information collected by the operations manager at Jensen Bearings Inc. is shown in Table 6.3.

TABLE 6.3 | OPERATIONS DATA FOR A FAMILY OF RETAINERS AT JENSEN BEARINGS, INC.

Overall Process Attributes	Average demand: 3,200/week (1,000 "L"; 2,200 "S") Batch size: 40 Number of shifts per day: 1 Availability: 8 hours per shift with two 30-minute lunch breaks	
Process Step 1	Press	Cycle time = 12 seconds Setup time = 10 min Up time = 100% Operators = 1 WIP = 5 days of sheets (Before Press)
Process Step 2	Pierce & Form	Cycle time = 34 seconds Setup time = 3 minutes Up time = 100% Operators = 1 WIP = 1,000 "L," 1,250 "S" (Before Pierce & Form)
Process Step 3	Finish Grind	Cycle time = 35 seconds Setup time = 0 minutes Up time = 100% Operators = 1 WIP = 1,050 "L," 2,300 "S" (Before Finish Grind)
Process Step 4	Shipping	WIP = 500 "L," 975 "S" (After Finish Grind)

	Average demand: 3,200/week (1,000 "L"; 2,200 "S")
	Batch size: 40
	Number of shifts per day: 1
Overall Process Attributes	Availability: 8 hours per shift with two 30-minute lunch breaks
Customer Shipments	One shipment of 3,200 units each week in trays of 40 pieces

Information Flow	All communications from customer are electronic:
	  180/90/60/30/day Forecasts
	  Daily Order
	All communications to supplier are electronic
	  4-Week Forecast
	  Weekly Fax
	There is a weekly schedule manually delivered to Press, Pierce & Form, and Finish Grind and a Daily Ship Schedule manually delivered to Shipping
	All material is pushed

a. Using data shown in Table 6.3; create a value stream map for Jensen Bearings Inc. and show how the data box values are calculated.

b. What is the takt time for this manufacturing cell?

c. What is the production lead time at each process in the manufacturing cell?

d. What is the total processing time of this manufacturing cell?

e. What is the capacity of this manufacturing cell?

SOLUTION

a. We use the VSM icons to illustrate in Figure 6.8 what a current state map would look like for Jensen Bearings Inc. The process characteristics and inventory buffers in front of each process are shown in the current state map of Figure 6.8. One worker occupies each station. The process flows shown at the bottom of Figure 6.8 are similar to the flowcharts discussed in Chapter 2, "Process Strategy and Analysis," except that more detailed information is presented here for each process. However, what really sets the

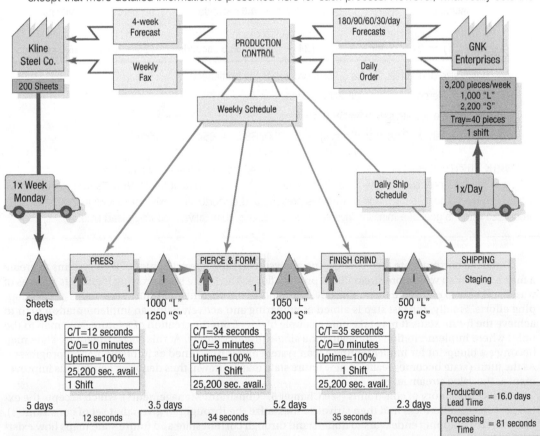

◀ **FIGURE 6.8**
Current State Map for a
Family of Retainers at Jensen
Bearings Incorporated

value stream maps apart from flowcharts is the inclusion of information flows at the top of Figure 6.8, which plan and coordinate all the process activities. The value stream maps are more comprehensive than process flowcharts and meld together planning and control systems (discussed in detail in Chapter 11, "Resource Planning") with detailed flowcharts (discussed in Chapter 2) to create a comprehensive supply chain view that includes both information and material flows between the firm and its suppliers and customers.

b. The cell's takt time is the rate at which the cell must produce units to match demand.

Daily Demand = [(1,000 + 2,200) pieces per week]/5 working days per week
= 640 pieces per day

Daily Availability = (7 hours per day) × (3,600 seconds per hour) = 25,200 seconds per day

Takt Time = Daily Availability/Daily Demand = (25,200 seconds per day)/640 pieces per day
= **39.375** seconds per piece

c. The production lead time (in days) is calculated by summing the inventory held between each processing step divided by daily demand.

Raw Material lead time = 5.0 days

WIP lead time between Press and Pierce & Form = (2,250/640) = 3.5 days

WIP lead time between Pierce & Form and Finish Grind = (3,350/640) = 5.2 days

WIP lead time between Finish Grind and Shipping = (1,475/640) = 2.3 days

Total Production Lead time = (5 + 3.5 + 5.2 + 2.3) = **16** days

d. The cycle time at each process is added to compute total processing time. The manufacturing cell's total processing time is (12 + 34 + 35) = **81** seconds.

e. The cell's capacity may be calculated by locating the bottleneck and computing the number of units that it can process in the available time per day at that bottleneck with the given batch size of 40 units.

Capacity at Press	Capacity at Pierce & Form	Capacity at Finish Grind
Cycle time = 12 seconds	Cycle time = 34 seconds	Cycle time = 35 seconds
Setup Time = (10 min * 60 seconds per min)/40 units per batch = **15.0 seconds**	Setup Time = (3 minutes * 60 seconds per minute)/40 units per batch = **4.5 seconds**	Setup Time = (0 minutes * 60 seconds per minute)/40 units per batch = **0.0 seconds**
Per Unit Processing Time = (12 + 15) = **27 seconds**	Per Unit Processing Time = (34 + 4.5) = **38.5 seconds**	Per Unit Processing Time = (35 + 0.0) = **35.0 seconds**

At a batch size of 40 units, Pierce & Form process is the bottleneck.

Availability at Pierce & Form = 25,200 seconds per day

Time at bottleneck (with setup) = 38.5 seconds

Capacity (Availability/Time at bottleneck) = 25,200/38.5 = **654** units per day

DECISION POINT
Although the total processing time for each retainer is only 81 seconds, it takes 16 days for the cumulative production lead time. Clearly *muda* or waste is present, and opportunities exist for reconfiguring the existing processes with the goal of eliminating inventories and reducing cumulative production lead time.

Once the current state map is done, the analysts can then use principles of lean systems to create a future state map with more streamlined product flows. The future state drawing highlights sources of waste and how to eliminate them. The developments of the current and future state maps are overlapping efforts. Finally, the last step is aimed at preparing and actively using an implementation plan to achieve the future state. It may take only a couple of days from the creation of a future state map to the point where implementation can begin for a single product family. At this stage, the future state map becomes a blueprint for implementing a lean system and is fine-tuned as implementation progresses. As the future state becomes reality, a new future state map is drawn, thus denoting continuous improvement at the value stream level.

Unlike the theory of constraints (see Chapter 5, "Constraint Management"), which accepts the existing system bottlenecks and then strives to maximize the throughput given that set of constraint(s), value stream mapping endeavors to understand through current state and future state maps how existing processes can be altered to eliminate bottlenecks and other wasteful activities. The goal is to bring the production rate of the entire process closer to the customer's desired demand rate. The benefits of applying this tool to the waste-removal process include reduced lead times and work-in-process inventories, reduced rework and scrap rates, and lower indirect labor costs.

The *Kanban* System

One of the most publicized aspects of lean systems, and the TPS in particular, is the *kanban* system developed by Toyota. **Kanban**, meaning "card" or "visible record" in Japanese, refers to cards used to control the flow of production through a factory. In the most basic *kanban* system, a card is attached to each container of items produced. The container holds a given percent of the daily production requirements for an item. When the user of the parts empties a container, the card is removed from the container and put on a receiving post. The empty container is then taken to the storage area, and the card signals the need to produce another container of the part. When the container has been refilled, the card is put back on the container, which is then returned to a storage area. The cycle begins again when the user of the parts retrieves the container with the card attached.

Figure 6.9 shows how a single-card *kanban* system works when a fabrication cell feeds two assembly lines. As an assembly line needs more parts, the *kanban* card for those parts is taken to the receiving post, and a full container of parts is removed from the storage area. The receiving post accumulates cards for assembly lines and a scheduler sequences the production of replenishment parts. In this example, the fabrication cell will produce product 2 (red) before it produces product 1 (green). The cell consists of three different operations, but operation 2 has two workstations. Once production has been initiated in the cell, the product begins on operation 1 but could be routed to either of the workstations performing operation 2, depending on the workload at the time. Finally, the product is processed on operation 3 before being taken to the storage area.

General Operating Rules

The operating rules for the single-card system are simple and are designed to facilitate the flow of materials while maintaining control of inventory levels.

1. Each container must have a card.

2. The assembly line always withdraws materials from the fabrication cell. The fabrication cell never pushes parts to the assembly line because, sooner or later, parts will be supplied that are not yet needed for production.

3. Containers of parts must never be removed from a storage area without a *kanban* first being posted on the receiving post.

4. The containers should always contain the same number of good parts. The use of nonstandard containers or irregularly filled containers disrupts the production flow of the assembly line.

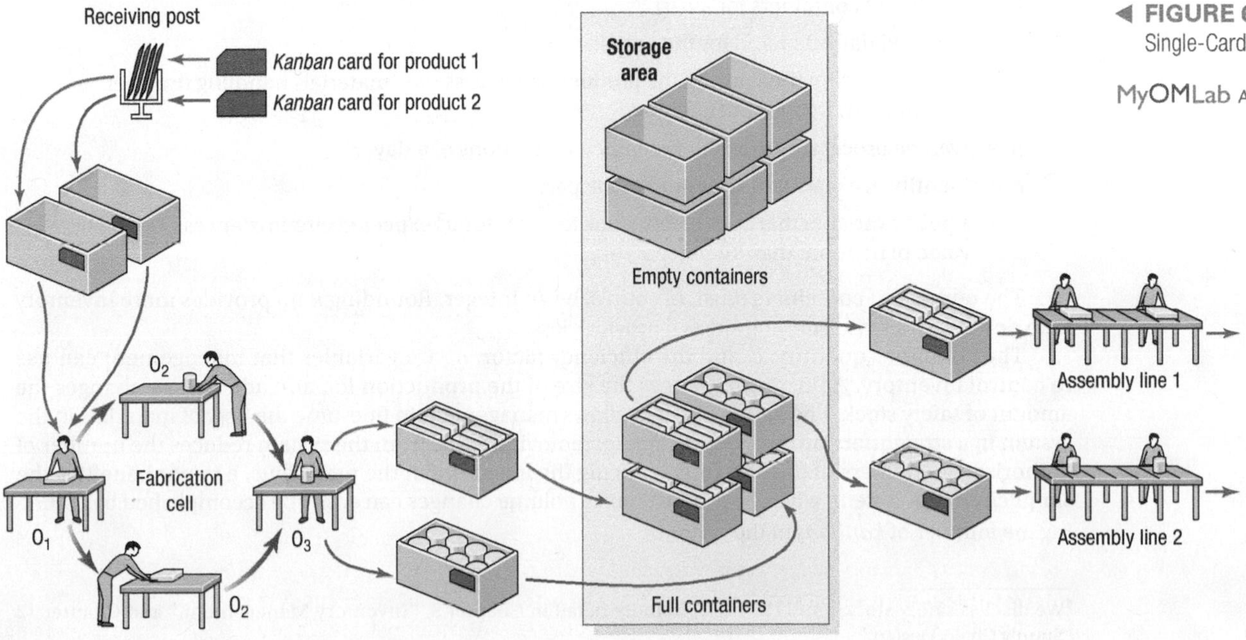

kanban

A Japanese word meaning "card" or "visible record" that refers to cards used to control the flow of production through a factory.

◀ **FIGURE 6.9**
Single-Card *Kanban* System

MyOMLab Animation

5. Only nondefective parts should be passed along to the assembly line to make the best use of materials and worker's time. This rule reinforces the notion of building quality at the source, which is an important characteristic of lean systems.

6. Total production should not exceed the total amount authorized on the *kanbans* in the system.

Toyota uses a two-card system, based on a withdrawal card and a production-order card, to control inventory quantities more closely. The withdrawal card specifies the item and the quantity the user of the item should withdraw from the producer of the item, as well as the stocking locations for both the user and the producer. The production-order card specifies the item and the quantity to be produced, the materials required and where to find them, and where to store the finished item. Materials cannot be withdrawn without a withdrawal card, and production cannot begin without a production-order card. The cards are attached to containers when production commences. By manipulating the number of withdrawal and production cards in play at any time, management can control the flow of materials in the production system.

Determining the Number of Containers

The number of authorized containers in the TPS determines the amount of authorized inventory. Management must make two determinations: (1) the number of units to be held by each container, and (2) the number of containers flowing back and forth between the supplier station and the user station. The first decision amounts to determining the size of the production lot.

The number of containers flowing back and forth between two stations directly affects the quantities of work-in-process inventory, which includes any safety stock inventory to cover for unexpected requirements.[4] The containers spend some time in production, in a line waiting, in a storage location, or in transit. The key to determining the number of containers required is to estimate the average lead time needed to produce a container of parts. The lead time is a function of the processing time per container at the supplier station, the waiting time during the production process, and the time required for materials handling. Little's Law, which says that the average work-in-process inventory (WIP) equals the average demand rate multiplied by the average time a unit spends in the manufacturing process, can be used to determine the number of containers needed to support the user station (see Supplement B, "Waiting Lines").

WIP = (average demand rate)(average time a container spends in the manufacturing process) + safety stock

In this application of determining the number of containers needed for a part, WIP is the product of κ, the number of containers, and c, the number of units in each container. Consequently,

$$\kappa c = \overline{d}(\overline{\omega} + \overline{\rho})(1 + \alpha)$$

$$\kappa = \frac{\overline{d}(\overline{\omega} + \overline{\rho})(1 + \alpha)}{c}$$

where

κ = number of containers for a part

$\overline{d}$ = expected daily demand for the part, in units

$\overline{\omega}$ = average waiting time during the production process plus materials handling time per container, in fractions of a day

$\overline{\rho}$ = average processing time per container, in fractions of a day

c = quantity in a standard container of the part

α = a policy variable that adds safety stock to cover for unexpected circumstances (Toyota uses a value of no more than 10 percent)

The number of containers must, of course, be an integer. Rounding κ up provides more inventory than desired, whereas rounding κ down provides less.

The container quantity, c, and the efficiency factor, α, are variables that management can use to control inventory. Adjusting c changes the size of the production lot, and adjusting α changes the amount of safety stock. The *kanban* system allows management to fine-tune the flow of materials in the system in a straightforward way. For example, removing cards from the system reduces the number of authorized containers of the part thus reducing the inventory of the part. Thus, a major benefit is the simplicity of the system, whereby product mix or volume changes can easily be accomplished by adjusting the number of *kanbans* in the system.

---

[4]We discuss safety stocks, and their use, in more detail in Chapter 9, "Inventory Management," and Chapter 12 "Supply Chain Design."

EXAMPLE 6.2	Determining the Appropriate Number of Containers

The Westerville Auto Parts Company produces rocker-arm assemblies for use in the steering and suspension systems of four-wheel-drive trucks. A typical container of parts spends 0.02 day in processing and 0.08 day in materials handling and waiting during its manufacturing cycle. The daily demand for the part is 2,000 units. Management believes that demand for the rocker-arm assembly is uncertain enough to warrant a safety stock equivalent of 10 percent of its authorized inventory.

a. If each container contains 22 parts, how many containers should be authorized?

b. Suppose that a proposal to revise the plant layout would cut materials handling and waiting time per container to 0.06 day. How many containers would be needed?

▲ **FIGURE 6.10**
OM Explorer Solver for Number of Containers

SOLUTION

a. If $\bar{d} = 2{,}000$ units / day, $\bar{\rho} = 0.02$ day, $\alpha = 0.10$, $\bar{\omega} = 0.08$ day, and $c = 22$ units,

$$\kappa = \frac{2{,}000(0.08 + 0.02)(1.0)}{22} = \frac{220}{22} = \textbf{10 containers}$$

b. Figure 6.10 from OM Explorer shows that the number of containers drops to **8**.

DECISION POINT

The average lead time per container is $\bar{\omega} + \bar{\rho}$. With a lead time of 0.10 day, 10 containers are needed. However, if the improved facility layout reduces the materials handling time and waiting time to $\bar{\omega} = 0.06$ day, only 8 containers are needed. The maximum authorized inventory of the rocker-arm assembly is κc. Thus, in part (a), the maximum authorized inventory is 220 units, but in part (b), it is only 176 units. Reducing $\bar{\omega} + \bar{\rho}$ by 20 percent reduces the inventory of the part by 20 percent. Management must balance the cost of the layout change (a one-time charge) against the long-term benefits of inventory reduction.

Other *Kanban* Signals

Cards are not the only way to signal the need for more production of a part. Other, less formal methods are possible, including container and containerless systems.

Container System Sometimes, the container itself can be used as a signal device: An empty container signals the need to fill it. Unisys took this approach for low-value items. Adding or removing containers adjusts the amount of inventory of the part. This system works well when the container is specially designed for a particular part and no other parts could accidentally be put in the container. Such is the case when the container is actually a pallet or fixture used to position the part during precision processing.

Containerless System Systems requiring no containers have been devised. In assembly-line operations, operators use their own workbench areas to put completed units on painted squares, one unit per square. Each painted square represents a container, and the number of painted squares on each operator's bench is calculated to balance the line flow. When the subsequent user removes a unit from one of the producer's squares, the empty square signals the need to produce another unit. McDonald's uses a containerless system. Information entered by the order taker at the cash register is transmitted to the cooks and assemblers, who produce the sandwiches requested by the customer.

Operational Benefits and Implementation Issues

To gain competitive advantage and to make dramatic improvements, a lean system can be the solution. Lean systems can be an integral part of a corporate strategy based on speed because they cut cycle times, improve inventory turnover, and increase labor productivity. Recent studies also show that practices representing different components of lean systems such as JIT, TQM, Six Sigma, total preventive maintenance (TPM), and human resource management (HRM), individually as well as cumulatively, improve the performance of manufacturing plants as well as service facilities. Lean systems also involve a considerable amount of employee participation through small-group interaction sessions, which have resulted in improvements in many aspects of operations, not the least of which is service or product quality.

Even though the benefits of lean systems can be outstanding, problems can still arise after a lean system has long been operational, which was witnessed recently in product recalls and a perceived shift away from tightly controlled quality that has always been the standard at Toyota. In addition, implementing a

After the pathology lab at the University of Pittsburgh Medical Center adopted a lean operations approach based on a line system versus a batch-and-queue system, the time it took to process samples dropped from days to just hours. Diagnoses were made more quickly as a result, and patients' stays at the hospital were shortened.

lean system can take a long time. We address below some of the issues managers should be aware of when implementing a lean system.

Organizational Considerations

Implementing a lean system requires management to consider issues of worker stress, cooperation and trust among workers and management, and reward systems and labor classifications.

The Human Costs of Lean Systems

Lean systems can be coupled with statistical process control (SPC) to reduce variations in output. However, this combination requires a high degree of regimentation and sometimes stresses the workforce. For example, in the TPS, workers must meet specified cycle times, and with SPC, they must follow prescribed problem-solving methods. Such systems might make workers feel pushed and stressed, causing productivity losses or quality reductions. In addition, workers might feel a loss of some autonomy because of the close linkages in work flows between stations with little or no excess capacity or safety stocks. Managers can mitigate some of these effects by allowing for some slack in the system—either safety stock inventories or capacity slack—and by emphasizing work flows instead of worker pace. Managers also can promote the use of work teams and allow them to determine their task assignments within their domains of responsibility.

Cooperation and Trust

In a lean system, workers and first-line supervisors must take on responsibilities formerly assigned to middle managers and support staff. Activities such as scheduling, expediting, and improving productivity become part of the duties of lower-level personnel. Consequently, the work relationships in the organization must be reoriented in a way that fosters cooperation and mutual trust between the workforce and management. However, this environment can be difficult to achieve, particularly in light of the historical adversarial relationship between the two groups.

Reward Systems and Labor Classifications

In some instances, the reward system must be revamped when a lean system is implemented. At General Motors, for example, a plan to reduce stock at one plant ran into trouble because the production superintendent refused to cut back on the number of unneeded parts being made. Why? Because his or her salary was based on the plant's production volume.

The realignment of reward systems is not the only hurdle. Labor contracts traditionally crippled a company's ability to reassign workers to other tasks as the need arose. For example, a typical automobile plant in the United States has several unions and dozens of labor classifications. Generally, the people in each classification are allowed to do only a limited range of tasks. In some cases, companies have managed to give these employees more flexibility by agreeing to other types of union concessions and benefits. In other cases, however, companies relocated their plants to take advantage of nonunion or foreign labor.

Process Considerations

Firms using lean systems typically have some dominant work flows. To take advantage of lean practices, firms might have to change their existing layouts. Certain workstations might have to be moved closer together, and cells of machines devoted to particular component families may have to be established. However, rearranging a plant to conform to lean practices can be costly. For example, many plants currently receive raw materials and purchased parts by rail, but to facilitate smaller and more frequent shipments, truck deliveries would be preferable. Loading docks might have to be reconstructed or expanded and certain operations relocated to accommodate the change in transportation mode and quantities of arriving materials.

Inventory and Scheduling

Manufacturing firms need to have stable master production schedules, short setups, and frequent, reliable supplies of materials and components to achieve the full potential of the lean systems concept.

Schedule Stability

Daily production schedules in high-volume, make-to-stock environments must be stable for extended periods. At Toyota, the master production schedule is stated in fractions of days over a 3-month period and is revised only once a month. The first month of the schedule is frozen to avoid disruptive changes in the daily production schedule for each workstation; that is, the workstations execute the same work schedule each day of the month (see Chapter 11, "Resource Planning," for more details on master production schedules and freezing). At the beginning of each month, *kanbans* are reissued for the new daily production rate. Stable schedules are needed so that production lines can be balanced and new assignments found for employees who otherwise would be underutilized. Lean systems used in high-volume, make-to-stock environments cannot respond quickly to scheduling changes because little slack inventory or capacity is available to absorb these changes.

Setups   If the inventory advantages of a lean system are to be realized, small lot sizes must be used. However, because small lots require a large number of setups, companies must significantly reduce setup times. Some companies have not been able to achieve short setup times and, therefore, have to use large-lot production, negating some of the advantages of lean practices. Also, lean systems are vulnerable to lengthy changeovers to new products because the low levels of finished goods inventory will be insufficient to cover demand while the system is down. If changeover times cannot be reduced, large finished goods inventories of the old product must be accumulated to compensate. In the automobile industry, every week that a plant is shut down for new-model changeover costs between $16 million and $20 million in pretax profits.

Purchasing and Logistics   If frequent, small shipments of purchased items cannot be arranged with suppliers, large inventory savings for these items cannot be realized. For example, in the United States, such arrangements may prove difficult because of the geographic dispersion of suppliers.

The shipments of raw materials and components must be reliable because of the low inventory levels in lean systems. A plant can be shut down because of a lack of materials. Similarly, recovery becomes more prolonged and difficult in a lean system after supply chains are disrupted, which is what happened immediately after 9/11.

Process design and continuous improvement are key elements of a successful operations strategy. In this chapter, we focused on lean systems as a directive for efficient process design and an approach to achieve continuous improvement. We showed how JIT systems, a popular lean systems approach, can be used for continuous improvement and how a *kanban* system can be used to control the amount of work-in-process inventory. Transforming a current process design to one embodying a lean systems philosophy is a constant challenge for management, often fraught with implementation issues. However, adopting appropriate tools and management approaches can facilitate such a transformation, as exemplified by firms like Aldi, Panasonic, and Toyota among others.

LEARNING GOALS IN REVIEW

Learning Goal	Guidelines for Review	MyOMLab Resources
① Describe how lean systems can facilitate the continuous improvement of processes.	See the section on "Continuous Improvement using a Lean Systems Approach," pp. 209–210. Review Figure 6.1 and the opening vignette on Aldi Corporation.	
② Identify the strategic supply chain and process characteristics of lean systems.	See the sub-sections on "Supply Chain Considerations in Lean Systems," p. 211, and "Process Considerations in Lean Systems," pp. 212–216. The subsection on "Toyota Production System," pp. 216–217, illustrates how one firm implements lean characteristics to gain strategic advantage over its competition.	**Video:** Lean Systems at Autoliv
③ Explain the differences between one worker, multiple machine (OWMM) and group technology (GT) approaches to lean system layouts.	The section "Designing Lean System Layouts," pp. 217–219, shows you how to differentiate between two different types of layouts used to implement line flows, when volumes are not high to justify a single line of multiple workers to a single product.	
④ Understand value stream mapping and its role in waste reduction.	The section "Value Stream Mapping," pp. 219–223, shows you how to construct value stream maps and identify waste in the processes. Review Example 6.1 for details on mapping and creating data boxes.	
⑤ Understand *kanban* systems for creating a production schedule in a lean system.	The section "The *Kanban* System," pp. 223–225, shows how firms like Toyota use simple visual systems to pull production and make exactly what the market demands. Example 6.2 shows how to calculate the number of *kanban* cards needed.	**OM Explorer Tutor:** 6.1: Calculate Number of Containers in a *Kanban* System **OM Explorer Solver:** Number of Containers
⑥ Explain the implementation issues associated with the application of lean systems.	The section "Operational Benefits and Implementation Issues," pp. 225–227, reviews organizational and process considerations needed to successfully deploy lean systems and gain their benefits.	**Video:** Lean Systems at Autoliv

Key Equations

The *Kanban* System

Number of containers:

$$\kappa = \frac{\bar{d}(\bar{\omega} + \bar{\rho})(1 + \alpha)}{c}$$

Key Terms

five S (5S) 214
group technology (GT) 218
heijunka 213
jidoka 212
JIT system 210
just-in-time (JIT) philosophy 209

kanban 223
lean systems 208
lot 211
mixed-model assembly 214
one worker, multiple machines (OWMM)
  cell 217

poka-yoke 213
pull method 212
push method 212
single-digit setup 211
takt time 213
value stream mapping (VSM) 220

Solved Problem 1

MyOMLab Video

Metcalf, Inc., manufacturers engine assembly brackets for two major automotive customers. The manufacturing process for the brackets consists of a cell containing a forming operation, a drilling operation, a finish grinding operation, and packaging, after which the brackets are staged for shipping. The information collected by the operations manager at Metcalf, Inc., is shown in Table 6.4.

TABLE 6.4 | OPERATIONS DATA FOR BRACKETS AT METCALF, INC.

Overall Process Attributes	Average demand: 2700/day Batch size: 50 Number of shifts per day: 2 Availability: 8 hours per shift with a 30-minute lunch break	
Process Step 1	Forming	Cycle time = 11 seconds Setup time = 3 minutes Up time = 100% Operators = 1 WIP = 4000 units (Before Forming)
Process Step 2	Drilling	Cycle time = 10 seconds Setup time = 2 minutes Up time = 100% Operators = 1 WIP = 5,000 units (Before Drilling)
Process Step 3	Grinding	Cycle time = 17 seconds Setup time = 0 minutes Up time = 100% Operators = 1 WIP = 2,000 units (Before Grinding)
Process Step 4	Packaging	Cycle time = 15 seconds Setup time = 0 minutes Up time = 100% Operators = 1 WIP = 1,600 units (Before Packaging) WIP = 15,700 units (Before Shipping)
Customer Shipments	One shipment of 13,500 units each week	
Information Flow	All communications with customer are electronic There is a weekly order release to Forming All material is pushed	

a. Using data shown in Table 6.4; create a value stream map for Metcalf, Inc., and show how the data box values are calculated.

b. What is the takt time for this manufacturing cell?

c. What is the production lead time at each process in the manufacturing cell?

d. What is the total processing time of this manufacturing cell?

e. What is the capacity of this manufacturing cell?

SOLUTION

a. Figure 6.11 shows the current value stream state map for Metcalf, Inc.

b. Daily Demand $=$ 2,700 units per day

Daily Availability $=$ (7.5 hours per day) $\times$ (3,600 seconds per hour) $\times$ (2 shifts per day)
$\qquad = $ 54,000 seconds per day

Takt Time $=$ Daily Availability/Daily Demand $=$ 54,000 seconds per day/2,700 units per day
$\qquad = $ **20** seconds per unit

c. The production lead time (in days) is calculated by summing the inventory held between each processing step divided by daily demand.

Raw Material lead time $= \lceil 4{,}000/2{,}700 \rceil = 1.48$ days

WIP lead time between Forming and Drilling $= \lceil 5{,}000/2{,}700 \rceil = 1.85$ days

WIP lead time between Drilling and Grinding $= \lfloor 2{,}000/2{,}700 \rfloor = 0.74$ day

WIP lead time between Grinding and Packaging $= \lceil 1{,}600/2{,}700 \rceil = 0.59$ day

Finished Goods lead time before Shipping $= \lceil 15{,}700/2{,}700 \rceil = 5.81$ days

The cell's total production lead time is: $1.48 + 1.85 + 0.74 + 0.59 + 5.81 = $ **10.47** days

d. The manufacturing cell's total processing time is $(11 + 10 + 17 + 15) = $ **53** seconds.

e. The cell's capacity may be calculated by locating the bottleneck and computing the number of units that it can process in the available time per day at that bottleneck.

▼ **FIGURE 6.11**
Current State Value Stream Map for Metcalf, Inc.

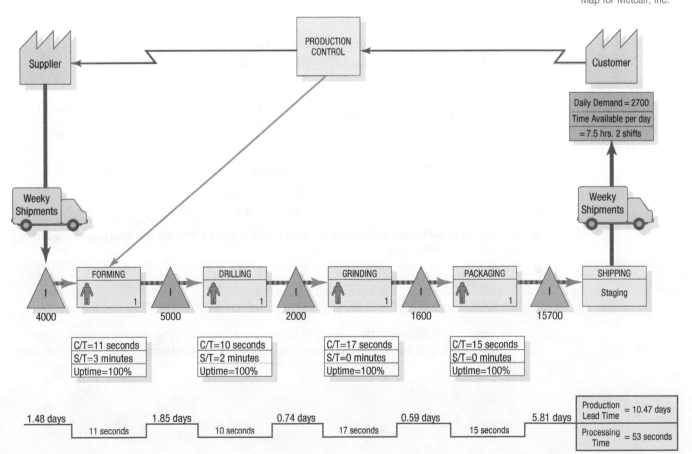

Capacity at Forming	Capacity at Drilling	Capacity at Grinding	Capacity at Packaging
Cycle time = 11 seconds	Cycle time = 10 seconds	Cycle time = 17 seconds	Cycle time = 15 seconds
Setup Time = (3 minutes * 60 seconds per minute)/ 50 units per batch = **3.6 seconds**	Setup Time = (2 minutes * 60 seconds per minute)/ 50 units per batch = **2.4 seconds**	Setup Time = **zero seconds**	Setup Time = **zero seconds**
Per Unit Processing Time = (11 + 3.6) = **14.6 seconds**	Per Unit Processing Time = (10 + 2.4) = **12.4 seconds**	Per Unit Processing Time = (17 + 0) = **17.0 seconds**	Per Unit Processing Time = (15 + 0) = **15.0 seconds**

a. At a batch size of 50 units, Finish Grinding process is the bottleneck

b. Availability at Grinding = 54,000 seconds per day

c. Time at bottleneck (with setup) = 17.0 seconds

d. Capacity (Availability/Time at bottleneck) = 54,000/17 = **3,176** units per day

Solved Problem 2

A company using a *kanban* system has an inefficient machine group. For example, the daily demand for part L105A is 3,000 units. The average waiting time for a container of parts is 0.8 day. The processing time for a container of L105A is 0.2 day, and a container holds 270 units. Currently, 20 containers are used for this item.

a. What is the value of the policy variable, α?

b. What is the total planned inventory (work-in-process and finished goods) for item L105A?

c. Suppose that the policy variable, α, was 0. How many containers would be needed now? What is the effect of the policy variable in this example?

SOLUTION

a. We use the equation for the number of containers and then solve for α:

$$\kappa = \frac{\bar{d}(\bar{\omega} + \bar{\rho})(1 + \alpha)}{c}$$

$$20 = \frac{3,000(0.8 + 0.2)(1 + \alpha)}{270}$$

and

$$(1 + \alpha) = \frac{20(270)}{3,000(0.8 + 0.2)} = 1.8$$

$$\alpha = 1.8 - 1 = \mathbf{0.8}$$

b. With 20 containers in the system and each container holding 270 units, the total planned inventory is 20(270) = **5,400** units.

c. If $\alpha = 0$

$$\kappa = \frac{3,000(0.8 + 0.2)(1 + 0)}{270} = 11.11, \text{ or } \mathbf{12} \text{ containers}$$

The policy variable adjusts the number of containers. In this case, the difference is quite dramatic because $\bar{\omega} + \bar{\rho}$ is fairly large and the number of units per container is small relative to daily demand.

Discussion Questions

1. Compare and contrast the following two situations:

   a. A company's lean system stresses teamwork. Employees feel more involved and, therefore, productivity and quality increase at the company. The problem is that workers also experience a loss of individual autonomy.

   b. A humanities professor believes that all students want to learn. To encourage students to work together and learn from each other—thereby increasing the involvement, productivity, and the quality of the learning experience—the professor announces that all students in the class will receive the same grade and that it will be based on the performance of the group.

2. Which elements of lean systems would be most troublesome for manufacturers to implement? Why?

3. List the pressures that lean systems pose for supply chains, whether in the form of process failures due to inventory shortages or labor stoppages, and so forth. Reflect on how these pressures may apply to a firm that is actually implementing lean philosophy in their operations.

4. Identify a service or a manufacturing process that you are familiar with, and draw a current state value stream map to depict its existing information and material flows.

Problems

The OM Explorer and POM for Windows software is available to all students using the 11th edition of this textbook. Go to **http://www.pearsonhighered.com/krajewski** to download these computer packages. If you purchased MyOMLab, you also have access to Active Models software and significant help in doing the following problems. Check with your instructor on how best to use these resources. In many cases, the instructor wants you to understand how to do the calculations by hand. At the least, the software provides a check on your calculations. When calculations are particularly complex and the goal is interpreting the results in making decisions, the software replaces entirely the manual calculations.

Strategic Characteristics of Lean Systems

1. Swenson Saws produces bow, frame, dovetail, and tenon saws used by craft furniture makers. During an 8-hour shift, a saw is produced every 6 minutes. The demand for bow, frame, and dovetail saws is about the same, but the demand for tenon saws is twice the demand for the other three.

   a. If mixed-model scheduling is used, how many of each saw will be produced before the cycle is repeated?

   b. Determine a satisfactory production sequence for one unit production. How often is this sequence repeated?

   c. How many of each saw does Swenson produce in one shift?

2. The Harvey Motorcycle Company produces three models: the Tiger, a sure-footed dirt bike; the LX2000, a nimble café racer; and the Golden, a large interstate tourer. This month's master production schedule calls for the production of 54 Goldens, 42 LX2000s, and 30 Tigers per 7-hour shift.

   a. What average cycle time is required for the assembly line to achieve the production quota in 7 hours?

   b. If mixed-model scheduling is used, how many of each model will be produced before the production cycle is repeated?

   c. Determine a satisfactory production sequence for the ultimate in small-lot production: one unit.

   d. The design of a new model, the Cheetah, includes features from the Tiger, LX2000, and Golden models. The resulting blended design has an indecisive character and is expected to attract some sales from the other models. Determine a mixed-model schedule resulting in 52 Goldens, 39 LX2000s, 26 Tigers, and 13 Cheetahs per 7-hour shift. Although the total number of motorcycles produced per day will increase only slightly, what problem might be anticipated in implementing this change from the production schedule indicated in part (b)?

3. The Farm-4-Less tractor company produces a grain combine (GC) in addition to both a large (LT) and small size tractor (SM). Its production manager desires to produce to customer demand using a mixed-model production line. The current sequence of production, which is repeated 30 times during a shift, is SM-GC-SM-LT-SM-GC-LT-SM. A new machine is produced every 2 minutes. The plant operates two 8-hour shifts. There is no downtime because the 4 hours between each shift are dedicated to maintenance and restocking raw material. Based on this information, answer the following questions.

   a. How long does it take the production cycle to be completed?

   b. How many of each type of machine does Farm-4-Less produce in a shift?

Value Stream Mapping

4. Figure 6.12 provides a new current state value stream map for the family of retainers at the Jensen Bearings, Inc., firm described in Example 6.1. This map depicts the value stream after Kline Steel agrees to accept daily orders for steel sheets and Jensen Bearings continues to deliver the finished goods on a daily basis.

FIGURE 6.12 ▶
New Current State Value Stream
Map at Jensen Bearings, Inc.

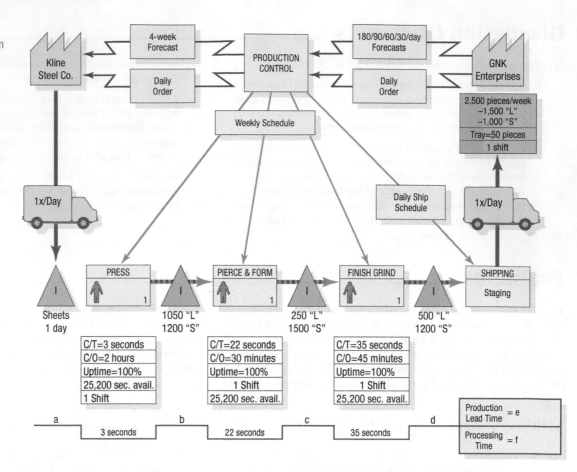

Calculate each component of the new value stream's reduced lead time.

a. How many days of raw material does the Bearing's plant now hold?

b. How many days of work in process inventory is held between Press and Pierce & Form?

c. How many days of work in process inventory is held between Pierce & Form and Finish Grind?

d. How many days of work in process inventory is held between Finish Grind and Shipping?

e. What is the new value steam's production lead time?

f. What is the new value stream's processing time?

5. Anguilla Manufacturing is interested in using the data collected during Value Stream Mapping to evaluate the current state performance of the capacity of its manual assembly line process under different batch size assumptions. The availability of processing per shift, after accounting for breaks and a mid-shift employee meeting, is 436 minutes. The current operating characteristics of each processing step are found in the table below. Note that each step can only process one part at a time and all steps must process the same sized batches.

	Saw	Sand	Drill	Assemble	Mark
Cycle time per part	20 seconds	15 seconds	30 seconds	25 seconds	10 seconds
Setup time per batch	3 minutes	4 minutes	0 minutes	3 minutes	8 minutes

a. Calculate the average processing time per unit and the capacity at each step assuming batch sizes of:

   i. 10 units

   ii. 20 units

   iii. 30 units

   iv. 40 units

b. Identify the bottleneck operation and the line's processing capacity for each batch size listed in part a.

c. Explain why batch sizes beyond 40 units will not increase the line's processing capacity further.

6. The manager at Ormonde, Inc., collected the value stream mapping data from the plant's most problematic manufacturing cell that fabricates parts for washing machines. This data is shown in Table 6.5. Using this data, calculate the current state performance of the cell and answer the following questions.

a. What is the cell's current inventory level?

b. What is the takt time for this manufacturing cell?

c. What is the production lead time at each process in the manufacturing cell?

d. What is the total processing time of this manufacturing cell?

e. What is the capacity of this manufacturing cell?

TABLE 6.5 | OPERATIONS DATA FOR ORMONDE, INC.

Overall Process Attributes	Average demand: 550/day Batch size: 20 Number of shifts per day: 3 Availability: 8 hours per shift with a 45-minute lunch break	
Process Step 1	Cutting	Cycle time = 120 seconds Setup time = 3 minutes Up time = 100% Operators = 1 WIP = 400 units (Before Cutting)
Process Step 2	Bending	Cycle time = 100 seconds Setup time = 5 minutes Up time = 100% Operators = 1 WIP = 500 units (Before Bending)
Process Step 3	Punching	Cycle time = 140 seconds Setup time = none Up time = 100% Operators = 1 WIP = 200 units (Before Punching) WIP = 1,000 units (After Punching)
Customer Shipments	One shipment of 2,750 units each week	
Information Flow	All communications with customer are electronic There is a weekly order release to Cutting All material is pushed	

The *Kanban* System

7. A fabrication cell at Spradley's Sprockets uses the pull method to supply gears to an assembly line. George Jitson is in charge of the assembly line, which requires 500 gears per day. Containers typically wait 0.20 day in the fabrication cell. Each container holds 20 gears, and one container requires 1.8 days in machine time. Setup times are negligible. If the policy variable for unforeseen contingencies is set at 5 percent, how many containers should Jitson authorize for the gear replenishment system?

8. You are asked to analyze the *kanban* system of LeWin, a French manufacturer of gaming devices. One of the workstations feeding the assembly line produces part M670N. The daily demand for M670N is 1,800 units. The average processing time per unit is 0.003 day. LeWin's records show that the average container spends 1.05 days waiting at the feeder workstation. The container for M670N can hold 300 units. Twelve containers are authorized for the part. Recall that ρ is the average processing time per container, not per individual part.

    a. Find the value of the policy variable, α, that expresses the amount of implied safety stock in this system.

    b. Use the implied value of α from part (a) to determine the required reduction in waiting time if one container was removed. Assume that all other parameters remain constant.

9. An assembly line requires two components: gadjits and widjits. Gadjits are produced by center 1 and widjits by center 2. Each unit of the end item, called a jit-together, requires three gadjits and two widjits, as shown in Figure 6.13. The daily production quota on the assembly line is 800 jit-togethers.

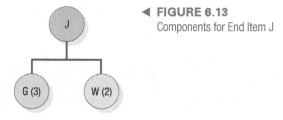

◄ **FIGURE 6.13**
Components for End Item J

The container for gadjits holds 80 units. The policy variable for center 1 is set at 0.09. The average waiting time for a container of gadjits is 0.09 day, and 0.06 day is needed to produce a container. The container for widjits holds 50 units, and the policy variable for center 2 is 0.08. The average waiting time per container of widjits is 0.14 day, and the time required to process a container is 0.20 day.

    a. How many containers are needed for gadjits?

    b. How many containers are needed for widjits?

10. Gestalt, Inc. uses a *kanban* system in its automobile production facility in Germany. This facility operates 8 hours per day to produce the Jitterbug, a replacement for the obsolete but immensely popular Jitney Beetle. Suppose that a certain part requires 150 seconds of processing at machine cell 33B and a container of parts average 1.6 hours of waiting time there. Management allows a 10 percent buffer for unexpected occurrences. Each container holds 30 parts, and 8 containers are authorized. How much daily demand can be satisfied

with this system? (Hint: Recall that ρ is the average processing time per container, not per individual part.)

11. A U.S. Postal Service supervisor is looking for ways to reduce stress in the sorting department. With the existing arrangement, stamped letters are machine-canceled and loaded into tubs with 375 letters per tub. The tubs are then pushed to postal clerks, who read and key zip codes into an automated sorting machine at the rate of 1 tub per 375 seconds. To overcome the stress caused when the stamp canceling machine outpaces the sorting clerks, a pull system is proposed. When the clerks are ready to process another tub of mail, they will pull the tub from the canceling machine area. How many tubs should circulate between the sorting clerks and the canceling machine if 90,000 letters are to be sorted during an 8-hour shift, the safety stock policy variable, α, is 0.18, and the average waiting time plus materials handling time is 25 minutes per tub?

12. The production schedule at Mazda calls for 1,200 Mazdas to be produced during each of 22 production days in January and 900 Mazdas to be produced during each of 20 production days in February. Mazda uses a *kanban* system to communicate with Gesundheit, a nearby supplier of tires. Mazda purchases four tires per vehicle from Gesundheit. The safety stock policy variable, α, is 0.15. The container (a delivery truck) size is 200 tires. The average waiting time plus materials handling time is 0.16 day per container. Assembly lines are rebalanced at the beginning of each month. The average processing time per container in January is 0.10 day. February processing time will average 0.125 day per container. How many containers should be authorized for January? How many for February?

13. Jitsmart is a retailer of plastic action-figure toys. The action figures are purchased from Tacky Toys, Inc., and arrive in boxes of 48. Full boxes are stored on high shelves out of reach of customers. A small inventory is maintained on child-level shelves. Depletion of the lower-shelf inventory signals the need to take down a box of action figures to replenish the inventory. A reorder card is then removed from the box and sent to Tacky Toys to authorize replenishment of a container of action figures. The average demand rate for a popular action figure, Agent 99, is 36 units per day. The total lead time (waiting plus processing) is 11 days. Jitsmart's safety stocky policy variable, α, is 0.25. What is the authorized stock level for Jitsmart?

14. Markland First National Bank of Rolla utilizes *kanban* techniques in its check processing facility. The following information is known about the process. Each *kanban* container can hold 50 checks and spends 24 minutes a day in processing and 2 hours a day in materials handling and waiting. Finally, the facility operates 24 hours per day and utilizes a policy variable for unforeseen contingencies of 0.25.

   a. If there are 20 *kanban* containers in use, what is the current daily demand of the check processing facility?

   b. If the muda or the waste in the system were eliminated completely, how many containers would then be needed?

VIDEO CASE   Lean Systems at Autoliv

Autoliv is a world-class example of lean manufacturing. This Fortune 500 company makes automotive safety components such as seat belts, airbags, and steering wheels, and has over 80 plants in more than 32 countries. Revenues in 2007 topped $6.7 billion. Autoliv's lean manufacturing environment is called the Autoliv Production System (APS) and is based on the principles of lean manufacturing pioneered by Toyota, one of the world's largest automobile manufacturers, and embodied in its Toyota Production System (TPS).

At the heart of Autoliv is a system that focuses on continuous improvement. Based on the "House of Toyota," Autoliv's Ogden, Utah, airbag module plant puts the concepts embodied in the house to work every day. The only difference between the Toyota house and the one at Autoliv is that the company has added a third pillar to its house to represent employee involvement in all processes because a culture of involvement, while the norm in Japan, is not always found in the United States.

Autoliv started its lean journey back in 1995. At that time, the Ogden plant was at manufacturing capacity with 22 work cells. Company managers acknowledge that, back then, Autoliv was "broken" and in need of significant and immediate change if it was to survive. This meant that everyone—from senior management to employees and suppliers—needed to be on-board with rebuilding the company. It was not that the company could not fulfill the needs of its automaker customers; however, with increasing demand for both reliable and cost-effective component supplies, pressure to change became obvious. Recognizing the value of Toyota's approach, senior management made the commitment to embark on its own journey to bring the transformative culture of lean manufacturing to Autoliv.

Autoliv employee folds an air bag in a Toyota-inspired production cell.

In 1998, *sensei* Takashi Harada arrived from Japan to spend three years teaching top company managers the principles, techniques, and culture of the lean system. This helped managers create an environment in which continuous improvement could be fostered and revered as an essential activity for long-term success. Because the environment was changing, it made it difficult at first for suppliers to meet Autoliv's constantly changing and unstable processes. It also made problems visible and forced the company to address and resolve the problems instead of finding ways to work around them as had been done in the past. Daily audits, monthly training, and more in-depth education programs were created to help focus attention on where changes needed to be made. Workers and management were organized into teams that were held accountable for common goals and tasked with working toward common success.

By 2004, the lean culture was integrated into the company, and it now hosts regular visits by other corporations who want to learn from Autoliv's journey and experiences. Compared to 1995, the space required for a typical work cell has been reduced by 88.5 percent, while the number of cells has grown over 400 percent. This has allowed Autoliv to dramatically increase its production capacity with minimal investment.

Lean concepts play out every day in the each plant. For example, everyone gathers at the start of the workday for pre-shift stretching and a brief meeting—this is part of the employee involvement pillar in the APS House. Then, workers head to one of 104 work cells on the plant floor. Heijunka Room team members deliver heijunka cards to each cell to communicate the work to be done in that cell. Lot sizes may vary with each card delivered to the cell. Everything the workers need to make the lot is in the cell and regularly replenished through the *kanban* card system. Every 24 minutes, another heijunka card comes to the cell to signal workers what they will build next. This is part of the JIT pillar in the house.

Since a culture of continuous improvement requires employees at every level to be responsible for quality, a worker may identify an "abnormal condition" during work execution that slows down the work of the cell, or stops it altogether. This is embodied in the right pillar of the Toyota house—jidoka, which Autoliv interprets as "stop and fix." This is a rare occurrence, however, since both Autoliv and its suppliers are expected to deliver defect-free products. When a supplier is new or has experienced quality issues, the supplier pays for inspection in Autoliv's receiving dock area until Autoliv is certain the supplier can meet quality expectations for all future deliveries. In this manner, workers in the cells know they can trust the integrity of the raw materials arriving through the *kanban* system into their cells for assembly. Jidoka may also come into play when a machine does not operate properly or an employee notices a process that has deviated from the standard. When workers "stop and fix" a problem at the point of its creation, they save the company from added cost as well as lost confidence in the eyes of the customer.

To help focus worker efforts daily, Autoliv has a blue "communication wall" that everyone sees as they head to their work site. The wall contains the company's "policy deployment," which consists of company-wide goals for customer satisfaction, shareholder/financial performance, and safety and quality. The policy deployment begins with the company-wide goals, which then flow down to the plant level through the plant manager's goals, strategies, and actions for the facility. These linked activities assure that Autoliv achieves its goals. By communicating this information—and more—in a visual manner, the central pillar of the APS House is supported. Other visual communication and management methods are in place as well. For example, each cell has an overhead banner that states how that cell is doing each month in the areas of safety, quality, employee involvement, cost, and delivery. These all tie into the policy deployment shown on the communication wall.

Another visual communication method is to use a "rail" for the management of the heijunka cards in each cell. The rail has color-coded sections. As each card is delivered, it slides down a color-coded railing to the team. At the end nearest the cell, the rail is green, indicating that any cards that fall into this area can be completed within normal working hours. The middle of the rail is yellow, indicating overtime for the cell that day. The end is red, meaning weekend overtime is required to bring work processes back into harmony with customer demand. As a heijunka card slides down the rail, it stops when it hits the end or stacks up behind another card. If the cell is not performing at the required pace to meet customer demand, the cards will stack up on the rail and provide a very visual cue that the cell is not meeting expectations. This provides an opportunity for cell team members as well as management to implement immediate countermeasures to prevent required overtime if the situation is not remedied.

All aisles and walkways surrounding cells are to be clear of materials, debris, or other items. If anything appears in those areas, everyone can quickly see the abnormality. As team members work together to complete their day's work, the results of their efforts are displayed boldly on each cell's "communi-cube." This four-sided rotating display visually tells the story of the cell's productivity, quality, and 5S performance. The cube also contains a special section for the management of *kaizen* suggestions for the team itself. These *kaizens* enable the team to continuously improve the work environment as well as drive the achievement of team results.

Autoliv's lean journey embodied in the Autoliv Production System has led to numerous awards and achievement of its policy deployment goals. Product defects have been dramatically reduced, inventory levels are lower, and inventory turnover is approaching world-class levels of 50. Employee turnover is close to 5 percent and remains well below that of other manufacturers in the industry. Yet the destination has not been reached. The company continues its emphasis on driving systemic improvement to avoid complacency and loss of competitive advantage. Best practices from sources beyond each immediate area of the organization are studied and integrated. And finding ways to engage and reward Autoliv's workforce in a maturing market is critical. Kaizen suggestions in the most recent year at the Ogden plant totaled 74,000, or nearly 60 per employee, indicating the culture of continuous improvement in Autoliv's APS House is alive and well.

QUESTIONS

1. Why is a visual management approach such an integral part of Autoliv's lean system?

2. Describe the JIT considerations presented in the chapter as they relate to Autoliv's manufacturing environment.

3. Which method of work flow is embodied in Autoliv's system? Why is this approach most suitable to its lean environment?

4. When Autoliv started its lean journey, a number of operational benefits and implementation issues had to be addressed. What were they, and how were they addressed?

CASE Copper Kettle Catering

Copper Kettle Catering (CKC) is a full-service catering company that provides services ranging from box lunches for picnics or luncheon meetings to large wedding, dinner, or office parties. Established as a lunch delivery service for offices in 1972 by Wayne and Janet Williams, CKC has grown to be one of the largest catering businesses in Raleigh, North Carolina. The Williams's divide customer demand into two categories: deliver only and deliver and serve.

The deliver-only side of the business delivers boxed meals consisting of a sandwich, salad, dessert, and fruit. The menu for this service is limited to six sandwich selections, three salads or potato chips, and a brownie or fruit bar. Grapes and an orange slice are included with every meal, and iced tea can be ordered to accompany the meals. The overall level of demand for this service throughout the year is fairly constant, although the mix of menu items delivered varies. The planning horizon for this segment of the business is short: Customers usually call no more than a day ahead of time. CKC requires customers to call deliver-only orders in by 10:00 A.M. to guarantee delivery the same day.

The deliver-and-serve side of the business focuses on catering large parties, dinners, and weddings. The extensive range of menu items includes a full selection of hors d'oeuvres, entrées, beverages, and special-request items. The demand for these services is much more seasonal, with heavier demands occurring in the late spring–early summer for weddings and the late fall–early winter for holiday parties. However, this segment also has a longer planning horizon. Customers book dates and choose menu items weeks or months ahead of time.

CKC's food preparation facilities support both operations. The physical facilities layout resembles that of a job process. Five major work areas consist of a stove–oven area for hot food preparation, a cold area for salad preparation, an hors d'oeuvre preparation area, a sandwich preparation area, and an assembly area where deliver-only orders are boxed and deliver-and-serve orders are assembled and trayed. Three walk-in coolers store foods requiring refrigeration, and a large pantry houses nonperishable goods. Space limitations and the risk of spoilage limit the amount of raw materials and prepared food items that can be carried in inventory at any one time. CKC purchases desserts from outside vendors. Some deliver the desserts to CKC; others require CKC to send someone to pick up desserts at their facilities.

The scheduling of orders is a two-stage process. Each Monday, the Williamses develop the schedule of deliver-and-serve orders to be processed each day. CKC typically has multiple deliver-and-serve orders to fill each day

of the week. This level of demand allows a certain efficiency in the preparation of multiple orders. The deliver-only orders are scheduled day to day, owing to the short-order lead times. CKC sometimes runs out of ingredients for deliver-only menu items because of the limited inventory space.

Wayne and Janet Williams have 10 full-time employees: two cooks and eight food preparation workers, who also work as servers for the deliver-and-serve orders. In periods of high demand, the Williamses hire additional part-time servers. The position of cook is specialized and requires a high degree of training and skill. The rest of the employees are flexible and move between tasks as needed.

The business environment for catering is competitive. The competitive priorities are high-quality food, delivery reliability, flexibility, and cost—in that order. "The quality of the food and its preparation is paramount," states Wayne Williams. "Caterers with poor-quality food will not stay in business long." Quality is measured by both freshness and taste. Delivery reliability encompasses both on-time delivery and the time required to respond to customer orders (in effect, the order lead time). Flexibility focuses on both the range of catering requests that a company can satisfy and menu variety.

Recently, CKC began to notice that customers are demanding more menu flexibility and faster response times. Small specialty caterers who entered the market are targeting specific well-defined market segments. One example is a small caterer called Lunches-R-Us, which located a facility in the middle of a large office complex to serve the lunch trade and competes with CKC on cost.

Wayne and Janet Williams are impressed by the lean systems concept, especially the ideas related to increasing flexibility, reducing lead times, and lowering costs. They sound like what CKC needs to remain competitive. However, the Williamses wonder whether lean concepts and practices are transferable to a service business.

QUESTIONS

1. Are the operations of Copper Kettle Catering conducive to the application of lean concepts and practices? Explain.

2. What, if any, are the major barriers to implementing a lean system at Copper Kettle Catering?

3. What would you recommend that Wayne and Janet Williams do to take advantage of lean concepts in operating CKC?

Source: This case was prepared by Dr. Brooke Saladin, Wake Forest University, as a basis for classroom discussion. Copyright © Brooke Saladin. Reprinted by permission.

Sean Dempsey/PA Wire/AP Images

Building on the success of Xbox 360, Xbox One was launched in 2013. Here, a gamer tries the Xbox One console at the Violin Factory in south London, ahead of its release in November.

PROJECT MANAGEMENT

XBOX 360

Anyone who has tried video gaming knows how entertaining and challenging it can be. What might not be known is that the total video game market is projected to be $111 billion for 2015. It is no wonder why companies such as Microsoft channel a lot of energy into the design and manufacture of video gaming consoles to satisfy that market. Microsoft's first offering was the Xbox in 2001 followed by the Xbox 360 in 2005, which has been touted to be the most influential product in the market because of its emphasis on digital media and online and multiplayer gaming. How did this trail-blazing product come into being?

Four years after the introduction of Xbox, Microsoft needed to quickly design, develop, and produce a new product. Sony's PlayStation 2 was dominating the video game market, and Microsoft needed a new product to compete with the impending release of PlayStation 3. Developing such a product is a project of massive proportions. The project consisted of four phases: (1) design, (2) analysis, (3) development, and (4) launch. The result was Xbox 360.

Design

The design of the Xbox 360 was a collaborative effort between Microsoft and many other firms, including Astro Studios in San Francisco, which designed the overall console and controller; IBM, which designed the processor chip; ATI, which designed the graphics chip; and a host of game design firms to develop games for the new product. A key element of the new product was the built-in Internet access that allowed gamers to access online games, buy game add-ons, and access multiplayer games developed exclusively for Xbox 360. Microsoft also included its primary manufacturers, Flextronics and Wistron, in the design process to optimize the production and assembly of the more than 1,000 parts contained in an Xbox 360.

Analysis

Getting an estimate of future sales for a new product is always difficult; however, in this case, the historic patterns for PlayStation 1, PlayStation 2, and Xbox were useful. Analysts found that the peak year for a PlayStation product was 4 years after its introduction and that the life cycle for those products is about 11 years. This information provided a basis for estimating the sales potential of Xbox 360, although actual sales may be limited due to supply constraints. Nonetheless, Microsoft realized that the potential was there to open a new generation of game consoles well ahead of the market.

Development

Microsoft worked closely with Flextronics, Wistron, and the various design firms to iron out manufacturing problems in the early phases of Xbox 360 production. Once initial production was underway, Microsoft brought on Celestica to add production capacity. The decision was made to focus manufacturing operations in China. All told, 10,000 workers in China would be involved in Xbox 360 production.

Launch

Microsoft's Xbox 360 gained an early lead in terms of market share due, in part, to its early launch date, which was one year ahead of its rivals PlayStation 3 and Wii. All told, the product was released in 36 countries in the first year of production, a Herculean effort requiring extensive coordination and a high level of project management skill. Sales of the Xbox 360 exceeded expectations with more than 10 million units sold in the first year alone; as of 2013, 80 million units were sold worldwide. Nonetheless, Microsoft experienced difficulties in getting the supply chain to meet customer demands in a timely fashion in the early days of the launch. The lesson to be learned is that projects can be planned and executed properly; however, the underlying infrastructure that delivers the product is equally important in the ultimate success of the venture.

The jobs of product designers and project managers do not end with the launch of a new product. Feedback from the market provides insight into new features for existing products or entirely new products. Subsequently, there was the Xbox 360 S in 2010, the Xbox 360 E in 2013, and the new generation Xbox One in 2013.

Source: David Holt, Charles Holloway, and Hau Lee, "Evolution of the Xbox Supply Chain," Stanford Graduate School of Business, Case: GS-49, (April 14, 2006); "Xbox 360," Wikipedia, the free encyclopedia, **http://en.wikipedia .org/wiki/Xbox_360**; Rob van der Meulen and Janessa Rivera, "Gartner Says Worldwide Video Market to Total $93 Billion in 2013," **http://www.gartner.com**, (October 29, 2013); Rick Marshall, "The History of the Xbox," **http://www.digitaltrends.com**, (May 12, 2013).

LEARNING GOALS *After reading this chapter, you should be able to:*

1 Explain the major activities associated with defining and organizing a project.

2 Describe the procedure for constructing a project network.

3 Develop the schedule of a project.

4 Analyze cost–time trade-offs in a project network.

5 Assess the risk of missing a project deadline.

6 Identify the options available to monitor and control projects.

Companies such as Microsoft are experts at managing projects such as Xbox 360. They master the ability to schedule activities and monitor progress within strict time, cost, and performance guidelines. A **project** is an interrelated set of activities with a definite starting and ending point, which results in a unique outcome for a specific allocation of resources.

Projects are common in everyday life as well as in business. Planning weddings, remodeling bathrooms, writing term papers, and organizing surprise parties are examples of small projects in everyday life. Conducting company audits, planning mergers, creating advertising campaigns, reengineering processes, developing new services or products, and establishing a strategic alliance are examples of large projects in business.

The three main goals of any project are (1) complete the project on time or earlier, (2) do not exceed the budget, and (3) meet the specifications to the satisfaction of the customer. When we must undertake projects with some uncertainty involved, it does not hurt to have flexibility with respect to resource availability, deadlines, and budgets. Consequently, projects can be complex and challenging to manage. **Project management**, which is a systemized, phased approach to defining, organizing, planning, monitoring, and controlling projects, is one way to overcome that challenge.

Projects often cut across organizational lines because they need the skills of multiple professions and organizations. Furthermore, each project is unique, even if it is routine, requiring new combinations of skills and resources in the project process. For example, projects for adding a new branch office, installing new computers in a department, or developing a sales promotion may be initiated several times a year. Each project may have been done many times before; however, differences arise with each replication. Uncertainties, such as the advent of new technologies or the activities of competitors, can change the character of projects and require responsive countermeasures. Finally, projects are temporary because personnel, materials, and facilities are organized to complete them within a specified time frame and then are disbanded.

Projects, and the application of project management, facilitate the implementation of strategy. However, the power of this approach goes beyond the focus on one project. Operations strategy initiatives often require the coordination of many interdependent projects. Such a collection of projects is called a **program**, which is an interdependent set of projects with a common strategic purpose. As new project proposals come forward, management must assess their fit to the current operations strategy and ongoing initiatives and have a means to prioritize them because funds for projects are often limited. Projects can be also used to implement changes to processes and supply chains. For example, projects involving the implementation of major information technologies may affect all of a firm's core processes and supporting processes as well as some of their suppliers' and customers' processes. As such, projects are a useful tool for improving processes and supply chains.

project

An interrelated set of activities with a definite starting and ending point, which results in a unique outcome for a specific allocation of resources.

project management

A systemized, phased approach to defining, organizing, planning, monitoring, and controlling projects.

program

An interdependent set of projects that have a common strategic purpose.

Defining and Organizing Projects

A clear understanding of a project's organization and how personnel are going to work together to complete the project are keys to success. In this section, we will address (1) defining the scope and objectives, (2) selecting the project manager and team, and (3) recognizing the organizational structure.

Defining the Scope and Objectives of a Project

A thorough statement of a project's scope, time frame, and allocated resources is essential to managing the project. This statement is often referred to as the *project objective statement*. The scope provides a succinct statement of project objectives and captures the essence of the desired project outcomes in the form of major deliverables, which are concrete outcomes of the project. Changes to the scope of a project inevitably increase costs and delay completion. Collectively, changes to scope are called *scope creep* and, in sufficient quantity, are primary causes of failed projects. The time frame for a project should be as specific as possible, as in "the project should be completed by January 1, 2017." Finally, although specifying an allocation of resources to a project may be difficult during the early stages of planning, it is important for managing the project. The allocation should be expressed as a dollar figure or as full-time equivalents of personnel time. A specific statement of allocated resources makes it possible to make adjustments to the scope of the project as it proceeds.

Selecting the Project Manager and Team

Once the project is selected, a project manager must be chosen. The qualities of a good project manager should be well aligned with the roles a project manager must play.

- *Facilitator.* The project manager often must resolve conflicts between individuals or departments to ensure that the project has the appropriate resources for the job to be completed. Successful project managers have good leadership skills and a *systems view*, which encompasses the interaction of the project, its resources, and its deliverables with the firm as a whole.

- *Communicator.* Project progress and requests for additional resources must be clearly communicated to senior management and other stakeholders in a project. The project manager must also frequently communicate with the project team to get the best performance.

- *Decision Maker.* Good project managers will be sensitive to the way the team performs best and be ready to make tough decisions, if necessary. The project manger must organize the team meetings, specify how the team will make decisions, and determine the nature and timing of reports to senior management.

Selecting the project team is just as important as the selection of the project manager. Several characteristics should be considered.

- *Technical Competence.* Team members should have the technical competence required for the tasks to which they will be assigned.

- *Sensitivity.* All team members should be sensitive to interpersonal conflicts that may arise. Senior team members should be politically sensitive to help mitigate problems with upper-level management.

- *Dedication.* Team members should feel comfortable solving project problems that may spill over into areas outside their immediate expertise. They should also be dedicated to getting the project done, as opposed to maintaining a comfortable work schedule.

Recognizing Organizational Structure

The relationship of the project manager to the project team is determined by the firm's organizational structure. Each of the three types of organizational structure described below has its own implications for project management.

- *Functional.* The project is housed in a specific department or functional area, presumably the one with the most interest in the project. Assistance from personnel in other functional areas must be negotiated by the project manager. In such cases, the project manager has less control over project timing than if the entire scope of the project fell within the purview of the department.

- *Pure Project.* The team members work exclusively for the project manager on a particular project. This structure simplifies the lines of authority and is particularly effective for large projects that consist of enough work for each team member to work full time. For small projects, it could result in significant duplication of resources across functional areas.

- *Matrix.* The matrix structure is a compromise between the functional and pure project structures. The project managers of the firm's projects all report to a program manager who coordinates resource and technological needs across the functional boundaries. The matrix structure allows each functional area to maintain control over who works on a project and the technology that is used. However, team members, in effect, have two bosses: the project manager and the department manager. Resolving these line-of-authority conflicts requires a strong project manager.

JB-2078/Alamy

The palm Jumeirah is an artificial archipelago in the shape of a palm tree extending into the Persian Gulf. The island has been created using 94 million cubic meters of sand and 7 million tons of rock. The island features themed hotels, three types of villas, apartment buildings, beaches, marinas, restaurants, and a variety of retail outlets. Projects of this magnitude must be carefully planned and organized.

Constructing Project Networks

After the project is defined and organized, the team must formulize the specific work to be accomplished and the relationships between the activities in the project. Constructing a project network involves two steps: (1) defining the work breakdown structure, and (2) diagramming the network.

Defining the Work Breakdown Structure

The **work breakdown structure (WBS)** is a statement of all work that has to be completed. Perhaps the single most important contributor to delay is the omission of work that is germane to the successful completion of the project. The project manager must work closely with the team to identify all activities. An **activity** is the smallest unit of work effort consuming both time and resources that the project manager can schedule and control. Typically, in the process of accumulating activities, the team generates a hierarchy to the work breakdown. Major work components are broken down to smaller tasks that ultimately are broken down to activities that are assigned to individuals. Figure 7.1 shows a WBS for a major project involving the relocation of a hospital. In the interest of better serving the surrounding community, the board of St. John's Hospital has decided to move to a new location. The project involves constructing a new hospital and making it operational. The work components at level 1 in the WBS can be broken down into smaller units of work in level 2 that could be further divided at level 3, until the project manager gets to activities at a level of detail that can be scheduled and controlled. For example, "Organizing and Site Preparation" has been divided into six activities at level 2 in Figure 7.1. We have kept our example simple so that the concept of the WBS can be easily understood. If our activities in the example are divided into even smaller units of work, it is easy to see that the total WBS for a project of this size may include many more than 100 activities. Regardless of the project, care must be taken to include all important activities in the WBS to avoid project delays. Often overlooked are the activities required to plan the project, get management approval at various stages, run pilot tests of new services or products, and prepare final reports.

Each activity in the WBS must have an "owner" who is responsible for doing the work. *Activity ownership* avoids confusion in the execution of activities and assigns responsibility for timely completion. The team should have a defined procedure for assigning activities to team members, which can be democratic (consensus of the team) or autocratic (assigned by the project manager).

Diagramming the Network

Network planning methods can help managers monitor and control projects. These methods treat a project as a set of interrelated activities that can be visually displayed in a **network diagram**, which consists of nodes (circles) and arcs (arrows) that depict the relationships between activities. Two

work breakdown structure (WBS)

A statement of all work that has to be completed.

activity

The smallest unit of work effort consuming both time and resources that the project manager can schedule and control.

network diagram

A network planning method, designed to depict the relationships between activities, that consists of nodes (circles) and arcs (arrows).

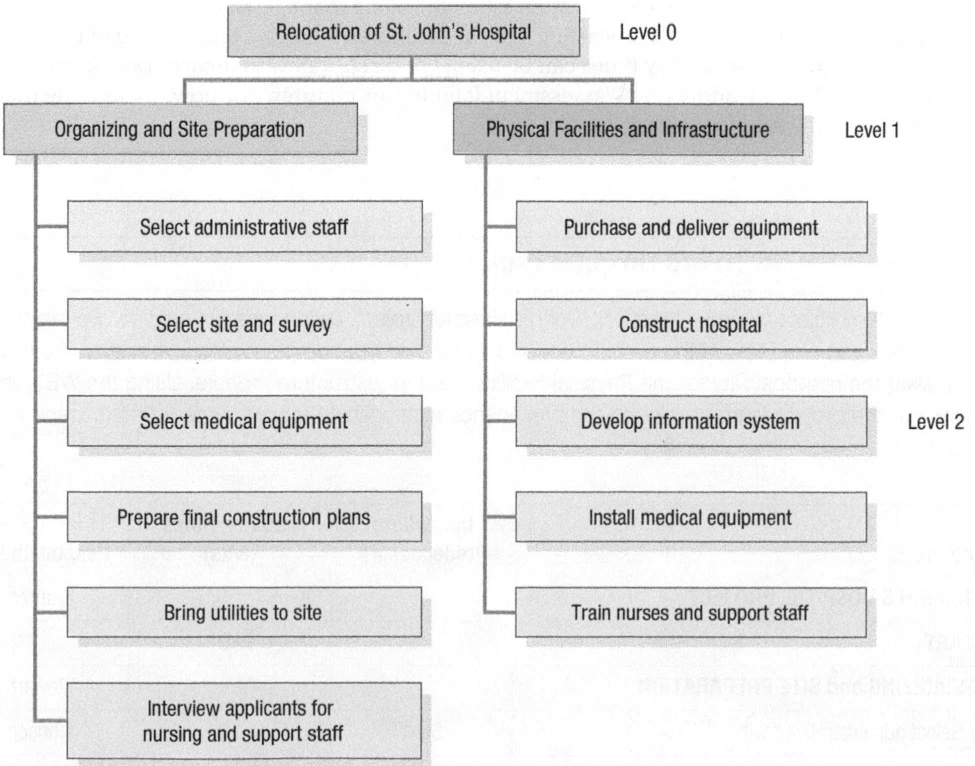

◀ **FIGURE 7.1**

Work Breakdown Structure for the St. John's Hospital Project

program evaluation and review technique (PERT)

A network planning method created for the U.S. Navy's Polaris missile project in the 1950s, which involved 3,000 separate contractors and suppliers.

critical path method (CPM)

A network planning method developed in the 1950s as a means of scheduling maintenance shutdowns at chemical-processing plants.

network planning methods were developed in the 1950s. The **program evaluation and review technique (PERT)** was created for the U.S. Navy's Polaris missile project, which involved 3,000 separate contractors and suppliers. The **critical path method (CPM)** was developed as a means of scheduling maintenance shutdowns at chemical-processing plants. Although early versions of PERT and CPM differed in their treatment of activity time estimates, today the differences are minor. For purposes of our discussion, we refer to them collectively as PERT/CPM. These methods offer several benefits to project managers, including the following:

1. Considering projects as networks forces project teams to identify and organize the data required and to identify the interrelationships between activities. This process also provides a forum for managers of different functional areas to discuss the nature of the various activities and their resource requirements.

2. Networks enable project managers to estimate the completion time of projects, an advantage that can be useful in planning other events and in conducting contractual negotiations with customers and suppliers.

3. Reports based on project networks highlight the activities that are crucial to completing projects on schedule. They also highlight the activities that may be delayed without affecting completion dates, thereby freeing up resources for other, more critical activities.

4. Network methods enable project managers to analyze the time and cost implications of resource trade-offs.

Diagramming the project network involves establishing precedence relationships and estimating activity times.

precedence relationship

A relationship that determines a sequence for undertaking activities; it specifies that one activity cannot start until a preceding activity has been completed.

Establishing Precedence Relationships A **precedence relationship** determines a sequence for undertaking activities; it specifies that one activity cannot start until a preceding activity has been completed. For example, brochures announcing a conference for executives must first be designed by the program committee (activity A) before they can be printed (activity B). In other words, activity A must *precede* activity B. For large projects, establishing precedence relationships is essential because incorrect or omitted precedence relationships will result in costly delays. The precedence relationships are represented by a network diagram, similar to what we used for analyzing line balancing problems (see Chapter 6, "Constraint Management").

Estimating Activity Times When the same type of activity has been done many times before, time estimates will have a relatively high degree of certainty. Several methods can be used to get time estimates in such an environment. First, statistical methods can be used if the project team has access to data on actual activity times experienced in the past (see MyOMLab Supplement H, "Measuring Output Rates,"). Second, if activity times improve with the number of replications, the times can be estimated using learning curve models (see Supplement I, "Learning Curve Analysis," in MyOMLab). Finally, the times for first-time activities are often estimated using managerial opinions based on similar prior experiences (see Chapter 8, "Forecasting"). If the estimates involve a high degree of uncertainty, probability distributions for activity times can be used. We discuss how to incorporate uncertainty in project networks when we address risk assessment later in this chapter. For now, we assume that the activity times are known with certainty.

MyOMLab

EXAMPLE 7.1	**Diagramming the St. John's Hospital Project**

Judy Kramer, the project manager for the St. John's Hospital project, divided the project into two major modules. She assigned John Stewart the overall responsibility for the Organizing and Site Preparation module and Sarah Walker the responsibility for the Physical Facilities and Infrastructure module. Using the WBS shown in Figure 7.1, the project team developed the precedence relationships, activity time estimates, and activity responsibilities shown in the following table:

Activity	Immediate Predecessors	Activity Times (wks)	Responsibility
ST. JOHN'S HOSPITAL PROJECT			Kramer
START		0	
ORGANIZING and SITE PREPARATION			Stewart
A. Select administrative staff	Start	12	Johnson

Activity	Immediate Predecessors	Activity Times (wks)	Responsibility
B. Select site and survey	Start	9	Taylor
C. Select medical equipment	A	10	Adams
D. Prepare final construction plans	B	10	Taylor
E. Bring utilities to site	B	24	Burton
F. Interview applicants for nursing and support staff	A	10	Johnson
PHYSICAL FACILITIES and INFRASTRUCTURE			Walker
G. Purchase and deliver equipment	C	35	Sampson
H. Construct hospital	D	40	Casey
I. Develop information system	A	15	Murphy
J. Install medical equipment	E, G, H	4	Pike
K. Train nurses and support staff	F, I, J	6	Ashton
FINISH	K	0	

For purposes of our example, we will assume a work week consists of five work days. Draw the network diagram for the hospital project.

SOLUTION

The network diagram, activities, and activity times for the hospital project are shown in Figure 7.2. The diagram depicts activities as circles, with arrows indicating the sequence in which they are to be performed. Activities A and B emanate from a *start* node because they have no immediate predecessors. The arrows connecting activity A to activities C, F, and I indicate that all three require completion of activity A before they can begin. Similarly, activity B must be completed before activities D and E can begin, and so on. Activity K connects to a *finish* node because no activities follow it. The start and finish nodes do not actually represent activities; they merely provide beginning and ending points for the network.

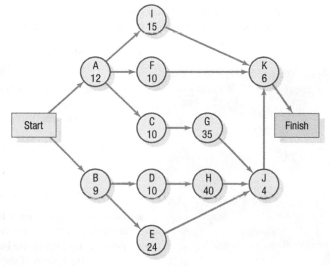

▲ **FIGURE 7.2**
Network Showing Activity Times for the St. John's Hospital Project

Developing the Project Schedule

A key advantage of network planning methods is the creation of a schedule of project activities that will help managers achieve the objectives of the project. Given a project network, managers can (1) estimate the completion time of a project by finding the critical path, (2) identify the start and finish times for each activity for a project schedule, and (3) calculate the amount of slack time for each activity.

Critical Path

A crucial aspect of project management is estimating the time of completion of a project. If each activity in relocating the hospital were done in sequence, with work proceeding on only one activity at a time, the time of completion would equal the sum of the times for all the activities, or 175 weeks. However, Figure 7.2 indicates that some activities can be carried on simultaneously, given adequate resources. We call each sequence of activities between the project's start and finish a **path**. The network describing the hospital relocation project has five paths: (1) A–I–K, (2) A–F–K, (3) A–C–G–J–K, (4) B–D–H–J–K, and (5) B–E–J–K. The **critical path** is the sequence of activities between a project's start and finish that takes the longest time

path
The sequence of activities between a project's start and finish.

critical path
The sequence of activities between a project's start and finish that takes the longest time to complete.

to complete. Thus, the activities along the critical path determine the completion time of the project; that is, if one of the activities on the critical path is delayed, the entire project will be delayed. The estimated times for the paths in the hospital project network are:

Path	Estimated Time (weeks)
A–I–K	33
A–F–K	28
A–C–G–J–K	67
B–D–H–J–K	69
B–E–J–K	43

earliest finish time (EF)

An activity's earliest start time plus its estimated duration, t, or $EF = ES + t$.

earliest start time (ES)

The earliest finish time of the immediately preceding activity.

latest finish time (LF)

The latest start time of the activity that immediately follows.

latest start time (LS)

The latest finish time minus its estimated duration, t, or $LS = LF - t$.

The activity string B–D–H–J–K is estimated to take 69 weeks to complete. As the longest, it constitutes the critical path. Because the critical path defines the completion time of the project, Judy Kramer and the project team should focus on these activities and any other path that is close in length to the critical path.

Project Schedule

The typical objective is to finish the project as early as possible as determined by the critical path. The project schedule is specified by the start and finish times for each activity. For any activity, managers can use the earliest start and finish times, the latest start and finish times (and still finish the project on time), or times in between these extremes if the activity is not on the critical path.

- **Earliest Start and Earliest Finish Times** The earliest start and earliest finish times are obtained as follows:

  1. The **earliest finish time (EF)** of an activity equals its earliest start time plus its estimated duration, t, or $EF = ES + t$.

     The **earliest start time (ES)** for an activity is the earliest finish time of the immediately preceding activity. For activities with more than one preceding activity, ES is the latest of the earliest finish times of the preceding activities.

     To calculate the duration of the entire project, we determine the EF for the last activity on the critical path.

- **Latest Start and Latest Finish Times** To obtain the latest start and latest finish times, we must work backward from the finish node. We start by setting the latest finish time of the project equal to the earliest finish time of the last activity on the critical path.

  1. The **latest finish time (LF)** for an activity is the latest start time of the activity that immediately follows. For activities with more than one activity that immediately follow, LF is the earliest of the latest start times of those activities.

  2. The **latest start time (LS)** for an activity equals its latest finish time minus its estimated duration, t, or $LS = LF - t$.

Aircraft construction is an example of a large project that requires a sound project schedule because of the capital involved. Here several 747's are under construction at Boeing's plant in Everett, Washington.

George Hall/Corbis

EXAMPLE 7.2	**Calculating Start and Finish Times for the Activities**

Calculate the ES, EF, LS, and LF times for each activity in the hospital project. Which activity should Kramer start immediately? Figure 7.2 contains the activity times.

SOLUTION

To compute the early start and early finish times, we begin at the start node at time zero. Because activities A and B have no predecessors, the earliest start times for these activities are also zero. The earliest finish times for these activities are

$$EF_A = 0 + 12 = 12 \text{ and } EF_B = 0 + 9 = 9$$

Because the earliest start time for activities I, F, and C is the earliest finish time of activity A,

$$ES_I = 12, ES_F = 12, \text{ and } ES_C = 12$$

Similarly,

$$ES_D = 9 \text{ and } ES_E = 9$$

After placing these ES values on the network diagram (see Figure 7.3), we determine the EF times for activities I, F, C, D, and E:

$$EF_I = 12 + 15 = 27, EF_F = 12 + 10 = 22, EF_C = 12 + 10 = 22,$$
$$EF_D = 9 + 10 = 19, \text{ and } EF_E = 9 + 24 = 33$$

The earliest start time for activity G is the latest EF time of all immediately preceding activities. Thus,

$$ES_G = EF_C = 22, ES_H = EF_D = 19$$
$$EF_G = ES_G + t = 22 + 35 = 57, EF_H = ES_H + t = 19 + 40 = 59$$

The project team can now determine the earliest time any activity can be started. Because activity J has several predecessors, the earliest time that activity J can begin is the latest of the EF times of any of its preceding activities: $EF_G, EF_H,$ or EF_E. Thus, $EF_J = 59 + 4 = 63$. Similarly, $ES_K = 63$ and $EF_K = 63 + 6 = 69$. Because activity K is the last activity on the critical path, the earliest the project can be completed is week 69. The earliest start and finish times for all activities are shown in Figure 7.3.

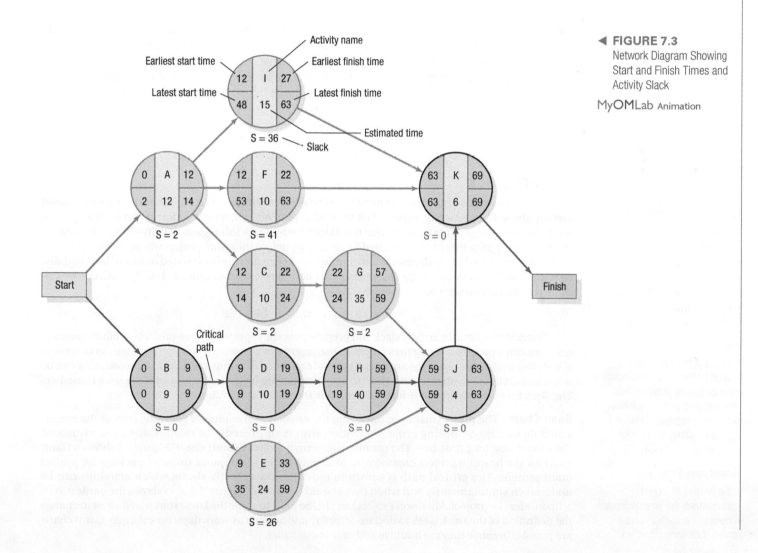

◀ **FIGURE 7.3**
Network Diagram Showing Start and Finish Times and Activity Slack

MyOMLab Animation

To compute the latest start and latest finish times, we begin by setting the latest finish activity time of activity K at week 69, which is its earliest finish time as determined in Figure 7.3. Thus, the latest start time for activity K is

$$LS_K = LF_K - t = 69 - 6 = 63$$

If activity K is to start no later than week 63, all its predecessors must finish no later than that time. Consequently,

$$LF_I = 63, LF_F = 63, \text{ and } LF_J = 63$$

The latest start times for these activities are shown in Figure 7.3 as

$$LS_I = 63 - 15 = 48, LS_F = 63 - 10 = 53, \text{ and } LS_J = 63 - 4 = 59$$

After obtaining LS_J, we can calculate the latest start times for the immediate predecessors of activity J:

$$LS_G = 59 - 35 = 24, LS_H = 59 - 40 = 19, \text{ and } LS_E = 59 - 24 = 35$$

Similarly, we can now calculate the latest start times for activities C and D:

$$LS_C = 24 - 10 = 14 \text{ and } LS_D = 19 - 10 = 9$$

Activity A has more than one immediately following activity: I, F, and C. The earliest of the latest start times is 14 for activity C. Thus,

$$LS_A = 14 - 12 = 2$$

Similarly, activity B has two immediate followers: D and E. Because the earliest of the latest start times of these activities is 9,

$$LS_B = 9 - 9 = 0$$

DECISION POINT

The earliest or latest start times can be used for developing a project schedule. For example, Kramer should start activity B immediately because the latest start time is 0; otherwise, the project will not be completed by week 69. When the LS is greater than the ES for an activity, that activity could be scheduled for any date between ES and LS. Such is the case for activity E, which could be scheduled to start anytime between week 9 and week 35, depending on the availability of resources. The earliest start and earliest finish times and the latest start and latest finish times for all activities are shown in Figure 7.3.

---

activity slack

The maximum length of time that an activity can be delayed without delaying the entire project, calculated as $S = LS - ES$ or $S = LS - EF$.

MyOMLab

Active Model 7.1 in MyOMLab provides additional insight on Gantt charts and their uses for the St. John's Hospital project.

Gantt chart

A project schedule, usually created by the project manager using computer software, that superimposes project activities, with their precedence relationships and estimated duration times, on a time line.

normal time (NT)

In the context of project management, the time necessary to complete an activity under normal conditions.

Activity Slack

The maximum length of time that an activity can be delayed without delaying the entire project is called **activity slack**. Consequently, *activities on the critical path have zero slack*. Information on slack can be useful because it highlights activities that need close attention. In this regard, activity slack is the amount of schedule slippage that can be tolerated for an activity before the entire project will be delayed. Slack at an activity is reduced when the estimated time duration of an activity is exceeded or when the scheduled start time for the activity must be delayed because of resource considerations. Activity slack can be calculated in one of two ways for any activity:

$$S = LS - ES \quad \text{or} \quad S = LF - EF$$

Computers calculate activity slack and prepare periodic reports for large projects, enabling managers to monitor progress. Using these reports, managers can sometimes manipulate slack to overcome scheduling problems. When resources can be used on several different activities in a project, they can be taken from activities with slack and given to activities that are behind schedule until the slack is used up. The slack for each activity in the hospital project is shown in Figure 7.3.

Gantt Chart   The project manager, often with the assistance of computer software, creates the project schedule by superimposing project activities, with their precedence relationships and estimated duration times, on a time line. The resulting diagram is called a **Gantt chart**. Figure 7.4 shows a Gantt chart for the hospital project created with Microsoft Project, a popular software package for project management. The critical path is shown in red. The chart clearly shows which activities can be undertaken simultaneously and when they should be started. Figure 7.4 also shows the earliest start schedule for the project. Microsoft Project can also be used to show the latest start schedule or to change the definition of the work week to declare Saturday and Sunday as work days, for example. Gantt charts are popular because they are intuitive and easy to construct.

	Task Name	Duration	Start	Finish	Predecessors
1	⊟ St John's Hospital Project	69 wks	Mon 9/12/11	Fri 1/4/13	
2	Start	0 wks	Mon 9/12/11	Mon 9/12/11	
3	⊟ Organizing and Site Prep	33 wks	Mon 9/12/11	Fri 4/27/12	
4	A. Select Staff	12 wks	Mon 9/12/11	Fri 12/2/11	2
5	B. Select Site	9 wks	Mon 9/12/11	Fri 11/11/11	2
6	C. Select Equipment	10 wks	Mon 12/5/11	Fri 2/10/12	4
7	D. Construction Plans	10 wks	Mon 11/14/11	Fri 1/20/12	5
8	E. Utilities	24 wks	Mon 11/14/11	Fri 4/27/12	5
9	F. Interviews	10 wks	Mon 12/5/11	Fri 2/10/12	4
10	⊟ Facilities and Infrastructure	57 wks	Mon 12/5/11	Fri 1/4/13	
11	G. Purchase Equipment	35 wks	Mon 2/13/12	Fri 10/12/12	6
12	H. Construct Hospital	40 wks	Mon 1/23/12	Fri 10/26/12	7
13	I. Information System	15 wks	Mon 12/5/11	Fri 3/16/12	4
14	J. Install Equipment	4 wks	Mon 10/29/12	Fri 11/23/12	8,11,12
15	K. Train Staff	6 wks	Mon 11/26/12	Fri 1/4/13	9,13,14
16	Finish	0 wks	Fri 1/4/13	Fri 1/4/13	15

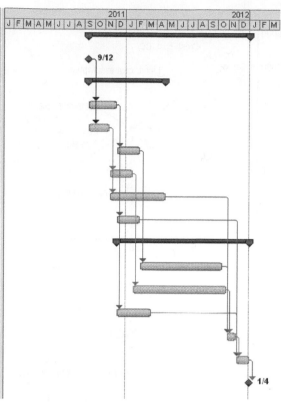

▲ **FIGURE 7.4**
MS Project Gantt Chart for the St. John's Hospital Project Schedule

Analyzing Cost–Time Trade-Offs

Keeping costs at acceptable levels is almost always as important as meeting schedule dates. In this section, we discuss the use of PERT/CPM methods to obtain minimum-cost schedules.

The reality of project management is that there are always cost–time trade-offs. For example, a project can often be completed earlier than scheduled by hiring more workers or running extra shifts. Such actions could be advantageous if savings or additional revenues accrue from completing the project early. *Total project costs* are the sum of direct costs, indirect costs, and penalty costs. These costs are dependent either on activity times or on project completion time. *Direct costs* include labor, materials, and any other costs directly related to project activities. *Indirect costs* include administration, depreciation, financial, and other variable overhead costs that can be avoided by reducing total project time: The shorter the duration of the project, the lower the indirect costs will be. Finally, a project may incur *penalty costs* if it extends beyond some specific date, whereas *an incentive* may be provided for early completion. Managers can shorten individual activity times by using additional direct resources, such as overtime, personnel, or equipment. Thus, a project manager may consider *crashing*, or expediting, some activities to reduce overall project completion time and total project costs.

Cost to Crash

To assess the benefit of crashing certain activities—from either a cost or a schedule perspective—the project manager needs to know the following times and costs:

1. The **normal time (NT)** is the time necessary to complete an activity under normal conditions.
2. The **normal cost (NC)** is the activity cost associated with the normal time.
3. The **crash time (CT)** is the shortest possible time to complete an activity.
4. The **crash cost (CC)** is the activity cost associated with the crash time.

Excavators work on the new Panama Canal project, which has international implications and massive costs.

Mark Eveleigh/Alamy

normal cost (NC)
The activity cost associated with the normal time.

crash time (CT)
The shortest possible time to complete an activity.

crash cost (CC)
The activity cost associated with the crash time.

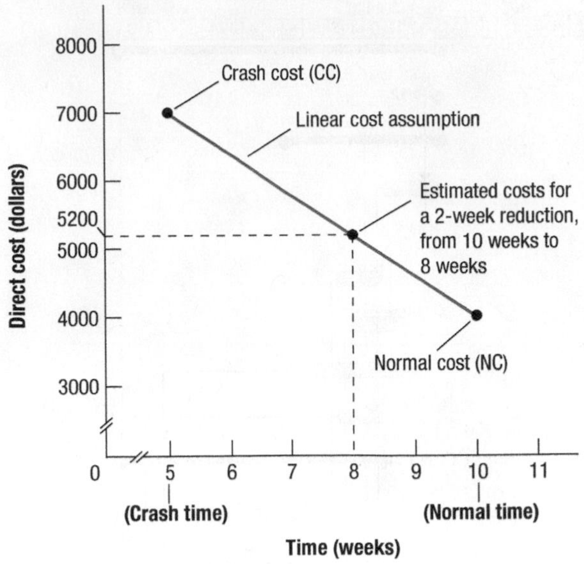

FIGURE 7.5
Cost–Time Relationships in
Cost Analysis

Our cost analysis is based on the assumption that direct costs increase linearly as activity time is reduced from its normal time. This assumption implies that for every week the activity time is reduced, direct costs increase by a proportional amount. For example, suppose that the normal time for activity C in the hospital project is 10 weeks and is associated with a direct cost of $4,000. Also, suppose that we can crash its time to only 5 weeks at a total cost of $7,000; the net time reduction is 5 weeks at a net cost increase of $3,000. We assume that crashing activity C costs $3,000 / 5 = $600 per week—an assumption of linear marginal costs that is illustrated in Figure 7.5. Thus, if activity C were expedited by 2 weeks (i.e., its time reduced from 10 weeks to 8 weeks), the estimated direct costs would be $4,000 + 2($600) = $5,200. For any activity, the cost to crash an activity by one week is

$$\text{Cost to crash per period} = \frac{CC - NC}{NT - CT}$$

Table 7.1 contains direct cost and time data, as well as the costs of crashing per week for the activities in the hospital project.

TABLE 7.1 | DIRECT COST AND TIME DATA FOR THE ST. JOHN'S HOSPITAL PROJECT

Activity	Normal Time (NT) (weeks)	Normal Cost (NC) ($)	Crash Time (CT) (weeks)	Crash Cost (CC) ($)	Maximum Time Reduction (week)	Cost of Crashing per Week ($)
A	12	$12,000	11	13,000	1	1,000
B	9	50,000	7	64,000	2	7,000
C	10	4,000	5	7,000	5	600
D	10	16,000	8	20,000	2	2,000
E	24	120,000	14	200,000	10	8,000
F	10	10,000	6	16,000	4	1,500
G	35	500,000	25	530,000	10	3,000
H	40	1,200,000	35	1,260,000	5	12,000
I	15	40,000	10	52,500	5	2,500
J	4	10,000	1	13,000	3	1,000
K	6	30,000	5	34,000	1	4,000
Totals		$1,992,000		$2,209,500		

Minimizing Costs

The objective of cost analysis is to determine the project schedule that minimizes total project costs. Suppose that project indirect costs are $8,000 per week. Suppose also that, after week 65, the Regional Hospital Board imposes on St. John's a penalty cost of $20,000 per week if the hospital is not fully operational. With a critical path completion time of 69 weeks, the hospital faces potentially large penalty costs unless the schedule is changed. For every week that the project is shortened—to week 65—the hospital saves one week of penalty *and* indirect costs, or $28,000. For reductions beyond week 65, the savings are only the weekly indirect costs of $8,000.

minimum-cost schedule

A schedule determined by starting with the normal time schedule and crashing activities along the critical path, in such a way that the costs of crashing do not exceed the savings in indirect and penalty costs.

The minimum possible project duration can be found by using the crash times of each activity for scheduling purposes. However, the cost of that schedule could be prohibitive. Project managers are most interested in minimizing the costs of their projects so that budgets are not exceeded. In determining the **minimum-cost schedule**, we start with the normal time schedule and crash activities along the critical path, whose length equals the length of the project. We want to determine how much we can add in crash costs without exceeding the savings in indirect and penalty costs. The procedure involves the following steps:

Step 1. Determine the project's critical path(s).

Step 2. Find the activity or activities on the critical path(s) with the lowest cost of crashing per week.

Step 3. Reduce the time for this activity until (a) it cannot be further reduced, (b) another path becomes critical, or (c) the increase in direct costs exceeds the indirect and penalty cost savings that result from shortening the project. If more than one path is critical, the time for an activity on each path may have to be reduced simultaneously.

Step 4. Repeat this procedure until the increase in direct costs is larger than the savings generated by shortening the project.

| EXAMPLE 7.3 | **Find a Minimum-Cost Schedule** |

Determine the minimum-cost schedule for the St. John's Hospital project. Use the information provided in Table 7.1 and Figure 7.3.

SOLUTION

The projected completion time of the project is 69 weeks. The project costs for that schedule are $1,992,000 in direct costs, 69($8,000) = $552,000 in indirect costs, and (69 − 65)($20,000) = $80,000 in penalty costs, for total project costs of $2,624,000. The five paths in the network have the following normal times:

A–I–K:	33 weeks
A–F–K:	28 weeks
A–C–G–J–K:	67 weeks
B–D–H–J–K:	69 weeks
B–E–J–K:	43 weeks

It will simplify our analysis if we can eliminate some paths from further consideration. If all activities on A–C–G–J–K were crashed, the path duration would be 47 weeks. Crashing all activities on B–D–H–J–K results in a project duration of 56 weeks. Because the *normal* times of A–I–K, A–F–K, and B–E–J–K are less than the minimum times of the other two paths, we can disregard those three paths; they will never become critical regardless of the crashing we may do.

STAGE 1

Step 1. The critical path is B–D–H–J–K.

Step 2. The cheapest activity to crash per week is J at $1,000, which is much less than the savings in indirect and penalty costs of $28,000 per week.

Step 3. Crash activity J by its limit of three weeks because the critical path remains unchanged. The new expected path times are

A–C–G–J–K: 64 weeks and B–D–H–J–K: 66 weeks

The net savings are 3 ($28,000) − 3($1,000) = $81,000. The total project costs are now $2,624,000 − $81,000 = $2,543,000.

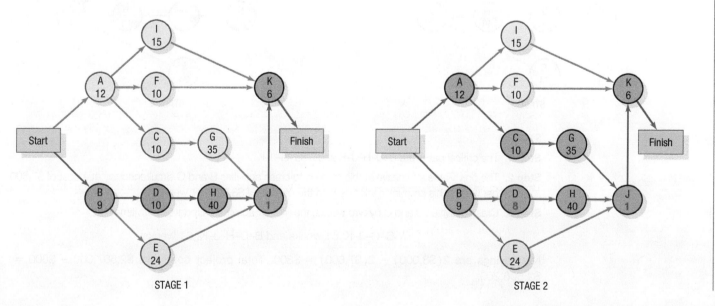

STAGE 1   STAGE 2

MyOMLab

Active Model 7.2 in MyOMLab provides additional insight on cost analysis for the St. John's Hospital project.

STAGE 2

Step 1. The critical path is still B–D–H–J–K.

Step 2. The cheapest activity to crash per week is now D at $2,000.

Step 3. Crash D by two weeks. The first week of reduction in activity D saves $28,000 because it eliminates a week of penalty costs, as well as indirect costs. Crashing D by a second week saves only $8,000 in indirect costs because, after week 65, no more penalty costs are incurred. These savings still exceed the cost of crashing D for a second week. Updated path times are

A–C–G–J–K: 64 weeks and B–D–H–J–K: 64 weeks

The net savings are $28,000 + $8,000 − 2($2,000) = $32,000. Total project costs are now $2,543,000 − $32,000 = $2,511,000.

STAGE 3

Step 1. After crashing D, we now have two critical paths. *Both* critical paths must now be shortened to realize any savings in indirect project costs. If one is shortened and the other is not, the length of the project remains unchanged.

Step 2. Our alternatives are to crash one of the following combinations of activities—(A, B), (A, H), (C, B), (C, H), (G, B), (G, H)—or to crash activity K, which is on both critical paths (J has already been crashed). We consider only those alternatives for which the cost of crashing is less than the potential savings of $8,000 per week. The only viable alternatives are (C, B) at a cost of $7,600 per week and K at $4,000 per week. We choose activity K to crash.

Step 3. We crash activity K to the greatest extent possible—a reduction of one week—because it is on both critical paths. Updated path times are

A–C–G–J–K: 63 weeks and B–D–H–J–K: 63 weeks

The net savings are $8,000 − $4,000 = $4,000. Total project costs are $2,511,000 − $4,000 = $2,507,000.

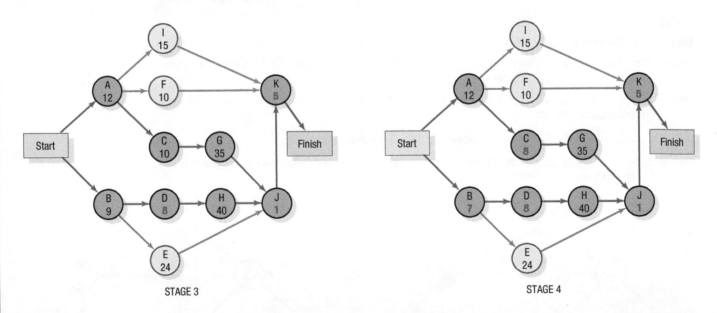

STAGE 4

Step 1. The critical paths are B–D–H–J–K and A–C–G–J–K.

Step 2. The only viable alternative at this stage is to crash activities B and C simultaneously at a cost of $7,600 per week. This amount is still less than the savings of $8,000 per week.

Step 3. Crash activities B and C by two weeks, the limit for activity B. Updated path times are

A–C–G–J–K: 61 weeks and B–D–H–J–K: 61 weeks

Net savings are 2($8,000) − 2($7,600) = $800. Total project costs are $2,507,000 − $800 = $2,506,200.

The following table summarizes the analysis:

Stage	Crash Activity	Time Reduction (weeks)	Resulting Critical Path(s)	Project Duration (weeks)	Project Direct Costs, Last Trial ($000)	Crash Cost Added ($000)	Total Indirect Costs ($000)	Total Penalty Costs ($000)	Total Project Costs ($000)
0	—	—	B–D–H–J–K	69	1,992.0	—	552.0	80.0	2,624.0
1	J	3	B–D–H–J–K	66	1,992.0	3.0	528.0	20.0	2,543.0
2	D	2	B–D–H–J–K A–C–G–J–K	64	1,995.0	4.0	512.0	0.0	2,511.0
3	K	1	B–D–H–J–K A–C–G–J–K	63	1,999.0	4.0	504.0	0.0	2,507.0
4	B,C	2	B–D–H–J–K A–C–G–J–K	61	2,003.0	15.2	488.0	0.0	2,506.2

DECISION POINT

Because the crash costs exceed weekly indirect costs, any other combination of activities will result in a net increase in total project costs. The minimum-cost schedule is 61 weeks, with a total cost of $2,506,200. To obtain this schedule, the project team must crash activities B, D, J, and K to their limits and activity C to eight weeks. The other activities remain at their normal times. This schedule costs $117,800 less than the normal-time schedule.

Assessing and Analyzing Risks

Risk is a measure of the probability and consequence of not reaching a defined project goal. Risk involves the notion of uncertainty as it relates to project timing and costs. Often, project teams must deal with uncertainty caused by labor shortages, weather, supply delays, or the outcomes of critical tests. In this section, we discuss risk management plans and the tools managers can use to analyze the risks, such as simulation and statistical analysis, which enable managers to estimate the probability of completing a project on time and the potential for near-critical paths to affect the project completion time.

Risk-Management Plans

A major responsibility of the project manager at the start of a project is to develop a **risk-management plan**, which identifies the key risks to a project's success and prescribes ways to circumvent them. A good risk-management plan will quantify the risks, predict their impact on the project, and provide contingency plans. Project risk can be assessed by examining four categories:

■ **Strategic Fit** The project may not be a good strategic fit in that it may not be clearly linked to the strategic goals of the firm.

■ **Service/Product Attributes** If the project involves the development of a new service or product, there may be market, technological, or legal risks. There is a chance that competitors may offer a superior product or a technological discovery may render the service or product obsolete before it even hits the market. There may also be a legal risk of potential lawsuits or liability that could force a design change after product development has begun.

■ **Project Team Capability** The project team may not have the capability to complete the project successfully because of the size and complexity of the project or the technology involved.

■ **Operations** There may be an operations risk because of poor information accuracy, lack of communication, missing precedence relationships, or bad estimates for activity times.

These risks should be identified and the significant ones should have contingency plans in case something goes wrong. The riskier a project is, the more likely the project will experience difficulties as Managerial Practice 7.1 shows.

Simulation PERT/CPM networks can be used to quantify risks associated with project timing. Often, the uncertainty associated with an activity can be reflected in the activity's time duration.

risk-management plan

A plan that identifies the key risks to a project's success and prescribes ways to circumvent them.

For example, an activity in a new product development project might be developing the enabling technology to manufacture it, an activity that may take from eight months to a year. To incorporate uncertainty into the network model, probability distributions of activity times can be calculated using two approaches: (1) computer simulation and (2) statistical analysis. With simulation, the time for each activity is randomly chosen from its probability distribution (see MyOMLab Supplement E, "Simulation"). The critical path of the network is determined, and the completion date of the project computed. The procedure is repeated many times, which results in a probability distribution for the completion date. We will have more to say about simulation when we discuss near critical paths later in this chapter.

MyOMLab

MANAGERIAL PRACTICE 7.1   San Francisco—Oakland Bay Bridge

San Francisco, California, has many noteworthy attractions: gardens, museums, Golden Gate Park, barking seals and seafood at Fisherman's Wharf, and the San Francisco Giants baseball team. The team was preparing to play in game 3 of the 1989 World Series against the Oakland Athletics when a 7.1 magnitude earthquake struck the Bay Area, minutes before the start of the game, resulting in the loss of many lives and billions of dollars in damage. Included in the damage was a 50-foot section of the upper deck of the Bay Bridge, which was closed until November 18, 1989, while the section was replaced. However, the Bay Bridge replacement project, which was needed to protect against future earthquakes, was not completed until September 12, 2013, at a cost of $6.4 billion, one of the most costly projects in the history of California. Are you wondering how that can happen? The answer lies at the heart of engaging in what we refer to as a risky project.

Aerial Archives/Alamy

The eastern span replacement of the San Francisco—Oakland Bay Bridge was built between 2002 and 2013. It is the largest public works project in California history. The construction project was complex; the span is engineered to withstand the largest earthquake expected over a 1,500 year period, and it is expected to last at least 150 years with proper maintenance. Projects such as this pose many risks for project managers.

The two major indicators of project performance are time and cost. Let's explore these two factors for the Bay Bridge replacement project.

Time. Shortly after the initial repair of the bridge, engineers determined that the eastern span of the bridge had to be made more earthquake resistant. Several design proposals were submitted. One proposal was to retrofit the existing bridge by replacing or supplementing the existing supports, doing little to change the appearance of the existing structure. However, the design was called into question for lack of robustness in an earthquake. The second type of design would replace the entire eastern span of the bridge. Debate arose as two designs emerged, one lacking esthetics but meeting the structural requirements and having a lower price tag, called the *freeway on stilts*, and the other the result of a contest having a more innovative and dramatic appearance but costing more. It was referred to as the *signature span*. Meanwhile, in 1997, there was political bickering about whether the bridge should be built to the north or the south of the existing bridge. One of the complaints was that with the existing placement and design the bridge would cast a shadow over prime development sites on Yerba Buena Island, which is within the province of San Francisco. Consequently, San Francisco restricted soil engineers' access to the proposed site for two years while a bridge design compromise was worked out. Finally the revised signature span proposal was accepted, and on January 29, 2002, construction began with an estimated completion date in 2007. However, in 2004, the governor of the State of California announced that insufficient funds were available for the signature span design and that the "freeway on stilts" should be constructed instead. After six months of delay, in 2005, additional funding was found and the original signature span design was reapproved. Once the project was in full swing, additional unforeseen hurdles such as technical challenges, permitting, weather, and design revisions caused long delays that added years to the original project deadlines. Consequently, because the project was extremely complex and involved an esthetically pleasing but seldom built design, securing accurate time estimates for the activities was nearly impossible.

Cost. As project delays mounted, costs increased. In 1997, the cost for the signature span design was estimated to be $1.5 billion. By 2002, when approval for the start of the project was obtained, the cost for steel rose dramatically, primarily because of a building boom in China. The entire project required 100,000 tons of structural steel; the total project cost was reestimated to be about $6.2 billion. Contractors were now considering uncertainties in construction costs due to the innovative design as well as the increase in steel costs in their cost estimates. Further, the delay in 2004 over the funding of the signature span design added an estimated $83 million to the cost of the project. Additional problems, including defective rods anchoring the roadway to earthquake safety structures, broken bolts connecting portions of the bridge deck to concrete columns, and water leaks due to a problem with the caulking between the steel guardrails and the roadway, added cost as well. All told, the project was estimated to cost $6.4 billion.

Projects of this size and complexity are inherently risky; contingency plans should cover the most likely disruptions. Schedule and budget problems are not unusual; however, the job of project managers is to manage the risks and minimize the deviations.

Sources: http://en.wikipedia.org/wiki/Eastern_span_replacement_of_the_San Francisco_Oakland Bay Bridge (2013); Rick Weinberg, "26: World Series halted by Bay Area earthquake," **http://sports.espn.go.com/espn25** (2013); Jason Dearen, "After 24 years, $6.4 Billion S.F. Bay Bridge Project Draws to Close," **http://cnsnews.com/ news/article** (2013); Jaxon Van Derbeken, "Bay Bridge's new problem: leaks," **http://www.sfgate.com/bayarea/article** (2014).

Statistical Analysis

The statistical analysis approach requires that activity times be stated in terms of three reasonable time estimates:

1. The **optimistic time** (a) is the shortest time in which an activity can be completed, if all goes exceptionally well.

2. The **most likely time** (m) is the probable time required to perform an activity.

3. The **pessimistic time** (b) is the longest estimated time required to perform an activity.

With three time estimates—the optimistic, the most likely, and the pessimistic—the project manager has enough information to estimate the probability that an activity will be completed on schedule. To do so, the project manager must first calculate the mean and variance of a probability distribution for each activity. In PERT/CPM, each activity time is treated as though it were a random variable derived from a beta probability distribution. This distribution can have various shapes, allowing the most likely time estimate (m) to fall anywhere between the pessimistic (b) and optimistic (a) time estimates. The most likely time estimate is the *mode* of the beta distribution, or the time with the highest probability of occurrence. This condition is not possible with the normal distribution, which is symmetrical, because the normal distribution requires the mode to be equidistant from the end points of the distribution. Figure 7.6 shows the difference between the two distributions.

Two key assumptions are required. First, we assume that a, m, and b can be estimated accurately. The estimates might best be considered values that define a reasonable time range for the activity duration negotiated between the project manager and the team members responsible for the activities. Second, we assume that the standard deviation, σ, of the activity time is one-sixth the range $b - a$. Thus, the chance that actual activity times will fall between a and b is high. Why does this assumption make sense? If the activity time followed the normal distribution, six standard deviations would span approximately 99.74 percent of the distribution.

Even with these assumptions, derivation of the mean and variance of each activity's probability distribution is complex. These derivations show that the mean of the beta distribution can be estimated by using the following weighted average of the three time estimates:

$$t_e = \frac{a + 4m + b}{6}$$

optimistic time (a)

The shortest time in which an activity can be completed, if all goes exceptionally well.

most likely time (m)

The probable time required to perform an activity.

pessimistic time (b)

The longest estimated time required to perform an activity.

FIGURE 7.6 ▶
Differences Between Beta and
Normal Distributions for Project
Risk Analysis

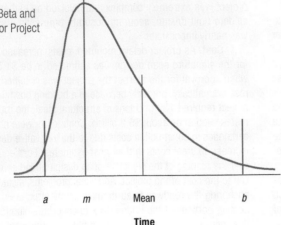

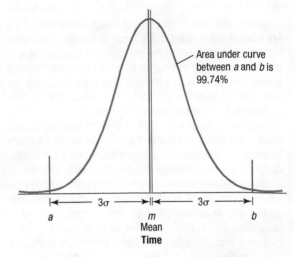

(a) **Beta distribution:** The most likely time (*m*) has the highest probability and can be placed anywhere between the optimistic (*a*) and pessimistic (*b*) times.

(b) **Normal distribution:** The mean and most likely times must be the same. If *a* and *b* are chosen to be 6σ apart, there is a 99.74% chance that the actual activity time will fall between them.

Note that the most likely time has four times the weight of the pessimistic and optimistic estimates. The variance of the beta distribution for each activity is

$$\sigma^2 = \left(\frac{b-a}{6}\right)^2$$

The variance, which is the standard deviation squared, increases as the difference between *b* and *a* increases. This result implies that the less certain a person is in estimating the actual time for an activity, the greater will be the variance.

| EXAMPLE 7.4 | **Calculating Means and Variances** |

Suppose that the project team has arrived at the following time estimates for activity B (Select site and survey) of the St. John's Hospital project:

$$a = 7 \text{ weeks}, m = 8 \text{ weeks}, \text{and } b = 15 \text{ weeks}$$

a. Calculate the expected time and variance for activity B.

b. Calculate the expected time and variance for the other activities in the project.

SOLUTION

a. The expected time for activity B is

$$t_e = \frac{7 + 4(8) + 15}{6} = \frac{54}{6} = 9 \text{ weeks}$$

Note that the expected time (9 weeks) does not equal the most likely time (8 weeks) for this activity. These times will be the same only when the most likely time is equidistant from the optimistic and pessimistic times. We calculate the variance for activity B as

$$\sigma^2 = \left(\frac{15-7}{6}\right)^2 = \left(\frac{8}{6}\right)^2 = 1.78$$

b. The following table shows expected activity times and variances for the activities listed in the project description.

	TIME ESTIMATES (WEEKS)			ACTIVITY STATISTICS	
Activity	Optimistic (*a*)	Most Likely (*m*)	Pessimistic (*b*)	Expected Time (t_e)	Variance (σ^2)
A	11	12	13	12	0.11
B	7	8	15	9	1.78
C	5	10	15	10	2.78
D	8	9	16	10	1.78
E	14	25	30	24	7.11
F	6	9	18	10	4.00
G	25	36	41	35	7.11
H	35	40	45	40	2.78
I	10	13	28	15	9.00
J	1	2	15	4	5.44
K	5	6	7	6	0.11

DECISION POINT

The project team should notice that the greatest uncertainty lies in the time estimate for activity I, followed by the estimates for activities E and G. These activities should be analyzed for the source of the uncertainties, and actions should be taken to reduce the variance in the time estimates.

Analyzing Probabilities

Because time estimates for activities involve uncertainty, project managers are interested in determining the probability of meeting project completion deadlines. To develop the probability distribution for project completion time, we assume that the duration time of one activity does not depend on that of any other activity. This assumption enables us to estimate the mean and variance of the probability distribution of the time duration of the entire project by summing the duration times and variances of the activities along the critical path. However, if one work crew is assigned two activities that can be done at the same time, the activity times will be interdependent and the assumption is not valid. In addition, if other paths in the network have small amounts of slack, one of them might become the critical path before the project is completed; we should calculate a probability distribution for those paths as well.

Because of the assumption that the activity duration times are independent random variables, we can make use of the central limit theorem, which states that the sum of a group of independent, identically distributed random variables approaches a normal distribution as the number of random variables increases. The mean of the normal distribution is the sum of the expected activity times on the path. In the case of the critical path, it is the earliest expected finish time for the project:

$$T_E = \sum (\text{Expected activity times on the critical path}) = \text{Mean of normal distribution}$$

Similarly, because of the assumption of activity time independence, we use the sum of the variances of the activities along the path as the variance of the time distribution for that path. That is, for the critical path,

$$\sigma_P^2 = \sum (\text{Variances of activities on the critical path})$$

To analyze probabilities of completing a project by a certain date using the normal distribution, we focus on the *critical path* and use the *z*-transformation formula:

$$z = \frac{T - T_E}{\sigma_P}$$

where

$$T = \text{due date for the project}$$

Given the value of z, we use the Normal Distribution appendix to find the probability that the project will be completed by time T, or sooner. An implicit assumption in this approach is that no other path will become critical during the time span of the project. Example 7.5, part (a), demonstrates this calculation for the St. John's Hospital project.

The procedure for assessing the probability of completing any activity in a project by a specific date is similar to the one just discussed. However, instead of the critical path, we would use the longest time path of activities from the start node to the activity node in question.

Near-Critical Paths

A project's duration is a function of its critical path. However, paths that are close to the same duration as the critical path may ultimately become the critical path over the life of the project. In practice, at the start of the project, managers typically do not know the activity times with certainty and may never know which path was the critical path until the actual activity times are known at the end of the project. Nonetheless, this uncertainty does not reduce the usefulness of identifying the probability of one path or another causing a project to exceed its target completion time; it helps to identify the activities that need close management attention. To assess the chances of near-critical paths delaying the project completion, we can focus on the longest paths in the project network keeping in mind that both duration and variance along the path must be considered. Shorter paths with high variances could have just as much a chance to delay the project as longer paths with smaller variances. We can then estimate the probability that a given path will exceed the project target completion time. We demonstrate that approach using statistical analysis in Example 7.5, part (b).

Alternatively, simulation can be used to estimate the probabilities. The advantage of simulation is that you are not restricted to the use of the beta distribution for activity times. Also, activity or path dependencies, such as decision points that could involve different groups of activities to be undertaken, can be incorporated in a simulation model much more easily than with the statistical analysis approach. Fortunately, regardless of the approach used, it is rarely necessary to evaluate every path in the network. In large networks, many paths will have both short durations and low variances, making them unlikely to affect the project duration.

EXAMPLE 7.5	Calculating the Probability of Completing a Project by a Given Date

MyOMLab

Active Model 7.3 in MyOMLab provides additional insight on probability analysis for the St. John's Hospital project.

Calculate the probability that St. John's Hospital will become operational in 72 weeks, using (a) the critical path and (b) near-critical path A–C–G–J–K.

SOLUTION

a. The critical path B–D–H–J–K has a length of 69 weeks. From the table in Example 7.4, we obtain the variance of path B–D–H–J–K: $\sigma_P^2 = 1.78 + 1.78 + 2.78 + 5.44 + 0.11 = 11.89$. Next, we calculate the z-value:

$$z = \frac{72 - 69}{\sqrt{11.89}} = \frac{3}{3.45} = 0.87$$

Using the Normal Distribution appendix, we go down the left-hand column until we arrive at the value 0.8 and then across until we arrive at the 0.07 column, which shows a tabular value of 0.8078. Consequently, we find that the probability is about 0.81 that the length of path B–D–H–J–K will be no greater than 72 weeks. Because this path is the critical path, there is a 19 percent probability that the project will take longer than 72 weeks. This probability is shown graphically in Figure 7.7.

b. From the table in Example 7.4, we determine that the sum of the expected activity times on path A–C–G–J–K is 67 weeks and that $\sigma_P^2 = 0.11 + 2.78 + 7.11 + 5.44 + 0.11 = 15.55$. The z-value is

$$z = \frac{72 - 67}{\sqrt{15.55}} = \frac{5}{3.94} = 1.27$$

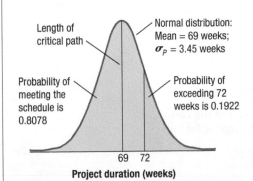

Length of critical path

Normal distribution: Mean = 69 weeks; σ_P = 3.45 weeks

Probability of meeting the schedule is 0.8078

Probability of exceeding 72 weeks is 0.1922

69   72

Project duration (weeks)

▲ **FIGURE 7.7**

Probability of Completing the St. John's Hospital Project on Schedule

The probability is about 0.90 that the length of path A–C–G–J–K will be no greater than 72 weeks.

DECISION POINT

The project team should be aware of the 10 percent chance that path A–C–G–J–K will exceed the target completion date of week 72. Although the probability is not high for that path, activities A, C, and G bear watching during the first 57 weeks of the project to make sure no more than 2 weeks of slippage occurs in their schedules. This attention is especially important for activity G, which has a high time variance.

Monitoring and Controlling Projects

Once project planning is over, the challenge becomes keeping the project on schedule within the budget of allocated resources. In this section, we discuss how to monitor project status and resource usage. In addition, we identify the features of project management software useful for monitoring and controlling projects.

Monitoring Project Status

A good tracking system will help the project team accomplish its project goals. Effective tracking systems collect information on three topics: (1) open issues, (2) risks, and (3) schedule status.

Open Issues and Risks
One of the duties of the project manager is to make sure that issues that have been raised during the project actually get resolved in a timely fashion. The tracking system should remind the project manager of due dates for open issues and who was responsible for seeing that they are resolved. Likewise, it should provide the status of each risk to project delays specified in the risk management plan so that the team can review them at each meeting. To be effective, the tracking system requires team members to update information periodically regarding their respective responsibilities.

Schedule Status
Even the best laid project plans can go awry. A tracking system that provides periodic monitoring of slack time in the project schedule can help the project manager control activities along the critical path. Periodic updating of the status of ongoing activities in the project allows the tracking system to recalculate activity slacks and indicate those activities that are behind schedule or are in danger of using up all of their slack. Managers can then focus on those activities and reallocate resources as needed.

Monitoring and controlling shipbuilding projects is critical to keeping these complex projects on schedule. Here a propeller is attached to an ocean-going vessel.

Monitoring Project Resources

Experience has shown that the resources allocated to a project are consumed at an uneven rate that is a function of the timing of the schedules for the project's activities. Projects have a *life cycle* that consists of four major phases: (1) definition and organization, (2) planning, (3) execution, and (4) close out. Figure 7.8 shows that each of the four phases requires different resource commitments.

We have already discussed the activities associated with the project definition and organization and project planning phases. The phase that takes the most resources is the *execution phase*, during which manager's focus on activities pertaining to deliverables. The project schedule becomes very important because it shows when each resource devoted to a given activity will be required. Monitoring the progress of activities throughout the project is important to avoid potential overloading of resources. Problems arise when a specific resource, such as a construction crew or staff specialist, is required on several activities with overlapping schedules. Project managers have several options to alleviate resource problems, including the following:

- *Resource Leveling.* The attempt to reduce the peaks and valleys in resource needs by shifting the schedules of conflicting activities within their earliest and latest start dates. Software packages such as MS Project have algorithms that move activities to avoid violating resource constraints.

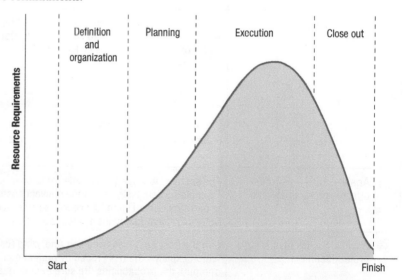

▲ **FIGURE 7.8**
Project Life Cycle

- *Resource Allocation.* The assignment of resources to the most important activities. Most popular project management software packages have a few priority rules that can be used to decide which activity a critical resource should be scheduled to perform when conflicts arise. For example, for all the activities requiring a given resource, assign the resource to the one with the earliest start time. An activity slack report identifies potential candidates for resource shifting—shift resources from high slack activities to those behind schedule.

- *Resource Acquisition.* The addition of more of an overloaded resource to maintain the schedule of an activity. Obviously, this tactic is constrained by the project budget.

Controlling Projects

Project managers have the responsibilities of accounting for the effective use of the firm's resources as well as managing the activities to achieve the time and quality goals of the project. The firm's assets include the physical assets, human resources, and financial resources. Physical assets are controlled by the timely maintenance of machines and equipment so that their failure does not delay the project. Inventories must be received, stored for future use, and replenished. Project managers are also responsible for human resource development. Projects provide a rich environment to develop future leaders; project managers can take advantage of the situation by assigning team members important activities to aid in their managerial development. Last, but not least, project managers must control the expenditures of the firm's financial resources. Most project management software packages contain accounting reports, budget reports, capital investment controls, and cash flow reports. Deviations from the project plan, often referred to as variances, must be periodically reported and analyzed for their causes.

close out

An activity that includes writing final reports, completing remaining deliverables, and compiling the team's recommendations for improving the project process.

Monitoring and controlling projects are ongoing activities throughout the execution phase of the project life cycle. The project **close out**, however, is an activity that many project managers forget to include in their consideration of resource usage. The purpose of this final phase in the project life cycle is to write final reports and complete remaining deliverables. An important aspect of this phase, however, is compiling the team's recommendations for improving the project process of which they were a part. Many team members will be assigned to other projects where they can apply what they learned.

LEARNING GOALS IN REVIEW

Learning Goal	Guidelines for Review	MyOMLab Resources
① Explain the major activities associated with defining and organizing a project.	Read the opener to the chapter, which shows the four major phases of the project to introduce the new XBOX 360 product, the introduction to the chapter, and the section "Defining and Organizing Projects," pp. 239–240.	**Video:** Project Management at the Phoenician
② Describe the procedure for constructing a project network.	Focus on the section "Constructing Project Networks," pp. 241–243, paying close attention to Example 7.1.	**SmartDraw** – free trial
③ Develop the schedule of a project.	Review the section "Developing the Project Schedule," pp. 243–247. The schedule is determined when activity slacks and the critical path are computed. Focus on Example 7.2 and Figure 7.3.	**Active Model Exercise:** 7.1: Gantt Chart **OME Solver:** Single Time Estimates **POM for Windows:** Single Time Estimates **MS Project** – free trial **Supplement H:** Measuring Output Rates **Supplement I:** Learning Curve Analysis
④ Analyze cost–time trade-offs in a project network.	The section "Analyzing Cost–Time Trade-offs," pp. 247–251, and Example 7.3 demonstrate how the relevant costs must be considered to minimize costs. Figure 7.5 explains a key assumption in the analysis. Solved Problem 1 contains a detailed solution.	**Active Model Exercise:** 7.2: Cost Analysis **POM for Windows:** Crashing
⑤ Assess the risk of missing a project deadline.	See the section "Assessing and Analyzing Risks," pp. 251–256, which explains the risks faced by project managers and how to compute the probabilities. Be sure to understand Examples 7.4 and 7.5 and Solved Problem 2.	**Active Model Exercise:** 7.3: Probability Analysis **OME Solver:** Three Time Estimates **POM for Windows:** Triple Time Estimates; Mean/Standard Deviation Given **Simquick Simulation Exercise:** Software Development Company **Supplement E:** Simulation
⑥ Identify the options available to monitor and control projects.	See the section "Monitoring and Controlling Projects," pp. 257–258.	**OME Solver:** Project Budgeting **POM for Windows:** Cost Budgeting

Key Equations

Developing the Project Schedule

1. Start and finish times:

    t = estimated time duration of the activity

    ES = latest of the EF times of all activities immediately preceding activity

    EF = ES + t

    LF = earliest of the LS times of all activities immediately following activity

    LS = LF − t

2. Activity slack:

    $$S = LS - ES \text{ or } S = LF - EF$$

Analyzing Cost–Time Trade-offs

3. Project costs:

    $$\text{Crash cost per period} = \frac{\text{Crash cost} - \text{Normal cost}}{\text{Normal time} - \text{Crash time}}$$

    $$= \frac{CC - NC}{NT - CT}$$

Assessing and Analyzing Risks

4. Activity time statistics:

    t_e = mean of an activity's beta distribution

    $$t_e = \frac{a + 4m + b}{6}$$

    σ^2 = variance of the activity time

    $$\sigma^2 = \left(\frac{b - a}{6}\right)^2$$

5. z-transformation formula:

    $$z = \frac{T - T_E}{\sigma_P}$$

    where

    T = due date for the project

    $T_E = \sum (\text{expected activity times on the critical path})$

    = mean of normal distribution of critical path time

    σ_P = standard deviation of critical path time distribution

Key Terms

activity 241
activity slack 246
close out 258
crash cost (CC) 247
crash time (CT) 247
critical path 243
critical path method (CPM) 242
earliest finish time (EF) 244
earliest start time (ES) 244
Gantt chart 246

latest finish time (LF) 244
latest start time (LS) 244
minimum-cost schedule 248
most likely time (m) 253
network diagram 241
normal cost (NC) 247
normal time (NT) 246
optimistic time (a) 253
path 243
pessimistic time (b) 253

precedence relationship 242
program 239
program evaluation and review
    technique (PERT) 242
project 239
project management 239
risk-management plan 251
work breakdown structure (WBS) 241

Solved Problem 1

MyOMLab Video

Your company has just received an order from a good customer for a specially designed electric motor. The contract states that, starting on the 13th day from now, your firm will experience a penalty of $100 per day until the job is completed. Indirect project costs amount to $200 per day. The data on direct costs and activity precedence relationships are given in Table 7.2.

TABLE 7.2 | ELECTRIC MOTOR PROJECT DATA

Activity	Normal Time (days)	Normal Cost ($)	Crash Time (days)	Crash Cost ($)	Immediate Predecessor(s)
A	4	1,000	3	1,300	None
B	7	1,400	4	2,000	None
C	5	2,000	4	2,700	None
D	6	1,200	5	1,400	A
E	3	900	2	1,100	B
F	11	2,500	6	3,750	C
G	4	800	3	1,450	D, E
H	3	300	1	500	F, G

a. Draw the project network diagram.

b. What completion date would you recommend?

SOLUTION

a. The network diagram, including normal activity times, for this procedure is shown in Figure 7.9. Keep the following points in mind while constructing a network diagram.

1. Always have start and finish nodes.
2. Try to avoid crossing paths to keep the diagram simple.
3. Use only one arrow to directly connect any two nodes.
4. Put the activities with no predecessors at the left and point the arrows from left to right.
5. Be prepared to revise the diagram several times before you come up with a correct and uncluttered diagram.

b. With these activity durations, the project will be completed in 19 days and incur a $700 penalty. Determining a good completion date requires the use of the minimum-cost schedule procedure. Using the data provided in Table 7.2, you can determine the maximum crash-time reduction and crash cost per day for each activity. For example, for activity A

$$\text{Maximum crash time} = \text{Normal time} - \text{Crash time}$$
$$= 4 \text{ days} - 3 \text{ days} = 1 \text{ day}$$

$$\text{Crash cost per day} = \frac{\text{Crash cost} - \text{Normal cost}}{\text{Normal time} - \text{Crash time}}$$

$$= \frac{CC - NC}{NT - CT}$$

$$= \frac{\$1,300 - \$1,000}{4 \text{ days} - 3 \text{ days}} = \$300$$

FIGURE 7.9 ▶
Network Diagram for the Electric
Motor Project

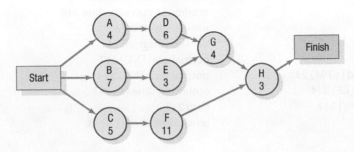

Activity	Crash Cost per Day ($)	Maximum Time Reduction (days)
A	300	1
B	200	3
C	700	1
D	200	1
E	200	1
F	250	5
G	650	1
H	100	2

Table 7.3 summarizes the analysis and the resultant project duration and total cost. The critical path is C–F–H at 19 days, which is the longest path in the network. The cheapest of these activities to crash is H, which costs only an extra $100 per day to crash. Doing so saves $200 + $100 = $300 per day in indirect and penalty costs. If you crash this activity for two days (the maximum), the lengths of the paths are now

A–D–G–H: 15 days, B–E–G–H: 15 days, and C–F–H: 17 days

The critical path is still C–F–H. The next cheapest critical activity to crash is F at $250 per day. You can crash F only two days because at that point you will have three critical paths. Further reductions in project duration will require simultaneous crashing of more than one activity (D, E, and F). The cost to do so, $650, exceeds the savings, $300. Consequently, you should stop. Note that every activity is critical. The project costs are minimized when the completion date is day 15. However, some goodwill costs may be associated with disappointing a customer who wants delivery in 12 days.

TABLE 7.3 | PROJECT COST ANALYSIS

Stage	Crash Activity	Time Reduction (days)	Resulting Critical Path(s)	Project Duration (days)	Project Direct Costs, Last Trial ($)	Crash Cost Added ($)	Total Indirect Costs ($)	Total Penalty Costs ($)	Total Project Costs ($)
0	—	—	C–F–H	19	10,100	—	3,800	700	14,600
1	H	2	C–F–H	17	10,100	200	3,400	500	14,200
2	F	2	A–D–G–H B–E–G–H C–F–H	15	10,300	500	3,000	300	14,100

Solved Problem 2

An advertising project manager developed the network diagram shown in Figure 7.10 for a new advertising campaign. In addition, the manager gathered the time information for each activity, as shown in the accompanying table.

Activity	TIME ESTIMATES (WEEKS)			Immediate Predecessor(s)
	Optimistic	Most Likely	Pessimistic	
A	1	4	7	—
B	2	6	7	—
C	3	3	6	B
D	6	13	14	A
E	3	6	12	A, C
F	6	8	16	B
G	1	5	6	E, F

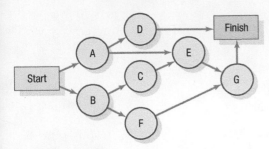

▲ FIGURE 7.10
Network Diagram for the
Advertising Project

a. Calculate the expected time and variance for each activity.

b. Calculate the activity slacks and determine the critical path, using the expected activity times.

c. What is the probability of completing the project within 23 weeks?

SOLUTION

a. The expected time and variance for each activity are calculated as follows:

$$t_e = \frac{a + 4m + b}{6}$$

Activity	Expected Time (weeks)	Variance (σ^2)
A	4.0	1.00
B	5.5	0.69
C	3.5	0.25
D	12.0	1.78
E	6.5	2.25
F	9.0	2.78
G	4.5	0.69

b. We need to calculate the earliest start, latest start, earliest finish, and latest finish times for each activity. Starting with activities A and B, we proceed from the beginning of the network and move to the end, calculating the earliest start and finish times:

Activity	Earliest Start (weeks)	Earliest Finish (weeks)
A	0	0 + 4.0 = 4.0
B	0	0 + 5.5 = 5.5
C	5.5	5.5 + 3.5 = 9.0
D	4.0	4.0 + 12.0 = 16.0
E	9.0	9.0 + 6.5 = 15.5
F	5.5	5.5 + 9.0 = 14.5
G	15.5	15.5 + 4.5 = 20.0

Based on expected times, the earliest finish for the project is week 20, when activity G has been completed. Using that as a target date, we can work backward through the network, calculating the latest start and finish times (shown graphically in Figure 7.11):

Activity	Latest Start (weeks)	Latest Finish (weeks)
G	15.5	20.0
F	6.5	15.5
E	9.0	15.5
D	8.0	20.0
C	5.5	9.0
B	0.0	5.5
A	4.0	8.0

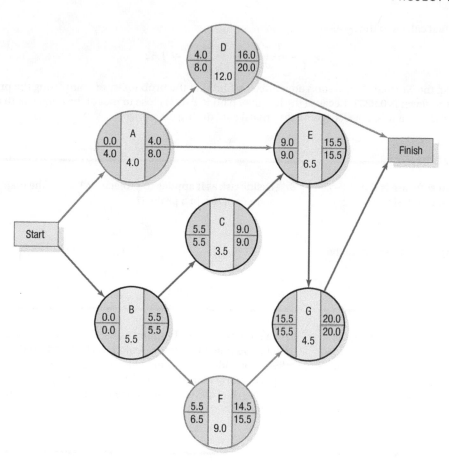

◀ FIGURE 7.11
Network Diagram with All
Time Estimates Needed to
Compute Slack

We now calculate the activity slacks and determine which activities are on the critical path:

| Activity | START (WEEKS) | | FINISH (WEEKS) | | | |
	Earliest	Latest	Earliest	Latest	Slack	Critical Activity
A	0.0	4.0	4.0	8.0	4.0	No
B	0.0	0.0	5.5	5.5	0.0	Yes
C	5.5	5.5	9.0	9.0	0.0	Yes
D	4.0	8.0	16.0	20.0	4.0	No
E	9.0	9.0	15.5	15.5	0.0	Yes
F	5.5	6.5	14.5	15.5	1.0	No
G	15.5	15.5	20.0	20.0	0.0	Yes

The paths, and their total expected times and variances, are

Path	Total Expected Time (weeks)	Total Variance (σ_P^2)
A–D	4 + 12 = 16	1.00 + 1.78 = 2.78
A–E–G	4 + 6.5 + 4.5 = 15	1.00 + 2.25 + 0.69 = 3.94
B–C–E–G	5.5 + 3.5 + 6.5 + 4.5 = 20	0.69 + 0.25 + 2.25 + 0.69 = 3.88
B–F–G	5.5 + 9 + 4.5 = 19	0.69 + 2.78 + 0.69 = 4.16

The critical path is B–C–E–G, with a total expected time of 20 weeks. However, path B–F–G is 19 weeks and has a large variance.

c. We first calculate the z-value:

$$z = \frac{T - T_E}{\sigma_P} = \frac{23 - 20}{\sqrt{3.88}} = 1.52$$

Using the Normal Distribution appendix, we find that the probability of completing the project in 23 weeks or fewer is 0.9357. Because the length of path B–F–G is close to that of the critical path and has a large variance, it might well become the critical path during the project.

Discussion Questions

1. One of your colleagues comments that software is the ultimate key to project management success. How would you respond?

2. Explain how to determine the slack for each activity in a project. Why is it important for managers to know where the slack is in their projects?

3. Define risk as it applies to projects. What are the major sources of risk in a project?

Problems

The OM Explorer and POM for Windows software is available to all students using the 11th edition of this textbook. Go to **http://www.pearsonhighered.com/krajewski** to download these computer packages. If you purchased MyOMLab, you also have access to Active Models software and significant help in doing the following problems. Check with your instructor on how best to use these resources. In many cases, the instructor wants you to understand how to do the calculations by hand. At the least, the software provides a check on your calculations. When calculations are particularly complex and the goal is interpreting the results in making decisions, the software replaces entirely the manual calculations.

Developing the Project Schedule

1. Consider the following data for a project to install a new server at the Northland Pines High School:

Activity	Activity Time (days)	Immediate Predecessor(s)
A	2	—
B	4	A
C	5	A
D	2	B
E	1	B
F	8	B, C
G	3	D, E
H	5	F
I	4	F
J	7	G, H, I

a. Draw the network diagram.

b. Calculate the critical path for this project.

c. How much slack is in each of the activities G, H, and I?

2. The following information is known about a project to upgrade a point-of-sale system at Kids and Tots Apparel.

Activity	Activity Time (days)	Immediate Predecessor(s)
A	7	—
B	2	A

Activity	Activity Time (days)	Immediate Predecessor(s)
C	4	A
D	4	B, C
E	4	D
F	3	E
G	5	E

a. Draw the network diagram for this project.

b. Determine the critical path and project duration.

c. Calculate the slack for each activity.

3. A project for improving a billing process has the following precedence relationships and activity times:

Activity	Activity Time (weeks)	Immediate Predecessor(s)
A	3	—
B	11	—
C	7	A
D	13	B, C
E	10	B
F	6	D
G	5	E
H	8	F, G

a. Draw the network diagram.

b. Calculate the slack for each activity. Which activities are on the critical path?

4. The following information is available about a project to organize an event to honor the mayor of West Allis at the Nathan Hale High School:

Activity	Activity Time (days)	Immediate Predecessor(s)
A	3	—
B	4	—
C	5	—
D	4	—
E	7	A
F	2	B, C, D
G	4	E, F
H	6	F
I	4	G
J	3	G
K	3	H

a. Draw the network diagram.

b. Find the critical path.

5. The following information has been gathered for a project to install a new machine lathe at Diamond Manufacturing, Inc:

Activity	Activity Time (weeks)	Immediate Predecessor(s)
A	4	—
B	7	A
C	9	B
D	3	B
E	14	D
F	10	C, D
G	11	F, E

a. Draw the network diagram.

b. Calculate the slack for each activity and determine the critical path. How long will the project take?

6. Consider the following information for a project to add a drive-through window at Crestview Bank.

Activity	Activity Time (weeks)	Immediate Predecessor(s)
A	5	—
B	2	—
C	6	—
D	2	A, B
E	7	B
F	3	D, C
G	9	E, C
H	11	F, G

a. Draw the network diagram for this project.

b. Specify the critical path.

c. Calculate the slack for activities A and D.

7. Consider the following data for a project to reorganize the office space at Platinum Financial Advisors:

Activity	Expected Time t_e (weeks)	Immediate Predecessor(s)
A	5	—
B	3	—
C	2	A
D	5	B
E	4	C, D
F	7	D

a. Draw the network diagram for this project.

b. Identify the critical path and estimate the project's duration.

c. Calculate the slack for each activity.

8. Paul Silver, owner of Sculptures International, just initiated a new art project. The following data are available for the project:

Activity	Activity Time (days)	Immediate Predecessor(s)
A	4	—
B	1	—
C	3	A
D	2	B
E	3	C, D

a. Draw the network diagram for the project.

b. Determine the project's critical path and duration.

c. What is the slack for each activity?

9. Reliable Garage is completing production of the J2000 kit car. The following data are available for the project:

Activity	Activity Time (days)	Immediate Predecessor(s)
A	2	—
B	6	A
C	4	B
D	5	C
E	7	C
F	5	C
G	5	F
H	3	D, E, G

a. Draw the network diagram for the project.

b. Determine the project's critical path and duration.

c. What is the slack for each activity?

10. The following information concerns a project to raise money for the Kids Against Crime Foundation:

Activity	Activity Time (days)	Immediate Predecessor(s)
A	10	—
B	11	—
C	9	A, B
D	5	A, B
E	8	A, B
F	13	C, E
G	5	C, D
H	10	G
I	6	F, G
J	9	E, H
K	11	I, J

a. Draw the network diagram for this project.

b. Determine the critical path and project completion time.

11. Consider a project to produce custom door moldings
 ⒟ for GMC Acadia cross-over vehicles, described in Table 7.4.

Analyzing Cost–Time Trade-offs

12. Table 7.5 contains information about an environmental clean-up project in the township of Hiles. Shorten the project three weeks by finding the minimum-cost schedule. Assume that project indirect costs and penalty costs are negligible. Identify activities to crash while minimizing the additional crash costs.

TABLE 7.5 | ENVIRONMENTAL PROJECT DATA

Activity	Normal Time (weeks)	Crash Time (weeks)	Cost to Crash ($ per week)	Immediate Predecessor(s)
A	7	6	200	None
B	12	9	250	None
C	7	6	250	A
D	6	5	300	A
E	1	1	—	B
F	1	1	—	C, D
G	3	1	200	D, E
H	3	2	350	F
I	2	2	—	G

13. The Advanced Tech Company has a project to design an integrated information database for a major bank. Data for the project are given in Table 7.6. Indirect project costs amount to $300 per day. The company will incur a $150 per day penalty for each day the project lasts beyond day 14.

 ⒟ = Difficult Problem

a. If you start the project immediately, when will it be finished?

b. You are interested in completing your project as soon as possible. You have only one option. Suppose you could assign Employee A, currently assigned to activity G, to help Employee B, currently assigned to activity F. Each week that Employee A helps Employee B will result in activity G increasing its time by one week and activity F reducing its time by one week. How many weeks should Employee A work on activity F?

TABLE 7.4 | PROJECT DATA FOR GMC ACADIA

Activity	Activity Time (weeks)	Immediate Predecessor(s)
START	0	—
A	3	START
B	4	START
C	4	B
D	4	A
E	5	A, B
F	6	D, E
G	2	C, E
FINISH	0	F, G

a. What is the project's duration if only normal times are used?

b. What is the minimum-cost schedule?

c. What is the critical path for the minimum-cost schedule?

TABLE 7.6 | DATABASE DESIGN PROJECT DATA

Activity	Normal Time (days)	Normal Cost ($)	Crash Time (days)	Crash Cost ($)	Immediate Predecessor(s)
A	6	1,000	5	1,200	—
B	4	800	2	2,000	—
C	3	600	2	900	A, B
D	2	1,500	1	2,000	B
E	6	900	4	1,200	C, D
F	2	1,300	1	1,400	E
G	4	900	4	900	E
H	4	500	2	900	G

14. You are the manager of a project to improve a billing process at your firm. Table 7.7 contains the data you will need to conduct a cost analysis of the project. Indirect costs are $1,600 per week, and penalty costs are $1,200 per week after week 12.

a. What is the minimum-cost schedule for this project?

b. What is the difference in total project costs between the earliest completion time of the project using "normal" times and the minimum-cost schedule you derived in part (a)?

TABLE 7.7 | DATA FOR THE BILLING PROCESS PROJECT

Activity	Immediate Predecessor(s)	Normal Time (weeks)	Crash Time (weeks)	Normal Cost ($)	Crash Cost ($)
A	—	4	1	5,000	8,000
B	—	5	3	8,000	10,000
C	A	1	1	4,000	4,000
D	B	6	3	6,000	12,000
E	B, C	7	6	4,000	7,000
F	D	7	6	4,000	7,000

15. Table 7.8 contains data for the installation of new equipment in a manufacturing process at Excello Corporation. Your company is responsible for the installation project. Indirect costs are $15,000 per week, and a penalty cost of $9,000 per week will be incurred by your company for every week the project is delayed beyond week 9.

   a. What is the shortest time duration for this project regardless of cost?

   b. What is the minimum total cost associated with completing the project in 9 weeks?

   c. What is the total time of the minimum-cost schedule?

TABLE 7.8 | DATA FOR THE EQUIPMENT INSTALLATION PROJECT

Activity	Immediate Predecessor(s)	Normal Time (weeks)	Crash Time (weeks)	Normal Cost ($)	Crash Cost ($)
A	—	2	1	7,000	10,000
B	—	2	2	3,000	3,000
C	A	3	1	12,000	40,000
D	B	3	2	12,000	28,000
E	C	1	1	8,000	8,000
F	D, E	5	3	5,000	15,000
G	E	3	2	9,000	18,000

16. The diagram in Figure 7.12 was developed for the project launch of Kitty Condo, a new product in the luxury cat cage market. Suppose that you, as project manager, are interested in finding ways to speed up the project at minimal additional cost. Determine the schedule for completing the project in 25 days at minimum cost. Penalty and project-overhead costs are negligible. Time and cost data for each activity are shown in Table 7.9.

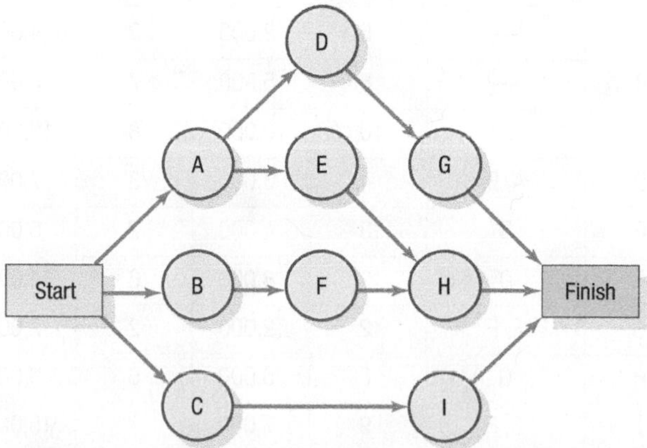

▲ FIGURE 7.12
Network Diagram for Kitty Condo

TABLE 7.9 | PROJECT ACTIVITY AND COST DATA

Activity	NORMAL		CRASH	
	Time (days)	Cost ($)	Time (days)	Cost ($)
A	12	1,300	11	1,900
B	13	1,050	9	1,500
C	18	3,000	16	4,500
D	9	2,000	5	3,000
E	12	650	10	1,100
F	8	700	7	1,050
G	8	1,550	6	1,950
H	2	600	1	800
I	4	2,200	2	4,000

17. You are in charge of a project at the local community center. The center needs to remodel one of the rooms in time for the start of a new program. Delays in the project mean that the center must rent other space at a nearby church at additional cost. Time and cost data for your project are contained in Table 7.10. Your interest is in minimizing the cost of the project to the community center.

a. Using the *normal times* for each activity, what is the earliest date you can complete the project?

b. Suppose the variable overhead costs are $50 per day for your project. Also, suppose that the center must pay $40 per day for a temporary room on day 15 or beyond. Find the minimum-cost project schedule.

TABLE 7.10 | DATA FOR THE COMMUNITY CENTER PROJECT

Activity	Normal Time (days)	Normal Cost ($)	Crash Time (days)	Crash Cost ($)	Immediate Predecessor(s)
START	0	0	0	0	—
A	10	50	8	150	START
B	4	40	2	200	START
C	7	70	6	160	B
D	2	20	1	50	A, C
E	3	30	3	30	A, C
F	8	80	5	290	B
G	5	50	4	180	D
H	6	60	3	180	E, F
FINISH	0	0	0	0	G, H

18. The information in Table 7.11 is available for a large fund-raising project.

a. Determine the critical path and the expected completion time of the project.

b. Plot the total project cost, starting from day 1 to the expected completion date of the project, assuming the earliest start times for each activity. Compare that result to a similar plot for the latest start times. What implication does the time differential have for cash flows and project scheduling?

TABLE 7.11 | FUND-RAISING PROJECT DATA

Activity	Activity Time (days)	Activity Cost ($)	Immediate Predecessor(s)
A	3	100	—
B	4	150	—
C	2	125	A
D	5	175	B
E	3	150	B
F	4	200	C, D
G	6	75	C
H	2	50	C, D, E
I	1	100	E
J	4	75	D, E
K	3	150	F, G
L	3	150	G, H, I
M	2	100	I, J
N	4	175	K, M
O	1	200	H, M
P	5	150	N, L, O

19. You are the project manager of the software installation project in Table 7.12. You would like to find the minimum-cost schedule for your project. There is a $1,000-per-week penalty for each week the project is delayed beyond week 25. In addition, your project team determined that indirect project costs are $2,500 per week.

a. What would be your target completion week?

b. How much would you save in total project costs with your schedule?

TABLE 7.12 | DATA FOR SOFTWARE INSTALLATION PROJECT

Activity	Immediate Predecessors	Normal Time (weeks)	Normal Cost ($)	Crash Time (weeks)	Crash Cost ($)
A	—	5	2,000	3	4,000
B	—	8	5,000	7	8,000
C	A	10	10,000	8	12,000
D	A, B	4	3,000	3	7,000
E	B	3	4,000	2	5,000
F	D	9	8,000	6	14,000
G	E, F	2	2,000	2	2,000
H	G	8	6,000	5	9,000
I	C, F	9	7,000	7	15,000

D = Difficult Problem

Assessing and Analyzing Risks

20. Jordanne King, the project manager for Webjets International, Inc., compiled a table showing time estimates for each of the activities of a project to upgrade the company's Web page, including optimistic, most likely, and pessimistic.

a. Calculate the expected time, t_e, for each activity.

b. Calculate the variance, σ^2, for each activity.

Activity	Optimistic (days)	Most Likely (days)	Pessimistic (days)
A	3	8	19
B	12	15	18
C	2	6	16
D	4	9	20
E	1	4	7

21. Recently, you were assigned to manage a project to remodel the seminar room for your company. You have constructed a network diagram depicting the various activities in the project (Figure 7.13). In addition, you have asked your team to estimate the amount of time that they would expect each of the activities to take. Their responses are shown in the following table:

Activity	TIME ESTIMATES (DAYS)		
	Optimistic	Most Likely	Pessimistic
A	5	8	11
B	4	8	11
C	5	6	7
D	2	4	6
E	4	7	10

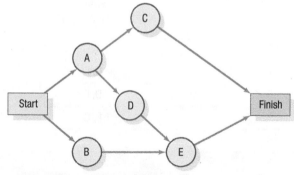

▲ FIGURE 7.13
Network Diagram for Problem 21

a. What is the expected completion time of the project?

b. What is the probability of completing the project in 21 days?

c. What is the probability of completing the project in 17 days?

22. In Solved Problem 2, estimate the probability that the noncritical path B–F–G will take more than 20 weeks. *Hint:* Subtract from 1.0 the probability that B–F–G will take 20 weeks or less.

23. The director of continuing education at Bluebird University just approved the planning for a sales training seminar. Her administrative assistant identified the various activities that must be done and their relationships to each other, as shown in Table 7.13.

TABLE 7.13 | ACTIVITIES FOR THE SALES TRAINING SEMINAR

Activity	Description	Immediate Predecessor(s)
A	Design brochure and course announcement	—
B	Identify prospective teachers	—
C	Prepare detailed outline of course	—
D	Send brochure and student applications	A
E	Send teacher applications	B
F	Select teacher for course	C, E
G	Accept students	D
H	Select text for course	F
I	Order and receive texts	G, H
J	Prepare room for class	G

Because of the uncertainty in planning the new course, the assistant also has supplied the following time estimates for each activity:

Activity	TIME ESTIMATES (DAYS)		
	Optimistic	Most Likely	Pessimistic
A	5	7	8
B	6	8	12
C	3	4	5
D	11	17	25
E	8	10	12
F	3	4	5
G	4	8	9
H	5	7	9
I	8	11	17
J	4	4	4

The director wants to conduct the seminar 47 working days from now. What is the probability that everything will be ready in time?

24. Gabrielle Kramer, owner of Pet Paradise, is opening a new store in Columbus, Ohio. Her major concern is the hiring of a manager and several associates who are animal lovers. She also has to coordinate the renovation of a building that was previously owned by a chic clothing store. Kramer has gathered the data shown in Table 7.14.

a. How long is the project expected to take?

b. Suppose that Kramer has a personal goal of completing the project in 14 weeks. What is the probability that it will happen this quickly?

TABLE 7.14 | DATA FOR THE PET PARADISE PROJECT

Activity	Description	Immediate Predecessor(s)	*A*	*m*	*b*
			TIME (WEEKS)		
A	Interview for new manager	—	1	3	6
B	Renovate building	—	6	9	12
C	Place ad for associates and interview applicants	—	6	8	16
D	Have new manager prospects visit	A	2	3	4
E	Purchase equipment for new store and install	B	1	3	11
F	Check employee applicant references and make final selection	C	5	5	5
G	Check references for new manager and make final selection	D	1	1	1
H	Hold orientation meetings and do payroll paperwork	E, F, G	3	3	3

25. The project manager of Good Public Relations gathered the data shown in Table 7.15 for a new advertising campaign.

a. How long is the project likely to take?

b. What is the probability that the project will take more than 38 weeks?

c. Consider the path A–E–G–H–J. What is the probability that this path will exceed 38 weeks?

TABLE 7.15 | ACTIVITY DATA FOR ADVERTISING PROJECT

Activity	Optimistic	Most Likely	Pessimistic	Immediate Predecessor(s)
	TIME ESTIMATES (WEEKS)			
A	8	10	12	START
B	5	8	17	START
C	7	8	9	START
D	1	2	3	B
E	8	10	12	A, C
F	5	6	7	D, E
G	1	3	5	D, E
H	2	5	8	F, G
I	2	4	6	G
J	4	5	8	H
K	2	2	2	H

26. Consider the office renovation project data in Table 7.16. A "zero" time estimate means that the activity could take a very small amount of time and should be treated as a numeric zero in the analysis.

a. Based on the critical path, find the probability of completing the office renovation project by 39 days.

b. Find the date by which you would be 90 percent sure of completing the project.

D = Difficult Problem

TABLE 7.16 | DATA FOR THE OFFICE RENOVATION PROJECT

Activity	TIME ESTIMATES (DAYS)			Immediate Predecessor(s)
	Optimistic	Most Likely	Pessimistic	
START	0	0	0	—
A	6	10	14	START
B	0	1	2	A
C	16	20	30	A
D	3	5	7	B
E	2	3	4	D
F	7	10	13	C
G	1	2	3	D
H	0	2	4	G
I	2	2	2	C, G
J	2	3	4	I
K	0	1	2	H
L	1	2	3	J, K
FINISH	0	0	0	E, F, L

Active Model Exercise

Active Model 7.1, Gantt Chart, appears in MyOMLab. It allows you to evaluate the sensitivity of the project time to changes in activity times and activity predecessors. In this exercise we use the data from Example 7.2 to develop a Gantt chart.

QUESTIONS

1. Activity B and activity K are critical activities. Describe the difference that occurs on the graph when you increase activity B versus when you increase activity K.

2. Activity F is not critical. Use the scroll bar to determine how many weeks you can increase activity F until it becomes critical.

3. Activity A is not critical. How many weeks can you increase activity A until it becomes critical? What happens when activity A becomes critical?

4. What happens when you increase activity A by one week after it becomes critical?

5. Suppose that building codes may change and, as a result, activity C would have to be completed before activity D could be started. How would this affect the project?

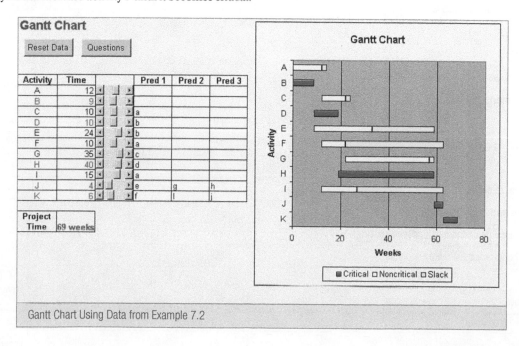

Gantt Chart Using Data from Example 7.2

| VIDEO CASE | Project Management at the Phoenician |

The Phoenician in Phoenix, Arizona, is part of Starwood's Luxury Collection and its only AAA Five Diamond Award resort in the southwestern United States. Sophistication, elegance, and excellence only begin to describe the guest experience at the hotel. Guests can dine in one of nine restaurants, relax poolside, play tennis, take in 27 holes of golf on three 9-hole courses, or relax with a variety of soothing spa treatments at the 22,000-square-foot Centre for Well-Being.

The Phoenician recently embarked on an ambitious $38 million spa and golf renovation program. The resort's golf and spa programs historically earned high marks from surveys in their industries over the years, but the environment was changing. Evidence of this change was seen in the explosive growth of new golf courses and spas in the Southwest region. Phoenix alone has over 275 golf courses, and the Southwest boasts the largest concentration of new luxury spas anywhere. The Phoenician's facilities, while world-class and highly rated, were more than 15 years old. The hotel's recently awarded Five Diamond status renewed emphasis on bringing every process and service at the property up to Five Diamond level.

The decision to renovate the golf course and existing spa became not a question of *whether* to undertake the projects, but *to what degree* they needed to be pursued. Key considerations centered on (1) whether to build basic facilities or commit to the grandiose luxury level, (2) having a domestic versus international reputation, and (3) developing creative packaging of the new facilities to attract loyal guests, such as a spa and golf "country club-like" membership program. Such a program would be limited to about 600 spa/golf memberships, with a one-time fee of $65,000 each.

The company's senior management considered three options for the Centre for Well-Being spa. First, the existing space in the heart of the resort could be renovated. This option would require relocating the spa to another part of the resort and offering limited treatments during this time, thereby reducing spa revenues significantly. With option 2, hilly terrain directly behind the resort could be carved out to create a new mountainside facility with sweeping vistas. This option meant the closure of one of the hotel's buildings housing 60 guest rooms and suites during the construction period. The existing spa could remain open, however. Under option 3, a parking structure on existing hotel property could be used, having the least impact on revenues. The first option was seen as a short-term fix, while the remaining two were viewed as having longer-term potential.

Additional discussion centered on the type of spa to be built. Recent acquisition of the Bliss spa brand for Starwood's W Hotels was an option, offering day spa amenities and an indulgence atmosphere. The second option was to remain a holistic resort spa with an emphasis on health and restoration. The third option was to become a destination spa with dedicated guest stays and week-long programs. Day spas are the fastest-growing category, with few destination spas.

The Phoenician management team, with assistance from Starwood Field Operations and Corporate offices, prepared an extensive analysis of strengths, weaknesses, opportunities, and threats to better understand the environment. The result of this analysis was used by the team to identify the set of activities necessary for each option. The Corporate Design and Construction group developed architectural and engineering plans, as well as the work breakdown structure and diagrams showing

Work Breakdown Structure	Activity Time (days)	Activity Precedence Relationships
Project Conception		
A. Kick-off meeting	2	
B. Creation of spa specifications	30	A
Geotechnical Investigation		
C. Preliminary site characterizations	10	B
D. Subsurface investigation	10	C
E. Laboratory testing	5	D
F. Geologic hazard assessments	10	E
Design Development		
G. Initial designs	70	B
H. Preliminary zoning compliance plan	15	C, G
I. Final designs	18	H
J. Owner approval of designs	5	I
Documentation and Cost Estimation		
K. Construction documentation and landscape package	80	F, I
L. Acquisition of contractor estimates and bids	90	J, K
Decision		
M. Owner approval of one of the three projects	60	L

the critical path for the possible project options. The work breakdown structure, activity times, and activity precedence relationships are shown in the table on the previous page.

QUESTIONS

1. Coordinating departments in a major project is always a challenge. Which departments within the Starwood organization likely played a role in each of the following project related activities?

   a. Defining and organizing the project

   b. Planning the project

   c. Monitoring and controlling the project

2. Many times, project decision makers do not rely solely on financial hurdles, such as return on investment or internal rates of return, but place a lot of emphasis on intangible factors. Which are the salient intangible factors associated with selecting one of the three options for the spa?

3. Timing is always a challenge in managing projects. Construct a network diagram for the spa selection process. How soon can the Phoenician management make a decision on the spa?

When the Phoenician, a luxury hotel in Phoenix, Arizona, sought to redesign its Center for Well-Being, its management team created a work breakdown structure in order to compare different project options and choose the best one.

CASE   The Pert Mustang

Roberts Auto Sales and Service (RASAS) consists of three car dealerships that sell and service several makes of American and Japanese cars, two auto parts stores, a large body shop and car painting business, and an auto salvage yard. Vicky Roberts, owner of RASAS, went into the car business when she inherited a Ford dealership from her father. She was able to capitalize on her knowledge and experience to build her business into the diversified and successful mini-empire it is today. Her motto, "Sell 'em today, repair 'em tomorrow!" reflects a strategy that she refers to in private as "Get 'em coming and going."

Roberts has always retained a soft spot in her heart for high-performance Mustangs and just acquired a 1965 Shelby Mustang GT 350 that needs a lot of restoration. She also notes the public's growing interest in the restoration of vintage automobiles. Roberts is thinking of expanding into the vintage car restoration business and needs help in assessing the feasibility of such a move. She wants to restore her 1965 Shelby Mustang to mint condition, or as close to mint condition as possible. If she decides to go into the car restoring business, she can use the Mustang as an exhibit in sales and advertising and take it to auto shows to attract business for the new shop.

Roberts believes that many people want the thrill of restoring an old car themselves, but they do not have the time to run down all the old parts. Still, others just want to own a vintage auto because it is different and many of them have plenty of money to pay someone to restore an auto for them.

Roberts wants the new business to appeal to both types of people. For the first group, she envisions serving as a parts broker for NOS ("new old stock"), new parts that were manufactured many years ago and are still packaged in their original cartons. It can be a time-consuming process to find the right part. RASAS could also machine new parts to replicate those that are hard to find or that no longer exist.

In addition, RASAS could assemble a library of parts and body manuals for old cars to serve as an information resource for do-it-yourself restorers. The do-it-yourselfers could come to RASAS for help in compiling parts lists, and RASAS could acquire the parts for them. For others, RASAS would take charge of the entire restoration.

Roberts asked the director of service operations to take a good look at her Mustang and determine what needs to be done to restore it to the condition it was in when it came from the factory more than 40 years ago. She wants to restore this car in time to exhibit it at the Detroit Auto Show. If the car gets a lot of press, it will be a real public relations coup for RASAS—especially if Roberts decides to enter this new venture. Even if she does not, the car will be a showpiece for the rest of the business.

Roberts asked the director of service operations to prepare a report about what is involved in restoring the car and whether it can be done in time for the Detroit show in 45 working days using PERT/CPM. The parts manager, the body shop manager, and the chief mechanic have provided the following estimates of times and activities that need to be done, as well as cost estimates:

a. Order all needed material and parts (upholstery, windshield, carburetor, and oil pump). Time: 2 days. Cost (telephone calls and labor): $100.

b. Receive upholstery material for seat covers. Cannot be done until order is placed. Time: 30 days. Cost: $2,100.

c. Receive windshield. Cannot be done until order is placed. Time: 10 days. Cost: $800.

d. Receive carburetor and oil pump. Cannot be done until order is placed. Time: 7 days. Cost: $1,750.

e. Remove chrome from body. Can be done immediately. Time: 1 day. Cost: $200.

f. Remove body (doors, hood, trunk, and fenders) from frame. Cannot be done until chrome is removed. Time: 1 day. Cost: $300.

g. Have fenders repaired by body shop. Cannot be done until body is removed from frame. Time: 4 days. Cost: $1,000.

h. Repair doors, trunk, and hood. Cannot be done until body is removed from frame. Time: 6 days. Cost: $1,500.

i. Pull engine from chassis. Do after body is removed from frame. Time: 1 day. Cost: $200.

j. Remove rust from frame. Do after the engine has been pulled from the chassis. Time: 3 days. Cost $900.

k. Regrind engine valves. Do after the engine has been pulled from the chassis. Time: 5 days. Cost: $1,000.

l. Replace carburetor and oil pump. Do after engine has been pulled from chassis and after carburetor and oil pump have been received. Time: 1 day. Cost: $200.

m. Rechrome the chrome parts. Chrome must have been removed from the body first. Time: 3 days. Cost: $210.

n. Reinstall engine. Do after valves are reground and carburetor and oil pump have been installed. Time: 1 day. Cost: $200.

o. Put doors, hood, and trunk back on frame. The doors, hood, and trunk must have been repaired first. The frame must have had its rust removed first. Time: 1 day. Cost: $240.

p. Rebuild transmission and replace brakes. Do so after the engine has been reinstalled and the doors, hood, and trunk are back on the frame. Time: 4 days. Cost: $2,000.

q. Replace windshield. Windshield must have been received. Time: 1 day. Cost: $100.

r. Put fenders back on. The fenders must have been repaired first, the transmission rebuilt, and the brakes replaced. Time: 1 day. Cost: $100.

s. Paint car. Cannot be done until the fenders are back on and windshield replaced. Time: 4 days. Cost: $1,700.

t. Reupholster interior of car. Must have received upholstery material first. Car must have been painted first. Time: 7 days. Cost: $2,400.

u. Put chrome parts back on. Car must have been painted and chrome parts rechromed first. Time: 1 day. Cost: $100.

v. Pull car to the Detroit Auto Show. Must have completed reupholstery of interior and have put the chrome parts back on. Time: 2 days. Cost: $1,000.

Roberts wants to limit expenditures on this project to what could be recovered by selling the restored car. She has already spent $50,000 to acquire the car. In addition, she wants a brief report on some of the aspects of the proposed business, such as how it fits in with RASAS's other businesses and what RASAS's operations task should be with regard to cost, quality, customer service, and flexibility.

In the restoration business there are various categories of restoration. A basic restoration gets the car looking great and running, but a mint-condition restoration puts the car back in original condition—as it was "when it rolled off the line." When restored cars are resold, a car in mint condition commands a much higher price than one that is just a basic restoration. As cars are restored, they can also be customized. That is, something is put on the car that could not have been on the original. Roberts wants a mint-condition restoration for her Mustang without customization. (The proposed new business would accept any kind of restoration a customer wanted.)

The total budget cannot exceed $70,000 including the $50,000 Roberts has already spent. In addition, Roberts cannot spend more than $3,600 in any week given her present financial position. Even though much of the work will be done by Roberts's own employees, labor and materials costs must be considered. All relevant costs have been included in the cost estimates.

QUESTIONS

1. Using the information provided, prepare the report that Vicky Roberts requested, assuming that the project will begin immediately. Assume 45 working days are available to complete the project, including transporting the car to Detroit before the auto show begins. Your report should briefly discuss the aspects of the proposed new business, such as the competitive priorities that Roberts asked about.

2. Construct a table containing the project activities using the letter assigned to each activity, the time estimates, and the precedence relationships from which you will assemble the network diagram.

3. Draw a network diagram of the project similar to Figure 7.3. Determine the activities on the critical path and the estimated slack for each activity.

4. Prepare a project budget showing the cost of each activity and the total for the project. Can the project be completed within the budget? Will the project require more than $3,600 in any week? To answer this question, assume that activities B, C, and D must be paid for when the item is received (the earliest finish time for the activity). Assume that the costs of all other activities that span more than one week can be prorated. Each week contains five work days. If problems exist, how might Roberts overcome them?

Source: This case was prepared by and is used by permission of Dr. Sue P. Siferd, Professor Emerita, Arizona State University (Updated September, 2007).

Michael Tercha/MCT/Newscom

9

INVENTORY MANAGEMENT

Associates remove returned DVDs from their mailing envelop and then inspect them at Netflix's Carol Stream, Illinois distribution facility. This facility serves subscribers in Chicago and surrounding communities.

Inventory Management at Netflix

Netflix is a $4 billion company specializing in delivering movies and TV programs directly to the homes of customers via streaming or DVD for a subscription fee. It employs more than 2,000 employees worldwide, has more than 44 million streaming customers in over 40 countries, and has 7 million DVD customers in the United States, which is the only DVD market for Netflix. The inventory, of course, comes in the form of DVDs (also blue ray discs). Netflix holds a DVD inventory valued at $2 billion; that amounts to about 89 million discs distributed across 39 warehouses located across the country. That inventory must be carefully managed: New releases of movies must be purchased in adequate quantities while older movies cannot simply be discarded because many customers like to see the "classics." The *composition* of the inventory of discs supports one of Netflix's competitive priorities, variety. However, if it were not for the fact that Netflix designed a process to minimize the lead time in processing customer requests for a disc, the inventory of discs needed to support variety would balloon to enormous proportions.

Another of Netflix's competitive priorities is delivery speed, as evidenced by its goal of delivering a disc by "the next business day." That is, once a customer has returned a disc in his possession, the next disc in his queue will be delivered in a day. This goal was necessary to compete against the bricks-and-mortar video stores where customers could get a movie the same day they wanted it. The *size* of the inventory helps support delivery speed. The inventory of discs consists of two parts: those discs in the possession of customers, and those in stock waiting for a request. Netflix had two options for processing a customer's request for a new disc once his disc is returned to the warehouse: (1) send the next disc in the customer's queue from the stockpiled inventory of discs, or (2) process the returned discs quickly and satisfy the customer's request for the next disc in his queue from those being returned that day. Each warehouse can handle 60,000 orders per day, so a good number of requests could be satisfied with in-transit returns. Netflix opted for the second option, thereby reducing the need for a larger stockpile of discs. The process at a typical warehouse is as follows:

1. ARRIVAL: Six nights a week, unmarked trucks arrive at the post office at around 3 A.M. to pick up cartons of returned discs. The trucks deliver the discs to the Netflix warehouse.

2. INSPECTION: Employees remove the returned discs from their mailing envelopes, confirm that the disc title matches the disc sleeve, clean the disc, check for cracks or scratches, place it back into the sleeve, and file the disc in one of two bins, one for damaged discs or discs in the wrong sleeve, and one for acceptable discs. Each employee does this process about 650 times per hour. After 65 minutes of inspection, a bell rings and the employees stand up for exercise drills.

3. INVENTORY: The discs are scanned into the inventory by a machine that reads 30,000 bar codes per hour. As soon as the barcode on the disc sleeve is scanned, the last renter receives an email confirming that the disc has been received and what disc that renter will receive next.

4. SORTING: Discs are scanned a second time to see if anyone has ordered them online. Ordered discs are sorted by ZIP code in preparation for shipment. Others are shelved for future use.

5. STUFFING: Outgoing discs are stuffed into new mailing envelopes and sent through a label machine that scans their bar codes and prints shipping addresses. Around 5 P.M., warehouse trucks are loaded with the cartons of discs and returned to the post office.

While it is clear that streaming will eventually overtake the business of shipping DVDs directly to the homes of customers, what lessons can we take away from Netflix's DVD process? First, properly managed inventories can support the competitive priorities of variety and delivery speed. Second, process design can help to reduce the need for excessive inventory investment. These are lessons that can be applied to most any business.

Sources: Christopher Borrelli, "How Netflix Gets Your Movies to Your Mailbox So Fast," Chicago Tribune (August 4, 2009); Tracy V. Wilson and Stephanie Crawford, "How Netflix Works," How Stuff Works, **http://electronics. howstufworks.com**; Rick Newman, "How Netflix (and Blockbuster) Killed Blockbuster," US News, **http://moneyusnews. com** (September 23, 2010); Netflix Annual Report 2013.

LEARNING GOALS *After reading this chapter, you should be able to:*

1 Identify the advantages, disadvantages, and costs of holding inventory.

2 Define the different types of inventory and the roles they play in supply chains.

3 Explain the tactics for reducing inventories in supply chains.

4 Use ABC analysis to determine the items deserving most attention and tightest inventory control.

5 Calculate the economic order quantity and apply it to various situations.

6 Determine the order quantity and reorder point for a continuous review inventory control system.

7 Determine the review interval and target inventory level for a periodic review inventory control system.

Inventory management, the planning and controlling of inventories to meet the competitive priorities of the organization, is an important concern for managers in all types of businesses. Effective inventory management is essential for realizing the full potential of any supply chain. The challenge is not to pare inventories to the bone to reduce costs or to have plenty around to satisfy all demands, but to have the right amount to achieve the competitive priorities of the business most efficiently. That is the strategy Netflix applied to their inventory of discs. This type of efficiency can only happen if the right amount of inventory is flowing through the supply chain—through suppliers, the firm, warehouses or distribution centers, and customers. Much of inventory management involves *lot sizing*, which is the determination of how frequently and in what quantity to order inventory. We make ample reference to the term **lot size**, which is the quantity of an inventory item management either buys from a supplier or manufactures using internal processes. In this chapter, we focus on the decision-making aspects of inventory management.

Inventories are important to all types of organizations, their employees, and their supply chains. Inventories profoundly affect everyday operations because they must be counted, paid for, used in operations, used to satisfy customers, and managed. Inventories require an investment of funds, as does the purchase of a new machine. Monies invested in inventory are not available for investment in other things; thus, they represent a drain on the cash flows of an organization. Nonetheless, companies realize that the availability of products is a key selling point in many markets and downright critical in many more.

So, is inventory a boon or a bane? Certainly, too much inventory on hand reduces profitability, and too little inventory on hand creates shortages in the supply chain and ultimately damages customer confidence. Inventory management, therefore, involves trade-offs. Let us discover how companies can effectively manage inventories across the organization.

inventory management

The planning and controlling of inventories to meet the competitive priorities of the organization.

lot size

The quantity of an inventory item management either buys from a supplier or manufactures using internal processes.

Inventory Trade-Offs

The value of inventory management becomes apparent when the complexity of the supply chain is recognized. The performance of numerous suppliers determines the inward flow of materials and services to a firm. The performance of the firm determines the outward flow of services or products to the next stage of the supply chain. The flow of materials, however, determines inventory levels. **Inventory** is a stock of materials used to satisfy customer demand or to support the production of services or goods. Figure 9.1 shows how inventories are created at one node in a supply chain through the analogy of a water tank. The flow of water into the tank raises the water level. The inward flow of water represents input materials, such as steel, component parts, office supplies, or a finished product. The water level represents the amount of inventory held at a plant, service facility, warehouse, or retail outlet. The flow of water from the tank lowers the water level in the tank. The outward flow of water represents the demand for materials in inventory, such as customer orders for a Huffy bicycle or service requirements for supplies such as soap, food, or furnishings. The rate of the outward flow also reflects the ability of the firm to match the demand for services or products. Another possible outward flow is that of scrap, which also lowers the level of useable inventory. Together, the difference between input flow rate and the output flow rate determines the level of inventory. Inventories rise when more material flows into the tank than flows out; they fall when more material flows out than flows in. Figure 9.1 also shows clearly why firms utilize Six Sigma and total quality management (TQM) to reduce defective materials: The larger the scrap flows, the larger the input flow of materials required for a given level of output.

inventory

A stock of materials used to satisfy customer demand or to support the production of services or goods.

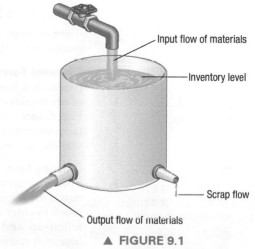
Input flow of materials

Inventory level

Scrap flow

Output flow of materials

▲ **FIGURE 9.1**
Creation of Inventory

A fundamental question in supply chain management is how much inventory to have. The answer to this question involves a trade-off between the advantages and disadvantages of holding inventory. Depending on the situation, the pressures for having small inventories may or may not exceed the pressures for having large inventories.

Pressures for Small Inventories

An inventory manager's job is to balance the advantages and disadvantages of both small and large inventories and find a happy medium between the two levels. The primary reason for keeping inventories small is that inventory represents a temporary monetary investment. As such, the firm incurs an opportunity cost, which we call the cost of capital, arising from the money tied up in inventory that could be used for other purposes. The **inventory holding cost** (or *carrying cost*) is the sum of the cost of capital plus the variable costs of keeping items on hand, such as storage and handling costs and taxes, insurance, and shrinkage costs. When these components change with inventory levels, so does the holding cost.

Companies usually state an item's holding cost per period of time as a percent of its value. The annual cost to maintain one unit in inventory typically ranges from 15 to 35 percent of its value. Suppose that a firm's holding cost is 20 percent. If the average value of total inventory is 20 percent of sales, the average annual cost to hold inventory is 4 percent [0.20(0.20)] of total sales. This cost is sizable in terms of gross profit margins, which often are less than 10 percent. Thus, the components of holding cost create pressures for small inventories.

Cost of Capital The cost of capital is the opportunity cost of investing in an asset relative to the expected return on assets of similar risk. Inventory is an asset; consequently, we should use a cost measure that adequately reflects the firm's approach to financing assets. Most firms use the *weighted average cost of capital (WACC)*, which is the average of the required return on a firm's stock equity and the interest rate on its debt, weighted by the proportion of equity and debt in its portfolio. The cost of capital usually is the largest component of holding cost, as high as 15 percent of inventory value, depending on the particular capitalization portfolio of the firm. Firms typically update the WACC on an annual basis because it is used to make many financial decisions.

Storage and Handling Costs Inventory takes up space and must be moved into and out of storage. Storage and handling costs may be incurred when a firm rents space on either a long- or short-term basis. An inventory holding cost is incurred when a firm could use storage space productively in some other way.

Taxes, Insurance, and Shrinkage More taxes are paid if end-of-year inventories are high, and the cost of insuring the inventories increases, too. Shrinkage takes three forms. The first, *pilferage*, or theft of inventory by customers or employees, is a significant percentage of sales for some businesses. The second form of shrinkage, called *obsolescence*, occurs when inventory cannot be used or sold at full value, owing to model changes, engineering modifications, or unexpectedly low demand. Obsolescence is a big expense in the retail clothing industry. Drastic discounts on seasonal clothing frequently must be offered on many of these products at the end of a season. Finally, *deterioration* through physical spoilage or damage due to rough or excessive material handling results in lost value. Food and beverages, for example, lose value and might even have to be discarded when their shelf life is reached. When the rate of deterioration is high, building large inventories may be unwise.

Pressures for Large Inventories

Given the costs of holding inventory, why not eliminate it altogether? Let us look briefly at the pressures related to maintaining large inventories.

Customer Service Creating inventory can speed delivery and improve the firm's on-time delivery of goods. High inventory levels reduce the potential for stockouts and backorders, which are key concerns of wholesalers and retailers. A *stockout* is an order that cannot be satisfied, resulting in loss of the sale. A *backorder* is a customer order that cannot be filled when promised or demanded but is filled later. Customers do not like waiting for backorders to be filled. Many of them will take their business elsewhere. Sometimes, customers are given discounts for the inconvenience of waiting.

Ordering Cost Each time a firm places a new order, it incurs an **ordering cost**, or the cost of preparing a purchase order for a supplier or a production order for manufacturing. For the same item, the ordering cost is the same, regardless of the order size. The purchasing agent must take the time to decide how much to order and, perhaps, select a supplier and negotiate terms. Time also is spent on paperwork, follow-up, and receiving the item(s). In the case of a production order for a manufactured item, a blueprint and routing instructions often must accompany the order. However, the Internet streamlines the order process and reduces the costs of placing orders.

---

inventory holding cost

The sum of the cost of capital and the variable costs of keeping items on hand, such as storage and handling, taxes, insurance, and shrinkage.

Using Operations to Create Value

MANAGING PROCESSES

Process Strategy and Analysis
Quality and Performance
Capacity Planning
Constraint Management
Lean Systems
Project Management

MANAGING CUSTOMER DEMAND

Forecasting
→ Inventory Management
Operations Planning and
   Scheduling
Resource Planning

MANAGING SUPPLY CHAINS

Supply Chain Design
Supply Chain Logistic Networks
Supply Chain Integration
Supply Chain Sustainability

---

ordering cost

The cost of preparing a purchase order for a supplier or a production order for manufacturing.

Setup Cost   The cost involved in changing over a machine or workspace to produce a different item is the **setup cost**. It includes labor and time to make the changeover, cleaning, and sometimes new tools or equipment. Scrap or rework costs are also higher at the start of the production run. Setup cost also is independent of order size, which creates pressure to make or order a large supply of the items and hold them in inventory rather than order smaller batches.

Labor and Equipment Utilization   By creating more inventory, management can increase workforce productivity and facility utilization in three ways. First, placing larger, less frequent production orders reduces the number of unproductive setups, which add no value to a service or product. Second, holding inventory reduces the chance of the costly rescheduling of production orders because the components needed to make the product are not in inventory. Third, building inventories improves resource utilization by stabilizing the output rate when demand is cyclical or seasonal. The firm uses inventory built during slack periods to handle extra demand in peak seasons. This approach minimizes the need for extra shifts, hiring, layoffs, overtime, and additional equipment.

Transportation Cost   Sometimes, outbound transportation cost can be reduced by increasing inventory levels. Having inventory on hand allows more full-carload shipments to be made and minimizes the need to expedite shipments by more expensive modes of transportation. Inbound transportation costs can also be reduced by creating more inventory. Sometimes, several items are ordered from the same supplier. Placing these orders at the same time will increase inventories because some items will be ordered before they are actually needed; nonetheless, it may lead to rate discounts, thereby decreasing the costs of transportation and raw materials.

Payments to Suppliers   A firm often can reduce total payments to suppliers if it can tolerate higher inventory levels. Suppose that a firm learns that a key supplier is about to increase its prices. In this case, it might be cheaper for the firm to order a larger quantity than usual—in effect delaying the price increase—even though inventory will increase temporarily. A firm can also take advantage of quantity discounts this way. A **quantity discount**, whereby the price per unit drops when the order is sufficiently large, is an incentive to order larger quantities. Supplement C, "Special Inventory Models," shows how to determine order quantities in such a situation.

setup cost

The cost involved in changing over a machine or workspace to produce a different item.

quantity discount

A drop in the price per unit when an order is sufficiently large.

MANAGERIAL PRACTICE 9.1   Inventory Management at Walmart

In the market for shaver blade replacements? A printer? First-aid supplies? Dog food? Hair spray? If so, you expect that the store you shop at will have what you want. However, making sure that the shelves are stocked with tens of thousands of products is no simple matter for inventory managers at Walmart, which has 10,700 Walmart stores and Sam's Club locations in 27 countries, employs more than 2.2 million associates, serves 245 million customers per week worldwide, and uses 100,000 suppliers. You can imagine in an operation this large that some things can get lost. Linda Dillman, then CIO at Walmart, recounts the story of the missing hair spray at one of the stores. The shelf needed to be restocked with a specific hair spray; however, it took three days to find the case in the backroom. Most customers will not swap hair sprays, so Walmart lost three days of sales on that product.

Knowing what is in stock, in what quantity, and where it is being held is critical to effective inventory management. Without accurate inventory information, companies can make major mistakes by ordering too much, not enough, or shipping products to the wrong location. Companies can have large inventories and still have stockouts of product because they have too much inventory of some products and not enough of others. Walmart, a $466 billion company with inventories in excess of $44 billion, is certainly aware of the potential benefits from improved inventory management and is constantly experimenting with ways to reduce inventory investment. The economics of retailing are circular: You order products, they are delivered, and you have 30 days to pay for it. The faster you sell the merchandise, the less it costs to finance. Ideally you want to sell it before the 30 days are up; the vendors would actually be financing your inventory. That is why reducing the amount of

An employee stacks a shipment of pet supplies at a Walmart distribution center in Fort Pierce, Florida. The 1.2-million-square-foot facility serves 45 Walmart stores on the east coast of Florida.

Paul J. Milette/Palm Beach Post/ZUMA Press/Newscom

inventory on hand is so important to a company that handles a lot of inventory. Knowing when to replenish inventory stocks and how much to order each time is critical when dealing with so much inventory investment. The application of technology is also important, such as using radio frequency identification (RFID) to track inventory shipments and stock levels at stores and warehouses throughout the supply chain (see Chapter 14, Supply Chain Integration). Of course, having a lot of technology will not help if there are not enough employees available to move the products from the storeroom to the shelves, as Walmart has found out. Cutting the hours of employees can cause stockouts even if the product is available in the stockroom. Nonetheless, one handheld RFID reader could have found the missing case of hair spray in a few minutes.

Source: Laurie Sullivan, "Walmart's Way," **http://Informationweek.com** (September 27, 2004), pp. 36–50; Bill Saporito, "The Trouble Lurking on Walmart's Empty Shelves," **http://business.time.com**, (April 9, 2013); Todd Traub, "Walmart Used Technology to Become Supply Chain Leader," *Arkansas Business* (July 2, 2012); and Walmart 2013 Annual Report.

Types of Inventory

Inventories can be classified in several ways. In this section we discuss accounting inventories and operational inventories.

Accounting Inventories

raw materials (RM)

The inventories needed for the production of services or goods.

work-in-process (WIP)

Items, such as components or assemblies, needed to produce a final product in manufacturing or service operations.

finished goods (FG)

The items in manufacturing plants, warehouses, and retail outlets that are sold to the firm's customers.

independent demand items

Items for which demand is influenced by market conditions and is not related to the inventory decisions for any other item held in stock or produced.

Inventory exists in three aggregate categories that are useful for accounting purposes. **Raw materials (RM)** are the inventories needed for the production of services or goods. They are considered to be inputs to the transformation processes of the firm. **Work-in-process (WIP)** consists of items, such as components or assemblies, needed to produce a final product in manufacturing. WIP is also present in some service operations, such as repair shops, restaurants, check-processing centers, and package delivery services. **Finished goods (FG)** in manufacturing plants, warehouses, and retail outlets are the items sold to the firm's customers. The finished goods of one firm may actually be the raw materials for another.

Figure 9.2 shows how inventory can be held in different forms and at various stocking points. In this example, raw materials—the finished goods of the supplier—are held both by the supplier and the manufacturer. Raw materials at the plant pass through one or more processes, which transform them into various levels of WIP inventory. Final processing of this inventory yields finished goods inventory. Finished goods can be held at the plant, the distribution center (which may be a warehouse owned by the manufacturer or the retailer), and retail locations.

An important distinction regarding the three categories of inventories is the nature of the demand they experience. For example, take finished goods, which are **independent demand items**—that is, items for which demand is influenced by market conditions and is not related to the inventory decisions for any other item held in stock or produced. Retailers, such as JCPenney and Dillards, deal with finished goods. Examples of independent demand items include:

- Wholesale and retail merchandise
- Service support inventory, such as stamps and mailing labels for post offices, office supplies for law firms, and laboratory supplies for research universities
- Product and replacement-part distribution inventories
- Maintenance, repair, and operating (MRO) supplies—that is, items that do not become part of the final service or product, such as employee uniforms, fuel, paint, and machine repair parts

Managing an independent demand inventory can be tricky because demand is influenced by external factors. For example, the owner of a bookstore may not be sure how many copies of the latest best-seller novel customers will purchase during the coming month. As a result, the manager may decide to stock extra copies as a safeguard. Independent demand, such as the demand for various book titles, must be *forecasted* using the techniques we discussed in Chapter 8, "Forecasting." There is, however, a whole different type of demand for certain items that must be considered.

Raw materials, work-in-progress, and finished goods inventories can all be stocked in the same facility. Modern warehouses allow for efficient inventory access.

Marcin Balcerzak/Shutterstock.com

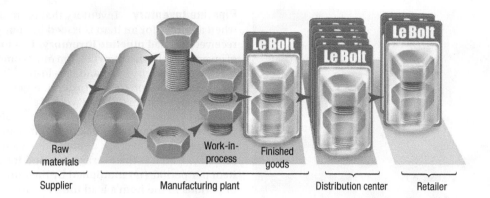

◀ **FIGURE 9.2**
Inventory of Successive
Stocking Points

Raw materials | Work-in-process | Finished goods

Supplier | Manufacturing plant | Distribution center | Retailer

Dependent demand items, consisting of raw materials and work-in-process inventories, are those items whose required quantity varies with the production plans for other items held in the firm's inventory. These items are required as components or inputs to a service or product. Dependent demand should be calculated, not forecasted, and exhibits a pattern very different from that of independent demand (see Chapter 11, "Resource Planning").

dependent demand items

Items whose required quantity varies with the production plans for other items held in the firm's inventory.

Operational Inventories

Inventories can also be classified by how they are created. In this context, inventory takes four forms: (1) cycle, (2) safety stock, (3) anticipation, and (4) pipeline. They cannot be identified physically; that is, an inventory manager cannot look at a pile of widgets and identify which ones are cycle inventory and which ones are safety stock inventory. However, conceptually, each of the four types comes into being in an entirely different way. Once you understand these differences, you can prescribe different ways to reduce inventory.

Cycle Inventory   The portion of total inventory that varies directly with lot size is called **cycle inventory**. Determining how frequently to order, and in what quantity, is called **lot sizing**. Two principles apply.

cycle inventory

The portion of total inventory that varies directly with lot size.

1. The lot size, Q, varies directly with the elapsed time (or cycle) between orders. If a lot is ordered every 5 weeks, the average lot size must equal 5 weeks' demand.

2. The longer the time between orders for a given item, the greater the cycle inventory must be.

lot sizing

The determination of how frequently and in what quantity to order inventory.

At the beginning of the interval, the cycle inventory is at its maximum, or Q. At the end of the interval, just before a new lot arrives, cycle inventory drops to its minimum, or 0. The average cycle inventory is the average of these two extremes:

$$\text{Average cycle inventory} = \frac{Q + 0}{2} = \frac{Q}{2}$$

This formula is exact only when the demand rate is constant and uniform. However, it does provide a reasonably good estimate even when demand rates are not constant. Factors other than the demand rate (e.g., scrap losses) also may cause estimating errors when this simple formula is used.

Safety Stock Inventory   To avoid customer service problems and the hidden costs of unavailable components, companies hold safety stock. **Safety stock inventory** is surplus inventory that protects against uncertainties in demand, lead time, and supply changes. Safety stocks are desirable when suppliers fail to deliver either the desired quantity on the specified date or items of acceptable quality, or when manufactured items require significant amounts of scrap or rework. Safety stock inventory ensures that operations are not disrupted when such problems occur, allowing subsequent operations to continue.

safety stock inventory

Surplus inventory that a company holds to protect against uncertainties in demand, lead time, and supply changes.

To create safety stock, a firm places an order for delivery earlier than when the item is typically needed.[1] The replenishment order therefore arrives ahead of time, giving a cushion against uncertainty. For example, suppose that the average lead time from a supplier is 3 weeks, but a firm orders 5 weeks in advance just to be safe. This policy creates a safety stock equal to a 2 weeks' supply $(5 - 3)$.

Anticipation Inventory   Inventory used to absorb uneven rates of demand or supply, which businesses often face, is referred to as **anticipation inventory**. Predictable, seasonal demand patterns lend themselves to the use of anticipation inventory. Uneven demand can motivate a manufacturer to stockpile anticipation inventory during periods of low demand so that output levels do not have to be increased much when demand peaks. Anticipation inventory also can help when suppliers are threatened with a strike or have severe capacity limitations.

anticipation inventory

Inventory used to absorb uneven rates of demand or supply.

---

[1]When orders are placed at fixed intervals, a second way to create safety stock is used. Each new order placed is larger than the quantity typically needed through the next delivery date.

Pipeline inventories result from moving items and materials from one location to another. Because trains offer an economical way to transport large quantities of goods, they are a favorite choice to reduce the costs of pipeline inventories.

Pipeline Inventory Inventory that is created when an order for an item is issued but not yet received is called **pipeline inventory**. This form of inventory exists because the firm must commit to enough inventory (on-hand plus in-transit) to cover the lead time for the order. Longer lead times or higher demands per week create more pipeline inventory. As such, the average pipeline inventory between two stocking points can be measured as the average demand during lead time, $\overline{D}_L$, which is the average demand for the item per period ($\overline{d}$) multiplied by the number of periods in the item's lead time (L) to move between the two points, or

$$\text{Pipeline inventory} = \overline{D}_L = \overline{d}L$$

The equation assumes that both $\overline{d}$ and L are constants and that L is not affected by the order or lot size, Q. Changing an item's lot size does not directly affect the average level of the pipeline inventory. Nonetheless, the lot size can *indirectly* affect pipeline inventory if it is related to the lead time. In such a case, pipeline inventory will change depending on the relationship of L to Q. Example 9.1 shows how this can happen.

pipeline inventory

Inventory that is created when an order for an item is issued but not yet received.

EXAMPLE 9.1	**Estimating Inventory Levels**

MyOMLab

Tutor 9.1 in MyOMLab provides a new example to practice the estimation of inventory levels.

A plant makes monthly shipments of electric drills to a wholesaler in average lot sizes of 280 drills. The wholesaler's average demand is 70 drills a week, and the lead time from the plant is 3 weeks. The wholesaler must pay for the inventory from the moment the plant makes a shipment. If the wholesaler is willing to increase its purchase quantity to 350 units, the plant will give priority to the wholesaler and guarantee a lead time of only 2 weeks. What is the effect on the wholesaler's cycle and pipeline inventories?

SOLUTION

The wholesaler's current cycle and pipeline inventories are

$$\text{Cycle inventory} = \frac{Q}{2} = \frac{280}{2} = 140 \text{ drills}$$

$$\text{Pipeline inventory} = \overline{D}_L = \overline{d}L = (70 \text{ drills/week})(3 \text{ weeks}) = 210 \text{ drills}$$

Figure 9.3 shows the cycle and pipeline inventories if the wholesaler accepts the new proposal.

FIGURE 9.3 ▶

Estimating Inventory Levels Using Tutor 9.1

1. Enter the average lot size, average demand during a period, and the number of periods of lead time:

Average lot size	350
Average demand	70
Lead time	2

2. To compute cycle inventory, simply divide average lot size by 2. To compute pipeline inventory, multiply average demand by lead time:

Cycle inventory	175
Pipeline inventory	140

DECISION POINT

The effect of the new proposal on cycle inventories is to increase them by 35 units, or 25 percent. The reduction in pipeline inventories, however, is 70 units, or 33 percent. The proposal would reduce the total investment in cycle and pipeline inventories. Also, it is advantageous to have shorter lead times because the wholesaler only has to commit to purchases 2 weeks in advance, rather than 3 weeks.

Inventory Reduction Tactics

Managers are always eager to find cost-effective ways to reduce inventory in supply chains. In this section we discuss the basic tactics (which we call *levers*) for reducing cycle, safety stock, anticipation, and pipeline inventories in supply chains. A primary lever is one that must be activated if inventory is to be reduced. A secondary lever reduces the penalty cost of applying the primary lever and the need for having inventory in the first place.

Cycle Inventory

The primary lever to reduce cycle inventory is simply to reduce the lot sizes of items moving in the supply chain. However, making such reductions in Q without making any other changes can be devastating. For example, setup costs or ordering costs can skyrocket. If these changes occur, two secondary levers can be used:

1. Streamline the methods for placing orders and making setups to reduce ordering and setup costs and allow Q to be reduced. This may involve redesigning the infrastructure for information flows or improving manufacturing processes.

2. Increase repeatability to eliminate the need for changeovers. **Repeatability** is the degree to which the same work can be done again. Repeatability can be increased through high product demand; the use of specialization; the devotion of resources exclusively to a product; the use of the same part in many different products; the use of *flexible automation*; the use of the *one-worker, multiple-machines* concept; or through *group technology*. Increased repeatability may justify new setup methods, reduce transportation costs, and allow quantity discounts from suppliers.

repeatability
The degree to which the same work can be done again.

Safety Stock Inventory

The primary lever to reduce safety stock inventory is to place orders closer to the time when they must be received. However, this approach can lead to unacceptable customer service unless demand, supply, and delivery uncertainties can be minimized. Four secondary levers can be used in this case:

1. Improve demand forecasts so that fewer surprises come from customers. Design the mechanisms to increase collaboration with customers to get advanced warnings for changes in demand levels.

2. Cut the lead times of purchased or produced items to reduce demand uncertainty. For example, local suppliers with short lead times could be selected whenever possible.

3. Reduce supply uncertainties. Suppliers are likely to be more reliable if production plans are shared with them. Put in place the mechanisms to increase collaboration with suppliers. Surprises from unexpected scrap or rework can be reduced by improving manufacturing processes. Preventive maintenance can minimize unexpected downtime caused by equipment failure.

4. Rely more on equipment and labor buffers, such as capacity cushions and cross-trained workers. These buffers are important to businesses in the service sector because they generally cannot inventory their services.

Anticipation Inventory

The primary lever to reduce anticipation inventory is simply to match demand rate with production rate. Secondary levers can be used to even out customer demand in one of the following ways:

1. Add new products with different demand cycles so that a peak in the demand for one product compensates for the seasonal low for another.

2. Provide off-season promotional campaigns.

3. Offer seasonal pricing plans.

Pipeline Inventory

An operations manager has direct control over lead times but not demand rates. Because pipeline inventory is a function of demand during the lead time, the primary lever is to reduce the lead time. Two secondary levers can help managers cut lead times:

1. Find more responsive suppliers and select new carriers for shipments between stocking locations or improve materials handling within the plant. Improving the information system could overcome information delays between a distribution center and retailer.

2. Change Q in those cases where the lead time depends on the lot size.

Inventories in supply chains are managed with the help of inventory control systems. These systems manage the levels of cycle, safety stock, anticipation, and pipeline inventories in a firm. Regardless of whether an item experiences independent or dependent demand, three important questions must be answered: What degree of control should we impose on an item? How much should we order? and When should we place the order? An approach called ABC analysis, which we address in the next section, helps with the first question. Inventory control systems respond to the last two questions. In selecting an inventory control system for a particular application, the nature of the demands imposed on the inventory items is crucial. In this chapter, we focus on inventory control systems for independent demand items, which is the type of demand the bookstore owner, other retailers, service providers, and distributors face. Even though demand from any one customer is difficult to predict, low demand from some customers for a particular item often is offset by high demand from others. Thus, total demand for any independent demand item may follow a relatively smooth pattern, with some random fluctuations. For items facing dependent demands, such as raw materials and work-in-process inventories, material requirements planning (MRP) systems are useful. We devote Chapter 11, "Resource Planning" to this important inventory control system.

In the remainder of this chapter we first address the question of what degree of control to impose on an item, and then answer the question of how much to order. In the last two sections we discuss and compare two inventory control systems: (1) the continuous review system, called a *Q* system, and (2) the periodic review system, called a *P* system.

ABC Analysis

stock-keeping unit (SKU)

An individual item or product that has an identifying code and is held in inventory somewhere along the supply chain.

ABC analysis

The process of dividing SKUs into three classes, according to their dollar usage, so that managers can focus on items that have the highest dollar value.

cycle counting

An inventory control method, whereby storeroom personnel physically count a small percentage of the total number of items each day, correcting errors that they find.

▼ **FIGURE 9.4**
Typical Chart Using ABC
Analysis

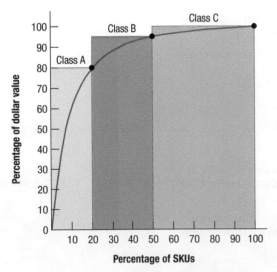

Thousands of items, often referred to as stock-keeping units, are held in inventory by a typical organization, but only a small percentage of them deserve management's closest attention and tightest control. A **stock-keeping unit (SKU)** is an individual item or product that has an identifying code and is held in inventory somewhere along the supply chain. **ABC analysis** is the process of dividing SKUs into three classes according to their dollar usage so that managers can focus on items that have the highest dollar value. This method is the equivalent of creating a *Pareto chart* except that it is applied to inventory rather than to process errors. As Figure 9.4 shows, class A items typically represent only about 20 percent of the SKUs but account for 80 percent of the dollar usage. Class B items account for another 30 percent of the SKUs but only 15 percent of the dollar usage. Finally, 50 percent of the SKUs fall in class C, representing a mere 5 percent of the dollar usage. The goal of ABC analysis is to identify the class A SKUs so management can closely control their inventory levels.

The analysis begins by multiplying the annual demand rate for an SKU by the dollar value (cost) of one unit of that SKU to determine its dollar usage. After ranking the SKUs on the basis of dollar usage and creating the Pareto chart, the analyst looks for "natural" changes in slope. The dividing lines in Figure 9.4 between classes are inexact. Class A SKUs could be somewhat higher or lower than 20 percent of all SKUs but normally account for the bulk of the dollar usage.

Class A SKUs are reviewed frequently to reduce the average lot size and to ensure timely deliveries from suppliers. It is important to maintain high inventory turnover for these items. By contrast, class B SKUs require an intermediate level of control. Here, less frequent monitoring of suppliers coupled with adequate safety stocks can provide cost-effective coverage of demands. For class C SKUs, much looser control is appropriate. While a stockout of a class C SKU can be as crucial as for a class A SKU, the inventory holding cost of class C SKUs tends to be low. These features suggest that higher inventory levels can be tolerated and that more safety stock and larger lot sizes may suffice for class C SKUs. See Solved Problem 2 for a detailed example of ABC analysis.

Creating ABC inventory classifications is useless unless inventory records are accurate. Technology can help; many companies are tracking inventory wherever it exists in the supply chain. Chips imbedded in product packaging contain information on the product and send signals that can be accessed by sensitive receivers and transmitted to a central location for processing. There are other, less sophisticated approaches of achieving accuracy that can be used. One way is to assign responsibility to specific employees for issuing and receiving materials and accurately reporting each transaction. Another method is to secure inventory behind locked doors or gates to prevent unauthorized or unreported withdrawals. This method also guards against accidentally storing newly received inventory in the wrong locations, where it can be lost for months. **Cycle counting** can also be used, whereby storeroom personnel physically count a small percentage of the total number of SKUs each day, correcting errors that they find. Class A SKUs are counted most frequently. A final method is to make logic error checks on each transaction reported and fully investigate any discrepancies. The discrepancies can include (1) actual receipts when no receipts are scheduled, (2) disbursements that exceed the current on-hand inventory balance, and (3) receipts with an inaccurate (nonexistent) SKU number.

Now that we have identified the inventory items deserving of most attention, we turn to the decision of how much to order.

Economic Order Quantity

Supply chain managers face conflicting pressures to keep inventories low enough to avoid excess inventory holding costs but high enough to reduce ordering and setup costs. *Inventory holding cost* is the sum of the cost of capital and the variable costs of keeping items on hand, such as storage and handling, taxes, insurance, and shrinkage. *Ordering cost* is the cost of preparing a purchase order for a supplier or a production order for the shop, while *setup cost* is the cost of changing over a machine to produce a different item. In this section, we will address the *cycle inventory*, which is that portion of total inventory that varies directly with lot size. A good starting point for balancing these conflicting pressures and determining the best cycle-inventory level for an item is finding the **economic order quantity (EOQ)**, which is the lot size that minimizes total annual cycle-inventory holding and ordering costs. The approach to determining the EOQ is based on the following assumptions:

economic order quantity (EOQ)

The lot size that minimizes total annual inventory holding and ordering costs.

1. The demand rate for the item is constant (for example, always 10 units per day) and known with certainty.

2. No constraints are placed (such as truck capacity or materials handling limitations) on the size of each lot.

3. The only two relevant costs are the inventory holding cost and the fixed cost per lot for ordering or setup.

4. Decisions for one item can be made independently of decisions for other items. In other words, no advantage is gained in combining several orders going to the same supplier.

5. The lead time is constant (e.g., always 14 days) and known with certainty. The amount received is exactly what was ordered and it arrives all at once rather than piecemeal.

The economic order quantity will be optimal when all five assumptions are satisfied. In reality, few situations are so simple. Nonetheless, the EOQ is often a reasonable approximation of the appropriate lot size, even when several of the assumptions do not quite apply. Here are some guidelines on when to use or modify the EOQ.

- **Do not use the EOQ**
  - If you use the "make-to-order" strategy and your customer specifies that the entire order be delivered in one shipment
  - If the order size is constrained by capacity limitations such as the size of the firm's ovens, amount of testing equipment, or number of delivery trucks

- **Modify the EOQ**
  - If significant quantity discounts are given for ordering larger lots
  - If replenishment of the inventory is not instantaneous, which can happen if the items must be used or sold as soon as they are finished without waiting until the entire lot has been completed (see Supplement C, "Special Inventory Models," for several useful modifications to the EOQ)

- **Use the EOQ**
  - If you follow a "make-to-stock" strategy and the item has relatively stable demand
  - If your carrying costs per unit and setup or ordering costs are known and relatively stable

The EOQ was never intended to be an optimizing tool. Nonetheless, if you need to determine a reasonable lot size, it can be helpful in many situations.

Calculating the EOQ

We begin by formulating the total cost for any lot size Q for a given SKU. Next, we derive the EOQ, which is the Q that minimizes total annual cycle-inventory cost. Finally, we describe how to convert the EOQ into a companion measure, the elapsed time between orders.

When the EOQ assumptions are satisfied, cycle inventory behaves as shown in Figure 9.5. A cycle begins with Q units held in inventory, which happens when a new order is received. During the cycle, on-hand inventory is used at a constant rate and, because demand is known with certainty and the lead time is a constant, a new lot can be ordered so that inventory falls to 0 precisely when the new lot is received. Because inventory varies uniformly between Q and 0, the average cycle inventory equals half the lot size, Q.

FIGURE 9.5 ▶
Cycle-Inventory Levels

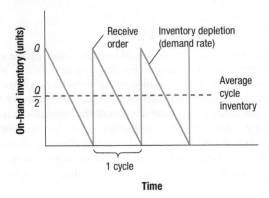

The annual holding cost for this amount of inventory, which increases linearly with Q, as Figure 9.6(a) shows, is

$$\text{Annual holding cost} = (\text{Average cycle inventory})(\text{Unit holding cost})$$

The annual ordering cost is

$$\text{Annual ordering cost} = (\text{Number of orders/Year})(\text{Ordering or setup cost})$$

The average number of orders per year equals annual demand divided by Q For example, if 1,200 units must be ordered each year and the average lot size is 100 units, then 12 orders will be placed during the year. The annual ordering or setup cost decreases nonlinearly as Q increases, as shown in Figure 9.6(b), because fewer orders are placed.

MyOMLab Animation

FIGURE 9.6 ▶
Graphs of Annual
Holding, Ordering,
and Total Costs

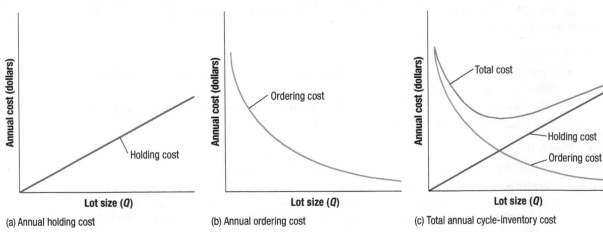

(a) Annual holding cost   (b) Annual ordering cost   (c) Total annual cycle-inventory cost

The total annual cycle-inventory cost,[2] as graphed in Figure 9.6(c), is the sum of the two cost components:

$$\text{Total cost} = \text{Annual holding cost} + \text{Annual ordering or setup cost}[3]$$

$$C = \frac{Q}{2}(H) + \frac{D}{Q}(S)$$

---

[2]Expressing the total cost on an annual basis usually is convenient (although not necessary). Any time horizon can be selected as long as D and H cover the same time period. If the total cost is calculated on a monthly basis, D must be monthly demand and H must be the cost of holding a unit for 1 month.

[3]The number of orders actually placed in any year is always a whole number, although the formula allows for the use of fractional values. However, rounding is not needed because what is being calculated is an average of multiple years. Such averages often are nonintegers.

where

C = total annual cycle-inventory cost

Q = lot size, in units

H = cost of holding one unit in inventory for a year, often expressed as a percentage of the item's value

D = annual demand, in units per year

S = cost of ordering or setting up one lot, in dollars per lot

---

EXAMPLE 9.2	The Cost of a Lot-Sizing Policy

A museum of natural history opened a gift shop two years ago. Managing inventories has become a problem. Low inventory turnover is squeezing profit margins and causing cash-flow problems.

One of the top-selling SKUs in the container group at the museum's gift shop is a bird feeder. Sales are 18 units per week, and the supplier charges $60 per unit. The cost of placing an order with the supplier is $45. Annual holding cost is 25 percent of a feeder's value, and the museum operates 52 weeks per year. Management chose a 390-unit lot size so that new orders could be placed less frequently. What is the annual cycle-inventory cost of the current policy of using a 390-unit lot size? Would a lot size of 468 be better?

MyOMLab

Tutor 9.2 in MyOMLab provides a new example of the application of ABC analysis.

SOLUTION

We begin by computing the annual demand and holding cost as

$$D = (18 \text{ units/week})(52 \text{ weeks/year}) = 936 \text{ units}$$

$$H = 0.25(\$60/\text{unit}) = \$15$$

The total annual cycle-inventory cost for the current policy is

$$C = \frac{Q}{2}(H) + \frac{D}{Q}(S)$$

$$= \frac{390}{2}(\$15) + \frac{936}{390}(\$45) = \$2,925 + \$108 = \$3,033$$

The total annual cycle-inventory cost for the alternative lot size is

$$C = \frac{468}{2}(\$15) + \frac{936}{468}(\$45) = \$3,510 + \$90 = \$3,600$$

DECISION POINT

The lot size of 468 units, which is a half-year supply, would be a more expensive option than the current policy. The savings in ordering costs are more than offset by the increase in holding costs. Management should use the total annual cycle-inventory cost function to explore other lot-size alternatives.

Figure 9.7 displays the impact of using several Q values for the bird feeder in Example 9.2. Eight different lot sizes were evaluated in addition to the current one. Both holding and ordering costs were plotted, but their sum—the total annual cycle-inventory cost curve—is the important feature. The graph shows that the best lot size, or EOQ, is the lowest point on the total annual cost curve, or between 50 and 100 units. Obviously, reducing the current lot-size policy $Q = 390$ can result in significant savings.

A more efficient approach is to use the EOQ formula:

$$EOQ = \sqrt{\frac{2DS}{H}}$$

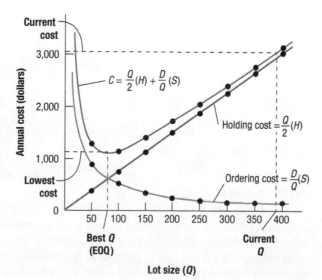

◀ **FIGURE 9.7**
Total Annual Cycle-Inventory Cost Function for the Bird Feeder

We use calculus to obtain the EOQ formula from the total annual cycle-inventory cost function. We take the first derivative of the total annual cycle-inventory cost function with respect to Q, set it equal to 0, and solve for Q. As Figure 9.7 indicates, the EOQ is the order quantity for which annual holding cost equals annual ordering cost. Using this insight, we can also obtain the EOQ formula by equating the formulas for annual ordering cost and annual holding cost and solving for Q. The graph in Figure 9.7 also reveals that when the annual holding cost for any Q exceeds the annual ordering cost, as with the 390-unit order, we can immediately conclude that Q is too high. A lower Q reduces holding cost and increases ordering cost, bringing them into balance. Similarly, if the annual ordering cost exceeds the annual holding cost, Q should be increased.

time between orders (TBO)

The average elapsed time between receiving (or placing) replenishment orders of Q units for a particular lot size.

Sometimes, inventory policies are based on the time between replenishment orders, rather than on the number of units in the lot size. The **time between orders (TBO)** for a particular lot size is the average elapsed time between receiving (or placing) replenishment orders of Q units. Expressed as a fraction of a year, the TBO is simply Q divided by annual demand. When we use the EOQ and express time in terms of months, the TBO is

$$TBO_{EOQ} = \frac{EOQ}{D} \, (12 \text{ months/year})$$

In Example 9.3, we show how to calculate TBO for years, months, weeks, and days.

EXAMPLE 9.3	**Finding the EOQ, Total Cost, and TBO**

MyOMLab

Tutor 9.3 in MyOMLab provides a new example to practice the application of the EOQ model.

MyOMLab

Active Model 9.1 in MyOMLab provides additional insight on the EOQ model and its uses.

FIGURE 9.8 ▶
Total Annual Cycle-Inventory Costs Based on EOQ Using Tutor 9.3

For the bird feeder in Example 9.2, calculate the EOQ and its total annual cycle-inventory cost. How frequently will orders be placed if the EOQ is used?

SOLUTION

Using the formulas for EOQ and annual cost, we get

$$EOQ = \sqrt{\frac{2DS}{H}} = \sqrt{\frac{2(936)(45)}{15}} = 74.94, \text{ or } 75 \text{ units}$$

Figure 9.8 shows that the total annual cost is much less than the $3,033 cost of the current policy of placing 390-unit orders.

Parameters

Current Lot Size (Q)	390	
Demand (D)	936	
Order Cost (S)	$45	
Unit Holding Cost (H)	$15	

Economic Order Quantity	75

Annual Costs

Orders per Year	2.4
Annual Ordering Cost	$108.00
Annual Holding Cost	$2,925.00
Annual Inventory Cost	$3,033.00

Annual Costs based on EOQ

Orders per Year	12.48
Annual Ordering Cost	$561.60
Annual Holding Cost	$562.50
Annual Inventory Cost	$1,124.10

When the EOQ is used, the TBO can be expressed in various ways for the same time period.

$$TBO_{EOQ} = \frac{EOQ}{D} = \frac{75}{936} = 0.080 \text{ year}$$

$$TBO_{EOQ} = \frac{EOQ}{D}(12 \text{ months/year}) = \frac{75}{936}(12) = 0.96 \text{ month}$$

$$TBO_{EOQ} = \frac{EOQ}{D}(52 \text{ weeks/year}) = \frac{75}{936}(52) = 4.17 \text{ weeks}$$

$$TBO_{EOQ} = \frac{EOQ}{D}(365 \text{ days/year}) = \frac{75}{936}(365) = 29.25 \text{ days}$$

DECISION POINT

Using the EOQ, about 12 orders per year will be required. Using the current policy of 390 units per order, an average of 2.4 orders will be needed each year (every 5 months). The current policy saves on ordering costs but incurs a much higher cost for carrying the cycle inventory. Although it is easy to see which option is best on the basis of total ordering and holding costs, other factors may affect the final decision. For example, if the supplier would reduce the price per unit for large orders, it may be better to order the larger quantity.

Managerial Insights from the EOQ

Subjecting the EOQ formula to *sensitivity analysis* can yield valuable insights into the management of inventories. Sensitivity analysis is a technique for systematically changing crucial parameters to determine the effects of a change. Table 9.1 shows the effects on the EOQ when we substitute different values into the numerator or denominator of the formula.

TABLE 9.1 | SENSITIVITY ANALYSIS OF THE EOQ

Parameter	EOQ	Parameter Change	EOQ Change	Comments
Demand	$\sqrt{\dfrac{2DS}{H}}$	↑	↑	Increase in lot size is in proportion to the square root of *D*.
Order/Setup Costs	$\sqrt{\dfrac{2DS}{H}}$	↓	↓	Weeks of supply decreases and inventory turnover increases because the lot size decreases.
Holding Costs	$\sqrt{\dfrac{2DS}{H}}$	↓	↑	Larger lots are justified when holding costs decrease.

As Table 9.1 shows, the EOQ provides support for some of the intuition you may have about inventory management. However, the effect of ordering or setup cost changes on inventories is especially important for *lean systems*. This relationship explains why manufacturers are so concerned about reducing setup time and costs; it makes small lot production economic. Actually, lean systems provide an environment conducive to the use of the EOQ. For example, yearly, monthly, daily, or hourly demand rates are known with reasonable certainty in lean systems, and the rate of demand is relatively uniform. Lean systems (see Chapter 6, "Lean Systems") may have few process constraints if the firm practices *constraint management* (see Chapter 5, "Constraint Management"). In addition, lean systems strive for constant delivery lead times and dependable delivery quantities from suppliers, both of which are assumptions of the EOQ. Consequently, the EOQ as a lot sizing tool is quite compatible with the principles of lean systems.

We now turn to a discussion of the two most common independent demand inventory control systems: the continuous review (*Q*) system and the periodic review (*P*) system.

continuous review (*Q*) system

A system designed to track the remaining inventory of a SKU each time a withdrawal is made to determine whether it is time to reorder.

reorder point (ROP) system

See continuous review (*Q*) system.

Retailers typically face independent demands for the products on their shelves. Thousands of customers may shop at a large store, each looking for a different selection of products. The products must be restocked from a distribution center in the region. Here shoppers look for bargains at a JCPenney store in the Glendale Galleria in California.

Continuous Review System

A **continuous review (*Q*) system**, sometimes called a **reorder point (ROP) system** or *fixed order-quantity system*, tracks the remaining inventory of a SKU each time a withdrawal is made to determine whether it is time to reorder. In practice, these reviews are done frequently (e.g., daily) and often continuously (after each withdrawal). The advent of computers and electronic cash registers linked to inventory records has made continuous reviews easy. At each review, a decision is made about a SKU's inventory position. If it is judged to be too low, the system triggers a new order. The **inventory position (IP)** measures the SKU's ability to satisfy future demand. It includes **scheduled receipts (SR)**, which are orders that have been placed but have not yet been received, plus on-hand inventory (OH) minus backorders (BO). Sometimes, scheduled receipts are called **open orders**. More specifically,

Inventory position = On-hand inventory + Scheduled receipts − Backorders

$$IP = OH + SR - BO$$

When the inventory position reaches a predetermined minimum level, called the **reorder point (*R*)**, a fixed quantity *Q* of the SKU is ordered. In a continuous review system, although the order quantity *Q* is

inventory position (IP)

The measurement of a SKU's ability to satisfy future demand.

scheduled receipts (SR)

Orders that have been placed but have not yet been received.

open orders

See scheduled receipts (SR).

reorder point (*R*)

The predetermined minimum level that an inventory position must reach before a fixed quantity *Q* of the SKU is ordered.

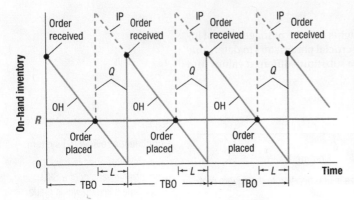

▲ FIGURE 9.9

Q System When Demand and Lead Time Are Constant and Certain

fixed, the time between orders can vary. Hence, Q can be based on the EOQ, a price break quantity (the minimum lot size that qualifies for a quantity discount), a container size (such as a truckload), or some other quantity selected by management.

Selecting the Reorder Point When Demand and Lead Time Are Constant

To demonstrate the concept of a reorder point, suppose that the demand for feeders at the museum gift shop in Example 9.3 is always 18 per week, the lead time is a constant 2 weeks, and the supplier always ships the exact number ordered on time. With both demand and lead time constant, the museum's buyer can wait until the inventory position drops to 36 units, or (18 units/week) (2 weeks), to place a new order. Thus, in this case, the reorder point, R, equals the *total demand during lead time*, with no added allowance for safety stock.

Figure 9.9 shows how the system operates when demand and lead time are constant. The downward-sloping line represents the on-hand inventory, which is being depleted at a constant rate. When it reaches reorder point R (the horizontal line), a new order for Q units is placed. The on-hand inventory continues to drop throughout lead time L until the order is received. At that time, which marks the end of the lead time, on-hand inventory jumps by Q units. A new order arrives just when inventory drops to 0. The TBO is the same for each cycle.

The inventory position, IP, shown in Figure 9.9 corresponds to the on-hand inventory, except during the lead time. Just after a new order is placed, at the start of the lead time, IP increases by Q, as shown by the dashed line. The IP exceeds OH by this same margin throughout the lead time.[4] At the end of the lead time, when the scheduled receipts convert to on-hand inventory, IP = OH once again. The key point here is to compare IP, not OH, with R in deciding whether to reorder. A common error is to ignore scheduled receipts or backorders.

EXAMPLE 9.4	**Placing a New Order When Demand and Lead Time Are Constant**

Demand for chicken soup at a supermarket is always 25 cases a day and the lead time is always 4 days. The shelves were just restocked with chicken soup, leaving an on-hand inventory of only 10 cases. No backorders currently exist, but there is one open order in the pipeline for 200 cases. What is the inventory position? Should a new order be placed?

SOLUTION

$$R = \text{Total demand during lead time} = (25)(4) = 100 \text{ cases}$$
$$IP = OH + SR - BO$$
$$= 10 + 200 - 0 = 210 \text{ cases}$$

DECISION POINT

Because IP exceeds R (210 versus 100), do not reorder. Inventory is almost depleted, but a new order need not be placed because the scheduled receipt is in the pipeline.

MyOMLab Animation

▼ FIGURE 9.10

Q System When Demand Is Uncertain

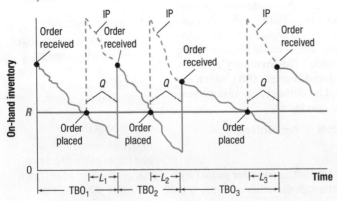

Selecting the Reorder Point When Demand Is Variable and Lead Time Is Constant

In reality demand is not always predictable. Figure 9.10 shows how the Q system operates when demand is variable and lead time is constant. The wavy downward-sloping line indicates that demand varies from day to day. Its slope is steeper in the second cycle, which means that the demand rate is higher during this time period. The changing demand rate means that the time between orders changes, so $TBO_1 \neq TBO_2 \neq TBO_3$. Example 9.5 shows the mechanics of the continuous review system when demand is variable and the lead time is constant.

---

[4]A possible exception is the situation when more than one scheduled receipt is open at the same time because of long lead times or larger than average demands during the lead time. Such is the case in Example 9.5.

EXAMPLE 9.5	Placing a New Order When Demand is Variable and Lead Time is Constant

A distribution center (DC) in Wisconsin stocks Sony plasma TV sets. The center receives its inventory from a mega warehouse in Kansas with a lead time (L) of 5 days. The DC uses a reorder point (R) of 300 sets and a fixed order quantity (Q) of 250 sets. The current on-hand inventory (OH) at the end of Day 1 is 400 sets, there are no scheduled receipts (SR), and there are no backorders (BO). Assume that all demands and receipts occur at the end of the day. The inventory position is compared to the reorder point after demands and receipts are accounted for. If necessary, an order is placed and the inventory position is updated. Given the demand schedule in the table below, determine when to order using a (Q) system.

SOLUTION
We use the following equation:

Inventory position (IP) = OH + SR − BO

Day	Demand	OH	SR	BO	IP	Q
1	50	400			400 + 0 = 400	
2	60	340			340 + 0 = 340	
3	80	260	**250** after ordering		260 < R before ordering 260 + **250** = 510 after ordering	**250** (due Day 8)
4	40	220	**250**		220 + **250** = 470	
5	75	145	**250**		145 + **250** = 395	
6	55	90	**250**		90 + **250** = 340	
7	95	0	**250** + **250** = 500 after ordering	5	0 + **250** − 5 = 245 < R before ordering 245 + **250** = 495 after ordering	**250** (due Day 12)
8	50	0 + **250** − 50 − 5 = 195	**250**		195 + **250** = 445	
9	45	195 − 45 = 150	**250**		150 + **250** = 400	
10	30	120	**250**		120 + **250** = 370	
11	50	70	**250**		70 + **250** = 320	
12	60	70 − 60 + **250** = 260	**250** after ordering		260 < R before ordering 260 + **250** = 510 after ordering	**250** (due Day 17)
13	40	260 − 40 = 220	**250**		220 + **250** = 470	
14	50	170	**250**		170 + **250** = 420	

DECISION POINT
The figure to the right shows the relationship between the on-hand quantity of TV sets and the inventory position. The IP at the DC drops below the reorder point of 300 sets for the first time on Day 3, triggering an order for 250 sets. On Day 7, demand exceeded the supply of TVs, generating a backorder of 5 sets. Notice that the calculation for IP accounts for the backorder as well as the fact that there are two scheduled receipts on the books once the new order is placed. This situation occurred because the reorder point was breached one day before the open order for 250 sets was received. On Day 8, the shipment of 250 sets arrives and the backorders are satisfied. Note that the on-hand inventory satisfies the demand for that day, as well as the backorders, from the shipment of 250 sets, leaving only 195 sets for inventory. The demands at the DC are fairly volatile and can cause the reorder point to be breached quite dramatically at times. This often happens with continuous review systems

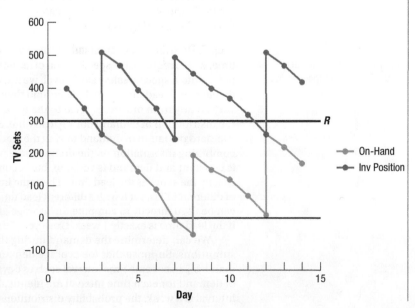

when customers place orders in large quantities, rather than one unit at a time. The customers of the DC could be large retailers who purchase large volumes of TV sets for sales promotions. Another possible reason is that the DC in this example performs all inventory transactions at the end of the day; even if shipments to customers were only one unit at a time, they were treated as one large shipment for purposes of inventory control. With today's technology and the use of product bar codes, the DC could continuously monitor inventory and replenishment orders would be placed just as the reorder point was reached.

As shown in Example 9.5, because of uncertainty, demands during the lead time are unpredictable and backorders or stockouts can occur. That is why managers add safety stock to hedge against lost sales. Consequently R is higher in Figure 9.10 than in Figure 9.9. It also explains why the on-hand inventory usually does not drop to 0 by the time a replenishment order arrives for well-designed continuous review systems. The greater the safety stock and thus the higher reorder point R, the less likely a stockout. In general

$$\text{Reorder point} = \text{Average demand during lead time} + \text{Safety stock}$$

$$= \bar{d}L + \text{safety stock}$$

where

$$\bar{d} = \text{average demand per week or day or month}$$

$$L = \text{constant lead time in weeks or days or months}$$

Because the average demand during lead time is variable, the real decision to be made when selecting R concerns the safety stock level. Deciding on a small or large safety stock is a trade-off between customer service and inventory holding costs. Cost minimization models can be used to find the best safety stock, but they require estimates of stockout and backorder costs, which are usually difficult to make with any precision because it is hard to estimate the effect of lost sales, lost customer confidence, future loyalty of customers, and market share because the customer went to a competitor. The usual approach for determining R is for management—based on judgment—to set a reasonable service-level policy for the inventory and then determine the safety stock level that satisfies this policy. There are three steps to arrive at a reorder point:

1. Choose an appropriate service-level policy.
2. Determine the distribution of demand during lead time.
3. Determine the safety stock and reorder point levels.

service level

The desired probability of not running out of stock in any one ordering cycle, which begins at the time an order is placed and ends when it arrives in stock.

Step 1: Service Level Policy   Select a **service level**, or **cycle-service level** (the desired probability of not running out of stock in any one ordering cycle), which begins at the time an order is placed and ends when it arrives in stock. The intent is to provide coverage over the **protection interval**, or the period over which safety stock must protect the user from running out of stock. For the Q system, the lead time is the protection interval. For example, in a bookstore the manager may select a 90 percent cycle-service level for a book. In other words, the probability is 90 percent that demand will not exceed the supply during the lead time. The probability of running short *during the protection interval*, creating a stockout or backorder, is only 10 percent ($100 - 90$) in our example. This stockout risk, which occurs only during the lead time in the Q system, is greater than the overall risk of a stockout because the risk is nonexistent outside the ordering cycle.

cycle-service level

See service level.

protection interval

The period over which safety stock must protect the user from running out of stock.

Step 2: Distribution of Demand during Lead Time   Determine the distribution of demand during lead time, which requires the specification of its mean and standard deviation. To translate a cycle-service level policy into a specific safety stock level, we must know how demand during the lead time is distributed. If demand and lead times vary little around their averages, the safety stock can be small. Conversely, if they vary greatly from one order cycle to the next, the safety stock must be large. Variability is measured by the distribution of demand during lead time. Sometimes, average demand during the lead time and the standard deviation of demand during the lead time are not directly available and must be calculated by combining information on the demand rate with information on the lead time. Suppose that lead time is constant and demand is variable, but records on demand are not collected for a time interval that is exactly the same as the lead time. The same inventory control system may be used to manage thousands of different SKUs, each with a different lead time. For example, if demand is reported *weekly*, these records can be used directly to compute the average and the standard deviation of demand during the lead time if the lead time is exactly 1 week. However, if the lead time is 3 weeks, the computation is more difficult.

We can determine the demand during the lead time distribution by making some reasonable assumptions. Suppose that the average demand, $\bar{d}$, is known along with the standard deviation of demand, σ_d, over some time interval such as days or weeks. Also, suppose that the probability distributions of demand for each time interval are identical and independent of each other. For example, if the time interval is a week, the probability distributions of demand are assumed to be the same each week (identical $\bar{d}$ and σ_d), and the total demand in 1 week does not affect the total demand in another week. Let L

be the constant lead time, expressed in the same time units as the demand. Under these assumptions, average demand during the lead time will be the sum of the averages for each of the L identical and independent distributions of demand, or $\bar{d} + \bar{d} + \bar{d} + \ldots = \bar{d}L$. In addition, the variance of the distribution of demand during lead time will be the sum of the variances of the L identical and independent distributions of demand, or

$$\sigma_d^2 + \sigma_d^2 + \sigma_d^2 + \ldots = \sigma_d^2 L$$

Finally, the standard deviation of the distribution of demand during lead time is

$$\sigma_{dLT} = \sqrt{\sigma_d^2 L} = \sigma_d \sqrt{L}$$

Figure 9.11 shows how the demand distribution of the lead time is developed from the individual distributions of weekly demands, where $\bar{d} = 75$, $\sigma_d = 15$, and $L = 3$. In this example, average demand during the lead time is $(75)(3) = 225$ units and $\sigma_{dLT} = 15\sqrt{3} = 25.98$.

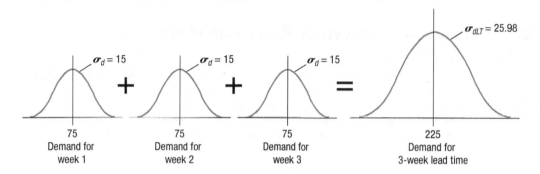

◀ **FIGURE 9.11**
Development of Distribution of Demand during Lead Time

Step 3: Safety Stock and Reorder Point   When selecting the safety stock, the inventory planner often assumes that demand during the lead time is normally distributed, as shown in Figure 9.12.

The average demand during the lead time is the centerline of the graph, with 50 percent of the area under the curve to the left and 50 percent to the right. Thus, if a cycle-service level of 50 percent were chosen, the reorder point R would be the quantity represented by this centerline. Because R equals the average demand during the lead time plus the safety stock, the safety stock is 0 when R equals this average demand. Demand is less than average 50 percent of the time and, thus, having no safety stock will be sufficient only 50 percent of the time.

To provide a service level above 50 percent, the reorder point must be higher than the average demand during the lead time. As Figure 9.12 shows, that requires moving the reorder point to the right of the centerline so that more than 50 percent of the area under the curve is to the left of R. An 85 percent cycle-service level is achieved in Figure 9.12 with 85 percent of the area under the curve to the left of R (in blue) and only 15 percent to the right (in pink). We compute the safety stock as follows:

$$\text{Safety stock} = z\sigma_{dLT}$$

where

$z =$ the number of standard deviations needed to achieve the cycle-service level

$\sigma_{dLT} =$ standard deviation of demand during the lead time

The reorder point becomes

$$R = \bar{d}L + \text{safety stock}$$

The higher the value of z, the higher the safety stock and the cycle-service level should be. If $z = 0$, there is no safety stock, and stockouts will occur during 50 percent of the order cycles. For a cycle-service level of 85 percent, $z = 1.04$. Example 9.6 shows how to use the Normal Distribution appendix to find the appropriate z value, safety stock, and reorder point.

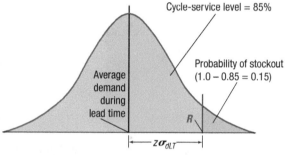

▲ **FIGURE 9.12**
Finding Safety Stock with Normal Probability Distribution for an 85 Percent Cycle-Service Level

EXAMPLE 9.6	**Reorder Point for Variable Demand and Constant Lead Time**

Let us return to the bird feeder in Example 9.3. The EOQ is 75 units. Suppose that the average demand is 18 units per week with a standard deviation of 5 units. The lead time is constant at 2 weeks. Determine the safety stock and reorder point if management wants a 90 percent cycle-service level.

MyOMLab

Tutor 9.4 in MyOMLab provides a new example to determine the safety stock and the reorder point for a Q system.

SOLUTION

In this case, $\sigma_d = 5$, $\bar{d} = 8$ units, and $L = 2$ weeks, so $\sigma_{dLT} = \sigma_d \sqrt{L} = 5\sqrt{2} = 7.07$. Consult the body of the table in the Normal Distribution appendix for 0.9000, which corresponds to a 90 percent cycle-service level. The closest number is 0.8997, which corresponds to 1.2 in the row heading and 0.08 in the column heading. Adding these values gives a z value of 1.28. With this information, we calculate the safety stock and reorder point as follows:

$$\text{Safety stock} = z\sigma_{dLT} = 1.28(7.07) = 9.05, \text{ or 9 units}$$
$$\text{Reorder point} = \overline{d}L + \text{Safety stock}$$
$$= 2(18) + 9 = 45 \text{ units}$$

DECISION POINT

The Q system for the bird feeder operates as follows: Whenever the inventory position reaches 45 units, order the EOQ of 75 units. Various order quantities and safety stock levels can be used in a Q system. For example, management could specify a different order quantity (because of shipping constraints) or a different safety stock (because of storage limitations).

Selecting the Reorder Point When Both Demand and Lead Time Are Variable

In practice, it is often the case that both the demand and the lead time are variable. Unfortunately, the equations for the safety stock and reorder point become more complicated. In the model below we make two simplifying assumptions. First, the demand distribution and the lead time distribution are measured in the same time units. For example, both demand and lead time are measured in weeks. Second, demand and lead time are *independent*. That is, demand per week is not affected by the length of the lead time.

$$\text{Safety stock} = z\sigma_{dLT}$$
$$R = (\text{Average weekly demand} \times \text{Average lead time in weeks}) + \text{Safety stock}$$
$$= \overline{d}\overline{L} + \text{Safety stock}$$

where

$$\overline{d} = \text{Average weekly or daily or monthly demand}$$
$$\overline{L} = \text{Average weekly or daily or monthly lead time}$$
$$\sigma_d = \text{Standard deviation of weekly or daily or monthly demand}$$
$$\sigma_{LT} = \text{Standard deviation of the lead time, and}$$
$$\sigma_{dLT} = \sqrt{\overline{L}\sigma_d^2 + \overline{d}^2\sigma_{LT}^2}$$

Now that we have determined the mean and standard deviation of the distribution of demand during lead time under these more complicated conditions, we can select the reorder point as we did before for the case where the lead time was constant.

| EXAMPLE 9.7 | **Reorder Point for Variable Demand and Variable Lead Time** |

The Office Supply Shop estimates that the average demand for a popular ball-point pen is 12,000 pens per week with a standard deviation of 3,000 pens. The current inventory policy calls for replenishment orders of 156,000 pens. The average lead time from the distributor is 5 weeks, with a standard deviation of 2 weeks. If management wants a 95 percent cycle-service level, what should the reorder point be?

SOLUTION

We have $\overline{d} = 12,000$ pens, $\sigma_d = 3,000$ pens, $\overline{L} = 5$ weeks, and $\sigma_{LT} = 2$ weeks.

$$\sigma_{dLT} = \sqrt{\overline{L}\sigma_d^2 + \overline{d}^2\sigma_{LT}^2} = \sqrt{(5)(3,000)^2 + (12,000)^2(2)^2} = 24,919.87 \text{ pens}$$

Consult the body of the Normal Distribution appendix for 0.9500, which corresponds to a 95 percent cycle-service level. That value falls exactly in the middle of the tabular values of 0.9495 (for a z value of 1.64) and 0.9505 (for a z value of 1.65). Consequently, we will use the more conservative value of 1.65. We calculate the safety stock and reorder point as follows:

$$\text{Safety stock} = z\sigma_{dLT} = (1.65)(24,919.87) = 41,117.79, \text{ or 41,118 pens}$$
$$\text{Reorder point} = \overline{d}\overline{L} + \text{Safety stock} = (12,000)(5) + 41,118 = 101,118 \text{ pens}$$

DECISION POINT

Whenever the stock of ball-point pens drops to 101,118, management should place another replenishment order of 156,000 pens to the distributor.

Sometimes, the theoretical distributions for demand and lead time are not known. In those cases, we can use simulation to find the distribution of demand during lead time using discrete distributions for demand and lead times. Simulation can also be used to estimate the performance of an inventory system. More discussion, and an example, can be found in MyOMLab.

Systems Based on the *Q* System

Two systems based on the *Q* system are the two-bin system and the base-stock system.

Two-Bin System   The concept of a *Q* system can be incorporated in a **visual system**, that is, a system that allows employees to place orders when inventory visibly reaches a certain marker. Visual systems are easy to administer because records are not kept on the current inventory position. The historical usage rate can simply be reconstructed from past purchase orders. Visual systems are intended for use with low-value SKUs that have a steady demand, such as nuts and bolts or office supplies. Overstocking is common, but the extra inventory holding cost is minimal because the items have relatively little value.

A visual system version of the *Q* system is the **two-bin system** in which a SKU's inventory is stored at two different locations. Inventory is first withdrawn from one bin. If the first bin is empty, the second bin provides backup to cover demand until a replenishment order arrives. An empty first bin signals the need to place a new order. Premade order forms placed near the bins let workers send one to purchasing or even directly to the supplier. When the new order arrives, the second bin is restored to its normal level and the rest is put in the first bin. The two-bin system operates like a *Q* system, with the normal level in the second bin being the reorder point *R*. The system also may be implemented with just one bin by marking the bin at the reorder point level.

Base-Stock System   In its simplest form, the **base-stock system** issues a replenishment order, *Q*, each time a withdrawal is made, for the same amount as the withdrawal. This one-for-one replacement policy maintains the inventory position at a base-stock level equal to expected demand during the lead time plus safety stock. The base-stock level, therefore, is equivalent to the reorder point in a *Q* system. However, order quantities now vary to keep the inventory position at *R* at all times. Because this position is the lowest IP possible that will maintain a specified service level, the base-stock system may be used to minimize cycle inventory. More orders are placed, but each order is smaller. This system is appropriate for expensive items, such as replacement engines for jet airplanes. No more inventory is held than the maximum demand expected until a replacement order can be received.

visual system

A system that allows employees to place orders when inventory visibly reaches a certain marker.

two-bin system

A visual system version of the *Q* system in which a SKU's inventory is stored at two different locations.

base-stock system

An inventory control system that issues a replenishment order, *Q*, each time a withdrawal is made, for the same amount of the withdrawal.

Calculating Total *Q* System Costs

Total costs for the continuous review (*Q*) system is the sum of three cost components:

Total cost = Annual cycle inventory holding cost + annual ordering cost
+ annual safety stock holding cost

$$C = \frac{Q}{2}(H) + \frac{D}{Q}(S) + (H)(\text{Safety stock})$$

The annual cycle-inventory holding cost and annual ordering cost are the same equations we used for computing the total annual cycle-inventory cost in Example 9.2. The annual cost of holding the safety stock is computed under the assumption that the safety stock is on hand at all times. Referring to Figure 9.10 in each order cycle, we will sometimes experience a demand greater than the average demand during lead time, and sometimes we will experience less. On average over the year, we can assume the safety stock will be on hand. See Solved Problems 4 and 6 at the end of this chapter for an example of calculating the total costs for a *Q* system.

Advantages of the *Q* System

The primary advantages of *Q* systems are the following:

1. The review frequency of each SKU may be individualized. Tailoring the review frequency to the SKU can reduce total ordering and holding costs.

2. Fixed lot sizes, if large enough, can result in quantity discounts. The firm's physical limitations, such as its truckload capacities, materials handling methods, and shelf space might also necessitate a fixed lot size.

3. The system requires low levels of safety stock for the amount of uncertainty in demands during the lead time.

Periodic Review System

periodic review (P) system

A system in which an item's inventory position is reviewed periodically rather than continuously.

MyOMLab Animation

▼ **FIGURE 9.13**
P System When Demand Is Uncertain

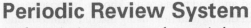

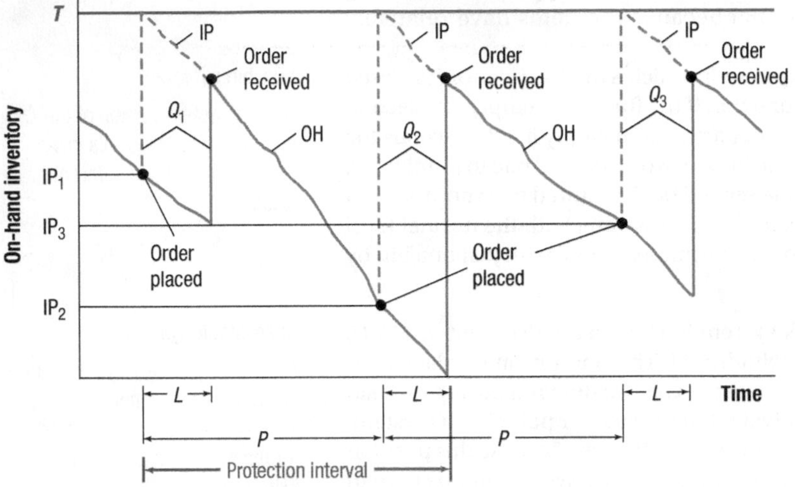

An alternative inventory control system is the **periodic review (P) system**, sometimes called a *fixed interval reorder system* or *periodic reorder system*, in which an item's inventory position is reviewed periodically rather than continuously. Such a system can simplify delivery scheduling because it establishes a routine. A new order is always placed at the end of each review, and the time between orders (TBO) is fixed at P. Demand is a random variable, so total demand between reviews varies. In a P system, the lot size, Q, may change from one order to the next, but the time between orders is fixed. An example of a periodic review system is that of a soft-drink supplier making weekly rounds of grocery stores. Each week, the supplier reviews the store's inventory of soft drinks and restocks the store with enough items to meet demand and safety stock requirements until the next week.

Under a P system, four of the original EOQ assumptions are maintained: (1) no constraints are placed on the size of the lot, (2) the relevant costs are holding and ordering costs, (3) decisions for one SKU are independent of decisions for other SKUs, and (4) lead times are certain and supply is known. However, demand uncertainty is again allowed for. Figure 9.13 shows the periodic review system under these assumptions. The downward-sloping line again represents on-hand inventory. When the predetermined time, P, has elapsed since the last review, an order is placed to bring the inventory position, represented by the dashed line, up to the target inventory level, T. The lot size for the first review is Q_1, or the difference between inventory position IP_1 and T. As with the continuous review system, IP and OH differ only during the lead time. When the order arrives at the end of the lead time, OH and IP again are identical. Figure 9.13 shows that lot sizes vary from one order cycle to the next. Because the inventory position is lower at the second review, a greater quantity is needed to achieve an inventory level of T.

EXAMPLE 9.8	Determining How Much to Order in a P System

Return to the distribution center (DC) in Example 9.5. Suppose that management wants to use a periodic review system for the Sony TV sets. The first review of the inventory is scheduled for the end of Day 2. Assume that all demands and receipts occur at the end of the day. On the scheduled review day, inventory replenishment orders are placed after the demands and receipts have been accounted for. The lead time is 5 days, and management has set $T = 620$ and $P = 6$ days. Given the demand schedule in the table below, determine how much to order (Q) using a P system.

SOLUTION
We use the following equations:

$$\text{Inventory Position (IP)} = \text{OH} + \text{SR} - \text{BO}$$

$$\text{Order Quantity (Q)} = T - \text{IP}$$

Day	Demand	OH	SR	BO	IP	Q
1	50	400			400	
2	60	340	**280** after ordering		340 before ordering 340 + **280** = 620 after ordering	620 − 340 = **280** (due Day 7)
3	80	260	**280**		260 + **280** = 540	
4	40	220	**280**		220 + **280** = 500	
5	75	145	**280**		145 + **280** = 425	
6	55	90	**280**		90 + **280** = 370	
7	95	90 + **280** − 95 = 275			275 + 0 = 275	
8	50	225	**395** after ordering		225 + 0 = 225 before ordering 225 + **395** = 620 after ordering	620 − 225 = **395** (due Day 13)

Day	Demand	OH	SR	BO	IP	Q
9	45	180	**395**		180 + **395** = 575	
10	30	150	**395**		150 + **395** = 545	
11	50	100	**395**		100 + **395** = 495	
12	60	40	**395**		40 + **395** = 435	
13	40	40 + **395** − 40 = 395			395 + 0 = **395**	
14	50	345	**275** after ordering		345 + 0 = 345 before ordering 345 + **275** = 620 after ordering	620 − 345 = **275** (due Day 19)

DECISION POINT

The figure to the right shows the relationship between on-hand inventory and the inventory position. The DC did not experience any backorders because on Day 7 the replenishment order arrived in the nick of time. Notice that the order quantities vary in size while the time between orders remains a constant. Compare the operation of the P system in this example to the Q system in Example 9.5. The Q system requires constant monitoring to determine when the order point is reached. However, the average daily inventory is only 188 sets, compared to 226 sets for the P system. Granted, the Q system experienced backorders because of some unexpectedly large orders. Nonetheless, it is a general rule that to gain the benefits of periodic ordering, the P system requires more inventory for the same level of protection against stockouts or backorders. We will see why this is the case as we develop the parameters for the P system.

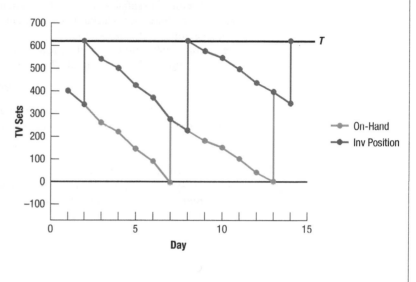

Selecting the Time between Reviews

To run a P system, managers must make two decisions: the length of time between reviews, P, and the target inventory level, T. Let us first consider the time between reviews, P. It can be any convenient interval, such as each Friday or every other Friday. Another option is to base P on the cost trade-offs of the EOQ. In other words, P can be set equal to the average time between orders for the economic order quantity, or TBO_{EOQ}. Because demand is variable, some orders will be larger than the EOQ and some will be smaller. However, over an extended period of time, the average lot size should be close to the EOQ. If other models are used to determine the lot size (e.g., those described in Supplement C, "Special Inventory Models"), we divide the lot size chosen by the annual demand, D, and use this ratio as P. It will be expressed as the fraction of a year between orders, which can be converted into months, weeks, or days as needed.

Selecting the Target Inventory Level When Demand Is Variable and Lead Time Is Constant

Now, let us calculate the target inventory level, T, when demand is variable but the lead time is constant. Figure 9.13 reveals that an order must be large enough to make the inventory position, IP, last beyond the next review, which is P time periods away. The checker must wait P periods to revise, correct, and reestablish the inventory position. Then, a new order is placed, but it does not arrive until after the lead time, L. Therefore, as Figure 9.13 shows, a protection interval of $P + L$ periods is needed. A fundamental difference between the Q and P systems is the length of time needed for stockout protection. A Q system needs stockout protection only during the lead time because orders can be placed as soon as they are needed and will be

Large, fixed capacity modes of transportation require defined schedules of operation. Such a situation supports the use of periodic review systems. Here ocean vessels await loads of petro-chemicals at the Vopak terminal in the Port of Rotterdam.

received L periods later. A P system, however, needs stockout protection for the longer $P + L$ protection interval because orders are placed only at fixed intervals, and the inventory is not checked until the next designated review time.

As with the Q system, we need to develop the appropriate distribution of demand during the protection interval to specify the system fully. In a P system, we must develop the distribution of demand for $P + L$ time periods. The target inventory level T must equal the expected demand during the protection interval of $P + L$ periods, plus enough safety stock to protect against demand uncertainty over this same protection interval. We assume that lead time is constant and that demand in one period is independent of demand in the next period. Thus, the average demand during the protection interval is $\overline{d}(P + L)$, or

$$T = \overline{d}(P + L) + \text{Safety stock for the protection interval}$$

We compute safety stock for a P system much as we did for the Q system. However, the safety stock must cover demand uncertainty for a longer period of time. When using a normal probability distribution, we multiply the desired standard deviations to implement the cycle-service level, z, by the standard deviation of demand during the protection interval, σ_{P+L}. The value of z is the same as for a Q system with the same cycle-service level. Thus,

$$\text{Safety stock} = z\sigma_{P+L}$$

Based on our earlier logic for calculating σ_{dLT} we know that the standard deviation of the distribution of demand during the protection interval is

$$\sigma_{P+L} = \sigma_d\sqrt{P + L}$$

Because a P system requires safety stock to cover demand uncertainty over a longer time period than a Q system, a P system requires more safety stock; that is, σ_{P+L} exceeds σ_{dLT}. Hence, to gain the convenience of a P system requires that overall inventory levels be somewhat higher than those for a Q system.

EXAMPLE 9.9	Calculating *P* and *T*

MyOMLab

Tutor 9.5 in MyOMLab provides a new example to determine the review interval and the target inventory for a *P* system.

Again, let us return to the bird feeder example. Recall that demand for the bird feeder is normally distributed with a mean of 18 units per week and a standard deviation in weekly demand of 5 units. The lead time is 2 weeks, and the business operates 52 weeks per year. The Q system developed in Example 9.5 called for an EOQ of 75 units and a safety stock of 9 units for a cycle-service level of 90 percent. What is the equivalent *P* system? Answers are to be rounded to the nearest integer.

SOLUTION

We first define D and then P. Here, P is the time between reviews, expressed in weeks because the data are expressed as demand *per week*:

$$D = (18 \text{ units/week})(52 \text{ weeks/year}) = 936 \text{ units}$$

$$P = \frac{EOQ}{D}(52) = \frac{75}{936}(52) = 4.2, \text{ or 4 weeks}$$

With $\overline{d} = 18$ units per week, an alternative approach is to calculate P by dividing the EOQ by $\overline{d}$ to get $75/18 = 4.2$, or 4 weeks. Either way, we would review the bird feeder inventory every 4 weeks. We now find the standard deviation of demand over the protection interval $(P + L = 6)$:

$$\sigma_{P+L} = \sigma_d\sqrt{P + L} = 5\sqrt{6} = 12.25 \text{ units}$$

Before calculating T, we also need a z value. For a 90 percent cycle-service level, $z = 1.28$ (see the Normal Distribution appendix). The safety stock becomes

$$\text{Safety stock} = z\sigma_{P+L} = 1.28(12.25) = 15.68, \text{ or 16 units}$$

We now solve for T:

$$T = \text{Average demand during the protection interval} + \text{Safety stock}$$
$$= \overline{d}(P + L) + \text{Safety stock}$$
$$= (18 \text{ units/week})(6 \text{ weeks}) + 16 \text{ units} = 124 \text{ units}$$

Selecting the Target Inventory Level When Demand and Lead Time Are Variable

A useful approach for finding *P* and *T* in practice is simulation. Given discrete probability distributions for demand and lead time, simulation can be used to estimate the demand during the protection interval distribution. The "*Demand During the Protection Interval Simulator*" in OM Explorer can be used to determine the distribution. Once determined, the distribution can be used to select a value for *T*, given a desired cycle-service level. More discussion, and an example, can be found in MyOMLab.

MyOMLab

Systems Based on the *P* System

Two systems based on the *P* system are the single-bin system and the optional replenishment system.

Single-Bin System   The concept of a *P* system can be translated into a simple visual system of inventory control. In the **single-bin system**, a maximum level is marked on the storage shelf or bin, and the inventory is brought up to the mark periodically—say, once a week. The single bin may be, for example, a gasoline storage tank at a service station or a storage bin for small parts at a manufacturing plant.

Optional Replenishment System   Sometimes called the optional review, min–max, or (s, S) system, the **optional replenishment system** is much like the *P* system. It is used to review the inventory position at fixed time intervals and, if the position has dropped to (or below) a predetermined level, to place a variable-sized order to cover expected needs. The new order is large enough to bring the inventory position up to a target inventory, similar to *T* for the *P* system. However, orders are not placed after a review unless the inventory position has dropped to the predetermined minimum level. The minimum level acts as the reorder point *R* does in a *Q* system. If the target is 100 and the minimum level is 60, the minimum order size is 40 (or $100 - 60$). Because continuous reviews need not be made, this system is particularly attractive when both review and ordering costs are high.

single-bin system

A system of inventory control in which a maximum level is marked on the storage shelf or bin, and the inventor is brought up to the mark periodically.

optional replenishment system

A system used to review the inventory position at fixed time intervals and, if the position has dropped to (or below) a predetermined level, to place a variable-sized order to cover expected needs.

Calculating Total *P* System Costs

The total costs for the *P* system are the sum of the same three cost elements for the *Q* system. The differences are in the calculation of the order quantity and the safety stock. As shown in Figure 9.13, the average order quantity will be the average consumption of inventory during the *P* periods between orders. Consequently, $Q = \overline{d}P$. Total costs for the *P* system are

$$C = \frac{\overline{d}P}{2}(H) + \frac{D}{\overline{d}P}(S) + (H)(\text{Safety stock})$$

See Solved Problem 5 at the end of this chapter for an example of calculating total *P* system costs.

Advantages of the *P* System

The primary advantages of *P* systems are the following:

1. The system is convenient because replenishments are made at fixed intervals. Fixed replenishment intervals allow for standardized pickup and delivery times. In contrast, individual items are ordered on their own best intervals with the *Q* system, which can differ widely.

2. Orders for multiple items from the same supplier can be combined into a single purchase order. This approach reduces ordering and transportation costs and can result in a price break from the supplier.

3. The inventory position, IP, needs to be known only when a review is made (not continuously, as in a *Q* system). However, this advantage is moot for firms using computerized record-keeping systems, in which a transaction is reported upon each receipt or withdrawal. When inventory records are always current, the system is called a **perpetual inventory system**.

Both the *Q* system and the *P* system have their advantages. Indeed, the advantages for one system become the disadvantages for the other. In conclusion, the choice between *Q* and *P* systems is not clear cut. Which system is better depends on the relative importance of its advantages in various situations.

perpetual inventory system

A system of inventory control in which the inventory records are always current.

LEARNING GOALS IN REVIEW

Learning Goal	Guidelines for Review	MyOMLab Resources
1 Identify the advantages, disadvantages, and costs of holding inventory.	We cover these important aspects of inventories in the section "Inventory Trade-offs," pp. 319–322. Focus on the pressures for small or large inventories and Figure 9.1.	**Video**: Inventory Management at Crayola
2 Define the different types of inventory and the roles they play in supply chains.	The section "Types of Inventory," pp. 322–324, explains each type of inventory and provides an example in Figure 9.2. Example 9.1 and Solved Problem 1 show how to estimate inventory levels. Be sure to understand the distinction between independent and dependent inventories.	**OM Explorer Tutor**: 9.1: Estimating Inventory Levels
3 Explain the tactics for reducing inventories in supply chains.	See the section "Inventory Reduction Tactics," pp. 325–326, for important approaches to managing inventory levels. The main tools for eliminating unneeded inventories are inventory control systems.	
4 Use ABC analysis to identify the items deserving most attention and tightest inventory control.	The section "ABC Analysis," pp. 326–327, shows a simple approach to categorizing inventory items for ease of management oversight. Figure 9.4 has an example. Solved Problem 2 demonstrates the calculations.	**OM Explorer Tutor**: 9.2: ABC Analysis **POM for Windows**: ABC Analysis
5 Calculate the economic order quantity and apply it to various situations.	See the section "Economic Order Quantity," pp. 327–331, for a complete discussion of the EOQ model. Focus on Figures 9.5, 9.6, and 9.7 to see how the EOQ model affects inventory levels under the standard assumptions and how the EOQ provides the lowest cost solution. Review Examples 9.2 and 9.3 and Solved Problem 3 for help in calculating the total costs of various lot-size choices. Table 9.1 reveals important managerial insights from the EOQ. See also the Active Model Exercise on p. 353.	**Active Model**: 9.1: Economic Order Quantity **OM Explorer Tutor**: 9.3: Finding EOQ and Total Cost **POM for Windows**: Economic Order Quantity (EOQ) Model **Tutor Exercise**: 9.1: Finding EOQ; Safety Stock; R, P, T at Bison College Bookstore
6 Determine the order quantity and reorder point for a continuous review inventory control system.	The section "Continuous Review System," pp. 331–337, builds the essence of the Q system from basic principles to more realistic assumptions. Be sure to understand Figures 9.10 and 9.12. Examples 9.4, 9.5, and 9.6 and Solved Problems 4 and 6 show how to determine the parameters Q and B under various assumptions.	**OM Explorer Solvers**: Inventory Systems Designer; Demand During Protection Interval Simulator; Q System Simulator **OM Explorer Tutor**: 9.4: Finding the Safety Stock and R **Tutor Exercise**: 9.1: Finding EOQ; Safety Stock; R,P,T at Bison College Bookstore **Tutorial on Inventory Management Systems**: Using Simulation to Develop Inventory Management Systems **Advanced Problems**: Office Supply Shop Simulation; Floral Shop Simulation Simquick Simulation Exercise
7 Determine the review interval and target inventory level for a periodic review inventory control system.	We summarize the key concepts in the section "Periodic Review System," pp. 338–341. Figure 9.13 shows how a P system operates while Examples 9.8 and 9.9 and Solved Problem 5 demonstrate how to calculate the parameters P and T.	**OM Explorer Solver**: Inventory Systems Designer; Demand During Protection Interval Simulator **OM Explorer Tutor**: 9.5: Calculating P and T **Tutor Exercise**: 9.1: Finding EOQ; Safety Stock; R,P,T at Bison College Bookstore **Tutorial on Inventory Management Systems**: Using Simulation to Develop Inventory Management Systems **Advanced Problem**: Grocery Store Simulation; Simquick Simulation Exercise

Key Equations

Types of Inventory

1.

2.

Economic Order Quantity

3. Total annual cycle-inventory cost = Annual holding cost + Annual ordering or setup cost:

$$C = \frac{Q}{2}(H) + \frac{D}{Q}(S)$$

4. Economic order quantity:

$$EOQ = \sqrt{\frac{2DS}{H}}$$

5. Time between orders, expressed in weeks:

$$TBO_{EOQ} = \frac{EOQ}{D}(52\,\text{weeks}/\text{year})$$

Continuous Review System

6. Inventory position = On-hand inventory + Scheduled receipts − Backorders:

$$IP = OH + SR - BO$$

7. Continuous review system:

Protection interval = Lead time (L)

Standard deviation of demand during the lead time (constant L) $= \sigma_{dLT} = \sigma_d \sqrt{L}$

Standard deviation of demand during the lead time (variable L) $= \sigma_{dLT} = \sqrt{\bar{L}\sigma_d^2 + \bar{d}^2\sigma_{LT}^2}$

Safety stock $= z\sigma_{dLT}$

Reorder point R for constant lead time $= \bar{d}L$ + Safety stock

Reorder point R for variable lead time $= \bar{d}\bar{L}$ + Safety stock

Order quantity = EOQ

Replenishment rule: Order EOQ units when IP $\leq R$

Total Q system cost: $C = \dfrac{Q}{2}(H) + \dfrac{D}{Q}(S) + (H)(\text{Safety stock})$

Periodic Review System

8. Periodic review system:

Review interval = Time between orders $= P$

Protection interval = Time between orders + Lead time $= P + L$

Standard deviation of demand during the protection interval $\sigma_{P+L} = \sigma_d\sqrt{P + L}$

Safety stock $= z\sigma_{P+L}$

Target inventory level (T) = Average demand during the protection interval + Safety stock

$$= \bar{d}(P + L) + \text{Safety stock}$$

Order quantity Target inventory level − Inventory position $= T - IP$

Replenishment rule: Every P time periods, order $T - IP$ units

Total P system cost: $C = \dfrac{\bar{d}P}{2}(H) + \dfrac{D}{\bar{d}P}(S) + (H)(\text{Safety stock})$

Key Terms

Solved Problem 1

A distribution center experiences an average weekly demand of 50 units for one of its items. The product is valued at $650 per unit. Inbound shipments from the factory warehouse average 350 units. Average lead time (including ordering delays and transit time) is 2 weeks. The distribution center operates 52 weeks per year; it carries a 1-week supply of inventory as safety stock and no anticipation inventory. What is the value of the average aggregate inventory being held by the distribution center?

SOLUTION

Type of Inventory	Calculation of Aggregate Average Inventory	
Cycle	$\dfrac{Q}{2} = \dfrac{350}{2}$	= 175 units
Safety stock	1-week supply	= 50 units
Anticipation	None	
Pipeline	$\bar{d}L$ = (50 units/week) (2 weeks)	= 100 units
	Average aggregate inventory	= 325 units
	Value of aggregate inventory	= $650(325)
		= $211,250

Solved Problem 2

Booker's Book Bindery divides SKUs into three classes according to their dollar usage. Calculate the usage values of the following SKUs and determine which is most likely to be classified as class A.

SOLUTION

The annual dollar usage for each SKU is determined by multiplying the annual usage quantity by the value per unit. As shown in Figure 9.14, the SKUs are then sorted by annual dollar usage, in declining order. Finally, A–B and B–C class lines are drawn roughly, according to the guidelines presented in the text. Here, class A includes only one SKU (signatures), which represents only 1/7, or 14 percent, of the SKUs but accounts for 83 percent of annual dollar usage. Class B includes the next two SKUs, which taken together represent 28 percent of the SKUs and account for 13 percent of annual dollar usage. The final four SKUs, class C, represent over half the number of SKUs but only 4 percent of total annual dollar usage.

SKU Number	Description	Quantity Used per Year	Unit Value ($)
1	Boxes	500	3.00
2	Cardboard (square feet)	18,000	0.02
3	Cover stock	10,000	0.75
4	Glue (gallons)	75	40.00
5	Inside covers	20,000	0.05
6	Reinforcing tape (meters)	3,000	0.15
7	Signatures	150,000	0.45

SKU Number	Description	Quantity Used per Year		Unit Value ($)		Annual Dollar Usage ($)
1	Boxes	500	×	3.00	=	1,500
2	Cardboard (square feet)	18,000	×	0.02	=	360
3	Cover stock	10,000	×	0.75	=	7,500
4	Glue (gallons)	75	×	40.00	=	3,000
5	Inside covers	20,000	×	0.05	=	1,000
6	Reinforcing tape (meters)	3,000	×	0.15	=	450
7	Signatures	150,000	×	0.45	=	67,500
					Total	81,310

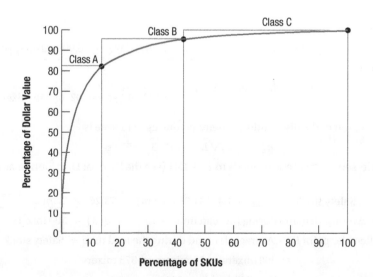

SKU #	Description	Qty Used/Year	Value	Dollar Usage	Pct of Total	Cumulative % of Dollar Value	Cumulative % of SKU	Class
7	Signatures	150,000	$0.45	$67,500	83.0%	83.0%	14.3%	A
3	Cover stock	10,000	$0.75	$7,500	9.2%	92.2%	28.6%	B
4	Glue	75	$40.00	$3,000	3.7%	95.9%	42.9%	B
1	Boxes	500	$3.00	$1,500	1.8%	97.8%	57.1%	C
5	Inside covers	20,000	$0.05	$1,000	1.2%	99.0%	71.4%	C
6	Reinforcing tape	3,000	$0.15	$450	0.6%	99.6%	85.7%	C
2	Cardboard	18,000	$0.02	$360	0.4%	100.0%	100.0%	C

Total $81,310

◀ **FIGURE 9.14**
Annual Dollar Usage for Class A, B, and C SKUs Using Tutor 9.2

Solved Problem 3

Nelson's Hardware Store stocks a 19.2 volt cordless drill that is a popular seller. Annual demand is 5,000 units, the ordering cost is $15, and the inventory holding cost is $4/unit/year.

a. What is the economic order quantity?

b. What is the total annual cost for this inventory item?

SOLUTION

a. The order quantity is

$$EOQ = \sqrt{\frac{2DS}{H}} = \sqrt{\frac{2(5,000)(\$15)}{\$4}} = \sqrt{37,500}$$

$$= 193.65, \text{ or } 194 \text{ drills}$$

b. The total annual cost is

$$C = \frac{Q}{2}(H) + \frac{D}{Q}(S) = \frac{194}{2}(\$4) + \frac{5,000}{194}(\$15) = \$774.60$$

Solved Problem 4

MyOMLab Video

A regional distributor purchases discontinued appliances from various suppliers and then sells them on demand to retailers in the region. The distributor operates 5 days per week, 52 weeks per year. Only when it is open for business can orders be received. The following data are estimated for a counter-top mixer:

Average daily demand $(\bar{d})$ = 100 mixers

Standard deviation of daily demand (σ_d) = 30 mixers

Lead time (L) = 3 days

Holding cost (H) = $9.40/unit/year

Ordering cost (S) = $35/order

Cycle-service level = 92 percent

The distributor uses a continuous review Q system.

a. What order quantity Q, and reorder point, R, should be used?

b. What is the total annual cost of the system?

c. If on-hand inventory is 40 units, one open order for 440 mixers is pending, and no backorders exist, should a new order be placed?

SOLUTION

a. Annual demand is

$$D = (5 \text{ days/week})(52 \text{ weeks/year})(100 \text{ mixers/day}) = 26,000 \text{ mixers/year}$$

The order quantity is

$$EOQ = \sqrt{\frac{2DS}{H}} = \sqrt{\frac{2(26,000)(\$35)}{\$9.40}} = \sqrt{193,167} = 440.02, \text{ or } 440 \text{ mixers}$$

The standard deviation of the distribution of demand during lead time is

$$\sigma_{dLT} = \sigma_d\sqrt{L} = 30\sqrt{3} = 51.96$$

A 92 percent cycle-service level corresponds to $z = 1.41$ (see the Normal Distribution appendix). Therefore,

$$\text{Safety stock} = z\sigma_{dLT} = 1.41(51.96 \text{ mixers}) = 73.26, \text{ or } 73 \text{ mixers}$$

$$\text{Average demand during the lead time} = \bar{d}L = 100(3) = 300 \text{ mixers}$$

$$\text{Reorder point } R = \text{Average demand during the lead time } + \text{ Safety stock}$$

$$= 300 \text{ mixers} + 73 \text{ mixers} = 373 \text{ mixers}$$

With a continuous review system, $Q = 440$ and $R = 373$.

b. The total annual cost for the Q systems is

$$C = \frac{Q}{2}(H) + \frac{D}{Q}(S) + (H)(\text{Safety stock})$$

$$C = \frac{440}{2}(\$9.40) + \frac{26{,}000}{440}(35) + (\$9.40)(73) = \$4{,}822.38$$

c. Inventory position $=$ On-hand inventory $+$ Scheduled receipts $-$ Backorders

$$IP = OH + SR - BO = 40 + 440 - 0 = 480 \text{ mixers}$$

Because IP (480) exceeds R (373), do not place a new order.

Solved Problem 5

Suppose that a periodic review (P) system is used at the distributor in Solved Problem 4, but otherwise the data are the same.

a. Calculate the P (in workdays, rounded to the nearest day) that gives approximately the same number of orders per year as the EOQ.
b. What is the target inventory level, T? Compare the P system to the Q system in Solved Problem 4.
c. What is the total annual cost of the P system?
d. It is time to review the item. On-hand inventory is 40 mixers; receipt of 440 mixers is scheduled, and no backorders exist. How much should be reordered?

SOLUTION

a. The time between orders is

$$P = \frac{EOQ}{D}(260 \text{ days/year}) = \frac{440}{26{,}000}(260) = 4.4, \text{ or } 4 \text{ days}$$

b. Figure 9.15 shows that $T = 812$ and safety stock $= (1.41)(79.37) = 111.91$, or about 112 mixers. The corresponding Q system for the counter-top mixer requires less safety stock.
c. The total annual cost of the P system is

$$C = \frac{\overline{d}P}{2}(H) + \frac{D}{\overline{d}P}(S) + (H)(\text{Safety stock})$$

$$C = \frac{(100)(4)}{2}(\$9.40) + \frac{26{,}000}{(100)(4)}(\$35) + (\$9.40)(1.41)(79.37)$$

$$= \$5{,}207.80$$

d. Inventory position is the amount on hand plus scheduled receipts minus backorders, or

$$IP = OH + SR - BO = 40 + 440 - 0 = 480 \text{ mixers}$$

The order quantity is the target inventory level minus the inventory position, or

$$Q = T - IP = 812 \text{ mixers} - 480 \text{ mixers} = 332 \text{ mixers}$$

An order for 332 mixers should be placed.

Continuous Review (Q) System		Periodic Review (P) System	
z	1.41	Time Between Reviews (P)	4.00 Days
Safety Stock	73	☑ Enter manually	
Reorder Point	373	Standard Deviation of Demand During Protection Interval	79.37
Annual Cost	$4,822.38	Safety Stock	112
		Average Demand During Protection Interval	700
		Target Inventory Level (T)	812
		Annual Cost	$5,207.80

◀ **FIGURE 9.15**
OM Explorer Solver for Inventory Systems

Solved Problem 6

Grey Wolf Lodge is a popular 500-room hotel in the North Woods. Managers need to keep close tabs on all room service items, including a special pine-scented bar soap. The daily demand for the soap is 275 bars, with a standard deviation of 30 bars. Ordering cost is $10 and the inventory holding cost is $0.30/bar/year. The lead time from the supplier is 5 days, with a standard deviation of 1 day. The lodge is open 365 days a year.

a. What is the economic order quantity for the bar of soap?

b. What should the reorder point be for the bar of soap if management wants to have a 99 percent cycle-service level?

c. What is the total annual cost for the bar of soap, assuming a Q system will be used?

SOLUTION

a. We have $D = (275)(365) = 100{,}375$ bars of soap; $S = \$10$; and $H = \$0.30$. The EOQ for the bar of soap is

$$\text{EOQ} = \sqrt{\frac{2DS}{H}} = \sqrt{\frac{2(100{,}375)(\$10)}{\$0.30}} = \sqrt{6{,}691{,}666.7}$$

$$= 2{,}586.83, \text{ or } 2{,}587 \text{ bars}$$

b. We have $\bar{d} = 275$ bars/day, $\sigma_d = 30$ bars, $\bar{L} = 5$ days, and $\sigma_{LT} = 1$ day.

$$\sigma_{dLT} = \sqrt{\bar{L}\sigma_d^2 + \bar{d}^2\sigma_{LT}^2} = \sqrt{(5)(30)^2 + (275)^2(1)^2} = 283.06 \text{ bars}$$

Consult the body of the Normal Distribution appendix for 0.9900, which corresponds to a 99 percent cycle-service level. The closest value is 0.9901, which corresponds to a z value of 2.33. We calculate the safety stock and reorder point as follows:

$$\text{Safety stock} = z\sigma_{dLT} = (2.33)(283.06) = 659.53, \text{ or } 660 \text{ bars}$$
$$\text{Reorder point} = \bar{d}\bar{L} + \text{Safety stock} = (275)(5) + 600 = 2{,}035 \text{ bars}$$

c. The total annual cost for the Q system is

$$C = \frac{Q}{2}(H) + \frac{D}{Q}(S) + (H)(\text{Safety stock})$$

$$= \frac{2{,}587}{2}(\$0.30) + \frac{100{,}375}{2{,}587}(\$10) + (\$0.30)(660) = \$974.05$$

Discussion Questions

1. What is the relationship between inventory and the nine competitive priorities we discussed in Chapter 1, "Using Operations to Create Value"? Suppose that two competing manufacturers, Company H and Company L, are similar except that Company H has much higher investments in raw materials, work-in-process, and finished goods inventory than Company L. In which of the nine competitive priorities will Company H have an advantage?

2. Suppose that a large discount retailer with a lot of purchasing power in a supply chain requires that all suppliers incorporate a new information system that will reduce the cost of placing orders between the retailer and its suppliers as well as between the suppliers and their suppliers. Suppose also that order quantities and lead times are related; the smaller the order quantity the shorter the lead time from suppliers. Assume that all members of the supply chain use a continuous review system and EOQ order quantities. Explain the implications of the new information system for the supply chain in general and the inventory systems of the supply chain members in particular.

3. Will organizations ever get to the point where they will no longer need inventories? Why or why not?

Problems

The OM Explorer and POM for Windows software is available to all students using the 11th edition of this textbook. Go to **http://www.pearsonhighered.com/krajewski** to download these computer packages. If you purchased MyOMLab, you also have access to Active Models software and significant help in doing the following problems. Check with your instructor on how best to use these resources. In many cases, the instructor wants you to understand how to do the calculations by hand. At the least, the software provides a check on your calculations. When calculations are particularly complex and the goal is interpreting the results in making decisions, the software replaces entirely the manual calculations.

Types of Inventory

1. A part is produced in lots of 1,000 units. It is assembled from 2 components worth $50 total. The value added in production (for labor and variable overhead) is $60 per unit, bringing total costs per completed unit to $110. The average lead time for the part is 6 weeks and annual demand is 3,800 units, based on 50 business weeks per year.

   a. How many units of the part are held, on average, in cycle inventory? What is the dollar value of this inventory?

   b. How many units of the part are held, on average, in pipeline inventory? What is the dollar value of this inventory? (*Hint:* Assume that the typical part in pipeline inventory is 50 percent completed. Thus, half the labor and variable overhead cost has been added, bringing the unit cost to $80, or $50 + $60/2).

2. Prince Electronics, a manufacturer of consumer electronic goods, has five distribution centers in different regions of the country. For one of its products, a high-speed modem priced at $350 per unit, the average weekly demand at *each* distribution center is 75 units. Average shipment size to each distribution center is 400 units, and average lead time for delivery is 2 weeks. Each distribution center carries 2 weeks' supply as safety stock but holds no anticipation inventory.

   a. On average, how many dollars of pipeline inventory will be in transit to each distribution center?

   b. How much total inventory (cycle, safety, and pipeline) does Prince hold for all five distribution centers?

3. Terminator, Inc., manufactures a motorcycle part in lots of 250 units. The raw materials cost for the part is $150, and the value added in manufacturing 1 unit from its components is $300, for a total cost per completed unit of $450. The lead time to make the part is 3 weeks, and the annual demand is 4,000 units. Assume 50 working weeks per year.

   a. How many units of the part are held, on average, as cycle inventory? What is its value?

   b. How many units of the part are held, on average, as pipeline inventory? What is its value?

Inventory Reduction Tactics

4. Ruby-Star Incorporated is considering two different vendors for one of its top-selling products which has an average weekly demand of 50 units and is valued at $75 per unit. Inbound shipments from vendor 1 will average 350 units with an average lead time (including ordering delays and transit time) of 2 weeks. Inbound shipments from vendor 2 will average 500 units with an average lead time of 1 week. Ruby-Star operates 52 weeks per year; it carries a 2-week supply of inventory as safety stock and no anticipation inventory.

   a. What would be the average aggregate inventory value of this product if Ruby-Star used vendor 1 exclusively?

   b. What would be the average aggregate inventory value of this product if Ruby-Star used vendor 2 exclusively?

   c. How would your analysis change if average weekly demand increased to 100 units per week?

5. Haley Photocopying purchases paper from an out-of-state vendor. Average weekly demand for paper is 150 cartons per week for which Haley pays $15 per carton. Inbound shipments from the vendor average 1000 cartons with an average lead time of 3 weeks. Haley operates 52 weeks per year; it carries a 4-week supply of inventory as safety stock and no anticipation inventory. The vendor has recently announced that they will be building a facility near Haley Photocopying that will reduce lead time to one week. Further, they will be able to reduce shipments to 200 cartons. Haley believes that they will be able to reduce safety stock to a 1-week supply. What impact will these changes make to Haley's average inventory level and its average aggregate inventory value?

ABC Analysis

6. Oakwood Hospital is considering using ABC analysis to classify laboratory SKUs into three categories: those that will be delivered daily from their supplier (Class A items), those that will be controlled using a continuous review system (B items), and those that will be held in a two-bin system (C items). The following table shows the annual dollar usage for a sample of eight SKUs. Rank the SKUs, and assign them to their appropriate category.

SKU Code	Dollar Value	Annual Usage
1	$0.01	1,200
2	$0.03	120,000
3	$0.45	100
4	$1.00	44,000

SKU Code	Dollar Value	Annual Usage
5	$4.50	900
6	$0.90	350
7	$0.30	70,000
8	$1.50	200

7. Southern Markets, Inc., is considering the use of ABC analysis to focus on the most critical SKUs in its inventory. Currently, there are approximately 20,000 different SKUs with a total dollar usage of $10,000,000 per year.

   a. What would you expect to be the number of SKUs and the total annual dollar usage for A items, B items, and C items at Southern Markets, Inc.?

b. The following table provides a random sample of the unit values and annual demands of eight SKUs. Categorize these SKUs as A, B, and C items.

SKU Code	Unit Value	Demand (Units)
A104	$2.10	2,500
D205	$2.50	30
X104	$0.85	350
U404	$0.25	250
L205	$4.75	20
S104	$0.02	4,000
X205	$0.35	1,020
L104	$4.25	50

8. New Wave Shelving's Inventory Manager would like to start using an ABC inventory classification system. The following table shows the annual inventory usage of all the 19 component items that the company holds. Assign them to their appropriate category.

SKU #	Description	Quantity Used Per Year	Dollar Value Per Unit
a-1	Steel panel	500	$ 25.00
a-2	Steel bumper	750	$ 135.00
a-3	Steel clamp	3500	$ 5.00
a-4	Steel brace	200	$ 20.00
b-1	Copper coil	1250	$ 260.00
b-2	Copper panel	1250	$ 50.00
b-3	Copper brace 1	250	$ 75.00
b-4	Copper brace 2	150	$ 125.00
c-1	Rubber bumper	8500	$ 0.75
c-2	Rubber foot	6500	$ 0.75
c-3	Rubber seal 1	1500	$ 1.00
c-4	Rubber seal 2	3500	$ 1.00
c-5	Rubber seal 3	1200	$ 2.25
d-1	Plastic fastener kit	1500	$ 3.50
d-2	Plastic handle	2000	$ 0.75
d-3	Plastic panel	1000	$ 6.50
d-4	Plastic bumper	2000	$ 1.25
d-5	Plastic coil	450	$ 6.00
d-6	Plastic foot	6000	$ 0.25

Economic Order Quantity

9. Yellow Press, Inc., buys paper in 1,500-pound rolls for printing. Annual demand is 2,500 rolls. The cost per roll is $800, and the annual holding cost is 15 percent of the cost. Each order costs $50 to process.

   a. How many rolls should Yellow Press, Inc., order at a time?

   b. What is the time between orders?

10. Babble, Inc., buys 400 blank cassette tapes per month for use in producing foreign language courseware. The ordering cost is $12.50. Holding cost is $0.12 per cassette per year.

   a. How many tapes should Babble, Inc., order at a time?

   b. What is the time between orders?

11. At Dot Com, a large retailer of popular books, demand is constant at 32,000 books per year. The cost of placing an order to replenish stock is $10, and the annual cost of holding is $4 per book. Stock is received 5 working days after an order has been placed. No backordering is allowed. Assume 300 working days a year.

   a. What is Dot Com's optimal order quantity?

   b. What is the optimal number of orders per year?

   c. What is the optimal interval (in working days) between orders?

d. What is demand during the lead time?

e. What is the reorder point?

f. What is the inventory position immediately after an order has been placed?

12. Leaky Pipe, a local retailer of plumbing supplies, faces demand for one of its SKUs at a constant rate of 30,000 units per year. It costs Leaky Pipe $10 to process an order to replenish stock and $1 per unit per year to carry the item in stock. Stock is received 4 working days after an order is placed. No backordering is allowed. Assume 300 working days a year.

   a. What is Leaky Pipe's optimal order quantity?

   b. What is the optimal number of orders per year?

   c. What is the optimal interval (in working days) between orders?

   d. What is the demand during the lead time?

   e. What is the reorder point?

   f. What is the inventory position immediately after an order has been placed?

Continuous Review System

13. Sam's Cat Hotel operates 52 weeks per year, 6 days per week, and uses a continuous review inventory system. It purchases kitty litter for $11.70 per bag. The following information is available about these bags.

> Demand = 90 bags/week
>
> Order cost = $54/order
>
> Annual holding cost = 27 percent of cost
>
> Desired cycle-service level = 80 percent
>
> Lead time = 3 weeks (18 working days)
>
> Standard deviation of *weekly* demand = 15 bags

Current on-hand inventory is 320 bags, with no open orders or backorders.

a. What is the EOQ? What would be the average time between orders (in weeks)?

b. What should R be?

c. An inventory withdrawal of 10 bags was just made. Is it time to reorder?

d. The store currently uses a lot size of 500 bags (i.e., $Q = 500$). What is the annual holding cost of this policy? Annual ordering cost? Without calculating the EOQ, how can you conclude from these two calculations that the current lot size is too large?

e. What would be the annual cost saved by shifting from the 500-bag lot size to the EOQ?

14. Consider again the kitty litter ordering policy for Sam's Cat Hotel in Problem 13.

a. Suppose that the weekly demand forecast of 90 bags is incorrect and actual demand averages only 60 bags per week. How much higher will total costs be, owing to the distorted EOQ caused by this forecast error?

b. Suppose that actual demand is 60 bags but that ordering costs are cut to only $6 by using the Internet to automate order placing. However, the buyer does not tell anyone, and the EOQ is not adjusted to reflect this reduction in S. How much higher will total costs be, compared to what they could be if the EOQ were adjusted?

15. In a Q system, the demand rate for strawberry ice cream is normally distributed, with an average of 300 pints *per week*. The lead time is 9 weeks. The standard deviation of *weekly* demand is 15 pints.

a. What is the standard deviation of demand during the 9-week lead time?

b. What is the average demand during the 9-week lead time?

c. What reorder point results in a cycle-service level of 99 percent?

16. Petromax Enterprises uses a continuous review inventory control system for one of its SKUs. The following information is available on the item. The firm operates 50 weeks in a year.

> Demand = 50,000 units/year
>
> Ordering cost = $35/order
>
> Holding cost = $2/unit/year
>
> Average lead time = 3 weeks
>
> Standard deviation of weekly demand = 125 units

a. What is the economic order quantity for this item?

b. If Petromax wants to provide a 90 percent cycle-service level, what should be the safety stock and the reorder point?

17. In a continuous review inventory system, the lead time for door knobs is 5 weeks. The standard deviation of demand during the lead time is 85 units. The desired cycle-service level is 99 percent. The supplier of door knobs streamlined its operations and now quotes a one-week lead time. How much can safety stock be reduced without reducing the 99 percent cycle-service level?

18. In a two-bin inventory system, the demand for three-inch lag bolts during the 2-week lead time is normally distributed, with an average of 53 units per week. The standard deviation of weekly demand is 5 units.

a. What is the probability of demand exceeding the reorder point when the normal level in the second bin is set at 130 units?

b. What is the probability of demand exceeding the 130 units in the second bin if it takes 3 weeks to receive a replenishment order?

19. You are in charge of inventory control of a highly successful product retailed by your firm. Weekly demand for this item varies, with an average of 200 units and a standard deviation of 16 units. It is purchased from a wholesaler at a cost of $12.50 per unit. You are using a continuous review system to control this inventory. The supply lead time is 4 weeks. Placing an order costs $50, and the inventory carrying rate per year is 20 percent of the item's cost. Your firm operates 5 days per week, 50 weeks per year.

a. What is the optimal ordering quantity for this item?

b. How many units of the item should be maintained as safety stock for 99 percent protection against stockouts during an order cycle?

c. If supply lead time can be reduced to 2 weeks, what is the percent reduction in the number of units maintained as safety stock for the same 99 percent stockout protection?

d. If through appropriate sales promotions, the demand variability is reduced so that the standard deviation of weekly demand is 8 units instead of 16, what is the percent reduction (compared to that in part [b]) in the number of units maintained as safety stock for the same 99 percent stockout protection?

20. Your firm uses a continuous review system and operates 52 weeks per year. One of the SKUs has the following characteristics.

> Demand (D) = 20,000 units/year
>
> Ordering cost (S) = $40/order
>
> Holding cost (H) = $2/unit/year
>
> Lead time (L) = 2 weeks
>
> Cycle-service level = 95 percent

Demand is normally distributed, with a standard deviation of *weekly* demand of 100 units.

Current on-hand inventory is 1,040 units, with no scheduled receipts and no backorders.

a. Calculate the item's EOQ. What is the average time, in weeks, between orders?

b. Find the safety stock and reorder point that provide a 95 percent cycle-service level.

c. For these policies, what are the annual costs of (i) holding the cycle inventory and (ii) placing orders?

d. A withdrawal of 15 units just occurred. Is it time to reorder? If so, how much should be ordered?

21. A company begins a review of ordering policies for its continuous review system by checking the current policies for a sample of SKUs. Following are the characteristics of one item.

Demand (D) = 64 units/week (Assume 52 weeks per year)

Ordering or setup cost (S) = $50/order

Holding cost (H) = $13/unit/year

Lead time (L) = 2 weeks

Standard deviation of *weekly* demand = 12 units

Cycle-service level = 88 percent

a. What is the EOQ for this item?

b. What is the desired safety stock?

c. What is the reorder point?

d. What are the cost implications if the current policy for this item is Q = 200 and R = 180?

22. Osprey Sports stocks everything that a musky fisherman could want in the Great North Woods. A particular musky lure has been very popular with local fishermen as well as those who buy lures on the Internet from Osprey Sports. The cost to place orders with the supplier is $30/order; the demand averages 4 lures per day, with a standard deviation of 1 lure; and the inventory holding cost is $1.00/lure/year. The lead time from the supplier is 10 days, with a standard deviation of 3 days. It is important to maintain a 97 percent cycle-service level to properly balance service with inventory holding costs. Osprey Sports is open 350 days a year to allow the owners the opportunity to fish for muskies during the prime season. The owners want to use a continuous review inventory system for this item.

a. What order quantity should be used?

b. What reorder point should be used?

c. What is the total annual cost for this inventory system?

23. The Farmer's Wife is a country store specializing in knick-knacks suitable for a farm-house décor. One item experiencing a considerable buying frenzy is a miniature Holstein cow. Average weekly demand is 30 cows, with a standard deviation of 5 cows. The cost to place a replenishment order is $15 and the holding cost is $0.75/cow/year. The supplier, however, is in China. The lead time for new orders is 8 weeks, with a standard deviation of 2 weeks. The Farmer's Wife, which is open only 50 weeks a year, wants to develop a continuous review inventory system for this item with a cycle-service level of 90 percent.

a. Specify the continuous review system for the cows. Explain how it would work in practice.

b. What is the total annual cost for the system you developed?

24. **(D)** Muscle Bound is a chain of fitness stores located in many large shopping centers. Recently, an internal memo from the CEO to all operations personnel complained about the budget overruns at Muscle Bound's central warehouse. In particular, she said that inventories were too high and that the budget will be cut dramatically and proportionately equal for all items in stock. Consequently, warehouse management set up a pilot study to see what effect the budget cuts would have on customer service. They chose 5-pound barbells, which are a high volume SKU and consume considerable warehouse space. Daily demand for the barbells is 1,000 units, with a standard deviation of 150 units. Ordering costs are $40 per order. Holding costs are $2/unit/year. The supplier is located in the Philippines; consequently, the lead time is 35 days with a standard deviation of 5 days. Muscle Bound stores operate 313 days a year (no Sundays).

Suppose that the barbells are allocated a budget of $16,000 for total annual costs. If Muscle Bound uses a continuous review system for the barbells and cannot change the ordering costs and holding costs or the distributions of demand or lead time, what is the best cycle-service level management can expect from their system?

It may be helpful to review MyOMLab Supplement E, "Simulation," before working Problem 25.

25. **(D)** The Georgia Lighting Center stocks more than 3,000 lighting fixtures, including chandeliers, swags, wall lamps, and track lights. The store sells at retail, operates 6 days per week, and advertises itself as the "brightest spot in town." One expensive fixture is selling at an average rate of 5 units per day. The reorder policy is Q = 40 and R = 15. A new order is placed on the day the reorder point is reached. The lead time is 3 business days. For example, an order placed on Monday will be delivered on Thursday. Simulate the performance of this Q system for the next 3 weeks (18 work days). Any stockouts result in lost sales (rather than backorders). The beginning inventory is 19 units, and no receipts are scheduled. Table 9.2 simulates the first week of operation. Extend Table 9.2 to simulate operations for the next 2 weeks if demand for the next 12 business days is 7, 4, 2, 7, 3, 6, 10, 0, 5, 10, 4, and 7.

a. What is the average daily ending inventory over the 18 days? How many stockouts occurred?

b. Using the same beginning inventory and daily demand data, simulate the inventory performance of the same item assuming a Q = 30, R = 20 system is used. Calculate the average inventory level and number of stockouts and compare with part (a).

TABLE 9.2 | FIRST WEEK OF OPERATION

Workday	Beginning Inventory	Orders Received	Daily Demand	Ending Inventory	Inventory Position	Order Quantity
1. Monday	19	—	5	14	14	40
2. Tuesday	14	—	3	11	51	—
3. Wednesday	11	—	4	7	47	—
4. Thursday	7	40	1	46	46	—
5. Friday	46	—	10	36	36	—
6. Saturday	36	—	9	27	27	—

(D) = Difficult Problem

Periodic Review System

26. Nationwide Auto Parts uses a periodic review inventory control system for one of its stock items. The review interval is 6 weeks, and the lead time for receiving the materials ordered from its wholesaler is 3 weeks. Weekly demand is normally distributed, with a mean of 100 units and a standard deviation of 20 units.

  a. What is the average and the standard deviation of demand during the protection interval?

  b. What should be the target inventory level if the firm desires 97.5 percent stockout protection?

  c. If 350 units were in stock at the time of a periodic review, how many units should be ordered?

27. In a P system, the lead time for a box of weed-killer is 2 weeks and the review period is 1 week. Demand during the protection interval averages 218 boxes, with a standard deviation of 40 boxes.

  a. What is the cycle-service level when the target inventory is set at 300 boxes?

  b. In the fall season, demand for weed-killer decreases but also becomes more highly variable. Assume that during the fall season, demand during the protection interval is expected to decrease to 180 boxes, but with a standard deviation of 50 boxes. What would be the cycle-service level if management keeps the target inventory level set at 300 boxes?

28. Suppose that Sam's Cat Hotel in Problem 10 uses a P system instead of a Q system. The average daily demand is $\bar{d} = 90/6 = 15$ bags and the standard deviation of *daily* demand is $\sigma_d = \dfrac{\sigma_{week}}{\sqrt{6}} = (15/\sqrt{6}) = 6.124$ bags.

  a. What P (in working days) and T should be used to approximate the cost trade-offs of the EOQ?

  b. How much more safety stock is needed than with a Q system?

  c. It is time for the periodic review. How much kitty litter should be ordered?

29. Your firm uses a periodic review system for all SKUs classified, using ABC analysis, as B or C items. Further, it uses a continuous review system for all SKUs classified as A items. The demand for a specific SKU, currently classified as an A item, has been dropping. You have been asked to evaluate the impact of moving the item from continuous review to periodic review. Assume your firm operates 52 weeks per year; the item's current characteristics are:

  Demand $(D) = 15{,}080$ units/year

  Ordering cost $(S) = \$125.00$/order

  Holding cost $(H) = \$3.00$/unit/year

Lead time $(L) = 5$ weeks

Cycle-service level $= 95$ percent

Demand is normally distributed, with a standard deviation of weekly demand of 64 units.

  a. Calculate the item's EOQ.

  b. Use the EOQ to define the parameters of an appropriate continuous review and periodic review system for this item.

  c. Which system requires more safety stock and by how much?

30. Using the same information as in Problem 21, develop the best policies for a periodic review system.

  a. What value of P gives the same approximate number of orders per year as the EOQ? Round to the nearest week.

  b. What safety stock and target inventory level provide an 88 percent cycle-service level?

31. Wood County Hospital consumes 1,000 boxes of bandages per week. The price of bandages is \$35 per box, and the hospital operates 52 weeks per year. The cost of processing an order is \$15, and the cost of holding one box for a year is 15 percent of the value of the material.

  a. The hospital orders bandages in lot sizes of 900 boxes. What *extra* cost does the hospital incur, which it could save by using the EOQ method?

  b. Demand is normally distributed, with a standard deviation of weekly demand of 100 boxes. The lead time is 2 weeks. What safety stock is necessary if the hospital uses a continuous review system and a 97 percent cycle-service level is desired? What should be the reorder point?

  c. If the hospital uses a periodic review system, with $P = 2$ weeks, what should be the target inventory level, T?

32. A golf specialty wholesaler operates 50 weeks per year. Management is trying to determine an inventory policy for its 1-irons, which have the following characteristics:

  Demand $(D) = 2{,}000$ units/year

  Demand is normally distributed

  Standard deviation of *weekly* demand $= 3$ units

  Ordering cost $= \$40$/order

  Annual holding cost $(H) = \$5$/units

  Desired cycle-service level $= 90$ percent

  Lead time $(L) = 4$ weeks

  a. If the company uses a periodic review system, what should P and T be? Round P to the nearest week.

  b. If the company uses a continuous review system, what should R be?

Active Model Exercise

Active Model 9.1, "Economic Order Quantity," appears in MyOMLab. It allows you to evaluate the sensitivity of the EOQ and associated costs to changes in the demand and cost parameters.

QUESTIONS

1. What is the EOQ and what is the lowest total cost?

2. What is the annual cost of holding inventory at the EOQ and the annual cost of ordering inventory at the EOQ?

3. From the graph, what can you conclude about the relationship between the lowest total cost and the costs of ordering and holding inventory?

4. How much does the total cost increase if the store manager orders twice as many bird feeders as the EOQ? How much does the total cost increase if the store manager orders half as many bird feeders as the EOQ?

5. What happens to the EOQ and the total cost when demand is doubled? What happens to the EOQ and the total cost when unit price is doubled?

6. Scroll through the lower order cost values and describe the changes to the graph. What happens to the EOQ?

7. Comment on the sensitivity of the EOQ model to errors in demand or cost estimates.

Economic Order Quantity (EOQ) Model

[Reset Data]   [Questions]

Annual demand rate, D	936	◄ ►
Order cost, S	45	◄ ►
Holding cost percent	25%	◄ ►
Unit price, P	60	◄ ►

	Optimal	Other
Order quantity, Q*	75	390
Maximum inventory	75	390
Average Inventory	37	195
Num orders per year	12.49	2.40

	Optimal	Other
Annual holding cost	$ 562.05	$ 2,925.00
Annual ordering cost	$ 562.05	$108.00
Total	$1,124.10	$3,033.00

Difference	$1,908.90
% Difference	169.82%

Inventory: Cost vs Quantity

(graph: Cost ($) on vertical axis from 0 to 4000, Order Quantity (Q) on horizontal axis from 0 to 500)

Legend: — Order cost   — Holding cost   — Total cost   --- EOQ

Inventory Management at Crayola

Managing inventory at Crayola is a fine balancing act. With the back-to-school period driving 42% of company demand for crayons, markers, paints, modeling compounds and other products, production starts in February so enough finished goods are in the 800,000 square foot warehouse in time to supply 3,600 Walmarts, 1,400 Targets, and thousands of other retailers in the United States for the fall school supply rush.

Crayola must supply customers with nearly 1,500 products, which requires an average inventory investment of $110 million. Finished goods inventory, shown here, must be stored in advance of seasonal demand peaks, such as the back-to-school period, which accounts for 42 percent of annual demand.

This means demand forecasts for raw materials in the master production schedule must be developed months before any of the finished products move to those retail customers. Lead times range from 60 days for domestic raw materials sources to upwards of 90 days for finished goods from suppliers outside the United States. As production ramps up for the back-to-school season well before the first day of classes, Crayola plans inventory levels for the entire year so that production remains reasonably steady. While the back-to-school season represents the lion's share of annual sales, holiday sales account for 35% of revenues, and the rest comes from spring sales. Crayola has over 1,500 SKUs, with close to 225 top sellers, so accurate forecasts are essential.

Historical sales patterns as well as orders generated by its U.S. sales divisions located in Easton, Pennsylvania (headquarters), Bentonville, Arkansas (near Walmart's headquarters), and Minneapolis (near Target's headquarters) help managers attain the accuracy needed. Marketing co-branding for the latest movies and comic books plays a role in creating the forecast for new SKUs and bundles, which must be coordinated to hit retailers the same time the movies and comics debut or the company risks missing the market and ending up with inventory that can't easily be sold.

Crayola's inventory holding costs run about 25%, and its average inventory value is $110 million. The company must assure there is warehouse space for finished goods as well as raw materials used in production. Pigments, clays, and packaging materials are moved from the warehouse and positioned close to the production lines, using a Kanban system to pull raw materials inventory as needed. Rail tanker cars from Louisiana and Pennsylvania carrying paraffin wax are delivered twice a week for crayon production. Since the rail cars feed directly into production, any disruption in delivery has the potential for shutting down production. Bad weather is a particular risk in this part of the company's supply chain since it can prevent the transport of goods during hurricanes or snowstorms.

Crayola attempts to source as many raw materials from domestic sources as possible. Cartons, clay, ink, labels and corrugated boxes come from the mid-Atlantic region of the United States, while those plastic components Crayola does not manufacture on site, such as nibs for markers, are sourced from Asia and can take up to 120 days to ship through the Panama Canal to the Port of Newark. Materials used in kits and bundles come from Korea, China, Vietnam and Brazil, and face similar shipping logistics.

When considering work-in-process inventories at Crayola, paints, markers, modeling clays, and many of the crayons coming off the production line are boxed into trays for use downstream in creating kits and bundles. These items are considered work-in-process items, even though the individual units are finished goods (i.e., a crayon or marker is completely manufactured once it comes off the line). The same is true for marker barrels, paint pots and other plastics. Specialized equipment is used to make these items which feed downstream production.

Recently, Crayola's leadership expected that actual demand for its popular Marker Maker© toy product might come in higher than the original forecast.

As a countermeasure, Crayola established duplicate capacities in China and the U.S. to meet the aggregate potential demand. In China, the company produced the original forecast and delivered to customers as planned. However, when the actual demand was 26% over the original forecast, Crayola could meet the surge in demand because it had positioned the long lead time ink bottles in its Pennsylvania plants and was able to mold the plastic parts using marker components from its core marker product. By utilizing existing machine capacity in its plants, reducing the lead time of ink bottles by making them in Pennsylvania, and by duplicating tooling, Crayola was able to ensure that its customers and consumers were satisfied during the holiday season.

QUESTIONS

1. Consider the pressures for small vs. large inventories. Which situation does Crayola seem to fit, and why?

2. Explain how both independent and dependent demand items are present at Crayola.

3. The Marker Maker© product recently experienced an unexpected surge in demand and the supply chain's agility was credited with helping to meet the crisis. We have discussed four ways to classify operational inventories by how they are created. Regarding the ways managers can use these inventories to satisfy demand, explain how Crayola can achieve the flexibility to adjust to unexpected demand surges.

EXPERIENTIAL LEARNING   Swift Electronic Supply, Inc.

It was a typical fall afternoon in Southern California, with thousands of tourists headed to the beaches to have fun. About 40 miles away, however, Steven Holland, the CEO of Swift Electronic Supply, Inc., faced a severe problem with Swift's inventory management.

An Intel veteran, Steven Holland worked in the electronic components distribution industry for more than 20 years. Seven years ago, he founded Swift Electronic Supply, Inc., an electronic distributor. After several successful years, the company is now troubled with eroding profit margins. Recent economic downturns further worsened the situation. Factors such as the growth of B2B e-commerce, the globalization of markets, the increased popularity of value-added services, and ongoing consolidations among electronic distributors affect the future of Swift.

To reverse these influences, Holland talked to a prestigious local university. After consultation, Holland found the most effective way to increase profitability is to cut inventory costs. As a starting point, he studied in detail a representative product, dynamic random access memory (DRAM), as the basis for his plan.

Industry and Company Preview

Owing to a boom in the telecommunications industry and the information technology revolution, electronics distributors experienced double-digit annual growth over the last decade. To cut the cost of direct purchasing forces, large component manufacturers such as Intel, Cisco, and Texas Instruments decided to outsource their procurement so that they could focus on product development and manufacturing. Therefore, independent electronic distributors like Swift started offering procurement services to these companies.

Swift serves component manufacturers in California and Arizona. Working as the intermediary between its customers and overseas original equipment manufacturers (OEMs), Swift's business model is quite simple. Forecasting customer demand, Swift places orders to a number of OEMs, stocks those products, breaks the quantities down, and delivers the products to its end customers.

Recently, due to more intense competition and declines in demand, Swift offered more flexible delivery schedules and was willing to accommodate small order quantities. However, customers can always shift to Swift's competitors should Swift not fulfill their orders. Steven Holland was in a dilemma: The intangible costs of losing customers can be enormous; however, maintaining high levels of inventory can also be costly.

Dram

Holland turned his attention to DRAM as a representative product. Previously, the company ordered a large amount every time it felt it was necessary. Holland's assistant developed a table (Table 9.3) that has 2 months of demand history. From Holland's experience, the demand for DRAM is relatively stable in the company's product line and it had no sales seasonality. The sales staff agrees that conditions in the current year will not be different from those of past years, and historical demand will be a good indicator of what to expect in the future.

The primary manufacturers of DRAM are those in Southeast Asia. Currently, Swift can purchase one unit of 128M DRAM for $10. After negotiation with a reputable supplier, Holland managed to sign a long-term agreement, which kept the price at $10 and allowed Swift to place orders at any time. The supplier also supplies other items in Swift's inventory. In addition, it takes the supplier of the DRAM 2 days to deliver the goods to Swift's warehouse using air carriers.

When Swift does not have enough inventory to fill a customer's order, the sales are lost; that is, Swift is not able to backorder the shortage because its customers fill their requirements through competitors. The customers will accept partial shipments, however.

It costs Swift $200 to place an order with the suppliers. This amount covers the corresponding internal ordering costs and the costs of delivering the products to the company. Holland estimates that the cost of lost sales amounts to $2 per unit of DRAM. This rough estimate includes the loss of profits, as well as the intangible damage to customer goodwill.

To simplify its inventory management system, Swift has a policy of maintaining a cycle-service level of 95 percent. The holding cost per day per unit is estimated to be 0.5 percent of the cost of goods, regardless of the product. Inventory holding costs are calculated on the basis of the ending inventory each day. The current balance is 1,700 units of DRAM in stock.

The daily purchasing routine is as follows. Orders are placed at the *beginning* of the day, before Swift is open for customer business. The orders arrive at the beginning of the day, 2 days later, and can be used for sales that day. For example, an order placed at the beginning of day 1 will arrive at Swift before Swift is open for business on day 3. The actual daily demand is always recorded at the *end* of the day, after Swift has closed for customer business. All cost computations are done at the end of the day after the total demand has been recorded.

TABLE 9.3 | HISTORICAL DEMAND DATA FOR THE DRAM (UNITS)

Day	Demand	Day	Demand	Day	Demand
1	869	21	663	41	959
2	902	22	1,146	42	703
3	1,109	23	1,016	43	823
4	947	24	1,166	44	862
5	968	25	829	45	966
6	917	26	723	46	1,042
7	1,069	27	749	47	889
8	1,086	28	766	48	1,002
9	1,066	29	996	49	763
10	929	30	1,122	50	932
11	1,022	31	962	51	1,052
12	959	32	829	52	1,062
13	756	33	862	53	989
14	882	34	793	54	1,029
15	829	35	1,039	55	823
16	726	36	1,009	56	942
17	666	37	979	57	986
18	879	38	976	58	736
19	1,086	39	856	59	1,009
20	992	40	1,036	60	852

Simulation

Holland believes that simulation is a useful approach to assess various inventory control alternatives. The historical data from Table 9.3 could be used to develop attractive inventory policies. The table was developed to record various costs and evaluate different alternatives. An example showing some recent DRAM inventory decisions is shown in Table 9.4.

1. Design a new inventory system for Swift Electronic Supply, Inc., using the data provided.

2. Provide the rationale for your system, which should include the decision rules you would follow to determine how much to order and when.

3. Simulate the use of your inventory system and record the costs. Develop a table such as Table 9.4 to record your results. Your instructor will provide actual demands on a day-to-day basis during the simulation.

TABLE 9.4 | EXAMPLE SIMULATION

Day	1	2	3	4	5	6	7	8	9	10
Beginning inventory position	1,700	831	1,500	391	3,000	3,232	2,315			
Number ordered	1,500		3,000	1,200			1,900			
Daily demand	869	902	1,109	947	968	917	1,069			
Day-ending inventory	831	−71	391	−556	2,032	2,315	1,246			
Ordering costs ($200 per order)	200		200	200			200			
Holding costs ($0.05 per piece per day)	41.55	0.00	19.55	0.00	101.60	115.75	62.30			
Shortage costs ($2 per piece)	0	142	0	1,112	0	0	0			
Total cost for day	241.55	142.00	219.55	1,312.00	101.60	115.75	262.30			
Cumulative cost from last day	0.00	241.55	383.55	603.10	1,915.10	2,016.70	2,132.45			
Cumulative costs to date	241.55	383.55	603.10	1,915.10	2,016.70	2,132.45	2,394.75			

CASE | Parts Emporium

Parts Emporium, Inc., is a wholesale distributor of automobile parts formed by two disenchanted auto mechanics, Dan Block and Ed Spriggs. Originally located in Block's garage, the firm showed slow but steady growth for 7 years before it relocated to an old, abandoned meat-packing warehouse on Chicago's South Side. With increased space for inventory storage, the company was able to begin offering an expanded line of auto parts. This increased selection, combined with the trend toward longer car ownership, led to an explosive growth of the business. Fifteen years later, Parts Emporium was the largest independent distributor of auto parts in the north central region.

Recently, Parts Emporium relocated to a sparkling new office and warehouse complex off Interstate 55 in suburban Chicago. The warehouse space alone occupied more than 100,000 square feet. Although only a handful of new products have been added since the warehouse was constructed, its utilization increased from 65 percent to more than 90 percent of capacity. During this same period, however, sales growth stagnated. These conditions motivated Block and Spriggs to hire the first manager from outside the company in the firm's history.

It is June 6, Sue McCaskey's first day in the newly created position of materials manager for Parts Emporium. A recent graduate of a prominent business school, McCaskey is eagerly awaiting her first real-world problem. At approximately 8:30 A.M., it arrives in the form of status reports on inventory and orders shipped. At the top of an extensive computer printout is a handwritten note from Joe Donnell, the purchasing manager: "Attached you will find the inventory and customer service performance data. Rest assured that the individual inventory levels are accurate because we took a complete physical inventory count at the end of last week. Unfortunately, we do not keep compiled records in some of the areas as you requested. However, you are welcome to do so yourself. Welcome aboard!"

A little upset that aggregate information is not available, McCaskey decides to randomly select a small sample of approximately 100 items and compile inventory and customer service characteristics to get a feel for the "total picture." The results of this experiment reveal to her why Parts Emporium decided to create the position she now fills. It seems that the inventory is in all the wrong places. Although an *average* of approximately 60 days of inventory

is on hand, the firm's customer service is inadequate. Parts Emporium tries to backorder the customer orders not immediately filled from stock, but some 10 percent of demand is being lost to competing distributorships. Because stockouts are costly, relative to inventory holding costs, McCaskey believes that a cycle-service level of at least 95 percent should be achieved.

McCaskey knows that although her influence to initiate changes will be limited, she must produce positive results immediately. Thus, she decides to concentrate on two products from the extensive product line: the EG151 exhaust gasket and the DB032 drive belt. If she can demonstrate significant gains from proper inventory management for just two products, perhaps Block and Spriggs will give her the backing needed to change the total inventory management system.

The EG151 exhaust gasket is purchased from an overseas supplier, Haipei, Inc. Actual demand for the first 21 weeks of this year is shown in the following table:

Week	Actual Demand	Week	Actual Demand
1	104	12	97
2	103	13	99
3	107	14	102
4	105	15	99
5	102	16	103
6	102	17	101
7	101	18	101
8	104	19	104
9	100	20	108
10	100	21	97
11	103		

A quick review of past orders, shown in another document, indicates that a lot size of 150 units is being used and that the lead time from Haipei is fairly constant at 2 weeks. Currently, at the end of week 21, no inventory is on hand, 11 units are backordered, and the company is awaiting a scheduled receipt of 150 units.

The DB032 drive belt is purchased from the Bendox Corporation of Grand Rapids, Michigan. Actual demand so far this year is shown in the following table:

Week	Actual Demand	Week	Actual Demand
11	18	17	50
12	33	18	53
13	53	19	54
14	54	20	49
15	51	21	52
16	53		

Because this product is new, data are available only since its introduction in week 11. Currently, 324 units are on hand, with no backorders and no scheduled receipts. A lot size of 1,000 units is being used, with the lead time fairly constant at 3 weeks.

The wholesale prices that Parts Emporium charges its customers are $12.99 for the EG151 exhaust gasket and $8.89 for the DB032 drive belt. Because no quantity discounts are offered on these two highly profitable items, gross margins based on current purchasing practices are 32 percent of the wholesale price for the exhaust gasket and 48 percent of the wholesale price for the drive belt.

Parts Emporium estimates its cost to hold inventory at 21 percent of its inventory investment. This percentage recognizes the opportunity cost of tying money up in inventory and the variable costs of taxes, insurance, and shrinkage. The annual report notes other warehousing expenditures for utilities and maintenance and debt service on the 100,000-square-foot warehouse, which was built for $1.5 million. However, McCaskey reasons that these warehousing costs can be ignored because they will not change for the range of inventory policies that she is considering.

Out-of-pocket costs for Parts Emporium to place an order with suppliers are estimated to be $20 per order for exhaust gaskets and $10 per order for drive belts. On the outbound side, the company can charge a delivery fee. Although most customers pick up their parts at Parts Emporium, some orders are delivered to customers. To provide this service, Parts Emporium contracts with a local company for a flat fee of $21.40 per order, which is added to the customer's bill. McCaskey is unsure whether to increase the ordering costs for Parts Emporium to include delivery charges.

QUESTIONS

1. Put yourself in Sue McCaskey's position and prepare a detailed report to Dan Block and Ed Spriggs on managing the inventory of the EG151 exhaust gasket and the DB032 drive belt. Be sure to present a proper inventory system and recognize all relevant costs.

2. By how much do your recommendations for these two items reduce annual cycle inventory, stockout, and ordering costs?

SPECIAL INVENTORY MODELS

Many real world problems require relaxation of certain assumptions on which the economic order quantity (EOQ) model is based. This supplement addresses three realistic situations that require going beyond the simple EOQ formulation.

1. Noninstantaneous Replenishment. Particularly in situations in which manufacturers use a continuous process to make a primary material, such as a liquid, gas, or powder, production is not instantaneous. Thus, inventory is replenished gradually, rather than in lots.

2. Quantity Discounts. Three annual costs are (1) the inventory holding cost, (2) the fixed cost for ordering and setup, and (3) the cost of materials. For service providers and for manufacturers alike, the unit cost of purchased materials sometimes depends on the order quantity.

3. One-Period Decisions. Retailers and manufacturers of fashion goods often face a situation in which demand is uncertain and occurs during just one period or season.

This supplement assumes you have read Chapter 9, "Inventory Management," and Supplement A, "Decision Making."

LEARNING GOALS *After reading this supplement, you should be able to:*

① Calculate the optimal lot size when replenishment is not instantaneous.

② Determine the optimal order quantity when materials are subject to quantity discounts.

③ Calculate the order quantity that maximizes the expected profits for a one-period inventory decision.

Noninstantaneous Replenishment

If an item is being produced internally rather than purchased, finished units may be used or sold as soon as they are completed, without waiting until a full lot is completed. For example, a restaurant that bakes its own dinner rolls begins to use some of the rolls from the first pan even before the baker finishes a five-pan batch. The inventory of rolls never reaches the full five-pan level, the way it would if the rolls all arrived at once on a truck sent by a supplier.

Figure C.1 depicts the usual case, in which the production rate, p, *exceeds* the demand rate, d. If demand and production were equal, manufacturing would be continuous with no buildup of cycle inventory. If the production rate is lower than the demand rate, sales opportunities are being missed on an ongoing basis. We assume that $p > d$ in this supplement.

FIGURE C.1 ▶
Lot Sizing with Noninstantaneous
Replenishment

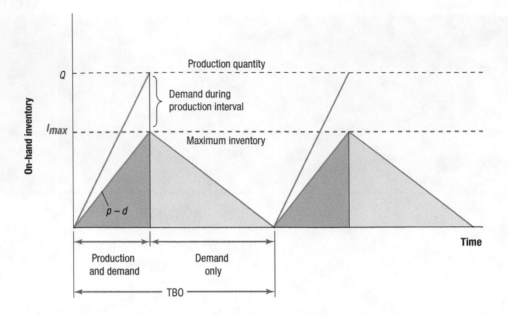

This chemical plant stores its products in stainless steel silos. The production of each product is scheduled to start when its silo is nearly empty.

Cycle inventory accumulates faster than demand occurs; that is, a buildup of $p - d$ units occurs per time period. For example, if the production rate is 100 units per day and the demand is 5 units per day, the buildup is 95 (or $100 - 5$) units each day. This buildup continues until the lot size, Q, has been produced, after which the inventory depletes at a rate of 5 units per day. Just as the inventory reaches 0, the next production interval begins. To be consistent, both p and d must be expressed in units of the same time period, such as units per day or units per week. Here, we assume that they are expressed in units per day.

The $p - d$ buildup continues for Q/p days because Q is the lot size and p units are produced each day. In our example, if the lot size is 300 units, the production interval is 3 days (300/100). For the given rate of buildup over the production interval, the maximum cycle inventory, I_{max}, is

$$I_{max} = \frac{Q}{p}(p - d) = Q\left(\frac{p - d}{p}\right)$$

Cycle inventory is no longer $Q/2$, as it was with the basic EOQ method; instead, it is $I_{max}/2$. Setting up the total annual cost equation for this production situation, where D is annual demand, and as before d is daily demand, we get

Total annual cost = Annual holding cost + Annual ordering or setup cost

$$C = \frac{I_{max}}{2}(H) + \frac{D}{Q}(S) = \frac{Q}{2}\left(\frac{p - d}{p}\right)(H) + \frac{D}{Q}(S)$$

economic production lot size (ELS)

The optimal lot size in a situation in which replenishment is not instantaneous.

Based on this cost function, the optimal lot size, often called the **economic production lot size (ELS)**, is

$$\text{ELS} = \sqrt{\frac{2DS}{H}}\sqrt{\frac{p}{p - d}}$$

Because the second term is a ratio greater than 1, the ELS results in a larger lot size than the EOQ.

EXAMPLE C.1	Finding the Economic Production Lot Size

A plant manager of a chemical plant must determine the lot size for a particular chemical that has a steady demand of 30 barrels per day. The production rate is 190 barrels per day, annual demand is 10,500 barrels, setup cost is $200, annual holding cost is $0.21 per barrel, and the plant operates 350 days per year.

a. Determine the economic production lot size (ELS).

b. Determine the total annual setup and inventory holding cost for this item.

c. Determine the time between orders (TBO), or cycle length, for the ELS.

d. Determine the production time per lot.

What are the advantages of reducing the setup time by 10 percent?

MyOMLab

Tutor C.1 in MyOMLab provides a new example to determine the ELS.

MyOMLab

Active Model C.1 in MyOMLab provides additional insight on the ELS model and its uses.

SOLUTION

a. Solving first for the ELS, we get

$$ELS = \sqrt{\frac{2DS}{H}}\sqrt{\frac{p}{p-d}} = \sqrt{\frac{2(10,500)(\$200)}{\$0.21}}\sqrt{\frac{190}{190-30}}$$

$$= 4,873.4 \text{ barrels}$$

b. The total annual cost with the ELS is

$$C = \frac{Q}{2}\left(\frac{p-d}{p}\right)(H) + \frac{D}{Q}(S)$$

$$= \frac{4,873.4}{2}\left(\frac{190-30}{190}\right)(\$0.21) + \frac{10,500}{4,873.4}(\$200)$$

$$= \$430.91 + \$430.91 = \$861.82$$

c. Applying the TBO formula to the ELS, we get

$$TBO_{ELS} = \frac{ELS}{D}(350 \text{ days/year}) = \frac{4,873.4}{10,500}(350)$$

$$= 162.4, \quad \text{or} \quad 162 \text{ days}$$

d. The production time during each cycle is the lot size divided by the production rate:

$$\frac{ELS}{p} = \frac{4,873.4}{190} = 25.6, \quad \text{or} \quad 26 \text{ days}$$

DECISION POINT

As OM Explorer shows in Figure C.2, the net effect of reducing the setup cost by 10 percent is to reduce the lot size, the time between orders, and the production cycle time. Consequently, total annual costs are also reduced. This adds flexibility to the manufacturing process because items can be made more quickly with less expense. Management must decide whether the added cost of improving the setup process is worth the added flexibility and inventory cost reductions.

Period Used in Calculations	Day ▼	
Demand per Day	30	
Production Rate/Day	190	
Annual Demand	10,500	
Setup Cost	$180	
Annual Holding Cost ($)	$0.21	● Enter Holding Cost Manually ○ Holding Cost As % of Value
Operating Days per Year	350	
Economic Lot Size (ELS)	4,623	
Annual Total Cost	$817.60	
Time Between Orders (days)	154.1	
Production Time	24.3	

◀ **FIGURE C.2**

OM Explorer Solver for the Economic Production Lot Size Showing the Effect of a 10 Percent Reduction in Setup Cost

Many hospitals join cooperatives (or co-ops) to gain the clout needed to garner price discounts from suppliers. Here a hospital pharmacist checks inventory records of supplies in preparation for placing an order.

Quantity Discounts

Quantity discounts, which are price incentives to purchase large quantities, create pressure to maintain a large inventory. For example, a supplier may offer a price of $4.00 per unit for orders between 1 and 99 units, a price of $3.50 per unit for orders between 100 and 199 units, and a price of $3.00 per unit for orders of 200 or more units. The item's price is no longer fixed, as assumed in the EOQ derivation; instead, if the order quantity is increased enough, the price is discounted. Hence, a new approach is needed to find the best lot size—one that balances the advantages of lower prices for purchased materials and fewer orders (which are benefits of large order quantities) against the disadvantage of the increased cost of holding more inventory.

The total annual cost now includes not only the holding cost, $(Q/2)(H)$, and the ordering cost, $(D/Q)(S)$, but also the cost of purchased materials. For any per-unit price level, P, the total cost is

$$\text{Total annual cost} = \text{Annual holding cost} + \text{Annual ordering or setup cost} + \text{Annual cost of materials}$$

$$C = \frac{Q}{2}(H) + \frac{D}{Q}(S) + PD$$

The unit holding cost, H, usually is expressed as a percent of the unit price because the more valuable the item held in inventory, the higher is the holding cost. Thus, the lower the unit price, P, the lower is H. Conversely, the higher P is, the higher is H.

The total cost equation yields U-shaped total cost curves. Adding the annual cost of materials to the total cost equation raises each total cost curve by a fixed amount, as shown in Figure C.3(a). The three cost curves illustrate each of the price levels. The top curve applies when no discounts are received; the lower curves reflect the discounted price levels. No single curve is relevant to all purchase quantities. The relevant, or feasible, total cost begins with the top curve, then drops down, curve by curve, at the price breaks. A price break is the minimum quantity needed to get a discount. In Figure C.3(a), two price breaks occur at $Q = 100$ and $Q = 200$. The result is a total cost curve, with steps at the price breaks.

▼ **FIGURE C.3**
Total Cost Curves with
Quantity Discounts

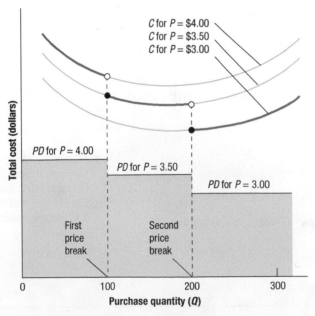

(a) Total cost curves with purchased materials added

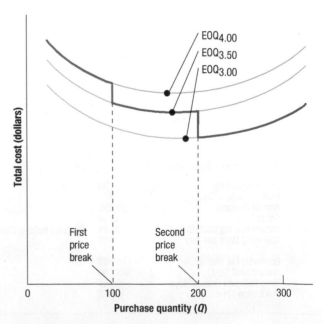

(b) EOQs and price break quantities

Figure C.3(b) also shows three additional points—the minimum point on each curve—obtained with the EOQ formula at each price level. These EOQs do not necessarily produce the best lot size for two reasons.

1. The EOQ at a particular price level may not be feasible. The lot size may not lie in the range corresponding to its per-unit price. Figure C.3(b) illustrates two instances of an infeasible EOQ. First, the minimum point for the $3.00 curve appears to be fewer than 200 units. However, the supplier's quantity discount schedule does not allow purchases of that small a quantity at the $3.00 unit price. Similarly, the EOQ for the $4.00 price level is greater than the first price break, so the price charged would be only $3.50.

2. The EOQ at a particular price level may be feasible but may not be the best lot size. The feasible EOQ may have a higher cost than is achieved by the EOQ or price break quantity on a lower price curve. In Figure C.3(b), for example, the 200-unit price break quantity for the $3.00 price level has a lower total cost than the feasible EOQ for the $3.50 price level. A feasible EOQ is always better than any feasible point on cost curves with higher price levels, but not necessarily those with lower levels. Thus, the only time we can immediately conclude, without comparing total costs, that a feasible EOQ is the best order quantity is when it is on the curve for the lowest price level. This conclusion is not possible in Figure C.3(b) because the only feasible EOQ is at the middle price level, $P = \$3.50$.

We must, therefore, pay attention only to feasible price–quantity combinations, shown as solid lines in Figure C.3(b), as we search for the best lot size. The following two-step procedure may be used to find the best lot size.

Step 1. Beginning with the lowest price, calculate the EOQ for each price level until a feasible EOQ is found. It is feasible if it lies in the range corresponding to its price. Each subsequent EOQ is smaller than the previous one because P, and thus H, gets larger and because the larger H is in the denominator of the EOQ formula.

Step 2. If the first feasible EOQ found is for the lowest price level, this quantity is the best lot size. Otherwise, calculate the total cost for the first feasible EOQ and for the larger price break quantity at each lower price level. The quantity with the lowest total cost is optimal.

EXAMPLE C.2	**Finding Q with Quantity Discounts at St. LeRoy Hospital**

A supplier for St. LeRoy Hospital has introduced quantity discounts to encourage larger order quantities of a special catheter. The price schedule is

Order Quantity	Price per Unit
0 to 299	$60.00
300 to 499	$58.80
500 or more	$57.00

The hospital estimates that its annual demand for this item is 936 units, its ordering cost is $45.00 per order, and its annual holding cost is 25 percent of the catheter's unit price. What quantity of this catheter should the hospital order to minimize total costs? Suppose the price for quantities between 300 and 499 is reduced to $58.00. Should the order quantity change?

SOLUTION

Step 1. Find the first feasible EOQ, starting with the lowest price level:

$$EOQ_{57.00} = \sqrt{\frac{2DS}{H}} = \sqrt{\frac{2(936)(\$45.00)}{0.25(\$57.00)}} = 77 \text{ units}$$

A 77-unit order actually costs $60.00 per unit, instead of the $57.00 per unit used in the EOQ calculation, so this EOQ is infeasible. Now, try the $58.80 level:

$$EOQ_{58.80} = \sqrt{\frac{2DS}{H}} = \sqrt{\frac{2(936)(\$45.00)}{0.25(\$58.80)}} = 76 \text{ units}$$

This quantity also is infeasible because a 76-unit order is too small to qualify for the $58.80 price. Try the highest price level:

$$EOQ_{60.00} = \sqrt{\frac{2DS}{H}} = \sqrt{\frac{2(936)(45.00)}{0.25(60.00)}} = 75 \text{ units}$$

This quantity is feasible because it lies in the range corresponding to its price, $P = \$60.00$.

Step 2. The first feasible EOQ of 75 does not correspond to the lowest price level. Hence, we must compare its total cost with the price break quantities (300 and 500 units) at the lower price levels ($58.80 and $57.00):

$$C = \frac{Q}{2}(H) + \frac{D}{Q}(S) + PD$$

$$C_{75} = \frac{75}{2}[(0.25)(\$60.00)] + \frac{936}{75}(\$45.00) + \$60.00(936) = \$57,284$$

$$C_{300} = \frac{300}{2}[(0.25)(\$58.80)] + \frac{936}{300}(\$45.00) + \$58.80(936) = \$57,382$$

$$C_{500} = \frac{500}{2}[(0.25)(\$57.00)] + \frac{936}{500}(\$45.00) + \$57.00(936) = \$56,999$$

The best purchase quantity is 500 units, which qualifies for the deepest discount.

DECISION POINT

If the price per unit for the range of 300 to 499 units is reduced to $58.00, the best decision is to order 300 catheters, as shown by OM Explorer in Figure C.4. This result shows that the decision is sensitive to the price schedule. A reduction of slightly more than 1 percent is enough to make the difference in this example. In general, however, it is not always the case that you should order more than the economic order quantity when given price discounts. When discounts are small, holding cost H is large, and demand D is small; small lot sizes are better even though price discounts are foregone.

FIGURE C.4 ▶

OM Explorer Solver for Quantity Discounts Showing the Best Order Quantity

	More	Fewer
Min. Amount Req'd for Price Point	Lot Sizes	Price/Unit
	0–299	$60.00
300	300–499	$58.00
500	500 or more	$57.00

Annual Demand	936
Order Cost	$45
Holding Cost (% or price)	25%

Best Order Quantity	300

Price Point	EOQ or Req'd Order for Price Point	Inventory Cost	Order Cost	Purchase Cost	Total Cost
$60.00	75	$562.50	$561.60	$56,160	$57,284
$58.00	300	$2,175	$140.40	$54,288	$56,603
$57.00	500	$3,563	$84.24	$53,352	$56,999

One-Period Decisions

One of the dilemmas facing many retailers is how to handle seasonal goods, such as winter coats. Often, they cannot be sold at full markup the next year because of changes in styles. Furthermore, the lead time can be longer than the selling season, allowing no second chance to rush through another order to cover unexpectedly high demand. A similar problem exists for manufacturers of other fashion goods.

This type of situation is often called the *newsboy problem*. If the newspaper seller does not buy enough newspapers to resell on the street corner, sales opportunities are lost. If the seller buys too many newspapers, the overage cannot be sold because nobody wants yesterday's newspaper.

The following process is a straightforward way to analyze such problems and decide on the best order quantity.

1. List the different levels of demand that are possible, along with the estimated probability of each.

2. Develop a *payoff* table that shows the profit for each purchase quantity, Q, at each assumed demand level, D. Each row in the table represents a different order quantity, and each column represents a different demand level. The payoff for a given quantity–demand combination depends on whether all units are sold at the regular profit margin during the regular season, which results in two possible cases.

    a. If demand is high enough ($Q \leq D$), then all units are sold at the full profit margin, p, during the regular season,

$$\text{Payoff} = (\text{Profit per unit})(\text{Purchase quantity}) = pQ$$

    b. If the purchase quantity exceeds the eventual demand ($Q > D$), only D units are sold at the full profit margin, and the remaining units purchased must be disposed of at a loss, l, after the season. In this case,

$$\text{Payoff} = \left(\begin{array}{c}\text{Profit per unit sold}\\\text{during season}\end{array}\right)(\text{Demand}) - \left(\begin{array}{c}\text{Loss per}\\\text{unit}\end{array}\right)\left(\begin{array}{c}\text{Amount disposed of}\\\text{after season}\end{array}\right)$$
$$= pD - l(Q - D)$$

3. Calculate the expected payoff for each Q (or row in the payoff table) by using the *expected value* decision rule. For a specific Q, first multiply each payoff in the row by the demand probability associated with the payoff, and then add these products.

4. Choose the order quantity Q with the highest expected payoff.

Using this decision process for all such items over many selling seasons will maximize profits. However, it is not foolproof, and it can result in an occasional bad outcome.

EXAMPLE C.3   Finding *Q* for One-Period Inventory Decisions

One of many items sold at a museum of natural history is a Christmas ornament carved from wood. The gift shop makes a $10 profit per unit sold during the season, but it takes a $5 loss per unit after the season is over. The following discrete probability distribution for the season's demand has been identified:

Demand	10	20	30	40	50
Demand Probability	0.2	0.3	0.3	0.1	0.1

How many ornaments should the museum's buyer order?

SOLUTION

Each demand level is a candidate for best order quantity, so the payoff table should have five rows. For the first row, where $Q = 10$, demand is at least as great as the purchase quantity. Thus, all five payoffs in this row are

$$\text{Payoff} = pQ = (\$10)(10) = \$100$$

This formula can be used in other rows but only for those quantity–demand combinations where all units are sold during the season. These combinations lie in the upper-right portion of the payoff table, where $Q \leq D$. For example, the payoff when $Q = 40$ and $D = 50$ is

$$\text{Payoff} = pQ = (\$10)(40) = \$400$$

The payoffs in the lower-left portion of the table represent quantity–demand combinations where some units must be disposed of after the season ($Q > D$). For this case, the payoff must be calculated with the second formula. For example, when $Q = 40$ and $D = 30$,

$$\text{Payoff} = pD = l(Q - D) = (\$10)(30) - (\$5)(40 - 30) = \$250$$

OM Explorer or POM for Windows can be used to analyze this problem. Using OM Explorer, we obtain the payoff table in Figure C.5.

MyOMLab
Tutor C.3 in MyOMLab provides a new example to practice the one-period inventory decision.

MyOMLab
Active Model C.3 in MyOMLab provides additional insight on the one-period inventory decision model and its uses.

▼ FIGURE C.5
OM Explorer Solver for One-Period Inventory Decisions Showing the Payoff Table

Profit	$10.00	(if sold during preferred period)
Loss	$5.00	(if sold after preferred period)

Enter the possible demands along with the probability of each occurring. Use the buttons to increase or decrease the number of allowable demand forecasts. NOTE: Be sure to enter demand forecasts and probabilities in all tinted cells, and be sure probabilities add up to 1.

<	>	

Demand	10	20	30	40	50
Profitability	0.2	0.3	0.3	0.1	0.1

Payoff Table

		Demand			
Quantity	10	20	30	40	50
10	100	100	100	100	100
20	50	200	200	200	200
30	0	150	300	300	300
40	−50	100	250	400	400
50	−100	50	200	350	500

Now we calculate the expected payoff for each Q by multiplying the payoff for each demand quantity by the probability of that demand and then adding the results. For example, for $Q = 30$,

$$\text{Payoff} = 0.2(\$0) + 0.3(\$150) + 0.3(\$300) + 0.1(\$300) + 0.1(\$300) = \$195$$

Using OM Explorer, Figure C.6 shows the expected payoffs.

DECISION POINT

Because $Q = 30$ has the highest payoff at $195, it is the best order quantity. Management can use OM Explorer or POM for Windows to do sensitivity analysis on the demands and their probabilities to see how confident they are with that decision.

FIGURE C.6 ▶
OM Explorer Solver Showing the Expected Payoffs for One-Period Inventory Decisions

Weighted Payoffs

Order Quantity	Expected Payoff
10	100
20	170
30	195
40	175
50	140

Greatest Expected Payoff   195

Associated with Order Quantity   30

The need for one-time inventory decisions also can arise in manufacturing plants when (1) customized items are made (or purchased) to a single order, and (2) scrap quantities are high. A customized item produced for a single order is never intentionally held in stock because the demand for it is too unpredictable. In fact, it may never be ordered again so the manufacturer would like to make just the amount requested by the customer—no more, no less. The manufacturer also would like to satisfy an order in just one run to avoid an extra setup and a delay in delivering goods ordered. These two goals may conflict if the likelihood of some units being scrapped is high. Suppose that a customer places an order for 20 units. If the manager orders 20 units from the shop or from the supplier, one or two units may have to be scrapped. This shortage will force the manager to place a second (or even third) order to replace the defective units. Replacement can be costly if setup time is high and can also delay shipment to the customer. To avoid such problems, the manager could order more than 20 units the first time. If some units are left over, the customer might be willing to buy the extras or the manager might find an internal use for them. For example, some manufacturing companies set up a special account for obsolete materials. These materials can be "bought" by departments within the company at less than their normal cost, as an incentive to use them.

LEARNING GOALS IN REVIEW

Learning Goal	Guidelines	MyOMLab Resources
❶ Calculate the optimal lot size when replenishment is not instantaneous.	See the section "Noninstantaneous Replenishment," pp. 359–361. Study Example C.1 and Solved Problem 1 for help on determining the ELS.	**Active Model:** C.1: Economic Production Lot Size **OM Explorer Solver:** Economic Production Lot size **OM Explorer Tutor:** C.1: Economic Production Lot Size **POM for Windows:** Economic Production Lot Size
❷ Determine the optimal order quantity when materials are subject to quantity discounts.	See the section "Quantity Discounts," pp. 362–364. Study Example C.2 and Solved Problem 2 for a step-by-step approach to determine the best order quantity.	**Active Model:** C.2: Quantity Discounts **OM Explorer Solver:** Quantity Discounts **OM Explorer Tutor:** C.2: Finding Q with Quantity Discounts **POM for Windows:** Quantity Discount Model
❸ Calculate the order quantity that maximizes the expected profits for a one-period inventory decision.	See the section "One-Period Decisions," pp. 364–366. Be sure to understand Example C.3 and Solved Problem 3.	**Active Model:** C.3: One-Time Inventory Decisions **OM Explorer Solver:** One-Period Inventory Decisions **OM Explorer Tutor:** C.3: One-Period Inventory Decisions **POM for Windows:** Decision Tables

Key Equations

Noninstantaneous Replenishment

1. Maximum cycle inventory: $I_{max} = Q\left(\dfrac{p-d}{p}\right)$

2. Total annual cost = Annual holding cost + Annual ordering or setup cost

$$C = \frac{Q}{2}\left(\frac{p-d}{p}\right)(H) + \frac{D}{Q}(S)$$

3. Economic production lot size: $\text{ELS} = \sqrt{\dfrac{2DS}{H}}\sqrt{\dfrac{p}{p-d}}$

4. Time between orders, expressed in years: $\text{TBO}_{\text{ELS}} = \dfrac{\text{ELS}}{D}$

Quantity Discounts

5. Total annual cost = Annual holding cost + Annual ordering or setup cost
   + Annual cost of material

$$C = \frac{Q}{2}(H) + \frac{D}{Q}(S) + PD$$

One-period Decisions

6. Payoff matrix: $\text{Payoff} = \begin{cases} pQ & \text{if } Q \leq D \\ pD - l(Q-D) & \text{if } Q > D \end{cases}$

Key Term

economic production lot size (ELS) 360

Solved Problem 1

Peachy Keen, Inc., makes mohair sweaters, blouses with Peter Pan collars, pedal pushers, poodle skirts, and other popular clothing styles of the 1950s. The average demand for mohair sweaters is 100 per week. Peachy's production facility has the capacity to sew 400 sweaters per week. Setup cost is $351. The value of finished goods inventory is $40 per sweater. The annual per-unit inventory holding cost is 20 percent of the item's value.

a. What is the economic production lot size (ELS)?
b. What is the average time between orders (TBO)?
c. What is the total of the annual holding cost and setup cost?

SOLUTION

a. The production lot size that minimizes total cost is

$$\text{ELS} = \sqrt{\frac{2DS}{H}}\sqrt{\frac{p}{p-d}} = \sqrt{\frac{2(100 \times 52)(\$351)}{0.20(\$40)}}\sqrt{\frac{400}{(400-100)}}$$

$$= \sqrt{456{,}300}\sqrt{\frac{4}{3}} = 780 \text{ sweaters}$$

b. The average time between orders is

$$\text{TBO}_{\text{ELS}} = \frac{\text{ELS}}{D} = \frac{780}{5{,}200} = 0.15 \text{ year}$$

Converting to weeks, we get

$$\text{TBO}_{\text{ELS}} = (0.15 \text{ year})(52 \text{ weeks/year}) = 7.8 \text{ weeks}$$

c.   The minimum total of setup and holding costs is

$$C = \frac{Q}{2}\left(\frac{p-d}{p}\right)(H) + \frac{D}{Q}(S) = \frac{780}{2}\left(\frac{400-100}{400}\right)(0.20 \times \$40) + \frac{5,200}{780}(\$351)$$

$$= \$2,340/\text{year} + \$2,340/\text{year} = \$4,680/\text{year}$$

Solved Problem 2

MyOMLab Video

A hospital buys disposable surgical packages from Pfisher, Inc. Pfisher's price schedule is $50.25 per package on orders of 1 to 199 packages and $49.00 per package on orders of 200 or more packages. Ordering cost is $64 per order, and annual holding cost is 20 percent of the per-unit purchase price. Annual demand is 490 packages. What is the best purchase quantity?

SOLUTION

We first calculate the EOQ at the *lowest* price:

$$EOQ_{49.00} = \sqrt{\frac{2DS}{H}} = \sqrt{\frac{2(490)(\$64.00)}{0.20(\$49.00)}} = \sqrt{6,400} = 80 \text{ packages}$$

This solution is infeasible because, according to the price schedule, we cannot purchase 80 packages at a price of $49.00 each. Therefore, we calculate the EOQ at the next lowest price ($50.25):

$$EOQ_{50.25} = \sqrt{\frac{2DS}{H}} = \sqrt{\frac{2(490)(\$64.00)}{0.20(\$50.25)}} = \sqrt{6,241} = 79 \text{ packages}$$

This EOQ is feasible, but $50.25 per package is not the lowest price. Hence, we have to determine whether total costs can be reduced by purchasing 200 units and thereby obtaining a quantity discount.

$$C = \frac{Q}{2}(H) + \frac{D}{Q}(S) + PD$$

$$C_{79} = \frac{79}{2}(0.20 \times \$50.25) + \frac{490}{79}(\$64.00) + \$50.25(490)$$

$$= \$396.98/\text{year} + \$396.68/\text{year} + \$24,622.50/\text{year} = 25,416.44/\text{year}$$

$$C_{200} = \frac{200}{2}(0.20 \times \$49.00) + \frac{490}{200}(\$64.00) + \$49.00(490)$$

$$= \$980.00/\text{year} + \$156.80/\text{year} + \$24,010.00/\text{year} = \$25,146.80/\text{year}$$

Purchasing 200 units per order will save $269.64/year, compared to buying 79 units at a time.

Solved Problem 3

Swell Productions is sponsoring an outdoor conclave for owners of collectible and classic Fords. The concession stand in the T-Bird area will sell clothing such as T-shirts and official Thunderbird racing jerseys. Jerseys are purchased from Columbia Products for $40 each and are sold during the event for $75 each. If any jerseys are left over, they can be returned to Columbia for a refund of $30 each. Jersey sales depend on the weather, attendance, and other variables. The following table shows the probability of various sales quantities. How many jerseys should Swell Productions order from Columbia for this one-time event?

Sales Quantity	Probability	Quantity Sales	Probability
100	0.05	400	0.34
200	0.11	500	0.11
300	0.34	600	0.05

SOLUTION

Table C.1 is the payoff table that describes this one-period inventory decision. The upper-right portion of the table shows the payoffs when the demand, D, is greater than or equal to the order quantity, Q. The payoff is equal to the per-unit profit (the difference between price and cost) multiplied by the order quantity. For example, when the order quantity is 100 and the demand is 200.

TABLE C.1 | PAYOFFS

			DEMAND, D				
Q	100	200	300	400	500	600	Expected Payoff
100	$3,500	$3,500	$ 3,500	$ 3,500	$ 3,500	$ 3,500	$ 3,500
200	$2,500	$7,000	$ 7,000	$ 7,000	$ 7,000	$ 7,000	$ 6,775
300	$1,500	$6,000	$10,500	$10,500	$10,500	$10,500	$ 9,555
400	$ 500	$5,000	$ 9,500	$14,000	$14,000	$14,000	$10,805
500	($ 500)	$4,000	$ 8,500	$13,000	$17,500	$17,500	$10,525
600	($1,500)	$3,000	$ 7,500	$12,000	$16,500	$21,000	$ 9,750

$$\text{Payoff} = (p - c)Q = (\$75 - \$40)100 = \$3,500$$

The lower-left portion of Table C.1 shows the payoffs when the order quantity exceeds the demand. Here the payoff is the profit from sales, pD, minus the loss associated with returning overstock, $l(Q - D)$, where l is the difference between the cost and the amount refunded for each jersey returned and $Q - D$ is the number of jerseys returned. For example, when the order quantity is 500 and the demand is 200,

$$\text{Payoff} = pD - l(Q - D) = (\$75 - \$40)200 - (\$40 - \$30)(500 - 200) = \$4,000$$

The highest expected payoff occurs when 400 jerseys are ordered:

$$\text{Expected payoff}_{400} = (\$500 \times 0.05) + (\$5,000 \times 0.11) + (\$9,500 \times 0.34)$$
$$+ (\$14,000 \times 0.34) + (\$14,000 \times 0.11) + (\$14,000 \times 0.05)$$
$$= \$10,805$$

Problems

The OM Explorer and POM for Windows software is available to all students using the 11th edition of this textbook. Go to **http://www.pearsonhighered.com/krajewski** to download these computer packages. If you purchased MyOMLab, you also have access to Active Models software and significant help in doing the following problems. Check with your instructor on how best to use these resources. In many cases, the instructor wants you to understand how to do the calculations by hand. At the least, the software provides a check on your calculations. When calculations are particularly complex and the goal is interpreting the results in making decisions, the software entirely replaces the manual calculations. The software also can be a valuable resource well after your course is completed.

Noninstantaneous Replenishment

1. Bold Vision, Inc., makes laser printer and photocopier toner cartridges. The demand rate is 625 EP cartridges per week. The production rate is 1,736 EP cartridges per week, and the setup cost is $100. The value of inventory is $130 per unit, and the holding cost is 20 percent of the inventory value. Bold Vision operates 52 weeks a year. What is the economic production lot size?

2. Sharpe Cutter is a small company that produces specialty knives for paper cutting machinery. The annual demand for a particular type of knife is 100,000 units. The demand is uniform over the 250 working days in a year. Sharpe Cutter produces this type of knife in lots and, on average, can produce 450 knives a day. The cost to set up a production lot is $300, and the annual holding cost is $1.20 per knife.

   a. Determine the economic production lot size (ELS).

   b. Determine the total annual setup and inventory holding cost for this item.

   c. Determine the TBO, or cycle length, for the ELS.

   d. Determine the production time per lot.

3. Suds's Bottling Company does bottling, labeling, and distribution work for several local microbreweries. The demand rate for Wortman's beer is 600 cases (24 bottles each) per week. Suds's bottling production rate is 2,400 cases per week, and the setup cost is $800. The value of inventory is $12.50 per case, and the annual holding cost is 30 percent of the inventory value. Suds's facilities operate 52 weeks each year. What is the economic production lot size?

4. One-Eyed Toad Pottery makes custom planters for up-scale clients. The average demand for planters is 20 per week. One-Eyed Toad's production facility has the capacity to make 25 planters per week. Setup cost is $1500. The value of finished goods inventory is $250 per planter. The annual per-unit inventory holding cost is 35 percent of the item's value.

   a. What is the economic production lot size (ELS)?

   b. What is the average time between orders (TBO)?

   c. What is the total of the annual holding cost and setup cost?

Quantity Discounts

5. The Bucks Grande exhibition baseball team plays 50 weeks each year and uses an average of 350 baseballs per week. The team orders baseballs from Coopers-Town, Inc., a ball manufacturer noted for six-sigma-level consistency and high product quality. The cost to order baseballs is $100 per order and the annual holding cost per ball is 38 percent of the purchase price. Coopers-Town's price structure is:

Order Quantity	Price per Unit
1–999	$7.50
1,000–4999	$7.25
5,000 or more	$6.50

a. How many baseballs should the team buy per order?

b. What is the total annual cost associated with the best order quantity?

c. Coopers-Town, Inc., discovers that, owing to special manufacturing processes required for the Buck's baseballs, it has underestimated the setup time required on a capacity-constrained piece of machinery. Coopers-Town adds another category to the price structure to provide an incentive for larger orders and thereby hopes to reduce the number of setups required. If the Bucks buy 15,000 baseballs or more, the price will drop to $6.25 each. Should the Bucks revise their order quantity?

6. To boost sales, Pfisher (refer to Solved Problem 2) announces a new price structure for disposable surgical packages. Although the price break no longer is available at 200 units, Pfisher now offers an even greater discount if larger quantities are purchased. On orders of 1 to 499 packages, the price is $50.25 per package. For orders of 500 or more, the price per unit is $47.80. Ordering costs, annual holding costs, and annual demand remain at $64 per order, 20 percent of the per-unit cost, and 490 packages per year, respectively. What is the new lot size?

7. The University Bookstore at a prestigious private university buys mechanical pencils from a wholesaler. The wholesaler offers discounts for large orders according to the following price schedule:

Order Quantity	Price per Unit
0 to 200	$4.00
201 to 2,000	$3.50
2,001 or more	$3.25

The bookstore expects an annual demand of 2,500 units. It costs $10 to place an order, and the annual cost of holding a unit in stock is 30 percent of the unit's price. Determine the best order quantity.

8. Mac-in-the-Box, Inc., sells computer equipment by mail and telephone order. Mac sells 1,200 flat-bed scanners per year. Ordering cost is $300, and annual holding cost is 16 percent of the item's price. The scanner manufacturer offers the following price structure to Mac-in-the-Box:

Order Quantity	Price per Unit
0 to 11	$520
12 to 143	$500
144 or more	$400

What order quantity minimizes total annual costs?

9. As inventory manager, you must decide on the order quantity for an item that has an annual demand of 2,000 units. Placing an order costs you $20 each time. Your annual holding cost, expressed as a percentage of average inventory value, is 20 percent. Your supplier has provided the following price schedule:

Minimum Order Quantity	Price per Unit
1	$2.50
200	$2.40
300	$2.25
1,000	$2.00

What ordering policy do you recommend?

10. Bold Vision, Inc. (from Problem 1), must purchase toner from a local supplier. The company does not wish to carry raw material inventory and therefore only purchases enough toner to satisfy the demand of each individual batch of cartridges. Each toner cartridge requires one pound of toner. The raw material supplier offers Bold Vision a purchase discount of $2.00 per pound if the company orders at least 2,000 pounds at a time. Should Bold Vision accept this offer and alter its toner purchase quantity?

One-Period Decisions

11. Downtown Health Clinic needs to order influenza vaccines for the next flu season. The Clinic charges its patients $15.00 per vaccination and each dose of vaccine costs the clinic $4.00 to purchase. The Center for Disease Control has a long standing policy of buying back unused vaccines for $1.00 per dose. The Clinic estimates the following probability distribution for the season's demand:

Demand	Probability
2,000	0.05
3,000	0.20
4,000	0.25
5,000	0.40
6,000	0.10

a. How many vaccines should the Clinic order to maximize its expected profit?

b. The Clinic is trying to determine if they should participate in a new Federal program in which the cost of each dose is reduced to $2.00. However, to participate in the program, they can charge no more than $10.00 per vaccine. On strictly a profit maximizing basis, should the Clinic agree to participate?

12. Dorothy's pastries are freshly baked and sold at several specialty shops throughout Perth. When they are a day old, they must be sold at reduced prices. Daily demand is distributed as follows:

Demand	Probability
50	0.25
150	0.50
200	0.25

Each pastry sells for $1.00 and costs $0.60 to make. Each one not sold at the end of the day can be sold the next day for $0.30 as day-old merchandise. How many pastries should be baked each day?

13. The Aggies will host Tech in this year's homecoming football game. Based on advance ticket sales, the athletic department has forecast hot dog sales as shown in the following table. The school buys premium hot dogs for $1.50 and sells them during the game at $3.00 each. Hot dogs left over after the game will be sold for $0.50 each to the Aggie student cafeteria, where they will be used in making hotdog casserole.

Sales Quantity	Probability
2,000	0.10
3,000	0.30
4,000	0.30
5,000	0.20
6,000	0.10

Use a payoff matrix to determine the number of hot dogs to buy for the game.

14. The Lake Sharkey BBQ Pit serves slow cooked beef brisket by the pound. Based on historical sales during the Labor Day weekend, management has forecasted brisket sales in pounds as shown in the following table. Lake Sharkey spends $14 to produce each pound of brisket for which it charges $23 per pound. Any unsold brisket at the end of the weekend is ground into chili which sells for $12 per pound. How many pounds of brisket should The Lake Sharkey BBQ Pit prepare for sale this Labor Day?

Demand in pounds	Probability
500	0.10
1000	0.40
1500	0.30
2000	0.15
2500	0.05

Ian Simpson/Alamy

10

OPERATIONS PLANNING AND SCHEDULING

In 1997 Cooper Tires purchased Avon Rubber PLC of Melksham, Wiltshire, in the United Kingdom. The Cooper facility in Melksham is a major employer in the region. Avon, heavily involved with Formula One racing since 1982, had been the sole supplier of tires for the British Formula Three Championship and, from 2009, its tires were re-branded "Cooper" as Cooper became the championship's sole sponsor. For its own part, Cooper became the official tire of the A1 Grand Prix for the initial season and was under contract to produce slick and treaded rain tires until 2008. It also became the official tire for two other championships: Champ Car Atlantic Championship and USF2000 National Championship. Cooper Tires remains a major source of racing tires worldwide.

Cooper Tire and Rubber Company

The Cooper Tire and Rubber Company is a $3.4 billion company with 13,000 employees worldwide. The company is the fourth-largest tire manufacturer in North America and the 11th largest globally. Rather than participating in both the original equipment and replacement tire markets as do its major competitors, Bridgestone, Goodyear Tire and Rubber, and Michelin, it focuses on producing and selling replacement tires for the passenger car, light truck, motorcycle, race car, commercial, and off-road vehicle markets worldwide. It has nine manufacturing facilities located in North America, Europe, and China and 40 distribution centers worldwide. Tires are distributed through independent dealers, regional retailers and wholesalers, and national retailers.

Cooper has three key strategic imperatives to guide operations: (1) Develop a competitive cost structure and improve profitability, (2) drive top-line profitable growth, and (3) build organizational capabilities. Indeed, while everything we have to offer in this text comes to bear in supporting these imperatives, let us see what Cooper has done regarding operations planning and scheduling, the topic of this chapter. We examine several press releases to gain insight into the nature of operations planning and scheduling at a large manufacturer.

October 1, 2008. Cooper Tire and Rubber Company announced it continues to adjust production schedules at its U.S. facilities primarily due to raw material shortages and soft demand in the North American market. This adjustment was largely due to the hurricanes, which hit the Gulf Coast. Raw materials were allocated to plants with critical customer demands and labor schedules were flexed at all plants while the raw materials shortages are allocated. By flexing work schedules Cooper attempted to avoid layoffs at any of the plants. The estimated impact of the production adjustments was $9 to $11 million.

October 5, 2009. Cooper Tire and Rubber Company announced plans to increase production capacity at its Texarkana, Arkansas, facility by changing to 24/7 operations and to add approximately 200 additional employees to meet a growing demand for its products. The shift in production took several months in 2010.

March 7, 2013. Cooper Tire and Rubber Company temporarily idled production at its Findlay, Ohio, plant due to high tire inventories and Cooper's implementation of a new software system. Cooper built the extra tires in 2012's fourth-quarter to offset any lost production in 2013. However, company officials said the expiration of tariffs on imported Chinese-made tires in the fall of 2012 resulted in higher-than-normal tire inventories, resulting in fewer orders. In its annual report, Cooper said that the tariff expiration was expected to affect sales and production in the first and possibly second quarter of 2013.

September 16, 2013. JDA Software Group and Cooper Tire and Rubber Company announced the implementation of JDA Production Scheduling—Discrete at its manufacturing facilities. With the size proliferation in original equipment tires, including the phasing out of 12-, 13-, and 14-inch tires and the increase in bigger tires and better designs, Cooper realized that the changes in designs and sizes would make it increasingly more difficult to meet the needs of its customers. Before the software change, the company operated with a manual, weekly planning cycle. The schedulers reviewed the demand data SKU by SKU to create a curing schedule for each plant. The curing process is a capacity-limited resource that controls the flow of tires in a plant. The scheduling process was time consuming and the data were not up to date by the time the schedule was completed. With the new software, the scheduling lead time was reduced by nine days; all of the plant constraints were automatically recognized, and inventory management was improved.

Cooper Tire's example shows us how employee hires, changes to workforce schedules, temporary use of undertime by idling a plant, and facility scheduling can be used to achieve its strategic initiatives.

Sources: http://coopertire.com/About-Us, 2014; http://coopertire.com/News/Corporate-News-Releases, (October 5, 2009); http://www.answers.com/topic/cooper-tire-rubber-company, 2014; http://www.bloomberg.com, (October 1, 2008); http://www.toledoblade.com, (March 7, 2013); JDA Software Group, "Case Study: Optimizing the Planning Schedule," (September 16, 2013).

LEARNING GOALS *After reading this chapter, you should be able to:*

1 Explain the rationale behind the levels in the operations planning and scheduling process.

2 Describe the supply options used in sales and operations planning.

3 Compare the chase planning strategy to the level planning strategy for developing sales and operations plans.

4 Use spreadsheets for sales and operations planning.

5 Develop workforce and workstation schedules.

Managing supply chains effectively requires more than just good demand forecasts or knowing how much to order and when. Demand is the first half of the equation, and the other half is supply. As Cooper Tires in the chapter opener has shown, the firm must develop plans to supply the resources needed to meet the forecasted demand. These resources include the workforce, materials, inventories, dollars, and equipment capacity.

Operations planning and scheduling is the process of making sure that demand and supply plans are in balance, from the aggregate level down to the short-term scheduling level. Operations planning and scheduling lies at the core of supply chain integration, around which plans are made up and down the supply chain, from supplier deliveries to customer due dates and services. Why is it so important? First, it requires managerial inputs from all of the firm's functions. Marketing provides inputs on demand and accounting provides important cost data and a firm's financial condition. Second, each function is affected by the plan. A plan that calls for expanding the workforce has a direct impact on the hiring and training requirements for the human resources function. As the plan is implemented, it creates revenue and cost streams that finance must deal with as it manages the firm's cash flows. Third, each department and group in a firm has its own workforce. Managers of these departments must make choices on hiring, overtime, and vacations. Finally, whether the business is an airline, hotel, computer manufacturer, or university, schedules are a part of everyday life. Schedules involve an enormous amount of detail and affect every process in a firm. For example, service, product, and employee schedules determine specific cash flow requirements, trigger the firm's billing process, and initiate requirements for the employee training process. Firms use the scheduling process to lower their costs and improve their responsiveness, affecting operations up and down the supply chain worldwide. Table 10.1 defines several types of plans related to operations planning and scheduling.

TABLE 10.1 | TYPES OF PLANS WITH OPERATIONS PLANNING AND SCHEDULING

Key Term	Definition
Sales and operations plan (S&OP)	A plan of future aggregate resource levels so that supply is in balance with demand. It states a company's or department's production rates, workforce levels, and inventory holdings that are consistent with demand forecasts and capacity constraints. The S&OP is time-phased, meaning that it is projected for several time periods (such as months or quarters) into the future.
Aggregate plan	Another term for the sales and operations plan.
Production plan	A sales and operations plan for a *manufacturing firm* that centers on production rates and inventory holdings.
Staffing plan	A sales and operations plan for a *service firm*, which centers on staffing and on other human resource-related factors.
Resource plan	An intermediate step in the planning process that lies between S&OP and scheduling. It determines requirements for materials and other resources on a more detailed level than the S&OP. It is covered in the next chapter.
Schedule	A detailed plan that allocates resources over shorter time horizons to accomplish specific tasks.

In this chapter, we begin by discussing the three levels of operations planning and scheduling: (1) sales and operations planning (S&OP), (2) resource planning, and (3) scheduling. We explain the purpose of aggregation in sales and operations planning and the various information inputs required for its development. We examine how S&OP relates with other plans and functional areas within the firm and describe the supply options and planning strategies for effective S&OP. We show how spreadsheets can help find good solutions. Then, we conclude with scheduling, including performance measures and some basic techniques for creating schedules. MyOMLab Supplement J, "Operations Scheduling," provides additional help with scheduling problems.

Levels in Operations Planning and Scheduling

Managers develop plans for their operations covering varying time spans, from the long term to the short term. These plans form a hierarchy: the long-term plans form an umbrella under which short-term plans exist. Sales and operations plans exist at Level 1 and represent the long-term operations plans. These plans form the basis for major outlays for materials and resources and consequently cannot be very specific regarding products or services. Resource plans exist at Level 2 and are more detailed than the sales and operations plans and cover a shorter term. The most detailed plans are the schedules in Level 3, which cover very short time horizons and relate to specific products and resources. Level 2 plans must be consistent with Level 1 plans, and Level 3 plans must be consistent with Level 2 plans.

MyOMLab

operations planning and scheduling

The process of balancing supply with demand, from the aggregate level down to the short-term scheduling level.

Level 1: Sales and Operations Planning

In this section, we explain why companies begin with plans that take a macro, or big-picture, view of their business. We also describe how these plans relate to their other plans and how the long-term plans ultimately are translated into detailed schedules ready for immediate action.

Aggregation   The sales and operations plan is useful because it focuses on a general course of action, consistent with the company's strategic goals and objectives, without getting bogged down in details. We must first aggregate, and then use the targets and resources from the plan to create effective, coordinated schedules. A company's managers must determine whether they can satisfy budgetary goals without having to schedule each of the company's thousands of products and employees individually. While schedules with such detail are the goal, the operations planning and scheduling process begins at the aggregate level.

In general, companies perform aggregation along three dimensions: (1) services or products, (2) workforce, and (3) time.

1. **Services or products** A group of customers, services, or products that have similar demand requirements and common process, workforce, and materials requirements is called a **product family**. Sometimes, product families relate to market groupings or to specific processes. A firm can aggregate its services or products into a set of relatively broad families, avoiding too much detail at this stage of the planning process. For instance, a manufacturer of bicycles that produces 12 different models of bikes might divide them into two groups, mountain bikes and road bikes, for the purpose of preparing the sales and operations plan. Common and relevant measurements should be used.

2. **Workforce** A company can aggregate its workforce in various ways as well, depending on its flexibility. For example, if workers at the bicycle manufacturer are trained to work on either mountain bikes or road bikes, for planning purposes management can consider its workforce to be a single aggregate group, even though the skills of individual workers may differ.

3. **Time** The planning horizon covered by a sales and operations plan typically is one year, although it can differ in various situations. To avoid the expense and disruptive effect of frequent changes in output rates and the workforce, adjustments usually are made monthly or quarterly. In other words, the company looks at time in the aggregate—months, quarters, or seasons—rather than in weeks, days, or hours.

Information Inputs   Just as it is needed to manage the demand side, consensus is needed among the firm's departments when decisions for the supply side are made. Information inputs are sought to create a sales and operations plan that works for all. Figure 10.1 lists inputs from each functional area. They must be accounted for to make sure that the plan is a good one and also doable. Such coordination helps synchronize the flow of services, materials, and information through the supply chain to best balance supply with customer demand.

product family

A group of services or products that have similar demand requirements and common process, labor, and materials requirements.

business plan

A projected statement of income, costs, and profits.

annual plan (or financial plan)

A plan for financial assessment used by a nonprofit service organization.

This plant is manufacturing bikes for Shinola, which makes three bike models along with other consumer goods such as watches and leather goods. The bikes would represent a product family for sales and operations planning purposes.

Jim West/Alamy

Related Plans   A financial assessment of the organization's near future—that is, for 1 or 2 years ahead—is called either a business plan (in for-profit firms) or an annual plan (in nonprofit service organizations). A **business plan** is a projected statement of income, costs, and profits. It usually is accompanied by budgets, a projected (pro forma) balance sheet, and a projected cash flow statement showing sources and allocations of funds. The business plan unifies the plans and expectations of a firm's operations, finance, sales, and marketing managers. In particular, it reflects plans for market penetration, new product introduction, and capital investment. Manufacturing firms and for-profit service organizations, such as a retail store, a firm of attorneys, or a hospital, prepare such plans. A nonprofit service organization, such as the United Way or a municipal government, prepares a different type of plan for financial assessment, called an **annual plan** or **financial plan**.

Figure 10.2 illustrates the relationships among the business or annual plan, constraint management, forecasting, operations strategy, sales and

◀ **FIGURE 10.1**
Managerial Inputs from
Functional Areas to Sales and
Operations Plans

operations plan, and the detailed plans and schedules derived from it. For *service providers* in the supply chain, top management sets the organization's direction and objectives in the business plan (in a for-profit organization) or annual plan (in a not-for-profit organization). This plan then provides the framework for developing the sales and operations plan, which typically focuses on staffing and other human resource–related factors at a more aggregate level. It presents the number and types of employees needed to meet the objectives of the business or annual plan. For *manufacturing firms* in the supply chain, top management sets the company's strategic objectives for at least the next year in the business plan. It provides the overall framework, along with inputs coming from operations strategy, forecasting, and capacity constraint management. The sales and operations plan specifies product family production rates, inventory levels, and workforce levels. Regardless of whether the firm is a service provider or a manufacturer, the sales and operations plan sets the stage for the two levels to follow.

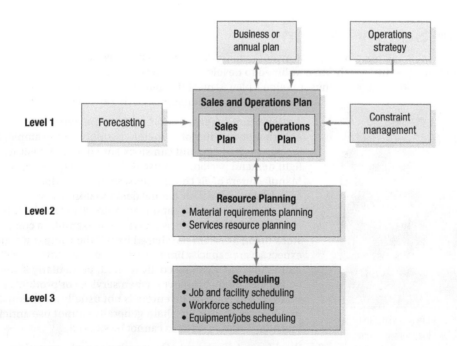

◀ **FIGURE 10.2**
The Relationship of Sales
and Operations Plans and
Schedules to Other Plans

MyOMLab Animation

Level 2: Resource Planning

The next planning level is *resource planning*, which is a process that takes sales and operations plans; processes time standards, routings, and other information on how services or products are produced; and then plans the timing of capacity and material requirements. It decomposes the aggregate quantities of product families, workforce, and time to arrive at the material and resource requirements implied in the sales and operations plan over a shorter time horizon. For a manufacturing firm, the resource plan gets specific as to individual products within each product family, purchased materials, and resources on a detailed level. A major input is the *master production schedule*, which specifies the timing and size of production quantities for each product in the product families. The *material requirements planning* process then derives plans for components, purchased materials, and workstations. For a service firm, the resource plan may specify the daily or weekly facility capacity requirements for service facilities or labor over the next several months. In essence, the resource planning activity provides due dates for the supply of materials, components, products, and other resources such as labor, space, vehicles, and dollars. This activity sets up Level 3, Scheduling. Because of its importance, we devote Chapter 11, "Resource Planning," to this topic.

Level 3: Scheduling

Scheduling takes the resource plan and translates it into specific operational tasks on a detailed basis. Facility schedules can be developed by assigning activities to facilities so as to utilize them efficiently. For example, surgeries for specific patients can be assigned to operating rooms so as to meet the needs of the patients while adhering to the capacity constraints of the operating rooms. Another important schedule is the *workforce schedule*, which details the specific work schedule for each category of employee. For example, a sales and operations plan might allocate 10 police officers for the day shift in a particular district; the resource plan may determine the police protection requirements for a typical week, and the workforce schedule might assign five of them to work Monday through Friday and the other five to work Wednesday through Sunday to meet the varying daily needs for police protection in that district. Finally, given the material requirements plan for a group of jobs in a manufacturing plant, the specific sequence of those jobs can be scheduled on a bottleneck machine. We will address scheduling problems later in this chapter. Thus, the sales and operations plan plays a key role in translating the strategies of the business plan into an operational plan for the manufacturing process.

As the arrows in Figure 10.2 indicate, information flows in two directions: from the top down (broad to detailed) and from the bottom up (detailed to broad). If a sales and operations plan cannot be developed to satisfy the objectives of the business or annual plan with the existing resources, the business or annual plan might need some adjustment. Similarly, if a feasible capacity requirements or material requirements plan cannot be developed, the sales and operations plan might need some adjustment. The planning process is dynamic, with periodic plan revisions or adjustments based on two-way information flows, typically on a monthly basis.

S&OP Supply Options

Developing sales and operations plans means making decisions. In this section, we concentrate on the supply options that ultimately are combined to develop a sales and operations plan. Given demand forecasts, operations managers must develop a plan to meet the demand. There are six options that can be used singly or in combination to arrive at a plan.

1. **Anticipation Inventory** *Anticipation inventory* can be used to absorb uneven rates of demand or supply. For example, a plant facing seasonal demand can stock anticipation inventory during light demand periods and use it during heavy demand periods. Manufacturers of air conditioners, such as Whirlpool, can experience 90 percent of their annual demand during just three months of a year. Extra, or anticipation inventory, also can help when supply, rather than demand, is uneven. For example, a company can stock up on a certain purchased item if the company's suppliers expect severe capacity limitations. Despite its advantages, anticipation inventory can be costly to hold, particularly if stocked in its finished state. Moreover, when services or products are customized, anticipation inventory is not usually an option. Service providers in the supply chain generally cannot use anticipation inventory because services cannot be stocked.

2. **Workforce Adjustment** Management can adjust workforce levels by hiring or laying off employees. The use of this alternative can be attractive if the workforce is largely unskilled or semiskilled and the labor pool is large. These conditions are more likely found in some countries than in others. However, for a particular company, the size of the qualified labor pool may limit the number of new employees that can be hired at any one time. Also, new employees must be trained, and the capacity of the training facilities

An employee stocks a Whirlpool air conditioner at a Lowe's store in Westborough, Massachusetts. The demand for window units is highly seasonal and also depends on variations in the weather. Typically, Whirlpool begins production of room air conditioners in the fall and holds them as inventory until they are shipped in the spring. Building anticipation inventory in the slack season allows the company to even out production rates over much of the year and still satisfy demand in the peak periods (spring and summer) when retailers are placing most of their orders.

themselves might limit the number of new hires at any one time. In some industries, laying off employees is difficult or unusual for contractual reasons (unions); in other industries, such as tourism and agriculture, seasonal layoffs and hirings are the norm.

3. **Workforce Utilization** An alternative to a workforce adjustment is a change in workforce utilization involving overtime and undertime. **Overtime** means that employees work longer than the regular workday or workweek and receive additional pay for the extra hours. It can be used to satisfy output requirements that cannot be completed on regular time. Overtime is expensive (typically 150 percent of the regular-time pay rate), and workers often do not want to work a lot of overtime for an extended period of time. Excessive overtime also can result in declining quality and productivity. On the other hand, it helps avoid the costly fringe benefits (such as health insurance, dental care, Social Security, retirement funds, paid vacations, and holidays) that come with hiring a new full-time employee. **Undertime** means that employees do not have enough work for the regular-time workday or workweek. For example, they cannot be fully utilized for eight hours per day or for five days per week. Undertime occurs when labor capacity exceeds demand requirements (net of anticipation inventory), and this excess capacity cannot or should not be used productively to build up inventory or to satisfy customer orders earlier than the delivery dates already promised.

   Undertime can either be paid or unpaid. An example of *paid undertime* is when employees are kept on the payroll rather than being laid off. In this scenario, employees work a full day and receive their full salary but are not as busy because of the light workload. Some companies use paid undertime (though they do not call it that) during slack periods, particularly with highly skilled, hard-to-replace employees or when there are obstacles to laying off workers. The disadvantages of paid undertime include the cost of paying for work not performed and lowered productivity.

4. **Part-Time Workers** Another option apart from undertime is to hire part-time workers, who are paid only for the hours and days worked. Perhaps they only work during the peak times of the day or peak days of the week. Sometimes, part-time arrangements provide predictable work schedules, but in other cases workers are not called in if the workload is light. Such arrangements are more common in low-skill positions or when the supply of workers seeking such an arrangement is sufficient. Part-time workers typically do not receive fringe benefits.

5. **Subcontractors** Subcontractors can be used to overcome short-term capacity shortages, such as during peaks of the season or business cycle. Subcontractors can supply services, make components and subassemblies, or even assemble an entire product.

6. **Vacation Schedules** A manufacturer can shut down during an annual lull in sales, leaving a skeleton crew to cover operations and perform maintenance. Hospital employees might be encouraged to take all or part of their allowed vacation time during slack periods. The use of this alternative depends on whether the employer can mandate the vacation schedules of its employees. In any case, employees may be strongly discouraged from taking vacations during peak periods or encouraged to take vacations during slack periods.

S&OP Strategies

Here we focus on supply options that define output rates and workforce levels. Two basic strategies are useful starting points in searching for the best plan.

Chase Strategy

The **chase strategy** involves hiring and laying off employees to match the demand forecast over the planning horizon. Varying the workforce's regular-time capacity to equate supply to demand requires no inventory investment, overtime, or undertime. The drawbacks are the expense of continually adjusting workforce levels, the potential alienation of the workforce, and the loss of productivity and quality because of constant changes in the workforce.

Level Strategy

The **level strategy** involves keeping the workforce constant (except possibly at the beginning of the planning horizon). It can vary its utilization to match the demand forecast via overtime, undertime (paid or unpaid), and vacation planning (i.e., paid vacations when demand is low). A constant workforce can be sized at many levels: Managers can choose to maintain a large workforce so as to minimize the planned use of overtime during peak periods (which, unfortunately, also maximizes the need for undertime during slack periods). Alternately, they can choose to maintain a smaller workforce and rely heavily on overtime during the peak periods (which places a strain on the workforce and endangers quality).

overtime

The time that employees work that is longer than the regular workday or workweek for which they receive additional pay.

undertime

The situation that occurs when employees do not have enough work for the regular-time workday or workweek.

chase strategy

A strategy that involves hiring and laying off employees to match the demand forecast.

level strategy

A strategy that keeps the workforce constant, but varies its utilization via overtime, undertime, and vacation planning to match the demand forecast.

Charles Buchanan/Daily Free Press/Associated Press

The greeting card business is highly seasonal, which poses problems for the producers of those cards. Hallmark strives to keep a level strategy to maintain some security for their workforce. Here a shopper is selecting a Valentine's Day card at a Hallmark store in Kinston, NC.

mixed strategy

A strategy that considers the full range of supply options.

These two "pure" strategies used alone usually do not produce the best sales and operations plan. It might not be best to keep the workforce exactly level or to vary it to exactly match forecasted demand on a period-by-period basis. The best strategy, therefore, usually is a **mixed strategy** that considers the full range of supply options. The chase strategy is limited to just hiring and laying off employees. The level strategy is limited to overtime, undertime, and vacation schedules. The mixed strategy opens things up to all options, including anticipation inventory, part-time workers, subcontractors, back-orders, and stockouts.

Constraints and Costs

An acceptable sales and operations plan must recognize relevant constraints or costs. Constraints can be either physical limitations or related to managerial policies. Examples of physical constraints might be machine capacities that limit maximum output or inadequate inventory storage space. Policy constraints might include limitations on the number of back-orders or the use of subcontractors or overtime, as well as the minimum inventory levels needed to achieve desired safety stocks. Ethical issues may also be involved, such as excessive layoffs or required overtime. Typically, many plans can contain a number of constraints. Table 10.2 lists the costs that the planner considers when preparing sales and operations plans.

Sales and Operations Planning as a Process

Sales and operations planning is a decision-making process, involving both planners and management. It is dynamic and continuing, as aspects of the plan are updated periodically when new information becomes available and new opportunities emerge. It is a cross-functional process that seeks a set of plans that all of a firm's functions can support. For each product family, decisions are made based on cost trade-offs, recent history, recommendations by planners and middle management, and the executive team's judgment.

Figure 10.3 shows a typical plan for a manufacturer. The plan is for one of the manufacturer's make-to-stock product families expressed in aggregate units. This simple format shows the interplay between demand and supply. The history on the left for January through March shows how forecasts are tracking actual sales and how well actual production conforms to the plan. The inventory projections are of particular interest to finance because they significantly affect the manufacturer's cash requirements. The last two columns on the top right show how current fiscal year sales projections match up with the current business plan.

This plan is projected out for 18 months, beginning with April. The forecast, operations, and inventory sections for the first 6 months are shown on a month-by-month basis. They then are shown on a

TABLE 10.2 | TYPES OF COSTS WITH SALES AND OPERATIONS PLANNING

Cost	Definition
Regular time	Regular-time wages paid to employees plus contributions to benefits, such as health insurance, dental care, Social Security, retirement funds, and pay for vacations, holidays, and certain other types of absences.
Overtime	Wages paid for work beyond the normal workweek, typically 150 percent of regular-time wages (sometimes up to 200 percent for Sundays and holidays), exclusive of fringe benefits. Overtime can help avoid the extra cost of fringe benefits that come with hiring another full-time employee.
Hiring and layoff	Costs of advertising jobs, interviews, training programs for new employees, scrap caused by the inexperience of new employees, loss of productivity, and initial paperwork. Layoff costs include the costs of exit interviews, severance pay, retaining and retraining remaining workers and managers, and lost productivity.
Inventory holding	Costs that vary with the level of inventory investment: the costs of capital tied up in inventory, variable storage and warehousing costs, pilferage and obsolescence costs, insurance costs, and taxes.
Backorder and stockout	Additional costs to expedite past-due orders, the costs of lost sales, and the potential cost of losing a customer to a competitor (sometimes called loss of goodwill).

Artic Air Company—April Sales and Operations Plan

Family: Medium window units (make-to-stock)   *Unit of measure:* 100 units

◀ **FIGURE 10.3**
Sales and Operations Plan for Make-to-Stock Product Family

SALES	HISTORY J	F	M	A*	M	J	J	A	S	3rd 3 Mos**	4th 3 Mos	Mos 13–18	Fiscal Year Projection ($000)	Business Plan ($000)
New forecast	45	55	60	70	85	95	130	110	70	150	176	275	$8,700	$8,560
Actual sales	52	40	63											
Diff for month	7	−15	3											
Cum		−8	−5											
OPERATIONS														
New Plan	75	75	75	75	75	85	85	85	75	177	225			
Actual	75	78	76											
Diff for month	0	3	1											
Cum		3	4											
INVENTORY														
Plan	85	105	120	125	115	105	60	35	40	198	321			
Actual	92	130	143											

DEMAND ISSUES AND ASSUMPTIONS
1. New product design to be launched in January of next year.

SUPPLY ISSUES
1. Vacations primarily in November and December.
2. Overtime in June–August.

* April is the first month of the planning horizon for this current plan. When next month's plan is developed, its first month in the planning horizon will be May, and the most recent month of the history will be April (with January no longer shown in the history).

** This column provides the sales, operations, and inventory totals for October through December. For example, the forecast of 150 units translates into an average of 50 units per month (or 150/3 = 50).

quarterly basis for the second 6 months. Finally, the totals for the last 6 months in the time horizon are given in just one column. This display gives more precision to the short term and yet gives coverage well into the future—all with a limited number of columns.

The medium window product family is a make-to-stock product that experiences highly seasonal demand. The operations plan is to build up anticipation inventory in the slack season of January through April, schedule vacations as much as possible in November and December, and use overtime in the peak season of June, July, and August. For example, the Operations plan increases monthly production from 75 to 85 for June through August, returns to 75 for September, and then drops to an average of only 59 (or 177/3) for October through December. Sales and operations plans use different formats depending on the production and inventory strategy. For an assemble-to-order strategy, the inventory does not consist of finished goods. Instead, it is inventory of standardized components and subassemblies built for the finishing and assembly operations. For a make-to-order strategy, the inventory section in the plan of Figure 10.3 is replaced by a section showing the planned and actual order backlog quantities.

Sales and operations plans for service providers are quite different. For one thing, their plan does not contain an inventory section, but focuses instead on the demand and supply of human resources. Forecasts are typically expressed in terms of employees required, with separate rows for regular time, overtime, vacations, part-time workers, and so on. Different departments or worker classifications replace product families.

The S&OP process itself, typically done on a monthly basis, consists of six basic steps. They are much like the forecasting process steps we discussed in Chapter 8, "Forecasting."

Step 1. Begin to "roll forward" the plan for the new planning horizon. Start preliminary work right after the month's end. Update files with actual sales, production, inventory, costs, and constraints.

Step 2. Participate in the forecasting and demand planning process to create the authorized demand forecasts. For service providers, the forecasts are staff requirements for each workforce group. For example, a director of nursing in a hospital can develop a workload index for a nursing staff and translate a projection of the month-to-month patient load into an equivalent total amount of nursing care time—and thus the number of nurses—required for each month of the year.

Step 3. Update the sales and operations plans for each family, recognizing relevant constraints and costs including availability of materials from suppliers, training facilities capable of handling only so many new hires at a time, machine capacities, or limited storage space. Policy constraints might include limitations on the number of backorders, or the use of subcontractors or overtime, as well as the minimum inventory levels needed to achieve desired safety stocks. Typically, many plans can satisfy a specific set of constraints.

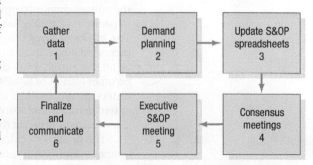

FUJIFILM Imaging Colorants makes inks and dyes, primarily for inkjet printer cartridges, and operates an effective S&OP process. It must coordinate between a U.S. finishing plant and a UK bulk manufacturing plant. Managers from all functions teleconference at the U.S. site with seven other UK managers. At this Partnership meeting (step 4 in the S&OP process), they review the demand, production, and inventory plans, as well as the projected working capital plan.

The planner searches for a plan that best balances costs, customer service, and workforce stability, which may necessitate revising the plan several times.

Step 4. Have one or more consensus meetings with the stakeholders on how best to balance supply with demand. Participants could include the supply chain manager, plant manager, controller, purchasing manager, production control manager, or logistics manager. The goal is one set of recommendations to present at the firm's executive sales and operations planning (S&OP) meeting. Where agreement cannot be reached, prepare scenarios of alternative plans. Also prepare an updated financial view of the total business by rolling up the plans for all product families into a spreadsheet expressed in total dollars.

Step 5. Present recommendations by product family at the executive S&OP meeting, which typically includes the firm's president and the vice presidents of functional areas. The plan is reviewed relative to the business plan, new product issues, special projects, and other relevant factors. The executives may ask for final changes to the plan, such as to balance conflicting objectives better. Acceptance of this authorized plan does not necessarily mean that everyone is in total agreement, but it does imply that everyone will work to achieve the plan.

Step 6. Update the plans to reflect the outcome of the executive S&OP meeting, and communicate them to the important stakeholders for implementation. Important recipients include those who do resource planning, covered in the next chapter.

Spreadsheets for Sales and Operations Planning

The sales and operations plan in Figure 10.3 does not show much on the supply options used in the operations plan or their cost implications. Here we discuss using spreadsheets that do just that. Supplement D, "Linear Programming," describes using the transportation method for production planning. Both spreadsheets and linear programming could be used on the side as a planner develops prospective plans in step 3 of the S&OP process.

Various spreadsheets can be used, including ones that you develop on your own. Here we work with the *Sales and Operations Planning with Spreadsheets* Solver in OM Explorer.

Spreadsheets for a Manufacturer

Figure 10.4 shows a plan for a manufacturer, which uses all supply options except overtime. The top part of the spreadsheet shows the *input values* that consist of the forecasted demand requirements and the supply option choices period by period. Vary these "levers" as you search for better plans.

The next part of the spreadsheet (in green) shows the *derived values* that follow from the input values. The first row of derived values is called *utilized time*, which is that portion of the workforce's regular time that is paid for and productively used. In any period, the utilized time equals the workforce level minus undertime and vacation time. For example, in period 1 the utilized time is 94 (or $120 - 6 - 20$). Given the utilized time of the workforce, the *inventory* can be calculated by subtracting the forecast from the utilized time, adding last periods ending inventory, and adding subcontracting time and backorders. In period 1, assuming last period's ending inventory is zero, the inventory is 70 (or $94 - 24 + 0 + 0 + 0$). The *hires* and *layoffs* rows can be derived from the workforce levels. In this example, the workforce is increased for period 2 from its initial size of 120 employees to 158, which means that 38 employees are hired. Because the workforce size remains constant at 158 throughout the rest of the planning horizon, no other hirings or layoffs happen. When additional alternatives, such as vacations, inventory, and backorders are all possible, the overtime and undertime cannot be derived just from information on forecasted demand and workforce levels. Thus, undertime and overtime are shown as input values (rather than derived values) in the spreadsheet, and the user must be careful to specify consistent input values.

The final part of the spreadsheet, the *calculated values* of the plan, shows the plan's cost consequences. Along with qualitative considerations, the cost of each plan determines whether the plan is

	1	2	3	4	5	6	Total
Inputs							
Forecasted demand	24	142	220	180	136	168	870
Workforce level	120	158	158	158	158	158	910
Undertime	6	0	0	0	0	0	6
Overtime	0	0	0	0	0	0	0
Vacation time	20	6	0	0	4	10	40
Subcontracting time	0	0	0	0	0	6	6
Backorders	0	0	0	4	0	0	4
Derived							
Utilized time	94	152	158	158	154	148	864
Inventory	70	80	18	0	14	0	182
Hires	0	38	0	0	0	0	38
Layoffs	0	0	0	0	0	0	0
Calculated							
Utilized time cost	$376,000	$608,000	$632,000	$632,000	$616,000	$592,000	$3,456,000
Undertime cost	$24,000	$0	$0	$0	$0	$0	$24,000
Overtime cost	$0	$0	$0	$0	$0	$0	$0
Vacation time cost	$80,000	$24,000	$0	$0	$16,000	$40,000	$160,000
Inventory cost	$2,800	$3,200	$720	$0	$560	$0	$7,280
Backorders cost	$0	$0	$0	$4,000	$0	$0	$4,000
Hiring cost	$0	$91,200	$0	$0	$0	$0	$91,200
Layoff cost	$0	$0	$0	$0	$0	$0	$0
Subcontracting cost	$0	$0	$0	$0	$0	$43,200	$43,200
Total cost	$482,800	726,400	632,720	636,000	632,560	675,200	$3,785,680

◀ FIGURE 10.4
Manufacturer's Plan Using a Spreadsheet and Mixed Strategy

satisfactory or whether a revised plan should be considered. When seeking clues about how to improve a plan already evaluated, we identify its highest cost elements. Revisions that would reduce these specific costs might produce a new plan with lower overall costs. Spreadsheet programs make analyzing these plans easy, and they present a whole new set of possibilities for developing sound sales and operations plans.

The plan in Figure 10.4 definitely is for a manufacturer because it uses inventory to advantage, particularly in the first two periods. It is a mixed strategy, and not just because it uses anticipation inventory, backorders, and subcontracting. The workforce level changes in period 2, but it does not exactly match the forecasted demand as with a chase strategy. It has some elements of the level strategy, because undertime and vacation time are part of the plan, but it does not rely exclusively on these supply options.

Care must be taken to recognize differences in how inputs are measured. The workforce level might be expressed as the number of employees, but the forecasted demand and inventory are expressed as units of the product. The OM Explorer spreadsheets require a common unit of measure, so we must translate some of the data prior to entering the input values. Perhaps the easiest approach is to express the forecasted demand and supply options as *employee-period equivalents*. If demand forecasts are given as units of product, we can convert them to employee-period equivalents by dividing them by the productivity of a worker. For example, if the demand is for 1,500 units of product and the average employee produces 100 units in one period, the demand requirement is 15 employee-period equivalents.

Spreadsheeets for a Service Provider

The same spreadsheets can be used by service providers, except anticipation inventory is not an option. You can unprotect the sheet and then hide the rows that are not relevant. It is useful not to hide the inventory row until the end, however, because positive or negative values signal an inconsistency in your plan. Whereas Figure 10.4 shows a good plan found after several revisions, here we illustrate with Example 10.1 how to find a good plan for a service provider beginning with the chase and level (ignoring vacations) strategies. These plans can provide insights that lead to even better mixed strategy plans.

EXAMPLE 10.1	Using the Chase and Level Strategies as Starting Points

The manager of a large distribution center must determine how many part-time stockpickers to maintain on the payroll. She wants to develop a staffing plan that minimizes total costs, and wants to begin with the chase strategy and level strategy. For the level strategy, she wants to first try the workforce level that meets demand with the minimum use of undertime and not consider vacation scheduling.

First, the manager divides the next year into six time periods, each one 2 months long. Each part-time employee can work a maximum of 20 hours per week on regular time, but the actual number can be less. Instead of paying undertime, each worker's day is shortened during slack periods. Once on the payroll, each worker is used each day, but they may work only a few hours. Overtime can be used during peak periods.

The distribution center's forecasted demand is shown as the number of part-time employees required for each time period at the maximum regular time of 20 hours per week. For example, in period 3, an estimated 18 part-time employees working 20 hours per week on regular time will be needed.

	1	2	3	4	5	6	Total
Forecasted demand*	6	12	18	15	13	14	78

*Number of part-time employees

Currently, 10 part-time clerks are employed. They have not been subtracted from the forecasted demand shown. Constraints and cost information are as follows:

a. The size of training facilities limits the number of new hires in any period to no more than 10.

b. No backorders are permitted; demand must be met each period.

c. Overtime cannot exceed 20 percent of the regular-time capacity (that is, 4 hours) in any period. Therefore, the most that any part-time employee can work is 1.20(20) = 24 hours per week.

d. The following costs can be assigned:

Regular-time wage rate	$2,000 per time period at 20 hours per week
Overtime wages	150 percent of the regular-time rate
Hires	$1,000 per person
Layoffs	$500 per person

Framed by thousands of ski poles, a part-time worker sorts and inventories new products in the receiving department of REI's distribution center in Sumner, Washington. REI employs a high percentage of part-time workers, many of whom are college students. They tend to be young people who participate in outdoor sports and are familiar with the equipment that REI sells.

MyOMLab

Tutor 10.1 in MyOMLab provides a new example for planning using the chase strategy with hiring and layoffs.

SOLUTION

a. Chase Strategy

This strategy simply involves adjusting the workforce as needed to meet demand, as shown in Figure 10.5. Rows in the spreadsheet that do not apply (such as inventory and vacations) are hidden. The workforce level row is identical to the forecasted demand row. A large number of hirings and layoffs begin with laying off four part-time employees immediately because the current staff is 10 and the staff level required in period 1 is only six. However, many employees, such as college students, prefer part-time work. The total cost is $173,500, and most of the cost increase comes from frequent hiring and layoffs, which add $17,500 to the cost of utilized regular-time costs.

	1	2	3	4	5	6	Total
Inputs							
Forecasted demand	6	12	18	15	13	14	78
Workforce level	6	12	18	15	13	14	78
Undertime	0	0	0	0	0	0	0
Overtime	0	0	0	0	0	0	0
Derived							
Utilized time	6	12	18	15	13	14	78
Hires	0	6	6	0	0	1	13
Layoffs	4	0	0	3	2	0	9
Calculated							
Utilized time cost	$12,000	$24,000	$36,000	$30,000	$26,000	$28,000	$156,000
Undertime cost	$0	$0	$0	$0	$0	$0	$0
Hiring cost	$0	$6,000	$6,000	$0	$0	$1,000	$13,000
Layoff cost	$2,000	$0	$0	$1,500	$1,000	$0	$4,500
Total cost	$14,000	30,000	42,000	31,500	27,000	29,000	$173,500

◀ **FIGURE 10.5**
Spreadsheet for Chase Strategy

b. Level Strategy

To minimize undertime, the maximum use of overtime possible must occur in the peak period. For this particular level strategy (other workforce options are possible), the most overtime that the manager can use is 20 percent of the regular-time capacity, w, so

$$1.20w = 18 \text{ employees required in peak period (period 3)}$$

$$w = \frac{18}{1.20} = 15 \text{ employees}$$

A 15-employee staff size minimizes the amount of undertime for this level strategy. Because the staff already includes 10 part-time employees, the manager should immediately hire five more. The complete plan is shown in Figure 10.6. The total cost is $164,000, which seems reasonable because the minimum conceivable cost is only $156,000 (78 employee-periods × $2,000/employee-period). This cost could be achieved only if the manager found a way to cover the forecasted demand for all 78-employee periods with regular time. The plan seems reasonable primarily because it involves the use of large amounts of undertime (15-employee periods), which in this example are unpaid.

MyOMLab
Tutor 10.2 in MyOMLab provides a new example for planning using the level strategy with overtime and undertime.

	1	2	3	4	5	6	Total
Inputs							
Forecasted demand	6	12	18	15	13	14	78
Workforce level	15	15	15	15	15	15	90
Undertime	9	3	0	0	2	1	15
Overtime	0	0	3	0	0	0	3
Derived							
Utilized time	6	12	15	15	13	14	75
Hires	5	0	0	0	0	0	5
Layoffs	0	0	0	0	0	0	0
Calculated							
Utilized time cost	$12,000	$24,000	$30,000	$30,000	$26,000	$28,000	$150,000
Undertime cost	$0	$0	$0	$0	$0	$0	$0
Overtime cost	$0	$0	$9,000	$0	$0	$0	$9,000
Hiring cost	$5,000	$0	$0	$0	$0	$0	$5,000
Layoff cost	$0	$0	$0	$0	$0	$0	$0
Total cost	$17,000	24,000	39,000	30,000	26,000	28,000	$164,000

◀ **FIGURE 10.6**
Spreadsheet for Level Strategy

DECISION POINT

The manager, now having a point of reference with which to compare other plans, decided to evaluate some other plans before making a final choice, beginning with the chase strategy. The only way to reduce costs is somehow to reduce the premium in period 3 for three overtime employee periods (3 employee-periods × $3,000/employee-period) or to reduce the hiring cost of five employees (5 hires × $1,000/person). Nonetheless, better solutions may be possible. For example, undertime can be reduced by delaying the hiring until period 2 because the current workforce is sufficient until then. This delay would decrease the amount of unpaid undertime, which is a qualitative improvement. See Active Model 10.1 for additional insights.

MyOMLab
Active Model 10.1 in MyOMLab shows the impact of changing the workforce level, the cost structure, and overtime capacity.

Scheduling

Scheduling is the last step in Figure 10.2. It takes the operations and scheduling process from planning to execution, and is where the "rubber meets the road." This important aspect of supply chain management is itself a process. It requires gathering data from sources such as demand forecasts or specific customer orders, resource availability from the sales and operations plan, due dates for resource or material requirements from resource planning activities, and specific constraints to be reckoned with from employees and customers. It then involves generating a schedule for the supply of resources or materials to meet the needs determined in resource planning. Here we cover job and facility scheduling, workforce scheduling, job sequencing at a workstation, and software support.

Job and Facility Scheduling

Schedules can be displayed in various ways. For different jobs or activities, schedules can simply list the job due dates, show in a table their start and finish times, or show in a graph their start and finish times. The *Gantt chart* uses the third approach. Figure 7.4 in Chapter 7, "Project Management," demonstrates how a "picture can be worth a thousand words" in managing projects. Associates not familiar with scheduling techniques can still grasp the essence of the plan by just looking at such a chart. This tool can be used to monitor the progress of work and to view the load on workstations or other facilities. The chart takes two basic forms: (1) The job or activity progress chart, which can be used to monitor and revise schedules, and (2) the workstation chart, which can be used to schedule the capacity of facilities.

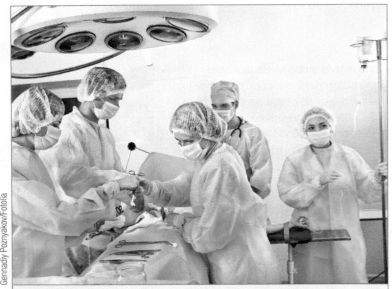

Gennadiy Poznyakov/Fotolia

Operating room represents a fixed capacity that must be scheduled carefully to avoid unused capacity. Any time not used by surgeons is time lost forever.

Gantt Progress Chart   The *Gantt progress chart* graphically displays the current status of each job or activity relative to its scheduled completion date. For example, suppose that an automobile parts manufacturer has three jobs under way, one each for Ford, Nissan, and Buick. The actual status of these orders is shown by the colored bars in Figure 10.7; the red lines indicate the desired schedule for the start and finish of each job. For the current date, April 21, this Gantt chart shows that the Ford order is behind schedule because operations has completed only the work scheduled through April 18. The Nissan order is exactly on schedule, and the Buick order is ahead of schedule.

Gantt Workstation Chart   Figure 10.8 shows a *Gantt workstation chart* of the operating rooms at a hospital for a particular day. Using the same notation as in Figure 10.7, the chart shows the load on the operating rooms and the nonproductive time. The time slots assigned to each doctor include the time needed to clean the room prior to the next surgery. The chart can be used to identify time slots for unscheduled emergency surgeries. It can also be used to accommodate requests to change the time of surgeries.

FIGURE 10.7 ▶
Gantt Progress Chart for an Auto
Parts Company

Current date

Job	4/17	4/18	4/19	4/20	4/21	4/22	4/23	4/24	4/25	4/26
Ford										
Nissan										
Buick										

⌐ Start activity

¬ Finish activity

▯ Scheduled activity time

▬ Actual progress

⊠ Nonproductive time

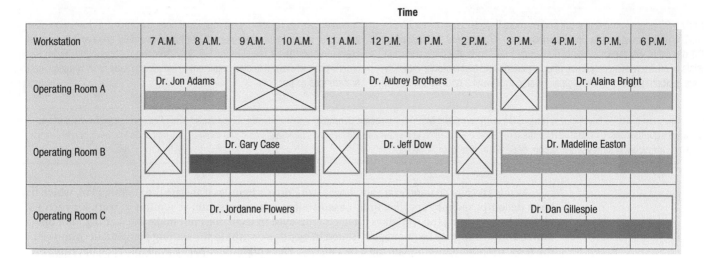

Workstation	7 A.M.	8 A.M.	9 A.M.	10 A.M.	11 A.M.	12 P.M.	1 P.M.	2 P.M.	3 P.M.	4 P.M.	5 P.M.	6 P.M.
Operating Room A	Dr. Jon Adams		⊠			Dr. Aubrey Brothers			⊠	Dr. Alaina Bright		
Operating Room B	⊠	Dr. Gary Case			⊠	Dr. Jeff Dow			⊠	Dr. Madeline Easton		
Operating Room C	Dr. Jordanne Flowers					⊠		Dr. Dan Gillespie				

For example, Dr. Flowers may be able to change the start of her surgery to 2 P.M. by swapping time slots with Dr. Gillespie in operating room C or by asking Dr. Brothers to start her surgery one hour earlier in operating room A and asking Dr. Bright to schedule her surgery for the morning in operating room C. In any event, the hospital administrator would have to get involved in rescheduling the surgeries.

▲ **FIGURE 10.8**
Gantt Workstation Chart for Operating Rooms at a Hospital

Workforce Scheduling

Another way to manage capacity is **workforce scheduling**, which is a type of scheduling that determines when employees work. Of particular interest are situations when not all employees work the same five days a week, and same eight hours per day. The schedule specifies the on-duty and off-duty periods for each employee over a certain time period, as in assigning postal clerks, nurses, pilots, attendants, or police officers to specific workdays and shifts. This approach is used when customers demand quick response and total demand can be forecasted with reasonable accuracy. In these instances, capacity is adjusted to meet the expected loads on the service system. Managerial Practice 10.1 shows how Air New Zealand derives its flight and crew schedules from higher-level plans.

workforce scheduling

A type of scheduling that determines when employees work.

MANAGERIAL PRACTICE 10.1   Scheduling at Air New Zealand

How important is scheduling to an airline company? Certainly, customer satisfaction regarding on-time schedule performance is critical in a highly competitive industry such as air transportation. In addition, airlines lose a lot of money when expensive equipment, such as an aircraft, is idle. Flight and crew scheduling, however, is a complex process. For example, Air New Zealand is a group of five airlines with a combined fleet of 105 aircraft, with another 21 more on order. The average utilization is 8:28 hours per day. It has undergone an $800 million upgrade to its long-haul service, refitting its Boeing 747 fleet and adding eight new Boeing 777-200 aircraft for flights to North America. It directly serves 50 ports—26 domestic and 24 international within 15 countries. It carries 13.4 million passengers annually, and its network incorporates flight times ranging from 15 minutes to 13 hours.

Operations planning and scheduling at the aggregate level begins with a market plan that identifies the new and existing flight segments that are needed to remain competitive. This general plan is further refined to a three-year plan and then is put into an annual budget in which flight segments have specific departure and arrival times. Twenty-six weeks prior to the day of operation, the timetable for all the flights Air New Zealand will fly is created. This is followed by the assignment of aircraft types to flights and the development of aircraft routes. Six weeks prior to the day of operation schedulers determine sequences of flights that can be flown in a feasible way at minimum cost. The two types of crews—pilots and attendants—each come with its own set of constraints. Pilots, for example, cannot be scheduled for

Operations planning and scheduling at an airline like Air New Zealand goes through several stages to match supply with demand, from aggregate plans to short-term schedules. Even after finalizing flights and crew roster schedules, severe weather conditions or mechanical failures can cause last-minute changes. Air New Zealand's long-term competitive strength depends on how well it performs this process.

Tupungato/Shutterstock

more than 35 hours in a 7-day week and no more than 100 hours in a 28-day cycle. They also must have a 36-hour break every 7 days and 30 days off in an 84-day cycle. Each pilot's tour of duty begins and ends at a crew base and consists of an alternating sequence of duty periods and rest periods, with duty periods including one or more flights. Finally, four weeks prior to the day of

operation, actual rosters for an individual crew member are developed. The scheduler must ensure that each flight has a qualified crew and that each crew member has a feasible tour of duty over the roster period. From the crew's point of view, it is also important to satisfy as many crew requests and preferences as possible.

Source: Rasmussen, Matias Sevel, Lusby, Richard M., and Ryan, David M., "A Subsequence Generation Approach for the Airline Crew Pairing Problem," **http://www.agifors. org/award/submissions2011/MatiasRasmussen**; "Service Scheduling at Air New Zealand," *Operations Management 10e Video Library* (Upper Saddle River, NJ: Prentice Hall, 2010); **http://www.airnewzealand.com** (May, 2014). See video in MyOMLab.

As the Air New Zealand example shows, workforce schedules translate the staffing plan, which has been decomposed into specific, time-based staff requirements, into schedules of work for each employee. Determining the workdays for each employee in itself does not make the staffing plan operational. Daily workforce requirements, stated in aggregate terms in the staffing plan and decomposed in the resource requirements plan, must be satisfied. The workforce capacity available each day must meet or exceed daily workforce requirements. If it does not, the scheduler must try to rearrange days off until the requirements are met. If no such schedule can be found, management might have to change the staffing plan and hire more employees, authorize overtime hours, or allow for larger backlogs.

Constraints The technical constraints imposed on the workforce schedule are the resources provided by the staffing plan and the requirements placed on the operating system. However, other constraints, including legal and behavioral considerations, also can be imposed. For example, Air New Zealand is required to have at least a minimum number of flight attendants on duty at all times. Similarly, a minimum number of fire and safety personnel must be on duty at a fire station at all times. Such constraints limit management's flexibility in developing workforce schedules.

The constraints imposed by the psychological needs of workers complicate scheduling even more. Some of these constraints are written into labor agreements. For example, an employer might agree to give employees a certain number of consecutive days off per week or to limit employees' consecutive workdays to a certain maximum. Other provisions might govern the allocation of vacations, days off for holidays, or rotating shift assignments. In addition, the preferences of the employees themselves need to be considered.

One way that managers deal with certain undesirable aspects of scheduling is to use a **rotating schedule**, which rotates employees through a series of workdays or hours. Thus, over a period of time, each person has the same opportunity to have weekends and holidays off and to work days, as well as evenings and nights. A rotating schedule gives each employee the next employee's schedule the following week. In contrast, a **fixed schedule** calls for each employee to work the same days and hours each week.

Developing a Workforce Schedule Suppose that we are interested in developing a workforce schedule for a company that operates seven days a week and provides each employee with two consecutive days off. In this section, we demonstrate a method that recognizes this constraint. The objective is to identify the two consecutive days off for each employee that will minimize the amount of total slack capacity, thereby maximizing the utilization of the workforce. The work schedule for each employee, then, is the five days that remain after the two days off have been determined. The procedure involves the following steps.

Step 1. From the schedule of net requirements for the week, derived from the resource plan in Level 2, find all the pairs of consecutive days, excluding the day (or days) with the maximum daily requirement. Select the unique pair that has the lowest total requirements for the two days. In some unusual situations, all pairs may contain a day with the maximum requirements. If so, select the pair with the lowest total requirements. Suppose that the numbers of employees required are

Monday: 8	Thursday: 12	Saturday: 4
Tuesday: 9	Friday: 7	Sunday: 2
Wednesday: 2		

The maximum daily requirement is 12 employees, on Thursday. The consecutive pair with the lowest total requirements is Saturday and Sunday, with $4 + 2 = 6$.

Step 2. If a tie occurs, choose one of the tied pairs, consistent with the provisions written into the labor agreement, if any. Alternatively, the tie could be broken by asking the employee being scheduled to make the choice. As a last resort, the tie could be broken arbitrarily. For example, preference could be given to Saturday–Sunday pairs.

Step 3. Assign the employee the selected pair of days off. Subtract the requirements satisfied by the employee from the net requirements for each day the employee is to work. In this example, the employee

---

rotating schedule

A schedule that rotates employees through a series of workdays or hours.

fixed schedule

A schedule that calls for each employee to work the same days and hours each week.

is assigned Saturday and Sunday off. After requirements are subtracted, Monday's requirement is 7, Tuesday's is 8, Wednesday's is 1, Thursday's is 11, and Friday's is 6. Saturday's and Sunday's requirements do not change because no employee is yet scheduled to work those days.

Step 4. Repeat steps 1 through 3 until all the requirements have been satisfied or a certain number of employees have been scheduled.

This method reduces the amount of slack capacity assigned to days with low requirements and forces the days with high requirements to be scheduled first. It also recognizes some of the behavioral and contractual aspects of workforce scheduling in the tie-breaking rules.

EXAMPLE 10.2	Developing a Workforce Schedule

The Amalgamated Parcel Service is open seven days a week. The schedule of requirements is

Day	M	T	W	Th	F	S	Su
Required number of employees	6	4	8	9	10	3	2

The manager needs a workforce schedule that provides two consecutive days off and minimizes the amount of total slack capacity. To break ties in the selection of off days, the scheduler gives preference to Saturday and Sunday if it is one of the tied pairs. If not, she selects one of the tied pairs arbitrarily.

MyOMLab

Tutor 10.3 in MyOMLab provides a new example to practice workforce scheduling.

SOLUTION

Friday contains the maximum requirements, and the pair S–Su has the lowest total requirements. Therefore, Employee 1 is scheduled to work Monday through Friday.

Note that Friday still has the maximum requirements and that the requirements for the S–Su pair are carried forward because these are Employee 1's days off. These updated requirements are the ones the scheduler uses for the next employee.

The day-off assignments for the employees are shown in the following table.

SCHEDULING DAYS OFF

M	T	W	Th	F	S	Su	Employee	Comments
6	4	8	9	10	3	2	1	The S–Su pair has the lowest total requirements. Assign Employee **1** to a Monday through Friday schedule and update the requirements.
5	3	7	8	9	3	2	2	The S–Su pair has the lowest total requirements. Assign Employee **2** to a Monday through Friday schedule and update the requirements.
4	2	6	7	8	3	2	3	The S–Su pair has the lowest total requirements. Assign Employee **3** to a Monday through Friday schedule and update the requirements.
3	1	5	6	7	3	2	4	The M–T pair has the lowest total requirements. Assign Employee **4** to a Wednesday through Sunday schedule and update the requirements.
3	1	4	5	6	2	1	5	The S–Su pair has the lowest total requirements. Assign Employee **5** to a Monday through Friday schedule and update the requirements.
2	0	3	4	5	2	1	6	The M–T pair has the lowest total requirements. Assign Employee **6** to a Wednesday through Sunday schedule and update the requirements.
2	0	2	3	4	1	0	7	The S–Su pair has the lowest total requirements. Assign Employee **7** to a Monday through Friday schedule and update the requirements.
1	0	1	2	3	1	0	8	Four pairs have the minimum requirement and the lowest total: S–Su, Su–M, M–T, and T–W. Choose the S–Su pair according to the tie-breaking rule. Assign Employee **8** to a Monday through Friday schedule and update the requirements.
0	0	0	1	2	1	0	9	Arbitrarily choose the Su–M pair to break ties because the S–Su pair does not have the lowest total requirements. Assign Employee **9** to a Tuesday through Saturday schedule and update the requirements.
0	0	0	0	1	0	0	10	Choose the S–Su pair according to the tie-breaking rule. Assign Employee **10** to a Monday through Friday schedule.

In this example, Friday always has the maximum requirements and should be avoided as a day off. The final schedule for the employees is shown in the following table.

FINAL SCHEDULE								
Employee	M	T	W	Th	F	S	Su	Total
1	X	X	X	X	X	off	off	
2	X	X	X	X	X	off	off	
3	X	X	X	X	X	off	off	
4	off	off	X	X	X	X	X	
5	X	X	X	X	X	off	off	
6	off	off	X	X	X	X	X	
7	X	X	X	X	X	off	off	
8	X	X	X	X	X	off	off	
9	off	X	X	X	X	X	off	
10	X	X	X	X	X	off	off	
Capacity, C	7	8	10	10	10	3	2	50
Requirements, R	6	4	8	9	10	3	2	42
Slack, C − R	1	4	2	1	0	0	0	8

DECISION POINT

With its substantial amount of slack capacity, the schedule is not unique. Employee 9, for example, could have Sunday and Monday, Monday and Tuesday, or Tuesday and Wednesday off without causing a capacity shortage. Indeed, the company might be able to get by with one fewer employee because of the total of eight slack days of capacity. However, all 10 employees are needed on Fridays. If the manager were willing to get by with only nine employees on Fridays or if someone could work one day of overtime on a rotating basis, he would not need Employee 10. As indicated in the table, the net requirement left for Employee 10 to satisfy amounts to only one day, Friday. Thus, Employee 10 can be used to fill in for vacationing or sick employees.

Sequencing Jobs at a Workstation

sequencing

Determining the order in which jobs or customers are processed in the waiting line at a workstation.

Another aspect of scheduling is sequencing work at workstations. **Sequencing** determines the order in which jobs are processed in the waiting line at a workstation. In this regard, the term "job" refers to either production orders or human customers. When combined with the expected processing times, the sequence allows you to estimate the start and finish times of each job and use a workstation Gantt chart to display the schedule.

priority sequencing rule

A rule that specifies the job or customer processing sequence when several jobs are waiting in line at a workstation.

Priority Sequencing Rules   One way to determine what job to process next is with the help of a **priority sequencing rule**. The following two priority sequencing rules are commonly used in practice.

- *First-Come, First-Served.* The job arriving at the workstation first has the highest priority under a **first-come, first-served (FCFS)** rule. This rule is "fair" in that each job is treated equally, with no one stepping ahead of others already in line. It is commonly used at service facilities and is the rule that was assumed in Supplement B, "Waiting Lines."

first-come, first-served (FCFS)

A priority sequencing rule that specifies that the job or customer arriving at the workstation first has the highest priority.

- *Earliest Due Date.* The job with the **earliest due date (EDD)** is the next one to be processed. The *due date* specifies when work on a job should be finished. Due dates are commonly used by manufacturers and suppliers in the supply chain. For example, a product cannot be assembled until all of its purchased and produced components are available. If these components were not already in inventory, they must be ordered prior to when the product assembly can begin. Their due date is the start date for assembling the product to be assembled. This simple relationship is fundamental to coordinating with suppliers and with the manufacturer's own shops in the supply chain. It is also the key to **expediting**, which is the process of completing a job sooner than would otherwise be done. Expediting can be done by revising the due date, moving the job to the front of the waiting line, making a special appeal by phone or e-mail to the supplier, adding extra capacity, or even putting a red tag on the job that says the job is urgent.

earliest due date (EDD)

A priority sequencing rule that specifies that the job or customer with the earliest due date is the next job to be processed.

Neither rule guarantees finding an optimal solution. Different sequences found by trial and error can produce better schedules. In fact, there are multiple performance measures for judging a schedule. A schedule that does well on one measure may do poorly on another.

Performance Measures   The quality of a schedule can be judged in various ways. Two commonly used performance measures are flow time and past due.

- *Flow Time.* The amount of time a job spends in the service or manufacturing system is called **flow time**. It is the sum of the waiting time for servers or machines; the process time, including setups; the time spent moving between operations; and delays resulting from machine breakdowns, unavailability of facilitating goods or components, and the like. Flow time is sometimes referred to as *throughput time* or *time spent in the system, including service*. For a set of jobs to be processed at a single workstation, a job's flow time is

$$\text{Flow time} = \text{Finish time} + \text{Time since job arrived at workstation}$$

When using this equation, we assume for convenience that the first job scheduled starts at time zero (0). At time 0, all the jobs were available for processing at the workstation.

- *Past Due.* The measure **past due** can be expressed as the amount of time by which a job missed its due date (also referred to as **tardiness**) or as the percentage of total jobs processed over some period of time that missed their due dates. Minimizing these past due measures supports the competitive priorities of cost (penalties for missing due dates), quality (perceptions of poor service), and time (on-time delivery).

expediting

The process of completing a job or finishing with a customer sooner than would otherwise be done.

flow time

The amount of time a job spends in the service or manufacturing system.

past due

The amount of time by which a job missed its due date.

tardiness

See past due.

EXAMPLE 10.3	Using the FCFS and EDD Priority Sequencing Rules

Currently a consulting company has five jobs in its backlog. The time since the order was placed, processing time, and promised due dates are given in the following table. Determine the schedule by using the FCFS rule, and calculate the average days past due and flow time. How can the schedule be improved, if average flow time is the most critical?

Customer	Time Since Order Arrived (days ago)	Processing Time (days)	Due Date (days from now)
A	15	25	29
B	12	16	27
C	5	14	68
D	10	10	48
E	0	12	80

SOLUTION

a. The FCFS rule states that Customer A should be the first one in the sequence, because that order arrived earliest—15 days ago. Customer E's order arrived today, so it is processed last. The sequence is shown in the following table, along with the days past due and flow times.

Customer Sequence	Start Time (days)		Processing Time (days)		Finish Time (days)	Due Date	Days Past Due	Days Ago Since Order Arrived	Flow Time (days)
A	0	+	25	=	25	29	**0**	15	**40**
B	25	+	16	=	41	27	**14**	12	**53**
D	41	+	10	=	51	48	**3**	10	**61**
C	51	+	14	=	65	68	**0**	5	**70**
E	65	+	12	=	77	80	**0**	0	**77**

The *finish time* for a job is its start time plus the processing time. Its finish time becomes the start time for the next job in the sequence, assuming that the next job is available for immediate processing. The days past due for a job is zero (0) if its due date is equal to or exceeds the finish time. Otherwise it equals the shortfall. The flow time for each job equals its finish time plus the number of days ago since the order first arrived at the workstation. For example, Customer C's flow time is its scheduled finish time of 65 days plus the 5 days since the order arrived, or 70 days. The days past due and average flow time performance measures for the FCFS schedule are

$$\text{Average days past due} = \frac{0 + 14 + 3 + 0 + 0}{5} = 3.4 \text{ days}$$

$$\text{Average flow time} = \frac{40 + 53 + 61 + 70 + 77}{5} = 60.2 \text{ days}$$

b. The average flow time can be reduced. One possibility is the sequence shown in the following table, which uses the Shortest Processing Time (SPT) rule, which is one of several rules developed more fully in MyOMLab Supplement J, "Operations Scheduling." (For still another possibility, see Solved Problem 3, which applies the EDD rule.)

MyOMLab

Customer Sequence	Start Time (days)		Processing Time (days)		Finish Time (days)	Due Date	Days Past Due	Days Ago Since Order Arrived	Flow Time (days)
D	0	+	10	=	10	48	0	10	20
E	10	+	12	=	22	80	0	0	22
C	22	+	14	=	36	68	0	5	41
B	36	+	16	=	52	27	25	12	64
A	52	+	25	=	77	29	48	15	92

$$\text{Average days past due} = \frac{0 + 0 + 0 + 25 + 48}{5} = 14.6 \text{ days}$$

$$\text{Average flow time} = \frac{20 + 22 + 41 + 64 + 92}{5} = 47.8 \text{ days}$$

This schedule reduces the average flow time from 60.2 to 47.8 days—a 21 percent improvement. However, the past due times for jobs A and B have increased.

DECISION POINT

Management decided to use a modified version of the second schedule, adding overtime when Customer B is processed. Further, Customer A agreed to extend its due date to 77 days, because in this case the advanced warning allowed it to reschedule its own operations with little problem.

Nataliya Hora/Shutterstock

Scheduling an automobile assembly line is a challenging task, and requires the help of sophisticated software. Even with robots doing much of the work, parts and components must be timed to arrive at the precise time the frame is available for assembly. Here robotic arms assemble a Skoda in a Czech factory.

Software Support

Computerized scheduling systems are available to cope with the complexity of workforce scheduling, such as the myriad constraints and concerns at Air New Zealand. In some types of firms, such as telephone companies, mail-order catalog houses, or emergency hotline agencies, employees must be on duty 24 hours a day, 7 days a week.

Sometimes a portion of the staff is part time, which allows management a great deal of flexibility but adds considerable complexity to the scheduling requirements. The flexibility comes from the opportunity to match anticipated loads closely through the use of overlapping shifts or odd shift lengths; the complexity comes from the need to evaluate the numerous possible alternatives. Management also must consider the timing of lunch breaks and rest periods, the number and starting times of shift schedules, and the days off for each employee. The programs select the schedule that minimizes the sum of expected costs of over- and understaffing.

Software is also available for sequencing jobs at workstations. They help firms design and manage the linkages between customers and suppliers in the supply chain. True integration requires the manipulation of large amounts of complex data in real time because the customer order work flow must be synchronized with the required material, manufacturing, and distribution activity. Coupled with the Internet and improved data storage and manipulation methods, such computer software has given rise to **advanced planning and scheduling (APS) systems**, which seek to optimize resources across the supply chain and align daily operations with strategic goals. A firm's ability to change its schedules quickly and still keep the goods and services flowing smoothly through the supply chain provides a competitive edge.

advanced planning and scheduling (APS) systems

Computer software systems that seek to optimize resources across the supply chain and align daily operations with strategic goals.

LEARNING GOALS IN REVIEW

Learning Goal	Guidelines for Review	MyOMLab Resources
① Explain the rationale behind the levels in the operations planning and scheduling process.	The section "Levels in Operations Planning and Scheduling," pp. 375–378, shows the various levels in a hierarchy of plans and how they relate to each other. There are two key figures in this section: Figure 10.1 shows the information inputs to the sales and operations plan, which is at the top of the hierarchy, and Figure 10.2 shows the levels of plans.	**Video:** Sales and Operations Planning at Starwood
② Describe the supply options used in sales and operations planning.	See the section "S&OP Supply Options," pp. 378–379, for the six ways managers can satisfy demands with the sales and operations plan.	
③ Compare the chase planning strategy to the level planning strategy for developing sales and operations plans.	"S&OP Strategies," pp. 379–382, explains the chase and level strategies, the related constraints and costs, and the process managers use to develop a sales and operations plan. Figure 10.3 shows what a sales and operations plan looks like.	**Active Model Exercise:** 10.1: Level Strategy **OM Explorer Tutors:** 10.1: Chase Strategy; 10.2: Level Strategy **Tutor Exercise:** 10.1: Results of Different Scenarios with a Level Strategy
④ Use spreadsheets for sales and operations planning.	See "Spreadsheets for Sales and Operations Planning," pp. 382–385, for a detailed discussion of how to use spreadsheets in S&OP. Example 10.1, pp. 383–385, demonstrates the procedure for doing S&OP for a service facility. See also Solved Problem 1, pp. 394–395.	**OM Explorer Solver:** Sales and Operations Planning with Spreadsheets **OM Explorer Tutor:** 10.4: Staffing Strategies with Spreadsheets
⑤ Develop workforce and workstation schedules.	The section "Scheduling," pp. 386–393, shows how to use Gantt charts, create workforce schedules, and sequence jobs at a workstation. Additional help can be found in Example 10.2, pp. 389–390, and Solved Problem 2, pp. 395–396, for workforce schedules, and Example 10.3, pp. 391–392, and Solved Problem 3, pp. 396–397, for sequencing jobs.	**Video:** Air New Zealand: Service Scheduling **OM Explorer Solvers:** Workforce Scheduler; Single-Workstation Scheduler **OM Explorer Tutor:** 10.3: Developing a Workforce Schedule **Tutor Exercise:** 10.2: Staffing for the Newest MBA Class **POM for Windows:** Scheduling **Case:** Food King

Key Terms

advanced planning and scheduling (APS) systems 393
aggregate plan 375
annual plan (or financial plan) 376
backorder and stockout cost 380
business plan 376
chase strategy 379
earliest due date (EDD) 390
expediting 391
first-come, first-served (FCFS) 390
fixed schedule 388

flow time 391
hiring and layoff cost 380
inventory holding cost 380
level strategy 379
mixed strategy 380
operations planning and scheduling 375
overtime 379
overtime cost 380
past due 391
priority sequencing rule 390
product family 376

production plan 375
regular time cost 380
resource plan 375
rotating schedule 388
sales and operations plan (S&OP) 375
schedule 375
sequencing 390
staffing plan 380
tardiness 391
undertime 379
workforce scheduling 387

Solved Problem 1

MyOMLab

Tutor 10.4 in MyOMLab provides another example for practicing sales and operations planning using a variety of strategies.

MyOMLab Video

The Cranston Telephone Company employs workers who lay telephone cables and perform various other construction tasks. The company prides itself on good service and strives to complete all service orders within the planning period in which they are received.

Each worker puts in 600 hours of regular time per planning period and can work as many as an additional 100 hours of overtime. The operations department has estimated the following staff requirements for such services over the next four planning periods:

Planning Period	1	2	3	4
Demand (hours)	21,000	18,000	30,000	12,000

Cranston pays regular-time wages of $6,000 per employee per period for any time worked up to 600 hours (including undertime). The overtime pay rate is $15 per hour over 600 hours. Hiring, training, and outfitting a new employee costs $8,000. Layoff costs are $2,000 per employee. Currently, 40 employees work for Cranston in this capacity. No delays in service, or backorders, are allowed. Use the spreadsheet approach to answer the following questions:

a. Prepare a chase strategy using only hiring and layoffs. What are the total numbers of employees hired and laid off?

b. Develop a staffing plan that uses the level strategy, relaying only on overtime and undertime. Maximize the use of overtime during the peak period so as to minimize the workforce level and amount of undertime.

c. Propose an effective mixed-strategy plan.

d. Compare the total costs of the three plans.

SOLUTION

a. The chase strategy workforce level is calculated by dividing the demand for each period by 600 hours, or the amount or regular-time work for one employee during one period. This strategy calls for a total of 20 workers to be hired and 40 to be laid off during the four-period plan. Figure 10.9 shows the "chase strategy" solution that OM Explorer's *Sales and Operations Planning with Spreadsheets* Solver produces. We simply hide any unneeded columns and rows in this general-purpose solver.

FIGURE 10.9 ▶
Spreadsheet for Chase Strategy

	1	2	3	4	Total
Inputs					
Forecasted demand	35	30	50	20	135
Workforce level	35	30	50	20	135
Undertime	0	0	0	0	0
Overtime	0	0	0	0	0
Derived					
Utilized time	35	30	50	20	135
Hires	0	0	20	0	20
Layoffs	5	5	0	30	40
Calculated					
Utilized time cost	$210,000	$180,000	$300,000	$120,000	$810,000
Undertime cost	$0	$0	$0	$0	$0
Overtime cost	$0	$0	$0	$0	$0
Hiring cost	$0	$0	$160,000	$0	$160,000
Layoff cost	$10,000	$10,000	$0	$60,000	$80,000
Total cost	$220,000	190,000	460,000	180,000	$1,050,000

b. The peak demand is 30,000 hours in period 3. As each employee can work 700 hours per period (600 on regular time and 100 on overtime), the workforce level of the level strategy that minimizes undertime is $30{,}000/700 = 42.86$, or 43 employees. This strategy calls for three employees to be hired in the first quarter and for none to be laid off. To convert the demand requirements into employee-period equivalents, divide the demand in hours by 600. For example, the demand of 21,000 hours in period 1 translates into 35 employee-period equivalents (21,000/600) and demand in period 3 translates into 50 employee-period equivalents (30,000/600). Figure 10.10 shows OM Explorer's spreadsheet for this level strategy that minimizes undertime.

	1	2	3	4	Total
Inputs					
Forecasted demand	35	30	50	20	135
Workforce level	43	43	43	43	172
Undertime	8	13	0	23	44
Overtime	0	0	7	0	7
Derived					
Utilized time	35	30	43	20	128
Hires	3	0	0	0	3
Layoffs	0	0	0	0	0
Calculated					
Utilized time cost	$210,000	$180,000	$258,000	$120,000	$768,000
Undertime cost	$48,000	$78,000	$0	$138,000	$264,000
Overtime cost	$0	$0	$63,000	$0	$63,000
Hiring cost	$24,000	$0	$0	$0	$24,000
Layoff cost	$0	$0	$0	$0	$0
Total cost	$282,000	258,000	321,000	258,000	$1,119,000

◀ **FIGURE 10.10**
Spreadsheet for Level Strategy

c.   The mixed-strategy plan that we propose uses a combination of hires, layoffs, and overtime to reduce total costs. The workforce is reduced by 5 at the beginning of the first period, increased by 8 in the third period, and reduced by 13 in the fourth period. Figure 10.11 shows the results.

	1	2	3	4	Total
Inputs					
Forecasted demand	35	30	50	20	135
Workforce level	35	35	43	30	143
Undertime	0	5	0	10	15
Overtime	0	0	7	0	7
Derived					
Utilized time	35	30	43	20	128
Hires	0	0	8	0	8
Layoffs	5	0	0	13	18
Calculated					
Utilized time cost	$210,000	$180,000	$258,000	$120,000	$768,000
Undertime cost	$0	$30,000	$0	$60,000	$90,000
Overtime cost	$0	$0	$63,000	$0	$63,000
Hiring cost	$0	$0	$64,000	$0	$64,000
Layoff cost	$10,000	$0	$0	$26,000	$36,000
Total cost	$220,000	210,000	385,000	206,000	$1,021,000

◀ **FIGURE 10.11**
Spreadsheet for Mixed Strategy

d.   The total cost of the chase strategy is $1,050,000. The level strategy results in a total cost of $1,119,000. The mixed-strategy plan was developed by trial and error and results in a total cost of $1,021,000. Further improvements are possible.

Solved Problem 2

The Food Bin grocery store operates 24 hours per day, 7 days per week. Fred Bulger, the store manager, has been analyzing the efficiency and productivity of store operations recently. Bulger decided to observe the need for checkout clerks on the first shift for a one-month period. At the end of the month, he calculated the average number of checkout registers that should be open during the first shift each day. His results showed peak needs on Saturdays and Sundays.

Day	M	T	W	Th	F	S	Su
Number of Clerks Required	3	4	5	5	4	7	8

Bulger now has to come up with a workforce schedule that guarantees each checkout clerk two consecutive days off, but still covers all requirements.

a.   Develop a workforce schedule that covers all requirements while giving two consecutive days off to each clerk. How many clerks are needed? Assume that the clerks have no preference regarding which days they have off.

b. Plans can be made to use the clerks for other duties if slack or idle time resulting from this schedule can be determined. How much idle time will result from this schedule, and on what days?

SOLUTION

a. We use the method demonstrated in Example 10.2 to determine the number of clerks needed. The minimum number of clerks is eight.

	DAY						
	M	**T**	**W**	**Th**	**F**	**S**	**Su**
Requirements	3	4	5	5	4	7	8*
Clerk 1	off	off	X	X	X	X	X
Requirements	3	4	4	4	3	6	7*
Clerk 2	off	off	X	X	X	X	X
Requirements	3	4	3	3	2	5	6*
Clerk 3	X	X	X	off	off	X	X
Requirements	2	3	2	3	2	4	5*
Clerk 4	X	X	X	off	off	X	X
Requirements	1	2	1	3	2	3	4*
Clerk 5	X	off	off	X	X	X	X
Requirements	0	2	1	2	1	2	3*
Clerk 6	off	off	X	X	X	X	X
Requirements	0	2*	0	1	0	1	2*
Clerk 7	X	X	off	off	X	X	X
Requirements	0	1*	0	1*	0	0	1*
Clerk 8	X	X	X	X	off	off	X
Requirements	0	0	0	0	0	0	0

*Maximum requirements

b. Based on the results in part (a), the number of clerks on duty minus the requirements is the number of idle clerks available for other duties:

	M	**T**	**W**	**Th**	**F**	**S**	**Su**
Number on duty	5	4	6	5	5	7	8
Requirements	3	4	5	5	4	7	8
Idle clerks	2	0	1	0	1	0	0

The slack in this schedule would indicate to Bulger the number of employees he might ask to work part time (fewer than 5 days per week). For example, Clerk 7 might work Tuesday, Saturday, and Sunday, and Clerk 8 might work Tuesday, Thursday, and Sunday. That would eliminate slack from the schedule.

Solved Problem 3

Revisit Example 10.3, where the consulting company has five jobs in its backlog. Create a schedule using the EDD rule, calculating the average days past due and flow time. In this case, does EDD outperform the FCFS rule?

SOLUTION

Customer Sequence	Start Time (days)		Processing Time (days)		Finish Time (days)	Due Date	Days Past Due	Days Ago Since Order Arrived	Flow Time (days)
B	0	+	16	=	16	27	**0**	12	**28**
A	16	+	25	=	41	29	**12**	15	**56**
D	41	+	10	=	51	48	**3**	10	**61**
C	51	+	14	=	65	68	**0**	5	**70**
E	65	+	12	=	77	80	**0**	0	**77**

The days past due and average flow time performance measures for the EDD schedule are

$$\text{Average days past due} = \frac{0 + 12 + 3 + 0 + 0}{5} = 3.0 \text{ days}$$

$$\text{Average flow time} = \frac{28 + 56 + 61 + 70 + 77}{5} = 58.4 \text{ days}$$

By both measures, EDD outperforms the FCFS (3.0 versus 3.4 days past due and 58.4 versus 60.2 days flow time). However, the solution found in part (b) of Example 10.3 still has the best average flow time of only 47.8 days.

Discussion Questions

1. List the types of costs incurred when employees are laid off. What costs are difficult to estimate in monetary terms? Suppose that a firm is facing a downturn in business, each employee has skills valued at $40,000 per year, and it costs $100,000 to lay off an employee. If business is expected to improve in one year, are layoffs financially justified? What is the "payback" period for the layoff decision?

2. In your community, some employers maintain stable workforces at all costs, and others furlough and recall workers seemingly at the drop of a hat. What are the differences in markets, management, products, financial position, skills, costs, and competition that could explain these two extremes in personnel policy?

3. Consider Managerial Practice 10.1 and the manner in which Air New Zealand schedules its flight crews. Relate each step in the process to the levels in the operations planning and scheduling process shown in Figure 10.2.

4. Explain why management should be concerned about priority systems in service and manufacturing organizations.

Problems

The OM Explorer and POM for Windows software is available to all students using the 11th edition of this textbook. Go to **http:// www.pearsonhighered.com/krajewski** to download these computer packages. If you purchased MyOMLab, you also have access to Active Models software and significant help in doing the following problems. Check with your instructor on how best to use these resources. In many cases, the instructor wants you to understand how to do the calculations by hand. At the least, the software provides a check on your calculations. When calculations are particularly complex and the goal is interpreting the results in making decision, the software entirely replaces the manual calculations.

S&OP Strategies

1. The Barberton Municipal Division of Road Maintenance is charged with road repair in the city of Barberton and the surrounding area. Cindy Kramer, road maintenance director, must submit a staffing plan for the next year based on a set schedule for repairs and on the city budget. Kramer estimates that the labor hours required for the next four quarters are 6,000, 12,000, 19,000, and 9,000, respectively. Each of the 11 workers on the workforce can contribute 500 hours per quarter. Payroll costs are $6,000 in wages per worker for regular time worked up to 500 hours, with an overtime pay rate of $18 for each overtime hour. Overtime is limited to 20 percent of the regular-time capacity in any quarter. Although unused overtime capacity has no cost, unused regular time is paid at $12 per hour. The cost of hiring a worker is $3,000, and the cost of laying off a worker is $2,000. Subcontracting is not permitted.

    a. Find a level staffing plan that relies just on overtime and the minimum amount of undertime possible. Overtime can be used to its limits in any quarter. What is the total cost of the plan and how many undertime hours does it call for?

    b. Use a chase strategy that varies the workforce level without using overtime or undertime. What is the total cost of this plan?

    c. Propose a plan of your own. Compare your plan with those in part (a) and part (b) and discuss its comparative merits.

2. Bob Carlton's golf camp estimates the following staff requirements for its services over the next 2 years.

Quarter	1	2	3	4
Demand (hours)	4,200	6,400	3,000	4,800
Quarter	5	6	7	8
Demand (hours)	4,400	6,240	3,600	4,800

Each certified instructor puts in 480 hours per quarter regular time and can work an additional 120 hours overtime. Regular-time wages and benefits cost Carlton $7,200 per employee per quarter for regular time worked up to 480 hours, with an overtime cost of $20 per hour. Unused regular time for certified instructors is paid at $15 per hour. There is no cost for unused overtime capacity. The cost of hiring, training, and certifying a new employee is $10,000. Layoff costs are $4,000 per employee. Currently, eight employees work in this capacity.

a. Find a staffing plan using the level strategy that allows for no delay in service. It should rely only on overtime and the minimum amount of undertime necessary. What is the total cost of this plan?

b. Use a chase strategy that varies the workforce level without using overtime or undertime. What is the total cost of this plan?

c. Propose a better plan and calculate its total cost.

3. Continuing Problem 2, now assume that Carlton is permitted to employ some uncertified, part-time instructors, provided they represent no more than 15 percent of the total workforce hours (regular, overtime, and part-time) in any quarter. Each part-time instructor can work up to 240 hours per quarter, with no overtime or undertime cost. Labor costs for part-time instructors are $12 per hour. Hiring and training costs are $2,000 per uncertified instructor, and there are no layoff costs.

a. Propose a low-cost, mixed-strategy plan and calculate its total cost.

b. What are the primary advantages and disadvantages of having a workforce consisting of both regular and temporary employees?

4. The Donald Fertilizer Company produces industrial chemical fertilizers. The projected manufacturing requirements (in thousands of gallons) for the next four quarters are 80, 50, 80, and 130, respectively. A level workforce is desired, relying only on anticipation inventory as a supply option. Stockouts and backorders are to be avoided, as are overtime and undertime.

a. Determine the quarterly production rate required to meet total demand for the year, and minimize the anticipation inventory that would be left over at the end of the year. Beginning inventory is zero.

b. Specify the anticipation inventory that will be produced.

c. Suppose that the requirements for the next four quarters are revised to 80, 130, 50, and 80, respectively. If total demand is the same, what level of production rate is needed now, using the same strategy as part (a)?

5. Management at the Kerby Corporation has determined the following aggregated demand schedule (in units):

Month	1	2	3	4
Demand	500	800	1,000	1,400
Month	5	6	7	8
Demand	2,000	3,000	2,700	1,500
Month	9	10	11	12
Demand	1,400	1,500	2,000	1,200

An employee can produce an average of 10 units per month. Each worker on the payroll costs $2,000 in regular-time wages per month. Undertime is paid at the same rate as regular time. In accordance with the labor contract in force, Kerby Corporation does not work overtime or use subcontracting. Kerby can hire and train a new employee for $2,000 and lay off one for $500. Inventory costs $32 per unit on hand at the end of each month. At present, 140 employees are on the payroll and anticipation inventory is zero.

a. Prepare a production plan that only uses a level workforce and anticipation inventory as its supply options. Minimize the inventory left over at the end of the year. Layoffs, undertime, vacations, subcontracting, backorders, and stockouts are not options. The plan may call for a one-time adjustment of the workforce before month 1 begins.

b. Prepare a production plan using a chase strategy, relying only on hiring and layoffs.

c. Prepare a mixed-strategy production plan that uses only a level workforce and anticipation inventory through month 7 (an adjustment of the workforce may be made before month 1 begins) then switches to a chase strategy for months 8–12.

d. Contrast these three plans on the basis of annual costs.

6. Gretchen's Kitchen is a fast-food restaurant located in an ideal spot near the local high school. Gretchen Lowe must prepare an annual staffing plan. The only menu items are hamburgers, chili, soft drinks, shakes, and French fries. A sample of 1,000 customers taken at random revealed that they purchased 2,100 hamburgers, 200 pints of chili, 1,000 soft drinks and shakes, and 1,000 bags of French fries. Thus, for purposes of estimating staffing requirements, Lowe assumes that each customer purchases 2.1 hamburgers, 0.2 pint of chili, 1 soft drink or shake, and 1 bag of French fries. Each hamburger requires 4 minutes of labor, a pint of chili requires 3 minutes, and a soft drink or shake and a bag of fries each take 2 minutes of labor.

The restaurant currently has 10 part-time employees who work 80 hours a month on staggered shifts. Wages are $400 per month for regular time and $7.50 per hour for overtime. Hiring and training costs are $250 per new employee, and layoff costs are $50 per employee.

Lowe realizes that building up seasonal inventories of hamburgers (or any of the products) would not be wise because of shelf-life considerations. Also, any demand not satisfied is a lost sale and must be avoided. Three strategies come to mind.

- Use a level strategy relying on overtime and undertime, with up to 20 percent of regular-time capacity on overtime.
- Maintain a base of 10 employees, hiring and laying off as needed to avoid any overtime.
- Utilize a chase strategy, hiring and laying off employees as demand changes to avoid overtime.

When performing her calculations, Lowe always rounds to the next highest integer for the number of employees. She also follows a policy of not using an employee more than 80 hours per month, except when overtime is needed. The projected demand by month (number of customers) for next year is as follows:

Jan.	3,200	July	4,800
Feb.	2,600	Aug.	4,200
Mar.	3,300	Sept.	3,800
Apr.	3,900	Oct.	3,600
May	3,600	Nov.	3,500
June	4,200	Dec.	3,000

a. Develop the schedule of service requirements (hours per month) for the next year.

b. Which strategy is most effective?

c. Suppose that an arrangement with the high school enables the manager to identify good prospective employees without having to advertise in the local newspaper. This source reduces the hiring cost to $50, which is mainly the cost of charred hamburgers during training. If cost is her only concern, will this method of hiring change Gretchen Lowe's strategy? Considering other objectives that may be appropriate, do you think she should change strategies?

7. A manager faces peak (weekly) demand for one of her operations, but is not sure how long the peak will last. She can either use overtime from the current workforce, or hire/lay off and just pay regular-time wages. Regular-time pay is $500 per week, overtime is $750 per week, the hiring cost is $2,000, and the layoff cost is $3,000. Assuming that people are available seeking such a short-term arrangement, how many weeks must the surge in demand last to justify a temporary hire? *Hint:* Use break-even analysis (see Supplement A, "Decision Making"). Let w be the number of weeks of the high demand (rather than using Q for the break-even quantity). What is the fixed cost for the regular-time option? Overtime option?

Spreadsheets for Sales and Operations Planning

8. Tax Prep Advisers, Inc., has forecasted the following staffing requirements for tax preparation associates over the next 12 months. Management would like three alternative staffing plans to be developed.

Month	1	2	3	4
Demand	5	8	10	13
Month	5	6	7	8
Demand	18	20	20	14
Month	9	10	11	12
Demand	12	8	2	1

The company currently has 10 associates. No more than 10 new hires can be accommodated in any month because of limited training facilities. No backorders are allowed, and overtime cannot exceed 25 percent of regular-time capacity on any month. There is no cost for unused overtime capacity. Regular-time wages are $1,500 per month, and overtime wages are 150 percent of regular-time wages. Undertime is paid at the same rate as regular time. The hiring cost is $2,500 per person, and the layoff cost is $2.000 per person.

a. Prepare a staffing plan utilizing a level workforce strategy, minimizing undertime. The plan may call for a one-time adjustment of the workforce before month 1.

b. Using a chase strategy, prepare a plan that is consistent with the constraint on hiring and minimizes use of overtime.

c. Prepare a mixed strategy in which the workforce level is slowly increased by two employees per month through month 5 and is then decreased by two employees per month starting in month 6 and continuing through month 12. Does this plan violate the hiring or overtime constraints set the company?

d. Contrast these three plans on the basis of annual costs.

9. Climate Control, Inc., makes expedition-quality rain gear for outdoor enthusiasts. Management prepared a forecast of sales (in suits) for next year and now must prepare a production plan. The company has traditionally maintained a level workforce strategy. All nine workers are treated like family and have been employed by the company for a number of years. Each employee can produce 2,000 suits per month. At present, finished goods inventory holds 24,000 suits. The demand forecast follows:

Month	1	2	3	4
Demand	25,000	16,000	15,000	19,000
Month	5	6	7	8
Demand	32,000	29,000	27,000	22,000
Month	9	10	11	12
Demand	14,000	15,000	20,000	6,000

Use the *Sales and Operations Planning with Spreadsheets* Solver in OM Explorer or develop your own spreadsheet models to address the following questions.

a. Management is willing to authorize overtime in periods for which regular production and current levels of anticipation inventory do not satisfy demand. However, overtime must be strictly limited to no more than 20 percent of regular-time capacity. Management wants to avoid stockouts and backorders and is not willing to accept a plan that calls for shortages. Is it feasible to hold the workforce constant, assuming that overtime is only used in periods for which shortages would occur?

b. Assume that management is not willing to authorize any overtime. Instead, management is willing to negotiate with customers so that backorders may be used as a supply option. However, management is not willing to carry more than 5,000 suits from one month to the next in backorder. Is it feasible to hold the workforce constant, assuming that a maximum backorder of 5,000 suits may be maintained from month to month?

c. Assume management is willing to authorize the use of overtime over the next four months to build additional anticipation inventory. However, overtime must be strictly limited to no more than 20 percent of regular-time capacity. Management wants to avoid stockouts and backorders and is not willing to accept a plan that calls for shortages. Is it feasible to hold the workforce constant, assuming that overtime is only used in months 1–4? If not, in which months would additional overtime be required?

10. The Kool King Company has followed a policy of no layoffs for most of the manufacturer's life, even though the demand for its air conditioners is highly seasonal. Management wants to evaluate the cost-effectiveness of this policy. Competitive pressures are increasing, and ways need to be found to reduce costs. The following demand (expressed in employee–month equivalents) has been forecast for next year:

Jan.	70	May	130	Sept.	110
Feb.	90	June	170	Oct.	60
Mar.	100	July	170	Nov.	20
Apr.	100	Aug.	150	Dec.	40

Additional planning data follow, with costs, inventory, and backorders expressed in employee–month equivalents:

Regular-time production cost	$1,500	Hire cost	$500/person
Overtime production cost	150% of regular-time production cost	Layoff cost	$2,000/person
Subcontracting cost	$2,500	Current backorders	10
Inventory holding cost	$100	Current inventory	0
Backorder cost	$1,000	Desired ending inventory	0
Maximum overtime	20% of regular-time capacity	Current employment	130 employees

Hiring costs are lower than layoff costs because the facility is located near a Technical Training School. Undertime is paid at the rate equivalent to regular-time production. Each employee who has been with the company at least one year also received 0.5 months of paid vacation. All 130 employees currently employed qualify for vacations next year, assuming that they remain on the workforce. Answer the following questions using *Sales and Operations Planning with Spreadsheets* Solver in OM Explorer, or an Excel spreadsheet that you developed on your own.

a. Develop an S&OP with the level strategy using overtime, undertime, and vacations as the only supply options. Use the maximum amount of overtime so as to minimize undertime. What is the total cost of this plan, and what are its advantages and disadvantages?

b. Develop an S&OP with the chase strategy. Part of your decision will be when and how many vacation periods to grant. What is the total cost of this plan, and what are its advantages and disadvantages?

c. Develop an S&OP with a lower cost than found with either the level or chase strategy, being open to the full range of supply options (including anticipation inventory). Subcontractors can supply up to 50 employee-month equivalents. What is the total cost of this plan, and what are its advantages and disadvantages?

11. Jane Dapna, the operations manager of Classico Inc., is using the *Sales and Operations Planning with Spreadsheets* Solver in OM Explorer to develop a five month production plan. Her initial plan is to maintain a level workforce and use overtime and backorders as shown below. Use the provided inputs to calculate the derived inputs: Utilized time, Inventory, Hires and Layoffs, and the associated costs. (*Hint:* Don't forget to express the forecasted demand and reactive alternatives as employee-period equivalents.)

Inputs								
Starting Workforce		20		Cost to Hire One Worker				$ 10,000.00
Wages per Worker per Period		$ 4,000.00		Cost to Lay Off One Worker				$ 20,000.00
Overtime Pay Percentage		150%		Initial Inventory Level				10
Subcontracting Cost per Period		0		Initial Backorders				0
				Inventory Cost				$ 100.00
				Backorder Cost				$ 250.00

Period	January	February	March	April	May		Total
Inputs							
Forecasted demand	20	30	40	30	20		140
Workforce level	20	20	20	20	20		100
Undertime	0	0	0	0	0		0
Overtime	0	0	10	20	0		30
Vacation time	0	0	0	0	0		0
Subcontracting time	0	0	0	0	0		0
Backorders	0	0	10	0	0		10
Derived							
Utilized time							100
Inventory							10
Hires							0
Layoffs							0
Calculated							
Utilized time cost							$ 400,000.00
Undertime cost							$ -
Overtime cost							$ 180,000.00
Vacation time cost							$ -
Inventory cost							$ 1,000.00
Backorders cost							$ 2,500.00
Hiring cost							$ -
Layoff cost							$ -
Subcontracting cost							$ -
Total cost							$ 583,500.00

Reminder: Express the forecasted demand and reactive alternatives as employee-period equivalents.

12. Gemini Inc. is using the *Sales and Operations Planning with Spreadsheets* Solver in OM Explorer to develop a five month production plan. Use the provided Derived outputs and Calculated costs to specify the model's inputs. (*Hint:* Don't forget that the forecasted demand and reactive alternatives are expressed as employee-period equivalents.)

Inputs						
Starting Workforce		20		Cost to Hire One Worker		$ 20,000.00
Wages per Worker per Period		$ 2,500.00		Cost to Lay Off One Worker		$ 5,000.00
Overtime Pay Percentage		150%		Initial Inventory Level		0
Subcontracting Cost per Period		0		Initial Backorders		10
				Inventory Cost		$ 100.00
				Backorder Cost		$ 250.00

Period	January	February	March	April	May		Total
Inputs							
Forecasted demand							165
Workforce level							130
Undertime							0
Overtime							35
Vacation time							0
Subcontracting time							0
Backorders							10
Derived							
Utilized time	20	20	30	30	30		130
Inventory	0	10	15	15	0		40
Hires	0	0	10	0	0		10
Layoffs	0	0	0	0	0		0
Calculated							
Utilized time cost	$ 50,000.00	$ 50,000.00	$ 75,000.00	$ 75,000.00	$ 75,000.00		$ 325,000.00
Undertime cost	$ -	$ -	$ -	$ -	$ -		$ -
Overtime cost	$ -	$ -	$ 56,250.00	$ 37,500.00	$ 37,500.00		$ 131,250.00
Vacation time cost	$ -	$ -	$ -	$ -	$ -		$ -
Inventory cost	$ -	$ 1,000.00	$ 1,500.00	$ 1,500.00	$ -		$ 4,000.00
Backorders cost	$ -	$ -	$ -	$ -	$ 2,500.00		$ 2,500.00
Hiring cost	$ -	$ -	$ 20,000.00	$ -	$ -		$ 20,000.00
Layoff cost	$ -	$ -	$ -	$ -	$ -		$ -
Subcontracting cost	$ -	$ -	$ -	$ -	$ -		$ -
Total cost	$ 50,000.00	$ 51,000.00	$ 152,750.00	$ 114,000.00	$ 115,000.00		$ 482,750.00

Reminder: Express the forecasted demand and reactive alternatives as employee-period equivalents.

Scheduling

13. Gerald Glynn manages the Michaels Distribution Center. After careful examination of his database information, he has determined the daily requirements for part-time loading dock personnel. The distribution center operates 7 days a week, and the daily part-time staffing requirements are

Day	M	T	W	Th	F	S	Su
Requirements	6	3	5	3	7	2	3

Find the minimum number of workers Glynn must hire. Prepare a workforce schedule for these individuals so that each will have two consecutive days off per week and all staffing requirements will be satisfied. Give preference to the S–Su pair in case of a tie.

14. Cara Ryder manages a ski school in a large resort and is trying to develop a schedule for instructors. The instructors receive little salary and work just enough to earn room and board. They receive free skiing and spend most of their free time tackling the resort's notorious double black-diamond slopes. Hence, the instructors work only 4 days a week. One of the lesson packages offered at the resort is a 4-day beginner package. Ryder likes to keep the same instructor with a group over the 4-day period, so she schedules the instructors for 4 consecutive days and then 3 days off. Ryder uses years of experience with demand forecasts provided by management to formulate her instructor requirements for the upcoming month.

Day	M	T	W	Th	F	S	Su
Requirements	7	5	4	5	6	9	8

a. Determine how many instructors Ryder needs to employ. Give preference to Saturday and Sunday off. (*Hint:* Look for the group of 3 days with the lowest requirements.)

b. Specify the work schedule for each employee. How much slack does your schedule generate for each day?

15. The mayor of Cambridge, Colorado, wanting to be environmentally progressive, decides to implement a recycling plan. All residents of the city will receive a special three-part bin to separate their glass, plastic, and aluminum, and the city will be responsible for picking up the materials. A young city and regional planning graduate, Michael Duffy, has been hired to manage the recycling program. After carefully studying the city's population density, Duffy decides that the following numbers of recycling collectors will be needed:

Day	M	T	W	Th	F	S	Su
Requirements	12	7	9	9	5	3	6

The requirements are based on the populations of the various housing developments and subdivisions in the city and surrounding communities. To motivate residents of some areas to have their pickups scheduled on weekends, a special tax break will be given.

a. Find the minimum number of recycling collectors required if each employee works 5 days a week and has two consecutive days off. Give preference to the S–Su pair when that pair is involved in a tie.

b. Specify the work schedule for each employee. How much slack does your schedule generate for each day?

c. Suppose that Duffy can smooth the requirements further through greater tax incentives. The requirements then will be eight collectors on Monday and seven on the other days of the week. How many collectors will be needed now? Does smoothing of requirements have capital investment implications? If so, what are they?

16. Little 6, Inc., an accounting firm, forecasts the following weekly workload during the tax season:

	DAY						
	M	**T**	**W**	**Th**	**F**	**S**	**Su**
Personal Tax Returns	24	14	18	18	10	28	16
Corporate Tax Returns	16	10	12	15	24	12	4

Corporate tax returns each require 4 hours of an accountant's time, and personal returns each require 90 minutes. During tax season, each accountant can work up to 10 hours per day. However, error rates increase to unacceptable levels when accountants work more than 5 consecutive days per week.

Hint: Read Supplement D before doing this problem. Let x_i = number for each working schedule, e.g., x_1 = number for Tuesday through Saturday.

a. Create an effective and efficient work schedule by formulating the problem as a linear program and solve using POM for Windows.

b. Assume that management has decided to offer a pay differential to those accountants who are scheduled to work on a weekend day. Normally, accountants earn $1,200 per week, but management will pay a bonus of $100 for Saturday work and $150 for Sunday work. What schedule will cover all demand as well as minimize payroll cost?

c. Assume that Little 6 has three part-time employees available to work Friday, Saturday, and Sunday at a rate of $800. Could these employees be cost effectively utilized?

17. Return to Problem 13 and the workforce schedule for part-time loading dock workers. Suppose that each part-time worker can work only 3 days, but the days must be consecutive. Formulate and solve this workforce scheduling problem as a linear program and solve it using POM for Windows. Your objective is to minimize total slack capacity. What is the minimum number of loaders needed now, and what are their schedules?

Hint: Read Supplement D before doing this problem. Let x_i = number of workers for each 3-day schedule, for instance, x_1 = number of workers for Tuesday through Thursday.

18. The Hickory Company manufactures wooden desks. Management schedules overtime every weekend to reduce the backlog on the most popular models. The automatic routing machine is used to cut certain types of edges on the desktops. The following orders need to be scheduled for the routing machine:

Order	Time Since Order Arrived (hours ago)	Estimated Machine Time (hours)	Due Date (hours from now)
1	6	10	12
2	5	3	8
3	3	15	18
4	1	9	20
5	0	7	21

The due dates reflect the need for the order to be at its next operation.

a. Develop separate schedules by using the FCFS and EDD rules. Compare the schedules on the basis of average flow time and average past due hours.

b. Comment on the performance of the two rules relative to these measures.

19. Currently a company that designs Web sites has five customers in its backlog. The day when the order arrived, processing time, and promised due dates are given in the following table. The customers are listed in the order of when they arrived. They are ready to be scheduled today, which is the start of day 190.

Customer	Time Since Order Arrived (days ago)	Processing Time (days)	Due Date (days from now)
A	10	20	26
B	8	12	50
C	6	28	66
D	3	24	58
E	2	32	100

a. Develop separate schedules by using the FCFS and EDD rules. Compare the schedules on the basis of average flow time and average days past due.

b. Comment on the performance of the two rules relative to these measures. Which one gives the best schedule? Why?

20. The Mowry Machine Shop still has five jobs to be processed as of 8 A.M. today (day 23) at its bottleneck operation. The day when the order arrived, processing time, and promised due dates are given in the following table. The jobs are listed in the order of arrival.

Job	Time Since Order Arrived (days ago)	Processing Time (days)	Due Date (days from now)
A	11	10	22
B	10	8	13
C	8	4	19
D	6	4	16
E	1	3	30

a. Develop separate schedules by using the FCFS and EDD rules. Compare the schedules on the basis of average flow time and average days past due.

b. Which rule gives the best schedule, in your judgment? Why?

Active Model Exercise

Active Model 10.1, "Level Strategy," appears in MyOMLab. It allows you to evaluate the effects of modifying the size of a constant workforce.

QUESTIONS

1. If we use the same number of workers in each period, what happens as the number of workers increases from 15?

2. If we use the same number of workers in each period, what happens as the number of workers decreases from 15?

3. Suppose the hiring cost is $1,100. What happens as the number of workers increases?

4. Suppose the overtime cost is $3,300. What happens as the number of workers increases?

5. Suppose the undertime cost is the same as the regular-time cost (i.e., paid undertime). What is the best number of workers to have in each month and still meet the demand?

6. If the overtime capacity increases to 30 percent, what is the minimum number of workers that meets the demand in every month?

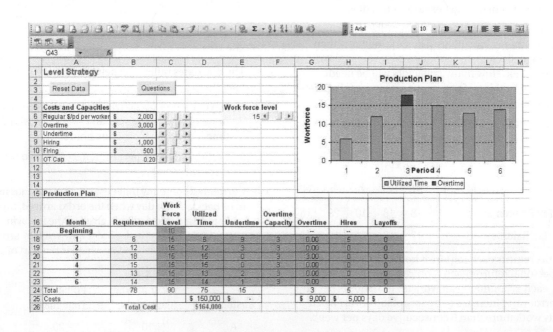

VIDEO CASE	Sales and Operations Planning at Starwood

Business travel often means staying overnight in a hotel. Upon arrival, you may be greeted by a doorman or valet to assist you with your luggage. Front desk staff awaits your check-in. Behind the scenes, housekeeping, maintenance, and culinary staff prepare for your stay. Making a reservation gives the hotel notice of your plan to stay, but even before your trip is ever conceived, the hotel is staffed and ready. How? Through a process called *sales and operations planning*.

Sales and operations planning is a process every organization performs to some degree. Called a staffing plan (or service resource plan if more detailed) in service organizations, the plan must strike the right level of customer service while maintaining workforce stability and cost control so as to achieve the organization's profit expectations. So where do companies begin? Let us take a look at Starwood Hotels and Resorts to see how it is done.

Starwood operates in more than 750 locations around the globe. At the highest levels, Starwood engages in sales and operations planning on an annual basis, with adjustments made as needed each month by region and by property. Budgeted revenues and other projections come from headquarters; the regions and individual properties then break down the forecasts to meet their expected occupancies. Typically, the director of human resources determines the staffing mix needed across divisions such as food and beverage service, rooms (including housekeeping, spa, and guest services), engineering, Six Sigma (see Chapter 3, "Quality and Performance"), revenue management, and accounting.

At the property level, general managers and their staff must provide input into next year's plan while implementing and monitoring activity in the current year. For most properties, payroll is close to 40 percent of budgeted revenues and represents the largest single expense the hotel incurs. It is also the most controllable expense. Many of Starwood's hotels and most resorts experience patterns of seasonality that affect demand for rooms and services. This seasonality, in turn, significantly affects the organization's staffing plan.

To determine the staffing levels, the company uses a proprietary software program that models occupancy demand based on historical data. The key drivers of staffing are occupied rooms and restaurant meals, called "covers." Starwood knows on a *per room* and *per cover* basis how many staff are required to function properly. When occupancy and covers are entered into the software program, the output models a recommended staffing level for each division. This recommendation is then reviewed by division managers and adjusted as needed to be sure staffing is in line with budgeted financial plans. Job fairs to recruit nonmanagement staff are held several times a year so a qualified candidate pool of both part-time and full-time staff is ready when needed. Most hotels maintain a pool of part-time workers who can contract or expand the hours worked if required by property guest levels. Vacations for management are scheduled for the low season. Overtime will be worked as needed, but is less desirable than scheduling the appropriate level of staff in each division.

The program also takes into account both the complexity and positioning of the property within Starwood. For example, a 400-room city hotel that is essentially a high-rise building is not as complex as a 400-room sprawling resort with golf, spa, convention, and other services not offered by the city hotel. Positioning also is important. A five-star resort hotel's customer service

A software program that forecasts occupancy based on historical data helps Starwood maintain proper staffing levels at its hotels. Managers know on a per-room, and "per-cover," basis how many hotel employees should be scheduled so that customers get good service.

expectations are much greater than a three-star airport hotel location and requires much higher ratios of staff to guests. Finally, if the hotel is a brand new property, historical data from similar properties is used to model staffing for the first year or two of operation.

Starwood attempts to modify demand and smooth out the peaks and valleys of its demand patterns. Many of the company's hotels experience three seasons: high, mid (called "shoulder"), and low season. Starwood, like its competitors, offers special rates, family packages, and weekend specials to attract different segments of the market during slower business periods. Staff is cross-trained to work in multiple areas, such as front reception and the concierge desk, so additional staff does not have to be added across seasons. Employees may also be temporarily redeployed among Starwood's properties to help out during peak periods. For example, when occupancy is forecast to be high in one region of the country, staff from areas entering their low season will be assigned to cover the demand.

QUESTIONS

1. At what points in the planning process would you expect accounting/finance, marketing, information systems, and operations to play a role? What inputs should these areas provide, and why?

2. Does Starwood employ a chase, level, or mixed strategy? Why is this approach the best choice for the company?

3. How would staffing for the opening of a new hotel or resort differ from that of an existing property? What data might Starwood rely upon to make sure the new property is not over- or understaffed in its first year of operation?

CASE | Memorial Hospital

Memorial Hospital is a 265-bed regional health care facility located in the mountains of western North Carolina. The mission of the hospital is to provide quality health care to the people of Ashe County and the six surrounding counties. To accomplish this mission, Memorial Hospital's CEO has outlined three objectives: (1) maximize customer service to increase customer satisfaction, (2) minimize costs to remain competitive, and (3) minimize fluctuations in workforce levels to help stabilize area employment.

The hospital's operations are segmented into eight major wards for the purposes of planning and scheduling the nursing staff. These wards are listed in Table 10.3, along with the number of beds, targeted patient-to-nurse ratios, and average patient census for each ward. The overall demand for hospital services remained relatively constant over the past few years even though the population of the seven counties served increased. This stable demand can be attributed to increased competition from other hospitals in the area and the rise in alternative health care delivery systems, such as health maintenance organizations (HMOs). However, demand for Memorial Hospital's services does vary considerably by type of ward and time of year. Table 10.4 provides a historical monthly breakdown of the average daily patient census per ward.

The director of nursing for Memorial Hospital is Darlene Fry. Each fall she confronts one of the most challenging aspects of her job: planning the nurse-staffing levels for the next calendar year. Although the average demand for nurses has remained relatively stable over the past couple of years, the staffing plan usually changes because of changing work policies, changing pay structures, and temporary nurse availability and cost. With fall quickly approaching, Fry is collecting information to plan next year's staffing levels.

The nurses at Memorial Hospital work a regular schedule of four 10-hour days per week. The average regular-time pay across all nursing grades is $12.00 per hour. Overtime may be scheduled when necessary. However, because of the intensity of the demands placed on nurses, only a limited amount of overtime is permitted per week. Nurses may be scheduled for as many as 12 hours per day, for a maximum of 5 days per week. Overtime is compensated at a rate of $18.00 per hour. In periods of extremely high demand, temporary part-time nurses may be hired for a limited period of time. Temporary nurses are paid $15.00 per hour. Memorial Hospital's policy limits the proportion of temporary nurses to 15 percent of the total nursing staff.

Finding, hiring, and retaining qualified nurses is an ongoing problem for hospitals. One reason is that various forms of private practice lure many nurses away from hospitals with higher pay and greater flexibility. This situation has caused Memorial to guarantee its full-time staff nurses pay for a minimum of 30 hours per week, regardless of the demand placed on nursing services. In addition, each nurse receives 4 weeks of paid vacation each year. However, vacation scheduling may be somewhat restricted by the projected demand for nurses during particular times of the year.

TABLE 10.3 | WARD CAPACITY DATA

Ward	Number of Beds	Patients per Nurse	Patient Census[*]
Intensive Care	20	2	10
Cardiac	25	4	15
Maternity	30	4	10
Pediatric	40	4	22
Surgery	5	[†]	[†]
Post-Op	15	5	8 (T–F daily equivalent)[‡]
Emergency	10	3	5 (daily equivalent)[‡]
General	120	8	98

[*]Yearly average per day

[†]The hospital employs 20 surgical nurses. Routine surgery is scheduled on Tuesdays and Fridays; five surgeries can be scheduled per day per operating room (bed) on these days. Emergency surgery is scheduled as needed.

[‡]Daily equivalents are used to schedule nurses because patients flow through these wards in relatively short periods of time. A daily equivalent of 5 indicates that throughout a typical day, an average of five patients are treated in the ward.

At present, the hospital employs 130 nurses, including 20 surgical nurses. The other 110 nurses are assigned to the remaining seven major areas of the hospital. The personnel department informed Fry that the average cost to the hospital for hiring a new full-time nurse is $400 and for laying off or firing a nurse is $150. Although layoffs are an option, Fry is aware of the hospital's objective of maintaining a level workforce.

After looking over the information that she collected, Darlene Fry wants to consider staffing changes in all areas except the surgery ward, which is already correctly staffed.

QUESTIONS

1. Explain the alternatives available to Darlene Fry as she develops a nurse-staffing plan for Memorial Hospital. How does each alternative plan meet the objective stated by the CEO?

2. Based on the data presented, develop a nurse-staffing plan for Memorial Hospital. Explain your rationale for this plan.

TABLE 10.4 | AVERAGE DAILY PATIENT CENSUS PER MONTH

Ward						MONTH						
	J	F	M	A	M	J	J	A	S	O	N	D
Intensive Care	13	10	8	7	7	6	11	13	9	10	12	14
Cardiac	18	16	15	13	14	12	13	12	13	15	18	20
Maternity	8	8	12	13	10	8	13	13	14	10	8	7
Pediatric	22	23	24	24	25	21	22	20	18	20	21	19
Surgery*	20	18	18	17	16	16	22	21	17	18	20	22
Post-Op†	10	8	7	7	6	6	10	10	7	8	9	10
Emergency†	6	4	4	7	8	5	5	4	4	3	4	6
General	110	108	100	98	95	90	88	92	98	102	107	94

Source: This case was prepared by Dr. Brooke Saladin, Wake Forest University, North Carolina, as a basis for classroom discussion. Copyright © Brooke Saladin. Reprinted with permission.

*Average surgeries per day on Tuesday and Thursday.

†Daily equivalents

12

SUPPLY CHAIN DESIGN

Geoffrey Robinson/Alamy

To compete with bricks-and-mortar competitors, Amazon has to have ample inventories at strategically located facilities to support the competitive priority of delivery speed. Here an employee in the Amazon fulfillment center In Milton Keynes, England is scanning inventory in preparation for Cyber Monday, 2012.

Amazon.com

mazon.com is a $76 billion company specializing in the online retail business. It has 96 fulfillment centers and employs 117,000 employees worldwide to deliver enormous volumes of packages of diverse products to an international clientele. On its busiest day in 2012, customers ordered more than 26.5 million items, or about 306 items per second, only 57 percent of which were in North America. Seasonality in demand patterns, customers demanding variety in product selection, and many brick-and-mortar stores offering stiff competition: if there is ever a situation where supply chain design is important, this is it.

Competing against the likes of Walmart, Target, and Best Buy is a challenging task. All have retail stores as well as an online presence. At brick-and-mortar retail stores customers can see the products they are interested in and experience instant gratification in obtaining the item the second it is bought. Also, Best Buy and Walmart, for example, use their store locations as distribution hubs for online orders, cutting their delivery times to two days or less, which is quicker than having them shipped from warehouses located across the country.

How can Amazon compete? There are four key competitive priorities for its supply chain: delivery speed, variety, customization, and low-cost operations. Amazon has achieved delivery speed by strategically locating its distribution facilities and adding more capacity, adding more than 1,300 robots to its line to help get packages out the door faster, increasing the items held in stock to support delivery speed while not over-investing in slow moving items, and working with manufacturers and distributors to ship products directly to customers for those items not in stock, a practice known as *drop shipping*. To further reduce the time between a customer's order and delivery of the products, Amazon has initiated a program to use the United States Postal Service to make Sunday home deliveries.

As for variety, customers shopping on Amazon.com have access to literally tens of millions of products. For example, a blank search of home and kitchen products on Amazon's website yields over 17 million hits, and that is only one of 38 departments a customer can shop. Only a fraction of these items are stocked in Amazon's warehouses, which puts a high priority on coordination with manufacturers and distributors. Customization is the ability to provide the specific, unique order each customer wants. The distribution process is initiated by a customer ordering from the Amazon.com website or an affiliate website. The system determines which distribution center to ship the item from or whether to use a drop shipper, who uses Amazon packaging and delivers the item directly to the customer. The decision is determined by product availability and transportation costs. Several items for an order may come from different sources, in which case they are amalgamated at transportation hubs before final delivery. Amazon is practicing *mass customization* and is using an *assemble-to-order* supply chain design. Finally, price is a major order winner for Amazon. Low prices are supported by low-cost operations in the supply chain. High volumes put a downward pressure on per-unit prices from manufacturers and distributors. Further, Amazon's revenues do not have to support operations at retail outlets, thereby saving the overhead associated with them. Finally, the high costs of transportation and shipping has forced Amazon to carefully design their supply chains with logistics in mind, such as the use of its own fleet in some of its major markets.

Supporting the four competitive priorities requires Amazon to design a supply chain that is agile and able to produce unique customer orders on a timely basis.

Sources: Mae Anderson and Anne D'Innocenzio, "Amazon vs. Stores: The Holiday Battle Heats Up," Associated Press, Naples Daily News (Thursday, November 28, 2013), pp. 2B; Jay Greene, "Amazon.com Cuts Deal with USPS," Associated Press, Naples Daily News (Tuesday, November 12, 2013), pp. 5A–5B; Mark Solomon, "Amazon Plans Revamp of U.S. Shipping with Mix of Private Fleet, Regional Carriers, and USPS," DC Velocity, (March 6, 2014), pp. 1–3; "Company Analysis: Team C2X 'Amazon.com,' " National Institute of Industrial Engineering, Powai, Mumbai, India (2012), pp. 3–20; Amazon.com 2013 Annual Report, **http://phx.corporate-ir.net** (2014).

LEARNING GOALS *After reading this chapter, you should be able to:*

1. Explain the strategic importance of supply chain design.

2. Identify the nature of supply chains for service providers as well as for manufacturers.

3. Calculate the critical supply chain performance measures.

4. Explain how efficient supply chains differ from responsive supply chains and the environments best suited for each type of supply chain

5. Explain the strategy of mass customization and its implications for supply chain design.

6. Analyze a make-or-buy decision using break-even analysis.

Amazon.com is an excellent example of how a supply chain can be successfully tailored to customer needs in a highly competitive market. A *supply chain* is the interrelated series of processes within a firm and across different firms that produces a service or product to the satisfaction of customers. More specifically, it is a network of service, material, monetary, and information flows that link a firm's customer relationship, order fulfillment, and supplier relationship processes to those of its suppliers and customers. It is important to note, however, that a firm such as Amazon may have multiple supply chains, depending on the mix of products it buys and sells. A supplier in one supply chain may not be a supplier in another supply chain because the product may be different or the supplier may simply be unable to negotiate a successful contract.

Creating an Effective Supply Chain

Creating an effective supply chain involves the recognition of external competitive pressures as well as internal organizational pressures from groups such as sales, marketing, and product development. These pressures are (1) dynamic sales volumes, (2) customer service and quality expectations, (3) service/product proliferation, and (4) emerging markets.

Dynamic sales volumes   One of the most costly operating aspects of supply chains is trying to meet the needs of volatile sales volumes. Often this involves excessive inventories, underutilized personnel, or more expensive delivery options to meet customer demands on time. While sometimes these volatile demands are caused by external sources such as the customers themselves, they are often caused internally by end-of-month sales promotions. Supply chain design should involve close collaboration between top-level managers across the organization so that unnecessary costly supply chain options are avoided. We will discuss the implications of supply chain dynamics in more depth in Chapter 14, "Supply Chain Integration."

Customer service and quality expectations   We have discussed customer service levels as they relate to an organization's internal inventories in Chapter 9, "Inventory Management." Here we focus on the organizational pressures emanating from the sales and marketing groups for superior service levels for the organization's customers. Questions such as "What service level should be guaranteed?" or "How speedy must our deliveries be?" need collaborative discussion from the sales, marketing, and finance groups. Customers are also demanding stricter conformance to service or product specifications and higher levels of quality. "What levels of quality are achievable and at what cost?" The answers to these questions impinge on the design of the supply chain, particularly its points of supply and the choice of suppliers.

Service/product proliferation   The sales and marketing groups provide the momentum to create new services or products because they are closely in touch with customers and their needs. The survival of any organization depends on the development of new markets. However, adding more services or products often adds complexity to the supply chain. It is not an unusual circumstance to find that a relatively large proportion of SKUs contribute only a small percentage of the revenues. Generally, these niche services or products have low volumes and therefore cost more to produce, market, and deliver. A thoughtful balance needs to be struck between the cost of operating the supply chain and the need to market new services and products.

Emerging markets   The increasing importance of emerging markets and the roles they play in the global market emphasizes the pressure on critical resources such as iron ore, agricultural commodities, and labor. For example, differing growth rates or internal strife across various emerging markets means that rising labor costs can quickly change the attractiveness of manufacturing facilities. Emerging markets also represent pools of new customers who demand products with lower price points. Such was the case with Gillette who produced a lost-cost razor as an entry to the Indian market. The health of the global economy often determines the need to examine the design of an organization's supply chains.

The design of an effective supply chain must be a collaborative effort from the CEO down if it is to meet the four pressures. All functional areas have a stake in an organization's supply chains. The firm's operations strategy and competitive priorities guide its supply chain choices. Figure 12.1 shows the three major areas of focus in creating an effective supply chain.

1. *Link Services or Products with Internal Processes.* Parts 1 and 2 of this text have shown how firms coordinate internal process decisions with the competitive priorities of the services or products covered in the operations strategy.

▼ **FIGURE 12.1**
Creating an Effective Supply Chain

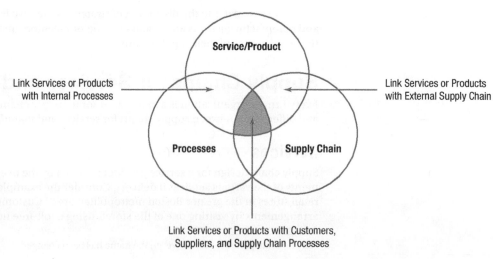

Link Services or Products with Internal Processes

Link Services or Products with External Supply Chain

Service/Product

Processes   Supply Chain

Link Services or Products with Customers, Suppliers, and Supply Chain Processes

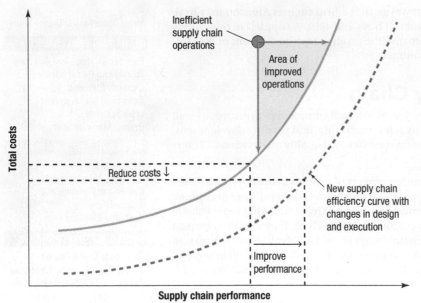

▲ **FIGURE 12.2**
Supply Chain Efficiency Curve

MyOMLab Animation

supply chain design

Designing a firm's supply chain to meet the competitive priorities of the firm's operations strategy.

2. *Link Services or Products with the External Supply Chain.* The competitive priorities assigned to the firm's services or products must be reflected in the design of the network of suppliers.

3. *Link Services or Products with Customers, Suppliers, and Supply Chain Processes.* The firm's processes that enable it to develop what customers want, interact with suppliers, deliver services or products, interact with customers, address environmental and ethical issues, and provide the information and planning tools needed to execute the operations strategy are the glue that binds the effective supply chain.

Supply chain management, the synchronization of a firm's processes with those of its suppliers and customers to match the flow of materials, services, and information with demand, is a critical skill in most organizations. A key part of supply chain management is **supply chain design**, which seeks to design a firm's supply chain to meet the competitive priorities of the firm's operations strategy. To get a better understanding of the importance of supply chain design, consider Figure 12.2, which conceptually shows the challenges facing supply chain managers. The blue line is an *efficiency curve*, which shows the trade-off between costs and performance for the current supply chain design if the supply chain is operated as efficiently as it can be. Now, suppose that your firm plots its actual costs and performance, as indicated by the red dot. It is far off of the efficiency curve, which is not an uncommon occurrence. Perhaps the performance is due to the four pressures mentioned above, which have been left unchecked for a period of time. The challenge is to move operations into the tinted area, as close to the blue curve as possible, which can be accomplished by better forecasting, inventory management, operations planning and scheduling, and resource planning, all of which we have already discussed in previous chapters. However, quantum steps in improvement can be obtained by improving the design of the supply chain in accordance with a sound operations strategy, which moves the curve as shown by the dashed red line. The goal is to reduce costs as well as increase performance.

What options are available to design a supply chain that best meets an organization's needs? Supply chain design options can be placed into four categories:

1. Strategic options, which include linking supply chain designs to competitive priorities, mass customization, and outsourcing decisions. These topics are discussed in this chapter.

2. Logistical network options, which include facility locations and inventory placement in the network of material flows. See Chapter 13, "Supply Chain Logistic Networks" for details.

3. Integration options, which include designs to mitigate supply chain dynamics and risk, supply chain collaboration to link major processes, and supplier selection. Chapter 14, "Supply Chain Integration," discusses this important set of issues.

4. Sustainability options, which include designs for environmental concerns and disaster relief. See Chapter 15, "Supply Chain Sustainability," for insights into the considerations managers must make in this important area.

Before we get into the discussion of strategic issues, we first differentiate supply chains for services and manufacturing firms and discuss the major inventory and financial measures firms use to monitor the performance of their supply chains.

Supply Chains for Services and Manufacturing

Every firm or organization is a member of some supply chain. In this section, we show the similarities and differences between supply chains for services and manufacturing.

Services

Supply chain design for a service provider is driven by the need to provide support for the essential elements of the various services it delivers. Consider the example of Flowers-on-Demand, a florist with 27 retail stores in the greater Boston metropolitan area.[1] Customers can place orders for customized floral arrangements by visiting one of the stores, using a toll-free number, or going to the florist's Web page.

---

[1]The florist depicted is real; however, the name has been changed.

The 800 number and the Web page are operated by a local Internet services company, which takes orders and relays them to the florist. The arrangements are produced at a distribution center, and deliveries are made using either local couriers, or FedEx, if the delivery is outside of the Boston area. Fresh flowers, flown in from all over the world, are used in the arrangements.

What differentiates Flowers-on-Demand from floral wire services, such as Teleflora or FTD, is that it assembles all the arrangements and can ship out-of-area orders for next-day delivery anywhere in the country. To do business, the florist must have a supply chain that provides retail stores, a delivery center, computers, point-of-sale equipment, and employees. It must purchase flowers that are sourced globally as well as arrangement materials, such as pots, baskets, greeting cards, and packing materials. The florist must arrange the flowers per the customer's order and ensure that the arrangement is delivered as specified by the customer, using local services or FedEx. The design of its supply chain must provide convenience, which is facilitated by the location of the retail outlets and the opportunity to place orders via the Internet or the toll-free number.

An employee at a warehouse for a commercial flower farm packages flowers for local delivery. The farm acts as a supplier to grocery stores and retail florists.

Figure 12.3 illustrates a simplified supply chain for the florist. Each of the suppliers, of course, has its own supply chain (not shown). For example, the supplier for the arrangement materials may get baskets from one supplier and pots from another. The suppliers in the florist's supply chain play an integral role in its ability to meet its competitive priorities, such as top quality, delivery speed, and customization.

Manufacturing

A fundamental purpose of supply chain design for manufacturers is to control inventory by managing the flow of materials. The typical manufacturer spends more than 60 percent of its total income from sales on purchased services and materials, whereas the typical service provider spends only 30 to 40 percent. Because materials comprise such a large component of the sales dollar, manufacturers can reap large profits with a small reduction in the cost of materials, which makes supply chain management a key competitive weapon.

The supply chain for a manufacturing firm can be complicated, as Figure 12.4 illustrates. However, the supply chain depicted is an oversimplification because many companies have hundreds, if not thousands, of suppliers. In this example, the firm is in the U.S. and deals with an international supply chain. In addition, it owns its distribution and transportation services. Suppliers are often identified by their position in the supply chain. Here, tier 1 suppliers provide major subassemblies that are assembled by the manufacturing firm, tier 2 suppliers provide tier 1 suppliers with components, and so on. Not all

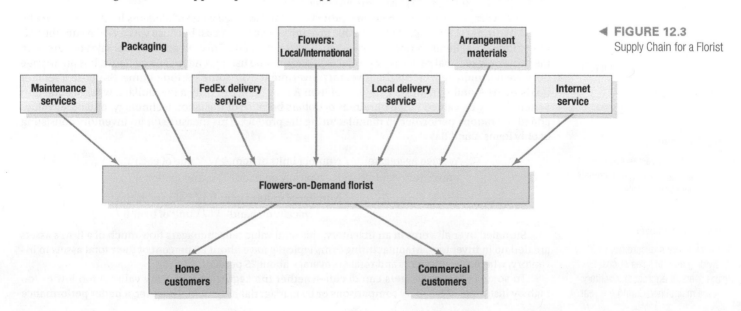

◀ FIGURE 12.3
Supply Chain for a Florist

companies have the same number of levels in their supply chains. For example, companies that engineer products to customer specifications normally do not have distribution centers as part of their supply chains. Such companies often ship products directly to their customers.

FIGURE 12.4 ▶

Supply Chain for a
Manufacturing Firm

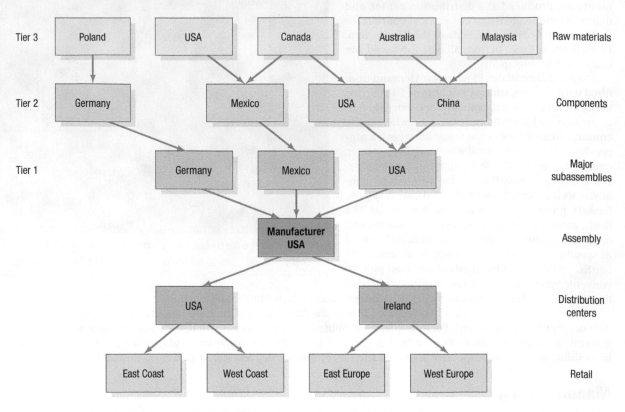

Measuring Supply Chain Performance

Regardless of whether the supply chain supports services or manufacturing, managers need performance measures to assess the implications of changes to supply chains. Before discussing the major supply chain design decisions, we define the typical inventory measures and financial measures used to monitor supply chain performance and evaluate alternative supply chain designs.

Inventory Measures

All methods of measuring inventory begin with a physical count of units, volume, or weight. However, measures of inventories are reported in three basic ways: (1) average aggregate inventory value, (2) weeks of supply, and (3) inventory turnover.

average aggregate inventory value

The total average value of all items held in inventory for a firm.

    The **average aggregate inventory value** is the total average value of all items held in inventory by a firm. We express the dollar values in this inventory measure at cost because we can then sum the values of individual items in raw materials, work-in-process, and finished goods. Final sales dollars have meaning only for final services or products and cannot be used for all inventory items. It is an average because it usually represents the inventory investment over some period of time. Suppose a retailer holds items A and B in stock. One unit of item A may be worth only a few dollars, whereas one unit of item B may be valued in the hundreds of dollars because of the labor, technology, and other value-added operations performed in manufacturing the product. This measure for an inventory consisting of only items A and B is

weeks of supply

An inventory measure obtained by dividing the average aggregate inventory value by sales per week at cost.

$$\begin{array}{l}\text{Average aggregate}\\ \text{inventory value}\end{array} = \left(\begin{array}{c}\text{Number units of item A}\\ \text{typically on hand}\end{array}\right)\left(\begin{array}{c}\text{Value of each}\\ \text{unit of item A}\end{array}\right) +$$

$$\left(\begin{array}{c}\text{Number of units of item B}\\ \text{typically on hand}\end{array}\right)\left(\begin{array}{c}\text{Value of each}\\ \text{unit of item B}\end{array}\right)$$

inventory turnover

An inventory measure obtained by dividing annual sales at cost by the average aggregate inventory value maintained during the year.

    Summed over all items in an inventory, this total value tells managers how much of a firm's assets are tied up in inventory. Manufacturing firms typically have about 25 percent of their total assets in inventory, whereas wholesalers and retailers average about 75 percent.

    To some extent, managers can decide whether the aggregate inventory value is too low or too high by historical or industry comparisons or by managerial judgment. However, a better performance measure would take demand into account because it would show how long the inventory resides in the firm. **Weeks of supply** is an inventory measure obtained by dividing the average aggregate inventory value by sales per week at cost. (In some low-inventory operations, days or even hours are a better unit of time for measuring inventory.) The formula (expressed in weeks) is

$$\text{Weeks of supply} = \frac{\text{Average aggregate inventory value}}{\text{Weekly sales (at cost)}}$$

Although the numerator includes the value of all items a firm holds in inventory (raw materials, WIP, and finished goods), the denominator represents only the finished goods sold—at cost rather than the sale price after markups or discounts. This cost is referred to as the *cost of goods sold.*

Inventory turnover (or *turns*) is an inventory measure obtained by dividing annual sales at cost by the average aggregate inventory value maintained during the year, or

$$\text{Inventory turnover} = \frac{\text{Annual sales (at cost)}}{\text{Average aggregate inventory value}}$$

The "best" inventory level, even when expressed as turnover, cannot be determined easily. A good starting point is to benchmark the leading firms in an industry.

Just looking at the size of an inventory does not reveal if it is a problem or an important element of a firm's strategy. Measures such as weeks of inventory or inventory turnover, relative to the industry, are needed. Here a distribution center is storing boxes of clothing, which have an industry average of about five turns per year.

Alistair Berg/Getty Images

EXAMPLE 12.1	*Calculating Inventory Measures*

The Eagle Machine Company averaged $2 million in inventory last year, and the cost of goods sold was $10 million. Figure 12.5 shows the breakout of raw materials, work-in-process, and finished goods inventories. The best inventory turnover in the company's industry is six turns per year. If the company has 52 business weeks per year, how many weeks of supply were held in inventory? What was the inventory turnover? What should the company do?

MyOMLab

Tutor 12.1 in MyOMLab provides a new example to practice the calculation of inventory measures.

◀ **FIGURE 12.5**
Calculating Inventory Measures Using *Inventory Estimator* Solver

Cost of Goods Sold	$10,000,000
Weeks of Operation	52

	Item Number	Average Level	Unit Value	Total Value
Raw Materials	1	1,400	$50.00	$70,000
	2	1,000	$32.00	$32,000
	3	400	$60.00	$24,000
	4	2,400	$10.00	$24,000
	5	800	$15.00	$12,000
Work in Process	6	320	$700.00	$224,000
	7	160	$900.00	$144,000
	8	280	$750.00	$210,000
	9	240	$800.00	$192,000
	10	400	$1,000.00	$400,000
Finished Goods	11	60	$2,000.00	$120,000
	12	40	$3,500.00	$140,000
	13	50	$2,800.00	$140,000
	14	20	$5,000.00	$100,000
	15	40	$4,200.00	$168,000
Total				$2,000,000

Average Weekly Sales at Cost	$192,308
Weeks of Supply	10.4
Inventory Turnover	5.0

SOLUTION

The average aggregate inventory value of $2 million translates into 10.4 weeks of supply and five turns per year, calculated as follows:

$$\text{Weeks of supply} = \frac{\$2 \text{ million}}{(\$10 \text{ million})/(52 \text{ weeks})} = 10.4 \text{ weeks}$$

$$\text{Inventory turns} = \frac{\$10 \text{ million}}{\$2 \text{ million}} = 5 \text{ turns/year}$$

DECISION POINT

The analysis indicates that management must improve the inventory turns by 20 percent. Management should improve its order fulfillment process to reduce finished goods inventory. Supply chain operations can also be improved to reduce the need to have so much raw materials and work-in-process inventory stock. It will take an inventory reduction of about 16 percent to achieve the target of six turns per year. However, inventories would not have to be reduced as much if sales increased. If the sales department targets an increase in sales of 8 percent ($10.8 million), inventories need only be reduced by 10 percent ($1.8 million) to get six turns a year. Management can now do sensitivity analyses to see what effect reductions in the inventory of specific items or increases in the annual sales have on weeks of supply or inventory turns.

Financial Measures

How the supply chain is designed and managed has a huge financial impact on the firm. Inventory is an investment because it is needed for future use. However, inventory ties up funds that might be used more profitably in other operations. Figure 12.6 shows how supply chain decisions can affect financial measures.

Total Revenue   Supply chain performance measures related to time, which is a critical dimension of supply chain operations, have financial implications. Many service providers and manufacturers measure the percent of on-time deliveries of their services or products to their customers, as well as services and materials from their suppliers. Increasing the percent of on-time deliveries to customers,

MyOMLab Animation

▼ **FIGURE 12.6**
How Supply Chain Decisions
Can Affect ROA

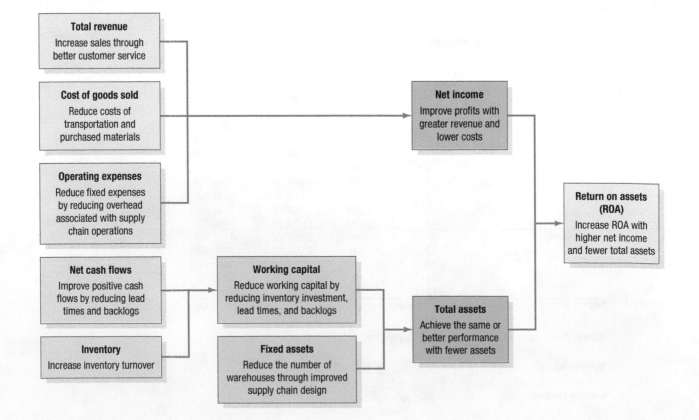

for example, will increase *total revenue* because satisfied customers will buy more services and products from the firm.

Cost of Goods Sold   Being able to buy materials or services at a better price and transform them more efficiently into services or products will improve a firm's *cost of goods sold* measure and ultimately its *net income*. These improvements will also have an effect on *contribution margin*, which is the difference between price and the variable costs to produce a service or good. Reducing production, material, transportation, and poor quality costs increases the contribution margin, allowing for greater profits. Contribution margins are often used as inputs to decisions regarding the portfolio of services or products the firm offers.

Operating Expenses   Selling expenses, fixed expenses, and depreciation are considered operating expenses. Designing a supply chain with minimal capital investment can reduce depreciation charges. Changes to the supply chain infrastructure can have an effect on overhead, which is considered a fixed expense.

Cash Flow   The supply chain design can improve positive net cash flows by focusing on reducing lead times and backlogs of orders. The Internet brings another financial measure related to cash flows to the forefront: *Cash-to-cash* is the time lag between paying for the services and materials needed to produce a service or product and receiving payment for it. The shorter the time lag, the better the *cash flow* position of the firm because it needs less working capital. The firm can then use the freed-up funds for other projects or investments. Redesigning the order placement process, so that payment for the service or product by the customer is made at the time the order is placed, can reduce the time lag. By contrast, billing the customer after the service is performed or the order is shipped increases the need for working capital. The goal is to have a negative cash-to-cash situation, which is possible when the customer pays for the service or product before the firm has to pay for the resources and materials needed to produce it. In such a case, the firm must have supplier inventories on consignment, which allows it to pay for materials as it uses them.

Working Capital   Weeks of inventory and inventory turns are reflected in another financial measure, *working capital*, which is money used to finance ongoing operations. Decreasing weeks of supply or increasing inventory turns reduces the working capital needed to finance inventories. Reductions in working capital can be accomplished by improving the customer relationship, order fulfillment, or supplier relationship processes. For example, reducing supplier lead times has the effect of reducing weeks of supply and increasing inventory turns. Matching the input and output flows of materials is easier because shorter-range, more reliable forecasts of demand can be used.

Return on Assets   Designing and managing the supply chain so as to reduce the aggregate inventory investment or fixed investments such as warehouses will reduce the *total assets* portion of the firm's balance sheet. An important financial measure is *return on assets* (*ROA*), which is net income divided by total assets. Consequently, reducing aggregate inventory investment and fixed investments, or increasing net income by better cost management, will increase ROA. Techniques for reducing inventory, transportation, and operating costs related to resource usage and scheduling are discussed in the chapters to follow.

We now turn to a discussion of several strategic options for supply chain design and their implications for a firm's performance.

Strategic Options for Supply Chain Design

A supply chain is, of course, a network of firms. Thus, each firm in the chain should design its own supply chains to support the competitive priorities of its services or products. Even though extensive technologies such as the Internet, computer-assisted design, flexible manufacturing, and automated warehousing have been applied to all stages of the supply chain, the performance of many supply chains remains dismal. A study of merging companies has shown that poor coordination and collaboration can drive inventory levels as much as 40 percent higher within a few months, and it can have similar effects on distribution costs, timeliness of delivery, and a variety of other metrics.[2] One possible cause for failures is that managers do not understand the nature of the demand for their services or products and, therefore, cannot design supply chains to satisfy those demands. Two distinct designs used to competitive advantage are *efficient supply chains* and *responsive supply chains*. Table 12.1 shows the environments that best suit each design.

---

[2]The study was conducted by the Boston Consulting Group in conjunction with Wharton University. See "Avoiding the Cost of Inefficiency: Coordination and Collaboration in Supply Chain Management," **https://knowledge .wharton.upenn.edu**, September 6, 2006.

TABLE 12.1 | ENVIRONMENTS BEST SUITED FOR EFFICIENT AND RESPONSIVE SUPPLY CHAINS

Factor	Efficient Supply Chains	Responsive Supply Chains
Demand	Predictable, low forecast errors	Unpredictable, high forecast errors
Competitive priorities	Low cost, consistent quality, on-time delivery	Development speed, fast delivery times, customization, volume flexibility, variety, top quality
New-service/product introduction	Infrequent	Frequent
Contribution margins	Low	High
Product variety	Low	High

Efficient supply chains need to keep logistical costs to a minimum. Here vessels loaded with containers berth at Singapore's Keppel Port, one of the world's most efficient, and busiest, sea ports.

Roslan Rahman/AFP/Getty Images

Efficient Supply Chains

The nature of demand for the firm's services or products is a key factor in the best choice of supply chain strategy. Efficient supply chains work best in environments where demand is highly predictable, such as demand for staple items purchased at grocery stores or demand for a package delivery service.

Common Designs   There is one popular design for efficient supply chains.

- *Make-to-stock* (MTS): The product is built to a sales forecast and sold to the customer from a finished goods stock. The end customer has no individual inputs into the configuration of the product and typically purchases the product from a retailer. Examples include groceries, books, appliances, and housewares. Figure 12.7 shows that these designs rely heavily on forecasts to move materials down the chain to the customer.

The focus of the MTS supply chain is on efficient service, material, monetary, and information flows; and keeping inventories to a minimum. Because of the markets the firms serve, service or product designs last a long time, new introductions are infrequent, and variety is small. Such firms typically produce for markets in which price is crucial to winning an order. Contribution margins are low and efficiency is important. Consequently, efficient supply chains have competitive priorities of low-cost operations, consistent quality, and on-time delivery.

Responsive Supply Chains

Responsive supply chains are designed to react quickly to hedge against uncertainties in demand. They work best when firms offer a great variety of services or products and demand predictability is low.

FIGURE 12.7 ▶
Supply Chain Design for
Make-to-Stock Strategy

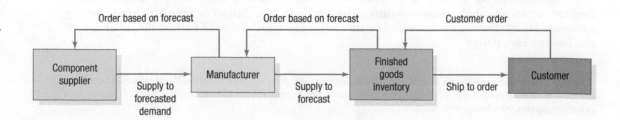

Order based on forecast   Customer order

```
┌──────────┐   Supply to   ┌──────────────┐  Supply as   ┌───────────┐              ┌──────────┐           ┌──────────┐
│Component │──────────────▶│ Standardized │   needed     │Fabrication│─────────────▶│ Assembly │──────────▶│ Customer │
│ Supplier │  forecasted   │  Component   │─────────────▶│           │              │          │           │          │
└──────────┘   demand      │  Inventory   │              └───────────┘              └──────────┘           └──────────┘
                           └──────────────┘
                                      Supply as needed
```

▲ **FIGURE 12.8**
Supply Chain Design for
Assemble-to-Order Strategy

Common Designs   There are three popular designs for responsive supply chains.

- *Assemble-to-order* (ATO): The product is built to customer specifications from a stock of existing components. Customers can choose among various standard components in arriving at their own products; however, they have no control over the design of the components. Assembly is delayed until the order is received. Examples include Dell's approach to customizing desktops and laptops and automobile manufacturers who offer a selection of options with each model. Figure 12.8 shows how an ATO supply chain is designed. Notice that much of the material flows are on an "as needed" basis, as opposed to the MTS design. We will return to this design when we address mass customization as a strategy.

- *Make-to-order* (MTO): The product is based on a standard design; however, component production and manufacture of the final product is linked to the customer's specifications. Examples include custom-made clothing, such as that offered by Land's End and Tommy Hilfiger, predesigned houses, and commercial aircraft, such as in the case of Boeing as depicted in Managerial Practice 12.1 (see pg. 498).

- *Design-to-order* (DTO): The product is designed and built entirely to the customer's specifications. This supply chain allows customers to design the product to fit their specific needs. Examples include large construction projects, women's designer dresses, custom-made men's suits, and original architecture house construction.

To stay competitive, firms in a responsive supply chain frequently introduce new services or products. Nonetheless, because of the innovativeness of their services or products, they enjoy high contribution margins. Typical competitive priorities for responsive supply chains are development speed, fast delivery times, customization, variety, volume flexibility, and top quality. The firms may not even know what services or products they need to provide until customers place orders. In addition, demand may be short-lived, as in the case of fashion goods. The focus of responsive supply chains is reaction time, which helps avoid keeping costly inventories that ultimately must be sold at deep discounts.

A firm may need to utilize both types of supply chains, especially when it focuses its operations on specific market segments or it can segment the supply chain to achieve two different requirements. For example, the supply chain for a standard product, such as an oil tanker, has different requirements than that for a customized product, such as a luxury liner, even though both are ocean-going vessels and both may be manufactured by the same company. You might also see elements of efficiency and responsiveness in the same supply chain. For example, Gillette uses an efficient supply chain to manufacture its products so that it can utilize a capital-intensive manufacturing process, and then it uses a responsive supply chain for the packaging and delivery processes to be responsive to retailers. The packaging operation involves customization in the form of printing in different languages. Just as processes can be broken into parts, with different process structures for each, supply chain processes can be segmented to achieve optimal performance.

Gillette uses both supply chain designs: efficient and responsive. The capital-intensive processes in its Boston factory support an efficient supply chain to keep costs down. Gillette uses a responsive supply chain for packaging and delivery to service its retail customers.

Designs for Efficient and Responsive Supply Chains

Table 12.2 contains the basic design features for efficient and responsive supply chains. The more downstream in an efficient supply chain that a firm is, the more likely

TABLE 12.2 | DESIGN FEATURES FOR EFFICIENT AND RESPONSIVE SUPPLY CHAINS

Factor	Efficient Supply Chains	Responsive Supply Chains
Operation strategy	Make-to-stock standardized services or products; emphasize high volumes	Assemble-to-order, make-to-order, or design-to-order customized services or products; emphasize variety
Capacity cushion	Low	High
Inventory investment	Low; enable high inventory turns	As needed to enable fast delivery time
Lead time	Shorten, but do not increase costs	Shorten aggressively
Supplier selection	Emphasize low prices, consistent quality, on-time delivery	Emphasize fast delivery time, customization, variety, volume flexibility, top quality

it is to have a line-flow strategy that supports high volumes of standardized services or products. Consequently, suppliers in efficient supply chains should have low capacity cushions because high utilization keeps the cost per unit low. High inventory turns are desired because inventory investment must be kept low to achieve low costs. Firms should work with their suppliers to shorten lead times, but care must be taken to use tactics that do not appreciably increase costs. For example, lead times for a supplier could be shortened by switching from rail to air transportation; however, the added cost may offset the savings or competitive advantages obtained from the shorter lead times. Suppliers should be selected with emphasis on low prices, consistent quality, and on-time delivery. Because of low capacity cushions, disruptions in an efficient supply chain can be costly and must be avoided. Figure 12.9 shows that firms with large batch, line, or continuous processes are more likely to be part of an efficient supply chain.

By contrast, firms in a responsive supply chain should be flexible and have high capacity cushions. WIP inventories should be positioned in the chain to support delivery speed, but inventories of expensive finished goods should be avoided. Firms should aggressively work with their suppliers to shorten lead times because it allows them to wait longer before committing to a customer order—in other words, it gives them greater flexibility. Firms should select suppliers to support the competitive priorities of the services or products provided, which in this case would include the ability to provide quick deliveries, customize services or components, adjust volumes quickly to match demand cycles, offer variety, and provide top quality. Figure 12.9 shows that firms with job or small batch processes are more likely to be a part of a responsive supply chain.

FIGURE 12.9 ►

Linking Supply Chain Design to Processes and Service/Product Characteristics

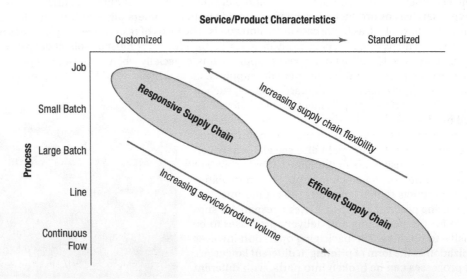

Poor supply chain performance often is the result of using the wrong supply chain design for the services or products provided. A common mistake is to use an efficient supply chain in an environment that calls for a responsive supply chain. Over time, a firm may add options to its basic service or product, or introduce variations, so that the variety of its offerings increases dramatically and demand for any given service or product predictability drops. Yet the firm continues to measure the performance of its supply chain as it always has, emphasizing efficiency, even when contribution margins would allow a responsive supply chain design. Consider Figure 12.10, which shows a generalized relationship between the annual volumes of a firm's stock-keeping units (SKUs) and their weekly demand variability. For this firm, some SKUs have high volume and low variability while some SKUs have low volume and high variability. To the extent that the volatility in demands is outside the control of the firm, hanging on to the firm's legacy supply chain may be too costly because of supply chain dynamics. Mapping the portfolio of products along the dimensions of annual volume and weekly demand variability may reveal better configurations of the supply chain. A firm may therefore have two distinctly different supply chain designs serving two different product groups. For example, SKUs with lower volumes and higher weekly variability may be best served with a responsive supply chain design, such as ATO or MTO. Doing so reduces the need for finished goods inventories where customer demands are very unpredictable. Alternatively, serving the high volume, low weekly demand variability SKUs with an efficient supply chain design such as build-to-stock would be better. Forecasts are more accurate and using a finished goods inventory is an effective strategy. Redesigning a supply chain is a costly endeavor and should only be contemplated when the dynamics cannot be sufficiently reduced by other means.

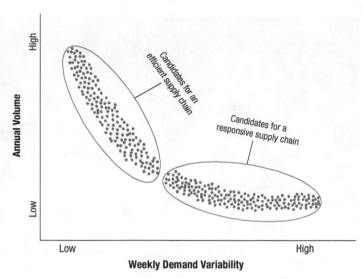

▲ **FIGURE 12.10**
Annual Volume versus Variability in Weekly Demands for a Firm's SKUs

Mass Customization

A firm's supply chain must be capable of addressing certain competitive priorities that will win orders from customers. Often customers want more than a wide selection of standard services or products; they want a personalized service or product and they want it fast. For example, suppose you want to paint your living room a new color. You need to complement all of the existing furnishings, wall decorations, and carpet. You go to your local paint retail store and select a color from a stack of books that spans every color of the rainbow. The store can give you all the paint you need in your selected color while you wait. How can the store provide that service economically? Certainly the store cannot stock thousands of colors in sufficient quantities for any job. The store stocks the base colors and pigments separately and mixes them as needed, thereby supplying an unlimited variety of colors without maintaining the inventory required to match each customer's particular color needs. The paint retailer is practicing a strategy known as *mass customization*, whereby a firm's highly divergent processes generate a wide variety of customized services or products at reasonably low costs. Essentially, the firm allows customers to select from a variety of standard options to create the service or product of their choice.

Competitive Advantages

A mass customization strategy has three important competitive advantages.

- *Managing Customer Relationships.* Mass customization requires detailed inputs from customers so that the ideal service or product can be produced. The firm can learn a lot about its customers from the data it receives. Once customers are in the database, the firm can keep track of them over time. A significant competitive advantage is realized through these close customer relationships based on a strategy of mass customization.

- *Eliminating Finished Goods Inventory.* Producing to a customer's order is more efficient than producing to a forecast because forecasts are not perfect. The trick is to have everything you need to produce the order quickly. A technology some firms use for their order placement process is a software system called a *configurator*, which gives firms and customers easy access to data relevant to the options available for the service or product. Dell uses a configurator that allows customers to design their own computer from a set of standard components that are in stock. Once the order is placed, the product is assembled and then delivered. Using sales promotions, the firm can exercise some control over the requirements for the inventory of components by steering customers away from options that are out of stock in favor of options that are in stock. This capability takes pressure off the supply chain while keeping the customer satisfied.

    Service providers also take advantage of mass customization to reduce the level of inventory. British Airways is trying to personalize the service of customers once they are on board. It has a software system that tracks the preferences of its most favored customers down to the magazines they read. This information allows the airline to more accurately plan what to pack on each flight. This information saves the airline a significant amount of money because it does not pack amenities passengers do not want.

- *Increasing Perceived Value of Services or Products.* With mass customization, customers can have it their way. In general, mass customization often has a higher value in the mind of the customer than it actually costs to produce. This perception allows firms to charge prices that provide a nice margin.

At My Twinn doll company, kids can create their own doll online. Artisans can even match the doll face to the child's face from a photo you supply. My Twinn continues to market clothing accessories as the doll "grows up" with its human twin.

Robert Gonzalez KRT/Newscom

Supply Chain Design for Mass Customization

How does mass customization affect the design of supply chains? We address three major considerations.

Assemble-to-Order Strategy The underlying process design is an assemble-to-order strategy. This strategy involves two stages in the provision of the service or product. Initially, standardized components are produced or purchased and held in stock. This stage is important because it enables the firm to produce or purchase these standard items in large volumes to keep the costs low. In the second stage, the firm assembles these standard components to a specific customer order. In mass customization, this stage must be flexible to handle a large number of potential combinations and be capable of producing the order quickly and accurately. For example, for My Twinn customized dolls, customers can choose from more than 325,000 different doll combinations. To ensure accuracy, the Web site takes the customer through the required choices and allows the customer to see the doll as the various options are chosen. As shown in Figure 12.8 when we introduced the ATO design, the customer order is transmitted to the fabrication and assembly operations and standardized purchased components are taken to the point of fabrication or assembly as needed for the order. Notice that there is no finished goods inventory.

Modular Design The service or product must have a modular design that enables the "customization" the customer desires. This approach requires careful attention to service or product designs so that the final service or product can be assembled from a set of standardized modules economically and quickly in response to a customer order.

Postponement Finally, successful mass customizers postpone the task of differentiating a service or product for a specific customer until the last possible moment. *Postponement* is a concept whereby some of the final activities in the provision of a service or product are delayed until the orders are received. Doing so allows the greatest application of standard modules before specific customization is done. Postponement is a key decision because it specifies where in the supply chain volume-oriented, standardized operations are separated from custom-oriented, assembly operations. Sometimes the final customization occurs in the last step.

The assemble-to-order strategy and postponement can be extended to supply chains. The costs of inventory and transportation often determine the extent to which a manufacturer uses postponement in the supply chain. With postponement, manufacturers can avoid inventory buildup. Some firms take advantage of a process called **channel assembly**, whereby members of the distribution channel act as if they were assembly stations in the factory. Distribution centers or warehouses can perform the last-minute customizing operations after specific orders have been received. Channel assembly is particularly useful when the required customizing has some geographical rationale, such as language differences or technical requirements. In general, beyond the inventory advantages, the advantage of postponement in the distribution channel is that the firm's plants can focus on the standardized aspects of the product, while the distributor can focus on customizing a product that may require additional components from local suppliers.

channel assembly

The process of using members of the distribution channel as if they were assembly stations in the factory.

Outsourcing Processes

All businesses buy at least some inputs to their processes (such as professional services, raw materials, or manufactured parts) from other producers. Most businesses also purchase services to get their products to their customers. How many of the processes that produce those purchased items and services should a firm own and operate instead? The answer to that question determines the extent of the firm's vertical integration. The more processes in the supply chain that the organization performs itself, the more vertically integrated it is. If it does not perform some processes itself, it must rely on **outsourcing**, or paying suppliers and distributors to perform those processes and provide needed services and materials. Some firms outsource important processes such as accounting, marketing, manufacturing, or distribution. Many firms outsource payroll, security, cleaning, and other types of services rather than employ personnel to provide these services. Outsourcing is a particularly attractive option to those firms that have low volumes. What prompts a firm to outsource? An outsourcing firm realizes that another firm can perform the outsourced process more efficiently and with better quality than it can. They opt to add external suppliers to their supply chains rather than to keep internal suppliers. However, the outsourcing decision is a serious one because the firm can lose the skills and knowledge needed to conduct the process. All learning about process advancements is left to the outsourcing partner, which makes it difficult to ever bring that process back into the firm.

> **outsourcing**
>
> Paying suppliers and distributors to perform processes and provide needed services and materials.

The strategy of globalizing a firm adds a new dimension to the development of supply chains and the use of outsourcing. Several strategies have emerged. **Offshoring** is a supply chain strategy that involves moving processes to another country. As such, offshoring is more encompassing than outsourcing because it also includes ownership of facilities and internal processes in other countries. Firms are motivated to initiate operations offshore by the market potential and the cost advantages it provides. The firm may be able to create new markets because of its presence in other countries and its ability to offer competitive prices due to its cost efficiencies. Competitive priorities other than low costs, such as delivery speed to distant customers, can drive the decision, too. However, the term "offshoring" was popular when labor costs and other factors were very favorable in Asia and many companies were conducting operations there. Over time, costs and business conditions have changed, which has spawned sourcing strategies that focus on key operational advantages. For example, **next-shoring** is a supply chain strategy that involves locating processes in close proximity to customer demand or product R&D. These processes may be outsourced or owned by the firm and may be in-country or offshore. This strategy is useful in situations where evolving demand from new markets places a premium on the ability to adapt products to different regions or to reduce logistics costs to the new market. Other strategies, such as *near-shoring* and *on-shoring*, are largely a reaction to the increasing costs of operations and logistics in Asia and focus on moving processes closer to the home operation.

> **offshoring**
>
> A supply chain strategy that involves moving processes to another country.

> **next-shoring**
>
> A supply chain strategy that involves locating processes in close proximity to customer demand or product R&D.

Decision Factors   The strategy to pursue is, of course, situational and depends on a number of factors.

- *Comparative Labor Costs.* Some countries such as China and India have traditionally held a huge edge when it comes to labor costs. In India, the salary for a computer programmer is much less than that of a programmer in the United States with comparable skills. In China, the average monthly wages are much less than those in Japan. However, the advantage of doing business in these and other low-wage countries is eroding as wages in those countries rise due to increased demands. In some cases, the labor-cost advantage may only be a short-term one because of local economic conditions, such as the lowered wage structures in the United States because of the recession of 2008.

- *Rework and Product Returns.* While labor wage rates may be low in a particular location, the quality of workmanship must also be considered. Internal rework costs and the cost of product returns may offset the advantage in wage rates.

- *Logistics Costs.* Even if labor costs are not favorable, it may still be less costly to outsource or move final assembly processes to other countries to reduce the logistical costs of delivering products to international customers. Moving processes closer to the customer and using more local suppliers reduces the cost of transporting the final product to its ultimate destination. Using shipping or air transportation can be costly because of their dependence on oil. The savings in logistical costs can offset the higher labor costs in those countries.

- *Tariffs and Taxes.* Some countries offer tax incentives to firms that do business within their borders. Tariffs can also be a stumbling block for firms looking to do business in a country. Sometimes they are high enough that the firm decides to assemble the products in that country rather than export the products in.

- *Market Effects.* Not to be overlooked is the potential advantage of next-shoring a process in a location where the presence of the firm can have a positive effect on local sales.

- *Labor Laws and Unions.* Some countries have fewer unions or restrictions on the flexible use of labor. The ability to use workers to perform a number of different tasks without restrictions can be important to firms trying to achieve flexibility in operations and reduce costs. Nonetheless, firms must be cognizant of local labor laws and customs and strive to achieve a high level of ethical behavior when doing business in other countries.

- *Internet.* The Internet reduces the transaction costs of managing distant partners or operations.

- *Energy Costs.* As technology advances and carbon-based energy sources deplete, comparative energy costs can be a major cost consideration.

Employees work on the Wuling minivan engine assembly line at the SAIC GM Wuling Automobile Co., Ltd. factory in Liuzhou, Guangxi Province, China. SAIC got a license to use GM's technical knowledge for the design and manufacture of automobiles.

- *Access to Low Cost Capital.* It is often easier and cheaper to buy equipment, buildings, and land at home than it is abroad.

- *Supply Chain Complexity.* Producing goods or services in another country requires the operation of two supply chains—one at home and one in the other country. With two supply chains to manage, issues of quality, meeting customer schedule commitments, and theft of intellectual property, among other things, become real concerns.

Potential Pitfalls   Even though outsourcing may appear to offer some big advantages, it also has some pitfalls that should be carefully explored before using this strategy.

- *Pulling the Plug Too Quickly.* A major mistake is to decide to outsource a process before making a good-faith effort to fix the existing one. We discussed many ways to improve processes in parts 1 and 2 of this text; these methods should be explored first. It is not always the case that outsourcing is the answer, even if local labor wages far exceed those of other countries. Make sure you really need to outsource to accomplish your operations strategy.

- *Technology Transfer.* Often an outsourcing strategy involves creating a *joint venture* with a company in another country. With a joint venture, two firms agree to jointly produce a service or product together. Typically, a transfer of technology takes place to bring one partner up to speed regarding the service or product. The danger is that the firm with the technology advantage will essentially be setting up the other firm to be a future competitor.

- *Process Integration.* Despite the power of the Internet, it is difficult to fully integrate outsourced processes with the firm's other processes. Time, distance, and communication can be formidable hurdles, especially if the supplier is on the other side of the world. Managing offshore processes will not be the same as managing processes located next door. Often considerable managerial time must be expended to coordinate offshore processes.

Managerial Practice 12.1 reveals outsourcing on a global scale can be challenging for management.

MANAGERIAL PRACTICE 12.1   Building a Supply Chain for the Dreamliner

Suppose that you had the freedom to totally design the supply chain for one of the most highly anticipated airliners of modern times. The airliner, the Boeing 787 Dreamliner, is a super-efficient commercial airplane that can carry up to 330 passengers on routes as long as 8,000 nautical miles at speeds up to 850 miles per hour. It is constructed with carbon-fiber composite materials, which are lightweight and not susceptible to corrosion or fatigue like aluminum. This plane uses 50 percent composite materials; Boeing used only 10 to 12 percent in the 777. Boeing's goal was to bring the most complex machine in mass production to market in just over 4 years, or 2 years less time than other projects. Boeing had two options for the design of the supply chain: (1) Produce about 50 percent of the plane in-house, including the wing and fuselage as in existing Boeing planes, and run the risk that production lead times will suffer because of capacity constraints; or (2) outsource about 85 percent of the plane, essentially only constructing the vertical fin in-house, and manage the global suppliers responsible for design as well as production of major components. Boeing selected option 2.

There are some good reasons for this choice. First, a number of big customers for the 787, such as India and Japan, require that significant portions of the aircraft must be manufactured in their countries. Using

The first Boeing 787 Dreamliner takes shape in the final assembly plant in Everett, Washington. The new commercial airplane is assembled with major components produced worldwide.

major contractors within those countries satisfies the requirement. Second, a shortage of high-quality engineering talent also puts pressure on outsourcing. Third, the sheer complexity of the airplane makes it necessary to share the load. Boeing, even with all of its resources, could not build all of the components and pieces in one facility or region. Finally, work on the plane can proceed concurrently, rather than sequentially, thereby saving time and money. For example, the modular design of the plane allows Boeing to utilize flexible tooling to move planes through the factory much more quickly. The suppliers design and deliver the subsystems on a just-in-time basis where they are "snapped" together by a smaller number of factory workers in a matter of days rather than a month, the typical time for a plane of that complexity.

Boeing chose to design its supply chain with 43 top-tier suppliers on three continents. Outsourcing so much responsibility requires a lot of managerial attention; you have to know what is going on in each factory at all times. As expected with something so complex, major glitches popped up like gremlins. The first Dreamliner to show up at Boeing's factory was missing tens of thousands of parts. Supplier problems ranged from language barriers to problems caused by some contractors who outsourced major portions of their assigned work and then experienced problems with their suppliers. The first fuselage section, the big multipart cylindrical barrel that encompasses the passenger seating area, failed in company testing, causing Boeing to make more sections than planned and to reexamine quality and safety concerns. Software programs designed by a variety of manufacturers had trouble talking to one another and the overall weight of the airplane was too high, especially the carbon-fiber wing. These and many other glitches caused major delays in the promised deliveries of the first 787s. The in-service date for the first commercial 787 was October 26, 2011, more than three years behind schedule. As of May 2014, 147 of the planes have been built.

Did the advantages of collaboration on such a large scale outweigh the loss of logistical and design control? The jury is still out on that question. The latest problem involved the design of the lithium ion batteries that supply power to the energy-hungry electrical systems, which caught fire in an auxiliary power unit of a Japan Airlines 787 on the ground at Boston's Logan International Airport on January 7, 2013. The batteries have since been redesigned; however, Boeing's customers are not happy with all of the delays. Nonetheless, Boeing has more than 1,031 orders for the Dreamliner.

Source: Elizabeth Rennie, "Beyond Borders," *APICS Magazine* (March 2007), pp. 34–38; Stanley Holmes, "The 787 Encounters Turbulence," *Business Week* (June 19, 2006), pp. 38–40; J. Lynn Lunsford, "Boeing Scrambles to Repair Problems with New Plane," *The Wall Street Journal* (December 7, 2007), p. A1; "Boeing 787 Dreamliner," **http:// en.wikipedia.org/wiki/Boeing_787_Dreamliner** (2014); Joan Lowry and Joshua Freed, "Lithium Batteries Are Central to Boeing's 787 Woes," Associated Press (January 18, 2013).

Vertical Integration

Outsourcing is one means to acquire processes a firm lacks or is unwilling to perform. Another approach is vertical integration whereby the firm purchases the processes it needs. Vertical integration can be in two directions. **Backward integration** represents a firm's movement upstream in the supply chain toward the sources of raw materials, parts, and services through acquisitions, such as a major grocery chain investing in its own plants to produce house brands of ice cream, frozen pizza dough, and peanut butter. Backward integration has the effect of reducing the risk of supply. **Forward integration** means that the firm acquires more channels of distribution, such as its own distribution centers (warehouses) and retail stores. It can also mean that the firm goes even farther by acquiring its business customers. A firm chooses vertical integration when it has the skills, volume, and resources to hit the competitive priorities better than outsiders can. Doing the work within its organizational structure may mean better control over quality and more timely delivery, as well as taking better advantage of the firm's human resources, equipment, and space. Extensive vertical integration is generally attractive when input volumes are high because high volumes allow task specialization and greater efficiency. It is also attractive if the firm has the relevant skills and views the processes that it is integrating as particularly important to its future success. However, care must be exercised that excessive vertical integration does not lead to a loss of focus for the firm in delivering value in its core business.

Management must identify, cultivate, and exploit its core competencies to prevail in global competition. Recall that core competencies reflect the collective learning of the organization, especially its ability for coordinating diverse processes and integrating multiple technologies. (See Chapter 1, "Using Operations to Create Value.") They define the firm and provide its reason for existence. Management must be constantly attentive to bolstering core competencies, perhaps by looking upstream toward its suppliers and downstream toward its customers and acquiring those processes that support its core competencies—those that allow the firm to organize work and deliver value better than its competitors. To do otherwise poses a risk that the firm will lose control over critical areas of its business.

backward integration

A firm's movement upstream toward the sources of raw materials, parts, and services through acquisitions.

forward integration

Acquiring more channels of distribution, such as distribution centers (warehouses) and retail stores, or even business customers.

Make-or-Buy Decisions

When managers opt for more vertical integration, by definition less outsourcing occurs. These decisions are sometimes called **make-or-buy decisions**, with a *make* decision meaning more vertical integration and a *buy* decision meaning more outsourcing. After deciding what to outsource and what to do in-house, management must find ways to coordinate and integrate the various processes and suppliers involved. Example 12.2 shows how break-even analysis, which can be found in Supplement A, "Decision Making," can be used for the make-or-buy decision.

make-or-buy decision

A managerial choice between whether to outsource a process or do it in-house.

EXAMPLE 12.2	Using Break-Even Analysis for the Make-or-Buy Decision

MyOMLab

Active Model A.2 in MyOMLab provides additional insight on the make-or-buy decision and its extensions.

MyOMLab

Tutor A.2 in MyOMLab provides a new example to practice break-even analysis on make-or-buy decisions.

Thompson manufacturing produces industrial scales for the electronics industry. Management is considering outsourcing the shipping operation to a logistics provider experienced in the electronics industry. Thompson's annual fixed costs of the shipping operation are $1,500,000, which includes costs of the equipment and infrastructure for the operation. The estimated variable cost of shipping the scales with the in-house operation is $4.50 per ton-mile. If Thompson outsourced the operation to Carter Trucking, the annual fixed costs of the infrastructure and management time needed to manage the contract would be $250,000. Carter would charge $8.50 per ton-mile. How many ton-miles per year would Thompson need to break even on these two options?

SOLUTION

From Supplement A, "Decision Making," the formula for the break-even quantity yields

$$Q = \frac{F_m - F_b}{c_b - c_m}$$

$$= \frac{1,500,000 - 250,000}{8.50 - 4.50} = 312,500 \text{ ton-miles}$$

DECISION POINT

Thompson management must now assess how many ton-miles of product will likely be shipped now and in the future. If that estimate is less than 312,500 ton-miles, the best option is to outsource the operation to Carter Trucking.

LEARNING GOALS IN REVIEW

Learning Goal	Guidelines for Review	MyOMLab Resources
❶ Explain the strategic importance of supply chain design.	Review Figures 12.1 and 12.2 for the big picture of supply chain strategy and design. The section "Creating an Effective Supply Chain," pp. 485–486, reveals the nature of designing supply chains that support competitive priorities and the pressures that impinge on supply chain design.	**Video**: Supply Chain Design at Crayola
❷ Identify the nature of supply chains for service providers as well as for manufacturers.	See the section "Supply Chains for Services and Manufacturing," pp. 486–488, for the similarities and differences of supply chains for service providers and manufacturers.	
❸ Calculate the critical supply chain measures.	"Measuring Supply Chain Performance," pp. 488–491, explains the important inventory and financial measures. Be sure to understand Example 12.1 and the Solved Problem. Use OM Explorer Solver: Financial Measures Analyzer for the Brunswick Distribution, Inc. case.	**Active Model**: A.2 **OM Explorer Solvers**: Inventory Estimator, Financial Measures Analyzer **OM Explorer Tutors**: A.1: Break-Even, Evaluating Products and Services; A.2: Break-Even Evaluating Processes; 12.1: Calculating Inventory Measures; F.4: NPV, IRR, Payback **POM for Windows**: Break-Even Analysis, Financial Analysis **Tutor Exercise**: 12.1: Calculating Inventory Measures Under Different Scenarios
❹ Explain how efficient supply chains differ from responsive supply chains and the environments best suited for each type of supply chain.	Review the section "Strategic Options for Supply Chain Design," pp. 491–495. Be sure to understand Tables 12.1 and 12.2.	

Learning Goal	Guidelines for Review	MyOMLab Resources
⑤ Explain the strategy of mass customization and its implications for supply chain design.	The section "Mass Customization," pp. 495–496, describes the competitive advantages and the implications for supply chain design. Be sure to understand the ATO responsive supply chain design, which is the basis for the mass customization strategy.	
⑥ Analyze a make-or-buy decision using break-even analysis.	Outsourcing, offshoring, and next-shoring are discussed in detail in the section "Outsourcing Processes," pp. 496–500. Be sure to review Example 12.2, which uses break-even analysis for the make-or-buy decision. Managerial Practice 12.1 shows how complex the outsourcing decision can become.	

Key Equations

Measuring Supply Chain Performance

1. Average aggregate inventory value = average inventory of each SKU multiplied by its value, summed over all SKUs held in stock.

2. Weeks of supply $= \dfrac{\text{Average aggregate inventory value}}{\text{Weekly sales (at cost)}}$

3. Inventory turnover $= \dfrac{\text{Annual sales (at cost)}}{\text{Average aggregate inventory value}}$

Outsourcing Processes

4. Make-or-buy break-even quantity: $Q = \dfrac{F_m - F_b}{c_b - c_m}$

Key Terms

average aggregate inventory value 488
backward integration 499
channel assembly 496
forward integration 499

inventory turnover 488
make-or-buy decision 499
next-shoring 497
offshoring 497

outsourcing 497
supply chain design 486
weeks of supply 488

Solved Problem

A firm's cost of goods sold last year was $3,410,000, and the firm operates 52 weeks per year. It carries seven items in inventory: three raw materials, two work-in-process items, and two finished goods. The following table contains last year's average inventory level for each item, along with its value.

MyOMLab Video

a. What is the average aggregate inventory value?
b. How many weeks of supply does the firm maintain?
c. What was the inventory turnover last year?

Category	Part Number	Average Level	Unit Value
Raw materials	1	15,000	$3.00
	2	2,500	5.00
	3	3,000	1.00
Work-in-process	4	5,000	14.00
	5	4,000	18.00
Finished goods	6	2,000	48.00
	7	1,000	62.00

SOLUTION

a.

Part Number	Average Level		Unit Value		Total Value
1	15,000	×	$3.00	=	$ 45,000
2	2,500	×	5.00	=	12,500
3	3,000	×	1.00	=	3,000
4	5,000	×	14.00	=	70,000
5	4,000	×	18.00	=	72,000
6	2,000	×	48.00	=	96,000
7	1,000	×	62.00	=	62,000
			Average aggregate inventory value	=	$360,500

b. Average weekly sales at cost $= \$3,410,000/52 \text{ weeks} = \$65,577/\text{week}$

$$\text{Weeks of supply} = \frac{\text{Average aggregate inventory value}}{\text{Weekly sales (at cost)}} = \frac{\$360,500}{\$65,577} = 5.5 \text{ weeks}$$

c. $\text{Inventory turnover} = \dfrac{\text{Annual sales (at cost)}}{\text{Average aggregate inventory value}} = \dfrac{\$3,410,000}{\$360,500} = 9.5 \text{ turns}$

Discussion Questions

1. Explain how a firm can reduce costs while improving the performance of its supply chain.

2. The Walmart retail chain sells standardized items and enjoys great purchasing clout with its suppliers, none of which it owns. The Limited retail chain sells fashion goods and owns Mast Industries, which is responsible for producing many of the items sold in The Limited stores. The Limited boasts that it can go from the concept for a new garment to the store shelf in 1,000 hours. Compare and contrast the implications for supply chain design for these two retail systems.

3. Canon, a Japanese manufacturer of photographic equipment, decided against offshoring and kept its manufacturing and new product development processes in Japan, which has relatively high labor costs. In contrast, GM, headquartered in the United States, has a joint venture with Shanghai Auto Industry Corporation (SAIC) to produce cars in China. Given our discussion of outsourcing, offshoring, next-shoring, and supply chain design, discuss how these two seemingly diverse decisions could be supportive of each company's operations strategy.

Problems

The OM Explorer and POM for Windows software is available to all students using the 11th edition of this textbook. Go to **http://www.pearsonhighered.com/krajewski** to download these computer packages. If you purchased MyOMLab, you also have access to Active Models software and significant help in doing the following problems. Check with your instructor on how best to use these resources. In many cases, the instructor wants you to understand how to do the calculations by hand. At the least, the software provides a check on your calculations. When calculations are particularly complex and the goal is interpreting the results in making decisions, the software replaces entirely the manual calculations.

Measuring Supply Chain Performance

1. EBI Solar uses a high-tech process to turn silicon wafers into tiny solar panels. These efficient and inexpensive panels are used to power low-energy, hand-held electronic devices. Last year, EBI Solar turned their inventory 4.5 times and had a cost of goods sold of $2.5 million. Assuming 52 business weeks per year:

   a. Express last year's average inventory in weeks of supply.

   b. After several supply chain improvement initiatives, inventory investment has dropped across all inventory categories. While EBI's cost of goods sold is not expected to change from last year's level, the value of raw materials has dropped to $100,500; work-in-process to $25,800; and finished goods to $16,200. Assuming 52 business weeks per year, express EBI's current total inventory level in weeks of supply and inventory turns.

2. Cyberphone, a manufacturer of cell phone accessories, ended the current year with annual sales (at cost) of $48 million. During the year, the inventory of accessories turned over six times. For the next year, Cyberphone plans to increase annual sales (at cost) by 25 percent.

   a. What is the increase in the average aggregate inventory value required if Cyberphone maintains the same inventory turnover during the next year?

   b. What change in inventory turns must Cyberphone achieve if, through better supply chain management, it wants to support next year's sales with no increase in the average aggregate inventory value?

3. Jack Jones, the materials manager at Precision Enterprises, is beginning to look for ways to reduce inventories. A recent accounting statement shows the following inventory investment by category: raw materials, $3,129,500; work-in-process, $6,237,000; and finished goods, $2,686,500. This year's cost of goods sold will be about $32.5 million. Assuming 52 business weeks per year, express total inventory as

   a. Weeks of supply

   b. Inventory turns

4. One product line at Spearman Fishing Industries has 10 turns per year and an annual sales volume (at cost) of $985,000. How much inventory is being held, on average?

5. The Bawl Corporation supplies alloy ball bearings to auto manufacturers in Detroit. Because of its specialized manufacturing process, considerable work-in-process and raw materials are needed. The current inventory levels are $2,470,000 and $1,566,000, respectively. In addition, finished goods inventory is $1,200,000 and sales (at cost) for the current year are expected to be about $48 million. Express total inventory as

   a. Weeks of supply

   b. Inventory turns

6. The following data were collected for a retailer:

Cost of goods sold	$3,500,000
Gross profit	$700,000
Operating costs	$500,000
Operating profit	$200,000

Total inventory	$1,200,000
Fixed assets	$750,000
Long-term debt	$300,000

Assuming 52 business weeks per year, express total inventory as

   a. Weeks of supply

   b. Inventory turns

7. Sapphire Aerospace operates 52 weeks per year, and its cost of goods sold last year was $6,500,000. The firm carries eight items in inventory: four raw materials, two work-in-process items, and two finished goods. Table 12.3 shows last year's average inventory levels for these items, along with their unit values.

   a. What is the average aggregate inventory value?

   b. How many weeks of supply does the firm have?

   c. What was the inventory turnover last year?

TABLE 12.3 | SAPPHIRE AEROSPACE INVENTORY ITEMS

Category	Part Number	Average Inventory Units	Value per Unit
Raw materials	RM-1	20,000	$1
	RM-2	5,000	5
	RM-3	3,000	6
	RM-4	1,000	8
Work-in-process	WIP-1	6,000	10
	WIP-2	8,000	12
Finished goods	FG-1	1,000	65
	FG-2	500	88

8. Dogs-R-Us and K-9, Inc. are two retail stores that cater to the needs of dog owners in the greater Charleston area. There is healthy competition between these two establishments. Both operate 52 weeks a year and both sell approximately the same type and dollar value of items. Table 12.4 provides the cost of goods sold, the average inventory level, and unit value of each item sold in the two stores.

   a. Compare the two retail stores in terms of average aggregate inventory value.

   b. Compare the two retail stores in terms of weeks of supply.

   c. Compare the two retail stores in terms of inventory turnover.

D = **Difficult Problem**

TABLE 12.4 | INVENTORY DATA FOR DOGS-R-US AND K-9, INC. STORES

	DOGS-R-US		K-9, INC.	
Cost of Goods Sold	**$560,000.00**		**$640,000.00**	
Category	**Average Inventory in Units**	**Value per Unit**	**Average Inventory in Units**	**Value per Unit**
Dog Beds	200	$55.00	140	$55.00
Dog Bones & Treats	1,200	$2.50	250	$2.50
Pet Feeders	50	$12.50	20	$12.50
Flea & Tick	350	$7.50	75	$7.50
Dog Kennels	10	$65.00	2	$65.00
Dog Pens	10	$220.00	3	$220.00
Patio Pet Doors	5	$120.00	2	$120.00
Dog Ramps	5	$150.00	2	$150.00
Pet Strollers	10	$40.00	2	$40.00
Pet Supplements	1,400	$4.50	150	$4.50
Dog Toys	250	$2.20	100	$2.20

Outsourcing Processes

9. A large global automobile manufacturer is considering outsourcing the manufacturing of a solenoid used in the transmission of its SUVs. The company estimates that annual fixed costs of manufacturing the part in-house, which include equipment, maintenance, and management, amounts to $6 million. The variable costs of labor and material are $5.00 per unit. The company has an offer from a major subcontractor to produce the part for $8.00 per unit. However, the subcontractor wants the company to share in the costs of the equipment. The automobile company estimates that the total cost would be $4 million, which also includes management oversight for the new supply contact.

   a. How many solenoids would the automobile company need per year to make the in-house option least costly?

   b. What other factors, besides costs, should the automobile company consider before revising its supply chain for SUVs?

10. Donegal Footwear is an international supplier of outdoor footwear for adventurous families. Currently, the company uses a logistical provider to provide warehouse services and handle packages destined for ground delivery. The contract calls for $9 million in annual fixed charges, which covers the provider's overhead and warehouse costs, and variable costs of $15 per package shipped. Recently, Donegal Footwear found a warehouse it could lease at a cost of $16 million per year, which includes lease costs, labor, and management oversight. Furthermore, the company found another provider who would deliver packages from the warehouse for $6.00 per package. Considering only costs, how many packages must Donegal Footwear ship to make the vertical integration into warehouse operations beneficial?

11. At the BlueFin Bank corporate headquarters, management was discussing the potential of outsourcing the processing of credit card transactions to DataEase, an international provider of banking operational services. Processing of the transactions at BlueFin has been a costly element of the annual profit and loss statement and the continual investment in equipment

to keep up to date has been draining capital reserves. Based upon initial study and negotiations, DataEase will charge $0.02 more per transaction than BlueFin's cost per transaction, and DataEase will want $12 million per year to cover equipment and overhead costs associated with the contract. BlueFin has yet to develop an estimate for the annual overhead and fixed costs associated with processing the transactions. These costs include supervision, administrative support, maintenance, equipment depreciation, and overhead. If BlueFin must process 20 million transactions per year, how high must those fixed costs be before it would pay to use DataEase?

12. A global manufacturer of electrical switching equipment (ESE) is considering outsourcing the manufacturing of an electrical breaker used in the manufacturing of switch boards. The company estimates that the annual fixed cost of manufacturing the part in-house, which includes equipment, maintenance, and management, amounts to $8 million. The variable cost of labor and materials are $11.00 per breaker. The company has an offer from a major subcontractor to produce the part for $16.00 per breaker.

   a. How many breakers would the electrical switching equipment company need per year to make the in-house option the least costly?

   b. Assume the subcontractor wants the company to share in the costs of the equipment. The ESE company estimates that the total annual cost would be $5 million, which also includes management oversight for the new supply contract. For this concession, the subcontractor will drop the per-unit price to $12.00. Under this assumption, how many breakers would the ESE company need per year to make the in-house option least costly?

   c. If the ESE manufacturer is expecting to use 1,500,000 breakers per year, which option (make in-house, use subcontractor without sharing in the cost of equipment, use subcontractor with sharing in the cost of equipment) is the least costly?

D = Difficult Problem

| VIDEO CASE | Supply Chain Design at Crayola |

Crayola LLC is a profitable wholly-owned subsidiary of Hallmark Cards of Kansas City, Missouri. The company's world headquarters are located in Easton, Pennsylvania and house marketing, sales, operations & manufacturing, finance, R&D, Internet services, customer care consumer affairs and corporate communications. Sales offices in Easton, Bentonville, Arkansas, and Minneapolis manage domestic accounts, while offices in Canada, Mexico, France, Italy, Japan, and Hong Kong handle international business. The Global Operations Division in Easton is responsible for the sourcing, quality, manufacturing, and logistics of Crayola products worldwide.

Two thirds of what Crayola sells globally is produced in its three Pennsylvania facilities in the Lehigh Valley. The "Forks I" plant is devoted to manufacturing crayons and markers, the "Forks II" plant handles plastic molding, and the Lehigh Valley Industrial Park (LVIP) plant creates paints, modeling compounds, activity kits, and Silly Putty®. A single 800,000 square foot distribution center in nearby Bethlehem, Pennsylvania handles finished goods for logistics to U.S. and international customers, and to global business units.

Each plant and its products have their own unique supply chains because the raw materials, suppliers and requirements all differ. For example, paraffin wax for crayons comes from sources in Louisiana and Pennsylvania via rail tanker cars twice a week, so proximity to the railroad is essential for the Forks I plant making crayons. All raw materials for each supply chain are first evaluated by independent board-certified toxicologists so Crayola can assure its products are not only of the highest quality, but also safe and non-toxic. Then, design hazard and risk assessments are done for all products during development to assure production meets the stringent standards set by the Art and Creative Materials Institute (ACMI).

Pete Ruggiero, Executive Vice President—Global Operations and his team have responsibility for designing supply chains that are innovative, resilient, responsive, and sustainable while assuring quality, ethics and cost considerations are met. Whenever the company's marketing division develops a new product kit that might contain paints, clays, crayons, markers or other products, the supply chain sourcing of the raw materials as well as the downstream production processes must be addressed to be sure the forecasted demand can be accommodated within the existing facilities. Not long ago, the company introduced an innovative new product called ColorWonder® that consists of pens that only write on the special paper they are packed with for sale. This required examining whether the existing supply chain could support the addition of producing the specialized ink markers, where to source the coated paper, and how to best create the kits containing both markers and paper.

Now in production, ColorWonder® is a best seller worldwide, with nearly 40 percent of Japanese sales coming from this product alone. Managers received feedback from the market that the pens in the kits were lasting longer than the paper, so the supply chain responded by creating separate paper packets so consumers may purchase just the paper after the initial pages in the kit are used. The result of this action has had a ripple effect on the demand for markers, which is now lower, since consumers are buying fewer full kits but more Color Wonder® books, so the supply chain and production had to adjust once again.

Another major challenge is the assembly of kits whose components are derived from diverse supply chains and assembled into finished products in the company's LVIP plant. An example is the popular Washable Deluxe Painting Kit®. The kit consists of paints and watercolors, paint brushes, smocks for the artist, and sponges for special effects. The company wants to

The Washable Deluxe Painting Kit, assembled at Crayola's Lehigh Valley Industrial Park plant, contains paints and watercolors produced in the USA and paint brushes, a smock, and a sponge produced in Asia. Demand for the kit has grown substantially in international markets, prompting a redesign of the supply chain so that Asian demand can be satisfied by Asian production facilities capable of producing and assembling the entire kit.

expand sales into the growing Asian market. The kit's paints and watercolors are made by Crayola in the U.S., but the paintbrushes come from China, the smocks come from Vietnam, and the sponges come from China. Labor costs for assembling the kits in the U.S. is a significant component, so if Crayola wants to sell the kits internationally, it needs to explore whether it makes sense to keep the existing supply chain design in place, or make a change to begin producing the kits closer to the growth in its international customer base. The lynchpin of this decision is that all components (including paint and watercolor trays historically manufactured in the United States) need to be made in Asia to make production efficient, and minimize duties and lead times. By producing the entire product—including its components and packaging—in Asia, Crayola is able to optimize its delivered cost to the markets. Producing this product in the U.S. and shipping it to Asia would be an impediment because of cost and lead time challenges.

QUESTIONS

1. Describe the text's four external and internal pressures on supply chain design as they relate to Crayola's supply chains for ColorWonder® and Washable Deluxe Painting Kit®.

2. Review the strategic implications of supply chains as described in the text. Does Crayola have efficient or responsive supply chains, or both? Explain your position.

3. Regarding the design of the Washable Deluxe Painting Kit® supply chain, Crayola must evaluate the strategy of next-shoring in Asia or retaining an existing network that involves the assembly of the kits in the U.S. Compare and contrast these two supply chain designs from perspective of the decision factors and pitfalls for outsourcing discussed in the text.

EXPERIENTIAL LEARNING | Sonic Distributors

Scenario

Sonic Distributors produces and sells music CDs. The CDs are pressed at a single facility (factory), issued through the company's distribution center, and sold to the public from various retail stores. The goal is to operate the distribution chain at the lowest total cost.

Materials (available from instructor)

Retail and distributor purchase order forms

Factory work order forms

Factory and distributor materials delivery forms

Inventory position worksheets

A means of generating random demand (typically a pair of dice)

Setup

Each team is in the business of manufacturing music CDs and distributing them to retail stores where they are sold. Two or more people play the role of retail outlet buyers. Their task is to determine the demand for the CDs and order replenishment stock from the distributor. The distributor carries forward-placed stock obtained from the factory. The factory produces in lot sizes either to customer order or to stock.

Tasks

Divide into teams of four or five.

Two or three people operate the retail stores.

One person operates the distribution center.

One person schedules production at the factory.

Every day, as play progresses, the participants at each level of the supply chain estimate demand, fill customer orders, record inventory levels, and decide how much to order or produce and when to place orders with their supplier.

Costs and Conditions

Unless your instructor indicates otherwise, the following costs and conditions hold.

Costs

Holding cost per unit per day	Retail outlets: $1.00/CD/day
	Distribution Center: $0.50/CD/day
	Factory: $0.25/CD/day
Pipeline inventory cost	Assume that pipeline cost can be ignored for this exercise (consider it zero).
Ordering cost (retailers and distributors)	$20/order
Factory setup cost (to run an order)	$50 (Note: Cost is per order, not per day, because even though successive orders from distributors are for the same item, the factory is busy fabricating other items between orders.)
Stockout (lost margin) cost	Retail Store: $8 per CD sale lost in a period

	$0 for backorders for shortages from the factory or shipping new orders
Shipping cost	Because other products are already being distributed through this chain and because CDs are light and take up little volume, consider the cost to be zero.

Conditions

Starting inventory	Retail stores each have 15 CDs
	Distribution center has 25 CDs
	Factory has 100 CDs
Lot-sizing restrictions	Retail outlets and distribution centers—no minimum order. Any amount may be stored. Factory production lot sizes and capacity—produce in minimum lots of 20. Maximum capacity: 200/day.
Outstanding orders	None

Delays

Ordering Delay. One day to send an order from a retail store to the distributor or from the distributor to the factory (i.e., 1 day is lost between placing an order and the recipient acting on it).

No delay occurs in starting up production once an order has been received (but 1 day is needed for delivery of an order from the distributor to the factory).

Delivery Delay. One-day shipping time between the distributor and a retail store or between the factory and the distributor (i.e., 1 day is lost between shipping an order and receiving it).

Run the Exercise

For simplicity's sake, assume all transactions take place simultaneously at the middle of the day. For every simulated day, the sequence of play goes as follows.

Retailers

a. Each retailer receives any shipment due in from its distributor (1 day after shipment) and places it in sales inventory (adds the quantity indicated on any incoming Material Delivery Form from the distributor—after its 1-day delay—to the previous day's ending inventory level on the Retailer's Inventory Position Worksheet). (*Note:* For the first day of the exercise, no order will come in.)

b. The retailers each determine the day's retail demand (the quantity of CDs requested) by rolling a pair of dice. The roll determines the number demanded.

c. Retailers fill demand from available stock, if possible. Demand is filled by subtracting it from the current inventory level to develop the ending inventory level, which is recorded. If demand exceeds supply, sales are lost. Record all lost sales on the worksheet.

d. Retailers determine whether an order should be placed. If an order is required, the desired quantity of CDs is written on a Retail Store Purchase Order, which is forwarded to the distributor (who receives it after a 1-day delay). If an order is made, it should be noted on the worksheet. Retailers may also desire to keep track of outstanding orders separately.

Distributor

a. The distributor receives any shipment due in from the factory and places the CDs in available inventory (adds the quantity indicated on any incoming Material Delivery Form from the factory—after its 1-day delay—to the previous day's ending inventory level on the distributor's inventory position worksheet).

b. All outstanding backorders are filled (the quantity is subtracted from the current inventory level indicated on the worksheet) and prepared for shipment. CDs are shipped by filling out a Distribution Center Material Delivery Form indicating the quantity of CDs to be delivered.

c. The distributor uses the purchase orders received from the retail stores (after the designated 1-day delay) to prepare shipments for delivery from available inventory. Quantities shipped are subtracted from the current level to develop the ending inventory level, which is recorded. If insufficient supply exists, backorders are generated.

d. The distributor determines whether a replenishment order should be placed. If an order is required, the quantity of CDs is written on a Distribution Center Purchase Order, which is forwarded to the factory (after a 1-day delay). If an order is made, it should be noted on the worksheet. The distributor may also desire to keep track of outstanding orders separately.

Factory

a. The factory places any available new production into inventory (adds the items produced the previous day to the previous day's ending inventory level on the Factory Inventory Position Worksheet).

b. All outstanding backorders are filled (the quantity is subtracted from the current inventory level indicated on the worksheet) and prepared for shipment. CDs are shipped by filling out a Factory Material Delivery Form, indicating the quantity of CDs to be delivered.

c. The factory obtains the incoming distributor's purchase orders (after the designated 1-day delay) and ships them from stock, if it can. These amounts are subtracted from the current values on the inventory worksheet. Any unfilled orders become backorders for the next day.

d. The factory decides whether to issue a work order to produce CDs either to stock or to order. If production is required, a Factory Work Order is issued, and the order is noted on the inventory worksheet. Remember that a setup cost applies to each *production* order. It is important to keep careful track of all production in process.

Remember, once an order has been placed, it cannot be changed and no partial shipments can be made. For each day, record your ending inventory position, backorder or lost sales amount, and whether an order was made (or a production run initiated). After everyone completes the transactions for the day, the sequence repeats, beginning at retailer step (a). Your instructor will tell you how many simulated days to run the exercise.

When the play is stopped, find the cumulative amount of inventory and other costs. You can do so by summing up the numbers in each column and then multiplying these totals by the costs previously listed. Use the total of these costs to assess how well your team operated the distribution chain.

Source: This exercise was developed by Larry Meile, Carroll School of Management, Boston College. Reprinted by permission.

CASE | Brunswick Distribution, Inc.

Alex Brunswick, CEO of Brunswick Distribution, Inc. (BDI), looked out his office window at another sweltering day and wondered what could have gone wrong at his company. He had just finished reviewing his company's recent financial performance and noticed something that worried him. BDI had experienced a period of robust growth over the last 4 years. "What could be going wrong?" he thought to himself. "Our sales have been growing at an average rate of 8 percent over the last 4 years but we still appear to be worse off than before." He sat back in his chair with a heavy sigh and continued reviewing the report on his desk.

Sales had risen consistently over the past 4 years but the future was uncertain. Alex Brunswick was aware that part of the past growth had largely been the result of a few competitors in the region going out of business, a situation that was unlikely to continue. Net earnings, however, had been declining for the last 3 years and were expected to decline next year.

Brunswick was determined to turn his company around within the next 3 years. He sat back from his desk and buzzed his personal assistant: "Gabrielle, could you ask Marianna and Bradley to come up?"

Background

The distribution business, in its simplest form, involves the purchase of inventory from a variety of manufacturers and its resale to retailers. Over the last 3 to 5 years, demands on inventory changed considerably; neither manufacturers nor retailers want to handle inventory, leaving distributors to pick up the slack. In addition, an increased tendency of retailers to order directly from manufacturers placed further strain on the profitability of distributorships in general.

After humble beginnings in a shed behind the house of Brunswick's grandmother, the company moved to a 10,000 square-foot leased facility. Ten years ago, BDI began distributing high-end appliance products to supplement its low-margin products. BDI entered into an agreement with KitchenHelper Corp., a large manufacturer of high-end kitchen appliances, located 35 miles from Moline, Illinois, to distribute KitchenHelper appliances to customers in the region. Over the years BDI enjoyed steady growth and expanded its area of coverage. Currently, Brunswick was covering an area with a radius of 200 miles from the company's main facility. Given the rapid growth, BDI purchased the leased facility and made additions to bring its capacity to 30,000 square feet.

The demise of several of its competitors resulted in the acquisition of new retailer customers and some new product lines. Traditional ordering in the retailer-distributor-manufacturer chain took place via fax or telephone. Brunswick considered implementing an Internet-based ordering system but was unsure of the potential operational and marketing benefits that it could provide.

Concerns

Market

Direct competition from distributors increased over the past 5 years. As a result, the most successful distributors adopted a value-added strategy to remain competitive. Retailers want dependable delivery to support sales promotions and promises to customers. They also want the freedom to hold sales promotions at any time as competitive conditions dictate and with only short notice to distributors. They also want the opportunity to choose from a wide variety of appliances. Nonetheless, many orders are won on the basis of price and lost on the basis of delivery problems.

Financial

Manufacturers commonly demand payment in 30 to 45 days and provide no financing considerations. Retailers, on the other hand, pay in 50 to 60 days. This difference often leaves BDI in a cash-poor situation that puts an unnecessary strain on its current operating loan. The company's borrowing capacity has almost been exhausted. Any additional financing will have to be sought from alternative sources. Given BDI's financial situation, any additional financing will be issued at a higher charge than the company's existing debt.

Operations

Inventory turnover also presented a problem for the past 5 years. In the past 2 years, however, a significant downturn in turnover occurred. This trend seems likely to continue.

Orders from retailers come in as their customers near completion of construction or renovations. Even though historical information provided a good benchmark of future sales, the changing market lessened the reliability of the information. The changes also affect BDI's ordering. Manufacturers require projections 60, 90, and 120 days out to budget their production. Sometimes penalties are assessed when BDI changes an order after it is placed with a manufacturer.

Strategic Issues

As Marianna and Bradley walked into Brunswick's office, he was still pondering the report. "Grab a seat," he grunted. They knew they were going to have a long day. Brunswick quickly briefed them on why he had summoned them, and they all immediately dove into a spirited discussion. Brunswick pointed out that BDI would need to be properly structured to deal with the recession and the reality of today's market. "We need to be well-positioned for growth as the market stabilizes," he said. To meet this challenge, BDI must evaluate a number of alternative options. Some of the possible options might include expanding current systems and, when necessary, developing new systems that interface with suppliers, customers, and commercial transportation resources to gain total asset visibility.

Before making any investment decision, Brunswick reminded them that BDI would have to evaluate any new capital requirements, as well as the expected contribution to the company's bottom line and market share, that any option might provide. Exhibit 1 shows the income statement for the current year.

Investing in New Infrastructure

Bradley Pulaski, vice president of operations, said, "Since Associated Business Distribution Corp. ceased operations 4 years ago, we have been inundated with phone calls and e-mails from potential customers across the Midwest looking for an alternative to ABD's services. These requests come not only from former ABD customers, but also from potential customers that have not dealt with either ABD or us in the past. We cannot adequately service this market from our current warehouse because the customers do not want to wait for lengthy deliveries. We are currently servicing some customers in that region; however, I do not think we can keep them much longer because of delayed deliveries. To take advantage of this opportunity, we would have to construct a new storage facility to complement our already strained resources and 'forward position' inventory to shorten our delivery times to customers on short notice. We are challenged by an inadequate infrastructure far too small for our requirements. We only have the Moline warehouse at this time." The addition of new facilities would provide BDI with

an opportunity for increased penetration in key industrial markets in the upper Midwest where the company has had a limited presence.

EXHIBIT 1 ▼

Company Income Statement ($000's)		
Revenue		33,074
Cost of Goods Sold		
Shipping costs	8,931	
Direct materials	5,963	
Direct labor and other	6,726	
Total	21,620	
Gross Profit		11,454
Operating Expenses		
Selling expenses	2,232	
Fixed expenses	2,641	
Depreciation	1,794	
Total	6,667	
Earnings before Interest and Taxes		4,787
Interest expense		838
Earnings before Taxes		3,949
Taxes @ 35%		1,382
Net Income		2,567

The financing resources for this option would be a challenge, given that BDI was approaching its credit limit with its principal bank. Additional financing from larger banks in Chicago, however, was not ruled out. It would be expensive (with current interest rates for long-term loans starting at 11 percent). According to Bradley, this option would cost $2 million for property and $10 million for plant and equipment. The new warehouse facilities would be depreciated over 20 years. The 20-year loan would be repaid with a single balloon payment at the end of the loan. With the additional infrastructure, BDI would be able to increase its annual sales by $4,426,000. In addition, delivery lead times to customers in the region would be reduced from 5 days to 2 days, which would be very competitive. Because of the added warehouse capacity, BDI could also increase the number of brands and models of appliances to better serve the retailers' needs for more variety. However, certain categories in the costs of goods sold would also increase. Total annual shipping costs, which include supplier deliveries to the warehouse as well as deliveries to the customer, would increase by $955,000. Annual materials costs (for the sold appliances) and labor costs would each increase by 6 percent. Total assets would increase from $30,170,000 to $43,551,000. This increase takes into account changes to inventory investment, which would become $7,200,000, accounts receivable, property, and plant and equipment.

Streamlining the Distribution System

Marianna Jackson, the vice president of logistics, stated, "I believe there is an opportunity to capitalize on the void left by our fallen rivals by utilizing a cost-efficient distribution system. We do not need a new facility; we can continue to serve the customers in the Midwest as best we can.

However, what we do need is an efficient distribution system. We are holding a considerable amount of stock that has not moved simply because of our inefficient inventory systems. One of our top priorities is working diligently with the inventory control department to keep what we need and dispose of what we do not need. This approach will allow us to use the space recovered from the unneeded items for automated warehouse equipment that will enable us to become more efficient. Everything we do and every dollar we spend affects our customers. We need to keep our prices competitive. Our cost of operations is our customers' cost. Our goal is to enable customers to spend their resources on readiness and the tools of their trade, not logistics. This option will not help us much with product variety or delivery speed; however, it will increase our on-time delivery performance and improve our flexibility to respond to changes in retailer orders to support their sales programs."

The option of having an integrated center, comprised of sophisticated automation systems, advanced materials handling equipment, and specially developed information technology, would provide BDI with both the versatility and capacity to offer improved products and services to Brunswick's customers. The system would support real-time ordering, logistics planning and scheduling, and after-sales service. When an order is received through a call center at Brunswick's offices in Moline, it will be forwarded to a logistics center for processing. The customer is given a delivery date based on truck availability. Orders would be grouped by destination so that trucks could be efficiently loaded to maximize the truck capacity. The order would then be scheduled for delivery and the customer notified of the estimated arrival. This new information technology would improve BDI's reliability in delivering the products when promised. The system also includes an automatic storage and retrieval system (AS/RS). The AS/RS selects a customer order and moves it to a dock for loading on a truck headed for the customer's location. The capital costs for this system would be $7 million, which would be depreciated over a 10-year period. The operating costs, including training, would run at $0.5 million each year. These costs would be considered fixed expenses by Brunswick. The improved system, however, would have tremendous cost savings. Marianna estimated that the system would save up to 16 percent in shipping expenses and 16 percent in labor expenses annually. Total assets would increase from $30,170,000 to $35,932,000 to account for changes in accounts receivables and equipment. Aggregate inventories would be only $4,500,000 because of the reduced need for safety stock inventories. BDI could finance this option using a 10-year loan at a 10 percent rate of interest. The loan would be repaid with a balloon payment at the end of the loan.

These savings would come from more efficient handling of customers' orders by the call center, better planning and scheduling of shipments, and improved communication with the warehouse and the customer, resulting in a dramatic reduction in the shipping costs in the supply chain. Additional savings would result from the reduction in personnel costs; fewer operators would be required. Marianna Jackson thought that BDI could maintain its current level of service with her option while becoming much more efficient.

The Decision

Alex Brunswick pondered the two options posed by Bradley Pulaski and Marianna Jackson. Bradley's option enabled the firm to increase its revenues by serving more customers. The capital outlay was sizable, however. Marianna's option focused on serving the firm's existing customers more efficiently. The value of that option was its dramatic reduction in costs; however, it was uncertain whether BDI could hold onto its current upper Midwest customers. Brunswick realized that he could not undertake both options, given the company's current financial position. Brunswick uses a 12 percent cost of capital as the discount rate when making financial decisions. How will each option affect the firm's operational and financial performance measures, which investors watch closely? Which supply chain design option would be better for the company? Use the Solver "Financial Measures Analyzer" for your analysis.

SUPPLY CHAIN
INTEGRATION

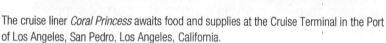

The cruise liner *Coral Princess* awaits food and supplies at the Cruise Terminal in the Port of Los Angeles, San Pedro, Los Angeles, California.

Ian Dagnall/Alamy

Coral Princess

Regardless of where you are right now, or what the weather is like in your home town, think of lounging on the deck of the *Coral Princess* somewhere in the Caribbean just after passing through the Panama Canal. The view is gorgeous, the breezes soft and cool; you find it difficult to contemplate that you and 1974 other guests are in a top-rated hotel with amenities that range from an outdoor movie theater to a casino with every game of chance a gambler ever wanted. If you want a wedding, there is a chapel. There is a swimming pool with a retractable glass dome, a cigar bar, and a complete TV studio.

While all those amenities sound good, there is one thing that all cruise liner guests look forward to and that is eating. There are five high-quality restaurants on board the *Coral Princess*. When the meals arrive in front of you, have you ever wondered how they got there? The supply of food, and its preparation, puts a tremendous strain on the coordination of supply chain processes for the *Coral Princess*. Here, four days at sea, the hotel manager just cannot call the suppliers and say that he forgot the carrots, the butter, and the sugar. Running out of stock is not an acceptable option. Pure volume is a complicating factor. On an average 15-day cruise, the *Coral Princess* will use 175 tons of food, including 43,200 eggs, 2,425 pounds of pasta, 7,245 pounds of rice, 84,000 pounds of vegetables, 13,000 pounds of chicken, 8,800 pounds of fish, and 10,500 pounds of beef. Two hundred galley employees prepare over 10,000 meals daily, all washed down with 3,800 bottles of wine and 12,000 bottles or cans of beer a cruise. Not everything is purchased, nor can all 175 tons of food be stored on board at one time. Certain items such as ice cream, dessert pastries, and breads are produced onboard to ensure their freshness. Other items must be restocked at selected ports on a schedule put in place long in advance of the cruise. While the guests are enjoying a port of call, the ship personnel are restocking the hold with food from suppliers in that area that have been proven to supply the best quality. Cruise ships must be very careful not to accept food that will cause sickness onboard.

Even a well-oiled wagon can run off the road, and so it can with the supply chain of a cruise ship. Good planning, including contingency plans, and quick reactions are desirable attributes. Natural disasters, such as hurricanes or earthquakes, cause cruise ships to reschedule their ports of call, which can disrupt the scheduled supply of food, boutique items, hotel supplies, and maintenance items. All of this requires close coordination up and down the supply chain. For example, the massive Japanese earthquake and tsunami of March 11, 2011, not only caused cruise ships to revise their itineraries, but it will also affect the supply chain for a very long time, given the scare from radiation getting into the food supply. Another example of a disruptive event is a strike at a port of supply for a cruise ship. A labor strike at the Ports of Los Angeles and Long Beach caused a massive congestion of 70 vessels waiting to be unloaded, thereby putting pressure on Princess Cruises' schedule for replenishing a cruise ship headed for Mexico. The solution was to use trucks to move part of the shipment in ocean freight containers to go by sea using a vessel at the Port of Oakland, 450 miles away, and the rest of the shipment by land using 53-foot trailers, timed so that both shipments would meet the cruise ship in Mexico. The two loads required considerable coordination for health inspections, security, customs clearance, and refrigerated equipment.

Cruise ships strive to provide the best possible experience for their guests. High levels of supply chain integration across multiple commodity groups and suppliers, as well as numerous ordering, delivery, and stocking points, are at the heart of that effort.

Source: Handout, *The Coral Princess Food & Beverage Department* (August 16, 2011); News archive at **http://www.princess.com/news/article**; Case Study Cruise Line Logistics-Princess Cruises, *Agility Logistics,* **http://www.agilitylogistics.com**.

Using Operations to Create Value

MANAGING PROCESSES

Process Strategy and Analysis
Quality and Performance
Capacity Planning
Constraint Management
Lean Systems
Project Management

MANAGING CUSTOMER DEMAND

Forecasting
Inventory Management
Operations Planning and
 Scheduling
Resource Planning

MANAGING SUPPLY CHAINS

Supply Chain Design
Supply Chain Logistic Networks
➤ **Supply Chain Integration**
Supply Chain Sustainability

LEARNING GOALS *After reading this chapter, you should be able to:*

1 Identify the major causes of disruptions in a supply chain.

2 Describe the four major nested processes in the new service or product development process.

3 Explain the five major nested processes in the supplier relationship process and use total cost analysis and preference matrices to identify appropriate sources of supply.

4 Identify the four major key nested processes in the order fulfillment process and use the expected value decision rule to determine the appropriate capacity of logistic resources.

5 Define the three major nested processes in the customer relationship process.

6 Explain how firms can mitigate the operational, financial, and security risks in a supply chain.

The development and delivery of services and products has become increasingly complex in today's global economy. The *Coral Princess*, one of several cruise liners owned and operated by the Princess Cruise Line, is an example of how a firm can excel at coordinating its supply chain for competitive advantage. To be effective, accurate inventory and demand information has to be available combined with considerable collaboration between the ship and its suppliers along the cruise itinerary. The Princess Cruise Line is successful at **supply chain integration**, which is the effective coordination of supply chain processes through the seamless flow of information up and down the supply chain. Supply chain integration provides each member of the supply chain visibility into the capacities and inventories of other members of the supply chain to aid in planning and scheduling. It facilitates collaboration between firms in a supply chain; in effect, it is an enabler of supply chain management and is at the core of reducing the risks of supply disruption.

supply chain integration
The effective coordination of supply chain processes through the seamless flow of information up and down the supply chain.

Supply chain integration involves internal as well as external processes. Figure 14.1 shows just how interconnected processes and firms in a supply chain can be. Think of a supply chain as a river that flows from raw material suppliers to consumers. For example, a ketchup factory gets its major supply from the tomato paste factories, which for the ketchup factory is a tier 1 supplier. In turn, the tomato paste factories get their major supplies from the tomato grading stations, which are tier 2 suppliers of the ketchup factory. Finally, the tomato growers ship their product directly to the tomato grading stations. The tier 1, tier 2, and tier 3 suppliers are all *upstream* from the ketchup factory, which means that they control the flow of supply to the ketchup factory. Suppose the tomato paste factory has a major process failure. The flow of tomato paste to the ketchup factory would dwindle to a trickle, as if someone built a dam across a river. Indeed, even those entities *downstream* from the ketchup factory could feel the effects after inventories of ketchup have been consumed. When a link in the supply chain fails, whether it is an internal process or one at a supplier, the rest of the chain feels the effects.

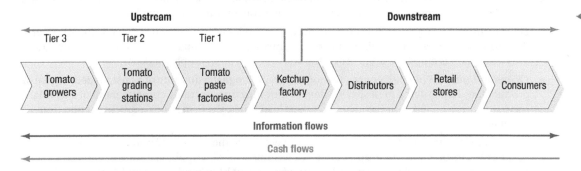

◀ **FIGURE 14.1**
Supply Chain for a Ketchup Factory

Mitigating the effects of supply chain disruptions is an important benefit of supply chain integration. Information flows, both upstream and downstream, provide visibility to supply chain members regarding supplies, capacities, and plans. Cash flows move upstream and are affected by pricing, promotional programs, supply contracts, and exchange rates. Every supply chain faces an undeniable risk in operational disruptions, security failures, and financial performance. Understanding the implications of these disruptions for supply chain performance is important for all employees in an organization.

In this chapter, we begin by discussing the nature and impact of disruptions to supply chain operations. We then explore the four major processes involved in supply chain integration and how they are linked internally and externally. We finish the chapter with a discussion of **supply chain risk management**, which is the practice of managing the risk of any factor or event that can materially disrupt a supply chain, whether within a single firm or across multiple firms.

supply chain risk management
The practice of managing the risk of any factor or event that can materially disrupt a supply chain, whether within a single firm or across multiple firms.

Supply Chain Disruptions

When a company expands from a local or regional presence to a more global one, supply chain strategy often needs to be adjusted. In a global arena, different products are directed to more diverse customers via different distribution channels, which require different supply chains. These supply chains are typically more complex and are exposed to both domestic and international disruptions. In this section, we identify the causes of supply chain disruptions, discuss how they cause supply chain dynamics, and show how supply chain integration can mitigate those effects.

Causes of Supply Chain Disruptions

Supply chain disruptions could result in cost increases, loss of reputation, civil and criminal penalties, bankruptcy, lost customers, or reduced revenue, profit, and market share. The more complex the supply chain, the less predictable the likelihood and the impact of a disruption, and the greater the risk to the effectiveness of the supply chain. Disruptions can emanate from outside the firm as well as inside the firm.

The Kinzua Viaduct Bridge in northwest Pennsylvania, constructed in 1882, was the longest railroad bridge in the world, spanning 2,053 feet and reaching a maximum height of 301 feet. It facilitated the flow of raw materials from the east to the great lakes regions. The trestle bridge was destroyed by a tornado in 2003. It takes reminders such as this to highlight the importance of integrated supply chains to avoid disrupting the flow of products and supplies.

Philip Scalia/Alamy

External Causes A firm has the least amount of control over its external customers and suppliers, who can periodically cause disruptions. Typical external disruptions include the following:

- *Environmental Disruptions.* Natural disasters, terrorism, political instability or war affecting supplier operations, regulatory changes, quotas, and strikes all can disrupt the normal flow of materials and services in a supply chain.

- *Supply Chain Complexity.* Increases in the dependencies between supply chain entities (suppliers, partners, and customers), increases in the number of supply chain entities, and changes in the configuration of the extended supply chain (the suppliers to suppliers) all have the potential to cause disruptions in the supply of materials, products, and services.

- *Loss of Major Accounts.* A loss of significant demand volume is the result of losing a large customer. This disruption is compounded when the firm has a concentrated customer base.

- *Loss of Supply.* Losing the supply of key materials or services can slow down or even stop the operations in a supply chain. Downtime due to equipment failures or quality issues is a common cause. This disruption is amplified if the firm is too consolidated in its supply markets.

- *Customer-Induced Volume Changes.* Customers may change the quantity of a customized service or product they had ordered for a specific date or they may unexpectedly demand more of a standard service or product. If the market demands short lead times, the firm needs a quick reaction from its suppliers.

- *Service and Product Mix Changes.* Customers may change the mix of items in an order and cause a ripple effect throughout the supply chain. For example, a major appliance store chain may change the mix of washing machines in its orders from 60 percent Whirlpool brand and 40 percent Kitchen Aid brand to 40 percent Whirlpool and 60 percent Kitchen Aid. This decision changes the production schedule of the Whirlpool plant that makes both brands, causing imbalances in its inventories. In addition, the tier 1 supplier that makes the face plates for the washing machines must change its schedules, thereby affecting *its* suppliers.

- *Late Deliveries.* Late deliveries of materials or delays in essential services can force a firm to switch its schedule from production of one product model to another. Firms that supply model-specific items may have their schedules disrupted. For example, the Whirlpool plant may find that a component supplier for its Model A washing machine could not supply the part on time. To avoid shutting down the assembly line, which is an expensive action, Whirlpool may decide to switch to Model B production. Suddenly, the demand on the suppliers of Model B-specific parts increases.

- *Underfilled Shipments.* Suppliers that send partial shipments do so because of disruptions at their own plants. The effects of underfilled shipments are similar to those of late shipments unless the underfilled shipment contains enough materials to allow the firm to operate until the next shipment.

Internal Causes A firm's own operations can be the culprit in what becomes the source of constant disruption in the supply chain. Typical internal disruptions include the following:

- *Internally Generated Shortages.* A shortage of parts manufactured by a firm may occur because of machine breakdowns, lengthy setup times, limited capacity and bottlenecks, or inexperienced workers. Internal shortages can cause a change in the firm's production schedule, thus affecting suppliers.

- *Quality Failures.* Product recalls, such as the record number of automobiles recalled by General Motors in 2013 and 2014, can cause huge costs and supply chain disruptions. Even if quality failures do not involve product recalls, they restrict the flow of services or products and negatively affect the performance of the supply chain.

- *Poor Supply Chain Visibility.* The inability to "see" the inventories and capabilities of suppliers and the inventories of customers, as well as the pipeline of materials and products, poses a risk to the performance of a firm. Often this risk arises because of a lack of collaborative planning and forecasting (see Chapter 8, "Forecasting").

- *Engineering Changes.* Changes to the design of services or products can have a direct impact on suppliers. For example, a major fast-food restaurant switching from Styrofoam packaging to biodegradable packaging for its sandwiches will affect the demand experienced by the suppliers of Styrofoam.

- *Order Batching.* Suppliers may offer a quantity discount, which gives an incentive to firms to purchase large quantities of an item less frequently, thereby raising the variability in orders to the supplier. Order batching may also result in transportation economies; larger orders may enable full-truckload shipments, thereby reducing the cost to ship materials but creating more variability in the supply chain.

- *New Service or Product Introductions.* A firm decides on the number of new service or product introductions, as well as their timing, and hence introduces a dynamic in the supply chain. New services or products may even require a new supply chain or the addition of new members to an existing supply chain. The more complex a service or product is, the greater is the risk of a disruption.

- *Service or Product Promotions.* A common practice of firms producing standardized services or products is to use price discounts to promote sales. Price discounting creates a spike in demand that is felt throughout the supply chain.

- *Information Errors.* Demand forecast errors can cause a firm to order too many or too few services and materials or can precipitate expedited orders that force suppliers to react more quickly to avoid shortages in the supply chain. In addition, errors in the physical count of items in stock can cause shortages (leading to panic purchases) or too much inventory (leading to a slowdown in purchases). Finally, communication links between buyers and suppliers can be faulty.

Supply Chain Dynamics

Why do these disruptions pose a risk to supply chain operations? Each firm in a supply chain depends on other firms for services, materials, or the information needed to supply its immediate external customer in the chain. Because firms are typically owned and managed independently, the actions of downstream supply chain members (positioned nearer the end user of the service or product) can affect the operations of upstream members. The reason is that upstream members of a supply chain must react to the demands placed on them by downstream members of the chain. These demands are a function of the policies downstream firms have for replenishing their inventories, the actual levels of those inventories, the demands of their customers, and the accuracy of the information they have to work with. As you examine the order patterns of firms in a supply chain, you will frequently see the variability in order quantities increase as you proceed upstream. This increase in variability is referred to as the **bullwhip effect**, which gets its name from the action of a bullwhip—the handle of the whip initiates the action; however, the tip of the whip experiences the wildest action. The slightest change in customer demands can ripple through the entire chain, with each member receiving more variability in demands from the member immediately downstream. A firm contributes to the bullwhip effect if the variability of the orders to its suppliers exceeds the variability of the orders from its immediate customers.

Figure 14.2 shows the bullwhip effect in a supply chain for facial tissue. The variability in the orders increases as you go upstream in the supply chain. Because supply patterns do not match demand

bullwhip effect

The phenomenon in supply chains whereby ordering patterns experience increasing variance as you proceed upstream in the chain.

MyOMLab Animation

▼ **FIGURE 14.2**
Supply Chain Dynamics for Facial Tissue

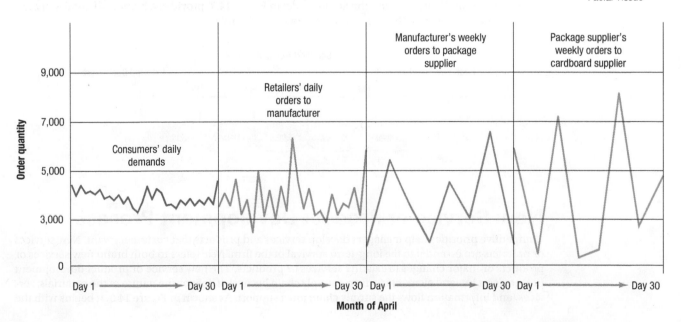

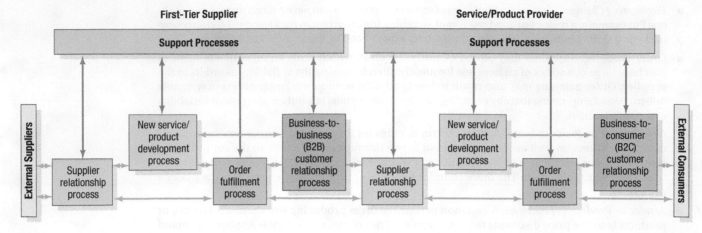

patterns, inventories accumulate in some firms and shortages occur in others. The firms with too much inventory stop ordering, and those that have shortages place expedited orders.

Integrated Supply Chains

Regardless of the supply chain design, minimizing supply chain disruptions begins with a high degree of functional and organizational integration. Such integration does not happen overnight; it must include linkages between the firm and its suppliers and customers, as shown in Figure 14.3. The new service or product development, supplier relationship, order fulfillment, and customer relationship processes, as well as their internal and external linkages, are integrated into the normal business routine. The firm takes on a customer orientation. However, rather than merely reacting to customer demand, the firm strives to work with its customers and suppliers so that everyone benefits from improved flows of services, materials, and information. The firm must also develop a better understanding of its suppliers' organizations, capacities, strengths, and weaknesses—and include its suppliers earlier into the design of new services or products.

SCOR model

A framework that focuses on a basic supply chain of plan, source, make, deliver, and return processes, repeated again and again along the supply chain.

Another integrative frame of reference is the *supply chain operations reference model*, known as *SCOR*, developed by the Supply Chain Council with the assistance of 70 of the world's leading manufacturing companies. Figure 14.4 shows that the **SCOR model** focuses on a basic supply chain of *plan*, *source*, *make*, *deliver*, and *return* processes, repeated again and again along the supply chain. The return processes handle the return of recyclable materials and defective products, which we will discuss in more detail in Chapter 15, "Supply Chain Sustainability." Much like our model shown in Figure 14.3, the SCOR model emphasizes that the design of an integrated supply chain is complex and requires a *process view*. We already provided some key insights into process design decisions in Part 1 and Part 2 of the text. These insights must be applied to the new service or product development, supplier relationship, order fulfillment, and customer relationship processes. Beyond that, these processes need to be integrated both within a firm and across the supply chain. It is important to know that an integrated supply chain, implied by Figure 14.3 and the SCOR model in Figure 14.4, provides a framework for the operating decisions in a firm and that these processes play a major role.

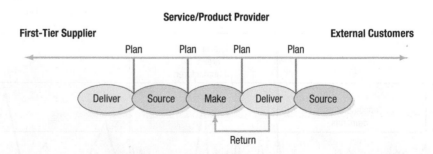

New Service or Product Development Process

Competitive priorities help managers develop services and products that customers want. New services or products are essential to the long-term survival of the firm. *New* refers to both brand new services or products or major changes to existing services or products. The new service or product development process is an integral element in a firm's supply chain because it defines the nature of the materials, services, and information flows the supply chain must support. As shown in Figure 14.5, it begins with the

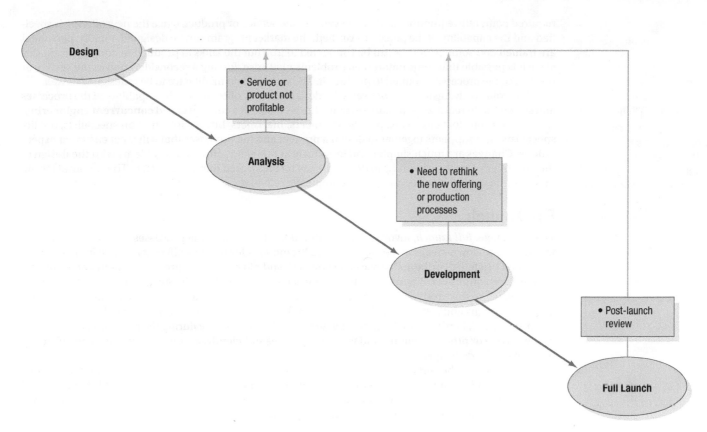

▲ **FIGURE 14.5**
New Service/Product
Development Process

consideration of the development strategy and ends with the launch of the new offering. There are four key nested processes, or stages, in the new service or product development process: design, analysis, development, and full launch. Here are some considerations for supply chain managers.

Design

The *design* stage is critical because it links the creation of new services or products to the corporate strategy of the firm and defines the requirements for the firm's supply chain. As we have already noted, the corporate strategy specifies the long-term objectives and the markets in which the firm wishes to compete. In the design stage, ideas for new offerings are proposed and screened for feasibility and market worthiness. These ideas specify how the customer connects with the service or manufacturing firm, the benefits and outcomes for the customer, and the value of the service or product. Proposals also specify how the new offering will be produced and delivered—an important consideration for the supply chain. Often critical choices must be made, such as the raw materials, degree of modularity in the design, or the nature of the logistical services needed to get the service or product to market. Even though many of the detailed specifics of the service or product and its processes have not yet been developed, the inputs of designers, engineers, suppliers, supply chain managers, and potential customers in this stage can avoid costly mistakes.

Analysis

The second stage, *analysis*, involves a critical review of the new offering and how it will be produced to make sure that it fits the corporate strategy, is compatible with regulatory standards, presents an acceptable market risk, and satisfies the needs of the intended customers. The resource requirements for the new offering must be examined from the perspective of the core capabilities of the firm and the need to acquire additional resources. The existing supply chain must be evaluated for its appropriateness for the new offering. If change is needed, the design might have to be revised (efficient or responsive) or new capabilities acquired by forming strategic partnerships with new firms. If the analysis reveals that the new offering has good market potential and that the firm has the capability (or can acquire it), the authorization is given to proceed to the next stage.

Development

The third stage, *development*, brings more specificity to the new offering. The required competitive priorities are used as inputs to the design (or redesign) of the processes that will be involved in delivering the new offering. The processes are analyzed, including those of suppliers; each activity is designed to meet its required competitive priorities and to add value to the service or product. Once the new offering is specified and the capability of the processes verified, the market program can be designed. Finally, personnel are trained and some pilot runs can be conducted to iron out the kinks in production and supply. At this stage it is possible that some unforeseen problems may arise, forcing a reconsideration of the service or product or the processes required to produce it. The supply chain might have to be redesigned as well.

To avoid costly mismatches between the design of a new offering and the capability of the processes and supply chain required to produce it, many firms engage in a concept called **concurrent engineering**, which brings product engineers, process engineers, marketers, buyers, information specialists, quality specialists, and suppliers together to design a product and the processes that will meet customer expectations. Changes are much simpler and less costly at this stage. However, problems with the design of the new offering or the capability to deliver it may be discovered during this stage. The proposal for the new offering may have to be scrapped or completely rethought.

concurrent engineering

A concept that brings product engineers, process engineers, marketers, buyers, information specialists, quality specialists, and suppliers together to design a product and the processes that will meet customer expectations.

Full Launch

The final stage, *full launch*, involves the coordination of many internal processes as well as those both upstream and downstream in the supply chain. Promotions for the new offering must be initiated, sales personnel briefed, distribution processes activated, and old services or products that the new offering is to replace withdrawn. A particular strain is placed on the supply chain during a period referred to as *ramp-up*, when the production processes must increase volume to meet demands while coping with quality problems and last-minute design changes. The more integrated the supply chain, the easier the ramp-up period. Flexibility in the supply chain is a desirable attribute during the ramp-up period. Later, as the service or product matures and volume increases sufficiently, a supply chain based on efficiency may have to be developed.

Regardless of the service or product, a post launch review should compare the competitive priorities of the supply chain to its competitive capabilities, perhaps signaling a need to rethink the original service or product idea or the supply chain. The review should also get inputs from customers, who may divulge their experiences and may share ideas for change.

Supplier Relationship Process

The nature of the service or product determines the design requirements for the upstream supply chain. The supplier relationship process, which focuses on the interaction of the firm with upstream suppliers, includes five major nested processes: (1) sourcing, (2) design collaboration, (3) negotiation, (4) buying, and (5) information exchange. For many firms, these processes are the organizational responsibility of **purchasing**, which is the activity that decides the suppliers to use, negotiates contracts, maintains information flows, and determines whether to buy locally.

purchasing

The activity that decides which suppliers to use, negotiates contracts, and determines whether to buy locally.

Sourcing

The sourcing process is involved in the selection, certification, and evaluation of suppliers and, in general, the management of supply contracts.

Supplier Selection   A starting point for selecting suppliers is to perform a total cost analysis. There are four key costs to consider for each supplier.

- *Material costs.* Negotiating with suppliers for the provision of a service or product results in a price per unit (or application of the service). Material costs equal annual requirements (D) multiplied by the price per unit, p.

$$\text{Annual material costs} = pD$$

- *Freight costs.* The costs of transporting the product or the equipment and personnel who will perform the service can vary greatly depending on the location of the supplier, the size of the shipments (full truckload shipments [TL] are cheaper per pound than less-than-truckload shipments [LTL]), the number of shipments per year, and the mode of transportation (air transportation is more expensive than truck or rail transportation).

- *Inventory costs.* Buyers interested in purchasing products must consider the shipping quantity and the lead time from the supplier. The shipping quantity, Q, will determine the cycle inventory the buyer must maintain until the next shipment of the product.

$$\text{Cycle inventory} = Q/2$$

The lead time, L, and the average requirements per day (or week) $\bar{d}$, will determine the level of the pipeline inventory, which also may be the responsibility of the buyer. Assuming a constant lead time,

$$\text{Pipeline inventory} = \bar{d}L$$

The buyer must pay inventory holding costs on the cycle and pipeline inventories. Annual inventory costs equal the sum of the cycle and pipeline inventories multiplied by the annual holding cost per unit, H. See Chapter 9, "Inventory Management" for a review of inventory holding costs and cycle and pipeline inventories.

$$\text{Annual inventory costs} = (Q/2 + \bar{d}L)H$$

- *Administrative costs.* Supply contacts must be monitored and frequent interactions with the supplier may be required. Administrative costs include the managerial time, travel, and other variable costs associated with interacting with a supplier. These costs may vary greatly depending on the location of the supplier; more distant suppliers typically require more administrative attention.

The total annual cost for a supplier is the sum of these costs:

$$\text{Total Annual Cost} = pD + \text{Freight costs} + (Q/2 + \bar{d}L)H + \text{Administrative costs}$$

EXAMPLE 14.1	Total Cost Analysis for Supplier Selection

Compton Electronics manufactures laptops for major computer manufacturers. A key element of the laptop is the keyboard. Compton has identified three potential suppliers for the keyboard, each located in a different part of the world. Important cost considerations are the price per keyboard, freight costs, inventory costs, and contract administrative costs. The annual requirements for the keyboard are 300,000 units. Assume Compton has 250 business days a year. Managers have acquired the following data for each supplier.

	ANNUAL FREIGHT COSTS		
	Shipping Quantity (Units/Shipment)		
Supplier	**10,000**	**20,000**	**30,000**
Belfast	$380,000	$260,000	$237,000
Hong Kong	$615,000	$547,000	$470,000
Shreveport	$285,000	$240,000	$200,000

	KEYBOARD COSTS AND SHIPPING LEAD TIMES			
Supplier	**Price/Unit**	**Annual Inventory Carrying Cost/Unit**	**Shipping Lead Time (Days)**	**Administrative Costs**
Belfast	$100	$20.00	15	$180,000
Hong Kong	$96	$19.20	25	$300,000
Shreveport	$99	$19.80	5	$150,000

Which supplier provides the lowest annual total cost to Compton?

SOLUTION

The average requirements per day are

$$\bar{d} = 300{,}000/250 = 1{,}200 \text{ keyboards.}$$

Each option must be evaluated with consideration for the shipping quantity using the following equation:

$$\text{Total Annual Cost} = \text{Material costs} + \text{Freight costs} + \text{Inventory costs} + \text{Administrative costs}$$
$$= pD + \text{Freight costs} + (Q/2 + \bar{d}L)H + \text{Administrative costs}$$

For example, consider the Belfast option for a shipping quantity of $Q = 10{,}000$ units. The costs are

Material costs $= pD = (\$100/\text{unit})(300{,}000 \text{ units}) = \$30{,}000{,}000$

Freight costs $= \$380{,}000$

Inventory costs $= (\text{cycle inventory} + \text{pipeline inventory})H = (Q/2 + \bar{d}L)H$

$$= (10{,}000 \text{ units}/2 + 1{,}200 \text{ units/day} (15 \text{ days}))\$20/\text{unit/year} = \$460{,}000$$

Administrative costs $= \$180{,}000$

Total Annual Cost $= \$30{,}000{,}000 + \$380{,}000 + \$460{,}000 + \$180{,}000 = \$31{,}020{,}000$

The total costs for all three shipping quantity options are similarly calculated and are contained in the following table.

	TOTAL ANNUAL COSTS FOR THE KEYBOARD SUPPLIERS		
	Shipping Quantity		
Supplier	**10,000**	**20,000**	**30,000**
Belfast	$31,020,000	$31,000,000	$31,077,000
Hong Kong	$30,387,000	$30,415,000	$30,434,000
Shreveport	$30,352,800	$30,406,800	$30,465,800

DECISION POINT

Notice that the shipping quantity plays an important role; the lowest cost for the Belfast supplier comes with a shipping quantity of 20,000 keyboards. Nonetheless, based on the total cost analysis, the Shreveport supplier will provide the lowest cost to Compton. Compton should choose a shipping quantity of 10,000 keyboards, which implies that there will be 30 shipments a year (or 300,000/10,000). While the Hong Kong supplier had the lowest price per keyboard, the Shreveport supplier could deliver the keyboards to Compton with the lowest overall cost, which includes logistics, inventory, and administrative costs.

While total cost is an important consideration in the selection of suppliers, other performance dimensions may also be important. The quality of a supplier's materials may be critical since hidden costs of poor quality may be high. Similarly, shorter lead-times and on-time delivery may allow the buying firm to maintain acceptable customer service with less inventory. So management must review the market segments it wants to serve and accordingly relate its supplier selection needs to the supply chain. Competitive priorities and order winners for the firm are a good starting point in developing a list of performance criteria to be used. For example, if you were a manager of a food-service firm, in addition to total costs, you would likely use on-time delivery and quality as top criteria for selecting suppliers. These criteria reflect the requirements that food-service supply chains need to meet.

green purchasing

The process of identifying, assessing, and managing the flow of environmental waste and finding ways to reduce it and minimize its impact on the environment.

Another criterion that is important in the selection of suppliers is environmental impact. Many firms are engaging in **green purchasing**, which involves identifying, assessing, and managing the flow of environmental waste and finding ways to reduce it and minimize its impact on the environment. Suppliers are being asked to be environmentally conscious when designing and producing their services or products. Claims such as *green, biodegradable, natural,* and *recycled* must be substantiated when bidding on a contract. In the not-too-distant future, this criterion could become an important one in the selection of suppliers. We will have more to say about this topic in Chapter 15, "Supply Chain Sustainability."

When faced with multiple criteria in the supplier selection problem, management can use a preference matrix as shown in Example 14.2. See Supplement A, "Decision Making" for a review of this approach.

EXAMPLE 14.2	**Using a Preference Matrix for Selecting Suppliers**

The management of Compton Electronics has done a total cost analysis for three international suppliers of keyboards (see Example 14.1). Compton also considers on-time delivery, consistent quality, and environmental stewardship in its selection process. Each criterion is given a weight (total of 100 points), and each supplier is given a score (1 = poor, 10 = excellent) on each criterion. The data are shown in the following table.

		SCORE		
Criterion	**Weight**	**Belfast**	**Hong Kong**	**Shreveport**
Total Cost	25	5	8	9
On-Time Delivery	30	9	6	7
Consistent Quality	30	8	9	6
Environment	15	9	6	8

SOLUTION

The weighted score for each supplier is calculated by multiplying the weight by the score for each criterion and arriving at a total. For example, the Belfast weighted score is

$$WS = (25 \times 5) + (30 \times 9) + (30 \times 8) + (15 \times 9) = 770$$

Similarly, the weighted score for Hong Kong is 740, and for Shreveport, 735. Consequently, Belfast is the preferred supplier.

DECISION POINT

Even though Belfast had a higher total cost based on the calculations in Example 14.1, it significantly outperformed the other suppliers on the criteria Compton considered very important. Given the weights placed on the criteria, it is clear that Compton is willing to pay extra for better delivery performance, quality, and environmental stewardship.

Supplier Certification and Evaluation Supplier certification programs verify that potential suppliers have the capability to provide the services or materials the buying firm requires. ISO 9001:2008 is one such program (see Chapter 3, "Quality and Performance," for more details). Nonetheless, certification typically involves site visits by a cross-functional team from the buying firm, which does an in-depth evaluation of the supplier's capability to meet cost, quality, delivery, and flexibility targets from process and information system perspectives. The team may consist of members from operations, purchasing, engineering, information systems, and accounting. Every aspect of producing the services or materials is explored. The team observes the supplier's processes in action and reviews the documentation for completeness and accuracy. Once certified, the supplier can be used by the purchasing department without its having to make background checks.

Certification does not give the supplier a free pass on future evaluation. Performance is regularly monitored and performance records are kept. Periodic visits by the certification team may take place. Recertification may be required after a certain period of time or if performance declines.

Design Collaboration

The design collaboration process focuses on jointly designing new services or products with key suppliers; it facilitates concurrent engineering by drawing key suppliers into the new service/product development process, particularly in the design and development stages. This process seeks to eliminate costly delays and mistakes incurred when many suppliers concurrently design service packages or manufactured components.

An approach that many firms are using in their design collaboration process is called **early supplier involvement**, which is a program that includes suppliers in the design phase of a service or product. Suppliers provide suggestions for design changes and materials choices that will result in more efficient operations and higher quality. In the automotive industry, an even higher level of early supplier involvement is known as **presourcing**, whereby suppliers are selected early in a product's concept

BIOTA's premium natural spring water originates from one of the world's highest protected alpine springs perched above Ouray, Colorado, and is packaged in the world's first biodegradable bottle. Made from corn, a 100 percent renewable resource, BIOTA bottles break down in approximately 80 days in a commercial composting environment.

PRNewsFoto/BIOTA Brands of America, Inc./AP Photos

early supplier involvement

A program that includes suppliers in the design phase of a service or product.

presourcing

A level of supplier involvement in which suppliers are selected early in a product's concept development stage and are given significant, if not total, responsibility for the design of certain components or systems of the product.

value analysis

A systematic effort to reduce the cost or improve the performance of services or products, either purchased or produced.

competitive orientation

A supplier relation that views negotiations between buyer and seller as a zero-sum game: Whatever one side loses, the other side gains, and short-term advantages are prized over long-term commitments.

development stage and are given significant, if not total, responsibility for the design of certain components or systems of the product. Presourced suppliers also take responsibility for the cost, quality, and on-time delivery of the items they produce.

Firms can also improve performance by engaging in **value analysis**, which is a systematic effort to reduce the cost or improve the performance of services or products, either purchased or produced. It is an intensive examination of the services, materials, processes, information systems, and flows of material involved in the production of a service or an item. Benefits include reduced production, materials, and distribution costs; improved profit margins; and increased customer satisfaction.

Negotiation

The negotiation process focuses on obtaining an effective contract that meets the price, quality, and delivery requirements of the supplier relationship process's internal customers. The nature of the relations maintained with suppliers can affect the quality, timeliness, and price of a firm's services and products. The firm's orientation toward supplier relations will affect the negotiation and design collaboration processes.

Competitive Orientation   The **competitive orientation** sees negotiations between buyer and seller as a zero-sum game: Whatever one side loses, the other side gains. Short-term advantages are prized over long-term commitments. The buyer may try to beat the supplier's price down to the lowest survival level or push demand to high levels during boom times and order almost nothing during recessions. In contrast, the supplier presses for higher prices for specific levels of quality, customer service, and volume flexibility. Which party wins depends largely on who has the most clout.

Purchasing power determines the clout that a firm has. A buyer has purchasing power when the purchasing volume represents a significant share of the supplier's sales or the purchased service or item is standardized and many substitutes are available. We refer to this condition as *economic dependency*. However, firms may have other sources of power in a relationship with suppliers. These sources include:

- *Referent*—the supplier values identification with the buyer. For example, the fact that a firm is supplying IBM may open the door for business with other customers.

- *Expert*—the buyer has access to knowledge, information, and skills desired by the supplier. For example, a supplier to UPS may get access to logistics planning skills possessed by UPS.

- *Reward*—the buyer has the ability to give rewards to the supplier. Often, the rewards may involve the promise for future business or the opportunity to become a partner sometime in the future.

- *Legal*—the buyer has the legal right to prescribe behavior for the supplier. For example, the buyer may demand strict compliance to the negotiated contract or else the matter will be taken to court.

- *Coercive*—the buyer has the ability to punish the supplier. For example, the buyer may threaten to cancel future business with the supplier unless the supplier adheres to the buyer's demands.

It should be noted that the buyer does not always possess the power in a relationship. Sometimes the supplier holds the power; consequently, the supplier could exercise these sources of power as well. Managerial Practice 14.1 shows how the exercise of power can go overboard.

MANAGERIAL
PRACTICE **14.1**   The Consequences of Power in an Automotive Supply Chain

General Motors (GM) is a $155 billion global company that designs, manufactures, markets, and distributes ten brands of vehicles and vehicle parts and sells financial services. It has 18,500 suppliers, 212,000 employees speaking 50 languages in 396 facilities in 37 countries touching six continents crossing 23 time zones, and 21,000 retail dealers worldwide. Imagine the complexity of the nested web of supply chains GM has to manage. To be successful in such an environment, a firm needs good supplier relations because economic and physical disruptions are very likely. Unfortunately for GM, the disruptions were *very* likely. In February 2014, GM issued a massive recall of 2.6 million vehicles designed and sold in the market 10 years earlier for a defective part implicated in at least 13 deaths. What went wrong?

To gain perspective, we must go back to the year 2000, when GM's profit margins were declining because of the rising costs of worker and retiree

benefit obligations and eroding market share. The Chevrolet Cobalt and the Saturn Ion, the "small-car hope" of the future and the very cars that were the subject of the recall 10 years later, were being designed. GM had planned to build those cars on a common platform with the Opel Astra in conjunction with Fiat. Building a compact car off a single global platform would have generated a profit even for an inexpensive $12,000 car; stamping out millions of similar models would have created economies of scale. However, the venture with Fiat failed. Given the gloomy financial picture, GM management decided that they had to find other ways to reduce costs. While GM never advocated building unsafe cars, the message "build them for less" reflected a culture of cutting costs and squeezing suppliers. Using the power it had over suppliers in the supply chain, GM began pressing its suppliers, including former parts division Delphi Automotive Plc, to shave pennies off the price of every part to

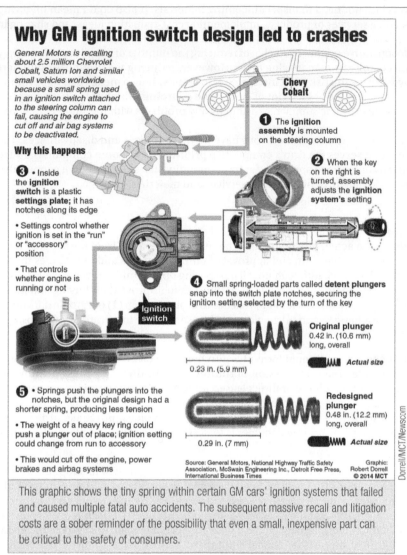

Why GM ignition switch design led to crashes

General Motors is recalling about 2.5 million Chevrolet Cobalt, Saturn Ion and similar small vehicles worldwide because a small spring used in an ignition switch attached to the steering column can fail, causing the engine to cut off and air bag systems to be deactivated.

Chevy Cobalt

❶ The **ignition assembly** is mounted on the steering column

❷ When the key on the right is turned, assembly adjusts the **ignition system's** setting

Why this happens

❸ • Inside the **ignition switch** is a plastic **settings plate**; it has notches along its edge

• Settings control whether ignition is set in the "run" or "accessory" position

• That controls whether engine is running or not

Ignition switch

❹ Small spring-loaded parts called **detent plungers** snap into the switch plate notches, securing the ignition setting selected by the turn of the key

Original plunger 0.42 in. (10.6 mm) long, overall

0.23 in. (5.9 mm)   *Actual size*

❺ • Springs push the plungers into the notches, but the original design had a shorter spring, producing less tension

• The weight of a heavy key ring could push a plunger out of place; ignition setting could change from run to accessory

• This would cut off the engine, power brakes and airbag systems

Redesigned plunger 0.48 in. (12.2 mm) long, overall

0.29 in. (7 mm)   *Actual size*

Source: General Motors, National Highway Traffic Safety Association, McSwain Engineering Inc., Detroit Free Press, International Business Times

Graphic: Robert Dorrell © 2014 MCT

Dorrell/MCT/Newscom

This graphic shows the tiny spring within certain GM cars' ignition systems that failed and caused multiple fatal auto accidents. The subsequent massive recall and litigation costs are a sober reminder of the possibility that even a small, inexpensive part can be critical to the safety of consumers.

had to give GM an immediate price reduction on current business. The price cuts amounted to millions of dollars. Those suppliers who won contracts had to agree on annual price cuts of 3 percent to 5 percent of the new business.

The part that spurred the recall was an ignition switch, costing between $2 and $5. A spring inside the part was loose enough to allow the ignition to switch out of the "on" position, shutting off the engine and power steering and disabling the air bags. The defect caused much damage and injury, including death. The part was initially produced in 2001 at Delphi's Mechatronics plant in Foley, Alabama, which had an expensive union contract. It is unclear as to how the pressure on prices played a role with respect to the failure of the switch; however, buckling under the pressure to cut costs in 2005, Delphi moved the plant to Metamoros, Mexico, where workers made the equivalent of $11 per day. Nonetheless, the ignition-switch fault was already known at GM by then.

From 2002 through 2005, GM had the worst supplier relations in the industry. Things went steadily downhill, and in 2009, GM filed for Chapter 11 bankruptcy. While there are many reasons for the downfall, two things are clear. First, GM lost perspective on its competitive priorities and focused almost exclusively on low-cost operations. It used the tremendous power it had to squeeze suppliers on price to the point they had to cut corners to stay in business. Second, GM forgot about the importance of good supplier relations, relying on a competitive orientation to maintain its own profit margins in light of burgeoning overhead costs.

GM has come out of 2009 much leaner and has shown that it has learned some of the hard lessons from the past. It has made sharp gains in supplier relations; it still has a long way to go. To garner better supplier relations, GM initiated the Strategic Supplier Engagement Program, which offers perks such as better access to GM purchasing and engineering executives, joint strategic planning on opportunities for growth, and training for those suppliers who are rated highly on key measures including cost containment and various cultural aspects such as open communication and technology sharing. GM will assign ratings to its 400 largest suppliers; those receiving a prime rating will have access to the new program. Apparently the "new" GM is now exercising *expert* power and *reward* power in its relationships with suppliers. It remains to be seen if GM will be able to shed all of its past negative reputation with its supply base.

match rock-bottom prices from Asia. Using *coercive* power, GM threatened to outsource the production overseas if suppliers could not match those low prices. Delphi, for example, relied on GM for 90 percent of its business; the leverage was enormous. Further, to bid on a new parts contract, suppliers

Sources: Naughton, Keith, David Welch, Jeff Green, and Mina Kimes, "GM's Flawed Cars Born as Engineers Pushed Suppliers for Low 'China Cost'," Bloomberg, **http://finance.yahoo.com** (March 21, 2014); Colias, Mike, "GM Takes Next Step to Strengthen Relationship with Suppliers," Automotive News, **http://www.autonews.com** (February 2, 2014); Wilson, Chris, "GM Leads Pack in Recalled Car Models," TIME, **http://time.com/45235** (April 1, 2014); GM Annual Report (2013), **http://www.gm.com**.

Cooperative Orientation   The **cooperative orientation** emphasizes that the buyer and the seller are partners, each helping the other as much as possible. A cooperative orientation means long-term commitment, joint work on quality and service or product designs, and support by the buyer of the supplier's managerial, technological, and capacity development. A cooperative orientation favors fewer suppliers of a particular service or item, with just one or two suppliers being the ideal number. As order volumes increase, the supplier gains economies of scale, which lowers costs. When contracts are large and a long-term relationship is ensured, the supplier might even build a new facility and hire a new workforce, perhaps relocating close to the buyer's plant. Suppliers become almost an extension of the buyer.

A cooperative orientation means that the buyer shares more information with the supplier about its future buying intentions. This forward visibility allows suppliers to make better, more reliable forecasts of future demand. The buyer visits suppliers' plants and cultivates cooperative attitudes. The buyer may even suggest ways to improve the suppliers' operations. This close cooperation with suppliers could

cooperative orientation

A supplier relation in which the buyer and seller are partners, each helping the other as much as possible.

even mean that the buyer does not need to inspect incoming materials. It also could mean involving the supplier more in designing services or products, implementing cost-reduction ideas, and sharing in savings.

One advantage of a cooperative orientation is that of reducing the number of suppliers in the supply chain, which reduces the complexity of managing them. However, reducing the number of suppliers for a service or item may increase the risk of an interruption in supply. It also means less opportunity to drive a good bargain unless the buyer has a lot of clout. **Sole sourcing**, which is the awarding of a contract for a service or item to only one supplier, can amplify any problems with the supplier that may crop up.

Both the competitive and cooperative orientations have their advantages and disadvantages. The key is to use the approach that serves the firm's competitive priorities best. Some companies utilize a mixed strategy, applying a competitive approach for its commodity-like supplies and a cooperative approach for its complex, high-valued, or high-volume services and materials.

sole sourcing

The awarding of a contract for a service or item to only one supplier.

Buying

The buying process relates to the actual procurement of the service or material from the supplier. This process includes the creation, management, and approval of purchase orders and determines the locus of control for purchasing decisions. Although not all purchasing opportunities involve the Internet, virtual marketplaces have provided firms with many opportunities to improve their buying and information exchange processes. Here we discuss four approaches to e-purchasing: (1) electronic data interchange, (2) catalog hubs, (3) exchanges, and (4) auctions, and close with the implications of choosing a locus of control.

Electronic Data Interchange A traditional form of e-purchasing is **electronic data interchange (EDI)**, a technology that enables the transmission of routine, standardized business documents from computer to computer over telephone or direct leased lines. Special communications software translates documents into and out of a generic form, allowing organizations to exchange information even if they have different hardware and software components. Invoices, purchase orders, and payments information are some of the routine documents that EDI can handle—it replaces the phone call or mailed document.

electronic data interchange (EDI)

A technology that enables the transmission of routine business documents having a standard format from computer to computer over telephone or direct leased lines.

Catalog Hubs **Catalog hubs** can be used to reduce the costs of placing orders to suppliers as well as the costs of the services or goods themselves. Suppliers post their catalog of items on the hub, and buyers select what they need and purchase them electronically. The hub connects the firm to potentially hundreds of suppliers through the Internet, saving the costs of EDI, which requires one-to-one connections to individual suppliers. Moreover, the buying firm can negotiate prices with individual suppliers for items such as office supplies, technical equipment, services, and so forth. The catalog that the buying firm's employees see consists only of the approved items and the prices the buyer has prenegotiated with its suppliers. Employees use their PCs to select the items they need, and the system generates the purchase orders, which are electronically dispatched to the suppliers.

catalog hubs

A system whereby suppliers post their catalog of items on the Internet and buyers select what they need and purchase them electronically.

Exchanges An **exchange** is an electronic marketplace where buying firms and selling firms come together to do business. The exchange maintains relationships with buyers and sellers, making it easy to do business without the aspect of contract negotiations or other types of long-term conditions. Exchanges are often used for "spot" purchases to satisfy an immediate need at the lowest possible cost. Commodity items such as oil, steel, or energy fit this category. However, exchanges can also be used for most any item, such as hotel or hospital supplies.

exchange

An electronic marketplace where buying firms and selling firms come together to do business.

Auctions An extension of the exchange is the **auction**, where firms place competitive bids to buy something. For example, a site may be formed for a particular industry, and firms with excess capacity or materials can offer them for sale to the highest bidder. Bids can either be closed or open to the competition. Industries where auctions have value include used autos, steel, and chemicals. Examples involving consumers include eBay and Priceline.com. An approach that has received considerable attention is the so-called *reverse auction*, where suppliers bid for contracts with buyers. Each bid is posted, so suppliers can see how much lower their next bid must be to remain in the running for the contract. Each contract has an electronic prospectus that provides all the specifications, conditions, and other requirements that are nonnegotiable. The only thing left to determine is the cost to the buyer. Savings to the buyer can be dramatic, sometime as much as 20 to 30 percent over typical contract prices.

auction

A marketplace where firms place competitive bids to buy something.

Locus of Control When an organization has several facilities (stores, hospitals, or plants, for example), management must decide whether to buy locally or centrally. This decision has implications for the control of supply chain flows.

Centralized buying has the advantage of increasing purchasing power by creating a situation where suppliers are economically dependent on the buyer. Savings can be significant, often on the order of 10 percent or more. Increased buying power can mean getting better service, ensuring long-term supply availability, or developing new supplier capability. Companies with overseas suppliers favor centralization because the specialized skills (e.g., understanding of foreign languages and cultures) needed to buy from foreign sources can be centralized in one location. Buyers also need to understand international commercial and contract law regarding the transfer of services and goods. Another trend that favors centralization is the growth of computer-based information systems and the Internet, which give specialists at headquarters access to data previously available only at the local level.

Probably the biggest disadvantage of centralized buying is loss of control at the local level. Centralized buying is undesirable for items unique to a particular facility. These items should be purchased locally whenever possible. The same holds for purchases that must be closely meshed with production schedules. Localized buying is also an advantage when the firm has major facilities in foreign countries because the managers there, often foreign nationals, have a much better understanding of the local culture than staff members at the home office. Also, centralized buying often means longer lead times.

Perhaps the best solution is a compromise strategy, whereby both local autonomy and centralized buying are possible. For example, the corporate purchasing group at IBM negotiates contracts on a centralized basis only at the request of local plants. Management at one of the plants then monitors the contract for all the participating plants.

Information Exchange

The information exchange process facilitates the exchange of pertinent operating information, such as forecasts, schedules, and inventory levels between the firm and its suppliers. New technology in the form of radio frequency identification facilitates the flow of inventory information. Beyond inventory information, the exchange of forecasts and other demand-related data facilitates integrating activities such as vendor-managed inventories.

Radio Frequency Identification   An important requirement for any information exchange process in a supply chain context is accurate information regarding the quantity and location of inventories. A new application of an old technology presents some tantalizing benefits. **Radio frequency identification (RFID)** is a method for identifying items through the use of radio signals from a tag attached to an item. The tag has information about the item and sends signals to a device that can read the information and even write new information on the tag. Data from the tags can be transmitted wirelessly from one place to another through electronic product code (EPC) networks and the Internet, making it theoretically possible to uniquely identify every item a company produces and track it until the tag is destroyed. The use of RFID has not come without controversy, however. There has been considerable concern over security and privacy issues. Theoretically, anyone with the appropriate reader can gather the data these chips emit and use it for nefarious actions. Nonetheless, Walmart, Target, Intel, Gillette, and the Department of Defense, among a number of large retailers, manufacturers, government agencies, and suppliers, are implementing RFID in their supply chains. The use of RFID data can increase a supplier's service level and reduce theft. Gillette is using RFID to reduce the amount of razor-blade theft, which amounts to as much as 30 percent of sales.

> **radio frequency identification (RFID)**
>
> A method for identifying items through the use of radio signals from a tag attached to an item.

Individual firms can use RFID within their own operations and avoid costly coordination with other firms in the supply chain. Benefits of using RFID internal to the firm are limited, however, and so is the investment. The larger potential gains come with application to the supply chain. To be successful, all members of the supply chain must benefit from the investment in RFID, not just the firm pushing the project. This is particularly true for global operations. Global data synchronization using industry standards is critical to ensure that accurate and consistent product information is exchanged between trading partners—a very challenging task.

Vendor-Managed Inventories   Reliable information regarding inventories up and down the supply chain allows firms to collaborate on effective ways to improve material flows. A tactic that requires a reliable information exchange process is **vendor-managed inventories (VMI)**, a system in which the supplier has access to the customer's inventory data and is responsible for maintaining the inventory level required by the customer. The inventory is on the customer's site, and often the supplier retains possession of the inventory until it is used by the customer. Companies such as Walmart and Dell leverage their market position to mandate VMI. Vendor-managed inventories have several key elements.

> **vendor-managed inventories (VMI)**
>
> A system in which the supplier has access to the customer's inventory data and is responsible for maintaining the inventory on the customer's site.

- *Collaborative Effort.* For VMI to succeed, the customers must be willing to allow the supplier access to their inventory information, which is facilitated by RFID but must be bolstered by information on forecasts, sales promotions, and other demand-related data. The implication is that the supplier assumes an important administrative role in the management of the inventory. Thus, an atmosphere of trust and accountability is required.

- *Cost Savings.* Suppliers and customers eliminate the need for excess inventory through better operational planning. VMI lowers costs by reducing administrative and inventory costs. Order placement costs are also reduced.

- *Customer Service.* The supplier is frequently on the customer's site and better understands the operations of the customer, improving response times and reducing stockouts.

- *Written Agreement.* It is important that both parties fully understand the responsibilities of each partner. Areas such as billing procedures, forecast methods, and replenishment schedules should be clearly specified. Further, the responsibility for obsolete inventory resulting from forecast revisions and changes in contract lengths should be included.

VMI can be used both by service providers as well as manufacturers. AT&T, Roadway Express, Walmart, Dell, Westinghouse, and Bose are among the companies that use it.

Order Fulfillment Process

The order fulfillment process produces and delivers the service or product to the firm's customers. There are four key nested processes: (1) customer demand planning, (2) supply planning, (3) production, and (4) logistics.

Customer Demand Planning

The customer demand planning (CDP) process facilitates the collaboration of a supplier and its customers for the purpose of forecasting customer requirements for a service or product. CDP is a business-planning process that enables sales teams (and customers) to develop demand forecasts as input to service-planning processes, production and inventory planning, and revenue planning. Forecasts must generally precede plans: It is not possible to make decisions on staffing levels, purchasing commitments, and inventory levels until forecasts are developed that give reasonably accurate views of demand over the forecasting time horizon. Chapter 8, "Forecasting," contains many practical tools for forecasting customer demands.

Supply Planning

The supply planning process takes the demand forecasts produced by the customer demand planning process, the customer service levels and inventory targets provided by inventory management, and the resources provided by sales and operations planning to generate a plan to meet the demand. Regardless of whether the firm is producing services or a product, this process is critical for effective execution in the supply chain. See Chapter 9, "Inventory Management," Chapter 10, "Operations Planning and Scheduling," and Chapter 11, "Resource Planning" for the details involving the preparation of effective supply plans at both the aggregate and detailed levels.

Production

The production process executes the supply plan to produce the service or product. Nonetheless, the production process must be integrated with the processes that supply the inputs, establish the demands, and deliver the product to the customers. For example, while customers can always shop for standardized Dell computer packages at retail stores like Best Buy and Walmart, order placement, buying, production, and logistics processes are tightly linked at Dell when a customized machine is being ordered directly from the computer manufacturer. Dell's supply chain is designed to support an assemble-to-order strategy, thereby providing speedy service with minimal inventories.

Integrating the supply-facing and customer-facing processes to the production process is as important to service firms as it is to manufacturing firms. The best firms tightly link their production process to suppliers as well as customers.

Logistics

A key aspect of order fulfillment is the logistics process, which delivers the product or service to the customer. Five important decisions determine the design and implementation of logistics processes: (1) degree of ownership, (2) facility location, (3) mode selection, (4) capacity level, and (5) amount of cross-docking.

- *Ownership.* The firm has the most control over the logistics process if it owns and operates it, thereby becoming a *private carrier.* Although this approach may help to better achieve the firm's competitive priorities, the cost of equipment, labor, facilities, and maintenance could be high. The firm could instead leave the distribution to a *third-party logistics provider* (3PL), negotiating with the carrier for specific services. Those services could involve taking over a major portion of the order fulfillment process. 3PLs typically provide integrated services, from transportation and packaging services to warehousing and inventory management, for corporate clients that need to get their products to market. They can help with the design of a client's supply chain and facilitate the flow of information up and down the supply chain.

- *Facility Location.* A critical decision affecting the effectiveness of supply chains is the location of facilities that serve as points of service, storage, or manufacture. Chapter 13, "Supply Chain Logistic Networks," provides a complete discussion of facility location choices.

- *Mode Selection.* The five basic modes of transportation are (1) truck, (2) train, (3) ship, (4) pipeline, and (5) airplane. The drivers for the selection should be the firm's competitive priorities. Trucks provide the greatest flexibility because they can go wherever roads go. Transit times are good, and rates are usually better than trains for small quantities and short distances. Rail transportation can move large quantities cheaply; however, the transit times are long and often variable. Water transportation provides high capacity and low costs and is necessary for overseas shipments of bulky items; however, the transit times are slow, and highway or rail transportation is often needed to get the product to its ultimate destination. Pipeline transportation is highly specialized and is used for liquids, gases, or solids in slurry form. Although it has limited geographical flexibility, transporting via pipeline requires no packaging, and the operating costs per mile are low. Finally, air transportation is the fastest and most costly mode per mile. Nonetheless, getting a product to the customer fast using air transportation may actually reduce total costs when the costs of inventory and warehouse handling are considered. The cost of the funds tied up in some in-transit inventories can be considerable. Firms can also use mixed modal transportation, whereby a given shipment may combine two or more different modes. For example, containers can be carried by trucks, trains, or ships over different portions of their transit and can often give the best tradeoffs between cost and delivery times.

The Trans Alaska Pipeline System traverses 800 miles from the North Slope of Alaska to the northern most ice-free port of Valdez, Alaska. The pipeline is 48 inches in diameter, has 11 pump stations, and has a maximum throughput of 2 million barrels per day.

- *Capacity.* The performance of a logistics process is directly linked to its capacity. The ownership decision and the modal selection decision are often intertwined because the question of how much capacity is needed must be resolved. If ownership of the equipment and facilities is under consideration, capital costs as well as variable operating costs must be weighed against the costs of obtaining the logistics services from a supplier. Making things more difficult is the fact that the requirements for the logistics process are rarely known with certainty. In such cases, management can use the *expected value decision rule* to evaluate capacity alternatives. The expected value of an alternative is calculated as follows:

> *Expected value of an alternative* = (probability of a level of demand occurring) multiplied by (payoff for using the alternative if that level of demand materialized) summed over all possible levels of demand.

See Supplement A, "Decision Making," for details on this approach. Example 14.3 demonstrates the use of the expected value decision rule for analyzing truck capacity.

| EXAMPLE 14.3 | Using the Expected Value Decision Rule for Truck Capacity |

Tower Distributors provides logistical services to local manufacturers. Tower picks up products from the manufacturers, takes them to its distribution center, and then assembles shipments to retailers in the region. Tower needs to build a new distribution center; consequently, it needs to make a decision on how many trucks to use. The monthly amortized capital cost of ownership is $2,100 per truck. Operating variable costs are $1 per mile for each truck owned by Tower. If capacity is exceeded in any month, Tower can rent trucks at $2 per mile. Each truck Tower owns can be used 10,000 miles per month. The requirements for the trucks, however, are uncertain. Managers have estimated the following probabilities for several possible demand levels and corresponding fleet sizes.

Requirements (miles/month)	100,000	150,000	200,000	250,000
Fleet Size (trucks)	10	15	20	25
Probability	0.2	0.3	0.4	0.1

Notice that the sum of the probabilities must equal 1.0. If Tower Distributors wants to minimize the expected cost of operations, how many trucks should it use?

SOLUTION

We use the expected value decision rule to evaluate the alternative fleet sizes where we want to minimize the expected monthly cost. To begin, the monthly cost, C, must be determined for each possible combination of fleet size and requirements. The cost will depend on whether additional capacity must be rented for the month. For example, consider the *10 truck fleet size* alternative, which represents a capacity of 100,000 miles per month.

C = monthly capital cost of ownership+variable operating cost per month + rental costs if needed:

$$C\,(100{,}000\,\text{miles/month}) = (\$2{,}100/\text{truck})(10\,\text{trucks}) + (\$1/\text{mile})(100{,}000\,\text{miles}) = \$121{,}000$$

$$C\,(150{,}000\,\text{miles/month}) = (\$2{,}100/\text{truck})(10\,\text{trucks}) + (\$1/\text{mile})(100{,}000\,\text{miles})$$
$$+ (\$2\,\text{rent/mile})(150{,}000\,\text{miles} - 100{,}000\,\text{miles}) = \$221{,}000$$

$$C\,(200{,}000\,\text{miles/month}) = (\$2{,}100/\text{truck})(10\,\text{trucks}) + (\$1/\text{mile})(100{,}000\,\text{miles})$$
$$+ (\$2\,\text{rent/mile})(200{,}000\,\text{miles} - 100{,}000\,\text{miles}) = \$321{,}000$$

$$C\,(250{,}000\,\text{miles/month}) = (\$2{,}100/\text{truck})(10\,\text{trucks}) + (\$1/\text{mile})(100{,}000\,\text{miles})$$
$$+ (\$2\,\text{rent/mile})(250{,}000\,\text{miles} - 100{,}000\,\text{miles}) = \$421{,}000$$

Next, calculate the expected value for the *10 truck fleet size* alternative as follows:

Expected Value (10 trucks) = 0.2($121,000) + 0.3($221,000) + 0.4($321,000) + 0.1($421,000) = $261,000

Using similar logic, we can calculate the expected costs for each of the other fleet-size options:

Expected Value (15 trucks) = 0.2($131,500) + 0.3($181,500) + 0.4($281,500) + 0.1($381,500) = $231,500

Expected Value (20 trucks) = 0.2($142,000) + 0.3($192,000) + 0.4($242,000) + 0.1($342,000) = $217,000

Expected Value (25 trucks) = 0.2($152,500) + 0.3($202,500) + 0.4($252,500) + 0.1($302,500) = $222,500

Using the expected value decision rule, Tower Distributors should use a fleet of 20 trucks.

DECISION POINT

The fleet size of 20 trucks means that Tower will have enough capacity to handle 90 percent of its requirements (sum of the probabilities for 100,000 miles, 150,000 miles, and 200,000 miles). Further, there will be a 50 percent chance that it will have excess capacity (sum of the probabilities for 100,000 miles and 150,000 miles). While the decision to invest in 20 trucks will minimize expected costs, it will also provide slack capacity 50 percent of the time, which is reflective of the relatively high cost for being short of capacity.

cross-docking

The packing of products on incoming shipments so that they can be easily sorted at intermediate warehouses for outgoing shipments based on their final destinations.

- *Cross-Docking.* Low-cost operations and delivery speed can be enhanced with a technique called **cross-docking**, which is the packing of products on incoming shipments so that they can be easily sorted at intermediate warehouses for outgoing shipments based on their final destinations; the items are carried from the incoming-vehicle docking point to the outgoing-vehicle docking point without being stored in inventory at the warehouse. The warehouse becomes a short-term staging area for organizing efficient shipments to customers. The benefits of cross-docking include reductions in inventory investment, storage space requirements, handling costs, and lead times, as well as increased inventory turnover and accelerated cash flow. Management must decide where cross-docking operations are best placed, given the overall flow of items and their destinations.

Customer Relationship Process

The customer relationship process addresses the interface between the firm and its customers downstream in the supply chain. The purpose of the customer relationship process, which supports *customer relationship management (CRM)* programs, is to identify, attract, and build relationships with customers and to facilitate the transmission and tracking of orders. Key nested processes include the marketing, order placement, and customer service processes.

Marketing

The marketing process focuses on such issues as determining the customers to target, how to target them, what services or products to offer and how to price them, and how to manage promotional campaigns. In this regard, **electronic commerce (e-commerce)**, which is the application of information and communication technology anywhere along the supply chain of business processes, has had a huge impact up and down the supply chain. There are two e-commerce technologies that relate to the marketing process: (1) business-to-consumer (B2C) and (2) business-to-business (B2B) systems.

Business-to-Consumer Systems   Business-to-consumer (B2C) systems, which allow customers to transact business over the Internet, are commonplace. B2C e-commerce offers a new distribution channel for businesses, and consumers can avoid crowded department stores with long checkout lines and parking-space shortages. Many of the advantages of e-commerce were first exploited by retail "e-businesses," such as Amazon.com, E*TRADE, and Autobytel. These three companies created Internet versions of traditional bookstores, brokerage firms, and auto dealerships. The Internet has changed operations, processes, and cost structures for even traditional retailers, and the overall growth in its usage has been dramatic. Today, anyone with an Internet connection can open a store in cyberspace. Even well-established retailers like Walmart have a web-based shopping presence through their site-to-store program, where customers can actually shop on the Internet and pick up their order at the closest store within a few days.

Business-to-Business Systems   The biggest growth, however, has been in business-to-business (B2B) e-commerce systems, or commerce between firms. In fact, business-to-business e-commerce outpaces business-to-consumer transactions, with trade between businesses making up more than 70 percent of the regular economy. These systems facilitate trade up and down the supply chain, making it easier to purchase or sell services or products. B2B systems can also help manage the flow of materials. For example, if a distributor is out of stock, the firm's central warehouse can be notified to immediately ship replenishment stock directly to the customer.

electronic commerce (e-commerce)

The application of information and communication technology anywhere along the supply chain of business processes.

Order Placement

The order placement process involves the activities required to execute a sale, register the specifics of the order request, confirm the acceptance of the order, and track the progress of the order until it is completed. Often the firm has a sales force that visits prospective and current customers to encourage a sale.

The Internet enables firms to reengineer their order placement process to benefit both the customer and the firm. The Internet provides the following advantages for a firm's order placement process.

- *Cost Reduction.* Using the Internet can reduce the costs of processing orders because it allows for greater participation by the customer. Customers can select the services or products they want and place an order with the firm without actually talking to anyone. This approach reduces the need for call centers, which are labor intensive and often take longer to place orders.

- *Revenue Flow Increase.* A firm's Web page can allow customers to enter credit card information or purchase-order numbers as part of the order placement process. This approach reduces the time lags often associated with billing the customer or waiting for checks sent in the mail.

- *Global Access.* Another advantage the Internet provides to firms is the opportunity to accept orders 24-hours a day. Traditional brick-and-mortar firms only take orders during their normal business hours. Firms with Internet access can reduce the time it takes to satisfy customers, who can shop and purchase at any time. This access gives these firms a competitive advantage over brick-and-mortar firms.

- *Pricing Flexibility.* Firms with their services and products posted on the Web can easily change prices as the need arises, thereby avoiding the cost and delay of publishing new catalogs. Customers placing orders have current prices to consider when making their choices. From the perspective of supply chains, Dell uses this capability to control for component shortages. Because of its direct-sales approach and promotional pricing, Dell can steer customers to certain configurations of computers for which ample supplies exist.

Sherwin Crasto/Reuters/Corbis

Many firms have outsourced their customer service processes, particularly if the service can be transacted over the phone. Here Indian employees at a call center in the southern city of Bangalore, India, provide service support to international customers.

Customer Service

The customer service process helps customers with answers to questions regarding the service or product, resolves problems, and, in general, provides information to assist customers. It is an important point of contact between the firm and its customers, who may judge the firm on the basis of their experiences with this process. The age-old tradeoff between cost and quality, however, enters the picture, especially for call centers. In an effort to reduce the cost of their customer service process, many firms have opted to replace human service agents with automated systems, which often require customers to wade through an exhausting sequence of options that sometimes only lead to frustration. Other firms are using Verbots®, or "verbal robots," which are supported by sophisticated artificial intelligence. They have personalities, ask and respond to questions, and in some cases are almost indistinguishable from humans over the phone. Nonetheless, most customers and others seeking information about a service or product prefer humans. Consequently, in consideration for the cost involved, many companies have expanded their supply chain by outsourcing the customer service process to an off-shore site where labor costs are low. In this regard, India has responded in a big way to the international need for low-cost call centers. Of course, the big risk in outsourcing the customer service process, or a part of it, is that the firm loses some control over a process that has direct interface with its customers. This consideration should be carefully weighed in the final analysis.

Supply Chain Risk Management

Now that we have discussed a framework for integrated supply chains, we can return to the causes of supply chain disruptions and how integrated supply chains can mitigate the risks of poor performance from unwanted dynamics. *Supply chain risk management* focuses on managing the risks posed by any factor or event that can materially disrupt a supply chain. In this section, we address the management of operational, financial, and security risks and reveal important performance measures for tracking supply chain operations.

Operational Risks

Operational risks are threats to the effective flow of materials, services, and products in a supply chain. The following options reduce the risk for operational disruptions and also minimize the bullwhip effect in supply chains.

- *Strategic alignment*—once an appropriate design is determined for the supply chain, make sure that all partners adhere to competitive priorities that are consistent with its strategic thrust. Misalignment of priorities, goals, and objectives can cause delays or disruptions in flows in a supply chain. Internal business functions should similarly be aligned.

- *Upstream/downstream supply chain integration*—working closely with customers and suppliers in CDP and the new service or product design collaboration process improves information flows and reduces surprises from demand spikes due to promotions or supply hang-ups because of poorly designed services or products. The integration should extend as far upstream in the supply chain as possible, beyond first and second-tier suppliers.

- *Visibility*—one source of dynamics in supply chains is the lack of visibility of end-user demand by suppliers upstream in the supply chain. To facilitate planning at all levels in the supply chain, point-of-sale (POS) data, which records actual customer purchases of the final service or product, can be shared with all suppliers. RFID can also be used to track quantities of inventory throughout the supply chain.

- *Flexibility and redundancy*—develop the right level of flexibility and redundancy across the supply chain to be able to absorb disruptions and adapt to change. Seek dual sources of critical materials and components, build in adequate capacity cushions, and adjust safety stocks and inventory levels to maintain desired flows.

- *Short replenishment lead times*—improving internal processes and working with suppliers to reduce lead times allows the firm to react quickly to a change in demand levels, thereby mitigating the bullwhip effect. In addition, shorter lead times leads to smaller pipeline inventories.

- *Small order lot sizes*—working on ways to reduce the costs associated with ordering, transporting and receiving inventory throughout the supply chain will reduce order lot sizes and thereby decrease the amount of fluctuation in the size of orders in the supply chain.

- *Rationing short supplies*—when a shortage exists, customers sometimes artificially inflate their orders to protect themselves, only to cancel them later when the shortage is relieved. To counteract this behavior, suppliers can ration short supplies to customers on the basis of their past sales, rather than their current orders.

- *Everyday low pricing (EDLP)*—promotional or discount pricing encourages spikes in demand. Using a stable pricing program such as EDLP, as is done by Walmart, discourages customers from buying excess stock at discounted prices so they can offer price promotions, a practice called *forward buying*. EDLP levels the demand spikes that are driven by price fluctuations.

- *Cooperation and trustworthiness*—being cooperative in solving supply issues and providing information that can be trusted serves to reduce costs for all members of the supply chain and mitigates the deleterious effects of supply chain dynamics.

Financial Risks

Financial risks are threats to the financial flows in a supply chain, such as prices, costs, and profits. Buyers may purchase services or products at an agreed fixed price. With a commitment made at a certain price, factors outside of the control of a buyer may threaten the profitability of the buyer. For example, market conditions could cause overcapacity at the supplier or oversupply of a product such that the price of the service or product plummets, which means that the buyer's profits will be lower than they could have been, and competitors purchasing these same items at a lower price could take advantage. Alternatively, even without changes in the supply of the service or product, the exchange rate in currencies between the buyer and seller could make the agreed price more expensive for the buyer. To show the effect of fluctuations in exchange rates, consider an Italian firm that supplies cotton to a firm in the United States. The currency chosen for the transaction was the U.S. dollar (USD). A contract in July 2012 called for $100,000 in shipments per month, to end in January 2013. In July 2012, the exchange rate was 1,589 ITL/USD, or equivalently 1,589,000 lira in revenues per month for the Italian supplier. However, by the end of the contract in January 2013, the dollar depreciated relative to the Italian lira; the exchange rate fell to 1,430 ITL/USD. Because the Italian supplier had to pay all of its expenses in lira, its profits fell 10 percent even though actual operating costs did not change. A similar situation can occur when service or product prices change during a supply contract because of market conditions.

How can financial risks in a supply chain be managed? One way is to reduce unnecessary costs in supply chain operations, both upstream and downstream, which we have already discussed in this text. This approach provides some protection against cost increases due to operational issues or exchange rates. Another way is to use a new low-cost source of supply, also known as *low-cost hopping*, which could benefit a firm in the short run. However, it is not conducive to effective supply chain integration over the long term. Perhaps the most often used approach to protect against financial risks is called **hedging**, which is a supply chain risk management strategy used in limiting or offsetting the probability of loss from fluctuations in the prices of commodities or currencies. In effect, hedging is a transfer of risk without buying insurance policies. One way to hedge in a supply chain is to take advantage of the flexibility in operations to reallocate production across facilities in different regions of the world to improve financial flows. This approach, referred to as *production shifting*, moves the production of products to countries where exchange rates or commodity prices are favorable. Production facilities must be flexible enough to change their production assignments, which could entail a different mix of products and shipping schedules.

Another way of hedging is to use a **futures contract**, which is a contractual agreement, generally made on the trading floor of a futures exchange, to buy or sell a particular commodity or financial instrument at a predetermined price in the future. Just like the price of blueberries at a grocery store, the prices of commodities such as metals and oil or currencies change on a weekly or daily basis. If the price goes up, the *buyer* of the futures contract makes money because he gets the product at the agreed-upon price and can now sell it at today's higher market price. If the price goes down, the futures *seller* makes money because he can buy the item at today's lower price and sell it to the futures buyer at the higher

hedging

A supply chain risk management strategy used in limiting or offsetting the probability of loss from fluctuations in the prices of commodities or currencies.

futures contract

A contractual agreement, generally made on the trading floor of a futures exchange, to buy or sell a particular commodity or financial instrument at a pre-determined price in the future.

agreed-upon price. Often, the commodity is not actually delivered to the buyer of a futures contract. To fulfill the contract, the seller of the futures contract only has to show proof that the item is at the warehouse; the contract can be settled between the two parties by paying the cash difference.[1]

The mechanics of setting up a futures contract is beyond the scope of this text; however, a simple example can demonstrate its use in a supply chain. Suppose that Action Pro, a manufacturer of cotton sporting apparel, wants to secure its supply of cotton for the next year. The price of cotton has been volatile because of global stockpiling by large Asian manufacturers. Action Pro is not interested in speculation and only wants to break even with a hedge against future cotton prices. It is now December, currency exchange rates have been stable, and the market price for cotton is $70 per 100 pounds (CWT). If the cotton price stayed at $70 Action Pro could make a reasonable profit; however, the cotton supplier is not willing to accept a fixed price because of the possibility of a rise in global cotton prices due to the Asian activity. Consequently, Action Pro entered into a contract with the supplier for 100,000 pounds of cotton per month starting in January at market prices. To counter the risk of higher cotton prices, Action Pro entered into a futures contract with a financial institution for 100,000 pounds of cotton per month at $70/ CWT. In this contract, Action Pro agrees to pay the financial institution $70/CWT in exchange for the institution paying Action Pro whatever the market price of cotton is each month.[2] Table 14.1 contains two snapshots that demonstrate how the hedge helped Action Pro break even with regard to cotton prices.

TABLE 14.1 | HEDGING THE MARKET PRICE OF COTTON

(a) It is now January and the market price of cotton has risen to $87/CWT.

Financial Result	Physical Result
Paid for 100,000 pounds of cotton on the futures contract for January at $70/CWT.	Purchased 100,000 pounds of cotton at market price of $87/CWT for January delivery.
Sold 100,000 pounds of cotton for cash at the new price of $87/CWT.	It now costs more than budgeted to produce the cotton apparel.
Financial profit = $87 − $70 = $17 / *CWT*.	**Physical loss in profits relative to budget** = $70 − $87 = −$17 / *CWT*.

The financial profit achieved by hedging has compensated for the increased price of cotton in the physical market. This means that Action Pro has been able to maintain their budgeted target of $70/CWT for their cotton supplies.

(b) It is now June and the market price of cotton has dropped to $65/CWT.

Financial Result	Physical Result
Paid $70/CWT for 100,000 pounds of cotton on the futures contract for the month of June.	Purchased 100,000 pounds of cotton at the market price of $65/CWT for June delivery.
Sold 100,000 pounds of cotton for cash at the new price of $65/CWT.	It is now less expensive to produce the cotton apparel.
Financial loss = $65 − $70 = −$5 / *CWT*.	**Physical increase in profits relative to budget** = $70 − $65 = $5 / *CWT*.

The financial loss is balanced by the increase in physical profits. Active Pro has achieved the budgeted cost of $70/CWT.

Security Risks

Security risks are threats to a supply chain that could potentially damage stakeholders, facilities, or operations; destroy the integrity of a business; or jeopardize its continuation. The actions that form the basis of these threats are intentional and are designed to do physical or financial damage. A supply chain is *secure* when it can fend off unauthorized acts that are designed to cause intentional harm or damage to the supply chain and the materials (human and otherwise) that flow through its processes. A risk is amplified if the threat has a high probability of occurrence and a high level of severity. Firms interested in achieving a high level of supply chain security have a big job; there are many elements in a typical supply

---

[1] For more information about futures contracts, see Kimberly Amadeo, "What Are Commodities Futures?" **http://useconomy.about.com.**

[2] This contract is actually called a "swap," which is a form of futures contract. To keep things simple, we will ignore the fees paid to the financial institution for services.

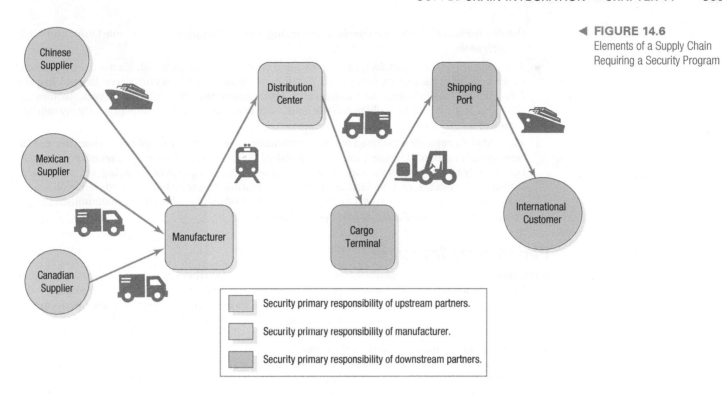

◀ **FIGURE 14.6**
Elements of a Supply Chain
Requiring a Security Program

chain and they are not all under the direct control of the firm. Figure 14.6 shows examples in a supply chain where security programs are needed.

Primary security responsibility shifts from suppliers, to the manufacturer, to downstream partners, and ultimately to the customer as the goods flow through the supply chain. Security programs should assess the severity of the threats, such as terrorism, cargo theft, hijacking, drug or contraband smuggling, undeclared hazardous goods, and government instability. These programs should also assess how vulnerable the supply chain is regarding procedures for security, physical access controls, container and trailer security, and information technology security, for example. Finally, the consequences of a breach in security to factors such as demand volume, the firm's competitive priorities, and the impact of lost business should be assessed. As the responsibility for security is paramount and distributed among many entities in a supply chain, it is clear that the more integrated a supply chain is, the more effective security measures can be.

While security programs vary in content depending on the application, here are some typical security activities:

- *Access control.* Check IDs of all visitors, vendors, drivers, and, in general, all participants in the supply chain. Employ real-time monitored systems that document entry, exit, and movement of materials and cargo.

- *Physical security.* Conduct random facility inspections and ensure compliance to established security standards. Monitor CCTV and alarm systems that allow for immediate real-time response. Perform penetration tests and audits of compliance.

- *Shipping and receiving.* Screen and validate the contents of the cargo being shipped and received. Provide advanced notification of the contents to

Security guards check truck drivers' paperwork as they enter the Seagrit Marine Terminal in Baltimore, Maryland. The guards can check the manifest against the items in the truck to prohibit the shipment of undocumented hazardous materials, illegal weapons, or other forms of contraband.

the destination country. Use specialized packing material, unique shipping markings, and high-security seals.

- *Transportation service provider.* Ensure the security of cargo while in transit via the use of locks and tamper-proof seals. Ensure that the carrier does not make stops in security "red zones." Require GPS tracking for the tractors and trailers and regular communication with the drivers. Require notification of the use of any subcontractors and make sure they adhere to the same security requirements as the primary carrier.

- *ISO 28000.* Recognizing the need of the international community for supply chain security, the International Standards Organization has established **ISO 28000:2007**, which is a set of requirements for a supply chain security management system that includes aspects of financing, manufacturing, information systems, and the facilities for packing, storing, and transferring goods between modes of transportation and locations. Certification in ISO 28000:2007 enables firms to demonstrate their compliance with stated security management policies.

ISO 28000:2007

A set of requirements for a supply chain security management system that includes aspects of financing, manufacturing, information systems, and the facilities for packing, storing, and transferring goods between modes of transportation and locations.

Performance Measures

It is important to monitor the performance of supply chains to see where improvements can be made or to measure the impact of disruptions. Supply chain managers monitor performance by measuring costs, time, quality, and environmental impact. Table 14.2 contains examples of commonly used performance measures for three supply chain processes. Managers periodically collect data on these measures and track them to note changes in level or direction. Statistical process control charts can be used to determine whether the changes are statistically significant.

Integrated supply chains are powerful tools for achieving competitiveness along many performance measures. Currently, concerns about security and the environment are prompting supply chain managers to take a careful look at their operations and those of their suppliers. In Chapter 15, "Supply Chain Sustainability," we take a look at the impact of environmental concerns on supply chains and how integrated supply chains can be used to relieve some of those concerns and still be profitable.

TABLE 14.2 | SUPPLY CHAIN MEASURES FOR CORE PROCESSES

Customer Relationship	Order Fulfillment	Supplier Relationship
■ Percent of orders taken accurately	■ Percent of incomplete orders shipped	■ Percent of suppliers' deliveries on time
■ Time to complete the order placement process	■ Percent of orders shipped on-time	■ Suppliers' lead times
■ Customer satisfaction with the order placement process	■ Time to fulfill the order	■ Percent defects in services and purchased materials
■ Customer's evaluation of firm's environmental stewardship	■ Percent of botched services or returned items	■ Cost of services and purchased materials
■ Percent of business lost because of supply chain disruptions	■ Cost to produce the service or item	■ Inventory levels of supplies and purchased components
	■ Customer satisfaction with the order fulfillment process	■ Evaluation of suppliers' collaboration on streamlining and waste conversion
	■ Inventory levels of work-in-process and finished goods	■ Amount of transfer of environmental technologies to suppliers
	■ Amount of greenhouse gasses emitted into the air	
	■ Number of security breaches	

LEARNING GOALS IN REVIEW

Learning Goal	Guidelines for Review	MyOMLab Resources
❶ Identify the major causes of disruptions in a supply chain.	See the section "Supply Chain Disruptions" pp. 545–548. Focus on understanding the causes for disruptions from external and internal sources and what it means to integrate the supply chain. Study Figure 14.1, which demonstrates the flows in a supply chain, and Figure 14.2, which shows how mild dynamics in consumer demand can result in wild fluctuations in supplier demand. Figure 14.3 shows the integrative model used in this text, while Figure 14.4 shows the SCOR model.	**Video**: Sourcing Strategy at Starwood
❷ Describe the four major nested processes in the new service and product development process.	The section "New Service or Product Development Process," pp. 548–550, discusses the four nested processes and how they are linked.	

Learning Goal	Guidelines for Review	MyOMLab Resources
③ Explain the five major nested processes in the supplier relationship process and use total cost analysis and preference matrices to identify appropriate sources of supply.	See the section "Supplier Relationship Process," pp. 550–558, for a discussion of the five nested processes. Focus on the "sourcing" process, which explains the total cost model and the preference matrix approach for finding an appropriate source of supply. Study Examples 14.1 and 14.2, along with Solved Problems 1 and 2.	**OM Explorer Tutor:** A.3: Preference Matrix **OM Explorer Solver:** Preference Matrix **POM for Windows:** Preference Matrix
④ Identify the four major nested processes in the order fulfillment process and use the expected value decision rule to determine the appropriate capacity of logistic resources.	Review the section "Order Fulfillment Process," pp. 558–560, which discusses the four key nested processes. Focus on Example 14.3, which shows how to use the expected value decision rule to choose the appropriate amount of truck capacity. Solved Problem 3 shows the set up and solution to a problem involving the expected value decision rule.	**OM Explorer Tutor:** A.5: Decisions Under Risk **OM Explorer Solver:** Decision Theory **POM for Windows:** Decision Tables
⑤ Define the three major nested processes in the customer relationship process.	The section "Customer Relationship Process," pp. 561–562, discusses the three major nested processes and how they link together.	
⑥ Explain how firms can mitigate the operational, financial, and security risks in a supply chain.	See the section "Supply Chain Risk Management," pp. 562–566, for the ways firms can mitigate the operational, financial, and security risks they face. Be sure to understand the practice of hedging and how exchange rate fluctuations and commodity price changes can be dealt with. Also study Figure 14.6 to understand the complexity of managing security risks in a supply chain.	

Key Equations

Supplier Relationship Process

1. Total Annual Cost $= pD +$ Freight costs $+ (Q/2 + \bar{d}L)H +$ Administrative costs

Order Fulfillment Process

2. *Expected value of an alternative* $=$ (probability of a level of demand occurring)(payoff for using the alternative if that level of demand materialized) summed over all possible levels of demand.

Key Terms

auction 556
bullwhip effect 547
catalog hubs 556
competitive orientation 554
concurrent engineering 550
cooperative orientation 555
cross-docking 560
early supplier involvement 554

electronic commerce (e-commerce) 561
electronic data interchange (EDI) 556
exchange 556
futures contract 563
green purchasing 552
hedging 563
ISO 28000:2007 566
presourcing 554

purchasing 550
radio frequency identification (RFID) 557
SCOR model 548
sole sourcing 556
supply chain integration 545
supply chain risk management 545
value analysis 554
vendor-managed inventories (VMI) 557

Solved Problem 1

Eagle Electric Repair is a repair facility for several major electric appliance manufacturers. Eagle wants to find a low-cost supplier for an electric relay switch used in many appliances. The annual requirements for the relay switch (D) are 100,000 units. Eagle operates 250 days a year. The following data are available for two suppliers, Kramer and Sunrise, for the part:

MyOMLab Video

Supplier	Freight Costs Shipping Quantity (Q)		Price/Unit (p)	Carrying Cost/Unit (H)	Lead Time (L) (days)	Administrative Costs
	2,000	10,000				
Kramer	$30,000	$20,000	$5.00	$1.00	5	$10,000
Sunrise	$28,000	$18,000	$4.90	$0.98	9	$11,000

Which supplier will provide the lowest annual total costs?

SOLUTION

The daily requirements for the relay switch are:

$$\bar{d} = 100{,}000/250 = 400 \text{ units.}$$

We must calculate the total annual costs for each alternative:

Total annual cost = Material costs + Freight costs + Inventory costs + Administrative costs

$$= pD + \text{Freight costs} + (Q/2 + \bar{d}L)H + \text{Administrative costs}$$

Kramer

$Q = 2{,}000$: $(\$5.00)(100{,}000) + \$30{,}000 + (2{,}000/2 + 400(5))(\$1) + \$10{,}000 = \$543{,}000$

$Q = 10{,}000$: $(\$5.00)(100{,}000) + \$20{,}000 + (10{,}000/2 + 400(5))(\$1) + \$10{,}000 = \$537{,}000$

Sunrise

$Q = 2{,}000$: $(\$4.90)(100{,}000) + \$28{,}000 + (2{,}000/2 + 400(9))(\$0.98) + \$11{,}000 = \$533{,}508$

$Q = 10{,}000$: $(\$4.90)(100{,}000) + \$18{,}000 + (10{,}000/2 + 400(9))(\$0.98) + \$11{,}000 = \$527{,}428$

The analysis reveals that using Sunrise and a shipping quantity of 10,000 units will yield the lowest annual total costs.

Solved Problem 2

Eagle Electric Repair wants to select a supplier based on total annual cost, consistent quality, and delivery speed. The following table shows the weights management assigned to each criterion (total of 100 points) and the scores assigned to each supplier (Excellent = 5, Poor = 1).

Criterion	Weight	Scores	
		Kramer	Sunrise
Total annual cost	30	4	5
Consistent quality	40	3	4
Delivery speed	30	5	3

Which supplier should Eagle select given these criteria and scores?

SOLUTION

Using the preference matrix approach, the weighted scores for each supplier are:

$$Kramer: \ WS = (30 \times 4) + (40 \times 3) + (30 \times 5) = 390$$
$$Sunrise: \ WS = (30 \times 5) + (40 \times 4) + (30 \times 3) = 400$$

Based on the weighted scores, Eagle should select Sunrise even though delivery speed performance would be better with Kramer.

Solved Problem 3

Schneider Logistics Company has built a new warehouse in Columbus, Ohio, to facilitate the consolidation of freight shipments to customers in the region. George Schneider must determine how many teams of dock workers he should hire to handle the cross-docking operations and the other warehouse activities. Each team costs $5,000 a week in wages and overhead. Extra capacity can be subcontracted at a cost of $8,000 a team per week. Each team, whether in-house or subcontracted, can satisfy 200 labor hours of work a week. The labor hour requirements for the new facility are uncertain. Management has estimated the following probabilities for the requirements:

Requirements (hours/wk)	200	400	600
Number of teams	1	2	3
Probability	0.20	0.50	0.30

How many teams should Schneider hire?

SOLUTION

We use the expected value decision rule by first computing the cost for each option for each possible level of requirements and then using the probabilities to determine the expected value for each option. The option with the lowest expected cost is the one Schneider will implement. We demonstrate the approach using the "one team" in-house option.

One Team In-House

$$C(200) = \$5,000$$
$$C(400) = \$5,000 + \$8,000 = \$13,000$$
$$C(600) = \$5,000 + \$8,000 + \$8,000 = \$21,000$$

Expected Value

$$(\text{One Team}) = 0.20(\$5,000) + 0.50(\$13,000) + 0.30(\$21,000) = \$13,800.$$

A table of the complete results is below.

In-House	Weekly Labor Requirements			Expected Value
	200 hrs	**400 hrs**	**600 hrs**	
One team	$5,000	$13,000	$21,000	$13,800
Two teams	$10,000	$10,000	$18,000	$12,400
Three teams	$15,000	$15,000	$15,000	$15,000

Based on the expected value decision rule, Schneider should employ two teams at the warehouse.

Discussion Questions

1. Supply chain dynamics can cause excessive costs and poor customer service. Explain how the redesign of a supply chain can help to mitigate the effects of supply chain dynamics.

2. Chrysler and General Motors vigorously compete with each other in many automobile and truck markets. When Jose Ignacio Lopez was vice president of purchasing for GM, he made it clear that his buyers were not to accept luncheon invitations from suppliers. Thomas Stalcamp, head of purchasing for Chrysler at the time, instructed his buyers to take suppliers to lunch. Rationalize these two directives in light of supplier relations and the impact on supply chain management.

3. Firms such as Walmart, General Electric, Chase Manhattan, and Boeing have a lot of influence in their respective supply chains because of the power they have. Explain how firms with a lot of power can influence supply chain integration.

4. We discussed the inventory and supply chain considerations such as small lot sizes, close supplier ties, and quality at the source in Chapter 6, "Lean Systems." What are the implications of these principles for supply chain integration?

Problems

The OM Explorer and POM for Windows software is available to all students using the 11th edition of this textbook. Go to **http://www.pearsonhighered.com/krajewski** to download these computer packages. If you purchased MyOMLab, you also have access to Active Models software and significant help in doing the following problems. Check with your instructor on how best to use these resources. In many cases, the instructor wants you to understand how to do the calculations by hand. At the least, the software provides a check on your calculations. When calculations are particularly complex and the goal is interpreting the results in making decisions, the software entirely replaces the manual calculations.

Supplier Relationship Process

1. Horizon Cellular manufactures cell phones for exclusive use in its communication network. Management must select a circuit board supplier for a new phone soon to be introduced to the market. The annual requirements are 50,000 units and

Horizon's plant operates 250 days per year. The data for three suppliers are in Table 14.3.

Which supplier and shipping quantity will provide the lowest total cost for Horizon Cellular?

TABLE 14.3 | DATA FOR SUPPLIERS TO HORIZON CELLULAR

| Supplier | Annual Freight Costs Shipping Quantity | | Price/Unit | Annual Holding Cost/Unit | Lead Time (Days) | Annual Administrative Cost |
	10,000	20,000				
Abbott	$10,000	$7,000	$30	$6.00	4	$10,000
Baker	$12,000	$9,000	$28	$5.60	7	$12,000
Carpenter	$9,000	$6,500	$31	$6.20	3	$9,000

2. Eight Flags operates several amusement parks in the Midwest. The company stocks machine oil to service the machinery for the many rides at the parks. Eight Flags needs 30,000 gallons of oil annually; the parks operate 50 weeks a year. Management is unsatisfied with the current supplier of oil and has obtained two bids from other suppliers. The data are contained in Table 14.4.

Which supplier and which shipping quantity will provide the lowest costs for Eight Flags?

TABLE 14.4 | DATA FOR SUPPLIERS TO EIGHT FLAGS

| Supplier | Annual Freight Costs Shipping Quantity | | | Price/Unit | Annual Holding Cost/Unit | Lead Time (wks) | Annual Administrative Cost |
	5,000	10,000	15,000				
Sharps	$5,000	$2,600	$2,000	$4.00	$0.80	4	$4,000
Winkler	$5,500	$3,200	$2,900	$3.80	$0.76	6	$5,000

3. The Bennet Company purchases one of its essential raw materials from three suppliers. Bennet's current policy is to distribute purchases equally among the three. The owner's son, Benjamin Bennet, just graduated from a business college. He proposes that these suppliers be rated (high numbers mean a good performance) on six performance criteria weighted as shown in the table. A total score hurdle of 0.60 is proposed to screen suppliers. Purchasing policy would be revised to order raw materials from suppliers with performance scores greater than the total score hurdle, in proportion to their performance rating scores.

| Performance Criterion | Weight | Rating | | |
		Supplier A	Supplier B	Supplier C
1. Price	0.2	0.6	0.5	0.9
2. Quality	0.2	0.6	0.4	0.8
3. Delivery	0.3	0.6	0.3	0.8
4. Production facilities	0.1	0.5	0.9	0.6
5. Environmental protection	0.1	0.7	0.8	0.6
6. Financial position	0.1	0.9	0.9	0.7

a. Use a preference matrix to calculate the total weighted score for each supplier.

b. Which supplier(s) survived the total score hurdle? Under the younger Bennet's proposed policy, what proportion of orders would each supplier receive?

c. What advantages does the proposed policy have over the current policy?

D = Difficult Problem

4. Beagle Clothiers uses a weighted score for the evaluation and selection of its suppliers of trendy fashion garments. Each supplier is rated on a 10-point scale (10 = highest) for four different criteria: price, quality, delivery, and flexibility (to accommodate changes in quantity and timing). Because of the volatility of the business in which Beagle operates, flexibility is given twice the weight of each of the other three criteria, which are equally weighted. The table below shows the scores for three potential suppliers for the four performance criteria. Based on the highest weighted score, which supplier should be selected?

Criteria	Supplier A	Supplier B	Supplier C
Price	8	6	6
Quality	9	7	7
Delivery	7	9	6
Flexibility	5	8	9

5. Bradley Solutions and Alexander Limited are two well-established suppliers of inexpensive tools. Weekend Projects is a national chain of retail outlets that caters to the occasional fixer-upper who would prefer to get the job done fast rather that investing in a well-appointed tool box. Weekend Projects wants to find a supplier for a particular tool set that promises to be a big seller. Expected annual sales are 100,000 units. Weekend's warehouses operate 50 weeks a year. Management collected data on the two suppliers, which are contained in the first table.

a. Which of the two suppliers would provide the lowest annual cost to Weekend Projects? What shipping quantity would you suggest?

b. Before management could make a decision, another option became available. Zelda Tools offered the tool set for only $8.00; however, the lead time is longer than the other two suppliers. Zelda is a new supplier and has not been in the industry very long. Additional data for Zelda are in the second table.

Management has begun to assess the administrative costs to manage the contract with Zelda. What is the lowest level of administrative costs at which Weekend Projects would be indifferent between using Zelda versus the option you chose in part (a)?

Supplier	Freight Costs Shipping Quantity			Price/Unit	Annual Holding Cost/Unit	Lead Time (wks)	Annual Administrative Cost
	10,000	25,000	50,000				
Bradley	$35,000	$25,000	$18,000	$8.10	$1.62	6	$10,000
Alexander	$40,000	$28,000	$19,000	$8.10	$1.62	4	$15,000

Supplier	Freight Costs Shipping Quantity			Price/Unit	Annual Holding Cost/Unit	Lead Time (wks)
	10,000	25,000	50,000			
Zelda	$45,000	$25,000	$17,000	$8.00	$1.60	7

6. Wanda Lux must select a supplier for a plastic bottle and proprietary dispenser for its new hair shampoo. Three suppliers have placed bids; at Wanda's request, all bids are for a shipping quantity of 20,000 bottles with annual requirements of 40,000 units. Wanda's factory operates 250 days a year. The first table (below) shows each supplier's price, estimated annual freight costs, and current lead times; management has added estimates for holding costs and administrative oversight costs for each supplier.

Beyond costs, however, Wanda has three other criteria considered important in the selection of a supplier. The second table (see below) shows all the criteria, their weights,

and the scores for all of them except total costs, where a score of 1 indicates "poor" and 10 indicates "superior." Because all three suppliers have done business with Wanda Lux before, management will assign a score of "10" to the supplier with the lowest total annual cost, a score of "8.5" for the next lowest cost, and a score of "7.0" for the worst cost of the three.

a. Which of the three suppliers will provide the lowest annual cost to Wanda Lux?

b. Given Wanda's criteria and weighting system, which supplier should Wanda award the contract to?

Suppliers	Freight Costs	Price/Unit	Annual Holding Cost Per Unit	Lead Time (days)	Annual Administrative Costs
Dover Plastics	$3,500	$5.10	$1.02	15	$4,000
Evan & Sons	$3,000	$5.05	$1.01	12	$6,000
Farley, Inc.	$4,500	$5.00	$1.00	20	$3,000

Criterion	Weight	Score		
		Dover	Evan	Farley
Total Cost	30	?	?	?
Consistent Quality	30	9	9	7
On-Time Delivery	20	8	9	9
Environment	20	8	7	7

7. Adelie Enterprises is exploring a new service to provide weekly delivery of grocery items to homes in the greater Greenwood area. The company's customers place Web-based orders and Adelie's team assembles and delivers the orders in specially designed cardboard boxes. Management, interested in locating a supplier that can provide boxes cheaply and

efficiently, has discovered that each potential supplier's ability to satisfy the company's requirements is influenced by the level of demand. The following table provides Adelie's vendor selection criteria, criterion weights, and rankings (1–10 with 10 being the highest) under the assumption that low, moderate, or high demand is generated for their service.

D = Difficult Problem

SUPPLIER RATING UNDER LOW, MODERATE, AND HIGH LEVELS OF DEMAND

		Local Supplier			National Supplier			International Supplier		
	Weight	Low	Moderate	High	Low	Moderate	High	Low	Moderate	High
Product Quality	0.35	8	6	5	7	7	7	6	6	6
Delivery Speed	0.15	9	7	3	6	6	6	4	5	7
Product Price	0.25	5	5	3	5	7	9	7	7	9
Environmental Impact	0.25	9	9	9	7	7	7	8	8	8

a. Which supplier should be selected if there is low demand for Adelie's new service? Which supplier should be selected under moderate demand assumptions? Under high demand assumptions?

b. Which supplier is selected if Adelie evaluates each alternative using a Maximin decision criterion (see Supplement A, "Decision Making")?

c. Which supplier achieves the highest expected ranking if the probability of low demand is 35 percent,

moderate demand is 45 percent, and high demand is 20 percent?

8. Adelie Enterprises (from Problem 7) has decided to drop **D** the international supplier from consideration. Furthermore, Adelie has decided to order boxes in lots of 10,000 to optimize the use of available storage space at its distribution facility. To more completely consider the cost/volume tradeoffs associated with selecting the local or national supplier, management has collected the following data. Adelie services its customers 250 days per year.

	Demand Level	Demand	Price/unit	Freight Cost/1,000	Carrying Cost/unit	Lead Time (days)	Administrative costs
Local Supplier	Low	50,000	$1.25	$20.00	$0.10	1	$15,000.00
	Moderate	100,000	$1.25	$20.00	$0.10	1	$15,000.00
	High	250,000	$1.25	$20.00	$0.10	1	$15,000.00
National Supplier	Low	50,000	$1.35	$120.00	$0.10	15	$12,500.00
	Moderate	100,000	$1.25	$120.00	$0.10	15	$12,500.00
	High	250,000	$1.00	$120.00	$0.10	15	$12,500.00

a. On purely a total cost basis, which supplier should be selected if there is low demand for Adelie's new service; which supplier should be selected under moderate demand assumptions; and which supplier should be selected under high demand?

b. Which supplier achieves the lowest expected cost if the probability of low demand is 35 percent, moderate demand is 45 percent, and high demand is 20 percent?

Order Fulfillment Process

9. Wingman Distributing Company is expanding its supply chain to include a new distribution hub in South Bend. A key decision involves the number of trucks for the facility. The particular model of truck Wingman is considering can be used 8,000 miles a month and will cost $1,500 a month in capital costs. In addition, each mile a truck is used costs $0.90 for maintenance. A local truck rental firm will rent trucks at a cost of $1.40 per mile. Given the distribution of likely requirements for trucks, management has come up with three alternatives to consider as shown in the table:

Monthly requirements (miles)	40,000	80,000	120,000
Probability	0.30	0.40	0.30
Fleet size (trucks)	5	10	15

Which fleet size will yield the lowest expected monthly costs for Wingman?

10. Sanchez Trucking has been experiencing delays at its warehouse operations. Management hired a consultant to find out why service deliveries to local businesses have taken longer than they should. The consultant narrowed down the problem to the number of work crews loading and unloading trucks. Each crew consists of six employees who work as a team on a variety of tasks; each employee works a full 40 hours a week. However, costs are also a concern. The consultant advised management that they could supplement work crews with short-term employees, at a higher cost, to cover unexpected needs on a weekly basis. Each work crew permanently hired by Sanchez costs $3,200 per week in wages and benefits, while a crew of short-term employees costs $5,000 per week. Complicating the decision is the fact that the weekly hourly requirements for work crews is uncertain because of the volatility in the number of deliveries to be made. Deliberating with management, the consultant arrived at the following data:

D = Difficult Problem

Requirements (labor hours)	720	960	1,200	1,440
Probability	0.2	0.4	0.3	0.1
Number of Crews	3	4	5	6

If the consultant wants to offer a solution that minimizes the expected weekly costs for Sanchez, how many work crews should Sanchez have on its permanent payroll?

11. Acadia Logistics anticipates that it will need more distribution center space to accommodate what it believes will be a significant increase in demand for its final-mile services. Acadia could either lease public warehouse space to cover all levels of demand or construct its own distribution center to meet a specified level of demand, and then use public warehousing to cover the rest. The yearly cost of building and operating its own facility, including the amortized cost of construction, is $12.00 per square foot. The yearly cost of leasing public warehouse space is $20.00 per square foot. The expected demand requirements follow:

Requirements (in sq. ft)	200,000	300,000	400,000	500,000
Probability	0.4	0.3	0.2	0.1

a. Calculate the expected value of leasing public warehouse space as required by demand.

b. Calculate the expected value of building a 200,000-square-foot distribution center and leasing public warehouse space as required if demand exceeds the need for 200,000 square feet of space.

c. Calculate the expected value of building a 300,000-square-foot distribution center and leasing public warehouse space as required if demand exceeds the need for 300,000 square feet of space.

d. Calculate the expected value of building a 400,000-square-foot distribution center and leasing public warehouse space as required if demand exceeds the need for 400,000 square feet of space.

e. Calculate the expected value of building a 500,000-square-foot distribution.

f. Which of the above decisions provides the minimized expected value?

12. Transworld Deliveries is expanding its contract home delivery service into the Northeastern United States. The company anticipates that to accommodate this expansion it will need between 25 and 40 staffed delivery vehicles. Transworld is currently moving 25 of its own vehicles, with drivers, into the Northeast. The daily cost of operating its own fleet is $820 per vehicle, while the daily cost of leasing a vehicle and driver is expected to be $1,200 per vehicle. The expected demand requirements follow:

Requirements (in vehicles)	25	30	35	40
Probability	0.25	0.25	0.25	0.25

Using an expected value approach, should Transworld purchase additional vehicles and hire additional drivers? If so, how many would you recommend?

Supply Chain Risk Management

13. Eastmark Electrical Equipment Manufacturers needs to secure its supply of copper for the next year. The price of copper is extremely volatile because of huge month-to-month variation in demand. Eastmark wants to break even with a hedge against future copper prices. Currently, the market price for copper is reasonably low at $3.25 per pound or $325 (CWT). Eastmark has entered into a contract with the supplier for 500,000 pounds of copper per month starting in January at market prices. Eastmark has also entered into a futures contract with a financial institution for 500,000 pounds per month at $3.25 per pound. CWT (hundredweight) is equal to 100 pounds in the United States.

a. Calculate the one month financial and the physical results if the market price of copper has risen to $4.50 per pound.

b. Calculate the one month financial and the physical results if the market price of copper has fallen to $3.00 per pound.

14. Refer to Problem 13 regarding Eastmark Electrical Equipment Manufacturers. Suppose the futures contact is still in force in February.

a. However, assume the firm has just lost a key client's business and only purchases 400,000 pounds of copper.

i. Calculate the one month financial and the physical results if the market price of copper has risen to $4.50 per pound. Calculate only the financial impact of copper transactions and disregard the loss of revenue due to business loss.

ii. Calculate the one month financial and the physical results if the market price of copper has fallen to $3.00 per pound. Calculate only the financial impact of copper transactions and disregard the loss of revenue due to business loss.

b. Now assume the firm has just received a new client's business and must purchase 800,000 pounds of copper.

i. Calculate the one month financial and the physical results if the market price of copper has risen to $4.50 per pound. Calculate only the financial impact of copper transactions and disregard the loss of revenue due to business loss.

ii. Calculate the one month financial and the physical results if the market price of copper has fallen to $3.00 per pound. Calculate only the financial impact of copper transactions and disregard the loss of revenue due to business loss.

VIDEO CASE | Sourcing Strategy at Starwood

Bath towels. Televisions. Fresh produce. Uniforms. On the surface, these items may not appear to have any relationship to each other. Sure, they exist in most households, even though they were probably bought independently of one another. Yet to the supply chain manager employed in the hospitality industry, they not only have a relationship, but their purchase can be critical to gaining a competitive advantage.

Just ask Paul Davis, vice president of strategic sourcing for Starwood's North American operations. With hundreds of hotels and resorts in the United States, Canada, and the Caribbean, Davis's goal is to create the hospitality industry's best supply chain organization. The items procured within his organization not only include replenishable goods such as fresh produce and food items but also extend to the sourcing of national contracts for nonperishable goods such as bath towels, electronics, staff apparel, energy, and contract services.

It is easy to confuse supply chain processes with the routine procurement of goods and services. Starwood's supply chain certainly does include contracting, but it is much more: It consists of the customer relationship, order fulfillment, and supplier relationship processes. Strong linkages exist among the company's upstream suppliers of services, materials, and information and the customers of Starwood's hotels and resorts. If the upstream relationships are not carefully managed, downstream delivery of consistency, quality, and value to Starwood's guests may suffer. As a result, significant effort is placed on the nested processes within the supplier relationship process such as design collaboration, sourcing, negotiation, contracting, and information exchange.

Any number of events will trigger the involvement of Paul Davis's supply chain team:

- Existing contracts expire.
- Individual hotel brands seek new products.
- Hotel property design teams generate ideas.
- New categories of products emerge and need evaluation.
- A particular hotel needs help with a local service contract.

When a product or service needs to be sourced, the specifications are driven by internal customers such as restaurant chefs, housekeeping, and maintenance. If the product or service does not already exist, domestic and international suppliers that might be able to create the item are researched, as are regional and local vendors. Sometimes, sourcing an existing item simply means renewing an agreement with a current supplier. Still other situations demand creating a new category that has not been sourced before or using a third party to help locate sources.

Due diligence is always performed by sending potential suppliers a "request for information" in either paper or electronic form. The responses returned by the suppliers are entered into a database and help Starwood to prequalify the suppliers. A good match is sought, requiring the suppliers to meet minimum requirements for financial viability, quality, scope of operations, references, and legal risk avoidance. With a suitable potential supplier candidate pool, Starwood then takes one of two paths. The first one is to conduct a reverse auction where preselected vendors bid against each other. This method is used with shorter-term contracts on commodity items that have low external customer visibility. Kitchen uniforms, hotel room door keys, and paint are sourced this way. The second option is to send out a request for proposals (RFP), which requires the vendor to put its best terms forward at the outset for consideration.

After review by the supply chain team, the vendor winning the auction or emerging from the RFP review activity as the best fit is engaged in negotiations. Throughout the supplier relationship building process, Starwood gets to know the vendors, but it becomes much more personal at this point as both parties move toward concluding their contract negotiations.

Starwood maintains a cooperative orientation toward its supplier relationships, building a partnership to maximize value for each party to ensure that each side is comfortable with the price, quality, and delivery requirements it has agreed upon in the contract negotiation process. When contract negotiations are complete, the different brands are notified and the buying and information exchange processes begin.

At this point, you might think the job of the supply chain team is done. Yet managing the existing supplier relationship after the contract ink dries is perhaps the most challenging task of all. The contract involving sourcing of bed linens and terrycloth items is a perfect example. Not long after the contract was finalized, an alternate supplier approached Starwood with an offer to supply comparable quality goods at a much lower cost. Supply chain managers had a choice to make: continue to work with the existing supplier or buy out the current supplier's contract and begin sourcing with the new one.

QUESTIONS

1. Should Starwood maintain a cooperative orientation or a competitive orientation with its suppliers for the kind of items described here?

2. What types of information should Starwood exchange with its bed linens and terrycloth supplier? What does Starwood risk by sharing too much information?

3. How would you approach the sourcing of bed linens and terrycloth items? That is, would you use a reverse auction or request for proposal? Under what circumstances would you change suppliers?

4. In addition to performing value analysis on the services its properties offer, Starwood evaluates the performance of its suppliers against contract metrics. Using the bed linens and terrycloth supplier as an example, describe some of the metrics Starwood should use.

CASE   Wolf Motors

John Wolf, president of Wolf Motors, just returned to his office after visiting the company's newly acquired automotive dealership. It was the fourth Wolf Motors dealership in a network that served a metropolitan area of 400,000 people. Beyond the metropolitan area, but within a 45-minute drive, were another 500,000 people. Each of the dealerships in the network marketed a different brand of automobile and historically had operated autonomously.

Wolf was particularly excited about this new dealership because it was the first "auto supermarket" in the network. Auto supermarkets differ from traditional auto dealerships in that they sell multiple brands of automobiles at the same location. The new dealership sold a full line of Chevrolets, Nissans, and Volkswagens.

Starting 15 years ago with the purchase of a bankrupt Dodge dealership, Wolf Motors had grown steadily in size and in reputation. Wolf attributed this success to three highly interdependent factors. The first was volume. By maintaining a high volume of sales and turning over inventory rapidly, economies of scale could be achieved, which reduced costs and provided customers with a large selection. The second factor was a marketing approach called the "hassle-free buying experience." Listed on each automobile was the "one price—lowest price." Customers came in, browsed, and compared prices without being approached by pushy salespeople. If they had questions or were ready to buy, a walk to a customer service desk produced a knowledgeable salesperson to assist them. Finally, and Wolf thought perhaps most importantly, was the after-sales service. Wolf Motors established a solid reputation for servicing, diagnosing, and repairing vehicles correctly and in a timely manner—the first time.

High-quality service after the sale depended on three essential components. First was the presence of a highly qualified, well-trained staff of service technicians. Second was the use of the latest tools and technologies to support diagnosis and repair activities. Third was the availability of the full range of parts and materials necessary to complete the service and repairs without delay. Wolf invested in training and equipment to ensure that the trained personnel and technology were provided. What he worried about, as Wolf Motors grew, was the continued availability of the right parts and materials. This concern caused him to focus on the supplier relationship process and management of the service parts and materials flows in the supply chain.

Wolf thought back to the stories in the newspaper's business pages describing the failure of companies that had not planned appropriately for growth. These companies outgrew their existing policies, procedures, and control systems. Lacking a plan to update their systems, the companies experienced myriad problems that led to inefficiencies and an inability to compete effectively. He did not want that to happen to Wolf Motors.

Each of the four dealerships purchased its own service parts and materials. Purchases were based on forecasts derived from historical demand data, which accounted for factors such as seasonality. Batteries and alternators had a high failure rate in the winter, and air-conditioner parts were in great demand during the summer. Similarly, coolant was needed in the spring to service air conditioners for the summer months, whereas antifreeze was needed in the fall to winterize automobiles. Forecasts also were adjusted for special vehicle sales and service promotions, which increased the need for materials used to prep new cars and service other cars.

One thing that made the purchase of service parts and materials so difficult was the tremendous number of different parts that had to be kept on hand. Some of these parts would be used to service customer automobiles, and others would be sold over the counter. Some had to be purchased from the automobile manufacturers or their certified wholesalers, and to support, for example, the "guaranteed GM parts" promotion. Still, other parts and materials such as oils, lubricants, and fan belts could be purchased from any number of suppliers. The purchasing department had to remember that the success of the dealership depended on (1) lowering costs to support the hassle-free, one price–lowest price concept and (2) providing the right parts at the right time to support fast, reliable after-sales service.

As Wolf thought about the purchasing of parts and materials, two things kept going through his mind: the amount of space available for parts storage and the level of financial resources available to invest in parts and materials. The acquisition of the auto supermarket dealership put an increased strain on both finances and space, with the need to support three different automobile lines at the same facility. Investment dollars were becoming scarce, and space was at a premium. Wolf wondered what could be done in the purchasing area to address some of these concerns and alleviate some of the pressures.

QUESTIONS

1. What recommendations would you make to John Wolf with respect to structuring the supplier relationship process for the Wolf Motors dealership network?

2. How might purchasing policies and procedures differ as the dealerships purchase different types of service parts and materials (for example, lubricants versus genuine GM parts)?

3. How can supply chain design and integration help John Wolf reduce investment and space requirements while maintaining adequate service levels?

NORMAL DISTRIBUTION

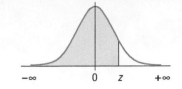

	.00	.01	.02	.03	.04	.05	.06	.07	.08	.09
.0	.5000	.5040	.5080	.5120	.5160	.5199	.5239	.5279	.5319	.5359
.1	.5398	.5438	.5478	.5517	.5557	.5596	.5636	.5675	.5714	.5753
.2	.5793	.5832	.5871	.5910	.5948	.5987	.6026	.6064	.6103	.6141
.3	.6179	.6217	.6255	.6293	.6331	.6368	.6406	.6443	.6480	.6517
.4	.6554	.6591	.6628	.6664	.6700	.6736	.6772	.6808	.6844	.6879
.5	.6915	.6950	.6985	.7019	.7054	.7088	.7123	.7157	.7190	.7224
.6	.7257	.7291	.7324	.7357	.7389	.7422	.7454	.7486	.7517	.7549
.7	.7580	.7611	.7642	.7673	.7704	.7734	.7764	.7794	.7823	.7852
.8	.7881	.7910	.7939	.7967	.7995	.8023	.8051	.8078	.8106	.8133
.9	.8159	.8186	.8212	.8238	.8264	.8289	.8315	.8340	.8365	.8389
1.0	.8413	.8438	.8461	.8485	.8508	.8531	.8554	.8577	.8599	.8621
1.1	.8643	.8665	.8686	.8708	.8729	.8749	.8770	.8790	.8810	.8830
1.2	.8849	.8869	.8888	.8907	.8925	.8944	.8962	.8980	.8997	.9015
1.3	.9032	.9049	.9066	.9082	.9099	.9115	.9131	.9147	.9162	.9177
1.4	.9192	.9207	.9222	.9236	.9251	.9265	.9279	.9292	.9306	.9319
1.5	.9332	.9345	.9357	.9370	.9382	.9394	.9406	.9418	.9429	.9441
1.6	.9452	.9463	.9474	.9484	.9495	.9505	.9515	.9525	.9535	.9545
1.7	.9554	.9564	.9573	.9582	.9591	.9599	.9608	.9616	.9625	.9633
1.8	.9641	.9649	.9656	.9664	.9671	.9678	.9686	.9693	.9699	.9706
1.9	.9713	.9719	.9726	.9732	.9738	.9744	.9750	.9756	.9761	.9767
2.0	.9772	.9778	.9783	.9788	.9793	.9798	.9803	.9808	.9812	.9817
2.1	.9821	.9826	.9830	.9834	.9838	.9842	.9846	.9850	.9854	.9857
2.2	.9861	.9864	.9868	.9871	.9875	.9878	.9881	.9884	.9887	.9890
2.3	.9893	.9896	.9898	.9901	.9904	.9906	.9909	.9911	.9913	.9916
2.4	.9918	.9920	.9922	.9925	.9927	.9929	.9931	.9932	.9934	.9936
2.5	.9938	.9940	.9941	.9943	.9945	.9946	.9948	.9949	.9951	.9952
2.6	.9953	.9955	.9956	.9957	.9959	.9960	.9961	.9962	.9963	.9964
2.7	.9965	.9966	.9967	.9968	.9969	.9970	.9971	.9972	.9973	.9974
2.8	.9974	.9975	.9976	.9977	.9977	.9978	.9979	.9979	.9980	.9981
2.9	.9981	.9982	.9982	.9983	.9984	.9984	.9985	.9985	.9986	.9986
3.0	.9987	.9987	.9987	.9988	.9988	.9989	.9989	.9989	.9990	.9990
3.1	.9990	.9991	.9991	.9991	.9992	.9992	.9992	.9992	.9993	.9993
3.2	.9993	.9993	.9994	.9994	.9994	.9994	.9994	.9995	.9995	.9995
3.3	.9995	.9995	.9995	.9996	.9996	.9996	.9996	.9996	.9996	.9997
3.4	.9997	.9997	.9997	.9997	.9997	.9997	.9997	.9997	.9997	.9998

Selected References

Chapter 1: Using Operations to Create Value

Chase, Richard B., and Uday M. Apte. "A History of Research in Service Operations: What's the Big Idea?" *Journal of Operations Management*, vol. 25, no. 2 (2007), pp. 375–386.

Collis, David J., and Michael G. Rukstad. "Can You Say What Your Strategy Is?" *Harvard Business Review*, vol. 86, no. 4 (2008), pp. 82–90.

Fitzsimmons, James A., and Mona Fitzsimmons. *Service Management*. New York: McGraw-Hill, 2005.

Gaimon, Cheryl. "The Management of Technology: A Production and Operations Management Perspective." *Production and Operations Management*, vol. 17, no. 1 (2008), pp. 1–11.

Hammer, Michael. "Deep Change: How Operational Innovation Can Transform Your Company." *Harvard Business Review*, vol. 82, no. 9 (2004), pp. 85–93.

Heineke, Janelle, and Mark Davis. "The Emergence of Service Operations as an Academic Discipline." *Journal of Operations Management*, vol. 25, no. 2 (2007), pp. 364–374.

Hill, Terry. *Manufacturing Strategy: Text and Cases*, 3rd ed. Homewood, IL: Irwin/McGraw-Hill, 2000.

Huckman, Robert S., and Darren E. Zinner. "Does Focus Improve Operational Performance? Lessons from the Management of Clinical Trials." *Strategic Management Journal*, vol. 29 (2008), pp. 173–193.

Jones, Daniel T., James P. Womack, and Daniel Roos. *The Machine That Changed the World: The Story of Lean Production—Toyota's Secret Weapon in the Global Car Wars That Is Now Revolutionizing World Industry*. New York: The Free Press, 2007.

Karmarkar, Uday. "Will You Survive the Services Revolution?" *Harvard Business Review*, vol. 82 (2004), pp. 100–108.

Kaplan, Robert S., and David P. Norton. *Balanced Scoreboard*. Boston, MA: Harvard Business School Press, 1997.

King Jr., Neil. "A Whole New World." *Wall Street Journal*, 244, no. 61 (September 27, 2004), pp. R1–R3.

Meyer, Christopher and Andre Schwager. "Understanding Customer Experience." *Harvard Business Review*, vol. 85 (2007), pp. 116–126.

Neilson, Gary L., Karla L. Martin, and Elizabeth Powers. "The Secrets to Successful Strategy Execution." *Harvard Business Review*, vol. 86, no. 6 (2008), pp. 60–70.

Ohno, Taiichi. *Toyota Production System: Beyond Large-Scale Production*. New York: Productivity Press, 1988.

Pande, Peter S., Robert P. Neuman, and Roland R. Cavanaugh. *The Six Sigma Way: How to Maximize the Impact of Your Change and Improvement Efforts*. New York: McGraw-Hill, 2014.

Pisano, G., and Shih, W. "Does America Really Need Manufacturing?" *Harvard Business Review*, vol. 90, no. 3 (2012), pp. 94–102.

Porter, Michael E. *Competitive Advantage*. New York: The Free Press, 1987.

Porter, Michael E., and Mark R. Kramer. "Strategy and Society: The Link Between Competitive Advantage and Corporate Social Responsibility." *Harvard Business Review*, vol. 84, no. 12 (2006), pp. 78–92.

Powell, Bill. "It's All Made in China Now." *Fortune* (March 4, 2002), pp. 121–128.

Safizadeh, M. Hossein, Larry P. Ritzman, Deven Sharma, and Craig Wood. "An Empirical Analysis of the Product-Process Matrix." *Management Science*, vol. 42, no. 11 (1996), pp. 1576–1591.

Skinner, Wickham. "Manufacturing—Missing Link in Corporate Strategy." *Harvard Business Review* (May/June 1969), pp. 136–145.

Simchi-Levi, D., and Peruvankal, J. "Is It Time to Rethink Your Manufacturing Strategy." *MIT Sloan Management Review*, vol. 53, no. 2 (2012), pp. 20–22.

Stanwick, Sarah D., and Peter A. Stanwick. "The Ethics of Outsourcing at Mattel." *Problems and Perspectives in Management*, vol. 8, no. 4 (2010), pp. 179–183.

Svensson, Peter. "GameStop to Sell Rain Checks for Wii." http://usatoday30.usatoday.com/tech/products/2007-12-14-1075661460_x.htm (December 14, 2007).

Voss, Chris, Aleda Roth, and Richard Chase. "Experience, Service Operations Strategy, and Services as Destinations: Foundations and Exploratory Investigation" *Production and Operations Management*, vol. 17, no. 3 (2008), pp. 247–266.

Ward, Peter T., and Rebecca Duray. "Manufacturing Strategy in Context: Environment, Competitive Strategy and Manufacturing Strategy." *Journal of Operations Management*, vol. 18 (2000), pp. 123–138.

Wiseman, Paul. "Despite China's Might, U.S. Factories Maintain Edge." http://www.cbsnews.com/news/despite-chinas-might-us-factories-maintain-edge-30-01-2011/ (January 31, 2011).

Supplement A: Decision Making

Clemen, Robert T., and Terence Reilly. *Making Hard Decisions with Decision Tools Suite*. Cincinnati, OH: South-Western, 2004.

Ragsdale, Cliff. *Spreadsheet Modeling & Decision Analysis: A Practical Introduction to Business Analytics*, 7th ed., Stamford, CT: Cengage Learning, 2014.

Velleman, J. "Deciding How to Decide." *Harvard Business Review*, vol. 91, no. 11 (2013), pp. 62–71.

Chapter 2: Process Strategy and Analysis

Andersen, Bjørn. *Business Process Improvement Toolbox*, 2nd ed. Milwaukee, Wisconsin: American Society for Quality, 2007.

Ahire, Sanjay L., and Manoj K. Malhotra. "Scripting a Holistic Rx for Process Improvement at Palmetto Health Imaging Centers." *Journal of Global Business and Organizational Excellence*, vol. 30, no. 2 (January/February 2011), pp. 23–35.

Baghai, Ramin, Edward H. Levine, and Saumya S. Sutaria. "Service-Line Strategies for U.S. Hospitals." *The McKinsey Quarterly* (July 2008), pp. 1–9.

Bhuiyan, Nadjia, Amit Baghel, and Jim Wilson. "A Sustainable Continuous Improvement Methodology at an Aerospace Company," *International Journal of Productivity and Performance Management*, vol. 55, no. 8 (2006), pp. 671–687.

Booth, Alan. "The Management of Technical Change: Automation in the UK and USA since 1950." *The Economic History Review*, vol. 62, no. 2 (May 2009), pp. 493–494.

Brink, Harold, Senthil Muthiah, and Rajan Naik. "A Better Way to Automate Service Operations." *McKinsey on Business Technology*, vol. 20 (Summer, 2010), pp. 1–10.

Carey, Susan. "Case of the Vanishing Airport Lines." *Wall Street Journal*, vol. 250, no. 33 (August 9, 2007), pp. B1–B4.

Chase, Richard B., and Uday M. Apte. "A History of Research in Service Operations: What's the Big Idea?" *Journal of Operations Management*, vol. 25 (2007), pp. 375–386.

Davenport, Thomas H. "The Coming Commoditization of Processes." *Harvard Business Review*, (June 2005), pp. 101–108.

Edmondson, Amy C. "The Competitive Imperative of Learning." *Harvard Business Review*, vol. 86 (July/August, 2008), pp. 1–13.

Fisher, Anne. "Get Employees to Brainstorm Online." *Fortune*, vol. 150, no. 11 (November 2004), p. 72.

Fisher, Marshall L. "Bob Hayes: Forty Years of Leading Operations Management into Uncharted Waters." *Production and Operations Management*, vol. 16, no. 2, (March/April 2007), pp. 159–168.

Fleming, John H., Curt Coffman, and James K. Harter. "Manage Your Human Sigma." *Harvard Business Review* (July/August 2005), pp. 101–108.

Greasley, A. "Using Process Mapping and Business Process Simulation to Support a Process-Based Approach to Change in a Public Sector Organisation." *Technovation*, vol. 26 (2006), pp. 95–103.

Grosskopf, Alexander, Gero Decker, and Mathias Weske. *The Process: Business Process Modelling Using BPMN*. Tampa, Florida: Meghan-Kiffer Press, 2009.

Grover, Varun, and Manoj K. Malhotra. "Business Process Reengineering: A Tutorial on the Concept, Evolution, Method, Technology, and Application." *Journal of Operations Management*, vol. 15, no. 3 (1997), pp. 194–213.

Hall, J. M., and M. E. Johnson. "When Should a Process Be Art, Not Science?" *Harvard Business Review*, vol. 87, no. 3 (2009), pp. 58–66.

Hammer, Michael. "Deep Change: How Operational Innovation Can Transform Your Company." *Harvard Business Review*, vol. 82, no. 4 (April 2004), pp. 85–93.

Hammer, Michael. "The Process Audit." *Harvard Business Review*, vol. 82, no. 4 (April 2007), pp. 111–123.

Hammer, Michael. "What Is Business Process Management?" *Handbook on Business Process Management*, vol. 1 (2010), pp. 3–16.

Hartvigsen, David. *SimQuick: Process Simulation with Excel*, 2nd ed. Upper Saddle River, NJ: Prentice Hall, 2004.

Hayes, Robert. *Operations, Strategy, and Technology: Pursuing the Competitive Edge*, Hoboken, NJ: Wiley, 2005.

Hill, Terry. *Manufacturing Strategy: Text and Cases*, 3rd ed. Homewood, IL: Irwin/McGraw-Hill, 2000.

Jack, Eric, and John Collis. "Strengthen and Tone: A Flexible Approach to Operations Can Build Some Serious Muscle." *APICS Magazine* (June 2006), pp. 35–38.

Jain, Rashmi, Angappa Gunasekaran, and Anithashree Chandrasekaran. "Evolving Role of Process Reengineering: A Perspective of Employers." *Industrial and Commercial Training*, vol. 41, no. 7 (2009), pp. 382–390.

Jensen, John B., Sanjay L. Ahire, and Manoj K. Malhotra. "Trane/Ingersoll Rand Combines Lean and Operations Research Tools to Redesign Feeder Manufacturing Operations." *Interfaces*, vol. 43, no. 4 (2013), pp. 325–340.

Jeston, John, and Johan Nelis. *Management by Process: A Roadmap to Sustainable Business Process Management*. Oxford, UK: Elsevier, 2008.

Johansson, Pontus, and Jan Olhager. "Linking Product-Process Matrices for Manufacturing and Industrial Service Operations." *International Journal of Production Economics*, vol. 104, (2006), pp. 615–624.

Karmarkar, Uday. "Will You Survive the Services Revolution?" *Harvard Business Review*, vol. 82, no. 6 (June 2004), pp. 100–107.

Kulpa, Margaret K., and Kent A. Johnson. *Interpeting the CMMI: A Process Improvement Approach*, 2nd ed. Boca Raton, FL: Auerbach Publications, 2008.

Kung, Peter, and Claus Hagen. "The Fruits of Business Process Management: An Experience Report from a Swiss Bank." *Business Process Management Journal*, vol. 13, no. 4 (2007), pp. 477–487.

La Ferla, Beverly. "Mapping the Way to Process Improvement." *IEE Engineering Management* (December 2004/January 2005), pp. 16–17.

Lee, Hau L. "The Triple-A Supply Chain." *Harvard Business Review* (October 2004), pp. 102–112.

Malhotra, Manoj K., and Larry P. Ritzman. "Resource Flexibility Issues in Multistage Manufacturing." *Decision Sciences*, vol. 21, no. 4 (1990), pp. 673–690.

Metters, Richard, Kathryn King-Metters, and Madeleine Pullman. *Successful Service Operations Management*. Mason, OH: South-Western, 2003.

Prajogo, Daniel. "The Implementation of Operations Management Techniques in Service Organisations." *International Journal of Operations & Production Management*, vol. 26, no. 12 (2006), pp. 1374–1390.

Rayport, Jeffrey F., and Bernard J. Jaworski. "Best Face Forward." *Harvard Business Review*, vol. 82, no. 12 (2003), pp. 47–58.

Rummler, Geary A., and Alan P. Brache. *Improving Performance*, 2nd ed. San Francisco: Jossey-Bass Inc., 1995.

Safizadeh, M. Hossein, Joy M. Field, and Larry P. Ritzman. "An Empirical Analysis of Financial Services Processes with a Front-Office or Back-Office Orientation." *Journal of Operations Management*, vol. 21, no. 5 (2003), pp. 557–576.

Safizadeh, M. Hossein, Larry P. Ritzman, and Debasish Mallick. "Revisiting Alternative Theoretical Paradigms in Manufacturing." *Production and Operations Management*, vol. 9, no. 2 (2000), pp. 111–127.

Scott, Bradley, S., Anne E. Wilcock, and Vinay Kanetkar. "A Survey of Structured Continuous Improvement Programs in the Canadian Food Sector." *Food Control*, vol. 20 (2009), 209–217.

Sehgal, Sanjay, B. S. Sahay, and S. K. Goyal. "Reengineering the Supply Chain in a Paint Company." *International Journal of Productivity and Performance Management*, vol. 55, no. 8 (2006), pp. 655–670.

Skinner, Wickham. "Operations Technology: Blind Spot in Strategic Management." *Interfaces*, vol. 14 (January/February 1984), pp. 116–125.

Swink, Morgan, and Anand Nair. "Capturing the Competitive Advantages of AMT: Design-Manufacturing Integration as a Complementary Asset." *Journal of Operations Management*, vol. 25 (2007), pp. 736–754.

Zomerdijk, Leonieke G., and Jan de Vries. "Structuring Front Office and Back Office Work in Service Delivery Systems." *International Journal of Operations & Production Management*, vol. 27, no. 1 (2007), pp. 108–131.

Chapter 3: Quality and Performance

Babbar, Sunil. "Service Quality and Business Ethics." *International Journal of Service and Operations Management*, vol. 1, no. 3 (2005), pp. 203–219.

Babbar, Sunil. "Teaching Ethics for Quality as an Innovation in a Core Operations Management Course." *Decision Sciences Journal of Innovative Education*, vol. 8, no. 2 (2010), pp. 361–366.

Besterfield, Dale. *Quality Improvement*, 9th ed. Upper Saddle River, NJ: Prentice Hall, 2012.

Cole, R. "What Really Happened to Toyota?" *MIT Sloan Management Review*, vol. 52, no. 4 (2011), pp. 29–35.

Cole, R., and M. Flynn. "Automotive quality reputation: Hard to Achieve, Hard to Lose, Still Harder to Win Back." *California Management Review*, vol. 52, no. 1 (2009), pp. 67–94.

Collier, David A. *The Service/Quality Solution*. New York: Irwin Professional Publishing; Milwaukee: ASQC Quality Press, 1994.

Crosby, Philip B. *Quality Is Free: The Art of Making Quality Certain*. New York: McGraw-Hill, 1979.

Deming, W. Edwards. *Out of the Crisis*. Cambridge, MA: Massachusetts Institute of Technology Center for Advanced Engineering Study, 1986.

Duncan, Acheson J. *Quality Control and Industrial Statistics*, 5th ed. Homewood, IL: Irwin, 1986.

Feigenbaum, A. V. *Total Quality Control: Engineering and Management*, 3rd ed. New York: McGraw-Hill, 1983.

Hartvigsen, David. *SimQuick: Process Simulation with Excel*, 2nd ed. Upper Saddle River, NJ: Prentice Hall, 2004.

Hoyle, David. *ISO 9000*, 6th ed. Oxford: Butler-Heinemann, 2009.

Kerwin, Kathleen. "When Flawless Isn't Enough." *BusinessWeek* (December 8, 2003), pp. 80–82.

Lucier, Gregory T., and Sridhar Seshadri. "GE Takes Six Sigma Beyond the Bottom Line." *Strategic Finance* (May 2001), pp. 41–46.

Mitra, Amitava. *Fundamentals of Quality Control and Improvement*, 3rd ed. Hoboken, NJ: Wiley & Sons, 2008.

Russell, J. P., and Dennis Arter. *ISO Lesson Guide to ISO 9001*, 3rd ed. Milwaukee: ASQC Quality Press, 2008.

Schwarz, Anne. "Listening to the Voice of the Customer Is the Key to QVC's Success." *Journal of Organizational Excellence* (Winter 2004), pp. 3–11.

Sester, Dennis. "Motorola: A Tradition of Quality." *Quality* (October 2001), pp. 30–34.

Srinivasan, A., and B. Kurey. "Creating a Culture of Quality." *Harvard Business Review*, vol. 92, no. 4 (2014), pp. 23–25.

Yannick, Julliard. "Ethics Quality Management." *Techne' Journal*, vol. 8, no. 1 (Fall 2004), pp. 117–135.

Chapter 4: Capacity Planning

Bakke, Nils Arne, and Ronald Hellberg. "The Challenges of Capacity Planning." *International Journal of Production Economics*, vols. 31–30 (1993), pp. 243–264.

Bower, J. L., and C. G. Gilbert. "How Managers' Everyday Decisions Create or Destroy Your Company's Strategy." *Harvard Business Review*, vol. 85, no. 2 (2007), pp. 72–79.

Hartvigsen, David. *SimQuick: Process Simulation with Excel*, 2nd ed. Upper Saddle River, NJ: Prentice Hall, 2004.

"Intel's $10 Billion Gamble." *Fortune* (November 11, 2002), pp. 90–102.

Klassen, Robert D., and Larry J. Menor. "The Process Management Triangle: An Empirical Investigation of Process Trade-offs." *Journal of Operations Management*, vol. 25 (2007), pp. 1015–1034.

Ritzman, Larry P., and M. Hossein Safizadeh. "Linking Process Choice with Plant-Level Decisions about Capital and Human Resources." *Production and Operations Management*, vol. 8, no. 4 (1999), pp. 374–392.

Tenhiala, A. "Contingency Theory of Capacity Planning: The Link Between Process Types and Planning Methods." *Journal of Operations Management*, vol. 29 (2011), pp. 65–77.

Supplement B: Waiting Lines

Buell, R., and M. Norton. "Think Customers Hate Waiting? Not so Fast." *Harvard Business Review*, vol. 89, no. 5 (2011), pp. 34.

Cooper, Robert B. *Introduction to Queuing Theory*, 3rd ed. Washington, DC: George Washington University, 1990.

Hartvigsen, David. *SimQuick: Process Simulation with Excel*, 2nd ed. Upper Saddle River, NJ: Prentice Hall, 2004.

Hillier, F. S., and G. S. Lieberman. *Introduction to Operations Research*, 9th ed. New York: McGraw-Hill, 2009.

Little, J. D. C. "A Proof for the Queuing Formula: $L = \lambda M$." *Operations Research*, vol. 9, (1961), pp. 383–387.

Morse, P. M. *Queues, Inventories and Maintenance*. New York: Dover Publications, 2004.

Chapter 5: Constraint Management

Brown, A. "Theory of Constraints Tapped to Accelerate BP's Gulf of Mexico Cleanup." *Industry Week* (March 18, 2011).

Corominas, Albert, Rafael Pastor, and Joan Plans. "Balancing Assembly Line with Skilled and Unskilled Workers." *Omega*, vol. 36, no. 6 (2008), pp. 1126–1132.

Goldratt, E. M., and J. Cox. *The Goal*. New York: North River Press, 2012.

McClain, John O., and L. Joseph Thomas. "Overcoming the Dark Side of Worker Flexibility." *Journal of Operations Management*, vol. 21, (2003), pp. 81–92.

Srikanth, Mokshagundam L., and Michael Umble. *Synchronous Management: Profit-Based Manufacturing for the 21st Century*, vol. 1. Guilford, CT: Spectrum Publishing Company, 1997.

Steele, Daniel C., Patrick R. Philipoom, Manoj K. Malhotra, and Timothy D. Fry. "Comparisons Between Drum-Buffer-Rope and Material Requirements Planning: A Case Study." *International Journal of Production Research*, vol. 43, no. 15 (2005), pp. 3181–3208.

Umble, M., E. Umble, and S. Murakami. "Implementing Theory of Constraints in a Traditional Japanese Manufacturing Environment: The Case of Hitachi Tool Engineering." *International Journal of Production Research*, vol. 44, no. 15 (2006), pp. 1863–1880.

Chapter 6: Lean Systems

Ansberry, Clare. "Hurry-Up Inventory Method Hurts Where It Once Helped." http://online.wsj.com/news/articles/SB1024952665607014520 (June 25, 2002).

Holweg, Matthias. "The Genealogy of Lean Production." *Journal of Operations Management*, vol. 25 (2007), pp. 420–437.

Immelt, J. "The CEO of General Electric on Sparking an American Manufacturing Renewal." *Harvard Business Review*, vol. 90, no. 3 (2012), pp. 43–46.

Klein, J. A. "The Human Costs of Manufacturing Reform." *Harvard Business Review* (March/April 1989), pp. 60–66.

Manufacturing Engineering Inc. "5S Solutions: Train-Implement-Sustain" http://www.mfgeng.com/5S.htm (2013).

Mascitelli, Ron. "Lean Thinking: It's about Efficient Value Creation." *Target*, vol. 16, no. 2 (Second Quarter 2000), pp. 22–26.

McBride, David. "Toyota and Total Productive Maintenance." http://www.emsstrategies.com/dm050104article2.html (May 2004).

Spear, Steven J. "Learning to Lead at Toyota." *Harvard Business Review* (May 2004), pp. 78–86.

Spear, Steven J., and H. Kent Bowen. "Decoding the DNA of the Toyota Production System." *Harvard Business Review* (September–October 1999), pp. 97–106.

Staats, B., and D. Upton. "Lean Knowledge Work." *Harvard Business Review*, vol. 89, no. 12 (2011), pp. 21–22.

Chapter 7: Project Management

Goldratt, E. M. *Critical Chain*. Great Barrington, MA: North River, 1997.

"A Guide to Project Management Body of Knowledge." Available from the Project Management Institute at www.pmi.org, 2013.

Hartvigsen, David. *SimQuick: Process Simulation with Excel*, 2nd ed. Upper Saddle River, NJ: Prentice Hall, 2004.

Kerzner, Harold. *Advanced Project Management: Best Practices on Implementation*, 2nd ed. New York: John Wiley & Sons, 2004.

Kerzner, Harold. *Project Management: A Systems Approach to Planning, Scheduling, and Controlling*, 11th ed. New York: John Wiley & Sons, 2013.

Lewis, J. P. *Mastering Project Management*, 2nd ed. New York: McGraw-Hill, 2007.

Mantel Jr., Samuel J., Jack R. Meredith, Scott M. Shafer, and Margaret M. Sutton. *Project Management in Practice*, 4th ed. New York: John Wiley & Sons, 2010.

Meredith, Jack R., and Samuel J. Mantel, *Project Management: A Managerial Approach*, 8th ed. New York: John Wiley & Sons, 2011.

Muir, Nancy C. *Microsoft Project 2010 for Dummies*. New York: John Wiley & Sons, 2010.

Nicholas, John M., and Herman Stein. *Project Management for Engineering, Business, and Technology*, 4th ed. London, U.K.: Routledge, 2012.

Srinivasan, Mandyam, Darren Jones, and Alex Miller. "CORPS Capabilities." *APICS Magazine* (March 2005), pp. 46–50.

Chapter 8: Forecasting

Armstrong, J. Scott. "Findings from Evidence-based Forecasting: Methods for Reducing Forecast Error." *International Journal of Forecasting*, vol. 22, no. 3 (2006), pp. 583–598.

Armstrong, J. Scott. (ed.). *Principles of Forecasting: A Handbook for Researchers and Practitioners*. Norwell, MA: Kluwer Academic Publishers, 2001. Also visit http://www.forecastingprinciples.com for valuable information on forecasting, including frequently asked questions, a forecasting methodology tree, and a dictionary.

Attaran, Mohsen, and Sharmin Attaran. "Collaborative Supply Chain Management." *Business Process Management Journal*, vol. 13, no. 13 (June 2007), pp. 390–404.

Cederlund, Jerold P., Rajiv Kohli, Susan A. Sherer, and Yuliang Yao. "How Motorola Put CPFR into Action." *Supply Chain Management Review* (October 2007), pp. 28–35.

Daugherty, Patricia J., R. Glenn Richey, Anthony S. Roath, Soonhong Min, Haozhe Chen, Aaron D. Arndt, and Stefan E. Genchev. "Is Collaboration Paying Off for Firms?" *Business Horizons* (2006), pp. 61–70.

Fildes, Robert, Paul Goodwin, Michael Lawrence, and Konstantinos Nikolopoulos. "Effective Forecasting and Judgmental Adjustments: An Empirical Evaluation and Strategies for Improvement in Supply-Chain Planning." *International Journal of Forecasting*, vol. 25, no. 1 (2009), pp. 3–23.

Lawrence, Michael, Paul Goodwin, Marcus O'Connor, and Dilek Onkal. "Judgmental Forecasting: A Review of Progress over the Last 25 Years." *International Journal of Forecasting* (June 2006), pp. 493–518.

Makridakis, S., R. Hogarth, and A. Gaba. "Why Forecasts Fail? What to Do Instead?" *MIT Sloan Management Review*, vol. 51, no. 2 (2010), pp. 83–90.

McCarthy, Teresa, Donna F. Davis, Susan L. Golicic, and John T. Mentzer. "The Evolution of Sales Forecasting Management: A 20-Year Longitudinal Study of Forecasting Practices." *Journal of Forecasting*, vol. 25 (2006), pp. 303–324.

Min, Hokey, and Wen-Bin Vincent Yu. "Collaborative Planning, Forecasting and Replenishment: Demand Planning in Supply Chain Management." *International Journal of Information Technology and Management*, vol. 7, no. 1 (2008), pp. 4–20.

Montgomery, David. "Flashpoints for Changing Your Forecasting Process." *The Journal of Business Forecasting* (Winter 2006–2007), pp. 35–42.

Saffo, Paul. "Six Rules for Effective Forecasting." *Harvard Business Review* (July–August 2007), pp. 1–30.

Smaros, Johanna. "Forecasting Collaboration in the European Grocery Sector: Observations from a Case Study." *Journal of Operations Management*, vol. 25, no. 3 (April 2007), pp. 702–716.

Smith, Larry. "West Marine: A CPFR Success Story." *Supply Chain Management Review* (March 2006), pp. 29–36.

Syntetos, Aris, Konstantinos Nikolopoulos, John Boylan, Robert Fildes, and Paul Goodwin. "The Effects of Integrating Management Judgement into Intermittent Demand Forecasts." *International Journal of Production Economics*, vol. 118, no. 1 (March, 2009), pp. 72–81.

Wikipedia. "Collaborative Planning, Forecasting, and Replenishment," http:en.wikipedia.org/wiki/Collaborative Planning Forecasting and Replenishment (April, 2011).

Chapter 9: Inventory Management

Arnold, Tony J. R., Stephen Chapman, and Lloyd M. Clive. *Introduction to Materials Management*, 7th ed. Upper Saddle River, NJ: Prentice Hall, 2012.

Axsäter, Sven. *Inventory Control*, 2nd ed. New York: Springer Science + Business Media, LLC, 2006.

Bastow, B. J. "Metrics in the Material World." *APICS—The Performance Advantage* (May 2005), pp. 49–52.

Benton, W. C. *Purchasing and Supply Chain Management*, 3rd ed. New York: McGraw-Hill, 2013.

Callioni, Gianpaolo, Xavier de Montgros, Regine Slagmulder, Luk N. Van Wassenhove, and Linda Wright. "Inventory-Driven Costs." *Harvard Business Review* (March 2005), pp. 135–141.

Cannon, Alan R., and Richard E. Crandall. "The Way Things Never Were." *APICS—The Performance Advantage* (January 2004), pp. 32–35.

Gaur, V., S. Kesavan, and A. Raman. "Retail Inventory: Managing the Canary in the Coal Mine." *California Management Review*, vol. 56, no. 2 (2014), pp. 55–76.

Hartvigsen, David. *SimQuick: Process Simulation with Excel*, 2nd ed. Upper Saddle River, NJ: Prentice Hall, 2004.

Operations Management Body of Knowledge. Falls Church, VA: American Production and Inventory Control Society, 2009.

Timme, Stephen G., and Christine Williams-Timme. "The Real Cost of Holding." *Supply Chain Management Review* (July/August 2003), pp. 30–37.

Walters, Donald. *Inventory Control and Management*, 2nd ed. West Sussex, England: John Wiley and Sons, Ltd, 2003.

Supplement C: Special Inventory Models

American Production and Inventory Control Society. *Operations Management Body of Knowledge Framework*, 3rd ed. Falls Church, VA: American Production and Inventory Control Society, 2011.

Arnold, Tony J. R., Stephen Chapman, and Lloyd M. Clive. *Introduction to Materials Management*, 7th ed. Upper Saddle River, NJ: Prentice Hall, 2012.

Axsäter, Sven. *Inventory Control*, 2nd ed. New York: Springer Science + Business Media, LLC, 2006.

Bastow, B. J. "Metrics in the Material World." *APICS—The Performance Advantage* (May 2005), pp. 49–52.

Benton, W. C. *Purchasing and Supply Chain Management*, 2nd ed. New York: McGraw-Hill, 2010.

Callioni, Gianpaolo, Xavier de Montgros, Regine Slagmulder, Luk N. Van Wassenhove, and Linda Wright. "Inventory-Driven Costs." *Harvard Business Review* (March 2005), pp. 135–141.

Cannon, Alan R., and Richard E. Crandall. "The Way Things Never Were." *APICS—The Performance Advantage* (January 2004), pp. 32–35.

Hartvigsen, David. *SimQuick: Process Simulation with Excel*, 2nd ed. Upper Saddle River, NJ: Prentice Hall, 2004.

Manikas, Andrew. "Fighting Pests with the EOQ," *APICS Magazine* (April 2007), pp. 34–37.

Timme, Stephen G., and Christine Williams-Timme. "The Real Cost of Holding." *Supply Chain Management Review* (July/August 2003), pp. 30–37.

Walters, Donald. *Inventory Control and Management*, 2nd ed. West Sussex, England: John Wiley and Sons, Ltd, 2003.

Chapter 10: Operations Planning and Scheduling

Chiang, Wen-Chyuan, Jason C. H. Chen, and Xiaojing Xu. "An Overview of Research on Revenue Management: Current Issues and Future Research." *International Journal of Revenue Management*, vol. 1, no. 1 (2007), pp. 97–128.

Dougherty, John R. "Lessons from the Pros." *APICS Magazine* (November/ December, 2007), pp. 31–33.

Dougherty, John R., and Christopher Gray. *Sales & Operations Planning— Best Practices*. Victoria, Canada: Trafford Publishing, 2006.

Esper, Terry L., Alexander E. Ellinger, Theodore P. Stank, Daniel J. Flint, and Mark Moon. "Demand and Supply Integration: A Conceptual Framework of Value Creation through Knowledge Management." *Journal of the Academy of Marketing Science*, vol. 38 (2010), pp. 5–18.

Gray, Christopher. *Sales & Operations Planning—Standard System*. Victoria, Canada: Trafford Publishing, 2007.

Gupta, Jatinder N. D., and Edward Stafford Jr. "Flowshop Scheduling Research after Five Decades." *European Journal of Operational Research*, vol. 169 (2006), pp. 699–711.

Jacobs, F. Robert, William Berry, and D. Clay Whybark. *Manufacturing Planning and Control Systems for Supply Chain Management*, 6th ed. New York: McGraw-Hill/Irwin, 2010.

Kelly, Erin L., and Phyllis Moen. "Rethinking the ClockWork of Work: Why Schedule Control May Pay Off at Work and at Home." *Advances in Developing Human Resources*, vol. 9, no. 4 (November 2007), pp. 487–605.

Maher, Kris. "Wal-Mart Seeks New Flexibility in Worker Shifts." *The Wall Street Journal* (January 3, 2007), p. A1.

Muzumdar, Maha, and John Fontanella. "The Secrets to S&OP Success." *Supply Chain Management* (April 2006), pp. 34–41.

Nakano, Mikihisa. "Collaborative Forecasting and Planning in Supply Chains: The Impact on Performance in Japanese Manufacturers." *International Journal of Physical Distribution & Logistics Management*, vol. 39, no. 2 (2009), pp. 84–105.

Olhager, Jan, and Erik Selldin. "Manufacturing Planning and Control Approaches: Market Alignment and Performance." *International Journal of Production Research*, vol. 45, no. 6 (2007), pp. 1469–1484.

Pinedo, Michael. *Planning and Scheduling in Manufacturing and Services*, 2nd ed. New York: Springer, 2009.

Quadt, Daniel, and Heinrich Kuhn. "A Taxonomy of Flexible Flow Line Scheduling Procedures." *European Journal of Operational Research*, vol. 178 (2007), pp. 686–698.

Rennie, Elizabeth. "All Fired UP: Why Food and Beverage Professionals Must Put S&OP on the Menu." *APICS Magazine* (July/August 2006a), pp. 32–35.

Rennie, Elizabeth. "Remote Possibilities: Improved Logistics Management Leads to Promising New Distribution Activities." *APICS Magazine* (July/August 2006b), pp. 36–37.

Singhal, Jaya, and Kalyan Singhal. "Holt, Modigliani, Muth, and Simon's Work and Its Role in the Renaissance and Evolution of Operations Management." *Journal of Operations Management*, vol. 25, no. 2 (March 2007), pp. 300–309.

Slone, Reuben, John T. Mentzer, and J. Paul Dittmann. "Are You the Weakest Link in Your Company's Supply Chain?" *Harvard Business Review* (October, 2007), pp.1–11.

Smith, Larry, Joseph C. Andraski, and E. Fawcett. "Integrated Business Planning: A Roadmap to Linking S&OP and CPFR." *Business Forecasting*, vol. 29, no. 4 (Winter 2011), pp. 1–17.

Takey, Flavia, and Marco A. Mesquita. "Aggregate Planning for a Large Food Manufacturer with High Seasonal Demand." *Brazilian Journal of Operations & Production Management*, vol. 3, no. 1 (2006), pp. 5–20.

Trottman, Melanie. "Choices in Stormy Weather: How Airline Employees Make Hundreds of Decisions to Cancel or Reroute Flights." *Wall Street Journal* (February 14, 2006), pp. B1–B3.

Wallace, Thomas F., and Robert A. Stahl. "Sales Forecasting: Improving Cooperation Between the Demand People and the Supply People." *Foresight*, no. 12 (Winter, 2009), pp. 14–20.

Wallace, Thomas F., and Robert A. Stahl. *Sales & Operations Planning: The How-To Handbook*, 3rd ed. Cincinnati, OH: T. F. Wallace & Company, 2008.

Supplement D: Linear Programming

Anderson, D. R., D. J. Sweeney, T. A. Williams, J. D. Camm, and R. Kipp Martin. *An Introduction to Management Science: A Quantitative Approach to Decision Making*, 13th ed. Cincinnati: South-Western, 2011.

Hillier, Fredrick S., and Mark S. Hillier. *Introduction to Management Science: A Modeling and Case Studies Approach with Spreadsheets*, 5th ed. Burr Ridge, IL: McGraw Hill, 2013.

Ragsdale, Cliff. *Spreadsheet Modeling & Decision Analysis: A Practical Introduction to Management Science*, 6th ed. Cincinnati, OH: South-Western, 2011.

Render, Barry, Ralph M. Stair, and Michael E. Hanna. *Quantitative Analysis for Management*, 12th ed. Upper Saddle River, NJ: Prentice Hall, 2014.

Winston, Wayne L., and S. Christian Albright. *Practical Management Science*, 4th ed. Belmont, CA: Duxbury Press, 2012.

Chapter 11: Resource Planning

Becker, Nathan. "iPad's Bill of Materials Close to first iPad." *Wall Street Journal Online* http://online.wsj.com/articles/SB10001424052748704893604576200132535033172 (March 14, 2011).

Bendoly, E., and M. Cotteleer. "Understanding Behavioral Sources of Process Variation following Enterprise System Deployment." *Journal of Operations Management*, vol. 26, no. 1 (2008), pp. 23–44.

Collins, David J., and Cynthia A. Montgomery. "Competing on Resources." *Harvard Business Review*, vol. 86, no. 7 (2008), pp. 140–150.

Davenport, Thomas H. "Putting the Enterprise into the Enterprise System." *Harvard Business Review* (July/August 1998), pp. 121–131.

Hendricks, Kevin B., Vinod R. Singhal, and Jeff K. Stratman. "The Impact of Enterprise Systems on Corporate Performance: A Study of ERP, SCM and CRM System Implementations." *Journal of Operations Management*, vol. 25, no. 1 (2007), pp. 65–82.

Jacobs, F. Robert, William Berry, and D. Clay Whybark. *Manufacturing Planning and Control Systems for Supply Chain Management*, 6th ed. New York: McGraw-Hill/Irwin, 2010.

Jacobs, F. Robert, and F. C. (Ted) Weston Jr. "Enterprise Resource Planning (ERP)—A Brief History." *Journal of Operations Management*, vol. 25, no. 2 (2007), pp. 357–363.

Mabert, Vincent A. "The Early Road to Materials Requirements Planning." *Journal of Operations Management*, vol. 25, no. 2 (2007), pp. 346–356.

McAfee, A., and E. Brynjolfsson. "Investing in the IT That Makes a Competitive Advantage." *Harvard Business Review*, vol. 86 (July/August 2008), pp. 98–107.

McCue, Andy. "Too Much Candy: IT Glitch Costs Cadbury." *BusinessWeek* (June 8, 2006).

Scalle, Cedric X., and Mark J. Cotteleer. *Enterprise Resource Planning (ERP)*. Boston, MA: Harvard Business School Publishing, 1999, No. 9-699-020.

Simons, Robert. "Choosing the Right Customer." *Harvard Business Review*, vol. 92, no. 3 (2014), pp. 48–55.

Wallace, Thomas F. *Sales & Operations Planning: The How-To Handbook*, 3rd ed. Cincinnati, OH: T. F. Wallace & Company, 2008.

Wallace, Thomas F., and Robert A. Stahl. *Master Scheduling in the 21st Century*. Cincinnati, OH: T. F. Wallace & Company, 2003.

Chapter 12: Supply Chain Design

Aron, Ravi, and Jitendra V. Singh. "Getting Offshoring Right." *Harvard Business Review* (December 2005), pp. 135–143.

de Waart, Dick, and Steve Kemper. "5 Steps to Service Supply Chain Excellence." *Supply Chain Management Review* (January/February 2004), pp. 28–35.

Duray, Rebecca. "Mass Customization Origins: Mass or Custom Manufacturing?" *International Journal of Operations and Production Management*, vol. 22, no. 3 (2002), pp. 314–328.

Ellram, Lisa M., and Baohong Liu. "The Financial Impact of Supply Management." *Supply Chain Management Review* (November/December 2002), pp. 30–37.

Fisher, Marshall L. "What Is the Right Supply Chain for Your Product?" *Harvard Business Review* (March/April 1997), pp. 105–116.

Flynn, Laurie J. "Built to Order." *Knowledge Management* (December 11, 2000), http://www.destinationkm.com.

Garber, Randy, and Suman Sarkar. "Want a More Flexible Supply Chain?" *Supply Chain Management Review* (January/February 2007), pp. 28–34.

George, Katy, Sree Ramaswamy, and Lou Rassey, "Next-shoring: A Ceo's Guide." *McKinsey Quarterly* (January 2014), pp. 1–8.

Glatzel, Christoph, Jocher Großpietsch, and Ildefonso Silva. "Is Your Top Team Undermining Your Supply Chain?" *McKinsey Quarterly* (January 2011), pp. 1–6.

Goel, Ajay K., Nazgol Moussavi, and Vats N. Srivastan. "Time to Rethink Offshoring?" *McKinsey on Business Technology: Innovations in IT Management*, no. 14 (Winter 2008), pp. 32–35.

Grey, William, Kaan Katircioglu, Dailun Shi, Sugato Bagchi, Guillermo Gallego, Mark Adelhelm, Dave Seybold, and Stavros Stefanis. "Beyond ROI." *Supply Chain Management Review* (March/April 2003), pp. 20–27.

Hartly-Urquhart, Roland. "Managing the Financial Supply Chain." *Supply Chain Management Review* (September 2006), pp. 18–25.

Hartvigsen, David. *SimQuick: Process Simulation with Excel*, 2nd ed. Upper Saddle River, NJ: Prentice Hall, 2004.

Hofman, Debra. "Supply Chain Measurement: Turning Data into Action." *Supply Chain Management Review* (November 2007), pp. 20–26.

Johnson, P., and M. Leenders. "Minding the Supply Savings Gaps." *MIT Sloan Management Review*, vol. 51, no. 2 (2010), pp. 25–31.

Lacity, M., and L. Willcocks. "Outsourcing Business Processes for Innovation." *MIT Sloan Management Review*, vol. 54, no. 3 (2013), pp. 63–69.

Lee, Hau L. "The Triple-A Supply Chain." *Harvard Business Review* (October 2004), pp. 102–112.

Lindgreen, A., and J. Vanhamme. "Go Configure: The Mix of Purchasing Practices to Choose for Your Supply Base." *California Management Review*, vol. 55, no. 2 (2013), pp. 72–96.

Malik, Yogesh, Alex Niemeyer, and Brian Ruwadi. "Building the Supply Chain of the Future," *McKinsey Quarterly* (January 2011), pp. 1–6.

Melnyk, S., E. Davis, R. Spekman, and J. Sandor. "Outcome-Driven Supply Chains." *MIT Sloan Management Review*, vol. 51, no. 2 (2010), pp. 33–38.

Rackly, Michael. "Guest Commentary: The Next Big thing in Manufacturing? On-Shoring," http://logisticsviewpoints.com (April 16, 2013).

Reeve, James M., and Mandyam M. Srinivasan. "Which Supply Chain Design Is Right for You?" *Supply Chain Management Review* (May/June 2005), pp. 50–57.

Roberts, Dexter. "China's Factory Blues." *BusinessWeek* (April 7, 2008), pp. 78–82.

Simchi-levi, D., Clayton, A., and Raven, B. "When One Size Does Not Fit All." *MIT Sloan Management Review*, vol. 54, no. 2 (2013), pp. 15–17.

Slone, Reuben E., John T. Mentzer, and J. Paul Dittmann. "Are You the Weakest Link in Your Supply Chain?" *Harvard Business Review* (September 2007), pp. 116–127.

Stackhouse-Kaeible, Steve. "Right Shoring: The Regionalization of the High-Tech Supply Chain," http://www.areadevelopment.com/HoghTechNanoElectronics/Q3-2013 (Q3/Summer 2013), pp. 1–4.

Stavrulaki, Euthemia, and Mark Davis. "Aligning Products with Supply Chain Processes and Strategy." *The International Journal of Logistics Management*, vol. 21, no. 1 (2010), pp. 127–151.

Tiede, Tom, and Kay Ree Lee. "What Is an Optimal Distribution Network Strategy?" *Supply Chain Management Review* (November 2005), pp. 32–39.

Zirpoli, F., and M. Becker. "What Happens When You Outsource Too Much?" *MIT Sloan Management Review*, vol. 52, no. 2 (2011), pp. 59–64.

Chapter 13: Supply Chain Logistic Networks

Agrawal, A., A. Meyer, A. De, and L. N. Van Wassenhove. "Managing Value in Supply Chains." *California Management Review*, vol. 56, no. 2 (2014), pp. 23–54.

Chittum, Ryan. "Location, Location, and Technology: Where to Put That New Store? Site-Selection Software May Be Able to Help." *Wall Street Journal* (July 18, 2005), p. R7.

Deeds, David. "Increasing the Rate of New Venture Creation: Does Location Matter?" *Academy of Management Executive*, vol. 18, no. 2 (2004), pp. 152–154.

"Doing Well by Doing Good." *The Economist* (April 22, 2000), pp. 65–67.

Galuszka, P. "The South Shall Rise Again." *Chief Executive* (November 2004), pp. 50–54.

Gavet, M. "How We Did It... The CEO of Ozon on Building an E-commerce Giant in a Cash-only Economy." *Harvard Business Review*, vol. 92, no. 7 (2014), pp. 38–41.

Hahn, E. D., and K. Bunyaratavej. "Services Cultural Alignment in Offshoring: The Impact of Cultural Dimensions on Offshoring Location Decisions." *Journal of Operations Management*, vol. 28, no. 3 (2010), pp. 186–193.

Lovelock, Christopher H., and George S. Yip. "Developing Global Strategies for Service Businesses." *California Management Review*, vol. 38, no. 2 (1996), pp. 64–86.

"Manager's Journal: Why BMW Cruised into Spartanburg." *Wall Street Journal* (July 6, 1992), p. A10.

"MapInfo Delivers Location Intelligence for Marco's Pizza." *Directions Magazine* (December 14, 2004), http://www.directionsmag.com/press.releases/?duty=Show&id=10790.

Melo, M. T., S. Nickel, and F. Saldanha-da-Gama. "Facility Location and Supply Chain Management a Review." *European Journal of Operational Research*, vol. 196, no. 2 (2009), pp. 401–412.

Rubinstein, Ed. "Chain Chart Their Course of Actions with Geographic Information Systems." *Nation's Restaurant News*, vol. 32, no. 6 (1998), p. 49.

Southerland, R., "The Science of Site Selection." *National Real Estate Investor* http://nreionline.com/technology/science-site-selection (October 11, 2002).

Chapter 14: Supply Chain Integration

Altug, M. S., and G. van Ryzin. "Is Revenue Sharing Right for Your Supply Chain?" *California Management Review*, vol. 56, no. 4 (2014), pp. 53–81.

Amadeo, Kimberly. "What are Commodities Futures?", http://useconomy.about.com (2014).

Anderson, J., J. Narus, and M. Wouters. "Tiebreaker Selling." *Harvard Business Review*, vol. 92, no. 3 (2014), pp. 90–96.

Anderson, J., J. Narus, and M. Wouters. "What You Can Learn from Your Customer's Customer." *MIT Sloan Management Review*, vol. 54, no. 2 (2013), pp. 75–82.

Bowersox, Donald. *Supply Chain Logistics Management*, 4th ed. New York: McGraw-Hill, 2012.

Brienzi, Mark, and Dr. Sham Kekre. "How Kodak Transformed Its Service Parts Supply Chain." *Supply Chain Management Review* (October 2005), pp. 25–32.

Chick, S. "Europe's Solution Factories." *Harvard Business Review*, vol. 92, no. 4 (2014), pp. 111–115.

Choi, T., and T. Linton. "Don't Let your Supply Chain Control Your Business." *Harvard Business Review*, vol. 89, no. 12 (2011), pp. 112–117.

Chopra, Sunil, and ManMohan S. Sodhi. "Looking for the Bang from the RFID Buck." *Supply Chain Management Review* (May/June 2007), pp. 34–41.

Chopra, Sunil, and Peter Meindl. *Supply Chain Management*, 5th ed. Upper Saddle River, NJ: Prentice Hall, 2012.

CME Group. "Managing Price Risk along the Steel Supply Chain," http://www.cmegroup.com/futures (2012).

Cook, Robert L., Brian Gibson, and Douglas MacCurdy. "A Lean Approach to Cross-Docking." *Supply Chain Management Review* (March 2005), pp. 54–59.

Doheny, Mike, Venu Nagali, and Florian Weig. "Agile Operations for Volatile Times," *McKinsey Quarterly*, http://www.mckinsey.com (May 2012).

Fleck, Thomas. "Supplier Collaboration in Action at IBM." *Supply Chain Management Review* (March 2008), pp. 30–37.

Freund, Brian C., and June M. Freund. "Hands-On VMI." *APICS—The Performance Advantage* (March 2003), pp. 34–39.

Fugate, Brian S., and John T. Mentzer. "Dell's Supply Chain DNA." *Supply Chain Management Review* (October 2004), pp. 20–24.

Gil, N. "Developing Cooperative Project Client-Supplier Relationships: How Much to Expect from Relational Contracts." *California Management Review*, vol. 51 no. 2 (2009), pp. 144–170.

Handfield, Robert B., and Kevin McCormack. "What you Need to Know about Sourcing from China." *Supply Chain Management Review* (September 2005), pp. 28–33.

Hartvigsen, David. *SimQuick: Process Simulation with Excel*, 2nd ed. Upper Saddle River, NJ: Prentice Hall, 2004.

Henke Jr., John W., and C. Zhang. "Increasing Supplier-Driven Innovation." *MIT Sloan Management Review*, vol. 51, no. 2 (2010), pp. 41–46.

Lee, Hau L. "The Triple-A Supply Chain." *Harvard Business Review* (October 2004), pp. 102–112.

Liker, Jeffrey K., and Thomas Y. Choi. "Building Deep Supplier Relationships." *Harvard Business Review* (December 2004), pp. 104–113.

Malik, Yogesh, Alex Niemeyer, and Brian Ruwadi. "Building the Supply Chain of the Future." *McKinsey Quarterly* (January 2011), pp. 1–10.

Maloni, M. J., and W.C. Benton. "Power Influences in the Supply Chain." *Journal of Business Logistics*, vol. 21 (2000), pp. 49–73.

Melnyk, Steven, Robert Sroufe, and Roger Calantone. "Assessing the Impact of Environmental Management Systems on Corporate and Environmental Performance." *Journal of Operations Management*, vol. 21, no. 3 (2003), pp. 329-351.

Miller, Jamey. "Shared Success: Working Together to Find the Value of VMI." *APICS Magazine* (November/December 2007), pp. 37-39.

Murphy-Hoye, Mary, Hau L. Lee, and James B. Rice, Jr. "A Real-World Look at RFID." *Supply Chain Management Review* (July/August 2005), pp. 18-26.

Randall, Taylor, Serguei Netessine, and Nils Rudi. "Should You Take the Virtual Fulfillment Path?" *Supply Chain Management Review* (November/December 2002), pp. 54-58.

Simchi-Levi, David, Ioannis M. Kyratzoglou, and Constantine G. Vassiliadis. "Supply Chains and Risk Management," MIT Forum for Supply Chain Innovation 2013, Massachusetts Institute of Technology.

Sullivan, Laurie. "Walmart's Way." *Informationweek.com* (September 27, 2004), pp. 37-50.

Thomke, S., and D. Reinertsen. "Six myths of Product Development." *Harvard Business Review*, vol. 90, no. 5 (2012), pp. 84-94.

Trent, Robert J. "What Everyone Needs to Know about SCM." *Supply Chain Management Review* (March 2004), pp. 52–59.

Tripathi, Abhishek, and Akash P. Wani. "Hedging: A Powerful Tool in Supply Chain manager's Arsenal," http://c2xnitie.wordpress.com (2013).

Wagner, Richard H. "An Interview with Dirk Brand: Hotel Manager of Queen Mary 2." *Beyondships.com* (December 2007), pp. 1-4.

Wallingford, Jeff. "Viewpoint: Managing Currency Risk in the Supply Chain." *Industry Week*, http://www.industryweek.com (June 25, 2012).

Chapter 15: Supply Chain Sustainability

Atasu, A. "So What If Remanufacturing Cannibalizes My New Product Sales." *California Management Review*, vol. 52, no. 2 (2010), pp. 56-77.

Beamon, Benita M. "Environmental and Sustainability Ethics in Supply Chain Management." *Science and Engineering Ethics*, vol. 11 (2005), pp. 221-234.

Beschorner, Thomas, and Martin Muller. "Social Standards: Toward an Active Ethical Involvement of Business in Developing Countries." *Journal of Business Ethics*, vol. 73 (2006), pp. 11-23.

Bonini, Sheila, Steven Gorner, and Alissa Jones. "How Companies Manage Sustainability." *McKinsey & Company Global Survey Results* (February 2010), pp. 1-8.

Carter, C. R., and M. M. Jennings. "The Role of Purchasing in Corporate Social Responsibility." *Journal of Business Logistics*, vol. 25, no. 1 (2004), pp. 145-186.

Conner, Martin P. "The Supply Chain's Role in Leveraging Product Life Cycle Management." *Supply Chain Management Review* (March 2004), pp. 36-43.

Curkovic, Sime, and Robert Sroufe. "Using ISO 14001 to Promote a Sustainable Supply Chain." *Business Strategy and the Environment*, vol. 20 (2011), pp. 71-93.

Day, J. M., I. Junglas, and L. Silva. "Information Flow Impediments in Disaster Relief Supply Chains." *Journal of the Association for Information Systems*, vol. 10, no. 8 (August 2009), pp. 637-660.

Drake, Matthew J., and John Teepen Schlachter. "A Virtue-Ethics Analysis of Supply Chain Collaboration." *Journal of Business Ethics*, vol. 82 (2007), pp. 851-864.

Ferguson, Mark. "Making Your Supply Chain More Sustainable by Closing the Loop." *The European Business Review* (November/December 2010), pp. 28-31.

Fiksel, Joseph, Douglas Lambert, Les B. Artman, John A. Harris, and Hugh M. Share. "Environmental Excellence: The New Supply Chain Edge." *Supply Chain Management Review* (July/August 2004), pp. 50-57.

"Global Responsibility," *RR Donnelley* (2010), pp. 1-21.

Golicic, S., C. Boerstler, and L. Ellram. "'Greening' Transportation in the Supply Chain." *MIT Sloan Management Review*, vol. 51, no. 2 (2010), pp. 47-55.

Handfield, Robert B., and David L. Baumer. "Managing Conflicts of Interest in Purchasing." *Journal of Supply Chain Management* (Summer 2006), pp. 41-50.

Handfield, Robert S., Walton, Robert Sroufe, and Steven Melnyk. "Applying Environmental Criteria to Supplier Assessment: A Study of the Application of the Analytical Hierarchy Process." *European Journal of Operational Research*, vol. 41, no. 1 (2002), pp. 70-87.

Hartvigsen, David. *SimQuick: Process Simulation with Excel*, 2nd ed. Upper Saddle River, NJ: Prentice Hall, 2004.

Hindo, Brian. "Everything Old Is New Again." *BusinessWeek* (September 25, 2006), pp. 64-70.

"How to Calculate the Weight Break," http://freightlogistics.wordpress.com (December 19, 2007).

Keating, B., A. Quazi, A. Kriz, and T. Coltman. "In Pursuit of a Sustainable Supply Chain: Insights from Weatpac Banking Corporation." *Research Online*, http://ro.uow.edu.au/infopapers/688 (2008).

Kulwiec, Ray. "Reverse Logistics Provides Green Benefits." *Target*, vol. 22, no. 3 (Third Issue 2006), pp. 11-20.

Lacy, Peter, Tim Cooper, Rob Hayward, and Lisa Neuberger. "A New Era of Sustainability," *UN Global Compact-Accenture CEO Study 2010* (June 2010), pp. 1-60.

Lai, K., T. Cheng, and A. Tang. "Green Retailing: Factors for Success." *California Management Review*, vol. 52, no. 2 (2010), pp. 6-32.

Lillywhite, Serena. "Responsible Supply Chain Management: Ethical Purchasing in Practice." *Brotherhood of St. Laurence* (October 2004), pp. 1-5.

Maon, Francois, Adam Lindgreen, and Joelle Vanhamme. "Supply Chains in Disaster Relief Operations: Cross-Sector Socially Oriented Collaborations." *Hull University Business School*, Research Memorandum 80 (April 2009), pp. 1-35.

Martha, Joseph, and Sunil Subbakrishna. "Targeting a Just-In-Case Supply Chain for the Inevitable Next Disaster." *Supply Chain Management Review* (September/October 2002), pp. 18-23.

Melnyk, Steven, E. W. Davis, R. E. Spekman, and J. Sandor. "Outcome Driven Supply Chains." *Sloan Management Review*, vol. 51, no. 2 (2010), pp. 33-38.

Meyer, Tobias A. "Increasing the Energy Efficiency of Supply Chains." *McKinsey Quarterly*, (August 2009), pp. 1-2.

Mollenkopf, Diane A., and David J. Closs. "The Hidden Value in Reverse Logistics." *Supply Chain Management Review* (July/August 2005), pp. 34-43.

New, S. "The Transparent Supply Chain." *Harvard Business Review*, vol. 88, no. 10 (2010), pp. 76-82.

Olcott, G., and N. Oliver. "Social Capital, Sensemaking, and Recovery: Japanese Companies and the 2011 Earthquake." *California Management Review*, vol. 56, no. 2 (2014), pp. 5-22.

Plambeck, Erica L. "The Greening of Walmart's Supply Chain." *Supply Chain Management Review* (July/August 2007), pp. 18-25.

Plambeck, Erica L, H. Lee, and P. Yatsko. "Improving Environmental Performance in Your Chinese Supply Chain." *MIT Sloan Management Review*, vol. 53, no. 2 (2012), pp. 43-51.

Rothenberg, S., and J. Ettlie. "Strategies to Cope with Regulatory Uncertainty in the Auto Industry." *California Management Review*, vol. 54, no. 1 (2011), pp. 126-145.

Sheffi, Y. "Driving Growth and Employment Through Logistics." *MIT Sloan Management Review*, vol. 54, no. 1 (2012), pp. 20-22.

Simchi-levi, D., W. Schmidt, and Y. Wei. "From Superstorms to Factory Fires." *Harvard Business Review*, vol. 92, no. 1 (2014), pp. 96-101.

"Social Accountability International—SA8000," http://www.sa-intl.org (2014).

Thomas, A., and L. Kopczak. "Life-Saving Supply Chains and the Path Forward." In H. Lee and C. Y. Lee (Eds.), *Building Supply Chain Excellence in Emerging Economies*. London: Springer Science and Business Media LLC, 2007, pp. 93-110.

Vandenbosch, M., and S. Sapp. "Opportunism Knocks." *MIT Sloan Management Review*, vol. 52, no. 1 (2000), pp. 17–19.

Van Wassenhove, L. "Humanitarian Aid Logistics: Supply Chain Management in High Gear." *Journal of the Operational Research Society*, vol. 57, no. 5 (2006), pp. 475–489.

Wagner, S. "A Strategic Framework for Spare Parts Logistics." *California Management Review*, vol. 54, no. 4 (2012), pp. 69–93.

Whybark, D. C. "Issues in Managing Disaster Relief Inventories." *International Journal of Production Economics*, vol. 108, no. 1 (July 2007), pp. 228–235.

Whybark, D. C., Steven A. Melnyk, Jamison Day, and Ed Davis. "Disaster Relief Supply Chain Management: New Realities, Management Challenges, Emerging Opportunities." *Decision Line* (May 2010), pp. 4–7.

Glossary

ABC analysis The process of dividing SKUs into three classes, according to their dollar usage, so that managers can focus on items that have the highest dollar value.

acceptable quality level (AQL) The quality level desired by the consumer.

acceptance sampling The application of statistical techniques to determine whether a quantity of material should be accepted or rejected based on the inspection or test of a sample.

action notice A computer-generated memo alerting planners about releasing new orders and adjusting the due dates of scheduled receipts.

activity The smallest unit of work effort consuming both time and resources that the project manager can schedule and control.

activity-on-node (AON) network An approach used to create a network diagram, in which nodes represent activities and arcs represent the precedence relationships between them.

activity slack The maximum length of time that an activity can be delayed without delaying the entire project, calculated as $S = LS - ES$ or $S = LF - EF$.

additive seasonal method A method in which seasonal forecasts are generated by adding a constant to the estimate of average demand per season.

advanced planning and scheduling (APS) systems Computer software systems that seek to optimize resources across the supply chain and align daily operations with strategic goals.

aggregate plan Another term for the sales and operations plan.

aggregation The act of clustering several similar services or products so that forecasts and plans can be made for whole families.

allowance time The time added to the normal time to adjust for certain factors.

annual plan (or financial plan) A plan for financial assessment used by a nonprofit service organization.

annuity A series of payments on a fixed amount for a specified number of years.

anticipation inventory Inventory used to absorb uneven rates of demand or supply.

appraisal costs Costs incurred when the firm assess the performance level of its processes.

assemble-to-order strategy A strategy for producing a wide variety of products from relatively few subassemblies and components after the customer orders are received.

assignable causes of variation Any variation-causing factors that can be identified and eliminated.

attributes Service or product characteristics that can be quickly counted for acceptable performance.

auction A marketplace where firms place competitive bids to buy something.

automation A system, process, or piece of equipment that is self-acting and self-regulating.

available-to-promise (ATP) inventory The quantity of end items that marketing can promise to deliver on specified dates.

average aggregate inventory value The total average value of all items held in inventory for a firm.

average outgoing quality (AOQ) The expected proportion of defects that the plan will allow to pass.

average outgoing quality limit (AOQL) The maximum value of the average outgoing quality over all possible values of the proportion defective.

back office A process with low customer contact and little service customization.

backlog An accumulation of customer orders that a manufacturer has promised for delivery at some future date.

backorder A customer order that cannot be filled when promised or demanded but is filled later.

backorder and stockout cost Additional costs to expedite past-due orders, the costs of lost sales, and the potential cost of losing a customer to a competitor (sometimes called loss of goodwill).

backward integration A firm's movement upstream toward the sources of raw materials, parts, and services through acquisitions.

balance delay The amount by which efficiency falls short of 100 percent.

Baldrige Performance Excellence Program A program named for the late secretary of commerce, Malcolm Baldrige, who was a strong proponent of enhancing quality as a means of reducing the trade deficit; organizations vie for an award that promotes, recognizes, and publicizes quality strategies and achievements.

bar chart A series of bars representing the frequency of occurrence of data characteristics measured on a yes-or-no basis.

base case The act of doing nothing and losing orders from any demand that exceeds current capacity, or incur costs because capacity is too large.

base-stock system An inventory control system that issues a replenishment order, Q, each time a withdrawal is made, for the same amount of the withdrawal.

batch process A process that differs from the job process with respect to volume, variety, and quantity.

benchmarking A systematic procedure that measures a firm's processes, services, and products against those of industry leaders.

bill of materials (BOM) A record of all the components of an item, the parent–component relationships, and the usage quantities derived from engineering and process designs.

bill of resources (BOR) A record of a service firm's parent–component relationships and all of the materials, equipment time, staff, and other resources associated with them, including usage quantities.

binding constraint A constraint that helps form the optimal corner point; it limits the ability to improve the objective function.

Black Belt An employee who reached the highest level of training in a Six Sigma program and spends all of his or her time teaching and leading teams involved in Six Sigma projects.

block plan A plan that allocates available space to operations and indicates their placement relative to each other.

bottleneck A capacity constraint resource (CCR) whose available capacity limits the organization's ability to meet the product volume, product mix, or demand fluctuation required by the marketplace.

brainstorming Letting a group of people, knowledgeable about the process, propose ideas for change by saying whatever comes to mind.

break-even analysis The use of the break-even quantity; it can be used to compare processes by finding the volume at which two different processes have equal total costs.

break-even quantity The volume at which total revenues equal total costs.

bullwhip effect The phenomenon in supply chains whereby ordering patterns experience increasing variance as you proceed upstream in the chain.

business plan A projected statement of income, costs, and profits.

c-chart A chart used for controlling the number of defects when more than one defect can be present in a service or product.

capacity The maximum rate of output of a process or a system.

capacity cushion The amount of reserve capacity a process uses to handle sudden increases in demand or temporary losses of production capacity; it measures the amount by which the average utilization (in terms of total capacity) falls below 100 percent.

capacity gap Positive or negative difference between projected demand and current capacity.

capacity requirement What a process's capacity should be for some future time period to meet the demand of customers (external or internal), given the firm's desired capacity cushion.

capacity requirements planning (CRP) A technique used for projecting time-phased capacity requirements for workstations; its purpose is to match the material requirements plan with the capacity of key processes.

capital intensity The mix of equipment and human skills in a process.

carbon footprint The total amount of greenhouse gasses produced to support operations, usually expressed in equivalent tons of carbon dioxide (CO_2).

cash flow The difference between the flows of funds into and out of an organization over a period of time, including revenues, costs, and changes in assets and liabilities.

catalog hubs A system whereby suppliers post their catalog of items on the Internet and buyers select what they need and purchase them electronically.

causal methods A quantitative forecasting method that uses historical data on independent variables, such as promotional campaigns, economic conditions, and competitors' actions, to predict demand.

cause-and-effect diagram A diagram that relates a key performance problem to its potential causes.

center of gravity A good starting point to evaluate locations in the target area using the load–distance model.

centralized placement Keeping all the inventory of a product at a single location such as a firm's manufacturing plant or a warehouse and shipping directly to each of its customers.

certainty The word that is used to describe that a fact is known without doubt.

channel One or more facilities required to perform a given service.

channel assembly The process of using members of the distribution channel as if they were assembly stations in the factory.

chase strategy A strategy that involves hiring and laying off employees to match the demand forecast.

checklist A form used to record the frequency of occurrence of certain process failures.

close out An activity that includes writing final reports, completing remaining deliverables, and compiling the team's recommendations for improving the project process.

closed-loop supply chain A supply chain that integrates forward logistics with reverse logistics, thereby focusing on the complete chain of operations from the birth to the death of a product.

closeness matrix A table that gives a measure of the relative importance of each pair of operations being located close together.

collaborative planning, forecasting, and replenishment (CPFR) A process for supply chain integration that allows a supplier and its customers to collaborate on making the forecast by using the Internet.

combination forecasts Forecasts that are produced by averaging independent forecasts based on different methods, different sources, or different data.

common causes of variation The purely random, unidentifiable sources of variation that are unavoidable with the current process.

competitive capabilities The cost, quality, time, and flexibility dimensions that a process or supply chain actually possesses and is able to deliver.

competitive orientation A supplier relation that views negotiations between buyer and seller as a zero-sum game: Whatever one side loses, the other side gains, and short-term advantages are prized over long-term commitments.

competitive priorities The critical dimensions that a process or supply chain must possess to satisfy its internal or external customers, both now and in the future.

complementary products Services or products that have similar resource requirements but different demand cycles.

component An item that goes through one or more operations to be transformed into or become part of one or more parents.

compounding interest The process by which interest on an investment accumulates and then earns interest itself for the remainder of the investment period.

concurrent engineering A concept that brings product engineers, process engineers, marketers, buyers, information specialists, quality specialists, and suppliers together to design a product and the processes that will meet customer expectations.

consistent quality Producing services or products that meet design specifications on a consistent basis.

constraint Any factor that limits the performance of a system and restricts its output. In linear programming, a limitation that restricts the permissible choices for the decision variables.

consumer's risk (β) The probability of accepting a lot with LTPD quality (a type II error).

continuous flow process The extreme end of high-volume standardized production and rigid line flows, with production not starting and stopping for long time intervals.

continuous improvement The philosophy of continually seeking ways to improve processes based on a Japanese concept called *kaizen*.

continuous review (Q) system A system designed to track the remaining inventory of a SKU each time a withdrawal is made to determine whether it is time to reorder.

control chart A time-ordered diagram that is used to determine whether observed variations are abnormal.

cooperative orientation A supplier relation in which the buyer and seller are partners, each helping the other as much as possible.

core competencies The unique resources and strengths that an organization's management considers when formulating strategy.

core process A set of activities that delivers value to external customers.

corner point A point that lies at the intersection of two (or possibly more) constraint lines on the boundary of the feasible region.

crash cost (CC) The activity cost associated with the crash time.

crash time (CT) The shortest possible time to complete an activity.

critical mass A situation whereby several competing firms clustered in one location attract more customers than the total number who would shop at the same stores at scattered locations.

critical path The sequence of activities between a project's start and finish that takes the longest time to complete.

critical path method (CPM) A network planning method developed in the 1950s as a means of scheduling maintenance shutdowns at chemical-processing plants.

critical ratio (CR) A ratio that is calculated by dividing the time remaining until a job's due date by the total shop time remaining for the job, which is defined as the setup, processing, move, and expected waiting times of all remaining operations, including the operation being scheduled

cross-docking The packing of products on incoming shipments so that they can be easily sorted at intermediate warehouses for outgoing shipments based on their final destinations.

cumulative sum of forecast errors (CFE) A measurement of the total forecast error that asses the bias in a forecast.

customer contact The extent to which the customer is present, is actively involved, and receives personal attention during the service process.

customer involvement The ways in which customers become part of the process and the extent of their participation.

customer population An input that generates potential customers.

customer relationship process A process that identifies, attracts, and builds relationships with external customers and facilitates the placement of orders by customers; sometimes referred to as *customer relationship management*.

customization Satisfying the unique needs of each customer by changing service or product designs.

cycle counting An inventory control method, whereby storeroom personnel physically count a small percentage of the total number of items each day, correcting errors that they find.

cycle inventory The portion of total inventory that varies directly with lot size.

cycle-service level See service level.

cycle time The maximum time allowed for work on a unit at each station.

decision theory A general approach to decision making when the outcomes associated with alternatives are often in doubt.

decision tree A schematic model of alternatives available to the decision maker, along with their possible consequences.

decision variables Variables that represent the choices the decision maker can control.

defect Any instance when a process fails to satisfy its customer.

degeneracy A condition that occurs when the number of nonzero variables in the optimal solution is less than the number of constraints.

delivery speed Quickly filling a customer's order.

Delphi method A process of gaining consensus from a group of experts while maintaining their anonymity.

demand management The process of changing demand patterns using one or more demand options.

dependent demand The demand for an item that occurs because the quantity required varies with the production plans for other items held in the firm's inventory.

dependent demand items Items whose required quantity varies with the production plans for other items held in the firm's inventory.

dependent variable The variable that one wants to forecast.

design-to-order strategy A strategy that involves designing new products that do not currently exist, and then manufacturing them to meet unique customer specifications.

development speed Quickly introducing a new service or a product.

discount rate The interest rate used in discounting the future value to its present value.

discounting The process of finding the present value of an investment when the future value and the interest rate are known.

diseconomies of scale Occurs when the average cost per unit increases as the facility's size increases.

distribution center A warehouse or stocking point where goods are stored for subsequent distribution to manufacturers, wholesalers, retailers, and customers.

double-sampling plan A sampling plan in which management specifies two sample sizes and two acceptance numbers; if the quality of the lot is very good or very bad, the consumer can make a decision to accept or reject the lot on the basis of the first sample, which is smaller than in the single-sampling plan.

drum-buffer-rope (DBR) A planning and control system that regulates the flow of work-in-process materials at the bottleneck or the capacity constrained resource (CCR) in a productive system.

earliest due date (EDD) A priority sequencing rule that specifies that the job or customer with the earliest due date is the next job to be processed.

earliest finish time (EF) An activity's earliest start time plus its estimated duration, t, or $EF = ES + t$.

earliest start time (ES) The earliest finish time of the immediately preceding activity.

early supplier involvement A program that includes suppliers in the design phase of a service or product.

economic order quantity (EOQ) The lot size that minimizes total annual inventory holding and ordering costs.

economic production lot size (ELS) The optimal lot size in a situation in which replenishment is not instantaneous.

economies of scale A concept that states that the average unit cost of a service or good can be reduced by increasing its output rate.

economies of scope Economies that reflect the ability to produce multiple products more cheaply in combination than separately.

electronic commerce (e-commerce) The application of information and communication technology anywhere along the supply chain of business processes.

electronic data interchange (EDI) A technology that enables the transmission of routine business documents having a standard format from computer to computer over telephone or direct leased lines.

elemental standard data A database of standards compiled by a firm's analysts for basic elements that they can draw on later to estimate the time required for a particular job, which is most appropriate when products or services are highly customized, job processes prevail, and process divergence is great.

employee empowerment An approach to teamwork that moves responsibility for decisions further down the organizational chart—to the level of the employee actually doing the job.

end item The final product sold to a customer.

enterprise process A companywide process that cuts across functional areas, business units, geographical regions, and product lines.

enterprise resource planning (ERP) systems Large, integrated information systems that support many enterprise processes and data storage needs.

environmental responsibility An element of sustainability that addresses the ecological needs of the planet and the firm's stewardship of the natural resources used in the production of services and products.

ethical failure costs Societal and monetary costs associated with *deceptively* passing defective services or products to internal or external customers such that it jeopardizes the well being of stockholders, customers, employees, partners, and creditors.

Euclidean distance The straight-line distance, or shortest possible path, between two points.

exchange An electronic marketplace where buying firms and selling firms come together to do business.

executive opinion A forecasting method in which the opinions, experience, and technical knowledge of one or more managers are summarized to arrive at a single forecast.

expediting The process of completing a job or finishing with a customer sooner than would otherwise be done.

exponential smoothing method A weighted moving average method that calculates the average of a time series by implicitly giving recent demands more weight than earlier demands.

external customers A customer who is either an end user or an intermediary (e.g., manufacturers, financial institutions, or retailers) buying the firm's finished services or products.

external failure costs Costs that arise when a defect is discovered after the customer receives the service or product.

external suppliers The businesses or individuals who provide the resources, services, products, and materials for the firm's short-term and long-term needs.

facility location The process of determining geographic sites for a firm's operations.

feasible region A region that represents all permissible combinations of the decision variables in a linear programming model.

financial responsibility An element of sustainability that addresses the financial needs of the shareholders, employees, customers, business partners, financial institutions, and any other entity that supplies the capital for the production of services or products or relies on the firm for wages or reimbursements.

finished goods (FG) The items in manufacturing plants, warehouses, and retail outlets that are sold to the firm's customers.

first-come, first served (FCFS) A priority sequencing rule that specifies that the job or customer arriving at the workstation first has the highest priority.

five S (5S) A methodology consisting of five workplace practices—sorting, straightening, shining, standardizing, and sustaining—that are conducive to visual controls and lean production.

fixed automation A manufacturing process that produces one type of part or product in a fixed sequence of simple operations.

fixed cost The portion of the total cost that remains constant regardless of changes in levels of output.

fixed order quantity (FOQ) A rule that maintains the same order quantity each time an order is issued.

fixed schedule A schedule that calls for each employee to work the same days and hours each week.

flexible flow The customers, materials, or information move in diverse ways, with the path of one customer or job often crisscrossing the path that the next one takes.

flexible (or programmable) automation A manufacturing process that can be changed easily to handle various products.

flexible workforce A workforce whose members are capable of doing many tasks, either at their own workstations or as they move from one workstation to another.

flow shop A manufacturer's operation that specializes in medium- to high-volume production and utilizes line or continuous flow processes.

flow time The amount of time a job spends in the service or manufacturing system.

flowchart A diagram that traces the flow of information, customers, equipment, or materials through the various steps of a process.

focus forecasting A method of forecasting that selects the best forecast from a group of forecasts generated by individual techniques.

focused factories The result of a firm's splitting large plants that produced all the company's products into several specialized smaller plants.

forecast A prediction of future events used for planning purposes

forecast error The difference found by subtracting the forecast from actual demand for a given period.

forward integration Acquiring more channels of distribution, such as distribution centers (warehouses) and retail stores, or even business customers.

forward placement Locating stock closer to customers at a warehouse, DC, wholesaler, or retailer.

front office A process with high customer contact where the service provider interacts directly with the internal or external customer.

future value of an investment The value of an investment at the end of the period over which interest is compounded.

futures contract A contractual agreement, generally made on the trading floor of a futures exchange, to buy or sell a particular commodity or financial instrument at a pre-determined price in the future.

Gantt chart A project schedule, usually created by the project manager using computer software, that superimposes project activities, with their precedence relationships and estimated duration times, on a time line.

geographical information system (GIS) A system of computer software, hardware, and data that the firm's personnel can use to manipulate, analyze, and present information relevant to a location decision.

graphic method of linear programming A type of graphic analysis that involves the following five steps: plotting the constraints, identifying the feasible region, plotting an objective function line, finding a visual solution, and finding the algebraic solution.

graphs Representations of data in a variety of pictorial forms, such as line charts and pie charts.

Green Belt An employee who achieved the first level of training in a Six Sigma program and spends part of his or her time teaching and helping teams with their projects.

green purchasing The process of identifying, assessing, and managing the flow of environmental waste and finding ways to reduce it and minimize its impact on the environment.

gross requirements The total demand derived from *all* parent production plans.

group technology (GT) An option for achieving line flow layouts with low volume processes; this technique creates cells not limited to just one worker and has a unique way of selecting work to be done by the cell.

hedging A supply chain risk management strategy used in limiting or offsetting the probability of loss from fluctuations in the prices of commodities or currencies.

heijunka The leveling of production load by both volume and product mix.

hiring and layoff cost Costs of advertising jobs, interviews, training programs for new employees, scrap caused by the inexperience of new employees, loss of productivity, and initial paperwork. Layoff costs include the costs of exit interviews, severance pay, retaining and retraining remaining workers and managers, and lost productivity.

histogram A summarization of data measured on a continuous scale, showing the frequency distribution of some process failure (in statistical terms, the central tendency and dispersion of the data).

holdout sample Actual demands from the more recent time periods in the time series that are set aside to test different models developed from the earlier time periods.

humanitarian logistics The process of planning, implementing, and controlling the efficient, cost-effective flow and storage of goods and materials, as well as related information, from the point of origin to the point of consumption for the purpose of alleviating the suffering of vulnerable people.

hurdle rate The interest rate that is the lowest desired return on an investment; the hurdle over which the investment must pass.

hybrid office A process with moderate levels of customer contact and standard services with some options available.

immediate predecessors Work elements that must be done before the next element can begin.

independent demand items Items for which demand is influenced by market conditions and is not related to the inventory decisions for any other item held in stock or produced.

independent variables Variables that are assumed to affect the dependent variable and thereby "cause" the results observed in the past.

industrial robot Versatile, computer-controlled machine programmed to perform various tasks.

interarrival times The time between customer arrivals.

intermediate item An item that has at least one parent and at least one component.

intermodal shipments Mixing the modes of transportation for a given shipment, such as moving shipping containers or truck trailers on rail cars.

internal customers One or more employees or processes that rely on inputs from other employees or processes to perform their work.

internal failure costs Costs resulting from defects that are discovered during the production of a service or product.

internal rate of return (IRR) The discount rate that makes the NPV of a project zero.

internal suppliers The employees or processes that supply important information or materials to a firm's processes.

inventory A stock of materials used to satisfy customer demand or to support the production of services or goods.

inventory holding cost The sum of the cost of capital and the variable costs of keeping items on hand, such as storage and handling, taxes, insurance, and shrinkage.

inventory management The planning and controlling of inventories to meet the competitive priorities of the organization.

inventory pooling A reduction in inventory and safety stock because of the merging of variable demands from customers.

inventory position (IP) The measurement of a SKU's ability to satisfy future demand.

inventory record A record that shows an item's lot-size policy, lead time, and various time-phased data.

inventory turnover An inventory measure obtained by dividing annual sales at cost by the average aggregate inventory value maintained during the year.

ISO 9001:2008 A set of standards governing documentation of a quality program.

ISO 140001:2004 Documentation standards that require participating companies to keep track of their raw materials use and their generation, treatment, and disposal of hazardous wastes.

ISO 28000:2007 A set of requirements for a supply chain security management system that includes aspects of financing, manufacturing, information systems, and the facilities for packing, storing, and transferring goods between modes of transportation and locations.

jidoka Automatically stopping the process when something is wrong and then fixing the problems on the line itself as they occur.

JIT system A system that organizes the resources, information flows, and decision rules that enable a firm to realize the benefits of JIT principles.

job process A process with the flexibility needed to produce a wide variety of products in significant quantities, with considerable divergence in the steps performed.

job shop A manufacturer's operation that specializes in low- to medium-volume production and utilizes job or batch processes.

Johnson's rule A procedure that minimizes makespan when scheduling a group of jobs on two workstations.

judgment methods A forecasting method that translates the opinions of managers, expert opinions, consumer surveys, and salesforce estimates into quantitative estimates.

judgmental adjustment An adjustment made to forecasts from one or more quantitative models that accounts for recognizing which models are performing particularly well in recent past, or take into account contextual information.

just-in-time (JIT) philosophy The belief that waste can be eliminated by cutting unnecessary capacity or inventory and removing non-value-added activities in operations.

kanban A Japanese word meaning "card" or "visible record" that refers to cards used to control the flow of production through a factory.

labor-limited environment An environment in which the resource constraint is the amount of labor available, not the number of machines or workstations.

latest finish time (LF) The latest start time of the activity that immediately follows.

latest start time (LS) The latest finish time minus its estimated duration, t, or $LS = LF - t$.

layout The physical arrangement of operations (or departments) relative to each other.

lead time The elapsed time between the receipt of a customer order and filling it.

lean systems Operations systems that maximize the value added by each of a company's activities by removing waste and delays from them.

learning curve A line that displays the relationship between processing time and the cumulative quantity of a product or service produced.

level strategy A strategy that keeps the workforce constant, but varies its utilization with overtime, undertime, and vacation planning to match the demand forecast.

line balancing The assignment of work to stations in a line process to achieve the desired output rate with the smallest number of workstations.

line flow The customers, materials, or information move linearly from one operation to the next, according to a fixed sequence.

line process A process that lies between the batch and continuous processes on the continuum; volumes are high and products are standardized, which allows resources to be organized around particular products.

linear programming A technique that is useful for allocating scarce resources among competing demands.

linear regression A casual method in which one variable (the dependent variable) is related to one or more independent variables by a linear equation.

linearity A characteristic of linear programming models that implies proportionality and additivity—there can be no products or powers of decision variables.

Little's law A fundamental law that relates the number of customers in a waiting-line system to the arrival rate and waiting time of customers.

load–distance method A mathematical model used to evaluate locations based on proximity factors.

lot A quantity of items that are processed together.

lot-for-lot (L4L) rule A rule under which the lot size ordered covers the gross requirements of a single week.

lot size The quantity of an inventory item management either buys from a supplier or manufactures using internal processes.

lot sizing The determination of how frequently and in what quantity to order inventory.

lot tolerance proportion defective (LTPD) The worst level of quality that the consumer can tolerate.

low-cost operation Delivering a service or a product at the lowest possible cost to the satisfaction of external or internal customers of the process or supply chain.

make-or-buy decision A managerial choice between whether to outsource a process or do it in-house.

make-to-order strategy A strategy used by manufacturers that make products to customer specifications in low volumes.

make-to-stock strategy A strategy that involves holding items in stock for immediate delivery, thereby minimizing customer delivery times.

makespan The total amount of time required to complete a group of jobs.

manufacturing resource planning (MRP II) A system that ties the basic MRP system to the company's financial system and to other core and supporting processes.

market research A systematic approach to determine external consumer interest in a service or product by creating and testing hypotheses through data-gathering surveys.

mass customization The strategy that uses highly divergent processes to generate a wide variety of customized products at reasonably low costs.

mass production A term sometimes used in the popular press for a line process that uses the make-to-stock strategy.

Master Black Belt Full-time teachers and mentors to several Black Belts.

master production schedule (MPS) A part of the material requirements plan that details how many end items will be produced within specified periods of time.

material requirements planning (MRP) A computerized information system developed specifically to help manufacturers manage dependent demand inventory and schedule replenishment orders.

mean absolute deviation (MAD) A measurement of the dispersion of forecast errors.

mean absolute percent error (MAPE) A measurement that relates the forecast error to the level of demand and is useful for putting forecast performance in the proper perspective.

mean squared error (MSE) A measurement of the dispersion of forecast errors.

methods time measurement (MTM) A commonly used predetermined data system.

metrics Performance measures that are established for a process and the steps within it.

minimum-cost schedule A schedule determined by starting with the normal time schedule and crashing activities along the critical path, in such a way that the costs of crashing do not exceed the savings in indirect and penalty costs.

mixed-model assembly A type of assembly that produces a mix of models in smaller lots.

mixed-model line A production line that produces several items belonging to the same family.

mixed strategy A strategy that considers the full range of supply options.

Modified Accelerated Cost Recovery System (MACRS) The only acceptable depreciation method for tax purposes that shortens the lives of investments, giving firms larger early tax deductions.

Monte Carlo simulation A simulation process that uses random numbers to generate simulation events.

most likely time (m) The probable time required to perform an activity.

MRP explosion A process that converts the requirements of various final products into a material requirements plan that specifies the replenishment schedules of all the subassemblies, components, and raw materials needed to produce final products.

multiple-dimension rules A set of rules that apply to more than one aspect of a job.

multiplicative seasonal method A method whereby seasonal factors are multiplied by an estimate of average demand to arrive at a seasonal forecast.

naïve forecast A time-series method whereby the forecast for the next period equals the demand for the current period, or Forecast $= D_t$

nearest neighbor (NN) heuristic A technique that creates a route by deciding the next city to visit on the basis of its proximity.

nested process The concept of a process within a process.

net present value (NPV) method The method that evaluates an investment by calculating the present values of all after-tax total cash flows and then subtracting the initial investment amount for their total.

network diagram A network planning method, designed to depict the relationships between activities, that consists of nodes (circles) and arcs (arrows).

new service/product development process A process that designs and develops new services or products from inputs received from external customer specifications or from the market in general through the customer relationship process.

next-shoring A supply chain strategy that involves locating processes in close proximity to customer demand or product R&D.

nominal value A target for design specifications.

nonnegativity An assumption that the decision variables must be positive or zero.

normal cost (NC) The activity cost associated with the normal time.

normal time (NT) In the context of project management, the time necessary to complete an activity under normal conditions.

normal time (NT) In the context of time study, a measurement found by multiplying the select time ($\bar{t}$), the frequency (F) of the work element per cycle, and the rating factor (RF).

normal time for the cycle (NTC) A measurement found by summing the normal time for each element.

objective function An expression in linear programming models that states mathematically what is being maximized or minimized.

offshoring A supply chain strategy that involves moving processes to another country.

one-worker, multiple-machines (OWMM) cell A one person cell in which a worker operates several different machines simultaneously to achieve a line flow.

on-time delivery Meeting delivery-time promises.

open orders See scheduled receipts (SR).

operating characteristic (OC) curve A graph that describes how well a sampling plan discriminates between good and bad lots.

operation A group of resources performing all or part of one or more processes.

operations management The systematic design, direction, and control of processes that transform inputs into services and products for internal, as well as external, customers.

operations planning and scheduling The process of balancing supply with demand, from the aggregate level down to the short-term scheduling level.

operations scheduling A type of scheduling in which jobs are assigned to workstations or employees are assigned to jobs for specified time periods.

operations strategy The means by which operations implements the firm's corporate strategy and helps to build a customer-driven firm.

optimistic time (a) The shortest time in which an activity can be completed, if all goes exceptionally well.

optional replenishment system A system used to review the inventory position at fixed time intervals and, if the position has dropped to (or below) a predetermined level, to place a variable-sized order to cover expected needs.

order fulfillment process A process that includes the activities required to produce and deliver the service or product to the external customer.

order qualifier Minimal level required from a set of criteria for a firm to do business in a particular market segment.

order winner A criterion customers use to differentiate the services or products of one firm from those of another.

ordering cost The cost of preparing a purchase order for a supplier or a production order for manufacturing.

organizational learning The process of gaining experience with products and processes, achieving greater efficiency through automation and other capital investments, and making other improvements in administrative methods or personnel.

outsourcing Paying suppliers and distributors to perform processes and provide needed services and materials.

overtime The time that employees work that is longer than the regular workday or workweek for which they receive additional pay.

overtime cost Wages paid for work beyond the normal workweek, typically 150 percent of regular-time wages (sometimes up to 200 percent for Sundays and holidays), exclusive of fringe benefits. Overtime can help avoid the extra cost of fringe benefits that come with hiring another full-time employee.

***p*-chart** A chart used for controlling the proportion of defective services or products generated by the process.

pacing The movement of product from one station to the next as soon as the cycle time has elapsed.

parameter A value that the decision maker cannot control and that does not change when the solution is implemented.

parent Any product that is manufactured from one or more components.

Pareto chart A bar chart on which factors are plotted along the horizontal axis in decreasing order of frequency.

part commonality The degree to which a component has more than one immediate parent.

past due The amount of time by which a job missed its due date.

path The sequence of activities between a project's start and finish.

payback method A method for evaluating projects that determines how much time will elapse before the total of after-tax flows will equal, or pay back, the initial investment.

payoff table A table that shows the amount for each alternative if each possible event occurs.

performance rating factor (RF) An assessment that describes *how much* above or below average the worker's performance is on each work element.

periodic order quantity (POQ) A rule that allows a different order quantity for each order issued but issues the order for predetermined time intervals.

periodic review (*P*) system A system in which an item's inventory position is reviewed periodically rather than continuously.

perpetual inventory system A system of inventory control in which the inventory records are always current.

pessimistic time (*b*) The longest estimated time required to perform an activity.

phase A single step in providing a service.

pipeline inventory Inventory that is created when an order for an item is issued but not yet received.

plan-do-study-act cycle A cycle, also called the Deming Wheel, used by firms actively engaged in continuous improvement to train their work teams in problem solving.

planned order release An indication of when an order for a specified quantity of an item is to be issued.

planned receipts Orders that are not yet released to the shop or the supplier.

planning horizon The set of consecutive time periods considered for planning purposes.

plants within plants (PWPs) Different operations within a facility with individualized competitive priorities, processes, and workforces under the same roof.

poka-yoke Mistake-proofing methods aimed at designing fail-safe systems that minimize human error.

postponement The strategy of delaying final activities in the provision of a product until the orders are received.

precedence diagram A diagram that allows one to visualize immediate predecessors better; work elements are denoted by circles, with the time required to perform the work shown below each circle.

precedence relationship A relationship that determines a sequence for undertaking activities; it specifies that one activity cannot start until a preceding activity has been completed.

predetermined data method A database approach that divides each work element into a series of micromotions that make up the element. The analyst then consults a published database that contains the normal times for the full array of possible micromotions.

preemptive discipline A rule that allows a customer of higher priority to interrupt the service of another customer.

preference matrix A table that allows the manager to rate an alternative according to several performance criteria.

present value of an investment The amount that must be invested now to accumulate to a certain amount in the future at a specific interest rate.

presourcing A level of supplier involvement in which suppliers are selected early in a product's concept development stage and are given significant, if not total, responsibility for the design of certain components or systems of the product.

prevention costs Costs associated with preventing defects before they happen.

priority rule A rule that selects the next customer to be served by the service facility.

priority sequencing rule A rule that specifies the job or customer processing sequence when several jobs are waiting in line at a workstation.

process Any activity or group of activities that takes one or more inputs, transforms them, and provides one or more outputs for its customers.

process analysis The documentation and detailed understanding of how work is performed and how it can be redesigned.

process capability The ability of the process to meet the design specifications for a service or product.

process capability index, C_{pk} An index that measures the potential for a process to generate defective outputs relative to either upper or lower specifications.

process capability ratio, C_p The tolerance width divided by six standard deviations.

process chart An organized way of documenting all the activities performed by a person or group of people, at a workstation, with a customer, or on materials.

process choice A way of structuring the process by organizing resources around the process or organizing them around the products.

process divergence The extent to which the process is highly customized with considerable latitude as to how its tasks are performed.

process failure Any performance shortfall, such as error, delay, environmental waste, rework, and the like.

process improvement The systematic study of the activities and flows of each process to improve it.

process simulation The act of reproducing the behavior of a process, using a model that describes each step.

process strategy The pattern of decisions made in managing processes so that they will achieve their competitive priorities.

process structure The process type relative to the kinds of resources needed, how resources are partitioned between them, and their key characteristics.

producer's risk (α) The risk that the sampling plan will fail to verify an acceptable lot's quality and, thus, reject it (a type I error).

product family A group of services or products that have similar demand requirements and common process, labor, and materials requirements.

production plan A sales and operations plan for a *manufacturing firm* that centers on production rates and inventory holdings.

product-mix problem A one-period type of planning problem, the solution of which yields optimal output quantities (or product mix) of a group of services or products subject to resource capacity and market demand constraints.

productivity The value of outputs (services and products) produced divided by the values of input resources (wages, costs of equipment, etc.).

program An interdependent set of projects that have a common strategic purpose.

program evaluation and review technique (PERT) A network planning method created for the U.S. Navy's Polaris missile project in the 1950s, which involved 3,000 separate contractors and suppliers.

project An interrelated set of activities with a definite starting and ending point, which results in a unique outcome for a specific allocation of resources.

project management A systemized, phased approach to defining, organizing, planning, monitoring, and controlling projects.

projected on-hand inventory An estimate of the amount of inventory available each week after gross requirements have been satisfied.

protection interval The period over which safety stock must protect the user from running out of stock.

pull method A method in which customer demand activates production of the service or item.

purchased item An item that has one or more parents but no components because it comes from a supplier.

purchasing The activity that decides which suppliers to use, negotiates contracts, and determines whether to buy locally.

push method A method in which production of the item begins in advance of customer needs.

quality A term used by customers to describe their general satisfaction with a service or product.

quality at the source A philosophy whereby defects are caught and corrected where they were created.

quality of life A factor that considers the availability of good schools, recreational facilities, cultural events, and an attractive lifestyle.

quantity discount A drop in the price per unit when an order is sufficiently large.

R-chart A chart used to monitor process variability.

radio frequency identification (RFID) A method for identifying items through the use of radio signals from a tag attached to an item.

random number A number that has the same probability of being selected as any other number.

range of feasibility The interval (lower and upper bounds) over which the right-hand-side parameter of a constraint can vary while its shadow price remains valid.

range of optimality The interval (lower and upper bounds) of an objective function coefficient over which the optimal values of the decision variables remain unchanged.

raw materials (RM) The inventories needed for the production of services or goods.

rectified inspection The assumption that all defective items in the lot will be replaced if the lot is rejected and that any defective items in the sample will be replaced if the lot is accepted.

rectilinear distance The distance between two points with a series of 90-degree turns, as along city blocks.

reduced cost How much the objective function coefficient of a decision variable must improve (increase for maximization or decrease for minimization) before the optimal solution changes and the decision variable "enters" the solution with some positive number.

reengineering The fundamental rethinking and radical redesign of processes to improve performance dramatically in terms of cost, quality, service, and speed.

regular time cost Regular-time wages paid to employees plus contributions to benefits, such as health insurance, dental care, Social Security, retirement funds, and pay for vacations, holidays, and certain other types of absences.

reorder point (R) The predetermined minimum level that an inventory position must reach before a fixed quantity Q of the SKU is ordered.

reorder point (ROP) system See continuous review (Q) system.

repeatability The degree to which the same work can be done again.

resource flexibility The ease with which employees and equipment can handle a wide variety of products, output levels, duties, and functions.

resource plan An intermediate step in the planning process that lies between S&OP and scheduling. It determines requirements for materials and other resources on a more detailed level than the S&OP.

resource planning A process that takes sales and operations plans; processes information in the way of time standards, routings, and other information on how services or products are produced; and then plans the input requirements.

revenue management Varying price at the right time for different customer segments to maximize revenues yielded by existing supply capacity.

reverse logistics The process of planning, implementing, and controlling the efficient, cost-effective flow of products, materials, and information from the point of consumption back to the point of origin for returns, repair, remanufacture, or recycling.

risk-management plan A plan that identifies the key risks to a project's success and prescribes ways to circumvent them.

rotating schedule A schedule that rotates employees through a series of workdays or hours.

route planning An activity that seeks to find the shortest route to deliver a service or product.

SA8000:2014 A list of standards covering nine dimensions of ethical workforce management.

safety stock inventory Surplus inventory that a company holds to protect against uncertainties in demand, lead time, and supply changes.

sales and operations plan (S&OP) A plan of future aggregate resource levels so that supply is in balance with demand. It states a company's or department's production rates, workforce levels, and inventory holdings that are consistent with demand forecasts and capacity constraints. The S&OP is time-phased, meaning that it is projected for several time periods (such as months or quarters) into the future.

salesforce estimates The forecasts that are compiled from estimates of future demands made periodically by members of a company's salesforce.

salvage value The cash flow from the sale or disposal of plant and equipment at the end of a project's life.

sample size A quantity of randomly selected observations of process outputs.

sampling plan A plan that specifies a sample size, the time between successive samples, and decision rules that determine when action should be taken.

scatter diagram A plot of two variables showing whether they are related.

schedule A detailed plan that allocates resources over short time horizons to accomplish specific tasks.

scheduled receipts (SR) Orders that have been placed but have not yet been received.

SCOR model A framework that focuses on a basic supply chain of plan, source, make, deliver, and return processes, repeated again and again along the supply chain.

select time ($\bar{t}$) The average observed time based only on representative times.

sensitivity analysis A technique for systematically changing parameters in a model to determine the effects of such changes.

sequencing Determining the order in which jobs or customers are processed in the waiting line at a workstation.

sequential-sampling plan A sampling plan in which the consumer randomly selects items from the lot and inspects them one by one.

service blueprint A special flowchart of a service process that shows which steps have high customer contact.

service facility A person (or crew), a machine (or group of machines), or both necessary to perform the service for the customer.

service level The desired probability of not running out of stock in any one ordering cycle, which begins at the time an order is placed and ends when it arrives in stock.

service system The number of lines and the arrangement of the facilities.

setup cost The cost involved in changing over a machine or workspace to produce a different item.

setup time The time required to change a process or an operation from making one service or product to making another.

shadow price The marginal improvement in Z (increase for maximization and decrease for minimization) caused by relaxing the constraint by one unit.

shortest processing time (SPT) A priority sequencing rule that specifies that the job requiring the shortest processing time is the next job to be processed.

shortest route problem A problem whose objective is to find the shortest distance between two cities in a network or map.

simple moving average method A time-series method used to estimate the average of a demand time series by averaging the demand for the n most recent time periods.

simplex method An iterative algebraic procedure for solving linear programming problems.

simulation The act of reproducing the behavior of a system using a model that describes the processes of the system.

single-bin system A system of inventory control in which a maximum level is marked on the storage shelf or bin, and the inventor is brought up to the mark periodically.

single-digit setup The goal of having a setup time of less than 10 minutes.

single-dimension rules A set of rules that bases the priority of a job on a single aspect of the job, such as arrival time at the workstation, the due date, or the processing time.

single-sampling plan A sampling plan whereby a decision is made to accept or reject a lot based on the results of one random sample from the lot.

Six Sigma A comprehensive and flexible system for achieving, sustaining, and maximizing business success by minimizing defects and variability in processes.

slack The amount by which the left-hand side of a linear programming constraint falls short of the right-hand side.

slack per remaining operations (S/RO) A priority sequencing rule that determines priority by dividing the slack by the number of operations that remain, including the one being scheduled.

social responsibility An element of sustainability that addresses the moral, ethical, and philanthropic expectations that society has of an organization.

sole sourcing The awarding of a contract for a service or item to only one supplier.

staffing plan A sales and operations plan for a *service firm,* which centers on staffing and other human resource-related factors.

standard deviation of the errors (σ) A measurement of the dispersion of forecast errors.

standard time (ST) A measurement found by incorporating the normal time and allowances; $ST = NTC(1 + A)$, where A equals the proportion of the normal time added for allowances.

statistical process control (SPC) The application of statistical techniques to determine whether a process is delivering what the customer wants.

steady state The state that occurs when the simulation is repeated over enough time that the average results for performance measures remain constant.

stock-keeping unit (SKU) An individual item or product that has an identifying code and is held in inventory somewhere along the supply chain.

stockout An order that cannot be satisfied, resulting in a loss of the sale.

straight-line depreciation method The simplest method of calculating annual depreciation; found by subtracting the estimated salvage value from the amount of investment required at the beginning of the project, and then dividing by the asset's expected economic life.

subassembly An intermediate item that is *assembled* (as opposed to being transformed by other means) from more than one component.

supplier relationship process A process that selects the suppliers of services, materials, and information and facilitates the timely and efficient flow of these items into the firm.

supply chain An interrelated series of processes within and across firms that produces a service or product to the satisfaction of customers.

supply chain design Designing a firm's supply chain to meet the competitive priorities of the firm's operations strategy.

supply chain integration The effective coordination of supply chain processes through the seamless flow of information up and down the supply chain.

supply chain management The synchronization of a firm's processes with those of its suppliers and customers to match the flow of materials, services, and information with customer demand.

supply chain processes Business processes that have external customers or suppliers.

supply chain risk management The practice of managing the risk of any factor or event that can materially disrupt a supply chain, whether within a single firm or across multiple firms.

support process A process that provides vital resources and inputs to the core processes and therefore is essential to the management of the business.

surplus The amount by which the left-hand side of a linear programming constraint exceeds the right-hand side.

sustainability A characteristic of processes that are meeting humanity's needs without harming future generations.

swim lane flowchart A visual representation that groups functional areas responsible for different subprocesses into lanes. It is most appropriate when the business process spans several department boundaries.

takt time Cycle time needed to match the rate of production to the rate of sales or consumption.

tardiness See past due.

teams Small groups of people who have a common purpose, set their own performance goals and approaches, and hold themselves accountable for success.

technological forecasting An application of executive opinion to keep abreast of the latest advances in technology.

theoretical minimum (TM) A benchmark or goal for the smallest number of stations possible, where the total time required to assemble each unit (the sum of all work-element standard times) is divided by the cycle time.

theory of constraints (TOC) A systematic management approach that focuses on actively managing those constraints that impede a firm's progress toward its goal.

throughput time Total elapsed time from the start to the finish of a job or a customer being processed at one or more work centers.

time-based competition A strategy that focuses on the competitive priorities of delivery speed and development speed.

time between orders (TBO) The average elapsed time between receiving (or placing) replenishment orders of Q units for a particular lot size.

time compression The feature of simulation models that allows them to obtain operating characteristic estimates in much less time than is required to gather the same operating data from a real system.

time series The repeated observations of demand for a service or product in their order of occurrence.

time-series analysis A statistical approach that relies heavily on historical demand data to project the future size of demand and recognized trends and seasonal patterns.

time study A work measurement method using a trained analyst to perform four basic steps in setting a time standard for a job or process: selecting the work elements (or nested processes) within the process to be studied, timing the elements, determining the sample size, and setting the final standard.

time value of money The concept that a dollar in hand can be invested to earn a return so that more than one dollar will be available in the future.

tolerance An allowance above or below the nominal value.

top quality Delivering an outstanding service or product.

total inventory The sum of scheduled receipts and on-hand inventories.

total quality management (TQM) A philosophy that stresses three principles for achieving high levels of process performance and quality: (1) customer satisfaction, (2) employee involvement, and (3) continuous improvement in performance.

tracking signal A measure that indicates whether a method of forecasting is accurately predicting actual changes in demand.

transportation method A more efficient solution technique than the simplex method for solving transportation problems.

transportation method for location problems A quantitative approach that can help solve multiple-facility location problems.

transportation problem A special case of linear programming that has linear constraints for capacity limitations and demand requirements.

traveling salesman problem A problem whose objective is to find the shortest possible route that visits each city exactly once and returns to the starting city.

trend projection with regression A forecasting model that is a hybrid between a time-series technique and the causal method.

two-bin system A visual system version of the Q system in which a SKU's inventory is stored at two different locations.

type I error An error that occurs when the employee concludes that the process is out of control based on a sample result that falls outside the control limits, when in fact it was due to pure randomness.

type II error An error that occurs when the employee concludes that the process is in control and only randomness is present, when actually the process is out of statistical control.

uncontrollable (or *random*) variables Random events that the decision maker cannot control.

undertime The situation that occurs when employees do not have enough work for the regular-time workday or workweek.

usage quantity The number of units of a component that are needed to make one unit of its immediate parent.

utilization The degree to which equipment, space, or the workforce is currently being used, and is measured as the ratio of average output rate to maximum capacity (expressed as a percent).

value analysis A systematic effort to reduce the cost or improve the performance of services or products, either purchased or produced.

value stream mapping (VSM) A qualitative lean tool for eliminating waste or *muda* that involves a current state drawing, a future state drawing, and an implementation plan.

variable cost The portion of the total cost that varies directly with volume of output.

variables Service or product characteristics, such as weight, length, volume, or time that can be measured.

variety Handling a wide assortment of services or products efficiently.

vendor-managed inventories (VMI) A system in which the supplier has access to the customer's inventory data and is responsible for maintaining the inventory on the customer's site.

visual system A system that allows employees to place orders when inventory visibly reaches a certain marker.

volume flexibility Accelerating or decelerating the rate of production of services or products quickly to handle large fluctuations in demand.

waiting line One or more "customers" waiting for service.

warranty A written guarantee that the producer will replace or repair defective parts or perform the service to the customer's satisfaction.

weeks of supply An inventory measure obtained by dividing the average aggregate inventory value by sales per week at cost.

weighted-distance method A mathematical model used to evaluate layouts (of facility locations) based on closeness factors.

weighted moving average method A time-series method in which each historical demand in the average can have its own weight; the sum of the weights equals 1.0.

work breakdown structure (WBS) A statement of all work that has to be completed.

work elements The smallest units of work that can be performed independently.

workforce scheduling A type of scheduling that determines when employees work.

work-in-process (WIP) Items, such as components or assemblies, needed to produce a final product in manufacturing or service operations.

work measurement The process of creating labor standards based on the judgment of skilled observers.

work sampling A process that estimates the proportion of time spent by people or machines on different activities, based on observations randomized over time.

work standard The time required for a trained worker to perform a task following a prescribed method with normal effort and skill.

$\bar{x}$-chart A chart used to see whether the process is generating output, on average, consistent with a target value set by management for the process or whether its current performance, with respect to the average of the performance measure, is consistent with past performance.

Name Index

Subject Index

Page numbers followed by "f" have figures. Page numbers followed by "t" have tables.

The act of reproducing the behavior of a system using a model that describes the processes of the system is called **simulation**. Once the model has been developed, the analyst can manipulate certain variables to measure the effects of changes on the operating characteristics of interest. A simulation model cannot prescribe what should be done about a problem. Instead, it can be used to study alternative solutions to the problem. The alternatives are systematically evaluated with the model, and the relevant operating characteristics are recorded. After all the alternatives have been tried, the best one is selected.

Simulation can be used in managing processes as well as whole supply chains. Various simulation models can help in understanding how a process performs dynamically over time and how well revised processes will work. Some of the changes that simulation can be used to assess include quality improvement ideas, capacity changes aimed at relieving bottlenecks, the layout of the process, or even changes that come from implementing lean systems ideas—in effect, all of the decision areas covered in Part 1. Simulation can also be used for many of the decisions related to managing supply chains (Parts 2 and 3), such as where to position inventory and in what quantities, or how different scheduling procedures work.

Waiting-line models (see Supplement B, "Waiting Lines") are not simulation models because they describe the operating characteristics with known equations. With simulation, the equations describing the operation characteristics are unknown. Using a simulation model, the analyst actually generates customer arrivals, puts customers into waiting lines, selects the next customer to be served by using some priority discipline, serves that customer, and so on. The model keeps track of the number in line, waiting time, and the like during the simulation and calculates the averages and variances at the end.

simulation

The act of reproducing the behavior of a system using a model that describes the processes of the system.

Reasons for Using Simulation Models

Simulation is useful when waiting-line models become too complex. Using simulation for analyzing processes may be based on other reasons as well. First, when the relationship between the variables is nonlinear or when the situation involves too many variables or constraints to handle with optimizing approaches, simulation models can be used to estimate operating characteristics or objective function values and analyze a problem.

LEARNING GOALS *After reading this supplement, you should be able to:*

1. Identify four reasons for using simulation models.
2. Perform a manual simulation using the Monte Carlo simulation process.
3. Create a simple simulation model with an Excel spreadsheet.
4. Describe the advanced capabilities of SimQuick.

Second, simulation models can be used to conduct experiments without disrupting real systems. Experimenting with a real system can be costly. For example, a simulation model can be used to estimate the benefits of purchasing and installing an automated processing system without first installing such a system. Also, the model could be used to evaluate different configurations or processing decision rules without disrupting production schedules.

Third, simulation models can be used to obtain operating characteristic estimates in much less time than is required to gather the same operating data from a real system. This feature of simulation is called **time compression**. For example, a simulation model of airport operations can generate statistics on airplane arrivals, landing delays, and terminal delays for a year in a matter of minutes on a computer. Alternative airport designs can be analyzed and decisions made quickly.

Finally, simulation is useful in sharpening managerial decision-making skills through gaming. A descriptive model that relates managerial decisions to important operating characteristics (e.g., profits, market share, and the like) can be developed. From a set of starting conditions, the participants make periodic decisions with the intention of improving one or more operating characteristics. In such an exercise, a few hours' "play" can simulate a year's time. Gaming also enables managers to experiment with new ideas without disrupting normal operations.

time compression

The feature of simulation models that allows them to obtain operating characteristic estimates in much less time than is required to gather the same operating data from a real system.

The Monte Carlo Simulation Process

The simulation process includes data collection, random-number assignment, model formulation, and analysis. This process is known as **Monte Carlo simulation**, after the European gambling capital, because of the random numbers used to generate the simulation events.

Monte Carlo simulation

A simulation process that uses random numbers to generate simulation events.

Data Collection

Simulation requires extensive data gathering on costs, productivities, capacities, and probability distributions. Typically, one of two approaches to data collection is used. Statistical sampling procedures are used when the data are not readily available from published sources or when the cost of searching for and collecting the data is high. Historical search is used when the data are available in company records, governmental and industry reports, professional and scientific journals, or newspapers. Example E.1 provides the data that Specialty Steel collected.

EXAMPLE E.1	Data Collection for a Simulation

The Specialty Steel Products Company produces items, such as machine tools, gears, automobile parts, and other specialty items, in small quantities to customer order. Because the products are so diverse, demand is measured in machine-hours. Orders for products are translated into required machine-hours, based on time standards for each operation. Management is concerned about capacity in the lathe department. Assemble the data necessary to analyze the addition of one more lathe machine and operator.

SOLUTION
Historical records indicate that lathe department demand varies from week to week as follows:

Weekly Production Requirements (hr)	Relative Frequency
200	0.05
250	0.06
300	0.17
350	0.05
400	0.30
450	0.15
500	0.06
550	0.14
600	0.02
	Total 1.00

To gather these data, all weeks with requirements of 175.00–224.99 hours were grouped in the 200-hour category, all weeks with 225.00–274.99 hours were grouped in the 250-hour category, and so on. The average weekly production requirements for the lathe department are

$$200(0.05) + 250(0.06) + 300(0.17) + \cdots + 600(0.02) = 400 \text{ hours}$$

Employees in the lathe department work 40 hours per week on 10 machines. However, the number of machines actually operating during any week may be less than 10. Machines may need repair, or a worker may not show up for work. Historical records indicate that actual machine-hours were distributed as follows:

Regular Capacity (hr)	Relative Frequency
320 (8 machines)	0.30
360 (9 machines)	0.40
400 (10 machines)	0.30

The average number of operating machine-hours in a week is

$$320(0.30) + 360(0.40) + 400(0.30) = 360 \text{ hours}$$

The company has a policy of completing each week's workload on schedule, using overtime and subcontracting if necessary. The maximum amount of overtime authorized in any week is 100 hours, and requirements in excess of 100 hours are subcontracted to a small machine shop in town. Lathe operators receive $10 per hour for regular time. However, management estimates that the cost for overtime work is $25 per hour per employee, which includes premium-wage, variable-overhead, and supervision costs. Subcontracting costs $35 per hour, exclusive of materials costs.

To justify adding another machine and worker to the lathe department, weekly savings in overtime and subcontracting costs should be at least $650. These savings would cover the cost of the additional worker and provide for a reasonable return on machine investment. Management estimates from prior experience that with 11 machines, the distribution of weekly capacity machine-hours would be

Regular Capacity (hr)	Relative Frequency
360 (9 machines)	0.30
400 (10 machines)	0.40
440 (11 machines)	0.30

Random-Number Assignment

Before we can begin to analyze this problem with simulation, we must specify a way to generate demand and capacity each week. Suppose that we want to simulate 100 weeks of lathe operations with 10 machines. We would expect that 5 percent of the time (5 weeks of the 100) we would have a demand for 200 hours. Similarly, we would expect that 30 percent of the time (30 weeks of the 100) we would have 320 hours of existing capacity with the 10 machines. However, we cannot use these averages of demand in our simulation because a real system does not operate that way. Demand may be 200 hours one week but 550 hours the next.

We can obtain the effect we want by using a random-number table to determine the amount of demand and capacity each week. A **random number** is a number that has the same probability of being selected as any other number (see the Table of Random Numbers at the end of this supplement for five-digit random numbers).

random number

A number that has the same probability of being selected as any other number.

The events in a simulation can be generated in an unbiased way if random numbers are assigned to the events in the same proportion as their probability of occurrence. We expect a demand of 200 hours 5 percent of the time. If we have 100 random numbers (00–99), we can assign 5 numbers (or 5 percent of them) to the event "200 hours demanded." Thus, we can assign the numbers 00–04 to that event. If we randomly choose numbers in the range of 00–99 enough times, 5 percent of the time they will fall in the range of 00–04. Similarly, we can assign the numbers 05–10, or 6 percent of the numbers, to the event "250 hours demanded." In Table E.1 we show the allocation of the 100 random numbers to the demand events in the same proportion as their probability of occurrence. We similarly assigned random numbers to the *capacity* events for 10 machines. The capacity events for the 11-machine simulation would have the same random-number assignments, except that the events would be 360, 400, and 440 hours, respectively.

TABLE E.1 | RANDOM-NUMBER ASSIGNMENTS TO SIMULATION EVENTS

			EVENT		
Weekly Demand (hr)	**Probability**	**Random Number**	**Existing Weekly Capacity (hr)**	**Probability**	**Random Numbers**
200	0.05	00–04	320	0.30	00–29
250	0.06	05–10	360	0.40	30–69
300	0.17	11–27	400	0.30	70–99
350	0.05	28–32			
400	0.30	33–62			
450	0.15	63–77			
500	0.06	78–83			
550	0.14	84–97			
600	0.02	98–99			

Model Formulation

Formulating a simulation model entails specifying the relationships among the variables. Simulation models consist of decision variables, uncontrollable variables, and dependent variables. *Decision variables* are controlled by the decision maker and will change from one run to the next as different events are simulated. For example, the number of lathe machines is the decision variable in the Specialty Steel Products problem in Example E.1. **Uncontrollable (or *random*) variables**, however, are random events that the decision maker cannot control. At Specialty Steel Products, the weekly production requirements and the *actual* number of machine-hours available are uncontrollable variables for the simulation analysis. Dependent variables reflect the values of the decision variables and the uncontrollable variables. At Specialty Steel Products, operating characteristics such as idle time, overtime, and subcontracting hours are dependent variables.

The relationships among the variables are expressed in mathematical terms so that the dependent variables can be computed for any values of the decision variables and uncontrollable variables. For example, in the simulation model for Specialty Steel Products, the methods of determining weekly production requirements and actual capacity availability must be specified first. Then, the methods of computing idle-time hours, overtime hours, and subcontracting hours for the values of production requirements and capacity hours can be specified.

uncontrollable (or *random*) variables

Random events that the decision maker cannot control.

EXAMPLE E.2 | **Formulating a Monte Carlo Simulation Model**

Formulate a Monte Carlo simulation model for Specialty Steel Products that will estimate idle-time hours, overtime hours, and subcontracting hours for a specified number of lathes. Design the simulation model to terminate after 20 weeks of simulated lathe department operations.

SOLUTION

Let us use the first two rows of random numbers in the random number table for the demand events and the third and fourth rows for the capacity events (see the Table of Random Numbers at the end of this supplement). Because they are five-digit numbers, we use only the first two digits of each number for our random numbers. The choice of the rows in the random-number table was arbitrary. The important point is that we must be consistent in drawing random numbers and should not repeat the use of numbers in any one simulation.

To simulate a particular capacity level, we proceed as follows:

Step 1. Draw a random number from the first two rows of the table. Start with the first number in the first row, then go to the second number in the first row, and so on.

Step 2. Find the random-number interval for production requirements associated with the random number.

Step 3. Record the production hours (PROD) required for the current week.

Step 4. Draw another random number from row 3 or 4 of the table. Start with the first number in row 3, then go to the second number in row 3, and so on.

Step 5. Find the random-number interval for capacity (CAP) associated with the random number.

Step 6. Record the capacity hours available for the current week.

Step 7. If CAP ≥ PROD, then IDLE HR = CAP − PROD.

Step 8. If CAP < PROD, then SHORT = PROD − CAP.

If SHORT ≤ 100, then OVERTIME HR = SHORT and SUBCONTRACT HR = 0.

If SHORT > 100, then OVERTIME HR = 100 and SUBCONTRACT HR = SHORT − 100.

Step 9. Repeat steps 1–8 until you have simulated 20 weeks.

Analysis

Table E.2 contains the simulations for the two capacity alternatives at Specialty Steel Products. We used a unique random-number sequence for weekly production requirements for each capacity alternative and another sequence for the existing weekly capacity to make a direct comparison between the capacity alternatives.

Based on the 20-week simulations, we would expect average weekly overtime hours (highlighted in orange) to be reduced by $41.5 - 29.5 = 12$ hours and subcontracting hours (highlighted in **blue**) to be reduced by $18 - 10 = 8$ hours per week. The average weekly savings would be

$$\text{Overtime: } (12\,\text{hours})(25/\text{hour}) = \$300$$
$$\text{Subcontracting: } (8\,\text{hours})(35/\text{hour}) = \underline{\quad 280}$$
$$\text{Total savings per week} = \$580$$

TABLE E.2 | 20-WEEK SIMULATION OF ALTERNATIVES

				10 MACHINES				11 MACHINES			
Week	Demand Random Number	Weekly Production (hr)	Capacity Random Number	Existing Weekly Capacity (hr)	Idle Hours	Overtime Hours	Subcontract Hours	Existing Weekly Capacity (hr)	Idle Hours	Overtime Hours	Subcontract Hours
1	71	450	50	360		90		400		50	
2	68	450	54	360		90		400		50	
3	48	400	11	320		80		360		40	
4	99	600	36	360		100	140	400		100	100
5	64	450	82	400		50		440		10	
6	13	300	87	400	100			440	140		
7	36	400	41	360		40		400			
8	58	400	71	400				440	40		
9	13	300	00	320	20			360	60		
10	93	550	60	360		100	90	400		100	50
11	21	300	47	360	60			400	100		
12	30	350	76	400	50			440	90		
13	23	300	09	320	20			360	60		
14	89	550	54	360		100	90	400		100	50
15	58	400	87	400				440	40		
16	46	400	82	400				440	40		
17	00	200	17	320	120			360	160		
18	82	500	52	360		100	40	400		100	
19	02	200	17	320	120			360	160		
20	37	400	19	320	——	80	——	360	——	40	——
				Total	490	830	360		890	590	200
				Weekly Average	24.5	41.5	18.0		44.5	29.5	10.0

This amount falls short of the minimum required savings of $650 per week. Does this outcome mean that we should not add the machine and worker? Before answering, let us look at Table E.3, which shows the results of a *1,000-week* simulation for each alternative. The costs (highlighted in lavender) are quite different from those of the 20-week simulations. Now the savings are estimated to be $1,851.50 − $1,159.50 = $692 and exceed the minimum required savings for the additional investment. This result emphasizes the importance of selecting the proper run length for a simulation analysis. We can use statistical tests to check for the proper run length.

TABLE E.3 | COMPARISON OF 1,000-WEEK SIMULATION

	10 Machines	**11 Machines**
Idle hours	26.0	42.2
Overtime hours	48.3	34.2
Subcontract hours	18.4	8.7
Cost	**$1,851.50**	**$1,159.50**

Simulation analysis can be viewed as a form of hypothesis testing, whereby the results of a simulation run provide sample data that can be analyzed statistically. Data can be recorded and compared with the results from other simulation runs. Statistical tests also can be made to determine whether differences in the alternative operating characteristics are statistically significant.

Even though a difference between simulation experiments may be statistically significant, it may not be *managerially* significant. For example, suppose that we developed a simulation model of a car wash operation. We may find by changing the speed of the car wash from 3 to 2.75 minutes per car that we can reduce the average waiting time per customer by 0.20 minute. Even though this may be a statistically significant difference in the average waiting time, the difference is so small that customers may not even notice it. What is managerially significant often is a judgment decision.

Simulation with Excel Spreadsheets

The manual simulation of the lathe process in Examples E.1 and E.2 demonstrates the basics of simulation. However, the simulation involves only one step in the process, two uncontrollable variables (weekly production requirements and the actual number of machine-hours available), and 20 time periods. It is important to simulate a process long enough to achieve **steady state**, so that the simulation is repeated over enough time that the average results for performance measures remain constant. Manual simulations can be excessively time-consuming, particularly if they include many subprocesses, many services or products with unique flow patterns, many uncontrollable variables, complex logic for releasing new jobs and assigning work, and the like.

Simulating these real-world situations manually can become too time-consuming and therefore requires a computer instead. Simple simulation models, say with one or two uncontrollable variables, can be developed using Excel. Its ability to generate random numbers—coupled with adding formulas elsewhere in the worksheet to specify relations between demand, customer served, inventory, and output—allow the Monte Carlo simulation approach to be implemented. Even more computer power comes from commercial, prewritten simulation software.

Simulation with Excel gets complex quickly, and you might want to skip this section on Excel and go directly to the section "Simulation with SimQuick Software," pp. E-9–E-10. SimQuick is a software package provided with MyOMLab that is powerful and quite appealing. You can download this software as well as a textbook full of examples on SimQuick's use.

The starting point in creating an Excel simulation is generating random numbers, the computer equivalent of using the Table of Random Numbers for manual simulations. Equally important is random-number assignment, which translates a random number into a value for an uncontrollable variable.

Generating Random Numbers

Random numbers can be created from 0 to 1 by entering the formula = RAND() into a cell of the Excel spreadsheet. This formula then can be copied to other cells in the spreadsheet as needed. Figure E.1 shows a table of 100 random numbers generated with the RAND() function in the range A3:J12. They were formatted to show four-digit numbers, although the format can be changed as desired. These random numbers are fractions from 0 to 1, rather than the two-digit integer numbers from 0 through 99 in Table E.1. If you attempt to replicate Figure E.1 or reopen an Excel file that was created earlier and saved, you will see a different set of random numbers. To use the same exact set or *stream* of random numbers, such as for experiments that compare the effectiveness of different policies, you should *freeze*

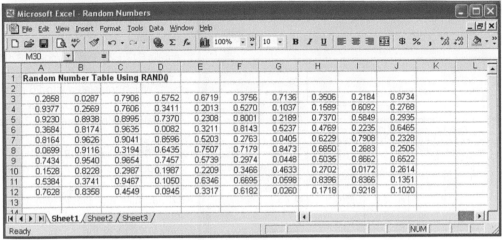

Microsoft® Windows®, and Microsoft Office® are registered trademarks of the Microsoft Corporation in the U.S.A. and other countries.
This book is not sponsored or endorsed by or affiliated with the Microsoft Corporation.

▲ **FIGURE E.1**
A Spreadsheet with 100 Random Numbers Generated with RAND( )

the random numbers. First, select with your mouse the cells holding the random numbers that you wish to freeze. For example, cover A3:J12 in Figure E.1. Next, click Edit/Copy in the menu at the top of your spreadsheet. Then, click Edit/Paste Special and choose the Values option. When you click OK, a copy of the numbers in these cells is pasted over the same cells with the = RAND() formulas in them. The result is that they are fixed in place and will not change from one use of the spreadsheet to the next. Each simulation is conducted with the same stream of random numbers. In fact, the numbers in Figure E.1 were frozen using this procedure.

Random-Number Assignment

A second capability that is needed for Excel simulations is to translate random numbers into values for the uncontrollable variables. It is equivalent to identifying the random-number interval in which a random number falls and then selecting the value of the uncontrollable variable assigned to that interval (see Table E.1 for the demand or capacity variables). In an Excel spreadsheet, the Lookup feature serves this purpose. Read about the VLOOKUP() function under Excel's Help Topics and check out the function by selecting Insert/Function/Lookup & Reference/VLOOKUP. Example E.3 demonstrates the use of both the VLOOKUP() and RAND() functions.

EXAMPLE E.3	Excel Simulation Model for BestCar Auto Dealer

The BestCar automobile dealership sells new automobiles. The dealership manager believes that the number of cars sold weekly has the following probability distribution:

Weekly Sales (cars)	Relative Frequency (probability)
0	0.05
1	0.15
2	0.20
3	0.30
4	0.20
5	0.10
	Total 1.00

The selling price per car is $20,000. Design a simulation model that determines the probability distribution and mean of the weekly sales.

SOLUTION

Figure E.2 simulates 50 weeks of sales at BestCar. A longer run length, say 500 or 1,000 weeks, would be prudent, but here we keep it small for demonstration purposes. The bottom right of the spreadsheet shows that

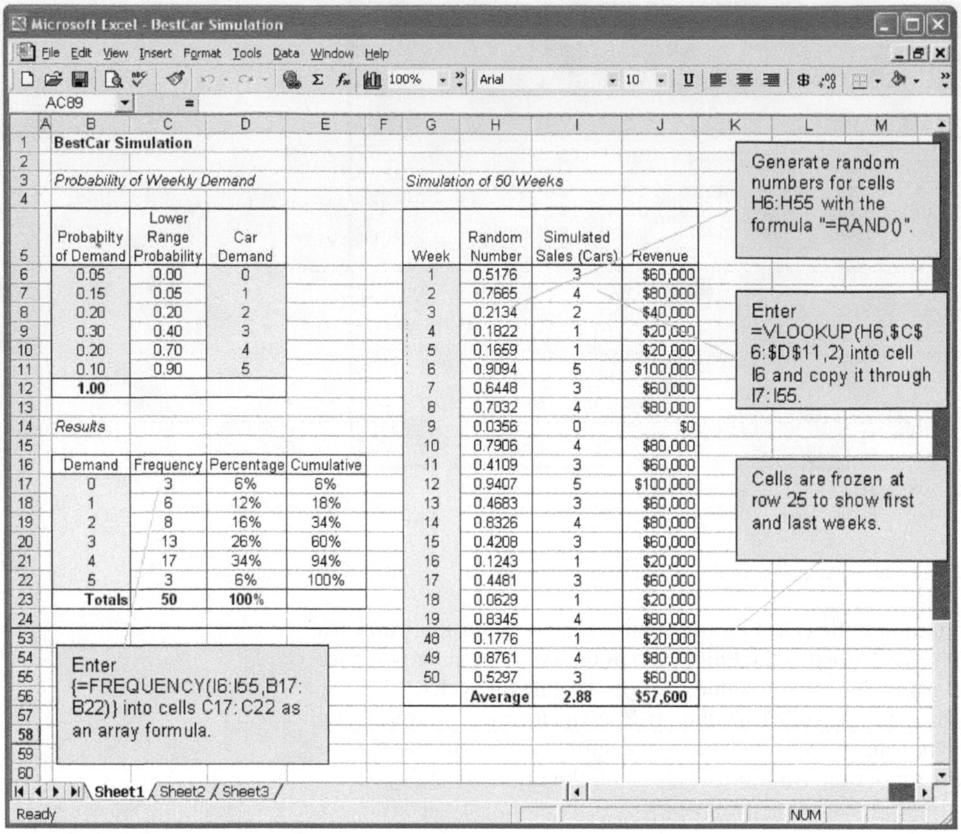

▲ FIGURE E.2
BestCar Simulation Model

Microsoft® Windows®, and Microsoft Office® are registered trademarks of the Microsoft Corporation in the U.S.A. and other countries. This book is not sponsored or endorsed by or affiliated with the Microsoft Corporation.

the average weekly sales is 2.88 cars, for $57,600 per week. The distribution of the simulated weekly demand is shown in cells B17:E22. For example, 13 of the 50 weeks experienced a demand for 3 cars, which translates into 26 percent of the weeks (see cell D20). The chance that sales are not more than 3 cars is 60 percent (see cell E20).

The first step in creating this spreadsheet is to input the probability distribution, including the cumulative probabilities associated with it. These input values are highlighted in yellow in cells B6:B11 of the spreadsheet, with corresponding demands in D6:D11. The lower range of cumulative probabilities is calculated in cells C6:C11 by entering 0 in C6 and then entering the formula "=C6 + B6" into cell C7 and copying it to cells C8:C11. The cumulative values provide a basis to associate random numbers to the corresponding demand, using the VLOOKUP( ) function. For example, the first random number for week 1 has the value 0.5176 and will result in a demand of three cars, because 0.5176 is greater than the lower range for a demand of three cars, but smaller than the lower range for demand of four cars. In a similar way, any random number with a value greater than 0.70 but smaller than 0.90 will correspond to a demand of four cars.

The next step is to create a table with four columns. Column G identifies each of the 50 weeks to be simulated in cells G6:G55. Column H generates the random numbers, one for each of the 50 weeks. To create the random numbers, we enter the formula "=RAND( )" into cell H6 of our spreadsheet and then copy it to the cells H7:H55. After generating the random numbers, we need to match these numbers with the corresponding demand values. We can do this by using the VLOOKUP function. We enter the formula "=VLOOKUP(H6, $C$6:$D$11,2)" into cell I6 and copy it through I7:I55. With this use of the VLOOKUP function, Excel's logic identifies (or "looks up") for each week's random number (in column H), which demand it corresponds to in the lookup array defined by $C$6:$D$11. Once it finds the probability range (defined by column C) in which the random number fits, it posts the car demand (in column D) for this range back into the week's sales (in column I). When searching the lookup array, it moves down through column C until it finds a cell that has a value greater than the random number. It goes back to the previous cell, gets the corresponding demand value from column D, and returns it to the cell in column I. The weekly revenue column is the fourth column in the simulation table, created in cells J6:J55 by multiplying the weekly demand values (column I) by average selling price ($20,000). The average car sales is calculated in cell I56 using the = AVERAGE(I6:I55) function, and the average revenue in cell J56 using the = AVERAGE(J6:J55) function. Note that Figure E.2 only shows the first 19 weeks and the last 3 weeks. This compression is possible using the Window/Freeze Panes option. Here, the window is frozen through week 19 (at start of row 25). You can scroll down or up to show just a few of the last weeks or most of them, depending on how much you want to display.

Finally, the results table is created at the lower left portion of the spreadsheet to summarize the simulation output. By entering the FREQUENCY function into cells C17:C22, we calculate the number of observations in each demand category out of a total of 50 observations. The function looks through the simulated demand values in cells I6:I55 and compares them to the demand categories in cells B17:B22, which are defined as the bin array of the FREQUENCY function. Percentage and cumulative columns next to the frequency column show the frequencies in percentage and cumulative percentage terms.

Simulation with Two Uncontrollable Variables

Simulations often involve two or more uncontrollable variables. For example, Figure E.3 shows an Excel simulation model of an inventory replenishment rule for futons. The weekly demand and lead time are both uncontrollable variables, and their probability distributions are input in the top of the spreadsheet, along with the inventory holding, ordering, and stockout cost parameters. There are two decision variables, the order size and reorder point. The order size is the quantity ordered each time a new order is placed with the supplier. The reorder point is the level to which the inventory is allowed to drop before a replenishment order is placed. The order size is set at 50 units in Figure E.3 and the reorder point is 35 units. The results of the simulation are summarized at the bottom of the spreadsheet. Of particular interest are the values of the dependent variables. The average holding cost is $44.91 per week, the average ordering cost is $3.20 per week, and the average stockout cost is $186.00 per week. The manager can try out different values of the order size and reorder point to seek a less costly result just by changing the input values of the two decision variables. The manager should notice the high stockout cost and might want to try a higher reorder point. The annotations in Figure E.3 show that the formulas become much more complex when the simulation model must reflect multiple decision and uncontrollable variables. For more information on the logic of inventory replenishment systems, see Chapter 9, "Inventory Management."

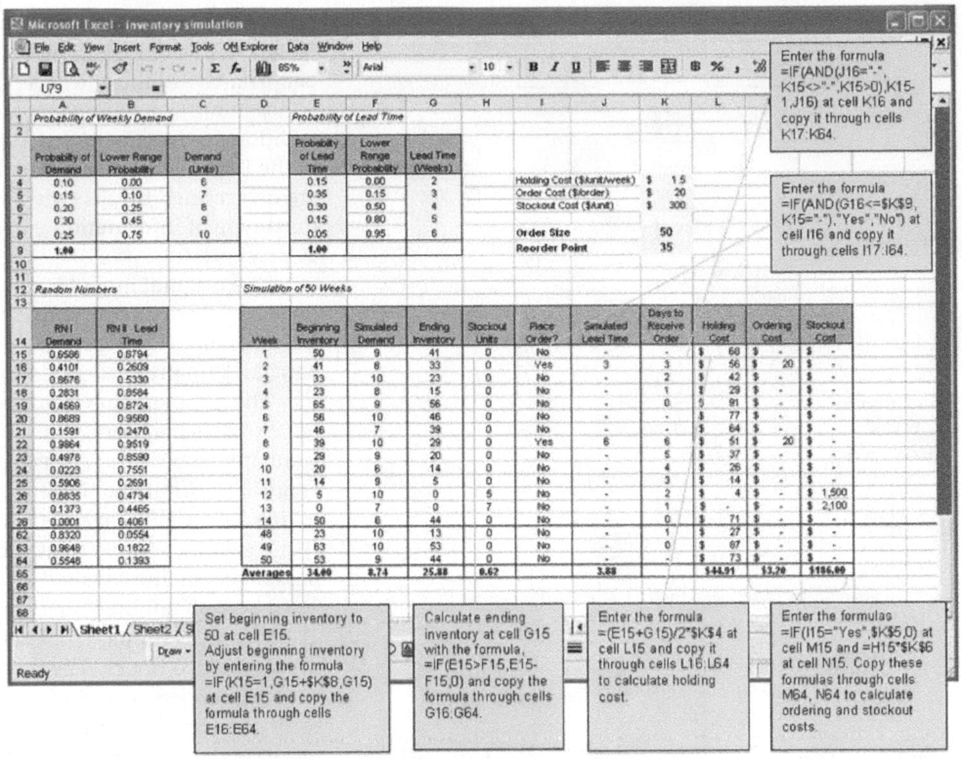

Microsoft® Windows®, and Microsoft Office® are registered trademarks of the Microsoft Corporation in the U.S.A. and other countries. This book is not sponsored or endorsed by or affiliated with the Microsoft Corporation.

▲ FIGURE E.3
Inventory Simulation Model

Simulation with SimQuick Software

Simulation of complex processes is possible with powerful PC-based packages, such as SimQuick (**http://www.nd.edu/~dhartvig/simquick/top.htm**), Extend (**http://www.imaginethatinc.com**), SIMPROCESS (**http://www.caciasl.com**), ProModel (**http://www.promodel.com**), and Witness (**http://www.lanner.com/corporate**). Here we illustrate process simulation with the SimQuick software (provided in MyOMLab).

MyOMLab

SimQuick is an easy-to-use package that is simply an Excel spreadsheet with some macros. Models can be created for a variety of simple processes, such as waiting lines, inventory control, and projects. Here we consider the passenger security process at one terminal of a medium-sized airport between the hours of 8 A.M. and 10 A.M. The process works as follows. Passengers arriving at the security area immediately enter a single line. After waiting in line, each passenger goes through one of two inspection stations, which involves walking through a metal detector and running any carry-on baggage through a scanner. After completing this inspection, 10 percent of the passengers are randomly selected for an additional inspection, which typically involves a more thorough search of each person's carry-on baggage. Two stations handle this additional inspection, and selected passengers go through only one of them. Management is interested in examining the effect of increasing the percentage of passengers who undergo the second inspection. In particular, they want to compare the waiting times for the second inspection when 10 percent, then 15 percent, and then 20 percent of the passengers are randomly selected for this inspection. Management also wants to know how opening a third station for the second inspection would affect these waiting times.

A first step in simulating this process with SimQuick is to draw a flowchart of the process using SimQuick's building blocks. SimQuick has five building blocks that can be combined in a wide variety of ways. Four of these types are used to model this process. An *entrance* is used to model the arrival of passengers at the security process. A *buffer* is used to model each of the two waiting lines, one before each type of inspection, as well as the passengers that have finished the process. Each of the four inspection stations is modeled with a *workstation*. Finally, the random selection of passengers for the second inspection is modeled with a *decision point*. Figure E.4 shows the flowchart.

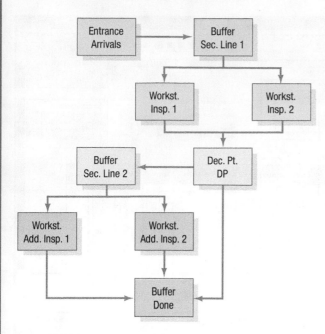

▲ **FIGURE E.4**
Flowchart of Passenger Security Process

Element Types	Element Names	Statistics	Overall Means
Entrance(s)	Door	Objects entering process	237.23
Buffer(s)	Line 1	Mean inventory	5.97
		Mean cycle time	3.12
	Line 2	Mean inventory	0.10
		Mean cycle time	0.53
	Done	Final inventory	224.57

FIGURE E.5 ▲
Simulation Results of Passenger Security Process

Information describing each building block is entered into SimQuick tables. In this model, three key types of information are entered: (1) when people arrive at the entrance, (2) how long inspections take at the four stations, and (3) what percentage of passengers are randomly selected for the additional inspection. All of this information must be entered into SimQuick in the form of statistical distributions. The first two types of information are determined by observing the real process from 8 A.M. and 10 A.M. The third type of information is a policy decision (10 percent, 15 percent, or 20 percent).

The original model is run 30 times, simulating the hours from 8 A.M. to 10 A.M. Statistics are collected by SimQuick and summarized. Figure E.5 provides some key results for the model of the current process as output by SimQuick (many other statistics are collected but not displayed here).

The numbers shown are averages across the 30 simulations. The number 237.23 is the average number of passengers that enter line 1 during the simulated two hours. The two mean inventory statistics tell us that, on average, 5.97 simulated passengers were standing in line 1 and 0.10 standing in line 2. Statistics on *cycle time*, interpreted here as the time a passenger spends at one or more SimQuick building blocks, tell us that the simulated passengers in line 1 waited an average of 3.12 minutes, while those in line 2 waited 0.53 minute. The final inventory statistic tells us that, on average, 224.57 simulated passengers passed through the security process in the simulated two hours. The next step is to change the percentage of simulated passengers selected for the second inspection to 15 percent, and then to 20 percent, and rerun the model. Of course, these process changes will increase the average waiting time for the second inspection, but by how much? The final step is to rerun these simulations with one more workstation and see its effect on the waiting time for the second inspection. All the details for this model (as well as many others) appear in the textbook *SimQuick: Process Simulation with Excel*, which is included, along with the SimQuick software, in MyOMLab.

Simulation programming can also be done in a variety of computer languages, including general-purpose programming languages such as VISUAL BASIC, FORTRAN, or C++. The advantage of general-purpose programming languages is that they are available on most computer systems. Special simulation languages, such as GPSS, SIMSCRIPT, and SLAM, are also available. These languages simplify programming because they have macroinstructions for the commonly used elements of simulation models. These macroinstructions automatically contain the computer instructions needed to generate arrivals, keep track of waiting lines, and calculate the statistics on the operating characteristics of a system.

MyOMLab

LEARNING GOALS IN REVIEW

Learning Goal	Guidelines for Review	MyOMLab Resources
❶ Identify four reasons for using simulation models.	Review the section "Reasons for Using Simulation Models," pp. 1–2, for four reasons why simulation is useful.	
❷ Perform a manual simulation using the Monte Carlo simulation process	See section "The Monte Carlo Simulation Process," pp. 2–6, which shows how random-number assignments are made for each random event. Focus on Table E.2. We also describe the model formulation process. Study Example E.2 to see how the eight steps are performed. Solved Problem 1 also provides an example.	**POM for Windows:** Simulation
❸ Create a simple simulation model with an Excel spreadsheet.	The section "Simulation with Excel Spreadsheets," pp. 6–9, simulates the sales at an automobile dealership. Of particular interest is the use of the formula = RAND( ) to generate a random number into a cell of the Excel spreadsheet. Figure E.2 is annotated to show how the spreadsheet works. Figure E.3 shows a more complicated simulation where there are two uncontrollable variables.	
❹ Describe the advanced capabilities of SimQuick.	In the section "Simulation with SimQuick Software," pp. 9–10, SimQuick, an easy-to-use package provided with MyOMLab, is illustrated with an example of a passenger security process. Several exercises are provided in MyOMLab for various chapters. Also study Solved Problem 2.	**SimQuick:** Process Simulation with Excel

Key Terms

Solved Problem 1

A manager is considering production of several products in an automated facility. The manager would purchase a combination of two robots. The two robots (named Mel and Danny) are capable of doing all the required operations. Every batch of work will contain 10 units. A waiting line of several batches will be maintained in front of Mel. When Mel completes its portion of the work, the batch will then be transferred directly to Danny.

$$\boxed{\text{Waiting line}} \rightarrow \text{Mel} \rightarrow \text{Danny}$$

Each robot incurs a setup before it can begin processing a batch. Each unit in the batch has equal run time. The distributions of the setup times and run times for Mel and Danny are identical. But because Mel and Danny will be performing different operations, simulation of each batch requires four random numbers from the table. The first random number determines Mel's setup time, the second determines Mel's run time per unit, and the third and fourth random numbers determine Danny's setup and run times, respectively.

Setup Time (Min)	Probability	Run Time per Unit (Sec)	Probability
1	0.10	5	0.10
2	0.20	6	0.20
3	0.40	7	0.30
4	0.20	8	0.25
5	0.10	9	0.15

Estimate how many units will be produced in an hour. Then, simulate 60 minutes of operation for Mel and Danny. The random numbers have already been selected in Table E.4 for each of the four uncontrolled variables. For example, the third column provides the random numbers for determining Mel's setup time for each batch, and the fifth column provides the random numbers for determining Mel's processing times.

SOLUTION

Except for the time required for Mel to set up and run the first batch, we assume that the two robots run simultaneously. The expected average setup time per batch is

$$[(0.1 \times 1\,\text{min}) + (0.2 \times 2\,\text{min})(0.4 \times 3\,\text{min})(0.2 \times 4\,\text{min})(0.1 \times 5\,\text{min})]$$
$$= 3\,\text{minutes or }180\,\text{seconds per batch}$$

The expected average run time per batch (of 10 units) is

$$[(0.1 \times 5\,\text{sec}) + (0.2 \times 6\,\text{sec}) + (0.3 \times 7\,\text{sec}) + (0.25 \times 8\,\text{sec}) + (0.15 \times 9\,\text{sec})]$$
$$= 7.15\,\text{seconds/units} \times 10\,\text{units/batch} = 71.5\,\text{seconds per batch}$$

Thus, the total of average setup and run times per batch is 251.5 seconds. In an hour's time, we might expect to complete about 14 batches ($3,600/251.5$ seconds $= 14.3$). However, this estimate is probably too high.

Keep in mind that Mel and Danny operate in sequence and that Danny cannot begin to do work until it has been completed by Mel (see batch 2 of Table E.4). Nor can Mel start a new batch until Danny is ready to accept the previous one. Refer to batch 6, where Mel completes this batch at time 25:50 but cannot begin the seventh batch until Danny is ready to accept the sixth batch at time 28:00.

Mel and Danny completed only 12 batches in one hour. Even though the robots used the same probability distributions and therefore have perfectly balanced production capacities, Mel and Danny did not produce the expected capacity of 14 batches because Danny was sometimes idle while waiting for Mel (see batch 2) and Mel was sometimes idle while waiting for Danny (see batch 6). This loss-of-throughput phenomenon occurs whenever variable processes are closely linked, whether those processes are mechanical, such as Mel's and Danny's, or functional, such as production and marketing. The simulation

TABLE E.4 | SIMULATION RESULTS FOR MEL AND DANNY

Batch No.	Start Time	Random No.	Setup	Mel Random No.	Process	Cumulative Time	Start Time	Random No.	Setup	Danny Random No.	Process	Cumulative Time
1	0:00	71	4 min	50	7 sec	5 min 10 sec	5:10	21	2 min	94	9 sec	8 min 40 sec
2	5:10	50	3 min	63	8 sec	9 min 30 sec	9:30	47	3 min	83	8 sec	13 min 50 sec
3	9:30	31	3 min	73	8 sec	13 min 50 sec	13:50	04	1 min	17	6 sec	15 min 50 sec
4	13:50	96	5 min	98	9 sec	20 min 20 sec	20:20	21	2 min	82	8 sec	23 min 40 sec
5	20:20	25	2 min	92	9 sec	23 min 50 sec	23:50	32	3 min	53	7 sec	28 min 00 sec
6	23:50	00	1 min	15	6 sec	25 min 50 sec	28:00	66	3 min	57	7 sec	32 min 10 sec
7	28:00	00	1 min	99	9 sec	30 min 30 sec	32:10	55	3 min	11	6 sec	36 min 10 sec
8	32:10	10	2 min	61	8 sec	35 min 30 sec	36:10	31	3 min	35	7 sec	40 min 20 sec
9	36:10	09	1 min	73	8 sec	38 min 30 sec	40:20	24	2 min	70	8 sec	43 min 40 sec
10	40:20	79	4 min	95	9 sec	45 min 50 sec	45:50	66	3 min	61	8 sec	50 min 10 sec
11	45:50	01	1 min	41	7 sec	48 min 00 sec	50:10	88	4 min	23	6 sec	55 min 10 sec
12	50:10	57	3 min	45	7 sec	54 min 20 sec	55:10	21	2 min	61	8 sec	58 min 30 sec
13	55:10	26	2 min	46	7 sec	58 min 20 sec	58:30	97	5 min	31	7 sec	64 min 40 sec

shows the need to place between the two robots sufficient space to store several batches to absorb the variations in process times. Subsequent simulations could be run to show how many batches are needed.

Solved Problem 2

Customers enter a small bank, get into a single line, are served by a teller, and finally leave the bank. Currently, this bank has one teller working from 9 A.M. to 11 A.M. Management is concerned that the wait in line seems to be too long. Therefore, it is considering two process improvement ideas: adding an additional teller during these hours or installing a new automated check-reading machine that can help the single teller serve customers more quickly. Use SimQuick to model these two processes. All the details for this model (as well as many others) appear in the book *SimQuick: Process Simulation with Excel*, which is included, along with the SimQuick software, in MyOMLab.

MyOMLab

SOLUTION

A first step in using SimQuick is to draw a flowchart of the process using SimQuick's building blocks. Figure E.6(a) shows that the one-teller bank (both the original and the variation with a check-reading machine) can be modeled with four building blocks: an entrance (modeling the arrival of customers at the bank), a buffer (modeling the waiting line), a workstation (modeling the teller), and a final buffer (modeling served customers). The two-teller variation can be modeled with five building blocks, as shown in Figure E.6(b).

Information describing each building block is entered into SimQuick tables. Three key pieces of information need to be entered: (1) when people arrive at the door, (2) how long the teller takes to serve a customer, and (3) the maximum length of the line. The first two pieces of information are described by statistical distributions. Each of the three models is run 30 times, simulating the hours from 9 A.M. to 11 A.M. Statistics are collected by SimQuick and summarized. Figure E.6 shows the key results for the model

FIGURE E.6A ▶
Flowchart for a One-Teller Bank

FIGURE E.6B ▶
Flowchart for a Two-Teller Bank

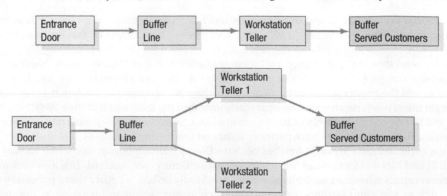

of the original one-teller process as output by SimQuick (many other statistics are collected, but they are not displayed here).

The numbers shown in Figure E.7 are averages across the 30 simulations. The service level for "Door" tells us that 90 percent of the simulated customers who arrived at the bank were able to get into "Line" (hence 10 percent found "Line" full and immediately left). The mean inventory for "Line" tells us that, on average, 4.47 simulated customers were standing in line. The mean cycle time tells us that simulated customers waited an average of 11.04 minutes in line.

When we run the model with two tellers, we find that the service level increases to 100 percent, the mean inventory in "Line" decreases to 0.37 customer, and the mean cycle time drops to 0.71 minute. These are all dramatic improvements. When we run the one-teller model with the faster check-reading machine, we find that the service level is 97 percent, the mean inventory in "Line" is 2.89 customers, and the mean cycle time is 6.21 minutes. These statistics, together with cost information, should help management select the best process.

▼ **FIGURE E.7**
Simulation Results of Bank

Element Types	Element Names	Statistics	Overall Means
Entrance(s)	Door	Service level	0.90
Buffer(s)	Line	Mean inventory	4.47
		Mean cycle time	11.04

Problems

The OM Explorer and POM for Windows software is available to all students using the 11th edition of this textbook. Go to **http://www.pearsonhighered.com/krajewski** to download these computer packages. If you purchased MyOMLab, you also have access to Active Models software and significant help in doing the following problems. Check with your instructor on how best to use these resources. In many cases, the instructor wants you to understand how to do the calculations by hand. At the least, the software provides a check on your calculations. When calculations are particularly complex and the goal is interpreting the results in making decisions, the software entirely replaces the manual calculations.

The Monte Carlo Simulation Process

1. Comet Dry Cleaners specializes in same-day dry cleaning. Customers drop off their garments early in the morning and expect them to be ready for pickup on their way home from work. The risk is, however, that the work needed on a garment cannot be done that day, depending on the type of cleaning required. Historically, an average of 20 garments has had to be held over to the next day. The outlet's manager is contemplating expanding to reduce or eliminate that backlog. A simulation model was developed with the following distribution for garments per day:

Number	Probability	Random Numbers
50	0.10	00–09
60	0.25	10–34
70	0.30	35–64
80	0.25	65–89
90	0.10	90–99

With expansion, the maximum number of garments that could be dry-cleaned per day is

Number	Probability	Random Numbers
60	0.30	00–29
70	0.40	30–69
80	0.30	70–99

In the simulation for a specific day, the number of garments needing cleaning (NGNC) is determined first. Next, the maximum number of garments that could be dry-cleaned (MNGD) is determined. If MNGD ≥ NGNC, all garments are dry-cleaned for that day. If MNGD < NGNC, then (NGNC − MNGD) garments must be added to the number of garments arriving the next day to obtain the NGNC for the next day. The simulation continues in this manner.

a. Assuming that the store is empty at the start, simulate 15 days of operation. Use the following random numbers, the first determining the number of arrivals and the second setting the capacity:

$$(49, 77), (27, 53), (65, 08), (83, 12), (04, 82),$$
$$(58, 44), (53, 83), (57, 72), (32, 53), (60, 79),$$
$$(79, 30), (41, 48), (97, 86), (30, 25), (80, 73)$$

Determine the average daily number of garments held overnight, based on your simulation.

b. If the cost associated with garments being held over is $25 per garment per day and the added cost of expansion is $200 per day, is expansion a good idea?

2. The Precision Manufacturing Company is considering the purchase of a numerical control (NC) machine and has narrowed the possible choices to two models. The company produces several products, and batches of work arrive at the NC machine every 6 minutes. The number of units in the batch has the following discrete distribution:

Number of Units in Batch	Probability
3	0.1
6	0.2
8	0.3
14	0.2
18	0.2

The distributions of the setup times and processing times for the two NC models follow. Assume that the work in a batch shares a single setup and that each unit in the batch has equal processing time. Simulate 2 hours (or 10 batch arrivals) of operation for the two NC machines. Use the following random numbers—the first one for the number of units in a batch, the second one for setup times, and the third one for run times:

(71, 21, 50), (50, 94, 63), (96, 93, 95), (83, 09, 49), (10, 20, 68), (48, 23, 11), (21, 28, 40), (39, 78, 93), (99, 95, 61), (28, 14, 48)

Which one would you recommend if both machines cost the same to purchase, operate, and maintain?

NC MACHINE 1			
Setup Time (min)	Probability	Run Time per Unit (sec)	Probability
1	0.10	5	0.10
2	0.20	6	0.20
3	0.40	7	0.30
4	0.20	8	0.25
5	0.10	9	0.15

NC MACHINE 2			
Setup Time (min)	Probability	Run Time per Unit (sec)	Probability
1	0.05	3	0.20
2	0.15	4	0.25
3	0.25	5	0.30
4	0.45	6	0.15
5	0.10	7	0.10

3. In Problem 2, what factors would you consider if the initial cost of NC Machine 1 was $4,000 less than that of NC Machine 2?

4. The 30 management professors at Omega University find out that telephone calls made to their offices are not being picked up. A call-forwarding system redirects calls to the management office after the fourth ring. A department office assistant answers the telephone and takes messages. An average of 90 telephone calls per hour is placed to the management faculty, and each telephone call consumes about one minute of the assistant's time. The calls arrive to a Poisson distribution, as shown in Figure E.8 (a), with an average of 1.5 calls per minute. Because the professors spend much of their time in class and in conferences, there is only a 40 percent chance that they will pick up a call themselves, as shown in Figure E.8 (b). If two or more telephone calls are forwarded to the office during the same minute, only the first call will be answered.

   a. Without using simulation, make a preliminary guess of what proportion of the time the assistant will be on the telephone and what proportion of the telephone calls will not be answered.

   b. Now, use random numbers to simulate the situation for one hour starting at 10:00 A.M. Table E.5 on the following page will get you started.

   c. What proportion of the time is the office assistant on the telephone? What proportion of the telephone calls is not answered? Are these proportions close to what you expected?

5. The management chair at Omega University is considering installing a voice-mail system. Monthly operating costs are $25 per voice-mailbox, but the system will reduce the amount of time the office assistant spends answering the telephone by 60 percent. The department has 32 telephones. Use the results of your simulation in Problem 4 to estimate the proportion of the assistant's time currently spent answering the telephone. The office assistant's salary (and overhead) is $3,000 per month. Should the management chair order the voice-mail system?

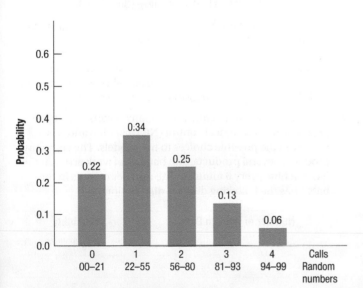

(a) Probabilities of numbers of telephone calls placed per minute

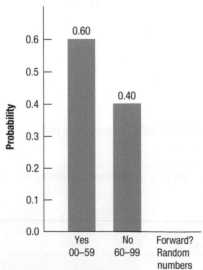

(b) Probability of forwarding a call

▲ **FIGURE E.8**
Probability Distributions for Omega University

TABLE E.5 | OFFICE ASSISTANT SIMULATION

Time	RN	Number of Calls Made	RN	1st Call Forwarded? (Yes/No)	RN	2nd Call Forwarded? (Yes/No)	RN	3rd Call Forwarded? (Yes/No)	RN	4th Call Forwarded? (Yes/No)	Number of Calls Not Answered	Assistant Idle (3)
10:00	68	2	30	Yes	54	Yes					1	
10:01	76	2	36	Yes	32	Yes					1	
10:02	68	2	04	Yes	07	Yes					1	
10:03	98	4	08	Yes	21	Yes	28	Yes	79	No	2	
10:04	25	1	77	No							0	✓
10:05	51	1	23	Yes							0	
10:06	67	2	22	Yes	27	Yes					1	
10:07	80	2	87	No	06	Yes					0	
10:08	03	0									0	✓
10:09	03	0									0	✓
10:10	33	1	78	No							0	✓

6. Weekly demand at a local E–Z Mart convenience store for 1-gallon jugs of low-fat milk for the past 50 weeks varied between 60 and 65 jugs, as shown in the following table. Demand in excess of stock cannot be backordered.

   a. Assign random numbers between 00 and 99 to simulate the demand probability distribution.

   b. E–Z Mart orders 62 jugs every week. Simulate the demand for this item for 10 weeks, using the random numbers 97, 2, 80, 66, 99, 56, 54, 28, 64, and 47. Determine the shortage or excess stock for each week.

Demand (jugs)	Number of Weeks
60	5
61	7
62	17
63	11
64	6
65	4
	Total 50

   c. What is the average shortage and the average excess stock for the 10 weeks?

7. The Brakes-Only Service Shop promises its customers same-day service by working overtime if necessary. The shop's two mechanics can handle a total of 12 brake jobs a day during regular hours. Over the past 100 days, the number of brake jobs at the shop varied between 10 and 14, as shown in the following table:

Demand (jobs)	Number of Days
10	10
11	30
12	30
13	20
14	10
	Total 100

   a. Assign random numbers between 00 and 99 to simulate the demand probability distribution for brake jobs.

   b. Simulate the demand for the next 10 days, using the random numbers 28, 83, 73, 7, 4, 63, 37, 38, 50, and 92.

   c. On how many days will overtime work be necessary? On how many days will the mechanics be underutilized?

   d. What percent of days, on average, will overtime work be necessary?

8. A machine center handles four types of clients: A, B, C, and D. The manager wants to assess the number of machines required to produce goods for these clients. Setup times for changeover from one client to another are negligible. Annual demand and processing times are uncertain; demand may be low, normal, or high. The probabilities for these three events are shown in the following tables:

CLIENT A			
Demand (units/yr)	Probability	Processing Time (hr/unit)	Probability
3,000	0.10	10	0.35
3,500	0.60	20	0.45
4,200	0.30	30	0.20

CLIENT B

Demand (units/yr)	Probability	Processing Time (hr/unit)	Probability
500	0.30	60	0.25
800	0.50	90	0.50
900	0.20	100	0.25

CLIENT C

Demand (units/yr)	Probability	Processing Time (hr/unit)	Probability
1,500	0.10	12	0.25
3,000	0.50	15	0.60
4,500	0.40	20	0.15

CLIENT D

Demand (units/yr)	Probability	Processing Time (hr/unit)	Probability
600	0.40	60	0.30
650	0.50	70	0.65
700	0.10	80	0.05

a. Explain how simulation could be used to generate a probability distribution for the total number of machine-hours required per year to serve the clients.

b. Simulate one year, using the following random numbers. Use random number 88 for client A's demand, 24 for client A's processing time, and so forth.

88, 24, 33, 29, 52, 84, 37, 92

Simulation with Excel Spreadsheets

9. The sales activity at BestCar (see Example E.3) has changed. Weekly sales are now estimated to be distributed as follows:

Weekly Sales (cars)	Relative Frequency (probability)
0	0.02
1	0.03
2	0.05
3	0.10
4	0.15
5	0.30
6	0.20
7	0.10
8	0.05
	Total 1.00

Create an Excel model that simulates 500 weeks at BestCar. It should calculate from the simulated experience the average number of cars and revenue per week and also a frequency table on car sales.

10. Keep the same weekly sales distribution for BestCar as in Example E.3, but assume that the price of cars is distributed as follows:

Sales Price (price/car)	Relative Frequency (probability)
$18,000	0.15
$20,000	0.35
$22,000	0.35
$24,000	0.10
$26,000	0.05
	Total 1.00

Create an Excel model that simulates 500 weeks at BestCar. It should calculate from the simulated experience the average number of cars and revenue per week and also a frequency table on car sales.

Table of Random Numbers

71509	68310	48213	99928	64650	13229	36921	58732	13459	93487
21949	30920	23287	89514	58502	46185	00368	82613	02668	37444
50639	54968	11409	36148	82090	87298	41396	71111	00076	60029
47837	76716	09653	54466	87987	82362	17933	52793	17641	19502
31735	36901	92295	19293	57582	86043	69502	12601	00535	82697
04174	32342	66532	07875	54445	08795	63563	42295	74646	73120
96980	68728	21154	56181	71843	66134	52396	89723	96435	17871
21823	04027	76402	04655	87276	32593	17097	06913	05136	05115
25922	07122	31485	52166	07645	85122	20945	06369	70254	22806
32530	98882	19105	01769	20276	59401	60426	03316	41438	22012
00159	08461	51810	14650	45119	97920	08063	70819	01832	53295
66574	21384	75357	55888	83429	96916	73977	87883	13249	28870
00995	28829	15048	49573	65277	61493	44031	88719	73057	66010
55114	79226	27929	23392	06432	50200	39054	15528	53483	33972
10614	25190	52647	62580	51183	31338	60008	66595	64357	14985
31359	77469	58126	59192	23371	25190	37841	44386	92420	42965
09736	51873	94595	61367	82091	63835	86858	10677	58209	59820
24709	23224	45788	21426	63353	29874	51058	29958	61220	61199
79957	67598	74102	49824	39305	15069	56327	26905	34453	53964
66616	22137	72805	64420	58711	68435	60301	28620	91919	96080
01413	27281	19397	36231	05010	42003	99865	20924	76151	54089
88238	80731	20777	45725	41480	48277	45704	96457	13918	52375
57457	87883	64273	26236	61095	01309	48632	00431	63730	18917
21614	06412	71007	20255	39890	75336	89451	88091	61011	38072
26466	03735	39891	26361	86816	48193	33492	70484	77322	01016
97314	03944	04509	46143	88908	55261	73433	62538	63187	57352
91207	33555	75942	41668	64650	38741	86189	38197	99112	59694
46791	78974	01999	78891	16177	95746	78076	75001	51309	18791
34161	32258	05345	79267	75607	29916	37005	09213	10991	50451
02376	40372	45077	73705	56076	01853	83512	81567	55951	27156
33994	56809	58377	45976	01581	78389	18268	90057	93382	28494
92588	92024	15048	87841	38008	80689	73098	39201	10907	88092
73767	61534	66197	47147	22994	38197	60844	86962	27595	49907
51517	39870	94094	77092	94595	37904	27553	02229	44993	10468
33910	05156	60844	89012	21154	68937	96477	05867	95809	72827
09444	93069	61764	99301	55826	78849	26131	28201	91417	98172
96896	43769	72890	78682	78243	24061	55449	53587	77574	51580
97523	54633	99656	08503	52563	12099	52479	74374	79581	57143
42568	30794	32613	21802	73809	60237	70087	36650	54487	43718
45453	33136	90246	61953	17724	42421	87611	95369	42108	95369
52814	26445	73516	24897	90622	35018	70087	60112	09025	05324
87318	33345	14546	15445	81588	75461	12246	47858	08983	18205
08063	83575	26294	93027	09988	04487	88364	31087	22200	91019
53400	82078	52103	25650	75315	18916	06809	88217	12245	33053
90789	60614	20862	34475	11744	24437	55198	55219	74730	59820
73684	25859	86858	48946	30941	79017	53776	72534	83638	44680
82007	12183	89326	53713	77782	50368	01748	39033	47042	65758
80208	30920	97774	41417	79038	60531	32990	57770	53441	58732
62434	96122	63019	58439	89702	38657	60049	88761	22785	66093
04718	83199	65863	58857	49886	70275	27511	99426	53985	84077

Selected References

Abdou, G., and S.P. Dutta. "A Systematic Simulation Approach for the Design of JIT Manufacturing Systems." *Journal of Operations Management*, vol. 11, no. 3 (1993), pp. 25–38.

Brennan, J.E., B.L. Golden, and H.K. Rappoport. "Go with the Flow: Improving Red Cross Bloodmobiles Using Simulation Analysis." *Interfaces*, vol. 22, no. 5 (1992), p. 1.

Christy, D.P., and H.J. Watson. "The Application of Simulation: A Survey of Industry Practice." *Interfaces*, vol. 13, no. 5 (October 1983), pp. 47–52.

Hartvigsen, David. *SimQuick: Process Simulation with Excel*, 2nd ed. Upper Saddle River, NJ: Prentice Hall, 2004.

ExtendSim 9.1, (http://www.extendsim.com) Imagine That Inc. San Jose, CA. (2014)

Law, A.M., and W.D. Kelton. *Simulation Modeling and Analysis*, 3rd ed. New York: McGraw-Hill, 2000.

Micro Analysis and Design Software, Inc. "Hospital Overcrowding Solutions Are Found with Simulation." *Industrial Engineering* (December 1993), p. 557.

Swedish, Julian. "Simulation Brings Productivity Enhancements to the Social Security Administration." *Industrial Engineering* (May 1993), pp. 28–30.

Winston, Wayne L. *Simulation Modeling Using @RISK: Updated for Version 4*. Belmont, CA: Wadsworth Publishing Company, 2001.

Winston, Wayne L. *Financial Models using Simulation and Optimization II: Investment*. Palisade Corporation, 2001.

F

FINANCIAL ANALYSIS

Many decisions in operations and supply chain management involve large capital investments. Automation, outsourcing decisions, capacity expansion, layout revisions, building a new distribution center, and installing a new ERP system are only a few examples. In fact, most of a firm's assets are tied up in the operations function. Therefore, management should seek high-yield capital projects and then assess their costs, benefits, and risks.

Such projects require strong cross-functional coordination, particularly with finance and accounting. The projects must fit in with the organization's financial plans and capabilities. If a firm plans to open a new production facility in 2019, it must begin lining up financing in 2015. The projects must also be subjected to one or more types of financial analysis to assess their attractiveness relative to other investment opportunities. This supplement presents a brief overview of basic financial analyses and the types of computer support available for making such decisions. See your finance textbook for a more comprehensive treatment of the subject.

LEARNING GOALS *After reading this supplement, you should be able to:*

1 Explain the time value of money concept.

2 Demonstrate the use of the net present value, internal rate of return, and payback methods of financial analysis.

3 Discuss the importance of combining managerial judgment with quantitative techniques when making investment decisions.

Time Value of Money

An important concept underlying many financial analysis techniques is that a dollar in hand today is worth more than a dollar to be received in the future. A dollar in hand can be invested to earn a return so that more than one dollar will be available in the future. This concept is known as the **time value of money**.

Future Value of an Investment

If $5,000 is invested at 10 percent interest for 1 year, at the end of the year the $5,000 will have earned $500 in interest and the total amount available will be $5,500. If the interest earned is allowed to accumulate, it also earns interest and the original investment will grow to $12,970 in 10 years. The process by which interest on an investment accumulates and then earns interest itself for the remainder of the investment period is known as **compounding interest**. The value of an investment at the end of the period over which interest is compounded is called the **future value of an investment**.

time value of money
The concept that a dollar in hand can be invested to earn a return so that more than one dollar will be available in the future.

compounding interest
The process by which interest on an investment accumulates and then earns interest itself for the remainder of the investment period.

future value of an investment
The value of an investment at the end of the period over which interest is compounded.

To calculate the future value of an investment, you first express the interest rate and the time period in the same units of time as the interval at which compounding occurs. Let us assume that interest is compounded annually, express all time periods in years, and use annual interest rates. To find the value of an investment one year in the future, multiply the amount invested by the sum of 1 plus the interest rate (expressed as a decimal). The value of a $5,000 investment at 12 percent per year, one year from now is

$$\$5,000(1.12) = \$5,600$$

If the entire amount remains invested, at the end of 2 years you would have

$$\$5,600(1.12) = \$5,000(1.12)^2 = \$6,272$$

In general,

$$F = P(1 + r)^n$$

where

F = future value of the investment at the end of n periods

P = amount invested at the beginning, called the principal

r = periodic interest rate

n = number of time periods for which the interest compounds

Present Value of an Investment

Let us look at the converse problem. Suppose that you want to make an investment now that will be worth $10,000 in one year. If the interest rate is 12 percent and P represents the amount invested now, the relation becomes

$$F = \$10,000 = P(1 + 0.12)$$

Solving for P gives

$$P = \frac{F}{(1 + r)^n} = \frac{10,000}{(1 + 0.12)^1} = \$8,929$$

present value of an investment

The amount that must be
invested now to accumulate to
a certain amount in the future at
a specific interest rate.

discounting

The process of finding the present value of an investment when
the future value and the interest
rate are known.

The amount that must be invested now to accumulate to a certain amount in the future at a specific interest rate is called the **present value of an investment**. The process of finding the present value of an investment when the future value and the interest rate are known is called **discounting** the future value to its present value. If the number of time periods n for which discounting is desired is greater than 1, the present value is determined by dividing the future value by the nth power of the sum of 1 plus the interest rate. The general formula for determining the present value is

$$P = \frac{F}{(1 + r)^n}$$

The interest rate is also called the **discount rate**.

discount rate

The interest rate used in
discounting the future value
to its present value.

Present Value Factors

Although you can calculate P from its formula in a few steps with most pocket calculators, you also can use a table. To do so, write the present value formula another way:

$$P = \frac{F}{(1 + r)^n} = F\left[\frac{1}{(1 + r)^n}\right]$$

Let $[1/(1 + r)^n]$ be the *present value factor*, which is called pf and which you can find in Table F.1. This table gives you the present value of a future amount of $1 for various time periods and interest rates. To use the table, locate the column for the appropriate interest rate and the row for the appropriate period. The number in the body of the table where this row and column intersect is the pf value. Multiply it by F to get P. For example, suppose that an investment will generate $15,000 in 10 years. If the interest rate is 12 percent, Table F.1 shows that pf = 0.3220. Multiplying it by $15,000 gives the present value, or

$$P = F(\text{pf}) = \$15,000(0.3220)$$

$$= \$4,830$$

TABLE F.1 | PRESENT VALUE FACTORS FOR A SINGLE PAYMENT

Number of Periods (n)	INTEREST RATE (r)																	
	0.01	0.02	0.03	0.04	0.05	0.06	0.08	0.10	0.12	0.14	0.16	0.18	0.20	0.22	0.24	0.26	0.28	0.30
1	0.9901	0.9804	0.9709	0.9615	0.9524	0.9434	0.9259	0.9091	0.8929	0.8772	0.8621	0.8475	0.8333	0.8197	0.8065	0.7937	0.7812	0.7692
2	0.9803	0.9612	0.9426	0.9246	0.9070	0.8900	0.8573	0.8264	0.7972	0.7695	0.7432	0.7182	0.6944	0.6719	0.6504	0.6299	0.6104	0.5917
3	0.9706	0.9423	0.9151	0.8890	0.8638	0.8396	0.7938	0.7513	0.7118	0.6750	0.6407	0.6086	0.5787	0.5507	0.5245	0.4999	0.4768	0.4552
4	0.9610	0.9238	0.8885	0.8548	0.8227	0.7921	0.7350	0.6830	0.6355	0.5921	0.5523	0.5158	0.4823	0.4514	0.4230	0.3968	0.3725	0.3501
5	0.9515	0.9057	0.8626	0.8219	0.7835	0.7473	0.6806	0.6209	0.5674	0.5194	0.4761	0.4371	0.4019	0.3700	0.3411	0.3149	0.2910	0.2693
6	0.9420	0.8880	0.8375	0.7903	0.7462	0.7050	0.6302	0.5645	0.5066	0.4556	0.4104	0.3704	0.3349	0.3033	0.2751	0.2499	0.2274	0.2072
7	0.9327	0.8706	0.8131	0.7599	0.7107	0.6651	0.5835	0.5132	0.4523	0.3996	0.3538	0.3139	0.2791	0.2486	0.2218	0.1983	0.1776	0.1594
8	0.9235	0.8535	0.7894	0.7307	0.6768	0.6274	0.5403	0.4665	0.4039	0.3506	0.3050	0.2660	0.2326	0.2038	0.1789	0.1574	0.1388	0.1226
9	0.9143	0.8368	0.7664	0.7026	0.6446	0.5919	0.5002	0.4241	0.3606	0.3075	0.2630	0.2255	0.1938	0.1670	0.1443	0.1249	0.1084	0.0943
10	0.9053	0.8203	0.7441	0.6756	0.6139	0.5584	0.4632	0.3855	0.3220	0.2697	0.2267	0.1911	0.1615	0.1369	0.1164	0.0922	0.0847	0.0725
11	0.8963	0.8043	0.7224	0.6496	0.5847	0.5268	0.4289	0.3505	0.2875	0.2366	0.1954	0.1619	0.1346	0.1122	0.0938	0.0787	0.0662	0.0558
12	0.8874	0.7885	0.7014	0.6246	0.5568	0.4970	0.3971	0.3186	0.2567	0.2076	0.1685	0.1372	0.1122	0.0920	0.0757	0.0625	0.0517	0.0429
13	0.8787	0.7730	0.6810	0.6006	0.5303	0.4688	0.3677	0.2897	0.2292	0.1821	0.1452	0.1163	0.0935	0.0754	0.0610	0.0496	0.0404	0.0330
14	0.8700	0.7579	0.6611	0.5775	0.5051	0.4423	0.3405	0.2633	0.2046	0.1597	0.1252	0.0985	0.0779	0.0618	0.0492	0.0393	0.0316	0.0254
15	0.8613	0.7430	0.6419	0.5553	0.4810	0.4173	0.3152	0.2394	0.1827	0.1401	0.1079	0.0835	0.0649	0.0507	0.0397	0.0312	0.0247	0.0195
16	0.8528	0.7284	0.6232	0.5339	0.4581	0.3936	0.2919	0.2176	0.1631	0.1229	0.0930	0.0708	0.0541	0.0415	0.0320	0.0248	0.0193	0.0150
17	0.8444	0.7142	0.6050	0.5134	0.4363	0.3714	0.2703	0.1978	0.1456	0.1078	0.0802	0.0600	0.0451	0.0340	0.0258	0.0197	0.0150	0.0116
18	0.8360	0.7002	0.5874	0.4936	0.4155	0.3503	0.2502	0.1799	0.1300	0.0946	0.0691	0.0508	0.0376	0.0279	0.0208	0.0156	0.0118	0.0089
19	0.8277	0.6864	0.5703	0.4746	0.3957	0.3305	0.2317	0.1635	0.1161	0.0829	0.0596	0.0431	0.0313	0.0229	0.0168	0.0124	0.0092	0.0068
20	0.8195	0.6730	0.5537	0.4564	0.3769	0.3118	0.2145	0.1486	0.1037	0.0728	0.0514	0.0365	0.0261	0.0187	0.0135	0.0098	0.0072	0.0053
21	0.8114	0.6598	0.5375	0.4388	0.3589	0.2942	0.1987	0.1351	0.0926	0.0638	0.0443	0.0309	0.0217	0.0154	0.0109	0.0078	0.0056	0.0040
22	0.8034	0.6468	0.5219	0.4220	0.3418	0.2775	0.1839	0.1228	0.0826	0.0560	0.0382	0.0262	0.0181	0.0126	0.0088	0.0062	0.0044	0.0031
23	0.7954	0.6342	0.5067	0.4057	0.3256	0.2618	0.1703	0.1117	0.0738	0.0491	0.0329	0.0222	0.0151	0.0103	0.0071	0.0049	0.0034	0.0024
24	0.7876	0.6217	0.4919	0.3901	0.3101	0.2470	0.1577	0.1015	0.0659	0.0431	0.0284	0.0188	0.0126	0.0085	0.0057	0.0039	0.0027	0.0018
25	0.7798	0.6095	0.4776	0.3751	0.2953	0.2330	0.1460	0.0923	0.0588	0.0378	0.0245	0.0160	0.0105	0.0069	0.0046	0.0031	0.0021	0.0014
26	0.7720	0.5976	0.4637	0.3607	0.2812	0.2198	0.1352	0.0839	0.0525	0.0331	0.0211	0.0135	0.0087	0.0057	0.0037	0.0025	0.0016	0.0011
27	0.7644	0.5859	0.4502	0.3468	0.2678	0.2074	0.1252	0.0763	0.0469	0.0291	0.0182	0.0115	0.0073	0.0047	0.0030	0.0019	0.0013	0.0008
28	0.7568	0.5744	0.4371	0.3335	0.2551	0.1956	0.1159	0.0693	0.0419	0.0255	0.0157	0.0097	0.0061	0.0038	0.0024	0.0015	0.0010	0.0006
29	0.7493	0.5631	0.4243	0.3207	0.2429	0.1846	0.1073	0.0630	0.0374	0.0224	0.0135	0.0082	0.0051	0.0031	0.0020	0.0012	0.0008	0.0005
30	0.7419	0.5521	0.4120	0.3083	0.2314	0.1741	0.0994	0.0573	0.0334	0.0196	0.0116	0.0070	0.0042	0.0026	0.0016	0.0010	0.0006	0.0004
35	0.7059	0.5000	0.3554	0.2534	0.1813	0.1301	0.0676	0.0356	0.0189	0.0102	0.0055	0.0030	0.0017	0.0009	0.0005	0.0003	0.0002	0.0001
40	0.6717	0.4529	0.3066	0.2083	0.1420	0.0972	0.0460	0.0221	0.0107	0.0053	0.0026	0.0013	0.0007	0.0004	0.0002	0.0001	0.0001	0.0000

$$P = \frac{F}{(1+r)^n} = F(pf)$$

where P = present value of a single investment
  F = future value of a single payment
  n = number of periods for which P is to be invested
  r = periodic interest rate
  pf = present value factor for $1 = 1/(1+r)^n$

Annuities

An **annuity** is a series of payments of a fixed amount for a specified number of years. All such payments are treated as happening at the end of a year. Suppose that you want to invest an amount at an interest rate of 10 percent so that you may draw out $5,000 per year for each of the next four years. You could determine the present value of this $5,000 four-year annuity by treating the four payments as single future payments. The present value of an investment needed now, in order for you to receive these payments for the next four years, is the sum of the present values of each of the four payments. That is,

$$P = \frac{\$5,000}{1 + 0.10} + \frac{\$5,000}{(1 + 0.10)^2} + \frac{\$5,000}{(1 + 0.10)^3} + \frac{\$5,000}{(1 + 0.10)^4}$$
$$= \$4,545 + \$4,132 + \$3,757 + \$3,415$$
$$= \$15,849$$

A much easier way to calculate this amount is to use Table F.2. Look for the factor in the table at the intersection of the 10 percent column and the fourth-period row. It is 3.1699. For annuities, this present value factor is called af to distinguish it from the present value factor for a single payment. To determine the present value of an annuity, multiply its amount by af to get

$$P = A(\text{af}) = \$5,000(3.1699)$$
$$= \$15,849$$

where

P = present value of an annuity

A = amount of the annuity received each year

af = present value factor for an annuity

Methods of Financial Analysis

You can now apply these concepts to the financial analysis of proposed investments. Three basic financial analysis techniques are as follow:

1. The net present value method
2. The internal rate of return method
3. The payback method

These methods work with *cash flows*. Cash flow is the cash that will flow into and out of the organization because of the project, including revenues, costs, and changes in assets and liabilities. Be sure to remember two points when determining cash flows for any project:

1. Consider only the amounts of cash flows that will change if the project is undertaken. These amounts are called incremental cash flows and are the difference between the cash flows with the project and without it.

2. Convert cash flows to *after-tax* amounts before applying the net present value, payback, or internal rate of return method to them. This step introduces taxes and depreciation into the calculations.

Depreciation and Taxes

Depreciation is an allowance for the consumption of capital. In this type of analysis, depreciation is relevant for only one reason: It acts as a tax shield. Depreciation is not a legitimate cash flow because it is not cash that is actually paid out each year. However, depreciation does affect how an accountant calculates net income, against which the income-tax rate is applied. Therefore, depreciation enters into the calculation, as a tax shield, only when tax liability is figured. Taxes must be paid on pretax cash inflows *minus* the depreciation that is associated with the proposed investment. U.S. tax laws allow either straight-line or accelerated depreciation.

Straight-Line Depreciation The **straight-line depreciation method** of calculating annual depreciation is the simplest and usually is adequate for internal planning purposes. First, subtract the estimated salvage value from the amount of investment required at the beginning of the project and then divide by the number of years in the asset's expected economic life. **Salvage value** is the cash flow

TABLE F.2 | PRESENT VALUE FACTORS OF AN ANNUITY

Number of Periods (n)	0.01	0.02	0.03	0.04	0.05	0.06	0.08	0.10	0.12	0.14	0.16	0.18	0.20	0.22	0.24	0.26	0.28	0.30
1	0.9901	0.9804	0.9709	0.9615	0.9524	0.9434	0.9259	0.9091	0.8929	0.8772	0.8621	0.8475	0.8333	0.8197	0.8065	0.7937	0.7812	0.7692
2	1.9704	1.9416	1.9135	1.8861	1.8594	1.8334	1.7833	1.7355	1.6901	1.6467	1.6052	1.5656	1.5278	1.4915	1.4568	1.4235	1.3916	1.3609
3	2.9410	2.8839	2.8286	2.7751	2.7232	2.6730	2.5771	2.4869	2.4018	2.3216	2.2459	2.1743	2.1065	2.0422	1.9813	1.9234	1.8684	1.8161
4	3.9020	3.8077	3.7171	3.6299	3.5460	3.4651	3.3121	3.1699	3.0373	2.9137	2.7982	2.6901	2.5887	2.4936	2.4043	2.3202	2.2410	2.1662
5	4.8534	4.7135	4.5797	4.4518	4.3295	4.2124	3.9927	3.7908	3.6048	3.4331	3.2743	3.1272	2.9906	2.8636	2.7454	2.6351	2.5320	2.4356
6	5.7955	5.6014	5.4172	5.2421	5.0757	4.9173	4.6229	4.3553	4.1114	3.8887	3.6847	3.4976	3.3255	3.1669	3.0205	2.8850	2.7594	2.6427
7	6.7282	6.4720	6.2303	6.0021	5.7864	5.5824	5.2064	4.8684	4.5638	4.2883	4.0386	3.8115	3.6046	3.4155	3.2423	3.0833	2.9370	2.8021
8	7.6517	7.3255	7.0197	6.7327	6.4632	6.2098	5.7466	5.3349	4.9676	4.6389	4.3436	4.0776	3.8372	3.6193	3.4212	3.2407	3.0758	2.9247
9	8.5660	8.1622	7.7861	7.4353	7.1078	6.8017	6.2469	5.7590	5.3282	4.9464	4.6065	4.3030	4.0310	3.7863	3.5655	3.3657	3.1842	3.0190
10	9.4713	8.9826	8.5302	8.1109	7.7217	7.3601	6.7101	6.1446	5.6502	5.2161	4.8332	4.4941	4.1925	3.9232	3.6819	3.4648	3.2689	3.0915
11	10.3676	9.7868	9.2526	8.7605	8.3064	7.8869	7.1390	6.4951	5.9377	5.4527	5.0286	4.6560	4.3271	4.0354	3.7757	3.5435	3.3351	3.1473
12	11.2551	10.5753	9.9540	9.3851	8.8633	8.3838	7.5361	6.8137	6.1944	5.6603	5.1971	4.7932	4.4392	4.1274	3.8514	3.6059	3.3868	3.1903
13	12.1337	11.3484	10.6350	9.9856	9.3936	8.8527	7.9038	7.1034	6.4235	5.8424	5.3423	4.9095	4.5327	4.2028	3.9124	3.6555	3.4272	3.2233
14	13.0034	12.1062	11.2961	10.5631	9.8986	9.2950	8.2442	7.3667	6.6282	6.0021	5.4675	5.0081	4.6106	4.2646	3.9616	3.6949	3.4587	3.2487
15	13.8651	12.8493	11.9379	11.1184	10.3797	9.7122	8.5595	7.6061	6.8109	6.1422	5.5755	5.0916	4.6755	4.3152	4.0013	3.7261	3.4834	3.2682
16	14.7179	13.5777	12.5611	11.6542	10.8378	10.1059	8.8514	7.8237	6.9740	6.2651	5.6685	5.1624	4.7296	4.3567	4.0333	3.7509	3.5026	3.2832
17	15.5623	14.2919	13.1661	12.1657	11.2741	10.4773	9.1216	8.0216	7.1196	6.3729	5.7487	5.2223	4.7746	4.3908	4.0591	3.7705	3.5177	3.2948
18	16.3983	14.9920	13.7535	12.6593	11.6896	10.8276	9.3719	8.2014	7.2497	6.4674	5.8178	5.2732	4.8122	4.4187	4.0799	3.7861	3.5294	3.3037
19	17.2260	15.6785	14.3238	13.1339	12.0853	11.1581	9.6036	8.3649	7.3658	6.5504	5.8775	5.3162	4.8435	4.4415	4.0967	3.7985	3.5386	3.3105
20	18.0456	16.3514	14.8775	13.5903	12.4622	11.4699	9.8181	8.5136	7.4694	6.6231	5.9288	5.3527	4.8696	4.4603	4.1103	3.8083	3.5458	3.3158
21	18.8570	17.0112	15.4150	14.0292	12.8212	11.7641	10.0168	8.6487	7.5620	6.6870	5.9731	5.3837	4.8913	4.4756	4.1212	3.8161	3.5514	3.3198
22	19.6604	17.6580	15.9369	14.4511	13.1630	12.0416	10.2007	8.7715	7.6446	6.7429	6.0113	5.4099	4.9094	4.4882	4.1300	3.8223	3.5558	3.3230
23	20.4558	18.2922	16.4436	14.8568	13.4886	12.3034	10.3711	8.8832	7.7184	6.7921	6.0442	5.4321	4.9245	4.4985	4.1371	3.8273	3.5592	3.3254
24	21.2434	18.9139	16.9355	15.2470	13.7986	12.5504	10.5288	8.9847	7.7843	6.8351	6.0726	5.4509	4.9371	4.5070	4.1428	3.8312	3.5619	3.3272
25	22.0232	19.5235	17.4131	15.6221	14.0939	12.7834	10.6748	9.0770	7.8431	6.8729	6.0971	5.4669	4.9476	4.5139	4.1474	3.8342	3.5640	3.3286
26	22.7952	20.1210	17.8768	15.9828	14.3752	13.0032	10.8100	9.1609	7.8957	6.9061	6.1182	5.4804	4.9563	4.5196	4.1511	3.8367	3.5656	3.3297
27	23.5596	20.7069	18.3270	16.3296	14.6430	13.2105	10.9352	9.2372	7.9426	6.9352	6.1364	5.4919	4.9636	4.5243	4.1542	3.8387	3.5669	3.3305
28	24.3164	21.2813	18.7641	16.6631	14.8981	13.4062	11.0511	9.3066	7.9844	6.9607	6.1520	5.5016	4.9697	4.5281	4.1566	3.8402	3.5679	3.3312
29	25.0658	21.8444	19.1885	16.9837	15.1411	13.5907	11.1584	9.3696	8.0218	6.9830	6.1656	5.5098	4.9747	4.5312	4.1585	3.8414	3.5687	3.3317
30	25.8077	22.3965	19.6004	17.2920	15.3725	13.7648	11.2578	9.4269	8.0552	7.0027	6.1772	5.5168	4.9789	4.5338	4.1601	3.8424	3.5693	3.3321
35	29.4086	24.9986	21.4872	18.6646	16.3742	14.4982	11.6546	9.6442	8.1755	7.0700	6.2153	5.5386	4.9915	4.5411	4.1644	3.8450	3.5708	3.3330
40	32.8347	27.3555	23.1148	19.7929	17.1591	15.0463	11.9246	9.7791	8.2438	7.1050	6.2335	5.5482	4.9966	4.5439	4.1659	3.8458	3.5712	3.3332

INTEREST RATE (r)

$$P = \frac{A}{(1+r)} + \frac{A}{(1+r)^2} + \cdots + \frac{A}{(1+r)^n} = A\sum_{j=1}^{n} 1/(1+r)^j = A(af)$$

where P = present value of an annuity

A = amount of annuity to be received at the end of each period

n = number of periods for which the annuity is received

r = periodic interest rate

af = annuity factor for an annuity of \$1 $= \sum_{j=1}^{n} 1/(1+r)^j$

MyOMLab

Tutor F.3 in MyOMLab
provides another example
to practice calculating the
straight-line depreciation for
an investment.

from the sale or disposal of plant and equipment at the end of a project's life.[1] The general expression for annual depreciation is

$$D = \frac{I - S}{n}$$

where

$$D = \text{annual depreciation}$$
$$I = \text{amount of the investment}$$
$$S = \text{salvage value}$$
$$n = \text{number of years of project life}$$

Accelerated Depreciation   If the tax shields come earlier, they are worth more. Tax laws allow just that with what is called *accelerated depreciation*. Since 1986, the only acceptable accelerated depreciation method in the United States is the **Modified Accelerated Cost Recovery System (MACRS)**. MACRS shortens the lives of investments, giving firms larger tax deductions. It creates six classes of investments, each of which has a recovery period or class life. Depreciation for each year is calculated by multiplying the asset's cost by the fixed percentage in Table F.3.[2] The following are examples of the first four classes:

Modified Accelerated Cost Recovery System (MACRS)

The only acceptable depreciation method for tax purposes that shortens the lives of investments, giving firms larger early tax deductions.

3-year class:	specially designed tools and equipment used in research
5-year class:	autos, copiers, and computers
7-year class:	most industrial equipment and office furniture
10-year class:	some longer-life equipment

Table F.3 does not show the 27.5- and 31.5-year classes, which are reserved for real estate. MACRS depreciation calculations ignore salvage value and the actual expected economic life. If there is salvage value after the asset has been fully depreciated, it is treated as taxable income.

TABLE F.3 | MACRS DEPRECIATION ALLOWANCES

	CLASS OF INVESTMENT			
Year	**3-Year**	**5-Year**	**7-Year**	**10-Year**
1	33.33	20.00	14.29	10.00
2	44.45	32.00	24.49	18.00
3	14.81	19.20	17.49	14.40
4	7.41	11.52	12.49	11.52
5		11.52	8.93	9.22
6		5.76	8.93	7.37
7			8.93	6.55
8			4.45	6.55
9				6.55
10				6.55
11				3.29
	100.0%	100.0%	100.0%	100.0%

Taxes   The income-tax rate varies from one state or country to another. Calculation of the tax total should include all relevant federal, state, and local income taxes. When doing a financial analysis, you may want to use an average income-tax rate based on the firm's tax rate over the past several years, or

---

[1]Disposal of property often results in an accounting gain or loss that can increase or decrease income tax and affect cash flows. These tax effects should be considered in determining the actual cash inflow or outflow from disposal of property.

[2]The table can be confusing because it allows a depreciation deduction for one more year than would seem appropriate for a given class. The reason is that MACRS assumes that assets are in service for only six months of the first year and six months of the last year. An asset in the second class still has a 5-year life, but it spans six calendar years.

you may want to base the tax rate on the highest tax bracket that applies to the taxpaying unit. The one thing you should never do is ignore taxes in making a financial analysis.

Analysis of Cash Flows

You now are ready to determine the after-tax cash flow for each year of the project's life. Use the following four steps to calculate the flow year by year:

1. Subtract the new expenses attributed to the project from new revenues. If revenues are unaffected, begin with the project's cost savings.

2. Next subtract the depreciation (D), to get pretax income.

3. Subtract taxes, which constitute the pretax income multiplied by the tax rate. The difference is called the net operating income (NOI).

4. Compute the total after-tax cash flow as NOI $+$ D, adding back the depreciation that was deducted temporarily to compute the tax.

EXAMPLE F.1   **Calculating After-Tax Cash Flows**

A local restaurant is considering adding a salad bar. The investment required to remodel the dining area and add the salad bar will be $16,000. The current year is 2015. Other information about the project is as follows:

1. The price and variable cost per salad are $3.50 and $2.00, respectively.

2. Annual demand should be about 11,000 salads.

3. Fixed costs, other than depreciation, will be $8,000, which cover the energy to operate the refrigerated unit and wages for another part-time employee to stock the salad bar during peak business hours.

4. The assets go into the MACRS 5-year class for depreciation purposes, with no salvage value.

5. The tax rate is 40 percent.

6. Management wants to earn a return of at least 14 percent on the project.

Determine the after-tax cash flows for the life of this project.

SOLUTION

The cash flow projections are shown in the following table. Depreciation is based on Table F.3. For example, depreciation in 2016, after the first year of the project, is $3,200 (or $16,000 × 0.20). The cash flow in 2021 comes from depreciation's tax shield in the first half of the year.

				YEAR			
Item	2015	2016	2017	2018	2019	2020	2021
Initial Information							
Annual demand (salads)		11,000	11,000	11,000	11,000	11,000	
Investment	$16,000						
Interest (discount) rate	0.14						
Cash Flows							
Revenue		$38,500	$38,500	$38,500	$38,500	$38,500	
Expenses: Variable costs		22,000	22,000	22,000	22,000	22,000	
Expenses: Fixed costs		8,000	8,000	8,000	8,000	8,000	
Depreciation (D)		3,200	5,120	3,072	1,843	1,843	922
Pretax income		$5,300	$3,380	$5,428	$6,657	$6,657	−$922
Taxes (40%)		2,120	1,352	2,171	2,663	2,663	−$369
Net Operating Income (NOI)		$3,180	$2,208	$3,257	$3,994	$3,994	−$553
Total cash flow (*NOI* + *D*)		$6,380	$7,148	$6,329	$5,837	$5,837	$369

Net Present Value Method

net present value (NPV) method

The method that evaluates an investment by calculating the present values of all after-tax total cash flows and then subtracting the initial investment amount for their total.

The **net present value (NPV) method** is used to evaluate an investment by calculating the present values of all after-tax total cash flows and then subtracting the original investment amount (which is already a present value) from their total. The difference is the project's net present value. If it is positive for the discount rate used, the investment earns a rate of return higher than the discount rate. If the net present value is negative, the investment earns a rate of return lower than the discount rate. Most firms set the discount rate equal to the *overall weighted average cost of capital*, which becomes the lowest desired return on investment. If a negative net present value results, the project is not approved. The discount rate that represents the lowest desired return on investment is thought of as a hurdle over which the investment must pass and is often referred to as the **hurdle rate**.

hurdle rate

The interest rate that is the lowest desired return on an investment; the hurdle over which the investment must pass.

Internal Rate of Return Method

internal rate of return (IRR)

The discount rate that makes the NPV of a project zero.

A related technique involves calculating the **internal rate of return (IRR)**, which is the discount rate that makes the NPV of a project zero. It is "internal" because it depends only on the cash flows of the investment, not on rates offered elsewhere. With this method, a project is acceptable only if the IRR exceeds the hurdle rate. The IRR is a single number that summarizes the merits of the investment. It can be used to rank multiple projects from best to worst, so it is particularly useful when the budget limits new investments in any year.

You can find the IRR by trial and error. Start with a low discount rate and calculate the NPV. If it exceeds 0, increase the discount rate and try again. The NPV will eventually go to 0 and later to a negative value. When the NPV is near 0, you have found the IRR.

Payback Method

payback method

A method for evaluating projects that determines how much time will elapse before the total of after-tax flows will equal, or pay back, the initial investment.

The other commonly used method of evaluating projects is the **payback method** which determines how much time will elapse before the total of *after-tax* cash flows will equal, or pay back, the initial investment.

The payback method is widely used, even though its advantages are somewhat ameliorated by its drawbacks. It can be quickly and easily applied and gives decision makers some idea of how long recovery of invested funds will take. Uncertainty surrounds every investment project. The costs and revenues on which analyses are based are best estimates, not actual values. An investment project with a quick payback is not considered as risky as one with a long payback. The payback method also has drawbacks. A major criticism is that it encourages managers to focus on the short run. A project that takes a long time to develop but generates excellent cash flows later in its life usually is rejected under the payback method. The payback method also has been criticized for its failure to consider the time value of money. For these reasons, we recommend that payback analysis be combined with a more sophisticated method such as NPV or IRR in analyzing the financial implications of a project.

EXAMPLE F.2	Calculating NPV, IRR, and Payback Period

What are the NPV, IRR, and payback period for the salad bar project in Example F.1?

SOLUTION

MyOMLab

Tutor F.4 in MyOMLab provides another example to practice calculating the NPV, IRR, and Payback for an investment.

Management wants to earn a return of at least 14 percent on its investment, so we use that rate to find the pf values in Table F.1. The present value of each year's total cash flow and the NPV of the project are as follows:

$$2016: \ \$6,380(0.8772) = \$5,596$$
$$2017: \ \$7,148(0.7695) = \$5,500$$
$$2018: \ \$6,329(0.6750) = \$4,272$$
$$2019: \ \$5,837(0.5921) = \$3,456$$
$$2020: \ \$5,837(0.5194) = \$3,032$$
$$2021: \ \$ \ \ 369(0.4556) = \$168$$

NPV of project

$$= (\$5,596 + \$5,500 + \$4,272 + \$3,456 + \$3,032 + \$168) - \$16,000$$
$$= \$6,024$$

Because the NPV is positive, the recommendation would be to approve the project.

To find the IRR, let us begin with the 14 percent discount rate, which produced a positive NPV. Incrementing at 4 percent with each step, we reach a negative NPV with a 30 percent discount rate. If we back up to 28 percent to "fine tune" our estimate, the NPV is $322. Therefore, the IRR is about 29 percent. The computer can provide a more precise answer with much less computation.

Discount Rate	NPV
14%	$6,025
18%	$4,092
22%	$2,425
26%	$977
30%	−$199

To determine the payback period, we add the after-tax cash flows at the bottom of the table in Example F.1 for each year until we get as close as possible to $16,000 without exceeding it. For 2016 and 2017, cash flows are $6,380 + $7,148 = $13,528. The payback method is based on the assumption that cash flows are evenly distributed throughout the year, so in 2018 only $2,472 must be received before the payback point is reached. In 2018 the cash flow is projected to be $6,329; consequently, as $2,472/$6,329 is 0.39, the payback period is 2.39 years.

Computer Support

The proliferation of microcomputers and the corresponding use of computer spreadsheets make it easy to evaluate projected cash flows with NPV, IRR, and payback period methods. The following computer output shows spreadsheet analysis for the salad bar in Example F.1. The analyst inputs the investment expenditure, depreciation method, discount rate, and pretax cash flows. If only cost savings are involved, the revenue row would be replaced by them and there would be no separate rows for variable costs and fixed costs. The computer then computes the depreciation, taxes, after-tax cash flows, NPV, IRR, and payback period.

OM Explorer makes it easy to evaluate projected cash flows with NPV, IRR, and payback period methods. Figure F.1 shows the output using the *Financial Analysis* Solver for the salad bar in Example F.1.

| | | | | | Net Present Value | | $ 6,024 | | ◀ FIGURE F.1 |
Investment amount (non lan   16,000

Investment amount (non lan	16,000	Net Present Value	$ 6,024
Investment (land)		Internal Rate of Return	29%
Starting year	2015	Payback Period	2.39 years
Depreciation type	5-Year MACRS ▼		

◀ FIGURE F.1
Financial Analysis Solver Output for Salad Bar

Years	5 ▲▼
Discount rate	14%
Tax Rate (as percent)	40%

	2016	2017	2018	2019	2020	2021
Revenue	38,500	38,500	38,500	38,500	38,500	
Expenses: Variable	22,000	22,000	22,000	22,000	22,000	
Expenses: Fixed	8,000	8,000	8,000	8,000	8,000	
Depreciation (D)	3200	5120	3072	1843	1843	922
Pre-tax income	5300	3380	5428	6657	6657	-922
Taxes (40%)	2120	1352	2171	2663	2663	-369
Net Operating Income (NOI)	3180	2028	3257	3994	3994	-553
Total Cash Flow (NOI + D)	6380	7148	6329	5837	5837	369

With such spreadsheets, the analyst no longer performs present value calculations by using formulas or tables but instead focuses on data collection and the evaluation of many different scenarios relating to a project. They are referred to as "what-if" analyses and allow an analyst to look at what would happen to financial performance if certain events or combinations of events were to occur.

Using Judgment with Financial Analysis

The precision and analytical detachment that come from using the NPV, IRR, or payback method can be deceiving. In fact, U.S. business has been accused of *managing by the numbers*, with a preference for short-term results from low-risk projects. Part of the problem lies with managers who are on the fast track to the top of their organizations. They occupy a rung on the ladder for a short time and then move up, and so they perceive it to be in their career interests to favor investments that give quick results. They establish short paybacks and high hurdle rates. They ignore or forgo long-term benefits from technological advances, innovative product plans, and strategic capacity additions. Over the long run, this narrow vision jeopardizes the firm's competitive advantage—and even its survival.

Managing by the numbers has a second cause. Projects with the greatest strategic impact are likely to be riskier and have qualitative benefits that cannot be easily quantified. Consider an investment in some of the newer types of flexible automation. Benefits can include better quality, quicker delivery times, higher sales, and lower inventory. The equipment might be reprogrammed to handle new products not yet conceived of by the firm. Enough might be learned with the new technology that subsequent investments will pay off at an even higher rate of return. The mistake is to ignore these benefits simply because they cannot be easily quantified. Including risks and qualitative factors as part of the analysis is far better than ignoring them. Using a preference matrix also may help an analyst recognize qualitative factors more explicitly.

The message is clear: Financial analysis is a valuable tool for evaluating investment projects. However, it can never replace the insight that comes from hands-on experience and sound managerial judgment. Managers must use their judgment, taking into account not only NPV, IRR, or payback data, but also how the project fits operations and corporate strategy.

LEARNING GOALS IN REVIEW

Learning Goal	Guidelines for Review	MyOMLab Resources
① Explain the time value of money concept.	The section "Time Value of Money," pp. 1–4, covers this concept, including the future value of an investment, present value of an investment, future value factors, and annuities.	**OM Explorer Tutors:** F1: Present Value of an Investment; F2: Present Value of an Annuity
② Demonstrate the use of the net present value, internal rate of return, and payback methods of financial analysis.	We explain these three methods in the section "Methods of Financial Analysis," pp. 4–9. Tables F.1 and F.2 make the calculations easy, with software such as *OM Explorer* or *POM for Windows* available for more complex problems that recognize taxes and cash flows over time.	**OM Explorer Tutors:** F3: Straight-Line Depreciation; F4: NPV, IRR, and Payback **OM Explorer Solver:** Financial Analysis **POM for Windows:** Financial Analysis
③ Discuss the importance of combining managerial judgment with quantitative techniques when making investment decisions.	See the last section "Using Judgment with Financial Analysis" on p. 10, which cautions against relying just on financial analysis without also bringing into play insight that comes from managerial judgment.	

Key Equations

Time Value of Money

1. Future Value of an Investment:

$$F = P(1 + r)^n$$

2. Present Value of an Investment:

$$P = \frac{F}{(1 + r)^n}$$

3. Present Value Factors:

$$P = F\left[\frac{1}{(1 + r)^n}\right]$$

4. Present Value of an Annuity:

$$P = A\,(\text{af})$$

Methods of Financial Analysis

5. Straight-Line Depreciation:

$$D = \frac{I - S}{n}$$

Key Terms

annuity 4
compounding interest 1
discounting 2
discount rate 2
future value of an investment 1

hurdle rate 8
internal rate of return (IRR) 8
Modified Accelerated Cost Recovery
   System (MACRS) 6
net present value (NPV) method 8

payback method 8
present value of an investment 2
salvage value 4
straight-line depreciation method 4
time value of money 1

Selected References

Brealey, Richard A., Stewart C. Meyers, and Alan J. Marcus. *Fundamentals of Corporate Finance*, 7e. New York: McGraw-Hill, 2012.

Hayes, Robert H., and William J. Abernathy. "Managing Our Way to Economic Decline." *Harvard Business Review* (July–August 1980), pp. 67–77.

Hodder, James E., and Henry E. Riggs. "Pitfalls in Evaluating Risky Projects." *Harvard Business Review* (January–February 1985), pp. 128–135.

Jordan, Bradford, Jeffrey Jaffe, Randolf Westerfield, and Stephen Ross. *Corporate Finance: Core Principles and Applications.* New York: McGraw-Hill Professional, 2013.

Luehrman, Timothy A. "What's It Worth? A General Manager's Guide to Valuation." *Harvard Business Review* (May–June 1997), pp. 132–142.

Ross, Stephen A., Randolph W. Westerfield, and Bradford D. Jordon. *Fundamentals of Corporate Finance* Standard Edition. Homewood, Ill.: McGraw-Hill/Irwin, 2012.

ACCEPTANCE SAMPLING PLANS

Acceptance sampling is an inspection procedure used to determine whether to accept or reject a specific quantity of material. As more firms initiate total quality management (TQM) programs and work closely with suppliers to ensure high levels of quality, the need for acceptance sampling will decrease. The TQM concept is that no defects should be passed from a producer to a customer, whether the customer is an external or internal customer. However, in reality, many firms must still rely on checking their materials inputs. The basic procedure is straightforward.

1. A random sample is taken from a large quantity of items and tested or measured relative to the quality characteristic of interest.

2. If the sample passes the test, the entire quantity of items is accepted.

3. If the sample fails the test, either (a) the entire quantity of items is subjected to 100 percent inspection and all defective items repaired or replaced or (b) the entire quantity is returned to the supplier.

We first discuss the tradeoffs involved in setting up acceptance sampling plans. We then address several attribute sampling plans.

LEARNING GOALS *After reading this supplement, you should be able to:*

1 Describe the tradeoffs between risk and quality level in the design of acceptance sampling plans.

2 Distinguish between single-sampling, double-sampling, and sequential-sampling plans, and describe the unique characteristics of each.

3 Develop an operating characteristic curve for a single-sampling plan, and estimate the probability of accepting a lot with a given proportion defective.

4 Select a single-sampling plan with a given acceptable quality level (AQL) and lot tolerance percent defective (LTPD).

5 Compute the average outgoing quality for a single-sampling plan.

Acceptance Sampling Quality and Risk Decisions

Acceptance sampling involves both the producer (or supplier) of materials and the consumer (or buyer). Consumers need acceptance sampling to limit the risk of rejecting good-quality materials or accepting bad-quality materials. Consequently, the consumer, sometimes in conjunction with the producer through contractual agreements, specifies the parameters of the plan. Any company can be both a producer of goods purchased by another company and a consumer of goods or raw materials supplied by another company.

Two levels of quality are considered in the design of an acceptance sampling plan. The first is the *acceptable quality level (AQL)*, or the quality level desired by the *consumer*. The producer of the item strives to achieve the AQL, which typically is written into a contract or purchase order. For example, a contract might call for a quality level not to exceed one defective unit in 10,000, or an AQL of 0.0001. The **producer's risk (α)** is the risk that the sampling plan will fail to verify an acceptable lot's quality and, thus, reject it—a type I error. Most often the producer's risk is set at 0.05, or 5 percent.

Although producers are interested in low risk, they often have no control over the consumer's acceptance sampling plan. Fortunately, the consumer also is interested in a low producer's risk because sending good materials back to the producer (1) disrupts the consumer's production process and increases the likelihood of shortages in materials, (2) adds unnecessarily to the lead time for finished products or services, and (3) creates poor relations with the producer.

The second level of quality is the **lot tolerance proportion defective (LTPD)**, or the worst level of quality that the consumer can tolerate. The LTPD is a definition of bad quality that the consumer would like to reject. Recognizing the high cost of defects, operations managers have become more cautious about accepting materials of poor quality from suppliers. Thus, sampling plans have lower LTPD values than in the past. The probability of accepting a lot with LTPD quality is the **consumer's risk (β)** or the type II error of the plan. A common value for the consumer's risk is 0.10, or 10 percent.

Sampling Plans

All sampling plans are devised to provide a specified producer's and consumer's risk. However, it is in the consumer's best interest to keep the average number of items inspected (ANI) to a minimum because that keeps the cost of inspection low. Sampling plans differ with respect to ANI. Three often-used attribute sampling plans are the single-sampling plan, the double-sampling plan, and the sequential-sampling plan. Analogous plans also have been devised for variable measures of quality.

Single-Sampling Plan

The **single-sampling plan** is a decision rule to accept or reject a lot based on the results of one random sample from the lot. The procedure is to take a random sample of size (n) and inspect each item. If the number of defects does not exceed a specified acceptance number (c), the consumer accepts the entire lot. Any defects found in the sample are either repaired or returned to the producer. If the number of defects in the sample is greater than c, the consumer subjects the entire lot to 100 percent inspection or rejects the entire lot and returns it to the producer. The single-sampling plan is easy to use but usually results in a larger ANI than the other plans. After briefly describing the other sampling plans, we focus our discussion on this plan.

Double-Sampling Plan

In a **double-sampling plan**, management specifies two sample sizes (n_1 and n_2) and two acceptance numbers (c_1 and c_2). If the quality of the lot is very good or very bad, the consumer can make a decision to accept or reject the lot on the basis of the first sample, which is smaller than in the single-sampling plan. To use the plan, the consumer takes a random sample of size n_1. If the number of defects is less than or equal to (c_1), the consumer accepts the lot. If the number of defects is greater than (c_2), the consumer rejects the lot. If the number of defects is between c_1 and c_2, the consumer takes a second sample of size n_2. If the combined number of defects in the two samples is less than or equal to c_2, the consumer accepts the lot. Otherwise, it is rejected. A double-sampling plan can significantly reduce the costs of inspection relative to a single-sampling plan for lots with a very low or very high proportion defective because a decision can be made after taking the first sample. However, if the decision requires two samples, the sampling costs can be greater than those for the single-sampling plan.

Sequential-Sampling Plan

A further refinement of the double-sampling plan is the **sequential-sampling plan**, in which the consumer randomly selects items from the lot and inspects them one by one. Each time an item is inspected, a decision is made to (1) reject the lot, (2) accept the lot, or (3) continue sampling, based on the cumulative results so far. The analyst plots the total number of defectives against the cumulative sample size, and if the number of defectives is less than a certain acceptance number (c_1), the consumer accepts the lot. If the number is greater than another acceptance number (c_2), the consumer rejects the lot. If the number is somewhere between the two, another item is inspected. Figure G.1 illustrates a decision to reject a lot after examining the 40th unit. Such charts can be easily designed with the help of statistical tables that specify the accept or reject cut-off values c_1 and c_2 as a function of the cumulative sample size.

---

producer's risk (α)

The risk that the sampling plan will fail to verify an acceptable lot's quality and, thus, reject it (a type I error).

lot tolerance proportion defective (LTPD)

The worst level of quality that the consumer can tolerate.

consumer's risk (β)

The probability of accepting a lot with LTPD quality (a type II error).

single-sampling plan

A sampling plan whereby a decision is made to accept or reject a lot based on the results of one random sample from the lot.

double-sampling plan

A sampling plan in which management specifies two sample sizes and two acceptance numbers; if the quality of the lot is very good or very bad, the consumer can make a decision to accept or reject the lot on the basis of the first sample, which is smaller than in the single-sampling plan.

sequential-sampling plan

A sampling plan in which the consumer randomly selects items from the lot and inspects them one by one.

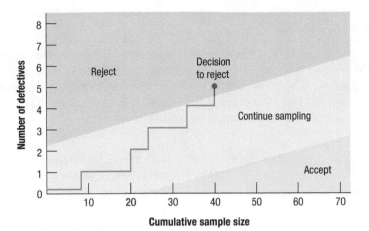

◀ **FIGURE G.1**
Cumulative Sample Size

The ANI is generally lower for the sequential-sampling plan than for any other form of acceptance sampling, resulting in lower inspection costs. For very low or very high values of the proportion defective, sequential sampling provides a lower ANI than any comparable sampling plan. However, if the proportion of defective units falls between the AQL and the LTPD, a sequential-sampling plan could have a larger ANI than a comparable single- or double-sampling plan (although that is unlikely). In general, the sequential-sampling plan may reduce the ANI to 50 percent of that required by a comparable single-sampling plan and, consequently, save substantial inspection costs.

Operating Characteristic Curves

Analysts create a graphic display of the performance of a sampling plan by plotting the probability of accepting the lot for a range of proportions of defective units. This graph, called an **operating characteristic (OC) curve**, describes how well a sampling plan discriminates between good and bad lots. Undoubtedly, every manager wants a plan that accepts lots with a quality level better than the AQL 100 percent of the time and accepts lots with a quality level worse than the AQL 0 percent of the time. This ideal OC curve for a single-sampling plan is shown in Figure G.2. However, such performance can be achieved only with 100 percent inspection. A typical OC curve for a single-sampling plan, plotted in red, shows the probability α of rejecting a good lot (producer's risk) and the probability β of accepting a bad lot (consumer's risk). Consequently, managers are left with choosing a sample size n and an acceptance number c to achieve the level of performance specified by the AQL, α, LTPD, and β.

operating characteristic (OC) curve

A graph that describes how well a sampling plan discriminates between good and bad lots.

Drawing the OC Curve

The sampling distribution for the single-sampling plan is the binomial distribution because each item inspected is either defective (a failure) or not (a success). The probability of accepting the lot equals the probability of taking a sample of size n from a lot with a proportion defective of p and finding c or fewer defective items. However, if n is greater than 20 and p is less than 0.05, the Poisson distribution can be used as an approximation to the binomial to take advantage of tables prepared for the purpose of drawing OC curves (see Table G.1 [pp. 11–14]). To draw the OC curve, look up the probability of accepting the lot for a range of values of p. For each value of p,

1. multiply p by the sample size n.
2. find the value of np in the left column of the table.
3. move to the right until you find the column for c.
4. record the value for the probability of acceptance, P_a.

When p = AQL, the producer's risk, α, is 1 minus the probability of acceptance. When p = LTPD, the consumer's risk, β, equals the probability of acceptance.

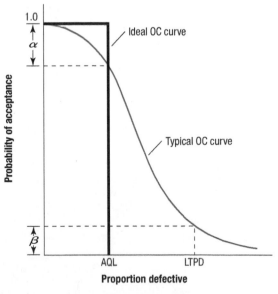

▲ **FIGURE G.2**
Operating Characteristic
Curve

EXAMPLE G.1	**Constructing an OC Curve**

MyOMLab

Tutor G.1 in MyOMLab provides another example to practice constructing an OC curve.

The Noise King Muffler Shop, a high-volume installer of replacement exhaust muffler systems, just received a shipment of 1,000 mufflers. The sampling plan for inspecting these mufflers calls for a sample size $n = 60$ and an acceptance number $c = 1$. The contract with the muffler manufacturer calls for an AQL of one defective muffler per 100 and an LTPD of six defective mufflers per 100. Calculate the OC curve for this plan, and determine the producer's risk and the consumer's risk for the plan.

SOLUTION

Let $p = 0.01$. Then, multiply n by p to get $60(0.01) = 0.60$. Locate 0.60 in Table G.1 (pp. 11–14). Move to the right until you reach the column for $c = 1$. Read the probability of acceptance: 0.878. Repeat this process for a range of p values. The following table contains the remaining values for the OC curve.

VALUES FOR THE OPERATING CHARACTERISTIC CURVE WITH $n = 60$ AND $c = 1$			
Proportion Defective (p)	**np**	**Probability of c or Less Defects (P_a)**	**Comments**
0.01 (AQL)	0.6	0.878	$\alpha = 1.000 - 0.878 = 0.122$
0.02	1.2	0.663	
0.03	1.8	0.463	
0.04	2.4	0.308	
0.05	3.0	0.199	
0.06 (LTPD)	3.6	0.126	$\beta = 0.126$
0.07	4.2	0.078	
0.08	4.8	0.048	
0.09	5.4	0.029	
0.10	6.0	0.017	

DECISION POINT

Note that the plan provides a producer's risk of 12.2 percent and a consumer's risk of 12.6 percent. Both values are higher than the values usually acceptable for plans of this type (5 and 10 percent, respectively). Figure G.3 shows the OC curve and the producer's and consumer's risks. Management can adjust the risks by changing the sample size.

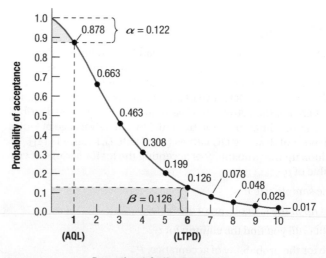

▲ **FIGURE G.3**

The OC Curve for Single-Sampling Plan with $n = 60$ and $c = 1$

Selecting a Single-Sampling Plan

Example G.1 raises the question: How can management change the sampling plan to reduce the probability of rejecting good lots and accepting bad lots? To answer this question, let us see how n and c affect the shape of the OC curve. In the Noise King example, a better single-sampling plan would have a lower producer's risk and a lower consumer's risk.

Sample Size Effect

What would happen if we increased the sample size to 80 and left the acceptance level, c, unchanged at 1? We can use Table G.1 (pp. 11–14). If the proportion defective of the lot is $p = \text{AQL} = 0.01$, then $np = 0.8$ and the probability of acceptance of the lot is only 0.809. Thus, the producer's risk is 0.191. Similarly, if $p = \text{LTPD} = 0.06$, the probability of acceptance is 0.048. Other values of the producer's and consumer's risks are shown in the following table:

n	Producer's Risk ($p = AQL$)	Consumer's Risk ($p = LTPD$)
60	0.122	0.126
80	0.191	0.048
100	0.264	0.017
120	0.332	0.006

These results, shown in Figure G.4, yield the following principle: *Increasing* n *while holding* c *constant increases the producer's risk* and *reduces the consumer's risk.* For the producer of the mufflers, keeping $c = 1$ and increasing the sample size makes getting a lot accepted by the customer tougher—only two bad mufflers will get the lot rejected. And the likelihood of finding those two defects is greater in a sample of 120 than in a sample of 60. Consequently, the producer's risk increases. For the management of Noise King, the consumer's risk goes down because a random sample of 120 mufflers from a lot with 6 percent defectives is less likely to have only one or fewer defective mufflers.

Acceptance Level Effect

Suppose that we keep the sample size constant at 60 but change the acceptance level. Again, we use Table G.1 (pp. 11–14).

c	Producer's Risk ($p = AQL$)	Consumer's Risk ($p = LTPD$)
1	0.122	0.126
2	0.023	0.303
3	0.003	0.515
4	0.000	0.706

The results are plotted in Figure G.5. They demonstrate the following principle: *Increasing* c *while holding* n *constant decreases the producer's risk* and *increases the consumer's risk.* The producer of the mufflers would welcome an increase in the acceptance number because it makes getting the lot accepted by the consumer easier. If the lot has only 1 percent defectives (the AQL) with a sample size of 60, we would expect only $0.01(60) = 0.6$ defect in the sample. An increase in the acceptance number from one to two lowers the probability of finding more than two defects and, consequently, lowers the producer's risk. However, raising the acceptance number for a given sample size increases the risk of accepting a bad lot. Suppose that the lot has 6 percent defectives (the LTPD). We would expect to have $0.6(60) = 3.6$ defectives in the sample. An increase in the acceptance number from one to two increases the probability of getting a sample with two or fewer defects and, therefore, increases the consumer's risk.

Thus, to improve Noise King's single-sampling acceptance plan, management should increase the sample size, which reduces the consumer's risk, *and* increase the acceptance number, which

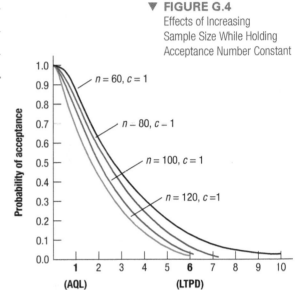

▼ **FIGURE G.4**
Effects of Increasing Sample Size While Holding Acceptance Number Constant

$n = 60, c = 1$
$n = 80, c = 1$
$n = 100, c = 1$
$n = 120, c = 1$

Probability of acceptance

(AQL)   (LTPD)

Proportion defective (hundredths)

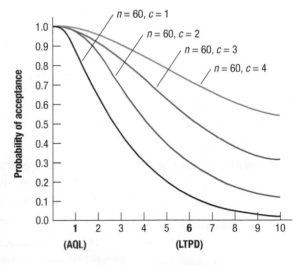

▲ **FIGURE G.5**
Effects of Increasing Acceptance Number While Holding Sample Size Constant

$n = 60, c = 1$
$n = 60, c = 2$
$n = 60, c = 3$
$n = 60, c = 4$

Probability of acceptance

(AQL)   (LTPD)

Proportion defective (hundredths)

reduces the producer's risk. An improved combination can be found by trial and error using Table G.1 (pp. 11–14). Alternatively, a computer can be used to find the best combination. For any acceptance number, the computer determines the sample size needed to achieve the desired producer's risk and compares it to the sample size needed to meet the consumer's risk. It selects the smallest sample size that will meet both the producer's risk and the consumer's risk. The following table shows that a sample size of 111 and an acceptance number of 3 are best. This combination actually yields a producer's risk of 0.026 and a consumer's risk of 0.10 (not shown). The risks are not exact because c and n must be integers.

	ACCEPTANCE SAMPLING PLAN DATA				
	AQL Based		**LTPD Based**		
Acceptance Number	**Expected Defectives**	**Sample Size**	**Expected Defectives**	**Sample Size**	
0	0.0509	5	2.2996	38	
1	0.3552	36	3.8875	65	
2	0.8112	81	5.3217	89	
3	1.3675	137	6.6697	111	
4	1.9680	197	7.9894	133	
5	2.6256	263	9.2647	154	
6	3.2838	328	10.5139	175	
7	3.9794	398	11.7726	196	
8	4.6936	469	12.9903	217	
9	5.4237	542	14.2042	237	
10	6.1635	616	15.4036	257	

Average Outgoing Quality

average outgoing quality (AOQ)

The expected proportion of defects that the plan will allow to pass.

rectified inspection

The assumption that all defective items in the lot will be replaced if the lot is rejected and that any defective items in the sample will be replaced if the lot is accepted.

average outgoing quality limit (AOQL)

The maximum value of the average outgoing quality over all possible values of the proportion defective.

We have shown how to choose the sample size and acceptance number for a single-sampling plan, given AQL, α, LTPD, and β parameters. To check whether the performance of the plan is what we want, we can calculate the plan's **average outgoing quality (AOQ)**, which is the expected proportion of defects that the plan will allow to pass. We assume that all defective items in the lot will be replaced with good items if the lot is rejected and that any defective items in the sample will be replaced if the lot is accepted. This approach is called **rectified inspection**. The equation for AOQ is

$$\text{AOQ} = \frac{p(P_a)(N - n)}{N}$$

where

$\quad p = $ true proportion defective of the lot
$\quad P_a = $ probability of accepting the lot
$\quad N = $ lot size
$\quad n = $ sample size

The analyst can calculate AOQ to estimate the performance of the plan over a range of possible proportion defectives to judge whether the plan will provide an acceptable degree of protection. The maximum value of the average outgoing quality over all possible values of the proportion defective is called the **average outgoing quality limit (AOQL)**. If the AOQL seems too high, the parameters of the plan must be modified until an acceptable AOQL is achieved.

EXAMPLE G.2	**Calculating the AOQL**

Suppose that Noise King is using rectified inspection for its single-sampling plan. Calculate the average outgoing quality limit for a plan with $n = 110, c = 3$, and $N = 1,000$. Use Table G.1 (pp. 11–14) to estimate the probabilities of acceptance for values of the proportion defective from 0.01 to 0.08 in steps of 0.01.

MyOMLab

Tutor G.1 in MyOMLab provides another example to practice calculating the AOQL for a single-sampling plan.

SOLUTION

Use the following steps to estimate the AOQL for this sampling plan:

Step 1. Determine the probabilities of acceptance for the desired values of p. These are shown in the following table. However, the values for $p = 0.03, 0.05$, and 0.07 had to be interpolated because the table does not have them. For example, P_a for $p = 0.03$ was estimated by averaging the P_a values for $np = 3.2$ and $np = 3.4$, or $(0.603 + 0.558)/2 = 0.580$.

Proportion Defective (p)	np	Probability of Acceptance (P_a)
0.01	1.10	0.974
0.02	2.20	0.819
0.03	3.30	$0.581 = (0.603 + 0.558)/2$
0.04	4.40	0.359
0.05	5.50	$0.202 = (0.213 + 0.191)/2$
0.06	6.60	0.105
0.07	7.70	$0.052 = (0.055 + 0.048)/2$
0.08	8.80	0.024

Step 2. Calculate the AOQ for each value of p.

For $p = 0.01: 0.01(0.974)(1000 - 110)/1000 = 0.0087$
For $p = 0.02: 0.02(0.819)(1000 - 110)/1000 = 0.0146$
For $p = 0.03: 0.03(0.581)(1000 - 110)/1000 = 0.0155$
For $p = 0.04: 0.04(0.359)(1000 - 110)/1000 = 0.0128$
For $p = 0.05: 0.05(0.202)(1000 - 110)/1000 = 0.0090$
For $p = 0.06: 0.06(0.105)(1000 - 110)/1000 = 0.0056$
For $p = 0.07: 0.07(0.052)(1000 - 110)/1000 = 0.0032$
For $p = 0.08: 0.08(0.024)(1000 - 110)/1000 = 0.0017$

The plot of the AOQ values is shown in Figure G.6.

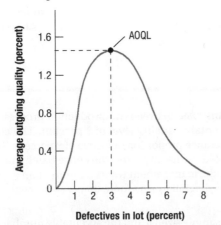

◄ **FIGURE G.6**

Average Outgoing Quality Curve for the Noise King Muffler Service

Step 3. Identify the largest AOQ value, which is the estimate of the AOQL. In this example, the AOQL is 0.0155 at $p = 0.03$.

LEARNING GOALS IN REVIEW

Learning Goal	Guidelines for Review	MyOMLab Resources
❶ Describe the tradeoffs between risk and quality in the design of acceptance sampling plans.	The section "Acceptance Sampling Quality and Risk Decisions," pp. 1–2, defines the acceptable quality level, with the producer's risk, and the lot tolerance proportion defective, with the consumer's risk, and the tradeoffs managers make in the design of acceptance sampling plans.	
❷ Distinguish between single-sampling, double-sampling, and sequential-sampling plans and describe the unique characteristics of each.	These three sampling plans are described in the section "Sampling Plans," pp. 2–3, along with their decision rules and impact on the average number of items inspected (ANI).	
❸ Develop an operating characteristic curve for a single-sampling plan and estimate the probability of accepting a lot with a given proportion defective.	We explain how to construct an operating characteristic curve in the section "Operating Characteristic Curves," pp. 3–4. Focus on Example G.1 which takes you through the whole process.	**OM Explorer Tutor:** G.1: Constructing an OC Curve **POM for Windows:** Operating Characteristic Curves
❹ Select a single-sampling plan with a given acceptable quality level (AQL) and lot tolerance percent defective (LTPD).	The section "Selecting a Single-Sampling Plan," pp. 5–6, shows how to choose the sample size and acceptance number, give the AQL, α, LTPD, and β parameters. Study the Solved Problem for a complete analysis of a single-sampling plan.	**OM Explorer Solver:** Single-Sampling Plans **POM for Windows:** Acceptance Sampling
❺ Compute the average outgoing quality for a single-sampling plan.	The section "Average Outgoing Quality," pp. 6–7, shows how to calculate the average outgoing quality of a single-sampling plan using rectified inspection. Example G.2 clearly shows the calculations involved.	**OM Explorer Tutor:** G.2: Calculating the AOQL

Key Equation

Average Outgoing Quality

Average outgoing quality:

$$\text{AOQ} = \frac{p(P_a)(N - n)}{N}$$

Key Terms

average outgoing quality (AOQ) 6
average outgoing quality limit (AOQL) 6
consumer's risk (β) 2
double-sampling plan 2

lot tolerance proportion defective
   (LTPD) 2
operating characteristic (OC) curve 3
producer's risk (α) 2

rectified inspection 6
sequential-sampling plan 2
single-sampling plan 2

Solved Problem

An inspection station has been installed between two production processes. The feeder process, when operating correctly, has an acceptable quality level of 3 percent. The consuming process, which is expensive, has a specified lot tolerance proportion defective of 8 percent. The feeding process produces in batch sizes; if a batch is rejected by the inspector, the entire batch must be checked and the defective items reworked. Consequently, management wants no more than a 5 percent producer's risk and, because of the expensive process that follows, no more than a 10 percent chance of accepting a lot with 8 percent defectives or worse.

   a. Determine the appropriate sample size, n, and the acceptable number of defective items in the sample, c.

   b. Calculate values and draw the OC curve for this inspection station.

   c. What is the probability that a lot with 5 percent defectives will be rejected?

SOLUTION

a. For AQL = 3 percent, LTPD = 8 percent, α = 5 percent, and β = 10 percent, use Table G.1 (pp. 11-14) and trial and error to arrive at a sampling plan. If n = 180 and c = 9,

$$np = 180(0.03) = 5.4$$

$$\alpha = 0.049$$

$$np = 180(0.08) = 14.4$$

$$\beta = 0.092$$

Sampling plans that would also work are $n = 200, c = 10$; $n = 220, c = 11$; and $n = 240, c = 12$.

b. The following table contains the data for the OC curve. Table G.1 (pp. 11-14) was used to estimate the probability of acceptance. Figure G.7 shows the OC Curve.

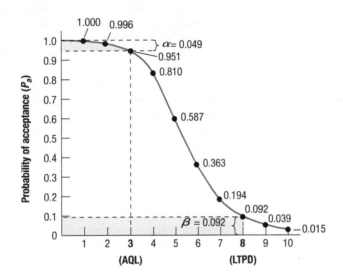

◀ **FIGURE G.7**
OC Curve

c. According to the table, the probability of accepting a lot with 5 percent defectives is 0.587. Therefore, the probability that a lot with 5 percent defects will be rejected is 0.413, or $1.00 - 0.587$.

Proportion Defective (p)	np	Probability of c or Less Defects (P_a)	Comments
0.01	1.8	1.000	
0.02	3.6	0.996	
0.03 (AQL)	5.4	0.951	$\alpha = 1 - 0.951 = 0.049$
0.04	7.2	0.810	
0.05	9.0	0.587	
0.06	10.8	0.363	
0.07	12.6	0.194	
0.08 (LTPD)	14.4	0.092	$\beta = 0.092$
0.09	16.2	0.039	
0.10	18.0	0.015	

Problems

The OM Explorer and POM for Windows software is available to all students using the 11th edition of this textbook. Go to **http://www.pearsonhighered.com/krajewski** to download these computer packages. If you purchased MyOMLab, you also have access to Active Models software and significant help in doing the following problems. Check with your instructor on how best to use these resources. In many cases, the instructor wants you to understand how to do the calculations by hand. At the least, the software provides a check on your calculations. When calculations are particularly complex and the goal is interpreting the results in making decisions, the software entirely replaces the manual calculations.

Operating Characteristic Curves

1. For $n = 200$, $c = 4$, AQL $= 0.5$ percent, and LTPD $= 4$ percent, find α and β.

2. Your company supplies sterile syringes to a distributor of hospital supplies. The contract states that quality should be no worse than 0.1 percent defective, or 10 parts in 10,000. During negotiations, you learned that the distributor will use an acceptance sampling plan with $n = 350$ to test quality.

   a. If the producer's risk is to be no greater than 5 percent, what is the lowest acceptance number, c, that should be used?

   b. The syringe production process averages 17 defective parts in 10,000. With $n = 350$ and the acceptance level suggested in part (a), what is the probability that a shipment will be returned to you?

   c. Suppose that you want a less than 5 percent chance that your shipment will be returned to you. For the data in part (b), what acceptance number, c, should you have suggested in part (a)? What is the producer's risk for that plan?

3. A buyer of electronic components has a lot tolerance proportion defective of 20 parts in 5,000, with a consumer's risk of 15 percent. If the buyer will sample 1,500 of the components received in each shipment, what acceptance number, c, would the buyer want? What is the producer's risk if the AQL is 10 parts per 5,000?

Selecting a Single-Sampling Plan

4. You are responsible for purchasing bearings for the maintenance department of a large airline. The bearings are under contract from a local supplier, and you must devise an appropriate acceptance sampling plan for them. Management has stated in the contract that the acceptable quality level is 1 percent defective. In addition, the lot tolerance proportion defective is 4 percent, the producer's risk is 5 percent, and the consumer's risk is 10 percent.

   a. Specify an appropriate acceptance sampling plan that meets all these criteria.

   b. Draw the OC curve for your plan. What is the resultant producer's risk?

   c. Determine the AOQL for your plan. Assume a lot size of 3,000.

5. The Sunshine Shampoo Company purchases the label that is pasted on each bottle of shampoo it sells. The label contains the company logo, the name of the product, and directions for the product's use. Sometimes the printing on the label is blurred or the colors are not right. The company wants to design an acceptance sampling plan for the purchased item. The acceptable quality level is five defectives per 500 labels, and the lot tolerance proportion defective is 5 percent. Management wants to limit the producer's risk to 5 percent or less and the consumer's risk to 10 percent or less.

   a. Specify a plan that satisfies those desires.

   b. What is the probability that a shipment with 3 percent defectives will be rejected by the plan?

   c. Determine the AOQL for your plan. Assume that the lot size is 2,000 labels.

6. Consider a certain raw material for which a single-sampling attribute plan is needed. The AQL is 1 percent, and the LTPD is 4 percent. Two plans have been proposed. Under plan 1, $n = 150$ and $c = 4$; under plan 2, $n = 300$ and $c = 8$. Are the two plans equivalent? Substantiate your response by determining the producer's risk and the consumer's risk for each plan.

7. You currently have an acceptance sampling plan in which $n = 40$ and $c = 1$, but you are unsatisfied with its performance. The AQL is 1 percent, and the LTPD is 5 percent.

   a. What are the producer's and consumer's risks for this plan?

   b. While maintaining the same 1:40 ratio of $c{:}n$ (called the *acceptance proportion*), increase c and n to find a sampling plan that will decrease the producer's risk to 5 percent or less *and* the consumer's risk to 10 percent or less. What producer's and consumer's risks are associated with this new plan?

   c. Compare the AOQLs for your plan and the current plan. Assume a lot size of 1,000 units.

8. For AQL $= 1$ percent, LTPD $= 4$ percent, and $n = 400$, what value(s) of the acceptance number, c, would result in the producer's risk and the consumer's risk *both* being under 5 percent?

9. For AQL $= 1$ percent and $c = 2$, what is the largest value of n that will result in a producer's risk of 5 percent? Using that sample size, determine the consumer's risk when LTPD $= 2$ percent.

10. For $c = 10$ and LTPD $= 5$ percent, what value of n results in a 5 percent consumer's risk?

11. Design a sampling plan for AQL $= 0.1$ percent, LTPD $= 0.5$ percent, producer's risk ≤ 5 percent, and consumer's risk ≤ 10 percent.

12. Design a sampling plan for AQL = 0.01 percent (100 parts per million), LTPD = 0.05 percent (500 ppm), producer's risk ≤ 5 percent, and consumer's risk ≤ 10 percent.

Observe the similarity of this problem to Problem 11. As AQL decreases by a factor of K, what is the effect on the sample size, n?

Average Outgoing Quality

13. Suppose that AQL = 0.5 percent, α = 5 percent, LTPD = 2 percent, β = 6 percent, and N = 1,000.

   a. Find the AOQL for the single-sampling plan that best fits the given parameter values.

   b. For each of the following experiments, find the AOQL for the best single-sampling plan. Change only the parameter indicated, holding all others at their original values.

      i. Change N to 2,000.

      ii. Change AQL to 0.8 percent.

      iii. Change LTPD to 6 percent.

   c. Discuss the effects of changes in the design parameters on plan performance, based on the three experiments in part (b).

14. Peter Lamb is the quality assurance manager at an engine plant. The summer intern assigned to Lamb is a student in operations management at a local university. The intern's

first task is to calculate the following parameters, based on the SPC information at the engine plant:

$$\text{AQL} = 0.02 \text{ percent}, \beta = 1 \text{ percent}, \alpha = 2 \text{ percent},$$
$$N = 1000, \text{LTPD} = 2.5 \text{ percent}$$

   a. Find the AOQL for the single-sampling plan that best fits the given parameter values.

   b. For each of the following experiments, find the AOQL for the best single-sampling plan. Change only the parameter indicated, holding all others at their original values.

      i. Change N to 2,000.

      ii. Change AQL to 0.3 percent.

      iii. Change LTPD to 4 percent.

   c. Discuss the effects of changes in the design parameters on plan performance, based on the three experiments in part (b).

TABLE G.1 | CUMULATIVE POISSON PROBABILITIES

c

np	0	1	2	3	4	5	6	7	8	9	10	11	12	13
.05	.951	.999	1.000											
.10	.905	.995	1.000											
.15	.861	.990	.999	1.000										
.20	.819	.982	.999	1.000										
.25	.779	.974	.998	1.000										
.30	.741	.963	.996	1.000										
.35	.705	.951	.994	1.000										
.40	.670	.938	.992	.999	1.000									
.45	.638	.925	.989	.999	1.000									
.50	.607	.910	.986	.998	1.000									
.55	.577	.894	.982	.998	1.000									
.60	.549	.878	.977	.997	1.000									
.65	.522	.861	.972	.996	.999	1.000								
.70	.497	.844	.966	.994	.999	1.000								
.75	.472	.827	.959	.993	.999	1.000								
.80	.449	.809	.953	.991	.999	1.000								
.85	.427	.791	.945	.989	.998	1.000								
.90	.407	.772	.937	.987	.998	1.000								
.95	.387	.754	.929	.984	.997	1.000								
1.0	.368	.736	.920	.981	.996	.999	1.000							
1.1	.333	.699	.900	.974	.995	.999	1.000							

$P(x)$

$$P(x \le c) = \sum_{x=0}^{x=c} \frac{\lambda^x e^{-\lambda}}{x!}$$

(continued)

TABLE G.1 (CONT.)

np	0	1	2	3	4	5	6	7	8	9	10	11	12	13
1.2	.301	.663	.879	.966	.992	.998	1.000							
1.3	.273	.627	.857	.957	.989	.998	1.000							
1.4	.247	.592	.833	.946	.986	.997	.999	1.000						
1.5	.223	.558	.809	.934	.981	.996	.999	1.000						
1.6	.202	.525	.783	.921	.976	.994	.999	1.000						
1.7	.183	.493	.757	.907	.970	.992	.998	1.000						
1.8	.165	.463	.731	.891	.964	.990	.997	.999	1.000					
1.9	.150	.434	.704	.875	.956	.987	.997	.999	1.000					
2.0	.135	.406	.677	.857	.947	.983	.995	.999	1.000					
2.2	.111	.355	.623	.819	.928	.975	.993	.998	1.000					
2.4	.091	.308	.570	.779	.904	.964	.988	.997	.999	1.000				
2.6	.074	.267	.518	.736	.877	.951	.983	.995	.999	1.000				
2.8	.061	.231	.469	.692	.848	.935	.976	.992	.998	.999	1.000			
3.0	.050	.199	.423	.647	.815	.916	.966	.988	.996	.999	1.000			
3.2	.041	.171	.380	.603	.781	.895	.955	.983	.994	.998	1.000			
3.4	.033	.147	.340	.558	.744	.871	.942	.977	.992	.997	.999	1.000		
3.6	.027	.126	.303	.515	.706	.844	.927	.969	.988	.996	.999	1.000		
3.8	.022	.107	.269	.473	.668	.816	.909	.960	.984	.994	.998	.999	1.000	
4.0	.018	.092	.238	.433	.629	.785	.889	.949	.979	.992	.997	.999	1.000	
4.2	.015	.078	.210	.395	.590	.753	.867	.936	.972	.989	.996	.999	1.000	
4.4	.012	.066	.185	.359	.551	.720	.844	.921	.964	.985	.994	.998	.999	1.000
4.6	.010	.056	.163	.326	.513	.686	.818	.905	.955	.980	.992	.997	.999	1.000
4.8	.008	.048	.143	.294	.476	.651	.791	.887	.944	.975	.990	.996	.999	1.000
5.0	.007	.040	.125	.265	.440	.616	.762	.867	.932	.968	.986	.995	.998	.999
5.2	.006	.034	.109	.238	.406	.581	.732	.845	.918	.960	.982	.993	.997	.999
5.4	.005	.029	.095	.213	.373	.546	.702	.822	.903	.951	.977	.990	.996	.999
5.6	.004	.024	.082	.191	.342	.512	.670	.797	.886	.941	.972	.988	.995	.998
5.8	.003	.021	.072	.170	.313	.478	.638	.771	.867	.929	.965	.984	.993	.997
6.0	.002	.017	.062	.151	.285	.446	.606	.744	.847	.916	.957	.980	.991	.996
6.2	.002	.015	.054	.134	.259	.414	.574	.716	.826	.902	.949	.975	.989	.995
6.4	.002	.012	.046	.119	.235	.384	.542	.687	.803	.886	.939	.969	.986	.994
6.6	.001	.010	.040	.105	.213	.355	.511	.658	.780	.869	.927	.963	.982	.992
6.8	.001	.009	.034	.093	.192	.327	.480	.628	.755	.850	.915	.955	.978	.990
7.0	.001	.007	.030	.082	.173	.301	.450	.599	.729	.830	.901	.947	.973	.987
7.2	.001	.006	.025	.072	.156	.276	.420	.569	.703	.810	.887	.937	.967	.984
7.4	.001	.005	.022	.063	.140	.253	.392	.539	.676	.788	.871	.926	.961	.980
7.6	.001	.004	.019	.055	.125	.231	.365	.510	.648	.765	.854	.915	.954	.976
7.8	.000	.004	.016	.048	.112	.210	.338	.481	.620	.741	.835	.902	.945	.971
8.0	.000	.003	.014	.042	.100	.191	.313	.453	.593	.717	.816	.888	.936	.966
8.2	.000	.003	.012	.037	.089	.174	.290	.425	.565	.692	.796	.873	.926	.960

(continued)

TABLE G.1 (CONT.)

							c							
np	0	1	2	3	4	5	6	7	8	9	10	11	12	13
8.4	.000	.002	.010	.032	.079	.157	.267	.399	.537	.666	.774	.857	.915	.952
8.6	.000	.002	.009	.028	.070	.142	.246	.373	.509	.640	.752	.840	.903	.945
8.8	.000	.001	.007	.024	.062	.128	.226	.348	.482	.614	.729	.822	.890	.936
9.0	.000	.001	.006	.021	.055	.116	.207	.324	.456	.587	.706	.803	.876	.926
9.2	.000	.001	.005	.018	.049	.104	.189	.301	.430	.561	.682	.783	.861	.916
9.4	.000	.001	.005	.016	.043	.093	.173	.279	.404	.535	.658	.763	.845	.904
9.6	.000	.001	.004	.014	.038	.084	.157	.258	.380	.509	.633	.741	.828	.892
9.8	.000	.001	.003	.012	.033	.075	.143	.239	.356	.483	.608	.719	.810	.879
10.0	0	.000	.003	.010	.029	.067	.130	.220	.333	.458	.583	.697	.792	.864
10.2	0	.000	.002	.009	.026	.060	.118	.203	.311	.433	.558	.674	.772	.849
10.4	0	.000	.002	.008	.023	.053	.107	.186	.290	.409	.533	.650	.752	.834
10.6	0	.000	.002	.007	.020	.048	.097	.171	.269	.385	.508	.627	.732	.817
10.8	0	.000	.001	.006	.017	.042	.087	.157	.250	.363	.484	.603	.710	.799
11.0	0	.000	.001	.005	.015	.038	.079	.143	.232	.341	.460	.579	.689	.781
11.2	0	.000	.001	.004	.013	.033	.071	.131	.215	.319	.436	.555	.667	.762
11.4	0	.000	.001	.004	.012	.029	.064	.119	.198	.299	.413	.532	.644	.743
11.6	0	.000	.001	.003	.010	.026	.057	.108	.183	.279	.391	.508	.622	.723
11.8	0	.000	.001	.003	.009	.023	.051	.099	.169	.260	.369	.485	.599	.702
12.0	0	.000	.001	.002	.008	.020	.046	.090	.155	.242	.347	.462	.576	.682
12.2	0	0	0.000	0.002	0.007	0.018	0.041	0.081	0.142	0.225	0.327	0.439	0.553	0.660
12.4	0	0	0.000	0.002	0.006	0.016	0.037	0.073	0.131	0.209	0.307	0.417	0.530	0.639
12.6	0	0	0.000	0.001	0.005	0.014	0.033	0.066	0.120	0.194	0.288	0.395	0.508	0.617
12.8	0	0	0.000	0.001	0.004	0.012	0.029	0.060	0.109	0.179	0.269	0.374	0.485	0.595
13.0	0	0	0.000	0.001	0.004	0.011	0.026	0.054	0.100	0.166	0.252	0.353	0.463	0.573
13.2	0	0	.000	.001	.003	.009	.023	.049	.091	.153	.235	.333	.441	.551
13.4	0	0	.000	.001	.003	.008	.020	.044	.083	.141	.219	.314	.420	.529
13.6	0	0	.000	.001	.002	.007	.018	.039	.075	.130	.204	.295	.399	.507
13.8	0	0	.000	.001	.002	.006	.016	.035	.068	.119	.189	.277	.378	.486
14.0	0	0	0	.000	.002	.006	.014	.032	.062	.109	.176	.260	.358	.464
14.2	0	0	0	.000	.002	.005	.013	.028	.056	.100	.163	.244	.339	.443
14.4	0	0	0	.000	.001	.004	.011	.025	.051	.092	.151	.228	.320	.423
14.6	0	0	0	.000	.001	.004	.010	.023	.046	.084	.139	.213	.302	.402
14.8	0	0	0	.000	.001	.003	.009	.020	.042	.077	.129	.198	.285	.383
15.0	0	0	0	.000	.001	.003	.008	.018	.037	.070	.118	.185	.268	.363
15.2	0	0	0	.000	.001	.002	.007	.016	.034	.064	.109	.172	.251	.344
15.4	0	0	0	.000	.001	.002	.006	.014	.030	.058	.100	.160	.236	..326
15.6	0	0	0	.000	.001	.002	.005	.013	.027	.053	.092	.148	.221	.308
15.8	0	0	0	0	.000	.002	.005	.011	.025	.048	.084	.137	.207	.291
16.0	0	0	0	0	.000	.001	.004	.010	.022	.043	.077	.127	.193	.275
16.2	0	0	0	0	.000	.001	.004	.009	.020	.039	.071	.117	.180	.259

(continued)

TABLE G.1 (CONT.)

								c						
np	0	1	2	3	4	5	6	7	8	9	10	11	12	13
16.4	0	0	0	0	.000	.001	.003	.008	.018	.035	.065	.108	.168	.243
16.6	0	0	0	0	.000	.001	.003	.007	.016	.032	.059	.100	.156	.228
16.8	0	0	0	0	.000	.001	.002	.006	.014	.029	.054	.092	.145	.214
17.0	0	0	0	0	.000	.001	.002	.005	.013	.026	.049	.085	.135	.201
17.2	0	0	0	0	.000	.001	.002	.005	.011	.024	.045	.078	.125	.188
17.4	0	0	0	0	.000	.001	.002	.004	.010	.021	.041	.071	.116	.176
17.6	0	0	0	0	0	.000	.001	.004	.009	.019	.037	.065	.107	.164
17.8	0	0	0	0	0	.000	.001	.003	.008	.017	.033	.060	.099	.153
18.0	0	0	0	0	0	.000	.001	.003	.007	.015	.030	.055	.092	.143
18.2	0	0	0	0	0	.000	.001	.003	.006	.014	.027	.050	.085	.133
18.4	0	0	0	0	0	.000	.001	.002	.006	.012	.025	.046	.078	.123
18.6	0	0	0	0	0	.000	.001	.002	.005	.011	.022	.042	.072	.115
18.8	0	0	0	0	0	.000	.001	.002	.004	.010	.020	.038	.066	.106
19.0	0	0	0	0	0	.000	.001	.002	.004	.009	.018	.035	.061	.098
19.2	0	0	0	0	0	0	.000	.001	.003	.008	.017	.032	.056	.091
19.4	0	0	0	0	0	0	.000	.001	.003	.007	.015	.029	.051	.084
19.6	0	0	0	0	0	0	.000	.001	.003	.006	.013	.026	.047	.078
19.8	0	0	0	0	0	0	.000	.001	.002	.006	.012	.024	.043	.072
20.0	0	0	0	0	0	0	.000	.001	.002	.005	.011	.021	.039	.066

Selected References

Besterfield, D.H. *Quality Improvement*, 9th ed. Englewood Cliffs, NJ: Prentice Hall, 2013.

Duncan, A. J. *Quality Control and Industrial Statistics*, 5th ed. Homewood, Ill: Irwin Professional Publication, 1986.

Montgomery, Douglas, C. *Introduction to Statistical Quality Control*, 7th ed. Hoboken, NJ: Wiley, 2013.

U.S. Department of Defense. *Military Standard (MIL-STD-414), Sampling Procedures and Tables for Inspection by Variables for Percent Defective.* Washington, D.C.: U.S. Government Printing Office, 1957.

U.S. Department of Defense. *Military Standard (MIL-STD-105), Sampling Procedures and Tables for Attributes.* Washington, D.C.: U.S. Government Printing Office, 1963.

This supplement focuses on measuring the volume of work produced per unit of time, called an output rate. The rate of output is influenced by operations strategy, process choice, technology, and job design. The first step in measuring an output rate is determining a normal level of performance. A **work standard** is the time required for a trained worker to perform a task following a prescribed method with normal effort and skill. Robots of the same type perform the same repetitive tasks with little variation in output rate, but human output is more difficult to evaluate because skill, effort, intellect, and stamina vary from one employee to another.

work standard

The time required for a trained worker to perform a task following a prescribed method with normal effort and skill.

LEARNING GOALS *After reading this supplement, you should be able to:*

1. Provide examples of the uses of work standards by managers.

2. Use the time study method for establishing a work standard.

3. Describe the elemental standard data method for creating a work standard.

4. Discuss the predetermined data method for developing work standards.

5. Use the work sampling method to estimate the proportion of time spent on an activity.

6. Discuss the managerial considerations of work measurement.

Work Standards

Managers use work standards in the following ways:

1. *Establishing Prices and Costs.* Managers can use labor and machine time standards to develop costs for current and new products, create budgets, determine prices, and arrive at make-or-buy decisions.

2. *Motivating Workers.* Standards can be used to define a day's work or to motivate workers to improve their performance. For example, under an incentive compensation plan, workers can earn a bonus for output that exceeds the standard.

3. *Comparing Alternative Process Designs.* Time standards can be used to compare different routings for an item and to evaluate new work methods and new equipment.

4. *Scheduling.* Managers need time standards to assign tasks to workers and machines in ways that effectively utilize resources.

5. *Capacity Planning.* Managers can use time standards to determine current and projected capacity requirements for given demand requirements. Workforce staffing decisions also may require time estimates.

6. *Performance Appraisal.* A worker's output can be compared to the standard output over a period of time to evaluate worker performance and productivity. A manager's performance can be measured by comparing actual costs to standard costs of a process.

Developing a Work Standard

The key to developing a work standard is defining *normal* performance. Suppose, for example, that the manager of a fast-growing company that manufactures frozen pizza wants to create a standard for pizza assembly. To assemble the pizza, a worker spreads sauce over the pizza shell, adds pepperoni and cheese, places the pizza in a box, and puts the assembled product on a cart for fast freezing. The entire process takes 20 seconds. At this pace, a worker could assemble 1,440 pizzas in an 8-hour day.

Before settling on 20 seconds as the standard, however, the manager must consider whether all the employees have the skills of the observed worker. He may be exceptionally energetic, experienced, and efficient. Moreover, the estimate of 20 seconds per pizza did not account for fluctuations in pace or scheduled rest periods. Generally, the time per unit observed over a short period for one employee should not be used as a standard for an extended period of time for all employees.

Methods for Measuring Output Rates

work measurement

The process of creating labor standards based on the judgment of skilled observers.

Management has several methods for measuring output rates. **Work measurement** is the process of creating labor standards based on the judgment of skilled observers. Managers often use informal methods to arrive at labor standards. They can develop simple estimates of the time required for activities or the number of employees needed for a job on the basis of experience and judgment. Formal methods of work measurement available to the manager include the following:

1. The time study method
2. The elemental standard data method
3. The predetermined data method
4. The work sampling method

The method chosen often depends on the purpose of the data. For example, when an analyst needs a high degree of precision in comparing actual work method results to standards, a stopwatch study or predetermined times might be required. Alternatively, an analyst who wants to estimate the percentage of time that an employee is idle while waiting for customers or materials requires a work sampling method. Moreover, an analyst may use more than one method to obtain needed work measurement information. In the remainder of this supplement, we assume that the worker has fully learned the work method under study.

Time Study Method

The method used most often for setting time standards for a job is called a *time study*, which consists of four steps.

Step 1: Selecting Work Elements

Each work element should have definite starting and stopping points to facilitate taking stopwatch readings. Work elements that take less than three seconds to complete should be avoided because they are difficult to time. The work elements selected should correspond to a standard work method that has been running smoothly for a period of time in a standard work environment. Incidental operations not normally involved in the task should be identified and separated from the repetitive work.

Step 2: Timing the Elements

After the work elements have been identified, the analyst times a worker trained in the work method to get an initial set of observations. The analyst may use either the *continuous method*, recording the stopwatch reading for each work element upon its completion, or the *snap-back method*, resetting the stopwatch to zero upon completion of each work element. For the latter method, the analyst uses two watches, one for recording the previous work element and the other for timing the current work element.

If the sample data include a single, isolated time that differs greatly from other times recorded for the same element, the analyst should investigate the cause of the variation. Time for an "irregular occurrence," such as a dropped tool or a machine failure, should not be included in calculating the average time for the work element. The average observed time based only on representative times is called the **select time** $(\bar{t})$. Irregular occurrences can be covered in the allowances that we discuss later.

select time $(\bar{t})$

The average observed time based only on representative times.

Step 3: Determining Sample Size

Typically, those who use the time study method to set standards want an average time estimate that is very close to the true long-range average most of the time. A formula, based on the normal distribution, allows the analyst to determine the sample size, n, required:

$$n = \left[\left(\frac{z}{p} \right) \left(\frac{\sigma}{\bar{t}} \right) \right]^2$$

where

n = required sample size

p = precision of the estimate as a proportion of the true value

$\bar{t}$ = select time for a work element

σ = standard deviation of representative observed times for a work element

z = number of normal standard deviations needed for the desired confidence

Typical values of z for this formula are as follows:

Desired Confidence (%)	z
90	1.65
95	1.96
96	2.05
97	2.17
98	2.33
99	2.58

For example, a 95% confidence level z value of 1.96 represents ± 1.96 standard deviations from the mean, leaving a total of 5 percent in the tails of the standardized normal curve. The precision of the estimate, p, is expressed as a proportion of the true (but unknown) average time for the work element.

EXAMPLE H.1	**Estimating the Sample Size in a Time Study**

A coffee cup packaging operation has four work elements. A preliminary study provided the following results:

MyOMLab

Tutor H.1 in MyOMLab provides another example of determining the sample size for a time study.

Work Element	Standard Deviation, σ (min)	Select Time, $\bar{t}$ (min)	Sample Size
1. Get two cartons	0.0305	0.50	5
2. Put liner in carton	0.0171	0.11	10
3. Place cups in carton	0.0226	0.71	10
4. Seal carton and set aside	0.0241	1.10	10

Work element 1 was observed only five times because it occurs once every two work cycles. The study covered the packaging of 10 cartons. Determine the appropriate sample size if the estimate for the select time for any work element is to be within 4 percent of the true mean 95 percent of the time.

SOLUTION

For this problem,

$$p = 0.04 \text{ and } z = 1.96$$

The sample size for each work element must be calculated, and the largest must be used for the final study so that all estimates will meet or exceed the desired precision.

$$\text{Work element 1: } n = \left[\left(\frac{1.96}{0.04} \right) \left(\frac{0.0305}{0.500} \right) \right]^2 = 9$$

$$\text{Work element 2: } n = \left[\left(\frac{1.96}{0.04} \right) \left(\frac{0.0171}{0.11} \right) \right]^2 = 58$$

$$\text{Work element 3: } n = \left[\left(\frac{1.96}{0.04} \right) \left(\frac{0.0226}{0.71} \right) \right]^2 = 3$$

$$\text{Work element 4: } n = \left[\left(\frac{1.96}{0.04} \right) \left(\frac{0.0241}{1.10} \right) \right]^2 = 2$$

DECISION POINT

All fractional calculations were rounded to the next largest integer. To be sure that all select times are within 4 percent of the true mean 95 percent of the time, we must have a total of 58 observations because of work element 2. Consequently, we have to observe the packaging of 48 (or 58 − 10) more cartons.

Step 4: Setting the Standard

performance rating factor (RF)

An assessment that describes *how much* above or below average the worker's performance is on each work element.

The final step is to set the standard. To do so, the analyst first determines the normal time for each work element by judging the pace of the observed worker. The analyst must assess not only whether the worker's pace is above or below average, but also a **performance rating factor (RF)** that describes *how much* above or below average the worker's performance is on each work element. Setting the performance rating requires the greatest amount of judgment. Usually, only a few workers are observed during a study. If the workers are fast, basing the standard on their average time would not be fair, particularly if a wage incentive plan is involved. Conversely, if the workers are slow, basing the standard on their normal time would be unfair to the company. Furthermore, workers may slow their pace when they are being observed in a time study. Thus, the analyst has to make an adjustment in the average observed time to estimate the time required for a trained operator to do the task at a normal pace. Analysts go through training programs to ensure consistency of ratings over many analyses.

normal time (NT)

In the context of time study, a measurement found by multiplying the select time ($\bar{t}$), the frequency (F) of the work element per cycle, and the rating factor (RF).

The analyst must also factor in the frequency of occurrence, F, of a particular work element in a work cycle. Some work elements may not be performed every cycle. The analyst finds the **normal time (NT)** for any work element by multiplying the select time ($\bar{t}$), the frequency (F) of the work element per cycle, and the rating factor (RF):

$$\text{NT} = \bar{t}(F)(\text{RF})$$

normal time for the cycle (NTC)

A measurement found by summing the normal time for each element.

Use $F = 1$ if the work element is performed every cycle, $F = 0.5$ if it is performed every other cycle, and so on. To find the **normal time for the cycle (NTC)**, the analyst sums the normal time for each element:

$$\text{NTC} = \sum \text{NT}$$

EXAMPLE H.2	Determining the Normal Time

MyOMLab

Tutor H.2 in MyOMLab provides another example of determining the normal times for a time study.

Suppose that 48 additional observations of the coffee cup packaging operation were taken and the following data were recorded:

Work Element	$\bar{t}$	F	RF
1	0.53	0.50	1.05
2	0.10	1.00	0.95
3	0.75	1.00	1.10
4	1.08	1.00	0.90

Because element 1 occurs only every other cycle, its average time per cycle must be half its average observed time. That is why $F_1 = 0.50$ for that element. All others occur every cycle. What are the normal times for each work element and for the complete cycle?

SOLUTION

The normal times are calculated as follows:

Work element 1: $\text{NT}_1 = 0.53(0.50)(1.50) = 0.28$ minute
Work element 2: $\text{NT}_2 = 0.10(1.00)(0.95) = 0.10$ minute
Work element 3: $\text{NT}_3 = 0.75(1.00)(1.10) = 0.83$ minute
Work element 4: $\text{NT}_4 = 1.08(1.00)(0.90) = \underline{0.97}$ minute

Total $= 2.18$ minutes

The normal time for the complete cycle is 2.18 minutes.

DECISION POINT

The normal time only tells us what the specific worker used for the study can do. It must be modified to get a useful measure of output for a group of workers.

We cannot use the normal time of 2.18 minutes for the cycle as a standard because it does not allow for fatigue, rest periods, or unavoidable delays that occur during an average workday. Hence, we must add some **allowance time** to the normal time to adjust for these factors. The **standard time (ST)** then becomes

$$ST = NTC(1 + A)$$

where

$$A = \text{proportion of the normal time added for allowances}$$

Most allowances range from 10 to 20 percent of normal time and cover factors that may be difficult to measure. However, work sampling, which we discuss later, can be used to estimate some of those factors.

allowance time

The time added to the normal time to adjust for certain factors.

standard time (ST)

A measurement found by incorporating the normal time and allowances; $ST = NTC(1 + A)$, where A equals the proportion of the normal time added for allowances.

EXAMPLE H.3	**Determining the Standard Time**

Management needs a standard time for the coffee cup packaging operation. Suppose that $A = 0.15$ of the normal time. What is the standard time for the coffee cup packaging operation, and how many cartons can be expected per 8-hour day?

MyOMLab

Tutor H.3 in MyOMLab provides another example of determining a standard time for a work method.

SOLUTION

For $A = 0.15$ of the normal time,

$$ST = 2.18(1 + 0.15) = 2.51 \text{ minutes/carton}$$

DECISION POINT

For an 8-hour day, this translates into a production standard of

$$\frac{480 \text{ minutes/day}}{2.51 \text{ minutes/carton}} = 191 \text{ cartons/day}$$

Management can now use that estimate to make production plans and cost estimates.

Overall Assessment of Time Study

Time study methods have some limitations. They should not be used to set standards for jobs in which the nature of the task is different each time, such as a student solving a problem, a professor preparing a lecture, or an automobile mechanic diagnosing the cause of a nonroutine problem. In addition, an inexperienced person should not conduct time studies because errors in recording information or in selecting the work elements to include can result in unreasonable standards. Finally, some workers may object to time study because of the subjectivity involved. Nonetheless, time studies conducted by an experienced observer usually provide a satisfactory, although imperfect, tool for setting equitable time standards.

Elemental Standard Data Method

If a plant requires thousands of work standards, the time and cost required for the time study method may be prohibitive. When a high degree of similarity exists in the work elements of certain jobs, analysts often use *elemental standard data* to derive standards for various jobs. In this method, analysts use a work measurement method, such as time study or management opinions, to compile standards for the common elements. The standards are stored in a database. If the time required for a work element depends on certain variable characteristics of the jobs, an equation that relates these characteristics to the time required can also be stored in a database. Once established, the database can provide the data needed to estimate the normal times for jobs requiring these work elements with varying characteristics. However, allowances still must be added to arrive at standard times for the jobs.

In addition to reducing the number of time studies or informed opinions needed, the elemental standard data method can help managers develop standards for new work before production begins. This feature is helpful in product costing, pricing, and production planning.

Although the use of the elemental standard data method reduces the need for time studies or opinions, they cannot be eliminated. The analyst should periodically use work measurement methods to check the standards developed by the elemental standard data method. Specifying all the job variables that affect times for each work element may be difficult; consequently, this method may not produce good estimates for the normal time.

Predetermined Data Method

The predetermined data method eliminates the need for time studies altogether. The analyst divides each work element into a series of micromotions common to a variety of tasks. The analyst then consults a published database that contains the normal times for these micromotions along with modifications for job variables. The normal time for any task can be developed by accessing the database.

methods time measurement (MTM)

A commonly used predetermined data system.

One of the most commonly used predetermined data systems is **methods time measurement (MTM)**. Actually, there are several MTM databases, but we focus on the most accurate, MTM-1. In MTM-1, the basic micromotions are reach, move, disengage, apply pressure, grasp, position, release, and turn. The normal times for these micromotions, modified for job variables, were developed by trained observers, who applied performance ratings to observations of motion picture studies of workers in various industrial settings.

Each micromotion is measured in time measurement units (TMUs). One TMU equals 0.0006 minute. Setting standards from predetermined data involves several steps.

1. Break each work element into its basic micromotions.

2. Find the proper tabular value for each micromotion. Tabular values account for mitigating factors such as weight, distance, size of object, and degree of difficulty.

3. Add the normal time for each motion from the tables to get the normal time for the total job.

4. Adjust the normal time for allowances to give the standard time.

For example, suppose that a worker must move an 18-pound object with both hands to an exact location 20 inches away. The hands are not in motion prior to the move. To find the TMU value for this action, we first go to Table H.1, which describes the *move* motion. The table allows for differences in weight, distance moved, and circumstances of the move. Note that case C describes the circumstances of

TABLE H.1 | MTM PREDETERMINED DATA FOR THE MOVE MICROMOTION

Distance Moved (in.)	Time TMU				WT. Allowance			
	A	**B**	**C**	**Hand in Motion B**	**Wt.(lb) Up to**	**Dynamic Factor**	**Static Constant (TMU)**	**Case and Description**
3/4 or less	2.0	2.0	2.0	1.7				
1	2.5	2.9	3.4	2.3	2.5	1.00	0	
2	3.6	4.6	5.2	2.9				
3	4.9	5.7	6.7	3.6	7.5	1.06	2.2	A Move object to other hand or against stop.
4	6.1	6.9	8.0	4.3				
5	7.3	8.0	9.2	5.0	12.5	1.11	3.9	
6	8.1	8.9	10.3	5.7				
7	8.9	9.7	11.1	6.5	17.5	1.17	5.6	B Move object to approximate or indefinite location.
8	9.7	10.6	11.8	7.2				
9	10.5	11.5	12.7	7.9	22.5	1.22	7.4	
10	11.3	12.2	13.5	8.6				
12	12.9	13.4	15.2	10.0	27.5	1.28	9.1	
14	14.4	14.6	16.9	11.4				
16	16.0	15.8	18.7	12.8	32.5	1.33	10.8	
18	17.6	17.0	20.4	14.2				
20	19.2	18.2	22.1	15.6	37.5	1.39	12.5	C Move object to exact location.
22	20.8	19.4	23.8	17.0				
24	22.4	20.6	25.5	18.4	42.5	1.44	14.3	
26	24.0	21.8	27.3	19.8				
28	25.5	23.1	29.0	21.2	47.5	1.50	16.0	
30	27.1	24.3	30.7	22.7				
Additional	0.8	.6	0.85				TMU per inch over 30 inches	

Source: MTM Association for Standards and Research, Des Plaines, IL. Reprinted by permission.

this move. Under column C, the entry for 20 inches is 22.1 TMUs. Now make adjustments for the weight of the object. The worker is using 2 hands, so the weight *per hand* is 9 pounds, which is greater than 7.5 pounds and less than 12.5 pounds in the weight allowance columns. The dynamic factor is 1.11, and the static factor is 3.9 TMUs. To find the final TMU value for this activity, we multiply the tabular TMU value for the distance moved by the dynamic factor and add the static factor: $22.1(1.11) + 3.9 = 28$ TMUs. Similar tables are available for other motions.

The predetermined data method offers some advantages over the other methods that we have discussed. First, standards can be set for new jobs before production begins, something that cannot be done with the time study method. Second, new work methods can be compared without conducting a time study. Third, a greater degree of consistency in the setting of time standards is provided because the sources of error in time studies, such as data recording errors, are reduced. Finally, this method lessens the problem of biased judgment because performance ratings are no longer needed in the derivation of a standard.

The predetermined data method also has its drawbacks. Work must be broken into micromotions, making this method impractical for products or services with low repeatability. Moreover, the sample of workers used to develop the predetermined data may not be representative of the workers in a particular facility.

Furthermore, performance time variations can result from a complex array of factors. For example, the time needed to move an object may depend on the shape of the object, but the MTM-1 charts do not recognize this factor. Also, the method assumes that the times associated with the micromotions simply can be summed to get the total time for a task. This assumption disregards the possibility that the actual time may depend on the specific *sequence* of motions. Finally, there is a danger that the method will be misused. Although the method appears to be easy to use, considerable training and experience are required to identify all the micromotions and accurately judge the mitigating factors of the motion.

Work Sampling Method

The *work sampling method* involves estimating the proportions of time spent by people and machines on activities, based on a large number of observations. These activities might include producing a service or product, doing paperwork, waiting for instructions, waiting for maintenance, or being idle. The underlying assumption is that the proportion of time during which the activity is observed in the sample will be the proportion of time spent on the activity in general. Data from work sampling also can be used to estimate how effective machines or workers are, estimate the allowances needed to set standards for use with other work measurement methods, determine job content, and help assess the cost of jobs or activities.

Work Sampling Procedure

Conducting a work sampling study involves the following steps:

1. Define the activities.
2. Design the observation form.
3. Determine the length of the study.
4. Determine the initial sample size.
5. Select random observation times using a random number table.
6. Determine the observer schedule.
7. Observe the activities and record the data.
8. Decide whether additional sampling is required.

A work sampling study should be conducted over a period of time that is representative of normal work conditions, in which each activity occurs a representative number of times. For example, if an activity occurs only once a week, the study should probably span several months. However, if the activity occurs continuously throughout the week and from week to week throughout the year, the study might cover only several weeks.

Sample Size

The goal of work sampling is to obtain an estimate of the proportion of time spent on a particular activity that does not differ from the true proportion by more than a specified error. That is, the analyst wants to take a sample, calculate the sample proportion, $\hat{p}$, and be able to say that the following interval contains the true proportion with a specified degree of precision:

$$\hat{p} - e \leq \hat{p} \leq \hat{p} + e$$

where

$\hat{p}$ = sample proportion (number of occurrences divided by the sample size)

e = maximum error in the estimate

The sample size affects the degree of precision that can be expected from work sampling for any desired level of statistical confidence. Work sampling involves estimating proportions, so the sampling distribution is the binomial distribution. However, large sample sizes are required for this method, and the normal approximation to the binomial distribution can be used to determine the appropriate sample size. Figure H.1 shows the confidence interval for a work sampling study. The maximum error can be computed as

$$e = z\sqrt{\frac{\hat{p}(1 - \hat{p})}{n}}$$

where

n = sample size

z = number of standard deviations needed to achieve the desired confidence

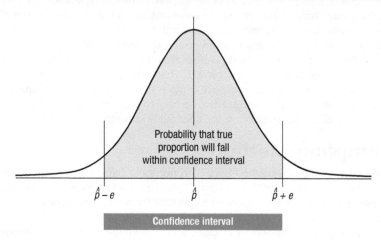

FIGURE H.1 ▶
Confidence Interval for a Work Sampling Study

Because n is in the divisor of the equation, as n increases, the maximum error decreases. To determine the proper sample size for a given error, the analyst uses the formula for e to solve for n:

$$n = \left(\frac{z}{e}\right)^2 \hat{p}(1 - \hat{p})$$

Initially, the analyst may have to make a reasonable guess for the proportion of time an activity takes, use the formula to determine n, and then compute an estimate of the proportion based on the sample. The new estimate for the proportion can be used in the formula for n to determine whether additional sampling is required.

Sampling Schedule

The times of day the analyst gathers the sample data should be selected at random over the length of the study. This method reduces the amount of bias in the data. For example, if employees know that they will be observed each day at 2:30 P.M., some of them may alter their behavior at that time. If that happens, the data will not represent actual performance. After determining the observation times to be used, the analyst can develop a schedule for the observer.

EXAMPLE H.4	**Using Work Sampling Data for Decision Making**

The hospital administrator at a private hospital is considering a proposal for installing an automated medical records storage and retrieval system. To determine the advisability of purchasing such a system, the administrator needs to know the proportion of time that registered nurses (RNs) and licensed vocational nurses (LVNs) spend accessing records. Currently, these nurses must either retrieve the records manually or have them copied and sent to their wards. A typical ward, staffed by eight RNs and four LVNs, is selected for the study.

a. The hospital administrator estimates that accessing records takes about 20 percent of the RNs' time and about 5 percent of the LVNs' time. The administrator wants 95 percent confidence that the estimate for each category of nurses falls within ±0.03 of the true proportion. What should the sample size be?

b. The hospital administrator estimates that the annual amortization cost and expenses for maintaining the new automated medical records storage and retrieval system will be $150,000. The supplier of the new system estimates that the system will reduce the amount of time the nurses spend accessing records by 25 percent. The total annual salary expense for RNs in the hospital is $3,628,000, and for LVNs it is

Activity					
	Accessing records	Attending to patients	Other support activities	Idle or break	Total observations
RN	124	258	223	83	688
LVN	28	251	46	19	344

◀ FIGURE H.2
Results of the Initial Study

$2,375,000. The hospital administrator assumes that nurses could productively use any time saved by the new system. The pilot work sampling study resulted in the data shown in Figure H.2. Should the administrator purchase the new system?

SOLUTION

a. Using estimates for the proportion of time spent accessing records of 0.20 for RNs and 0.05 for LVNs, an error of ± 0.03 for each, and a 95 percent confidence interval ($z = 1.96$), we recommend the following sample sizes:

$$\text{RN: } n = \left(\frac{1.96}{0.03}\right)^2 (0.20)(0.80) = 683$$

$$\text{LVN: } n = \left(\frac{1.96}{0.03}\right)^2 (0.05)(0.95) = 203$$

Eight RNs and four LVNs can be observed on each trip. Therefore, $683/8 = 86$ (rounded up) trips are needed for the observations of RNs, and only $203/4 = 51$ (rounded up) trips are needed for the LVNs. Thus, 86 trips through the ward will be sufficient for observing both nurse groups. This number of trips will generate 688 observations of RNs and 344 observations of LVNs. It will provide many more observations than are needed for the LVNs, but the added observations may as well be recorded as the observer will be going through the ward anyway.

b. Before using the estimates from the work sampling study, we must be sure that additional sampling is not required. Figure H.2 shows that RNs accessed records 124 times and LVNs only 28 times. The computer output shows that the proportion of working time spent on accessing records is 0.1802 for the RNs and 0.0814 for the LVNs. Thus, the original estimates were off the mark. The computer uses the new estimates for the proportions in the same formulas we used in part (a) to revise the sample sizes. However, the new sample sizes are *smaller* than those already used, so no additional sampling is required. If the sample sizes were too small for the proportions found, additional sampling would have to be performed. In addition, the confidence interval shows the range possible in the "true" proportions, based on the results of the pilot study. For example, the actual proportion of time spent by the RNs on accessing records could be as low as 0.15 and as high as 0.21.

				CONFIDENCE INTERVAL		
Workgroup	Total Obs.	Activity Obs.	Proportion of Total	Lower	Upper	Required Sample Size
RN	688	124	0.1802	0.15151	0.2090	631
LVN	344	28	0.0814	0.05250	0.1103	320

Because the nurses will not be using the system all the time, we accept the supplier's estimate of 25 percent to determine the value of the time spent accessing records. Estimated annual net savings from the purchase of the automatic medical records storage and retrieval system are

$$\text{Net savings} = 0.25[(\$3,628,000)(0.18) + (\$2,375,000)(0.08)] - \$150,000$$
$$= \$60,760$$

DECISION POINT
The confidence intervals indicate that the true proportions could be as low as 0.15 for RNs and 0.05 for LVNs. If that "worst-case" situation occurred, the net savings would be

$$\text{Net savings} = 0.25[(\$3,628,000)(0.15) + (\$2,375,000)(0.05)] - \$150,000$$
$$= \$15,737$$

Based on the results of the work sampling study, the new system appears to be a good investment, provided the nurses can spend the time saved productively on other duties.

Overall Assessment of Work Sampling

The work sampling method is used frequently to estimate the proportion of time that people or machines spend on particular activities because it offers certain advantages over other methods. No special training is required for the observers, no stopwatches are needed, and several studies can be conducted simultaneously. In addition, workers themselves often prefer this method of work measurement because it typically is directed at the activities of groups rather than individuals.

The major disadvantage to work sampling is the large number of brief observations required to provide a reasonable degree of precision for the estimate. Unlike the other methods discussed, this method usually is not used for setting standards for repetitive, well-defined jobs.

Managerial Considerations in Work Measurement

In light of new technologies and management philosophies, managers should carefully evaluate work measurement techniques to ensure that they are used in ways that are consistent with the firm's competitive priorities. Balancing the need to manage processes and supply chains and the need for employee involvement is a difficult task. Traditional work measurement techniques sometimes are viewed as repressive and not conducive to good management–employee relations. Nonetheless, management needs the data in order to measure outputs and the results of process improvements.

Technological change is another reason to reexamine work measurement techniques. For example, when a firm increases its level of automation, its methods of work measurement must also change. The need to use traditional work measurement techniques to develop work standards is less for automated processes because many computer-controlled machines can gather data on their processes. Hence, standards for machines can be set without having to sample unit processing times. Application of the techniques discussed in this supplement can then focus on less prevalent activities that are largely controlled by the pace of workers.

LEARNING GOALS IN REVIEW

Learning Goal	Guidelines for Review	MyOMLab Resources
❶ Provide examples of the uses of work standards by managers.	The section "Work Standards," pp. 1–2, identifies six different uses for work standards.	
❷ Use the time study method for establishing a work standard.	See the section "Time Study Method," pp. 2–5, and study Examples H.1–H.3. Also review Solved Problem 1.	**OM Explorer Tutors:** H.1: Time Study Sample Size; H2: Normal Time; H3: Standard Time **OM Explorer Solver:** Measuring Output Rates (Time Study) **POM for Windows:** Time Study Sample Size
❸ Describe the elemental standard data method for creating a work standard.	The section "Elemental Standard Data Method," p. 5, describes the method and its uses.	
❹ Discuss the predetermined data method for developing work standards.	The section "Predetermined Data Method," pp. 6–7, discusses the method and its advantages and disadvantages.	
❺ Use the work sampling method to estimate the proportion of time spent on an activity.	See the section "Work Sampling Method," pp. 7–10, to understand how to use this method for work measurement. Study Example H.4 and Solved Problem 2.	**OM Explorer Solver:** Measuring Output Rates (Work Sampling) **POM for Windows:** Work Sampling (sample size)
❻ Discuss the managerial considerations of work measurement.	See the section "Managerial Considerations in Work Measurement," p. 10.	

Key Equations

Time Study Method

1. Required sample size in a time study: $n = \left[\left(\frac{z}{p}\right)\left(\frac{\sigma}{\bar{t}}\right)\right]^2$

2. Normal time for a work element: $NT = \bar{t}(F)(RF)$

3. Normal time for the cycle: $NTC = \sum NT$

4. Standard time: $ST = NTC(1 + A)$

Work Sampling Method

5. Required sample size in a work sampling study: $n = \left(\frac{z}{e}\right)^2 \hat{p}(1 - \hat{p})$

Key Terms

allowance time 5
methods time measurement (MTM) 6
normal time (NT) 4

normal time for the cycle (NTC) 4
performance rating factor (RF) 4
select time ($\bar{t}$) 2

standard time (ST) 5
work measurement 2
work standard 1

Solved Problem 1

For a time study of a health insurance claims-adjusting process, the analyst uses the continuous method of recording times. The job is divided into four work elements. Shown in Figure H.3 are the performance rating factors, RF, and the continuous method recorded times, r, for each work element.

Operation: *Insurance claim processing*		Date: *10/09/15*			Observer: *Jennifer Johnson*					
		Observations								
Work Element		1	2	3	4	5	$\bar{t}$	RF	σ
1. Check form completion and signatures	t	0.50	0.55	0.45	0.60	0.50	0.52	1.1	0.0570
	r	0.50	3.30	5.70	8.20	10.85			
2. Enter claim amounts, check math	t	0.20	0.15	0.25	0.35	0.25	0.24	1.2	0.0742
	r	0.70	3.45	5.95	8.55	11.10			
3. Determine proportion of claim to be disallowed	t	0.75	0.60	0.55	0.70	0.65	0.65	1.2	0.0791
	r	1.45	4.05	6.50	9.25	11.75			
4. Generate form letter, enter data for check	t	1.30	1.20	1.10	1.10	1.30	1.20	0.9	0.1000
	r	2.75	5.25	7.60	10.35	13.05			

◀ **FIGURE H.3**
Time Study Data for Insurance Claim Processing

a. Calculate the normal time for this job.

b. Calculate the standard time for this job, assuming that the allowance is 20 percent of the normal time.

c. What is the appropriate sample size for estimating the time for element 2 within ± 10 percent of the true mean with 95 percent confidence?

SOLUTION

a. To get the normal time for this job, we must first determine the observed time, t, for each work element for each cycle. We calculate the time for each observation by finding the difference between successive recorded times, r. For example, the time for the fifth observation of the first work element is the difference between the recorded time when that element was completed (at 10.85 minutes) and the time when the fourth observation of the fourth work element was completed (at 10.35 minutes): 10.85 minutes − 10.35 minutes = 0.50 minute. Similarly, the time for the fifth observation of the second work element is 11.10 minutes − 10.85 minutes = 0.25 minute. With no extreme variation in the observed times for the work elements, they are representative of the process. All the data can be used for calculating the average observed time, called the select time, $\bar{t}$, and the standard deviation of the observed times, σ. The results of those calculations are given in Figure H.3. Every work element occurs during every cycle, so the frequency, F, equals 1. The normal times are calculated as

$$NT_1 = \bar{t}(F)(RF)$$

Work element 1: $NT_1 = (0.52)(1)(1.1) = 0.572$ minute

Work element 2: $NT_2 = (0.24)(1)(1.2) = 0.288$ minute

Work element 3: $NT_3 = (0.65)(1)(1.2) = 0.780$ minute

Work element 4: $NT_4 = (1.20)(1)(0.9) = \underline{1.080 \text{ minutes}}$

$$\text{Total} = 2.720 \text{ minutes}$$

b. Standard time = (Normal time per cycle) (1.0 + Allowances), or

$$ST = NTC(1.0 + A) = 2.72(1.0 + 0.2)$$

$$= 3.264 \text{ minutes}$$

c. The appropriate sample size for 95 percent confidence that the select time for work element 2 is within ± 10 percent of the true mean is

$$n = \left[\left(\frac{z}{p}\right)\left(\frac{\sigma}{\bar{t}}\right)\right]^2 = \left[\left(\frac{1.96}{0.10}\right)\left(\frac{0.0742}{0.24}\right)\right]^2$$

$$= 36.72, \text{ or } 37 \text{ observations}$$

Solved Problem 2

A library administrator wants to determine the proportion of time the circulation clerk is idle. The following information was gathered randomly by using work sampling:

Day	Number of Times Clerk Busy	Number of Times Clerk Idle	Total Number of Observations
Monday	8	2	10
Tuesday	7	1	8
Wednesday	9	3	12
Thursday	7	3	10
Friday	8	2	10
Saturday	6	4	10

If the administrator wants a 95 percent confidence level and a degree of precision of ± 4 percent, how many more observations are needed?

SOLUTION

The total number of observations made was 60. The clerk was observed to be idle 15 times. The initial estimate of the sample proportion is $\hat{p} = 15/60 = 0.25$. The required sample size for a precision of ± 4 percent is

$$n = \frac{z^2 \hat{p}(1 - \hat{p})}{e^2} = \frac{(1.96)^2(0.25)(0.75)}{(0.04)^2}$$

$$= 450.19, \text{ or } 451 \text{ observations}$$

As 60 observations have already been made, an additional 391 are needed.

Problems

The OM Explorer and POM for Windows software is available to all students using the 11th edition of this textbook. Go to **http://www.pearsonhighered.com/krajewski** to download these computer packages. If you purchased MyOMLab, you also have access to Active Models software and significant help in doing the following problems. Check with your instructor on how best to use these resources. In many cases, the instructor wants you to understand how to do the calculations by hand. At the least, the software provides a check on your calculations. When calculations are particularly complex and the goal is interpreting the results in making decisions, the software entirely replaces the manual calculations.

Time Study Method

1. During a time study in a machine shop, five observations of a milling operation performed by an operator whose rating factor is 95 percent yielded the following times (in minutes): 40, 48, 48, 46, and 42. The allowance for this type of operation is 15 percent.

   a. Determine the normal time for this operation.

   b. Determine the standard time for this operation.

2. The manager of Stetson and Stetson Company is trying to develop a time standard for the powder filling and packing operation. This operation has five work elements, each of which is performed once every cycle. The allowance for each work element is 18 percent. The operation was studied for 20 cycles, and the following summary data were obtained:

Work Element	Select Time (minutes)	Standard Deviation (minutes)
1	0.40	0.021
2	0.20	0.011
3	0.31	0.018
4	0.15	0.005
5	1.25	0.085

   a. Determine the standard time for the filling and packing operation. Assume the rating factor $= 1.0$.

   b. Determine the sample size necessary if the estimate of the select time for the work elements is to be within ± 3 percent of the true mean 95 percent of the time.

   c. Is the sample size chosen to determine the standard time adequate? If not, how many additional cycles should be observed?

3. A time study involving the preparation of hamburgers at Bill's fast-food restaurant used the snap-back method to obtain the data (in minutes) shown in Table H.2. Allowances typically constitute 15 percent of normal time. The schedule calls for 300 hamburgers to be prepared during the lunch rush. If each part-time employee works 190 minutes per day, how many employees will be needed?

4. A cook at Bill's restaurant (see Problem 3) has devised a new method of quickly flipping and pressing hamburgers that he believes will save time in cooking the second side of hamburgers (work element 3 in Table H.2). The cook asked a peer to conduct a time study for this work element, with the results shown in Table H.3. This cook is renowned for superior strength and speed in hamburger flipping and pressing. The rating factor for this study is 1.2. Allowances typically constitute 15 percent of the normal time.

TABLE H.2 | TIME STUDY RESULTS OF HAMBURGER PREPARATION

Work Element	OBSERVATION					$\bar{t}$	F	RF	NT
	1	2	3	4	5				
1. Prepare patty	0.45	0.41	0.50	0.48	0.36		1	0.9	
2. Cook first side	0.85	0.81	0.77	0.89	0.83		1	1.2	
3. Flip, press, and cook other side	0.60	0.55	0.59	0.58	0.63		1	1.2	
4. Assemble	0.31	0.24	0.27	0.26	0.32		1	1.0	
						Normal time per cycle (NTC) $=$			

TABLE H.3 | WORK ELEMENT 3 TIME STUDY

Work Element	OBSERVATION									
	1	2	3	4	5	6	7	8	9	10
Revised Work Element 3	0.45	0.31	0.50	0.48	0.39	0.31	0.44	0.29	0.33	0.40

   a. What is the average of select times for revised work element 3? For the revised normal time?

   b. What is the revised normal time per cycle? The revised standard time?

   c. The managers seem very interested in this revised method for work element 3. They say that if they could be sure the average of the select times for this study was within ± 13 percent of the true average time for this new method, they could afford to buy health insurance for the part-time cooks. How many observations would be required to be 98 percent confident that the average of select times for this study was within ± 13 percent of the true mean?

   d. The cook is not only quick with a spatula, but also quick with a calculator and a bit suspicious of management's motives. If the average of the select times found in part (c) were inflated by 13 percent, how many cooks would Bill's restaurant need?

5. The information (in minutes) shown in Table H.4 (see next page) pertains to a package filling operation at the Black Sheep Wool Company. When three bags are full, the third work element involves transporting the three bags down the line. What is the normal cycle time for this operation?

6. A time analyst for the Super-Fast speedway pit crew observed the mechanic in charge of changing both front tires during

a pit-stop practice session. The mechanic's job is divided into six work elements and a preparation time between drills. The element times (in seconds) for the first six cycles are shown in Table H.5.

a. Calculate the normal time for changing tires.

b. What sample size is appropriate for estimating the average time for work element 3 within ± 1 percent of the true mean with 99 percent confidence?

c. What is the standard time for changing tires if the allowance is 20 percent?

7. A time study has been conducted on a cellular telephone assembly operation. The data shown in Table H.6 (in minutes) were obtained. A standard time within ± 3 percent of the true mean with 95 percent confidence is desired.

a. Calculate the standard time for the assembly operations.

b. How many more observations will be required?

8. Consider the recorded observations of 10 cycles of the cup packaging operation, shown in Figure H.4 (see next page).

a. Determine the select times for each work element, the normal time for the cycle, and the standard time per package.

b. Suppose that we want a sample size that gives an average time within ± 5 percent of the true average 95 percent of the time. Did we make enough observations? If not, how many more should we make?

c. Suppose that all we wanted was a precision of ± 10 percent. How many additional observations would we need?

TABLE H.4 | TIME STUDY RESULTS OF THE PACKAGE FILLING OPERATION

| Work Element | OBSERVATION | | | | | | | | | | | | | |
	1	2	3	4	5	6	7	8	9	10	11	12	F	RF
1. Fill bag	0.20	0.22	0.24	0.18	0.20	0.21	0.22	0.19	0.24	0.18	0.19	0.25	1.00	1.2
2. Sew closed	0.40	0.38	0.37	0.41	0.41	0.40	0.36	0.37	0.41	0.42	0.39	0.36	1.00	0.8
3. Transport			0.82			0.84			0.73			0.85	0.33	1.1

TABLE H.5 | PIT CREW TIME STUDY DATA

| Work Element | OBSERVATION | | | | | | | |
	1	2	3	4	5	6	F	RF
1. Wait for car lift	2.9		3.2		2.6		0.5	1.0
2. Remove lugs	3.3	3.8	3.6	3.8	4.0	4.3	1.0	0.9
3. Switch tires	6.4	7.1	6.8	7.3	6.2	6.4	1.0	1.2
4. Tighten lugs	4.1	3.8	3.5	4.9	3.5	4.2	1.0	0.8
5. Move to right side	3.8	—	4.3	—	3.2	—	0.5	1.2
6. Clear away for drop	—	2.1	—	2.7	—	2.0	0.5	0.9

TABLE H.6 | CELLULAR TELEPHONE TIME STUDY DATA

| Work Element | OBSERVATION | | | | | | | |
	1	2	3	4	5	6	7	8	F	RF
1. Assemble unit	0.78	0.70	0.75	0.80	0.79	0.82	0.81	0.80	1.0	1.2
2. Insert batteries	0.20	0.21	0.16	0.19	0.23	0.25	0.24	0.26	1.0	1.0
3. Test	0.61	0.60	0.55	0.57	0.63	0.61	0.62	0.60	1.0	0.9
4. Package	0.41	0.36	0.45	0.37	0.39	0.40	0.43	0.44	1.0	1.1

Operation: *Coffee cup packaging*		Date: *1/23*			Observer: *B. Larson*							

FIGURE H.4
Cup Packaging Operation

Work Element		**Observations** 1	2	3	4	5	6	7	8	9	10	$\bar{t}$	F	RF
1. Get two cartons	t													
	r	0.48		4.85		9.14		13.53		17.83			0.5	1.05
2. Put liner in carton	t													
	r	0.59	2.56	4.94	6.82	9.25	11.23	13.61	15.50	17.93	19.83		1.0	0.95
3. Place cups in carton	t													
	r	1.33	3.24	5.65	7.51	9.98	11.93	14.29	16.24	18.64	20.55		1.0	1.10
4. Seal carton, set aside	t													
	r	2.43	4.39	6.72	8.60	11.10	13.04	15.38	17.32	19.74	21.68		1.0	0.90
Normal time for cycle:														
Allowances (% of total time): 15 %						Standard time:					minutes per piece		

Work Sampling Method

9. Management in a large hospital is planning to install a computer to reduce the time spent by nurses doing paperwork. First, management needed to know how much time nurses spend doing paperwork in order to estimate the potential savings from the computer installation. A work sampling study comprising 500 observations taken at random over a week yielded the following data:

Activity	Number of Observations
Attending to patients	180
Moving between stations	40
Consulting with doctors	60
Taking a break or idle	50
Doing paperwork	170

   a. Estimate the proportion of time that the nurses spend doing paperwork.

   b. Construct a 95 percent confidence interval for your estimate.

   c. If an hour of a nurse's time costs the hospital $40, estimate the annual savings in cost if the installation of the computer cuts time spent on paperwork by 80 percent. Assume 24 hours per day, 365 days per year of operation.

10. The manager of a loading dock is concerned about the time spent by her crew in nonproductive activities (e.g., waiting for paperwork, idle time, and the like.). Although she is not sure what the true proportion of nonproductive time is, she believes that it is close to 20 percent. If the manager wants to use work sampling to estimate this proportion with 95 percent confidence, a maximum error of 3.5 percent, how many samples should he or she take?

11. Mayor Jonathan (Johnny) Johnson of Graft City is running for reelection. At a big rally in the city park, volunteers will assemble signs reading "A vote for Johnny is a vote for Graft" to be placed on front lawns and city property. To ensure that the rally will go smoothly, the mayor directs the public works department to conduct a preliminary time study to estimate the rate of work and number of city workers that will be needed to make signs during the rally. The results (in seconds) are shown in Figure H.5.

Operation: *Yard sign assembly*		Date: *9/27*			Observer: *public works employee*							

FIGURE H.5
Results of Preliminary Time Study

Work Element		**Observations** 1	2	3	4	5	6	7	8	9	10	$\bar{t}$	F	RF
1. Get stake and sign	t													
	r	8	39	70	107	142	181	207	254	282	312		1.0	1.05
2. Put glue on stake	t													
	r	14	46	75	112	151	185	214	259	285	316		1.0	0.8
3. Place sign, four staples	t													
	r	25	60	90	126	168	196	236	270	298	338		1.0	0.9
4. Check assem., set aside	t													
	r	30	64	97	132	176	199	245	276	303	343		1.0	1.2
Normal time for cycle:														
Allowances (% of total time): 25%						Standard time:					seconds per piece		

a. Because of the chaos and uncontrolled environment at the city park rally, allowances will be 25 percent of the normal time. Determine the normal time for the cycle and the standard time.

b. The mayor does not like to leave things to chance. Suppose that he wants 99 percent confidence that each work element's average time from the study is within ± 5 percent of the true average. Did the public works department make enough observations? If not, how many more should be made?

12. The information systems department of Universal Life Insurance Company wants to determine the proportion of time that the data entry operator is idle. The following information was gathered randomly using work sampling:

Date	Number of Times Clerk Busy	Number of Times Clerk Idle	Total Number of Observations
8/22	11	2	13
8/23	12	3	15
8/24	11	3	14
8/25	12	4	16
8/26	13	1	14
8/27	13	3	16
8/28	6	6	12

If the department wants a 99 percent confidence level and a degree of precision of ± 0.01, how many more observations are needed?

13. The manager of the Valley Forge post office is interested in the amount of time that window clerks spend on ancillary services such as selling special issue stamp sets or commemorative T-shirts and helping customers with passport applications. Three clerks, each earning $36,000 per year, staff the windows. When they are not needed at the window, they sort mail for the carriers. The results of a preliminary work sampling study are shown in Table H.7, where entries reflect number of occurrences.

a. For a degree of precision of ± 0.05, what is the sample size adequate for special stamp sets? For T-shirts? For passports? What proportion of time do the clerks spend on each activity?

b. If a machine to sell special stamps could be purchased outright for $3,500, would you recommend buying it? Discuss.

14. As manager of an encoding department in a bank, you are concerned about the amount of time your encoder clerks have to spend cleaning their machines because of malfunctions. You obtained a proposal to modify the design of the machines to reduce the number of malfunctions. The modification will reduce the amount of time spent cleaning the machines by 75 percent. You employ 20 encoder clerks at an average salary of $36,000 for working 2,000 hours per year. To help you decide whether the proposal is worth considering, you had a pilot work sampling study made, which provided the following results:

Activity	Observations
Processing checks	52
Cleaning machine	15
Other duties	25
Breaks	8
	Total 100

a. Estimate the value of the annual labor savings from modifying the encoding machine design.

b. Construct a 95 percent confidence interval for your estimate. Would you suggest a larger sample size? Why? (*Hint:* Base your confidence interval on the normal approximation to the binomial distribution where the standard error is $\sigma_p = \sqrt{\hat{p}(1 - \hat{p})/n}$.

TABLE H.7 | VALLEY FORGE WORK SAMPLING DATA

Day	Selling Postage	Priority Mail	Special Stamp Sales	T-Shirt Sales	Passports	Other	Total
1	6	1	1			2	10
2	6	1		1	1	1	10
3	9			1			10
4	6	1	1		1	1	10
5	8			1		1	10
6	7	2	1				10
7	7	1		1	1		10
8	6	1	1			2	10
9	8	1				1	10
10	6	3		1			10

The following problem requires prior reading of MyOMLab Supplement E, "Simulation."

15. You have been asked by your boss to make a presentation at the next management committee meeting on the methodology of work sampling and its use in your machine shop. A consultant has recommended this method to management for use in estimating the proportion of nonproductive time for production equipment, such as a punch press. The committee members want an insider to brief them on this method. Sampling in real time is not possible during the meeting, so you decide to develop a chart that is a "virtual representation" of use of the punch press in the "real machine" shop. The chart will cover all time intervals during the five working days of the week. To develop this virtual representation of the actual operation, you ask an assistant to observe it each day of the week and record running, setup, idle, and breakdown times along a time line from 8:00 A.M. to 5:00 P.M. After making the observations, your assistant summarized his or her findings in a chart, as shown in Figure H.6. You intend to use this chart to simulate work sampling, thereby executing a work sampling plan in minutes that would normally take a week. You can then compare the proportions of time devoted to different activities estimated from the sample with the actual proportions and explain how to obtain estimates corresponding to any desired confidence level and within any specified maximum error.

a. Use a random number table to select 20 times during the week you will "observe" the punch press. Use a random number first to select the day and then use another random number to select the time of day. Omit the time period 12 P.M. to 1 P.M. each day because that is lunchtime, during which the machine will be shut down. Put these 20 times in an observation schedule.

b. Using your observation schedule, determine from Figure H.6 what the machine is doing at these times. Determine the sample proportion of the time spent in each category.

c. What are the actual proportions of time spent in each category from Figure H.6? How do they compare with the sample estimates?

d. Determine the sample size needed to ensure accuracy within ± 4 percent with 95 percent confidence.

e. Based on your experiment, what can you tell management about sample sizes and the accuracy of the estimates?

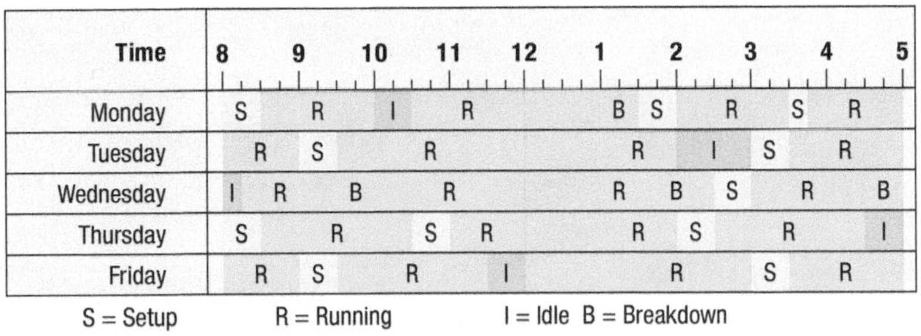

◀ **FIGURE H.6**
Chart of Observations

Selected References

Aft, Lawrence S. *Work Measurement and Methods Improvement.* Hoboken, NJ: John Wiley & Sons, 2000.

Ellis, Christian M., and Lea A.P. Tonkin. "Mature Teams Rewards and the High-Performance Workplace: Change and Opportunity." *Target,* vol. 11, no. 6 (1995).

Gephart, Martha A. "The Road to High Performance." *Training and Development,* vol. 49 (June 1995), pp. 29–44.

Groover, Mikell. Work Systems: And the Methods, Measurement, and Management of Work. Upper Saddle River, NJ: Prentice Hall, 2007.

Meyers, Fred and Jim R. Stewart, *Motion and Time Study for Lean Manufacturing,* 3rd ed. Upper Saddle River, NJ: Prentice Hall, 2002.

Sherman, Stratford. "Levi's: As Ye Sew, So Shall Ye Reap." *Fortune* (May 12, 1997), pp. 104–116.

Wiersma, Eelke. "Conditions That Shape the Learning Curve: Factors That Increase the Ability and Opportunity to Learn." *Management Science,* vol. 53, no. 12 (December 2007), pp. 1903–1915.

D = Difficult Problem

LEARNING CURVE ANALYSIS

In today's dynamic workplace, change occurs rapidly. Where there is change, there also is learning. With instruction and repetition, workers learn to perform jobs more efficiently and thereby reduce the number of direct labor hours per unit. Like workers, organizations learn.

Organizational learning involves gaining experience with products and processes, achieving greater efficiency through automation and other capital investments, and making other improvements in administrative methods or personnel. Productivity improvements may be gained from better work methods, tools, product design, or supervision, as well as from individual worker learning. These improvements mean that existing standards must be continually evaluated and new ones set. The *Selected References* at the end of the supplement show that learning curves apply to a wide variety of settings, ranging from software development to energy technology development.

organizational learning

The process of gaining experience with products and processes, achieving greater efficiency through automation and other capital investments, and making other improvements in administrative methods or personnel.

LEARNING GOALS *After reading this supplement, you should be able to:*

1. Explain the concept of a learning curve and how volume is related to unit costs.

2. Develop a learning curve using the logarithmic model.

3. Identify ways to use learning curves for managerial decision making.

4. Discuss the key managerial considerations in the use of learning curves.

The Learning Curve Concept

The learning effect can be represented by a line called a *learning curve*, which displays the relationship between the total direct labor per unit and the cumulative quantity of a product or service produced. The learning curve relates to a repetitive job or task and represents the relationship between experience and productivity: The time required to produce a unit decreases as the operator or firm produces more units. The curve in Figure I.1 is a learning curve for one process. It shows that the process time per unit continually decreases until the 140th unit is produced. At that point learning is negligible and a standard time for the operation can be developed. The terms *manufacturing progress function* and *experience curve* also have been used to describe this relationship, although the experience curve typically refers to total value-added costs per unit rather than labor hours. The principles underlying these curves are identical to those of the learning curve, however. Here we use the term *learning curve* to depict reductions in either total direct labor per unit or total value-added costs per unit.

FIGURE I.1 ▶
Learning Curve, Showing the
Learning Period and the Time
When Standards Are Calculated

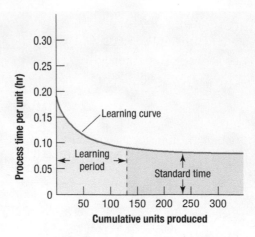

Background

The learning curve was first developed in the aircraft industry prior to World War II, when analysts discovered that the direct labor input per airplane declined with considerable regularity as the cumulative number of planes produced increased. A survey of major airplane manufacturers revealed that a series of learning curves could be developed to represent the average experience for various categories of airframes (fighters, bombers, and so on), despite the different amounts of time required to produce the first unit of each type of airframe. Once production started, the direct labor for the eighth unit was only 80 percent of that for the fourth unit, the direct labor for the twelfth was only 80 percent of that for the sixth, and so on. In each case, each doubling of the quantity reduced production time by 20 percent. Because of the consistency in the rate of improvement, the analysts concluded that the aircraft industry's rate of learning was 80 percent between doubled quantities of airframes. Of course, for any given product and company, the rate of learning may be different.

Learning Curves and Competitive Strategy

Learning curves enable managers to project the manufacturing cost per unit for any cumulative production quantity. Firms that choose to emphasize low price as a competitive strategy rely on high volumes to maintain profit margins. These firms strive to move down the learning curve (lower labor hours per unit or lower costs per unit) by increasing volume. This tactic makes entry into a market by competitors difficult. For example, in the electronics component industry, the cost of developing an integrated circuit is so large that the first units produced must be priced high. As cumulative production increases, costs (and prices) fall. The first companies in the market have a big advantage because newcomers must start selling at lower prices and suffer large initial losses.

However, market or product changes can disrupt the expected benefits of increased production. For example, Douglas Aircraft management assumed that it could reduce the costs of its new jet aircraft by following a learning curve formula and committing to fixed delivery dates and prices. Continued engineering modification of its planes disrupted the learning curve, and the cost reductions were not realized. The resulting financial problems were so severe that Douglas Aircraft was forced to merge with McDonnell Company.

Developing Learning Curves

In the following discussion and applications, we focus on direct labor hours per unit, although we could as easily have used costs. When we develop a learning curve, we make the following assumptions:

- The direct labor required to produce the $n + 1$ unit will always be less than the direct labor required for the nth unit.

- Direct labor requirements will decrease at a declining rate as cumulative production increases.

- The reduction in time will follow an exponential curve.

In other words, the production time per unit is reduced by a fixed percentage each time production is doubled. We can use a logarithmic model to draw a learning curve. The direct labor required for the nth unit, k_n, is

$$k_n = k_1 n^b$$

where

k_1 = direct labor hours for the first unit

n = cumulative numbers of units produced

$b = \dfrac{\log r}{\log 2}$

r = learning rate (as a decimal)

We can also calculate the cumulative average number of hours per unit for the first n units with the help of Table I.1. It contains conversion factors that, when multiplied by the direct labor hours for the first unit, yield the average time per unit for selected cumulative production quantities.

TABLE I.1 | CONVERSION FACTORS FOR THE CUMULATIVE AVERAGE NUMBER OF DIRECT LABOR HOURS PER UNIT

80% Learning Rate (n = cumulative production)						90% Learning Rate (n = cumulative production)					
n		n		n		n		n		n	
1	1.00000	19	0.53178	37	0.43976	1	1.00000	19	0.73545	37	0.67091
2	0.90000	20	0.52425	38	0.43634	2	0.95000	20	0.73039	38	0.66839
3	0.83403	21	0.51715	39	0.43304	3	0.91540	21	0.72559	39	0.66595
4	0.78553	22	0.51045	40	0.42984	4	0.88905	22	0.72102	40	0.66357
5	0.74755	23	0.50410	64	0.37382	5	0.86784	23	0.71666	64	0.62043
6	0.71657	24	0.49808	128	0.30269	6	0.85013	24	0.71251	128	0.56069
7	0.69056	25	0.49234	256	0.24405	7	0.83496	25	0.70853	256	0.50586
8	0.66824	26	0.48688	512	0.19622	8	0.82172	26	0.70472	512	0.45594
9	0.64876	27	0.48167	600	0.18661	9	0.80998	27	0.70106	600	0.44519
10	0.63154	28	0.47668	700	0.17771	10	0.79945	28	0.69754	700	0.43496
11	0.61613	29	0.47191	800	0.17034	11	0.78991	29	0.69416	800	0.42629
12	0.60224	30	0.46733	900	0.16408	12	0.78120	30	0.69090	900	0.41878
13	0.58960	31	0.46293	1,000	0.15867	13	0.77320	31	0.68775	1,000	0.41217
14	0.57802	32	0.45871	1,200	0.14972	14	0.76580	32	0.68471	1,200	0.40097
15	0.56737	33	0.45464	1,400	0.14254	15	0.75891	33	0.68177	1,400	0.39173
16	0.55751	34	0.45072	1,600	0.13660	16	0.75249	34	0.67893	1,600	0.38390
17	0.54834	35	0.44694	1,800	0.13155	17	0.74646	35	0.67617	1,800	0.37711
18	0.53979	36	0.44329	2,000	0.12720	18	0.74080	36	0.67350	2,000	0.37114

EXAMPLE I.1   **Developing a Learning Curve**

A manufacturer of diesel locomotives needs 50,000 hours to produce the first unit. Based on past experience with similar products, the rate of learning is 80 percent.

a. Use the logarithmic model to estimate the direct labor required for the 40th diesel locomotive and the cumulative average number of labor hours per unit for the first 40 units.

b. Draw a learning curve for this situation.

MyOMLab

Tutor I.1 in MyOMLab presents another example of the use of learning curves.

SOLUTION

a. The estimated number of direct labor hours required to produce the 40th unit is

$$k_{40} = 50,000(40)^{(\log 0.8)/(\log 2)} = 50,000(40)^{-0.322} = 50,000(0.30488)$$

$$= 15,244 \text{ hours}$$

We calculate the cumulative average number of direct labor hours per unit for the first 40 units with the help of Table I.1. For a cumulative production of 40 units and an 80 percent learning rate, the factor is 0.42984. The cumulative average direct labor hours per unit is 50,000(0.42984) = 21,492 hours.

b. Plot the first point at (1, 50,000). The labor time of the second unit (the first doubling) is 80 percent of the first, so multiply 50,000(0.80) = 40,000 hours. Plot the second point at (2, 40,000). The labor time for the fourth unit (second doubling) is 80 percent of the second, so multiply 40,000(0.80) = 32,000 hours. Plot the point (4, 32,000). The result is shown in Figure I.2.

FIGURE I.2 ▶

The 80 Percent Learning Curve

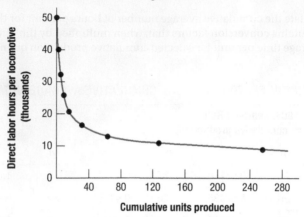

DECISION POINT

Management can now use these estimates to determine the labor requirements to build the locomotives.

Using Learning Curves

Learning curves can be used in a variety of ways. Let us look briefly at their use in bid preparation, financial planning, and labor requirement estimation.

Bid Preparation

Estimating labor costs is an important part of preparing bids for large jobs. Knowing the learning rate, the number of units to be produced, and wage rates, the project manager can arrive at the cost of labor by using a learning curve. After calculating expected labor and materials costs, the project manager adds the desired profit to obtain the total bid amount.

Financial Planning

Learning curves can be used in financial planning to help the financial planner determine the amount of cash needed to finance operations. Learning curves provide a basis for comparing prices and costs. They can be used to project periods of financial drain, when expenditures exceed receipts. They can also be used to determine a contract price by identifying the average direct labor costs per unit for the number of contracted units. In the early stages of production the direct labor costs will exceed that average, whereas in the later stages of production the reverse will be true. This information enables the financial planner to arrange financing for certain phases of operations.

Labor Requirement Estimation

For a given production schedule, the analyst can use learning curves to project direct labor requirements. This information can be used to estimate training requirements and develop production and staffing plans.

EXAMPLE I.2	Using Learning Curves to Estimate Labor Requirements

The manager of a custom manufacturer has just received a production schedule for an order for 30 large turbines. Over the next 5 months, the company is to produce 2, 3, 5, 8, and 12 turbines, respectively. The first unit took 30,000 direct labor hours, and experience on past projects indicates that a 90 percent learning curve is appropriate; therefore, the second unit will require only 27,000 hours. Each employee works an average of 150 hours per month. Estimate the total number of full-time employees needed each month for the next 5 months.

SOLUTION

The following table shows the production schedule and cumulative number of units scheduled for production through each month:

Month	Units per Month	Cumulative Units
1	2	2
2	3	5
3	5	10
4	8	18
5	12	30

We first need to find the cumulative average time per unit using Table I.1 and the cumulative total hours through each month. We then can determine the number of labor hours needed each month. The calculations for months 1–5 follow.

Month	Cumulative Average Time per Unit	Cumulative Total Hours for All Units
1	30,000(0.95000) = 28,500.0	(2)28,500.0 = 57,000
2	30,000(0.86784) = 26,035.2	(5)26,035.2 = 130,176
3	30,000(0.79945) = 23,983.5	(10)23,983.5 = 239,835
4	30,000(0.74080) = 22,224.0	(18)22,224.0 = 400,032
5	30,000(0.69090) = 20,727.0	(30)20,727.0 = 621,810

Calculate the number of hours needed for a particular month by subtracting its cumulative total hours from that of the previous month.

Month 1:   57,000 −   0 =   57,000 hours
Month 2: 130,176 − 57,000 =   73,176 hours
Month 3: 239,835 − 130,176 = 109,659 hours
Month 4: 400,032 − 239,835 = 160,197 hours
Month 5: 621,810 − 400,032 = 221,778 hours

The required number of employees equals the number of hours needed each month divided by 150, the number of hours each employee can work.

Month 1:   57,000/150 =   380 employees
Month 2:   73,176/150 =   488 employees
Month 3: 109,659/150 =   731 employees
Month 4: 160,197/150 = 1,068 employees
Month 5: 221,778/150 = 1,479 employees

DECISION POINT

The number of employees needed increases dramatically over the 5 months. Management may have to begin hiring now so that proper training can take place.

Managerial Considerations in the Use of Learning Curves

Although learning curves can be useful tools for operations planning, managers should keep several things in mind when using them. First, an estimate of the learning rate is necessary in order to use learning curves, and it may be difficult to get. Using industry averages can be risky because the type of work and competitive niches can differ from firm to firm. The learning rate depends on factors such as process complexity and the rate of capital additions. The simpler the process, the less pronounced the learning rate. A complex process offers more opportunity than does a simple process to improve work methods and material flows. Replacing direct labor hours with automation alters the learning rate, giving less opportunity to make reductions in the required hours per unit. Typically, the effect of each capital addition on the learning curve is significant.

Second, another important estimate, if the first unit has yet to be produced, is that of the time required to produce it. The entire learning curve is based on it. The estimate may have to be developed by management using past experiences with similar products.

Third, learning curves provide their greatest advantage in the early stages of new service or product production. As the cumulative number of units produced becomes large, the learning effect is less noticeable.

Fourth, learning curves are dynamic because they are affected by various factors. For example, a short service or product life cycle means that firms may not enjoy the flat portion of the learning curve for very long before the service or product is changed or a new one is introduced. In addition, organizations utilizing team approaches will have different learning rates than they had before they introduced teams. Total quality management and continual improvement programs also will affect learning curves.

Finally, managers should always keep in mind that learning curves are only approximations of actual experience.

LEARNING GOALS IN REVIEW

Learning Goal	Guidelines for Review	MyOMLab Resources
① Explain the concept of a learning curve and how volume is related to unit costs.	See "The Learning Curve Concept," pp. 1–2, to understand the relationship between experience and productivity and how volume, or the number of repetitions, plays a role.	
② Develop a learning curve using the logarithmic model.	We show in the section "Developing Learning Curves," pp. 2–3, how the time for the nth unit can be calculated directly from the formula (using your calculator) and how Table I.1 can be used to calculate the cumulative average time per unit. Study Example I.1 to master this concept.	**OM Explorer Tutor:** I.1: Learning Curves **OM Explorer Solver:** Learning Curve Analysis **POM for Windows:** Display Times Given a Coefficient; Find Learning Coefficient Given Two Times
③ Identify ways to use learning curves for managerial decision making.	The section "Using Learning Curves," pp. 4–5, illustrates some of the uses of the learning curves. Example I.2 demonstrates how to project the cumulative hours required for a project for different time segments. Study the Solved Problem as an application of learning curves to estimate labor requirements.	**OM Explorer Tutor:** I.1: Learning Curves **OM Explorer Solver:** Learning Curve Analysis
④ Discuss the key managerial considerations in the use of learning curves.	See the section "Managerial Considerations in the Use of Learning Curves," pp. 5–6.	

Key Equation

Developing Learning Curves

Labor time for the nth unit:

$$k_n = k_1 n^b$$

Key Term

organizational learning 1

Solved Problem

The Minnesota Coach Company has just been given the following production schedule for ski-lift gondola cars. This product is considerably different from any others the company has produced. Historically, the company's learning rate has been 80 percent on large projects. The first unit took 1,000 hours to produce.

Month	Units	Cumulative Units
1	3	3
2	7	10
3	10	20
4	12	32
5	4	36
6	2	38

a. Estimate how many hours would be required to complete the 38th unit.

b. If the budget only provides for a maximum of 30 direct labor employees in any month and a total of 15,000 direct labor hours for the entire schedule, will the budget be adequate? Assume that each direct labor employee is productive for 150 work hours each month.

SOLUTION

a. We use the learning curve formulas to calculate the time required for the 38th unit:

$$b = \frac{\log r}{\log 2} = \frac{\log 0.8}{\log 2} = \frac{-0.09691}{0.30103} = -0.322$$

$$k_n = k_1 n^b = (1{,}000 \text{ hours})(38)^{-0.322}$$

$$= (1{,}000 \text{ hours})(0.3099) = 310 \text{ hours}$$

b. Table I.1 gives the data needed to calculate the cumulative number of hours through each month of the schedule. Table I.2 shows these calculations.

TABLE I.2 | CUMULATIVE TOTAL HOURS

Month	Cumulative Units	Cumulative Average Time per Unit	Cumulative Total Hours Month for All Units
1	3	1,000(0.83403) = 834.03 hr/u	(834.03 hr/u)(3u) = 2,502.1 hr
2	10	1,000(0.63154) = 631.54 hr/u	(631.54 hr/u)(10u) = 6,315.4 hr
3	20	1,000(0.52425) = 524.25 hr/u	(524.25 hr/u)(20u) = 10,485.0 hr
4	32	1,000(0.45871) = 458.71 hr/u	(458.71 hr/u)(32u) = 14,678.7 hr
5	36	1,000(0.44329) = 443.29 hr/u	(443.29 hr/u)(36u) = 15,958.4 hr
6	38	1,000(0.43634) = 436.34 hr/u	(436.34 hr/u)(38u) = 16,580.9 hr

The cumulative amount of time needed to produce the entire schedule of 38 units is 16,580.9 hours, which exceeds the 15,000 hours budgeted. By finding how much the cumulative total hours increased each month, we can break the total hours into monthly requirements. Finally, the number of employees required is simply the monthly hours divided by 150 hours per employee per month. The calculations are shown in Table I.3.

TABLE I.3 | DIRECT LABOR EMPLOYEES

Month	Cumulative Total Hours for Month	Direct Labor Workers by Month
1	2,502.1 − 0 = 2,502.1 hr	(2,502.1 hr)/(150 hr) = 16.7, or 17
2	6,315.4 − 2,502.1 = 3,813.3 hr	(3,813.3 hr)/(150 hr) = 25.4, or 26
3	10,485.0 − 6,315.4 = 4,169.6 hr	(4,169.6 hr)/(150 hr) = 27.8, or 28
4	14,678.7 − 10,485.0 = 4,193.7 hr	(4,193.7 hr)/(150 hr) = 27.9, or 28
5	15,958.4 − 14,678.7 = 1,279.7 hr	(1,279.7 hr)/(150 hr) = 8.5, or 9
6	16,580.9 − 15,958.4 = 622.5 hr	(622.5 hr)/(150 hr) = 4.2, or 5

The schedule is feasible in terms of the maximum direct labor required in any month because it never exceeds 28 employees. However, the total cumulative hours are 16,581, which exceeds the budgeted amount by 1,581 hours. Therefore, the budget will not be adequate.

Problems

The OM Explorer and POM for Windows software is available to all students using the 11th edition of this textbook. Go to **http://www.pearsonhighered.com/krajewski** to download these computer packages. If you purchased MyOMLab, you also have access to Active Models software and significant help in doing the following problems. Check with your instructor on how best to use these resources. In many cases, the instructor wants you to understand how to do the calculations by hand. At the least, the software provides a check on your calculations. When calculations are particularly complex and the goal is interpreting the results in making decisions, the software entirely replaces the manual calculations.

Developing Learning Curves

1. Mass Balance Company is manufacturing a new digital scale for use by a large chemical company. The order is for 40 units. The first scale took 60 hours of direct labor. The second unit took 48 hours to complete.

   a. What is the learning rate?

   b. What is the estimated time for the 40th unit?

   c. What is the estimated total time for producing all 40 units?

   d. What is the average time per unit for producing the last 10 units (#31–#40)?

2. Cambridge Instruments is an aircraft instrumentation manufacturer. It has received a contract from the U.S. Department of Defense to produce 30 radar units for a military fighter plane. The first unit took 85 hours to produce. Based on past experience with manufacturing similar units, Cambridge estimates that the learning rate is 93 percent. How long will it take to produce the 5th unit? The 10th? The 15th? The final unit?

Using Learning Curves

3. A large grocery corporation has developed the following schedule for converting frozen food display cases to use CFC-free refrigerant:

Week	Units
1	20
2	65
3	100
4	140
5	120

   Historically, the learning rate has been 90 percent on such projects. The budget allows for a maximum of 40 direct labor employees per week and a total of 8,000 direct labor hours for the entire schedule. Assume 40 work hours per week. If the first unit took 30 hours to convert, is this schedule feasible? If not, how can it be altered? Are additional costs involved in altering it?

4. Freddie and Jason have just opened the Texas Toothpick, a chain-saw sharpening and repair service located on Elm Street. The Texas Toothpick promises same-week repair service. Freddie and Jason are concerned that a projected dramatic increase in demand as the end of October nears will cause service to deteriorate. Freddie and Jason have had difficulty attracting employees, so they are the only workers available to complete the work. Safety considerations require that they each work no more than 40 hours per week. The first chain-saw sharpening and repair required 7 hours of work, and an 80 percent learning curve is anticipated.

Week	Units	Cumulative Units
October 2–6	8	8
October 9–13	19	27
October 16–20	10	37
October 23–27	27	64

a. How many total hours are required to complete 64 chain saws?

b. How many hours of work are required for the week ending on Friday the 13th?

c. Will Freddie and Jason be able to keep their same-week service promise during their busiest week just before Halloween?

5. The Bovine Products Company recently introduced a new automatic milking system for cows. The company just completed an order for 16 units. The last unit required 15 hours of labor, and the learning rate is estimated to be 90 percent on such systems. Another customer has just placed an order for the same system. This customer, who owns many farms in the Midwest, wants 48 units. How many total labor hours will be needed to satisfy this order?

6. You are in charge of a large assembly shop that specializes in contract assignments. One of your customers has promised to award you a large contract for the assembly of 1,000 units of a new product. The suggested bid price in the contract is based on an average of 20 hours of direct labor per unit. You conduct a couple of test assemblies and find that, although the first unit took 50 hours, the second unit could be completed in just 40 hours.

a. How many hours do you expect the assembly of the third unit to take?

b. How many hours do you expect the assembly of the 100th unit to take?

c. Is the contract's assumption about the average labor hours per unit valid or should the price be revised?

7. The personnel manager at Powerwest Inc. wants to estimate the direct and cumulative average direct labor hours for producing 30 locomotive train units during the next year. He estimates from past experience that the learning rate is 90 percent. The production department estimates that manufacturing the first unit will take 30,000 hours. Each employee averages 200 hours per month. The production rate forecast is as follows:

Month	Production Rate (units)	Month	Production Rate (units)
January	2	July	2
February	3	August	4
March	2	September	3
April	4	October	3
May	3	November	1
June	2	December	1

a. How many direct hours are required to produce the 30th unit?

b. How many total hours are needed to produce all 30 units?

c. What is the maximum number of employees required next year?

d. If the learning rate were changed to 0.85, what would be the impact on the total hours and the number of employees needed to produce 30 units?

8. The Really Big Six Corporation will hire 1,000 new accountants this year. Managers are considering whether to make or to buy office furniture for the new hires. Big can purchase office furniture for $2,000 per accountant, or it can make the desks itself. Equipment to assemble furniture can be scrounged from the company's carpentry shop. That old equipment has already been fully depreciated. Materials cost $500 per desk, and labor (and benefits) costs $30 per hour. Big hired a local shop to build a prototype desk. That desk required 100 hours of labor. If the learning curve is 90 percent, should Big make or buy the desks?

9. Although the learning curve never completely levels off to a horizontal line, if work standards are to be developed, there must be a point at which, for all practical purposes, learning is said to have stopped. If we have an 80 percent learning curve and say that the learning effect will be masked by other variables when the improvement in successive units is less than 0.5 percent, at about what unit number can the standard be set?

10. The Compton Company is manufacturing a solar grain dryer that requires methods and materials never before used by the company. The order is for 80 units. The first unit took 46 direct labor hours, whereas the 10th unit took only 24 direct labor hours.

a. Estimate the rate of learning that occurred for this product.

b. Use the learning rate in part (a) to estimate direct labor hours for the 80th unit.

11. The Hand-To-Mouth Company (HTM) has $200,000 in cash, no inventory, and a 90 percent learning curve. To reduce the complexity of this problem, ignore the hiring and training costs associated with dramatically increased production. Employees are paid $20 per hour every Friday for that week's work. HTM has received an order to build 1,000 oak desks over the next 15 weeks. Materials cost $400 per desk. Suppliers make deliveries each Monday and insist on cash upon delivery. The first desk takes 100 hours of direct labor to build. HTM will be paid $1,500 per desk 2 weeks after the desks are delivered. Should HTM take this order?

Week	Units	Week	Units	Week	Units
1	2	6	24	11	88
2	4	7	64	12	100
3	8	8	128	13	100
4	12	9	128	14	100
5	14	10	128	15	100
				Total	1,000

Selected References

Anzanello, M.J., and F.S. Foglatto. "Learning Curve Modeling of Work Assignments in Mass Customized Assembly Lines." *International Journal of Production Research*, vol. 45, no. 13 (2007), pp. 2919–2938.

Biskup, Dirk. "A State-of-the-Art Review on Scheduling with Learning Effects." *European Journal of Operations Research*, vol. 188, no. 2 (July 2008), pp. 315–329.

Ferioli, F., K. Schoots, and B.C.C. van der Zwaan. "Use and Limitations of Learning Curves for Energy Technology Policy: A Component-Learning Hypothesis." *Energy Policy*, vol. 37, no. 7 (July 2009), pp. 2525–2535.

Kull, Thomas J., Ken Boyer, and Roger Calantone. "Last-Mile Supply Chain Efficiency: An Analysis of Learning Curves in Online Ordering. "*International Journal of Operations & Production Management*, vol. 27, no. 4 (2007), pp. 409–434.

Neij, Lena. "Cost Development of Future Technologies for Power Generation—A Study Based on Experience Curves and Complementary Bottom-Up Assessments." *Energy Policy*, vol. 36, no. 6 (June 2008), pp. 2200–2211.

Nemet, Gregory F. "Beyond the Learning Curve: Factors Influencing Cost Reductions in Photovoltaics." *Energy Policy*, vol. 34, no.17 (November 2006), pp. 3218–3232.

Pendharkar, Parag C., and Girish H. Subramanian. "An Empirical Study of ICASE Learning Curves and Probability Bounds for Software Development Effort." *European Journal of Operational Research*, vol. 183, no. 3 (December 2007), pp. 1086–1096.

Wiersma, Eelke. "Conditions that Shape the Learning Curve: Factors that Increase the Ability and Opportunity to Learn." *Management Science*, vol. 53, no. 12 (December 2007), pp. 1903–1915.

OPERATIONS SCHEDULING

This supplement focuses on **operations scheduling**, which involves assigning jobs to workstations or employees to jobs for specified time periods. Effective scheduling helps managers achieve the full potential of their processes and supply chains. Chapter 10, "Operations Planning and Scheduling," covers the basics of scheduling—Gantt charts, workforce scheduling, two rules (FCFS and EDD) for sequencing work at a single workstation, and two commonly used performance measures (flow time and past due). Here, we deepen your understanding with additional performance measures and priority sequencing rules, a discussion of scheduling multiple workstations, and a discussion of scheduling a two-station flow shop.

operations scheduling

A type of scheduling in which jobs are assigned to workstations or employees are assigned to jobs for specified time periods.

LEARNING GOALS *After reading this supplement, you should be able to:*

1. Define new performance measures (beyond flow time and past due) for evaluating a schedule.

2. Determine schedules for a single workstation using the EDD, SPT, CR, and S/RO priority sequencing rules.

3. Determine schedules for a two-station flow shop using Johnson's rule.

4. Provide several labor assignment rules useful in developing schedules in a labor-limited environment.

Performance Measures for Scheduling Processes

The scheduling techniques we discuss in this supplement cut across the various process types found in services and manufacturing. Many service firms are characterized by a *front-office process* with high customer contact, divergent work flows, customization, and, consequently, a complex scheduling environment. Often customer demands are difficult to predict, which puts a high premium on scheduling employees to handle the varied needs of customers. At the other extreme in the service industry, a *back-office process* has low customer involvement, uses more line work flows, and provides standardized services. Inanimate objects are processed; these processes take on the appearance of manufacturing processes.

Manufacturing processes also benefit from operations scheduling techniques. Our discussion of the operations scheduling techniques in this supplement has application for job, batch, and line processes in services as well as in manufacturing. Schedules for continuous processes can be developed with *linear programming* (see Supplement D, "Linear Programming"). Although the scheduling techniques in this supplement provide some structure to the selection of good schedules, many alternatives typically need to be evaluated. How can we select the schedule that is best in a given situation? Reliable performance measures are needed.

We already covered two important performance measures in Chapter 10, "Operations Planning and Scheduling." *Flow time* is the time a job spends in the service or manufacturing system, and *past due* (tardiness) is the amount of time by which a job missed its due date. In this regard, a *job* is the object receiving service or being manufactured. For example, a job may be a customer waiting for service at a state licensing bureau or it may be a batch of pistons waiting for a manufacturing process. These two performance measures can be insufficient for choosing a good schedule, depending on the competitive priorities of a process. Additional performance measures follow:

makespan

The total amount of time required to complete a group of jobs.

- **Makespan.** The total amount of time required to complete a group of jobs is called **makespan**. Minimizing makespan supports the competitive priorities of cost (lower inventory) and time (delivery speed).

$$\text{Makespan} = \text{Time of completion of last job} - \text{Starting time of the first job}$$

total inventory

The sum of scheduled receipts and on-hand inventories.

- **Total Inventory.** This performance measure is used to measure the effectiveness of schedules for manufacturing processes. The sum of *scheduled receipts* and *on-hand inventories* is the **total inventory**.

$$\text{Total inventory} = \text{Scheduled receipts for all items} + \text{On-hand inventories of all items}$$

Minimizing total inventory supports the competitive priority of cost (inventory holding costs).

- **Utilization.** The degree to which equipment, space, or the workforce is currently being used, measured as the ratio of the average output rate to maximum capacity, is called *utilization*. Maximizing the utilization of a process supports the competitive priority of cost (slack capacity).

These performance measures often are interrelated. For example, minimizing the average flow time tends to increase utilization. Minimizing the makespan for a group of jobs tends to increase utilization. Understanding how flow time, makespan, past due, and utilization interact can make the selection of good schedules easier.

job shop

A manufacturer's operation that specializes in low- to medium-volume production and utilizes job or batch processes.

In this supplement we focus on scheduling approaches used in two environments: (1) divergent flow processes and (2) line flow processes. A manufacturer's operation with divergent flows is often called a **job shop**, which specializes in low- to medium-volume production and utilizes *job* or *batch* processes. The *front office* would be the equivalent of a job shop for a service provider. Jobs in divergent flow processes are difficult to schedule because of the variability in job routings and the continual introduction of new jobs to be processed. A manufacturer's operation with line flows is often called a **flow shop**, which specializes in medium- to high-volume production and utilizes *line* or *continuous flow* processes. The *back office* would be the equivalent of a flow shop for a service provider. Tasks are easier to schedule because the jobs have a common flow pattern through the system. Nonetheless, scheduling mistakes can be costly in either situation.

flow shop

A manufacturer's operation that specializes in medium- to high-volume production and utilizes line or continuous flow processes.

Job Shop Scheduling

Operations schedules are short-term plans designed to implement the sales and operations plan. Often, several jobs must be processed at one or more workstations. Typically, a variety of tasks can be performed at each workstation. If schedules are not carefully planned to avoid bottlenecks, waiting lines may develop. For example, Figure J.1 depicts the complexity of scheduling a manufacturing process. When a job order is received for a part, the raw materials are collected and the batch is moved to its first operation. The colored arrows show that jobs follow different routes through the manufacturing process, depending on the product being made. At each workstation, the next job to process is a decision because the arrival rate of jobs at a workstation often differs from the processing rate of the jobs at a workstation, thereby creating a waiting line. In addition, new jobs can enter the process at any time, thereby creating a dynamic environment. Such complexity puts pressure on managers to develop scheduling procedures that will handle the workload efficiently.

Priority Sequencing Rules

Just as many schedules are feasible for a specific group of jobs in queue at a particular set of workstations, numerous methods can be used to generate schedules. They range from straightforward manual methods, such as manipulating Gantt charts, to sophisticated computer models for developing optimal schedules. One way to generate schedules in job shops is by using *priority sequencing rules*, which allows the schedule for a workstation to evolve over a period of time. The decision about which job to process next is made with simple priority rules whenever the workstation becomes available for further processing. The priority rule determines a sequence of jobs through the workstation, thereby generating a schedule in real time. One advantage of this method is that last-minute information on operating conditions can be incorporated into the schedule as it evolves.

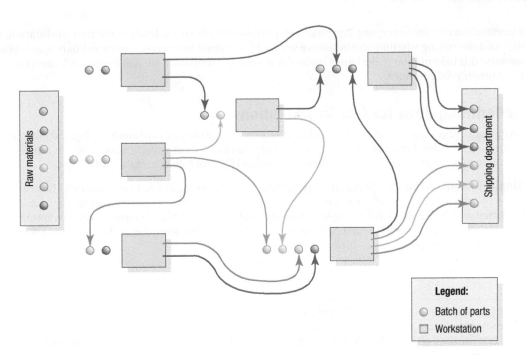

Legend:
○ Batch of parts
□ Workstation

We already covered two important priority rules in Chapter 10, "Operations Planning and Scheduling." The *first-come, first-served (FCFS)* rule gives the job arriving at the workstation first the highest priority. The *earliest due date (EDD)* rule gives the job with the earliest due date based on assigned due dates the highest priority. Such rules can be applied by a worker or incorporated into a computerized scheduling system that generates a dispatch list of jobs and priorities for each workstation. Additional priority sequencing rules follow:

- *Critical Ratio.* The **critical ratio (CR)** is calculated by dividing the time remaining until a job's due date by the total shop time remaining for the job, which is defined as the setup, processing, move, and expected waiting times of all remaining operations, including the operation being scheduled. The formula is

$$CR = \frac{\text{Due date} - \text{Today's date}}{\text{Total shop time remaining}}$$

The difference between the due date and today's date must be in the same time units as the total shop time remaining. A ratio less than 1.0 implies that the job is behind schedule, and a ratio greater than 1.0 implies that the job is ahead of schedule. The job with the lowest CR is scheduled next.

- *Shortest Processing Time.* The job requiring the **shortest processing time (SPT)** at the workstation is processed next.

- *Slack per Remaining Operations.* Slack is the difference between the time remaining until a job's due date and the total shop time remaining, including that of the operation being scheduled. A job's priority is determined by dividing the slack by the number of operations that remain, including the one being scheduled, to arrive at the **slack per remaining operations (S/RO)**.

$$S/RO = \frac{(\text{Due date} - \text{Today's date}) - \text{Total shop time remaining}}{\text{Number of operations remaining}}$$

The job with the lowest S/RO is scheduled next. Ties are broken in a variety of ways if two or more jobs have the same priority. One way is to arbitrarily choose one of the tied jobs for processing next.

Although the priority sequencing rules seem simple, the actual task of scheduling hundreds of jobs through hundreds of workstations requires intensive data gathering and manipulation. The scheduler needs information on each job's processing requirements: the job's due date; its routing; the standard setup, processing, and expected waiting times at each operation; whether alternative workstations could be used at each operation; and the inputs from internal or external suppliers at each operation. In addition, the scheduler needs to know the job's current status: its location (waiting in line for a workstation or being processed at a workstation), how much of the operation has been completed, the actual arrival and departure times at each operation or waiting line, and the actual processing and setup times. The scheduler or software uses the priority sequencing rules to determine the processing sequence of jobs at

critical ratio (CR)

A ratio that is calculated by dividing the time remaining until a job's due date by the total shop time remaining for the job, which is defined as the setup, processing, move, and expected waiting times of all remaining operations, including the operation being scheduled.

shortest processing time (SPT)

A priority sequencing rule that specifies that the job requiring the shortest processing time is the next job to be processed.

slack per remaining operations (S/RO)

A priority sequencing rule that determines priority by dividing the slack by the number of operations that remain, including the one being scheduled.

a workstation and the remaining information for estimating job arrival times at the next workstation, as well as determining whether an alternative workstation should be used when the primary one is busy. Because this information may change throughout the day, computers are needed to track the data and to maintain valid priorities.

Scheduling Jobs for One Workstation

Any priority sequencing rule can be used to schedule any number of workstations. For the purpose of illustrating the rules, however, we focus on scheduling several jobs at a single workstation. We divide the rules into two categories: (1) single-dimension rules and (2) multiple-dimension rules.

single-dimension rules

A set of rules that bases the priority of a job on a single aspect of the job, such as arrival time at the workstation, the due date, or the processing time.

Single-Dimension Rules   Some priority sequencing rules (e.g., FCFS, EDD, and SPT) base a job's priority assignment only on information about the jobs waiting for processing at the individual workstation. We call these rules **single-dimension rules** because they determine priority based on a single aspect of the job, such as arrival time at the workstation, the due date, or the processing time. We begin with an example of single-dimension rules.

| EXAMPLE J.1 | **Comparing the EDD and SPT Rules** |

MyOMLab

Tutor J.1 in MyOMLab presents another example of scheduling a single workstation using the EDD and SPT rules.

MyOMLab

Active Model J.1 in MyOMLab adds insight into scheduling a single workstation.

The Taylor Machine Shop rebores engine blocks. Currently, five engine blocks are waiting for processing. At any time, the company has only one engine expert on duty who can do this type of work. The engine problems have been diagnosed, and the processing times for the jobs have been estimated. Expected completion times have been agreed upon with the shop's customers. The accompanying table shows the current situation. Because the Taylor Machine Shop is open from 8:00 A.M. until 5:00 P.M. each weekday, plus weekend hours as needed, the customer pickup times are measured in business hours from the current time. Determine the schedule for the engine expert by using (a) the EDD rule and (b) the SPT rule. For each rule, calculate the average flow time, average hours early, and average hours past due. If average past due is most important, which rule should be chosen?

Engine Block	Business Hours Since Order Arrived	Processing Time, Including Setup (hrs)	Business Hours Until Due Date (customer pickup time)
Ranger	12	8	10
Explorer	10	6	12
Bronco	1	15	20
Econoline 150	3	3	18
Thunderbird	0	12	22

SOLUTION

a. The EDD rule states that the first engine block in the sequence is the one with the closest due date. Consequently, the Ranger engine block is processed first. The Thunderbird engine block, with its due date furthest in the future, is processed last. The resulting schedule is shown in the following table, along with the flow times, the hours early, and the hours past due.

Engine Block Sequence	Hours Since Order Arrived	Begin Work		Processing Time (hr)		Finish Time (hr)	Flow Time (hr)	Scheduled Customer Pickup Time	Actual Customer Pickup Time	Hours Early	Hours Past Due
Ranger	12	0	+	8	=	8	20	10	10	2	—
Explorer	10	8	+	6	=	14	24	12	14	—	2
Econoline 150	3	14	+	3	=	17	20	18	18	1	—
Bronco	1	17	+	15	=	32	33	20	32	—	12
Thunderbird	0	32	+	12	=	44	44	22	44	—	22

The flow time for each job is its finish time, plus the time since the job arrived.[1] For example, the Explorer engine block's finish time will be 14 hours from now (8 hours waiting time before the engine expert started to work on it plus 6 hours processing). Adding the 10 hours since the order arrived at this workstation (before the processing of this group of orders began) results in a flow time of 24 hours. You might think of the sum of flow times as the total *job hours* spent by the engine blocks since their orders arrived at the workstation until they were processed.

The performance measures for the EDD schedule for the five engine blocks are

$$\text{Average flow time} = \frac{20 + 24 + 20 + 33 + 44}{5} = 28.2 \text{ hrs}$$

$$\text{Average hours early} = \frac{2 + 0 + 1 + 0 + 0}{5} = 0.6 \text{ hr}$$

$$\text{Average hours past due} = \frac{0 + 2 + 0 + 12 + 22}{5} = 7.2 \text{ hrs}$$

b. Under the SPT rule, the sequence starts with the engine block that has the shortest processing time, the Econoline 150, and it ends with the engine block that has the longest processing time, the Bronco. The schedule, along with the flow times, early hours, and past due hours, is contained in the following table:

Engine Block Schedule	Hours Since Order Arrived	Begin Work		Processing Time (hr)		Finish Time (hr)	Flow Time (hr)	Scheduled Customer Pickup Time	Actual Customer Pickup Time	Hours Early	Hours Past Due
Econoline 150	3	0	+	3	=	3	6	18	18	15	—
Explorer	10	3	+	6	=	9	19	12	12	3	—
Ranger	12	9	+	8	=	17	29	10	17	—	7
Thunderbird	0	17	+	12	=	29	29	22	29	—	7
Bronco	1	29	+	15	=	44	45	20	44	—	24

The performance measures are

$$\text{Average flow time} = \frac{6 + 19 + 29 + 29 + 45}{5} = 25.6 \text{ hrs}$$

$$\text{Average hours early} = \frac{15 + 3 + 0 + 0 + 0}{5} = 3.6 \text{ hrs}$$

$$\text{Average hours past due} = \frac{0 + 0 + 7 + 7 + 24}{5} = 7.6 \text{ hrs}$$

DECISION POINT

The EDD rule is better than the SPT rule with respect to average past due (keeping promises to customers), but worse with respect to average flow time for the set of jobs in this example. Management's choice depends on which performance measure it values the most. More experimentation should be conducted before a final choice is made.

---

[1]Flow time, as a performance measure in its traditional use, does not count the time a job spends "outside the system under our control." Our "system" in this supplement is the single workstation (or two workstations in the case of Johnson's rule in the next section). Arrival time here relates to when the job was first available for processing at the workstation. Adding the time since the order arrived at the workstation to the job's finish time departs from conventions used in early research on static problems, which assumed that no jobs arrive during the time span covered by the resulting schedule. With traditional assumptions, a job's finish time and flow time are identical and SPT will always have the best flow time performance. With our definition of flow time, the SPT rules do not necessarily produce the best flow time performance, such as when the job with the shortest processing time arrived at the workstation well before the other jobs.

As the solution of Example J.1 shows, the EDD schedule gave better customer service, as measured by the average hours past due, and a lower maximum hours past due (22 versus 24). However, the SPT schedule provided a lower average flow time. In general, the SPT priority rule will push most jobs through the system to completion more quickly than will the other rules. Speed can be an advantage—but only if jobs can be delivered sooner than promised and revenue collected earlier. If they cannot, the completed job must stay in finished inventory. Consequently, the priority rule chosen can help or hinder the firm in meeting its competitive priorities.

Researchers have studied the implications of the single-dimension rules for various performance measures. In most of these studies, all jobs were considered to be independent (in contrast to the parent-component dependencies in MRP environments), and the assumption was made that sufficient capacity generally was available. These studies found that the EDD rule performs well with respect to the percentage of jobs past due and the variance of hours past due. For any set of jobs to be processed at a single workstation, it minimizes the maximum of the past due hours of any job in the set. The EDD rule is popular with firms that are sensitive to achieving due dates, which usually are the basis for setting priorities using MRP systems.

Often referred to as the *world champion*, the SPT rule tends to minimize the mean flow time (assuming time since arrival is 0 for all jobs) and the percentage of jobs past due. It also tends to maximize shop utilization. For the single-workstation case, the SPT rule always will provide the lowest mean finish time. However, it could increase total inventory because it tends to push all work to the finished state. In addition, it tends to produce a large variance in past due hours because the larger jobs might have to wait a long time for processing. Also, it provides no opportunity to adjust schedules when due dates change. The advantage of this rule over others diminishes as the load on the shop increases.

Finally, though the FCFS rule is considered fair to the jobs (or customers), it performs poorly with respect to all performance measures. This result is to be expected because FCFS does not acknowledge any job (or customer) characteristics. However, FCFS usually is the only acceptable choice for service processes where the customer is present and demand leveling options such as appointments or reservations are not used.

Multiple-Dimension Rules   Priority rules, such as CR and S/RO, incorporate information about the remaining workstations at which the job must be processed, in addition to the processing time at the present workstation or the due date considered by single-dimension rules. We call these rules **multiple-dimension rules** because they apply to more than one aspect of the job. Example J.2 demonstrates their use for scheduling jobs.

multiple-dimension rules

A set of rules that apply to more than one aspect of a job.

EXAMPLE J.2	Scheduling Jobs with the CR and S/RO Rules

MyOMLab

Tutor J.2 in MyOMLab presents another example of scheduling a single workstation using the CR and S/RO rules.

The first five columns of the following table contain information about a set of four jobs that just arrived (end of Hour 0 or beginning of Hour 1) at an engine lathe. They are the only ones now waiting to be processed. Several operations, including the one at the engine lathe, remain to be done on each job. Determine the schedule by using (a) the CR rule and (b) the S/RO rule. Compare these schedules to those generated by FCFS, SPT, and EDD.

Job	Processing Time at Engine Lathe (hours)	Time Remaining Until Due Date (days)	Number of Operations Remaining	Shop Time Remaining (days)	CR	S/RO
1	2.3	15	10	6.1	2.46	0.89
2	10.5	10	2	7.8	1.28	1.10
3	6.2	20	12	14.5	1.38	0.46
4	15.6	8	5	10.2	0.78	−0.44

SOLUTION

a. Using CR to schedule the machine, we divide the time remaining until the due date by the shop time remaining to get the priority index for each job. For job 1,

$$CR = \frac{\text{Time remaining until the due date}}{\text{Shop time remaining}} = \frac{15}{6.1} = 2.46$$

By arranging the jobs in sequence with the lowest critical ratio first, we determine that the order of jobs to be processed by the engine lathe is 4, 2, 3, and finally 1, assuming that no other jobs arrive in the meantime.

b. Using S/RO, we divide the difference between the time remaining until the due date and the shop time remaining by the number of remaining operations. For job 1,

$$S/RO = \frac{\text{Time remaining until the due date } - \text{ Shop time remaining}}{\text{Number of operations remaining}} = \frac{15 - 6.1}{10} = 0.89$$

Arranging the jobs by starting with the lowest S/RO yields a 4, 3, 1, 2 sequence for the jobs.

DECISION POINT
Note that the application of the two priority sequencing rules gives two different engine lathe schedules. Moreover, the SPT schedule, based on processing times (measured in hours) at the engine lathe only, is 1, 3, 2, and 4. No preference is given to job 4 in the SPT schedule, even though it may not be finished by its due date. The engine lathe schedule using the EDD rule is 4, 2, 1, and 3. For illustration purposes, we assume that the FCFS sequence is 1, 2, 3, and 4. All four jobs arrived at the workstation at the end of Hour 0, so the finish times and flow times are identical for all five rules. The following table shows the comparative performance of the five priority sequencing rules at the engine lathe:

PRIORITY RULE SUMMARY					
	FCFS	**SPT**	**EDD**	**CR**	**S/RO**
Average flow time	17.175	16.100	26.175	27.150	24.025
Average early time	3.425	6.050	0	0	0
Average past due	7.350	8.900	12.925	13.900	10.775

The S/RO rule is better than the EDD rule and the CR rule, but it is much worse than the SPT rule and the FCFS rule for this example. However, EDD, CR, and S/RO all have the advantage of allowing schedule changes when due dates change. These results cannot be generalized to other situations because only four jobs are being processed.

Research studies have shown that S/RO is better than EDD with respect to the percentage of jobs past due, but worse than SPT and EDD with respect to average flow times. These studies also indicate that CR results in longer flow times than SPT, but CR also results in less variance in the distribution of past due hours. Consequently, even though the use of the multiple-dimension rules requires more information, no choice is clearly best. Each rule should be tested in the environment for which it is intended.

Scheduling Jobs for Multiple Workstations

Priority rules can be used to schedule more than one operation. Each operation is treated independently. When a workstation becomes idle, the priority rule is applied to the jobs waiting for that operation, and the job with the highest priority is selected. When that operation is finished, the job is moved to the next operation in its routing, where it waits until it again has the highest priority. At any workstation, the jobs in the waiting line change over a period of time, so the choice of a priority rule can make quite a difference in the processing sequence. Schedules can be evaluated with the performance measures already discussed.

Identifying the best priority rule to use at a particular operation in a process is a complex problem because the output from one operation becomes the input to another. The priority rule at a workstation determines the sequence of work the workstation will perform, which in turn determines the arrival of work at the next workstation downstream. Computer *simulation* models are effective tools to determine which priority rules work best in a given situation. Once the current process is modeled, the analyst can make changes to the priority rules at various operations and measure the impact on performance measures, such as past due, flow time, and utilization. SimQuick, a simulation modelling software package useful for analyzing scheduling problems, can be found in MyOMLab.

MyOMLab

Flow Shop Scheduling

Consider a two-station flow shop. Suppose that the flow shop has several jobs ready for processing at the first of two workstations and that the routings of all jobs are identical. In the scheduling of two or more workstations in a flow shop, the makespan varies according to the sequence chosen. Determining a production schedule for a group of jobs to minimize the makespan has two advantages:

1. The group of jobs is completed in minimum time.
2. The utilization of the two-station flow shop is maximized. Utilizing the first workstation continuously until it processes the last job minimizes the idle time on the *second* workstation.

Johnson's rule

A procedure that minimizes makespan when scheduling a group of jobs on two workstations.

Johnson's rule is a procedure that minimizes makespan when scheduling a group of jobs on two workstations. S.M. Johnson showed that the sequence of jobs at the two stations should be identical and that the priority assigned to a job should, therefore, be the same at both. The procedure is based on the assumption of a known set of jobs, each with a known processing time and available to begin processing on the first workstation. The procedure is as follows.

Step 1. Scan the processing times at each workstation and find the shortest processing time among the jobs not yet scheduled. If two or more jobs are tied, choose one job arbitrarily.

Step 2. If the shortest processing time is on workstation 1, schedule the corresponding job as early as possible. If the shortest processing time is on workstation 2, schedule the corresponding job as late as possible.

Step 3. Eliminate the last job scheduled from further consideration. Repeat steps 1 and 2 until all jobs have been scheduled.

EXAMPLE J.3	Scheduling a Group of Jobs on Two Workstations Using Johnson's Rule

MyOMLab

Tutor J.3 in MyOMLab presents another example of using Johnson's rule for scheduling a two-station flow shop.

The Morris Machine Company just received an order to refurbish five motors for materials handling equipment that were damaged in a fire. The motors have been delivered and are available for processing. The motors will be repaired at two workstations in the following manner.

> Workstation 1: Dismantle the motor and clean the parts.
> Workstation 2: Replace the parts as necessary, test the motor, and make adjustments.

The customer's shop will be inoperable until all the motors have been repaired, so the plant manager is interested in developing a schedule that minimizes the makespan and has authorized around-the-clock operations until the motors have been repaired. The estimated time to repair each motor is shown in the following table:

Motor	TIME (HR)	
	Workstation 1	Workstation 2
M1	12	22
M2	4	5
M3	5	3
M4	15	16
M5	10	8

SOLUTION

The logic for the optimal schedule is shown in the following table:

	ESTABLISHING A JOB SEQUENCE	
Iteration	Job Sequence	Comments
1	M3	The shortest processing time is 3 hours for M3 at workstation 2. Therefore, M3 is scheduled as late as possible.
2	M2 M3	Eliminate M3 from the table of estimated times. The next shortest processing time is 4 hours for M2 at workstation 1. M2 is therefore scheduled first.
3	M2 M5 M3	Eliminate M2 from the table. The next shortest processing time is 8 hours for M5 at workstation 2. Therefore, M5 is scheduled as late as possible.
4	M2 M1 M5 M3	Eliminate M5 from the table. The next shortest processing time is 12 hours for M1 at workstation 1. M1 is scheduled as early as possible.
5	M2 M1 M4 M5 M3	The last motor to be scheduled is M4. It is placed in the last remaining position, in the middle of the schedule.

DECISION POINT

No other schedule of jobs will produce a shorter makespan. To determine the makespan, we can draw a Gantt chart, as shown in Figure J.2. In this case, refurbishing and reinstalling all five motors will take 65 hours. This schedule minimizes the idle time of workstation 2 and gives the fastest repair time for all five motors. Note that the schedule recognizes that a job cannot begin at workstation 2 until it has been completed at workstation 1.

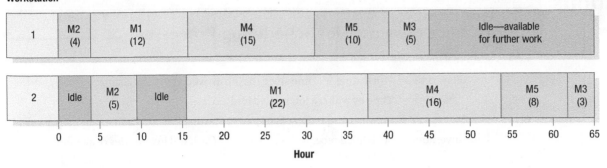

Workstation

▲ **FIGURE J.2**
Gantt Chart for the Morris Machine Company Repair Schedule

Labor-Limited Environments

Thus far, we have assumed that a job never has to wait for lack of a worker. The limiting resource has been the number of machines or workstations available. More typical, however, is a **labor-limited environment** in which the resource constraint is the amount of labor available, not the number of machines or workstations. In this case, workers are trained to work on a variety of machines or tasks to increase the flexibility of operations.

In a labor-limited environment, the scheduler not only must decide which job to process next at a particular workstation but also must assign workers to their next workstations. The scheduler can use priority sequencing rules to make these decisions, as we used them to schedule engine blocks in Example J.1. In labor-limited environments, the labor-assignment policies, as well as the priority sequencing rules, affect performance. The following examples provide some labor-assignment rules.

- Assign personnel to the workstation with the job that has been in the system longest.
- Assign personnel to the workstation with the most jobs waiting for processing.
- Assign personnel to the workstation with the largest standard work content.
- Assign personnel to the workstation with the job that has the earliest due date.

The manufacturing scheduling process is a key element of an integrated supply chain. Advanced planning and scheduling (APS) systems attempt to link the scheduling process to demand data and forecasts, supply chain facility and inventory decisions, and the capability of suppliers so that the entire chain can operate as efficiently as possible. A firm's ability to change its schedules quickly and still keep the supply chain flowing smoothly provides a competitive edge.

labor-limited environment

An environment in which the resource constraint is the amount of labor available, not the number of machines or workstations.

LEARNING GOALS IN REVIEW

Learning Goal	Guidelines for Review	MyOMLab Resources
1 Define new performance measures (beyond flow time and past due) for evaluating a schedule.	Review makespan, total inventory, and utilization in the section "Performance Measures for Scheduling Processes" on pp. 1–2.	
2 Determine schedules for a single workstation using the EDD, SPT, CR and S/RO priority sequencing rules.	Study the critical ratio (CR), shortest processing time (SPT), and slack per remaining operations (S/RO) in the "Job Shop Scheduling" section on pp. 2–7. Review Examples J.1 and J.2 (pp. 4–6), including how the performance measures are calculated. See also Solved Problem 1 and Solved Problem 2 on pp. 10–12.	**Active Model:** J.1: Job Shop Scheduling **OM Explorer Tutors:** J.1: Comparing EDD and SPT Rules; Scheduling with CR & S/RO **OM Explorer Solver:** Single-Machine Scheduler **POM for Windows:** Scheduling **SimQuick Simulation Exercises**
3 Determine schedules for a two-station flow shop using Johnson's rule.	Review the section "Flow Shop Scheduling," pp. 7–9, which discusses Johnson's rule and demonstrates its use in Example J.3. See also Solved Problem 3 on pp. 12–14.	**OM Explorer Tutor:** J.3: Scheduling a Two-Station Flow Shop **OM Explorer Solver:** Two Machine Scheduler **POM for Windows:** Scheduling
4 Provide several labor assignment rules useful in developing schedules in a labor-limited environment.	The section "Labor-Limited Environments," p. 9, discusses four labor assignment rules.	

Key Equations

Performance Measures for Scheduling Processes

1. Performance measures:

$$\text{Flow time} = \text{Finish time} + \text{Time since the job arrived at the workstation}$$

$$\text{Past due} = \text{Time by which a job missed its due date}$$

$$\text{Makespan} = \text{Time of completion of last job} - \text{Starting time of the first job}$$

$$\text{Total inventory} = \text{Scheduled receipts for all items} + \text{On-hand inventories of all items}$$

Job Shop Scheduling

2. Critical ratio:

$$\text{CR} = \frac{\text{Due date} - \text{Today's date}}{\text{Total shop time remaining}}$$

3. Slack per remaining operations:

$$\text{S/RO} = \frac{(\text{Due date} - \text{Today's date}) - \text{Total shop time remaining}}{\text{Number of operations remaining}}$$

Key Terms

critical ratio (CR) 3
flow shop 2
job shop 2
Johnson's rule 8

labor-limited environment 9
makespan 2
multiple-dimension rules 6
operations scheduling 1

shortest processing time (SPT) 3
single-dimension rules 4
slack per remaining operations (S/RO) 3
total inventory 2

Solved Problem 1

The Neptune's Den Machine Shop specializes in overhauling outboard marine engines. Some engines require replacement of broken parts, whereas others need a complete overhaul. Currently, five engines with varying problems are awaiting service. The best estimates for the labor times involved and the promise dates (in number of days from today) are shown in the following table. Customers usually do not pick up their engines early.

Engine	Time Since Order Arrived (days)	Processing Time, Including Setup (days)	Promise Date (days from now)
50-hp Evinrude	4	5	8
7-hp Johnson	6	4	15
100-hp Mercury	8	10	12
50-hp Honda	1	1	20
75-hp Nautique	15	3	10

a. Develop separate schedules by using the SPT and EDD rules.

b. Compare the two schedules on the basis of average flow time, percentage of past due jobs, and maximum past due days for any engine.

SOLUTION

a. Using the SPT rule, we obtain the following schedule:

Repair Schedule	Days Since Order Arrived	Processing Time	Finish Time	Flow Time	Promise Date	Actual Pickup Date	Days Early	Days Past Due
50-hp Honda	1	1	1	2	20	20	19	—
75-hp Nautique	15	3	4	19	10	10	6	—
7-hp Johnson	6	4	8	14	15	15	7	—
50-hp Evinrude	4	5	13	17	8	13	—	5
100-hp Mercury	8	10	23	31	12	23	—	11
		Total		83				

Using the EDD we obtain this schedule:

Repair Schedule	Days Since Order Arrived	Processing Time	Finish Time	Flow Time	Promise Date	Actual Pickup Date	Days Early	Days Past Due
50-hp Evinrude	4	5	5	9	8	8	3	—
75-hp Nautique	15	3	8	23	10	10	2	—
100-hp Mercury	8	10	18	26	12	18	—	6
7-hp Johnson	6	4	22	28	15	22	—	7
50-hp Honda	1	1	23	24	20	23	—	3
		Total		110				

b. Performance measures are as follows:

Average flow time is 16.6 (or 83/5) days for SPT and 22.0 (or 110/5) days for EDD. The percentage of past due jobs is 40 percent (2/5) for SPT and 60 percent (3/5) for EDD. For this set of jobs, the EDD schedule minimizes the maximum days past due, but has a greater flow time and causes more jobs to be past due.

Solved Problem 2

The following data were reported by the shop floor control system for order processing at the edge grinder. The current date is day 150. The number of remaining operations and the total work remaining include the operation at the edge grinder. All orders are available for processing, and none have been started yet. Assume the jobs were available for processing at the same time.

Current Order	Processing Time (hr)	Due Date (day)	Remaining Operations	Shop Time Remaining (days)
A101	10	162	10	9
B272	7	158	9	6
C105	15	152	1	1
D707	4	170	8	18
E555	8	154	5	8

a. Specify the priorities for each job if the shop floor control system uses slack per remaining operations (S/RO) or critical ratio (CR).

b. For each priority rule, calculate the average flow time per job at the edge grinder.

SOLUTION

a. We specify the priorities for each job using the two priority sequencing rules.

$$S/RO = \frac{(\text{Due date} - \text{Today's date}) - \text{Shop time remaining}}{\text{Number of operations remaining}}$$

$$E555: S/RO = \frac{(154 - 150) - 8}{5} = -0.80[1]$$

$$B272: S/RO = \frac{(158 - 150) - 6}{9} = 0.22[2]$$

$$D707: S/RO = \frac{(170 - 150) - 18}{8} = 0.25[3]$$

$$A101: S/RO = \frac{(162 - 150) - 9}{10} = 0.30[4]$$

$$C105: S/RO = \frac{(152 - 150) - 1}{1} = 1.00[5]$$

The sequence of production for S/RO is shown in the preceding brackets.

$$CR = \frac{\text{Due date} - \text{Today's date}}{\text{Shop time remaining}}$$

$$E555:CR = \frac{154 - 150}{8} = 0.50[1]$$

$$D707:CR = \frac{170 - 150}{18} = 1.11[2]$$

$$B272:CR = \frac{158 - 150}{6} = 1.33[3]$$

$$A101:CR = \frac{162 - 150}{9} = 1.33[4]$$

$$C105:CR = \frac{152 - 150}{1} = 2.00[5]$$

The sequence of production for CR is shown in the preceding brackets.

b. We are scheduling a set of jobs at a single machine, so each job's finish time equals the finish time of the job just prior to it in sequence plus its own processing time. Further, all jobs were available for processing at the same time, so each job's finish time equals its flow time. Consequently, the average flow times at this single machine are

$$S/RO: \frac{8 + 15 + 19 + 29 + 44}{5} = 23.30 \text{ hours}$$

$$CR: \frac{8 + 12 + 19 + 29 + 44}{5} = 22.4 \text{ hours}$$

In this example, the average flow time per job is lower for the CR rule, which is not always the case. For example, the critical ratios for B272 and A101 are tied at 1.33. If we arbitrarily assigned A101 before B272, the average flow time would increase to $(8 + 12 + 22 + 29 + 44)/5 = 23.0 \text{ hours}$.

Solved Problem 3

The Rocky Mountain Arsenal, formerly a chemical warfare manufacturing site, is said to be one of the most polluted locations in the United States. Cleanup of chemical waste storage basins will involve two operations.

Operation 1: Drain and dredge basin.

Operation 2: Incinerate materials.

Management estimates that each operation will require the following amounts of time (in days):

STORAGE BASIN	A	B	C	D	E	F	G	H	I	J
Dredge	3	4	3	6	1	3	2	1	8	4
Incinerate	1	4	2	1	2	6	4	1	2	8

Management's objective is to minimize the makespan of the cleanup operations. All storage basins are available for processing right now. First, find a schedule that minimizes the makespan. Then calculate the average flow time of a storage basin through the two operations. What is the total elapsed time for cleaning all 10 basins? Display the schedule in a Gantt machine chart.

SOLUTION

We can use Johnson's rule to find the schedule that minimizes the total makespan. Four jobs are tied for the shortest process time: A, D, E, and H. E and H are tied for first place, while A and D are tied for last place. We arbitrarily choose to start with basin E, the first on the list for the drain and dredge operation. The 10 steps used to arrive at a schedule are as follows:

1. Select basin E first (tied with basin H); put it at the front.

    E — — — — — — — — —

2. Select basin H next; put it toward the front.

    E H — — — — — — — —

3. Select basin A next (tied with basin D); put it at the end.

    E H — — — — — — — A

4. Put basin D toward the end.

    E H — — — — — — D A

5. Put basin G toward the front.

    E H G — — — — — D A

6. Put basin C toward the end.

    E H G — — — — C D A

7. Put basin I toward the end.

    E H G — — — I C D A

8. Put basin F toward the front.

    E H G F — — I C D A

9. Put basin B toward the front.

    E H G F B — I C D A

10. Put basin J in the remaining space.

    E H G F B J I C D A

Several optimal solutions are available to this problem because of the ties at the start of the scheduling procedure. However, all have the same makespan. The schedule would be as follows:

Basin	OPERATION 1		OPERATION 2	
	Start	Finish	Start	Finish
E	0	1	1	3
H	1	2	3	4
G	2	4	4	8
F	4	7	8	14
B	7	11	14	18
J	11	15	18	26
I	15	23	26	28
C	23	26	28	30
D	26	32	32	33
A	32	35	35	36
				Total 200

The makespan is 36 days. The average flow time is the sum of incineration finish times divided by 10, or 200/10 = 20 days. The Gantt machine chart for this schedule is given in Figure J.3.

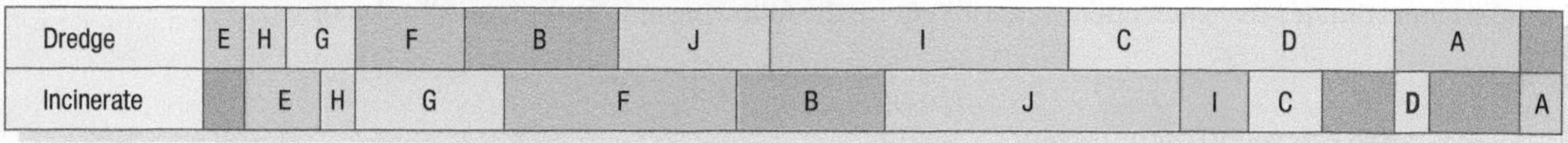

FIGURE J.3 ▶
Schedule for
Storage Basin

Discussion Question

1. Suppose that two alternative approaches for determining workstation schedules are available. One is an optimizing approach that can be run once a week on the computer. The other approach utilizes priority sequencing rules to determine the schedule as it evolves. Discuss the advantages and disadvantages of each approach and the conditions under which each approach is likely to be better.

Problems

The OM Explorer and POM for Windows software is available to all students using the 11th edition of this textbook. Go to **http://www.pearsonhighered.com/krajewski** to download these computer packages. If you purchased MyOMLab, you also have access to Active Models software and significant help in doing the following problems. Check with your instructor on how best to use these resources. In many cases, the instructor wants you to understand how to do the calculations by hand. At the least, the software provides a check on your calculations. When calculations are particularly complex and the goal is interpreting the results in making decisions, the software entirely replaces the manual calculations.

Job Shop Scheduling

1. The Hickory Company manufactures wooden desks. Management schedules overtime every weekend to reduce the backlog on the most popular models. The automatic routing machine is used to cut certain types of edges on the desktops. The following orders need to be scheduled for the routing machine:

Order	Time Since Order Arrived (hr)	Estimated Processing Time (hr)	Due Date (hr from now)
1	12	10	12
2	10	3	8
3	7	15	18
4	3	9	20
5	1	7	21

The due dates reflect the need for the order to be at its next operation.

a. Develop separate schedules by using the FCFS, SPT, and EDD rules.

b. Compare the schedules on the basis of average flow time, the average early time, and average past due hours for any order.

c. Comment on the performance of the two rules relative to these measures.

2. The drill press is a bottleneck operation. Currently, five jobs are waiting to be processed. Following are the available operations data. Assume that the number of remaining operations and the shop time remaining include the processing at the drill press.

Job	Time Since Order Arrived (hr)	Processing Time (hr)	Time to Due Date (wk)	Operations Remaining	Shop Time Remaining (wk)
AA	24	4	10	3	4
BB	16	8	16	4	6
CC	14	13	21	10	9
DD	12	6	23	3	12
EE	10	2	12	5	3

a. Specify the priority for each job if the shop floor control system uses each of the following priority rules: SPT, S/RO, EDD, and CR.

b. For each priority rule, calculate the average flow time per job at the drill press.

c. Which of these priority rules would work best for priority planning with an MRP system? Why?

3. The machine shop at Bycraft Enterprises operates 24 hours a day and uses a numerically controlled (NC) welding machine. The load on the machine is monitored, and no more than 24 hours of work is released to the welding operators in one day. The data for a typical set of jobs are shown in Table J.1. Management has been investigating scheduling procedures that would reduce inventory and increase customer service in the shop. Assume that at 9:00 A.M. on Monday the NC welding machine was idle. Also assume that job "arrival times" are the "release times" to the workstation.

TABLE J.1 | MANUFACTURING DATA

Job	Release Time	Lot Size	Processing Time (hr/unit)	Setup Time (hr)	Due Date
1	9:00 A.M. Monday	50	0.06	4	9:00 P.M.. Monday
2	10:00 A.M. Monday	120	0.05	3	10:00 P.M. Monday
3	11:00 A.M. Monday	260	0.03	5	11:00 P.M. Monday
4	12:00 P.M. Monday	200	0.04	2	2:00 A.M. Tuesday

a. Develop schedules for the SPT and EDD priority rules, and draw a Gantt machine chart for each schedule.

b. For each schedule in part (a), calculate the average flow time per job and the average past due hours per job.

4. The repair manager at Standard Components needs to develop a schedule for repairing eight Dell PCs. Each job requires analysis using the same diagnostic system. Furthermore, each job will require additional processing after the diagnostic evaluation. The manager does not expect any rescheduling delays, and the jobs are to move directly to the next process after the diagnostic work has been completed. The manager has collected the following processing time and scheduling data for each repair job:

Job	Time Since Order Arrived (days)	Processing Time (days)	Due Date (days from now)	Shop Time Remaining (days)	Operations Remaining
1	10	1.25		2.5	5
2	9	2.75	5	3.5	7
3	7	2.50	7	4.0	9
4	6	3.00	6	4.5	12
5	5	2.50	5	3.0	8
6	4	1.75	8	2.5	6
7	3	2.25	7	3.0	9
8	1	2.00	5	2.5	3

a. Compare the relative performance of the FCFS, SPT, EDD, S/RO, and CR priority rules in terms of the percent of jobs past due, average days past due, and maximum days past due. (*Hint*: The time since an order was placed is needed just to establish the sequence for the FCFS rule, because all performance measures deal with past due statistics.)

b. Discuss the selection of one of the rules for this company. What criteria do you consider most important in the selection of a rule in this situation?

5. Eight jobs must be processed on three machines in the sequence M1, M2, and M3. The processing times (in hours) are as follows:

		JOB						
		1	2	3	4	5	6	7	8
Machine 1		2	5	2	3	1	2	4	2
Machine 2		4	1	3	5	5	6	2	1
Machine 3		6	4	5	2	3	2	6	2

Machine M2 is a bottleneck, and management wants to maximize its use. Consequently, the schedule for the eight jobs, through the three machines, was based on the SPT priority rule on M2. The proposed schedule is 2, 8, 7, 3, 1, 4, 5, and 6.

a. It is now 4:00 P.M. on Monday. Suppose that processing on M2 is to begin at 7:00 A.M. on Tuesday. Use the proposed schedule to determine the schedules for M1 and M3 so that job 2 begins processing on M2 at 7:00 A.M. on Tuesday. Draw Gantt charts for M1, M2, and M3. What is the makespan for the eight jobs?

b. Find a schedule that utilizes M2 better and yields a shorter makespan.

6. The last few steps of a production process require two operations. Some jobs require processing on M1 before processing on M3. Other jobs require processing on M2 before M3. Currently, six jobs are waiting at M1 and four jobs are waiting at M2. The following data have been supplied by the shop floor control system:

Job	PROCESSING TIME (HR)			
	M1	M2	M3	Due Date (hr from now)
1	6	—	4	13
2	2	—	1	18
3	4	—	7	22
4	5	—	3	16
5	7	—	4	30
6	3	—	1	29
7	—	4	6	42
8	—	2	10	31
9	—	6	9	48
10	—	8	2	40

a. Schedule this shop by using the following rules: SPT, EDD, S/RO, and CR.

b. Discuss the operating implications of each of the schedules you developed in part (a). Assume all jobs arrived at the same time.

D = Difficult Problem

Flow Shop Scheduling

7. Refer to the Gantt machine chart in Figure J.4.

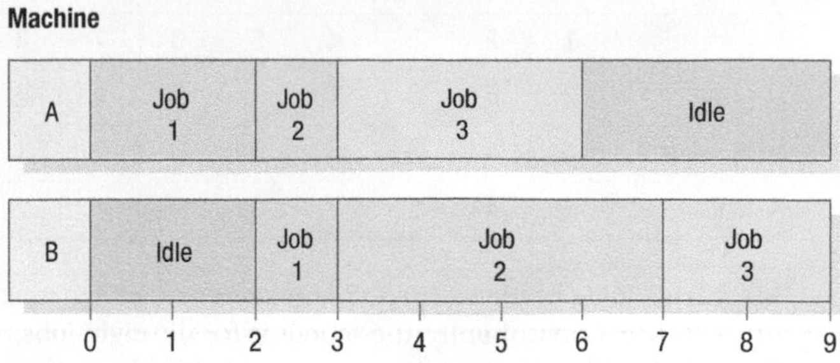

Machine

▲ FIGURE J.4
Gantt machine chart

   a. Suppose that a routing requirement is that each job must be processed on machine A first. Can the makespan be improved? If so, draw a Gantt chart with the improved schedule. If not, state why.

   b. Suppose that the machine sequence has no routing restriction; in other words, jobs can be processed in any sequence on the machines. Can the makespan in the chart be improved in this case? If so, draw a Gantt chart with your schedule. If not, state why.

8. A manufacturer of sails for small boats has a group of custom sails awaiting the last two processing operations before the sails are sent to the customers. Operation 1 must be performed before operation 2, and the jobs have different time requirements for each operation. The hours required are as follows:

	JOB									
	1	2	3	4	5	6	7	8	9	10
Operation 1	1	5	8	3	9	4	7	2	4	9
Operation 2	8	3	1	2	8	6	7	2	4	1

   a. Use Johnson's rule to determine the optimal schedule.

   b. Draw a Gantt chart for each operation.

9. McGee Parts Company is under tremendous pressure to complete a government contract for six orders in 31 working days. The orders are for spare parts for highway maintenance equipment. According to the government contract, a late penalty of $1,000 is imposed each day the order is late. Owing to a nationwide increase in highway construction, McGee Parts has received many orders for spare parts replacement and the shop has been extremely busy. To complete the government contract, the parts must be deburred and heat treated. The production control manager has suggested the following schedule:

	DEBUR		HEAT TREAT	
Job	Start	Finish	Start	Finish
1	0	2	2	8
2	2	5	8	13
3	5	12	13	17
4	12	15	17	25
5	15	16	25	30
6	16	24	30	32

   a. Use Johnson's rule to determine the optimal schedule.

   b. Draw a Gantt chart for each operation.

10. Carolyn Roberts is the operations manager of the machine shop of Reliable Manufacturing. She has to schedule eight jobs that are to be sent to final assembly for an important customer order. Currently, all eight jobs are in department 12 and must be next routed to department 22. All jobs arrived at the same time. Jason Mangano, supervisor for department 12, is concerned about keeping his inventory low and is adamant about processing the jobs through his department on the basis of shortest processing time. Pat Mooney, supervisor for department 22, pointed out that if Mangano were more flexible the orders could be finished and shipped earlier. The processing times (in days) for each job in each department follow:

	JOB							
	1	2	3	4	5	6	7	8
Department 12	2	4	7	5	4	10	8	2
Department 22	3	6	3	8	2	6	6	5

   a. Determine a schedule for the operation in each department. Use the SPT priority sequencing rule for department 12 and the same sequence for department 22. What is the average flow time for department 12? What is the makespan through both departments? What is the total number of job-days spent in the system?

   b. Find a schedule that will minimize the makespan through both departments, and then calculate the average flow time for department 12. What is the total number of job-days spent in the system?

   c. Discuss the trade-offs represented by these two schedules. What implications do they have for centralized scheduling?

11. **Penultimate Support Systems** makes fairly good speaker and
D equipment support stands for music groups. The assembly
process involves two operations: (1) fabrication, or cutting
aluminum tubing to the correct lengths, and (2) assembly,
with purchased fasteners and injection-molded plastic parts.
Setup time for assembly is negligible. Fabrication setup time
and run time per unit, assembly run time per unit, and the
production schedule for next week follow. All jobs arrived at
the same time. Organize the work to minimize makespan,
and create a Gantt chart. Can this work be accomplished
within two 40-hour shifts?

		FABRICATION		ASSEMBLY
Model	Quantity	Setup (hr)	Run Time (hr/unit)	Run Time (hr/unit)
A	200	2	0.050	0.04
B	300	3	0.070	0.10
C	100	1	0.050	0.12
D	250	2	0.064	0.60

Active Model Exercise

Active Model J.1, "Job Shop Scheduling," appears in MyOMLab. It
allows you to evaluate the application of single-dimension priority
rules for scheduling jobs at one workstation.

QUESTIONS

1. Which rule minimizes the average job flow time in the
system for this example?

2. Use the scroll bars to change the five processing times and
the five due dates. Does the same rule always minimize the
average flow time and average past due?

3. Which rule minimizes the average hours past due for this
example?

4. Use the scroll bar to change the processing time for
the Thunderbird and to modify the due date for the
Thunderbird. Does the same rule always minimize the
average hours past due?

5. Which rule minimizes the average hours early for this
example?

6. Use the scroll bar to change the processing time for the
Econoline and to modify the due date for the Econoline.
Does the same rule always minimize the average hours past
due?

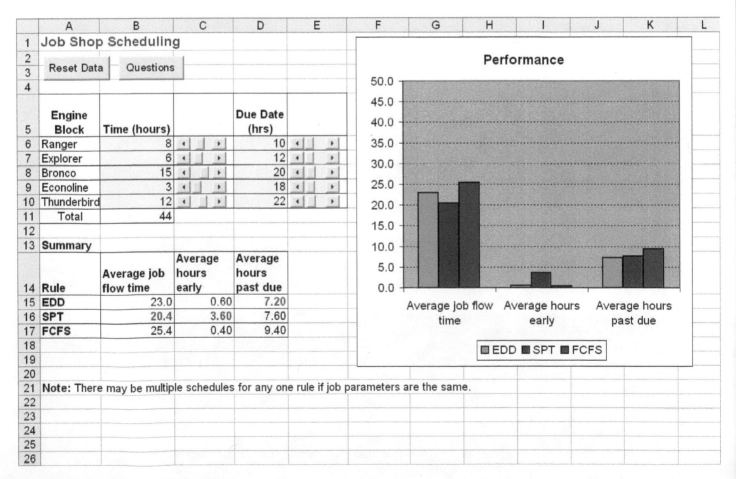

Job Shop Scheduling Using Data from Example J.1

D = Difficult Problem

Selected References

Baker, Kenneth R. and Dan Trietch. *Principles of Sequencing and Scheduling.* Hoboken, NJ: John Wiley & Sons (2009).

Hartvigsen, David. *SimQuick: Process Simulation with Excel,* 2nd ed. Upper Saddle River, NJ: Prentice Hall (2004).

Jacobs, F. Robert, William Berry, and D. Clay Whybark. *Manufacturing Planning and Control Systems for Supply Chain Management,* 6th ed. New York: McGraw-Hill/Irwin (2011).

LaForge, R. Lawrence, and Christopher W. Craighead. "Computer-Based Scheduling in Manufacturing Firms: Some Indicators of Successful Practice." *Production and Inventory Management Journal* (First Quarter 2000), pp. 29–34.

Pinedo, Michael. *Scheduling: Theory, Algorithms, and Systems,* 4th ed. New York: Springer Publishing Co. (2012).

In any organization, processes are grouped together into departments (or operations). How these groupings are positioned relative to each other is called a *layout*. In this supplement we demonstrate an approach to layout design that positions those departments close together that have strong interactions between them. It involves three basic steps, whether the design is for a new layout or for revising an existing layout: (1) gather information, (2) develop a block plan, and (3) design a detailed layout. We illustrate these steps with the Office of Budget Management (OBM), which is a major division in a large state government.

LEARNING GOALS *After reading this supplement, you should be able to:*

1. Identify the information requirements for designing a layout.

2. Develop and evaluate a block plan for a layout.

3. Describe what is needed to arrive at a detailed layout plan.

Step 1: Gather Information

OBM consists of 120 employees assigned to six different departments. Workloads have expanded to the extent that 30 new employees must be hired and somehow housed in the space allocated to OBM. The goal is to improve communication among people who must interact with each other effectively, creating a good work environment.

Three types of information are needed to begin designing the revised layout for OBM: (1) space requirements by center, (2) closeness factors, and (3) constraints on the relative locations of departments.

Space Requirements

OBM has grouped its processes into six different departments: (1) administration, (2) social services, (3) institutions, (4) accounting, (5) education, and (6) internal audit. The exact space requirements of each department, in square feet, are as follows:

Department	Area Needed (ft^2)
1. Administration	3,500
2. Social services	2,600
3. Institutions	2,400
4. Accounting	1,600
5. Education	1,500
6. Internal audit	3,400
	Total 15,000

Management must tie space requirements to capacity and staffing plans; calculate the specific equipment and space needs for each center; and allow circulation space, such as aisles and the like. At OBM, a way must be found to include all 150 employees in its assigned area. Consulting with the managers and employees involved can help avoid excessive resistance to change and make the transition smoother.

Closeness Factors

closeness matrix

A table that gives a measure of the relative importance of each pair of operations being located close together.

The layout designer must also know which departments need to be located close to one another. The table below shows OBM's **closeness matrix**, which gives a measure of the relative importance of each pair of operations being located close together. The metric used depends on the type of processes involved and the organizational setting. It can be a qualitative judgment on a scale from 0 to 10 that the manager uses to account for multiple performance criteria, as in OBM's case. Only the right-hand portion of the matrix is used. The closeness factors are indicators of the need for proximity based on an analysis of information flows and the need for face-to-face meetings. They give clues as to which departments should be located close together. For example, the most important interaction is between the administration and internal audit departments for OBM; it is given a score of 10 as shown in the first row and last column. Thus, the designer should locate departments 1 and 6 close together, which is not the arrangement in the current layout. A blank for a department above the diagonal in the matrix means that there is no need to be positioned close to the corresponding department. For example, Social Services does not need to be positioned close to Internal Audit.

CLOSENESS FACTORS						
Department	**1**	**2**	**3**	**4**	**5**	**6**
1. Administration	—	3	6	5	6	10
2. Social Services		—	8	1	1	
3. Institutions			—	3	9	
4. Accounting				—	2	
5. Education					—	1
6. Internal Audit						—

At a manufacturing plant, the closeness factor could be the number of trips (or some other measure of materials movement) between each pair of operations per day. Closeness factors can be gleaned by conducting a statistical sampling, polling supervisors and materials handlers, or, in a manufacturing setting, using the routings and ordering frequencies for typical items made at the plant.

Constraints

Frequently, certain operations need to be located in specific areas because of technical or physical constraints. For example, moving a computer center could involve costly rerouting of cables or power sources and moving air conditioning units. In a manufacturing setting, moving massive equipment could be prohibitive because the new location would have to be reinforced for the added weight or upgraded to handle new power and waste disposal requirements. In a similar vein, the information gathered for OBM includes constraints that depend not on the relative location of department pairs but on the *absolute* location of a single department. OBM has two such constraints.

1. Education (department 5) should remain where it is because it is next to the office library.

2. Administration (department 1) should remain where it is because that location has the largest conference room, which administration uses often. Relocating the conference room would be costly.

Step 2: Develop a Block Plan

The space available for a layout can be represented in a **block plan**, which allocates available space to operations and indicates their placement relative to each other. To describe a new facility layout, the plan need only provide the facility's dimensions and space allocations. When an existing facility layout is being modified, the current block plan is also needed. OBM's available space is 150 feet by 100 feet, or 15,000 square feet. The designer could begin the design by dividing the total amount of space into six equal blocks (50 × 50, or 2,500 square feet each). The equal-space approximation shown in Figure K.1 is sufficient until the detailed layout stage, when larger departments (such as administration) are assigned more space than smaller departments.

Having gathered the needed information in step 1, the next step is to develop a block plan that best satisfies performance criteria and area requirements. The most elementary way to do so is by trial and error, creating several alternative plans starting with the current layout. Because success depends on the designer's ability to spot patterns in the data, this approach does not guarantee the selection of the best or even a nearly best solution. When supplemented by the use of a computer to evaluate solutions, however, research shows that such an approach compares quite favorably with more sophisticated computerized techniques.

Weighted-Distance Method

When *relative* locations are a primary concern, such as for effective information flow, communication, material handling, and stockpicking, the weighted-distance method can be used to compare alternative block plans. The **weighted-distance method** is a mathematical model used to evaluate layouts based on closeness factors. A similar approach, called the *load-distance method*, can be used to evaluate facility locations. We have discussed the load-distance method in Chapter 13, "Supply Chain Logistic Networks," along with two measures used for distance: Euclidean and rectilinear. For this supplement, and our presentation of the weighted-distance method, we will only use the rectilinear measure for distance. *Rectilinear distance* measures the distance between two points with a series of 90-degree turns, as along city blocks. The distance traveled in the *x*-direction is the absolute value of the difference between the *x*-coordinates. Adding this result to the absolute value of the difference between the *y*-coordinates gives

$$d_{AB} = |x_A - x_B| + |y_A - y_B|$$

where

d_{AB} = distance between points A and B
x_A = x-coordinate of point A
y_A = y-coordinate of point A
x_B = x-coordinate of point B
y_B = y-coordinate of point B For assistance in calculating rectilinear distances, see Tutor 13.1 in MyOMLab.

The objective of the weighted-distance method is to select a layout that minimizes the total weighted distances that objects (e.g., people, vehicles, products) must travel between departments (e.g., offices, machines, centers, operations) identified on a block plan. The distance between two departments is expressed by assigning the departments to blocks in a block diagram and counting the number of blocks between them in a rectilinear fashion.

Evaluating Block Plans

The layout designer seeks to minimize the weighted-distance (*wd*) score by locating departments that have high closeness ratings close together. To calculate a layout's *wd* score, we simply multiply the closeness factors by the distances between departments. The sum of those products becomes the layout's final *wd* score—the lower the better.

block plan

A plan that allocates available space to operations and indicates their placement relative to each other.

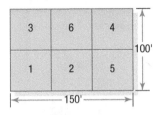

▲ **FIGURE K.1**
Current Block Plan for the Office of Budget Management

weighted-distance method

A mathematical model used to evaluate layouts (of facility locations) based on closeness factors.

MyOMLab
Tutor 13.1 in MyOMLab provides an example to calculate rectilinear distance measures.

EXAMPLE K.1	Calculating the Weighted-Distance Score

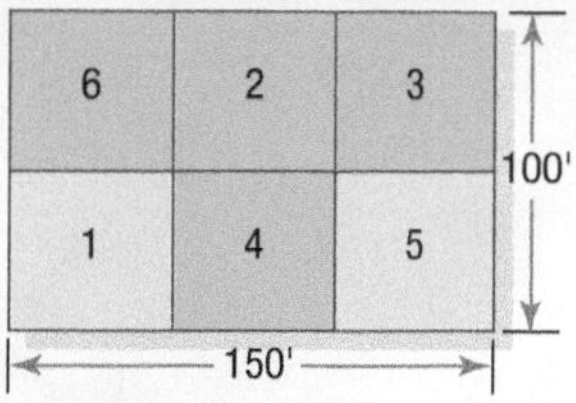

▲ **FIGURE K.2**
Proposed Block Plan

MyOMLab

Active Model K.1 in MyOMLab allows evaluation of the impact of swapping OBM departmental positions.

Current Plan

Proposed Plan

The initial block plan in Figure K.2 was developed using trial and error. A good place to start was to recognize the constraints and fix Departments 1 and 5 in their current locations. Then, the department pairs that had the largest closeness factors were positioned. The rest of the layout fell into place rather easily.

How much better, in terms of the *wd* score, is the proposed block plan shown in Figure K.2 than the current plan shown in Figure K.1?

SOLUTION

The accompanying table lists each pair of departments that has a nonzero closeness factor in the closeness matrix. For the third column, calculate the rectilinear distances between the departments in the *current* layout. For example, departments 3 and 5 in the current plan are in the upper-left corner and bottom-right corner of the building, respectively. Using rectilinear distances, the distance between the centers of these blocks is three units (two horizontally and one vertically). For the fourth column, we multiply the weights (closeness factors) by the distances, and then add the results for a total *wd* score of 112 for the current plan. Similar calculations for the *proposed* plan produce a *wd* score of only 82. For example, between departments 3 and 5 is just one unit of distance (one vertically and zero horizontally).

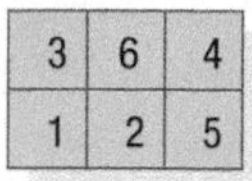

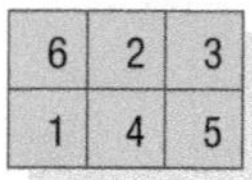

Department Pair	Closeness Factor (*w*)	CURRENT PLAN		PROPOSED PLAN	
		Distance (*d*)	Weighted-Distance Score (*wd*)	Distance (*d*)	Weighted-Distance Score (*wd*)
1, 2	3	1	3	2	6
1, 3	6	1	6	3	18
1, 4	5	3	15	1	5
1, 5	6	2	12	2	12
1, 6	10	2	20	1	10
2, 3	8	2	16	1	8
2, 4	1	2	2	1	1
2, 5	1	1	1	2	2
3, 4	3	2	6	2	6
3, 5	9	3	27	1	9
4, 5	2	1	2	1	2
5, 6	1	2	2	3	3
			Total 112		Total 82

To be exact, we could multiply the two *wd* total scores by 50 because each unit of distance (block) in the block plan represents 50 feet. However, the relative difference between the two totals remains unchanged.

DECISION POINT

The *wd* score for the proposed layout makes a sizeable drop from 112 to 82, an almost 27 percent improvement, but management would have to determine if the improvement outweighs the cost of relocating four of the six departments (i.e., all departments but 1 and 5). Nonetheless, there may be even better layouts.

OM Explorer and POM for Windows can help identify some even more attractive proposals. For example, one option is to modify the proposed plan by switching the locations of Departments 3 and 4. OM Explorer's output in Figure K.3 shows that the *wd* score for this second revision not only drops to 80, but requires that only three departments be relocated compared with the original layout in Figure K.1. Perhaps this second proposed plan is the best solution.

◉ Rectilinear Distances   ○ Euclidean Distances

◀ **FIGURE K.3**
Second Proposed Block Plan
(Analyzed with *Layout* Solver)

Department Pair	Closeness Factor	Distance	Score
1, 6	10	1	10
3, 5	9	1	9
2, 3	8	1	8
1, 3	6	1	6
1, 5	6	2	12
1, 4	5	3	15
1, 2	3	2	6
3, 4	3	2	6
4, 5	2	1	2
2, 4	1	1	1
2, 5	1	2	2
5, 6	1	3	3
Total			80

6	2	4
1	3	5

Step 3: Design a Detailed Layout

After finding a satisfactory block plan, the final step translates it into a detailed representation, showing the exact size and shape of each department, the arrangement of elements within the department (e.g., desks, machines, and storage areas); and the location of aisles, stairways, and other service space. These visual representations can be two-dimensional drawings, three-dimensional models, or computer-aided graphics. This step helps decision makers discuss the proposal and problems that might otherwise be overlooked. Such visual representations can be particularly important when evaluating high customer-contact processes.

LEARNING GOALS IN REVIEW

Learning Goal	Guidelines for Review	MyOMLab Resources
❶ Identify the information requirements for designing a layout.	Review the section "Step 1: Gather Information, pp. 1–3. Be sure to understand the meaning of space requirements, closeness factors, and constraints.	
❷ Develop and evaluate a block plan for a layout.	Study the section "Step 2: Develop a Block Plan," pp. 3–5. Review the weighted-distance method and how to use it to evaluate proposed block plans. Be sure to understand Exercise K.1 and the Solved Problem. See also the Active Model Exercise, p. 9, which demonstrates the weighted-distance method.	**Active Model:** K.1: Weighted-Distance Method **OM Explorer Tutor:** 13.1: Distance Measures **OM Explorer Solver:** Layout **POM for Windows:** Layout
❸ Describe what is needed to arrive at a detailed layout plan.	The section "Step 3: Design a Detailed Layout," p. 5, discusses the activities that need to take place to arrive at a detailed layout plan.	

Key Equation

Step 2: Develop a Block Plan

Rectilinear distance: $d_{AB} = |x_A - x_B| + |y_A - y_B|$

Key Terms

block plan 3   closeness matrix 2   weighted-distance method 3

Solved Problem

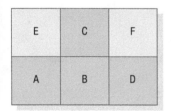

E	B	F
A	C	D

▲ **FIGURE K.4**
Current Layout

A defense contractor is evaluating its machine shop's current layout. Figure K.4 shows the current layout, and the table shows the closeness matrix for the facility measured as the number of trips per day between department pairs. Safety and health regulations require departments E and F to remain at their current locations.

		TRIPS BETWEEN DEPARTMENTS					
Department	**A**	**B**	**C**	**D**	**E**	**F**
A	—	8	3		9	5
B		—		3		
C			—		8	9
D				—		3
E					—	3
F						—

a. Use trial and error to find a better layout.

b. How much better is the proposed layout than the current layout in terms of the *wd* score?

SOLUTION

a. In addition to keeping departments E and F at their current locations, a good plan would locate the following department pairs close to each other: A and E, C and F, A and B, and C and E. Figure K.5 was worked out by trial and error and satisfies all these requirements. Start by placing E and F at their current locations. Then, because C must be as close as possible to both E and F, put C between them. Place A below E, and B next to A. All of the heavy traffic concerns have now been accommodated. Department D, located in the remaining space, does not need to be relocated.

E	C	F
A	B	D

▲ **FIGURE K.5**
Proposed Layout

		CURRENT PLAN		**PROPOSED PLAN**	
Department Pair	**Number of Trips (1)**	**Distance (2)**	***wd* Score (1) × (2)**	**Distance (3)**	***wd* Score (1) × (3)**
A, B	8	2	16	1	8
A, C	3	1	3	2	6
A, E	9	1	9	1	9
A, F	5	3	15	3	15
B, D	3	2	6	1	3
C, E	8	2	16	1	8
C, F	9	2	18	1	9
D, F	3	1	3	1	3
E, F	3	2	6	2	6
			wd = 92		*wd* = 67

b. The table reveals that the *wd* score drops from 92 for the current plan to 67 for the revised plan, a 27 percent reduction.

Problems

The OM Explorer and POM for Windows software is available to all students using the 11th edition of this textbook. Go to **http://www.pearsonhighered.com/krajewski** to download these computer packages. If you purchased MyOMLab, you also have access to Active Models software and significant help in doing the following problems. Check with your instructor on how best to use these resources. In many cases, the instructor wants you to understand how to do the calculations by hand. At the least, the software provides a check on your calculations. When calculations are particularly complex and the goal is interpreting the results in making decision, the software entirely replaces the manual calculations.

Step 2: Develop a Block Plan

1. Baker Machine Company is a job shop that specializes in precision parts for firms in the aerospace industry. Figure K.6 shows the current block plan for the key manufacturing centers of the 75,000-square-foot facility. Refer to the following closeness matrix. What is the change in the weighted distance, *wd*, score if Baker exchanges the locations of the tool crib and inspection.

3	4	2
1	5	6

◀ **FIGURE K.6**
Current Layout

CLOSENESS MATRIX

Center	\multicolumn{6}{c}{Trips between Centers}
	1	2	3	4	5	6
1. Burr and grind	—	8	3		9	5
2. Numerically controlled (NC) equipment		—	3			
3. Shipping and receiving			—		8	9
4. Lathes and drills				—		3
5. Tool crib					—	3
6. Inspection						—

2. Baker Machine (see Problem 1) is considering two alternative layouts. Compare the *wd* scores of the two block plans in Figure K.7 to determine which alternative layout is better.

3	6	4
5	1	2

◀ **FIGURE K.7(a)**
Alternative Layout 1

3	1	4
5	6	2

◀ **FIGURE K.7(b)**
Alternative Layout 2

3. The head of the information systems group at Conway Consulting must assign six new analysts to offices. The following closeness matrix shows the expected frequency of contact between analysts. The block plan in Figure K.8 shows the available office locations (1–6) for the six analysts (A–F). Assume equal-sized offices.

CLOSENESS MATRIX

Analyst	\multicolumn{6}{c}{Contacts between Analysts}
	A	B	C	D	E	F
Analyst A	—		6			
Analyst B		—		12		
Analyst C			—	2	7	
Analyst D				—		4
Analyst E					—	
Analyst F						—

1	2	3
4	5	6

◀ **FIGURE K.8**
Conway Consulting's Block Plan

Evaluate the *wd* scores of the three alternative layouts in Figures K.9(a), K.9(b), and K.9(c) and determine which is best.

B	C	D
A	E	F

◀ **FIGURE K.9(a)**
Alternative Layout 1

C	B	D
A	F	E

◀ **FIGURE K.9(b)**
Alternative Layout 2

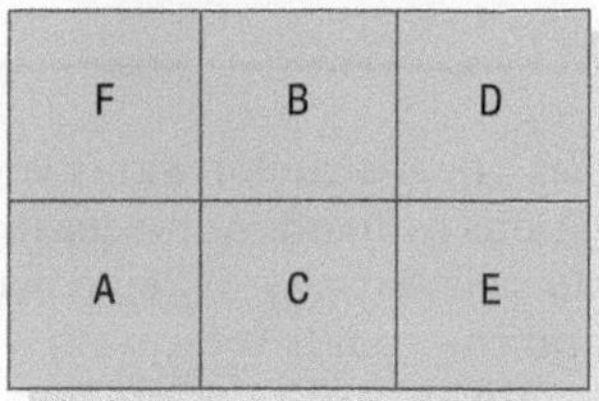

◀ FIGURE K.9(c)
Alternative Layout 3

4. Richard Garber is the head designer for Matthews and Novak Design Company. Garber has been called in to design the layout for a newly constructed office building. From statistical samplings over the past three months, Garber developed the following closeness matrix for daily trips between the department's offices.

	TRIPS BETWEEN OFFICES					
Office	A	B	C	D	E	F
A	—	25	90			185
B		—			105	
C			—		125	125
D				—	25	
E					—	105
F						—

a. If other factors are equal, which two offices should be located closest together?

b. Figure K.10 shows an alternative layout for the department. What is the total weighted-distance score for this plan?

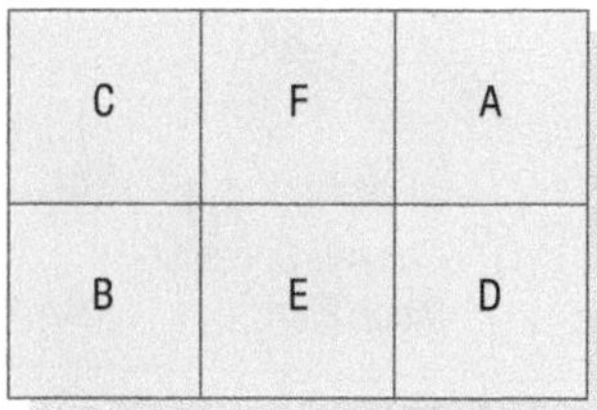

◀ FIGURE K.10
Alternative Block Plan

c. Use the explicit enumeration method of the POM for Windows software to find the block plan that minimizes the total weighted-distance score.

5. A firm with four departments has the following closeness matrix and the current block plan shown in Figure K.11.

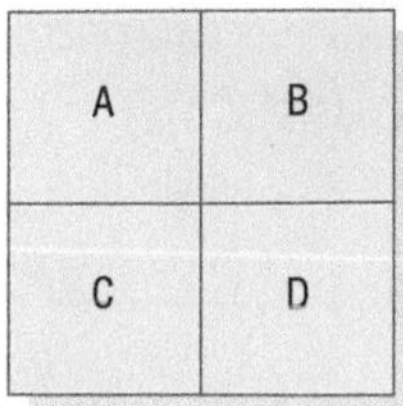

◀ FIGURE K.11
Current Block Plan

a. What is the weighted-distance score for the current layout?

CLOSENESS MATRIX

	Trips between Departments			
Department	A	B	C	D
A	—	12	10	8
B		—	20	6
C			—	0
D				—

b. Develop a better layout. What is its total weighted-distance score?

6. The department of engineering at a university in New Jersey must assign six faculty members to their new offices. The following closeness matrix indicates the expected number of contacts per day between professors. The available office spaces (1–6) for the six faculty members are shown in Figure K.12. Assume equal-sized offices. The distance between offices 1 and 2 (and between offices 1 and 3) is 1 unit, whereas the distance between offices 1 and 4 is 2 units.

CLOSENESS MATRIX

	Contacts Between Professors					
Professor	A	B	C	D	E	F
A	—		4			
B		—		12		10
C			—	2	7	
D				—		4
E					—	
F						—

a. Because of their academic positions, Professor A must be assigned to office 1, Professor C must be assigned to office 2, and Professor D must be assigned to office 6. Which faculty members should be assigned to offices 3, 4, and 5, respectively, to minimize the total weighted-distance score?

b. What is the weighted-distance score of your solution?

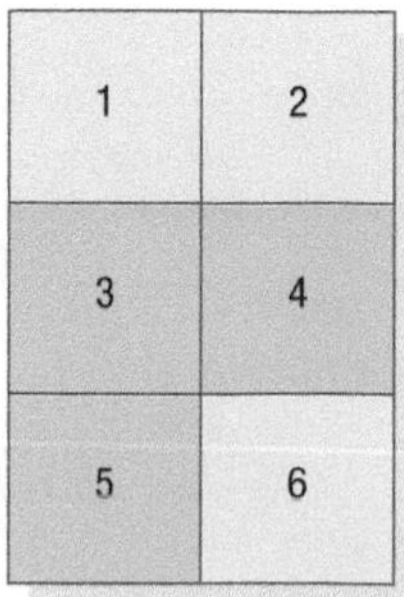

◀ FIGURE K.12
Available Space

Active Model Exercise

Active Model K.1, "Weighted-Distance Method," for Example K.1 appears in MyOMLab. It allows you to see the effects of performing paired swaps of departments.

QUESTIONS

1. What is the current total weighted-distance score?

2. Use the swap button one swap at a time. If the swap helps, move to the next pair. If the swap does not help, hit the swap button once again to put the departments back. What is the minimum weighted-distance score after all swaps have been tried?

3. Look at the two data tables, and use the yellow-shaded column to put departments in spaces. What space assignments lead to the minimum cost? What is this cost?

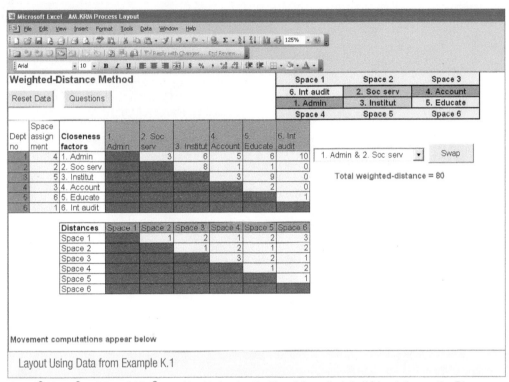

Layout Using Data from Example K.1

Microsoft® Windows®, and Microsoft Office® are registered trademarks of the Microsoft Corporation in the U.S.A. and other countries. This book is not sponsored or endorsed by or affiliated with the Microsoft Corporation.

Selected References

Anglin, Jeromy. "Implications of Office Layout and Building Design for Social Networks," **http://jeromyanglin.blogspot.com.au** (2010).

Birchfield, John C. and John Birchfield, Jr. *Design and Layout of Foodservice Facilities*, 3rd ed. Hoboken, NJ: John Wiley & Sons, 2008.

Gibbs, Tony. "5 Highly Efficient Office Layouts," www.business2community.com (October 25, 2012).

Greene, Jack. *Plant Layout and Facility Planning*, 2nd ed. CreateSpace Independent Publishing Platform 2013.

Safizadeh, M. Hossein, Joy M. Field, and Larry P. Ritzman. "An Empirical Analysis of Financial Services Processes with a Front-Office or Back-Office Orientation." *Journal of Operations Management*, vol. 21, no. 5 (2003), pp. 557–576.

Tooren, Wouter. "How to Create Office Layouts that Stimulate Collaboration," www.united-academics.org/journal (2012).

Zomerdijk, Leonieke G. and Jan de Vries. "Structuring Front Office and Back Office Work in Service Delivery Systems." *International Journal of Operations & Production Management*, vol. 27, no. 1 (2007), pp. 108–131.